WORLD CHRISTIANITY

WORLD CHRISTIANITY

Critical Concepts in Religious Studies

Edited by
Elizabeth Koepping

Volume III

Routledge
Taylor & Francis Group
LONDON AND NEW YORK

First published 2011
by Routledge
2 Park Square, Milton Park, Abingdon, OX14 4RN

Simultaneously published in the USA and Canada
by Routledge
270 Madison Avenue, New York, NY 10016

Routledge is an imprint of the Taylor & Francis Group, an informa business

Typeset in Times NR MT by Graphicraft Limited, Hong Kong
Printed and bound in Great Britain by MPG Books Group, UK

British Library Cataloguing in Publication Data
A catalogue record for this book is available from the British Library

British Library Cataloguing in Publication Data
A catalogue record for this book is available from the British Library

Library of Congress Cataloging-in-Publication Data
World Christianity : critical concepts in religious studies / edited by Elizabeth Koepping.
p. cm.
Includes bibliographical references and index.
ISBN 978-0-415-46827-5 (set) – ISBN 978-0-415-47291-3 (1) –
ISBN 978-0-415-47290-6 (2) – ISBN 978-0-415-47289-0 (3) –
ISBN 978-0-415-47288-3 (4) 1. Christianity.
I. Koepping, Elizabeth.
BR121.3.W67 2010
270.09–dc22
2010006472

ISBN 978-0-415-46827-5 (Set)
ISBN 978-0-415-47289-0 (Volume III)

Publisher's Note

References within each chapter are as they appear in the original complete work

CONTENTS

VOLUME III

Acknowledgements ix

Introduction to Volume III 1

PART 14
Living texts **11**

53 Coptic cultural nationalism **13**
S. S. HASAN

54 Ritual, history and identity in Goa **21**
ALEXANDER HENN

55 Fellowship in contemporary religion and ethics: report on oral enquiry into beliefs of village people in Catholic diocese of Zhouzi **38**
YOU XILIN AND CHEN LIANGUO

56 The imitation of Christ in Bicol, Philippines **61**
FENELLA CANNELL

PART 15
Discerning theology in context **81**

57 The status of Christian women in Kerala **83**
SUSAN VISVANATHAN

58 Contested masculine spaces in Greek Orthodoxy **94**
ELENI SOTIRIU

59 **Gender and change in an African immigrant church: an anthropologist and a (former) prophetess reflect** 106
DEIDRE HELEN CRUMBLEY AND
GLORIA MALAKE CLINE-SMYTHE

60 **Excerpt from 'Faith, fashion and family: religion, aesthetics, identity and social organization in Strasbourg'** 127
ATWOOD D. GAINES

61 **The feminization and professionalization of ordained ministry within the Mâ'ohi Protestant church in French Polynesia** 149
GWENDOLINE MALOGNE-FER

PART 16
Relating to place 163

62 **Experiencing spirit: religious processes of interaction and unification in Aboriginal Australia** 165
FIONA MAGOWAN

63 **Excerpt from 'Religion as resistance in Jamaican peasant life: the Baptist Church, Revival worldview and Rastafari Movement'** 181
JEAN BESSON

64 **Structural obstacles to grassroots pastoral practice: the case of a base community in urban Brazil** 195
MANUEL A. VÁSQUEZ

65 **Inuit Pentecostal and evangelical movements in the Canadian Eastern Arctic: the case of the healing the land rituals developed by the Canada Awakening Ministries** 212
FRÉDÉRIC LAUGRAND AND JARICH OOSTEN

66 **'Culture' as a tool and an obstacle: missionary encounters in post-Soviet Kyrgyzstan** 230
MATHIJS PELKMANS

67 **The Faith-healers of the Assemblies of God in Burkina Faso: taking responsibility for diseases related to 'living together'** 253
PIERRE-JOSEPH LAURENT

CONTENTS

PART 17
Texts biblical and local 273

68 The fundamentals of fertility: cosmology and conversion in a southwestern Nigerian Town 275
ELISHA P. RENNE

69 Jesus Christ as trickster in the religion of contemporary Bushmen 298
MATHIAS GUENTHER

70 Conversion to Protestantism among urban immigrants in Taiwan 317
HSING-KUANG CHAO

71 Christianity as a new religion: charisma, minor founders, and indigenous movements 329
MARK R. MULLINS

PART 18
Internal and external structures 343

72 The hidden sphere of religious searches in the Soviet Union: independent religious communities in Leningrad from the 1960s to the 1970s 345
OLGA TCHEPOURNAYA

73 American evangelicalism in Zimbabwe 357
PAUL GIFFORD

74 Excerpt from 'The persistence of apocalypticism within a denominationalizing sect: the apocalyptic fringe groups of Seventh-day Adventism 374
RONALD LAWSON

75 Native evangelism in Central Mexico 389
HUGO G. NUTINI

PART 19
Cross-national Pentecostalism past and present 407

76 'Heathendom' and the powers of darkness: on the role of the Devil in the preaching of the missionaries of the Norddeutsche Missionsgesellschaft in the nineteenth century and the contemporary African churches 409
BIRGIT MEYER

77 The transnationalisation of Brazilian Pentecostalism: the Universal Church of the Kingdom of God **423**
PAUL FRESTON

78 Certain knowledge: the encounter of global fundamentalism and local Christianity in urban south India **443**
LIONAL CAPLAN

79 Joana's story: syncretism at the actor's level **463**
ANDRÉ DROOGERS

ACKNOWLEDGEMENTS

The publishers would like to thank the following for permission to reprint their material:

Oxford University Press for permission to reprint S. S. Hasan, 'Coptic Cultural Nationalism', in *Christians versus Muslims in Modern Egypt: The Century-Long Struggle for Coptic Equality* (Oxford University Press, 2003), pp. 201–208.

Peter Lang GmbH for permission to reprint Alexander Henn, 'Ritual, History and Identity in Goa', in Alexander Henn and Klaus-Peter Köpping (eds), *Rituals in an Unstable World: Contingency, Hybridity, Embodiment* (Peter Lang, 2008), pp. 205–224.

CTBI (Churches Together in Britain and Ireland) for permission to reprint You Xilin and Chen Lianguo, 'Fellowship in Contemporary Religion and Ethics: Report on Oral Enquiry into Beliefs of Village People in Catholic Diocese of Zhouzi', *China Study Journal*, Spring/Summer 2007, 68–84.

Wiley Blackwell for permission to reprint Fenella Cannell, 'The Imitation of Christ in Bicol, Philippines', *Journal of The Royal Anthropological Institute*, 1995, 1, 377–394.

Oxford University Press, India for permission to reprint Susan Visvanathan, 'The Status of Christian Women in Kerala', in Arvind Sharma (ed.), *Women in Indian Religions* (Oxford University Press, 2002), pp. 189–200.

Sage Publications for permission to reprint Eleni Sotiriu, 'Contested Masculine Spaces in Greek Orthodoxy', *Social Compass*, 2004, 51, 4, 499–510.

New York University Press for permission to reprint Deidre Helen Crumbley and Gloria Malake Cline-Smythe, 'Gender and Change in an African Immigrant Church: An Anthropologist and a (Former) Prophetess Reflect', in Jacob K. Olupona & Regina Gemignani (eds), *African Immigrant Religions in America* (New York University Press, 2007), pp. 158–181.

Anthropological Quarterly for permission to reprint Atwood D. Gaines, Excerpt from 'Faith, Fashion and Family: Religion, Aesthetics, Identity and Social Organization in Strasbourg', *Anthropological Quarterly*, 1985, 58, 2, 47–62.

Continuum for permission to reprint Gwendoline Malogne-Fer, 'The Feminization and Professionalization of Ordained Ministry within the Mâ'ohi Protestant Church in French Polynesia', in I. Jones *et al.* (eds), *Women and Ordination in the Christian Churches: International Perspectives* (T&T Clark, a Continuum imprint, 2008), pp. 177–188.

Brill for permission to reprint Fiona Magowan, 'Experiencing Spirit: Religious Processes of Interaction and Unification in Aboriginal Australia', in Peggy Brock (ed.), *Indigenous Peoples and Religious Change* (Brill, 2005), pp. 157–175.

Palgrave Macmillan for permission to reprint Jean Besson, excerpt from 'Religion as Resistance in Jamaican Peasant Life: The Baptist Church, Revival Worldview and Rastafari Movement', revised by author 2009, originally published in Barry Chevannes (ed.), *Rastafari and Other African-Caribbean Worldviews* (Palgrave Macmillan, 1995; Rutgers University Press, 1998), pp. 47–63.

Oxford University Press for permission to reprint Manuel A. Vásquez, 'Structural Obstacles to Grassroots Pastoral Practice: The Case of a Base Community in Urban Brazil', *Sociology of Religion*, 1997, 58, 1, 53–68.

Frédéric Laugrand and Jarich Oosten for permission to reprint Frédéric Laugrand and Jarich Oosten, 'Inuit Pentecostal and Evangelical Movements in the Canadian Eastern Arctic: The Case of the Healing the Land Rituals Developed by the Canada Awakening Ministries', revised by authors 2009, originally published in *Numen*, 2007, 54, 229–269.

Wiley-Blackwell for permission to reprint Mathijs Pelkmans, '"Culture" as a Tool and an Obstacle: Missionary Encounters in Post-Soviet Kyrgyzstan', *Journal of the Royal Anthropological Institute* (N.S.), 2007, 13, 881–899.

Sage Publications for permission to reprint Pierre-Joseph Laurent, 'The Faith-healers of the Assemblies of God in Burkina Faso: Taking Responsibility for Diseases Related to "Living Together"', *Social Compass*, 2001, 48, 3, 333–351.

Oxford University Press for permission to reprint Hsing-Kuang Chao, 'Conversion to Protestantism Among Urban Immigrants in Taiwan', *Sociology of Religion*, 2006, 67, 2, 193–204.

Wiley-Blackwell for permission to reprint Elisha P. Renne, 'The Fundamentals of Fertility: Cosmology and Conversion in a Southwestern Nigerian Town', *Journal of the Royal Anthropological Institute* (N.S.), 2002, 8, 551–569.

Oxford University Press for permission to reprint Olga Tchepournaya, 'The Hidden Sphere of Religious Searches in the Soviet Union: Independent Religious Communities in Leningrad from the 1960s to the 1970s', *Sociology of Religion*, 2003, 64, 3, 377–388.

Taylor & Francis Ltd. for permission to reprint Ronald Lawson, excerpt from 'The Persistence of Apocalypticism within a Denominationalizing Sect: The Apocalyptic Fringe Groups of Seventh-day Adventism', in Thomas Robbins and Susan Palmer (eds), *Millennium, Messiahs, and Mayhem: Contemporary Apocalyptic Movements* (Routledge, 1997), pp. 207–221, 225–226.

Ethnology for permission to reprint Hugo G. Nutini, 'Native Evangelism in Central Mexico', *Ethnology*, 2000, 39, 1, 39–54. Copyright by The University of Pittsburgh.

Berg Publishers for permission to reprint Paul Gifford, 'American Evangelicalism in Zimbabwe', in *Christianity and Hegemony* (Berg, 1992), pp. 121–143.

Trinity Journal of Church and Theology for permission to reprint Birgit Meyer, '"Heathendom" and the Powers of Darkness: On the Role of the Devil in the Preaching of the Missionaries of the Norddeutsche Missionsgesellschaft in the Nineteenth Century and the Contemporary African Churches', revised by author 2010, originally published in *Trinity Journal of Church and Theology*, 1997, 7, 1–2, 15–27.

Hurst & Co. for permission to reprint Paul Freston, 'The Transnationalisation of Brazilian Pentecostalism: The Universal Church of the Kingdom of God', in A. Corten and R. Marshall-Fratani (eds), *Between Babel and Pentecost: Transnational Pentecostalism in Africa and Latin America* (Hurst & Co., 2001), pp. 196–215.

Taylor & Francis Books UK for permission to reprint Lional Caplan, 'Certain Knowledge: The Encounter of Global Fundamentalism and Local Christianity in Urban South India', in Wendy James (ed.), *The Pursuit of Certainty: Religious and Cultural Formulations* (Routledge, 1995), pp. 92–110.

Rowman and Littlefield for permission to reprint André Droogers, 'Joana's Story: Syncretism at the Actor's Level', in S. Greenfield and A. Droogers (eds), *Reinventing Religions: Syncretism and Transformation in Africa and the Americas* (Rowman and Littlefield, 2001), pp. 145–162.

Disclaimer

INTRODUCTION TO VOLUME III

Contemporary World Christianity: living the texts

The use of anthropology and sociology in historical studies was clearly evident in the readings in Volume II, almost all of which critically interrogated texts written between hard covers, in archives and bundles of letters, notes in margins and meetings. Hearing voices from the past on expected belief, gender, ethnicity and rank entails the historian or social scientist listening to the silences, reading between the lines, as they note the absence of certain voices and the contested presence of others. But that past is still with us. For example, the lens of authority and control can shed light on tensions between institutionally recognized leaders and 'travelling religious salesmen', not dissimilar to those between 'dangerous' nomads and 'predictable' farmers. Wandering Jesuit missioners in eighteenth-century Germany; church-planting Christian film-exhibitors in contemporary India; travelling nineteenth-century American tent-missions; evangelicals who want to 'bring Christ to prisons' already served by chaplains: differences of time and place and scale there may be, but there are also clear sociological similarities.

Crucial to this volume is that all the texts are drawn from fieldwork, discussions and mutual interrogations between researcher and local teacher-informants. Nineteen of the twenty-seven writers are anthropologists and eight rather more sociologists of religion, a pattern which inevitably continues in the final volume. As indicated in the General introduction, doing fieldwork does not eliminate the problem of re-presenting one's own love or loathing, ideological or personal blinkers being readily available for scholar and reader alike. Yet in long-drawn-out participation and ideally even more extended reflection there may be a little more chance for the anthropologist to act on Gadamer's caution that 'Researchers need to free themselves through reflection from that which otherwise and unbeknownst oppresses us'.[1] While the idea that anthropologists 'give people a voice' may seem patronizing, Fernandez[2] means, rather, enabling existing voices to be heard by otherwise deaf institutions and scholars.

One common point emerging from many of the readings is the frequent irrelevance of boundaries delineating traditions.[3] For the rural half of the world's population, living together in reasonable amity is the default mode: as villages were the world for most of human history, that style represents normality. Ideological divisions of orthodoxy may be feasible in town, but long-term rural cohabiting tends towards orthopraxy, with doctrinal diktats (if heard) of distant or transitory gatekeepers an irrelevant vanity. Forty years ago in parts of Borneo, wholeness for villagers lay in locality refracted by the Christian–Muslim–local palette, not 'Christian versus Muslim versus local' but rather as the Trinity represents facets of God. Now, urban divisions and worldly certainties encroach on courteous co-living in a pattern repeated worldwide. Essentialized religion was critiqued in Volume II; Volume III is able to challenge this even more consistently.

Part 14: Living texts

To reduce the multi-layered nature of relations comprising ordinary everyday life to just a couple of essentialized 'texts', a 'particular culture' and a 'generalized Christianity', is to fall into multiple traps; but how common it is! As noted in the General Introduction to these volumes, 'it is the faults and fissures that seem to mark out the landscape of collective selfhood',[4] rather than an overall consensus on fundamentals. As with 'culture', so is it with 'Christianities'. These may well share certain core elements: the centrality of Christ as Son/Mediator, God the Creator/Father and Sanctifier/Spirit; markers of acceptance, commonly including Baptism, and markers of spiritual community, commonly including Eucharist; a particular compilation and view of the Bible; love for the neighbour. Each item is variously understood by those whose identity includes Christianity, whether ritual specialists or not, and each category, each cluster is characterized by contests and rifts as well as consensus and amity. These readings by social scientists address this multiplicity.

The Copts of Egypt, one of the oldest continuously Christian communities in the world, are increasingly a church in diaspora. Whether in Europe, Australia or America, they make great efforts to retain the young, knowing that while ascription by birth may be enough to maintain community ties in the short term, teaching and global networking is essential for healthy survival. As the anthropologist Hasan explains (Chapter 53), Christian life in Egypt has its tensions, which Copts manage by teaching the faith using modern technology and strengthening community within given constraints. 'Christianity in Egypt' has two texts, cultural and religious, which are continually lived in relation to Islam, gender politics, local and state politics, chain migration and diaspora networks. They may 'bring the outsider home', but may also entice the insider to leave.

Living the texts in Goa is rather less fragile now than in the sixteenth century – but just as interesting. Henn, also an anthropologist, writes here of a festival jointly performed by Hindus and Catholics, and a Hindu festival with Christian elements (Chapter 54). Festivals may be framed by invocations to Christian figures – the Trinity, the Virgin Mary and local saints – and then move to the Hindu equivalent. An unknowing observer, or indeed a cleric, might well assume this to be a 'syncretic heresy': yet all attending identify 'their' segments and each competes with and complements the other. As Henn puts it, 'essentialist *and* hybrid views and practices are the rule . . . in religious and cultural encounter'.

You and Chen's article on Catholics in the Shaanxi Province of China (Chapter 55) sets out fifteen villagers' views on the relation between belief and ethics at a time when the state has ceased to 'inculcate ethical principles' and the migration to the cities has robbed the countryside of an entire age cohort. Fellowship, not doctrine, should become the basis of church life, say the mainly young adherents, the creative rule of 'love for fellow humans' drawn from Chinese as well as Christian ethical principles outweighing obedience to church rules.

The final paper in Part 14 (Chapter 56) also discusses a Christianity which, like the Goan, has been lived *in situ* for nearly five centuries – as long as Christianity in inner Latvia and Estonia. And in the Philippines, the specific Christianity Cannell presents is that lived by lowland Bicol people. Intimate links to their local saint and, through their 'imitations of Christ', to Christ himself allow both ordinary Catholics and Catholic shamans to access the full round of available support, from the kindly local spiritual forces to the loving power of Christ. Both are considered essential for healing and for the engendering of positive social relations within Bicol communities.

Part 15: Discerning theology in context

These readings may all seem to be about gender and (if fashion were female) women: Syrian Orthodox and Mar Thoma women in Kerala; Greek Orthodox men and women in Greece; menstrual rites in the Church of the Lord (Aladura) in the United States; faith and fashion in Strasbourg; and women's ministry in Tahiti. Yet beneath any surface links lie deeper levels of ecclesiology: the church as an institution, and the understanding of God as Creator, Mediator and Sanctifier or, in more gendered language, Father, Son and Spirit.

Arundhati Roy's *The God of Small Things* shapes Visvanathan's paper on Christian women in Kerala (Chapter 57): she works with the Syrian and Mar Thoma Christians whose male-dominated wealthy elite are the foundation of Roy's book. Her informants are rather poorer, though the Syrians have hopes through education of finding high-paid jobs worldwide. Paraiyar fisher-wives, while also educated (Kerala is the most literate state in India), live with deprivation and debts, not hope. Visvanathan's use of Roy in framing her paper reminds us that a novel can alert the keen-eyed reader to the structure of belief or preferment as set out by Soyinka or Masrui, Wa' Thiongo, Achebe or Trollope.

Sotiriu focuses on the Greek Orthodox altar as a male space, and the way Mary, Mother of God, is a model for women not paralleled by that of Christ for men (Chapter 58). Yet women do not follow all rules controlling them in the sanctuary and, given that few men attend church and the (married) priest is an almost feminine figure, there is some room for working with and around rules, though the theological demand that the priest represent the male Christ excludes women from the altar. In acquiescing to their exclusion from Mount Athos (currently contested by non-Greeks), women, says Sotiriu, accept their exclusion, thereby subordinating female ecclesial tensions within Orthodoxy to Greek identity.

The Aladura church was founded in Nigeria in 1930 and within forty-five years had expanded worldwide, become part of the World Council of Churches (WCC), and recognized the public ministry of women, usually that of a married couple. Chapter 59 is methodologically valuable (quite apart from the important exploration of menstrual rites and female ministry, especially in America) in that both writers, Cline-Smythe, an anthropologist, and Crumbley, a (former) Aladura Prophetess, discuss the setting up of the project together. Crumbley, critical of certain Aladura aspects before the work began, explains the reasons for her eventual departure.

Gaines (Chapter 60) looked at the effect of 'religious ideology' on the aesthetics of dress and furnishing in Roman Catholic and French Protestant Strasbourg, inspired by Weber, Goffman and Geertz in response to his mixed-faith informants' unerring capacity to ascribe religious affiliation by 'presentation of self' alone. As he makes clear, this is not a matter of wealth but of faith tradition, and it is indeed through discussion of theology acted out in ritual spaces, daily clothing and furnishing that Gaines reaches his conclusions.

French Tahiti was missionized by the London Missionary Society in the late eighteenth century and then by French Protestants (Chapter 61); 40 per cent of the population are still Protestant. Links to other Protestants in Oceania alerted Tahitian women to the ordination of women but not all ministers' wives were keen as up till then they had an important 'derived ministry' from their husband, marriage being obligatory for pastors. Once ordained, women experience problems in parish structures and with pastor's wives. For reasons of theology or rather sociology, they end up doing the same 'non-parish ministry' – schools and hospitals – which they did as laywomen. Such outcomes are in no way peculiar to churches in Oceania.

Christianities, as all other religious traditions, reflect and interact with their social context, hence the variety of expressions. Adherents may interrogate each context in which they must also live as social beings; they may be captured by it. Where there is a tension, it is shared by all traditions, categories and strands, gender being but one pattern illustrating the point.

Part 16: Relating to place

The point has repeatedly been made that Christianities, like other religious traditions with a universal spread, are local; each manifestation must therefore be considered *as it is in situ*. If an exported Christianity survives yet fails to localize, it may well be as a 'tribal faith' for expatriates linked by the memory of shared 'culture and blood' to a mythologized 'other place'. Contextualization, the liturgical and pastoral use of local language, symbolic systems and attitudes in socio-political context, is avoided, if not rejected, in such niches – though local influence will seep in. Inculturation, the creative response to faith from within the deepest ideological core of a community (*not* done by outsiders), which must be routinized to endure, may elicit no interest among, indeed be rejected by, local and imported gatekeepers, who oppose it with the spectre of 'syncretism' or deviation. A local Christianity is the outcome of negotiation between the various local constituencies and ideologies and the local and incoming gospel-bearers. All enduring mission is and has been primarily that of local people, even if some mission history suggests otherwise. A crucial variable is power and authority.

Magowan makes a difference between 'interact' and 'enmesh' as options for two systems in one place, in her case Yolngu Aboriginal and Christian religiosity (Chapter 62). Against anthropologists who feel Christianity cannot 'fit' Aboriginal and Yolngu ideology, she argues that it indeed does, just as for the Atlanta Baptists with whom these volumes began. Once foreign, it has been inculturated as another Christianity: Yolngu. She firmly avoids the often-made claims that people live either a doctrine-based EuroAmerican-style Christianity or a ritual-imagery religiosity inimical to that faith, claims which show a lamentable ignorance of human flexibility, finagling, faith and rationality. Besson's chapter on Baptists in Jamaica (Chapter 63), part of wider research on Rastafarians, also shows the relation between Christian ideas of order, ecclesiology, the heavens and the Trinity, and the local world of mediating spirits whose intentions are not always kind. It was founded for or by emancipated slaves, but church-going Baptist villagers, who still worked on estates and were thoroughly 'supervised' by their local minister, resisted by remaining equally committed to their Afro-Caribbean heritage.

While Magowan and Besson write of Christian communities which evolved more than a century ago, albeit both influenced by missionaries who acquired land, Vasquez's 'base Christian community' started in response to Vatican II and liberation theology (Chapter 64). He argues that the subsequent problems for such a group on the edge of Rio, unable fully to localize, had less to do with inadequate planning or inept people than with external economic constraints in Brazil and a radical change of direction in the Vatican, highlighting the need always to place the small picture within the large. Laugrand and Oosten, researching in Arctic Quebec, describe 'healing the land rites by Evangelical and Pentecostal ministries' (Chapter 65). This was the past practice of shamans, but is now done within the Christian framework, in order that imbalance resulting from wrong acts can be restored. After a major 'land healing' by Fijian visitors (the Inuit being part of a world indigenous circuit), a combined Anglican–Pentescostal Communion was held to celebrate the past as a source of wisdom as well as suffering, and to take collective responsibility for the future.

Kyrgyzstan, a broadly Muslim country, is now 1 per cent Christian and rising. Missions imbued the much-used Soviet use of fixed ethnicity and culture with the new faith, which maintains and reframes traditions such as circumcision, presenting itself as 'more compatible with Kirghiz culture' than Islam. 'Culture', identity and contextualization thread through Pelkmans's text (Chapter 66). Also working in a mixed-tradition area, Laurent sees identity and deliverance from local demons as at the core of Christian faith-healers in Burkino Faso (Chapter 67). Conversion may accompany healers' work of harnessing a two-strand – Christian and local – combination of knowledge and skill, and while the result may displease theologically orthodox Pentecostals, members and affiliates appear perfectly at ease, boundary-making and maintenance not being their job.

Part 17: Texts biblical and local

Local texts for being a person in community or specific enclaves thereof, and of being community in a nation, may interweave with, appropriate or oppose biblical texts. Each verse is used with a partiality clearly reflecting individual and group identity, intentions and needs as people review, re-envision and cherry-pick to oppose particular arguments or shore up particular views. Internal fissures in any 'group' and contradictions in any 'text' make this especially easy. The process is not different in a Christian community in Middle America than an indigenous religion village overlaid with Christianity in Borneo, inherent contradictions being present in all inscribed texts and all people having inherent tendencies to negotiation and scepticism. Naturally, any comparison must be done in an orderly fashion, rather than between (my) coherent theory and (your) inchoate praxis! There is just as much to be learnt about the actual use of the bible in so-called 'secular' EuroAmerica as assumedly 'still sacred' elsewhere, and a relative dearth of material.[5]

Renne explains in her discussion of fertility and faith among contemporary Yoruba Christians (Chapter 68) that assuming modernity, urban living and good education automatically means abandoning a biblically based faith is just not the case, as evidenced by a considerable proportion of American Christians as well as Nigerian Yoruba. Scientific descriptions concerning the start of life are evident among her informants, as are those of the Bible (especially the Old Testament) which support Yoruba understanding of creation and conception. As elsewhere, socio-religious views of the most exclusive nature and biological facts easily exist together, for they each answer different questions or present different facets of the speaker's life.

Jesus as Trickster is a familiar figure in anthropological literature, but Guenther (Chapter 69) goes beneath the sometimes superficial phrases to engage in a discussion about the relationship between Jesso Kreste and the great //Gauwa trickster and the theological and biblical interpretations used by Calvinist Bushmen. He notes, and this is important, that while those who accept the new faith separate //Ghawa, Satan and Christ clearly, others are less consistent. The latter comment caustically on sermons from their own position, much as did Rebera's Indian women in Volume I (Chapter 6). Guenther then suggests the Bushman Christ may usefully illuminate his context-bound pastiche of a EuroAmerican Christ.

Recent Taiwanese Protestants, writes Chao in his initial exploration of a little-researched topic (Chapter 70), appear to have two core texts: the Bible as literal Truth, and a slightly more flexible attitude to the eradication of alternative religious practices, including ancestor reverence, than other Presbyterian or Baptist-linked groups, those being the churches he studied. Yet both churches demand the removal of family altars before baptism into these pragmatically grounded communities which offer support to the growing numbers of urbanizing Taiwanese, and both expect the study of the Bible to be a major obligation of membership.

While the Bible and the local way of being a Christian person provide two texts in every context, Mullins's discussion of the texts involved in New Christian Movements in Japan (Chapter 71) sets up a third written text, rather similar to that provided for the main American New Christian church, the Mormons, by their nineteenth-century founder Joseph Smith. These added revelations similarly become part of church teaching, followers of new Tokyo churches such as Christ Heart Church citing the founder's name along with the names of the Trinity and according quasi-biblical authority to his writing. Making an explicit break from imported mission churches, these New Christian Movements in Japan regard themselves as unfolding the 'real' text of Christ through their Japanese heritage and, in common with some New Religious Movements in Japan closer to Buddhism than Christianity (such as Odoro Shuukyou), finding linguistic parallels between Japanese and New Testament words.

Part 18: Internal and external structures

A continuous theme of these volumes has been the identity of persons and communities in the round, taking special note of the local ordering and valorizing of ethnic, class, caste and gender constellations within the broad area of religion. A specific Christianity arises and evolves in the particularity of its context over time and, as regularly occurs with people and ideas, expands to other communities and contexts. Or, squeezed beyond endurance by internal and external stresses, and lacking sufficient local interest and commitment, it fails to survive.

Good intentions do not of themselves make for survival, for any new religious group needs to relate to and even be validated by local or national secular power and laws, which is unavoidable if it is to grow beyond a handful of secretive people. As we have also seen, relations between person, persuasion and polity, between internal 'structure and communitas', strife and striving, are part of that tension between divine euphoria and the demands of organization. While a tightly embedded religious system can serve as a support for a strong, even domineering, state – at the risk of being tarred by that brush – the imagined or real potential for religion to be used as a shorthand for resistance amid civic stress or as an equally shorthand method to sidestep or subvert the ballot box can swiftly see it restricted or proscribed.

Such internal and external pressures regularly take their toll, leaving apparently 'failed' movements. While the Hidden Christians (Kakure Kristian) in Japan maintained their very specific Christian identity embedded in Shinto and Buddhist thought over more than two centuries of repression, from 1634 to 1874, their end seems near as members increasingly have become become Buddhist or Catholic over the last thirty years. And where exogamy rules exclude close kin as spouses (or a community such as Shakers rejects procreation) very small tightly knit religious communities tend to die out. Cargo Cults, Cathars Gnostics, Kakure Kristian, Levellers and Münzerites all bubbled with textual passions and committed people yet collapsed or died away, though their ideas remain in the memory bank.

The first two papers in this part illustrate specific aspects of religion and the state. Tchepournaya discusses the Orthodox-oriented independent and secret religious groups in the anti-religious Soviet Union of the 1960s and 1970s (Chapter 72). Typical of totalitarian contexts, church-involvement represented both resistance to the state and a restatement of Russian identity. Gifford's discussion of churches in Zimbabwe (Chapter 73) makes clear that churches, in this case evangelical, relate not only to the country in which they work but, globalization and colonialism sharing some similarities, the country whence they come, religion and power crossing borders. The case shows how a state can use religion while being itself an object of worship.

Nutini and Lawson also discuss relatively new Christian groups, Lawson's Seventh Day Adventists, an American-origin church from 1860 to 1863 stemming from millennial Baptists and the prophetess Ellen White, and two Mexican churches, one small Evangelical and a larger Pentecostal one. Lawson (Chapter 74) discusses the maintenance of a church structure despite 'failed' apocalypticism and opposition to the state, both of which had a 'shelf-life' problem. One way the Adventist seminary teaching manages this is by clear avoidance – not the only denomination to deal thus with awkward doctrine. One of Nutini's two churches (Chapter 75) began in 1936, the other recently. The latter is non-liturgical, gender and class egalitarian, stresses liberal ethical behaviour between and beyond the group, Baptism but not Communion and does not proselytize. The earlier Pentecostal 'Light of the World' is tightly-organized, hierarchical overall but locally egalitarian, had a founder-to-son succession, does not social welfare beyond the church yet proselytizes. One link between them is the opposition their presence arouses among Roman Catholics and Protestants: one difference, suggests Nutini, may be survival.

Part 19: Cross-national Pentecostalism past and present

The growth of Pentecostalism is often attributed to its power over the intermediate 'spirit world' of demons and devils, enabling people who feel threatened to be both affirmed in their locality and made safe by bringing local spiritual forces under Christian control. There is certainly some truth in this view, for the wish for and success of healing amid sorcery or fate-inspired sickness is indeed an important element in conversion or affiliation. Yet there are problems too. An 'either/or' view may be feasible where Pentecostal communities interact mainly within their group, but is less easy (and likely to arouse antagonism) in multi-religious contexts, where attending each other's festivals was a pleasant part of fulfilling the normal obligations of community life. Yet, as with other traditions, laity interact with rather than suffer under rules, individuals or groups balancing the salvific benefits of exclusivity with the immediate effects of sociability, the value of maintaining ties to previous church traditions and being firmly committed to the new. One thing is clear. A Pentecostal member follows an often complex path with surprising origins[6] which, as with any tradition, may affirm the person's identity vis-à-vis the family or the state as well as in relation to God.

Meyer (Chapter 76) shows that the 'Devil-focus' in Ghanaian Pentecostal-oriented churches, far from being a recent American import, is rooted in work of the nineteenth-century North German Mission Society missionaries who brought Lutheran Pietist images of both Devil and witches. The Devil, not God, linked local Ewe and the German traditions, defence against Evil being more vital (or more obviously the job of religion) than support from a distant and uninterested Creator. The expansion of the Pentecostal movement is to a large extent linked to their capacity to heal and, provided healing in the new system is effective, to diabolize traditional religion. The Devil, given central place by the missionaries from their belief system and by the Ewe from theirs, represents the past and the present, or the past in the present.

The polycentric nature of Pentecostalism, says Freston (Chapter 77), led to its growth and influence being ignored by academia because its greatest regions of strength – Latin America, especially Brazil, and Africa – are beyond Western control. The Universal Church of the Reign of God is poorly regarded in Brazil, partly due to the poverty and powerlessness of its local adherents. Seen by Evangelical as well as Roman Catholic opponents as an unsatisfactory mélange of Evangelical, archaic Catholic and Afro-American elements, it has nevertheless, or perhaps because of this, expanded quickly overseas, initially in Latin America and then globally. Its global reach has similarities to 'ethnic churches' discussed elsewhere, most members beyond Latin America being Portuguese from Africa or Europe, or others with Hispanic or Lusophone links. Its mission to Portugal echoes that of African pastors re-missionizing Britain.

South Indian Pentecostalism in Chennai/Madras is the subject of Caplan's paper from his long fieldwork there (Chapter 78). Both Roman Catholic and Church of South India (CSI) churches take the Bible with faith, and follow the path of social activism and ties to other faiths. Caplan insists the American-imported Pentecostalism goes for certainty, obedience and firm boundaries, and that in satisfying explanation for and help through misfortune, which mainline churches and the urban elite ignore (as they ignore Grace), Pentecostal churches will continue to increase.

The final paper, by the anthropologist Droogers (Chapter 79), once again illustrates the dangers, indeed the futility, of essentializing 'denominations'. His paper challenges us not to forget that individuals, each with their own life-story sets of ongoing choices, make up a 'church', and that they do this to a considerable extent irrespective of brand name, text or prelates. Joana was Pentecostal and now chooses to identify as Roman Catholic. Some may regard her frame of religious reference as eclectic at best; but 'multiple-discourse' religion is, with different labels, arguably the norm for people in any faith tradition.

Notes

1 H.-G. Gadamer, in J. Habermas, D. Henrich and J. Taubes (eds) *Hermeneutik und Ideologiekritik*, Frankfurt, 1971, p. 296, quoted in E. Koepping, *Food Friends and Funerals*, Berlin: LIT, 2008, p. 187.
2 J. Fernandez, 'Anthropology as a Vocation: Listening to Voices', in E. Schultz and R. Lavenda (eds) *Current Anthropology: A Perspective on the Human Condition*, New York: Oxford University Press, [1987] 2004.
3 Also attested in (for example) J. Openshaw, *Bauls of Bengal*, Cambridge: Cambridge University Press, 2005 for Hindu–Muslim; C. Corneille, *Many Mansions*, Maryknoll, NY: Orbis, 2002, for varied Christian–other traditions; E. Koepping, *Food Friends and Funerals*, Berlin: LIT, 2008, for rural Muslim–Christian–localized traditions.
4 C. Geertz, *Available Light*, Princeton: Princeton University Press, 2000, p. 250.
5 One excellent text is T. Jenkins, *Religion in Everyday English Life*, Oxford: Berghahn, 1999.
6 W. Hollenweger, 'Common Witness between Catholics and Pentecostals', in *Pneuma*, vol. 18/2, 1996.

Part 14

LIVING TEXTS

53

COPTIC CULTURAL NATIONALISM

S. S. Hasan

Source: S. S. Hasan, *Christians versus Muslims in Modern Egypt: The Century-Long Struggle for Coptic Equality*, Oxford: Oxford University Press, 2003, pp. 201–8.

One of the hypotheses informing this work is that the church under Pope Shenuda has capitalized on the great value placed on religious identity in fin de siècle Egypt, to outbid the state for the loyalty of its beleaguered Christian citizens. It has done so by organizing a plethora of communal activities, by clericalizing laymen on a massive scale and above all by nurturing a potent religious culture. The numerous religio-cultural activities of the Bishopric of Youth aim, in part, to imbue the faithful with the conviction that the church is the social space where one receives one's true identity and that spaces that exclude it are a negation of the Coptic patrimony.

The cultural space that was created, under Pope Shenuda, and was meant to be complementary to the place of worship, was not destined only for the young. He created many forums, other than the Sunday schools, where adults, who felt excluded from Egyptian public life and from the informal social networks that sprang up among Muslims in the workplaces and in their residential neighborhoods, could get together with their co-religionists. In these forums, all subjects were discussed, from ethics and canonic law, the history of local saints and martyrs, to the contemporary problems facing the Copts.

Explaining the fundamentals of the revived faith in his book *Hayat al-Iman* (A Life of Faith), Shenuda writes that it is no longer sufficient for Copts to maintain their links to the mother church merely by attending a weekly prayer session; they must familiarize themselves with their religious patrimony as well, through the study of theological and canonical issues specific to the Orthodox Church: It is their "duty," he insists, to enter into a series of "apprenticeships," which will enable them to graduate to ever higher levels of faith[1]—levels once attainable only by those with a priestly or monastic vocation. For this new discipline, the pope stresses that perseverance is key. And indeed the seminaries, not so long ago limited to priest-hopefuls or would-be monks, are overflowing with laymen who sometimes (as in the case of the theological seminary in Minya, which I attended) travel long distances by train, just to get this *Kulturbuildung*.

This kind of socialization "from the cradle to the grave" is in its pedagogical guise an entirely new phenomenon, one that was viewed negatively by previous generations of Orthodox clerics, who considered it a form of secularization—a "Protestant deformation" of the Coptic religious patrimony. Indeed, it is without question a venture in religious modernization, which equips the church not only to take on Muslim supremacists but also to hold its own against the Egyptian Catholic and Protestant churches, which looked down on it in the past as archaic.

The church has sponsored all kinds of groups, including Bible, hagiography, Coptic archeology study groups, as well as groups for the study of Coptic canticles. Musicologists familiar with the history of the canticles have been placed in charge of modern laboratories for the work of recapturing the old tunes and of creating archives for them, as well as of recording them for sale.

Coptic liturgical music is among the oldest in the world. The chants existed as part of an oral tradition going back to ancient times. They were passed on by one generation of cantors to another. Dr. Rāghīb Muftaḥ, the head of the music and hymns department of the Institute of Higher Coptic Studies, resolved to save this Coptic musical heritage from oblivion, by recording and transcribing it into a western notation system—an endeavor that began seven decades prior to my research. In 1927, when he was still a young agricultural engineer active in the Sunday School Movement, Muftaḥ met a British ethnomusicologist, Earnest Newlandsmith, who had stopped in Egypt on his way back from Palestine. Newlandsmith was himself a Protestant clergyman's son with strong monastic proclivities (he used to refer to himself as the "hermit of Mt. Carmel").[2] The two young men, who shared a common interest in Coptic music, became friendly and Muftaḥ invited Newlandsmith to share his accommodations in his boathouse on the Nile. Muftaḥ spent nine winters, sitting cross-legged on the floor with the Englishman, learning, under his guidance, the western system of musical notation. Since there were no recordings as yet of Coptic liturgical music, they had to hire singers to come to the boathouse and chant the scores for them. Day in and day out, the Englishman went on laboriously scribbling down the chants of the blind master cantor Mualim Michael Jirjis al-Batanuni, while Muftaḥ tried to record them on the old-fashioned reels of tape that Newlandsmith had brought him from England. Together, they went on to transcribe enough music to fill the sixteen volumes of text, which have recently been acquired by the Library of Congress.[3]

The culmination of Muftaḥ's lifework was the publication in 1998 of a 1,200-page manuscript containing the complete musical scores of the liturgy of St. Basil and its accompanying words, translated from the Coptic into English and Arabic. When I met him when he was 94, he was still working, on the liturgical music of St. Cyril, which had almost been lost half of century earlier, due to the death of the last surviving cantor who knew the music.

This lifework, begun seventy-one years ago, required a singleness of purpose that was nothing short of monastic asceticism. Like the celibate founder of the Sunday School Movement, Ḥabīb Jirjis, Muftaḥ gave himself up entirely to it: he lived as "a monk in the world," though later, in old age, he sought out a female companion; his marriage was, by his own admission, "never consummated." He himself declared that he had married because he began to feel the weight of his age "I just needed someone to look after me"[4]—a statement that in the context of Egypt's male chauvinist culture shocked no one.

Taped canticles along with the taped hymns and the videos of the lives of church heroes—the Egyptian saints and martyrs—have been very successfully commercialized during the reign of Pope Shenuda. Their sale provides the many churches throughout Egypt with a considerable revenue.[5]

The formation of new song repertoires in Coptic, which are often used at the inaugural ceremonies, such as welcoming canticles for visiting bishops,[6] is a very good example of the usefulness of religious ritual for cultural nationalism. A traditional practice, the singing of church canticles at the beginning of Mass, is modified, ritualized, and institutionalized for a new purpose, namely, to mobilize the Coptic masses. By generating a sense of pride in their ancient heritage, it creates an esprit de corps. These are new songs, using the same idioms as the old canticles, often composed by professors at the Coptic Institute and then transferred via musicologists to a choral repertoire. Sung in unison at inaugural meetings, they have become a tradition of great symbolic force. The songs, which reflect the historical background and culture of the Coptic people, are for them what "The Star-Spangled Banner" is for Americans. They not only proclaim their religious identity, but also extol the sovereignty of their church, which has fought a fierce battle, since time immemorial, to maintain its independence from western Christendom.

The videotaped legends of the saints and martyrs have also become a potent cultural agent linking the different age groups and generations. I have seen children barely out of kindergarten, solemnly watching together with their parents and toothless grandparents a video about Barsum the Naked, the Egyptian hermit who lived alone in a cave with a snake he had tamed, and whose only clothes were his long hair and beard.[7]

In many of the families with whom I stayed during my fieldwork in the different dioceses, the only music the children were allowed to listen to up until the age of eighteen, when they finished high school and went off to universities in the big towns, were the canticles and hymns. The only films they were allowed to watch on television were these dramatized epics of the local saints and martyrs.[8]

Mention must also be made of the multiplicity of small church-sponsored printing workshops. The plethora of new religious publications is not just the product of big institutions. Aside from the papacy and the Department of Youth and all the diocesan bishoprics, which have acquired their own publishing houses, as have many of the churches and monasteries, many small groups like the diaconal groups, the groups of consecrated laymen and woman (*mukarasin*), the Sunday school groups and all manner of church-related voluntary groups have their own publications. These church-sponsored printing workshops have, since the advent of Shenuda, produced thousands of new publications that explain in simple language designed for mass consumption the historical roots of certain ritual practices, the stories of the ancient monastic church fathers and of the Egyptian martyrs, who gave their life for the survival of the church at the time of Roman persecution, as well as emphasizing the importance of regular participation in prayer—all of which are designed to turn religion into the predominate referent of identity for Copts.

But, of all the church-sponsored cultural groups, perhaps none are more important than the ones that have been put in charge of the resurrection of the Coptic language. It is part of the genius of the Sunday School Movement that it grasped the intimate connection between a private-property language and a sense of belonging to a nation. By 1961, it had succeeded in getting the education committee of the Communal Council to make the instruction of the Coptic language mandatory for all Sunday schools throughout the country.[9] And it is as a nation that the Coptic clergy thinks of the Coptic community—even though, unlike the Maronites in Mount Lebanon, they do not aspire to separate statehood, because it is realistically impossible to achieve. The Copts, unlike the Maronites, are not concentrated in one geographic area, nor do they even have a majority in any single city (in Assiut and Minya, they form no more than approximately 30 percent of the inhabitants). In referring to the Copts, in their conversations with me, the clergy either talked about *Sha'bina* (our people) or *al-Ummah al-Qibṭiyah* (the Coptic nation).

This sense of the Copts as a distinct entity is antagonistic to the view of Christianity as solely a religion, held by the ancien régime upper class. Indeed, its members even object to the terms *community* or *minority*. On several occasions when I, out of habit, slipped into such usage, to explain what I had come to study, I was sharply upbraided by one or the other of my interviewees, who insisted that the Copts were not a community distinguishable from their Muslim compatriots: both were Egyptian—different only, through one of those contingencies of birth, in religion; just as some Americans, they would add, worshiped in a synagogue and others in a church.[10]

In encouraging Coptic etymologists, philologists, grammarians, and lexicographers to work on the reconstruction, by scientific reasoning, of what was in effect a protolanguage, Pharaonic written with the help of a Greek alphabet, the church was engaging in activities central to the political identity of the Copts. Some of the Sunday School visionaries had gone all the way to the great libraries of Europe, where they devoted their best years to the compilation of word lists for monolingual dictionaries and to the study of the etymology of Coptic words. Bishop Gregorios, had, in his youth, gone to the University of London to write a 538-page doctoral dissertation—in an old-fashioned copperplate handwriting—on the etymology of Greek words in the Coptic language. To complete such a monumental task, he must have been moved by great passion, the kind of passion that sustains revolutionary activities. Later, as the bishop of Advanced Coptic Research, he devoted himself to the translation of ancient Coptic texts, transliterating the words into Roman script and tracing their etymology to the Greek and demotic languages.[11]

The importance the church attaches to the resurrection and transmission of the ancient Coptic language is evidenced by the diocesan bishops, with fantastically busy schedules, who take time out to teach Coptic themselves (I attended such courses in both Akhmim and Minya), and that Archbishop Bishoi, who is probably the bishop with the heaviest load of responsibilities, because he doubles up as the pope's vicar in most domestic matters, drives up all the way from the port town of Damietta to Cairo to teach a lesson once a week at the papal seminary. In one of those lessons, which I attended, professors, like Dr. Emile, although far more versed in the subject matter than the bishop, sat humbly at his feet, while he spent over an hour on a ponderous explanation of a single sentence.

Coptic was never successfully vernacularized the way Hebrew was by the indomitable pioneers who came to Palestine in the 1920s (Ben Yehuda, the father of vernacular Hebrew, is said to have refused to exchange a single word of Russian with his visiting old mother, even though she was not conversant in any other tongue). Nonetheless, or perhaps because of this, Coptic is potent as a tool of solidarity. The fact that even the high clergy have only a rudimentary grasp of that language and that their legions of church-servants have succeeded in passing on no more than a few words to the Sunday school children is unimportant, because it suffices for the community to use sacral words—many of them Greek words incorporated into the Coptic language—like *Kyrie Eleison* (Lord, have mercy), which is repeated forty-one times in the course of a single prayer—or to refer to their bishops as *Anba* (a change introduced by the Sunday School generation, from the previous use of the Hebrew word *Abba*), together with the reintroduction of ancient Coptic titles like *absalomos, aganostos*, and so on for the male deacons, and of ancient names of Greek derivation, like Phoebe, Anastasia, and so on for the female *mukarasat*, or to greet each other, over the telephone, with the word *Agape*, or on Easter Sunday with *Christos Anesti* (Christ is risen)—Greek words unintelligible to their Muslim compatriots—to maintain a sense of distinctiveness from the Other. This is their revenge against the Muslims, who exclude them from their social networks in the workplace, the universities, and the residential neighborhoods.

The fact that Coptic is reserved mainly for canticles, hymns, and a few prayers, particularly those used in the week of the Passion, only consolidates the astonishing power of the Orthodox clergy in Egypt: through their superior knowledge of a sacral language, they are looked up to by the faithful—not just as mediators between the Arabic vernacular, into which the mass has been translated, and Coptic, but as mediators between heaven and earth.

It is presumably for this reason that the Sunday School Movement in the 1940s and '50s succeeded in interesting the Copts in their language, while the secular nationalistic *al-Ummah al-Qibṭīyah* movement did not. The community's confidence in the sacredness of their language is tied to the conception of their church as cosmically central to Christianity in its role as the church of origin. Secular nationalists, like the lawyer and founder of *al-Ummah al-Qibṭīyah*, Ibrahim Hilal, could not compete with those who are linked to a supraterrestial order through the medium of a sacred language.

Coptic cultural nationalism remained a powerful current at the end of the twentieth century and its political ramifications may be gauged by the way the government and the local press reacted to a church-sponsored project to build a Coptic university in Egypt. Shenuda's meetings, in his papal headquarters, with a number of well-to-do Copts from the diaspora, to discuss the financing of such an institution as well as the possibility of recruiting Coptic expatriate professors "to help educate their younger brothers at home" were lambasted in the press as a "seditious" scheme. Predictably, the government was able to enlist the support of a Coptic member of Parliament, Gamal As'ad, who described it as a "dangerous" project that threatened to ignite sectarian conflict in Egypt.[12]

The question whether the Copts are to be allowed to set up such a privately endowed institution remains unresolved, despite the many compromises offered by the supporters of the project—down to the very name of the university, Coptic-Egyptian University, from which they were willing to delete the word *Coptic.* All of this failed to win government acquiescence, even though the Muslims have a similar institution in the Islamic university, al-Azhar, and even though the government itself insists on religious labeling on personal identification cards—a practice that works to the detriment of the Christian minority.[13]

The church is not merely reacting to the exclusivism of the Muslims by creating a compensatory private space for Christians. It is trying to reverse the secularizing trend of the first half of the twentieth century, which had made possible the political integration of the Copts. Secularism is a danger to the Coptic patrimony, in its view, almost as great as Islam. The church's attempt to mobilize the Coptic masses around a religio-cultural platform may be read, therefore, as a defeat of the secular upper class, whose disdain for all forms of religiosity is well captured by a statement the late Magdi Wahba made to me: "Tout les deux sont des bandes d'abruties" (Both of them [the religious Muslims and Copts] are a bunch of morons).

It is a sign of the growing prestige of the church that toward the end of the century, even the secular ancien régime aristocracy had felt compelled to pay homage to the pope. For example, Magdi Wahba described to me a meeting with the pope, to which he had been invited as a member of the Coptic Archeological society, on some matter relating to the preservation of Coptic Church antiquities. He had brought along his oldest son, Murad, and had had to pinch him, he told me laughingly, to get him to kiss the pope's hand. The young man, in whose hearing this was said, winked at me and jestingly remarked: "Je ne suis pas un lache comme mon pere!" (I am not a coward like my father). Similarly, shortly after his appointment to the post of secretary general of the United Nations was announced, Boutrous Boutrous Ghālī felt compelled to visit the papacy, ostensibly to obtain the pope's blessing for his new mission. Such a show of humility by the upper class would have been unimaginable prior to the advent of Shenuda to the papal throne. These two men, whom I knew well since they were friends of my parents, are both agnostics. They married outside the church—an abomination in the eyes of the Orthodox clergy—and both to Jews at that, a worse abomination. (The Egyptian Orthodox Church still holds to the traditional view of the culpability of the Jews in the killing of Jesus.)

Someone who marries outside the church is considered to be engaged in fornication (*zena*) and is an outcast, as evident in the story told to me by a Greek-Egyptian friend, Lela Petrides. Soon after her marriage, her husband, a Coptic physician of the Orthodox faith, was killed in an automobile accident on the desert road to Alexandria. When the police bearing his bloodied corpse woke her up at seven in the morning, she ran in tears to the neighboring papal headquarters to ask for their help. But the church refused to bury him, because he had married outside his faith (even though she was Greek-Orthodox, she would have had to convert to Egyptian Orthodoxy to be married in the Egyptian Orthodox church, which she refused to do on principle). So she turned in her despair to her own church, which at the beginning also refused to bury him, since he was not Greek, but finally gave in to her tears and put him to rest in the Greek cemetery.

The church has also spared no effort to catch the new upper middle class of successful, well-to-do physicians, engineers, businessmen, travel agents, real estate people, and the like, who have replaced the ancien régime aristocracy and are too preoccupied with advancing their careers to have time for religion, even if they consider the church a nice place to send their wives to on Sundays with the children. These grandees do not deign to mingle with the ordinary people in the general meetings of their local churches. So special meetings, accompanied by prayers and sermons, have been designed for them, both at the diocesan and papal level. The meetings with the pope, which take place both at the patriarchatal and in the Monastery of Bishoi, his weekend retreat, are often organized by profession: groups of prominent journalists, medical doctors, university professors, engineers, and the like are invited in turn.

In one such meeting with a group of well-known Coptic doctors, which a doctor friend of mine, ʻAkil Yūsuf, described to me, the pope at the end of the meeting asked each one to write down what he was prepared to do for the church. Some offered to contribute money, others volunteered their time in church-run clinics, and he himself put down "technical help only"—and indeed he treats bishops, priests, and monks for free in his private practice at the Anglo-American hospital.

All in all, the pope has succeeded in gaining the support of this new upper middle class, because, with a few exceptions such as Akil Yūsuf, whose grandfather was minister of Defense during the heyday of liberal nationalism in Egypt, they are nouveau riche of humble social origins and therefore share the same religio-cultural idiom as the clergy.

Notes

1 See Anba Shenuda, *Hayat al-Iman* (Cario, 1986).
2 Raymond Stock, "Preserving Pharaohs' Psalms," in *Egypt Today* (April 1997).
3 Ibid.
4 Ibid.
5 This information is based on my interviews with church-servants in charge of the duplication and sales of tapes at the Bishopric of Youth and in the different churches throughout the dioceses.
6 For example, when I visited the Abu Talat summer resort with Bishop Tackla in July 1993, the youngsters gathered around him on his arrival and sang such a song. The same thing happened when I visited Nazlit Ebeid in December 1992 with Bishop Arsanios.
7 I observed this during my stay with three families close to the church that were putting me up overnight in Aswan, Tima, and Kafr al-Sheihk.
8 Ibid.
9 Wakin, *A Lonely Minority*, p. 154.
10 This was said to me by both Fakhri Abd al-Nur and Magdi Wahba in the aforementioned interviews.
11 Interview with Bishop Gregorios, (Cairo, February 1992).
12 *Egyptian Gazette.* January 14, 1997.
13 Ibid.

54

RITUAL, HISTORY AND IDENTITY IN GOA

Alexander Henn

Source: Alexander Henn and Klaus-Peter Köpping (eds), *Rituals in an Unstable World: Contingency, Hybridity, Embodiment*, Frankfurt: Peter Lang, 2008, pp. 205–24.

The problem

Jagar[1] or *jagrana* rituals mark a distinct mode of religiosity in Indian Hinduism.[2] The name derives from the Sanskrit notion of *jagr* or 'wakefulness' (Turner 1966: 5174) and refers to religious night vigils that are seasonally celebrated in honor of local deities, saints, ancestors or tutelary beings. The rituals are part of temple, village or domestic festivals and have a special appeal in that they enact a ludic genre of *bhakti*[3] religiosity that combines serious religious ritual, namely sacrifice, invocation and prayer, with joyful entertainment in the form of music, singing, dancing and, in some regions, also mask and theatre plays.

The focus in this chapter is on *jagar* rituals celebrated in the villages of the Indian state of Goa by members of traditional small farmer, agricultural laboring and fishing castes, many of whom earn their living today in the service sector or through temporary labor migration to the Persian Gulf states. The Goan *jagare* are conspicuous for the fact that they transgress the realm of Hinduism and also form a part of the local Catholic liturgy. More precisely, four variations of *jagar* are celebrated in Goa today: 1) one that is performed exclusively by Hindus; 2) one that is performed exclusively by Catholics; 3) one that is jointly performed by Hindus and Catholics; and 4) one that is performed by Hindus but nevertheless includes Catholic elements. Variations 3 and 4, on which I shall concentrate in this chapter, are characterized by distinctly hybrid features in which their practitioners perform a syncretic mode of worship that pays religious homage simultaneously to Hindu and Christian divinities and sacredness. In addition, the linguistic and literary structures of the prayers and songs also show hybrid patterns by making parallel use of Konkani and Portuguese, Sanskrit and

Latin, and by referring to sacred texts and mythological plots from both the Hindu-Indian and the Luso-Catholic traditions. It is not uncommon, therefore, for the celebrants to start the ceremonies by invoking the Christian Trinity – "Deu Bapa, Deu Putra ani Ispirita Santa" – followed by invocations of Saibini Mai, the Virgin Mary, and a list of Catholic patron saints, only to change over at some point to further invocations of Maha Dev, Narayana, Ganesha, Lakshmi and other pan-Indian Hindu gods and goddesses, followed by Sateri and Shanta Durga, the most prominent local incarnations of Hindu female divinity, and finally an equally long list of Hindu *gramadevata* or village gods. These invocations or *namana* mark the beginning and end of the ceremonies and frame the ludic performances. These are exclusively presented by men and boys on a temporary stage or a central village square that marks a sacred space (*mand*) for the time of the ritual. The performances themselves take the form of a series of theatrical plays that combine song, dance and costumes with rudimentary theatrical acting. Though again alluding eclectically to Hindu and Christian themes and genres, especially the Hindu epics *Mahabharata* and *Ramayana* and the lore of Catholic hagiography, the plays are not confined to religious motifs, nor do they follow any master narrative, but enact a series of short stories presenting an enormous variety of mythical themes, historical episodes and day-to-day scenes from village life.

Although presenting a distinct case of religious syncretism and cultural hybridity, it is important to note that the rituals do not produce any confusion among their practitioners and audiences regarding religious identity. Indeed, although Hindus and Catholics perform the ceremonies jointly, they consciously, and at times even jealously, maintain certain distinctions and a certain distance between one another. Hence, in all villages, the two religious groups act discretely and present a different cultural habitus in the ceremonies. These distinctions are clearly marked even when homage is being paid to divine or saintly beings whose identity indeed oscillates between Hindu and Catholic, for instance, by presenting different types of offerings to them, such as oil in the case of Hindus and candles in the case of Catholics. In fact, in many villages one can even observe a certain competition between Hindus and Catholics over the leadership or other organizational aspects of the ceremonies. Moreover, in a number of villages the political self-assertion of Hindus in recent years can be seen to have initiated a kind of 'Hinduization' which implies the gradual removal of Catholic elements from the *jagar* ceremonies, for instance, by changing the dates or sites of the performances from those that have significance to Catholics to ones that are important to Hindus, or by inserting Hindu deities and other Hindu elements into otherwise predominantly Catholic texts and performances.

These Goan ceremonies thus present an intriguingly complex case of inter-religious and intercultural practice that resists theoretical reductionism in two ways. First, they cannot be restricted to the classical idea that rituals enact cultural intelligibilities that demarcate religions and cultures as bounded "meaning systems" (Geertz 1966). Nor, secondly, can they be resolved into the post-modern idea that religious beliefs and cultural practices by necessity reject theological orthodoxies and cultural boundary-marking, but instead produce hybridity and flux as the ontic state or "predicament of culture" (Clifford 1988). As Pnina Werbner puts it with a slightly different focus, "cultural hybridity masks an elusive paradox. [It] is celebrated as powerfully interruptive and yet theorized as commonplace and pervasive" (Werbner 2000: 1). Interestingly, a number of writings confirming that co-optations of essentialist *and* hybrid views and practices are the rule rather than the exception in processes of religious and cultural encounter also support the observation that rituals play an important role in what is variously called 'acculturation' (Assayag and Tarabout 1977), 'syncretism' (Shaw and Stewart 1994), or 'hybridity' (Werbner 2000, Bhabha 1994). Nevertheless little has been said so far why it is precisely in and through rituals that people seem to indulge in the paradox of simultaneously asserting and subverting religious identities by confirming and transgressing cultural boundaries respectively.

The historical narrative

To begin with, the background to the hybridity in Goa is obvious: for more than 450 years, from 1510 to 1961, the coastal region that constitutes today the Indian federal state of Goa was under Portuguese colonial rule and Catholic hegemony. Mass conversion campaigns, conducted by the missionaries of various Catholic orders, and accompanied by the extensive destruction of temples and mosques, led in the sixteenth and seventeenth centuries to a massive exodus of Hindus and Muslims and a steady growth in the number of Christians. This demographic shift reached a peak in the first half of the eighteenth century, when Christians constituted more than 90% of Goa's population (Srivastava 1990). The adoption of the Portuguese language, Portuguese dress and food habits, Portuguese styles of architecture, music, arts and sports by upper-caste converts led to the development of specific Lusitanian features in both public and private life. However, radical though the impact of Portuguese colonialism and Catholic proselytism was on Goan society and culture, it was never able to achieve the declared ambition of the foreign rulers of transforming the Asian colony into a sort of overseas Portugal. Instead, hegemonic aspirations were contested by a small but powerful section of Hindu society which asserted its considerable economic and political influence throughout the colonial period (Pearson 1973; De Souza 1975). More important still, economic, political and demographic changes kept cultural power relations in Goa fluid. Of crucial importance here was the growing economic crisis in the Asian colony, which, ever since the mid-nineteenth century, resulted in the mass emigration of Goan

Catholics to British India and elsewhere. In the twentieth century, the demographic shift was accelerated by political reforms which gradually improved the political and social situation of Hindus in Goa and eventually granted them the right to practice their religion again. This liberalization was fostered as much by constitutional changes back in Portugal (which was declared a republic in 1910) as by the rise of the nationalist movement in British India (which gained independence in 1947) and encouraged Hindus to (re-)migrate to Goa. Returning, first gradually, then in large numbers to the Portuguese-dominated area, Hindus brought about a revival of Hindu culture in Goa and since 1910 they have constituted a religious majority there. In 1961, Goa was liberated from Portuguese domination by the Indian Army and subsequently, in 1987, integrated as a separate state into the Indian Union (Newman 1988). In the post-colonial period, fundamental social and political changes, in particular the establishment of a secular and democratic constitution, laid the groundwork for a pluralistic culture in the new state, whose little over one million inhabitants are divided today into roughly 65% Hindus, 29% Christians and 5% Muslims (Government of Goa 1996: 16).[4]

Like the history of Hinduism in general, the history of the *jagar* rituals shifted in Goa. Archival as well as ethnographic evidence indicates that *jagar* rituals had been celebrated as part of Hindu temple festivals before the advent of the Portuguese.[5] Some time during the sixteenth and seventeenth centuries, Jesuit missionaries transformed the *jagar* into a Catholic rite, henceforth pronounced *zagor*, that became part of the annual church festivals celebrated in honor of local patron saints. More precisely, the missionaries assimilated the performative and ludic style of the Hindu *jagar*, substituted its Hindu content with Catholic meanings, in particular replacing the invocations of Hindu deities and village gods by invocations of the Christian Trinity and Catholic saints. In addition, in the same period all Hindu rituals, including the life-cycle ceremonies for births, marriages and deaths, were banned and suppressed in the Portuguese-controlled territories. The transformation from *jagar* to *zagor* thus enacted a form of iconoclastic appropriation that was widespread in contemporary religious conquests, taking the form of the assimilation of literary styles of religious Hindu texts in the production of Indian-language 'translations' of Christian hagiographies, catechisms and bibles, which, paradoxically, went together with the mass destruction of Hindu books and texts in so-called *autos-da-fe* or acts-of-faith (Henn forthcoming). In addition, the transformation of the *jagar* genre also had its parallel in the construction of Catholic churches, chapels and crosses at the sites of already destroyed Hindu temples, shrines and images, often using rubble from them in the new construction (Mitterwallner 1983). As with iconoclastic violence in general, however, paradoxically, and in a distinct way, the destruction did not annihilate so much as confirm the power and preserve the memory of what had been destroyed precisely because it had been considered worthy of destruction. Like the Christian texts that had assimilated Hindu literary styles and the churches that had replaced the Hindu temples, therefore, the Catholic *zagor* that had replaced the Hindu *jagar* also became predestined for syncretistic worship.

In response, the local Church and state authorities started a campaign in the eighteenth century attempting to ban the *zagor* and other Catholic practices that had assimilated Hindu traits by defaming them as "superstitious", "immoral" and "pagan" customs (Henn 2003: 134f.). Although variously repeated throughout the nineteenth centuries and persecuted by severe punishments, the subsequent renewal of the ban in 1905 indicates that a number of villages had long resisted the suppression of their *zagor*:

> We reconfirm all that had been ordered earlier regarding the superstitious and immoral entertainment of the so-called Zagor and we keep up the prohibition, issued likewise by our predecessors, to show the Most Sacred Sacrament and to perform processions in those communities in which it [the *zagor*] took place. And knowing that this ceremony is of pagan origin, the priests shall be neither reluctant nor hesitant to ask the worldly authorities for its suppression and to enforce ecclesiastical punishments against the excuses and deceptions used by some persons not to have the measures applied that prohibit this [ceremony]. The hidden and almost dark spot at which the Zagor is performed at late hours, the gathering of people of both sexes and all generations for so many hours during the night, suffices, apart from anything else, to prohibit this barbaric entertainment.
>
> (Decreto Diocesano, issued 1905, cit. Albuquerque 1922: 249; translation and additions A.H.).

The impression that, by the turn of the twentieth century, the *zagor* ceremonies had developed into a serious case of political subversion against Portuguese-Catholic rule is also supported by the ethnographic evidence. Thus older *zagor* activists remember that by then the ceremonies had become a popular platform for political criticism, propagating, for instance, the activities and ideas of the emerging *satyagraha* movement, which was agitating for India's independence from colonial rule. As a countermove, the government forces in Goa, despite their partial withdrawal from Church politics in the eighteenth century, intensified their control of the *zagor* ceremonies by introducing a special censorship to prevent any manifestation of anti-colonial activities, such as mentioning Mahatma Gandhi, Jawaharlal Nehru or any other spokesmen of the Indian nationalist movement. Nevertheless, people still remember, with a degree of satisfaction, that the *zagor* practitioners still found ways to undermine the censorship, for instance, by using a specially camouflaged form of Konkani that was understood by Goan villagers, but not Portuguese officials.

Nonetheless the complete suppression of the Catholic *zagor* would only have been a matter of time, had it not ironically been for the re-strengthening of Hinduism in Goa, which prevented this. More precisely, two developments lead to the survival of the *jagrana* tradition in late-colonial Goa. This was first the gradual repopulation of predominantly Catholic areas by Hindus. In particular, in the village Siolim in Bardes, the returning Hindus became active participants in the local *zagor* rituals, thus initiating the most conspicuous example of a public ritual jointly performed by Hindus and Catholics in Goa today. Although the local mythology cited by Catholics today alludes to some initial animosities between the two communities, with Hindus being accused of the 'robbery of the (sacred) coconuts' representing certain ancestors honoured in the ceremonies, the joint performance of the Siolim *zagor* by Hindus and Catholics has become an established and popular festivity that attracts thousands of devotees and spectators from both religious communities every year (Gomez 1991).

A similar historical development is documented for the *zagor* ceremonies performed by the ethnic group of Goan Gaude, most of whom live in the provinces of Tiswadi and Ponda. There is evidence that a large part of the Gaude population were converted to Catholicism by Jesuit and Franciscan missionaries in the sixteenth and seventeenth centuries and, as a consequence, transformed their traditional *jagar* into a Catholic ceremony. Yet though they had been subjected to mass conversion and enjoyed little Christian education, the Gaude remained only a marginally Christianized group in Goa. This caught the attention of the Hindu reform movement, the Arya Samaj, which, in the late nineteenth century, started a campaign to bring people whose ancestors had once converted to Islam or Christianity back into the fold of Hinduism (Jaffrelot 1994). In Goa, the *suddhi* or 'purification' ceremonies, held to reconvert Catholics to Hinduism, were prepared and organized by the prelate of a Vaishnavite monastery, who toured the villages of the Gaude with a troop of Hindu priests and monks singing devotional *bhakti* songs, performing *puja* sacrifices and preaching on ancient Hindu texts (Kakodkar 1988: 250). Moreover, by promising possible converts their protection against opposition from the Portuguese and Catholic authorities, Arya Samaj activists eventually succeeded in reconverting the considerable number of 7815 Catholic Gaude in a series of *suddhi* ceremonies in 1927 (Kakodkar 1988: 253).

These two historical events, the return of Hindus to predominantly Catholic areas and the re-conversion of Catholics to Hinduism, had important effects on the *zagor* tradition. First, the total extinction of the ceremonies intended by the Catholic Church was prevented by the fact that returning or re-converted Hindus, who henceforth participated in or continued respectively the local *zagores*, were no longer subject to the power of the sanctions of the Catholic Church. Secondly, henceforth the surviving *zagores* acquired the hybrid or syncretic aspects described at the beginning of this chapter. Nevertheless, it should be emphasized that neither in Siolim nor among the Gaude did the syncretic practices effect a blurring of the religious identities of the people who were participating in them. Instead, the Siolim *zagor* shows – though vicariously for other rituals in Goa in which members of both religious communities take part – that Hindus and Catholics consciously act discretely, even while indulging in common worship and invoking divinities and saints who formally belong to the opposite tradition. Similarly, the Gaude self-confidently emphasize their 'newly' achieved Hindu identity today while at the same time paying homage to the Christian Trinity and Catholic saints, who clearly remain of religious significance to them, even after their reconversion to Hinduism. In general, the two cases thus reveal that people indeed simultaneously assert and undermine their own religious identities, both stressing and transgressing the boundaries between Hinduism and Catholicism, thus rendering obsolete any theoretical position in trying to reduce their doing either to an essentialist or hybrid perspective.

The ritual performance

In order to account for these complexities, we must examine the ritual performance itself, which arguably constitutes historical memory and shapes identities in ways that differ from those of the historical narrative. The ritual modalities come to the fore in various performative devices, analysis of which may begin by looking at the prayer that opened the *zagor* ceremonies in the Gaude village of Kakra (Tiswadi Province) in 1994. The prayer was recited by the oldest woman of the leading Gaude clan in the *devace khud* or 'gods' room' of her house, in which images and idols of the deities, saints and ancestors mentioned in the prayer were displayed. Densely crowded into the room, the other members of the Gaude clan and most of the performers of the *zagor* play being performed, some already dressed in their costumes, followed the prayer and afterwards proceeded in solemn procession to the ceremonial house at the central village square, where the public ceremonies started. The prayer was as follows:

> "Devu, we ask you, Ganv Mai, we ask you, Kuris, we ask you, Bautis, we ask you;
>
> Here is our Odil, we ask you and pray to you, guide us well (to the ceremonial house) and bring us back well;
>
> Guide them (the performers) well and bring them back well, without all obstacles;
>
> This is your ceremony, you created it; let it be well;
>
> If we have committed mistakes, forgive us;
>
> And we ask you too, Fatorpekarin, with folded hands,

> And Sateri and Ravalnath and Vetal Devu, that all these men may return well and the ceremony may work well;
>
> Here at your feet, the whole *dhajan* (literally the 'ten person', viz. the village council) has gathered; they too shall come back well.

At this point, another person interrupted the prayer leader, saying: "Pray also to this god", upon which the prayer leader asked, "What is his name?". The person answered: "Jhariveilo", 'The-One-From-The-Spring'. The prayer leader continued:

> "We have prayed. If we have forgotten you, forgive us;
>
> We are ignorant, you are knowledgeable;
>
> What you once did, we are doing now;
>
> You have planted the *maddi* (the ritual poles) and constructed the *mand* (the ceremonial house);
>
> Like this it shall happen also now"

In detail, the prayer thus pays homage to the following beings: Devu, God, the generic Konkani notion of whom resonates in both the Sanskrit *deva* and the Latin *deus;* Ganv Mai, literally the 'village mother' or village goddess, whose Sanskritized name is also *gramadevi*; Kuris, the creolized version of the Portuguese *cruz*, referring here to the patron saint of the nearby town of Santa Cruz,[6] who is embodied in a large stone cross in the central village square of Kakra; Bautis, i.e. San João Baptista or St. John the Baptist; Odil, the 'ancestor'; Fatorekarin, the Hindu family goddess of the Gaude clan, whose temple is in the South Goan town of Fatorpa, from where the Gaude claim descent; Sateri, the most widespread Hindu female deity in Goa and *gramadevi* of Santa Cruz, whose temple was destroyed during the early period of Christianization and was rebuilt only in the nineteenth century; Ravalnath and Vetal, two popular male Hindu village gods, who once had temples in Santa Cruz, which were also destroyed, and of whom Ravalnath is regularly remembered when the annual procession carrying the idol of Sateri through Santa Cruz stops at the site of his former temple for prayers; and finally Jhariveilo, the 'tutelary god', who guards one of Kakra's natural springs and also marks the boundary between *ran,* the wilderness, and *vado,* the village territory.

What should particularly be noted about this *omnium gatherum* of divine and saintly beings is its cosmological ambition, that is, the attempt by those who are praying to pay homage to all the deities and saints who presently are and historically were of significance to them and their village. This ambition is grounded in the belief that gods or saints may become unforgiving and inflict hazards and evils on people when they are ritually neglected, something that plays a critical role in the performance of the ritual. Hence, the domestic prayer was only the prelude to the elaborate *namana* hymns, which were intoned little later in the ceremonial house by a chorus of men paying homage to a much larger series of divinities and saints, including in particular the Christian Trinity, Jesus, the Saviour, the Twelve Apostles, various manifestations of the Virgin Mary, St. Francis Xavier and numerous other Catholic patron saints, as well as the Hindu deities Ganesha, Krishna and Shanta Durga, and a similarly numerous series of the Hindu deities of neighbouring villages and regions of Goa. Even this does not conclude the long list, which in Kakra, as well as in other villages, may easily include several dozen divine and sacred beings. The *namana* hymn that closes the ceremonies at sunrise after the night-long dancing and singing finally ended by paying homage to:

> *baslele sabhek*, 'all [sacred and human beings] sitting in the assembly;[7]
>
> *tihthis koti*, the proverbial '33 million gods' living in India; and, finally,
>
> *cuklya maklya deva*, 'all the other deities' whom one might possibly have forgotten.

The *namana* hymns are very old texts, handed down orally and nowadays often also in hand-written manuscripts from 'originals' dating back to the times when the Christian missionaries transformed, as it were, the Hindu *jagar* into the Catholic *zagor*. Their word-for-word recitation marks one of the indispensable elements of *jagar* or *zagor* performances, notwithstanding the fact that the historical vicissitudes of the *jagrana* tradition have left their marks on them. Hence, many of the *namana* texts – and also the ancient texts recited in the ludic part – are cryptic and make it difficult, if not impossible, fully to decode or reconstruct their meanings today, due to the fact that their heteroglossic combination of Konkani and Portuguese, occasionally shot through with Marathi, Sanskrit and even Latin insertions, shows a multitude of semantic gaps, syntactical muddles and grammatical flaws. Therefore, the singers recite a considerable part of the hymns using a phonetic rather than semantic memory, repeating the words and articulating the sounds without fully understanding their meaning. Moreover, the texts reflect the theological shifts that have affected the *jagar* / *zagor* genre throughout its history, in particular the late- and post-colonial renaissance of Hinduism, revealing the insertion of Hindu elements into their otherwise primarily Christian content. Interestingly, though, a closer examination indicates that these changes were not carried out randomly, but followed a pattern that consciously retained certain performative traits, while changing the contents of the texts. One illustration of this is a passage in the *namana* hymns of Kakra that reveals the insertion of the elephant-headed Hindu god

Ganesha, here called Gajanan, just after the invocation of Deva, Deva Bapa ani Ispirta Santa, that is, the Christian God and the Holy Spirit. The exact wording of the insertion reads: *Varnea vrate Gajanan jhala, sant ani bhagevanta,* a cryptic passage that can only approximately be translated as: 'Worship is done, Ganesha comes, the Holy One and Saintly One'. Comparing this passage with the *namana* text from the neighboring village, from which the Kakra people claim to have 're-learned' the *namana* after their *zagor* ceased for a certain period following the reconversion of their parents to Hinduism in 1928, reveals a slight but interesting variation. Hence, the text of the neighboring village reads: *Varnea vrate igrojan jhala, sant ani bhagevanta,* which can be translated as: 'In order to worship, come to the Church, the Holy One and Saintly One'.[8] What is conspicuous here is not so much the insertion of the Hindu God into the text, but the way this is done. The text recited in Kakra differs by just a single word from the text from the neighboring village, in which *igrojan* is replaced by Gajanan, and, more strikingly even, the substitute words are phonetically similar.

The fact that this interpolation into the traditional text of the *namana* obviously takes special care to modify its performative structure only minimally suggests a conscious strategy. The performance of the texts, it is evident, is given equal significance to the meanings of the texts. The ritual, in other words, has its *raison d'être* as much in what it does as in what it signifies, while the phonetic structure and intonation of the *namana* are as important and critical as its meaning. This equivalence, if not the primacy of the performance in relation to the semantics, becomes generally visible in the Konkani word *devukar* for 'ritual' which combines Devu, God, with *kar,* the root of the word 'to do'. Conversely, despite its etymological affinity with 'name', the *namana* enacts more than the textual naming or invocation, that is, the practical embodiment or evocation of divine and saintly beings. Putting it in semiotic terms, the hymns do not so much articulate symbolic references to the gods and saints as effect iconic or indexical embodiments of them. These embodiments take different, albeit often related and overlapping forms. One form is spatial in nature, which means that it associates divine and saintly beings with distinct spaces and localities. Enacting this form of embodiment, the *jagar / zagor* evokes all the deities, saints and ancestors who are considered the owners, inhabitants or protectors of the village's territory, its central and liminal localities, its quarters, boundaries, fields and waters, as well as its wilderness, forests and seas, and also its vicinity, neighbourhood and the places of origin of its people. In this way, the *namana* hymns, and the ritual performance in general, are turned, as it were, into a virtual journey or pilgrimage through the sacred landscape that constitutes, structures and embeds the village realm.

Another form of embodiment is iconic. This form associates divine and sacred beings with images and material and natural objects, some of which are thought to share similarities or affinities with what they stand for.

Ranging from anthropomorphic images and idols representing gods and saints, via crosses and shrines (*gumti*) standing for patron saints and village deities, to natural objects such as coconuts, trees and rocks signifying ancestors and tutelary beings, the *jagar* / *zagor* evokes a multitude of iconic embodiments. The corporeal essence of this form of embodiment is perhaps best represented by two particular religious figures. One is St. Francis Xavier, the patron saint of Goa as a whole, who is simply addressed as *khud,* the 'body', a reference to his mummy, which is preserved in a sarcophagus of glass in the cathedral of Old Goa. The other is the Hindu goddess Sateri, also venerated as Bhumika, the Earth Goddess, who is embodied in sacred anthills – an allusion to the fact that the soil of the village is actually the body of the *gramadevi* herself.

The most important form of embodiment, however, is performative, a form that associates divine and sacred beings with the enactment of the ritual itself. More precisely, the *jagar* / *zagor* practitioners take the bodily activities of the ritual, that is, the drumming, dancing and singing – arguably, in precisely that order – to evoke the presence and effect the protective forces of the gods, saints and ancestors. This being so, it is in particular the sacred oil lamp – placed at the centre of the sacred space that marks the stage, right between the chorus of the men singing the *namana* hymns and the dancers performing individually or in groups the *songe* or 'characters' of the play – that embodies the gods and saints during the ceremonies. Strikingly, therefore, in most villages, the dancers always face the oil lamp during their performance, thus turning their backs on their human audience sitting around or in front of the 'stage'.

The performative *praesentia* of sacred and social beings becomes most palpable where the religious and ludic parts of the ceremonies meet. In the village of Siolim, the *omnium gatherum* of deities and saints honoured in the ritual is presided over by the local god Zagoryo, who, as indicated by his name, embodies the entire ritual and represents one of the characters on the stage. In fact, the scene of Zagoryo, who is also called Bhovor, 'The-Turning-One', and who is represented by a dancer turning slowly around his own axis, marks the climax of Siolim's *zagor* play in which otherwise Firanghi Raja ani Sayid, 'the Foreign (European) King and his Local Adversary', Maloni, 'the Gardeners', and Mhar ani Mharin, 'the Dalit and his Wife', are performed.

Although the *zagor* plays of Kakra and other Gaude villages do not have a central mimetic embodiment of the divine, they do act out a number of divine and semi-divine beings on stage, such as Gairama, the lady associated with Bhumi Mai, the Hindu 'Earth Mother'; Rusari Mai, the Catholic 'Mother of the Rosary', who 'visits the temples and churches of all neighbouring villages'; Lakshmi Kansatli Nar, the Hindu 'Rice Goddess', who 'protects the patty fields of the village'; and Semotri, 'the Wandering Ascetic', who is also called Shambu and whose costume and wild dance clearly alludes to the great Hindu god Shiva. The mimetic embodiment of these divine and semi-divine beings is completed by the multitude of ludic 'characters' that are variously introduced by Gorasher, the 'Trickster', who takes on different disguises. Occupational and caste positions mark the largest group of characters, among others Madval ani Madvalin, 'the Washermen and his Wife'; Perni, 'the Pearl Vendor; Vadar, 'the Stonemason'; Kalyar ani Kalyarin, 'the Tinker and his Wife'; Sambar, 'the Spice Vendor'; Govli, 'the Milkman'; Mhalo, 'the Barber'; Poder, 'the Baker'; Capekar, 'the Flower Vendor', and Gosavi, 'the Beggar and Fortune Teller'. Another group of characters consists of mythological figures, precarious kinship relations and often ridiculed social authorities, such as Hariscandra ani Caramati, 'the Hindu King and his Wife', Mama ani Batco, 'the Uncle', who is murdered by his 'Nephew'; Nikandar ani Porpoti, 'the Tax Collector and Village Barker'; Bhamon, the local Hindu Brahman; and in several variations Soldad Portugalre, 'Portuguese soldiers'. The stories of Josepha ani Soldad Portugalre, 'the Catholic Girl and the Portuguese Soldiers', Tendli ani Dadlo, 'the Hindu Woman and the Male Visitor', and Mari Bejel ani Firgin, 'the Catholic Girl and the (European) Stranger', are all variations on the common theme of illegitimate gender relations and amorous adventures. Finally, the *jagar* play presents a variety of characters who, from one perspective or another, mark 'strangers', such as Hindustan Dadlo ani Hindustan Bail, 'the Indian Man and the Indian Wife'; Firanghi, 'the Frank', who has become synonymous with the historical European; Hapshi, 'the (Black) African'; Khan Saib, 'the Muslim Merchant'; Paklo, the historical 'Portuguese'; and in some villages also Hippie, the popular term for the international tourists who have been frequenting Goa's beaches since the 1960s. By linking the gods, saints and ancestors evoked in the *namana* hymns and numerically presented on stage to this multitude of ludic characters, the performances gradually populate the sacred space of the stage, as it were, with all the divine, saintly, ancestral, mythological, authoritative and social persons that historically constituted and presently constitute the village world.

As mentioned earlier, the plays are performed by sumptuously costumed boys and men presenting a combination of dance, song and some theatrical acting. The songs are usually sung as a kind of dialogue between the dancers and the chorus of men sitting on the *mand*, who also play the cymbals and drums. However, although the stories therefore enact a series of sketches that present comic and dramatic stories that the audiences enjoy, strikingly they are not central to the quality of a *jagar / zagor* performance. Instead, when people are asked what makes a good *jagar / zagor*, they point to the vitality of the drumming and dancing, rather than the contents of the songs and sketches. In fact, it is argued that the more enthusiastically and tirelessly the performers beat the drums, move their dancing bodies and sing songs throughout the night, the more it can be expected that the sacred beings will stay awake too and protect the village from all manner of evil for the whole of the coming year. The most essential value of the ritual, in other words, is its very activity, which is mimetically transformed into divine bliss. The notion of *devukar*, of 'doing in the name of God', it can be argued, is qualified here by the notion of *mimesis*, which renders ritual an *imitatio dei* or imitation of god. Or, putting it differently yet again, notwithstanding its affinity to theatre, the *mimesis* of the *jagar / zagor* has its value not in what it represents, but in imitating action for action's sake. All the drumming and dancing and singing has eventually only one purpose: not to fall asleep, but to stay awake.

The tautological value of the action alluded to here is ultimately a reference to the subtleties of the Hindu theology that are expressed in the notion of *lila* or 'God's play'. According to the Indologist Norvin Hein (1995), the earliest scriptural evidence of *lila* is found in the Vedantra Sutra, an ancient Hindu text ascribed to the third century B.C., in which the author defends the belief in a divine Creator from the objection that this contradicts the idea of Divinity as all-embracing and omniscient, since creation reveals the need of something. The author replies that creativity and activity do not necessarily emanate from the intention to satisfy any need, but may also be the outcome of an absolutely purposeless, playful joy in action, in which sense God's acts of creation are to be understood. Realized in manifold ways in Hindu mythology, iconography and theatre, *lila* thus marks an ambiguous view of the activity of the gods and its effects on the world: although playful, meaningless and therefore as fickle and unreliable as Maya, the mundane world, the *lila* of the gods, is nevertheless what creates this world and keeps it going.

Conclusion

Returning to the problem posed at the start of how essentialist *and* hybrid perspectives and practices coexist in a situation of religious and cultural encounter, the Goan case suggests the intersection of two different representational and experiential modalities: the historical narrative and the ritual performance.[9] Both modalities realize experiences, articulations and practices that *in toto* mark the religious identities and cultures of Hindus and Catholics, though for various reasons they differ in their negotiation of the relationship between the two religious traditions. One significant difference lies in their different constructions of temporality and history. Itself a complex conceptual construct, the historical narrative can be simplified in two essential ways: first, it represents history as a linear succession of events, while secondly, it is organized as a plot or intelligible whole that governs the succession of events (Ricoeur 1980: 169, 170, passim). The historical narrative thus realizes the "genuine historical time" that characterizes the modern perception of history, following which what comes next necessarily overrides and modifies what had gone before, thus excluding the possibility of a co-temporality of past and present (Koselleck 1984: 58, passim). In the Goan case, it represents the identities of Hindus and Catholics by referring to historical events – in particular, conversions, encounters and migrations – which are taken to inscribe irreversible distinctions between the two communities. These demarcations hold true, even where some sort of reversibility seemed possible, for instance, through the re-conversion of Catholics to Hinduism or the revival of Hinduism in formerly predominantly Catholic areas, since, even then, the polarity between the two traditions persisted and could be overcome only through radical transformations.[10] More generally, the historical narrative tells of the origins, values and continuities that constituted and still constitute Catholicism and Hinduism as syndicated and separate religious traditions.

Ritual performance, in contrast, conceptualizes and communicates temporality and identity by performative operations whose coordination relies on neither the linear sequence of events, nor the logocentric organization of a plot. Instead, the ritual performance realizes a representational and experiential modus whose logic is localistic, objective and practical. In semiotic terms, it articulates meanings through the spatial and graphic embodiment and the mimesis that is realized in the icon and the index, rather than the logocentric convention that governs the symbol (Jacobson 1965). Thus, in the Goan ritual, gods, saints and ancestors are invoked not only by reference to their name, but also their manifestation in space, image and other iconic forms and, more importantly still, by the mimetic enacting of their qualities. In doing so, the ritual effects a *praesentia* of the divine and saintly beings that re-presents and re-enacts events who (are taken to) have manifested themselves in the past. Interestingly, these performative operations do nothing to blur the religious distinctions between Hindus and Catholics. However, unlike the temporal logic of the narrative, which constitutes the distinctions between the incisive and transformative events which, by definition, render their co-temporality impossible – that is, always only permits one to be either a Hindu or a Catholic – the performative logic of the ritual constitutes the distinctions with reference to bodily manifestations which may coexist in space and time, i.e. that permit belonging to a certain territory, or the embodiment in a certain iconic form, to overrule belonging to a different religious tradition.

In general, therefore, the Goan case emphasizes political and theoretical assumptions about the relationship between the ritual and social worlds, that is, between religion and politics. In political terms, it demonstrates that one and the same ritual may both affirm and subvert the identities and values that are valid in the socio-political world. Hence, while Hindus and Catholics self-consciously articulate their respective religious identities and cultural distinctions in the ritual, they strikingly subvert the political meaning of conversions and counteract the politically correct intercourse between the different religions by paying homage to deities and saints and by participating in modes of worship that formally belong to the 'other' religious tradition. In theoretical terms, the Goan case therefore suggests that ritual performance constitutes historical memory (Assmann 1988) and cultural identities in relative autonomy from the socio-political world, thus marking a kind of parallelism that paradoxically reminds of the pre-modern times when religion and politics marked two competing, but equivalent and above all inseparable domains of society and culture. This being the case, it stresses both theories that see ritual performance as being in a close representational (Tambiah 1979) or transformative (Schieffelin 1998) relationship with the social world, thus emphasising its potential autonomy, and theories that claim the existence of a fundamental rupture between ritual performance and sociopolitical meanings (Humphrey and Laidlaw 1994), thus emphasizing its potentially catalytic affirmative and subversive functions.

Notes

1 For convenience, diacritical signs have been omitted.
2 *Jagrana* ceremonies are performed in many parts of India and are especially popular in the western Himalayas (Gaborieau 1975), Rajasthan (Thiel-Horstmann 1985), Gujarat and Punjab (Erndl 1993) and Goa (Khedekar 1983, Verenkar 1991, Gomes and Shirodkar 1999, Henn 2003, 2004).
3 Literally translated as 'participation' or 'devotion', *bhakti* characterizes a form of Hindu piety that favors an intimate relationship with a personalized god and, to some extent, constitutes a demotic counter-current to certain aspects of Brahmanical theology and temple religiosity.
4 For a general overview of Goa's colonial and post-colonial political history, see Pearson 1987, Esteves 1986.
5 The first archival documentation of a *jagar* ritual in Goa dates from a Portuguese tax list valid for the period 1567–1585 (Foral de Salcete 1990; see also Henn 2003: 123).
6 Santa Cruz is the parish to which Kakra belongs.
7 Sabha, 'assembly' or 'society', refers to all human and divine *ganvkars*, that is, 'genuine villagers' of Kakra who have the right to sit in the sacred space in which the *zagor* is performed.
8 The text continues by paying homage to the Church itself: 'Let us honor Mother Church, let us respect the Church; Mother Church teaches the lessons, let us learn her lessons', so that the epithets of the 'Holy One' and 'Saintly One' may be attributable to the personified Church itself.
9 On narration and performance, see Bauman 1997.
10 It is this narrative logic which older theories of acculturation and syncretism used to mark hybridity as a generally transformative and temporary phenomenon.

Bibliography

Albuquerque, Manuel J. S. de 1922: Sumario Cronologico de Decretos Diocesanos do Arcebispado. Desde 1775 até 1922, Rachol 1922: Paroco de Rachol

Assayag, Jackie, and Gilles Tarabout G. 1997: Présentations, in: Altérité et Identité. Islam et Christianisme en Inde, Paris: EHESS

Assmann, Jan 1988: Kollektives Gedächtnis und kulturelle Identität, in: Jan Assmann und Tonio Hölscher (eds.): Kultur und Gedächtnis, Frankfurt: Suhrkamp
Clifford, James 1988: The Predicament of Culture: Twentieth-Century Ethnography, Literature, and Art, Cambridge (Mass.): Harvard University Press
De Souza, Teotonio R. 1975: Glimpses of Hindu Dominance of Goan Economy in the 17th Century, in: Indica 1975/12: 27–35
Erndl, M. Kathleen 1993: Victory to the Mother: The Hindu Goddess of Northwest India in Myth, Ritual, and Symbol, New York: Oxford University Press
Esteves, Sart, 1986: Politics and Political Leadership in Goa, Delhi: Sterlin
Foral de Salcete (1567–1585) 1990: in: Purabhilekh-Puratatva 8,2: 33–71
Gaborieau, Marc 1975: La Transe Rituelle Dans L'Himalaya Central: Folie, Avatar, Meditation, in: Purusartha 2:147–172
Geertz, C. 1966: Religion as a Cultural System, in: M. Banton (ed.): Anthropological Approaches to the Study of Religion, London: Tavistock
Government of Goa 1996: Directorate of Planning and Statistics and Evaluation: Statistical Pocket Book of Goa 1993–94, Panaji 1996: Government Printing Press
Hein, Norvin 1995: Lila, in: William Sax (ed.): The Gods at Play: Lila in South Asia, Oxford: Oxford University Press
Henn, Alexander (forthcoming): Jesuit Rhetorics: Translation and Conversion in Early-Modern Goa, in: Ivo Strecker, Christian Meyer and Felix Girke (eds.): The Constitutive Interplay Between Rhetoric and Culture, Berghahn Books
—— 2003: Wachheit der Wesen: Politik, Ritual und Kunst der Akkulturation in Goa, Münster 2003: Lit
Homi, Bhabha 1994: The Location of Culture, London: Routledge
Humphrey, Caroline, and James Laidlaw 1994: The Archetypal Actions of Ritual: A Theory of Ritual Illustrated by the Jain Rite of Worship, Oxford: Clarendon Press
Jaffrelot, Christophe 1994: Les (re)conversions a l'Hinduisme (1885–1990): Politisation et diffusion d'une 'invention de la tradition', in: Archives de Sciences Sociales des Religions 87: 73–98
Kakodkar, Archana 1988: Shuddhi: Reconversion to Hinduism in Goa, in: P. P. Shirodkar, (ed.): Goa: Cultural Trends, Panjim 1988: Directorate of Archives, Archaeology and Museum
Khedekar, V. 1983: Rythm and Revelry, The Folk Performers in: Saryn Doshi (ed.): Goa: Cultural Pattern, Bombay: Marg Publications
Koselleck, Reinhart 1984: Vergangene Zukunft: Zur Semantik geschichtlicher Zeiten, Frankfurt: Suhrkamp
Mitterwallner, Gritli von 1983: Testimonials of Heroism: Memorial Stones and Structures, in: Saryn Doshi (ed.): Goa: Cultural Pattern, Bombay: Marg Publications
Newman, Robert 1988: Konkani Mai Ascends the Throne: The Cultural Basis of Goan Statehood, in: South Asia 11,1: 1–24
Pearson, Michel 1987: The Portuguese in India, Cambridge: Cambridge University Press
Schieffelin, Edward, L. 1998: Problematizing Performance, in: Felicia Hughes-Freeland(ed): Ritual, Performance, Media, pp. 194–207, London: Routledge
Shaw, R. and C. Stewart 1994: Introduction: Problematizing Syncretism, in: C. Stewart and R. Shaw (eds.): Syncretism / Anti-Syncretism. The Politics of Religious Synthesis, London and New York: Routledge, pp. 1–26

Srivastava, Harish C. 1990: Demographic History and Human Resources, in: T. De Souza (ed.): Goa Through the Ages: An Economic History, Vol. II, Delhi: Concept Publishing House

Tambiah, S. J., 1979: A Performative Approach to Ritual, in: Proceedings of the British Academy, 65: 113–167, London: Oxford University Press

Thiel-Horstmann, Monika 1985: Nächtliches Wachen: Eine Form indischen Gottesdienstes, Bonn: Indica et Tibetica

Turner, R. L. 1966: A Comparative Dictionary of the Indo-Aryan Language, London: Oxford University Press

Verenkar, Sham 1991: Goenchea Lokvedacho Rupkar, Panjim: Goa Konkani Academy

Werbner, Pnina 2000: Introduction: The Dialectics of Cultural Hybridity, in: P. Werbner and T. Modood (eds.): Debating Cultural Hybridity: Multi-Cultural Identities and the Politics of Anti-Racism, London and New Jersey: Zed Books

55

FELLOWSHIP IN CONTEMPORARY RELIGION AND ETHICS

Report on oral enquiry into beliefs of village people in Catholic diocese of Zhouzi

You Xilin and Chen Lianguo

Source: *China Study Journal*, (Spring/Summer 2007), 68–84.

This is a preliminary report on an oral enquiry into the religious beliefs of Catholics in the diocese of Zhouzhi. The report makes clear the following points:

1 The nature of the knowledge which today's Catholics have of their faith and its impact on their lives is becoming increasingly related to its ethical element. The strange manifestations of a witchcraft culture which formerly persisted in the propagation of this kind of Christianity have now receded into a secondary position. This not only shows the positive approach that religion is taking towards contemporary society but also demonstrates the important distinction between religion and superstitions, which persist in confusing the area of natural cause and effect with that of ethics and belief.

2 The process of the modernization of Chinese society is hastening the breakdown of the functioning of society in rural areas. Not long after the patriarchal clan system lost its position as the controller of ethical standards at the beginning of the 20th century, the people's commune system unified ethical standards to a greater extent than ever before. However, the changes wrought by the modernization programme at the end of the 20th century brought about the dissolution of the entire structure of early modern society and, at the same time, this inevitably had the effect of steadily stripping the political authority of its function of

inculcating ethical principles. At the same time, to make matters worse, the growing process of urbanization brought with it a large-scale movement of the rural population. The fact that large numbers of the rural population have migrated into the towns not only created a 'wasteland' in the country they left behind and changed the basis of traditional production in the villages; it also led to the break-up of rural families, and thus shook traditional ethics to the core. This is how it came about that there is an ethical vacuum in China's agricultural villages nowadays. The individual loneliness to be found in China's rural villages nowadays is something that never existed before. The circumstances of people's lives, and their dire spiritual plight, have combined to produce a need for new ethical principles.

3 For any new ethical principles to fill this gap, they must, in practice, have a traditional content. And the most important element of this is certainly not going to be any theoretical concept, but rather the tradition of fellowship. There are various different kinds of ethical fellowship.

4 The capacity of Christianity to transcend blood relationships gives it an especially useful advantage in China's rural villages, which has enabled it, at the present time, to take on the function of an ethical fellowship. In general, this includes: providing assistance in disasters and mediating in human relationships, especially where religious faith is involved, or in matters related to human behaviour where it is not easy for ordinary social institutions to intervene, such as alleviating depression, providing spiritual support or consoling the bereaved. In such ethical or moral activities (such as talking about romance, or being a good person), Christianity is itself also being influenced by Chinese ethical principles.

The natural environment of Zhouzhi and an outline of its society, economy and spiritual civilization

Zhouzhi diocese enjoys an extremely important status in China because of its religious personalities, its geography and its history: it is not only one of the earliest places in China to have been reached by Christian missionaries, but is also the location of the look-out tower of one of the birthplaces of Daoism, and the location of the Famen temple, a Buddhist holy place. The Catholic diocese of Zhouzhi is the only *national* diocese in Shaanxi province – the significance of 'national' being that it was a priest of Chinese nationality who was the main driving force in the missionary work and administration of the diocese. The diocese was established in the early 1930s, having previously been known as the Guanzhong diocese and before that as the diocese of Shanshaan. The cathedral church of Guanzhong diocese was formerly in Tongyuan township in Gaolu, in Shaanxi province, a township previously known as Tongyuanfang. At first, the Shanshaan diocese had incorporated within its jurisdiction the missionary areas of Shaanxi and Shanxi provinces. The diocese of Zhouzhi was established for missionary purposes in the early part of the 1930s. Church affairs within the diocese were all managed by Chinese personnel, which is why it was known historically as 'the only Chinese diocese in Shanxi and Shaanxi'. Its administrative boundaries include Mei district (xian), Zhouzhi district and Hu district south of the Wei river, and Wugong district, Fufeng district, the town of Xingping and the area (qu) of Yangling north of the Wei river, making a total of five districts, one town and one area, which between them had a total Catholic population in 1999 of over 50,000 people. The Catholics of Zhouzhi diocese thus occupy a significant position among the Catholics of Shaanxi province. In terms of their numbers, the Catholics of Zhouzhi diocese make up over a quarter of the Catholics of that province. The Catholics of Zhouzhi diocese are considered to have the strongest faith and the highest educational standards of all the Catholics in Shaanxi province. There are also Catholics now living in other dioceses who came originally from the diocese of Zhouzhi; for example, many Catholic university graduates from Zhouzhi have gone to live and work in Xi'an, where they formed a distinct group. Many of these people, who found work in Xi'an and have now lived there for a long time, have become members of Xi'an diocese.

The faith of the Catholics of Zhouzhi diocese can be traced back almost to the Ming and Qing periods of the early part of the 17th century, when the missionaries in Shaanxi were members of the Franciscan order. The most remarkable of these men was Father Fang Dewang. It was reckoned at that time that he was probably a contemporary of Xu Guangqi. It is said of him that he performed a number of miracles in Central China and elsewhere, that he once blessed a tiger, and that, when he died, he was buried on the bank of the Shuang river. To express their gratitude to him for his services in saving people's lives by trapping tigers, a temple, called 'Old Father Fang's Temple', was built in memory of his achievements. Church people called him Saint Fang, while people outside the church called him 'dear old Fang'.

When Zhouzhi diocese was first established, its first acting pastor was Father Zhang Zhinan. He was succeeded by Gao Qizheng, who was in turn followed by Gao Zhengyi, and the first Chinese bishop to take office was Bishop Li Baiyu. As Zhang Zhinan, Gao Qizheng and Gao Zhengyi had all been priests undertaking the duties of bishop, they were all called administrators or acting bishops. Worth noting is that, in 1625, the 'monument to the arrival in China of the Nestorian religion from the West', renowned in both China and the West, was unearthed in Zhouzhi diocese, in the district of Zhouzhi. This was a great event in the history of the Catholic Church in China, and also for the Catholic Church worldwide. It would seem from the inscription on this monument that there was a history of Shaanxi people believing in Catholicism for a long period of recorded history, possibly going back as far as the Zhenyuan period of the Tang dynasty (year 635 of the Western calendar). Zuo Baihao, in his book *Research on Christianity in China* (vol. 1, p 471), states that, on the basis of previously discovered records and documents, it is clear that a Nestorian cathedral had already been established in Zhouzhi during the Yuan Mongol dynasty.

(1) Natural environment and social economy

The five counties over which the diocese of Zhouzhi has jurisdiction are scattered about the centre of the Guanzhong plain, which is half way along the 800-mile long Qin river. The terrain is flat, with abundant natural resources, and the people live lives that are basically peaceful and carefree. There are people living in the mountainous regions who have not yet solved the problems of how to stay warm and have enough to eat, but in the counties of Hu, Zhouzhi, Mei and some other counties and towns, the economy is comparatively advanced. In Huxian, Zhouzhixian and Meixian, in particular, which are south of the Wei river, where the terrain is lower-lying than it is on the north side, water is in plentiful supply. The farmers in these three counties rely for their income mainly on fruit trees and vegetables. They are much more prosperous than farmers in the counties of Wugong and Fufeng which lie north of the Wei river. Zhouzhi county, in particular, is famous throughout China for its Mihou peaches: this is because of the very sticky nature of the soil, which retains moisture and suits the cultivation of such trees, unlike the soil in the counties and towns to the north of the river, which does not suit the cultivation of peaches so well. The cultivation of these peaches is extremely costly, but their selling price is also high and they are thus a source of endless wealth for the people of Zhouzhi. Hu county, to the east of Zhouzhi, is very nearby, and while the amount of land available there is not great, the terrain is level, which is convenient for irrigation, and most of the people there are well off. The Guanzhong area is known as 'being as golden as Zhouzhi and as silvery as Hi county'. The land area of Mei county is comparatively spacious and contains many beauty spots. Its inhabitants rely on growing such economically valuable commodities as apple trees and pear trees for a livelihood, and live fairly prosperous lives.

Relatively speaking, the economic potential of the counties of Wugong and Fufeng, which are both north of the Wei river, is more limited, by virtue of the fact that they are on the Loess plateau, and the people who live there suffer from a serious shortage of water. As far as half of the cultivable area of Wugong is concerned, the weather dictates whether the people there have anything to eat or not: in the year 2000, two-thirds of the rice crop was lost in the drought and it was impossible to grow cash crops of any kind. Where the water supply cannot be guaranteed, newly planted trees either die or produce only weak growth. Where it is impossible to get cash crops to grow, many people, in addition to cultivating their fields, get work with teams of builders, to earn a little 'salt and vinegar' money. Sometimes they work for a whole year without earning a cent: either the team leader just does not give them anything, or he will make off with the proceeds of the workers' sweat and blood. Large groups of young labourers go and spend the whole year in town working on public building projects, which not only leaves the villages deserted but also contributes to the decline of traditional farming methods, and causes the destruction or breakdown of the family as the basis of traditional ethical principles. Most of those who stay behind in the villages are elderly people, or women with children, and the crisis affecting the quality of life and morale of these weaker individuals is thus further intensified.

Yangling is famous throughout China as a model farming area. It is also known as the 'agriculture specialist' township. The North West Science and Technology University for Agriculture and Forestry, where large numbers of able persons from all over the country have received training in various aspects of agriculture, is located in Yangling, which has become an important educational centre.

Xingping, which is a town at district level under the administrative district of Xianyang, also has a fairly prosperous economy. The people there depend mainly on the cultivation of vegetables for their living. The hothouse vegetables of Xingping are extremely well known throughout Guanzhong (i.e. the area of the central plain in Shaanxi). The vegetables are grown in heated sheds, and come in many different varieties. They are not limited to a particular season and can be supplied to people at any time throughout the year, according to their needs. This also brings in a small income for the people of Xingping, with the result that, in economic terms, their income is quite high.

(2) Situation regarding 'Spiritual Civilization'

The five counties, one town and one district for which the diocese of Zhouzhi has administrative responsibility are situated on the Guanzhong plain, where communications are relatively easy and, by comparison with the mountain districts, the economy is relatively prosperous. For this reason, as far as the people's cultural level is concerned, the standard of education and its overall quality are both relatively high. To speak only of Catholic believers, there are very few people who cannot read or write. The Catholics take a particular interest in the education of women and children. In many cases, the children of believers are university graduates and some have even gone on to obtain Masters and Ph.D. degrees. Priests and nuns also pay special attention to the people's cultural knowledge and school education. In many of the areas where churches for the herdsmen are situated, pre-school education is available, in some cases entirely free of cost and, in others, at reduced rates. The sisters who provide this teaching are very conscientious, responsible and generally welcomed. In agricultural villages, nuns and priests teach the believers songs during leisure time after people have finished work, both for their pleasure and also to train them musically. The church also pays special attention to ethical and moral, ideology and cultural education. Apart from improving relations between neighbours, this has brought about a clear improvement in people's self-discipline and behaviour, and also in their carrying out good works.

In addition, in the area of medical treatment and health, the majority of parishes in the Zhouzhi diocese have clinics run by religious sisters, as a way of providing a service for large numbers of people. These clinics usually provide their services either free of charge or for only a small fee for sick people who are poor. When treating their patients, the sisters are attentive to every detail, they ask whether the patient is too hot or too cold, and do not confine themselves to treating their physical ailments but treat their emotional problems as well, which may be related to their attitude to life, their purpose in life and also the principles of morality and the need to follow one's conscience.

In the township and the various counties and districts administered by the Zhouzhi diocese, numerous citizenship courses are available at beginners' and upper Middle School levels. An ordinary young person who is able to study up to upper Middle School level differs from his or her parents and grandparents in their understanding of the faith. In the past, their parents would have placed the emphasis on having faith for its own sake, taking the view that believers were people whose faith was the source of their redemption, like Abraham of whom the Old Testament says that subsequent generations would speak of him with respect as their 'father in faith'. The present generation, however, understand their faith as a very positive and dynamic way of life. People who make up the new generation think that being a believer should not simply be a matter of putting the emphasis on 'faith' by itself. What is much more important is that we should emphasise 'love': it is through faith that 'love' grows and has its being, and this should not remain fixed or static. It is a characteristic of this type of faith that in every situation the fact that one has faith will always produce a decisive response. And, to a certain degree, if young people have this kind of attitude, it will spread to and influence their parents' generation too. There are even some people of the parents' generation, and also some new converts to the church, who have already absorbed and this way of thinking and put it into practice. This will also produce a further reaction in individual cases in the future.

It is for this reason that, in the Catholic groups with which we have come into contact, young people are in the majority. This is very different from the out-of-date impression that people had of the Catholic Church that it was 'a church for the elderly', 'a church for women and children' and 'a church that is closed and conservative'.

During the course of the enquiries we conducted in Catholic towns and villages, concerning matters which are most universally relevant in farming villages, such as payment of the agricultural tax and other taxes, keeping the law, etc, the Catholics, in general, came out well; in the Catholic villages, there was almost no one who had broken the law or committed any wrongdoing. When we asked them about this, they attributed it to the precepts which Jesus Christ gave to His church; it was their view that, while the law of the state only pursued people for crimes committed against other people, the Ten Commandments of God pursued people even for their innermost thoughts, and focused on any hurt caused, whether physical or spiritual. Any injury caused to another person had to be paid for, otherwise the sin could not be forgiven by God. Also, at a deeper level, people were expected to put right their own consciences, to avoid thoughts of sexual impurity and greed, and to exercise self-control in eating, drinking and sexual desire. Such precepts of the church have served as a cause of moderation at a time when secular pleasurable pursuits have already become fashionable in our towns and villages.

Account of oral enquiry into beliefs of fifteen villagers

The villagers in question were distributed between Wudong county (four persons, A–D), Yangling district (ten persons, E–N) and Zhouzhi county (one person, O). The personal details of those questioned are shown in Table 1.

Wugong County

A. 65 years of age; Party member; chairperson, Village Women's Federation; educational standard: completed primary education

When young, she left Henan with her father and mother to escape from disaster.

On their way from Henan, her parents died. When she herself begged for food in a village, she was taken in by someone and brought up as a

Table 1

Gender:	Male:	6 people	40% total
	Female:	9 people	60% total
Age:	10–16 years	4 people	26.7% total
	17–50 years	11 people	73.3% total
Occupation	Peasants	8 people	
	Demobilized (ex-military)	1 person	
	Cadres	2 people	
Party Affiliation	No affiliation	9 people	
	Communist	2 people	

prospective daughter-in-law. After Liberation, she became a member of the Communist Party and then chairperson of the Women's Federation. She had some medical knowledge and often acted as midwife to the local women.

Record of conversation: I am an honest woman. After Liberation, the government helped me to live a settled and steady life and also accepted me as a member of the Party, and I am extremely grateful for all that. But during the Cultural Revolution, I saw with my own eyes many examples of people madly telling lies and doing evil things. I was very afraid but couldn't say anything. All I could do was parrot the views of other people. When the Cultural Revolution came to an end, there was a Catholic woman in my village whom I was training to be a midwife. After some time, we became close friends. She was a very good person, was very kind to other people and was a much stronger person than me. I was very curious, and asked her why she performed so many acts of kindness. She told me that this was what her church asked of her: it was what Christianity was all about. Later on, she told me a whole host of things about church teaching and, although I didn't understand, it made me feel good. Afterwards, I went to a place where there was a priest and attended Mass with her a few times, and had a feeling of great warmth. Then I started to believe; I was baptized and received into the church. After I came to belief, I felt much more peaceful in my heart and performed some acts of kindness myself, and I was able to feel the contentment of being loved by other people.

B. Farmer, 74 years of age, male, illiterate. When he was young, his family was poor and his elder brother was sent by his parents to live with a family in Xianyang. It was only quite recently that he had managed to trace him

Record of conversation: In my family, there were originally two brothers, but in 1929, there was a famine in Shaanxi and many people starved to death. My parents were unable to support both my brother and myself and sent my elder brother off to live with other people to avoid starvation. Later, just before my parents died, they told me that I should try to find my brother. I did not succeed in doing so, however, until just a few years ago. I felt that, sooner or later during my lifetime, my brother and I ought to be reunited. Although my wife was a Catholic, I couldn't be bothered to become a Catholic myself. I felt that Catholics were all good people, but I was a good person as well, so it was all right not being a Catholic. But later, I thought to myself that this was not the way things were. My wife believed in God, and when she died, she would go to heaven. Where would I go when I died? Just before she died, my wife took me by the hand and said: 'Papa, shouldn't you also be a believer? If you become a Catholic, we should be able to see each other again in heaven.' When I heard her say that, I thought that what she said was right, and so I became a Catholic. After doing so, I felt that my previous way of thinking had been very childish. After becoming a Catholic, I learnt many more things: the priest taught us how to sing, study scripture, undertake acts of kindness and help other people. He also told us we must love God in heaven and people on earth. Just loving God without loving our fellow men was wrong: because man was made in the image of God, loving man was also loving God. After I entered the church, everyone said that I changed. I also feel that I have become stronger and life is much more interesting.

C. Female, 45 years of age, farmer.
Has not attended school but is able to read

This person fled from Henan as a young child in search of food. She was taken in and brought up by the Party Secretary of her father's former military unit. Later on, when she was married, the bridegroom came to live with her in the same house.

Record of conversation: After my father died, his military unit held a very solemn funeral ceremony, but afterwards hardly any family members ever came to see me. I had no relatives in that place and, because I was an orphan, my father's family did not want to have anything to do with me. In our village, there was a Catholic woman who, up to that time, had been no more than a nodding acquaintance of mine. After my father died, however, she noticed that I always had a hangdog look about me and often came to visit me and offer me comfort. When I most needed help, she came along and provided it. I felt that she was a very good person and, whenever I had time, I would go and seek her out. On one occasion when I went to see her, she said she had to go out to go to Mass and suggested that I should go with her. I was afraid and didn't dare to go, but she said there was nothing to worry about, so I went. Afterwards, I felt that the priest was very pleasant, the congregation was very friendly and the atmosphere was good, so I went to Mass many times and was eventually received into the church. After becoming a Catholic, I felt very good about it and my fellow parishioners treated me in a very friendly way. I felt that my life was full of sunshine and, spiritually, I had something to live for.

D. Male, now dead, died at age of 58

During his life, he served in the army, but became a farmer after being demobilized. After becoming a Catholic, he served as a catechist. He died while helping to construct a church roof in a village. When the person who wrote down his story was a small child, this man came frequently to his house and told him the story of how he had become a Catholic, which is how it came about that he is in a position to narrate his story in such detail.

Record of D's story: When I was a young man, I was a soldier. Later on, when I was demobilized, I returned home and became a farmer. For a long time, my mind was extremely troubled. I thought that at my time of life I needed to find a true God whom I could trust. For this reason, I sought out books on Daoism, Buddhism and Catholicism and studied them all. I found the books on Catholicism clear, self-explanatory and easy to read. I frequently met with people who were Catholics, and I could see their faith from the way they behaved. I came to see even more clearly the benefit of believing in their religion, which was, in fact, that it guided people in the direction of becoming good and perfect human beings. At that time, my reputation for studying Catholic books was well known to everyone in the village, and although at that stage I hadn't yet become a Catholic everyone treated me as though I had. The Party Secretary in my village had previously always thought of me as a demobbed revolutionary soldier but now that it was public knowledge that I was preparing to become a Catholic this had a bad effect on my reputation, and he hurried over to talk to me about it. We discussed the matter for a whole morning but he failed to convince me and said: 'The weather forecast for tomorrow is that it is going to be fine, but, if your God is a true god, get him to send down some rain.' I realised that he was deliberately making things difficult for me, but I also knew that God was all-powerful, and could do anything He wanted. So I begged Him to send down a shower for all the village to see. While I prayed, I felt full of faith. Early the next day, the sun was shining and the village headman came and cross-examined me about it, but I told him that the day had not yet ended. I suggested that we talk about it again at the end of the day and went back to my room and said some more prayers. At mid-day, a heavy shower started falling from the sky and it continued falling for a good three hours. I nearly went berserk! I didn't think of going to poke fun at the village headman but went straight to the priest's house to ask to be baptized. After that, no one in the village ever again made fun of me for being a Catholic.

After being baptized, I thought that God had been too kind to me, and, when I could spare time from my farming, I went round to all the villages to spread the gospel. Now I lead a steady life, I have an open mind and everything is fine.

Yangling district

E. Male, 70 years of age, Party member.
Was a cadre in his work unit

Record of conversation: My experience of becoming a Catholic was that this was a big turning point in my life. Before I retired, I worked conscientiously in my work unit and I was often commended for being a model worker.

I was a delegate to the National People's Congress, but after I retired, my circumstances changed. Before retirement, I was still someone who counted for something in my work unit. People often got me to do a few jobs, and when I went out, there were often people I recognized, or even people I didn't recognize, who would nod their heads and ask after my health. But after I retired, the situation changed completely. The respect that people had for me was no longer to be seen. Not long afterwards, when I had an illness and found it difficult to move about, not even my relations had the slightest bit of patience with me. During that period of my life, my feelings were in tatters. Afterwards, I happened to meet a priest, who, when he got to know me, often came to pay me a visit and offer me some comfort. This enabled me to see a ray of light through the darkness of my soul. Gradually, at the invitation of the priest, I began to attend some of the activities at the church. For example, participating in the scripture readings, going to gatherings, etc. Through being introduced to the church, I came to feel the warmth of the great family that it is. What specially moved me was that Father Wang actually carried me on his back up and down the stairs: I felt that I had discovered genuine warmth and happiness, and at that point I joined the church. After joining the church, I felt that my frame of mind had become much more tolerant, and I felt much healthier physically. Truly, I felt that the church was an exceptionally good thing.

F. Farmer, 43 years of age, male. After the death of his wife, he single-handedly looked after three children, in circumstances of extreme hardship

Record of conversation: I once heard that a number of people in our village were joining the Catholic Church. I felt in my heart that that was very strange. However, it seemed to me that they were all people who were very good to others. If they could join the Catholic Church, they must have their reasons for doing so. Not long after that, a young religious sister came to our village. In due course, she called at my home. She was very sympathetic about our circumstances, and, from then on, whenever she came to the village, she usually came to our house to help us with our household chores. She would teach my children a few Chinese characters and songs, and as time went on, I felt that the way in which she, and the other Catholics, treated our whole family was very sincere. On one occasion, I couldn't resist asking them what it was that made them come and visit such a poor family as ours. The sister and the other Catholics said that it was what Jesus wanted them to do. Jesus wanted everyone to love one another and help each other. When I heard this, I felt that the Catholic religion must be good, so all my children and I joined the church. Since we did that, the children have become much more obedient than they were before.

G. Male, 15 years of age, lower middle school student. Prior to his becoming a Catholic, his attainment at school left much to be desired, as did his discipline. Since joining the church, he has taken a turn for the better at school, and his attainment has distinctly improved

Record of conversation: When I was at school, I used to beat up other children, I was rowdy and I always came bottom of the class. However, I never felt I did anything wrong. Later on, I came into contact with an 'auntie' who was a Catholic catechist who was, I felt, a very loving person and there was never any suggestion in the way in which she treated me of her blaming me or finding fault with me in any way. In dealing with my faults and shortcomings, she always showed me in a kindly way how I could improve my behaviour, encouraged me to do good deeds and get rid of the cowardliness and shamefulness in my heart. She frequently told me things about helping other people and having respect for my fellow pupils, and also talked to me about the whys and wherefores of respecting my teacher and working hard at my studies. Gradually, I changed a lot, and after a time I came to think that, if my 'auntie' was so good, her church must be even better. So I joined the church, and after that, my attainments and my behaviour improved enormously. My teacher was amazed and asked me what had made me stop beating up my fellow pupils and stop being rowdy in class. I told her it was because I had become a Catholic. I once found a scarf in the school playground. If this had happened before, I would definitely have kept it for myself. Now, however, it was as though there was a force urging me to hand it over to the teacher. To sum up, since joining the church, life seems much happier.

H. Male, junior middle school pupil

Record of conversation: When I was at school, in the eyes of my fellow pupils, I was a person who never looked up, who didn't have anything to do with his fellow pupils, and had no interest in them. My school results were just ordinary, and in the eyes of my teacher, I was a very ordinary pupil. Near where I lived, there were several people who had recently converted to Catholicism and their children often played with me. They were often visited by a religious sister and a priest, who taught them to sing songs and be kind to other people, which I thought was very strange. Later, there was an occasion when their children and I were having a game together and a priest came to visit them. The children were very pleased to see him and the impression I had of him was that he was very kind and warm-hearted towards them, and also very knowledgeable. From then on, whenever the priest came, I went regularly to listen to him expounding the scriptures and learning from him how to sing songs. Previously, I had been told that Catholic priests and nuns were such bad people but now I realised things were totally different. I saw for myself that people within the church were all so good to each other, and so I joined the church myself. Once when it snowed during the autumn, the snow was piled very deep outside our front door, making it difficult for anyone to go in or come out. So I went to sweep away the snow outside our door and then, when I had finished, I noticed that the snow outside our neighbours' houses still lay as deep as ever. It occurred to me that, in our daily lives, we should do good turns for other people and help them, so I made up my mind to sweep the snow away from the whole of our section of the road. After a while, all the neighbours joined in and between us we eventually cleared the snow away from the whole of our section of the road. This was something the like of which had never happened before I was received into the church. When the neighbours saw my parents, they all remarked on what a difference being converted to Catholicism made to children.

I. Female, 42 years of age, military service. Previously, had lived with her husband in an army camp, but the husband had now changed his occupation and returned to his village

Record of conversation: I used to be in the army acting as back-up for my husband and I felt that there wasn't much pressure in my life, but afterwards, when we returned home, I discovered that everybody was frantically thinking up ways of making money. Everyone was on the make, so I went off and bought an old car and started running it as a taxi. Business was quite good and I could make 50 or 60 yuan a day. There was one occasion when a customer wanted to go to a place I had never been to before: I was brave enough to take him there for the 15 yuan fare. On the way back, however, I lost the way. I drove along a narrow road scarcely wide enough to allow a man to pass through, leading to a high precipice. In order to climb high enough along the road to afford a clear view in every direction, I continued driving up the hill when, through a momentary lapse of concentration, the taxi skidded off the road right to the edge of the precipice. I could see that I and the taxi were about to fall a good ten metres or so over the edge. I hurriedly said a prayer to God to keep me safe, and vowed that, if my prayer was answered, I would definitely believe in Him and try to find Him. Then a miracle happened: the taxi, which was right on the edge of the slope, stopped slipping down. I got out of the taxi and managed to get it back up on the road. From then on, every time I was about to go out in the taxi, I prayed for God's protection and begged Him to help me find Him. Some time later, I happened to pass by a church. I went inside to have a look and thought there was a very good atmosphere about it. After meeting the priest and parishioners a number of times, I found that they had boundless love for others which far exceeded that of Daoist temples. I felt that, in the midst of my darkness, there was a force urging me to join the church, and that is what

I did. What's worth mentioning is that both my life and my business have improved considerably, my income has increased, and the affection between my husband, my children and myself has grown and been further strengthened.

J. Female, 40 years of age, village doctor, undertakes minor operations

Record of conversation: I am a village doctor, and I often come across sick people who are impoverished, either financially or spiritually, and in my experience, it is the spiritually impoverished, who do not have the consolation of warm affection or love, who are the worst affected. I once met a sick person who looked as though he was suffering great pain, and, after examining him, I decided to put him on a drip. It was by then already getting late and I needed to get someone to look after him. However, his wife came along and, after taking a look at him, she said, first of all, that she had to go and pick up her children and then, later, that she had other matters to go and attend to, so she wouldn't be able to look after him during the evening, having said which she suddenly went off, as much as to say it's best for everyone to look after himself. Apart from the fact that the man had had nothing to eat all afternoon, I had no alternative but to get a meal ready for him, then settle him down comfortably, tell him how to change his needle and leave him by himself in the sick room to look after himself for the night. I agonized a lot about whether I should leave him to look after himself for a whole night: I was a woman with a family and home of my own and – especially in a rural village – if a woman stayed overnight with a man, this could easily give rise to damaging gossip. The man was aware of this himself and did his best to persuade me to go home and not to bother about him. When I left him and was getting ready to go home, I said goodbye to him and clearly saw that, although he bore a smile on his face, there were tears welling up in his eyes. For the whole of that night, I felt distinctly uneasy.

Some time after that, I met several religious sisters and saw how they looked after sick and elderly people and cared for those who were weak, having total disregard for the disdainful looks of other people, and even seeing the funny side of emptying bedpans and cleaning up excrement, to the extent that I felt ashamed and guilty about my own inadequacies. Gradually, I came to realize that it was our Lord Jesus who had called them to act as they did. Their prime reason and motivation for doing so was to communicate the love of Jesus to their fellow human beings, and so I felt I had no option but to join the church myself. After doing so, I felt that I had the huge amount of courage required to devote all my energy to helping others. I would never again be afraid of the idle talk of others. To the extent that I could, I reduced or waived altogether the medical fees I charged to people who were hard up, I showed my concern for people in need of spiritual consolation and encouraged people in pain to come and see me and then go away afterwards with joy in their hearts. After I began to act in this way, so far from there being any deterioration in the efficacy of my treatment, it actually improved. It was clear to me that this was due to the intervention of Jesus.

K. Female, 10 years of age, attends primary school. Before becoming a Catholic, was naughty and troublesome, her progress in school was poor, and she frequently provoked her family to anger. After becoming a Catholic, she suddenly became like a young grown up, stopped misbehaving and started helping other members of the family with the housework, and her school results have improved

Report of conversation: The house we live in is close to a church. Before I became a Catholic, I was very naughty and often made my family angry. My grandma was always scolding me for being so naughty. Just to annoy her, I deliberately threw my toys, and also my brother's things, out into the courtyard. My grandma picked them all up and was very cross. When she had finished doing that, I threw everything outside again. Every day, I would do this many times until all my family and my grandma kept scolding me. I was very fat and my grandma tried to get me not to eat so much, but I would deliberately go on eating till I nearly burst just to annoy her, and I made her so cross that she scolded me every time I had a meal. I was also very mischievous at school and often annoyed my teacher and made her angry. Later on, when my grandma was scolding me again, I once ran out of the door and, when I was outside, ran around for a while with no intention of going back indoors, then, quite by chance, crossed the road to the church and squeezed my way inside. Wow! There were quite a lot of children in there and the funny thing was that, when they saw me, instead of scolding me or bullying me, they were very friendly and started to play with me, which I thought was very unusual. In our class, whenever a new boy joined the class, everyone would start teasing him. After a while, after we came out of school every day, when I had nothing else to do, I used to go into the church and play games. The priest and the sisters used to talk to us about looking after our fellow pupils, being respectful towards our teacher and polite towards our families and so on. Then I began to feel for the first time that I had done lots of things that were wrong and gradually stopped being naughty to my grandma. One morning, when I got up early, I discovered that my young brother had once again moved all my things. I got very angry with him and we had a fight. Later on, however, when I went out to play, I remembered what the priest and the sisters had said and was sorry. I ran back indoors and made up with my brother. He said that his head was sore, so I took him to the church clinic and asked the sister to give me some tablets for him to take when we got home. When the rest of the family came home, they said I was learning more and more all the time. Then I decided to be a good girl and to learn from Jesus and the priest and sisters, and I became a Catholic. Since then, my teacher has been astonished at what I have shown I can do!

L. Female, 10 years of age, studying at primary school

Record of conversation: Before I became a Catholic, in our house, only my grandma was a Catholic and the rest of the family didn't believe anything. My grandma treated everyone very well, and my Mum and Dad treated her with great respect. Although they didn't believe in religion, they knew that this was a place in which people loved one another, and whenever my grandma went to church she took me with her. After a while, I became very friendly with the priest and the sisters, and also with the children who often went and played at the church. I could feel that the people at the church were all very good people, and not snobbish like the people in the street. We did good things with the other children at the church and learnt to sing songs. The sister talked to us about how Jesus loved little children, about people having to help each other, and about how we were not only our parents' children but also the children of our heavenly Father, and so on. Once when some new members had asked to be baptized, I also joined the church with them.

I have always been a good girl at school, and, as I often helped other pupils, my teacher made me a member of the life committee. I think that from now on I shall be able to do lots of good works with the help of Jesus' teachings.

M. Female, 60 years of age. Housewife, illiterate

Record of conversation: I became a believer because of the influence of my daughter-in-law, who became a Catholic not very long ago. Before that, things were very bad. My son and my husband were constantly having rows with me and it was so bad that it disturbed the household dog and the chickens. For several years, because I was so mad at my daughter-in-law, I was constantly ill and frequently in hospital. My doctor told me I should try to control my anger, but I just couldn't do it. Last year, all of a sudden, I realized that my daughter-in-law and I had for some time not been quarrelling with each other, and that she had been much nicer towards me. Early every morning, when she had finished her housework, she went out. When I asked her where she was going, she said she was going to church, which surprised me a lot. I said to her that there were plenty of monasteries and temples nearby: why did she go to the church instead of to one of those other places? She said 'Ma, don't you know that churches are good places? If you go there, the priests teach you how to be good – how to tespect the elderly and do good deeds – it's a good place to go to. One day, when we have a chance, I'll take you there and you can see for yourself!' At last, I understood why she had recently been so much more pleasant towards me! I thought that, if she could learn to be good, and stop making me angry, then I shouldn't interfere even if she went to the cinema every day. I shall tell her to go if she likes, and I shan't tell her off if she does!

It's very strange, but ever since she started going to church she has been more and respectful towards me and my husband. I was truly amazed, and I decided to go to the church myself and have a look. So one day, my daughter-in-law took me there. There were quite a number of people there, both young and old. They read the scriptures, sang hymns and listened to the priest preaching his sermon, and it was all very interesting. The priest saw that it was my first visit to the church and he told my daughter-in-law she should take me there more often. I went more and more frequently and I gradually came to realise that the founder of the church, our Lord Jesus, wanted to teach everyone to honour God, love their fellow men, and help and have respect for each other. I felt that this was a good teaching and so I came to believe. Now our household is a very harmonious one and we are all in good health, and we owe these blessings to Our Lord.

N. Female, seventy years of age. Housewife

Record of conversation: I accepted Catholicism when I was in hospital. At that time, there were, in the ward that I was in, an old woman, a child and a young girl with no one to look after them. The old woman was unable to control her bowels and other movements and, as time went on, the nurse got very impatient and the ward stank to high heaven. The day came, some time later, when some strangers came into the ward and tidied up the old woman and give her a wash. When they had finished, they asked her how she was and, thereafter, they came to assist her and give her a wash every day. At first, we thought that the strangers must be her daughter and other relations. As time went on, however, we eventually found out that those people were Catholic lay people who were coming to the hospital to do some good deeds in their spare time, and when they heard about the old woman in our ward, they came along to pay her a visit. Up to that point, I had heard that Catholicism was a foreign religion and that its priests and religious sisters were all imperialist running dogs, but now I could see that the situation was very different – they were all very good people! Subsequently, the strangers got to be on very good terms with all the people in our ward, and they told us that it was at the bidding of Jesus that they were helping other people like that. They came every day to tidy up the old woman, give her a body wash and look after her right up to just over a month before she died. No one, not even her own daughter, had done for the old woman what those people did for her. I thought that the fact that they were able to do all this for someone they didn't even know showed that the religion they believed in must be a very wonderful thing. When I came out of hospital, I went and looked them up. They took me to their church to meet their priest, who was very nice and had a kindly face. From then on, I often went to the church and started studying the scriptures and listening to the priest's sermons and eventually I was baptized as a Catholic. I feel that it cannot be said of a woman of my age that, in the final reckoning, my life has been lived in vain, for I have found the true God! My soul is filled to the brim. My life is a happy one, and I should think that this is a blessing I have received from our Lord!

Zhouzhi County

O. Female, 40 years of age. Farmer

Record of conversation: My experience of being a Catholic is different from other people's. Next door to where we used to live, there was a man who died after drinking fertilizer. Despite this I used to see him frequently standing in front of me. As well as this, for a long while, I was often fainting. When I came to, my husband and I would talk a lot about this, and what we said was always related to the neighbour of ours who had died by taking fertilizer. After a while, my husband took me to hospital to see what was wrong with me. The doctor said I wasn't ill, but I continued to frequently lose consciousness, would mimic the man or would see him standing in front of me. Some time later, someone suggested that I go and consult a Catholic priest about it all. I did so, and the priest blessed me, blessed our house and gave me a bottle of holy water to sprinkle about the house. Strangely enough, my illness never came back. I felt that the Catholic priest had saved me and that Catholicism was the true religion, so I had myself baptized and became a Catholic. Now, my husband, our children and I are all Catholics, and, although our faith is constantly the cause of interference on the part of our relatives, we believe the choice we have made is the right one. Now, we have a very happy family life and our children are all happy and healthy.

Analysis of reports

Although our team interviewed only fifteen persons, the fact that these were separate individual accounts means that their value from the point of view of carrying out research into the interviewees' spiritual beliefs, and the relatively objective and wide-ranging standardization of the statistics, are all the more penetrating and important.

1. Among the fifteen persons interviewed, the motivation and crucial factor in their coming to have faith was, in the great majority of cases, of an ethical nature. Belief in Christianity itself had almost shrunk into the background. Of the persons interviewed, there were only three who related something to do with answers to prayer: D spoke of his determination to believe having been strengthened by an answer to his prayer for rain, I spoke of her taxi skidding to the edge of a precipice and being prevented from

slipping over the top through prayer, as a result of which she subsequently prayed for God's protection whenever she went out in the taxi, and O spoke of getting rid of sightings of a dead man as a result of taking holy water. These three examples, which all link faith with the natural law of cause and effect (though the latter two cases also have a link with mental psychology, that is to say, with individual consciousness of self) hark back to a pre-modern outlook associated with witchcraft. On the other hand, in the backgrounds to the cases of D and I, there was an ethical connection both before and after they accepted faith in Christianity. In the case of D, it was because he was 'seriously troubled in his mind' that he needed to find a true God whom he could trust, which is what prompted him to start reading books on Daoism, Buddhism and Catholicism. It was also because, having had contacts with people who were Catholics, he 'could see even more clearly the effects of being a Catholic, namely that it did in fact lead people towards what was good and perfect', from which it follows that he was already close to becoming a Catholic. As for I, she herself said that, when she was inside the church, she felt that 'it had a very good atmosphere about it', and also that 'the priest and the parishioners had a selfless love for other people which Daoist temples could not begin to compare with'. She also said that she felt that, in the midst of her darkness, there was a force that was urging her to join the church, which is what she proceeded to do. Thus, at this point, one could say, that the response to her prayer strengthened her motivation to accept the Catholic faith rather than it being the crucial event that actually caused her to accept it. If it is borne in mind that, in China's farming villages, they still maintain practices not entirely different from the ancient arts of witchcraft referred to by M (and the practice of divination to be seen on street corners in our cities is based on the same kind of folk religious belief – linked to what still survives of the art of witchcraft – as exists in our farming villages), then the proportion of farming people in our group for whom answers to prayer figured as the motive for their becoming Catholics must be reckoned to be very small. At the same time, it is conspicuously obvious that Christianity survives mainly by virtue of its ethical nature, as was the case in regions where there were similar villages in days gone by. This is also the principal difference between modern religions and the heterodox supernatural religions, which have as their special characteristic the crazy phenomenon of the art of witchcraft.

2. The ethical content in the conversions to Catholicism as told in our oral histories may be divided into the following types:

(i) Offering support in life's vicissitudes and mediating in disputes between individuals

F was a down and out widower trying to bring up three children, and a religious sister helped him with his housework and gave lessons to his children. This was an illustration of the way in which the church can practise mutual love and mutual help for a large family. E was an old man who had retired from work and was ill, and was cold-shouldered by society. A priest spoke to him in a kindly way, however, and invited him to join the church congregation and, for this reason, he 'felt the warmth of everybody in the church'. What particularly moved him was that the priest carried him up and down the stairs, which made him feel that he had discovered genuine warmth and happiness, as a result of which he had become a member of the church. M had entered the church after his daughter had changed from being bitterly sarcastic to being tolerant, kind and filial in her behaviour after she had become a Catholic etc.

The above circumstances are generally representative of the contents of the oral interviews undertaken by our group.

(ii) The progression from being an ethical person who turns towards goodness and practises good works to the higher level of loving one's neighbour and adopting a religious belief

Providing real ethical support is not by any means a monopoly of religion. It is work that can be undertaken by all kinds of secular groups as well. However, the substance of the ethical content of our oral enquiries went beyond social assistance of a merely external, materialistic nature and entered into the spiritual world of contemporary people. Spiritual experience of this kind could be divided into two stages: first came respect for special ethical qualities, which in turn ascended to respect fot the faith background to those ethical qualities, and then generally went on finally to the sublimation of these qualities into belief in Christianity, involving its concept of 'love'. The ethical qualities associated with Christian believers, and the example of their genuinely ethical behaviour in practice, had become the most important motivating force for the spread of Christianity. It was not the propagation of Christian doctrine that occupied the most important position in this regard: what was much mote important was the fusion of the universal love and the spirit of forgiveness which are implicit in Christianity with traditional Chinese ethical culture. For the persons interviewed by our group, the emphasis in their understanding of Christianity was, in almost every case, on the ethic of universal love as exemplified in such phrases as 'loving others', 'giving assistance to others without regard for oneself', 'being a good person'.

In her work as a midwife, A compared herself unfavourably with a religious believer she knew who 'was a very good person, very kind to others and much stronger' than she was. She was very curious about this, and asked the midwife why she performed so many acts of kindness; E made special mention of the fact that what specially moved him was that Father Wang had offered to carry him on his back up and down stairs; as far as J was concerned, the religious sisters had overcome the concerns that she had been unable to overcome, in that they had disregarded other people's disdainful looks and were even been able to see the funny side of cleaning up excrement and emptying bedpans: in doing all these things, they had made her feel ashamed and guilty about her own inadequacies; N had seen with her own eyes a situation in which, when an old woman in hospital had been given the cold shoulder by her own daughter and by the nurses, some Catholic lay people doing voluntary work at the hospital had taken on a dirty, menial task which no ordinary person would ever willingly undertake, and, because of her respect for their ethical values, she had come to believe in Jesus.

(iii) Acting as a spiritual companion in support of the lonely and distressed

Offering spiritual comfort is an area of ethical activity where it is difficult for present day social bodies to get involved. It is also an area which approximates most closely to religious faith. In particular, at times when businessmen live in circumstances in which the ethics of secular society are neglected or despised, the ethical concern shown by religion always shows itself overwhelmingly superior. Thus, when C's father died and she was taken in by the Party Secretary of her father's original army unit, she was ignored by everybody, and it was only a lay Catholic who, when she saw how sad and distressed she was, often came and helped and looked after her. E, a retired member of the National People's Congress, with the privileged social status of a former model worker, had fallen to the level of being a man without contacts on the fringes of a fickle world, who later became ill, found it difficult to get about and was, to an even worse degree than before, left to his own devices by his son and daughter; then, when his loneliness and suffering had reached its lowest point, a priest and his church took pity on him, resulting in him regarding the church as his spiritual paradise.

3. The oral enquiry undertaken by our group makes it clear that Christian ethics and China's traditional ethics are, between them, producing a twofold influence and change. On the one hand, Christianity, which is in the process of adapting its ethical principles so as to transform them into the main force within China's traditional culture, is actually evolving into an ethical body. (Belief in the doctrine of redemption made no impression whatsoever in our records of interview.) On the other hand, the concept of universal love associated with Christianity, even though in today's Chinese farming villages this was in the context of ethical practice, showed itself as possessing an even greater attraction than the lower form of love associated with China's traditional blood relationships. Especially today, when the commercial culture is becoming more developed, neither the ethics of blood relationships nor the customs of the masses can sustain morality. Within the

context of the popular ethical saying that 'at the sick man's bedside, there is no such thing as a filial son', the superiority of religious ethics may be able, to a certain degree, to fill an ethical gap.

4. As stated earlier, the attraction and influence of Christian ethics in China's farming villages today is not primarily the result of the preaching of its religious teaching, but is rather its implementation of ethical principles; in particular, it is its function as a source of ethical fellowship which has arisen as a result of the way in which the church relies on its tradition. The initiatives taken by relatives and friends in showing concern for, and calling upon, them were an essential element in the conversions of the people we interviewed. It is especially corporate activities such as the worship services in church, the sharing, the singing of hymns of praise and activities such as helping other people (or doing good deeds), which provide ethical fellowship in our local districts today. Because of its superior underpinning by a background of religious faith, this kind of ethical fellowship based on religion, in the circumstances of today in which the population of China's farming villagers has become scattered, is especially cohesive and effective.

The status of the patriarchal clan system in exercising its traditional control over the Chinese ethical system began to decline in the early pan of the 20th century. The unprecedented uniformly ethical system which took its place in the New China was based on the administrative structure of the People's Communes and what was, at that time, the strong teaching authority of the ruling political Party. However, from the end of the 20th century and the advent of the modernization programme onwards, China's farming villages on the one hand lost the strong backing of Party ethics and the commune system that went with them but at the same time plunged into the commodity and market economy to an extent and a depth that was without precedent. This pattern of events has brought about a situation in which China's agricultural villages have become an empty space, in which a split has developed between the old and the new, and in which the farmers, after freeing themselves from both the commune and the family clan system, find themselves in a state of crisis about which form of ethics to fall back on. Co-existing with Christian fellowship, there are other religious bodies such as Buddhism and Daoism, and there are also the fellowships offered by the revitalised patriarchal clans, such as the secret societies all over the country. They are all, between them, competing for believers. Of course, the biggest institutional resources are still those of the village councils, which are communes under a different name, and, apart from these, there are the new financial bodies such as the business enterprises being set up by our small towns and villages, which could be the basis for the emergence of a new ethical structure in the future.

To make a prediction on the basis of the general pattern of modernization, the modernization of Chinese society cannot put the clock back to the era of people's communes and the level of integration between politics and religion which prevailed at that time: both the Party and the state are likely to stick with the divisions which characterize modern society and will hand over the function of teaching about ethics to the educational, cultural and other fellowships at the various different levels of society. The fellowship of Christian ethics will, for this reason, go on preserving an appropriate space in which it can continue to survive and develop.

(Translated by Lawrie Breen)

56

THE IMITATION OF CHRIST IN BICOL, PHILIPPINES

Fenella Cannell

Source: *Journal of Royal Anthropological Institute*, 1 (1995), 377–94.

This article considers the way in which the local practice of Catholicism in Bicol, centred here on a miraculous image of a 'dead Christ', is linked to the healing of spirit-caused sickness. I argue that the relationship of people in S. Ignacio to their saint is one of identification, in which ritual and daily life echo each other, and devotional acts often take the form of 'imitations' of Christ which create intimacy with him and access power in the world. Healers also 'imitate' Christ as one of a range of ways in which they seek to manage relationships with the spirits, and the dead Christ himself also stands as a shamanic exemplar. I suggest that this approach to the mediation of hierarchy is probably one of the historical continuities in Bicolano culture, which has often been pejoratively described as 'merely' imitative of the West.

In this article, I examine religious and healing practices in one area of Bicol, a province of Southern Luzon, Philippines. Bicolanos, in common with Filipino populations in other lowland provinces, are overwhelmingly Roman Catholic, and the religious practices I discuss centre on a particular saint-cult, that of the *Amang Hinulid* (or *Ama*), a miraculous wooden figure of Christ-taken-down-from-the-cross whom I refer to in English as the 'dead Christ'. Healing seances are also an extremely important part of Filipino life in both rural and urban settings. They involve communication with spirits, and take complex forms which bridge the distinction often made in the literature between 'spirit mediumship' and 'shamanism'.[1]

Since the publication of *Ecstatic religion* (Lewis 1971), if not before, writers with quite contrasting theoretical interests have tended to stress how mediumship and possession can be oppositional to 'world religions'. This partly reflects the widespread historical fact of hostility between missionaries (or other agents of conversion) and local mediums, shamans or other practitioners, which applies to the history of the Philippines as to so many other contexts. However, the ethnography of Southeast Asia has tended to focus *either* on mediumship and possession as a discourse of the marginalized in relation to, especially, Islam (e.g. Ong 1987) *or* on areas marginal to the state, where mediumship and shamanship retain a central importance in the construction of (an oppositional) identity (e.g. Atkinson 1989; Tsing 1993).[2]

Because Christianity is the least widespread 'world religion' in Southeast Asia, its relation to mediumship has been less discussed than that of Islam. This article provides ethnography on the Philippine case, and contrasts with the existing literature in concentrating on the extent to which idioms are shared between Catholicism and healing. The argument pursues similarities between the ways in which Bicolanos think of and enact relations with a saint and with spirits. In each case, relations with these supernaturals are created, and hierarchy is represented as attenuated, through notions of 'pity' and through processes involving an 'imitation of Christ', who is locally identified with the cult image of the *Ama*.

The people with whom I did my fieldwork live in a *barangay* (community) of just over 200 families,[3] which I call 'S. Ignacio'. The main occupations are rice-farming and small-scale fishing, but S. Ignacio suffers from the typical regional problems of poverty to an even greater degree than some other *barangays*, because of the local pressure on farmland. The appearance of the *barangay* is rural and agricultural; green paddy fields stretch out beyond the family houseplots which lie on either side of the unsurfaced village road. Under severe economic pressures, however, men and women in S. Ignacio turn their hand to any small retailing or service-providing venture which will improve the family's cash resources; selling fish, making snack foods, even turning old car tyres into flowerpots and rubber shoes. Few such ventures provide any permanent or significant increase in wealth. The possible routes to a different kind of life – larger capital sums, college education and migration abroad – are beyond the reach of almost everyone in S. Ignacio.

Like many Bicolano communities, S. Ignacio is rural, but not isolated. A short stretch of road separates it from the outlying houses of the adjacent small town, whose modest market, town hall, wooden-seated cinema and church are all used by people in S. Ignacio. Many townspeople are also farmers, although they may hold more land than villagers.

To the casual visitor, the Christian, lowland Philippines present a confusingly 'Westernized' appearance, particularly in contrast to some other parts of Southeast Asia. While there are many modest local homes made of wood or bamboo, the most permanent and most striking buildings are either large Spanish-built stone churches, or private houses and public structures built in concrete to American-derived designs. Most people wear Western-style clothes and American influences on popular films and music, though often filtered through the Filipino entertainment industries of the capital, are clearly evident.

While what it means to live with these landscapes and patterns of consumption are complex issues (see Miller 1987), I am here concerned to critique a very powerful stereotype of lowland culture, found in both academic and non-academic accounts. This view puzzles over a lack of cultural authenticity in the lowlands, and emphasizes its permeability to influences from the two colonial periods: Spanish rule between 1607 and 1898, and American rule between 1899 and 1946. University staff in Bicol, for instance, felt that local healing styles had been corrupted by American movies about 'demonic possession', while in the *barangay* people would often explain to me that local culture was mostly an accretion of layers: 'The Spanish brought religion, the Americans brought democracy'.[4]

A second theme of this article is therefore to oppose the idea that Bicol culture is 'imitative' in this sense of being merely derivative, by exploring the distinctiveness of the meaning of 'imitation' itself in the context of saint-cult and spirit-mediumship. I argue that the 'imitations of Christ' here examined are themselves suggestive of consistent ways of representing hierarchy as accessible to a process of negotiation and reduction. It is these *processes*, rather than a fixed cultural *content*, which may constitute historical continuities between the Spanish and the post-American periods.

The 'dead Christ' and Bicolano funerals

Elsewhere, I have described the cult of the *Amang Hinulid* at greater length (Cannell 1991: 220–339), and it will suffice here to give a somewhat condensed version of my argument before proceeding to the material on mediums and healing.

The phrase *Amang Hinulid* (often abbreviated to *Ama*) means, literally, 'the father who is laid out in death'. This phrase provides the essential information about the local cult figure in the area where I worked. The *Ama* is an almost life-size, carved wooden image of Jesus after he has been taken down from the Cross, realistically painted with the wounds of the crucifixion and with drooping, half-closed eyes and a sorrowful expression. It is another of the legacies of Spanish colonialism that the *Ama* has 'mestizo' (European) features, which Bicolanos constantly compare to the dark complexion and 'low noses' by which they deprecatingly identify themselves.

The precise history of the image is hard to determine, but it may have been brought from Mexico at the turn of the century.[5] The miraculous history of the *Ama*, however, is given much greater local priority than its physical derivation, and this account is often told and is quite clear. The image was found as a shapeless piece of wood by a childless woman who, in a significant phrase, is said to have 'adopted' it (Bicol, *inampon niya si Ama.*) She 'took care of' the image, which began to assume a recognizable human shape, and gradually grew from child to adult. The miracles took a new turn when the *Ama* began to walk about in the area, recruiting pilgrims and devotees. It was through their labour and donations that the shrine was built, and this has always been known as the *Ama's* place or the 'house' of the *Ama.*[6] For some time, the *Ama* continued to appear in the region, attracting pilgrims rather as Christ travelled around teaching and gathering disciples. The *Ama* is now said to be 'too old' for such energetic pursuits, but he still works miracles by healing sickness and granting other kinds of 'help' (*tabang*).

The *Ama* is thus a highly personalized and humanized figure with a constantly-changing life-course of his own. He is also in a literal sense integrated into a Bicol family, although, due to the quirks of inheritance, this is no longer the immediate family of the woman who first 'adopted' him. It is a distinctive feature of Filipino Catholicism that most images of 'saints' (and I follow local usage in calling the *Ama* a 'saint') are not kept in churches, but are privately owned by local families and kept in family homes except during the processions of religious festivals. Families talk habitually of 'adopting' and 'bringing up' their saints, who are therefore in some ways like children of the family. In other ways, however, they are also parental figures, patrons of the family and traditionally holders of the riceland passed down according to parent-child inheritance customs.

When people speak of Christ in S. Ignacio, there is always a sense that they know who he is; he is in local reference the saint-*Ama*, powerful but deeply familiar. For instance, the story of the life of the *Ama* is explicitly identified with the life of Christ, as this is known through local, popular religious texts.[7] Inside his 'house' the *Ama* lies in a kind of glass coffin, dressed in wigs of human hair and clothing complete down to the underwear, also donated by his devotees.[8] His nail-marked feet are exposed at the open end of the coffin for people to kiss, and are constantly rubbed with perfumes by the visitors. Notes with petitions and thanks, ironically referred to in Bicol as 'love-letters to the *Ama*' are tucked around his draperies and under his pillow.

The shrine of the *Ama* marks the boundary between the town and S. Ignacio. It is an important location for both town and *barangay* people and is much visited by both. Some older women from S. Ignacio are in constant attendance there, and say novenas for pilgrims for a small payment. Pilgrims from further afield arrive on Fridays, especially on the first Friday of the month, but above all during the period of Lent leading up to Good Friday, which is appropriately enough the most important festival of the 'dead Christ'. Many of the visitors have made vows to the *Ama*, which range from the simple promise of a visit to complex obligations to perform a Passion-play, or to sing the Bicol-language text of the Passion story (*Pasion*) at his shrine, each Lent for a period of many years. Large numbers of local healers are among the regular visitors to the shrine, where they often buy or are given water or objects which have been in contact with the image, and which are used therapeutically in healing seances.

The Catholic church in the Philippines has emphasized Christ's birth and resurrection (Christmas and Easter Sunday) as the two key festivals of the calendar. However, in contemporary Bicol it is Good Friday, the day of Christ's death, which is instead the most conspicuous and emotional day of religious activity,[9] and one regional focus for this activity is the *Ama.* Although each Bicolano *barangay* has its own patron saint, the *Ama* is in many ways the most important sacred figure in the area, constantly spoken of and intimately known. This intimacy, as I will show, is not only due to the placing of saints within Bicolano families, but is also constantly enacted in three interwoven contexts: ordinary people's funeral practices, the performance of the most popular local religious text – the Bicol *Pasion* – and the rituals of Holy Week, which I will argue create a Bicolano wake and funeral for the *Ama.*

Anyone living in a Bicolano *barangay* is likely to attend a dozen or more funerals per year. To walk in the funeral procession (*dapit*) of a relative or neighbour is an important duty and sign of respect, as is helping out at wakes. Western-style medical care is expensive, and premature deaths from chronic and acute infectious diseases or complications of childbirth are frequent. In a poor *barangay* such as S. Ignacio, funerals provoke people to painful and conscious reflections on their own poverty.

The pattern of activity which follows a death in Bicol is predictable. The home of the bereaved family becomes the centre of a wake, which may last up to a week. During this time, the house itself is extended with bamboo poles and a canvas canopy, and is then known as 'the dead person's place' (*sa gadan*); the deceased is not referred to by name. Nowadays the body is almost always commercially embalmed[10] and then displayed in an open coffin, and neighbours join the bereaved family in keeping vigil.

All funerals pass through the town church for the saying of a blessing or a Mass. However, the priest is not usually present at the most emotional episodes of the funeral. These are the moments of the *manambitan*, or ritual weeping. The first eerie wail of the most closely bereaved is heard at the moment of death itself. There are two other occasions for ritual weeping: one when the body is taken from the house to be closed into its coffin and carried to the church, and one when the body is about to be placed in the cemetery tomb, and the coffin lid is opened briefly for the last time.

At these moments, the chief mourners of the deceased, who are usually glazed, pale and passive after the long vigil, will suddenly fling themselves into a passion of grief, wrestling with the coffin-bearers to open the lid again, or to pull back the coffin from the mouth of the tomb.[11] At the same time, they will cry out in a way simultaneously conventionalized and harrowing, calling on the dead person and screaming that it is too soon to let him or her go; that they remember the love and help the deceased gave to the living; that they will follow their dead mother or their dead child, or their wife dead in childbirth, and not abandon them alone in the desolate cemetery.[12]

The *manambitan* always brings tears to the eyes of those who hear it, yet at every funeral I witnessed, those not most closely connected to the deceased would turn hurriedly away from the scene at the tombs, wiping away tears almost angrily. Too much contact with grief and absorption in mourning can threaten the health and well-being of the living, drawing them after the dead. This danger also threatens the bereaved on the third day after death, when the soul of the dead is likely to return to the house of its living kin. Similar post-mortem visits are said in many parts of Southeast Asia to be due to the envy of the dead for the living (see, for example, Gibson 1986; Metcalf 1982). In Bicol, however, the explanation given is that the dead person pities (*herak*) their relatives left behind, and tries misguidedly to comfort them. For their part, living people say that 'pity' is what they feel at the cemetery, and it is presumably this emotion which must be so carefully controlled by the bereaved. For the living, the 'pity' of the dead and your own 'pity' for them lead to equally dangerous kinds of proximity.

In this part of Bicol, the pivotal events of Holy Week are constructed as though the rituals surrounding the *Ama* were one enormous wake and funeral. Over the last period of Lent, activity at the shrine intensifies; as pilgrims gather from all over the region in the 'house' of the *Ama* to keep vigil, distribute food and pray, it is as though they were an unusually large gathering of friends, followers and relatives at the wake of some deceased dignitary. By contrast, the main church in the centre of town is almost deserted between Holy Wednesday (when there is a preliminary procession) and the Good Friday services.

By the night of Holy Thursday, the shrine is packed with people and filled with the sound of voices singing the Passion-text. Outside the shrine, the drama is made explicit at temporary altars constructed of painted board like stage-flats, which are changed at intervals to show succeeding scenes of Christ crucified and then taken down dead for burial. On Good Friday itself, the religious activities centre on the great procession, in which the figure of the *Ama* is taken down from his coffin for the only time in the year. He is dressed as an honoured corpse, with a binding-cloth tying up his jaw. A sigh and a shout from the waiting crowd goes up as his body is placed inside a special decorated and glass-sided funeral bier. Local men struggle for a place pulling the bier. The pilgrims follow the *Ama*, who is accompanied by the town's funeral bands playing a dirge, and by a gradually increasing cortège of other saints' images, brought out from the houses of their owners as the procession circles the town, pausing at the church. Other images, such as the patron saints of *barangays*, are placed along the route as though they were spectators paying their last respects.

Just as the two *manambitan* of an ordinary funeral mark the removal of the body from the house and the moment when it is placed in the tomb, so cries and high emotions mark the taking of the *Ama* from his house, on his own *dapit* or funeral procession.[13] People comment on the occasion as if it were a funeral, noting how many 'friends' of the *Ama* have joined the procession, and inspecting the face of the dead Christ. 'Pity the poor *Ama*, he looks so pale and wan!' remarked one of my companions. 'Of course', replied another, 'for he's dead now'.

Of course, in one sense the *Ama* is always dead, and in another sense dies yearly on Good Friday. His body, rather than being consigned to the cemetery, is eventually brought back in procession and reinstated in his 'house'. But despite these differences, the idea that the *Ama* is essentially a *dead* Christ – Christ at the moment after death – neither crucified nor yet buried and resurrected, is made extremely clear.[14]

What emphasized this for me was the ceremony called the 'bathing of the Father' (*pagparigos ki Ama*), which is a highly popular part of the Good Friday rituals, and is also sometimes held on the first Friday of each month, out of Lent. Although a Mass may be held on the same day, the priest again is not really involved. Instead, the family who own the image and shrine of the *Ama*, together with a large crowd of pious people and male and female healers, gently remove the clothing of the *Ama*, sponge him all over with perfumed water (keeping towels carefully placed over the groin as though to save the image's modesty) and re-dress him. The mixture of tenderness and proprietorship with which this is done is remarkable to see. It is as though the attendants were laying out the corpse of a much-loved and respected relative, and the procedures they use closely resemble those which were common in Bicol before commercial embalming became widespread. The integration of the 'saint'-*Ama* into the Bicol family thus extends even to the gentle and respectful treatment of his 'dead' body.

If the Bicol funeral involves the danger of 'pity' between dead and living, and the Good Friday ritual presents the funeral of the *Ama*, a further link between them is made by the Bicol-language *Pasion*. This text tells the story of the suffering, death and resurrection of Christ interspersed with moral homilies, and was originally intended by the Spanish church as an aid to conversion. It was translated into Tagalog (and then other Filipino languages) very early in the Christianization of the Philippines, as part of the Church policy that evangelization should make use of native languages in the islands.[15] The text is now published in local languages by presses in Manila, and sold in every province.

The Passion text, its meanings and mode of performance have become highly indigenized and in various locations and historical periods have taken on significances very different from those intended by the Church (Ileto 1979; Rafael 1988). It is written in verse, and the story is hauntingly sung by relays of paired singers, to tunes which have many local variations. The correct 'reading' and harmonization are matters of skill, practice and nuanced improvization.

In Lent, the *Pasion* is read in private households as a devotional act. Since the text is long, it needs an all-night vigil to complete it, a scene which in several ways resembles the co-operative neighbourliness of a wake. Pilgrims at the house of the *Ama* read the *Pasion* intensively in Holy Week, often as one of the vows for recovery from sickness as mentioned above.

In this context, it is significant that when I asked people which parts of the *Pasion* were most important, the episode which was most often mentioned was that of the burial of Christ. This passage comes at the low point in most people's energy during the vigil, in the early hours of the morning, and is marked by a change of tune which tends to awaken those who have dozed off, as well as those in neighbouring houses. Tune and content combine visibly to move all those who hear it. It recounts how Mary and the mourners were filled with pity (*herak*) and painful feelings as they looked at Christ's body; how Mary clung to the body of Christ as it was placed in the stone tomb and would hardly release it; how the angels bent down from heaven in order to join in the funeral procession of Christ (the *dapit*).

The passage shares, in ways difficult to convey in translation, both the vocabulary and the narrative structure of an ordinary funeral in Bicol. The emotional moment of farewell at the tomb evokes the last *manambitan* in any Bicolano cemetery, just as the language used in the text (*dapit*, *herak*) is exactly that of all Bicol burials and bereavements. The *Pasion* thus closes the circle of resemblances and identifications between the Christ of the Passion, the dead Christ, and the Bicolano dead. It is for that reason, I suggest, that everyone I asked described this passage not only as the most significant, but as *pinakamakahibi*, the part which makes you weep the most.

That every *barangay* funeral is partly identified with Christ's funeral is further supported by what we know about the nature of religious devotions in Bicol and elsewhere in the lowlands. This identification is not a simple assimilation of church teaching. Local women, for instance, often talked about the parallels between their experience of the deaths of their children, and Mary's feelings as described in the 'burial' passage. But they did not regard the Virgin Mother as the model of womanhood, as has been suggested for European Catholicism (Warner 1976). Instead of feeling that they should be like her, they remarked that she was rather like them.

A similar process of identification underlies the performances of the passion play (*tanggal*) in Bicol. The *tanggal* is performed by a group of people again in fulfilment of a vow to the *Ama* linked to recovery from illness. The play is not only based on the passion text, but on its familiar woodcut drawings of Christ, Mary and others, which it literally brings to life.

The passion players must endure three nights and two days with little sleep to complete a performance; several players also go without food. The physical hardship is described as a 'sacrifice' (*sacrificio*) – but this has little to do with sin, repentance or reparation. Instead, the players feel that by embodying the persons from the passion story, and sharing some of their sufferings, they will move closer to them and thus also share in some of their powers. The players, like the readers of the *Pasion* keeping vigil, or the performers of any other devotional act, always say that they feel light, well and happy after it, and exhaustion leaves no mark. As Zialcita has put it, discussing the devotees in another part of the lowlands who undergo voluntary flagellation or even nailing to a Cross: 'By becoming Christ's intimate, the flagellant believes that Christ will grant his request' (1986: 59). However, this search for an 'intimacy' with Christ by imitation is not confined, at least in Bicol, to flamboyant self-punishment, but inflects many areas of daily experience.

Healers and the imitation of Christ

I have described how the shrine of the dead Christ and the 'bathing of *the Ama*' are a focus not only for ordinary people in S. Ignacio, but also for healers. In fact, the *Ama* and the healers are connected both by the idea of pity (*herak*) and by the imitation of the particular dead Christ who dominates the local imagination.

Sickness in Bicol can have a number of different kinds of causes, and is treatable by different specialists. I have already mentioned the difficulty poor people have in affording Western medicine, but even when there is cash to pay for it, it is not appropriate to every case.

The spirits, or 'people we cannot see' (*tawo na dai ta nahihiling*, in contrast to *tawo pareho ta*, 'people like us') are an important source of both sickness and healing. Some detail on spirits and healers is necessary here, in order to show how people's dealings with the *tawo* and the *Ama* are connected. The *tawo* are said to inhabit an invisible world which overlaps with our own visible one; one is thus very likely to blunder into these 'people' accidentally when going about one's daily business. Their retaliatory actions (*naigo*) are the main cause of minor ailments, especially among children.[16] *Tawo* may also become romantically attached to 'people like us', and/or feel a protective 'pity' (*herak*) for human trouble and poverty. Spirits approach future spirit-mediums from these motives; they offer assistance in healing as a gift which will bring the healer popularity and the gifts of patients, though healers themselves may experience the assumption of their vocation as coercion. They resist at first, only to become 'used to' their spirit-companions (*saro* or *sanib*) over time. The 'pity' of a spirit-companion, however (like the pity of the dead discussed above), is a dangerous thing, for both often threaten to carry the healer away from their troubles to live in the spirit-world.

A person 'accompanied' (made sick) by spirits may be suffering either from their anger or their troublesome 'pity', and displays symptoms of soul-loss or occasionally of possession. If the healer cannot negotiate successfully, the patient's soul too may stay in the invisible world, and the patient will die, though they are said to be lost or 'taken' rather than to be 'dead' in the normal sense.

It appears that spirits were thought of as ambivalent powers even in pre-colonial times (Rafael 1988: 190). Contemporary Bicolanos, however, also inherit a history of church disapproval of healing practices which were defined as superstitious, or worse, and the latent suspicion that possession might be demonic. This, no doubt, largely explains why many people attend healers regularly, but claim that while some spirits are good, others are un-Catholic 'evil beings'. This ambivalence also takes the form of a historical claim that healers nowadays are 'weaker' than those of the recent past, who used to refuse possession by spirit-companions and heal instead 'with their own voices'. The rhetoric, therefore, which is reminiscent of Eliade's (1989) shamanism-spirit mediumship contrast, is that current possession-centred practice has declined from a more powerful 'shamanic' past, and this decline is explicitly associated by *barangay* people with a disapproval of possession as both weak and un-Catholic.

This chain of associations is in fact somewhat misleading. To oppose possession and Catholicism disguises the fact that many healers are possessed, and almost every one of them stresses her Catholic faith, and uses Catholic symbols and props in healing. Some may also say that their spirit-companions are good Catholic beings, although others play this down.

The actual situation is complex and extremely varied, healing techniques in Bicol being highly idiosyncratic.[17] There are many healers who are always possessed in seance by their spirit-companion; the *tawo* then effectively runs the session and, speaking through the medium, heals the patient. There are fewer mediums who are never possessed; some of these use divination only, while others specialize in techniques of 'calling' the spirits and talking to them 'in their own voices', and are able to see them while they remain invisible to everyone else. Yet a number of these 'shamanic' healers may also use possession occasionally, when they judge it appropriate.

While it is quite possible that there has been a rise in the number of healers using possession (or possession only) in recent years, the shamanism-mediumship contrast is therefore not so much of a historical divide as local people claim, but rather constitutes two ends of a spectrum of styles. In fact, the evidence indicates that both modes of dealing with spirits already existed in the pre-Spanish Philippines (Alcina 1960 [1688]; Cullemar 1986: 17–23), although it is hard to know exactly how each was practised and understood. Moreover, these contrasting styles have little to do with therapeutic efficacy; possessed healers are common and very successful. They are only therapeutically 'weaker' in confrontation with those rare patients themselves possessed by an aggressive spirit; a medium should shun the possibility that this will enter her body, while 'shamanic' healers can negotiate with it 'in their own voice' with less danger.

Similarly, observers of Bicol healing might at first assume that elements borrowed from Christianity serve only to control and contain the movements of spirits and souls; crosses[18] marked on the patient's pulse-points, for example, certainly keep the soul in the body and the *tawo* out of it. This impression is reinforced by the standard story of the origin of the *tawo*:

> When God created the world, they say, he decided to bless everything (with sprinkled water, as a priest does at the end of Mass). He gathered all the people and animals together, but some of the people hid among the tree-trunks of the forests, and so they did not come within the area reached by the blessing. Hence, they remained invisible.

This story is quoted to explain why healers must be careful not to stay for the blessing when they attend Mass; for if they should happen at that moment to be possessed by one of the *tawo*, the spirit will be fixed within them by the blessing, and their own soul will not be able to return to their body. An invisible person would then be locked into a visible body, and vice versa. The logic here seems to be that the priest (or God) appears as an agent who fixes souls in position, while the activities of spirits involve their free passage between the visible and invisible worlds. Christian symbolism can then also make boundaries when 'copied' by the healers.

However, this too is an over-simplification for at least two reasons. First, while it is true that spirits are associated with a powerful tendency towards movement between worlds (as is evident from their threats to 'take' healers with them out of pity), Christianity is not of course the healers' only resource. What healers always combine with the use of Christian symbols is an emphasis on their ability to negotiate with and persuade the spirits who are making their patients sick. All healers will talk about these themes at length. Healers 'in their own voices' clearly demonstrate their skills in seance. Possessed healers, however, also do so at one remove; although the spirit-companion *saro* is the negotiator in a seance, the healer herself must cultivate her rapport with her *saro*, and this too requires negotiating skills.[19] The classic form of a conversation in a seance is that the healer will first discover the identity of the disease-causing spirit and its reason for 'accompanying' the patient, whether grievance or 'pity'. She will then appeal to the spirit to show a more helpful 'pity' by healing the sufferer. The tone may be commanding, teasing or propitiatory, depending on the circumstances.

Secondly, while all healers use Catholic props and gestures, these are not the only way in which Catholicism enters into Bicolano healing practice; on the contrary, the power of Christianity, and in particular here of the *Ama*, is closely implicated in what one might loosely call the shamanic tradition in Bicol, in which it is not only the spirits but the healers who are associated with the power to move between worlds. Quite ordinary people will sometimes tell stories of journeys to the land of the spirits or the dead (not sharply distinguished in many contexts[20]) from which they return unscathed and spiritually strengthened. Healers themselves may refer to such stories to illustrate their own powers to withstand and negotiate with the 'invisible people'.[21]

The ways in which healers approach the 'dead Christ' have several aspects, but all are aimed at creating an intimacy with him through which they share in his power. When healers gather at the shrine for the bathing of the image, they often collect water, oil or other objects which have been in contact with the body of the *Ama*, or borrow the clothes of the image. These are used in healing, but they are not simply boundary-markers clamping down the movements of the spirits. They are also ways in which the healer draws closer to the *Ama* through physical proximity and contact.

One young man I knew invoked the idea of direct possession, when he suddenly assumed the posture of Christ on the cross during a rather casual tea-time divination session. I have known other healers say that they were possessed by sacred figures and saints, but this degree of literal-mindedness is not usual; the young man was, I think, regarded as rather hubristic by most people.

It is more common for healers to tell stories of encounters with Christ and other holy figures, who give them gifts of amulets (*anting*) which are used in healing. These encounters may form an episode in one of the 'shamanistic' stories I have mentioned, part of the out-of-body voyage of the healer's soul. Conversely, the healer may have a mysterious visitor to her house, who is understood later to be Mary or the *Ama.*

The clearest form of identification with Christ, however, is common to almost all the healers of whom I have any knowledge, and this too is a kind of shamanistic-voyage story. It will be recalled that people first become healers at the insistence of the spirits, who 'pity' their troubles, and decide to become their spirit-companions and help them to heal.[22] People cannot resist the will of the spirits, though they may try ignoring their advances at first. The definitive moment comes when the spirit-companion 'accompanies' the healer's soul on an inaugural voyage to the spirit-world, leaving the healer's body behind as though unconscious or dead. As my friend Tiang Delia described it:

> It was as if I was dead, but they tell me I cured all kinds of people . . . when I had my consciousness again, the house was all full of people whom they said I had cured: they said I went walking about all over the place, but I knew nothing about it.

All these experiences, however, are phrased in a characteristic and standardized way. They always last three days, and they often begin on a Friday, or even (as Delia's did) on Good Friday itself. Clearly, the healers are replicating a kind of death and resurrection. In that sense, they are identifying with and repeating the experience of Christ, and evoking the *Ama* who is locally identified as Christ. The healer's unconscious body reproduces the state of the body of the 'father laid out in death' in his shrine. Anxious relatives and patients cluster round the unconscious novice healer as pilgrims do around the *Ama* during the 'bathing of the father' (or as mourners do around a real corpse).

This identification is strengthened by linguistic echoes; the same terms which link the Bicol *Pasion*-text to the stories of the *Ama* also link it to healers' tales. The novice healer Tiang Delia 'walking around', for instance, recalls Christ 'walking around' (*kalakawan*), which is the term used in religious texts to describe Christ's travels when he was performing the miracles. It is also noticeable that healers stress that their vocation is a 'sacrifice' (*sacrificio*), tiring and often thankless. Like the performers in the Passion play (which is also a *sacrificio*), they are becoming Christ's intimates by a process of identification with his experiences.

One strand of local rhetoric in Bicol, presumably reflecting Church antagonism to the spirits, links possession and the *tawo* and opposes them to non-possession and the *Ama.* I have argued that this is not an accurate description of healing practice; for example, a healer may be possessed by a spirit, a saint, or neither. Moreover, although the spirits are an ambivalent power, they cannot be neglected, and have not been replaced by the *Ama*; for most people, the two co-exist as sources of help and healing.

Healers, like other people, sometimes define 'proper' Catholicism and dealings with the spirits as potentially contradictory. However, their multifarious healing styles represent attempts (with almost as many fine variants as there are healers) not to choose between these powers, but to effect a rapprochement between them.[23] A healer's replication of Christ's death and resurrection endows her with power in relation to the *tawo*, but is also a 'shamanic' journey undertaken in the company of her *saro* or spirit-companion.

The creation of this rapprochement is no easy task, a point to which I return below. However, it is the continued relevance of both sources of power in Bicol which seems to explain why it is to the *dead* Christ (and not to the risen Christ of the Church) that healers and patients in S. Ignacio turn.

The equation of death and resurrection with a shamanic voyage is only one instance of the way in which the distinction between the afterlife and the invisible world of the spirits is often elided in Bicol (the case of 'dead' persons who have been 'taken' to live with the *tawo* is another).[24] The *Ama*, or dead Christ, is from this perspective a figure who is continuously performing the shamanic journey between life and death, or the visible and invisible worlds. But while healers in Bicol are always in negotiation with a repertoire of powers, the *Ama* performs this feat without calling on, or succumbing to, any more overwhelming power than his own. For this reason, I suggest, he serves for Bicolano healers as their shamanic exemplar.

Conclusion: the 'imitation' of 'Christ' in Bicol

I have looked in this article at themes of imitation, identification and power in the connected practices of local Catholicism and Bicolano healing. I began by exploring how people relate to the 'dead Christ' through a series of identifications with him. In Europe, the 'imitation of Christ' is a tradition which began in devotional mysticism and the attempt to experience Christ more closely (Koenigsberger & Mosse 1971: 102). In that sense, it stands for the long argument in European Christianity and Europe's converted colonies, between the church and local believers, about access to divine power and the power to define who shall mediate it, to the literature on which this ethnography also contributes (see Leach 1972; Bynum 1987; Christian 1989; 1992; Stirrat 1992). As incorporated in the Counter-Reformation Catholicism of Loyola, however, the 'imitation of Christ' became a form of mediation whose aim was the reduction of the heart to a proper state of Christian conformity and oneness with Christ through knowledge of oneself as a mortal and a sinner.

In Bicol, the imitation of Christ is something different; it is (as in the Passion play) an identification with Christ which does not primarily produce repentance but an intimate closeness with the *Ama.* Bicol healers also seek intimacy with the spirits, though more cautiously.

Imitation in Bicol is thus part of the management of relations between humans and supernaturals, and by humans between supernaturals of different kinds. These relations are conducted in idioms of asymmetrical reciprocity, which have most often been noted in the literature on the lowland Philippines when they refer to patronage, debt and obligation (Hollnsteiner 1970: 65–88; Szanton 1972: 126; Kerkvliet 1990: 243; Rafael 1988: 123). In this case, however, one of the most distinctive idioms is that of pity.[25] Both the *Ama* and the spirits approach people by 'pitying' them. The 'pity' of the *Ama* is seen as an unequivocal good; it may be solicited through prayer and promises, and adequate returns are made by the holding of Passion plays, readings and the performance of vows. The 'pity' of the spirits is less clearly solicited and more equivocal, carrying dangers as well as benefits for both patient and healer. This 'pity' must be managed by healers, through the rhetorical techniques of negotiation, through 'shamanic' magical prowess, or by the use of protective techniques borrowed from Catholic practice. In this repertoire, the sense in which every healer 'imitates Christ' is a key component. In the case of both dealings with the *Ama* and dealings with the spirits (especially with spirit-companions, who build up a relationship with healers over time), hierarchical relations are represented as constantly in process, with the subordinate party always drawing in (and drawing towards) the superior, although never entirely closing the gap.

At the same time, the healers' imitation of Christ cuts both ways; it does not merely elevate the *Ama* to a position separate from and superior to the realm of the spirits. Instead, it identifies him as himself a 'shamanic' figure associated with the control over movement between human and non-human worlds which is the distinguishing feature of such practitioners in the Philippine lowlands and beyond.

Ileto (1979) and Rafael (1988) provide two elegant historical studies of the Philippines' colonial encounters, for the end and the beginning of the Spanish periods respectively. Like Scott (1985: 96–126), both assume that Filipino culture constitutes the self through exchanges of indebtedness and gratitude with others, and vitally so with superiors, with whom one must place oneself in a debt relation in order to ensure a degree of protection. Rafael argues that an attempt to establish such relations with the Spanish determined much of the tenor of early Spanish-Filipino encounters. Filipinos re-constructed contexts such as confession, which were understood by the church as a one-way process of instruction to converts, as opportunities for the creation of (asymmetrical) two-way relations of reciprocity with social superiors.

The imperative to exchange was not only practical but also existential. The opposite of patronage and protection is not only exposure to material harm, but also the exposure of the self to predation or to effacement and total exclusion from social relationships.

The material discussed here shows some of the analogous processes in contemporary Bicol.[26] If pity describes the initiative of saint or spirits in instituting relations with humans, then verbal negotiation and identificatory imitation describe some of the human devices for instituting and managing such relationships, and domesticating dealings with superior powers.

There are undoubtedly comparisons to be made here with more 'egalitarian' highland Philippine societies such as the Ilongot as described by Renato Rosaldo (1980). The Ilongot say that aggression and potential hierarchy must be managed through a gradual and careful closing of distance (for instance, between two feuding parties) and then by public oratory and negotiation. The two parties will then 'become used to' each other, a phrase which is also used to describe love between men and women.[27] Many of the same idioms are used by spirit-mediums in Bicol to describe how they gradually build relationships with their spirit-companions, which can be seen as an exercise in the *reduction* of hierarchy rather than, as in the Ilongot case, the *avoidance* of it.

Much social history of the Philippines remains to be written. It is therefore inevitable that general conclusions about the relationship between changes in these idioms over time, and shifts in political context, should remain speculative. However, it is perhaps worth noting a comparison with part of Ileto's (1979) account of the Tagalog provinces at the turn of the century. A series of 'millenarian' peasant uprisings formed part of the successful Philippine revolution against the Spanish, and the initial resistance to the new American regime. Ileto's central point is that these revolutionary activities drew on images and understandings taken from the *Pasyon*, the Tagalog-language counterpart of the Bicol *Pasion* text described above. Thus, what had begun as a Spanish text of conversion was translated into an idiom of subversion.

The point I would draw out here, however, is a different one. It is clear from Ileto's account that the peasant leaders were men whose actions made sense to themselves and others because of a highly elaborated version of what I have been calling the imitation of Christ, in this case the Christ of the Passion-text. Stories about these leaders were cast within the framework and language of the stages of the life of Christ, and resurrections of those who died or disappeared were expected. This identification was integrated with a confident command of those sources of power which broadly belong to the Filipino and wider Southeast-Asian magical and 'shamanic' tradition. All the rebels possessed *anting*, the magical objects which are often the gifts of spirits, and most considered themselves adepts in techniques which would make them invulnerable to bullets.

Ileto's peasant leaders incorporated a conjunction of these two kinds of power at a particular political moment. Or, to put it slightly differently, they managed almost to erase the contradictions which arose because Catholic deities and non-Catholic spirits had to co-exist in the Spanish Philippines, by embodying a Christ who was truly Christ but was also a magical hero, the best 'shaman'. It is little wonder that they expected success from this prodigious achievement. By contrast in Bicol, the most permanent embodiment of this idea remained not human practitioners but the carved figure of the 'dead Christ' himself.

The political contexts of Ileto's study and my own are very different. In 1989, the Philippines had been independent for more than forty years, though American influence on policy was still a key issue. I have barely touched here on Bicolano perceptions of America, or on the influence of American Protestant missions, despite which both saints and spirits remain figures of crucial importance in daily life. But although the relationship between political change and religious representation is never a direct one, the contrast between the degree of resolution in Filipino imitations of Christ in revolutionary and non-revolutionary periods is probably not accidental. If 'imitation' in Bicol is understood as part of the representation of power relations, rather than as a symptom of lowland permeability to Western culture, this article would argue not only for the distinctiveness but also for the historical continuity of the ways in which that mediation has been effected in the Philippine lowlands.

Notes

Fieldwork was conducted between March 1988 and December 1989 with the assistance of an ESRC state studentship. I revisited Bicol in August 1992 with the help of grants kindly made available by the British Academy and the Evans Fund of Cambridge University. Earlier versions of this article were presented at the ASA decennial conference in Oxford in July 1993 and at the LSE departmental seminar in January 1994, and I have benefited from the comments of the participants. I should especially like to thank William Christian, Chris Fuller and John Peel for comments on drafts of this article.

1 Eliade makes a well-known contrast between true shamanism and 'spontaneous mediumship' (1989: 347). In the latter, which he considers typical of Southeast Asia, communion with spirits is less controlled than in the true shamanism of north Asia. While not accepting the view that Southeast Asian practice is a deviation from a 'true' form, I adopt Eliade's shamanism/possession distinction here for the purposes of clear description, since it captures one aspect of Bicolano rhetoric about different kinds of healing.
2 Space precludes my referring here to all the comparative literature on mediumship, saint-cults, 'syncretisms' and so on. Further references, and a longer account of the *Ama* and Bicol healers, are given in Cannell (1991). Ong's book (1987) explores spirit-possession as oppositional to capitalism as well as in tension with Malay Islam, a dimension which I do not address here. A recent Philippine ethnography of shamanship (but not Catholicism) is Magos (1986), and of 'syncretism' (but not healing) is Elesterio (1989). Dumont's interesting Visayan ethnography (1992) does not address these themes.
3 A *barangay* is the smallest unit of local government, constituting a 'village' in rural areas, and a subdivision of a town in urban ones. For convenience, I pluralize the word here using a final 's' as in English, but the correct Bicol plural would be *mga barangay.*
4 This view of the lowlands as deficient in cultural resistance and authenticity occurs in writers of very different intentions, theoretical backgrounds and political positions, and in journalism, guide-books and school text-books as well as social science writing. It has informed both sociological writing on the problems of 'modernization' and some Filipino nationalist critiques of over-dependency on American culture. A handful of contrasting examples are Lynch (1984), Davis (1973), Venco (1984), Mulder (1991), Mayuga & Yuson (1984), Constantino (1978).
5 This is my own supposition and that of local historian Danny Gerona (personal communication, see also Gerona 1990). The links between the Philippines and Mexico were established by the Spanish galleon trade, and a number of Filipino images came from Mexico (Zialcita, personal communication.) Alternatively, the image may have been made, as many are, by Filipino craftsmen in Manila. My estimate of the date of the image is based on the impressions of older people in S. Ignacio.
6 The chapels in which saints' images are kept are usually referred to in this way, by a Bicol phrase equivalent to *chez* in French; thus no distinction is made between *ki Maring* (Maria's place) and *ki S. Ignacio* (Saint Ignacio's place.) The word used for house is the one in normal usage, *harong.*
7 In Bicol, the most important popular religious text is the Bicol-language passion story or *Pasion.*
8 Some of the income from the shrine accrues to the family who own the *Ama*, and disputes may arise as to whether funds have been correctly divided.
9 Compare Father Frank Lynch, an American Jesuit and ethnographer of Bicol, who followed church teaching in seeing Easter as the climactic event of the year (Lynch c.1965: 123).
10 I discuss the full significance of embalming, and its probable historical importance in Cannell (1991: 242–50).

11 Bicolano cemeteries are arranged like some continental European Catholic cemeteries. They contain standing concrete structures much like filing cabinets, in which the dead are buried in a series of stacked 'drawers'. These spaces are rented from the Church for a fee, and eventually secondary burial is meant to follow. Wealthy families, however, purchase their own tomb plots.

12 Cemeteries (*kampusanto*) are places which people think of as lonely, neglected and frightening. They are not visited except on All Souls' Day, and are situated outside the town away from the church.

13 The parallels are followed in small particulars too. For example, a house cannot be swept out while a corpse lies within, nor can the shrine of the *Ama* be cleaned during Holy Week.

14 On a return visit to Bicol in summer 1992, I was told of some conflict between a new priest and the family who own the *Ama*. The priest had suggested that the *Ama* be taken to the church on Holy Wednesday, and that Good Friday be celebrated with a Mass there. Resistance to this relocation took the form of the *Ama* appearing in people's dreams asking 'Why do you want to bury me already (i.e. on Wednesday) *when I am not yet dead?*' The *Ama* was not moved to the church.

15 The Bicol version of the Passion, at least as a complete text, did not appear until relatively late, and it seems that the Tagalog version was used in the province until a translation was published (Javellana 1988: 11–20; Rafael 1988: 194). The Bicol version currently in use is Hernandez (1984 [1866]).

16 For a discussion of the nature of the 'people', their resemblances to and differences from other Southeast Asian spirits, and the history of mediumship in the lowland Philippines, see Cannell (1991: 75–220).

17 For instance, one healer used eggs and other objects for divination, prayers, amulets and protective signs. Another belonged to a small group who used 'syncretic' costumes modelled on archbishops' outfits, but decorated with pink sequins, and danced while possessed.

18 These are marked in ashes from paper on which prayers and spells (using Latin and Spanish words and Christian signs) have been written before it is burnt. Patients may also drink these ashes in water.

19 Healers and spirit-companions grow to have such a close relationship over time that the spirit's negotiating skill and personality cling around the healer. Healers will deal with their spirit-companions with gradually increasing confidence as the two 'become used to' each other.

20 See Cannell (in preparation).

21 The deliberate seeking of these adventures seems to have been mostly a male form of prowess; however, both men and women may modestly present themselves as having had power thrust upon them by the will of the *tawo.*

22 Even healers who are not normally possessed usually say that the spirits approached them in the same way, but later agreed to let them heal without acting as medium to the spirit-companion.

23 An individual healer's choice of style may of course reflect the way in which she wants to be seen in relation to Catholicism by her patients (or even by the priest), as well as other factors concerning status, personal history, and so on. This level of explanation of variation is beyond the scope of the present article, but see Cannell (1991).

24 For a full explanation of this elision between the spirit-world and the afterlife, see Cannell (in preparation).

25 Ileto (1979: 230) also discusses pity (Tagalog, *awa*) as an idiom which draws on the language of the Passion texts and interacts with the language of indebtedness.

26 There are, of course, many others, and debt is a primary determining fact of life in contemporary rural areas.

27 I intend to explore elsewhere the relation of these idioms to the wider discussion of 'the idea of power' in Southeast Asia (Anderson 1972; Errington 1989).

References

Alcina, F. 1960 [1688]. *The Muñoz text of Alcina's history of the Bisayan islands*; transliteration of the Spanish by Victor Baltazar. Chicago: Univ. of Chicago, Dept of Anthropology, Philippine Studies Program.

Anderson, B. 1972. The idea of power in Javanese culture. In *Culture and politics in Indonesia*, (eds) C. Holt *et al.* Ithaca: Cornell Univ. Press.

Atkinson, J. M. 1989. *The art and politics of Wana shamanship.* Berkeley: Univ. of California Press.

Bynum, C. W. 1987. *Holy feast and holy fast: the religious significance of food to medieval women.* Berkeley: Univ. of California Press.

Cannell, F. 1991. Catholicism, spirit mediums and the ideal of beauty in a Bicolano community, Philippines. Thesis, Univ. of London.

—— in preparation. Fear and the fate of the soul in Bicol. In *Anthropology of fear* [provisional title] (eds) R. Barnes *et al.*

Christian, W. A. 1989. *Person and God in a Spanish valley*; new revised edn. Princeton: Univ. Press.

—— 1992. *Moving crucifixes in modern Spain.* Princeton: Univ. Press.

Constantino, R. 1978. *Neocolonial identity and counter consciousness: essays in cultural decolonization.* London: Merlin Press.

Cullemar, E. T. 1986. *Babaylanism in Negros 1896–1907.* Quezon City: New Day.

Davis, W. G. 1973. *Social relations in a Philippine market: self interest and subjectivity.* Berkeley: Univ. of California Press.

Dumont, J.-P. 1992. *Visayan vignettes: ethnographic traces of a Philippine island.* Chicago: Univ. of Chicago Press.

Elesterio, F. G. 1989. *Three essays in Philippine religious culture.* Manila: De La Salle Univ. Press.

Eliade, M. 1989. *Shamanism: archaic techniques of ecstasy.* Harmondsworth: Penguin.

Errington, S. 1989. *Meaning and power in a Southeast Asian realm.* Princeton: Univ. Press.

Gerona, D. M. 1990. *From epic to history: a brief introduction to Bicol history.* Naga: Ateneo de Naga Univ. Press.

Gibson, T. 1986. *Sacrifice and sharing in the Philippine highlands: religion and society among the Buid of Mundoro.* London: Athlone Press.

Hernandez, T. 1984 [1866]. *Casaysayhan can mahal na Pasion ni Jesucristo Cagurangnanta: na sucat ipaglaad nin puso nin siisay man na magbasa* ('Pasion Bicol'); trans. T. Hernandez. Manila: U.S.T. Press.

Hollnsteiner, M. R. 1970. Reciprocity in the lowland Philippines. In *Four readings in Philippine values* (eds) F. Lynch & A. de Guzman (IPC Pap. 2). Quezon City: Ateneo de Manila Univ. Press.

Ileto, R. 1979. *Pasyon and revolution: popular movements in the Philippines, 1840–1910.* Manila: Ateneo de Manila Univ. Press.

Javellana, R. B. 1988. *Casaysayhan nang Pasiong Mahal ni Jesucristong Panginoon Natin na sucat ipag-alab nang puso nang sinomang babasa*; with an introduction, annotations and translation of the 1882 edition. Manila: Ateneo de Manila Univ. Press.

Kerkvliet, B. J. 1990. *Everyday politics in the Philippines: class and status relations in a central Luzon village.* Berkeley: Univ. of California Press.

Koenigsberger, H. G. & G. L. Mosse 1971. *Europe in the sixteenth century.* London: Longman.

Leach, E. 1972. Melchisedech and the emperor: icons of subversion and orthodoxy. In *Structuralist interpretations of Biblical myth* (eds) E. Leach & D. A. Aycock. Cambridge: Univ. Press.

Lewis, I. M. 1971. *Ecstatic religion: an anthropological study of spirit possession and shamanism.* Harmondsworth: Penguin.

Lynch, F. c.1965. Folk Catholicism in the Philippines. Typescript, Library of Institute of Philippine Culture, Ateneo de Manila University, Quezon City.

—— 1984. Social acceptance reconsidered. In *Philippine society and the individual: selected essays in honor of Frank Lynch, 1947–76* (eds) A. A. Yengoyan & P. Q. Makil. Ann Arbor: Univ. of Michigan Press.

Magos, A. P. 1986. The ideological basis and social context of *ma-aram* practice in a Kinaray-a society. Thesis, Univ. of the Philippines, Manila.

Mayuga, S. & A. Yuson 1984. *Insight guides: Philippines.* Hong Kong: APA Productions (Prentice-Hall, Harrap).

Metcalf, P. 1982. *A Borneo journey into death: Bornean eschatology from its rituals.* Philadelphia: Univ. of Pennsylvania Press.

Miller, D. 1987. *Material culture and mass consumption.* Oxford: Blackwell.

Mulder, N. 1991. The cultural process of lowland Christian Filipino society. Draft paper presented to the European Conference on Philippine Studies, Amsterdam, 1991.

Ong, A. 1987. *Spirits of resistance and capitalist discipline: factory women in Malaysia.* Albany: State Univ. of New York Press.

Rafael, V. 1988. *Contracting colonialism: translation and Christian conversion in Tagalog society under early Spanish rule.* Manila: Ateneo de Manila Univ. Press.

Rosaldo, R. 1980. *Ilongot head-hunting 1883–1974: a study in society and history.* Stanford: Univ. Press.

Scott, W. H. 1985. *Cracks in the parchment curtain, and other essays in Philippine history.* Quezon City: New Day Publishers.

Stirrat, R. L. 1992. *Power and religiosity in a post-colonial setting: Sinhala Catholics in contemporary Sri Lanka.* Cambridge: Univ. Press.

Szanton, M. C. B. 1972. *A right to survive: subsistence marketing in a lowland Philippine town.* Quezon City: Ateneo de Manila Univ. Press.

Tsing, A. L. 1993. *In the realm of the diamond-queen: marginality in an out-of-the-way place.* Princeton: Univ. Press.

Venco, S. A. 1984. Another look at inculturation. *Philipp. Stud.* **32**, 44–51.

Warner, M. 1976. *Alone of all her sex: the myth and cult of the Virgin Mary.* New York: Knopf.

Zialcita, F. N. 1986. Popular interpretations of the Passion of Christ. *Philipp. sociol. Rev.* **34**, 56–62.

Part 15

DISCERNING THEOLOGY IN CONTEXT

57

THE STATUS OF CHRISTIAN WOMEN IN KERALA

Susan Visvanathan

Source: Arvind Sharma (ed.), *Women in Indian Religions*, Oxford: Oxford University Press, 2002, pp. 189–200.

When I read Arundhati Roy's book *The God of Small Things*, I felt a deep sense of sadness. It mingled with my laughter. She was a good anthropologist except that her data was not out there. It was in her family, her courtyard, in her bones. It is not easy to be a hybrid—neither this nor that, or half this or half that. But rather than splicing her in two and saying 'Which half of you is Syrian Christian?' as if magical severings of beautiful women is a routine act of the sociologist, I would like to comment on her book and what it says about the status of Christian women in India, specifically Syrian Christian women in Kerala.

Firstly, Roy is very clear that rules are social constructs. People who break them receive severe punishment—ostracism, death, guilt, alienation, pain. These are felt so deeply by the subject that they know in no small measure they do not belong to the society. Every act of theirs is an underlining of the fact that they are rebels, and by that fact rendered marginal. Not surprisingly then, Roy uses adultery and incest as the two major petards with which to hoist her novel. Funnily enough, the lawyer Sabu Thomas who wanted to take Roy to court for obscenity only wished to see her punished on the court of adultery. Incest, which follows in the next couple of pages, is so subtly rendered that it probably bypassed Sabu Thomas' English completely.

I had met Mary Roy in 1981 during the course of my field-work.

My friends Markose and Susan Vellapally were very closely attached to Mrs Roy, since Markose had been a consultant lawyer while the property case and the inheritance act of the Travancore Christians were being contested by Mrs Roy. She invited me for dinner. She lived in a beautiful house built by the famed Laurie Baker, attached to the school which Mrs Roy owned—Corpus Christi. All the rich plantation owners who could not bear to send their children away from Kottayam were her clients. Mrs Roy offered a substantial education for rich children.

We had a marvellous dinner which she told me was cooked on methane gas harvested from the children's toilets. And a light and delicate souffle appeared, topped with honey collected from the school gardens. Mrs Roy told me that she had recently met Mrs Gandhi and asked for a ticket to stand in the elections but had been refused. (Most Syrian Christian, being landed merchants, never vote left, and it is nice that the late E.M.S. Namboodripad described Mary Roy as a strong woman, stronger than Ammu as portrayed in the book). I went away after meeting some other friends of the Vellapally's —all landowners who spent their holidays in America or the Greek Isles. They seemed to have no connection with the middle class, conservative and orthodox Christians whom I had chosen to study. These urbane upper-class Christians were educated in exclusive schools in the Nilgiris, and in colleges in New Delhi. They were part of India's elite who are at home everywhere and at home nowhere—cultured, intelligent people with lesions all their own. Warner had described this for the '30s in America brilliantly—the club, excesses of wealth and entertainment, adultery and divorce, some alcoholism. It was nothing very aberrant—in this circle it was normal to fall in and out of love, and to spend a lot on good books, furnishings, wine, complicated chicken recipes. Their lives never seemed painless or empty, it was just different from the conservatism of the middle-class morality of the people I was studying. The latter would just laugh and say 'Oh! the rich'. It conveyed everything.

One day I dropped in to see Mrs Roy thinking that I would follow the clue that she was descended from a Bishop's line—in fact, one of the key proponents of reformation in the Church in the 1930s. Maybe she had some old letters, papers, some early hymns or sermons, but when we went in she was lying down, and her face was turned to the wall. There was no electricity and when she turned to us, she had no mask on—it was a face tormented by some grief. I still remember recoiling from the agony in her eyes. I do not think it was the lack of a fan, or her asthma. It was a corrosive and terrible grief that made me stop in my tracks.

I was twenty-five, and not very good at handling grief. My patriarchal and repressive father who had caused me various existential crises was after all a *normal* patriarch. It was unlike the female-centred house Arundhati writes about. So, since Mary Roy was in no position on that hot afternoon to discuss her family's role in the Mar Thoma movement, with the anthropologist's *élan* at hiding professional interests, I pretended that it was just a social visit.

I could not fit her into my data. The 'Mary Roy case' came into its own in 1984, but it was the other two women who fought the case (single and helpless) who fitted into my frame. Mary Roy was too much like the Delhi-ites I knew and *didn't* then study: modern, feminist and, in some odd way, individualist.

When I read Arundhati Roy's book, a lot of things fell into place. The younger Roy defined pathology as the normalcy of her life, and etched these in a language both friendly, well crafted and yet excessive. She had the qualities of a good mimic, and so brought to life the nuances and cadences of what it meant to be on the margins. One Malayali critic said 'I wept reading what a sad and bitter life these children had led'.

Somewhere fiction and fact merged so that nobody knew any more what the actual position of Christian women in Kerala was. Even today, nobody admits to falling in love with their servants. For a woman to feel so intensely for a lower-caste man (*adima*) is unthinkable. A philosopher teaching in Delhi has said that he has stopped telling people that he is originally from Ayamennam because of the excitement generated by Roy's book! Malayalis have, however, generally been pleased that Roy wrote this book because, as one theologian Mathai Zachariah told me, 'She has done a service to humanity in general and to the Syrian Christian community in particular'. What is this service? It is to unveil the hypocrisy by which people have lived their lives. It is to state that so-called pathologies are 'normal'—that one can love someone who is not of one's own class or caste. Love him because he is so beautiful, so noble, so true, so proud, so unreal.

The problem of class certainly distinguishes the interpretation of Christianity by the women of Kerala. If the plantation owners of Kottayam represents the life that Roy's book depicts accurately, we see that the absence of the father is substituted by the strong patriarchal presence of the son, the inheritor of property. The sister Ammu is problematic because Syrian Christians have no place for the daughter once she is married off. Mary Roy's class contention that daughters must inherit an equal share of the father's property was immediately countered by the writing of wills by a Syrian Christian patriarch. Even the priests of many of the Syrian Christian churches come out against the Supreme Court judgement of 1984 saying that it would affect the patriarchal bases of Christianity.

The Christian women of Kerala who belong to the St Thomas tradition are generally articulate and strong-willed. Matriarchy persists in the institution of motherhood and mother-in-lawhood because, while men define the aspects of the external world and the relationship to it, it is women who control the inner spheres of the house.

It is this tension between assertive patriarchy and the implicit matriarchal compulsions which are bound to exist when sons are close to their mothers and avoid their fathers that I wish to delineate. Certainly while the father is alive, he makes the decisions about how income is spent, or whom his offspring will marry, or who may expect to inherit what. Yet, there is no doubt that women's sexual and emotional bonds with their husbands do allow them to have some say in the nature of proceedings. It is true that this is offered only as an 'opinion', not even as 'advice', but men do listen even if seemingly absent-mindedly or impatiently. The final decision on any important event is taken by the patriarch seemingly alone, or in the shared and cooperative wisdom of other lineage members. But, as much as my data have shown, Syrian Christian ethos, however patrilineal, is very subtly loving and protective of daughters.

Dowry, which is the greatest scourge of this high-status community, expresses the deep sense of obligation that fathers feel for their daughters. It is love, terror, misery—to give away a daughter, to hope that she falls in the right hands, to consider mortgaging one's property, borrow from relatives, give away a daughter-in-law's *stridhanam* so that one may be assured that she marries well, lives well. This anguish is shared by mother and daughter in equal terms. Women certainly do not have the courage to refuse the terms of marriage—the payment of *stridhanam*. This is why I have termed it as groom-price (Visvanathan, 1993). In a logical process called 'the redistribution of father's wealth', women also tend to see stridhan as their *avakasham* or right, their 'pre-mortem inheritance'.

What I wish to affirm is that mothers, sisters, daughters and wives play very significant roles in men's lives. The oppression lies in that whatever they say or think or feel is deemed to be insignificant. Yet, this does not mean that they do not have influence or cannot affect men's dispositions.

The relationship of mother-in-law to daughter-in-law has perhaps the greatest immediacy of all. After all, daughters and sisters must be married out. Wives influence husbands in the subterranean mode. Mothers and sons have a teasing light-hearted affectionate relationship which can be utilized to good effect as sons grow older and take over from the deceased patriarch. Mothers, as widowed mothers, wield the greater influence over their sons who are by title and responsibility the heads of the household. Yet, the power of women and the authority of their sons are qualitatively different, as Michelle Rosaldo has so vividly argued.

Women do have authority over daughers-in-law. This they express through every symbolic form of encounter—language interaction and silence. If the woman submits to the will of her mother-in-law, peace reigns in the household. Friendship, amity and cooperation revolve around the sharing of that scarce variable—the figure of the son-husband. It is in this dual and hyphenated sense that men live their lives. Veena Das has shown how men resolve this tension in the case of Punjabi kinship. Amongst the Syrian Christians, the relationship of love, contempt and desire mingle in the attitude of a man to his wife—frequently he refers to her in direct conversation as 'mollae' or daughter.

Emotional relationships are ambiguous. People say one thing, yet often experience something quite different. What interests me are the intricacies of intimacy in patriarchy. What is it that allows women to consent to patriarchy? Why do Syrian Christian women (across denominational schisms) accept the superiority of male wisdom, power and authority as if these can never be questioned? How do they create their own enclaves where their destiny as 'dependents' can be played out?

It is the daughter-in-law who traverses this path with so much tact and care. In this respect, it is important to go back to the ceremony of marriage to know what is expected of a bride. To a great extent, the Syrian Christians have remained self-consciously endogamous, except for a few rule-breakers. Sons see from their parents' marriage how supportive women are to their husbands' aims and ambitions, how, given the greatest cleavages by opinion or circumstance, women still stand by their husbands in an attitude of complete devotion and trust. Divorce is still almost unheard of even in the '90s except amongst those who have married out of the community. Christian patience, love and fortitude are invariably built in the contract of marriage. The men, in return, provide shelter, dignity and identity to women in society where single status is seen to be a state of virginal frustration and personal deprivation.

Marriage is thus seen to be a sacramental and permanent bond, and is entered into only after much discussion over the merits, demerits and compatibility of the partners-to-be, by members of the extended family. It is believed that if the families are compatible, then the individuals concerned are bound to have a happy marriage. While not admitting to a belief in destiny, the Syrian Christians definitely believe in God's will and, within that framework, all negotiations are always possible.

Once the betrothal takes place, the stridhanam is exchanged, the date is fixed and the wedding guests invited—the excitement of a traditional marriage is the most palpable thing in the household. Gifts are usually unilateral forms of presentation, as Vatuk has described it for north India where the hierarchies of wife-givers and wife-takers are clearly established. The pleasure of giving a daughter and gifts of gold to the groom's family is enacted, even though in reality the bride's parent may feel the pinch of both in very real terms.

The marriage service

The Syrian Christians, specifically the Yakoba, have rites which use Syrian liturgical and ritual paraphernalia, and the marriage ceremony consists of two interlinked events. The 'blessing of the rings' is the first. It is actually a ceremonial betrothal. The 'blessing of the crowns' is the ceremonial act of uniting man and woman, and symbolizes the inherent homology between Christ the King and the groom, and between the Church and the bride. This establishes the dominantly male symbolism of Pauline Christianity, which privileges spiritual love rather than erotic love. Because of this homology, marriage is a mystery, carrying within it implicitly the nature of grace.

Recently I attended a Syrian Christian wedding. The young couple were mediated by the presence of six priests and one bishop, by their parents and father's sisters on either side. An anthropologist colleague said at the end of the ceremony: 'They (the bride and groom) are still standing so far apart!'

Of course, the young people, modern and cosmopolitan though they were, felt embarrassed by the pageantry, the spectacle of it all. Custom demanded that they keep up a stance of reserve in front of their elders. In the modern contexts of the nuclear family, this reserve would perhaps immediately disappear insomuch as the husband allows it. In the extended family, the demeanour of detachment and controlled affection would be steadfastly maintained. In fact, Syrian Christians feel very threatened when husbands and wives express affection in public. Tender glances, leave alone any demonstration of passion, such as being enclosed with the spouse for long periods of time would put a great deal of strain on the emotions of parents, siblings and offspring. Sexuality is controlled by the expectation that time, space and other social relationships will mediate the expression of desire.

In an odd rendering of passivity as power, the woman is seen to be constantly searching for the groom. Christ represents the completeness of virtue in a man, who is seen to be the sun, while the woman is the day.

This passivity, this dependence of the Christian institution of marriage is based upon the desire of a woman in a patriarchal society to bear legitimate children, preferably sons, and to share the privileges of her husband's property which she may not necessarily own in tandem.

After the 'blessing of the crowns' (a ritual circling a gold chain and cross over the heads of bride and groom), the tying of the *tali*, or marriage locket, and the placing of the *mantrakodi* (cloth bought by the groom) over her head takes place. At this juncture, the girl's attendant who is usually her father's sister is substituted by the groom's sister. She now 'belongs' to them.

The next ritual is the joining of hands of bride and groom. The verses that follow articulate that the woman must leave her family for her husband. He must love her and have kindness. Even if he is naked, he must clothe her. As she loves her own life, she must love him. Even if he goes thirsty, he must give her a drink. Keeping the commandments, she must live with him in love and tenderness. The bride and groom must say the creed *visvasa pramanam* together, articulating their faith in Christian precepts.

The service concludes with the formal signing of the contract of marriage. The bride changes into the new sari the groom had placed over her head during the marriage ceremony. This is the first material gift that he makes to her, bonding her through the intimacy of clothing.

Just as the case of the Syrian Christian cannot be self-explanatory of Christian community and culture everywhere in India, so also the ethnographic uniqueness of the Syrian Christian expresses its cultural alienation from other Christian communities in Kerala itself.

A picture of direct contrast would be the lives of the women of the fishing community in Kerala, specifically those who belong to the Latin Christian community. The argument here is that men's occupations affect the lives of women.

The scenario today

Syrian Christian women are generally prosperous—wives of merchants, bankers, white-collar professionals, capitalists and trawler-owners, farmers and landowners. Whatever the class oscillations among them, they see themselves as an aristocracy. They might not be an elite, but they have the self perceptions of being one. They might do all the housework themselves, or hire maidservants to do their chores (which is practically non-existent now), but they are always cushioned by the memory of their community identity. Hard work is not seen to be demeaning. In fact, Syrian Christian women have been the backbone of the hospital system in many parts of the world by providing nursing and paramedical care. They are seen to be efficient, educated, clean, wellmannered, from good families and ready to work long hours for little pay either out of poverty and helplessness, or Christian virtue. Once married, they may give up their professions as teachers, nurses, secretaries or lab assistants and settle down to keeping house with equal vivaciousness. For those who require a salary to maintain the home in the style they are used to, the double burden of career and domestic chores is systematically handled. The leisured among them, who have servants and do not need to go out to work, nevertheless take pride in cooking and serving, and in nurturing their children. A certain boredom sets in during late middle age when the children are grown, married, and settled professionally in distant cities. Husbands never tend to 'retire' and remain active in their offices, the Church associations, their clubs. The silence of a leisured middle age is one of the most painful and deafening of all life's circumstances. It is spent waiting for the post, for telephone calls, for the possibility of a journey to America or to Allahabad to visit children, for the husband's return from office or club, for the evangelical workers' visit, for friends from the local 'prayer meeting' group. The earlier stamping and scuffling of growing children, the groans and demands of ageing parents-in-law, the shared responsibilities of parenting was a busy and noisy affair. The nostalgia for years gone by is captured by the incessant phrase *pillar valiyuda ayegi poyi* (the children are grown). Old age has its own attendant pleasures—the spiritualism, the delicacy of dependence and helplessness between two partners who have never dreamed of breaking their bond or living apart (unthinkable among the Syrian Christians even now) and the exquisite and subtle curiosity of 'waiting for the bridegroom' (death/Christ). The final answer to that question 'What is it like?' is a time of mediation, prayer, and even longing.

I will contrast this briefly with the wives of the fishermen. The data were collected in the summer of 1998 in Alleppey district. Of course, women's position cannot be understood segmentally in such traditional societies—their lives are conjoined with those of the men.

The fishermen of Ponappra are an active educated set—Christian and Marxist—comfortable with the vocation associated with the friends of Jesus. In the same breath, they are *malysia thozhilaligal*—fish workers.

The women of the fishing community are used to hunger, deprivation and to the thought of death. They are often in debt in terms of sums which are staggering to the average middle-class Syrian Christian peasant, banker or merchant. When the catch is good, the men bring home money to pay debts, gold ornaments for their wives, a new pet for the children or an expensive tape deck and, of course, alcohol. But, there are many days when the sea delivers nothing. It is truly empty.

Every time fishermen take out a boat to sea with forty men on board, it costs them up to a lakh of rupees. There is the cost of hiring the boat from the *modulali* (lord or capitalist overlord) as well as the cost of buying or hiring an outboard motor, the cost of diesel for running the boat out to sea for 6–12 hours, and the costs of feeding the *thozhiyalali* (workers) for this time. Tea alone comes to Rs 40 per person. The fishermen often suffer from vomiting and are unable to eat anything while out at sea. One of them said 'Love the sea? Are you joking? We are not on a beach. This is our work. It has its dangers. Some of us don't return.' In case they come back empty-handed, each fisherman is thousands in debt for that one day. They say they can come back empty-handed for ten days at a time before their luck takes a turn. They have known what it is to go without food for three days at a time. Yet, they assert to the generosity of their community. If a men gets ten baskets of fish, he gives two to the poor as alms, and two to the agent. The value of the remaining six he keeps.

But the ideal situation of catching ten baskets does not often happen. Because of sustained trawler overfishing, the sea is now emptying species by species. The fishermen live in decent dwellings in Ponappra—neat two- or three-room homes which they have put up with the aid of loans from the Church or the government. They remain unfinished, however, because of lack of funds.

The women among this specific local community do not often or necessarily participate in the catching or merchandising of fish. Some do wait at the beach, particularly if they are fishermen's widows, and buy fish as it comes fresh off the nets, which they then sell. Most fishermen deal with an agent (commission agent) who takes over immediately from them when they come in with the haul. These men are from upper-class Latin Christian households, profiteers who live in comfortable and stable houses some distance from the beach. There is some tension between the fishermen and the agents. The fishermen feel themselves unable to handle the constraints of the market; they do not really feel that, in practical matters, they have a union. The fishermen see themselves as innocent victims of the market and of the state. 'We have no union: anybody can join and anybody can leave.' This would come as a surprise to Tom Kocherry and others who lead the fishermen's struggle, who keep records of the union networking at a global level. The fishermen of

Ponappra look to the skies, and pray to different Gods that govern their particular religion.

I will not go into the relationship between poverty, literacy, health and political awareness. Clearly this community feels the pulverizing quality of financial oscillation in a way that other people cannot imagine. If the haul is good, there is a great deal of money which can be shared between forty men, and goes into paying costs and debts. If it is bad, then there is only hunger. But as they say, someone will always give an empty-handed fisherman a few fish for his family to fry.

The anthropology of subsistence societies or the culture of poverty has to handle the emotional mechanisms by which people orient themselves to wealth and degradation in equal measure. One thing they do realize is that the very basis of their life as communities, as families, as conjugal units is threatened by an ecological disaster such as overkill.

It is now difficult to imagine the status of the Latin Christian women who have to share the burden of their husbands' tribulations—the dangerousness of the sea, the poverty of their work, their illiteracy, their indebtedness to the moneylender landlords. Many women weave coir ropes to supplement their income. This is a laborious process of shaping the coir into rope by using their hands, and then plaiting it into strands. It is monotonous back-breaking labour. They sit upright with their legs stretched out, a pile of raw material at their side. Their hands are calloused. For four to six hours of work, they are paid approximately seven rupees. In spite of their degradation, they are somehow hopeful. The Church represents a very positive element in their life. It provides them with loans, helps them save money in a Church-sponsored credit thrift society. The priest who is most supportive to their cause and has helped organize the fishermen's movement in Ponappra tells a story that is woman-centred.

> My father and grandfather were away for long periods—they were in the Navy. So I grew up with my mother. We were very poor. And because of our poverty, our wealthier relatives were ungenerous and unkind. I grew up with the fishermen's sons. It was they who gave me my sense of being, my sense of place. I was really one of them. But then, as I grew older, my hatred for those who had been so contemptuous of our poverty became the blinding force in my life. I became part of a group of young men who were so wild, so terrible that one day my mother said that she cursed the day she had become mother to one such as I. That hurt me very much. It was the turning point of my life. And priesthood was the other side of the coin.

So this man, highly educated, theologically motivated, with a story somewhat like that of Frances of Assissi, trains bands of committed young people who work for the fishermen. Such priests are many. And many wives of fishermen wish their sons to go for a theological training. They will be released from their poverty, they will work for their people.

Ponappra cannot be understood without looking at the story of coir, and the place of the Church. Both the coir and the Church are central about women's location in the fishermen's community. The Church is substantially trying to organize the labour of women by providing them with wooden frames for weaving coir, where their earnings per day can go up from Rs 7 to Rs 25. There is also an understanding that with the ecological degradation of the sea, the community of fishers may be doomed to extinction. Problems of health and literacy are very high. One solution the highly motivated priests feel is to diversify coir and handicrafts production. They also feel that there is a movement, but not a union. Whether it is wages, ecological concerns or conjugal solidarity, women are centrally concerned. The axes of their lives centre around their husbands, the poverty they share and the daily terror of existence.

I use the fishermen's case as a very preliminary statement of the problem of women in Christianity in India. Class, language and region play a significant part in the interpretation of Christianity. The myths of conversion provide completely different bases to Christian ideology and life. Thus, the analyses of women in Christianity must seek to articulate the subject position of women in a very patriarchal system. Whatever transformations are to occur in their status can only be provided by the impetus that the Church and the power-holders in a community set forward. The very ideology of Pauline Christianity subjugates women, whether of upper status or poor. If Christianity is seen to be a radical transformative movement affecting the lives of the poor, then women impoverished by patriarchal Christianity must see in themselves the voice of power that the oppressed always signified for Jesus.

Bibliography

Ardener, Edwin, 1986, The Problem of Power in Leela Dube, *et. al.*, *Visibility and Power*, Oxford University Press, Delhi.

Arendt, Hannah, 1958, *The Human Condition*, University of Chicago Press, Chicago.

Das, Veena, 1976, *Masks and Faces* in *Contributions to Indian Sociology*, n.w. vol. 10, no. 1.

Dernet, J. D. M., 1970, *Law in the New Testament*, Darton, Longman and Todd, London.

Illich, Ivan, 1981, *Shadow Work*, Marion Boyars, London.

—— 1982, *Gender*, Pantheon, New York.

Mies, Maria, 1986, *Patriarchy and Accumulation on a World Scale*, Zed, London.

Mies, Maria, Veronika Benrhold-Thomsen and Claudia von Werlhoff, 1988, *Women: The Last Colony*, Zed Books, London.

Roy, Arundhati, 1997, *The God of Small Things*, Flamingo, London.
Rosaldo, Michelle and Louise Lamphere (eds), 1974, 'Woman', *Culture and Society*, Stanford University Press, California.
Showalter, Elaine (ed.), 1989, *Speaking of Gender*, RKP, New York.
Visvanathan, Susan, 1993, *The Christians of Kerala*, Oxford University Press, Madras.
—— 1994, The Fishing Struggle in Kerala, *Seminar*, November.
Warner, Lloyd W., 1975, *Family of God*, Greenwood Press, Connecticut.

58

CONTESTED MASCULINE SPACES IN GREEK ORTHODOXY

Eleni Sotiriu

Source: *Social Compass*, 51(4) (2004), 499–510.

Beginning in 1976 with the first international symposium (Agapia, Romania) on the role and participation of women in the church, women members of various local Orthodox Churches began to raise the question of the possibility of their access to ordained ministry. Such questions were prompted by interest in the women's movement in the West. Yet feminism and Orthodoxy seem to be antithetical terms. Indeed, feminist theology and spirituality are treated by the majority of male Orthodox ecclesiasts as the result of a defective Western theology and as something to be expiated. The Ecumenical Movement, however, produced an urgent need for a serious encounter of Orthodoxy with feminism. This need culminated in the Ecumenical Patriarch convening in 1988 an inter-Orthodox Symposium in Rhodes (Greece) which, in its attempt to clearly articulate the Orthodox position on the women's issue, reached important conclusions. Since then, two more international conferences on the same issue have taken place (Damascus, 1996; Constantinople, 1997). Nevertheless, apart from the fact that women's ordained ministry is still treated in Orthodoxy as "a casus irrealis" (Schmemann, 1999: 3), we are lacking any formal responses.

This article focuses on the key controversies surrounding women and Orthodoxy in contemporary Greece. It examines women's exclusion from the ministerial and sacramental orders of the church. Women, however, are excluded not only from the Altar—the focal point of ordinations—but also from another sacred space occupying a central place in the Greek religious landscape, that of Mount Athos. The fact that a lifting of the ban of women from the latter has been called for by the European Parliament makes it an issue of heated debate as yet to be treated in scholarly literature. As is the case of veiling in Turkey (Göle, 1996) or that of South Korean weddings as rites of modernization (Kendall, 1996), the issues under discussion present an engendered dialogue between "modernity" and "tradition", two concepts which, rather than being mutual antipodes, are jointly manipulated in the construction of both individual and collective identities and refuel patriarchal gender relations in Greece. In the discussion of gender relations "modernity" implies an egalitarian gender system while "tradition" is equated with asymmetrical gender relations and male hierarchy and control. Women, particularly those belonging to the educated and political elite, are forcing an encounter of Orthodoxy with modernity, but this is in practice mitigated by the re-appropriation of a tradition which juxtaposes church and state ideology and makes women modern nationalist icons. This "nationalization" of women hinders their potential for leadership in the religious sphere by subsuming their individuation under the umbrella of a generalized Greek Orthodox identity which projects the male perspective. Ultimately, a discussion of their exclusion becomes a discussion of Greek identity as Greeks blend tradition and modernity in an attempt to redefine self and other in Europe's cultural landscape.

Trouble in paradise: the exclusion of women from the altar

Surveying the arguments for and against the ordination of Orthodox women in the church is like traversing an ambiguous terrain. Although the theological schools have recently undergone a process of "feminization", since more and more women are now studying theology and an increasing number of women are included in the academic staff, very few of these women have voiced a concern regarding their participation in the priesthood. Indeed, many lay women and men would find such a suggestion as flirting with absurdity, while the majority of monastics would even go so far as to characterize it as blasphemous, against the holy tradition, and a by-product of the fallen West. Thus, the issue of women's ordination and its many related themes are debated not so much at a grass-roots level, but rather within a small circle of women, many of whom are living and working in the Greek diaspora and are more engaged in the ecumenical dialogue. The discussion of "women's issues" has been integrated into the inter-Orthodox dialogue mainly by the need to project to the non-Orthodox world an image of a religion which is not backward and stagnating, as many think of Orthodoxy in the West, but which can successfully address the challenges of modernity in its own way.

This need is also coupled with that of articulating an Orthodox "otherness" not only vis-à-vis Protestantism, which permits women's ordination, but also vis-à-vis Roman Catholicism, which maintains a conservative stance on the matter. Greek Orthodoxy claims generally to possess a more authentic tradition that involves unbroken continuity and, thus, is in need of no or minimal revision. To this effect, the focal point of related discussions has not been so much on the women's way to priesthood, but rather on the women's position in the early church, their role as deaconesses and the potential restoration of that order. As a result, the issues have been debated mostly through a scriptural and historical perspective rather than through a contemporary and critical one. Hence, Orthodox theologians of both sexes are quick to point out that women receive in the church an equal amount of reverence to men as martyrs, saints and even *isapostoloi* (equal-to-the apostles) and that there hardly exists a day in the ecclesiastical calendar without celebrating the memory of at least one of these remarkable women. In this context, references are frequently made to the Church Fathers as supporting the ontological unity of mankind and egalitarianism between men and women mainly at the eschatological level. Above all, such theologians evoke the exalted position occupied by the *Theotokos* (the Mother of God). She is venerated above all saints and provides the main model for the ministry and role of women both in church and society. It is worth noting that the Mother of God is revered as the "new Eve", representing sanctified humanity through obedience to God's will. The typological reclamation of Eve by Mary and the degradation of the former is, however, regarded by Topping (1983: 10) as the result of the misogynistic theology of the Church Fathers. In her view, both Mary and the female saints are extolled in part at the expense of Eve; they both cancel the fall of their archetypal mother. Moreover, female saints earned their position in the Orthodox cosmos because of their male-like qualities and their ability to overcome the impediments of their "feminine nature". In Orthodox iconography, Mary is depicted either in her motherhood role holding the figure of Christ or as the receptor of the power of the Holy Spirit (the icon of Annunciation). Thus, in both iconic and typological terms she typifies appropriate models of behaviour for women in a way that Christ does not for men.

Attempts, however, to answer feminist questions such as why any modern woman would embrace such conservative models are met with perplexity. Some scholars (Hirschon, 1978; du Boulay, 1986) have argued that such models are not as oppressive to women as feminists had supposed. In Orthodoxy, there exists a sharp distinction between theory and practice; in the latter, women may find a complementary egalitarianism ingratiating an ideology that symbolically affirms their submission to male power and authority. While such theories may prove that women lack no agency or suffer from a kind of "false consciousness" by emulating the conservative religious models on offer, it would be misleading to think that such models are the only ones in society and culture, though they still remain the dominant ones. The sexual dimorphism offered by the "daughters of Eve" and "Mothers of God" images runs parallel or at best is hidden under those offered by modernity. Women may work and be more sexually liberated today, but still they are expected to be "ladies of the house" and to "mother" (Faubion, 1993: 176). Antithetical as it may sound to many, they are Orthodox and "modern" at once, revealing one or other aspect of their identity or even mingling the two as the situation dictates. Thus, they create ad hoc interpretations of Orthodoxy that makes it more adaptable to their individual circumstances. In this way, they acquire a piety of their own which often defies the official rules of the church. For example, many women in the course of my fieldwork at a convent located in a Greek urban locality admitted that they were kissing the icons, lighting candles or receiving the "*antidoron*" (consecrated bread) while they were menstruating, because they just felt "a need for it". Such practices indicate a more "muted" female model of piety that runs against the official prescriptions concerning women's ritual impurity. Interest in the abolition of rituals and practices connected to women's impurity—such as prayers associated with miscarriage, abortion, postpartum mothers, the assumptions preventing women from partaking in the sacrament of Holy Communion when they are menstruating and the churching of infants (whereby female babies are not brought into the sanctuary and as girls are excluded from being altar servers)—has been expressed by women for a long time. Nonetheless, these matters still remain undecided.

Because discussions on women's status touch on almost every aspect of Orthodox theology, they best exemplify the ambiguities and contradictions inherent in the tradition and point to the already mentioned gap between theory and praxis. While women are getting more and more involved in lay ministry through their increased participation in the church's educational, administrative and philanthropic activities, mainly at the parish level in a role which has been termed as "supportive diakonia" (Limouris, 1992a: 30), their main position still remains that of an indispensable helper to the male ordained clergy, but a helper nonetheless. Their exclusion from the most sacred part of liturgical space—the Altar which paradoxically lies under the protection of the Mother of God depicted in the apse of all church buildings—is surmounted only by old non-menstruating women or professed nuns when it needs cleaning. Moreover, women are excluded from the minor orders of readers and chanters. These practices are overlooked only in the complete absence of men, as is the case of women's monasteries. This matter has been discussed in inter-Orthodox meetings and constitutes now a fairly uncontroversial possibility.

Thus, women's overall position is slowly improving. This is not only the result of the ongoing dialogue within the church, but also the accomplishment of ordinary women who disregard church rules and establish new practices more favourable to them. As religious actors they carve a space of their own not so much through overt social movements or external signs of difference—as, for example, Islamist women (cf. Göle, 1996)—but rather through common everyday practice. This is most evident in the case of church prescriptions concerning the manner of women's dress. Many women attend church wearing trousers, to the point that the current Archbishop Christodoulos has called for the relaxation of such prescriptions. A sign of improvement in the role and spiritual worthiness of women can also be seen in the exceptional position that some abbesses (such as Evgenia Kleidara of the Saint Raphael Monastery, Lesvos) occupy as "spiritual mothers", a role that in the past was reserved only for males. They are valued not only for their spiritual guidance and their philanthropic work, but also as the custodians of sacred, miraculous relics and powerful intercessors on behalf of the believers to those saints to whom the relics belong and to God. Of great interest is that women who became nuns in past centuries were uneducated and had few opportunities in society, while in the last few decades more and more Greek educated women are entering monasticism, reviving the institution and attracting converts from the West.

What, however, is striking among Greek Orthodox women at a grass-roots level is that they appear to lack strong sentiments against the discrimination and impediments that the male church hierarchy has imposed on their religious life. This may be due to two main reasons. The first is that Orthodoxy, as it is practised, reveals strong feminine tendencies, bringing it closer to women than to men. This is attested by the fact that the church attendance of men, as well as their role in ritual activities outside the church, is minimal compared to that of women. Moreover, anticlericalism as a sentiment runs higher in men. Women feel closer to the parish priest because his appearance, the place he serves and the values he embodies belong to the sphere that Greek society has termed "feminine". The second key factor is the flexibility characterizing Orthodoxy, which possesses a "magic tool", namely the principle of "*oikonomia*", used primarily in the Canon Law but applied generally as well. This shows its potential for adaptation and refers to a mild application of rules out of philanthropic concerns and especially when it is believed that the strict application of these rules would accentuate problems. "*Oikonomia*" thus allows things to happen that would be otherwise unacceptable. These exceptions do not become the rule, but they are tolerated under special circumstances and give to the church a "popular tinge".

Because of this the Orthodox Church appears to be less rigorist than the Roman Catholic Church concerning women's ordination. The current Archbishop Christodoulos, when he was Metropolitan of Demetrias in 1986, had ordained the abbess of the convent of St Spyridon (Promiri, Magnesia) into the diaconate. She was given the right to administer the sacrament of Holy Communion to the nuns in the absence of an ordained male clergyman. In this case, the revival of the old office of the deaconess was deemed necessary due to the inaccessibility of the place, particularly in the winter months. Although deaconesses existed in the West until at least the 11th century, the institution was considered mainly to be "Eastern" (Theodorou, 1992: 210). It flourished particularly in the 4th, 5th and 6th centuries when the deaconesses were held in high honour. Such women were selected out of the order of virgins dedicated to God or from the order of widows who were married only once. They were at least 40 years of age and had the necessary education to fulfil their catechetical duties. Their ordination was analogous to that of deacons and was considered of higher rank than that of sub-deacon. Deaconesses were important ceremonial, instructional and social-care intermediaries between the male hierarchy and the female church members. From the 9th century onwards, the order fell gradually in decline, though in Greece it never ceased to exist completely. Attempts to restore it began in 1911, when the later canonized Bishop Nektarios (Kephalas) ordained nuns into the diaconate, and continues up to the present day. In 1952 a School of Deaconesses was established in Athens to prepare women to assist the clergy, but no graduates were ever ordained. Nevertheless, the restitution of the female diaconate is seen by the great majority of scholars and ecclesiasts in a positive light. The Rhodes inter-Orthodox Symposium called for the revival of deaconesses, but such a call has produced no real action so far. This order is not an innovation endangering tradition, as many would think of women priests, but it certainly goes against the traditionalism of the male hierarchy, who fear that "giving an inch may lead to the taking of a mile" on the part of women and be used as a step towards access to the sacramental priesthood. The issue of women's ordination to any ecclesial office is treated with caution because it is first and foremost seen "as the product of feminism" (Kollontai, 2000: 172), which is considered to contain incongruous elements to those of Orthodoxy.

Thus, if the office of deaconess may seem a target within reach, women's admission to the priesthood remains an almost absolute impossibility. The main objections stem from the "iconic" character of the priesthood, from views about women's "nature" and their specific charismas and spirituality, and from the appeal to tradition. The "iconic" argument is based on the identity of the priest as an icon of Christ and defends the significance of the maleness of priests by stating that the priest should be "male as to express his likeness faithfully" (Harrison, 1999: 181). Moreover, this "iconism" is connected to another, that of the Church as Bride encountering Christ the Bridegroom and "not the Bride of the Bride" (Limouris, 1992b: 269). In the complex "iconic" symbolism, the priest's maleness is important because he is not merely representing Christ but "is a living icon" and "truly acts" in the place of Him. The woman's "iconic" relationship is with the Holy Spirit and the *Theotokos.* Her function is "Pneumatocentric" as an "exceptional bearer of the special charismas" of the Holy Spirit and as such is contrasted to the "Christocentric" function of the priesthood (Pheidas, 1992: 182, 192–193). Consequently, women are seen as having distinct roles which are thought of as equal and complementary to that of men, but at the same time supportive of a hierarchical structure, seen as reflecting the order of creation. Moreover, women's ordination to the priesthood is perceived as contravening their "natural gifts" and as "a betrayal on their part of their nature as a woman" (Chrysostomos, 1992: 130). The "tradition" argument further reinforces such positions, since it is based on Pauline teachings concerning the place of woman under man's authority and stresses the normative character of the apostolic era. Thus, since Christ did not choose any woman to be an apostle and the apostles never ordained women as priests, women should be excluded from the priesthood. More importantly, if women were to function as priests, such a function would have been exercised by the Mother of God.

All in all, the overall picture is one of rejection of women's ordination. Proponents of the opposite stance are few and far between. Most women scholars seem to be satisfied that a platform exists now for the discussion of important concerns affecting women without calling for their ordination and refuting the male traditionalism of the church. In fact, such a demand is seen not only as a product of feminist theology and spirituality but also as the result of Western Christian views which promote the "heresy of clericalism" by considering ordained ministry as the only meaningful way of service to the church (Karras, 1998: 33–34). It is thus refreshing to find at least one prominent male theologian, Farantos (2000: 152, 154), supporting women's ordination. He has argued that no dogmatic reason exists for their exclusion from sacramental priesthood and that such a role is more fitting to them because Christianity is a religion of love that finds its fullest expression in the feminine sphere, particularly that of motherhood. Stronger voices come mostly by way of female Orthodox scholars who work outside Greece, like Behr-Sigel (2001), calling for the transcendence of the masculine/feminine categories in the church which are secondary to humanity.

In Greece the main bearers of tradition are women, both by their greater participation in the religious sphere and by their motherhood role. Paradoxically, however, they are considered incompatible with the exercise of the priesthood. The 2000-year-old boundary that exists between the Altar and women is fortified by the appropriation of contrasted spiritual images of womanhood by Orthodox hierarchs and theologians and by appeals to authenticity and a male-produced tradition. The same arguments, more or less, have been also used to secure women's exclusion from Mount Athos. Only this time, these arguments have been moved from the religious to encompass the national level as well.

On swaying skirts, cats and the beast: the Mount Athos *avaton*

On 8 August 1982 the Greek newspaper *Avriani* published an article entitled "Skirts Will Sway on the Holy Mountain", revealing supposed plans by the then newly elected socialist government of Greece to lift the ban imposed on the female sex on Mount Athos. While this article turned out to be a "false alarm", the realization of such a proposal came almost 21 years later from outside Greece and invited a polemic by both the Athonite monastic community and the state. On 14 January 2003 the European Parliament voted a non-binding resolution contesting the prohibition of women's entry in the

Mount Athos peninsula and called for its revocation (Article 98). The so-called "*avaton*" is viewed by many female Euro-deputies, notably those of northern origin, who were the first to raise the issue, as an encroachment upon European human rights legislation. The monastic community and the state in Greece were quick to respond to what was in this case perceived as a common threat: the European Union. Given that Greece, up until recently, was the only Orthodox member state of the European Union and that Orthodoxy is the indissoluble cement of Greek identity, the approval of such a resolution was seen as an impending injury to Greekness. The religious alterity of Greece is that kind of otherness that has a long-standing history reaching back to the 1054 schism between Rome and Constantinople and produces among (West) Europeans images of backwardness, anachronism and irrationality. Conversely, the Catholic and Protestant countries of the European Union are seen by many Orthodox Greeks as conforming to stereotypes of irreligion and immorality.

It is against this background that the poignant rejection by both the Greek government and the *Iera Epistasia*, the governing council of the Athonite community, of the above-mentioned resolution should be understood. Both their responses centred on the special status of Athos as approved and confirmed by the Greek Constitution (Article 105) and mandated by international treaties concerning the incorporation of Greece into the EEC (1981). Mount Athos constitutes a self-governed part of the Greek state, whose sovereignty is justified on religious and spiritual grounds. The entire Athonite peninsula is the private property of the 20 monasteries that reside there, and its territory is constitutionally exempt from expropriation. Thus, the monks argued that the "*avaton*" has strong legal foundations and that any lifting on the ban would mean an infringement of their freedom of religious expression. These objections were also fully supported by the Greek state. In fact, the Culture Minister, Evangelos Venizelos, alluded to the double standards followed by the European Parliament, pointing out that the Vatican, although a member of the Council of Europe as a state, is represented solely by men. In his view, the European Parliament should confront such issues with "tolerance" and "a pluralistic attitude". Thus, both the state and the monks appealed to the nearly one-millennium-old tradition of the "*avaton*" which for religious, cultural, ecclesiastical and national reasons should remain unchanged. The argument based on legalities is intended mainly for "outside consumption", calling upon the rationality of non-Orthodox Europeans. The other two strategies, based on tradition and the need to protect Orthodoxy, are mainly directed to "insiders", appealing to values and sensitivities that are deeply ingrained into the Greek soul. In fact, the pinpointing of the Vatican case by Venizelos was not accidental but was intended to heighten these very sensitivities. Further, it is on the intermingling of factors belonging to the last two strategies that the undertone of the "*avaton*" as a gender issue rests.

Concerning the Greek women's stance on this controversial issue, the Euro-Deputy Anna Karamanou was the only one who voted in favour of lifting the prohibition on female visitors to Athos. She is currently the strongest advocate of such a position as well as of women's ordination. She argues (2003) that the ban on women was established a thousand years ago, in the period of the "dark Middle Ages", and reflects the social conditions of the time. This cannot be valid under the currently prevailing perceptions of human rights and gender equality, she says. This prohibition also contrasts with the message found in the Gospels. The monks' appeal to tradition is an "alibi" for treating even their own mothers as "children of a lesser God". Fotini Pipili, a prominent journalist, also accepts these views and was the first to demand that the issue be debated in the Greek parliament. She argued that the current restoration of the monasteries of Mount Athos has been achieved through the money of European taxpayers of both sexes and thus women cannot be excluded any longer. Yet another well-known journalist and MP, Liana Kanelli, is a militant opponent of such views. According to her, the prohibition should be upheld on the grounds that places of great symbolic value have often become places of entertainment in the wake of urbanization and modernization. This development cannot be regarded as progress. It is interesting also that most Orthodox lay women in Greece and from other Eastern European countries do not support the lifting of the ban (Clark, 2000: 5–6). In the case of Greece, this is not only due to strong adherence to religious tradition but also to an interplay of several discourses about religion, gender and national identity.

Here I will focus mainly on the "tradition" argument and on the symbolism informing the rhetorical strategies of both the Athonite community and the state, for they render transparent the dilemmas faced by women producing their "non-action" on the matter. The "tradition" argument rests principally on the "mythology" associated with the place. The Athonite peninsula is regarded as the "Garden of the Virgin" given to the Mother of God by her Son. According to legend, the Virgin, travelling on a ship to Cyprus, was blown ashore on the mountain. She was so overwhelmed by its beauty that she prayed to her Son to grant it to her. Since then, the Mother of God has been the patron and protectress of what has become known as the "Holy Mountain". Conforming to the legend, the ban on women, female animals and all female images was introduced in 1060 AD. In its long history the "*avaton*" has been violated many times, mainly in exceptional circumstances and under the principle of "*oikonomia*". Currently, a relaxation of the rule exists only for cats due to the divine providence of the Virgin who, according to the monks, "provided" them in order to keep the snake population of Mount Athos at bay. Women's curiosity about Mount Athos can only be satisfied by sailing at a distance of 500m from the shore. Any attempt to move closer can be penalized by imprisonment for a period ranging from two months to a year. Considering that the Mother of God alone of all her sex is represented on Mount Athos, any demand for the lifting of the ban is conceived of as a rivalry against the most venerated holy figure of Orthodoxy and, as such, a sign of the gravest irreverence. This "mythology" has secured an exclusionary purified social space and bestowed it with "holiness". While for the monks the place became holy because of the appearance of the Virgin there, according to popular thinking both Mount Athos and the Athonite monks owe their "holiness" to the exclusion of women. Indeed, Athonite monks are viewed as a particular kind of *Gemeinschaft* ranking higher in "holiness" than the rest of the male monastics in Greece, who are situated in the "Garden of Eve" (meaning the secular world). Women's entrance in Mount Athos will mean that the place will no longer be a locus of spiritual radiance. Women should be exorcized as the Devil. In fact, women became the "folk devil" of the Holy Mountain. There is an apparent process of "devilizing" women which is achieved not only through their obvious association with Eve and the Devil, whom the monks claim appears to them often in the shape of a woman arousing their sexual desires, but also through women's association with the ills of the West. Behind any attempt threatening the status quo lie the great anti-Orthodox enemies, i.e. the European Union and the Vatican, which in the minds of many monks are equated with the apocalyptic Beast. In the end, any "feminist endeavour" on the part of women is seen as the result of the fallen and inimical West. Although the association of women with the Beast is not explicit in the discourse of Athonite monks, I do not think it is far-fetched to suggest it.

The exclusion of women is secured not only by these negative associations. Rather, it is on the symbolic play of their dimorphic identity that the success of these strategies is based. Apart from Eve, there is also the tenacious association of women with the Virgin Mary. While the Virgin Mary is the protectress of Mount Athos at the local level, she is also the protectress of the whole of the Greek nation, a fact visibly revealed by the simultaneous celebration of many feasts connected with her and important national events. All these suggest an analogy between female identity and Greekness. It is in this context that the difficulty of women to reconcile nationalist assumptions with feminist demands should best be understood. To ask for the abolition of the "*avaton*" would thus be seen as betraying their identity as women, as Orthodox and as Greek. In fact, women are held "hostage" to their identity. Situated within the logic of nationalism, women's long exclusion from Athos is turned into an advantage, a proof of their necessity for the nation and consequently for Orthodoxy's own existence.

Gendered tradition

For Greece and Orthodoxy, the Altar and Mount Athos remain the "last bastions of masculinity" (Clark, 2000: 4). The male exclusivity of both has been defended by various arguments which invite dualities and oppositions producing unsurpassable dilemmas for women and hindering their role as a collective agent of social change. Tradition, whether holy or cultural, instead of being treated as a "dynamic" principle, has been equated with the male hierarchy of the church, and the male monastics and the state have been turned into its rigorous guardians. The questioning of such gender-based segregation has come from outside in the form of the ecumenical dialogue for women's exclusion from the priesthood and in the form of the EU's objection to the prohibition of women's entrance in Mount Athos. The reason for this is that the male hierarchy of both church and state manage to stress the superiority of national and, concomitantly, of religious identity over gender identity. Women seem to accept these male-generated discourses as authentic cultural formations. In this way, they become the "celebrants" not of their own womanhood, but of their exclusive Greek Orthodox identity.

References

Behr-Sigel, Elisabeth (2001) "Women", in K. Parry *et al.* (eds) *The Blackwell Dictionary of Eastern Christianity*, pp. 515–519. Oxford: Blackwell.

Chrysostomos, Metropolitan of Myra (1992) "Priesthood and Women in Ecclesiological Perspective", in G. Limouris (ed.) *The Place of the Woman in the Orthodox Church and the Question of the Ordination of Women*, pp. 117–132. Katerini: Tertios.

Clark, Victoria (2000) *Why Angels Fall: A Journey through Orthodox Europe from Byzantium to Kosovo.* London: Macmillan.

du Boulay, Juliet (1986) "Women – Images of Their Nature and Destiny in Rural Greece", in J. Dubisch (ed.) *Gender and Power in Rural Greece*, pp. 139–168. Princeton, NJ: Princeton University Press.

Farantos, Megas (2000) *Orthodoxia kai Theologia* [Orthodoxy and Theology]. Athens: Privately published.

Faubion, James D. (1993) *Modern Greek Lessons: A Primer in Historical Constructivism.* Princeton, NJ: Princeton University Press.

Göle, Nilüfer (1996) *The Forbidden Modern: Civilization and Veiling.* Ann Arbor: University of Michigan Press.

Harrison, Nonna Verna (1999) "Orthodox Arguments Against the Ordination of Women as Priests", in T. Hopko (ed.) *Women and Priesthood*, pp. 165–187. Crestwood, NY: St Vladimir's Seminary Press.

Hirschon, René (1978) "Open Body, Closed Space: The Transformation of Female Sexuality", in S. Ardener (ed.) *Defining Females: The Nature of Women in Society*, pp. 66–88. London: Croom Helm.

Karamanou, Anna (2003) "Statement – January 20, 2003", http://www.karamanou.gr/dir/press/art/en/st03_2001_en.htm (accessed 15 January 2004).

Karras, Valerie (1998) "Women in the Eastern Church: Past, Present and Future", *Sourozh* 71: 33–39.

Kendall, Laurel (1996) *Getting Married in Korea: Of Gender, Morality, and Modernity.* Berkeley: University of California Press.

Kollontai, Pauline (2000) "Contemporary Thinking on the Role and Ministry of Women in the Orthodox Church", *Journal of Contemporary Religion* 15: 165–179.

Limouris, Gennadios, ed. (1992a) *The Place of the Woman in the Orthodox Church and the Question of the Ordination of Women.* Katerini: Tertios.

Limouris, Gennadios (1992b) "Orthodox Reactions to Non-Orthodox Positions in Support of the Ordination of Women", in G. Limouris (ed.) *The Place of the Woman in the Orthodox Church and the Question of Ordination*, pp. 265–285. Katerini: Tertios.

Pheidas, Vlassios (1992) "The Question of the Priesthood of Women", in G. Limouris (ed.) *The Place of the Woman in the Orthodox Church and the Question of Ordination*, pp. 157–196. Katerini: Tertios.

Schmemann, Alexander (1999) "Preface to the 1982 Edition", in T. Hopko (ed.) *Women and Priesthood*, pp. 3–4. Crestwood, NY: St Vladimir's Seminary Press.

Theodorou, Evangelos (1992) "The Institution of Deaconesses in the Orthodox Church and the Possibility of Its Restoration", in G. Limouris (ed.) *The Place of the Woman in the Orthodox Church and the Question of Ordination*, pp. 207–238. Katerini: Tertios.

Topping, Eva C. (1983) "Patriarchal Prejudice and Pride in Greek Christianity: Some Notes on Origins", *Journal of Modern Greek Studies* 1: 7–17.

59

GENDER AND CHANGE IN AN AFRICAN IMMIGRANT CHURCH

An anthropologist and a (former) prophetess reflect

Deidre Helen Crumbley and Gloria Malake Cline-Smythe

Source: Jacob K. Olupona and Regina Gemignani (eds), *African Immigrant Religions in America*, New York: New York University Press, 2007, pp. 158–81.

> According to the Founder and First Primate of the Church—Prophet Dr Josiah Ositelu, God told him from the beginning of his ministry that He . . . has called both men and women into his ministry and should therefore not refuse or reject female disciples. Ministerial hierarchy in the Church therefore has men and women at parity. Both women Ministers and Laities are actively involved in the activities of all the diverse ministries and councils.
>
> "Women: The Church of the Lord Organisation."[1]

The African Diaspora in the New World has occurred in two major waves of migration. The first, shaped by the trans-Atlantic slave trade, was a consequence of forced migration to supply labor to expanding European nation-states. The recent African migration is a voluntary response to turbulent change in contemporary postcolonial Africa.[2] Both have entailed more than the movement of human bodies from one geopolitical space to another; both have entailed the movement of ideas, values, traditions, and institutions.

The slavery context of the first wave of Africans constrained the New World transfer of religious practices to varying degrees. The current transfer of African religious practices to American soil, occurring more than one hundred years after the Emancipation Proclamation, demonstrates greater exercise of religious autonomy and agency. African religious institutions are arriving whole and intact—open to adaptation, but on their own terms.

The decade between 1992 and 2002 saw half a million Africans immigrate to the United States. More than 75,000 of these were Nigerian, the largest group of Africans to immigrate in that period.[3] Some Nigerians have brought their religious institutions with them, further diversifying the already pluralistic religious landscape of twenty-first-century America. One of these is the Church of the Lord (Aladura) (CLA), an indigenous expression of Christianity that emerged among the Yoruba people of southwestern Nigeria. CLA is also part of a larger phenomenon of African Instituted Churches, discussed later in this chapter.

The Church of the Lord (Aladura) was founded in 1930 in Nigeria by Josiah Olunowo Ositelu, a Yoruba man from the town of Ogere and a former Anglican catechist-in-training before his vision and "call" to a new ministry. Like other Aladura or "owners of prayer," CLA selectively combines Yoruba and Christian religious traditions, but, unlike many Aladura churches, the Church of the Lord (Aladura) ordains women. This Church was not destined to remain a purely African phenomenon. Within twenty years of its founding, it had expanded beyond Nigeria into Anglophone Liberia and Sierra Leone.

In the 1960s, CLA spread to its first non-English speaking African country, Francophone Togo, then to South London, in Britain, and to Atlanta and Philadelphia, in the United States. In 1975, the Church of the Lord (Aladura) became a member of the World Council of Churches (WCC), and twenty years later, in 1994, the Church was formally registered in Germany. The German mission of CLA has flourished through the endeavors of the youngest son of the Church founder, the current CLA Primate Dr. Rufus Okikiolaolu Olubiyi Ositelu, who has earned two doctorates, one in computer science and the other in religion and theology.[4] Today, CLA has "stations" or branches in the United States, the most active ones located in Wooster, Massachusetts and Providence, Rhode Island. There are also two branches in New York City, one of which is located in Brooklyn, on Munro Street, the same street on which one also finds an "assembly" of Christ Apostolic Church (CAC), the first major Aladura church to emerge in Nigeria.

The Church of the Lord (Aladura), then, has become an international phenomenon. Further information about its beliefs, practices, history, and mission can be accessed globally at its World Wide Web Internet homepage, which states:

> Through the Internet, God has made a way for the Gospel of Christ to go out quickly around the world. We are honoured to be included among His messengers.[5]

The Church of the Lord (Aladura) Web site serves as a source of general information and a medium of evangelism. It is also a window on CLA gender practices.

Aim, approach, and methods

This Web site provides the point of departure for pursuing the threefold aim of this study. The first is to explore gender dynamics of CLA in its American context. The second is to incorporate into this investigation the female experience of CLA faith and gender practices. The third is to consider the implications of our findings for the study of gender in African Immigrant Religion (AIR) in the United States.

The rational for privileging the female voice in this study is that while Western intellectual categories help to critically assess social phenomena cross-culturally and to analyze gender categories within particular ethnographic contexts, the perspectives of actual culture bearers are crucial for developing nuanced interpretative frameworks, categories of analysis, and alternative research designs.[6] Thus, this article is coauthored by a Western-trained academic and an African faith practitioner. The resulting interpretative framework reflects social-scientific concern with structures and protocols of power, as well as valued perspectives of meaning and motivation shared by believers.

Deidre Helen Crumbley is a sociocultural anthropologist whose work has focused on religion and gender in Africa and, more recently, in the African Diaspora.[7] Gloria Malake Cline-Smythe, originally from Freetown Sierra Leone, rose to the level of senior prophetess in the Church of the Lord (Aladura) and was made supervisor of the East Coast CLA, except for the New York branches. Still, the anthropologist is not without her own faith and cultural background, and the prophetess is lacking neither in academic credentials nor in critical intellectual skills. Deidre Crumbley was raised in a female-founded African American "holy-sanctified" storefront church in the inner city of Philadelphia, and, in addition to her doctorate in anthropology, she holds a master of theological studies degree from divinity school. Gloria Cline-Smythe graduated with honors from Fourah Bay University, with a major in English and literature and a minor in theology. She has long aspired to expand her rich spiritual life to include formal theological training in a master of divinity program to better prepare for her ministry. In her secular profession, she has pursued successful careers in local and federal government on both sides of the Atlantic.

The first contact between the two women occurred through e-mail on 10 August 2003. Primate Rufus Ositelu referred Dr. Crumbley to the prophetess when the anthropologist expressed her desire to conduct research on gender dynamics in the CLA mission in America. Electronic media have continued to be central to the interaction between these two women, for whom the CLA Web page served as a point of departure for discussions about gender and church expansion. They also speak regularly by telephone, discussing and debating the collection and interpretation of data. Lengthy quotations from the prophetess are taken directly from her written notes.

Apart from the incorporation of twenty-first-century information technology into data collection methods, this investigation employs a conventional social-scientific case-study approach. Furthermore, at its inception, the interaction between the two women conformed to the traditional anthropologist-informant model. The prophetess enjoyed the "the opportunity of brain teasing" that "got me working on something I had not given thought to for some time." She delights in the intellectual banter between them and responds to the anthropologist's role of devil's advocate with grace, despite the directness of some rather personal questions.

As the research project proceeded, it became clear that, because of her university training and familiarity with social-scientific models of religion, Gloria Cline-Smythe was a source not only of rich data but also of analysis and critique. Thus, one of the first statements she made to Dr. Crumbley was that she wanted to make one thing perfectly clear: the Church of the Lord (Aladura) does not consist of uneducated people without resources, adding, "We have passed that." Prophetess Cline-Smythe pointed out that CIA's parishioners possess the wherewithal to emigrate from the continent and arrive in the United States able to compete successfully in the American context. Many have arrived with professional training and degrees that can stand them in good stead anywhere in the world. She insisted that her African church not be represented as the faith of backwards people from a backwards continent. Once convinced that this research project would avoid stereotypic representations of Africans and reductionistic interpretations of their faith, she agreed to be interviewed and eventually became coauthor of this essay.

The research contributions of Cline-Smythe required the anthropologist to change her view of the prophetess from informant to consultant and eventually to colleague. These shifts produced new perspectives on gender in African immigrant religion in general, and on menstrual blood avoidance in particular. Gender has been a research focus since Dr. Crumbley began her study of Aladura churches in Nigeria. For her, gender represents a conceptual problem; however, it is not "an issue" for her coauthor. Indeed, the anthropologist worked hard to retain the gender focus of this research project before realizing that the topic of gender and menstrual taboos would have to be approached as more than a matter of power relations if the collaboration was to be fruitful.

This research project, then, blurs conventional methodological and interpretive boundaries between the researcher and the researched. Furthermore, the inception and evolution of this study over its two-year duration highlights the interactive and constantly changing nature of knowledge production, in at least two ways. First, as is elaborated in the epilogue to this chapter, shifts took place in the prophetess's institutional relationship to the Church of the Lord (Aladura). These shifts reflect the challenges facing an African Instituted Church when it becomes an African Immigrant Church in America; these shifts also reflect the intersection of the personal and public, while underscoring the fact that academic research occurs within everyday human existence. As such, academic research is vulnerable to the unpredictable imponderables of life.

Second, the cyberspace point of departure for this study grew directly out of an encounter between the anthropologist and the primate of the Church of the Lord (Aladura). In part, the CLA link titled "Women" came into existence as a response to a criticism of the Web site made at the Third International Interdisciplinary Conference of the African Christian Diaspora in Europe, held at the Hirschluch Conference Centre near Berlin, 11–15 September 2003.[8] At this conference, Deidre Crumbley made the comment that the Church of the Lord (Aladura) Web site had failed to address one of CLA's most outstanding features, the ordination of women. Given the public nature of this criticism, the primate might have stood on his dignity and merely taken offense. Instead, his response was one of concerted constructive action, for, the month after the Hirschluch Conference, a new link titled "Women" had been added to the CLA homepage.

Concepts, categories, and language

The Church of the Lord (Aladura) is an institutional expression of the Aladura movement, which emerged out of an early-twentieth-century prayer and prophet-healing movement among the Yoruba people of southwestern Nigeria. CLA members, like other Christians, believe that Jesus Christ is the Son of God, that the Bible is the "Word of God," and that the Holy Ghost is the Spirit of God that guides and dwells with believers. In addition, Aladura also believe that witchcraft is real but is rendered ineffective by Christian faith and Holy Ghost protection, that Holy Ghost power can be evoked to address life's vicissitudes, and that fervent prayer, holy water, vigils, fasting, the burning of candles, and recitation of particular psalms can heal human bodies and situations. Aladura also celebrate and express the presence of divine spirit through holy dance and glossolalia, that is, speaking in unknown tongues.

As an Aladura church, the Church of the Lord (Aladura) is a Yoruba expression of the continentwide phenomenon of indigenous Christianity known as African Instituted/Initiated Churches.[9] African Instituted Churches (AICs) throughout sub-Saharan Africa selectively incorporate African and Christian cultural and religious traditions into their religious beliefs, practices, and organizational processes. In its U.S. diasporan context, the Church of the Lord (Aladura) is a "religion on the move";[10] it is also an example of African Immigrant Religions (AIR), which includes not only AICs but also African Islam and African traditional religions.

To avoid the interpretive baggage of terms such as "menstrual taboo" and "ritual pollution," these phrases have been intentionally replaced in this essay by "menstrual rites" and "ritual menstrual practices." Rejecting commonsense associations of menstrual blood with unhygienic dirtiness, classical anthropological interpretation associates "menstrual taboo" with the symbolic reassertion of gender rules in socially ambiguous situations.[11] To understand the coexistence of CLA menstrual rites with female ordination and office parity requires attention to notions of the sacred and the profane in the particular culture context, as well as the nuances of performance through which women specialists negotiate their identities as women and as leaders of their faith.[12]

CLA gender rules and structures

The Church of the Lord (Aladura), from its early history, placed women in positions of explicit leadership. In 1966, the ordained female ministry was established by the founder as a divine injunction; the founder added, "And as long as the church exists it shall not cease." The second primate, Adeleke Adejobi, writes:

> We firmly believe in the doctrine of the Priesthood of all believers (male and females alike). . . . We believe that God calls men and women who surrender their lives to Him and obey His Divine calling. . . . In this new life one's nationality or race or education or social position is unimportant; such things mean nothing. Whether a person has Christ is what matters, and He is equally available to all.[13]

The schema of CLA offices explicitly identifies offices of equal rank for men and women:

- Primate (unitary office)
- Provisional head (unitary office)
- Apostle/Reverend Mother Superior
- Bishop/Reverend Mother
- Archdeacon/Archdeaconess
- Senior Prophet/Senior Prophetess—Senior Evangelist/Senior Pastor
- Prophet/Pastor/Prophetess—Evangelist/Pastor/Lady Evangelist (Grades I)
- Prophet/Pastor/Prophetess—Evangelist/Pastor/Lady Evangelist (Grades II)
- Probationary Ministers (male and female)
- Disciples (male and female)

Only the primate and the provisional head are unitary offices, and, to date, these offices have been held by male clergy. However, as Primate Adejobi pointed out, there is nothing in the Church constitution that forbids a woman from becoming primate, so, theoretically, a woman may hold any CLA office up to and including the primacy. Male and female clergy holding the same office are assigned the same duties and responsibilities.[14] For example, section 6 of Article V, "Ministers and Officers," describes the duties of the senior prophet/senior prophetess as follows: "In addition to his/her pastoral functions, he/she shall perform some other administrative duties as may be assigned to him/her by the Primate or Provisional Head or the Diocese Overseer."[15]

Having a female body, however, places at least three constraints on women's access to holy space and ritual objects. First, ordained women may not perform the four sacraments of communion, marriage, baptism, and funerals until they reach the age of sixty and no longer menstruate. The explanation for this policy, provided by the current primate, Dr. Rufus Ositelu, is that when women are postmenopausal, the effect of menstrual blood on the elements of the communion—the bread/flesh and wine/blood of Christ—is no longer problematic. It should be noted that the prohibition against performing the four sacraments also applies to "Probationary Ministers" who "shall not perform Baptism, Holy Communion, Holy Wedlock and funerals."[16] Second, as expressed in the Church constitution, women must sit outside the church sanctuary during their menstrual cycles.[17] Third, Primate Adejobi writes, women are excluded from arbitration of doctrine: "We opine that, when St. Paul said, "I do not permit a woman to teach" (Timothy 2:11–14) . . . this is not an absolute denial of a woman's chance to preach, but it forbids a woman to be the ultimate arbiter of doctrine."[18] Primate Adejobi explained that the basis of the prohibition against women arbitrating doctrine is that Jesus and the twelve disciplines, founders of the Christian faith, were male.

CLA members who have female bodies, then, each month, must avoid holy things and spaces; are not able to perform the four sacraments until they no longer menstruate; and are excluded from doctrinal arbitration. Still, their access to formal "political" power is in sharp contrast to their ritual or "ceremonial" leadership. Other studies have emphasized the latter among AICs in general and Aladura churches in particular.[19]

Cyberspace images of gender

As the 6,177th visitor to the Church of the Lord Web site, http://www.aladura.de/, on Wednesday, November 15, 2004, Dr. Crumbley encountered a site that was available in several Western languages, including Spanish, German, and French. The home page has ten links that introduce visitors to CLA beliefs, practices, national and international organizational structures, ecumenical affiliations, youth activities, contact information, outreach ministries, and the annual Mt. Tabieorar pilgrimage, held in the hometown of the founder. There is also a link that connects to the World Council of Churches Web site, attesting to the "ecumenical outlook" of CLA, which has been a WCC member since 1975. Another important link reflecting the global mission of CLA is an article on "missions in reverse," that is, the role of African Instituted Churches not only in propagating the gospel worldwide but also in revitalizing Western Christianity.[20]

Other than the "Women" link, there are no direct references to gender issues or women's place in the life and history of CLA, with the exception of contact information for Spr. Mother Barbara Ositelu.[21] The "Women" Web page begins with the quotation that opens this chapter, followed by a list of the various church bodies on which CLA women sit. These range from the highest executive bodies, such as the Supreme Council of Prelates, the Primate in Council, and the Board of Trustees, to ministries such as Teaching, Social, Music, and Drama. Also included are organizations solely for women, such as Mother's Union Band and the Council of Deaconesses.

Prophetess Cline-Smythe responded to the Web site, generally, by commending the primate for expanding it to include a link that addressed the place of women in the Church of the Lord (Aladura). Her response to its treatment of the topic was that, had there been time and space, there was so very much more that could have been written about women in church history and current affairs. She would love to see the inclusion of stories about the women who had been instrumental in spreading CLA to Liberia, Sierra Leone, Britain, and the United States.

In sum, the Church Web site reiterates CLA's women-inclusive structures that not only support the ordination of women but also explicitly assign women the same rank and responsibilities as men. But how are CLA gender rules experienced in the everyday institutional life of the Church, especially in its American context? This question is addressed by documenting the lived-reality of CLA gender practices through the life and work of a senior clergywoman who has participated in CLA organizational processes on both sides of the Atlantic.

Sierra Leonean beginnings

The prophetess was not always a member of the Church of the Lord (Aladura). She was raised in the Methodist Church at a time when Aladura churches were not an established part of the Sierra Leonean religious landscape. The transplanting of this Nigerian Church was effected through the joint mission of Primate Adejobi and his ordained wife, Reverend Mother Superior Olive Adejobi, when they were young and in the early stages of their clerical careers,

> In 1948, Apostle Adejobi took the bold step of venturing out from Nigeria with his beautiful young bride, Olive; later she was to become the Reverend Mother Superior and also Vice Provost of Aladura Theological Seminary and Prophets/Prophetesses Training Institute. The inclusion of his wife in his ministry brought a different light to the Church's acceptance of women in the work of the

> mission. They became partners, and, in this way, many women were brought into the fold of the Church, first in Freetown and later in other major cities and towns of the Republic of Sierra Leone.
>
> The mission was first based at Dove's Cot, a little area in the east end of the city. Later, land was acquired, first at Wilberforce for the setting up of a seminary and later, on Williams Street, where the headquarters were established. To complete the early acquisition of property, bearing in mind the growth and development of the mission, land was bought on the hillside of Freetown that could accommodate the Church's own Holy Mount as well as a mini-cathedral. The Mount became the base for the spiritual development of ministers and, later, of laity found ready for such training. Regular meditation, Bible study, and ["spiritual exercises" that include] rolling and praying, as well as time for seclusion for preparation of ordination or anointment, are all carried out there.

Gloria Malake Cline-Smith was raised in the Methodist faith, and came to the Church of the Lord (Aladura) as an adult, after visiting the church during a lunch break one afternoon in Freetown at a time when her ex-husband was having a problem at work:

> It was the first time I had had anything to do with a church of "the praying people" (Aladura). I was captivated by my first experience of just walking into the church . . . to find someone who never knew me nor had ever had the opportunity to talk to me . . . to tell me the reason for my coming to the church that day. I found it bewildering, [but] as each of the prophecies came true, my faith in the God of the Church of the Lord (Aladura) became stronger.

Not only did she join the Church of the Lord (Aladura), but she began to ascend its national and international hierarchies.

> Time saw me grow through the ranks of laity to the position of international deaconess as well as assistant secretary to then Primate Reverend Dr. E. O. A. Adejobi. . . . [Being] the assistant secretary to the primate afforded me the opportunity to learn more about the Church, its administration, and its relationship with other church bodies like the World Council of Churches in Geneva, and others. I became a part of the local planning sessions for international forum . . . arranging our own international assemblies held once every three years in any country which felt like hosting it. In my national church, I served on the Education Board, the Board of Trustees, various Unions, and organizations of the church.

These various roles allowed her to interact with the clergy of other denominations, including Aladura denominations, causing her to realize that in many of them, because she is female, she never could be ordained or hold high office.

As an ordained CIA minister, she found her spiritual life in Sierra Leone further enriched by evangelical outreach, extended periods of prayer, and Bible study. She also supported parishioners as they drew on their faith to negotiate life's vicissitudes.

> I loved to pioneer branches—a challenge that not many people are cut out for. The planting of new branches of the Church took a lot of time and patience to get it operational. I found the practice of fasting and midnight struggles, beach prayers and struggles, most effective, as much as outside preaching from street to street within an area. The Bible had to be the basis for everything preached because a new convert had to have something tangible he could fall back on. The support demonstrated by the congregation, which is generally divided into Bands or Unions, is commendable. They fasted with whomever needed special prayers and equally shared in the outcome. If it turned out to be negative, they were quick to give encouragement and lend their committed time and support.

The female members with whom she worked had special needs, which the Church of the Lord (Aladura) in Sierra Leone addressed directly:

> The common needs, which brought many women together, kept them in groups within the Church. Childbearing, being a very important aspect of an African woman's life, stable homes, dedicated husbands, peace in one's home, astute business attributes, and the success of one's profession or career were some of the reasons that brought women and kept them together until their prayers were heard. As more women proved the power of prayer through God's miracles in their lives, so word of the work spread. It was and has continued to be that men were brought into the Church through their wives. Some [women] have stayed and nurtured their families through the years, and become formidable pillars where others have moved on to other things but still remember the blessings derived from their years within the walls of the [CLA].

While becoming increasingly involved in CLA, the prophetess held prestigious posts in Freetown's local government.

> At the time I came into the mission, I was a local government officer, serving as Secretary to the Mayor of Freetown. I had professional British training . . . as a secretary, and as the years progressed,

> I pursued a degree program [at] the University of Sierra Leone, majoring in English language and literature with a minor in theology. I graduated with a Second class in 1987 and returned to my local government position, but this time in an administrative position serving as city manager. Several foreign governments gave me the opportunity of receiving training to equip me for this position including the U.S.A. government through Operation Crossroads Africa I combined my church work with my regular work without problems, and from time to time invited my colleagues to attend functions at our church at which I preached.

Coming to America: CLA's American mission

Prophetess Cline-Smythe observed that, for reasons of history and contemporary circumstances, many of the first Church of the Lord (Aladura) branches in the United States were founded by Liberians. CLA was planted in Liberia about the same time it arrived in Sierra Leone through the missionary efforts of Apostle Samuel Oduwale and his wife, Delicia. Together they worked to spread the faith in the capital, Monrovia, and eventually in America, in part because of the close relationship between Liberia and the United States. Liberia was founded in 1822 to repatriate freed slaves from the United States, and it has maintained strong links with the United States and enjoyed special political and economic concessions. Unsurprisingly, many Liberians came to the United States for further studies and because it offered better prospects. Among African immigrants, Prophetess Cline-Smythe observed, disproportionately large populations of Liberians are found in Philadelphia, Pennsylvania; Providence, Rhode Island; and Worcester and Roslindale, Massachusetts. Those who were CLA members in Liberia wanted to worship in the traditions of the Church of the Lord (Aladura) in this new American context. As in Liberia, the husband-and-wife missionary team of the Oduwales was central to the spread of the CLA in America. However,

> after the death of her husband, Samuel, in the early 1960s, the Reverend Mother Delicia Oduwale moved to Philadelphia, where she founded the St. Samuel Chapel. Another Liberian, Archdeaconess Marie Cooper, of CLA Bronx, New York, also with her husband, provided spiritual nurturing for many who came to their church on Monroe Street, in the Bronx. The years have taken their toll on these female pioneers, but the churches, no matter how few their members, stand as a testimony to their hard work.

Because of the unrest associated with the civil war in Sierra Leone, the prophetess immigrated to the United States in 1991. Before leaving Freetown, she made a solemn vow that if her emigration was successful, she would pioneer a CLA branch in America.

> The payment and fulfillment of vows is taken as a sacred trust between a member and God, particularly when that vow is made under very trying circumstances. Such was the situation I found myself in when I arrived in this country [after] a ten-year [civil] war and an abusive marital relationship, which I had regularly committed into God's hands. I had fallen ill on the flight here. My recovery took a very long time, and when finally I fully recovered, I realized something was missing in me. I had been regularly attending church services near where I lived, but it was never fulfilling. I started looking around for a church with drums and clapping and a real pentecostal flavor but could find none. Then, one day, I bumped into an old school friend who had migrated to this country in the late sixties and . . . she invited me to her church.

This church was very far from her home, and with limited funds and transportation, she found it difficult to be an active participant. The prophetess, along with a few of the women living in her area, began praying and worshipping by phone, which "meant we all tied up the lines of the various homes we lived in and offended, in no small way, the various family members we were living with." Then, one night, she had a dream "in which I was reminded of my vow that if the Lord got me out of my troubles and I set my feet in this white man's land safe and sound, I would plant a church for His glory." Thus, her CLA mission in America was born, and as overseer of her region she would be intimately involved with the planning and development of not one but several congregations. Though the work was "fraught with difficulties from its inception," it was a "joy to see all the paperwork taken to Ogere, the International spiritual headquarters of the mission in Nigeria, and to be proudly received by the late third primate, Dr. Gabriel Ositelu."

Challenges to CLA in America

The prophetess identifies six challenges that face the Church of the Lord (Aladura) clergy in the American mission—none of which relate to CLA gender dynamics. First, she describes CLA in America as not only a "church of immigrants" but also a "church of migrants." Many CLA members are recent arrivals to the United States and are in the process of regularizing their immigration status. They are often "on their way elsewhere," and they want to relocate for several reasons, including wanting to live in a less urban setting, wishing to compete for jobs where there are fewer Africans with similar qualifications, and wanting to start their own "white-garment church" in an area where such African churches are few and far between. Regardless of their reason for leaving the Washington, D.C., area, the impact of such departures on the CLA mission is the same; when parishioners are "on their way elsewhere," it is difficult for clergy to develop a faith community that is financially self-sustaining, socially cohesive, and institutionally loyal.

A second challenge is a utilitarian approach to the Church. For example, worshippers visiting the parish in May, fasting and praying that their visa be regularized, by January may have relocated to Tennessee with green card in hand! The prophetess notes sadly:

> I found, to my disappointment, quite a few episodes which regularly reminded me of the Parable of the Ten Lepers. As soon as issues were resolved, they were gone—no forwarding address, no telephone number, nothing. In other words, the Church became used for the fulfillment of desires, and it was dropped subsequently as hot potatoes.

A third challenge facing the clergy is the experiential and communication gap between mission clergy in the Diaspora and clergy policymakers back in Africa. In the prophetess's CLA province back in Sierra Leone, clergy are required to minister full time and cannot hold another job; however, in America, where stations are financially unreliable, if CIA clergy do not hold a secular job, they cannot keep a roof over their head. Thus, CLA mission clergy in America can find their finances stretched and their lives stressful as they work full-time jobs while trying to spread the gospel in a strange land. Representatives of the primate, who serve as mentors to CLA clergy, are similarly constrained in their duties by a lack of time and financial support.

CLA clergy in the American mission are pioneering churches far from the support of extended family networks, in a society where they are lumped into a racial minority and perceived as a religious oddity. They also face the challenge of finding a way to make this experience "real" for church leaders who live in African nations under familiar laws, within traditional kinship networks, and in socially familiar contexts where their culture and their faith traditions are normative. The experiential gap between mission clergy in the Diaspora and clergy policymakers in Africa is keenly felt when clergy are expected to comply with the policy of sending one-third of church income to the Nigerian headquarters. This is difficult to do when the stability of fledgling parishes is so financially unpredictable. Add to this the task of staying on top of annual income tax remittances to the Internal Revenue Service, and the financial pressure on clergy is further exacerbated.

A fourth challenge involves interaction with local authorities. These include compliance with municipal codes, fear of immigration enforcement, and the effect of these on church attendance and quality of worship.

> Fear of law enforcement, in whatever form, keeps people away, particularly when the issues they are praying for are related to their [immigration] status being regularized. . . . Fear of reprisals, if people go into spirit and start shrieking or praying in a loud voice, is also a problem area. In the past, it was easy to godfather a church in the basement of homes, a school room, et cetera, but now there are basic requirements which must be provided; they [include] being in compliance [with] the Americans with Disabilities Act, having parking lots demarcating space for physically challenged persons.

A fifth problem is that stable and loyal communities tend to consist of older members. While the Rhode Island CLA branch is the most active and loyal, the average age of its members is sixty-five. Many of the children of leaders of CLA members in Africa join other Churches when they come to America. Just because someone was CLA in Africa does not mean that he or she can be depended upon to join and support CLA in America. The challenge is how to build on the stability of established elder members, retain younger CLA members once they have come to America, and attract other immigrant Africans and nonimmigrant Americans.

A final concern is about passing on valued gender practices to young men in the American mission of the CLA. Cooperation between female clergy and a trustworthy male is essential: "Tradition . . . dictates that during a female minister's monthly cycle, she cannot go into the inner altar to light up the candles and set the altar up for service. Therefore, she needs a Deacon or a Curate to ensure that, at that time of the month, the cleanliness of God's house is maintained." This requires a close and mutually respectful relationship between the presiding female priest and the man who works with her. The problem is twofold. First, the number of young men who attend CLA churches here in America is low. Second, many have grown up in America and not in Africa, where, as CLA members, they would have been regularly exposed to male and female clergy ministering together. This observation implies that the parity and inclusivity of CLA gender rules, though not perfectly enacted, nonetheless provide ideals to which one can aspire and to which one can be held accountable. It also implies that such ideals are not normative in American gender practices in either secular or religious institutions.

Negotiating CLA gender practices in America

The issue of gender was not mentioned among the problem areas just described. Only when the anthropologist pressed the matter did the prophetess address it. On these occasions, she graciously complied by offering richly nuanced insights and humorously related anecdotes. These provided a valuable window into the lived experience of being female in the Church of the Lord (Aladura) in America.

Women in leadership positions in African Immigrant Churches, such as the Church of the Lord (Aladura), are faced with the challenges of tradition and culture in the discharge of their duties as female ministers:

> Tradition dictates that in the presence of men, women are supposed to be submissive and obedient and to play a subservient role. However, the [Church of the Lord] empowers women to be leaders and gives each of us the same administrative powers . . . given to men; but, in reality, a woman needs to draw a fine line between being the effective minister . . . yet a respectful woman, who does not disregard the societal position of a man who many need chiding for infractions done.
>
> Our mothers in the church, such as retired Reverend Mother Olive Adejobi, wife of the second primate of the church, the late Dr. Emmanuel O. A. Adejobi, was hardly ever known to publicly administer punishment to male ministers when once they were out of seminary and in the field. She had to find recourse of meting out whatever deterrents through other means such as disciplinary committees, et cetera. She . . . was always committed to upholding the tradition of a woman's place to that of a man in whatever she did but at the same time respecting [one's] anointing as an ordained female minister of God.

Not all CLA female clergy have successfully negotiated the subtleties of CLA gender practices. Catherine Kamara, the first Sierra Leonean woman to train for the CLA ministry, the first CLA archdeaconess, and CLA representative to the World Council of Churches, was a role model to CLA women in Sierra Leone. Today, however, she heads her own church in England and is no longer affiliated with the Church of the Lord, due to irreconcilable differences associated with her strength of personality. Here, when the anthropologist asked how the prophetess, also a strong personality, handled this situation, Prophetess Cline-Smythe, in keeping with her ability to look reality squarely in the face and laugh at it, chuckled as she related that she, and women like her working in the United States, have been referred to as "these recalcitrant American women" who are "no more African women." Nevertheless, because "it is the women who stick" and see things through, changed male attitudes were inevitable, no matter the difficulty.

Honoring the menstrual rites in America

The prophetess values the menstrual rites of CLA and continues to practice them here in America, not only at CLA parishes but also when she visits American churches. She did the same when growing up in the Methodist Church in Sierra Leone, where her parents did not permit her to take communion when menstruating. This practice was common in "established" churches when she was growing up. Even today, she observes, some female members of Anglican churches in Africa do not approach the altar area, or even the sanctuary itself, when menstruating. In her home in the Washington, D.C., area, when she menstruates, she has a male household member drape her personal altar with a white cloth; then, after her menses, she "reconsecrates" her altar using Psalm 24. She observed, "As educated as I am, at this time of the month, I think of my self as unclean"; yet, she made it clear that this sense of being "unclean" does not diminish her sense of value to herself or her anointment.

She admits that it will require Holy Ghost guidance to communicate the value of CLA menstrual practice to non-Africans. CLA menstrual rituals are not a matter that clergy immediately broach with non-African newcomers, because, if they are put off by what is too culturally alien, they may "miss the religious experience of a lifetime"—namely the profound intimacy of "communing with God as friend to friend," an event full of "power and beauty." The prophetess has not had such experiences in the mission church of her youth or in contemporary mainline churches. She is quick to add, however, that such intimate encounters with God are not limited to CLA, but they do require "correct parameters"—namely a community of faith that regularly and fervently fasts, prays, and studies scriptures "together and on one accord."

Conclusions and implications

While the case-study approach of this study does not lend itself to generalizations, its findings help to advance the threefold aim of this study. Regarding the first aim of exploring gender in the Church of the Lord (Aladura) in the American context, the case of the Oduwales in America suggests that married ordained partnerships continue to be a missionary strategy. At the same time, being a single clergywoman did not prevent the prophetess from being assigned as regional overseer for the East Coast of the United States. Future research should explore the translation of women-inclusive CLA organizational structures into the American mission field, as well as subtler gender expectations that women should be discreet about disciplining male clergy in public. Tension between the need to show deference to men and the desire to be true to one's anointment could give rise to frustrations that lead women, like Catherine Kamara, to leave CLA when they have so much to contribute to its future expansion in Africa and abroad.

The second aim of the investigation was to incorporate into the research project the female voice from within the faith community. The voice of a senior clergywoman enriched the study with unique perspectives on female roles and symbolic life in CLA. The anthropologist had followed menstrual rites while conducting fieldwork in the Church of the Lord, but her cultural background did not prepare her to see menstrual rites in terms other than compliance. Menstrual rites "stood out" for her, becoming a major intellectual problem and research focus. Menstrual rites did not "stand out" for the prophetess. For her, they are part of a life of faith that also includes a highly valued life of devotion, duties, and status of ordained clergy on a par with those of men and a committed life of evangelical outreach. As such, gender is not a concept to be lifted out and analyzed separately but a daily reality to be lived and negotiated within the context of faith and mission. While remaining committed to the analysis of power and inequity, the anthropologist has expanded her understanding of menstrual rituals as more than a measure of power and control. The menstrual rites in the Church of the Lord are best understood in light of meanings and values associated with Church doctrine, its vision, and the cultural legacies of its members.

Prophetess Cline-Smythe is neither oblivious to nor in denial of the challenges that face her as a CLA clergywoman; however, she has directed her limited time and resources to honoring her "anointing" and to keeping her vow to propagate the gospel in America, which she has exceeded by being an area supervisor. Of course, one might argue that this response is the consequence of false consciousness fostered by internalized sexism. This explanation, however, suggests a lack of intellectual self-awareness and human agency on the part of the prophetess that the anthropologist, after working with her over the past two years, finds unacceptably inaccurate.

Regarding the third aim of this study, its larger implications for studying gender in African Immigrant Religions (AIRs), a methodological approach that incorporates the voices and collaboration of women can yield enlightening perspectives and productive applications. These include refined intellectual categories of knowledge for future academic research and fostering dialogue among CLA women and men about issues that could fester and explode if left unaddressed. Another application is the role of women's voices in establishing an information-based dialogue between immigrant communities and American institutions as they struggle to understand and appreciate each other's gender practices in religiously plural twenty-first-century America.

Epilogue

When this essay was first conceived, its subtitle was "An Anthropologist and Prophetess Reflect." By the end of the two-year research period, the qualifier "former" had to be added to it. Gloria Malake Cline-Smythe insisted on this revision because she had ceased to serve in her capacity as a regional overseer in the American mission of the Church of the Lord (Aladura). This decision was neither sudden nor made lightly; it has entailed soul searching, a strong sense of loss, and still unresolved sentiments. The "prophetess"—still referred to this way because she continues to speak forth the gospel and prophesy to those seeking spiritual guidance—is clear about her new direction. She has become active in the Lutheran Church, which she initially visited out of ecumenical curiosity, having had little exposure to this denomination in Africa.

She came to love the Lutheran liturgy, and, coming from the CLA experience, where clerical gender parity is normative, she was at ease with Lutheran gender practices. The Anglican liturgy is also beautiful, she observed, but while it has finally ordained women, it has unresolved issues about accepting women in higher posts, such as bishop. Additionally, the Lutheran church she attends has a "praise and worship" devotional service, during which she plays African drums, sings, and claps, reminiscent of enlivened CLA worship. When asked to describe the exact nature of her relationship to CLA, she responded, "I just don't know." When describing what it is like to be estranged from CLA, she says, "I feel in my very bones . . . a part of myself is missing."

What, then, could have led to such extreme measures, and what are the implications of this outcome for both the mission of CLA in America and the study of African immigrant religion? The reasons, in the end, come down to three points, two of which are addressed in the earlier "Challenges to the CLA in America" section. These two are the instability of local congregations and the communication gap between mission clergy in the Diaspora and those in the African headquarters. The "migrant immigrants" who make up these churches cannot be depended upon to provide the financial support needed to maintain the church, especially after one-third of its income is sent back to CLA headquarters in Nigeria. The prophetess made commitments of time and resources willingly and aggressively pursued the building of the CLA Church in America until CLA headquarters decided that she should relocate and start a mission in the state of Texas. At this point, the communication gap became unbridgeable.

In Nigeria, there is no social security to fall back upon, but there are traditional extended family structures and land tenure practices that make it possible for elders to have housing and food when they no longer can work. In the United States, such traditional social practices have given way to state and corporate structures so that, without a solid retirement plan and social security benefits, most American workers cannot be sure of meeting their basic needs in their old age. The prophetess was unable to communicate these contingencies to the Nigerian headquarters, where the response to her hesitation was to refer her to the biblical model of Abraham faithfully following God's command to leave his home and family in Haran for "a land that I will show thee."[22]

The America imagined by people outside the country is often a land of milk and honey; outsiders seem to be unaware of America as a land of working poor where many middle-class professionals are just a couple of paychecks away from being homeless and without medical coverage. A government job with the income, benefits, and security like that now held by the prophetess is very difficult for an immigrant African woman with dependents to find in America. It took her a long time to secure this post, after an extended period of temporary secretarial assignments.

Additionally, she is just a few years from retirement, and, as indicated in her narrative, she has had health challenges since her arrival in this country. While coauthoring this article, she was diagnosed with a life-threatening disease. Though her spirit and her faith are strong, such realities are sobering, and they reinforce what she has come to realize, namely that "This is my life we are talking about." She had to find a way to answer her call and still find a way to survive as a recent African immigrant in America.

She is happy in the Zion Evangelical Lutheran church, and Zion appears to be happy with the expression of African Christian spirituality she brings to this community of faith. The congregation is located in Tacoma Park, on the border between Washington, D.C., and Maryland, in the heart of an immigrant neighborhood "where Africans abound." About 70 percent of the approximately 250 members of Zion are of African descent, mainly Africans, with some West Indians and a few African Americans. The remaining members are white Americans, of whom a few are originally from Germany. Zion also has an African Outreach program, and through the Lutheran Church the prophetess may be able to realize a longheld dream of attending seminary and thereby better serving the propagation of the gospel.

It should be noted that no formal letter of termination from CLA headquarters has been presented to her, but then she was never "posted from Africa." She had already immigrated to America when she was asked to oversee the CLA churches in her region. Thus, her work with the CLA mission in America had as much to do with the completion of a personal vow as the performance of a clerical assignment.

The implications of this turn of events are important for future growth of the Church of the Lord (Aladura) in America. No matter how much CLA missionaries in America love the CLA faith and spirituality, as does the prophetess, they need support to do the work of church-building. This includes concessions based on a realistic appreciation of the institutional, financial, and personal challenges that face CLA clergy as Africans immigrants in America. If these realities are not taken into consideration, these frontline warriors for African Instituted Churches in the Diaspora could be lost to other denominations. This is especially the case when, as with this Lutheran congregation, other denominations sincerely welcome cultural diversity and provide its bearers with support and security.

The turn of events in the church life of the prophetess raises conceptual and methodological questions in the field, as well. How are scholars to address the religious practices of African immigrants who join established American denominations? Do their lives of faith cease to be of scholarly concern because they are not in African religious institutions? Finally, what methods are to be followed to access and interpret their religious contribution to American religious pluralism today? Although she is no longer active in the Church of the Lord (Aladura), the Aladura spirituality that Gloria Cline-Smythe brings to the Lutheran Church will impact this mainline denomination from within. As such, her story provides an important vehicle for interpreting Africa immigrant religion in America on the level of individual faith.

This article is dedicated to those African men and women who have selflessly dedicated their efforts and resources to establishing the Church of the Lord (Aladura) in America, Britain, Germany, and throughout the CLA Diaspora.

Notes

1 This quotation is taken from the Church of the Lord (Aladura) Web site, available online at http://vww.aladura.de/women.htm (accessed 8 November 2004).

2 Roswith Gerloff, "Africa as the Laboratory of the World: The Africa Christian Diaspora in Europe as Challenge to Mission and Ecumenical Relations," in R. Gerloff, ed., *Mission Is Crossing Frontiers: Essays in Honor of Bongani A. Mazibuko* (Pietermaritzburg: Cluster Publications, 2003), 343.

3 U.S. Department of Homeland Security, *Yearbook of Immigration Statistics 2002* (Washington, D.C.: U.S. Government Printing Office, 2003), 12–14, 17–18.

4 Rufus Okikiolaolu Olubiyi Ositelu, *African Instituted Churches* (New Brunswick, N.J.: Transaction Publishers, 2002), 200.

5 "Partner in Progress (PIP): The Church of the Lord Organisation," Church of the Lord (Aladura) Web site, available online at http://www.aladura.de/pip.htm (accessed 18 November 2004).

6 I. Amadiume, *Male Daughters, Female Husbands: Gender and Sex in an African Society* (Atlantic Highlands, N.J.: Zed Books, 1987), 15, 28–29, 31–68, 89; I. Amadiume, *Reinventing Africa: Matriarchy, Religion and Culture* (London and New York: Zed Books, 1997), 110, 119, 123–130, 191–192; N. Nzegwu, "Gender Equality in a Dual Sex System: The Case of Onitsha," *Canadian Journal of Law and Juris Prudence* 7 no. 1 (1994): 84–95; O. Oyewumi, *The Invention of Women* (Minneapolis: University of Minnesota Press, 1997), ix–xiii, 13–15, 29, 31, 46–49, 58–62.

7 Deidre Helen Crumbley, "Also Chosen: Jews in the Imagination of a Black Storefront Church," *Anthropology and Humanism* 25, no. 1 (April 2000): 6–23. See also Deidre Helen Crumbley, "On Being First: Dogma, Disease, and Domination in the Rise of an African Church," *Religion* 30, no. 2 (2000): 169–184; Deidre Helen Crumbley, "Patriarchs, Prophets, and Procreation: Sources of Gender Practices in Three African Churches," *Africa* 73, no. 4 (2003): 584–605.

8 "Women: The Church of the Lord Organisation," The Church of the Lord (Aladura) Web site, available online at http://www.aladura.de/women.htm (accessed 18 November 2004).

9 Allan Anderson, *African Reformation: African Initiated Christianity in the 20th Century* (Trenton: African World Press, 2001), 10. See also Ositelu, *African Instituted Churches*, 74–75.

10 Gerloff, "Africa as the Laboratory of the World," 365–367.

11 Mary Douglas, *Purity and Danger: An Analysis of the Concepts of Pollution and Taboo* (London: Routledge and Kegan Paul 1966), 1–5, 113.

12 For example, in the Igbo traditions of southeastern Nigeria, Professor Ogbu Kalu observes an association of menstrual blood with a sacred and powerful "other." Here, the phrase "*ifu nso*" is used to refer to menstrual blood. Literally it means "seeing" (*ifu*), "a holy or sacred thing" (*nso*) (personal correspondence, 8 December 2004). Abraham Akrong describes how similar beliefs prevent female religious specialists in Ghana from engaging in ritual activity when menstruating. These beliefs suggest that a god, on coming suddenly upon menstruating women in his or her shrine, might mistake the power in menstrual blood for an unknown force. Striking out against the trespasser, the god might accidentally kill the menstruating women. Interview with Abraham Akrong, University of Ghana, Legon, interviewed in Hirschluch, Germany, 13 September 2003. Also see Thomas C. T. Buckley and Alma Gottlieb, "A Critical Appraisal of Theories of Menstrual Symbolism," in T. C. T. Buckley and A. Gottlieb, eds., *Blood Magic: The Anthropology of Menstruation* (Berkeley: University of California Press, 1988), 23–50.

13 E. O. A. Adejobi, *The Observances and Practices of the Church of the Lord (Aladura) in the Light of Old Testament and New Testament* (Nigeria: Enterprise Du Chez, 1976), unpaginated preface.

14 *Year 2000 Revised Constitution of the Church of the Lord (Aladura) World Wide* (Shagamu, Nigeria: Grace Enterprises, 2001), 10–18, 60–61.

15 Ibid., 17.

16 Ibid., 18.

17 Ibid., 62.

18 Adejobi, *The Observances and Practices of the Church of the Lord (Aladura)*, preface.

19 B. Jules-Rosette, "The Arcadian Wish: Toward a Theory of Contemporary African Religion," in B. Jules-Rosette, ed., *The New Religions of Africa* (Norwood, N.J.: Ablex, 1979), 219–229, B. Jules-Rosette, "Women in Indigenous African Cults and Churches," in F. C. Steady, ed., *The Black Woman Cross-Culturally* (Cambridge: Schenkman Publishing, 1981), 185–207; Deidre Helen Crumbley, "Impurity and Power: Women in Aladura Churches," *Africa* 62, no. 4 (1992): 6–23.

20 "Artikel: The Church of the Lord Organisation," Church of the Lord (Aladura) Web site, available online at http://www.aladura.de/artikel.htm (accessed 18 November 2004).

21 "Info: The Church of the Lord Organisation," Church of the Lord (Aladura) Web site, available online at http://www.aladura.de/news.htm (accessed 18 November 2004).

22 Genesis 12:1.

60

Excerpt from 'FAITH, FASHION AND FAMILY

Religion, aesthetics, identity and social organization in Strasbourg'

Atwood D. Gaines

Source: *Anthropological Quarterly*, 58(2) (1985), 47–62.

Introduction: religion and social action

Researchers have been concerned for some time with the nature of the relationship between religion and the social and/or economic order. Many writers, following Max Weber, have been concerned specifically with the relationship of a certain form of Christianity, Calvinism, and a certain form of economic activity, capitalism. Other research has looked at other aspects of the relationship of forms of Christianity to the social order.

Underwood (1952) noted the rather striking difference among American Catholics and Protestants with respect to their positions on social issues and their abilities or lack thereof (Protestants) in enlisting solid, religious group support around particular social issues.

For Alsace itself, Weber himself showed striking differences in the attendence of Protestants and Catholics in academic and professional schools of the University of Strasbourg (1954). Juillard (1968) pointed out differences between rural Catholics and Protestants with respect to work, land inheritance and hygiene. Elsewhere, I have noted differences in belief in and reliance on magic (the "Miraculous"), a formulation which uses Weber's notion of the Reformation as a "disenchantment," a move away from the "enchanted" worldview of Medieval Europe described by Erickson (1976) (Gaines n.d., b).

Other researchers have suggested that there are systematic differences in the manifestations of psychopathology between Catholics and Protestants in America and Europe (see Parsons 1969; Opler 1959; Zola 1966). Also, authors see differences in concepts of self and self presentation in medical (Gaines 1982, 1984) and secular contexts (Lee 1959) and the patterning of dysphoric affect in the Meditteranean tradition (Gaines and Farmer n.d.)

However, aside from some of the studies above, researchers have concentrated on seemingly purely economic activities without recognizing that other domains of activity may be substantially affected or determined by religious ideology. Likewise, the possibility has been overlooked that religious ideology affects certain areas of life which in turn shape economic life. Researchers have thus tended to neglect other aspects of social life affected by religious ideology. The present article focuses on two such dimensions of social life: aesthetics and social organization.

The approach combines several strands of interpretive research: Weber's interest in the relationship of forms of Christianity to economic life; Geertz's (1968, 1973b) related insights clarifying how religions provide not only systems of worship but also motivational structures influencing behavior in secular contexts; and interactionism's concern for the role of actors' definition of the situation in human behavior (Schutz 1967; Blumer 1969; Gaines 1979a, 1982). The research is part of and a contribution to the larger research effort concerning the relationship of ideology to social action.

The domains under study, only apparently unrelated, are seen here as deriving from particular religious ideologies, viewed as cultural systems (Geertz 1973b). It is certain that both areas have considerable significance vis-à-vis economic affairs, which also should be seen as parts of total cultural systems. While the present paper suggests a relationship between religious ideology on the one hand and aesthetics and social organization on the other, it is not focally concerned with this relationship.

Religion and society in Alsace

During research (in 1974 and 1981) on ethnic identity in Alsace (see Gaines 1979, n.d., a,b), I was puzzled by informants' responses to questions about the ethnic identity of others. Specifically, my informants almost always seemed to know the religion of unacquainted others and about those of whom I had asked, but as frequently failed to exhibit comparable knowledge concerning the ethnicity of these others. An explanation for the informants' ascriptive abilities appeared as important to pursue.

As explained below, decor and dress necessarily became the objects of inquiry. These objects included the interior of the homes as well as the person of our informants and others. Our concern is with personal dress and decoration as well as the manner in which they choose to decorate their homes environments for, as we shall see, faith determines fashion.

Aspects of 'lay aesthetics' (i.e., nonprofessional, lay artistic manipulations of the self and objects of the environment over which the self has control), such as taste, I shall label "style" (since it is the same in French and English, it seems an appropriate choice). The analysis shows that asthetic systems expressed as style form the basis on which Strasbourgeois ascribe unacquainted others' religious affiliation.

In the investigation of home environments, it was also found that social organization differed among the two categories of religious affiliation. The description of the families thus entails focusing on both style and social interactions and the bases of these interactions. We will find that Catholics maintain intense ties, especially between daughters and mothers after marriage. Essentially, we find embedded social networks (see Bott 1957) among Catholics and loose networks among Protestants. We see differences, too, with membership in voluntary associations.

The analyses begin with a presentation of ethnographic descriptions of three families. The families are used as ideal types, after Weber, though they are real people and families. A Protestant family is first presented. This presentation is followed by that of a Catholic family. The comparison of these two families in terms of aesthetics and social organization begins in the presentation of the third family which contains a self-defined Protestant, my informant for this otherwise Catholic family. She provides a synthetic and critical viewpoint from within the social and cultural system of Strasbourg.

After the descriptions of the families, the relationship between style and social identity (religious) is scrutinized. The analysis of family social organization follows. The article concludes with a brief discussion of the implications of this study for conceptualizations of the impact of modernization of family social organization. Before presenting the ethnographic material on the families, the research setting will be included.

Families in Strasbourg

A Catholic family

Both M. and Mme. Metzger were born and raised in Strasbourg. They have two children. One, a daughter, is married and lives with her husband just four doors down the road from her parents. The second child, a boy, is twelve years old and lives at home.

The family is Roman Catholic and generally attends Mass at the Cathedral on Sundays, although sometimes they will "attend services" by watching the televised broadcast of the Mass from the Cathedral. The members of the Metzger family consider themselves to be 'fairly' religious and feel that religion is an important influence on their lives, but not one which dominates them.

M. Metzger owns a book store in town on the rue des Soeyrs. Jean-Paul, M. Metzger's son-in-law, works with him selling books, most of which are travel, children's and popular books. There are several salesgirls who work in the store weekends and after school. These are Metzger's godchildren, children of some old friends.

Mme. Metzger is a housewife as is her married daughter, Michèle. Michèle usually visits her mother once a day, sometimes more frequently.

Many meals are shared by the two households. The two women talk about a variety of topics including neighbors, remedies and recipes. The two often *faire shopping* together at both the neighborhood markets and department stores, especially Jung's in the city's center.

Outside the family, the Metzgers have some associational involvements. The family, including the married daughter, belongs to the *Club Mediterranée,* a vacation club. Their annual vacation is taken together in the South of France. Mme. Metzger is sometimes involved in church activities doing volunteer organizational work. But most of their social life involves family and friends, two couples of whom are *parrain* and *marraine* (godfather and godmother) to the Metzger children.

The Metzger family lives in a well-appointed three bedroom apartment which they own. The apartment is situated southwest of the city center in the *Quartier des Musiciens.* The family has decorated their apartment with both color and flair. The walls of the living and dining areas are covered in pastel green fabric. These rooms are trimmed with a rococco design in gold painted stucco.

The design of the furniture of these rooms matches that of the walls; matching material covering them and trimmed with a gold border. Lacquered tables and chests complete the decor of the room. Some of these are white, while other such articles are deep blues and reds. Some of these pieces of furniture are of Chinese designs and reflect Mme. Metzger's taste for the Oriental. This taste is not uncommon in Strasbourg because of several of the city's traditional industries, *Hannong faience* (china) and *imprimerée indienne*, Southeast Asian and Chinese designs printed on textiles. Several prints of religious subjects adorn the walls of the living area and are complemented by some portraits painted by local artists.

The Metzger reflect a sense of flair and fashion in their personal style as well. Mme. Metzger generally wears the currently required ensemble of expensive wool slacks with a blouse or sweater. She wears jewelry, gold and silver, such as necklaces, rings and bracelets. She also uses no small amount of makeup and her look is crowned by a stylish coiffeur that is the work of a *salon de beauté* near the Cathedral. The daughter of the Metzger's dresses in much this same way, as do many women, some of whom are more properly called girls. Both Metzger women have an affinity for bright and gay colors.

M. Metzger also shows concern for his appearance. He usually wears tailored, light-colored suits of French and Italian design. He wears some jewelry, a decorative watch, a bracelet and several jeweled rings. The well-kept appearance of his hair suggests that he does not simply go to the equivalent of a barber. The son of the family is generally well-dressed but is young enough to alter that at a moment's notice.

The general idea of clothing for the Metzgers', in tune with French fashion, is the well-tailored look of clothes which fit the contours of the body. This intent, however is not found with members of the Protestant family.

A Protestant family

Contrasting with the Metzger family on several levels of analysis as well as in religious affiliation is the Protestant (Reformed) Koechlin family. The Koechlins have been life-long residents of the city and now live in south Strasbourg. Like the Metzgers, the Koechlin family has a married daughter, but they have two other children as well, a younger son and daughter.

The married daughter, Dominique, lives with her husband at some distance from the parental home. Dominique's husband is a musician in the local symphony in which he plays violin. She is a doctoral candidate in chemistry at the University of Strasbourg and also works part-time as a chemist.

Two or three times a month the Koechlin family attends church at St. Peter's (formerly a Catholic military church which was bought from the Germans at the turn of the century). The younger children attend with them, but sit apart from their parents. Dominique sees her parents at church from time to time.

M. Koechlin owns a small glass (manufacturing) company that employs ten persons. None of these employees have any real or fictive familial ties with the Koechlin family. M. Koechlin inherited the firm from his father, but only after expressing his interest in doing so and after having taken courses of study in commerce and the technical aspects of the firm's product at the local university's commercial and technical schools.

Mme. Koechlin does not work now, although she has in the past both before and during her marriage. Mme. Koechlin spends much of her time with various volunteer groups such as the Red Cross, the local equivalent of the P.T.A., a neighborhood improvement society and the church. Her time there is devoted to the planning and organizational aspects of the parish, including obtaining lecturers for the parishioners and scheduling activities in the evening for them. She also spends time helping out at a mission located in the Foyer La Grange. This mission helps to feed the poor and indigent of Strasbourg.

M. Koechlin is also involved in these programs, but to a lesser extent because he is working and because he is often away in Paris for business reasons. Trips to Paris for permits and licenses are required because of the highly centralized character of government in France. M. Koechlin is very resentful since "such things should be done in Strasbourg and not require a wasteful sojourn to Paris."

Dominique, the married daughter, visits her parents once or twice a month when she invites them for lunch or dinner or when she and her husband are invited to her parents' home. These meetings are aside from those which might occur at church.

The parental home, which the Koechlins own, has two stories and has three bedrooms, spacious living, dining and kitchen areas. The interior walls of the home are painted stark white. Most of the furnishings appointed around the living and dining areas are dark natural wood; the stuffed chairs and couch are dark brown. A few paintings adorn the interior of the Koechlin home; all of these are either still-lifes or landscapes. There is nothing gold or silver. Recall that we saw portraits and much gold and silver color at the Metzger's.

Both M. and Mme. Koechlin dress well but one would not say fashionably, at least not in terms of French fashion. His untailored suits are of German block design and are gray, brown, black or other dark colors. He wears no accessories save a watch and wedding band, nor does his hair reflect the kind of care shown by that of M. Metzger. M. Koechlin's shoes are substantial looking and have not the trim, sleek and supple appearance of the footwear of M. Metzger.

Mme. Koechlin dresses in clothes with clean crisp lines and simple designs. She favors muted tones rather than bright colors. She wears little makeup or jewelry. A wedding band and simple earrings suffice. Her hair is usually tied in a bun at the back of her head, a style which seems not to need the assistance of the coiffeur. Their style is one of a somber simplicity.

The Hoffman family is the third family to be considered. The Hoffmann family, or at least Mireille Hoffmann, my principle contact with this family, presented me with what seemed to be a very serious problem. The problem related to the models of appearance fashioned from informants' comments. As will be seen, Mlle. Hoffmann first poses and then gets out of what could have been a real mess, not just a muddle, in my models of aesthetics and religious affiliation in Strasbourg.

A 'Protestant' in a Catholic family

I was introduced to Mlle. Hoffmann by another informant, Iris Schmidt. Schmidt is Catholic (Schmidt, double 't,' is a Protestant name) and between the two, there was an apparent contrast of styles. Mlle. Hoffmann 'looked' Protestant, according to the model I had in mind which I learned from other informants, including Iris Schmidt. She wore her hair long, barely combed and unstyled. She wore black corduroy pants, (loosely worn), hiking boots, an oversized grey pullover sweater, and didn't wear makeup—the kind of minimal concern for personal appearance 'characteristic' of Protestants. I asked to interview her at some later time. She agreed and extended an invitation for lunch at her house the following week. (As relates to social organizational differences, I note here that the very fact of the invitation further suggested Mile. Hoffmann was a Protestant. As I learned after some months into the research, Protestants always invited me into their homes immediately, while with Catholics a lot of hard work and time was required to get such an invitation.)

The following week at the appointed time, we met and she drove me to her home in Illkirch-Grafenstaden, a contigious suburb south of Strasbourg. Once at her home, we began to talk and I was surprised to learn that the Hoffmann family was Catholic. I learned this from two sources: first, the decor of the house, and second, later in the interview, Mlle. Hoffmann's statement to that effect. Although the family is not as well off as the Metzgers or the Koechlins, the decor reflected certain attempts at a conception of 'luxury': gold frames on the pictures (of people), wall hangings, gold and silver colored lamps with glass ornaments, figurines, etc. In this we recognize that the stylistic differences not only relate to the use of precious metals and stones or simulations thereof, but also the sheer number of items involved in decorative schemes.

I continued to pose questions and she responded with somber reflection to each "so as to make sure everything is right, at least as far as I know." The interview (in English, which Hoffmann taught in an elementary school in Strasbourg) continued for some six hours with time out for lunch, prepared and shared with us by her mother. Mireille's mother, however, was not in the least interested in being interviewed. During lunch she would answer my questions with polite responses that varied from "I don't know" to "I've heard that said but I wouldn't really know about it." She was more than a bit annoyed that her daughter had invited me, a perfect stranger, into the home and was even willingly talking with me.

Some time after lunch I concluded asking questions on topical areas of interest to me. I was still somewhat confused about the apparent contradiction Mlle. Hoffmann presented. I said, in response to her query of other topics I might be interested in asking about, "I am interested in the Alsatians, their culture and ethnic issues in Strasbourg, but that I am also interested in differences that might exist between members of the different religious denominations." Clearly intrigued, Mlle. Hoffmann's eyes widened and she asked: "Well then, what do you think of me?" I replied that she seemed "like a Protestant in a Catholic family," to which she quickly replied: "That is exactly what I am." She then went on to talk about her adolescence with respect to the religious issues just raised.

MH: Ever since I was a little girl, I've admired Protestant girls. They were curious like I was and wanted to learn about things (she owns nearly 500 scholarly books—far more than any French graduate student I ever met.) In their families they could talk about most anything, but that was not true in my family. There were lots of things that my parents felt we (she and her siblings) should not know (or talk about). So, I began to spend as much time as I could with my girlfriends.

Q: Protestant girlfriends?
MH: Yes.
Q: Could you tell the difference between a Protestant girl and a Catholic girl at school when you were young?
MH: Oh, yes, and we all wore uniforms.
Q: Then how could you tell the difference?
MH: By the way they looked, their hair (styles and cuts), the way they wore their uniforms, the way they walked, just everything. Of course today they don't wear uniforms and they can wear more makeup so it's not (so) difficult.
Q: Not (so) difficult for what?
MH: To recognize Catholics and Protestants if you're not used to doing it.
Q: I see. So what happened with you and your friends?
MH: I bacame like them. I became like a Protestant. Look, as you can see, I don't look like a Catholic girl, I look like a Protestant girl.

Related to social organization, Mireille also discussed visiting patterns at my suggestion. She talked about her sister who is married and lives just down the street. The sister, several years Mireille's senior, visits their mother almost everyday of the week.

MH: If she (the sister) doesn't come by, then my brother-in-law does.
Q: Why do you think they visit so often?
MH: I don't really know. If I were married, I wouldn't live near my mother and father, and I wouldn't come by so often. I think it is strange that they see so much of one another. I don't see any reason for it. But all of my family think I am weird, too.

After discussing the visiting patterns of her family (and her opposition to them), she took me over to the living room window out of which could be seen a large gathering of people of all ages. "There they are. The parents, their children, the grandchildren, cousins and whatever. You can see them all there once or twice a week. That's true of all the other families on this street. Except there are two families here (on the street) where these gatherings don't occur." She turned to me and said with an air of discovery, "And those two families are Protestant!"

As if to confirm the veracity of her statements about the 'weirdness' of familial interaction and matrifocal social organization, Mireille left Strasbourg three weeks after our interview. She had applied several years earlier for a teaching post at a North African university. To her delight and her parents' chagrin, the position had finally come up to her.

Aesthetics and religious identity

Here I want to consider an aspect of religious identity in Strasbourg: 'style.' Style may be considered as a cultural system (see Geertz 1973a, b). Here the term refers to the ideas, conceptions and assumptions, and their meaningful symbolic manifestations, with and by which people are led to select and to decorate the objects in their immediate personal and experimental environment in a particular *mode* (i.e., after a certain fashion). The objects which are the focus of action based upon particular aesthetic ideas may be animate or inanimate.

Seen in this way, the objects which receive the decorative attention of a group or a given individual may be that particular group or individual or other people, as well as the animate (e.g., pets) and inanimate objects in the surrounding environment and over which individuals have some control and to which they have access. Considered as a cultural system, style is both patterned and learned. The representations of this cultural system are probably influenced by economic factors as well as others including availability. But the economic base cannot be seen as allowing or disallowing the expression of aesthetics, but rather as affecting the degree to which it is expressed. In our sample, the economic level of any one family does not allow a great advantage over any of the others; the aesthetic taste of the Metzger's is not more complicated, further elaborated than that of the Koechlins because they have more money. In fact, the Koechlins have considerably more money.

In Strasbourg, style is a cultural system, a religious system that is learned, patterned, shared and recognized by the members of the social system. It is aesthetics, or style, that forms the bases for the public recognition of an individual's religious affiliation in urban contexts. It is noteworthy that these same stylistic differences also are to be found in the countryside.

Country style

The traditional dress of the provincial villages historically has reflected this dichotomy. I was shown a book by M. Herzlich, a salesman, in which were pictured in color the traditional costumes of each of the major cities and villages of Alsace. Religious differences were quite apparent.

Apparent was the variation in the traditional dress among the different villages. Those of the Protestant villages were in colors of brown, grey, black, dark blue—subdued colors all. These colors stood in contrast to those of the costumes of similar design in the Catholic villages.

In the villages designated as Catholic, there was a noticeable lack of the somber mood projected by Protestant costumes. The costumes were in bright and gay colors and used contrasts of colors to great effect, e.g., black with white trim, red with black trim, red with white trim, etc. In areas like that of Strasbourg where one finds individuals of different faiths in one locale, distinctions are still maintained in the traditional dress of the area. The traditional folk costume of the area of Strasbourg has three basic colors: red, black, and white. (One thinks here of Turner's article [1966] on these colors which he says are primary and fundamental, and Berlin and Kay's evolutionary argument [1969] which suggests that these three colors form the basic color triad from which, in a fixed sequence, other color terms develop, such as green and yellow.)

City styles

In the costume of Strasbourg, males wear black pants, and a red vest with rows of gold buttons worn over a white shirt. The square-cut coat is black, as are the shoes and hat. A bow tie is worn which may be either black or plaid. The traditional dress of the females is a good deal more complicated than that of the males.

The women's costume is composed of low-heel black leather shoes, often with felt bows, worn with white stockings and a calf-length full skirt bordered in decorative ribbon. On the waist is worn a black bodice over which is tied a ribbon in one of several colors. Over the bodice and under the ribbon a woman wears an embroidered silk apron. A white blouse is worn and is topped by a black shawl, again in embroidered silk.

The whole costume is topped off by the famous *schlumpfkappe.* These give viewers the appearance of a sort of hat or bonnet, which they are not. Schlumpfkappe are very wide ribbons tied and pinned to the head of the wearer. Their skillful arrangement gives the appearance of bonnets. In Strasbourg and the surrounding area, the schlumpfkappe are plain black satin, but elswwhere in Alsace one finds many other colors. An example is the white-with-red-rose color scheme of the schlumpfkappe of the village of Willgottheim (Bas Rhin).[1]

Having seen several performances of the *Ballet Folklorique* groups in Strasbourg during the summer tourist season, I had noted that a few things in the costume varied, i.e., variations appeared with respect to the color of the long skirts worn by the women and the ribbons worn tied around their waists.

I questioned some of the dancers performing at the Palais de Rohan about the significance of the colors of the long skirts. I was told that at one time long ago, the skirts in and around Strasbourg were red. Some time ago other colors appeared. Now, one color, green, is worn by Protestant females. The other colors are worn by Catholic females. Also, the ribbon tied around the skirt and bodice is green or black if the wearer is Protestant, and red, or one of a few other colors, if she is Catholic. For males, the bow tie is plaid if the wearer is Catholic, and black if Protestant. (Though the latter information was told to me by several informants, it does not seem to reflect the actual pattern of use.)

Lutherans, Calvinists and aesthetics

It is this sort of contrast which shows the Metzgers on one side and the Koechlins and Mlle. Hoffmann on the other. This stylistic dichotomoy is another dimension that can be added to Weber's notion of ascetic Protestantism (Weber 1954). However, on my examples I employed as a model a Reformed family, that of M. and Mme. Koechlin. It is appropriate to ask, then, whether or not their style, a rather somber aesthetic, is also found among the more numerous Lutherans of the city of Strasbourg.

My data indicate that this difference in style between Catholics and Protestants does indeed extend to the Lutherans, who are not included in Weber's system of classification as 'ascetic' Protestants. (I have elsewhere pointed out aspects of Lutheranism which render it much like Calvinism in its worldly orientation, even though its without the notion of predestination [see Gaines n.d.,b]). My informants also agreed with this.

Mlle. Hoffmann, in her remarks concerning the recognition of religious affiliation based on stylistic differences between Catholics and Protestants, did not differentiate between Lutheran and Reformed Protestants. Nor did M. Herzlich (who is Catholic) indicate that the traditional dress styles of the villages could be divided into three groups (Catholic, Lutheran and Reformed). Rather, he pointed out only two aesthetic divisions. The separation of traditional dress into only two color systems again makes this point. We can specify more precisely the nature of the differences in aesthetics between the two groups following the conventions of M. Herzlich.

M. Herzlich suggested that what one discerns in another's appearance is somber simplicity in both use of color and form among the Protestants and gay colors and elaboration in Catholics' dress. He believed the Protestants dressed simply (and drably) while Catholics were more creative and colorful: "Since slacks are in fashion for women, Catholic girls wear them very tightly, Protestants wear them loose fitting. The same with men's clothes, especially young men. Protestants men and women don't wear a lot of jewelry, Catholics [men and women] usually do [he wears four rings] if they can afford to. Catholic women wear makeup, Protestant women don't wear much." But again M. Herzlich did not distinguish between or among different sorts of Protestants.

Origins of aesthetic traditions

Now that we have established these aesthetic differences, an interesting question to ask is why they exist. I think the answer lies in the aesthetic milieu of the respective places of worship for each group. It seems that there is a parallel between the aesthetic involution, and their distinguishing means of dress. The decoration of church interiors displays wealth in the form of color (purples, reds, silver, gold, etc.) and precious stones, cloth, furs and metals.

It does not seem illogical to point to the connection between personal decorative styles and those observable in a given group's place of worship.

The aesthetics of the House of the Lord among Catholics appears to be the model of and for, as well as the means for, the maintenance of the aesthetic. The wealth—literal and in terms of color—displayed serves as a model of and for aesthetics for Catholics. My Catholic informants, however, did not see the connection. Although they saw the parallel which struck me, they were unsure of a relationship.

The Protestant sense of aesthetics minimizes both color and evidence of wealth. That it does so *is recognized* by Protestant informants as having a religious (theological) basis. In Calvinist doctrine, icons and elaborate sacred decoration are seen as detracting from the contemplation of divinity. Attention to fashion in the home or on one's person is seen by informants as wasteful and without point.

Also, Protestants (by which was meant Lutherans and Calvinists), as one Reformed informant, Pastor Frankel, pointed out, do not like (and he cringed) to represent Christ. He said that the Catholics do it all the time, in parades, statues, etc. Here we see a tendency toward representations of people, often in great distress, among the Catholics and a tendency to represent nature among Protestants. Note that this recalls the genre of painting found in the Catholic and Protestant homes described earlier.

In Catholic Churches, one sees no lack of imagery. There are stories told in stained glass and numerous chapels, each with a figure or figures of saints (or paintings thereof) adorned in precious stone, or metal or both. Also, and I think this has important psychological consequences, there is no lack of displays of violence in the form of martyred saints; here one carrying his head after an execution, there one pierced with a number of arrows, another with his heart torn from his body, and so on.[3]

In Alsace, we see representations of Ste. Odile, Alsace's patron saint, in her blindness. There is also a modern reliquary of sorts on Mount Ste. Odile near the statue of the saint that overlooks the province. There we find a large stone cross of rose limestone (from which the Catherdral is also made). In that cross is the heart, the actual heart, of Msgr. Reusch. The Monseigneur did not die in the 12th or 13th century. He died in the late 1960s.

But in St. Peter's Reformed Church virtually nothing in the way of decoration is to be found, save a small wooden lectern for Pastor Werrn and a large but bare and simple wooden cross which flanks the lectern. There are no statues, stained glass or precious metal ornaments. Pastor Werrn looks out over unpainted wooden pews.

Nearly the same ascetic aesthetic prevails in a nearby Lutheran church. But here we find a bit more in the way of decoration; a chalice, a candlestick, and some black curtains flanking a stone altar (the former and the latter because of communion). Again, there are no stained glass windows with images.

For the Reformed Church, it should be noted that the sparse decoration does not derive from a lack of funds. As the Pastor told me, his parishioners are drawn mostly from the highest levels of Protestant society in Strasbourg. He accurately described his congregation as consisting of "the true grande bourgeoisie." Pastor Werrn himself, unassisted by a cohort of altar boys, holds forth every Sunday in a dark business suit; there are no robes of rich cloth and elegant trimming here.

At St. Peter's we find not only the Koechlins in attendance, but also the two leading Alsatian families of Strasbourg. One of these is the Dollfuss family which, thanks to Pastor Wernn, I was able to interview. The Dollfuss family is one of the wealthiest in Strasbourg and in Alsace. Given their exhalted status and financial standing (they are multimillionaires) it is of interest to compare their style with the other Alsatians mentioned above.

Language, aesthetics and identity

As concerns ethnic identification of unacquainted others in Strasbourg and Alsace, we find that language competence is the feature of paramount importance. The ascription of ethnic affiliation among the unacquainted is not possible in Strasbourg because French ethnics do not perceive differences in physiognomy as a central criterion of differentiation. The Alsatians use it only to deny membership to people whose appearance suggests ancestry from outside of the province, e.g., Asian or African ancestry (see Gaines 1979; n.d.,a for an extended treatment of ethnicity in Alsace). For these reasons the folk categories of self-and other-ascription in Strasbourg have to do with religious rather than ethnic identity among the unacquainted.

When the criteria affecting the ascription of one's ethnic affiliation are seen from this perspective, several problems which confronted me in my research disappear. First, as noted above, that while Strasbourgeois often knew the religion of acquaintances or unacquainted others, they less often knew of others' ethnic affiliation. The second problem was that most French ethnic visitors and residents of the city, including several long-time residents as well, did not know that the Strasbourgeois are overwhelmingly ethnic Alsatians.

Most Strasbourgeois do not appear to be different in their sense of style or decoration, except in matters concerning folk arts and crafts, from the French sojourner or resident. They do recognize that some Alsatians are Protestant. Another component of this misattribution of ethnicity concerns language use which has been mentioned earlier. Briefly, it may be recalled that almost all urban Alsatians learn French as their first language. As a consequence, they speak it fluently without accent. Only the country-born people have Alsatian accents. As a consequence, since the French rely almost exclusively on the use of language (French) as a marker of belonging, they are led to assume that the French speaking urban Alsatians are French ethnics (Gaines 1979, n.d., a). We may now turn to the analysis of these aspects of family social organization and its relationship to religious affiliation.

Family social organization

Social networks

Bott (1957) characterized social networks as embedded and loose. If embedded, networks were characterized as those where friend, neighbors, workmates and relatives were all the same people. Conversely, the networks were loose if these various roles were filled with different people.

In looking at occupational contexts, we may note that M. Metzger employs his son-in-law. In this way an economic relationship is embedded in the kinship network. This domain is reinforced by the employment of children of Metzger's old friends, who are godmother and godfather to his children and for some of whom he serves as godfather.

As noted, the kinship idiom does not appear in the economic relations of M. Koechlin. Nor does this idiom appear in the case of the Hoffmanns. But, because he and his daughter are school teachers employed by the state, as are teachers of all grade levels in France, his position could not be comparable to that of the others. The descriptions thus begin only to highlight the embedded character of networks in Catholic areas. Among Catholic informants, it was seen as right and fair that one hire one's relatives. However, it was seen as unseemly nepotism by Protestants.

Family visiting and interaction

Another feature of the organization of the families is the visiting patterns of the married daughters noted both in the descriptions of the families and in Mlle. Hoffmann's remarks. In each case the pattern of visting was seen as normal and usual. The informal and frequent visits by the daughters of the Metzger and Hoffmann families are seen as normal and proper to them (with the exceptions of one member of the Hoffmann family as noted). Likewise, the Koechlin family sees nothing unusual about their relationship with their daughter. This relationship is comparatively formal and involves relatively infrequent visiting.

It seems in this case, then, that proximity itself is a result of ideological considerations. Proximity is not the responsible factor for the frequent visits nor is distance an appreciable factor in the pattern of infrequent visiting observed for the Koechlins. Even if the actual patterns were to vary, it would not alter the fact of the ideological or cultural system, the way things should be, in conforming with the patterns exemplified above (see Schneider 1965 for this distinction but related to a cultural e.g., symbolic, analysis of American kinship).

A woman's room

The patterns noted above are not unique. They are general and representative of the two religious groups. There is a variation of the Catholics' pattern I can note here. Strasbourg, because it is the major city in Haut Rhin and a university center, attracts many people from other cities and villages in France and Alsace itself. I collected a number of cases concerning single women in Strasbourg from another area which showed that they return home for any reason, mild illness, weekends, holidays, or simply because they want to return. What is striking about these women away from home is that their room in their family home is always kept as their room regardless of the length of time they are or were away.

One informant was Dominique Hesse, who lived in the apartment next to the Cathedral where I lived for 6 months of the research. Mlle. Hesse was a nursing student in Strasbourg. Periodically, I would want to ask Mlle. Hesse if she could help me on some problem or matter of interpretation. Frequently she was absent from her apartment. I would later ascertain that she had been home, to a suburb of the southern Alsatian city of Colmar, because of her illness or rest or just to visit. There was no problem with these visits as her room was maintained for her in her absence. All this despite the fact that she had 'lived away from home' for over five years.

The same situation prevailed with the Schmidt family, whose daughter Iris was mentioned earlier. Mlle. Schmidt was not living at home in 1974 after having spent 1973 teaching (1st grade) in the countryside. Generally, she returned home for the summers but this summer was different. Although her room had been kept as it was during her years at home (till age 22) four years before, she did not want to live there in 1974. There was a very good reason for this, although unknown to Mme. and M. Schmidt.

Iris had decided to marry a student at the Catholic Theological Institute at the University. The student, whom we will call Raymond, was a Canadian and was already a priest. He was finishing his doctorate at the University but while living in Canada. He would come to Strasbourg periodically; I believe he came four times during the year (1974), to take care of various bits of business relating to the work on his doctorate (which he finished in January 1975).

Naturally, he also came to see Iris and visit what he knew were future parents-in-law though they were unaware of this future relationship. He was considered by them as a friend of the family and nothing more. That is how Iris met him.

The major problem for Raymond and Iris was that if it were discovered that he intended to leave the priesthood and to marry, and in fact that he was already seeing a woman, he would not receive his doctorate. During the year I watched the development of a massive cover-up. Iris also told me that the discovery of the relationship would mean the end of her "reputation" and that of her family too, as people think "only the worst kind of girl would get involved with a priest" because she would be said to have, "led him astray and into sin."

To conclude this vignette I can relate that one day I spent the morning with M. and Mme. Schmidt at their home and had later that day met with Iris. Over a cup of coffee I mentioned to her that her mother was again painting (she was an inveterate painter and quite good) and that she had set up an easel in Iris' room and had hung and placed paintings everywhere in it. Iris was quite shocked. "*La vache*" (the cow) she said, "That's *my* room."

Later that same day, she told her mother, in no uncertain terms, (I later heard from Mme. Schmidt) to put "her" room back the way it was. Mme. Schmidt complied. (I have always suspected that Mme. Schmidt did in fact know that her daughter had some sort of plan and was actually testing her.)

In this simple example, we note that there was considerable attachment to her place in the family home and a sort of tacit agreement that it would always be hers. She was visably upset when this agreement was violated. Yet Iris knew perfectly well that she would never live there again as Raymond's doctorate was intended to take advantage of an offer of a position in a philosophy department of a secular Canadian university. The example clearly shows that while actual behavior may vary because circumstances vary, there is an underlying ideology of some consistency.

Husbands, wives and mothers

It seems to me that the pattern for males is somewhat different. The women's situation seems to reflect a matrifocal tendency I did not see with Protestant informants (except for one who had a Catholic mother whom she said felt neglected if she didn't visit her every week. For the mother this was still not enough). For males it seems that they are to act more independently. I think however, that they leave home later than one is accustomed to seeing in the U.S. and, more important, they seem to become enmeshed in their wife's mother's home life, as we saw occurred with Mlle. Hoffmanns's brother-in-law.

The material presented above seems to have relevance to some theoretical issues relating to the family and modernization as well as to the distinctiveness of two Christian traditions. By way of conclusion, a discussion of some issues follows.

Conclusion

Family and modernization

It has been generally assumed by sociologists, and recently challenged by some anthropologists, that the extended family was a victim of industrialization, that modernization in the West caused a breakdown of the 'traditional' extended family. A review of the literature relating to family and social networks and this research, however, indicates the presence of extended families in modern urban situations.

For instance, we find effectively functioning extended families among urban Italians in Firth's (1956) study in London, and among Londoners themselves in Bethnal Green (Young and Wilmott 1957) before their move to the housing estate. Chombart de Lauwe's study (1952) of Paris finds that Parisian neighborhoods are essentially closed social worlds with interaction and ties of aid and dependence occurring primarily within them. One notes too the older findings of the Lewis group which saw rural Mexicans moving to the city increasing, rather than decreasing, their kinship ties and interactions (Fox 1977). And, too, there is Bott's work (1957) that demonstrates the embedded character of urban social networks for working-class families in London.

The research presented here also suggests that these patterns are typical urban patterns for particular groups, not holdovers from the peasant or pre-industrial days. Rather, such patterns of familism are related to specific religious traditions in the society, whether whole or part society, to which the people belong. Researchers concerned with the affect of modernization on the 'traditional' family structure have neglected to consider or recognize specific traditions.

The argument about the relationship of family to industrialization and its consequence, urbanization, may be miscast. The relationship important for an analysis of dynamics may not be one which exists between particular religious, and hence, particular ideological systems and their related forms of family structure and organization in the West. Arguments like Laslett's (1972), which seek to show the historical demise of the extended family, focus on residential groups as obtained from historical records. As the Catholics in this research demonstrate, it is clearly not necessary for an extended family to *live* together in order to *stay* together.

On the contemporary scene, Bott's argument (1957) states that embedded or loose knit social networks are related to and form conjugal roles. But she fails to recognize that both are refractions of a religious ideology. In her case it was Anglicanism, the English version of Catholicism.

Voluntarism

A particularly important aspect, which we have but glimpsed here in this article, is the difference between Catholic and Protestant membership in voluntary associations. Sources suggest that familism of the kind found in Catholic countries or among Catholics in other areas precludes membership in voluntary asociations. Thus in Italy we find a paucity of such associational membership (Banfield 1958) as we do in France (Rose 1954) and Spain (Pitt-Rivers 1961). The same appears to be true of all Mediterranean societies and the descendents thereof (e.g., Mexico, Central and Latin American countries). (See Rubel 1976 for a discussion of the development of voluntary associations among Anglos but not Chicanos in the same Texas town.)

The lack of voluntary associations may have implications for political stability as well. Widespread voluntarism, as in the United States, may be seen as creating and sustaining a myriad of cross-cutiing ties of loyalty. Very likely these would positively affect political stability in countries where it is found and, conversely, its absence would seem to promote political instability. Such instability might be compensated for periodically by authoritarian regimes of the right or left.

In Catholicism, instead of associations of unrelated others, the family is the center of one's interests, efforts and attention. The family is a sacred unit. All those of this unit are seen as strangers, and implicitly or explicitly as enemies by their very definition as non-kin (see Campbell 1966). It is the (sacred) family that is the referent for conceptions of honor and shame and the unit supported or threatened by patronage ties (the extension of kin ties), expressions of virility (procreation and continuation of the family), and the institution of motherhood (reflecting Mariology, fertility, nurturance) (see Banfield 1958; Campbell 1966; Gaines 1982; Gilmore 1983; Peristiany 1965; Pitt-Rivers 1961).

Perhaps Aries (1962) is close to the point when he suggests that the nuclear family arose after the Renaissance in Western Europe. The following period is the Protestant Reformation and may be as directly related to the development of the nuclear family units in the West as it was to a new European worldview (Protestant) (Weber 1954; Erickson 1976).

These differences of a profound nature suggest for Europe, then, that there are at least two major ideological or cultural areas, Northern European Protestant and Mediterranean (see Gaines 1982, 1984, n.d. a, Gilmore 1983). It has been the reflections of these two Western traditions that we have found in Strasbourg.

Summary

This article has suggested two additional areas of social action which may be seen to differentiate among forms of Christian belief. These areas, aesthetics and social organization may be added to the list compiled by other researchers which include responses to modernization, social action, education, work, inheritance, orientations toward the miraculous, and illness symptomatology. The results were seen as having some implications for theories about the relationship of family to modernization or urbanization and for conceptualizations of two distinct culture areas in the West.

An interpretive approach was utilized because, as in the biological theory and practice of Biomedicine (see Gaines and Hahn 1982; Hahn and Gaines 1985; Mishler *et al.*, 1980), an anthropological emphasis on the putatively material (such "things" as social structure, ecology, economy, or "world systems", etc.) often leads researchers astray and away from the semantic nature and source of human action.

The research has utilized real people and families as ideal types in order to make its comparisons. Such comparisons demonstrated that the observable differences are not due to ethnic differences (as they are all Alsatians) in this plural society, nor are they due to economic, educational or even ecological differences. The differences derive from distinct religious ideologies that have been internalized and act as guides of and for social action in secular and religious contexts. The research confirms, as Geertz (1973a) has suggested, that religions do indeed "instill long lasting moods and motivations."

Notes

1 One informant told me that women wearing flowered schlumpfkappe are unmarried, while those who wear the solid colors are married. However, I have seen young girls much too young to be married wearing solid black or red schlumpfkappe. The significance of the different patterns actually derives from the identification of each with a particular village, usually, but not always, that of the wearer.

2 We note that the symbol of the American (and Protestant) businessman, is the drab, somber, gray flannel suit. The reader may more easily apprehend the differences in style discussed here by envisioning an Italian or Mexican furniture and comparing that image with a Scandinavian furniture store.

3 See Gaines and Farmer (n.d.) for a detailed analysis of suffering and sainthood in the Mediterranean tradition.

References cited

ARIES, PHILLIPE
1962 —Centuries of childhood. R. Baldick, trans. New York: Random House.
BANFIELD, EDWIN C.
1958 —The moral basis of a backward society. New York: Free Press.

BERLIN, BRENT, and PAUL KAY
1969 —Basic color terms: Their university and evolution. Berkeley: University of California Press.
BOTT, ELIZABETH
1957 —Family and social network. London: Tavistock.
BLUMER, HERBERT
1969 —Symbolic interactionism. Englewood Cliffs, New Jersey: Prentice-Hall, Inc.
CAMPBELL, JOHN K.
1966 —Honour, family and patronage. Oxford: Oxford University Press.
CHOMBART, DE LAUWE, PAUL-HENRI, *et al.*
1952 —Paris er l'Agglomeration Parisienne. Paris: Presses Universitaire de France. (2 volumes).
ERICKSON, CAROLLY
1976 —The medieval vision. Oxford: Oxford University Press.
FIRTH, RAYMOND
1956 —Two studies of kinship in London. London: Athlone.
FOX, RICHARD
1977 —Urban anthropology. Englewood Cliffs, New Jersey: Prentice-Hall.
GAINES, ATWOOD D.
1979a —Les Strasbourgeois. Paper presented at the Southwestern Anthropological Association Meeting. Santa Barbara, California.
1979b —Definitions and diagnoses. Culture, Medicine, and Psychiatry 3(4): pp. 381–418.
1982 —Cultural definitions, behavior and the person in American psychiatry. *In* Cultural Conceptions of Mental Health and Therapy. A. Marsella and G. White, eds. Dordrecht, Holland: D. Reidel Publishing Co., pp. 157–192.
1985 —The once-and the twice-born: Person and practice among Christian and secular psychiatrists. *In* Physicians of Western Medicine: Anthropological Approaches to Theory and Practice. R. A. Hahn and A. D. Gaines, eds. Dordrecht, Holland: D. Reidel Publishing Co.
n.d.a. —Ethnicity as a cultural system: Race, Language and culture in Strasbourg. MS.
n.d.b —The Word and the Cross: Cultural identity and paradox in Alsace. MS.
GAINES, ATWOOD D., and PAUL E. FARMER, JR.
n.d. —Visible saints: Social cynosure and dysphoria in the Mediterranean tradition. Culture, Medicine, and Psychiatry. (In press.)
GAINES, ATWOOD D., and ROBERT A. HAHN, eds.
1982 —Physicians of Western medicine: Five cultural studies. Special Issue. Culture, Medicine and Psychiatry 6(3).
GEERTZ, CLIFFORD
1968 —Islam observed. Chicago: University of Chicago Press.
1973a —The interpretation of cultures. New York: Basic Books.
1973b —Religion as a cultural system. *In* The Interpretation of Cultures. New York: Basic Books, pp. 87–125.
GILMORE, DAVID
1983 —Anthropology of the Mediterranean area. Annual Review of Anthropolgy. Palo Alto: Annual Review Press, pp. 175–205.

GOLDE, GUNTER

1975 —Catholics and Protestants: Agricultural modernization in two German villages. New York: Academic Press.

HAHN, ROBERT, and ATWOOD D. GAINES, eds.

1985 —Physicians of Western medicine: Anthropological approaches to theory and practice. Dordrecht, Holland: D. Reidel Publishing Co.

INSTITUT NATIONAL de la STATISTIQUE et des ÉTUDES ÉCONOMIQUES (INSEE)

1977 —Annuaire statistique de la France. 82e Volume. Paris: INSEE.

JUILLARD, ÉTIENNE

1968 —Catholiques et Protestants dans les Campagnes Bas-Rhinoises. *In* Problezms Alsaciens Vus par un Géographe. E. Juillard. Strasbourg: La Faculté des Lettres de l'Universitié de Strasbourg.

LASLETT, PETER

1972 —Household and family in past time. Cambridge: Cambridge University Press.

LEE, DOROTHY

1959 —View of the self in Greek culture. *In* Freedom and Culture. D. Lee. Englewood Cliffs, New Jersey: Prentice-Hall.

OPLER, M. K.

1959 —Cultural differences in mental disorders: An Italian and Irish contrast in the schizophrenias-USA. *In* Culture and Mental Health. M. K.Opler, ed. New York: Macmillan.

PARSONS, ANNE

1969 —Abstract and concrete images in paranoid delusions. *In* Belief, Magic and Anomie. Anne Parsons. New York: Free Press, pp. 204–211.

PERISTIANY, J. G., ed.

1965 —Honour and shame: The values of Mediterranean society. London: Weidenfeld and Nicholson.

PITT-RIVERS, JULIAN

1961 —The people of the Sierra. Chicago: University of Chicago Press.

ROSE, A. M.

1954 —Voluntary associations in France. *In* Theory and Method in the Social Sciences. A. M. Rose, ed. Minneapolis: University of Minnesota Press.

RUBEL, ARTHUR

1976 —Across the tracks. Austin: University of Texas Press.

SCHNEIDER, DAVID

1968 —American kinship: A cultural account. Englewood Cliffs, New Jersey: Prentice-Hall.

SOMBART, WERNER

1915 —The quintessence of capitalism. New York. E.P. Dutton and Co.

SCHUTZ, ALFRED

1967 —Collected papers: The problems of social reality. The Hague: Martinus Nijhoff.

TAWNEY, R. H.

1954 —Religion and the rise of capitalism. New York: Mentor Books.

TURNER, VICTOR W.

1966 —Colour classification in Ndembu ritual. *In* Anthropological Approaches to the Study of Religion. M. Banton, ed. London: Tavistock.

UNDERWOOD, KENNETH
1962 —Protestant and Catholic Boston: Beacon Press.
WEBER, MAX
1954 —The Protestant ethic and the spirit of capitalism. New York: C. Scribner.
YOUNG, MICHAEL, and PETER WILMOTT
1957 —Family and kinship in east London. Middlesex, England: Penguin.
ZOLA, I. K.
1966 —Culture and symptoms. American Sociological Review 3:615–630.

61

THE FEMINIZATION AND PROFESSIONALIZATION OF ORDAINED MINISTRY WITHIN THE MÂ'OHI PROTESTANT CHURCH IN FRENCH POLYNESIA[1]

Gwendoline Malogne-Fer

Source: I. Jones, J. Wootton and K. Thorpe (eds), *Women and Ordination in the Christian Churches: International Perspectives*, New York: T&T Clark, a Continuum imprint, 2008, pp. 177–88.

The Evangelical Church of French Polynesia (EEPF) – renamed the Mâ'ohi Protestant Church (EPM)[2] in 2004 – makes up approximately 40 per cent of the population (estimated at 250,000 inhabitants in 2002) despite a relative decline in church membership and a pluralization of the Polynesian religious landscape. It is a Protestant church in the Reformed tradition, whose origins are found in the London Missionary Society (1797–1863) and the Paris Society for Evangelical Missions (1863–1963). While the mission field afforded French women an opportunity to exercise significant responsibility, the arrival of Protestantism in Polynesia had effects upon the position of Polynesian women which were both paradoxical and hard to evaluate: on the one hand emancipation through equal access to instruction and baptism; on the other reinforced control of sexuality and family norms.

The decision to authorize women to become ministers is a recent one (1995), but has met with a certain degree of success, since of the last four cohorts of trainee ministers at theological college, women make up more than half of their number (10 out of 18). I propose to study here the conditions in which the debate on women's ordained ministry has come to light in French Polynesia, the attendant consequences in terms of the modification of the exercise of ordained ministry, and the incomplete nature of the process.[3] In French Polynesia, women's ordination has to be understood within a twofold dynamic: the Protestant Church's autonomy in relation to French missionaries and women's equal access to the different ministries recognized by the Church.[4] Women's access to ordained ministry should also be considered within the wider context of far-reaching institutional, economic and social changes taking place in Polynesian society.

Since the 1960s, and the establishment of the Pacific Nuclear Centre at Moruroa and Fangataufa (in the Tuamotu Gambier archipelago), an economy which was previously based on agriculture and fishing has now become dependent on tertiary activities (such as tourism, commerce and administration) and state subsidies. The development of these tertiary sectors, both private and public, which provide a large amount of employment for women, has facilitated a rapid increase in women's salaries.[5] This increase has been accompanied by an improvement in the level of education and a sharp decline in the birth rate within a short space of time.[6]

The admission of women to ordained ministry within the Mâ'ohi Protestant Church

Regional and international context

The EEPF achieved autonomy in 1963, which meant that it was no longer overseen by French missionaries but by Polynesian ministers. Church autonomy formed part of a global process of decolonization (the autonomy of churches having a duty to anticipate and accompany colonial independence) a process which, in French Polynesia, has not been completed due to the setting up of the Pacific nuclear testing centre. Within the contemporary Protestant Church its autonomous position encouraged a stance against the French presence on Polynesian soil.[7]

The church's organizational autonomy allowed it to sit as a fully-fledged church on different international or regional bodies, notably the World Council of Churches (WCC) and the Pacific Conference of Churches (PCFC) established in 1966, which brings together the Protestant and Anglican churches in the Pacific region.

The Church's autonomy led to a greater involvement in the ecumenical movement. The WCC, whose mission is to bring churches together and foster reconciliation between them, is also very active in relation to gender equality. In 1969 the WCC urged churches to send women to represent member churches, and this enabled some ministers' wives to attend ecumenical meetings and to become aware of the legitimacy of equality demands. It was at these international meetings that the ministers' wives discovered that some churches in the Pacific region, culturally and geographically close to their own, had ordained women as ministers; the first church to ordain women was the United Church of Papua New Guinea and the Solomon Islands in 1976.[8] Throughout the 1980s and 1990s a number of other Protestant churches allowed women to become ministers: the Kiribati Protestant Church (1984)[9], the Free Wesleyan Church of Tonga (1990) and in particular the Evangelical Church of New Caledonia and the Loyalty Islands (in 1991), with which the EPM maintains close relations due to the strong Tahitian Protestant community in Nouméa.[10]

The accession of women to the ordained ministry: a debate between two moments in history (1981 and 1995)

The question of women's ordained ministry was first raised in 1981 in connection with one particular case, that of a minister's wife who had obtained the same theology degree as her husband from the Pacific Theological College in Fiji.[11] At the time of the husband's ordination, the synod took the decision not to ordain his wife because this dual ordination would have upset the traditional functioning of the 'pastoral couple' (*le couple pastoral*). In 1995 the EEPF synod – under pressure from some ministers' wives active in the ecumenical movement – authorized the admission of women to the ministry, arguing that 'nothing in the Bible forbids women from becoming ministers'.[12] This position led to the arguments of those opposed to women's ordination being classed as culturally rather than theologically based, and hence inadmissible.

In fact, those ministers who came out in favour of women's ordination tended to see their own position as proof of their theological prowess, and that it was thanks to the teaching they had received at theological college that they understood and accepted the Church's decision. The reactions of clergy wives (not all of whom were involved in ecumenical organizations) were much more qualified because some saw in this a direct competition with the wife's ministry, which up to 1995 was the sole channel by which women could attain the highest levels of responsibility within the Church. The accession of women to ordained ministry reinforced the tensions between the older church members, attached to traditional interpretations of the Bible and the younger generation, notably young clergy, keen to promote a more contextualized reading of the Bible.

The conditions in which the question of women's ordination was raised emphasize that access to degree-level theological training constituted an essential step for the admission of women to ordained ministry. In France, the work of Jean-Paul Willaime demonstrated that in Reformed and Lutheran Protestantism, women's admission to ordained ministry came about thanks to women's admission to theology faculties.[13] These conclusions are akin to the work of Catherine Marry, who noted that in numerous professional spheres, higher education was key to the feminization of higher-level professions.[14] The fact that women were eligible to study theology, albeit initially justified by their involvement as wives in their husbands' ministries, subsequently played an instrumental role in the transformation of a derived ministry into a fully-fledged one.

Challenge to the traditional 'pastoral couple'

The decision taken in 1995 authorizing women to become ministers only partially challenges that of 1981, in so far as the Church (whilst upholding the obligation for ministers to marry) refused to allow both members of a couple to become ordained ministers. The obligation to marry dates from 1806, from the requirement for missionaries of the London Missionary Society to marry before departing for Tahiti, to prevent marriages between Englishmen and Tahitian women.[15] Marriage subsequently became a requirement for those Polynesians wishing to convert to Protestantism and become *'etâretia* (church members). Thus it was proof of a successful conversion no less than of the stability of conjugal relations.

Today, the obligation to marry remains in place for ministers, who have a duty to be a role model for their parishioners. The pastoral couple is widely believed to be the only model able to ensure the proper running of the parish, with the minister's wife overseeing the women of the parish while the minister looks after the whole parish. Wives are neither ordained nor paid by the Church but nevertheless carry out a 'derived ministry' not linked to their ecclesiastical status (they are lay people) but rather to their marital status. The ordination ceremony is meaningful in two senses – the minister is ordained, but his wife (who is generally involved in every stage of her husband's vocation and training, and who accompanies him at the ceremony), is not ordained. Throughout the 1980s ministers' wives built up their 'derived ministry', through access to the same classes as their husbands at theological college (1977), through attendance at clergy meetings and also because some of them carried out duties which were paid by the Church (as manager of young women's accommodation, or as teachers or librarians in Protestant primary and secondary schools). At the same time, the institutionalization of women's activities at parish level reinforced the position of ministers' and deacons' wives – most commonly as Chair of the Women's Committee, which is responsible in every parish for organizing the annual meeting of women church members and for Women's Sunday (every third Sunday). The ordination of women thus challenges the functioning of the traditional 'pastoral couple': where a woman becomes an ordained minister, there is no defined role for her husband. This change affects marital relations as well as the *modus operandi* of ordained ministry.

The feminization and professionalization of ordained ministry

A further important development was the professionalization of the ordained ministry to which women were seeking access. As Jean-Paul Willaime has written, professionalization is defined as

> le processus par lequel un métier s'autonomise par rapport à l'institution dans laquelle il s'exerce et s'auto-légitime à partir de la

> competence qu'il met en œuvre. Le professionel est un expert dans un domaine spécialisée et c'est sa qualité d'expert qui est la principale source de légitimité [the process by which a profession becomes autonomous in relation to the institution in which it is performed and defines its own legitimacy by the competence it displays. The professional is an expert in a specialized field and it is this expert quality which is the primary means of legitimacy].[16]

In the past three decades, the EEPF has instigated just such a process of professionalization in ordained ministry. The first stage of this process began during the 1970s with the untangling of family and parochial interests. No longer did pastors minister in their home parish, or continue to work on the land alongside their pastoral duties as a 'pastor-farmer'. Instead they became full-time ministers, with their authority derived from their theological college training rather than their family connections. However, if the professionalization of ordained ministry in the EEPF did not actually begin with women's ordination, the entry of women to the ministry did (as in France)[17] mark a new stage in the process. This has been manifested in the raising of educational standards, the emergence of specialized ministries and the exclusion from political office of those in church leadership positions.

Pastoral training rather than parish support

In 1995 the EEPF authorized women to become ordained ministers. In 1997 the first candidate entered theological college and was ordained in August 2003 after spending four years at theological college and two years on work-placement in a parish. The admission of women to ordained ministry in 1995 coincided with greater priority being given to pastoral training and a change in theological college entrance requirements. Since 1996, entry into theological college has required the baccalauréat, whilst a parallel entry process or probationary year is provided for those without a baccalauréat. The latter must attend evening classes for a year and take an exam which is more or less selective depending on the numbers of direct entrants to the theological college. The backgrounds of the students differ along gender lines: young women entrants tend to be single and baccalauréat-holders, while men are married, without a baccalauréat, and sent by their home parish. These differences should be viewed in light of the higher level of academic success being achieved by girls – not only in French Polynesia but in many countries – which may be explained by a number of factors: girls adjust better to school work, have a greater respect for discipline, and work harder as a means of avoiding domestic chores during adolescence when, in Polynesian homes, parental pressure to help with housework is exerted more strongly on girls than on boys.[18]

Table 1 Theological college entrants.

Students	*Women*	*Men*
1997–2001 (total)	1	3
Baccalauréat candidates	1	–
Single candidates	1	–
1999–2003 (total)	3	2
Baccalauréat candidates	3	–
Single candidates	3	–
2001–5 (total)	3	2
Baccalauréat candidates	2	1
Single candidates	3	1
2003–7 (total)	3	1
Baccalauréat candidates	2	–
Single candidates	3	–

The requirement of the baccalauréat for entry into theological college is a source of argument and discontent in the parish since it is perceived to favour young women. The transformation of scholarly capital into social capital recognized by parishes is not a given. The question asked by many parishioners – 'is vocation about faith or about qualifications?' – sets faith in opposition to the academic knowledge being delivered by the French education system. By implication, young women who place value upon their school education are, at the same time, distancing themselves from their parish activities. The debate over whether vocation is a matter of academic knowledge or personal faith serves to undermine young women. The admission of women to ordained ministry is felt to pose an intellectualizing threat to church ministry. Women with the baccalauréat on the other hand, view their academic success as a confirmation of a vocation which is not recognized by their parish.

Non-parish ministry: ideally feminine ministries?

Non-parish ministries target communities which cannot be defined in terms of geography and which are not involved in any parish: young people in schools, hospital patients, prisoners, etc. The emergence of these ministries is one factor challenging the parish framework as the exclusive model for ecclesiastical organization in the context of heavy migration (from the archipelagos to Tahiti) and increasing urbanization in Tahiti, which now accounts for up to 70 per cent of the population.[19] In many cases non-parish ministry suits female ministers particularly well for at least two reasons, the first is entirely negative: women's ordained ministry is by no means accepted in parishes and is potentially fraught with difficulties. Non-parish ministry provides an opportunity to balance the opposition between the synod authorization of women's ordination and the marked apprehension of parishioners.

The second reason is that non-parish ministry – such as school and hospital chaplaincy – corresponds with the activities and sectors traditionally open to women, such as the education of young children and care for the sick. As such, in 2005, three out of the first seven women ministers (ordained or on placement), carried out non-parish ministry (journalist, accountant, chaplain) and one was a minister in one of French Polynesia's two non-geographical parishes: which serves the *hakka*-speaking Protestant Chinese community in Tahiti. The Church's very first ordained woman minister is currently the chaplain at the Pirae Protestant high-school, thus tying her back into her former role as a primary school teacher. Moreover, when women are asked about their professional aspirations, the most common answer is to be a theological college teacher.

The separation of political and religious spheres

The professionalization of ordained ministry was reinforced by a ruling of the synod, applied for the first time in 2001, which required church ministers to choose between their church position and their political position. This ruling was taken initially in 1996 when church leaders called for a peaceful demonstration against the resumption of nuclear testing. They then realized that a significant number of deacons, who were also territorial or municipal counsellors in the Gaston Flosse political party, were not able to take part in the demonstration. Once church leaders realized how much political parties were making use of church structures (in particular the *'âmuira'a,* parish subgroups bringing together parishioners according to geography or family background), they ruled for a separation of political involvement and official church positions. In the main this decision was poorly received since it undermined both the traditional position of those who held the dual roles of deacon and municipal counsellor, and the way of life on the Austral Islands where church and village interests were closely intertwined.

An incomplete process

The feminization of ordained ministry is an incomplete process which has encountered three major obstacles: 'Doublebind' mechanisms or contradictory demands; potential institutional marginalization; and lastly a theological and cultural renewal, initiated by the Church's Theological Commission, which is at odds with the process of ministerial professionalization.

Differentialists vs. egalitarians – the insoluble dilemma

As women assume the same ecclesiastical responsibilities as men, the tension inherent in the dialogue between equality and difference becomes highly visible. Eleni Varikas recalls the dilemma facing women when they attain positions which were previously exclusively male domains: i.e. to adapt to masculine norms and run the risk of 'becoming' ('*devenir*') like the men or to bring to bear a feminine specificity which condemns them to be simply 'imperfect men' ('*hommes imparfaits*').[20]

The accession of women to ordained ministry was at the outset claimed by clergy wives on egalitarian grounds: equal access to ministerial training and equal capability of men and women. On the other hand, male ministers, and in particular the Church's leaders charged with representing and also reforming the Church as an institution, insist on the promotion of gender difference: women are expected to be ministers in a different way, working in closer relationship with and more attentive to their parishioners; to embody a new, less authoritative and more relational form of ministry. The promotion of their gender identity means that female theological students are called to remain different from their male counterparts despite undertaking the same responsibilities as them.

This call conflicts with the expectations of parishioners, who continue to want a married man, assisted by his wife. They cite parish organization (more particularly the existence of a Women's Committee, usually chaired by the minister's wife) as the justification for keeping the traditional 'pastoral couple'.

The conflicting expectations between parish integration and the demand for a feminine identity are being played out at the level of dress-codes, which play a determining role in the process of integration or exclusion in parishes. The parishioners of Papeete, who did not wish to receive female theological students on work-placement in their parish, expressed their disagreement by asking the students not to dress like a minister – in navy-blue suit – but in a white dress like a woman; in fact, like a minister's wife. The theological students meanwhile waver between the desire to display a certain femininity, and due respect for traditional dress-codes. The issue of hat-wearing seems to have been the most awkward for these young women, who associate it with the clothes worn by elderly people. All this has led to some delicate negotiations.

Institutional marginalization

Ordained women ministers are frequently responsible for non-parish ministries (school chaplaincy, accountancy and/or church journalism) or for non-Polynesian parishes. Consequently they are more rarely to be found within the leadership structures of the Church, elected by parishioners, than their colleagues. They are similarly absent from the Theological Commission. The fact that women are marginalized within the institution causes them to identify (and be identified) more closely with new forms of religious practice which are themselves less institutionalized.

In contrast to church leaders who desire women to have a 'different' kind of ministry, women ministers themselves are more preoccupied with matters such as being accepted by parishioners rather than with reforming the church institution early in their ministry. However, there are some female ministers who have combined the desire for institutional renewal, with another more personal objective, that of staying true to themselves, and thus are developing another, radically desacralized vision, of pastoral ministry and the Church. Women are frequently responsible for managing relations with non-Polynesian or non-Christian communities in French Polynesia and often find themselves, as a result, on the margins of the Church as institution. And yet, this precarious position reflects the religious pluralization which is a mark of contemporary familial evolution – including at the level of the individual family unit.[21] These women, as a result of their background and their marital situation, are already familiar with interfamily religious plurality (their husbands are sometimes non-practising or, more rarely, non-believers). They thus develop a more ecumenical approach in their ministry, mixing more easily with non-Protestant people (school chaplaincy lessons are delivered to all pupils irrespective of their religion) or non-practising people. They are also keen to accept invitations from other churches, notably Protestant ones (Pentecostals and Adventists).

Theological tensions: liberation of the Mâ'ohi people/liberation of the Mâ'ohi women

The feminization of the clergy is accompanied by a transformation in both the *modus operandi* and the legitimization of church ministries, which come into conflict with the Church's official theological position. While the professionalization of ministry places emphasis on theological training and heralds the deterritorialization of religious belonging, recent work carried out by the Theological Commission advocates a return to the land (*te fenua*) and to the Tahitian language (*Reo Mâ'ohi*) as the only way to an authentic Polynesian Protestantism.

Since 1988 the Theological Commission, chaired by a lay person, Turo Raapoto (a doctor in linguistics), has been producing pamphlets which sketch the contours for a 'theology of liberation' or 'theology of the land' which are based around Mâ'ohi culture, Mâ'ohi land and the Mâ'ohi language. Whilst translating the Bible into Tahitian, English missionaries recognized that the language had an almost sacred quality and this was the proof that God wanted to meet the Mâ'ohi people in their language and their culture.[22] This theological renewal goes beyond the initial objective, which was to 'decolonize' the theologies of the South by promoting the emergence of contextual theologies. This theological position does not stop at the promotion of cultural expressions since it accords a religious dimension to an exclusively cultural process. By multiplying the references to the pre-missionary period, a period during which women did not have access to the *marae* (open-air cultic sites at that time), the theological renewal lends weight to the opinions of those opposed to women's ordination who find reasons from within this cultural register for disqualifying women from ministerial ordination. In this way, the question of equality between men and women becomes an imported issue, which places the emancipation of women at the heart of the process of acculturation.

The approach of the Theological Commission, composed almost exclusively of men, underlines the impossibility of simultaneously considering the liberation of the Mâ'ohi people and that of Mâ'ohi women. This commission is composed essentially of male ministers who work in Tahitian language parishes and go from parish to parish teaching in *Reo Mâ'ohi.* So whilst from the early missionary days women have had access to biblical knowledge and to the transmission of that knowledge, notably by becoming Sunday School teachers, the work of the Theological Commission reveals that women still do not have full access to the creation of new theological knowledge.

Conclusion

At its most basic level, the feminization of the clergy simply means the numerical presence of women ministers in roles which were hitherto undertaken exclusively by men. However, at another level this term also points to a transformation of the ways in which ordained ministry is exercised. Women ministers particularly move away from the traditional pastoral couple model – which required the wife to carry out unpaid voluntary work alongside her spouse – in that their husbands play little or no part in their wives' pastoral mininstries.

At the same time as giving women entry to ordained ministry, the Church made the baccalauréat an entry criterion for theological college. This move to professionalize the ministry, favouring academic training over parish support and developing non-parish ministry, is at odds with the Church's ways of working and with parishioners' expectations.

At an institutional level, pastors not based in a parish remain the most often marginalized, if for no other reason than their exclusion from decision-making processes, which continue to operate along the lines of territorial-based representation. Above all professionalization of mininstry should in principle have been accompanied by a refocusing around the heart of the profession, i.e. theological training. However, women ministers, more of whom have the baccalauréat than their male counterparts, have had no opportunity to be involved in the work of the Theological Commission. The uncomfortable position of women ministers – holders of a French qualification but felt to lack parish experience – underlines the Church's ambiguous position on education. Whilst it requires the baccalauréat the Church is promoting the knowledge delivered by an education system rooted in a colonial context which it otherwise rejects.

At parish level, most parishioners continue to prefer their future ministers to be married men. Debates surrounding the conjugal status of women ministers (questions of celibacy, marriage, role of the husband) underline the tensions between a privatization of women ministers' conjugal lives and the maintenance of traditional models of authority based on the marital exemplar. Women ministers challenge the pastoral couple model by overturning the very hierarchy of the sexes which underpins it. Henceforth the requirement for them to marry before they may be ordained is losing legitimacy and is the focus for disquiet and debate.

The Church, conscious of these contradictions, remains for now hesitant in the light of two radically different options. The first of these, the product of a pastoral seminar in 2005, aims to strengthen the traditional pastoral couple model via the reintroduction of the requirement for all entrants to theological college to be married. The second option, discussed at the August 2006 synod, relates to a relaxation of the rules to enable the ordination of both marriage partners, thereby substituting (or juxtaposing) the '*couple pastoral*' model with that of the '*couple de pasteurs*'. Discussions relating to the marital situation of ministers are thus at present ongoing.

Notes

1 The original conference paper upon which this chapter is based was translated from the French by Stephen Brown. Additional translation for this revised version was by Alison Jones.

2 EEPF: L'église évangélique de Polynésie française; EPM: L'église protestante mâ'ohi.

3 This communication stems from a sociological thesis carried out under the supervision of Danièle Hervieu-Léger and defended in June 2005 at the Ecole des hautes études en sciences sociales in Paris. The method deployed is that of semi-directed interviews carried out in Tahiti between October 2000 and August 2002.

4 Women already had access to the diaconal ministry (since 1947) and the ministry of evangelist (the officializing of this ministry dates from the 1970s). Whilst many women have became evangelists, very few have chosen diaconal ministry, which is essentially defined as a ministry of authority (the council of deacons being the sole decision-making body in the parish).

5 The level of employment previously at 28 per cent in 1962 had increased to 47 per cent by 1996, a figure which is close to that of mainland France. (ISPF [Institut statistique de la Polynésie française] et ministère polynésien du tourisme, de l'environnement et de la condition féminine, *Vahine en chiffres* (Papeete: ISPF, 2002).)

6 The average number of children per woman which stood at 4.2 at the beginning of the 1960s had reduced to 2.1 by 2004 (ISPF, *Année 2004 des résultants incertains* (Papeete: ISPF, 2004), p. 67.

7 G. Malogne-Fer, 'L'EEPF et les essais nucléaires: de la prise de conscience chrétienne à la prise de position publique (1963–1982)', in J.-M. Regnault (ed.), *François Mitterrand et les territoires français du Pacifique (1981–1988*) (Paris: Les indes savants, 2003), pp. 205–14.

8 This is the first church in the Pacific region, apart from the churches of Australia and New Zealand. (See C. Forman, 'Women in the Churches of Oceania', in D. O'Brien and S. Tiffany (eds), *Rethinking Women's Roles. Perspectives from*

the Pacific (Berkeley and Los Angeles, CA: University of California Press, 1984), pp. 153–72 (p. 169).

9 M. K. Tenten, 'The Relationship between Katekateka and Women's Ordination in the Kiribati Protestant Church', in K. Johnson and J. A. Filemoni-Tofaeono (eds), *Weavings: Women Doing Theology in Oceania* (Suva, Fiji: Weavers, South Association of Theological Schools and Institute of Pacific Studies University of the South Pacific, 2003), pp. 32–42.

10 T. Wete, 'Women as "Life-Giver": Toward a Renewed Understanding of Women's Ministry and Leadership in the Evangelical Church of New Caledonia and the Loyalty Islands', unpublished Masters dissertation, Pacific Theological College, Suva, Fiji, 2003.

11 The Pacific Theological College was established as part of the PCFC initiative: from 1966 the college has trained future ministers from the Oceania region.

12 Paraphrase taken from an interview with John Doom, previous church general secretary, on 3 May 2001. The full quotation reads: 'L'accession des femmes au ministère pastoral n'est pas une décision de l'église mais un réflexion théologique, il n'y a aucun texte qui interdit les femmes au ministère pastoral' [The accession of women to pastoral ministry is not a decision for the church to make but rather a theological reflection, there is no text which forbids women from becoming ministers].

13 J.-P. Willaime, 'L'Accès des femmes au pastorat et la sécularisation du rôle du clerc dans le protestantisme', *Archives de sciences sociales des religions*, 95 (1996), pp. 29–45.

14 C. Marry, *Les Femmes ingénieurs: Une révolution silencieuse* (Paris: Belin, 2004).

15 J. Davies, *The History of the Tahitian Mission, 1799–1830*, ed. C. W. Newbury (Cambridge: Cambridge University Press, 1961), pp. xxxix, 91.

16 J.-P. Willaime, *Profession: pasteur. Sociologie de la condition du clerc à la fin du XXe siècle* (Genève: Labor et Fides, 1986), p. 217.

17 J.-P. Willaime, 'Les Pasteures et les mutations contemporaines du rôle du clerc', *CLIO: Histoire, femmes et sociétés*, 15 (2002), pp. 69–83 (p. 77).

18 In the 20–29 age group included in the census of 1996, young women holding the baccalaureate or a higher education degree represented 21.7 per cent of the total of young women in this bracket as opposed to 16.7 per cent for boys. In 2002 the figures were 34.3 per cent for young women and 23 per cent for young men respectively (Source: ISPF).

19 ISPF, 2003.

20 E. Varikas, 'Egalité', in H. Hirata, F. Laborie *et al.* (eds), *Dictionnaire critique du féminisme* (Paris: Presses Universitaires de France, 2000), pp. 54–60 (p. 56).

21 Within Polynesian families, the coexistence of different religions has increased markedly within the generation: a survey carried out in 2000 in Tahiti by the Louis Harris Institute and published in *La Tahiti dépêche de Tahiti* in September 2000 shows that 55 per cent of present-day couples have the same religion, whilst the percentage was 84 per cent for the parents of those questioned.

22 For a history of translation of the Bible into Tahitian see J. Nicole, *Au Pied de l'écriture, histoire de la traduction de la Bible en tahitien* (Papeete: Haere po no Tahiti, 1988).

Bibliography

Davies, J., *The History of the Tahitian Mission, 1799–1830*, ed. C. W. Newbury (Cambridge: Cambridge University Press, 1961).

Forman, C., *The Island Churches of the South Pacific* (New York: Orbis, 1982).
——, 'Women in the Churches of Oceania', in D. O'Brien and S. Tiffany (eds), *Rethinking Women's Roles. Perspectives from the Pacific* (Berkeley and Los Angeles, CA: University of California Press, 1984), pp. 153–72.
Kutimeni Tenten, M., 'The Relationship between Katekateka and Women's Ordination in the Kiribati Protestant Church', in K. Johnson and J.-A. Filemoni-Tofaeono (eds), *Weavings: Women Doing Theology in Oceania* (Suva, Fiji: Weavers, South Association of Theological Schools and Institute of Pacific Studies, University of the South Pacific, 2003), pp. 32–42.
ISPF (Institut statistique de la Polynésie française) et ministère polynésien du tourisme, de l'environnement et de la condition féminine, *Vahine en chiffres* (Papeete: ISPF, 2002).
——, *Année 2004 des résultats incertains* (Papeete: ISPF, 2005), p. 67.
Malogne-Fer, G., 'L'EEPF. et les essais nucléaires: de la prise de conscience chrétienne à la prise de position publique (1963–1982)', in J. M. Regnault (ed.), *François Mitterrand et les territoires français du Pacifique (1981–1988)* (Paris: Les indes savants, 2003), pp. 205–14.
——, 'Quand les femmes prennent la parole: démocratisation institutionnelle et professionnalisation des ministères au sein de l'église évangélique de Polynésie française', unpublished doctoral dissertation, Paris: l'Ecole des hautes etudes en sciences sociales, 2005.
——, *Les femmes dans l'église protestante mâ'ohi: religion, genre et pouvoir en Polynésie française* (Paris: Editions Karthala, 2007).
Marry, C., *Les Femmes ingénieurs. Une révolution silencieuse* (Paris: Belin, 2004).
Nicole, J., *Au Pied de l'écriture, histoire de la traduction de la Bible en tahitien* (Papeete: Haere po no Tahiti, 1988).
Varikas, E., 'Egalité', in H. Hirata, F. Laborie *et al.* (eds), *Dictionnaire critique du féminisme* (Paris: Presses Universitaires de France, 2000), pp. 54–60.
Wete, T., 'Women as "Life-Giver": Toward a renewed understanding of women's ministry and leadership in the Evangelical Church of New Caledonia and the Loyalty Islands', unpublished Masters dissertation, Suva, Fiji: Pacific Theological College, 2003.
Willaime, J.-P., *Profession: pasteur. Sociologie de la condition du clerc à la fin du XX*[e] *siècle* (Geneva: Labor et Fides, 1986).
——, 'L'Accès des femmes au pastorat et la sécularisation du rôle du clerc dans le protestantisme'. *Archives de sciences sociales des religions*, 95 (1996), pp. 29–45.
——, 'Les Pasteures et les mutations contemporaines du rôle du clerc', *CLIO: Histoire, femmes et sociétés* 15 (2002), pp. 69–83.

Part 16

RELATING TO PLACE

62

EXPERIENCING SPIRIT

Religious processes of interaction and unification in Aboriginal Australia

Fiona Magowan

Source: Peggy Brock (ed.), *Indigenous Peoples and Religious Change*, Leiden, Netherlands Brill, 2005, 157–75.

Anthropologists have often highlighted the dominant, civilizing and Christianizing approaches of missionization in Aboriginal Australia that have radically altered traditional ways of life.[1] In some analyses, colonizing regimes have been aligned with missionary intent, and spheres of Aboriginal religion and Christianity have been viewed as incommensurable due to contrasting notions of the sacred.[2] While the contexts and historical conditions in which Aboriginal Christianity emerged were foreign to Australia's inhabitants, more recently, there has been a re-reading of the Aboriginal landscape and spirituality along the lines of that occurring in southern Africa where "a dynamic process of symbolic interaction and innovation" has emerged with the introduction of Christianity.[3]

In this paper, I question the extent to which Yolngu Christianity and ancestral religion in north east Arnhem Land in the Northern Territory of Australia can be said to be wholly exclusive religious domains.[4] I draw upon Whitehouse's work on doctrinal and imagistic modes of religiosity in order to explore the relationship between the cognitive dynamics of Yolngu religious practices. Whitehouse argues that although both doctrinal and imagistic modes of religiosity can be found within the same religious context, they do not always converge but where they do they are the product of "multiple historically contingent causes."[5] Whitehouse also asserts that in Melanesia there is a definite tendency for doctrinal and imagistic modes of religiosity to *interact* rather than to become *enmeshed* whereas, in other parts of the world, they may be "so enmeshed that the analytical distinction seems to break down."[6] It is important to stress that the terms doctrinal, imagistic, interacting and enmeshed or unified are not used lightly here because each refers to a particular mode of religiosity and the way in which they relate to one another. Where doctrinal and imagistic modes of religiosity *interact* in Melanesia (as in missionary approaches to Christianity and ancestral rituals in Arnhem Land), this implies the maintenance of discrete boundaries between the two modalities, whereas in Yolngu Christianity the terms *enmesh* or *unify* imply a singular religious modality.

In Yolngu Christianity these two modes of religiosity do more than interact, they become part of one another because they have embodied simultaneity obfuscating the analytical distinction between them. This process of enmeshing or unification occurs because bodily states of heightened feeling are routinized in *both* ancestral and Christian domains. Of course, the historical contexts and social conditions of Yolngu enculturation to Christianity have radically differed from the processes of ancestral ritual transmission, yet, verbal and non verbal expressions of Yolngu Christians about their religious experiences in both domains are made in the same vein, unifying the two modalities. Thus, I consider how affective and sensory processes orient Yolngu Christian thought and bodily awareness across ancestral *and* Christian contexts.

Both the doctrinal and imagistic modes are associated with distinct patterns of "codification, transmission, cognitive processing and political association."[7] The doctrinal mode is characterized by frequently repeated rituals and teachings whereby ritual behavior becomes habituated through the ability to carry out procedures without reflection and the emphasis is on verbal transmission through oratory which opens up the possibility for a standardized creed.[8] Thus, doctrinal knowing is transmitted and codified for adherents in a structured, regulated body of belief, reinforced by ritual repetition over time. However, a problem identified in the doctrinal mode is the tendency towards the "tedium effect" as adherents get bored with the entrenched routine of ritual procedures resulting in the need to recreate constantly the excitement of spiritual revelation.[9]

In contrast to doctrinal systems, the imagistic mode of religiosity is peculiar to certain small-scale or regionally-fragmented ritual traditions and cults that tend to process religious belief as "multivocal iconic imagery, encoded in memory as distinct episodes, and producing highly cohesive and particularistic social ties."[10] The imagistic mode is based on internal mental processes of inner rumination as well as extreme sensual and emotional stimulation.[11]

Knowledge transmission in a missionary domain

In the early days of Christianity in Arnhem Land the doctrinal mode of religiosity was prevalent and early missionary endeavors presented a contradiction between the ideal of free will and the intent to bring Gospel teachings to the region. Missions were established along the Arnhem Land coast, at Goulburn Island (1961), Milingimbi (1923), Yirrkala (1935), and Galiwin'ku (1942). The missionary, Theodor Webb, Methodist superintendent from 1926–1939 at Yirrkala, posited that "if Yolngu chose to live in a European way, it must be by *choice*" but the choices open to Yolngu at that time were ones continually influenced by relations of power and missionary modes of religious teaching.[12] Nonetheless, Webb was a fair and just man and he mediated between the government and missionary agendas. When Yolngu massacred Japanese fishermen in Caledon Bay, the government planned a punitive expedition to which Webb strongly objected. Webb also believed that Christianity could and should be introduced to Yolngu through the context of their culture. However, World War II also made Yolngu realize that the professed behavior of Christians preached by the missionaries was not the sole modus operandi of Europeans as "servicemen introduced alcohol on a large scale and petrol sniffing when alcohol ran out."[13] In viewing the strength of military power from the Air Force base at Milingimbi followed by machine-gunnings from the Japanese, Yolngu concluded that they could never say, "No!" to Europeans because they were too powerful. So, the ideal of "choice" was something of an illusion.[14]

Over the years in different parts of Australia, missionaries have adopted radically different approaches to imparting religious doctrine, resulting in varying degrees of acceptance, rejection and adherence to Christianity. Furthermore, they have variously engaged in or distanced themselves from indigenous ritual forms and indigenous expressions of Christianity. The majority of missionaries in north east Arnhem Land presented a disciplined doctrinal system in which Yolngu could work and act with a sense of respect and dignity. This was not always the case in other parts of Australia where "corporal punishment and the withholding of food were not uncommon disciplinary measures."[15] In Hermannsburg, Pastor Albrecht reports how he gave a boy a hiding for staying away from the dormitory for four nights and although the Arrernte threatened him and then asked him to punish the children with three strokes at most, he refused.[16] The kinds of punishments that some missionaries such as Albrecht meted out were foreign to Aboriginal belief and practice.[17] Discipline was generally formal and often highly ritualized arising out of transgressions not only against a person but against the social body. Misdemeanors that required payback killings such as wife-stealing or murder constituted serious assaults on the social body and the strength of its relations. Like Arrernte, Yolngu engagements with the missionaries meant they also had to reconceptualize their world by responding and adapting to new ideology and practice that were passed on in unfamiliar ways. For example, when Ella and Harold Shepherdson set up the Galiwin'ku mission in 1942 approximately 700–800 Yolngu were present in the town. Morning prayer was held each day at 6.30am, five days a week and at 8am the bell rang to signal the start of work and school. This routinization meant that Christianity became the appropriate template for life and living in return for material benefits such as flour, sugar and other staples as well as clothes. The repetitive and formulaic structure of events also meant that Yolngu missionaries could instill codes of "proper behavior" and teach Methodism as a way of both thinking *and* acting. Yolngu learned a practical Christianity formulated as a Protestant work ethic underpinned by mutual respect and love.

Some missionaries began by learning the local language and translating select passages of Scripture and some hymns into a chosen dialect. They also taught English language, reading and writing with the aims of conveying the Gospel and the content of hymns, prayers and liturgy. However, for the older population who did not learn to read or speak English, the Scriptures retained their opacity. The first Yolngu Christians, Birrinydjawuy (Andrew) and Makarrwaḻa (Harry), helped facilitate the doctrinal mode of religiosity in Arnhem Land. Their experience of living in Darwin meant that they understood something about European ways and they became vital to the work of the missionaries, Theodor Webb and Harold Shepherdson. Makarrwala's son, Batangga, went to Galiwin'ku with the Shepherdsons and he and his elder brother, Wili Walalipa, were instrumental in assisting the Shepherdsons in training Yolngu children in Sunday School and providing interpretations of the Scriptures in Yolngu language in church. Their interpreting roles on Sunday were part of a broader doctrinal system of discipline and repetition that instilled an orderly structure and routine to everyday life. Yolngu were thus apparently being subjected to foreign regimes of work and bodily control.

However, the doctrinal mode of teaching introduced Yolngu to a lifestyle that was already partially inscribed in their relationships in the form of practical care. In the eyes of Yolngu, missionaries were practicing the very foundations of the ancestral law: the rule of *djägamirr*—caring for or looking after one another. This paradigm of care was manifest in the development of gardens, a sawmill and teaching trade skills; and these modes of learning were mirrored by the system of transmitting ancestral knowledge handed down by uncles or grandfathers, such as learning how to hunt or fish and how to paint or make ritual objects. As in Christianity, ancestral practice went further than just learning "how to", it was also a sign of relationship, of reciprocity and respect that meant each was beholden to the other and entangled in the web of Yolngu spiritual life itself. Whitehouse and Barker have argued that the abstracted and universalizing principles of Christianity do not make sense to another culture until there is some introduction to a corresponding reality.[18] In Yolngu mission life, the principle of *djägamirr* converged between the ancestral and Christian realms, so this doctrinal aspect of religiosity partially reinforced existing Yolngu principles of sociality and relationality.

Whilst there was a degree of convergence between the ancestral and Christian domains there were also states of distinction. While, on Galiwin'ku, Rev. Harold Shepherdson was relatively successful in combining practical care with spiritual teaching and instilling a work ethic, there was still a cognitive divide between the Yolngu and *balanda* (white) domains.[19] Harris reports that in Milingimbi Yolngu operated in two separate domains,

> the *balanda* domain, or that of the cash economy and modern technology [which operated] mainly between 8.00am and 5.00pm Monday to Friday . . . and a Yolngu domain where the vernacular is always spoken, all the time; the Aboriginal worldview and social priorities reign.[20]

This segregation meant that when the missionaries withdrew, their authority and material benefits were transferred to the government and distributed locally in weekly welfare checks, Yolngu church attendance declined. However, Yolngu did continue the model of church life. Today, the bell announces the two services held on the island at 10am and 7.30pm on Sundays. Morning prayer takes place at 6am on most weekdays and members of the Bible translation team lead lunchtime prayer meetings.

With the departure of the missionaries, Christianity was not rejected but the form of worship changed with regular prayer meetings being held around campfires with families gathered on sheets in a circle in the dark. Scriptural images held great interest for Yolngu as they perceived many convergences between Christianity and the ancestral law: including the memorial feast for the dead imaging the Eucharist; the use of geometric forms of painting traditionally used for water and blood to depict Christ's blood;[21] vernacular stories of a flood and a man called Noah and ideas about the Ark of the Covenant analogous to the sacred objects held by clan leaders.[22]

Transmission of knowledge in the ancestral domain

Yolngu did not strive to place all Christian elements that did not cohere to the Ancestral Law into a hyper-logical system, although there was a "highly conscious use of sacred symbols."[23] Consequently, if Christian ideology was incomplete or contradictory, this could be accommodated in the schema for ancestral knowledge that was also partial, fragmentary and based on individual ascriptions to place and ancestral identity. Furthermore, what could not be understood was relegated to "the inside", a Yolngu concept that relates the power of spiritual affect to degrees of secrecy. The more secret the information, the higher the levels of religious status and knowledge required before information can be revealed.[24] The transmission and dissemination of Yolngu religious knowledge stands in stark contrast to Christian doctrine where all are equal in the eyes of God and have unrestricted access to that knowledge. In the ancestral domain, it is the fear of what is not known or the fear of revealing knowledge that one does not have the authority to tell that characterizes the imagistic mode. In Yolngu cosmology, aspects of the deepest knowledge of the ancestral law are held firstly by senior clan leaders and by a very few senior women. Younger men and women may know more but may not be able to show or to tell that they know and young women and children generally hold "outside" levels of knowledge that are public for all to hear and to tell. Yolngu knowledge may be contrasted with Pomio Kivung of Papua New Guinea on whom Whitehouse, in part, bases his argument. The mainstream Pomio Kivung "experience of religious understanding tends to be focused on what one explicitly knows and can articulate, rather than on what one dimly conceptualises, profoundly fears, and cannot express logically."[25]

Restrictions upon knowledge then tie Yolngu together in a social network of obligation, expectation and power relating to the right to know, the right to show that one knows and the right to tell. This knowledge is founded on images, laws and actions of the ancestral world in which all animals, plants, and all living and non-living entities are related to humans. Yolngu order all these things into two halves or moieties known as Dhuwa and Yirritja to which each person belongs. The activities and travels of the Dhuwa and Yirritja ancestors fashioned the landscape and deposited humans at various places along their way. Consequently, the spiritual effects of the ancestors are still felt within the ground, waters and air. As in Baktaman religion, in Yolngu society, natural species "enter individually into larger ritual contexts, each of them as a separate more or less dense symbol carrying an aura of connotations."[26] Due to the levels of restriction placed upon "knowing" the characteristics, form and spiritual effects of the ancestors, Yolngu can experience ancestral revelations in a multiplicity of iconic ways. The very act of non-disclosure opens up the potential for multiple possibilities of imagining the impact of the ancestral environment in social and ritual contexts.

The complexity of disclosure and non-disclosure as a form of hierarchical knowledge in Yolngu life is made more intricate by the fact that the ancestral law is not only handed down as a set of rules but also as a series of images that are suggested in esoteric and polysemic song language and enacted in dance. While funerals are the common form of transmitting knowledge, rituals are never performed the same way twice since each song series is egocentrically determined by the identity of the deceased. Consequently, repetition only goes so far as songs are ordered to take the spirit of the deceased to their homeland in a particular genealogical line. Yolngu knowledge provides an iconic template of song words and related dance such as the shark, crocodile, kangaroo or other ancestor at their particular homelands. While the form and shape of the song's rhythm, melody and text will be recognized on each subsequent performance, its rendition will be unique to the context in which it is performed. Thus, Yolngu draw upon a polyvocal set of images that are intimately related to personhood and country and that necessitate the production and reproduction of immutable social webs of belonging.

The processes of transmission between missionization and ancestral cosmology reflect the distinction that Whitehouse makes between doctrinal and imagistic dynamics of religious experience and the discreteness between them suggests an apparent incommensurability. If this argument takes into account the question posed by Ranger as to whether there are limits to the possibility of the appropriation of Christianity by non-Western peoples, the process of transmission on its own would appear to support observations about the lack of fit between the two systems.[27] Indeed, Yengoyan has argued that the Pitjantjatjara do not convert as "the 'basic axioms' of the spiritual and sacred life are such that Christian doctrine simply does not provide the intellectual or spiritual underpinnings which relate to Aboriginal life."[28] Yet in Arnhem Land this is not the case as Yolngu Christians have brought the two domains together in an embodied simultaneity.

To counter any essentializing tendency of an absolute separation between the two modes of religiosity, Whitehouse has also offered the qualification that "none of the features of our respective modes of religiosity is mutually exclusive because doctrinal systems tend to be replete with ritual imagery," and "all ritual imagery is susceptible to interpretation in ways that are doctrine like."[29] Indeed, routine depends partly on the individual's ability to organize the inner reflections of autobiographical and personal memories in their spiritual life. Consequently, there can be no hard and fast separation between the doctrinal and the imagistic, since "the encoding of religious and ritual representations in semantic memory always presupposes the prior formation of episodic memories."[30] Despite these qualifications, Whitehouse notes that in Melanesia they "tend to retain a certain discreteness with regard to the domains in which they operate, interacting rather than becoming thoroughly enmeshed."[31]

Religious processes of unification

In the last part of this chapter, I explore how the flow of emotion from the ancestral to the Christian domains unites the doctrinal and imagistic modes through religious experiences based on Whitehouse's concepts of memory.[32] Rather than arbitrarily delineating features that might be considered either doctrinal or imagistic in this enmeshed form of religiosity, I argue that emotion is central to Yolngu experiences of ecology, spirituality and the body in both ancestral and Christian spheres. I avoid labeling this unified form of religiosity in order to view it from a plurality of perspectives for it is, "only by keeping alive a sense of the always varying, alternating ways in which experience is actually lived that we can avoid the epistemological trap of constructing a theory of knowledge out of one aspect or moment of experience and privileging it over all others."[33] As Jackson and Karp note, different schemas relating to the religious body "should be seen as descriptive of the varying ways human beings experience the world according to widely varying needs and interests."[34] Whitehouse also bases his distinction between doctrinal and imagistic modes partly on a dichotomy between "semantic" and "episodic" (or "autobiographical") memory originally posited by psychologists.[35] He argues that episodic memory is critical to internal cognitive processing in the imagistic mode as, "Episodic memory refers to mental representations of personally experienced events, conceptualized as unique episodes in one's life."[36] Furthermore, the vast array of unique episodes that each person can recall, tend to have a distinctive emotional salience and/or set of sensory associations."[37] In the imagistic mode emotions may run the gamut from joy to pain but what is significant about this form of religious cognition is that these emotional experiences "generate enduring autobiographical ('or episodic') memories of unique episodes."[38] The ability to remember is combined with "[often extreme] affective and sensory stimulation . . . in which enduring episodic memories are activated."[39]

Young men who participate in the Gunapipi or Djungguwan revelatory rituals or the Ngulmark and Mandiyala initiation rituals experience physical pain and psychological trauma induced by senior leaders in order to instill respect for deep knowledge about ritual objects and the ancestral law. Yolngu women similarly develop their own body of episodic memory through a process of self-harm. While only senior women may show that they can cry for their deceased loved ones, younger and older women may cut themselves with sharp sticks and stones to show their sorrow and love for the deceased. However, attempts to curtail these practices have been made by ministers at funerals by leading the mourners in prayer and telling women that they may sing crying-songs for the deceased but should not hurt themselves. For some women, these traumatic episodes leave physical scars and the action of inducing pain and bodily harm is a means of showing love for the deceased mirroring the respect produced through pain in revelatory rituals for young men. Women's emotional understanding of songs is developed through the heightened states of grief and feeling that are further structured through dancing at funerals. These songs are derived from men's singing and they must know the images conjured by the song text to be able to respond accurately to rhythmic cues to change dance steps. The coherence of Biblical stories and their meanings were also fulfilled through intense and highly emotive religious experiences. The excitation expressed in singing, dancing and heightened states of praise meant women especially would shake and cry out to God. They also gave visions and prophecies in polyvocal images for the church. This form of worship was also embodied in Yolngu ancestral ways of thinking. These imagistic practices are, as Whitehouse notes, "codified in ritual choreography rather than as a body of teachings [and are] transmitted by groups of ritual participants rather than proselytizing individuals."[40]

The problem of embodying restricted knowledge and of intimating the possibility of not-knowing through the non-verbal mode of dance means that knowledge of the ancestral law spreads slowly amongst those who have the authority to know. However, as women become proficient in dancing so younger women may also listen to the corpus of song texts by sitting close to senior women, hearing the images that they visualize through song. These younger women are too "*gora*" "ashamed" or "embarrassed" to cry until they are recognized as being senior enough to have the right to show that they know the songs and have the authority to sing them.

Templates for these forms of ritual action are based on what Whitehouse terms "semantic memory"—a way of cognizing how to act in any given situation that may be reproduced on subsequent occasions.[41] This form of memory is necessary for routinized behavior patterns to be established such as those evidenced in the doctrinal mode. While semantic memory refers to "mental representations of a general, propositional nature"[42] Whitehouse further argues, per Cohen, that semantic memory is derived from episodic memories by generalizing and abstracting them.[43] It is through the repeated development and accumulation of episodic memory that one can piece together the information required to act appropriately. In Yolngu Christianity, both these forms of memory interact bringing together the doctrinal and imagistic modes within one emotive and experiential religious mode. Although the form of Yolngu church services may sometimes take a doctrinal structure highlighting an "argument-centred religious discourse,"[44] the spiritual effects of Yolngu religious engagement present a continuum across Christian and ancestral domains.[45]

In Arnhem Land, Yolngu Christian leaders often reflect on their moral condition in relation to their ancestral identities, bodily discipline and spiritual ecology. Yolngu share a common concern for moral accountability to one another in the ancestral law that is felt through the landscape and seascape, represented in ritual songs and dances and ties people together in a mutual understanding of the spiritual fiber of Yolngu being. Knowing oneself as ancestrally bound to other people and places by spiritual essence (*märr*) begins with the knowledge that the fiber of the ancestral self is dreamt from the land and painted onto the ritual body in ochres of the earth that evoke the color of red clouds at sunset and the person's lifeblood from the land. These color-pulses of moral fiber are also the life force of river veins and their *märr* echoes through the landscape in ritual song and is pounded into the earth in the feet of dancers. This flow of ancestral life-force between the living and the dead is shared between clans and manifest in the shapes and forms of different animals, communicating a common mode of religious understanding. One man, Djanggirrawuy, commented to John Rudder,[46]

> If he loses [a man dies] and passes away and lies back on his elbow *likan ngaylil dipthun . . .* like [a] broken branch, sing *mayku* (*barrukala dharpa* [paperbark tree]). Instead of saying, "He's gone", I sing the song that says, "he's resting in peace," and in that song mention

> the places and announce with my spirit where his spirit has gone . . . Next I sing *guku* [my spirit turning into *guku* (honeybee) and flying]. The song tells where he's started and then his journey as *guku*. Then sing *mokuy* [spirit being named] Murayana. Same thing . . . After *mokuy*, singing about "*märr*" called Yaliyali and Räjta . . . By singing the song, it's like praying how much we love that *mokuy* (dead person). Our love is long like the long string. It doesn't help the *mokuy* (dead person), it helps our beliefs. We perform in a special way making ceremony (*bunggul*) and song (*manikay*) so we feel comfort instead of hard feelings or jealousy.

As I have noted previously, these song images structure funeral rituals and provide the foundations for episodic memories to be recalled when mourners feel the agony of loss expressed in extreme states of grief. Yolngu feelings for the deceased are joined by the string of one's spirit that flows into and through the land and men in particular can access *märr* through sacred objects, songs and dances. Reid reports how one man was able to invoke his own personal power to heal family members,

> My own power is from my mother's Dreaming, the Octopus Dreaming. The Octopus is really an Aborigine from a very long time ago [that is, a *wangarr* or totemic being] . . . When I concentrate hard I can bring up [mobilise] this power from the Octopus . . . when I do the Octopus dance . . . I can feel the power filling me. It is a personal power. It can be passed down as my father's [as well as mother's] was to me when he died, or from mother to daughter. These Octopus beings . . . protect me with this power. When two people tried to hurt me by pointing the bone the power told me it was going to happen . . . I can prevent any evil attacks. The *marrnggitj's* [Yolngu healer's] power for healing has the same name. It is called *ganydjarr* or *mirritjal*.[47]

When Yolngu participate in Christian worship some are acutely aware of the extension of bodily feelings and thoughts that they bring to the new context but they warn about the source of spiritual affect and intent. A Galiwin'ku church elder, the late George Dayngumbu commented,

> When I dance in a ceremony, who am I singing about? God or somebody else? I challenge lots of young boys: "You've been baptised, changed your life, and you went to that ceremony, but you've still got that mark of Jesus. You went to that ceremony and you were washed with that blood, but that blood belongs to Jesus!" They know what's going on, but they're scared to say: [they're] full of fear.[48]

Despite warnings such as this by leaders, emotional states extend from one context to the next and underscore people's relationships to spiritual powers. For example, fear is embedded in Yolngu cosmology arising from the power of healers, *marrngitj*, and sorcerers, *galka.* Warner notes,

> There is a kind of warfare between the forces which do good and those which do harm to man. The latter are related to an organized set of concrete techniques embodied in the person of the black magician, while an entirely different set gives practical expression, in the personality of the white magician, to those forces which control the effects of black magic.[49]

Fear in traditional contexts, often stems from the knowledge that retribution is related to transgressive acts such as inappropriate behavior at sacred sites.[50] Certain ancestral sites can bring about sickness simply by virtue of being there, such as walking through a Yingapungapu ritual sculpture when the transgressor may lose his strength and his bones will break.[51] Inappropriate invocation of ancestral power can also cause illness: one man said he had invoked the power of the octopus while dancing and kicking up the dirt with great energy. While the power itself is not dangerous, since it can be used for healing, it can cause harm if released without due ritual restraint.[52] The power of sacred objects can also afflict people if handled by those without authority. In one instance when a young man returned to Galiwin'ku after drinking in Darwin, he removed a ritual object from the sacred shade in the *Ngärra* fertility ritual. The women and children screamed and ran away and the leader of the ceremony told me that he should be killed for his actions.

Appreciating the traditional context in which spiritual power operates is critical to understanding processes of spiritual embodiment and adaptation in the Christian context. Former Moderator of the Northern Territory Synod and minister on Galiwin'ku, Rev. Dr. Djiniyini Gondarra commented,

> God is revealing himself in different forms to particular clans—in terms that are important and meaningful to each one. To one group, he says: "I am the Warungul power!" Warungul is a very sharp spear used for spearing people, but Jesus is saying: "I am that now! It is no longer for spearing a man—that is a two edged sword for me" [i.e. God's word]. To another, he has been revealing himself as a tongue of fire! That is very, very sacred! You cannot speak about that in public, but we have been using that during the revival . . . we're talking the faith of Jesus and saying that "tongues of fire" is the Holy Spirit—stolen in the ceremony.[53]

In Yolngu reinterpretations it is not the mode of religious transmission that is central but the spiritual force seen to be involved in it and how these forces are experienced, invoked and embodied. It is not surprising then that in a Christian context, knowledge of the spiritual is essentially conveyed via participant-centered performance as much as it is in leader-centered teaching and Yolngu have developed a wide range of performance through which they dance out their faith to counter feelings of doubt or fear. Youth groups from various homelands practice dance actions to American gospel choruses on cassette, Sydney's Hillsong ministries, music from Israel or Ireland. Yet others have attended workshops in Brisbane to learn Christian dance with tambourines and streamers. The flow of these dances reveals knowledge and feelings about a spiritual relationship between the Holy Spirit, the individual and their accountability to God and one another. A late church elder and Council Chairman remarked,

> Because I'm a good musician, I'm not going to play in the ceremony and then go and play in the church! That's not the way! As a group we sing to bring healing, to bless people, to give people strength through praising God—and the people can *feel* the singing. That's why we formed the group Dhurrkay Praise. We sing praise [to God] for the sick people and a lot of people have been healed—without touching them . . . the children *know* by singing. We read the Bible in our mind—but the Yolngu way is to worship God . . . and sing to the Lord himself.[54]

The emphasis on feeling is an extension of ideas of spiritual affect emanating from an ancestral mode of religiosity. In ancestral performance Yolngu will speak of the feelings of spiritual presence as a cold wind on the skin that is felt in the heart and some may shiver in response. In a Christian context, the same feeling can occur when people are praying or laying on hands and they say that the power of the Holy Spirit is conveyed through touch that feels very cold on the skin. Just as touch can mediate the power of the Holy Spirit, so too, the power of the Holy Spirit can counter feelings of fear through sound and movement. Speaking of how children have been used to bring prophetic messages to the congregation in Christian dances, one man commented,

> Many times the Lord has used them to bring a message to the church. One of the messages that came was through this song, Turn Your Eyes Upon Jesus. It came at a time when a lot of people were very frightened and there were payback killings going on and rumours about that sort of thing and a lot of trouble in the community. The message of Turn Your Eyes Upon Jesus was something that was given by God . . . It changed the focus from what the Devil was doing to what God was doing and it really made a difference in the community.[55]

Like the power of touch, the effects of prophetic dances are spoken of as clear, sweet sounds in the heart. Some say they "feel" a vibration as if coming from the ground. Consequently, the spiritual dialogue between Christianity and the ancestral law has manifested in a mixture of musical genres unifying religious knowledge and experience. These songs and dances use clapsticks and didjeridu to speak of Jesus in ancestral images, focusing mainly on the power of His blood, death and resurrection. This unification of feelingful performances of Christianity through ancestral understanding in Arnhem Land contrasts to Christian practices elsewhere in Australia. For example, regarding the United Aborigines Mission in Halls Creek, McDonald comments, "Present day missionaries wish there could be more Aboriginal cultural content in their church services, that didgeridoos and boomerang clapsticks could be introduced along with Aboriginal languages in singing, and that more of the Dreamtime stories were known."[56]

Appreciating the bodily extensions of spiritual feeling from the ancestral realm to Christianity is particularly complex as Yolngu Christians hold a multiplicity of perspectives about their involvement in the tenets and requirements of the ancestral law. As funerals tend to take place with little time between them, everyone in the community is involved in ancestral singing or dancing in some regard. Thus, as Yolngu Christians believe in the assurance that Jesus protects and will participate in many aspects of funerals, they also hold a healthy regard for abstaining from aspects of ancestral *märr* that lead to fear. Singing and dancing is an embodied modality of spiritual performativity through which individuals *come to feel* what might be considered acceptable or unacceptable engagement with different aspects of ancestral practice.

Conclusion

I have outlined how missionary Christianity brought new doctrinal modes of instruction that were foreign to Yolngu thinking whilst ancestral ritual highlighted imagistic modes of religiosity. However, I have also argued that these domains should not only be viewed as interacting whilst retaining discrete forms but that in Yolngu Christianity they become a unified mode of spiritual thought and bodily feeling. Yolngu Christianity brings the two domains of the ancestral law and Christianity together as extensions of bodily feeling and expression in the landscape and seascape whereby Yolngu have been able to reconcile the historically disjunctive nature of the two religious modalities.

In Yolngu Christianity both modes of religiosity are intimately intertwined. Yolngu have developed, adapted, codified and transformed missionary Christianity into a body-centered, affective and sensory spiritual practice that relates both to Christian doctrine and to the ancestral law. Fear of the spiritual effects of sorcery and the power of Jesus regulate embodied simultaneity between culture and the Gospel. As I have shown, spiritual attack is the potential to be gripped by fear and it is an ever-present danger. While fear can be manifest in the power of dangerous ancestral places, Yolngu Christians perceive the power of God in the land and sea bringing good and healing forces. As a person's ancestral identity cannot be separated from the land and sea, a tension exists between personal sanctification in baptism and the nature of power in the body and in the landscape. In these contexts, religious modalities are conjoined by a continuity of "potent substances and energies of the body"[57] where religious feeling is dialectically situated in relation to a wide range of spiritual and emotional effects that operate from ancestral performance to Christian worship.

This process stands in contrast to Melanesian forms of Christianity which operate in the doctrinal mode and "are largely denuded of any full-blown imagistic dimensions."[58] The distinction between Melanesia and Arnhem Land perhaps lies partly in the historical context and approach by missionaries to Yolngu Christianity and partly in the ways in which Yolngu have extended concepts of the body, personhood and feeling from indigenous cosmology to Christianity.[59] Thus, I have tried to avoid drawing hard and fast distinctions between doctrinal and imagistic modes of religiosity within Yolngu Christianity as it is in a flow of emotion that the sense of the spiritual self emerges. This is not to say that contradictions, distinctions and conflicts do not occur. However, the sense of the spiritual self is continually being assessed, renewed and reconsidered as Yolngu are continually in a process of reconstructing values and attitudes towards the world from experiences of the past to "the problems and exigencies which comprise their social [and spiritual] existence in the here and now."[60]

Notes

1 Jo Woolmington, "The Civilization/Christianization Debate and the Australian Aborigines," *Aboriginal History* 10 (1986), 90–98; Michelle Dewar, *The "Black War" in Arnhem Land: Missionaries and the Yolngu 1908–40* (Darwin: Australian National University North Australia Research Unit, 1992); John Harris, *One Blood: 200 Years of Aboriginal Encounter with Christianity: A Story of Hope* (Sutherland, NSW: Albatross Books, 1990).

2 David Trigger, *Whitefella Comin': Aboriginal Responses to Colonialism in Northern Australia.* (Cambridge: Cambridge University Press, 1992); William Edwards, "Recovering Spirit: Exploring Aboriginal Spirituality". The Charles Strong Memorial Trust Lecture. (University of South Australia. Unpublished paper, 2001); Lynne Hume, "The Dreaming in Contemporary Aboriginal Australia" in *Indigenous Religions: A Companion*, ed. G. Harvey (London: Continuum, 2000).

3 See Terence Ranger, this volume.

4 Yolngu is the name for the people of the north east Arnhem Land region. It is the term they use to refer to themselves.

5 Harvey Whitehouse, *Arguments and Icons: Divergent Modes of Religiosity.* (Oxford: Oxford University Press, 2000), 2.

6 Whitehouse, *Arguments and Icons*, 149.

7 Whitehouse, *Arguments and Icons*, 1.
8 Harvey Whitehouse, "Cognition and Culture" (Inaugural Lecture, Queen's University Belfast, 1 June, 2004).
9 Whitehouse, *Arguments and Icons*, 49.
10 Whitehouse, *Arguments and Icons*, 1.
11 Whitehouse, "Cognition".
12 John Harris, *One Blood* (Sutherland: Albatross Books, 1990), 801.
13 John Blacket, *Fire in the Outback: the untold story of the Aboriginal revival movement that began on Elcho Island in 1979* (Sutherland, Albatross Books, 1997), 56.
14 Blacket, 56.
15 Jacqueline Van Gent "Changing Concepts of Embodiment and Illness among the Western Arrernte at Hermannsburg Mission," *The Journal of Religious History* 27 no. 3 (2003), 332. See Van Gent this volume.
16 Albrecht 1927 cited in Van Gent, 333.
17 Other forms of punishment and payback spearings were a part of peace-making ceremonies in north east Arnhem Land and elsewhere.
18 Whitehouse, *Arguments and Icons*, 41; John Barker "Introduction: Ethnographic Perspectives on Christianity in Oceanic Societies" in *Christianity in Oceania: Ethnographic Perspectives*, ed. J. Barker, (Lanham: University Press of America, 1990), 16.
19 The Yolngu term *balanda* is derived from the Indonesian word for 'Hollander' following Dutch contact with the Arnhem Land coast.
20 Stephen Harris, *Culture and Learning: Tradition and Education in north east Arnhem Land.* (Darwin: N.T. Department of Education, 1980), 132.
21 Robert Bos, "Didgeridoo Theology" *Nungalinya Occasional Bulletin.* (Casuarina: Nungalinya College, 1980), 3, 4.
22 Djiniyini Gondarra, *Father you Gave us the Dreaming* (Casuarina: Nungalinya College, n.d.)
23 Bos, 4.
24 The state of being 'inside' or 'outside' with regard to knowledge of the ancestral law is relative to context and is derived from a continuum of restrictions pertaining to ritual knowledge and authority. See Howard Morphy, *Ancestral Connections: Art and an Aboriginal System of Knowledge.* (Chicago: Chicago University Press, 1991).
25 Whitehouse, *Arguments and Icons*, 63–64. While this is true for the mainstream Pomio Kivung, localised Kivung splinter groups also transmit religious knowledge in ways that more closely resemble the traditional Yolngu model (Whitehouse, pers.comm.).
26 Barth cited in Whitehouse, *Arguments and Icons*, 64; Frederick Barth, *Ritual and Knowledge Among the Baktaman of New Guinea.* (New Haven: Yale University Press 1975), 189.
27 Ranger, 2.
28 Aram Yengoyan, "Religion, Morality and Prophetic Traditions: Conversion among the Pitjantjatjara of Central Australia," In *Conversion to Christianity. Historical and Anthropological Perspectives on a Great Transformation*, ed. R. Hefner (Berkeley: University of California Press, 1993), 234.
29 Whitehouse, *Arguments and Icons*, 149.
30 Whitehouse, *Arguments and Icons*, 149.
31 Whitehouse, *Arguments and Icons*, 159.
32 Whitehouse, *Arguments and Icons.*
33 William James cited in Michael Jackson and Ivan Karp, *Personhood and Agency: The Experience of Self and Other in African Cultures.* (Washington: Smithsonian Institution Press, 1990), 17.

34 Jackson and Karp, 17.
35 Jackson and Karp, 5; E. Tulving, "Episodic and Semantic Memory" in *Organization of Memory*, eds E. Tulving and W. Donaldson (New York: Academic Press, 1972).
36 Whitehouse, *Arguments and Icons*, 5.
37 Whitehouse, *Arguments and Icons*, 7. The process by which this emotive recollection occurs is due to a form of episodic remembering that, following Brown and Kulik (1982), Whitehouse terms "flashbulb" memory. One of the unique features of flashbulb memory is "emotional excitation" (Whitehouse, *Arguments and Icons*, 8) and both episodic and semantic memory rely strongly on affective and sensory processes (Whitehouse 1996). Harvey Whitehouse 'Jungles and Computers: Neuronal Group Selection and the Epidemiology of Representations.' *Journal of the Royal Anthropological Institute* (NS), 1, (1996): 99–116.
38 Whitehouse, "Jungles," 112.
39 Gilbert Herdt, "Spirit Familiars in the Religious Imagination of Sambia Shamans," In *The Religious Imagination in New Guinea*, eds G. H. Herdt and M. Stephen, (New Brunswick: Rutgers University Press, 1989). Whitehouse, "Jungles", (1996).
40 Whitehouse, *Arguments and Icons*, 158.
41 Whitehouse, *Arguments and Icons*, 5–12.
42 Whitehouse, *Arguments and Icons*, 5.
43 Whitehouse, *Arguments and Icons*, 6.
44 Whitehouse, *Arguments and Icons*, 170.
45 A series of publications edited by Harvey Whitehouse are currently underway to review the potential dynamics of modes of religiosity. *Ritual and Memory: Toward a Comparative Anthropology of Religion* eds H. Whitehouse and J. Laidlaw (California: Altamira Press, 2004), 179–184.
46 John Rudder, "Yolngu Cosmology" Unpublished PhD thesis. (Canberra: Australian National University, 1990), 60.
47 Janice Reid, *Sorcerers and Healing Spirits: Continuity and Change in an Aboriginal Medical System* (NSW: Pergamon Press, 1983), 34.
48 Blacket, 248.
49 William Lloyd Warner, *A Black Civilization: A Social Study of an Australian Tribe* (Gloucester, Mass.: Peter Smith, 1958), 193.
50 While the power itself is morally neutral the purpose to which it is put can cause concern, Reid, 35.
51 Howard Morphy, "Yingapungapu – Ground Sculpture as Bark Painting." In *Form in Indigenous Art*, ed. P. J. Ucko, (Canberra: Australian Institute of Aboriginal Studies, 1977).
52 Reid, 51.
53 Blacket, 248.
54 Blacket, 262.
55 Interview with the author, fieldnotes, March 2000.
56 Heather MacDonald, *Blood, Bones and Spirit: Aboriginal Christianity in an East Kimberley Town.* (Melbourne: Melbourne University Press, 2001), 61.
57 MacDonald, 16.
58 Whitehouse, *Arguments and Icons*, 159.
59 Yolngu Christianity is not unique in this regard as other charismatic forms of Christianity, such as Pentecostalism, may demonstrate a similar tendency.
60 Jackson and Karp, 28.

63

Excerpt from 'RELIGION AS RESISTANCE IN JAMAICAN PEASANT LIFE
The Baptist Church, Revival worldview and Rastafari Movement'

Jean Besson

Source: originally published in Barry Chevannes (ed.), *Rastafari and Other African-Caribbean Worldviews*, London: Macmillan, 1995; Chapel Hill, NC: Rutgers University Press, 1998, pp. 47–63; revised by author, 2009.

The Baptist Church as a formal symbol of resistance

Following the capture of Jamaica from the Spanish by the British in 1655, the island was rapidly transformed into a sugar and slave plantation society under British rule (Patterson 1973:15–27). By 1700 Jamaica was the world's leading sugar producer and, in the eighteenth century, the very centre of New World plantation slavery and the most important colony in the British Empire (Walvin 1983:35; Williams 1970:152, 154).

In eighteenth-century Jamaica, the Anglican or 'Established' Church was the only church allowed by law to function in the island, and as the official religion of the slave masters, the Established Church supported the status quo of slavery and was as inefficient and corrupt as the plantation society that it served. At this time the planters' church also completely neglected the spiritual welfare of the slaves. Near the end of the eighteenth century, however, the abolition movement and the religious revival in England led to Nonconformist missionaries being sent to Jamaica, and this missionary activity had a greater impact on the slave population. The Established Church was violently opposed to the preaching of these missionaries, which they regarded as a threat to the slave system (Patterson 1973:40–1, 207–9).

In 1813 the Baptist Missionary Society in England sent out its first missionary to Jamaica, the Reverend John Rowe, who took up residence in

Falmouth, Trelawny's capital, in 1814. Following Rowe's death two years later from yellow fever, Falmouth was without a Baptist missionary until 1827. In that year the Reverend Thomas Burchell, stationed in St James, established the Falmouth Baptist Church, whose first pastor was Burchell's assistant, the Reverend James Mann. In 1830 Mann died of malaria, having established two other Baptist churches in Trelawny at Rio Bueno and Stewart Town. Mann was replaced in Falmouth, in 1830, by the Reverend William Knibb, an outspoken opponent of the Established Church and slavery. Knibb's congregation consisted largely of Trelawny's plantation slaves (Knibb Sibley 1965; Patterson 1973:211; Wright 1973).

Following the so-called 'Baptist War' slave rebellion in Jamaica's western parishes in 1831, Knibb, regarded by the plantocracy as one of the ringleaders of the rebellion, was arrested and briefly imprisoned. In 1832, as a deputy for the Baptist Church in Jamaica, Knibb contributed to the anti-slavery campaign in Britain, and in the Falmouth Baptist Church on 1 August 1838, Knibb celebrated the full emancipation of the slaves. Following emancipation, Knibb negotiated the first wage settlement in Jamaica with the Trelawny plantocracy on behalf of the former slaves. With another Baptist minister, the Reverend James Phillippo, Knibb also initiated the island's church-founded Free Village System within a context of acute plantation-peasant land and labour conflict. Trelawny was the vanguard of this village movement, under the sponsorship of Knibb (Besson 1984b; Knibb Sibley 1965; Mintz 1974:160; Wright 1973).

A crucial role of the Nonconformist post-slavery village system was the provision of freehold land to the ex-slaves, through the purchase and subdivision of properties by the churches. This was especially significant as many planters refused to sell land to the former slaves (Besson 1984a:64–5).

In November of that year Knibb was able to tell Hoby and the Birmingham abolitionist, Joseph Sturge, of the purchase of 500 acres in his 'cousin Dexter's' district for the founding of Trelawny's first free village. This property was the coffee plantation of Alps in the Stewart Town area in the south-east of the parish, where the Baptist missionary, the Reverend Benjamin Dexter, was stationed. This village, now renamed Alps but originally called New Birmingham after Joseph Sturge's hometown, was laid out around a Baptist chapel, providing accommodation for 550 persons, and a school. Founded with the assistance of Dexter, under the sponsorship of Knibb, it was settled by ex-slaves from the former Alps estate. By January 1839 over seventy families had purchased land and were erecting homes in this new village. Along with Sligoville, Jamaica's first free village, founded by Phillippo in the St Catherine hills, Alps provided a model for the Jamaican free village system. As my research in 1983 confirmed, the Baptist Church still provides the formal focus of Alps village (Besson 1984b:7, 17–18).

By 1845 Trelawny had twenty-three free village communities (Paget 1964:51). These included Refuge (originally named Wilberforce), Kettering and Granville, founded in 1838, 1841 and 1845 respectively by Knibb and studied by me in 1983 (Besson 1984b). These three villages were established through the subdivision of properties purchased through the Baptist Church, on marginal mountainous land bordering or surrounded by sugar plantations, to absorb ex-slaves from these estates.

Refuge, situated six miles east of Falmouth where Knibb's church was located, was founded, like Alps, in the year of full emancipation (1838). The records note the founding of the village, on some ninety acres of mountainous land purchased and subdivided by Knibb, around a Baptist chapel, accommodating 1,500 persons, and a school. The Baptist Church continues to provide the formal framework of Refuge village today. As in the case of Alps, originally called New Birmingham, Refuge's original name of Wilberforce – after the abolitionist William Wilberforce – reflects the Nonconformist anti-slavery stance and the emancipation theme (Besson 1984b:10, 13–15).

The free village of Kettering, named after William Knibb's hometown, was founded by Knibb in 1841 on a former pimento estate bordering Duncans town three miles east of Refuge. The village was laid out in 400 building lots, which were sold to ex-slaves, around a Baptist Church and school. On Kettering Hill, in the centre of the village, the freed slaves of the Baptist Church built Knibb a large stone house in gratitude for his efforts on their behalf in the abolitionist cause. Here Knibb made his home until his death in 1845. Today, nearly one hundred and fifty years after Knibb's death, the Baptist Church persists as an active force in contemporary Kettering village (Besson 1984b:15–16).

The free village of Martha Brae, the main context of my long-term research in Trelawny, was established by ex-slaves on the ruined site of the former planter town of Martha Brae, which had been the first capital of Trelawny but was eclipsed around 1800 by the new town and port of Falmouth (Besson 1984b:8–10). Unlike the other four villages studied, there is no record of the Baptist Church having founded Martha Brae. However, my research reveals several clues that suggest that Martha Brae is a variant on the Baptist Church-founded village theme (Besson 1987b:114–15). Both documentary evidence and oral history strongly suggest that the village was founded in the early post-emancipation era, probably in the 1840s. In addition, names of Martha Brae residents appear in the membership book of the Falmouth Baptist Church kept by William Knibb himself. The location of Martha Brae, just one mile south of Falmouth in the heartlands of the Trelawny plantations from which Knibb drew his congregation, would also have made its post-emancipation settlement of direct concern to Knibb.

The presence of a Baptist prayer house in Martha Brae, 'Class 5' of the Falmouth Baptist Circuit, which the oldest villagers remember as always being there, is also a central clue. In addition, the villagers are strongly Baptist in formal faith and regularly attend the William Knibb Memorial Baptist Church in Falmouth. Moreover the Baptist prayer house in Martha Brae, in disrepair in the 1970s, was renovated in 1986 under the supervision of the Falmouth Baptist Church; and in November of that year the prayer house was reopened at a large village function attended by members of the William Knibb Memorial Baptist Church and the Vice-President of the Jamaica Baptist Union (Besson 1987b:123).

In the five Trelawny villages studied, then, the Baptist Church is the formal symbol of the free village established and perpetuated in the face of colonial orthodox Christianity and the plantation system, a system that still encompasses Trelawny's fertile land today.

The paradox of Baptist religious resistance

The Baptist missionaries in Jamaica were reformers, however, not revolutionaries. The slaves were their potential converts and the free villages were both captive congregations and reservoirs of labour for the plantations. Thus, as seen above, Trelawny free villages such as Alps, Kettering and Refuge were laid out around a Baptist church; Granville was founded around a Baptist prayer house, later replaced by a Baptist church; while Martha Brae village also developed around a Baptist prayer house linked to the Falmouth Baptist Church.

While absorbing dispossessed ex-slaves from surrounding plantations such as Green Park, Carrickfoyle, Merrywood and Maxfield, Granville also provided a labour supply for these estates. Martha Brae was even closer to Falmouth than Granville, and was situated on the borders of Holland and Irving Tower plantations, while Refuge adjoined Oxford plantation (Besson 1984b).

The role of the Baptist free villages as reservoirs of plantation labour was made explicit by Knibb himself, in response to a question by the Select Committee of the House of Commons in 1842, using the example of Kettering village (adjoining the town of Duncans) in Trelawny founded by Knibb the previous year:

> Q.: Has it (the settlement of free villages) not a tendency to diminish the supply of labour to the estates?
>
> Knibb: During the time they are building their house, but not afterwards; but perhaps the Committee will understand it better when I inform them that whenever I had to do with buying a place for a free village, I have tried to select a spot surrounded by a number of estates.

In Trelawny's contemporary free villages, which persist today hemmed in on marginal land by two vast corporate sugar plantation 'centrals' and several 'properties' or large farms that have replaced the former slave plantations, many villagers still work as labourers on these surrounding estates.

In addition to providing captive congregations and reservoirs of labour, the post-emancipation communities may also have been subject to social control by the Baptist Church through the regulation of access to village land. Mintz cites a case, recorded in 1952 in the Baptist village of Sturge Town in St Ann parish neighbouring Trelawny, which suggests such social control. The case concerns a Sturge Towner who:

> walked twenty-two miles each time he went to his fields, which he rented. He was anxious to acquire the right to work a piece of church property in Sturge Town. But he was not a faithful member of the local church and did not get the use of the land. This is by no means to claim that church membership was a condition for economic or social assistance; but it seems likely that churchgoing improves one's community standing and, accordingly, one's local economic opportunities.
>
> (Mintz 1974:175)

Mintz is unable to establish the extent of such incidents in the earlier history of Sturge Town, but oral history in contemporary Granville suggests that membership and status in the Baptist Church was, indeed, a relevant factor in the internal differentiation of the post-emancipation villages. According to Granville villagers, the subdivision of the Granville lands was delegated by Knibb to a Baptist Class Leader, a position that the villagers also refer to in explaining why Knibb's 'land butcher' had access to the largest and best portion of land in the new village of Granville. This oral tradition is supported by the fact that the contemporary descendants of Knibb's surveyor hold inherited rights to the best portion of the Granville lands (Besson 1984b:11–12).

In his summation of the features of Jamaican church-founded villages, Mintz concludes, citing Cumper, that to some extent, in the context of constituted authority, the 'minister became a substitute – an altogether preferable substitute – for the estate owner, the overseer, the slave driver, the judge, and the custos' (Mintz 1974:179).

This paradox of the Baptist missionaries in Jamaica, as both challengers and perpetuators of the status quo, is paralleled by the Methodist missionaries of eighteenth and nineteenth century Nevis, where, on the one hand, Olwig (1990:94, 99) argues, 'the Methodist notion of brotherhood . . . had quite revolutionary [*sic*] implications when applied to British West Indian plantation society'; while on the other hand the missionaries, in providing the slaves with 'a more divine purpose to live for', were 'instituters of social order in colonial society'.

In Jamaica, this paradox in the role of the Baptist missionaries was fully perceived by the slaves and their descendants, who responded with a paradox of their own: supporting the Baptist Church in a formal context, while remaining committed to their African-Caribbean traditions. In the contemporary Trelawny villages, this paradox can be clearly seen. For within the formal framework of Baptist free village life, the villagers have evolved an African-Caribbean peasant culture in response and resistance to imposed colonial culture and the plantation system (cf. Mintz 1974:132–3). This peasant life-style is rooted in the tradition of slave resistance, which was very pronounced in Trelawny at the heart of Caribbean plantation slave society and manifested itself through slave rebellion, marronage and proto-peasant culture-building (Besson 1984b, 1987b, 1992; cf. Mintz 1971, 1974:131–250). The following section briefly delineates this peasant culture of resistance, by way of background to elucidating the co-existence of Revival and Rastafari with Baptist Christianity in Trelawny's post-slavery peasant communities.

The peasant culture of resistance

At the heart of the peasant culture of resistance in Trelawny's Baptist villages is a customary form of land use, tenure and transmission known as 'family land' (Besson 1984b, 1987b, 1988a). The roots of this institution, which is widely found in Caribbean post-slavery peasant communities, lie in proto-peasant culture-building on the slave plantations (Besson 1989b, 1992). There, wherever possible, the slaves established customary rights of use, tenure and transmission in relation to slave village yards and plantation backland provision grounds, as the basis of proto-peasant economies and communities. This customary tenurial system, which included both male and female slaves and their descendants, drew on the symbolic as well as economic significance of land in Caribbean plantation slave society, and transformed the principles of colonial legal freehold within the formal framework of the plantation.

After emancipation, this proto-peasant kin-based tenurial system mushroomed into the customary institution of family land in those Caribbean peasant communities, including Jamaica's Baptist land settlements, established by ex-slaves purchasing small landholdings.

These family land estates and their unrestricted descent lines, which were more significant in Caribbean peasant communities than the colonial nuclear family upheld by both Established and Nonconformist Christianity, form the basis of identity and continuity in Trelawny's Baptist villages today. For example, the two Baptist deacons in Refuge are members of the village's two most central family lines. One of these Old Families traces its ancestry four ascending generations from the oldest living members to an African slave woman, one of three sisters brought from Africa into slavery, who worked on Oxford estate bordering the village, and who was subsequently one of the original ex-slave settlers of Refuge who purchased land from Knibb. The other central family line traces its ancestry four ascending generations from the oldest living members to an African-born slave couple and their son, a Creole slave on nearby Hyde Hall estate, who was also one of the original ex-slave settlers of Refuge who purchased land from Knibb. Both of these Old Families have transformed this purchased land to family land, with family burial grounds (Besson 1984b:13–15). Similar themes of family land and family lines, embedded in oral tradition, can be identified in Granville, Kettering, Alps and Martha Brae. Moreover, the creation of family land from purchased land continues wherever possible in Trelawny's contemporary Baptist villages, in the face of persisting land monopoly not only by plantations but also by the mining and tourist industries (Besson 1984b, 1987b, 1988a).

Women as well as men are central to this peasant culture of resistance: as transmitters and trustees of family land, and as crucial agents in socialization, cultivation, marketing, kinship networks, marriage systems and mutual aid. Women also play a central role in the Revival cult, which is an important dimension of the peasant culture of resistance (Besson 1993). Like family land and other aspects of the peasant economy and community, the Revival worldview – which co-exists with the Baptist Church in Trelawny's villages – is rooted in African-Caribbean proto-peasant cultural resistance. Emerging from the Myalist traditions evolved in slavery, Revival, like family land with which it is closely interrelated, can also be seen as reflecting African continuities within the context of a dynamic process of Caribbean culture-building (Besson 1987b, 1988b, 1993), as the following section shows.

The Revival worldview: African-Caribbean cultural resistance

On the Jamaican slave plantations, where the slaves were untouched by Christianity until the arrival of the Nonconformist missionaries in the late eighteenth century, the slaves forged a new African-Caribbean cosmology following the shattering of their African religions. This creative process of Caribbean culture-building and cultural resistance drew on the African baseline beliefs in witchcraft, medicine, ancestral cults, and a pantheon of gods and spirits, remoulding them within the slave plantation system. At the heart of this recreated worldview were the magico-religious cults of Obeah and Myalism (Patterson 1973:182–207; cf. Mintz 1970).

Obeah was 'essentially a type of sorcery' using 'charms, poisons, and shadow catching' (Patterson 1973:188). Involving clients and an Obeahman, it was practised at an individual level for protection, punishment, or revenge. Obeah was also instrumental in slave rebellions, and in this and other respects, such as the manipulation of spirits, overlapped with Myalism (Alleyne 1988:84; Patterson 1973:186–95).

Myalism was centred around community rituals including spirit possession and the Myal dance, which honoured the African-derived minor spirit deities of the Myal pantheon (rather than the distant Supreme Deity) and the departed ancestors who, it was believed, could possess the living.

Integral also to Myalism was the belief in a dual spirit or soul. One spirit, the *duppy*, was believed to leave the body at death and, after remaining for a few days at the place of death or burial, to journey to join the ancestors. Elaborate funeral ritual was practised to effect and mark this transition. Another spirit was believed to be the shadow of the living person, which could be caught and harmed through Obeah and restored by Myalmen. Myalism, which was both a belief system and a religious organization, was modelled on West African secret cult societies, and initiation ceremonies symbolizing death and the restoration to life were also performed. The Myal cult united the slaves in resistant response to slavery and European values, and was thought to protect their communities from external and internal harm (Alleyne 1988:85–8, 102–3; Patterson 1973:190–5; Schuler 1980:32–3).

Schuler argues that Myalism, which appeared in Jamaica around the middle of the eighteenth century (Robotham 1988:35), 'appears to have been the first religious movement in Jamaica which addressed itself to the entire slave society, rather than to the microcosms of separate African groups' (Schuler 1979a:129). As such, it may be seen as either the basis of a pan-African solidarity (Schuler 1979a:129) or, perhaps more accurately, of an African-Jamaican identity (cf. Robotham 1988:35). Consistent with both of these perspectives, Alleyne (1988:88–9) contends that 'Myalism was the broadest reference' of slave religion in Jamaica, 'and serves as a cover term for all religious observances that developed from African religions'; and that 'Myalism must be viewed along a diachronic continuum of change beginning in Africa, and along a continuum of synchronic variation within the population at any one particular time'.

From the late eighteenth century these African-derived beliefs merged with Christianity, as Nonconformist proselytizing replaced the neglect of the slaves by the planters' Established Anglican Church (Patterson 1973: 207–15). As noted previously, of particular significance was the teaching of the Black Baptists George Lisle and Moses Baker, American ex-slaves, and the subsequent arrival of British Baptist missionaries. As seen above, the slaves embraced the Baptist faith at a formal level and attended the Baptist Church, which provided an added dimension to plantation life. However, the slaves also remained committed to their Myalist traditions. As a result, two variants of Baptist faith emerged: the 'Orthodox' form, taught by the missionaries and practised by the slave congregations in the churches; and the 'Native' or 'Black' Baptist variant, incorporating and controlled by Myalism, taught by Negro Class Leaders in the proto-peasant context on the slave plantations. This latter variant played a central role in the 1831 slave rebellion, the so-called 'Baptist War', led by the Native Baptist Class Leader, 'Daddy' Sam Sharpe, a domestic slave in Montego Bay, St James (neighbouring Trelawny), which hastened the abolition of slavery (Alleyne 1988:90–1; Patterson 1973:211–12, 273; Schuler 1980:34–7; Turner 1982:94).

After emancipation, this parallel commitment continued among the former slaves. Orthodox Baptist faith provided the formal framework of free village life (Mintz 1974:157–79); while the Native Baptist variant, rooted in Myalism, formed 'the core of a strong, self-confident counterculture' against the persisting plantation system (Schuler 1980:44), and the basis of a Black ethnicity (Robotham 1988:35–6). In the 1860s, Native Baptist beliefs, reinforced by the Myalist Revival of the 1840s and 1850s, and by the religion of post-emancipation African indentured immigrants, contributed to and controlled the Great Evangelical Revival (Alleyne 1988:99–100; Patterson 1973:187–8, 214–15; Schuler 1980:40–1, 104–5). This produced a new African-Christian variant, 'Revival', which is the basis of Jamaica's Revival cults, Revival Zion and Pukumina (or Pocomania), today. Alleyne (1988) describes these contemporary religious forms as 'important points in the continuum of religious differentiation created by the meeting of Myalism and Christianity' (p. 96); with Pukumina being the closer of the two to Myalism, and Revival Zion being nearer to Baptist Christianity (p. 101).

The parallel themes of Orthodox Baptist Christianity and Myalism were very pronounced among Trelawny's proto-peasants and post-emancipation peasantry who, as seen above, were at the heart of Baptist proselytizing in Jamaica and who were also at the centre of the island's Myal movement (Schuler 1980:35, 40–1, 43). These parallel themes form the basis of the dual commitment to the Baptist Church and Revival worldview in Trelawny's contemporary peasant communities. The increasing 'creolization' of Baptist beliefs through Myalism, which occurred within the slavery and post-slavery contexts and generated the Native Baptist variant and the Great Revival, provides the roots of the Revival worldview in Trelawny villages today.

Evidence of the existence of African-Jamaican religion within the context of Baptist free villages dates back to the post-emancipation era (Mintz 1974:157–79). From the perspective of the Baptist Church, this was regarded as 'backsliding':

> 'backsliding' sometimes took the form of religious innovation, innovation that involved in some ways the restoration of the more traditional (or 'African') religious forms that had been supplanted by Christianity.
>
> (Mintz 1974:177–8)

For example, in the case of Sturge Town founded by the Baptist missionary John Clark in the parish of St Ann (neighbouring Trelawny), Underhill's observations include the following in 1861, around the time of the Great Revival:

> STURGE TOWN TABERNACLE. Rev. John Clark, pastor . . . (It is necessary to mention that this church is a secession from the church under the native minister, Mr McLaggan, and arose out of certain

> occurrences connected with Obeahism, in which the minister and some of the members were involved) . . . There are about 700 persons in Sturge Town; all attend either the Tabernacle or Mr McLaggan's . . . Very few backsliders . . . People are not getting rid of religion, though it is not as it was twenty years ago. A little before and after freedom there was more piety, everybody 'was going to chapel' . . .
> (Underhill 1861:312–13, cited in Mintz 1974:168)

Mintz notes that Underhill's description suggests 'that, while the Baptist Church still wielded considerable influence in the village, new forces had arisen which were causing change in various ways', including the provision of 'competing faiths' (Mintz 1974:168).

In my comparative study of land, kinship and identity in five Trelawny villages in 1983 (Besson 1984b), Revival cults were observed as coexisting with the Baptist Church in at least three of these free village communities: Refuge, Granville and Martha Brae. In the case of Refuge, the Revival leader was the daughter of an elderly woman whose membership of the Baptist Church was the longest in the village, and the daughter had built her Revival cult house in their yard. In Martha Brae, where a study based on participant-observation in the Revival Zion cult was conducted by me in 1983 and followed up thereafter (Besson 1993), it was found that individuals who attended the Baptist Church also participated in Revival Zion. For, as I have argued previously:

> rather than providing competing faiths [from the perspective of the villagers], church and cult in Martha Brae share the same adherents to a large extent and have complementary roles. The Baptist Church provides a formal faith and moral guidelines for daily Christian life, while Revival Zion cosmology orders the villagers' entire world, including relations between the living and the dead, and promotes inter-community solidarity. Furthermore, both have complementary functions in village funerary ritual and mutual aid.
> (Besson 1987b:123)

In 1983 there were two Revival 'Bands' in Martha Brae, both led by women, and fieldwork focused on the oldest and most active of these groups, led by Mrs K. (Besson 1993). Her leading role as prophetess and healer was supported by her husband's role as chaplain, pastor or preacher, and by a secretary who is female. The cult house is beside the Ks' house in their yard, which is marked by a tall flag-pole believed to be instrumental in attracting the Revival spirit pantheon. Made of corrugated iron sheets, the cult house is furnished with wooden benches, a holy altar, and several goat-skinned drums – symbols of resistance from the slavery past (Campbell 1985:25). Other ritual symbols include bottles of holy water, believed to aid mediation with the spirits; vases of crotons representing the spirit world; and doves, kept outside the cult house in the yard. Revival meetings, attended by both men and women, but especially women, are held three nights a week, each lasting for several hours.

Revival cosmology in Martha Brae closely parallels that outlined by Chevannes in the preceding chapter for the traditional Revival worldview. Revival in Martha Brae is essentially a spirit possession cult related to a cosmology of an integrated world of living beings, God, the spirits and the dead. While the unseen portion of this world includes the Christian Trinity, the total spirit pantheon is Africa-derived (cf. Patterson 1973:182–207; Schuler 1979a:133). Likewise, spirit possession and baptism through immersion (the latter taking place on trips to a Revival 'Bands' at Lethe on the Great River in St James), stem, as Schuler notes of Myal, 'from an African and not a Christian or European tradition' (1979a:133). The spirits, including the spirits of the dead, are thought to cause good fortune and misfortune and to be open to influence for good or evil. The latter is believed to be effected through an Obeahman, while the former is the true role of Revival.

Spirit possession in Revival – believed to be induced through drumming, dancing, the singing of Revival hymns and 'trouping' around a basin of holy water, and culminating in trance and sometimes glossolalia – is seen as enabling communication with the spirits for protection, prophesy and healing. Individual members of the congregation experience different stages of possession, the most intense being manifested by the 'Leadress', Mrs K. It is believed that the spirit world may also be revealed to individuals through visions in dreams (Besson 1988a:51, 1993; cf. Chevannes, Chapter 2, this volume). Contact with the Revival spirit pantheon is perceived as a source of both power and of danger, and this is reflected in the symbolic colours of red and white associated with the cult: white symbolizing the sacred spirit world; red standing for the power and the danger involved in spirit contact. Revival turbans (cf. Chevannes, Chapter 5, this volume) therefore tend to be red or white; and women especially also dress, when possible, in red and white for Revival meetings.

The Revival Zion worldview in Martha Brae may also be seen as African-Caribbean cultural resistance, rooted in the slavery and post-emancipation past. As seen above, Myalism united the slaves against slavery and European values and was thought to protect the slave communities from harm; while the Native Baptist variant was the basis of a Black ethnicity and significant in the 'Baptist War' slave rebellion, which included Trelawny slaves. In the post-emancipation period, Myal and the Great Revival were central to the counter-cultures of resistance that emerged against the persisting plantation system, which retained its stranglehold in Trelawny (Besson 1981, 1987b:113, 124; Robotham 1988:35–6; Schuler 1980). Revival Zion continues this role in contemporary Martha Brae, integrating the peasant community, and is perceived as protecting it against misfortune from neo-colonial society, the spirits and the dead.

Revival Zion in Martha Brae also promotes inter-community solidarity, as did Myal, Native Baptism and the Great Revival in the past. Historically, the 'Baptist War' and the emergence of a Black ethnicity are obvious examples of this theme, another being the way in which this shared body of ritual and belief 'drew semi-autonomous plantation slave villages or free villages together" (Schuler 1979a:128). In Martha Brae, Revival Zion links the village with Revival 'Bands' in other village communities – both elsewhere in Trelawny and in other parishes, especially neighbouring St Ann and St James. Visits are made by Martha Brae Revivalists to 'Bands' in these other communities and are reciprocated by visits to Martha Brae. In the summer of 1983, four such visits to Martha Brae took place (Besson 1993).

The Revival worldview is also reflected in the elaborate rituals surrounding death in Martha Brae (cf. Chevannes, Chapter 2, this volume) and here continuity may be seen with African-derived death rituals on the slave plantations (Besson 1987b:124; Patterson 1973:195–8). The contemporary rituals, consisting especially of the 'lyke-wake' and 'Nine Night' wake, mark and are believed to effect the transition of the *duppy* of the deceased to join the spirits of the dead; while the tombing is thought to complete this process of transition (cf. Hertz 1960). Should these 'rites of passage' (van Gennep 1960) be incomplete, it is believed that the restless, unplaced *duppy* will wander among the living causing harm. One such reputed case is well known in Granville and Martha Brae.

In Martha Brae, Revival mortuary ritual also comforts the bereaved and symbolizes community solidarity. Grave-digging is also a community responsibility, the only payment being rum to keep the *duppy* at bay (cf. Chevannes, Chapter 2, this volume). Despite this communal service, mortuary ritual entails large expenditures by the bereaved and this is generally organized through the village Friendly Society, which regulates ritual mutual aid. The Society also officiates at funerals and holds annual fund-raising 'Anniversaries'.

The Baptist Church plays a complementary role to the Revival cult in such mortuary ritual and mutual aid in Martha Brae. Funeral services are often held in the William Knibb Memorial Baptist Church in Falmouth, following village wakes and before proceeding back to Martha Brae for the burial – where the Falmouth Baptist minister may also officiate. The fund-raising Anniversaries may also be held at the Baptist Church or William Knibb Memorial School, situated between Falmouth and Martha Brae.

Burial also reflects the interrelationship of the Revival cult and Baptist Church in Trelawny's post-slavery villages; for the graves that are the focus of Revival ritual are located on Baptist free village land. Such land has also often been transformed into family land estates, with family burial grounds linking the living and the dead of the Revival worldview. In contemporary Martha Brae burial is in the village cemetery rather than in family land yards, but oral history indicates that in the post-emancipation past interment was in the yard, the change being due to health regulations regarding proximity to the urban settlement of Falmouth. In Granville, one mile further inland from Falmouth than Martha Brae, the traditional pattern of yard burial continues undisturbed. The same is true of Refuge, six miles east of Falmouth and three miles west of Duncans. In Kettering, adjoining Duncans, the transformation of the traditional burial pattern that occurred over time in Martha Brae is reflected here spatially, for family land burial persists in those parts of Kettering furthest from Duncans town, while other Kettering burials now take place in the Duncans cemetery. In Alps, the most remote of the five communities studied and Trelawny's first free village, the family burial grounds are the most extensive (Besson 1984b:18–19).

These family burial grounds, which symbolize the family lines at the heart of Trelawny's post-slavery peasant communities, have been a central feature in the transformation of Baptist freehold land to family land. The family burial grounds also reflect the embedding of the Revival worldview and the peasant culture of resistance in the formal framework of the Baptist free village land settlements – where the Rastafari movement is also now emerging.

References

Alleyne, Mervyn (1988) *Roots of Jamaican Culture.* London: Pluto Press.

Besson, Jean (1984a) 'Family Land and Caribbean Society: Toward an Ethnography of Afro-Caribbean Peasantries', pp. 57–83 in Elizabeth M. Thomas-Hope (ed.), *Perspectives on Caribbean Regional Identity.* Monograph Series No. 11. Centre for Latin American Studies, University of Liverpool: Liverpool University Press.

Besson, Jean (1984b) 'Land Tenure in the Free Villages of Trelawny, Jamaica: A Case Study in the Caribbean Peasant Response to Emancipation', *Slavery & Abolition*, 5(1): 3–23.

Besson, Jean (1987b) 'Family Land as a Model for Martha Brae's New History: Culture-Building in an Afro-Caribbean Village', pp. 100–32 in Charles V. Carnegie (ed.), *Afro-Caribbean Villages in Historical Perspective.* ACIJ Research Review No. 2. Kingston, Jamaica: African-Caribbean Institute of Jamaica.

Besson, Jean (1988a) 'Agrarian Relations and Perceptions of Land in a Jamaican Peasant Village', pp. 39–61 in John S. Brierley and Hymie Rubenstein (eds), *Small Farming and Peasant Resources in the Caribbean.* Manitoba Geographical Studies 10. Winnipeg: University of Manitoba.

Besson, Jean (1989b) 'Review of OLWIG, Karen Fog, *Cultural Adaptation and Resistance on St. John: Three Centuries of Afro-Caribbean Life.* Gainesville: University Presses of Florida, 1985', *Plantation Society in the Americas*, 2(3): 345–8 (May).

Besson, Jean (1992) 'Freedom and Community: The British West Indies', in Seymour Drescher and Frank McGlynn (eds), *The Meaning of Freedom: The Anthropology and History of Post-Slavery Societies.* Pittsburgh: University of Pittsburgh Press, pp. 183–219.

Besson, Jean (1993) 'Reputation and Respectability Reconsidered: A New Perspective on Afro-Caribbean Peasant Women', in Janet Momsen (ed.), *Women and Change: A Pan-Caribbean Perspective*, London: James Currey and Bloomington: Indiana University Press, pp. 15–37.

Campbell, Horace (1985) *Rasta and Resistance: From Marcus Garvey to Walter Rodney.* London: Hansib.

Chevannes, Barry (ed.) 1995 *Rastafari and Other African-Caribbean Worldviews.* The Hague: Institute of Social Studies.

Chevannes, Barry 1995 'New Approaches to Rastafari' in Chevannes (ed.) *Rastafari and other African-Caribbean World Views.* The Hague: Institute of Social Studies.

Knibb Sibley, Inez (1965) *The Baptists of Jamaica 1793–1965.* Kingston: Jamaica Baptist Union.

Mintz, Sidney. W. (1971) 'The Caribbean as a Socio-Cultural Area', in M. M. Horowitz (ed.), *Peoples and Cultures of the Caribbean.* New York: Garden City.

Mintz, Sidney. W. (1974) *Caribbean Transformations.* Chicago: Aldine.

Mintz, Sidney. W. (1989) *Caribbean Transformations.* New York: Columbia University Press, Morningside Edition.

Olwig, Karen Fog (1990) 'The Struggle for Respectability: Methodism and Afro-Caribbean Culture on 19th Century Nevis', *Nieuwe West-Indische Gids/New West Indian Guide*, 64(3&4): 93–114.

Paget, Hugh (1964) 'The Free Village System in Jamaica', *Caribbean Quarterly*, 10(1): 38–51.

Patterson, Orlando (1973) *The Sociology of Slavery: An Analysis of the Origins, Development and Structure of Negro Slave Society in Jamaica.* London: Granada (first published 1967).

Robotham, Don (1974) 'Agrarian Relations in Jamaica', in Carl Stone and Aggrey Brown (eds), *Essays on Power and Change in Jamaica.* Kingston: Institute of Social and Economic Research, University of the West Indies.

Robotham, Don (1977) *The Notorious Riot: The Socio-economic and Political Bases of Paul Boate's Revolt.* ISER Working Paper Series, Number 28. Kingston: Institute of Social and Economic Research, University of the West Indies.

Robotham, Don (1988) 'The Development of a Black Ethnicity in Jamaica', pp. 23–38 in Lewis Rupert and Patrick Bryan (eds), *Garvey: His Work and Impact.* Mona, Jamaica: ISER and Extra-Mural Dept., University of West Indies.

Schuler, Monica (1979a) 'Afro-American Slave Culture', pp. 121–55 in Michael Craton (ed.), *Roots and Branches: Current Directions in Slave Studies.* Toronto: Pergamon Press.

Schuler, Monica (1979b) 'Myalism and the African Religious Tradition in Jamaica', pp. 65–79 in Margaret E. Crahan and Franklin Knight (eds), *Africa and the Caribbean: The Legacies of a Link.* Baltimore and London: Johns Hopkins University Press.

Schuler, Monica (1980) *'Alas, Alas, Kongo': A Social History of Indentured African Immigration Into Jamaica, 1841–1865.* Baltimore and London: Johns Hopkins University Press.

Turner, Mary (1982) *Slaves and Missionaries: The Disintegration of Jamaican Slave Society, 1787–1834.* Urbana: University of Illinois Press.

Walvin, James (1983) *Slavery and the Slave Trade: A Short Illustrated History.* London: Macmillan.

Williams, Eric (1970) *From Columbus to Castro: The History of the Caribbean 1492–1969.* London: André Deutsch.

Wright, Philip (1973) *Knibb, 'The Notorious': Slaves' Missionary 1803–1845* London: Sidgwick and Jackson.

64

STRUCTURAL OBSTACLES TO GRASSROOTS PASTORAL PRACTICE

The case of a base community in Urban Brazil

Manuel A. Vásquez

Source: *Sociology of Religion*, 58(1) (1997), 53–68.

At their conference in Medellín in 1968, the Latin American Catholic bishops, seeking to concretize Vatican II calls to dialogue with modernity, adopted a preferential option for the poor as the church's guiding pastoral principle. This decision paved the way for progressive Catholic forces in the region to form a "popular church" (*igreja popular*),[1] a set of pastoral and institutional initiatives designed to serve those at the margins of society. Chief among these initiatives were base ecclesial communities (*comunidades eclesiais de base*, or CEBs): small neighborhood-based groups in which poor people, inspired by biblical themes of justice, solidarity, and liberation, struggle to transform society as both a precondition and a sign of the coming reign of God.

Nowhere did CEBs attain a higher level of maturity than in Brazil, where, with support from a prominent progressive sector of the hierarchy, they became an important source of institutional renewal for the church and also a major democratizing force as the country emerged from military dictatorship in the late 1970s (Bruneau 1986; Della Cava 1989). Nevertheless, some scholars have recently noted that despite the CEBs' claim to be a "church born of the people," base communities attract only a small fraction of Brazil's religiously active population (Burdick 1992, 1993; Drogus 1992; Daudelin 1992). Some of these accounts also point to the contrasting example of Pentecostalism, which despite its often politically conservative message, has expanded rapidly among the poor, the CEBs' intended audience.

Readings of the base communities' failure to mobilize a larger segment of the poor in Brazil have tended to focus on contradictions in the CEBs' pastoral-pedagogical method and on personal failings, such as elitism or vanguardism, of pastoral agents (Burdick 1993; Mariz 1994). While such explanations may illuminate some aspects of CEB life, they fail to take into account the larger ecclesial and socio-economic processes that condition religious activity at the local level. Transformations in the global Catholic Church and in the life conditions of the poor, far beyond the control of individual actors, also shape the fate of CEBs. By examining the trajectory of a particular CEB, and especially its recent difficulties, I hope to point to some of the broader institutional and structural obstacles to the popular church's efforts to reach poor Brazilians.

This essay focuses on a CEB near Rio de Janeiro. I trace the community's evolution, reconstructing the factors that led to its apparent decline. This decline, I argue, was what Raymond Boudon (1979, 1981) calls a "perverse unintended consequence" (*effet perverse*), an "emergent effect" generated by the "overturning" and/or "reversion" of the goals of local action by larger institutional and structural processes. Boudon uses the term "perverse unintended consequences" to describe effects not explicitly sought by the agent of a particular act. These effects result from the agent's location within overarching and interdependent systems of interaction that shape his/her range of action and the outcome of this action. Therefore, although people's choices and strategies may follow logically from their goals, the effects of their actions appear paradoxical or "perverse" given the larger context.

Applying Boudon's theoretical construct to the case study, I contend that activities, pastoral strategies, and modes of organization which sought to empower and mobilize CEB participants had precisely the opposite effect in the light of larger external processes. These processes, including a conservative Vatican offensive and Brazil's economic crisis in the 1980s, created obstacles for the production and reception of the base community's message in the neighborhood and exacerbated tensions and contradictions within the CEB, triggering its decline. I conclude the essay by placing the case study within recent debates about the fate of CEBs and arguing for the need to situate local religious action within its proper institutional, structural, and systemic contexts.

A case study: Pedra Bonita[2]

The CEB that will be the focus of this paper is located in a small working-class neighborhood I will call Pedra Bonita, at the periphery of Nova Iguaçu, a sprawling urban district at the northwestern edge of Rio de Janeiro. Nova Iguaçu suffers socio-economic problems such as overpopulation, inadequate housing, lack of basic services, high crime, and poverty.[3] In response to these conditions, the diocese of Nova Iguaçu, under the leadership of well-known progressive bishop Adriano Hipólito, has been at the forefront in the implementation of the option for the poor, vigorously applying the popular church's pastoral-pedagogical method (Mainwaring 1986; Lernoux 1980).

Pedra Bonita's base ecclesial community, like many others throughout Brazil, originated in the organizing activities of a pastoral agent.[4] In the early 1970s, Father Claúdio, a diocesan priest who had worked extensively with Catholic Action in his native France,[5] came to Pedra Bonita seeking to purchase a plot of land to build a church in the neighborhood (*bairro*). Claúdio introduced a pastoral methodology that would remain unchanged for more than a decade. After he left in 1973, a succession of three French priests, all with strong ties to Catholic Action, ministered to the community, building on his pastoral groundwork. Claúdio's first step was to visit the most established families in the area and celebrate mass in their houses. This strategy allowed him to build a small group of five women who held weekly meetings to study the gospels. This *grupo de reflexão do Evangelho*, as it was called, became the community's first building block and its core, as each of its members became a leader in the evangelization teams that operated in the various sectors of the *bairro.*

Claúdio used the *grupo de reflexão* and the evangelization teams to train local lay leaders according to the pedagogical model of reflection-action-reflection.[6] Every Friday, he met with the women coordinating the evangelization teams to discuss and prepare the activities for the following week. The next Tuesday the women went out to evangelize among their neighbors, always taking care to link prepared readings with everyday life in the *bairro.* The following Friday the women met to reflect on their evangelizing experience and to prepare for yet another week of activities.

Claúdio's strategy proved highly successful. Each evangelization group attracted between 18 and 30 women. Before long, the sons and daughters of these women had formed catechism groups which, during the community's peak years in the late 1970s, prepared up to 40 youngsters at a time to receive their first communion. The level of lay involvement was so high that Pedra Bonita became a model for surrounding neighborhoods. This remarkable degree of mobilization, however, did not occur overnight. It required repeated house calls by the pastoral agents, who invited and even coaxed the women to set aside their daily responsibilities and attend the Bible meetings.

As the French priests' pastoral work began to take hold, a relatively stable ecclesial community emerged. Father Miguel, the last of the French priests, characterizes the early base community as a flexible "polycentered web," with some of the threads serving as the structural support for a whole array of activities, groups, and levels of involvement. The central threads converged in a "nucleus" or informal "directorate" consisting of the families of the five women who founded the community.

Once the CEB had taken shape, Claúdio introduced some important liturgical innovations, stressing spontaneous participation in various pedagogic and liturgical exercises. Laura, one of the five women who founded the CEB, recalls how the priest left all preparations for the mass to an ad hoc group of by people. They decided what would be done, setting up a informal rotation of duties that allowed continuity without reification of roles at the core.

> We would do everything for the mass . . . we were a liturgy team, only we did not call ourselves that. When the time came we would have things ready. 'Dona Otília, you're going to do the first reading of the Bible. Dona Cléa, you'll do the second. Vitória will read the Gospel.' The priest would just help people to speak and discover.

Instead of delivering a traditional sermon, Claúdio sought ways to encourage participation from the barely literate population, borrowing from Paulo Freire's pedagogical method. According to Gabriela, Laura's youngest daughter,

> Father Claúdio was sensitive to the difficulty people had in reading, people of the Northeast who came here. He would take the gospel reading and write it in a big brown poster and place it in the front of the room during the mass. And then people would read each word slowly, discussing it, linking it with our reality. People would even decorate the gospel text. He even had to bring paper so that people could draw what they understood from the readings. And it was a long process to make people understand that the end was not just to illustrate the gospels, but to read it, to enjoy it, and to link it with our lives.

Claúdio also began to encourage the five families in the CEB nucleus to form a group of the *Ação Católica Operária* (Workers' Catholic Action, or ACO).[7] Originally conceived as a conservative, clerically-controlled alternative to secular workers' movements, the ACO in Brazil, like Catholic Action more generally, became radicalized as its pastoral agents came into contact with working people's precarious life conditions. A key element in this radicalization was the adoption of the see-judge-act method, in which small groups reflect on a given reality, evaluate it in light of biblical and church teachings, and then act in accord with this evaluation. This process encouraged Catholic Action activists to uncover the social roots as well as the religious implications of problems in their lives.

As the CEB leaders who formed the ACO team in Pedra Bonita used the see-judge-act method to reflect on life in the neighborhood, they began to identify and understand the causes behind pressing problems such as the lack of running water, electricity, bus service to Rio, and schools. This realization, in turn, led to increasing political activism among core CEB members. According to Ernesto, a longtime member of both the base community and

ACO, people in the CEB nucleus "would initially come together to talk about the difficulties of life in the *bairro*, not knowing what the ACO was." As time went by they became "politically literate [*alfabetizado politicamente*]." They began to "awaken [*acordar*] to the discrimination and repression that [poor] people confront when [they] demand [their] rights."

The transition to political action was neither automatic nor smooth. Since the various Catholic Action movements were still subject to persecution by the military government in the early 1970s (Mainwaring 1986), when Pedra Bonita's ACO was forming, the group could not declare its identity openly. It met behind closed doors and only in the houses of the participating families. Although this secrecy enabled the group to survive the repression that dismantled all trade unions and opposition parties, it set the families in the ACO, who also formed the core of the CEB, apart from the rest of both the base community and the neighborhood. They were perceived as a highly politicized, and thus potentially dangerous, group within what was fundamentally a religious community.

As the military began to relax its grip on power, beginning in 1974, the ACO team emerged as the hegemonic force within Pedra Bonita's base community. Members of the group organized and led neighborhood-wide demonstrations at the city hall in Nova Iguaçu and the governor's mansion in Rio, which brought a school, bus service, and potable water to the area. The ACO group became a vanguard within the base community, seeking to "show the people that it is us, the neighbors, who have to struggle to gain our rights," as Ernesto puts it.

The rise of the ACO movement was a turning point for Pedra Bonita's CEB, for it encouraged the five families that had formed the base community nucleus to link religious matters with everyday concerns in the neighborhood. New ecclesial and liturgical practices spoke to the situation in the *bairro*, transcending the traditional view of religion as just the realm of prayer and the contemplative life. The connection between religion and politics in the base community reached its full maturity in 1982, with the formation of Pedra Bonita's Neighborhood Association, which became the main vehicle for local struggles (*reivindicações*), such as efforts to bring a health center to the neighborhood and to pave its main streets. The association also linked Pedra Bonita's community activists with other grassroots organizations in Nova Iguaçu.

It is important to note that the base community's political activism did not signal the abandonment of religious practices or its "original and enduring religious nature" (Levine 1992: 46). Community members continued to prepare mass, teach catechism, and meet in evangelization groups while also lobbying for better social services through the ACO and the neighborhood association. The balance between religious and political activities came from a reading of the Bible that tied Christian symbols, events, and teachings to the life of the poor in the community. Ernesto, for instance, asserts that there is

> a close link between Christ and today's worker. Today's worker is crucified by the system. Christ is a companion [*companheiro*] who is fighting on the worker's side, because he came to get rid of the oppression of people of his time, because he wanted to make an alliance with the world. So just as the worker now fights for justice, so did Jesus Christ. He said: 'Those who are hungry for justice will be satisfied.' And we too are hungry for justice, for a just wage. He also said: 'I came so that all have life and life in abundance.' So we fight for life. No one came to the world to suffer, not to have a house, not to have education for his children, not to have a place where his children could play. And injustice takes all that away from the worker.

During the late 1970s, Pedra Bonita's CEB continued to expand, adding new groups and movements. Developing parallel to the more politically-engaged current of the base community (the CEB-ACO nucleus) was a more traditional religious group: the Society of Saint Vincent de Paul. In Pedra Bonita, the *Vicentinos*, as this group is known, number ten to twelve persons. The leaders of this lay movement are among the poorest members of the base community. They are also older than most of the ACO activists.

Vicentino practice is intensely spiritual. It is supported by two main pillars: the cult of the saints expressed in prayer and ritual activities and the Holy Spirit, as the force that unifies and inspires the group. Rather than linking faith to political struggle for communal betterment, as the ACO does, the *Vicentinos* focus on personal conversion and renewal. Their social outreach is more "assistential," modelled along the lines of traditional Catholic charities. Every week *Vicentinos* prepare food packages, purchased with money contributed by group members, and distribute them to the poorest families in the community. They also visit the sick and destitute in the neighborhood, praying with them, reading the Bible with them, and more generally providing encouragement in hard times.

For ACO members, this kind of work raises some troubling questions. In Ernesto's opinion, the *Vicentinos* "are still too attached to the cult of the saints. They don't want to go out and confront present reality, or to link faith and life. You have to take your faith inside your union, association, workplace." Ana, his wife, concurs, adding that the *Vicentinos* "concentrate on giving away the fish that is already caught. They don't concern themselves with discussing with the poorest families the causes of the problems they are facing, making them reflect on the causes and consequences of the unemployment they are suffering." Tina, the president of the *Vicentinos*, acknowledges that some of the members in her group "sometimes don't participate in other movements, and that obstructs [*atrapalha*] community work. But I, as a *Vicentina*, participate in all neighborhood activities. I'm in the liturgy group."

Some members of the CEB nucleus in the ACO recognize the merits of the *Vicentinos's* social and pastoral work. According to Vitória, "The *Vicentinos* are very important in the neighborhood because they really work hard at visiting people, something that we [the ACO] haven't paid enough attention to." Thus, despite mutual suspicions, the two currents managed to work together for the benefit of the base community: while the ACO concentrated more on political activism, the *Vicentinos* focused on spiritual matters. Moreover, although the ACO's vision dominated CEB life, the informal rotation of liturgical activities set up by Claúdio allowed the *Vicentinos* to contribute actively to the base community. With the consolidation of the two currents, the *Vicentinos* and the CEB-ACO nucleus, the picture that emerged toward the early 1980s was of a complex, highly differentiated community capable of holding in productive tension two seemingly opposing forms of religiosity and approaches to social-pastoral action.[8] The balance between these two currents was maintained until 1981, when pastoral changes in the diocese and the parish collided with the ACO's *modus operandi.* These changes, combined with socio-economic transformations in the Brazilian society, generated a period of decline in Pedra Bonita's CEB.

In 1981, the French pastoral agents who had been working the area for more than 10 years returned to France and were replaced by Irish priests of the Order of the Holy Spirit. The latter, intent on giving "each community its independent type of life" and increasing the decision-making power of CEB members, took a more distant pastoral approach. In the Irish priests' view, Pedra Bonita's CEB had achieved sufficient maturity after the initial push provided by the French. Father Patrício, an Irish priest and the community's current pastoral agent, compares CEBs to a car:

> you [the pastoral agent] are driving the car, the car is doing everything, the engine is going, the wheels are going around, and all you do is to get your finger in the steering wheel. So, here . . . we strongly insist that the community do everything. We have as little presence as possible.

This approach generated discontent among some community members, especially among ACO activists in the CEB nucleus. In Teresa's opinion, "the French priests had us spoiled, they were so good with the people." They were good because, in Gabriela's words,

> They had a [pastoral] method which took them to our homes. They would bike around the neighborhood visiting, inviting people to come. They would participate in our moments of happiness and sorrow. And you know, Brazilian people are very hospitable. They like to be visited in their homes, to strike up conversations. And the Irish seem to be colder. They only come to say mass twice a month and leave quickly.

Patrício believes that Father Jaime, the first Irish priest to arrive in Pedra Bonita, sought to address problems of dependence and favoritism within the CEB. It appears that the French priests favored some ACO families in the CEB, giving them a monthly stipend to augment their meager incomes. This had made the base community dependent on external aid and blocked efforts at self-sufficiency through tithing. In addition, the French priests' emphasis on the ACO pastoral method had led to a concentration of initiatives in the hands of a few activists. This concentration of responsibilities in the CEB nucleus was a necessary organizational phase before the CEB could turn its attention to the world at large. Through its *pastoral de grupos pequenos* (small group pastoral approach), CEBs worked with selected individuals among the poor to be trained, with a consciousness-raising pedagogy, as lay leaders. These leaders would later on act as "organic intellectuals,"[9] or as Catholic activists say, *fermento de massa* (leaven), educating and inspiring those around them to become involved in building the reign of God. The ultimate objective of forming small groups like CEBs was thus to evangelize and mobilize the popular masses.

The Irish priests had misgivings about this transition from a *pastoral de grupos pequenos* to a *pastoral de massa.* Like the French priests, they also hoped to evangelize the larger community, but they favored different methods. The Irish priests wanted to open up the community, to avoid, in Father Patrício's words, the danger of it becoming "a small sect . . . taken over by one or two families who [were] stronger." As a first step, the Irish priests shifted to the base community the responsibility for evangelization and raising money for the parish fund. To involve the whole community in the tasks of self-maintenance and expansion, they proposed the construction of a new, bigger church in the neighborhood.

Unfortunately, this strategy generated "perverse unintended consequences" as the church construction project diverted dwindling resources from evangelization work, and bread-and-butter struggles, tasks vital to the CEB's well-being. The collapse of the Brazilian economy and the structural adjustment and neo-liberal policies adopted to resolve the crisis beginning in the mid-1980s placed a tremendous pressure on the working poor, limiting their leisure time and their capacity to contribute financially to their communities (Oliveira 1993). This added pressure has had a particularly deleterious effect on women, the backbone of the base communities (Benería and Feldman 1992). As a result of a sharp decline in industrial productivity and the concomitant loss of blue-collar jobs, the vast majority of which were occupied by men, women entered the labor force in greater numbers (especially in the informal sector of the economy, where they do not enjoy any job security), often becoming the main breadwinners in the household. Also, a combination of sharply declining wages and high inflation increased pressure on households to "self-exploit" more (Smith and Wallerstein 1992), that is, to stretch and preserve their dwindling resources, avoiding any investment in extra-household activities, including those connected to the CEB. As a result, women spend more time and energy at home mending and repairing their meager belongings and shopping for cheaper staples in an effort to reduce household expenses. The constant concern for making ends meet takes a heavy toll: At the end of the day people have little energy for extra-household activities in the base community.

Otília's case provides an example of the powerful influence of the economic crisis. As one of the CEB's founders, she played a key role in the formation of one of the most successful and durable evangelization groups in Pedra Bonita. She was known for her dynamic style of leadership and her willingness to set aside her seamstress work at home and attend community meetings. This willingness, however, has been severely undermined by the fact that her husband, an electrician, was laid off from his job at a neighboring construction company. For more than two years he has been practically unemployed, with only occasional odd jobs in the district. So, whereas before Otília's sewing work served to supplement her husband's steady income, now she and her 20 year-old daughter have become the main breadwinners in the household. Faced with this pressure, feeling "tired" of the wear and tear of pastoral visits and "despairing" over the "great suffering of families around [her]," she decided to pass the leadership of her group to another woman, who could not keep up with the visiting routine. In the absence of consistent lay work and without the direct involvement of the priest, the evangelization group, the essential instrument of community growth, all but collapsed.

Teresa, another CEB leader, highlights the economic situation's implications for community action. For her, the inability of people to participate has to do with

> [t]he social side of things: the need people have to work at the sewing machine, washing clothes, that doesn't give time to go to there [the community]. The need to work takes time away from the community. There are several [women] who can't take time off. If they don't work that day, they will not have anything to eat at home. The woman has to stay home washing clothes to be able to provide some change [*trocado*] for household expenses since her husband doesn't make enough money to buy bread.

In addition to re-allocating financial and logistical responsibilities, the Irish priests, following directives from the diocese of Nova Iguaçu, implemented pastoral and organizational changes in the community. In response to pressures generated by a conservative Vatican offensive,[10] the diocese sought to regularize the practices of base communities and their links with the hierarchy. This effort provided viable institutional spaces for CEBs to continue their work in the face of increasing reluctance from the National Conference of Brazilian Bishops to support progressive grassroots initiatives.

These spaces, however, came only at the cost of re-centralizing authority in clerical hands.[11]

Before the diocesan changes, CEBs in Nova Iguaçu, while receiving assistance from the hierarchy, had operated with a great deal of autonomy. This had created significant pastoral heterogeneity at local levels. Activities within each base community depended more on the personal approach of the pastoral agent, which was itself determined by the specific character and needs of the neighborhood. Thus, while diocesan changes in response to Vatican pressure legitimized the existence of base communities by making them part of the church's institutional structure, they also increased hierarchical supervision and control over progressive grassroots pastoral work.[12] This, in turn, allowed the clergy to force heterodox local beliefs and practices to conform to official orthodoxy. This transformation was in line with the aims of the Vatican restoration offensive.

One way to understand the underlying logic of the diocesan changes would be to characterize them as part of a process of "romanization" of CEB practices and discourses. Romanization has been used to describe a process, beginning in the middle of the last century, whereby the Catholic hierarchy in Latin America sought to regiment popular Catholicism by, among other things, attempting to take control over local religious sites (i.e., chapels and shrines) — until then mostly in the hands of the laity — and to force local practice to conform to Roman orthodoxy (Oliveira 1985; Della Cava 1970). The hierarchy also placed a strong emphasis on liturgy and the sacraments, making the clergy the only legitimate holders of sanctioned religious goods (Bourdieu 1971; Maduro 1982).

The case of Pedra Bonita illustrates how the recent Vatican drive reflects a trend towards a new romanization. Among the changes the Irish priests introduced was a renewed stress on the importance of liturgy in CEB life.[13] The strategy they chose to implement this emphasis was twofold. First, the priests sent community members to the diocesan training center in Nova Iguaçu, where they took short courses on the proper ways to assist with and, in the priest's absence, to conduct liturgical celebrations. In this manner, the diocese would strengthen its lay leadership, while at the same time creating lay agents capable of reproducing orthodox liturgical practices on their own. The second aspect of the strategy was the adoption of *A Folha*, a diocesan publication with the weekly service, as the heart of the liturgical celebration. The French priests used *A Folha* more as a pedagogical aid than a strict guide. The Irish pastoral agents, in contrast, made it the defining nexus between priest and community. Vitória noticed this change:

> Before, with the [French] priests, we reflected on the gospels, they would have us say what we understood when reading it. Now he [the Irish priest] only reads the *Folha* and the gospel text and gives a sermon. People don't speak up their minds [*não se colocam*]

In Pedra Bonita this new strategy had negative consequences. For one thing, it challenged the *ad hoc* rotation of liturgical functions among the community nucleus. Laura expresses her disappointment with the new strategy:

> With the [French] priests . . . we were the ones who prepared mass. The gospel text was read, but it was reflected on by the people. Each one would speak a little about what that reading meant, what Jesus Christ wanted to say with it. And people linked it with the life of the worker. And then when Father Jaime arrived he ended all that. He said that we had to organize a liturgy group, take a course to know how to read [*A Folha*] right. So he undid [*desmanchou*] our work, a work that was done for years. We had been working in that fashion for years. We also know that Jesus never took a course at the university to do his work.

The stress on correct liturgical etiquette had also a chilling effect on older, less literate CEB members, who felt that they could not live up to the new "orthopraxis." Laura recalls an episode where Father Jaime scolded Otília, who had prepared mass as she had always done under the French, for not reading the gospel text properly.

> [Father Jaime said:] 'Look! You have a comma there, you have to read using the comma. Periods and commas must be used when reading.' We found this absurd because Otília has not gone beyond second or third grade, just like me. Despite that, I'm capable of reading, slowly, in my own fashion, but I'm capable of reading during mass. Even more when those who hear me are just like me. But then people were ashamed of reading incorrectly, stuttering, letter by letter. And [so] they went to take the [liturgy] course.

Most of the members of the original base community nucleus resisted the pastoral changes introduced by the first Irish priests and politely refused to attend liturgy courses. To many, the courses symbolized a diversion of CEB energy and resources from social action to mere formalities. Father Jaime took the refusal to participate as a willful tactic of a militant political vanguard within the CEB-ACO nucleus to undermine his pastoral work. The *Vicentinos*, on the other hand, reacted favorably to Father Jaime's proposals, as they resonated with the group's emphasis on the ritual and devotional aspects of Christian life. This confluence of approach, along with the increasing tension between the ACO and the priest, made the *Vicentinos* the new hegemonic group in the base community.

As noted earlier, during the ACO's hegemonic period the *Vicentinos* had participated actively in the base community through the informal rotation of liturgical roles set up by the French priests. Thus, even though one group was predominant, the other contributed to and was included in the life of the community. This balance was broken, however, with the *Vicentinos*' ascendancy through the standardization and "professionalization" of the liturgy preparation.

Tensions came to a head during a meeting where Father Jaime tried to form a community council [*conselho comunitário*] in Pedra Bonita, as part of the diocesan plan to establish a more orderly division of labor within CEBs and to bring them under closer clerical supervision. Each movement or group within a CEB would choose a representative. These representatives would form a community council charged with planning, coordinating, and overseeing CEB work. In turn, representatives of each of the community councils in a given parish would form a *conselho paroquial*, thereby connecting each CEB to the diocesan hierarchical structure. Within each base community different specialized groups would assume specific pastoral tasks: baptism, catechism, and liturgy. People in the various groups would receive special training to carry out their functions properly.

The formation of the community council, which had appeared to be a natural step for a mature community, had disastrous effects. During the planning meeting, Father Jaime asked the participants to identify the group they were representing in order to draw up a list for the community council. When Laura indicated that she came from ACO, Jaime refused to acknowledge the movement. Presumably, Jaime wanted to marginalize the ACO because its members were the ones opposing the pastoral changes. This refusal led the main families in the CEB-ACO nucleus to retrench, withdrawing their support from the new community council. Without the participation of these key activists in the nucleus, the community's web began to unravel. The council, rather than serving to coordinate community activities, became an instance of "overbureaucratization," where functions and tasks were well-defined but there were no committed individuals to carry them out. Isolated from the rest of the base community and at loggerheads with the priest, the CEB-ACO nucleus lost its effectiveness, and many core members became disenchanted with the church more generally. This left the CEB's neighborhood outreach and social projects without anyone to execute them, plunging the entire community into a crisis characterized by declining membership and diminishing participation in CEB activities.

Conclusion

The decline of the CEB in Pedra Bonita resulted from the isolation and demobilization of the core of base community activists. This disempowerment had two sources. First, an economic crisis brought a drastic deterioration of life conditions for the Brazilian poor, which in turn limited their capacity to participate in the long process of consciousness-raising and social activism demanded by CEBs and reduced financial resources needed to make the base community self-sustaining. As I argued above, beginning in the mid-1980s, poor people in Pedra Bonita, as in other working-class neighborhoods in urban Brazil, were increasingly forced to spend all their energies to insure their daily survival. Under these conditions, the Irish priests' demands for the laity to assume full responsibility for CEB life in Pedra Bonita, especially for the construction of a new church, could not be adequately met, producing a pastoral vacuum that eventually led to the base community's decline. This vacuum was aggravated by the Irish priests' more distant pastoral approach and their hostility to the ACO.

The second source of community disempowerment stems from pastoral shifts in the diocese in response to conservative pressure from the Vatican. These shifts, designed to rationalize and standardize local pastoral practices through the formation of an institutionally-sanctioned community council and through an emphasis on proper ritual, undermined the autonomy of grassroots initiatives. Furthermore, they delegitimated the *ad hoc* forms of organizations already developed by laypeople in the base community. This, in turn, generated divisions within the CEB between those who received formal liturgical training (mostly the *Vicentinos*) and those who stressed a more spontaneous approach linking faith and everyday life (those in the original CEB-ACO nucleus). Divisions and mistrust between the two sectors already existed, due in part to the ACO group's militancy and secrecy during the military regime. Father Jaime's characterization of the CEB-ACO nucleus as an intransigent, radical fringe not interested in liturgical matters encouraged greater mistrust from the neighborhood at large, making the work of the CEB-ACO nucleus more difficult.

These pastoral shifts highlight the limits of grassroots innovation in the context of a hierarchical and global church whose institutional interest is to reproduce itself by reinforcing the structures already in place. Even when the bishop is sympathetic to grassroots renewal, as was the case with Hipólito in Nova Iguaçu, the weight of these structures, as part of an all-encompassing edifice, often suffocates the vitality and creativity of local pastoral initiatives. As Christian Smith (1995: 8) notes in a recent essay, "the Roman Catholic Church, to which most CEBs belong, is itself a profoundly nondemocratic institution, based on centralized hierarchy, top-down authority, and orthodoxy-through-discipline." The contradictions between this institutional structure and the CEBs' democratic ideals creates tensions which often cannot be resolved at the local level.

Pedra Bonita's case shows how the interplay of global dynamics in the religious field (i.e., the Vatican "restoration") and in society at large (i.e., the national economic crisis, itself the result of Brazil's insertion in a changing capitalist world-system) created obstacles for progressive pastoral work on the ground. This interplay magnified tensions within the community (between the priest and the CEB-ACO nucleus and between the latter and the *Vicentinos*) and, in Boudon's words, "overturned" the CEB's original emancipatory impetus.

In this sense, Pedra Bonita's case contradicts recent readings of the CEBs' crisis of participation which focus predominantly on internal contradictions in their pastoral-pedagogical methodology. John Burdick (1993) and Cecilia Mariz (1994), for example, argue that the CEBs' emphasis on a rational analysis of reality, literacy, and class-based activism to change social structures fails to resonate with the everyday experience and worldview of the poor. They contend that poor Brazilians continue to live in an "enchanted" world of saints and miracles, to rely mainly on oral forms of expression, and to be concerned primarily with personal affliction and household problems where questions of identity, gender, and race are paramount. Burdick, in particular, argues that the CEBs' pastoral-pedagogical method, based on notions such as consciousness-raising and the organic intellectual, leads logically to intellectual elitism and political vanguardism. Further, Burdick (1993: 47) claims that CEB activists embrace this elitism, willingly deploying their newly-found political awareness to exclude the non-literate, "alienated" masses. This exclusion, in turn, explains the failure of CEBs to attract and mobilize more poor Brazilians.

It is true that CEB pastoral-pedagogical methodology can be potentially elitist, as the concentration of responsibility on the base community nucleus in Pedra Bonita shows. However, we also saw in the informal rotation of liturgical activities how this concentration does not result necessarily in exclusion or the formation of a rigid hierarchical structure in the CEB.[14] It is only in the context of larger ecclesial and socio-economic changes beginning in the mid-1980s that this concentration led to intra-CEB divisions and ultimately to a breakdown of grassroots pastoral initiatives.[15] The formation of a permanent vanguard, such as the ACO group which later became isolated and exhausted, and thus unable to energize community life, was neither the logical result nor the intended objective of CEB members. Rather, the decline of Pedra Bonita's CEB was an unwanted effect generated by changes within the institutional church and in the life conditions of the poor. While these changes are part of global processes beyond local actors' control, they nonetheless exert a powerful impact on micro-practices, limiting the viability and appeal of certain religious choices, forms of organization, and strategies.

The complexity of Pedra Bonita's case highlights the need to study micro-macro links in the sociology of religion, particularly when one is focusing on grassroots movements (cf. Levine 1992: 317–352). While it is important to recognize the richness and relative autonomy of local religious practices, it is also necessary to place them within the institutional and systemic dynamics in which they are embedded. More specifically, future work on local religious activity, and thus on the trajectory of grassroots movements such as CEBs, should pay attention to the impact on everyday life of large-scale processes as diverse as economic restructuring, the crisis of the welfare state, increasing levels of social fragmentation and violence, the crisis of socialism and other modern emancipatory projects, and the reformulation of the Catholic Church's mission. Failure to take such factors into account may result in decontextualized and ahistorical readings, which tend to explain the emergence of complex and often paradoxical collective phenomena, such as the failure of CEBs to mobilize larger segments of the poor, only as the outcome of the rational and intentional behavior of individual actors.

Notes

1 The term "popular" has several meanings in Latin America. Progressive Catholics in Brazil use it to mean "of the people," especially of the organized poor sectors of society. I follow this usage, while recognizing that the term is contested within Brazilian Catholicism.

2 Between January and June 1991 I conducted 16 open-ended interviews with base community members and two with priests who served Pedra Bonita (one French and one Irish). I also observed CEB meetings and activities during this time. I conducted follow-up research in the neighborhood in summer 1995.

3 In 1981 Nova Iguaçu's population was estimated at 1.6 million.

4 Some scholars have argued that base ecclesial communities represented mainly a strategic institutional response to the shortage of priests throughout Latin America (Bruneau 1986). While this reading accurately represents the goals of some church leaders, it fails to capture the theological and pastoral motivations of many priests, nuns, and lay activists. For them, CEBs were a vehicle to implement the new ecclesiologies developed in Vatican II and Medellín.

5 Founded in 1867 in Italy, Catholic Action was initially a conservative movement designed to counter socialism.

6 This pedagogy represents a reformulation of the see-judge-act method under the influence of Brazilian educator Paulo Freire. Freire's work on literacy in the 1960s led him to propose a consciousness-raising method that became the backbone of pastoral work in CEBs (cf., Freire 1972).

7 The interpenetration of the ACO and the CEB is particular to Pedra Bonita. This fact, however, does not make the case study atypical. Although ACO and CEBs are distinct phenomena, all base communities adapt in one form or another the see-judge-act pastoral-pedagogic methodology developed by Catholic Action (cf., Texeira 1988).

8 W. E. Hewitt (1988) has proposed a CEB typology that arranges base communities in a "continuum, ranging from the most organizationally basic devotional groups to the most complex, politically active." Based on this heuristic classification, Pedra Bonita would constitute what he calls a "classical or ideal-type CEB" which engages in neighborhood improvement projects and in both "traditional" and "innovative" religious activities.

9 Progressive Catholic intellectuals adapted the term "organic intellectual" from Italian Marxist Antonio Gramsci (1971), via the work of Brazilian educator Paulo Freire (1972).

10 The conservative drive gathered momentum in the early 1980s with John Paul II's papacy. Broadly, it seeks to re-establish the universality and unity of the church by restoring the symbolic power of the priest's office and by reaffirming the unchangeability of Catholic values. In concrete terms, the drive has weakened

the position of progressive bishops, theologians, and pastoral agents in influential national churches such as Brazil's (Lernoux 1989; Della Cava 1989).

11 Recent Vatican documents affirm the value of CEBs but only under the hierarchy's close supervision. For instance, *The Instruction on Christian freedom and liberation* (1986) states that "The new basic communities . . . are a source of great hope for the Church. Their fidelity to their mission will depend on how careful they are to educate their members in the fullness of the Christian faith through listening to the Word of God, fidelity to the teaching of the Magisterium, to the hierarchical order of the Church, and to the sacramental life" (#69).

12 There is increasing evidence throughout Latin America of the constraining effects of the restoration movement at the grassroots, particularly in parishes where progressive Catholic pastoral strategies had held sway. See, for example, Peña 1992 on Peru and Williams and Peterson 1996 on El Salvador.

13 In his opening address to the fourth CELAM conference in Santo Domingo, John Paul II (1993:56–57) stated that CEBs "must be stamped with a clear ecclesial identity and find in the eucharist, presided over by a priest, the center of their life and communion among their members, in close union with their pastors and full harmony with the church's magisterium."

14 In fact, exclusion in Pedra Bonita's CEB resulted not from the "vanguardist" strategy of the ACO core, but rather from the more conservative efforts at "romanization."

15 For the Brazilian popular church, Pedra Bonita's case calls for a revision of its small group pastoral-pedagogical method. A method which had proved successful in the repressive years of the military regime begins to produce negative unintended consequences in the 1980s. As economic pressure begins to mount on both the *fermento* (leaven) and the mass, the connection between the two grows more fragile. This fact, added to the Vatican restoration drive and the persistence of political clientelism despite the transition to civilian rule, renders the CEB strategy for popular mobilization increasingly ineffective.

References

Benería, L., and F. Shelly, eds. 1992. *Unequal burden.* Boulder, CO: Westview Press.

Bedoyere, M. 1958. *The Cardijn story.* London: Longman, Green, and Co.

Boudon, R. 1979. *The logic of social action.* London: Routledge and Kegan Paul.

——. 1981. *The unintended consequences of social action.* New York: St. Martin's Press.

Bourdieu, P. 1971. Génese et structure du champ religieux. *Reveu Française de Sociologie* 12: 295–334.

Bruneau, T. 1986. Brazil: The Catholic Church and base Christian communities. In *Religion and political conflict in Latin America*, edited by D. Levine, 106–123. Chapel Hill: University of North Carolina Press.

Burdick, J. 1992. Rethinking the study of social movements. In *The making of social movements in Latin America*, edited by A. Escobar and S. Alvarez, 171–184. Boulder, CO: Westview Press.

——. 1993. *Looking for God in Brazil.* Berkeley: University of California Press.

Congregation for the doctrine of the faith. 1986. *Instruction on Christian freedom and liberation.* Washington, DC: United States Catholic Conference.

Daudelin, J. 1992. L'Eglise progressiste au Brésil: La fin d'une mythe? In *L'Amérique et les Amériques*, edited by J. Zylberberg. Quebec: Presses de l'Université de Laval.

Della Cava, R. 1970. *Miracle at Joazeiro.* New York: Columbia University Press.

——. 1989. The "People's Church," the Vatican, and abertura. In *Democratizing Brazil*, edited by A. Stepan, 143–167. New York: Oxford University Press.

Drogus, C. 1992. Popular movements and the limits of political mobilization at the grassroots in Brazil. In *Conflict and competition*, edited by E. Cleary and H. Stewart-Gambino, 63–86. Boulder, CO: Lynne Rienner.

Freire, P. 1972. *A pedagogy of the oppressed.* New York: Herder & Herder.

Gramsci, A. 1971. *Selections from the prison notebooks.* New York: International Publishers.

Hewitt, W. 1988. Christian Base Communities (CEBs): Structure, orientation, and sociopolitical thrust. *Thought* 63: 162–175.

John Paul II. 1993. Opening address to Fourth General Conference of the Latin American Episcopate. In *Santo Domingo and Beyond*, edited by A. Hennelly, 41–60. Maryknoll, NY: Orbis.

Lernoux, P. 1980. *Cry of the people.* New York: Penguin Books.

——. 1989. *People of God.* New York: Viking Press.

Levine, D. 1992. *Popular voices in Latin American Catholicism.* Princeton, NJ: Princeton University Press.

Maduro, O. 1982. *Religion and social conflict.* Maryknoll, NY: Orbis Books.

Mainwaring, S. 1986. *The Catholic Church and politics in Brazil: 1916–1985.* Stanford, CA: Stanford University Press.

Mariz, C. 1994. *Coping with poverty.* Philadelphia, PA: Temple University Press.

Oliveira, J. 1993. *O traço da desigualdade social no Brasil.* Rio de Janeiro: IBGE.

Oliveira, P. 1985. *Religião e dominação de classe.* Petrópolis: Vozes.

Peña, M. 1992. The sodalitium vitae movement in Perú: A rewriting of liberation theology. *Sociological Analysis* 53: 159–173.

Smith, C. 1995. The spirit and democracy: Base Communities, Protestantism, and democratization in Latin America. In *Religion and democracy in Latin America*, edited by W. H. Swatos, 1–25. New Brunswick, NJ: Transaction Publishers.

Smith, J., and I. Wallerstein. 1992. *Creating and transforming households.* Cambridge: Cambridge University Press.

Teixeira, F. 1988. *A gênese das CEBs no Brasil.* São Paulo: Paulinas.

Williams, P., and A. Peterson. 1996. Evangelicals and Catholics in El Salvador: Evolving religious responses to social change. *Journal of Church and State.*

65

INUIT PENTECOSTAL AND EVANGELICAL MOVEMENTS IN THE CANADIAN EASTERN ARCTIC

The case of the healing the land rituals developed by the Canada Awakening Ministries

Frédéric Laugrand and Jarich Oosten

Source: originally published in *Numen*, 54 (2007), 229–69; revised by authors, 2009.

Introduction

Inuit religious movements are not a recent phenomenon. After Christianity was introduced in the Canadian Eastern Arctic at the end of the 19th century, many leaders and shamans started their own religious movements (Blaisel, Laugrand, Oosten 1999). Usually these movements were repressed by local and governmental agencies, and soon Inuit perceived that shamanism and Christianity did not go together. The context of Christianity still provided scope for the combination of new and old traditions. Suluk's movement in Arviat in the 1940s and Armand Tagoona's church in Qamanittuaq in the 1970s testify to the creativity of Inuit developing their own forms of Christianity. Since the early 1970s, the rapid development of Pentecostal and Evangelical movements has given a new dynamics to Inuit Christianity.[1]

In this paper we focus our analysis on these contemporary forms of Inuit religiosity. We explore the development of Evangelical and Pentecostal movements in the Canadian Eastern Arctic, i.e., in Nunavik (Northern Quebec) and Nunavut focusing on the views of the participants and their practices (see Oosten 2005), and examine in more detail recent developments, notably the case of the healing the land rituals developed by the Canada Awakening Ministries[2] with the collaboration of a group from Fiji. Finally we discuss some of the basic patterns characterizing these new Christian movements. Although these movements are quite modern, they shape old and new features in a variety of ways. They claim to introduce discontinuity with the past as well as new forms of solidarity integrating modern ideologies in a Christian perspective. They claim to heal society providing space and context for the preservation of local views, models, and practices in a Christian framework. We will see that the relation to land as well as connections to shamanism remain central issues in contemporary Inuit discourses and forms of Pentecostalism.

Although most of the new religious movements strongly oppose shamanic traditions, some practices evoke these very traditions, especially to elders who have witnessed shamanic practices in the past. How can such a perception be explained? How do these new movements integrate Christianity and traditional beliefs today? We do not wish reduce these movements to modern and capitalistic ideology in a Weberian perspective but instead focus on problems of transition and transformation. How do Pentecostal and Evangelical movements manage to preserve that which they break from, to use an expression from Robbins (2004:5)[3].

Networks and globalisation: the Fijian connection

Pentecostal and Evangelical movements often encourage their adherents to travel abroad and bring in outsiders to preach. Thus Canada Awakening Ministries[4] promoted a few trips of Inuit new converts to Greenland in 2002 where they facilitated the building of a new church in Nuuk. In 2003 sixteen Inuit were brought to Israel and in 2004 twenty of them visited the same country again. In 2006 another trip was organized as the 7th Annual Inuit Ministries Holy Land Pilgrimage to Israel. During these trips Christian and Inuit traditions are integrated, notwithstanding the shamanic connotations of the latter. Thus the Inuit drum is presented as "the heartbeat of life" and a bone carving of an Inuit drum dancer as "a symbol of peace, joy and celebration." A Fijian Healing the Land Team was organized to restore the natural resources in the Fiji area and a trip of Fijians and Inuit to Israel in 2006 was planned. It was decided that in July 2006 the Fijian Healing the Land team would travel to Nunavut to heal the land[5].

Robbins (2004:5) indicated that lack of good descriptions of rituals is one of the greatest lacunas in research on Pentecostalism and Evangelism over the world. As for Inuit, it is not always clear to what extent Pentecostal and evangelical rituals really exercise a great appeal on them. Also, very little is known about the content of these practices. Therefore it is worthwhile to examine the healing the land rituals that were developed by Canada Awakening Ministries and show how they combine features from the past with more contemporary elements. A Fijian Healing the Land Team was organized to restore the natural resources in the Fiji area and a trip of Fijians and Inuit to Israel in 2006 was planned. It was decided that in July 2006 the Fijian Healing the Land team would travel to Nunavut to heal the land.

Robbins (2004:5) indicated that lack of good descriptions of rituals is one of the greatest lacunas in research on Pentecostalism and Evangelism over the world. As for Inuit, it is not always clear to what extent Pentecostal and evangelical rituals really exercise a great appeal on them. Also, very little is known about the content of these practices. Therefore it is worthwhile to examine the healing the land rituals that were developed by Canada Awakening Ministries and show how they combine features from the past with more contemporary elements.

a) Healing the land

In connecting a transformation of people to a transformation of the land, the Canada Awakening Ministries evokes old Inuit traditions about the connection of the health of people and that of the land. Several Inuit Elders stated that when the land became too hot by the transgressions of people they might shift their residence.

Maggie Akpahatak, the pastor from Aupaluk, related:

> Many people, including our government leaders, don't see any connection between prayer and repentance with the healing of the land, but indigenous peoples have long understood the connection that there is between people and land. What people do in a particular area can either defile or pollute the land, or it can cleanse and bringing healing to it. How people speak and act can determine the productivity of the land on which they live.

Armbruster described on the website of Canada Awakening Ministries how ancient Thule archaeological sites at Resolute Bay were cleansed through prayer. Thule people are presented as "a very controlled, male dominant people" who abused their women routinely. The website describes how Allie and Susan Salluviniq, respectively the town foreman and the mayor of Resolute Bay began to heal the land by praying:

> When these legal 'gatekeepers' begin to take responsibility for the sins that have defiled that part of the earth where they now have legal authority, you can be sure that something will happen to the land itself. The land will become healed so that the dry, barren desolate areas will begin to become productive, and will support the inhabitants that live there.

The quotations show the close connection between religion and politics. The legal gatekeepers, the dignitaries in the administrative system, should accept their responsibility to integrate their politic and religious perspective. Then the land can begin to heal. The healing will bear fruit in the reappearance of animals. In October 2005, Armbruster thus reports the observations of a few Inuit hunters: "They found that every caribou cow had at least one calf, and that some had more than one. It is very unusual and uncommon to see a whole herd of caribou cows with even one calf." Ambruster also related how the land around Rankin Inlet was cleansed during Thanksgiving week-end of 2005. At a traditional meeting place, where game had become scarce, about ten miles north of Rankin Inlet, the land was cleansed of its defilements by partaking of communion with one another, and applying the power of the blood of Jesus to the land itself. Again the ritual is not just perceived as a religious act and Armbruster has to find some "legal authority" that takes responsibility for the transformation:

> I realize that there needs to be a legal authority to do this by the gatekeepers and people in authority where one is praying. In view of the fact that Veronica Dewar is a prominent leader among the Inuit, and the Past President of the Inuit Women's Association, I believe that her presence among us added to the legal authority to what we were doing.

Again success became visible. Veronica Dewar informed Armbruster on Christmas day of 2005 that there were lots of caribou around Rankin Inlet. The healing of the land not only involved the return of animals, even trees and plants were returning to a once barren land at Resolute Bay:

> I am told that now in some places, even in the High Arctic, edible berries are beginning to grow as well. . . . There has never been a berry season in the High Arctic-only desolate wilderness. [. . .] Larry Audlaluk and Susan Salluviniq even shared with me how that trees are now starting to appear above the ground that were once buried and below the surface. . . .
>
> Could it be that the treeless Arctic tundra was once covered with trees, and was once like a garden, and that it will once again be covered with trees, and become like a garden once again?

Minerals and land resources would be affected positively as well, and the website concludes that we see that there are signs on the earth that God is healing the land in response to the prayers of His people.

b) Reconciliation at Rankin Inlet

In July 2006 the Fijian Healing Land arrived in Nunavut and first stopped in Rankin Inlet. The first step was to diagnose the causes of the wounds of the land. According to Ambruster not only the original inhabitants of the land, but also the newcomers would have to be involved:

> The original inhabitants have a legitimate claim to a special relationship with the land, but often they hold resentments towards the later groups, and the types of changes that they have brought in building buildings and changing the landscape in ways that the originals did not approve.

In Armbruster's perspective the reconciliation of the land thus requires a reconciliation of the groups concerned:

> In Rankin Inlet, on the morning of Monday, July 10, some of the descendants of the original inhabitants of the area began to humble themselves, and to repent of the bitterness and anger they that held in their hearts towards the descendants of the later inhabitants. On that same morning . . . , the later people and their descendants began to repent to the original inhabitants for not having observed proper protocol, of having simply come into the area, and doing their own thing without even asking for permission. Many tears were shed as representatives from both groups began to embrace one another. . . .
>
> Some 30 believers showed up who wanted to bring cleansing to the land where it had become defiled through past conflicts and violence.
>
> Then a ritual of reconciliation was celebrated within a circle of stones marking the site of an ancient dwelling.
>
> The original inhabitants then did what had never been done many years previously, and that was to officially welcome the later groups to this area. They welcomed them to come and join them inside the circle where they were standing inside of one of the original dwellings.
>
> This time, the later groups came into the circle with a legal authority and permission that would enable the two groups to enter into their inheritance together, to see the land cleansed and healed, and to produce enough to provide for all.

Thus the original inhabitants are endowed with a "legal authority" to welcome the newcomers on the land. By standing in the stone circles they represent their ancestors and nullify the tensions of the past. At the end of the ceremony newcomers and original inhabitants embraced each other.

The reconciliation of the two parties is not sufficient and a relation between the land and Christ has to be made.

> The two groups then partook of Communion with one another, and then, together, with the land itself as David Aglukark, one of the original inhabitants symbolically applied the blood of Jesus to the land, and Tagak Curley, one of the later inhabitants, is waiting to apply the bread which speaks of the Body of Jesus Christ which was broken for us.

Then prayers were put into a hole:

> "People then put their prayer requests into the hole as well, which contained their heart's desires, and what they wanted to see God do for the land that they had inherited from their fathers. A stone memorial was then erected right on this historic site.

Water, oil and salt were applied to the land:

> The water speaks of "living water" (John 7:37, 38), the oil speaks of the anointing which destroys the yoke (Isaiah 10:27), and the salt is to be a preservative agent against corruption and defilement (Matthew 5:13).

The mixture of oil, salt and water is blessed by the Fijian delegation before it is applied to the land.

> The water, oil and salt had previously been spiritually cleansed through the word of God and prayer, and set apart as a healing agent to bring a cleansing of the land's defilements, and a healing to the land.

Thus the reconciliation between newcomers and original inhabitants was followed by a healing of the land in four steps: 1) applying the bread and wine to the land, 2) putting prayers into a hole, 3) erecting a stone monument and, 4) the application of oil water and salt to the land as a healing agent. The first step requires a cooperation of aboriginal people and newcomers who have just been reconciled. The second step builds on the important tradition prayer, and a physical connection between the land and the prayers is made by putting them into a hole. The third step evokes the Inuit tradition of making *inuksuit* (stone markers) on the land that now become an emblem of the healing of the land. The final step involves the relation between the Fijians and the land embedding the ritual in a global perspective encompassing North and South. Within two days the land was abounding with caribou:

> According to the wildlife manager in Rankin Inlet, some 15,000 of them showed up right at the spot where the forgiveness and

> cleansing had taken place, and where the healing of the land had been prayed for. Local residents stated that the caribou in this number had not been seen in the area for some four years.

c) Healing at Pangnirtung

The Fiji Healing the Land Team flew to Pangnirtung on July 13, 2006. That same evening a group of believers drove through a place

> where drug dealings are alleged to have taken place, and in an area near there, in previous generations, shamanistic practices had taken place, and in some cases, curses had been released that needed to be broken. Strong prayers and intercession was waged right from that very spot.

Creating a healing circle to cleanse the land

On Saturday evening of July 15, Fijian pastor Vuniani invited the original inhabitants and later people (including White people) to come to the front in two groups facing each other. Then he invited Armbruster to take over the meeting and a general repentance of all participants for their attitudes and behaviour towards members of the other group followed. Armbruster emphasizes that even though outsiders were present (including a plane load of 12 Greenlanders who had come to Pangnirtung for this Healing the Land Conference, and one or two representatives from a number of communities in Baffin Island): "The people and leadership of Pangnirtung clearly saw this as their Conference. It was done under their authority, and with their blessing. They took ownership of both the Conference and the follow-up afterwards." As in Rankin Inlet, the repentance was followed by embracements between the members of the two groups. The following morning, Sunday morning of July 16, Anglican and Full Gospel Churches joined in a Communion. The Healing the Land Team washed the feet of all the spiritual leaders of the community. Armbruster reports that after a sermon about the crippled man at the pool of Bethesda, a miracle happened: "A man called, Jeetaloo, who had been bound to a wheelchair for some four years, for the first time got out of his wheelchair and walked!"

In Pangnirtung the land was also cleansed with oil, water and salt. Armbruster argues that the land already belonged to the Lord because he had created Pangnirtung and the whole procedure of cleansing was much less elaborate. It took place within the gym. Soil of the land was collected in a bucket and mixed with water, salt and the oil. It was "prayed over by the Fiji Healing the Land Team to be given back to the Lord while the leaders and elders of Pangnirtung gathered around to give their agreement and approval."

Apparently the defilement of the land was not seen in terms of long term conflicts as in Rankin Inlet but in a short-term perspective relating to the community today. On July 17 Loie Mike wrote: "Our land was defiled by you and me. Whenever you and I commit idolatry, adultery, shedding of innocent blood, breaking of covenants, and hold back our tithes and offerings, we defile the land, and it needs healing."

During the final evening service with the Fiji Team in Pangnirtung, on Thursday evening of July 20, a beautiful rainbow appeared over the whole community. Fijian pastor Vuniani pointed out that the rainbow was a sign of the covenant that God had made with man to remove the curse, and of his promise never to let the earth by cursed by a universal flood ever again.

The need for moral reform

Solving social problems is high on the Pentecostal agenda. Members of the Full Gospel Church do not drink alcohol, discourage smoking tobacco and are not permitted to substitute marriage with common-law relationships.

Political leaders, such as Tagak Curley elected in Rankin Inlet, have campaigned against the inclusion of sexual orientation in the Human Rights Act. Tibetts (2003) reported, "James Arreak said he was testifying on behalf of Inuit elders who oppose a 'gay tidal wave.' The Inuit, explained Mr. Arreak, strongly oppose same-sex marriage because it violates survival through procreation. "Inuit values would say that gay people cannot create life, that they cannot produce a child."

Pentecostal Inuit have also campaigned for the restoration of religious instruction in the schools (Bell 2004). In Nunavik, many people and at least three communities, notably Salluit, contested the teaching of Darwin's theory in local schools arguing that this theory about evolution off ends Inuit traditional beliefs.21

During the Arviat Men's Event that took place in Arviat in August 2004, David Aglukark, Tagak Curley and James Arreak extensively discussed marriages and intergenerational relationships, emphasizing the need for the protection of the institutions of marriage and the family.

At The Youth of Puvirnituq Event in 2004 Pastors E. Sallualuk, Q. Tookaluk, and J. Alloloo addressed the young people.

> The youth were exhorted to become violent in the spirit against the evil spirits of suicide and lust that had been attacking them from without, and against the attitudes of bitterness and unforgiveness that had been attacking them from within. . . .
>
> While youth were crying out to the Lord, one night, this young girl . . . came up to plead with her fellow youth to forgive their parents, to let the past go, to no longer hang on to the old resentments and bitterness. In between sobs, she spoke passionately and

> powerfully, and her words hit home with her fellow young people. Parents were also exhorted to reach out to their youth and children, and to turn their hearts to their children, so that the hearts of the children would be restored to the fathers. . . .
>
> Many of the youth began to weep as they wondered what to do next. . . . Then it happened. Many of the youth did not walk, but literally ran to their parents to fling themselves toward them as they were sitting in their chairs or standing. They were completely wholehearted to release forgiveness, and to hold nothing back.[6]

A relative of a young man who attempted to commit suicide that very night requested the people to pray for that man and the next day he returned to tell the people that his relative had not only survived, but was even fully recovered.[7]

The Third Promise Keeper Event "Gender and Generations Healed" held in Rankin Inlet on the 2005 Thanksgiving Weekend was dedicated to the topic of "Marriages of Integrity." Social problems were discussed such as healing the gap between the generations. Fathers were encouraged to create bonds with their children, and a plea was made to retain the wholeness of the family and avoid separation victimizing the children:

> Each family member is unique and special, and yet each needs to be connected in order to achieve their own destiny and purpose in life. . . . This is how the world will be changed — one family at a time — as each comes into oneness, wholeness and healing rather than to normalize and legalize our promiscuity and disconnectedness and isolationism from one another[8].

Pentecostal and Evangelical movements also often provide new opportunities for women to develop public leadership, hence the good relationships between these groups and the Pauktuutit Inuit Women's Association. They wish to involve more women in religious activities. Since 2006, a Linking Hearts Annual Women's Conference is organized with invited women leaders from other Canadian regions.

All these intitiatives aim to promote the constitution of solid Pentecostal communities. In contrast to Pentecostal movements in Africa, studied by Meyer (1999), Inuit groups do not so much emphasize a global community but a healthy local group.

Redefining connections to the past

Transformation of a community also implies redefining connections to the past. This is an old tradition. Inuit elders have always emphasized that one's wrongdoings would affect the life of children and grandchildren. Conversely, the misfortunes of people are often related to the deeds of their ancestors and namesakes. Therefore Pentecostal and Evangelical perceptions that many contemporary problems are linked to the sins of the previous generations have great appeal for Inuit.

> Since those sins committed in previous generations are still affecting our generation today, this generation can break that curse and defilement by identifying with the sins of our fathers, and repenting for them. We might say "Well I was not there when these things happened,' or that 'I didn't do those things personally.'

Thus transformation implies connecting to the past as well as redefining it. This ambiguity of the past is a structural feature of the modern discourse. The *inummariit*, the true Inuit of the past, represent a generation that was able to survive out on the land without modern technology, but they are also associated with taboos and superstitions that should be rejected.

Today, many elders favour a revalorization of the past. The Nunavut Government followed suit in coining the notion of *Inuit qaujimajatuqangit* (Inuit Traditional knowledge). Inuit should reconnect to the *inummariit*, their ancestors and their way of life. The Pentecostal and Evangelical movements connect to this problem of redefining the past focusing not only on the *inummariit* but also on external agents such as whalers and traders. The Fiji Healing the Land team therefore also visited two places with strong historical connotations: Marble Island, an island northeast of Rankin Inlet, associated with whalers as well as with traditional practices, and Kekerten, an island in Cumberland Sound, where the Scottish whalers had a station.

a) Marble Island

On July 11, 2006, some twenty-five Inuit from Rankin Inlet, eleven members of the *Healing the Land Team* from Fiji, and Roger and Marge Armbruster travelled by boat from Rankin Inlet to Marble Island located at a distance of some 25–30 miles to cleanse and heal the land. Armbruster summarizes an origin myth of the island relating that an old woman made ta wish that the ice would be transformed into marble so that her spirit could live on in that island. Armbruster does not question the existence of such a spirit, but wonders about its moral nature:

Clearly, we can see that this refers to some kind of an ancestral spirit that is alleged to live on this strange island of pure white rock which it is said to have first materialized as if by magic. The question needs to be asked, "Is this spirit motivated by fear of by love?"

Armbruster explains that people who go to the island are told that they must crawl a few feet in respect of the old woman's spirit:

> In fact, some legends have it that if people do not bow down and "crawl" to show respect for this ancestral spirit, that they will die within two years. I do not know if these myths were created by some of the original shamans, but I do know that not all of the shamans were plugged into the dark side of the spirit world. Some were true prophets of God who prepared the way for the coming of the gospel, and used their spiritual authority to encourage their people to accept the teachings of the Bible.

Armbruster does not reject the shamanic past completely but integrates it in his Christian perspective postulating that shamans prepared the way for the coming of the Gospel. According to him, part of Marble Island's special place is due to old Inuit traditions, another part results from the presence of the white people. Armbruster refers to the James Knight expedition of 1719 that was wrecked on the island and all members of the expedition died on the island. He adds a long list of disasters relating to Marble Island and emphasises the many forms of sicknesses and diseases which were brought to that place by the whalers who took Inuit wives and begot many children:

> As a result, as the children born to these relationships grew up, imagine their identity crisis, as the children were part Inuit and part non-Inuit. Without their non-Inuit fathers not there to raise them, and to love them, the children suffered, and many had to struggle to accept themselves, and to believe that they were just as valuable as children who had fathers, and whose parents were both Inuit. Further, the mothers could not have felt other than used, exploited and without self-esteem. There was no equality in the relationships.

Armbruster identifies four particular areas "that bring defilement to the land, and that affects the environment in which we live today": "1. Idolatry, witchcraft, or the worship of ancestral spirits or the impersonal gods of nature; 2. Adultery, or any kind of sexual sin or perversion; 3. The shedding of innocent blood; 4. The breaking of treaties and covenants."

When the group arrived, "nobody came on to the island crawling, or intimated that the spirit that controlled this island could bring a curse upon those who had come here, because they knew that the power of blessing is greater than the power of cursing." Armbruster specifies that the healing ritual required the healing experience already acquired by the *Fiji Healing the Land Team* under the legal authority of the indigenous tribal chiefs throughout Fiji as well as the presence of descendants of the original inhabitants of the land, descendants of the people who have practiced shamanism, and white people such as Roger and Marge Armbruster, who could identify with the descendants of European and American whalers. The ritual of the cleansing of the land is not described on the website, but it was probably done very much in the same way as in Rankin by applying the bread and wine representing the flesh and blood of Christ to the land.

According to Armbruster, the land cannot be cleansed by money, but only "by the shedding of blood, for life is in the blood." He thus explains that, "It will ultimately either be the blood of the family who sinned, or it will be the blood of Jesus which continually cleanses us from *all* sin whenever it is applied," but that, "Justice demands that sin be atoned by blood." After the ritual a Fijian and an Inuk reported that "a tarp of defilement that had covered the land was being lifted as the land was cleansed." Finally, a memorial was made by piling stones so it "would serve for the next generation but also as a sign of blessing to God."

b) Kekerten

When the Fiji Team arrived in Pangnirtung in July 2006, the issue was raised that some of the main problems in the community went back to the sins of adultery committed when people still lived in Kekerten Island in Cumberland Sound, some fifty kilometres south of Pangnirtung. Present-day elders in Pangnirtung acknowledge that at the time of the whalers many Inuit men would allow their wives have sexual intercourse with the whalers in exchange for tobacco and cigarettes.

Loie Mike related that present problems went back to a shamanic curse which was effected in 1970 when people exceeded their whalequotas. "Local Inuit say that since that time, the number of whales diminished even more, and they have never since been as plentiful as they once were." A collective trip to Kekerten Historic Park was organized on July 19, 2006, involving some forty people and eight boats. Besides three Fijians, the group included young believers and elders. The whole group gathered together within the foundations of one of the original storehouses in a circle and the healing process was led by the leader of the *Fiji Healing the Land Team.*" The group assembled in a circle around the original flag pole that that had been erected in the island beside the largest station house in 1857.

A prayer was spoken and two elders explained what had happened in Kekerten island. Armbruster reports:

> The stories were told about how the Inuit women were used by the whalers for their own sexual gratification. However, the fault was not only with the whalers. The Inuit men realized that their fathers had allowed their wives to be exploited for sexual purposes by the whalers, sometimes in exchange only for something like tobacco.

The group divided into two sub-groups, a male and a female one, each group being asked to repent.

> the male descendants of these Inuit men who allowed their wives to be used by the whalers in exchange only for tobacco got down on their knees in front of the women present, and repented for their sin, and the sin of their fathers. They realized that their father's sin was also their sin, in that sexual sin had persisted until this day. . . . a woman elder is standing in front of the men to release forgiveness, and to speak on behalf of her own grandmother and great grandmother in releasing the men for having allowed the women to be used. She very humbly released total forgiveness, and also acknowledged and repented on behalf of the women who had sinned as well.

In the first stage of the ritual men and women repented and apologized to each other.

In the second stage, Armbruster together with the Anglican Minister from Pangnirtung, repented "on behalf of the European and American whalers for their horrendous exploitation of the Inuit, for not having observed proper protocol and respect and for having used their women."

> After the identificational repentance by the men, and release of forgiveness by the women, both husbands and wives began to embrace one another, and to talk about things in private if they had any issues between them that needed to be repented of.

The collective repentance was followed by individual exchange as husbands and wives discussed the issues they had between them and repented their wrongdoings.

In the next stage of the ritual the shamanic curse was reversed and transformed into a blessing:

> Further, the Inuit identified with the sins of their fathers wherever they had put curses on the land, such as with the shaman who had cursed those government officials who charged an Inuk man for surpassing the quota on whales during the 1970s, resulting in a further depletion of the whales. That curse was changed into a blessing, so that the curse would be reversed, and transformed into a blessing, and a returning of the whales in greater number.

Pastor Vuniani read out aloud with the participants, Deuteronomy 33:13–16a, 19 and Psalm 148:7–10, that stress the richness of the resources from the earth. Finally as in preceding cleansings of the land water, oil and salt that had been prayed over and sanctified unto the Lord were applied to the land. In this case they were poured on to a pile of rocks in Kerkerten Historical site:

> Now the curse was reversed and the water around Kekerten changed to its original dark colour, and a new kind of fish was seen in the water.

Discussion and conclusions

Evangelical and Pentecostal movements in Nunavut have developed in close cooperation between religious leaders in the North and Pentecostal and Evangelical organisations down South. They have a strong social commitment focusing on the solving of social problems in the North.

The Healing circles that developed in the 1990s (Lepage 1997; Arnakaq 1999) were also closely connected to the new movements, and today their leaders often play an important role in the expanding Pentecostal and Evangelical movements. The Healing Circles focused on human suffering. They present the past as a source of wisdom as well as of suffering. By reconnecting to the old traditions people can be healed from their pain and suffering. The causes of suffering are often attributed to the coming of white men and the institutions they introduced. Angaangaq who organizes healing circles recalls that "When the white men arrived, they made Inuit small." He emphasized that

> The complexity of social problems is deep and disturbing. Why are there so many? One of the greatest reasons is that Inuit are being put down by the people who came up north. T ey did not come to serve Inuit, they came to take over. And of course when someone takes over your life, you lose your own identity. You lose your own security. You lose your own traditions. We are clinging on to them.
> (Suvaguuq 2004:37)

Pentecostal and Evangelical churches apply a similar reasoning and tend to develop similar concepts of regeneration. Many of their leaders are "reborn" and only became religious leaders after deeply sufferring from the severe social problems affecting modern Nunavut.

Today, a close network of political and religious leaders supports the evangelical movements and churches in local communities. Although evangelism has spread rapidly in the Eastern Arctic, its institutional basis remains weak. Many Inuit still attend large scale services and meetings, but that does not imply that they will leave their old churches. The Evangelical and Pentecostal movements have a strong appeal, but they also evoke strong resistance and elders associate marked features of these movements with shamanic traditions. They also object to being too religious. Especially in the last ten years the Canada Awakening Ministries, supported by the Sentinel Group, has developed an ambitious program to connect North and South, political and religious order and to transform the land and society into a new religious and political order. The covenant signed at Parliament Hill on June 21 testifies to these ambitions. It illustrates how evangelical leaders claim the role of representatives of the First Nations. This ambition is clearly expressed in the rituals of healing the land. Armbruster tries to give a legal foundation to these rituals by involving administrative authorities, but it is quite clear that the consent of the communities is not really required. The evangelical leaders themselves organize the rituals and decide how the various significant categories aboriginal people, newcomers, men, women etc. will be represented. These healing rituals evoke traditional rituals as well as Western traditions. Rituals of cleansing the land appear to already have existed before the coming of Christianity. Thus missionary E. J. Peck reports that the Nunagisaktut carried the confessions of the people to Sedna and in doing so prepared the land for hunting (Laugrand, Oosten and Trudel 2006). In the traditional rituals people had to respect the land and to adapt to it. Thus people had to follow the rules of the location, crawl to Marble Island, give pieces of meat at specific river crossings, avoid specific places etc. In the Pentecostal rituals we find an inverse approach. Precisely these rules are abolished and the land is subordinated to the new religious and political order. In this respect the Pentecostal rituals evoke Western traditions where explorers claimed the land by hoisting the national flag on a pole inserted in the land. In this way the land was subordinated to the political order represented by the newcomers, and the relations of the original inhabitants to the land were subordinated to this new order. In the Pentecostal rituals the new order is a transcendental order subordinating the land to Christ. The relevant groups are defined in terms of modern ideology (such as autochthones and allochthones, men and women) and they confess and apologize to each other. Only after these confessions and apologies can the land be cleansed. Legal authorities should be present to authorize the proceedings. The application of the bread and wine, representing the flesh and blood of Christ, the elements of water, salt and oil effect this transformation that is then objectifyed in the erection of a stone monument as a lasting memorial of this transformation of the land. The ritual operates with a modern ideology that is affected through a ritual of repentance. Men and women, newcomers and original inhabitants have to become each other's equals and repent all actions that deviated from this course. Thus the new transcendent moral order implies a cleansed land inhabited by equal individuals that respect each other as equals. The building of Inuksuit (cairns of stones), now interpreted as a sign of a new covenant, connects the new ritual to the old tradition and a divine sign (a rainbow, the lifting of the tarp etc.) confirm that the ritual is accepted by God. Thus the ritual brings together traditional, legal, political and religious dimensions.

The rituals fit perfectly into the modern ideology of the Canadian state and thus they can easily be perceived as a bridge from the present state of suffering of the aboriginal people to a new political and religious order that harmoniously unifies modern Christian and political ideals. The rituals play on the old ideals of confession and repentance, the use of *inuksuit* as markers, the close relationship between the health of society and that of the land. In this respect, they provide a recognizable idiom that allows for the transition to a modern political structure. In their emphasis on global relationships they connect Inuit to Fijians and Israel testifying to a new order of mobility where all nations meet in the context of this new transcendent order.

Notes

1 Studies of Inuit Pentecostalism in Nunavik are rare. Some information is provided by Dorais 2001; 1997, and Fletcher and Kirmayer 1997. Stuckenberger 2005 provides a case study of it in Broughton Island.

2 The Anglican Church worked in the region from 1929, and stressed the work of the Holy Spirit from the beginning. CAM was founded in 1978 by Roger and Marge Armbruster, and become a dominant factor in the development of Evangelical and Pentecostal movements in the Canadian Arctic. Other ministries tend to connect to this ministry

3 According to Robbins, Pentecostal and Evangelical relationships with traditional cultures are marked by both rejection and preservation. Our paper contributes to this debate that has especially developed among Africanists (see Mary 1999; Laurent 2003). For books on Pentecostal movements see for example Corten 1995; Coleman 2000; Freston 2001. Willaime 1999 and Robbins 2004 provide excellent overviews of the extensive literature.

4 http://www.canadaawakening.com/northwinds/northwindhome.html>. Consulted on March 18, 2007.

5 On Pentecostalism in Fijian villages, see Newland 2004.

6 http://www.threecordministries.org/Arctic_Adventures.htm>. Consulted on March 18, 2007.

7 http://www.canadaawakening.com/pages/Fall%202004%20Reports/PuvirnituqYouth.html>. Consulted on March 18, 2007.

8 http://www.canadaawakening.com/2005%20Reports/December%2005/genderandgenerations.html>. Consulted on March 18, 2007.

References

Anonymous
2006 "Darwin Put on Ice in Northern Quebec Community." CBC News, May 19.

Arnakaq Allattangit, M.
1999 "Healing Circles. Mamisarniup missanut nalunaijaijuq." Inuktitut 85: 33–39.

Bell, Jim
2004 "Fundamentalists Seek Foothold in Legislature." Nunatsiaq News, February 13.

Coleman, Simon
2000 The Globalisation of Charismatic Christianity: Spreading the Gospel of Prosperity. Cambridge: CUP.

Comaroff, Jean, and John L. Comaroff
1993 (ed.) Modernity and its Malcontents: Ritual and Power in Postcolonial Africa. Chicago: Chicago University Press.
Corten, Andre
1995 Le pentecôtisme au Brésil. Emotion du pauvre et romantisme théologique. Paris: Karthala.
Dorais, Louis-Jacques
1997 "Pratiques et sentiments religieux à Quaqtaq: continuité et modernité." Etudes Inuit Studies 21(1–2):255–267.
2001 Quaqtaq. Modernity and Identity in an Inuit Community. Toronto: University of Toronto Press.
Fletcher, Christopher M., and Laurence Kirmayer
1997 "Spirit Work: Nunavimmiut Experiences of Affliction and Healing." Etúdes Inuit Studies 21(1–2):189–208.
Freston, P.
2001 Evangelicals and Politics in Asia, Africa and Latin America. Cambridge: CUP.
Laugrand, Frédéric
2002 Mourir et renaître. La réception du christianisme par les Inuit de l'Arctique canadien,
1890–1940. Québec and Leiden: Presses de l'Université Laval and CNWS.
Laugrand, Frédéric, Jarich Oosten, and Maaki Kakkik
2003 Keeping the Faith. Iqaluit: Nunavut Arctic College.
Laugrand, Frédéric, Jarich Oosten, and Francois Trudel
2006 Apostle to the Inuit. The Journals and Ethnographic Notes of Edmund James
Laurent, Pierre-Joseph
2003 Les pentecôtistes du Burkina-Faso. Mariage, pouvoir et guérison. Paris: Karthala.
Lepage, Eva
1997 "Healing circles in Nunavik. Mamisarniq Nunavimmit." Inuktitut 81: 49–58.
Mary, André
1999 "Culture pentecôtiste et charisme visionnaire au sein d'une Eglise indépendante africaine." Archives de sciences sociales des religions 105(1):29–50.
Meyer, Birgit
1999 Translating the Devil: Religion and Modernity Among the Ewe in Ghana. Edinburgh: UP.
Newland, Lynda
2004 "Turning the Spirits into Witchcraft: Pentecostalism in Fijian Villages." Oceania 75(1):1–18.
Oosten, Jarich
2005 "Ideals and Values in the Participants' View of their Culture: A View from the Inuit Field." Social Anthropology 13(2):185–198.
Oosten, Jarich and Frédéric Laugrand
1999 (ed.) Transition to Christianity. (Inuit Perspectives on the 20th century, vol. 1.) Iqaluit: Nunavut Arctic College.
2001 Travelling and Surviving on Our Land. (Inuit Perspectives on the 20th century, vol. 2.) Iqaluit: Nunavut Arctic College.

2002 Inuit Qaujimajatuqangit: Shamanism and Reintegrating Wrongdoers. (Inuit Perspectives on the 20th century, vol. 4.) Iqaluit: Nunavut Arctic College.

Oosten, Jarich, Frédéric Laugrand, and Wim Rasing
1999 (ed.) Perspectives on Traditional Law: Interviewing Inuit Elders. vol. 2. Iqaluit: Nunavut Arctic College.

Robbins, Joel
2004 "The Globalization of Pentecostal and Charismatic Christianity." Annual Review of Anthropology 33:117–143.

Stuckenberger, Nicole
2005 Community at Play. Social and Religious Dynamics in the Modern Inuit Community of Qikiqtarjuaq. Utrecht: Rien Rabbers.

Suvaguuq
2004 "The Nuluaq Project: Bringing People Together to Heal the Hurt." Suvaguuq, National Newsletter on Inuit Social and Cultural Issues, XV, 2; 4 pages.

Tibetts, Janice
2003 "Same-Sex marriage 'alien to us,' Inuit tell commons committee." National Post, May 1.

Willaime, Jean-Paul
1999 "Le pentecôtisme: contours et paradoxes d'un protestantisme.

66

'CULTURE' AS A TOOL AND AN OBSTACLE

Missionary encounters in post-Soviet Kyrgyzstan

Mathijs Pelkmans

Source: *Journal of the Royal Anthropological Institute*, (N.S.) 13 (2007), 881–99.

The relatively large number of converts from Islam to evangelical Christianity in post-Soviet Kyrgyzstan is exceptional in the Muslim world and has challenged local confidence that Islam is an inseparable element of Kyrgyz nationality. I argue that part of the missionary success stems from unexpected synergies between communist cultural legacies and new evangelical approaches. Both communists and evangelicals attempted to advance their ideals by disconnecting religion and culture. But although these efforts delivered tangible results, they also had the (unintended) consequence of folklorizing and objectifying 'culture', thereby partly re-inscribing the ethnic boundaries that they intended to overcome.

In May 2004 an American evangelical missionary invited me to attend the circumcision feast (*sunnet toi*) of an Uzbek pastor's son in the south of Kyrgyzstan.[1] The host and his family had made extensive preparations for their numerous guests, including twenty-five foreign missionaries and about a hundred Kyrgyz and Uzbek Christians.[2] In many respects the celebrations resembled similar non-Christian festivities. The guests were seated at long tables covered with typical party food: fried bread, colourful candy, melons, nuts, rice dishes, mineral water, and soda, though no alcoholic drinks. Professional musicians played local instruments as well as a Yamaha synthesizer, once in a while interrupting the music to announce the arrival of new guests. Less usual were the dance ensembles that performed throughout the day, featuring missionaries and representatives of various ethnic groups – Uyghur, Kyrgyz, and Uzbek. Speeches were made. An American missionary spoke of the biblical origin of circumcision, arguing that although in Kyrgyzstan circumcision is often thought of as a Muslim custom, it had biblical roots. He cited passages from the Bible that described the 'covenant of circumcision' between Abraham and God (Genesis 17: 9–11), insisting that such similarities between Central Asian and Hebrew customs highlighted that Christianity should be seen as an Eastern instead of a Western religion.

What made this celebration special was that it simultaneously employed and challenged locally popular ideas of culture and religion. The celebration was provocative because the Christian participants actively appropriated cultural markers – circumcision itself as well as 'national' dresses, foods, dances, and music – that in Kyrgyzstan are usually associated with Muslimness. From an evangelical perspective, this Kyrgyz-Uzbek atmosphere was the feast's prime attraction. It ostensibly demonstrated that missionaries were sensitive to local culture and showed that Christianity was compatible with Central Asian cultural identities. At the same time, the conspicuous role of foreign missionaries in financing, organizing, and consuming the event raised pertinent questions concerning the nature of this 'identity'. A remark by an American missionary during the festivities was telling in this respect: 'I know that missionaries have often been accused of destroying culture. But if you look here, I would say that we are doing the exact opposite'.

Statements such as these underscore the argument that the employment of culture by indigenous rights groups, national elites, international NGOs, and missionaries have infused 'culture' with new ethnographic importance, while complicating its analytical use (Hann 2002; Kaneff & King 2004). That is, the divergent uses of 'culture' by various interest groups highlight that there is no underlying stable core to the concept. Therefore, as Gupta and Ferguson have argued, recognition of the contingent nature of what counts as culture requires that analysis focuses on the 'processes rather than essences [that] are involved in present experiences of cultural identity' (1992: 9). Moreover, since much is at stake in defining and defending the meaning of cultural identity, it is crucial to examine 'the processes through which the state, conflicting groups and/or elites, and people in general tend to appropriate "culture" in pushing particular agendas' (Andrade 2002: 236). While some authors have celebrated the empowering potential of 'culture' for indigenous movements, others have insisted that it is a 'double-edged sword: both a weapon of the weak and yet a potentially dangerous tool for nationalisms and oppression' (Kaneff & King 2004: 16). In post-Soviet Kyrgyzstan, where missionaries, national elites, individual Muslims, and new Christian Kyrgyz compete over the definition of 'culture', these oppressive and empowering elements of 'culture' need to be analysed in specific social contexts.

Although this short discussion highlights the unstable nature of 'culture', it is equally important to note that what counts as culture cannot be freely confiscated, appropriated, or created. The history of Christian missions has abundantly demonstrated that cultural translations of biblical messages often have unforeseen consequences (e.g. Jordan 1993; Keane 1996; Meyer 2002; Orta 2004). In this article I analyse such unintended consequences, but also aim to explain why, in this post-Soviet context, the cultural endeavours of evangelical missionaries found acceptance among certain layers of the Muslim Kyrgyz population. This question is particularly relevant because Christian missions have often found themselves incapable of making significant inroads among Muslims (Sharkey 2005: 47).

The communist attacks on Muslim structures and the socio-economic disruptions that occurred after the collapse of socialism account in part for the relative evangelical success in Kyrgyzstan (Pelkmans, Vaté & Falge 2005). Beyond such structural factors, however, I suggest that only by analysing the particular ways in which culture is appropriated, defended, and mobilized is it possible to capture the dynamics and implications of post-socialist religious encounters. What makes the case at hand especially interesting is that the notions of culture applied by evangelicals build upon seventy years of Soviet cultural politics that simultaneously objectified ethno-national categories and fostered a folkloristic understanding of culture (Peyrouse 2004; Slezkine 2000).[3] My central argument is that unexpected synergies between communist cultural legacies and new evangelical cultural appropriations are particularly relevant in explaining the attraction of Christianity as well as the unintended consequences of evangelical efforts. Despite the seemingly unbridgeable difference between Soviet 'atheizers' and Christian evangelizers, their efforts at cultural appropriation (or their efforts to apply culture) show striking similarities. Both communists and evangelicals endeavoured to disentangle the ties between religion and culture. Ironically, in doing so they unavoidably folklorized and objectified 'culture', setting the stage for the emergence of new lines of inclusion and exclusion, sometimes along the ethnic boundaries they intended to overcome.

Religious and national categories in Soviet Kyrgyzstan

Estimates of the number of Kyrgyz converts to Christianity vary widely from 10,000 to 100,000 (Iarkov 2002: 84; Murzakhalilov 2004). My own estimate – based on oral information, internet data, and church visits throughout the country – would be around 20,000 Kyrgyz converts.[4] If this estimate is roughly correct, then approximately one per cent of the titular Kyrgyz population has converted to Christianity. Since these new Kyrgyz Christians are not evenly distributed over Kyrgyzstan's territory, but live concentrated in the north and especially in urban areas, conversion has in certain locations become a phenomenon that is both socially visible and threatening to many Kyrgyz.

To appreciate the challenge that evangelical Christianity poses to established ideas about culture and nationality, it is crucial to review how the relationship between religious and ethnic categories developed during Soviet times. It has by now been well documented that the Soviet regime did not act as a 'breaker of nations', but rather served to channel and institutionalize ethno-national categories in specific ways (Hirsch 2005; Pelkmans 2006; Slezkine 2000). What is important to point out here is that Soviet nationalities policies also greatly influenced the trajectories of religious categories. The following discussion, taken from historian Lemercier-Quelquejay, between a Soviet 'atheizer' and a young Kyrgyz member of the Komsomol (Communist Union of Youth), provides a telling example of the ethno-religious dilemma in the late Soviet period: '"Why do you pretend to be a Muslim?" a Soviet anti-religious lecturer, Dorazhnov, asked a young member of the Kirghiz Komsomol. The answer was: "Because I am a Kirghiz"' (1984: 22). Lemercier-Quelquejay used this two-line dialogue to illustrate the tight connection between ethno-national and religious categories in Central Asia in the 1980s. Because of this tight connection, she contended, it was not uncommon that devoted communists and atheists would also stress that they were Muslim. In effect, what had developed – and was labelled as such in Soviet literature – was the formation of non-believing, 'atheist Muslims' (1984: 22).

Rather than attributing the continued relevance of the label 'Muslim' to the presumed strength of pre-Soviet religious traditions, it is more fruitful to point out that the links between religious and ethnic identification were inadvertently perpetuated by Soviet national and cultural politics. Whereas the Soviet regime de-legitimized religious structures and repressed most aspects of religion's public manifestations, the regime ironically also encoded religious identities through its nationality politics. Kemal Karpat shows that in Soviet Central Asia the appeal of newly created national categories derived (in part) from 'the incorporation of many elements of the religious culture in the emerging "national" cultures [which gave] the adherents of the latter a sense of the historical continuity, strength, and durability of their cultures' (1993: 416). Importantly, this process also backfired: the incorporation of religious elements in ethnic definitions also enshrined the position of Islam. Shahrani writes in an article on identity dynamics in Central Asia: 'The modern concept of nationalities has provided "legitimate" basis through which some of the most critical traditional notions of *Muslim* Turkestani identities and loyalties are communicated, and in which traditional values are reinvested' (1984: 35, emphasis original). Following Shahrani, it may be said that the creation of Central Asian 'nations' was facilitated and given legitimacy by the mobilization and institutionalization of local Muslim registers. Vice versa, it may also be said that Islam continued to be an important frame of reference because of this amalgamation of religious and national categories.

The relaxations on religious expression in the late 1980s and the sudden independence of Kyrgyzstan in 1991 led to a renewed interest in cultural and religious roots, much like elsewhere in the post-socialist world. As the political leadership looked for nation-binding themes, and large layers of the population explored their 'national religion', the ethno-religious amalgamation – the connection between Kyrgyz and Muslim identity – achieved a visible and public profile. At the same time, this 'ethnicization' of religion (Saroyan 1997: 95) invited critical responses from within, and recruitment attempts from the outside. This has been very true for the Muslim-Kyrgyz composite, which has become more vulnerable in the post-atheist era. Although most Kyrgyz continue to conceive of their ethnic identity as inseparable from Islam, this claim is now increasingly under attack. In fact, the challenge posed by the anti-religious lecturer who asked 'why do you *pretend* to be a Muslim?' has returned with renewed force. The interrogators are no longer atheists (who have ceased to exist, at least in public) but Christian and Muslim 'believers'. Both speak of the Kyrgyz as 'people who *call* themselves Muslim', but 'in fact' are only superficially so. Moreover, both groups view the pairing of religious and ethnic identity as unfortunate, because in their view faith should transcend ethnic or national categories. Clearly there are differences between both groups as well. Many newly pious Muslims (Hefner 2005) interpret the identification of Islam with Kyrgyz tradition as a perversion of their faith. Thus, their anti-syncretism challenges aspects of 'Kyrgyz culture' – like weddings, funerals, and healing practices – that are seen as incompatible with Islam, and that prevent people from becoming 'true Muslims' (see also McBrien 2006). By contrast, evangelical Christians direct their primary criticism not at culture but at religion, claiming that Islam not only is a false religion but also distorts Kyrgyz culture. Instead, they propose a Christianity which they see as culturally consistent with Kyrgyz ways of life.

Evangelical logics

Official sources in Kyrgyzstan claim that there are about 1,000 foreign missionaries active in the Kyrgyz Republic (population five million), of whom 700 are Protestant Christians (Mamaiusupov 2003: 305–6; Murzakhalilov 2004: 84). The actual numbers may be still higher, because not all missionaries register with the authorities. Many short-term missionaries, for example, do not have the time (nor face the necessity) to undergo the protracted registration procedures. Others are registered as development workers, even though they acknowledge that missionary work is a major part of their activities.[5] This interest in Kyrgyzstan reflects a broader trend of increased evangelical attention for post-communist as well as Muslim societies. In the early 1990s post-communist societies were considered to be 'virgin fields' in which it was an 'exciting time to be ministering as God is bringing in the harvest'.[6] Likewise, since the first Gulf war and especially after 9/11, evangelical interest to work among Muslims – considered the largest group of 'unreached people' – has sharply increased (Love 2000).[7] As a post-communist and Muslim region, Central Asia combines the attractions of both evangelical dreams. Moreover, of the Central Asian republics Kyrgyzstan stands out as the most liberal one. In the words of a commentator: 'Kyrgyzstan is what the US Center for World Missions is calling the most open Muslim country'.[8]

Missionaries arrive from countries as diverse as the United States and Ukraine, South Korea and Germany. They have ties to denominations like the Mennonite Brethren, Southern Baptists, Evangelical Lutherans, and various Pentecostal churches, which differ in their theology and missionary approach. Some of these missionaries establish churches along strictly defined denominational lines and maintain close contact with their congregations at home. A significant group of long-term missionaries, however, aims to escape denominational categorization and present themselves as non-denominational or as evangelical. My focus is on this group of long-term missionaries who are involved in promoting and assisting the emergence of what they called a *Kyrgyz* church. Associated with four American and German organizations – Youth with a Mission (YWAM), Asian Alliance, Central Asian Partnership, and Logos – these approximately 100 missionaries all know each other and frequently co-operate in specific mission activities.[9] Most significantly for the purpose of this article, they all see a so-called 'ethnic barrier' as the main obstacle to the conversion of the Kyrgyz. In the words of one missionary associated with Logos:

> Initial negative attitudes of Kyrgyz towards Christianity should in most cases be attributed not to Islamic conviction, but to people's quest for national identity. At the religious level they connect their national identity with Islam and traditional beliefs. A change towards another religion will therefore be seen as betrayal of the nation . . . In order to weaken the argument that Christianity is a religion of Russians or Germans, it is crucial that a Kyrgyz stays a Kyrgyz after his conversion.
>
> (Zweininger 2002: 89, translation MP)

What is at issue here are the ties between belief, religion, and ethno-national identity, which the evangelicals aim to untangle and reassemble. To many evangelical Christians, the term 'religion' has negative connotations, as it reeks of ritualized performance and of clerical hierarchies. To them, religion is only the *form* or the social cover, and should always be secondary to the real issue: belief in the fundamental tenets of the Christian message. This stance is grounded in the evangelical Christian discomfort with the relation between spirit and matter and the resulting effort to maintain or produce, as Keane (2007: 28) phrased it, 'discrete boundaries between materiality and meaning'. In this particular missionary encounter the stress on meaning – on the fundamentals of Christianity – has been combined with an internal critique of previous 'imperialistic' roles played by missionaries, triggering renewed attention to 'cultural contextualization' as a precondition to missionary success.[10] Analysis of evangelical missionary work in Kyrgyzstan reveals three – often implicit – basic logics that underlie their activities. Respectively I have termed these 'de-Russifying Christianity', 'de-Islamizing Kyrgyz culture', and 'Kyrgyzifying Christianity'.

The first theme addresses the Russian connotations of Christianity, as reflected in common parlance among Muslim Kyrgyz that 'Jesus is a Russian God'. This conflation of Christianity with Russianness can be traced back to the incorporation of Kyrgyzstan into the Russian Empire in the mid-nineteenth century as well as to Soviet anti-religious propaganda. As a result, Christianity came to be associated with people worshipping icons and crossing themselves, and with bearded priests dressed in long black cassocks uttering religious formulas. Among Kyrgyz these images often arouse negative emotions. As an acquaintance told me while referring to Orthodox Christian practices: 'All this is barbaric to us'. De-Russifying Christianity is not only crucial for overcoming such negative stereotypes, it also allows evangelical missionaries to exhibit their dissimilarity from Orthodox Christianity. Part of this 'de-Russification' comes naturally, as the services of evangelical congregations are very different from Orthodox services and show none of the Orthodox symbols and signs. In fact, the absence of visual religious symbols in evangelical churches allow missionaries to claim that they are not just proposing a different religion – a different branch of Christianity – but that they are a 'gathering of believers', who have *overcome* religion. Religion, in this line of thinking, is just 'form': at best it distracts, at worst it leads people astray. Thus, because of its Russian 'religious' connotations, some evangelicals avoid the word 'Christian' altogether, and instead talk about 'followers of Jesus'.

While the visual characteristics of evangelical churches and services may be sufficiently different from Russian Orthodoxy, missionaries have taken more active steps to adjust Christian *language*. This is not simply an issue of translation into Kyrgyz. In fact, many urban Kyrgyz are more fluent in the Russian than in the Kyrgyz language. But even if some Kyrgyz converts prefer to go to Russian-language services, the ethnic connotations of many Christian terms still arouse negative sentiments. To counter this problem, evangelicals often employ what they call 'Central Asian Russian' in their writings. This is standard Russian with the difference that Christian names and terms have been replaced with Turkic or Arabic equivalents. Thus, the Russian word *Biblia* is substituted with the Arabic *Injil* (Gospel or New Testament) or *Yiyk Kitebi*, which literally means 'holy book'. Likewise, the name for Jesus, known by most Kyrgyz as 'the Russian God' *Isus Khristos*, has become *Isa* or *Isa Mashayak* (Jesus the Saviour). The word for church is equally problematic. The Russian word *tserkov* as well as its Kyrgyz derivative *tsirkö* both indicate an Orthodox church. Because of these connotations the word 'church' is preferably avoided, and the term favoured instead is *jiin* (meeting), or less frequently *syiyny üiü* (house of prayer). These innovations reduce associations with Russianness and offer the additional advantage that Kyrgyz Christians can speak in public about religious affairs without revealing their religious affiliation. At the same time, though, these discursive techniques provoke accusations of deception. In particular, voices in the national media have repeatedly criticized the use of Islamic vocabulary by missionaries as an attempt to hide Christianity in Islamic guise and thus mislead people into conversion.[11]

A second crucial element in evangelical efforts is to 'de-Islamize' Kyrgyz culture. It is telling that evangelical Christians rarely speak of Kyrgyz people as Muslims point blank, except to prove to their donors that they are working among the largest group of so-called 'unreached people'. More often, they characterize Kyrgyz people as *having* a Muslim tradition, a Muslim background, or Muslim customs. And when talking about the religious situation in Kyrgyzstan, phrases like 'communist oppression', 'spiritual vacuum', and 'religious degeneration' predominate. In conversations they further trivialize Islam in Kyrgyzstan by insisting that it only has a superficial influence on Kyrgyz culture or by insisting that Islam in Kyrgyzstan is 'just about identity', an identity that makes sense only in opposition to Russians. Implicitly, like the previously mentioned Soviet atheizer (see above), these missionaries basically ask Kyrgyz people 'why they pretend to be Muslim'. There appears to be a twofold logic behind the described discursive practices. By implying that Kyrgyz are not *real* Muslims, they create the possibility of a directed dialogue in which the missionaries may raise their objections: you drink alcohol, you don't pray five times daily, those are actually shamanic healing practices, etcetera. In such dialogical encounters, the discursive practices function to dissociate the respondent from Islam. Moreover, by dissociating local religious practices from Islam, the evangelicals imply that there is only one true Islam, which they see as dogmatic by nature.[12] In essence, by stressing an essentialist core to Islam – with which very few Kyrgyz identify – evangelicals are able to argue that Islam and Kyrgyz 'culture' are incompatible. This way, they tempt people to make a decisive choice. And Christianity, they suggest, is far more in line with Kyrgyz ways of life.

This brings us to the third element – Kyrgyzifying Christianity. I repeatedly heard missionaries say that it is a common misunderstanding to see Christianity as a Western religion. Instead, they insisted, Christianity is an Eastern religion, and therefore by nature more in line with Eastern cultures than with European or American ones. One American missionary (linked to YWAM) told me that the Bible had captivated him since he read it for the first time, yet that translating its messages to contemporary North American life was often challenging. 'But when I came here', he continued, 'it was amazing. For these people reading the Bible must be like reading about their own forefathers, about their own culture!' A significant number of young American missionaries claimed to value the preservation of Kyrgyz culture among converts. After having attended a festive service in a Kyrgyz-led church in Bishkek, a YWAM missionary who speaks Kyrgyz told me how pleased he was with the use of Kyrgyz cultural idioms in the service: 'The way they were dancing in the church and then went outside and slaughtered a cow. I love that, they were not asked to do anything that was not part of their heritage, of their culture'. Similar ideas surfaced in other practices. The set-up in several churches, for example, was arranged to stress Kyrgyzness. Everyone, including the pastor, sat on felt carpets (*shyrdaks*) on the floor; the elderly received seats of honour, whereas young people sat near the entrance. The songs were in Kyrgyz, accompanied by music played on 'typical' Kyrgyz instruments. The intentionality behind such arrangements may be seen from the comment of a German missionary to Kyrgyzstan, who wrote that church services 'are deliberately designed to be as culturally relevant as possible' (Rempel 1999: 6).

So what is happening here? The missionaries want to carry across the message that Jesus is for everyone and that all cultures are equal, or equally special. But the contextualization of Christian messages, and the resulting stress on 'local culture' in missionary discourse and church activities, raises questions concerning the involved definition of culture. As the examples presented above showed, in the hands of evangelicals, Kyrgyz 'culture' implied a selective rendering of national symbols and signs, with an obvious emphasis on the visual and oral through music, dance, and public displays. In short, the kind of culture that evangelicals promoted was Kyrgyz in form and Christian in content. Indeed, there were clear parallels with Soviet uses of culture as condensed in the communist slogan 'national in form and socialist in content'. Both communists and evangelicals heralded the external manifestations of 'national cultures' as evident in dressing-styles, cuisine, handicraft, and the like, while simultaneously advancing specific ideologies. Like in the communist parallel, the culture promoted by evangelical Christians was of a folkloristic nature. And like in the communist parallel, there was always the risk that 'form' would take predominance over 'content'.[13]

Challenging identity: employing culture in the 'Church in Bishkek'

The relevance of discussing missionary practices is, of course, dependent on the question of how the ideas advanced by missionaries are interpreted, appropriated, and modified by Kyrgyz Christians. As Terence Ranger argued for the African context, the common tendency to focus exclusively on missionaries, and to see missionaries and local Christians as opposing categories, fails to recognize the complexity of missionary encounters and of religious change (1987*a*: 182–3). Instead, he argued, 'we should see mission churches as much less alien and independent churches as much less "African"'

(1987*b*: 31, quoted in Meyer 2004: 454–5). Since this article focuses on evangelical Christians who actively try to 'contextualize' religious messages and practices, tend to de-emphasize denominational differences, and aim to foster the emergence of a 'Kyrgyz church', assuming a straightforward division between missionaries and local Christians would be particularly problematic.[14] Indeed, although some of the missionaries led their own 'missionary church', they also actively supported 'independent churches' by providing financial support and technical assistance, facilitating study visits, and providing theological training.

One 'independent' church – the 'Church in Bishkek' – received particular attention from missionaries, precisely because it embodied the promise of becoming a truly 'Kyrgyz' church. Although not officially linked to a missionary organization, the church received substantial donations from individual missionaries and missionary organizations. The leaders of the church had extensive contacts with missionaries of the previously mentioned organizations (YWAM and CAPS in particular) and its services were almost always attended by several foreigners. At the same time, the wish to be (seen as) 'independent' meant that leaders of the 'Church in Bishkek' publicly stressed difference between their church and missionary churches; they were also critical of foreign missionaries who failed to appreciate the cultural specificities of Kyrgyzstan. A focus on this church, then, can provide important insights into the possibilities and limitations of the cultural endeavours undertaken by missionaries and selectively appropriated as well as enhanced by Kyrgyz evangelicals. To sketch the origins and development of this church, I will start by introducing its founder and senior pastor.

Pastor Tamaz had undergone a tumultuous spiritual journey, which he eagerly described to me.[15] Born in the provincial town of Naryn (East Kyrgyzstan), he had moved to Bishkek to study at a *madrasah* in the early 1990s. While studying at the *madrasah*, Tamaz heard about Kyrgyz people who had converted to Christianity. Outraged by the possibility, he and a friend decided to investigate the situation. Having arrived at the church, his friend entered into a heated debate with the Baptist pastor. Tamaz stood by and observed his friend becoming ever more enraged, while the pastor retained his calm posture and replied patiently and convincingly to the questions and accusations. Tamaz presented the event as a turning-point in his life. Soon after he gave up his studies at the *madrasah* and joined the Baptist church instead. In the following years Tamaz climbed the church hierarchy. He served first as group leader and eventually as pastor leading a congregation across the border in Kazakhstan. However, disagreement over the doctrine of eternal security (in salvation) led to his excommunication from the church.[16] Subsequently Tamaz founded a church in Bishkek together with a Korean missionary. Although it had presumably been agreed that Tamaz would lead the church, once the congregation had grown to fifty members the missionary decided that he himself would be pastor. Tamaz felt abused and claimed that the 'disrespectful' way he was treated characterized a general pattern: foreign missionaries tend to use Kyrgyz believers to do the hard work (evangelizing) and subsequently impose their faulted Western ideas. Nevertheless, Tamaz was hopeful for the future. He explained that while years ago Kyrgyz pastors 'scolded each other like small children', they had finally come to realize that they could survive without the assistance of foreigners.

In 1998, Tamaz decided to set up his own independent church. Starting with a dozen believers who gathered in his apartment, the church had steadily expanded. In 2004 the church had some 200 regular attendants at the central church in Bishkek, and another 300 people attending six daughter churches. The name of the central church – Church in Bishkek – may be confusing given the fact that there were as many as fifty Protestant churches in the city. Nevertheless, the name was carefully chosen. 'Church in Bishkek', according to Tamaz, was similar to the names of New Testament churches like the 'Church in Antiocha' or the 'Church in Jerusalem'.[17] Thus, the name indicated a symbolic return to biblical models of Christianity and reflected the wish that denominational differences would disappear in the future. Instead, the church Tamaz envisioned would be a church for all believers and fit within Kyrgyz culture.

Constructing a Christian self

The spoken word occupies a central place in evangelical Christianity. In her study of fundamentalist Baptists in the US, Harding shows convincingly that conversion was both produced and revealed through distinctive speech patterns. In this process, she argued, 'listeners become public speakers of the Gospel' (1987: 16). A related question relevant to the purpose of this article is to what extent this principle produces continuity in discourse between foreign missionaries and Kyrgyz church members. In this section I will show that the ideas about culture promoted by foreign missionaries tended to be replicated in self-portrayals and conversion accounts, not least because these ideas allowed Kyrgyz Christians to counter allegations of national betrayal. The importance of speech – of recounting conversion stories in particular – also means that the stories I was told were in no sense 'hidden scripts' that needed to be painstakingly solicited; they were public statements repeated for potentially interested audiences. They were simultaneously narrations of experiences and invitations for the listener to accept Christ (see also Harding 1987). In my discussion I focus on this first aspect in order to illustrate how conversion stories connect ideas of cultural and ethnic belonging with notions of faith.[18] The story of Mirgul, a member of the Church in Bishkek, is illustrative of how converts carve out Christian space in Kyrgyz society and how they constitute themselves as culturally specific persons.

Almost immediately after we started talking, Mirgul stressed that she did not belong to any particular religion or denomination. In her view, religions hinder people from finding the truth: 'God told me that he didn't create religions – he didn't create Islam. The only thing you need is faith'. She continued by describing how 'religion' had hindered her when she was a child. Her parents had died at an early age and Mirgul was raised by her grandparents in a village in Talas province, 200 kilometres southwest of Bishkek. As she told it, being deprived of parental love had caused an 'emptiness in her heart' which made her sensitive to existential issues. At that time she considered herself a Muslim and was proud of it. Whenever she was afraid, she would repeat the phrase *la ilaha illa llah wa* (there is no god but God), which her grandmother had taught her. Also, she felt protected by the magical power of stones she collected at the burial site of the Kyrgyz hero Manas. Mirgul may well have discussed these and other instances to show how 'hopeless' her previous beliefs had been, because she concluded: 'At that time I wanted to believe so badly, but [my religion] didn't give me anything'.

Mirgul's rendering of her pre-conversion background explicitly challenged what she disapprovingly called 'religion'. First, she stressed that her conversion was not about religion or religious practice – which she saw as human inventions – but about truth and faith, as reflected in her search for the meanings of life and death. Second, she depicted the religious ideas taught by her grandmother as ineffective superstitions. Her story thus strongly resembled the discourse of missionaries on 'folk Islam', which, intentionally or not, functioned to trivialize the Muslim affiliation of Kyrgyz.

Mirgul's doubts concerning the effectiveness of her native religion grew more intense after an encounter with a German 'believer' (probably a Mennonite), whom she met after she had moved to Bishkek. She described this person as very different from other people, standing out in honesty and emotional stability. Although she enjoyed his stories about Jesus, she was convinced that they were not meant for her because she was not a German. None the less, she continued to think about Jesus and even approached an elderly Russian Orthodox woman to enquire if she could be baptized. The lady dismissed the idea, saying: 'Girl, you are a Muslim! Anyway, baptism is only for the very young'.

Some time after this disappointing encounter, Mirgul visited her sister and other relatives in Talas province. Mirgul's sister told her about a new group of Christians which included some Kyrgyz. Together they decided to attend a service: 'We entered, and for the first time in my life I experienced that atmosphere. I was in awe to find such a place, such people . . . Afterwards it was as if I had wings. The only thing in my head was that Jesus is alive'. Not long thereafter Mirgul returned to Bishkek. Although she considered herself a believer at the time, in retrospect she recognized that she continued 'to live in sin', enmeshed in the 'worldly life' of the city.

This second part of Mirgul's story described the obstacles to finding and accepting the truth – obstacles which she located both in herself and in the social environment. For Mirgul, the faith of the German believer was unattainable because she was not a German. The negative response of the Russian Orthodox woman further affirmed that differences between Christians and Muslims were inborn and ethnically fixed. Only when Mirgul met a Kyrgyz believer was she able to find 'the truth'. But having overcome this 'ethnic barrier' and knowing 'the truth' was not the same as accepting it. The attractions of city life – presented as social pressures in other conversion narratives – kept her from leading a 'holy life' herself.

Mirgul discussed extensively the circumstances under which she finally became a *true* believer. She had travelled to Kazakhstan to assist in selling the apartment of a relative. After several weeks, a potential buyer finally came forward: 'She was a beautiful lady, about sixty years of age, very richly dressed . . . She said that she had been to Mecca and that she was a Muslim . . . She was also president of all the *ekstrasensy* (visionaries) in central Kazakhstan'. The woman agreed to buy the apartment but negotiated that she would start using it immediately and would deliver the money within fifteen days. When the woman delayed making payments, Mirgul threatened to call the police.

> Then [this lady] started shouting that she would paralyse me and turn me into an invalid, so that I would never again be able to move my arms and feet. And she would do it that very night. You see, she worshipped Satan to bring this harm to me . . . Right then and there – on the street while snow was falling – I accepted Christ as the Lord, as Saviour. It was as if I was drunk. I felt so good and strong, and I easily fell asleep . . . The next morning I met the woman again. She stood there, shivering as if sick, and without a word she handed me the money. It turns out that when she [used her magic that very night] she was struck by horrible pains. I was so happy. Since then my life completely changed. My friends, that world, it fell away . . . It has been five years since and I still thank God every single day.

Whereas in the first two sections of her story Mirgul described the social and psychological factors that played a role in her conversion, here she staged the active presence of Jesus. She positioned her own conversion experience at the epicentre of the struggle between powers of good and evil, in which she managed to survive only with Jesus' help. Tellingly, evil was represented by a Muslim woman who employed 'occult' powers which – symbolically at least – referred back to the 'superstitious' beliefs Mirgul had held in her youth.

The relation between faith, culture, and religion was important not only in Mirgul's coming to faith, but also in the way she practised it as a believer. Mirgul insisted that she had remained fully Kyrgyz and that her customs all stayed the same:

> The only things I disposed of are the occult practices of Kyrgyz people. I no longer worship trees, water, or stones. But for the rest everything stayed the same. We [Christians] have circumcision, we have wedding customs that include the *kalym* [bride-price] and we have all kinds of national celebrations.

Mirgul also explained that she continued to attend funerals of her non-converted relatives. During such funerals she would pray in her own way, but would complete the prayers like the others with '*omen*'.[19] She explained that some new believers start copying foreigners, something to which she objected: 'We don't need American culture. We need Kyrgyz culture'. A little later she added: 'I think that our culture should be a biblical culture. We didn't change our nationality. Instead of [having] religion we now believe. That is all'.

Mirgul was an enthusiastic and compelling narrator. This may well have been the reason why church members introduced me to her in the first place. Significantly, her story closely paralleled stories of converts who were less vocally apt. Stories typically started with a pre-conversion stage in which one was left unsatisfied with available religious beliefs and practices, followed by a move to a city and/or a personal crisis. Subsequently the person had an encounter with believers, dealt with obstacles related to family or social environment, experienced a crisis and miraculous recovery, and finally found joy of assured salvation through Christ.[20] This spiritual journey served not only to highlight the sincerity of conversion, but also to criticize the corruptions of worldly life in post-socialist Kyrgyzstan.

However, the selective reading of such stories was clear: potential converts face difficult obstacles but the rewards are worth the pain. Moreover, the implication was that one could accept Jesus and still be a true Kyrgyz. Of course, the message did not ease the social exclusion experienced by most converts, but it *did* provide them with a self-image and a vocabulary that could be used to counter negative reactions. In part, then, the insistence on Kyrgyzness may be seen as a way to neutralize negative reactions of people who accuse converts of selling or betraying the nation, just as it can be seen as a conversion strategy that makes conversion to Christianity acceptable and imaginable. Still, the employed concept of Kyrgyzness as well as the extent to which believers could participate in 'Kyrgyz culture' had limitations. It did not allow full participation in social life, and was not necessarily accepted by non-believers.

Folklorization and deception

The selective reading of Kyrgyzness corresponded closely to the cultural endeavours undertaken by the Church in Bishkek, and especially to the critical connection between cultural 'form' and Christian 'content'. It was almost standard practice at church celebrations or life-cycle rituals to make the events look as Kyrgyz as possible. For example, during one Christian fundraising event (co-organized by the church) dancers were dressed in 'traditional' clothing, while the musician who played the *komuz* (stringed instrument) wore a *kalpak* (felt hat) and *chapan* (long black coat). In the lobby were stalls that sold Christian Kyrgyz handicraft like small *shyrdaks* (felt rugs) with texts in English like 'North, South, West, East, Jesus is for everyone' and 'Pray for Kyrgyzstan'. A central place was reserved for a nativity scene in which Joseph wore a *kalpak* and Mary a 'traditional' Kyrgyz dress.

Such cultural displays may be described as 'folkloristic', in the sense of being systematic attempts to convey notions of tradition and authenticity through stylized displays of culture. Obviously these displays had limited significance in social life, something which Mirgul's story already indicated. It was possible to attend funerals, but not to pray in the same way as Muslims. Likewise, though evangelical codes did not proscribe attending parties, the ban on consuming alcohol limited participation in common forms of conviviality.[21] And although Mirgul stressed that 'everything stayed the same', conversion to her new faith did not only require her to denounce the spiritual ideas held by Muslim Kyrgyz, but also meant that, as she put it, her previous 'friends, that world, it fell away'.

The performances and commodities revealed the tendency to treat 'culture' as a set of free-floating images and signs that could be attached to a new set of morals and worldview. Discomfort with this understanding of culture partly explained negative reactions of several Muslim Kyrgyz acquaintances to pictures that I showed them of the events organized to celebrate the five-year mark of the Church in Bishkek. For this special event a yurt (*boz-üi*) was erected in the church-yard, the worship group was dressed in brightly coloured shiny Kyrgyz dresses, and many men wore *kalpaks*. The pictures also showed the slaughtering of a cow and several sheep, an open-air prayer meeting in the yard, and people praying with arms outstretched. For my acquaintances these visual images signified Kyrgyzness. They were astounded to learn that the people in the pictures were Christians, for what they saw in the photographs indicated Kyrgyzness and could not possibly have had anything to do with Christianity. Since several of them had previously mentioned that abandoning Islam implies a betrayal of Kyrgyz nationality, I asked them to revisit that statement after having seen the pictures of Kyrgyz Christians. One of them said, 'Well yes, they dress like Kyrgyz, they act like Kyrgyz, but still . . . inside they must be different'. My acquaintances would not easily give up their convictions about the ties between religion and nationality. One of them exclaimed: 'Dressing up like that is plain deception'. According to him, this 'abuse of Kyrgyz culture' was even worse than becoming a Russian – an Orthodox Christian.

Thus, at least two limitations followed from the evangelical uses of 'culture'. On one hand, the displays were not necessarily accepted by non-Christians, for whom the appropriation of Kyrgyz styles was sometimes a sign of superficiality or of cultural theft. On the other hand, the extensive cultural displays did not mean that believers could fully participate in social life. After having converted, their social world often became centred on other Christians. Precisely because of these challenges and difficulties, there was an inherent tendency to assign a more active role to 'cultural form'.

Cultural objectification and ethnocentrism

The evangelical attempt to disconnect faith, religion and culture runs into its own limits here. There is an unavoidable contradiction in disconnecting Christianity from 'Russian culture' and then abundantly displaying Kyrgyzness. One obvious consequence of this valorization of Kyrgyz culture was that people of different ethnic background became less attracted to the services. Several female Russian believers told me about their disillusionment with the churches that they used to attend. The services had been in Russian and were attended by Tatars, Koreans, Russians, and Kyrgyz alike. One of the women said: 'Suddenly everything had to change into Kyrgyz: the new pastor was a Kyrgyz, we had to sing Kyrgyz songs, etcetera. Just because they think that Russian [language] would make people think of icons and church bells'.

Apart from such 'earthly' exclusionary effects, the objectification of culture also formed the basis for a new ethnocentric cosmology. At the end of a service at the Church in Bishkek, Pastor Tamaz announced the performance of an *Isachi*. The term *Isachi*, he explained, was derived from *Manaschi*, or narrator of the famous Kyrgyz Manas epic. The *Isachi* in question, a woman wearing a pink and black 'national Kyrgyz dress', was seated on a felt carpet on the podium. She closed her eyes for a moment, then lifted her hands with palms up, and started reciting. Her sitting posture and arm movements, as well as the rhythm and intonation of her voice, strongly resembled performances by *manaschis*. The story she told, however, was that of the life of *Isa* (Jesus). Several people I spoke to after the service, including two Kyrgyz-speaking American missionaries, were full of praise for this remarkable performance. One of them commented that this was such a perfect example of the way the 'good news' can be contextualized, presenting it in a form that was recognizable to Kyrgyz people. When I met Pastor Tamaz again, he mentioned that another five *Isachis* were in training, and would soon be able to perform all over Kyrgyzstan.

Pastor Tamaz's efforts were not just attempts to contextualize Christian messages, but also reflected what he imagined to be God's plans with the Kyrgyz. Tamaz had become convinced that the Kyrgyz were descendants of one of the lost tribes of Israel.[22] He based this view on certain similarities between the Old Testament and the Manas epic. This epic tells the story of the hero Manas, who managed to integrate feuding Kyrgyz tribes into one nation and to defeat its enemies. Aside from the fact that the Manas epic pays as much attention to bloody battles and etiquette as the Old Testament does, Pastor Tamaz was especially intrigued by several more specific similarities. One of these was a semblance of personal names. The hero Manas has a father called Jakyp, which resembles the biblical story of Jacob, who adopts as his native son his grandson Manasseh (Genesis 48:5). Moreover, this grandfather-grandson adoption corresponded to the Kyrgyz custom to allow grandparents to adopt their first-born grandson. The hero Manas, according to Tamaz, was at times 'like David, who also had forty commanders of whom three stood out', and at others like Jesus, because it was likewise predicted that Manas 'would come to save his people'. Moreover, Tamaz continued, 'After Jesus was born, all infants were killed. When Manas was born they also killed all the children his age'. To Tamaz such similarities indicated that the Manas epic was rooted in the Bible. The biblical stories had been orally transmitted within the Jewish Manasseh tribe (the Kyrgyz, that is), meanwhile being changed and transformed into what is now known as the Manas epic.

Tamaz was not the only one to cherish these views. One of his friends, an American missionary associated with YWAM, had written a booklet titled *Ak Kalpak* in which he documented what he called 'God's fingerprints' on Kyrgyz culture, paying particular attention to the similarities between the Manas epic and the Old Testament. The booklet was translated in Kyrgyz and distributed by the 'Church in Bishkek'.[23] Moreover, in June 2004, Asian Alliance (mentioned above) organized a public event, titled 'Who is Manas?', in which (mostly foreign) evangelical Christians approvingly discussed similarities between the characters in the epic and the Bible.

While this cross-fertilization between missionaries and the Church in Bishkek forms an important backdrop to the story, it is equally important to note that the 'lost tribe' thesis was controversial within evangelical circles. Some Kyrgyz Christians and foreign missionaries had second thoughts about the ideas that Pastor Tamaz was propagating so actively. For example, a German lecturer of Central Asian church history at a theological seminary in Bishkek pointed out that even though he considered the similarities to be remarkable, they could just as well be the result of interaction between Kyrgyz bards and Nestorian monks in medieval times. However, Tamaz and his followers were convinced that such cynical remarks would be proven false in the future. Certain that the Kyrgyz were actually Israelites, Tamaz foresaw a special role for the Kyrgyz in the last wave of missionary activity before the second coming of Christ. According to Tamaz, the Kyrgyz are more charismatic, spiritually predisposed, and energetic than Europeans and Americans. The latter might have organizational qualities but are unable to ignite the passion in others.

> It seems to me that God needs humble, open-minded people. Not like Germans or Dutch, who have a lot of money and a technocratic way of thinking. They may have big plans, but they are not able to establish large churches [i.e. attract many believers]. Simple Kyrgyz people can achieve much more. Probably God meant it to be that way. Because otherwise people would say, 'oh well, it is just because of those rich Americans, that is why they [converted]'.

In January 2004, at a national evangelical convention, Tamaz expressed these ideas to a broad audience of Kyrgyz pastors. His ideas met with strong opposition from several pastors, who threatened to excommunicate him because they felt that his preoccupation with Kyrgyz history was distorting Christian teachings. But the controversy subsided and Tamaz continued to popularize his idea of the Kyrgyz as a lost tribe of Israel. Just before I left the country in August 2004, Tamaz arranged a nationwide competition to search for hidden similarities between the Manas epic and the Bible and had this broadcast on regional and national television channels. The emphasis on the Manas epic and the idea of 'spiritual superiority' based on biological descent go a long way in infusing Kyrgyz Christianity with new 'racial overtones'. Ironically, this Kyrgyz Christian ethnocentrism was a logical, if unintended, outcome of evangelical attempts to contextualize biblical messages in a post-Soviet context.

The core of the evangelical message is that people should pursue a personal relationship with God, and that Jesus died for people from all nations. The efforts to disconnect the Christian message from its Russian connotations and to prove that it is possible to remain Kyrgyz after conversion were part of this ideal. But although the intent was to disconnect the biblical message from its Russian cultural connotations so that it would be accessible to Kyrgyz as well, these efforts created new divisions within the community of believers. Ironically, dissolving one ethnic barrier meant that new boundaries were created in the process. This is so because actually practised faith, even in the case of evangelical Christianity with its stress on personal salvation, is deeply social. Therefore, 'form' and 'content' can never be durably separated.

Culture and religion

Almost a century ago, Émile Durkheim made his classic argument that religion expresses collective realities, indeed that 'the idea of society is the soul of religion' (2002 [1912]: 48). Durkheim saw religion as 'an eminently social thing' (2002 [1912]: 38), a view that still forms the basis of many anthropological studies of religion. But how does this principle hold in relation to religious groups that stress individual relations with God, operating in a country that has experienced seventy years of state atheism? As I outlined above, the social nature of religion took specific forms in the Soviet Union, whose narrow religious and ethno-territorial policies encouraged the fusion of ethnic and religious categories. In a way, the recent surge of ethnic imagery and the disappearance of Soviet ideology have made these connections even more important.

The continued importance of the ethno-religious connection is one of the reasons why many (secular) Muslim Kyrgyz resent the influx of Protestant missions and why the conversion of Kyrgyz people is so much feared: they pose a threat to familiar patterns of belonging and non-belonging. These fears have started to resonate in national politics. Whereas in the early 1990s evangelical missionaries were welcomed as agents of Western values, in recent years the government has made attempts to limit the activities of missionaries and to undermine the basis of the most successful churches. National media outlets have also grown increasingly negative about the missionary 'invasion', portraying evangelical churches as 'totalitarian cults' using hypnosis and psychological manipulation to brainwash their members.[24] The most frequently expressed fear by reporters and state officials is that these churches may destabilize the nation by introducing foreign religions based on ideas alien to Kyrgyz culture.[25]

Received notions become increasingly dear to people only when they lose their self-evident nature. In line with this I suggest that the increased stress on the ethno-religious connection reflects its vulnerability and that the relative success of evangelical Christians (as well as of scripturalist Muslims) is related to the effects of the Soviet pairing of ethnic and religious labels. Though on the surface this pairing secured the position of Islam in Soviet Kyrgyzstan, it simultaneously undermined its viability in the post-Soviet context. In particular, the conflation of religious and ethno-national categories ignored and partly excluded other aspects of religious life (such as belief, morality, aesthetics) as well as different personal motivations (devotion, existential questions) which became increasingly important in destabilized post-Soviet contexts. Phrased differently, the very success of the amalgamation of Muslimness with Kyrgyzness partly carried its own demise as it made the constituting parts seem shallow to people who started reconsidering them in the 1990s. While notions of Muslimness and Kyrgyzness were previously positioned against an atheist ideology and a Russian 'other', these negative frames of reference became less relevant after the collapse of the Soviet Union. For many, this raised the troubling question of what else was involved in their Muslimness beyond Kyrgyzness.

This lack of clarity concerning the position of Islam is one of the reasons why evangelical Christianity managed to make significant inroads in Kyrgyzstan. Evangelical Christians challenged people's religious affiliation by stressing differences between religion, culture, and faith. Like the Soviets they aimed to stress differences between 'form' and 'content', while simultaneously advancing stereotypic views of 'real' Islam. In the context of post-Soviet decline and existential uncertainty the evangelical emphasis on individuality – on salvation through an individual relation with Christ – proved attractive. Evangelical logics dictated that people would be able to see this message of salvation once they had overcome the 'ethnic barrier'. But despite their proclaimed intention to disconnect faith from religion and culture, and despite the emphasis on individuality and private faith, evangelicals ended up strengthening these cultural connections in new ways. While foreign missionaries viewed Kyrgyz cultural displays as effective means (the form) of transmitting biblical messages (the content), the case of Tamaz clearly indicated that 'form' and 'content' did not remain conveniently separated. His insistence on viewing the Kyrgyz as a lost tribe of Israel demonstrated the importance of finding Kyrgyz authenticity in Christianity, thus blending 'form' and 'content' in the idea of a chosen nation. In spirit, this historical narrative resonated with Soviet ideas of culture and ethnicity as primordial features, but also reflected the need to respond to accusations of national betrayal befalling Kyrgyz who abandoned Islam. As such, the incursions of evangelical Christianity underline that actually practised religion is deeply social and tightly entwined with ideas of belonging, even if the proposed combinations between ethnicity, culture, and religion are entirely novel.

Notes

This article is based on fieldwork in Kyrgyzstan between August 2003 and September 2004, carried out in the context of the project 'Religion and Civil Society after Socialism' at the Max Planck Institute for Social Anthropology, Halle, Germany.

1 I employ the terms 'Uzbek' and 'Kyrgyz' in the way that they are used locally. This means that the terms refer to official ethno-national categorizations as inscribed in passports and other documents, which are locally seen as based on biological descent.
2 The term 'evangelical' denotes a range of Protestant denominations that emphasize the authority of the Bible and the importance of evangelization. I prefer the term 'evangelical' over 'Protestant' because it underscores differences with mainstream Protestant groups that are less engaged in missionary activities.
3 The term 'folklore' is generally used to indicate 'traditional customs, tales, sayings, or art forms preserved among a people' (*Webster's Ninth New Collegiate Dictionary*). In this article, however, 'folklore' indicates selective appropriations of cultural forms for representative purposes.
4 Estimatmg the number of Kyrgyz Christians is not a straightforward matter. For example, should one include children of Kyrgyz Christians, or Kyrgyz who were baptized but no longer attend church? Though important for understanding the impact of evangelical Christianity in Kyrgyzstan, I did not include them in this estimate.
5 Such missionaries often call themselves 'tent-makers', a term which refers to the missionary activities of the apostle Paul, who combined his religious service with the profession of making tents (Acts 18: 1–5).
6 *http://www.wccpc.org/our_mission_work_files/MarkPalmer.doc*, last accessed 28 November 2005.

7 An indication of this increased interest is that the widely circulated *International Journal of Frontier Missions* devoted seven issues to Islam between 1994 and 2005, but none in the ten years prior to 1994.

8 *http://www.wccpc.org/our_mission_work_files/MarkPalmer.doc*, last accessed 28 November 2005. The range of missionary activity varies greatly among the Central Asian republics.

9 Of these organizations only YWAM is internationally known. Central Asian Partnership has an all-American staff linked to the Southern Baptists. Asian Alliance is registered as a Kyrgyz NGO, though most associates are Americans linked to various denominations. Logos is a German organization with a Mennonite background.

10 An overview of the ongoing discussions can be retrieved from the *International Journal of Frontier Missions*. During the 1990s, especially, many articles discussed the 'imperialist' legacy and designed new ways to dissociate evangelical efforts from its colonial and imperialistic connotations.

11 Negative portrayals of missionaries and converts (as well as newly pious Muslims) are intimately linked to secular fears of 'the religious'. See McBrien and Pelkmans (forthcoming 2008).

12 The involved stereotyping was, for example, evident in the words of a German missionary who confided in me: 'You can't disconnect Islam from the *sharia*. If [Muslims] have it their way they would be cutting off hands again'.

13 Slezkine (2000) describes the precarious relation between 'national form' and 'socialist content' during the Soviet period, pointing at the inherent tendency of 'national form' to take predominance.

14 See Wanner (2004) for a similar argument. She shows that in Ukraine the 'mission field' is characterized by numerous alliances and rifts that cross-cut an imagined division between foreign missionaries and local evangelical believers.

15 To guarantee anonymity, I have replaced the names of my interlocutors with pseudonyms.

16 The doctrine of eternal security, though existing in various forms, basically adopts the idea 'once saved, always saved'. Tamaz had adopted this stance but clashed with the leaders of the Baptist church, who argued that people who stray from God's path can lose their salvation.

17 Since 'Church in Bishkek' was a confusing name in everyday communication, members would generally refer to the church by mentioning the name of the street.

18 The account is based on two interview sessions in August 2003.

19 In Kyrgyzstan Muslims say '*omen*' and make an accompanying gesture of the hands along the face when ending a prayer, a meal, or, for example, passing a graveyard. Evangelical Christians translated the term conveniently as 'amen'.

20 Coleman (2002: 96) notices a similar uniformity in conversion stories in her study of Russian evangelicals.

21 It should be stressed that though the majority of the population in Kyrgyzstan are Muslim, they regularly consume large quantities of alcohol at most social events. These practices are generally not perceived as incompatible with a Muslim affiliation, except among a growing minority of newly pious Muslims (McBrien 2006). Evangelical churches generally discouraged the consumption of alcohol and many banned it altogether.

22 The 'lost tribe' myth has parallels in many corners of the earth. Colonizers and missionaries implemented the myth in the Pacific and Amazonia to understand or remake indigenous histories. While the myth has often served to obscure indigenous histories and limit local agency, in some cases it proved instrumental in the construction of cultural identity (Friedman 1992: 196; Kirsch 1997).

23 The booklet was written in 2002 and the Kyrgyz translation appeared in 2004. It was not officially published but circulated widely in Kyrgyz evangelical circles.

24 The (translated) titles of the following articles, taken from a major Kyrgyz newspaper, speak for themselves: 'Beware the foreign preachers' (*Vechernii Bishkek*, 8 September 2000), 'Psychological terror or dark totalitarian sect' (*Vechernii Bishkek*, 10 November 2000).

25 For example, an analyst at the State Committee of Religious Affairs declares that new religious movements negatively impact ethnic relations because they destabilize the 'way of life, traditions and mentality of [the] nations and nationalities of Kyrgyzstan' (Murzakhalilov 2004: 86).

References

Andrade, X. 2002. 'Culture' as stereotype: public uses in Ecuador. In *Anthropology beyond culture* (eds) R. Fox & B. King, 235–57. Oxford: Berg.

Coleman, H. 2002. Becoming a Russian Baptist: conversion narratives and social experience. *The Russian Review* **61**, 94–112.

Durkheim, É. 2002 [1912]. The elementary forms of the religious life. In *A reader in the anthropology of religion* (ed.) M. Lambek, 34–49. Oxford: Blackwell.

Friedman, J. 1992. Myth, history, and political identity. *Cultural Anthropology* **7**, 194–210.

Gupta, A. & J. Ferguson. 1992. Beyond 'culture': space, identity, and the politics of difference. *Cultural Anthropology* **7**, 6–23.

Hefner, R. 2005. Introduction: modernity and the remaking of Muslim politics. In *Remaking Muslim politics* (ed.) R. Hefner, 1–36. Princeton: University Press.

Hirsch, F. 2005. *Empire of nations: ethnographic knowledge and the making of the Soviet Union*. Ithaca, N.Y.: Cornell University Press.

Iarkov, A. 2002. *Ocherk istorii religii v Kzrgzystane*. Bishkek: Tsentr OBSE v Bishkeke.

Jordan, D. 1993. The glyphomancy factor: observations on Chinese conversion. In *Conversion to Christianity: historical and anthropological perspectives on a great transformation* (ed.) R. Hefner, 285–303. Berkeley: University of California Press.

Kaneff, D. & A. King 2004. Introduction: owning culture. *Focaal: European Journal of Anthropology* **44**, 3–19.

Karpat, K. 1993. The old and new Central Asia. *Central Asian Survey* **12**, 415–25.

Keane, W. 1996. Materialism, missionaries, and modern subjects in colonial Indonesia. In *Conversion to modernities: the globalization of Christianity* (ed.) P. van der Veer, 137–70. New York: Routledge.

—— 2007. *Christian moderns: freedom and fetish in the mission encounter*. Berkeley: University of California Press.

Kirsch, S. 1997. Lost tribes: indigenous people and the social imaginary. *Anthropological Quarterly* **70**: **2**, 58–67.

Lemercier-Quelquejay, C. 1984. From tribe to umma. *Central Asian Survey* **3**: **3**, 15–38.

Love, R. 2000. Disciplining all Muslim peoples in the twenty-first century. *International Journal of Frontier Missions* **17**: **4**, 5–12.

McBrien, J. 2006. Listening to the wedding speaker: discussing religion and culture in Southern Kyrgyzstan. *Central Asian Survey* 25, 341–57.

—— & M. PELKMANS forthcoming 2008. Turning Marx on his head: missionaries, 'extremists', and archaic secularists in post-Soviet Kyrgyzstan. *Critique of Anthropology*.

MAMAIUSUPOV, O. 2003. *Voprosy (problemy) religii na perekhodnom periode*. Bishkek.

MEYER, B. 2002. Christianity and the Ewe nation: German Pietist missionaries, Ewe converts and the politics of culture. *Journal of Religion in Africa* **32**, 167–99.

—— 2004. Christianity in Africa: from African Independent to Pentecostal-Charismatic Churches. *Annual Review of Anthropology* **33**, 447–74.

MILLER, F. J. 1990. *Folklore for Stalin: Russian folklore and pseudofolklore of the Stalin era*. Armonk, N.Y.: M.E. Sharpe.

MURZAKHALILOV, K. 2004. Proselytism in Kyrgyzstan. *Central Asia and the Caucasus: Journal of Social and Political Studies* **25**: **1**, 83–7.

ORTA, A. 2004. *Catechizing culture: missionaries, Aymara, and the 'new evangelization'*. New York: Columbia University Press.

PELKMANS, M. 2006. *Defending the border: identity, religion, and modernity in the Republic of Georgia*. Ithaca, N.Y.: Cornell University Press.

—— V. VATÉ & C. FALGE 2005. Christian conversion in a changing world: confronting issues of inequality, modernity, and morality. *Max Planck Institute for Social Anthropology report* 2004–2005.

REMPEL, H. 1999. Research paper on the church in Naryn, Kyrgyzstan, submitted to Prof. R. P. Prigodich. Denver Seminary, Denver, Colorado. Unpublished MS.

SAROYAN, M. 1997. *Minorities, mullahs, and modernity: reshaping community in the late Soviet Union*. (Research Series **95**). University of California.

SHAHRANI, M. 1984. 'From tribe to umma': comments on the dynamics of identity in Muslim Soviet Central Asia. *Central Asian Survey* **3**: **3**, 27–38.

SHARKEY, H. 2005. Empire and Muslim conversion: historical reflections on Christian missions in Egypt. *Islam and Christian-Muslim Relations* **16**, 43–60.

SLEZKINE, Y. 2000. The USSR as a communal apartment, or how a socialist state promoted ethnic particularism. In *Stalinism: new directions* (ed.) S. Fitzpatrick, 313–47. London: Routledge.

WANNER, C. 2004. Missionaries of faith and culture: evangelical encounters in Ukraine. *Slavic Review* **63**, 732–55.

67

THE FAITH-HEALERS OF THE ASSEMBLIES OF GOD IN BURKINA FASO

Taking responsibility for diseases related to 'living together'

Pierre-Joseph Laurent

Source: *Social Compass*, 48(3) (2001), 333–51.

Prayers for deliverance from demons—harmful spirits—have always been part of the ritual of the Assemblies of God in Burkina Faso. However, the practice of making these prayers as a group on a weekly basis occurred and spread only during the 1980s, at the same time as the appearance of the phenomenon of faith-healers, minor prophets on the margins of Pentecostal orthodoxy.[1]

The faith-healer can be defined as a member of the faithful who has received the gift of healing from the Holy Spirit, and frequently other gifts are added, depending on the case, such as the gift of insight (into the causes of sickness), of speaking in tongues (often in glossolalia), power, interpretation and prophecy. Normally the faith-healer is an ardent proselytizer. While many members of the Assemblies of God refer to the faith-healer as a prophet, it seems to me that the term faith-healer is more appropriate. In *mooré*, the language of the Mossi, it would be *wend nor ressa* (God's interpreter) or *wend nam tern tuumd da* (the one who does God's work).

The faith-healer plays an ambiguous role. He is desirable in order to stir up excitement in a community, but he is still feared because if he has a wide reputation he may steal the show from the pastor. Faith-healers we encountered, though they defended themselves fiercely, were actually professional curers. They earned their living thanks to the reputation that their spiritual gifts made for them. Of course, their discussions gloss over any personal interest they may have in the relationship with their "patients", of even the most subtle kind. To the contrary: they profess to be disinterested in any form of remuneration, and this attests the truth of their gifts and powers.

The Church of the Assemblies of God in Burkina Faso played an important role in the expansion of the Pentecostal movement on the African continent. Pastors of the *mossi* have frequently been given charge of missions of this church in neighbouring countries. It is also true that the church's influence on sister churches in Africa has been great. Since the beginning of the 20th century, beginning with the mother church, today located in Springfield, Missouri (USA), many missions have been sent to the African continent. Their church doctrine is characterized above all by the importance of the experience of the presence of God. Church members receive a baptism in the Holy Spirit, after which God may be felt as intensely present. All this leads to a new relation to the Divine. This experience of the power of God is transmitted to the faithful who in return discover new ways of understanding and living in the world.

It would be a mistake to treat the Church of the Assemblies of God in Burkina Faso as a "new religious movement". It has a very long history—which begins in 1921—and it has many long-time members whose membership should be resituated in its context. In rural areas primarily, Protestants had long symbolized[2] a certain modernity, and for the well-off they were the image of the modernity of the poor. In villages, the Assemblies of God offered to the faithful a space of freedom within which they could try to put in practice, privately, some new ways of living, and where they could also accumulate goods.[3]

That is hardly the whole story. Burkina Faso, or rather the villages which comprise it, is undergoing many more diverse influences than formerly. When we come to the 1980s, we can observe the beginnings of new churches, primarily in urban areas. This new phenomenon was caused by new motivations which did not for all that cancel out the previous ones.[4] In cities, in the outskirts of cities, and eventually in villages, the worship of the Assemblies of God grew like wildfire, at the same time that healing and curing cults appeared, at a time when the Holy Spirit was more and more frequently invoked. Church faithful, alerted in dreams by God, began to find that they had received gifts of power.

It is no accident that the majority of faith-healers emerged at that time as well. These events coincided, in Burkina Faso, with a severe crisis regarding family ties, and the speed with which this crisis worsened was related to the rapid implementation of development plans created by the neo-liberal party (PAS). Their effect, for a large part of the population, had to do with reductions in State support for schools and health care, and by the promotion, among the peasantry, of a particular farming model. The country suffered a 50 percent devaluation of the CFA franc. The plantation economy in coastal countries (hevea, cacao, coffee, bananas) became less prosperous, and this led to reactionary development of certain autochthonous ideologies, in

Ivory Coast above all. The reaction led to the return to Burkina Faso of a large number of Burkinans who had migrated, but who now fled xenophobia. Finally, this was also the time at which the AIDS epidemic declared itself with great virulence in urban and rural areas, resulting, as with the Black Death, in many violent social upheavals.

These large-scale rents in the social fabric led to similarly violent changes in the nature of social identity. They would eventually give rise, among other things, to a real crisis of sorcery, or at least a sharp rise in the number of possession cases, which involved for the most part sicknesses related to "living together". The Pentecostals were among those groups who tried to manage this disturbing trend.

The thesis that I shall defend argues that the healing services offered by the Assemblies of God—which does its recruiting essentially among the urban poor and rural peasants—are mainly based on a therapeutic technique which is composed of two parts, and which as a whole is capable of taking charge of various ailments related to the rapid transformations of the relationships between individuals and the people around them, or between people and the groups they belong to.[5] The novelty is related to the therapeutic attitude. This plays out like a co-operation between the wolf and the lamb, that is, between the pastors and the faith-healers, who co-operate without eliminating all competition and antagonism, since one group characterizes the other as false prophets.[6] We are nonetheless in the presence of a complex response, plural and plurivocal, which is capable of treating diseases linked to the clarification of principles which ruled the ancient forms of making oneself secure, upon which even the converted still depend. We are dealing with a form of modernity, then, one in which the group which has chosen to be faithful becomes in a way the group which is leaving the ancient co-dependent group, whether this be relatives, neighbours, or friends. Here, the accumulation of goods, in a universe where all are dependent (that of the gift, the debt, and where there is help to be asked for, but also that of fear, grudges and revenge), causes fear on the part of the one who gathers and also on the part of the one who has nothing. The first fears thieves, and the second thinks he has been unjustly excluded. In general, those who aspire to accumulate goods end up leaving the village, in order to go to live in a more anonymous environment or to seek new protections for themselves, even against their families, their neighbours and their friends. It is precisely at this point in the process of change that the conversion offered by the Assemblies of God comes into play.

In this sense the collective deliverance meeting and the individual prayers of faith-healers are not opposed to each other, but form a whole which must be analysed as such. Through a subtle interpenetration of the two parts of the therapeutic technique—at first official, concerning the collective prayers for deliverance, and then in the prayers of the faith-healers—new configurations are created, or rather reconstructions of identities[7] are made according to the singular maladies which members of the faithful suffer from. This works best once one realizes that deliverance equals a conversion which opens us up to other possible personalities, and first of all to a readjustment of our relationships with others.

Categories of thought: multiple identity, demonization, modernity

African societies are in the process of transforming rapidly and they certainly need to be analysed in the spirit of an open and dynamic style of thought.[8] The consciousness of sin, or the idea of beating one's breast is reinforced through the attempts to follow the doctrine of the Assemblies of God[9] (among other things), but these doctrines are not powerful enough to replace ancient forms of inward acceptance of laws and principles and of relationships with other persons. This situation leads to a "well-tempered" conversion which I will describe with the help of two particularities of the notion of the person.

In the first place, a belief in the "millenarian reign of Jesus" or in the promise of a thousand years of happiness, through the institution of a kingdom on earth[10] leads to a more optimistic vision of eschatology or of the consciousness of fault, and therefore guilt is less important than in concepts of a Last Judgement in which an inexorable division between the saved and the damned is made. In this sense a belief in the millenarian reign is still primarily related to a popular conception which hopes for happiness more than it fears suffering divine wrath (*dies irae*). This doctrinal point takes on all its meaning when it is set beside the hope for an eternal life which is itself opposed to any metempsychosis of ancestral souls. What is promised here is not a return to the earth. We will be finished with the bitter struggle for life that is the lot of the peasant, who believes that he suffers too much. Salvation from this point on means eternal life. In addition to that, it is a rejection of the conditions under which peasants live. The demonization of ancient customs by the Pentecostalists is related to the unbearable life these customs are part of, which began to get worse (pain, misery, lack of schools, lack of health care etc.). The figure of the devil therefore expresses a great fear, that of recognizing oneself only too well in the peasant beside you, always too close. People feared falling back into misery if their own conversions to a form of modernity failed to hold good. The demonization of *mossi* traditions by the Pentecostal Churches appears, from that point, as its own ghost.

Second, diseases also relate to the figure of the devil, in the sense of a possession caused by one or more harmful spirits. In addition, the idea of being possessed implies the notion of a person as lastingly composed of more than one decision-making agent (in the sense of a multiple self). This multiple self means that the person can keep intact the possibility of reaching out to those around him or her, as well as the possibility of denying guilt and thus reducing the feeling of guilt.[11]

As a result, the belief in a millenarian reign and in the permanence of a self made up of more than one decision-making agent moderates the feeling of belonging to a simple Western type of modernity, while these conceptions lead to the working out of new forms of life in common. To support this suggestion, I will describe several aspects of two healing/curing rituals practised within the Assemblies of God: private exorcism, conducted by a faith-healer, and collective deliverance ceremonies. The point will be to show that these two therapeutic attitudes, apparently opposed, are in reality one form, whose subtle interweaving explains much about the success of Pentecostal Churches.

First therapeutic procedure: exorcism by faith-healers

Here we are discussing exorcism sessions conducted by a faith-healer (minor prophet), or possibly by his assistants, at his house. The session may last a half hour.[12]

Processes of legitimation: steps in initiation and first miracles

The faith-healer attributes the origin of his gifts to certain dramatic events which permit him to see the world in a different way. He appears to be motivated by the decision to choose life, though he has experienced death. Each opportunity to cure another person becomes an opportunity for him to remember that determining moment, his true initiation, when the choice to live was made, while in a state of super-power and super-nature. It is his force, his conviction, and thus his faith which he transmits to the sick people he examines. From this, he produces a new and original life-story which gives him at one and the same time a new identity and a healing power. He relates this to his victory over sickness (even over the people who wished him ill) and to his initiatory quest-voyage. The story ends with baptism into the Holy Spirit, which anyone can obtain, and which constitutes conversion. Baptism allows one to believe in a new destiny, and it is this which, transformed into a narrative, possesses therapeutic virtue.

Provoking confessions

The word for purity in the *mooré* language (*peelem*) expresses the idea of whiteness. It is related to the idea of non-aggression. Confession, a necessary preliminary step prior to exorcism, is nothing more than the admission of weakness made by the sick person, followed by his or her statement of allegiance to the faith-healer. The sick person, who is purifying him- or herself, admits defeat, and agrees to discard old obsolete protections, which have been defeated by a superior power,[13] in order to become able to give him- or herself up to God's power, and equally to the faith-healer, who, making up any deficiency, takes responsibility for the battle against the evil spirits. In other words, it is a matter of an act of faith, of the patient's belief in the healer's power and in the operations which he or she will perform on behalf of the sick person, so that the latter may recover his or her own identity through conversion to new protections, those furnished by a strong God, stronger than the strongest sorcerers.

The gift of insight

The gift of insight is essentially the ability of the faith-healer to diagnose the ailment of the patient. The healer's reputation rests on the delicacy and sensitivity with which he or she is able to understand the sick person, although the environment may be one in which multiple transformations may occur. Naming the sickness is the essential first step toward exorcism. This implies a classification of sicknesses, actual contemporary problems which express themselves in a culturally coded manner, especially when they are connected to harmful mismanagement of the individual's relationships with those around him or her.

Initially, "indexed sicknesses" (to employ the *mossi* expression) carry the meaning of being ascribable to someone. The harmful effects usually have to do with someone who is part of the social world of the sick person, some neighbour, relative, or friend whose presence has become unbearable. It is a matter of the difficulty of living together, which gets expressed through eruptions of jealousy, resentment or hatred. These give rise to the various individual profiles of possession cases and concern something like persecution complexes. Such ailments, closely connected to a social and economic environment which is undergoing rapid transformation, make up a significant portion of possession cases, correlated with the rise of the new power, already "trans-national", which is represented by the Holy Spirit.

Second, possession, or rather this other voice, the voice of the genie, echoes problems which more directly imply a person who is guilty of some excesses or failure to observe some prohibition (cf. the genie of alcohol, the genie of laziness, of adultery . . .). These latter sicknesses are not strongly distinguished from the previous category. Both imply genies and multiple selves. But they still constitute a different transformation, based on the notions of purity and uncleanness. We cannot speak here of real guilt, or of a strong consciousness of sin, but we should speak rather in this context of fear, fear of vengeance from an intransigent judgement which remembers the nature of the transgression and applies the punishment required. The patient and even the faith-healer can fall under this judgement if they do not follow the prescribed steps: respect assures protection, and transgression leads to sickness, even to death.

A third major category comprises natural sicknesses or sicknesses of God (in this sense, that only God knows the future). Most sick persons in this category will go to consult nurses and/or *tiim moor soaba* (traditional practitioners). Along the therapeutic itinerary, already described several times, the sufferers can at any moment in the quest for health decide to put themselves completely in the hands of God's power and the miraculous force of the Holy Spirit which, *hic et nunc*, saves people from incurable sicknesses, promises success in examinations, and makes jobs easier to find.

The field of action for faith-healers is thus enormous and has to do with a certain accumulation of functions. First there is the function of the doctor (taken over when medicine proves unable to cure the sufferer). There is also the function of the seer (*baga*) and the healer or curer (*tiim moor soaba*). However, the faith-healers themselves recognize a greater effectiveness for their cures when it is a matter of "sicknesses from genies" in their terms. The faith-healers therefore are closer to seers (*baga* and *kinkirbaga*), though they do not use the same techniques nor do they treat the same sicknesses. It is important to note that miraculous cures are usually counted up at collective deliverance meetings at which the power of prayer is even more effective (see below).

A third person who erases guilt

Genies are at fault in the first two categories of illnesses. The nature of a composite self made up of more than one agent (not unified)—here genies provoke the transgression—makes it the case that no person is ever really brought before his judges, nor consequently before God, and even the idea of a tenuous (or non-existent) Alliance with God moderates the consciousness of sin. In other words, one does not accuse oneself, but on the contrary, one makes accusations. And if there is an accusation, it must be psychically and socially bearable. Thus, in traditional *mossi* society, regarding relatively minor offences, the important thing is to punish without destroying, that is, without ruining the social respectability on which individual survival depends, just as the survival of the group does. It is appropriate then to use customary designations which are socially acceptable for indicating the guilty party. This principle of prudence aims at preserving, according to the particular case, a family, a line of descent, or a village, to the extent that a "custom-based understanding" (*wum taaba*: an understanding) creates relationships of dependence with those around us, based on the fear of the other, which at the same time guarantees each other's security.[14]

As the faith-healer listens to this other voice (which is also that of the possessed patient) to which he attaches such importance, the figure of the genie becomes central. In this type of possession it is the *zina* (evil spirit) type of genie who does the possessing. This refers to the unhappy spirit of an individual excluded from the realm of the ancestors (*kiim kuulogo*), and so from any possibility of a return to the land of the living,[15] following upon a non-natural death, that is, death caused by someone. As if to obtain revenge for the evil intentions which have been directed, with or without their agreement, at the living person, the genie enters the body of a person and takes control by capturing two decision-making functions. The *zina* can either take advantage of an individual's weakness (lack of protection, failure to observe prohibitions etc.) or be sent by someone. This person, in exchange for having his desire for vengeance satisfied, which happens when the possession is successful, offers the *zina* a new life (a new body). In order to do this, he arranges for the genie to be able to get at the victim through sorcerous manipulations (*sônia*) which are intended to bring about the weakening of the victim's protections (protections for various parts of his body).

The faith-healer joins battle and confronts the evil spirits. During the battle, he or she has visions which are so many attempts to name the ailments and make them easier to understand. The faith-healer is the only one who speaks at this point in the process. The patient keeps silent because he or she has had his or her own voice stolen by genies who can nonetheless accuse their victim without compromising him or her. The patient indicates approval or disapproval of what is being said by movements of the body.

This genie-voice, the voice of evil spirits or demons, has a strange power to set free the one who is possessed, through the expression of resentments, grudges or pent-up hatred. This other voice, which is no longer the voice which properly belongs to the individual, can be approached through a conception of the multiple self. This way of looking at things furnishes an excuse which renders the person innocent of his or her own errors, but it also permits further accusations without getting caught up in the vicious circle of vengeance. The other voice has its own therapeutic effectiveness, through allowing the individual and those around him or her to identify, name and understand sicknesses, and thus to adapt to that which is at stake in the complexity which knots together all their destinies, in an economic and social environment where the group one belongs to is a source of security as much as of obligation.

It is appropriate to situate the analysis in a context of partial elucidation, of "between oneself", where accumulation is desired, but rarely attained. This is where the genie symbolizes the other essentially—the other than oneself, certainly, but also the others, that is the other people around the sick person who are experienced as a burden, but who of course cannot be removed, even if their death is often wished for as part of the expression of feelings of jealousy (which leads us back in the direction of sorcery); for survival, or the hope of reconciliation, always comes from the others. Confronted with a situation in which the invading presence of others becomes more unbearable every day (the desires of individual subjects—of modernity—being expressed more and more openly), the faith-healers of the Assemblies of God try to respond through the substitution of a conversion to faith in another power. The conversion must leave a person capable of existing within the hybrid context of today's *mossi* society, in which the customary forms of living together, demonized certainly to soma degree, still play a role. Strategies of survival, for the majority of people, demand (and will for some time) that people find a *modus vivendi* within their group, doing this in spite of the new strengthening of the individual side.

Deliverance as conversion

For the patient, the prayer of exorcism is the essential moment of the experience of divine Power. For the one who has been purified, and who in consequence has put him- or herself in the hands of God (and in the hands of the healer), this is the crucial test, the test of fear, of dread, of anguish: now the sufferer is naked, without protection from the revelation of the causes of his suffering, or from the exposure of the (customary) ways of "living together", in which success consists in keeping everyone at a certain distance from oneself. At the point of self-abandon, the sufferer experiences the fear of emptiness (of meaninglessness) and can only give him- or herself up to the protective power of God (and thus to the power of the faith-healer). The exorcism becomes here the moment of becoming conscious of the necessity of a conversion to a possible other person. This is variously expressed amid crying and screaming. The confrontation between the faith-healer and the patient leads to the working out of a syncretism which is able to produce a new synthesis between the security provided by those around the sufferer and the desire to live independently.[16]

Second therapeutic procedure: prayers for collective deliverance

The best-known collective deliverance rituals of today often originated with small prayer groups begun by individual pastors. This kind of collective prayer is usually found in urban settings, even if rural churches are involved now—though the rural churches are welcoming a growing number of city folk who are always looking for greater effectiveness in the rituals. Church members who have received spiritual gifts (faith-healers or pastors) lead the prayers. Each well-known ceremony may draw more than 300 people to a ceremony that lasts nearly four hours (the ceremonies often alternate with regular Sunday worship). So much for a quick sketch of the chief components of the second therapeutic procedure put in operation by the Assemblies of God.

The assembly's preparation for the battle

For as much as an hour, sometimes, the assembly, encouraged by the zeal of the organizers, sings praises to the Lord. These hymns concern four major themes: praise to God, the power of God, God's infinite knowledge including the personal problems of each one, and God's victory over the demons.

Obviously, they intend little by little to whip up an atmosphere of exaltation which is propitious to manifestations of the Spirit, and which prepares each one of the faithful to do battle. The songs also mention aspects of Pentecostal doctrine which play a role in divine healing, above all a faith in the God of miracles who is still able to accomplish, as it is written in Scripture, what he accomplished 2000 years ago.

The preaching attempts to clarify the main thrust of the ritual: those who have been possessed, we are told, will be delivered. In order to make that particular ceremony unique and special, the pastor begins to describe it as such, telling the faithful that they are indeed lucky to be able to participate *hic et nunc* in the victory of the Spirit over the demons. "There are evil spirits which speak to you, but today, right now, at this moment, we know that the Saviour, Christ, will cure those who suffer from them." Most often the preaching sketches out in broad terms what is about to take place, the steps of the ritual of deliverance. The argument bears at first upon two observations: there are evil spirits within you, and Jesus is alive. The preacher draws this conclusion: Jesus and Satan cannot live together within the same territory. Then the preacher presents, with long demonstrations and many Biblical passages cited in support, the three steps of the battle which he is trying to make understandable by saying the following: "The Spirit is among you. Jesus lives in our hearts. The victory therefore is within us." Each participant thus is told that he or she must become involved in the ritual if victory is to be won. The preparation for battle against the evil spirits is collective, but the victory remains personal and forms part of the experience of conversion, in the sense of self-abandon before the Divine power (they say: "I give myself to the Lord").

Unmasking the impure and detecting demons

The one who possess the gifts of the Holy Spirit can unmask impure persons, thanks to the superiority which the immediate relation to God confers—a relation which, if it is not attended by a certain temperance, can rapidly lead to totalitarian sorts of excess,[17] through the evocation of a jealous God who can tolerate neither competition nor disobedience. I have suggested that in this connection we speak of the provoking of a confession ("inverted") by contrast with the Christian practices with which we ourselves are familiar.

Thus, in the following passage, a famed faith-healer reminds us of what is at stake in deliverance, the process through which, only thinly disguised, a guilty party will be accused before the assembly of not having observed certain prohibitions.

> He came to see me at my place but I knew I could do nothing for him. I gave up the battle then and he left again. Then God revealed to me that someone was still drinking alcohol, still smoking and

> chasing girls. That means that though he had sinned, he had not confessed in the name of Jesus, before God. Nonetheless he is here today among us and he has not told everything. I'm asking him to leave. It is necessary that someone like that confess his sins before being present for the prayers of deliverance.

Head lowered, a man suddenly gets up and leaves. Despite the semantics of confession employed, it's obvious that what is being done here is an attempt to make up the lack of an admission of guilt. Everything happens, in many ways, as if a third person took on the responsibility for recognizing the sin, in place of a person who was inclined to deny responsibility, whether thanks to a multiple self, or by blaming others for his troubles. Thus, thanks to a divine revelation, the faithful inspired by the gifts of healing can also run down the list of sins and non-observance of prohibitions, pointing out the one guilty of these transgressions before the whole assembly. This description obviously goes beyond the notion of guilt.

The moderator tries to create a general climate of suspicion.

> You who drink alcohol, you who smoke cigarettes, you who have had an abortion, I ask you to leave. The people I am speaking of can go out and get right with God, in the name of Jesus. That is why I have stopped the singing. If you don't leave—there is no problem,

he explains, in a tone heavy with menace which suggests the vengeance of God irritated by the disorder human disobedience always causes.

Concerning the relationship between individual exorcism (a consultation with a patient at the home of the faith-healer) and the collective deliverance ceremony (which takes place in the temple, before the assembly gathered together, in the presence of pastors and faithful inspired by gifts of healing), we will observe that the faith-healer has established a prior relationship with the majority of patients during individual consultations. By this means, the sick know the reasons for their troubles before they get to the collective deliverance. Either they have been cured through prayer (set free) by the faith-healer and have been invited to come testify before the assembly, or else the individual exorcism did not work completely and the healer has to fall back on the power of group prayer.

As a result we are led to grasp these two procedures both as integral parts of a single unified therapeutic technique, which draws its effectiveness from the complementarity of various types of specific action which each part can bring forth out of its own particular resources. And due to this structure, sick people who attend deliverance ceremonies without first going through the step of making a private visit to the faith-healer are generally considered to be insufficiently prepared to go through the collective ceremony successfully. Unmasked, they are sent back to see the faith-healer so that they can be confessed, purified and converted. The rundown of ailments at the collective meeting does not have from that point the same function as an individual exorcism (cf. the first therapeutic procedure). It is less a matter, here, of proceeding to diagnose the ailments each patient is suffering from, than of recalling collectively the reasons which have been given already to each patient in order that they may be able to understand their problems. In other words, the naming of the causes of the suffering becomes a preliminary step which normally is accomplished "in private", in a confrontation between the faith-healer and the patient. If any reinforcement is necessary in order for the patient to be able to believe in this revelation which he or she has been given, namely, that another life is possible if conversion is accepted, that extra force must be found in the collective prayers for deliverance.

To this end, the listing of illnesses at the collective meeting takes the form of a full-dress battle plan which takes shape progressively. Nothing is left to chance. Everyone's role is precisely determined. The meticulous organization leads to a sort of codification of emotions, and various established categories of bodily ailments are filled in. From this point four major categories of participants are clearly established.

First, the group of the sick and suffering are identified. There is no question of diagnosing all the maladies they suffer from at this point, but each patient is reminded of the reasons which were previously given to them as means of understanding their problems.

The arrangement of the ritual requires the identification of the participants, and that they be sorted out into broad categories of ailments. The benches they are sitting on have been up till now set out in no particular arrangement in the church, but when the moderator orders it, the benches are lined up in four rows. The first two rows follow the distinction which has been established between two main types of possession (see above). Then there are persons who have something to ask for (examinations which they face, admission contests, requests for employment etc.), and lastly "those who went to the hospital and did not find the answer to their problems" who had, that is, "sicknesses of God".

Second, a group of witnesses is identified. A pastor takes their names and makes a list. The things they are going to talk about are announced. These faithful have experienced divine healing, and have been asked to return to testify before the assembly. They will testify to their gratitude toward God's power, and also, by their presence alone, they will testify to the truth of the miraculous power of the Spirit.

Third, the choir of church women, accompanied by a youth orchestra composed of percussion instruments, sings hymns to God. The pastor explains that during the deliverance, "God wants us to glorify him." He suggests that "If we praise God, a benediction will come down on us", bringing to light a well-understood conception of gift and counter-gift in the relation between God and the faithful.

Fourth, the group of exorcists/healers is put in place. Their job is to establish the relation between the sufferers and the Holy Spirit. The moderator calls to his aid those prominent members of the Pentecostal Church who may be present at the assembly. Officially, they do not take part in the healing or cures; they only lay on their hands and Jesus acts. Nevertheless, they occupy the key third-person position upon the path toward divine Power, where, by a semantic leap, the power of God is equated with the power embodied by the exorcists or the faith-healers.

The presence of the Spirit and the battle against spirits which cause suffering

The status and roles of the four principal groups participating have been carefully established and are now known to all. The tension has reached a fever pitch. The ceremony has been going on for about three hours. The wait becomes unbearable. The crowd, standing, shouts and claps loudly.

This is the moment when a pastor or one of the faithful begins to speak in tongues. Possessed by the Spirit, his voice becomes another voice, that of the divinity which speaks directly to the assembly in that moment. When one speaker in tongues stops to catch his breath, another faithful—also inspired by the Spirit—interprets the glossolalic episode. "God says he is the supreme chief, that he hears prayers, and will answer them." The voices of the crowd become more muted, and the voice of the Spirit is there among them. Humans and the divinity are side by side, almost touching . . . Something miraculous is about to happen in the radiance of this brief experience of the presence of God among men. Divinity expresses itself through the human voice in the middle of a babbling crowd of voices.

Faith at this precise moment means nothing other than the true experience of a collective emotion linked to manifestations of the Holy Spirit. Faith looks back, as well, on these supernatural occasions, at the memory of conversion experiences. This memory is intensely felt as a dramatic moment of self-abandon, that is a becoming conscious of the defeat of ancient protective powers which nonetheless controlled one's relationships with others.[18] The cries, the tears, the shaking, all express anguish before the unnameable emptiness of a glimpsed future, which the hope for a new world, which has been declared but is not yet revealed, does not yet reassure. The primary demand of faith, which is hammered in by the organizers of the ceremony of collective deliverance, consists in reminding the sufferers over and over that they must, without any other guarantees, give themselves up to the all-powerful protection of the "Great God", in order to have faith in the possible establishment of other relationships among the faith community.

For the battle against harmful spirits (genies, demons), two groups act together to conduct the deliverance: the praisers and the exorcists. The first give glory to God, recalling the importance of faith and obedience, while the second group calls for the intervention of the Holy Spirit. Apparently even before battling the evil spirits, the ritual must establish a dynamic equilibrium between gifts (praise given by men and Power given by God) and debts (God's silence in the face of the suffering of his creatures, the prayers for power and for the breaking of chains on the part of men) in the relationship between humans and the divinity, with God, formidable, feared, powerful.

Deliverance now takes on a quite individual character, which seems anyway to be its true nature. Even if the preparatory phase of the ceremony is collective (presenting the advantage, in relation to the prayers of the faith-healers, of compounding emotions and feelings of power), the battle itself, as the preacher promises in his opening remarks, remains an individual experience. "God is the Eternal God, he acts within you, if you have faith you will be saved." The healers come close to each participant and lay their hands on them, demanding that the demons come out of their victims. Cries begin to ring out. The exorcist summons the demons to depart in the name of God. "Out, out, in the name of Jesus, or I'll burn you!" Many sufferers, faced with the psychic violence of the battle, collapse. They are then carried by young assistants toward the altar and laid out on braided mats which are quickly covered with people lying down. The demons resist and the battle rages more fiercely than before. Little groups of exorcists form and begin to bear down on tough cases. Women collapse uttering rending screams. Some shake, some are seized by convulsions, some enter a trance state. Two or three assistants grapple with those in convulsion, holding their arms and legs down until they can be bound with ropes.

We note in this place that the speech of the spirit—that other speech (of the other-than-myself) which liberates the possessed patients during the exorcism, freeing them from being the author of their own suffering—that speech is lost here, covered over by the tumult of a crowd which is collectively involved in a battle which each patient wages against him- or herself, or against the dramatic consciousness of his or her condition such as it will appear to him or her from now on.

Result of divine intervention: praise, thanks and testimony

Without further ado, the moderator of the ceremony interrupts the battle and declares: "The Power has acted, you possess it, and so you are cured." Immediately, in the grip of a vision, a faith-healer states the result of the battle: "We know that 24 people have been delivered." The logic of this statement will be quickly passed over in favour of testimonies (*kasseto*). Adroitly, the moderator will not talk directly to those persons who are supposed to have been cured at the end of the battle just concluded, but rather, in a more general way, to persons who have been cured previously. At this point he can refer to a prearranged list of witnesses.

From that point, it appears that it is less important to establish the tangible proof of divine intervention than to provide all the participants with what they need in order to assign a positive result to the battle. This sort of inventory is aimed at the faithful, who are on the lookout for signs which confirm divine intervention, and who are particularly apt to credit God with the even the tiniest changes in their suffering or their conditions, in the hope of confirming most of all for themselves the solid foundation of their conversions, and their allegiance to the new Power.

Officially, witnesses are invited to give glory to God and to His power; the list contains names of persons who have been delivered from evil spirits or miraculously cured from "sicknesses of God". Nonetheless another justification could be suggested. These narratives could be seen as part of the follow-up to the process of the cure, in which testimony is one step among others. What is more, this final phase of the therapeutic process as begun in the deliverance ritual ends up with the testimony of those who received a miraculous cure, and they confirm the effectiveness of the Power. At that point the testimony of the witness itself also has therapeutic power, linked to mimetic effects which I would arrange in this manner: someone, who is just like me, was cured; so why not me? The testimonies accentuate the apparent truthfulness of the collective and personal experience of the power of the Spirit.

The effectiveness of a dual therapeutic arrangement

We shall try to show through a discussion of the two therapeutic techniques at work within the Assemblies of God that deliverance is actually part of a process which involves much more of the entire faith community, and which lasts much longer, than Assembly doctrine wishes to admit. For example, a patient's visit to a faith-healer, whether before or after attendance at a collective deliverance meeting, is an important step in diagnosis, but also an important first step in beginning the process of the cure, or in following it up, making sure the patient is not doing those things which he or she has been forbidden to do, and still following a holy and therefore pure life path. Pentecostalist cures are considered miraculous and thus immediate, but on the practical level they are connected to an act of faith, to a conversion to another person who the sufferer might become, perhaps rapidly, but most often progressively.

Looking more closely, curing and healing practices—quite apart from the official rhetoric which sticks to descriptions of miraculous events in which cures happen *hic et nunc*—occur as part of a long period of treatment of patients, which takes place on an individual basis with the faith-healer, and in collective fashion within the community of the faithful. This is all made possible by the interpenetration of two therapeutic techniques, one which is authoritative in the sense of ritual prescription, which allows lesser spirits to express themselves, which takes account of the alibis and excuses which can be offered by a self which is composed of multiple agents (which thus has characteristics connected to traditional conceptions of living together), and the other authoritative in an official sense, which takes account of God's omnipotence.

The dual therapeutic position of Pentecostal healing is based upon the following facts. The leaders of the Church are afraid of the faith-healers, and believe that they are obliged to contain them as best they can. Any popular outburst such as a too-exclusive appropriation of the evangelical Spirit by one of the faithful in an overzealous mood can lead to schismatic tensions. In other words, the Holy Spirit, institutionally speaking, remains a two-edged sword which is always capable of challenging all forms of authority. Thus, while the Spirit installs the leaders of the Church—homologically, the law of God becomes the law of the pastors—the Spirit makes them weak as well, by leaving the permanent possibility that a faith-healer (a minor prophet) will become established within the community, become authorized to speak to the faithful, without control, without restriction, because he has been chosen by God. But over and above this institutional antagonism, a pragmatic collaboration frequently occurs between pastors and certain faith-healers. From this there arises an original form of actions, which are coherent, effective, well adapted to the transformations of the contexts of ordinary life, and more closely intertwined in terms of techniques than official Pentecostal doctrine is able to admit.

In this sense, the collective deliverance meetings and the individual prayers of faith-healers are not opposed to one another but form a single whole which must be analysed as such. Thanks to the subtle manner in which they are interwoven, these two aspects of the faith-healing process combine to form a single therapeutic technique. This technique is a response to the elucidation of the older traditional forms of seeking social and economic security, which have been demonized, but which must nonetheless be held in reserve in case of certain difficulties, or as part of some eventual inclusion in a form of modernity, and it is precisely this wavering back and forth between two relationships which are hostile to all others, which becomes unbearable, unless some other form of conversion intervenes.[19]

The force of divine healing here consists in mixing the official doctrine of the Assemblies of God—that which demonizes the older forms of thinking as part of an introduction to a type of modernity—with relatively subtle arrangements, as regards the relation to the law, permitted through the concept of a multiple self (here revealed by the spirit under possession)—which can still be discussed in the intimacy (and the authority) of a meeting between the faith-healer and the patient. This allows the aspirations of the faithful to be taken into consideration, as well as their many social and material limitations, which could take the form, for example, of separation from those around them, without perhaps going as far as denying them. This very subtle arrangement of social relationships is made possible thanks to a doctrine which includes a belief in Jesus' millenarian reign and in the permanence of a concept of the notion of the person based on a notion of the multiple self, a doctrine which, without admitting as much, comes up with a normative cultural mixture which echoes the transformations undergone by the society. To some extent, it seems to me possible to speak in this connection of a popular conception (already "trans-nationalized" to a great extent) of modernity.

So it is essentially at the moment of individual exorcism that the voice of the spirit (one's own other voice) is most clearly expressed. The faith-healer carefully listens to and questions this voice, which sometimes leads to the accusation of a guilty party, thanks in part to an atmosphere of confidentiality. We are in the presence, therefore, of the more official part of the therapeutic apparatus of the Assemblies of God. This part of the therapy can, if necessary, dare to stray from doctrinal purity, in order to suggest a mixture, which cannot of course be admitted to have occurred, of traditional and Pentecostal methods, in order to cater to the expectations of certain patients, adding the nuances which answer these expectations. The other part of the process, the collective ceremony, is obliged to be more orthodox in its details, since it is based on an experience of the divine Power, and furnishes testimony to the effectiveness of this power. So the organizers of the collective ceremony keep open the possibility of referring a given patient to a private session, if they feel this is necessary. The moderator of the collective deliverance meeting does nothing more than this when he excludes a member from the assembly on grounds that he or she is impure. In this way the organizers can take charge of this person once again in private, in an ad hoc fashion and according to a more syncretic procedure, which would be less presentable in the eyes of Pentecostal institutions, which, fearing any loss of effectiveness of the Spirit which might be caused by mixing in other ritual, have demonized (or have appeared to do so) all the custom-based practices.

In other words, private, individual exorcism—monopolized by the faith-healers practising at the margins of the institutional Church—has essentially to do only with diagnosis and eventually the designation of a guilty party, while the collective ceremony has to do with something unsaid, that is, the result of diagnoses established earlier on the basis of private visits (see above). In this way, most patients know the causes of their troubles before submitting themselves to the power of collective prayer. And it is precisely those who have not understood these causes that the moderator of the collective deliverance meeting tries to unmask. These patients, who do not know the causes of their suffering since their persecutors have not been identified, cannot hope to be cured, since they have not given themselves to God, nor to the faith-healer. This situation must lead back toward conversion, which would connect up the recognition of the uselessness of previously used protections with purity, obedience and belief in a new power.

Through divine cures and healing, the Assemblies of God are able to give coherent explanations for many cases of ailments and suffering which actually involve various pathologies of "living together". These arise in the context of a society which is buffeted by many rapid changes. We have before us here a context in which the coercive power of social customs has been diminished, but which at the same time has not quite been counterbalanced by a mass assumption of membership in new forms of living together (citizenship for example). In other words, the principles which govern civil society have not erased those of the "village peace" (*wum taaba*: the understanding). In these gaps in authority, new norms coming from different sources of power which co-exist (power of custom, local elected officials, the State etc.) pile up and get in each other's way, casting doubt on each other's legitimacy and opening the way for campaigns to uphold a certain position, image or identity, which can sometimes turn violent. Pentecostalists enter this no man's land, and they respond to these temporary identity crises with novel solutions, closely enough attuned to the preoccupations of some groups within the population to calm the apprehensions they feel. Pentecostahsm responds by offering these people new forms of symbolization and thus of appropriation of what they have lived through.

Notes

1 In 1999, on the occasion of their 85th anniversary, the Assemblies of God boasted 32 million members from 158 different countries ("Where we've been" A/G online USA, 2000, p. 2). The most important faith communities are located in Brazil, which has no less than 13 million members (E. L. Nascimento, "Praise the Lord and Pass the Catsup", *News from Brasil*, cover story, 1995). There are 2.5 million members in the United States, 1 million converts in Nigeria, Peru and Korea (N. Luca, "Pentecôtisme en Corée", *Archives de Sciences Sociales des Religions* 105, 1999, pp. 99–123). This is without counting the churches in Mexico and Argentina (A. Corten, *Le pentecôtisme au Brésil. Emotion du pauvre et romantisme théologique*, Paris, Karthala, 1995, p.75). In Burkina Faso, there are more than a half-million members.

2 The earliest missionaries landed in Burkina Faso in 1921.

3 P.-J. Laurent, "Prosélytisme religieux, intensification agricole et organisation paysanne. Le rôle des Assemblées de Dieu dans l'émergence de la Fédération *Wend-Yam* au Burkina Faso", in J.-P. Jacob and P. Lavigne Delville, *Les associations paysannes: organisation et dynamiques*, Paris, APAD-IUED-Karthala, 1994, pp. 155–179.

4 P.-J. Laurent, "L'Eglise des Assemblées de Dieu du Burkina Faso. Histoire, transitions et recompositions identitaires", *Archives de Sciences Sociales des Religions* 105, 1999, pp. 71–97.

5 On all this, see: P.-J. Laurent, *Sémantique populaire du détournement dans les associations de développement en pays mossi (Burkina Faso)*, Nouveaux Cahiers de l'IUED, Geneva and Paris, PUF, no. 8, January 2000; P.-J. Laurent, "Entre ville et campagne. Le big man local ou la 'gestion coup d'Etat' de l'espace public", *Politique africaine* 80, Dec. 2000, pp. 169–182.

6 The logic of segmentation, in which the power stakes are always in the control of the healing business and leadership of the faithful, opposes the pastors,

legitimized by the Pentecostal institutions, to initiates who have been baptized in the Spirit, afterward receiving, without intermediary or control, messages from the Divine authorizing them also to speak in public and sometimes tempting them to found their own church.

7 In the sense of a birth, or a cohabitation, employing the terms used by R. Bastide, *Les religions africaines au Brésil*, Paris, PUF, 1995 (2nd edition).

8 Cf.G. Balandier, *Sociologie actuelle de l'Afrique noire*, Paris, PUF, 1955, p. 489.

9 As Andreas Zempléni was able to show, it seems less a question of a transition from persecution complexes to guilt complexes, although this can occur under certain circumstances (cf. the case of the "old man in the wagon"; P.-J. Laurent, "Conversions aux Assemblées de Dieu du Burkina Faso. Modernité et socialité", *Journal des Africanistes* 68[n°1–2], 1998, pp. 67–98), than a question of co-existence, which of course has to be resituated in an environment of transformation of forms of persecution and guilt. See, regarding this debate: M. Auge, *Génie du paganisme*, Paris, Gallimard, 1982, p. 80; M. Douglas, *De la souillure. Essais sur la notions de pollution et de tabou*, Paris, Maspero, 1971, p. 194; M.-C. Ortigues and E. Ortigues, *Oedipe africain*, Paris, L'Harmattan, 1984; C. Piault (ed.), *Prophétisme et thérapeutique. Albert Atcho et la communauté de Bregbo*, Paris, Hermann, 1975; P. Ricoeur, *Finitude et culpabilité. II: La symbolique du mal*, Paris, Aubier, 1960; A. Zempléni, "De la persécution à la culpabilité", in C. Piault (ed.), *Prophétisme et thérapeutique. Albert Atcho et la communauté de Bregbo*, Paris, Hermann, 1975, pp. 153–218.

10 In the Book of Revelation (ch. 20) the Apostle announces that God will put Satan in chains for 1000 years.

11 On this topic, see M. Douglas: "L'idée du 'moi' multiple permet des disculpations douces comme des fictions polies", in Douglas, "La connaissance de soi", in *Comment pense les institutions*, Paris, La Découverte/MAUSS, 1999, p. 160.

12 For fuller details see: P.-J. Laurent, *La guérison divine Ethnographie d'une Eglise Pentecôtiste (les Assemblées du Dieu du Burkina Faso)*, Paris.

13 This is related to the *auto-da-fé*. In some cases the faith-healer can go on to destroy in the fire the old protections, proving thereby their ineffectiveness.

14 The notion of an understanding (*wum taaba*) is related to the idea of a custom-based understanding which should be sharply distinguished from civil peace (in the sense of a common foundation for the "common good"). On this topic, see: P.-J. Laurent, *Une association de développement en pays mossi. Le don comme ruse*, Paris, Karthala, chapter 8, pp. 243–260.

15 A return in the sense of a metempsychosis, in which the spirit of a single ancestor can live in more than one body.

16 Regarding conversion experiences: A. Mary and H. Piault, "Parcours de conversion", *Journal des africanistes* 68(1–2), 1999, p. 335.

17 Which in certain ways recall the excesses of the Inquisition in the history of Western Christianity.

18 Ultimately, none other than the old world displaced.

19 In another context, it is quite interesting to note that in his work devoted to the Bwiti of the Fang of Gabon, a "syncretic cult par excellence" André Mary shows that their "system of the world is not opposed to the system of ancestry and lineal descent because the Bwiti do not attempt to tear the individual away from his belonging to a family, and do not demand that he seek his salvation or personal destiny outside the community and its development", A. Mary, *Le défi du syncrétisme. Le travail symbolique de la religion d'Eboga (Gabon)*, Paris, EHESS, 1999, p. 180.

Part 17

TEXTS BIBLICAL AND LOCAL

68

THE FUNDAMENTALS OF FERTILITY

Cosmology and conversion in a southwestern Nigerian town

Elisha P. Renne

Source: *Journal of the Royal Anthropological Institute*, (N.S.) 8 (2002), 551–69.

> In the beginning when God created the heavens and the earth. . . .
>
> (Genesis 1: 1)

> Let us not mix up heaven and earth, the global stage and the local scene, the human and the nonhuman. . . .
>
> (Latour 1993: 3)

The assumption that distinct dichotomies such as modern and traditional or secular and religious exist, parodied by Latour (1993) in his admonition that they should not be mixed, has recently been critiqued in several studies of religion and the nation-state (van der Veer & Lehman 1999). By presuming that secularism is associated with modernity – whereby religious belief and practices are believed to diminish in importance in both public and private spheres – social analysts have failed to realize the continuing impact of religion on political movements associated with the modern nation-state. Yet some political thinking is grounded in biblical texts, for example in narratives about chosenness, rebirth, and messianic deliverance. As van der Veer and Lehman (1999: 8) have observed, it is important 'to revitalize discussion of religion's place in modern society, which theories of secularization have brought to a dead end'.

This is a particularly appropriate subject for re-examination in many post-colonial settings as ideas about chosenness and messianic deliverance underwrote colonial activities in these places – for both colonial officials and missionaries. Furthermore, in many African societies, reading and writing – often initially of biblical texts (Peel 2000: 223) – came to be a marker of a modern identity. This article examines the consequences of 'becoming modern' (or 'enlightened'; Peel 1978), which, in towns throughout southwestern Nigeria, has been associated with conversion to Christianity and with the acquisition of literacy. Yet while many women and men in southwestern Nigeria view conversion to Christianity as reflecting their sense of being 'modern', few would describe their religious practices as distinct from their individual social lives or from the public and political life of the villages, towns, and cities in which they live. These 'modern hybrids' (Asad 1999: 179) – individuals who are both 'modern' and religious – cannot be characterized as reflecting a shift from communal 'traditional' religious beliefs and practices to 'modern' Christianity as both are (or have been) critical to the political and social life of their communities. Furthermore, these 'modern hybrids' should not be characterized simphstically as examples of religious syncretism (Shaw & Stewart 1994), since they represent neither a fixed blending of religious beliefs (traditional and Christian), nor a unidirectional trend from community-wide religious practice to private, secularized practice. As Hefner (1993: 27) has noted, the multiple consequences of the conversion process must be taken into account.

In considering the particular consequences of converting to Christianity and becoming 'modern' in southwestern Nigeria, I focus on one aspect of religious doctrine, specifically beliefs about the genesis of life. Beliefs about cosmology and fertility – like religious beliefs more generally – have been assumed to shift from spiritual, supernatural explanations to more secular, scientific ones. Like assumptions about modernization and nationalism which presume that citizens practise religion privately, distinct from public, political life, social analysts theorizing fertility transition (e.g. as described by Greenhalgh 1995: 5–8) have assumed that modern citizens with Western education will view fertility distinctly from religious beliefs. For them, fertility may be controlled through human agency, enabling women to have fewer children. This thinking is said to contrast with that of 'traditional' people, for whom fertility is believed to have a spiritual origin and is consequently outside of human control (Caldwell & Caldwell 1987). There is an implicit assumption in theories of fertility change that converts will observe a privatized, compartmentalized sort of Christianity which will be tolerant of state population policies (e.g. see Federal Republic of Nigeria 1988) that exhort people to have smaller families. Grounded in beliefs about biology and human control of fertility, the beliefs about fertility underwriting these programmes are seen as separate from religious beliefs about creation and birth. A focus on fertility provides a means for examining these assumptions about the separation of secular and religious beliefs in social life.

This study is based on research conducted in the small Ekiti Yoruba town of Itapa-Ekiti, in southwestern Nigeria, whose residents became Christian converts for various reasons, primarily in the 1930s. Their acceptance of Christianity and reading of biblical texts have altered the cosmological bases for their conceptualizations of fertility. However, scriptural doctrine did not bring about a total re-evaluation of local beliefs about fertility, but instead reinforced earlier beliefs maintained by some. The first part of the article focuses on beliefs about the basis of life and fertility. While thinking about fertility has been affected by conversion to Christianity, there is evidence that fertility was in itself an important factor in legitimating the conversion process, as may be seen from interactions between early Christians and traditionalists which are discussed in the second part of the article. In the article's final section, I discuss the consequences of one aspect of conversion, namely scriptural literacy, for thinking about fertility through an examination of people's interpretations of Bible stories associated with barrenness and extraordinary births.[1] Their recounting of the stories of Sarah and Hannah offer important insights into the ways in which local knowledge about fertility intersects with biblical accounts of the same topic, reflecting specific social concerns (see Beidelman 1963; Bowen 1992; Delaney 1998).[2] In some cases, elements associated with Yoruba beliefs and practices are accentuated in the narrative, while in others, elements derived specifically from Christian doctrine are emphasized. How these stories have been interpreted by Ekiti Yoruba women and men offers an invaluable perspective on the processes whereby forms of 'modern hybrids' are constructed, altered, and reconstructed, as well as on how the fundamental bases of fertility are understood and explained in particular social contexts.

Fertility and religious belief

Fertility has been a central concern of religious belief and ritual practice throughout southwestern Nigeria, where special streams, attributed with fertility-enhancing qualities, are the sites of ritual offerings made by infertile women (Oguntuyi 1979; Ojo 1966; Owomoyela 1988). In his discussion of the 'life-giving myth' as an underlying basis for ritual practices, Hocart (1970*a* [1936]: 33) stressed the importance of fertility and of having 'many progeny' in these 'life-giving' rituals. In Hocart's view, these rituals were performed in order to *do* something, for example 'to transfer life from one thing to another', rather than to express a moral stance associated with the 'health of the soul' (Hocart 1970*b* [1952]: 26).

None the less, there is a moral aspect to the practice of these rituals as they represent spiritual sources of fertility and, alternately, infertility, which may be good or bad. Various water deities (*orìṣa*), such as *Ọsun* and *Yẹmọja*, worshipped as sources of fertility (Awolalu 1979: 46–7), are described as white, cool, and self-contained, whereas witches or *ajẹ*, described as dangerous night-flying, anti-social beings (Apter 1992), are castigated as those who may 'turn the uterus' of women, leading to their infertility (Renne 1997). Witchcraft provides a way for people both to explain the misfortune of infertility and to find a possible avenue for obtaining fertility – through divination, and by assuaging witches through sacrifices and anti-witchcraft medicine. Alternately, sacrifice and prayer – whether to *orișa* (deities) or *imọlẹ* (nature spirits) – provide moral justification for bountiful fertility as a spiritual blessing, and also as a source of protection against infertility.

Yet spiritual sources of fertility and associated rituals may be reassessed when other myths of creation reflecting different cosmologies are perceived as offering more effective or alternative life-giving practices. One such reassessment of cosmological beliefs and the bases of fertility occurred with the introduction of Christianity to Ekiti Yoruba towns in the first half of the twentieth century. Christianity's life-giving efficacy – associated with certain benefits of colonial missions, including immunization and treatment programmes (Oguntuyi 1979) – provided persuasive evidence for these new beliefs, later reinforced by church-sponsored maternity clinics (Adetunji 1992: 1171).[3] Yet Christian cosmology and conversion were not accepted by all, particularly by those whose social status and political power rested on worshipping localized deities. The subsequent disputes over these competing cosmological claims and their associated life-giving powers have continued into the twenty-first century, suggesting a situation of ongoing dialogue, as Peel (1990) has argued. While Christianity and Islam[4] presently prevail in the town, people have maintained traditional religious practices[5] in various ways. Women may participate in Christian revivals (*isogi*), attend faith maternity clinics, bathe in or drink spirit water from particular streams, and consult diviners – not because they are 'irrational' victims of a confused cosmology, but because of the moral precedence of fertility and of having children.

Ideas about the creation

> So God made the dome, and divided the waters. . . .
>
> (Genesis 1: 7)

Before discussing local interpretations of fertility, I will describe three local explanations of the beginning of life on earth – and of the fundamental origins of fertility. One version of the story of the world's creation was given by Alameku, a man who is the head of the town's diviners and traditional healers:

> In the beginning of the creation, the whole of the world was full of water, no soil at all. It was the soil that followed and it was just a small quantity, which a hen was asked to spread on the surface of the water. And this was how the soil took over from the water and everything became solidified as the hen spread the soil, the water was gradually displaced. At the . . . time of creation, the sky was so low, it was not as high as we have it today; people would just take

> water from the sky and drink. People did touch the sky then, you wash yourself, your hands, and your clothes just as you like. But it was when people began to throw stones unnecessarily at the sky and people were no longer using the sky wisely that the sky moved up to the present location.[6]
>
> Then Adam and Eve were the first parents, and they married and gave birth to a baby boy and later a girl. When they both grew up for marriage, God ordered them that they should marry – so two children from the same womb married themselves and that was how they began to procreate and continue to marry themselves . . . Traditionally in the past, our forefathers used to refer to the period of Creation as *Igba Iya Kan Baba Kan* [the Time of One Mother, One Father] . . . It was the Bible that called it the period of Adam and Eve but traditionally it was the period of *Iya Kan Baba Kan.*
>
> (Interview: Itapa-Ekiti, 1998)

This description coincides with a creation myth recounted by a Christian Ekiti Yoruba woman who similarly describes the work of God in the creation of the world and the duplicity of humans in explaining their present fallen state:

> After God had created everything in the world, the sea, trees, and earth – just everything in the world – so he decided to create man who is going to be the ruler and king of everything he had created. It's a result of this that he created Adam and put him in the Garden of Eden. He created him from his own image. Later, he decided that Adam should have a helper who will be helping him in doing many things, so he created Eve out of Adam and kept the two of them in the Garden of Eden. It was in this garden that Satan came to deceive them and they know each other – that was how the world started to increase in number. Adam and Eve gave birth to children and we are the children up to today.
>
> (Interview: Itapa-Ekiti, 1992)

There are several similarities and differences in these myths, particularly in emphasis. While the biblical story of Adam and Eve is mentioned in both versions, Alameku also makes a point of equating local knowledge about the mythic past – 'the time of one father, one mother' – to the time of Adam and Eve. None the less, they share other themes, including the idea of a watery expanse, out of which were created the land and sea;[7] the peopling of the earth through the intercession of God; humans' initial link with heaven; their dispensation from work, and later travails. More importantly, both renditions of creation myths attribute fertility – the ability to conceive and to give birth – ultimately to God. By considering local understandings of the word 'fertility' itself, this aspect of its meaning may be seen more clearly.

Ideas about fertility and procreation

> Then God said, 'Let the earth put forth vegetation: plants yielding seed, and fruit trees of every kind . . .'.
>
> (Genesis 1: 11)

There is no one word in Yoruba that corresponds exactly to the English word 'fertility'. A word which is sometimes used is *iṣeabiamọ*, the act of giving birth to a child. Other words which are used tend to refer specifically to things associated with fertility, such as fruit, soil, or particularly fecund animals. For example, *oleso*, fertility or fruitfulness, is derived from the word *eso*, fruit. Thus a new bride might be saluted, ' "*A so eso asogbo*!" – May the bride be fruitful!' (Abraham 1962: 592). Similarly, the term *ọlọọra*, literally owner of fertile earth, derived from *ọra* (Abraham 1962: 525), may be used to convey the idea of fertility. The term *ẹlẹdẹ*, pig, is also used to describe certain women who are 'full of children', referring to the pig's birth of multiple piglets. With the exception of the word *iṣeabiamọ*, which implies a certain agency on the part of women, the other terms associated with fertility make reference to God-given aspects of the natural world – fruit, soil, and animals. As in the three creation myths cited, fertility is made possible by God, often conceptualized as God's breathing life into an inanimate body.[8]

Townswomen often gave more general explanations of God's role in the creation of a child when asked how a child was conceived and formed within a woman's body. For example, one woman said, 'It is the work of God because I heard that God made man with earth in his own image. So I think that it is still the same way that the child will be formed.' Yet this woman's statement that conception is the 'work of God' does not necessarily preclude thinking about the rebirth of spirits – which has important implications for understandings of fertility. For the rebirth both of ancestral spirits in descendants and of recalcitrant spirits referred to as *abiku* – children who are 'born to die', delivered to women who have suffered multiple child deaths – are still said to occur. The spirits of *abiku* children, like all children, are believed to come from an otherworldly realm, but unlike most children, when they come into this world they maintain contact with their friends in the other[9] and repeatedly return to them (i.e. die and are reborn).

However, with conversion to Christianity, attendance at maternity clinics, and a reduction in infant and child mortality, these ideas about *abiku* spirit children and the rebirth of ancestral spirits have diminished (Adetunji 1996: 1564). Furthermore, the concept *of abiku* has been reinterpreted by some, who now equate the pregnancies aborted by young women with *abiku* born-to-die children, as explained by one traditional healer:

> Actually *abiku* are no longer common except for *abiku* born to young women. This type of *abiku* is caused by aborting pregnancies . . . No

> matter how powerful a herbalist is, the moment a woman has lost the number of children in her through abortion, she can never get pregnant again. This is what *abiku* is today.
>
> (Interview: Itapa-Ekiti, 1997)

The thinking here relates to two ideas about fertility. Firstly, several women mentioned the idea that women have a certain number of pregnancies allotted to them in their lifetimes and that 'if you cannot give birth to all the babies in your stomach, it can cause disease'. This idea is reflected in the healer's point about a woman losing 'the number of children in her'. Secondly, it is the repeated instances of a child conceived that 'goes back' – in this case through repeated abortions – that is being described as an *abiku*. Although women's role in this process is somewhat different – in the past mothers of *abiku* were not necessarily responsible for their children 'going back' – ultimately these repeated conceptions and deaths come to the same thing: childlessness and infertility.

Thus while beliefs about spiritual rebirth and communications with ancestral spirits through divination clearly have changed in some ways, in other ways they have not. Ideas persist that a woman's fertility is limited and that ultimately fertility comes from somewhere else. Now people would be more likely to say that fertility comes 'from God' rather than the spirit world or from a particular *imọlẹ* or deity. Yet women continue to rely on bathing in and drinking water from particular streams (*omi imọlẹ*) to enhance fertility and to prevent miscarriages and infertility, though they have added the holy water (*omi mimọ*), prayed over in various churches, to this arsenal of cures.

The importance of ritual water for fertility

> And God said. 'Let the waters bring forth swarms of living creatures . . .'.
>
> (Genesis 1: 20)

This association of ever-flowing water with life-giving regeneration and fertility in Yoruba society is suggested by Ojo (1966: 164–5):

> Generally perennial streams were believed to be inhabited by spirits that never died. In order to induce them to impart this quality to infants, among whom the death-rate was much higher than in any other age-group, the river spirits were worshipped and the water prescribed for sick infants and also expectant mothers. There was always a stream so regarded in every locality in the past.

Such streams in Itapa may be associated with healing and with enhancing fertility,[10] as one older woman explained:

Q: Which stream in Itapa is it where women go to get pregnant?
A: Otele Stream.
Q: What do they do there?
A: A woman who was unable to get pregnant will go to that stream with some other women whose husband owns that stream and some *etutu* [sacrifice as atonement] will be done. And part of the water will be given to the woman to drink and it was believed that she will get pregnant before the year runs out.
Q: What special spirit is associated with this stream?
A: I don't know but the people believe that there is no woman who will drink from the water who will not get pregnant.

(Interview: Itapa-Ekiti, 1992)

Ideas about the regenerative power of certain types of water, and particularly its capacity to promote safe deliveries and healthy children, have been drawn on by women attending church-sponsored maternity clinics in Ekiti. At Christ Apostolic Church (CAC) maternity clinics at Ẹfọn Alaiye, for example, holy water is used although neither traditional nor modern medications are given. 'Instead, prayers would be said and sanctified water taken in response to almost all their health problems, including pregnancy care and child birth' (Adetunji 1992: 1173).[11] At the CAC Faith Maternity Clinic at Ado-Ekiti, pregnant women attend a faith medicine healing revival every Monday. One Itapa woman who attended described events there, which consisted of clapping and singing, praying, an examination (by a trained nurse), and finally drinking water that had had prayers spoken over it. 'We use the power of Christ throughout,' she explained.

Giving birth at a faith-healing clinic combines the sanctifying aspects of prayer with the pragmatics of life-giving holy water use. Yet, while practitioners at CAC and Holy Apostolic clinics discourage it, some women may supplement their attendance with registration at modern maternity clinics. As Adetunji (1996: 1565) explains, women may seek to increase their options for 'both natural and supernatural protections' and the likelihood of having access to a midwife when necessary. In certain circumstances, the importance of giving birth takes precedence over other, ideological, claims.

Reinterpreting the moral bases of fertility

> God made the two great lights – the greater light to rule the day and the lesser light to rule the night . . .
>
> (Genesis 1: 16)

This point, that the act of giving birth to a child is of primary importance, has interesting implications for the moral interpretation of the sources of fertility. For example, the images of Ekiti women attending faith-healing church clinics suggest a re-evaluation of the moral basis of these respective sources of fertility. Yet the use of water associated with spirit (from prayers) suggests a certain symbolic overlap with women using water from spirit streams. In cases of infertility, infant death, or illness, an unsuccessful practice may be jettisoned in favour of another, successful one (Peel 2000: 228). In other words, the evaluation of what is considered moral practice may be affected by misfortune (see Beidelman 1982: 138). This point is well illustrated by a particularly poignant case of maternal and infant death experienced by one of Itapa's early Christian converts, Joel Ajayi (1911–46):

> I, Joel Ajai and my friend Ajakara went to the chairman's house to buy a book called ABD [see Peel 2000]. We bought these two books for 6d. Both of us agreed to be Christians. It was not long when we fought and my friend went back to idol worshipping. He told lies against me, [saying] that I used to make fun of all the idol worshippers. They decided to kill me and they sent to my senior brother who stayed at Oye . . . [who] begged them with 6 kegs of palm-wine but they still insisted on killing me.
>
> I got married to an Itaji woman. It was during these problems that she . . . fell sick and died after 11 months. I did not have enough time to take care of her because I was sent out of my father's house for 1 year and 1 month because of my Christianity. There was no relative who came near me after the death of my wife. It was only the Christians who came near so that we could carry the dead body to Itaji. But the people of Itaji refused to accept the dead body.
>
> After the sixth time that they have rejected the body, I carried her home to bury her. It was only her bones that we packed inside a bag and buried. It was Emanu Oke and myself who did the burial. The only child that the woman bore for me died after the death of her mother. After all these, so many trials and problems came on me. (Kayọde n.d.).

The Job-like adversity faced by Joel Ajayi, rather than raising sympathy, confirmed the widespread moral condemnation of Christianity in Itapa during the 1920s and early 1930s. The death of Ajayi's wife and child confirmed for many the effective 'goodness' of local deities and the ineffectual 'badness' of Christ in protecting his followers. This is not to say that Christians did not make counter-claims as to the efficacy of the power of their faith in promoting life, as was described in one history of Itapa (Owoẹyẹ 1999: 4):

> In 1905 there was a serious fight, with combat between the Christians led by Pa Ojobaru [one of the founders of the Methodist Church in Itapa] and the traditionalists at a spot called Uta Yeye (a flat rock near the back of the Methodist church). This was to test the power between

> the two groups . . . In the process, there was victimization in various forms, but these Christian leaders began to wield power, and it was possible to have the first baby born in the church in 1905. The child was named Epedola, meaning 'the curses become fortune/honour'.

This early success – the birth of a child in church – was illusory as it was only with the eventual prosperity of Christian converts, mainly secured through mission education and health initiatives, that conversion to Christianity became widespread in Itapa in the 1930s. However, this particular conflation of worldly well-being (including fertility) with the morality of particular cosmologies supports the more general belief in divine intervention in successful childbearing. This way of thinking has specific implications not only for how some Ekiti women and men think of fertility, but also for how ideas about controlling fertility are perceived. For as Delaney (1991: 52) has noted: 'One learns much about theories of conception from ideas and practices relating to contraception.'

Controlling fertility

> God blessed them, and God said to them, 'Be fruitful and multiply, and fill the earth and subdue it . . .'.
>
> (Genesis 1: 28)

When Itapa women are asked how many children they would like to have, some say that this number is 'up to God'. Such responses have been attributed to a lack of Western education (Caldwell 1980) or to unfamiliarity with certain types of numeracy (van de Walle 1992). One of the explanations given by women for this response, however, reflects the beliefs about fertility which were discussed above. According to one woman, people cannot make such decisions because ultimately one's fertility (and the number of children a woman will bear) is 'the work of God'. This way of thinking about fertility is associated with traditional religious beliefs about creation and procreation, as well as with certain Christian interpretations of the Bible which view human attempts to intervene in God-given fertility as fundamentally immoral. It should not be surprising, then, that some Christian women said that they did not approve of using modern family planning methods to control their fertility for just this reason, for example:[12]

> I disapprove of it because of my belief in Jesus Christ. So if I wanted to limit my child I will be staying without having fun with anybody. Because if any born-again Christian does it, it is a sin to the person. And our Bible taught us that we should not kill and we should not try the evil spirit's power.
>
> (Interview: Itapa-Ekiti, 1992)

> Two people from here who have done family planning have died because of it . . . they didn't believe in Jesus, that's why they did family planning.
>
> (Interview: Itapa-Ekiti, 1992)

These views are supported by interpretations of the Bible as the literal words of God, describing events that took place long ago but which still have relevance for believers and for women concerned about their fertility. Indeed, several stories in the Bible recount God's participation in conception, as Frye (1982: 182) has noted:

> A closely related theme [in the Bible] is that of the birth of a son to a mother so late in her life that the birth is a miracle, or at least an act of special grace. This theme appears in the birth of Isaac from the old Sarah (Genesis 21), and is suggested in the birth of Samuel from Hannah.

These two stories were known by several women and men in Itapa, through classes in Bible knowledge taught in school (Adefọlarin 1988), through attendance at church services, and/or through private readings of the Bible. In the following section, several versions of these stories are given, along with examples of similar situations experienced by local Ekiti Yoruba townspeople in recent times.

Biblical discourse and miraculous births

Excerpts from the story of Abraham, Sarah, and the extraordinary birth of Isaac (Genesis 17: 16–19)[13] are recounted by one 52-year-old Christian man from Itapa-Ekiti:

> Sarah was the wife of Abraham . . . Abraham and Sarah were unable to give birth to a baby, they both began to challenge God and sent petitions to him that God should fulfil his promises of children. At that old age, they became tired of their lives and their faith in the Lord had almost been driven into the ocean; there were challenges, . . . particularly from the neighbourhood and even his wife (Sarah) no longer menstruated.[14] Abraham was still not hopeless of having children because God had made a covenant with him that he would increase his offspring; but until that time, the promises were not fulfilled.
>
> In order for Sarah to know the source of the problem of childlessness, whether it had to be traced to the husband or herself, . . . she tested Abraham with their maidservant, Hagar, so that Abraham could have sex with her. If pregnancy occurred, it meant

> that Abraham was gay and hearty . . . Abraham had carnal relations with the maidservant and pregnancy occurred through Hagar and she gave birth to a baby, Ismael. Sarah became very sad within herself, now realizing that it was she who had the problem of having children and not Abraham. She began to question how could God have brought her, a barren woman, to such a man of faith . . .
>
> So Sarah was filled with sorrow, even now that she could no longer direct the maidservant as she used to do in the past; Hagar now had a more domineering attitude in Abraham's house than Sarah . . . Sarah was the subject of ridicule to Hagar, Sarah no longer enjoyed a moment of joy in the home. It was in the course of this situation of unhappiness that three angels visited the home of Abraham . . . The angels told Abraham and his wife that by this time next year they would both rejoice together on the birth of a new child . . . Both the husband and wife burst into laughter but the angels said they were not joking with them. Before the end of a year after the prophesy, Sarah gave birth to a baby boy named Isaac.
>
> (Interview: Itapa-Ekiti, 2000)

He also told the story of Hannah's miraculous delivery of Samuel (see Samuel 1: 1–28):

> Hannah's life story was another similar story of barren women in the Bible. Hannah was the wife of Elkanah. Elkanah in his case married two wives, unlike Abraham, who was legitimately married to one wife. The second wife of Elkanah was Peninnah and she gave birth to many children. In the traditional setting, in this kind of marriage situation [there] used to set in seeds of discord. In the same manner, Peninnah began to pride herself before Hannah, she would not allow Hannah to have access to her children and she would be making mockery of Hannah. Hannah couldn't even send Peninnah s children on domestic errands.[15]
>
> This situation of childlessness troubled the mind of Hannah for a long time. There used to be an annual festival whereby Christians[16] would got to Shiloh to offer prayer to God . . . At Shiloh, everyone would have conversations with God, sending petitions unto God on their problems . . . During this time of festivity, each household used to go with food, based on their capacity . . . Elkanah killed a goat for the family, he gave a portion to Hannah and seven portions to Peninnah because she would take one portion [for] each [child], too. This condition further increased the sadness of Hannah.
>
> . . . This was how Eli the priest at Shiloh prayed for Hannah, that God would grant her petition. Before the next Shiloh festival, her

> prayer had been answered by giving birth to a child, Samuel . . . To fulfil her vow, when the child was no longer sucking breast the child was dedicated in the church for the work of God. Samuel worked in the Lord throughout his life. We should learn that when we make a vow with God, it must always be fulfilled, just like Hannah.
>
> (Interview: Itapa-Ekiti, 2000)

These two renditions of the biblical stories of Sarah and Hannah include several themes that resonate with traditional religious ideas about fertility and faith. One of the prominent themes in these two stories as well as in other biblical stories of miraculous births[17] is the role of God in controlling both barrenness and fertility (Metzger & Murphy 1991: 19n). For example, Hannah's unhappiness was partly caused by her co-wife who mocked her 'because the Lord had closed her womb' (1 Samuel 1: 6). Similarly, in the story of Abraham and Sarah in Gerar, God is said to have first closed and then opened the wombs of Abimelech's wife and female slaves (Genesis 20: 17–18). These stories are similar to ideas and practices associated with local religious beliefs described earlier, including the worship of particular deities such as Yẹmọja (Apter 1992: 98) and Ọsun (Ojo 1966: 164–5) who have the power to bring about conception and birth. In both instances, the importance of patience, prayer, and faith in a Supreme Being – Jehovah, Allah, Olodumare – or in local deities was viewed as critical to being blessed with a conception. When Ekiti Yoruba women say that the number of children they will bear is ultimately 'up to God', they are reflecting this belief.

Another theme mentioned in both stories is the discord between women when one wife has children and the other does not. Hannah was taunted by Peninnah, 'her rival [who] used to provoke her severely' (1 Samuel 1: 6), much as Hagar 'looked with contempt on her mistress' (Genesis 16: 4), Sarah, for her failure to conceive. While the story of Hannah documents the tensions of polygynous marriage, a common theme in Yoruba literature (Ṣoyinka 1963), folk tales (Renne 1995; cf. Jackson 1982), and proverbs (Owomoyela 1988), the tensions between Sarah, Abraham's wife, and Hagar, the maidservant who, through the birth of Ismael, became a *de facto* co-wife, are the subject of Yoruba oral and written narratives as well. Indeed, when a wife is infertile, tremendous pressure may be put on the husband by his family to marry another wife. At times a barren wife may tacitly agree to her husband's taking an 'outside wife' (Karanja 1987), whose subsequent issue may be raised as a foster-child by his lawful wife. Such a practice was followed by Sarah, who said to Abraham, 'You see that the Lord has prevented me from bearing children; go in to my slave-girl; it may be that I shall obtain children by her' (Genesis 16: 2).[18] Sarah subsequently regretted her decision and 'dealt harshly with her [Hagar], and she ran away from her' (Genesis 16: 6). This treatment of this theme of discord between 'co-wives' is also referred to in the division of Elkanah's sacrifice at Shiloh, where Peninnah and her more numerous children received a larger portion than Hannah. Interpreted through the sacrifice of a goat in the narrative above, the competition between co-wives over their husband's provision of resources for their children is a frequent source of friction in polygynous households.[19]

Another element of these stories, similarly practised in Ekiti Yoruba society, is the giving of special names to the children of these miraculous births so as to honour God and mark their extraordinary status. Thus Samuel's name may refer to the phrase, 'I have asked him of [possibly lent him to] the Lord' (Metzger & Murphy 1991: 342n), while the name Isaac derives from the Hebrew word for laughter. Similarly, Ekiti Yoruba children born after many years of barrenness may be called by such names as Oluwaremilekun ('the Lord wiped away my tears') and Oluwasina ('the Lord has opened up the way').

Thus aspects of biblical accounts of barrenness and births coincide in several ways with the experiences and understandings of fertility by Ekiti Yoruba women and men. However, the particular emphases and interpretations revealed in the telling of these two stories sometimes reflect specifically local understandings of barrenness and fertility. For example, in the narrative given above, Sarah is depicted as wanting to find out who was at fault for the couple's childlessness: 'In order for Sarah to know the source of the problem of childlessness, whether it had to be traced to the husband or herself . . . she tested Abraham with their maidservant, Hagar . . .' The biblical text does not indicate that this testing was an aspect of Sarah's motivation. But it clearly is a motive in Ekiti Yoruba marital relations which may be seen in descriptions of contemporary examples of miraculous fertility in present-day Itapa-Ekiti.

Interpreting miraculous births in a southwestern Nigerian town

One 60-year-old Muslim man cited two cases of women in Itapa-Ekiti who delivered children after being considered hopelessly barren, including the following example:

> There was a woman in Itapa who after several years of childlessness, with countless numbers of husbands, finally gave birth to two children, after she had lived with six different men. She delivered for the sixth husband, who was [actually] the first husband.
>
> Many families are so much in a hurry, they are not patient. Instead of holding to their Creator for their wants, women would be blaming their husbands for being impotent and their husbands blaming their wives for infertility. Although the same thought came to both Sarah and Abraham by agreeing with one another that Abraham should have a sexual relationship with Hagar, it was to test the ability of Abraham.

> That woman I referred to just now had little faith; she had married and re-married strong men, particularly men who had given birth to children, particularly male children, hoping she would get children but it was not so. This was because God has not destined her to have children from any other person apart from her own destined husband . . . The funniest thing was that the husband did not marry any other wife and he did not hesitate to take the wife back. Both lived happily for a long time before they died. We should all know that nothing is impossible with God if only we remain steadfast with him in our services to him.
>
> (Interview: Itapa-Ekiti, 2000)

In this account, the narrator stresses the antagonism between husband and wife over their inability to conceive and bear a child, reflecting the vital importance of fertility in marital and wider kinship relations. Their need for proof relates to ideas about moral virtue and fecundity. If a woman has difficulties getting pregnant, people will make aspersions about her character, saying that she has 'spoiled herself' through promiscuity or numerous abortions. Under such circumstances, a barren wife might go to some length to prove that a husband was the cause of the problem.

However, there is another aspect of this behaviour which has specifically local implications. A wife might want her husband to try his luck with another woman, not only to ascertain who was at fault, but also to enhance her own chances of a desired pregnancy, as was explained by a 40-year-old Christian woman:

> [Sarah] persuaded Abraham and her maidservant to sleep together so that at least a child could be born to their family. In the same vein, [in] our society today, women still allow their husbands to do that sort of thing. This is because, in the traditional way, the birth of a child from another woman could help to open the womb of the rightful wife. There have been cases of this in our society . . .
>
> Take, for example, one woman in Itapa gave birth to five children and all of them were female children. The husband was annoyed, accusing the wife that she was the one causing the problem of having female children all of the time. The wife was equally accusing the husband. The husband then went to marry another wife and the new wife conceived. Just about three months after, the older wife also conceived. To the dismay of nearly everyone, the new wife gave birth to a male child. But when the older wife at home delivered, she also delivered a baby boy!
>
> The same with Abraham and Sarah, they were not patient . . . The mistake could be traced to Sarah, for her asking the husband to have sexual dealings with Hagar . . . after which at last this woman was

> sent away. This further shows that God did not cherish that a man should marry more than one woman. This was a practical example when Abraham was asked to send away the illegitimate wife, Hagar.
>
> (Interview: Itapa-Ekiti, 2000)

This reading of the story of Abraham and Sarah also illustrates another aspect of this tension between co-wives, namely the preference of many women for monogamous marriage so as to preclude such problems. Hence, the woman draws the conclusion from this story that Sarah was to blame for the discord in her household, since 'God did not cherish that a man should marry more than one woman'.

The importance of faith in and prayer to God as exemplified by Hannah was cited in two other examples of extraordinary fertility that occurred in Itapa, although in both cases these women's infertility was explained in terms of local knowledge. In the first case, the speaker clearly distinguished her own experience from that recounted in the Bible:

> [T]here was a family which was faced with this kind of ordeal of childlessness. They got their problem from their immediate home, as they were bewitched. Though they believed in fervent prayer, their prayers were roadblocked by the evil doers; the major difference is that those who faced such problems in the Bible did not count the problem of [put the blame on] any person but [they] waited for the work of God. But today people would blame their childlessness on witches and witchcraft in their homes, though there were cases whereby witches did confess saying that they have caused the childlessness of certain women or men or that they have caused the evil in individual homes. There are even cases whereby some witches would, out of jealousy, cause some evil in some homes. This was actually the case of the family I am talking about because the person who perpetrated the fruitlessness of marriage in their house later confessed; and she confessed that she had blocked the vagina with a broken pot (*apaadi*). This was after so many years of prayers that the woman confessed. And just within the next one year of this confession, the woman got her vagina opened and she carried a pregnancy and later gave birth to a baby, Oluwafẹranmi (God loves me). The woman and the family came to give this testimony in our church; and she promised that since she has accepted Christ as her personal saviour, that nothing of the world can snatch her, the husband and the baby from God, that they would worship God through their lifetime.
>
> (Interview: Itapa-Ekiti, 2000)

The second example, also revealed by the afflicted woman in a church service, was related to the belief that some people are born as *emere*, special beings with supernatural powers, who, like the *abiku* mentioned earlier, belong to their own spirit-world 'club'. In this case, it was not the woman herself who continually died and returned to heaven as *abiku* children are said to do; rather, she continually gave birth to children in heaven, as one man explained:

> There was another Christian family who was unable to procreate about eight years after their marriage, people far and near began to talk among themselves about why this woman was unable to get pregnant. Some people were putting the blame on the husband and others on the wife. But after about seven years, a group of children in the church who claimed that they were in the same *emere* group with the woman said that the group members were not ready to give her a child, that the children that she could have given birth to on earth were being born in heaven. The whole church was amazed and the woman cried bitterly . . . She promised that she would not keep company with such evil spirits again. She did not leave the church because of this situation, but instead she became closer to God and decided to put on more of the whole armour of God. Now, the family has given birth to children.
>
> (Interview: Itapa-Ekiti, 2000)

References to witch-like beings and other forms of extraordinary spirituality are found in the Bible. Indeed, several verses refer to Satan (e.g. Job 2: 1–7) as well as to angels (e.g. Genesis 19: 1), beings who, like *emere* and *abiku*, travel between two separate realms – heaven and earth. However, the devil and angels are not directly associated with the control of fertility in the Bible, hence the above-cited man's distinction between people's attributions of infertility to God in the Bible and to witches in Ekiti (Apter 1992). None the less, these aspects of biblical narratives reinforce, rather than counter, certain ideas about fertility and the presence of supernatural beings associated with traditional religious beliefs and practices. It is not surprising that the early Yoruba historian Samuel Johnson (1921: 7) attributed the origins of the Yoruba people to Upper Egypt (where they had 'some knowledge of Christianity') based on the evidence of biblical similarities: '[This] might offer a solution of the problem of how it came about that traditional stories of the creation, the deluge, of Elijah, and other scriptural characters are current among them, and indirect stories of our Lord, termed "son of Moremi [Mary]".' Indeed, from this perspective, it would be difficult to discern which set of beliefs were the 'traditional' Ekiti Yoruba ones and which were the 'modern' Christian ones.

Conclusion

And on the seventh day God finished the work that he had done. . . .
(Genesis 2: 2)

For many women and men in southwestern Nigeria, fertility is considered to be the work of God, whether one is talking with women who continue to bathe in special streams, with women attending the Christ Apostolic Church who rely on water 'full of the power of prayer', or with women giving birth in hospitals who approve of and use contraceptive methods. These distinctive practices suggest that some women's assessments of the efficacy and moral basis of these sources of life-giving fertility have changed with the introduction of primary schools in the 1920s, widespread conversion to Christianity in the 1930s, and the establishment of mission hospitals in neighbouring towns in the 1940s. Yet the insistence of various women that they rely solely on the 'power of Christ', or that all women who drink special stream water will get pregnant, suggests an ongoing dialogue about this spiritual efficacy, morality, and fertility instead of a uniform shift from a 'traditional' religious view to a 'modern' secular one. Rather, women's varying views about their fertility represent 'a process of impassioned communication, whose outcome, while conditioned by the assumptions, interests and resources of the participants, is in the fullest sense the product of their interaction' (Peel 1990: 339).

Furthermore, their views counter assumptions associated with modernization theory, made by population specialists and development planners, that once women and men became literate and monogamous, and converted to Christianity – i.e. became 'Westernized' – they would uniformly interpret fertility in a secular way. This association should not be surprising considering that Western education came to many parts of southwestern Nigeria through missionaries whose teachings were based on the Bible, reinforcing a new identity for many Ekiti Yoruba women and men as modern citizens of the Nigerian state and as practising Christians. Many of the educated young people of Itapa-Ekiti use a Western scientific or bio-medical egg and sperm[20] model to explain procreation, and confine matters of religion to a separate domain which they think of as being unconnected with matters of fertility and child-bearing. Yet others within the same age-group and educational category continue to see procreation as 'the work of God', with religious practice embracing a much wider range of their social and moral considerations, including those to do with health and procreation matters. It is ironic to think that converts to Christianity in southwestern Nigeria would see the world as unaffected by these biblical texts, when understandings of cosmology and fertility in the West reflect a range of biblical interpretations of creation (Delaney 1998). Indeed, beliefs about cosmology and fertility (and its control) are contested issues in the United States and elsewhere, as evidenced in debates about evolution, creationism, and abortion. Rather than assuming that modernity implies secular thinking about the fundamentals of life and fertility, the varieties of ways that these cosmological narratives have influenced people's beliefs and practices should not be overlooked.

Notes

1 Six individuals were interviewed by Mr Owoẹyẹ in July 2000 about the stories of Sarah and Hannah and about any examples of similar cases from their own experiences. These tape-recorded interviews were conducted in Yoruba and translated into English by Mr Owoẹyẹ. Additionally, written responses to these questions made by two women were included in this discussion.

2 These studies, which examine local people's understanding and applications of biblical or Qur'anic narratives to their particular social context, differ from other anthropological approaches to the study of scriptural texts. While structural analyses of the Bible as a collection of related myths predominate (Aycock 1992; Carroll 1977; Leach 1969; Leach & Aycock 1983; Pocock 1975), some studies have focused on how biblical texts may be understood by comparing certain themes from cross-cultural (e.g. the mark of Cain and fratricide; Schapera 1955) and historical perspectives (e.g. the meaning of Sarah's seminal emission; van der Horst 1990). Other studies have been concerned with understanding the implications of biblical narratives on social relations and cultural patterns – such as kingship and gender (Feeley-Harnik 1990). Finally, a study by Barber (1988) focuses on a Yoruba scriptural text, based largely on Ifa divination texts, that incorporates biblical and Qur'anic elements within it.

3 For example, during the 1940s, archival references mention that a Wesley Mission nursing sister was supervising a Methodist Missionary Dispensary at Ikọle-Ekiti (about 12 km east of Itapa) while a Mission doctor supervised the dispensary set up at Ilupeju-Ekiti (about 2 km to the west; Matthews 1941).

4 While the town has a small Muslim population as well as Christians, this article focuses on biblical narratives, partly because many Muslim as well as Christian women and men have been exposed to Bible reading through attendance at local schools. Indeed, as one Muslim man remarked, 'The Bible and Qur'an are carbon copies, they are from the same source, from the same father and mother. I can say this because I can read both. Every reference made in the Qur'an was . . . analysed in the Bible' (Interview: Itapa-Ekiti, 2000).

Similarly, in one prominent Ifa divination priest's commentary, he viewed the Yoruba scriptural text, *Iwe Odu Mimọ*, 'as a text "which could replace the Bible and the Qur'an", and these two were treated throughout as virtually interchangeable' (Barber 1988: 200).

5 The phrases 'traditional religion' and 'Traditionalists' are used here and throughout this article to refer to local polytheistic religious worship. While they are hardly ideal, they are the phrases townspeople use when speaking of indigenous religion in English.

6 This portion of his story coincides with the well-known version of the Yoruba creation myth, presented by Idowu (1962: 19).

7 Frye (1982: 39) notes the pervasiveness of water in many creation myths.

8 For example, in one Yoruba creation myth cited by Idowu (1962), the high-divinity Orisanla is responsible for shaping the forms of humans while Olodumare is responsible for animating them with a spirit. The Old Testament also refers to God's intervention: 'Then the Lord God formed man of the dust of the ground, and breathed into his nostrils the breath of life; and man became a living soul' (Genesis 2: 7).

9 This 'other world' has been imagined in several ways. Oguntuyi (1979: 35).

10 Feeley-Harnik (1990: 168) suggests several biblical examples of associations made between water and conception.

11 These church-sponsored, faith-based maternity clinics have become popular since the 1980s, when many people joined Pentecostal churches. While women attribute their attendance at these faith-based maternity clinics to their religious beliefs, economic and other practical concerns have contributed to particular practices. For example, Adetunji (1992: 1173) noted that while some women preferred to attend the local faith maternity clinics, they did so rather late in their pregnancies in order to avoid the 2 km trek to required antenatal meetings to bathe in the River Oni.

12 This is not to say that other Christian and Muslim women did not approve of family planning methods to control their fertility.

13 'The story of a formerly barren woman who bears unusual offspring late in life as a special favor from God appears several times in the Bible . . . The unusual birth was thought to be symbolic of the importance of the person in later life' (Metzger & Murphy 1991: 341n).

14 Genesis 18: 11: 'Now Abraham and Sarah were old, advanced in age; it had ceased to be with Sarah after the manner of women.'

15 This interpolation of the biblical text was explained by one man:

> One thing is common to our people. The moment a woman is childless, she would not be authorized to send children from another family on errands . . . The fear is that her childless condition may force her to kill their children . . . The parents of such children would accuse her, asking her not to kill their children, that she should not make them childless like they are. Only those who have faith in the Lord could stomach such a situation.
>
> (Interview: Itapa-Ekiti, 2000)

16 This narrator appears to have associated both Old and New Testament stories with Christianity, reflecting a conflation made by the Muslim man referred to in note 4 (above) that 'The Bible and Qur'an are . . . from the same source'.

17 For example, see Rebekah (Genesis 25: 21), Rachel (Genesis 30: 22–4), the mother of Samson (Judges 13: 2–5), and Elizabeth (Luke 1: 5–17).

18 'According to ancient custom, a wife could give her maid to her husband and claim the child as her own (30.3, 9 [e.g. in the stories of Jacob, Rachel, and Bilhah; Jacob, Leah, and Zilpah])' (Metzger & Murphy 1991: 19n).

19 The proverb, *Orogun ki i jogun orogun*, 'A co-wife does not inherit from a co-wife', cleverly captures this sense of competition over resources – the word *orogun*, co-wife, is unrelated to the word *ogun*, inheritance (Owomoyela 1988: 303).

20 Martin's (1991) point about the gendered associations made by scientists in accounts of reproductive biology illustrates the difficulty of distinguishing scientific, secular thinking from broader cultural concepts.

References

Abraham, R. C. 1962. *Dictionary of modern Yoruba*. London: Hodder & Stoughton.

Adefọlarin, A. 1988. *Christian religious knowledge: Old Testament for senior secondary schools*. Lagos: Landmark Publications Ltd.

Adetunji, J. 1992. Church-based obstetric care in a Yoruba community, Nigeria. *Social Science & Medicine* **35**, 1171–8.

—— 1996. Preserving the pot and water: a traditional concept of reproductive health in a Yoruba community, Nigeria. *Social Science & Medicine* **43**, 1561–7.

Apter, A. 1992. *Black kings and critics*. Chicago: University Press.

Asad, T. 1999. Religion, nation-state, secularism. In *Nation and religion: perspectives on Europe and Asia* (eds) P. van der Veer & H. Lehmann, 178–203. Princeton: University Press.

Awolalu, J. O. 1979. *Yoruba beliefs and sacrificial rites*. London: Longman.

Aycock, A. 1992. Potiphar's wife: prelude to a structural exegesis. *Man* (N.S.) **27**, 479–94.

Barber, K. 1988. Discursive strategies in the texts of Ifa and in the 'Holy Book of Odu' of the African Church of Orunmila. In *Self-assertion and brokerage: early cultural nationalism in West Africa* (eds) P. F. de Moraes Farias & K. Barber, 196–224. Birmingham: Centre of West African Studies.

Beidelman, T. O. 1963. A Kaguru version of the sons of Noah: a study in the inculcation of the idea of racial superiority. *Cahiers d'Études Africaines* **12**, 474–90.

—— 1982. *Colonial evangelism: a sociohistorical study of an East African mission at the grassroots*. Bloomington: Indiana University Press.

Bowen, J. 1992. Elaborating scriptures: Cain and Abel in Gayo society. *Man* (N.S.) **27**, 495–516.

Caldwell, J. C. 1980. Mass education as a determinant of the timing of fertility decline. *Population and Development Review* **6**, 225–55.

—— & P. Caldwell 1987. The cultural context of high fertility in sub-Saharan Africa. *Population and Development Review* **13**, 409–37.

Carroll, M. P. 1977. Leach, Genesis, and structural analysis: a critical evaluation. *American Ethnologist* **4**, 663–77.

Delaney, C. 1991. *The seed and the soil: gender and cosmology in Turkish village society*. Berkeley: University of California Press.

—— 1998. *Abraham on trial: the social legacy of biblical myth*. Princeton: University Press.

Federal Republic of Nigeria 1988. *Republic of Nigeria policy on population for development, unity, progress and self-reliance*. Lagos: Government Printing Office.

Feeley-Harnik, G. 1990. Naomi and Ruth: building up the house of David. In *Text and tradition: the Hebrew Bible and folklore* (ed.) S. Niditch, 163–84. Atlanta: Scholars Press.

Frye, N. 1982. *The great code: the Bible and literature*. New York: Harcourt Brace Jovanovich.

Greenhalgh, S. 1995. Anthropology theorizes reproduction: integrating practice, political economic, and feminist perspectives. In *Situating fertility: anthropology and demographic inquiry* (ed.) S. Greenhalgh, 3–28. Cambridge: University Press.

Hefner, R. 1993. Introduction: world building and the rationality of conversion. In *Conversion to Christianity: historical and anthropological perspectives on a great transformation* (ed.) R. Hefner, 3–44. Berkeley: University of California Press.

Hocart, A. M. 1970*a* (1936). *Kings and councillors*. Chicago: University Press.

—— 1970*b* (1952). *The life-giving myth*. London: Methuen.

Idowu, E. G. 1962. *Olodumare: Cod in Yoruba belief*. London: Longman.

Jackson, M. 1982. *Allegories in the wilderness*. Bloomington: Indiana University Press.
Johnson, S. 1921. *The history of the Yorubas*. Lagos: C.S.S. Bookshops.
Karanja, W. 1987. 'Outside wives' and 'inside wives' in Nigeria. In *The transformation of African marriage* (eds) D. Parkin & D. Nyamwaya, 247–61. Manchester: University Press.
Kayọde, E. O. n.d. Ipilese isin Igbagbo ni ilu Itapa 1901 [The origins of Christianity in the town of Itapa-Ekiti, 1901]. Unpublished manuscript, Itapa-Ekiti.
Latour, B. 1993. *We have never been modern* (trans. C. Porter). Cambridge, Mass.: Harvard University Press.
Leach, E. 1969. *Genesis as myth and other essays*. London: Jonathan Cape.
—— & D. A. Aycock 1983. *Structuralist interpretations of biblical myth*. Cambridge: University Press and Royal Anthropological Institute.
Martin, E. 1991. The egg and the sperm: how science has constructed a romance based on stereotypical male-female roles. *Signs* **16**, 485–501.
Matthews, B. 1941. Handing over notes, Ekiti Division, 25/8/41, Ikole District, Ondo Prof 1/2, File OP37a. Ibadan: Nigerian National Archives.
Metzger, B. & R. Murphy (eds) 1991. *The new Oxford annotated Bible*. New York: Oxford University Press.
Ministry of Health, Ondo State 1953. Minhealth 1/1, File 3189. Ibadan: Nigerian National Archives.
Oguntuyi, A. 1979. *History of Ekiti*. Ibadan: Bisi Books.
Ojo, G. R. O. 1966. *Yoruba culture*. London: University of London.
Owoẹyẹ, K. 1999. *A history of Itapa-Ekiti*. Ann Arbor: Kolossos Printers.
Owomoyela, O. 1988. *A kìì: Yoruba proscriptive and prescriptive proverbs*. Lathan, Md.: University Press of America.
Peel, J. D. Y. 1978. *Ọlaju*: a Yoruba concept of development. *Journal of Development Studies* **14**, 139–65.
—— 1990. The pastor and the *babalawo*: the interaction of religions in nineteenth-century Yorubaland. *Africa* **60**, 338–69.
—— 2000. *Religious encounter and the making of the Yoruba*. Bloomington: Indiana University Press.
Pocock, D. F. 1975. North and south in the book of Genesis. In *Studies in social anthropology* (eds) J. Beattie & G. Lienhardt, 273–84. Oxford: Clarendon Press.
Renne, E. 1995. *Cloth that does not die*. Seattle: University of Washington Press.
—— 1997. Local and institutional interpretations of IUDs in southwestern Nigeria. *Social Science & Medicine* **44**, 1141–8.
Schapera, I. 1955. The sin of Cain. *Journal of the Royal Anthropological Institute of Great Britain and Ireland* **85**, 33–43.
Shaw, R. & C. Stewart 1994. Introduction: problematizing syncretism. In *Syncretism/anti-syncretism: the politics of religious synthesis* (eds) C. Stewart & R. Shaw, 1–26. London and New York: Routledge.
Ṣoyinka, W. 1963. *The lion and the jewel*. London: Oxford Unversity Press.
van de Walle, E. 1992. Fertility transition, conscious choice, and numeracy. *Demography* **29**, 487–502.
van der Horst, P. 1990. Sarah's seminal emission: Hebrews 11 : 11 in the light of ancient embryology. In *Greeks, Romans, and Christians* (eds) D. Balch, E. Ferguson & W. Meeks, 287–302. Minneapolis: Fortress Press.

van der Veer, P. & H. Lehmann 1999. Introduction. In *Nation and religion: perspectives on Europe and Asia* (eds) P. van der Veer & H. Lehmann, 3–14. Princeton: University Press.
Verger, P. 1968. La société *ẹgbẹ orun* des *abiku. Bulletin IFAN* (Série B) **30**, 1448–87.

69

JESUS CHRIST AS TRICKSTER IN THE RELIGION OF CONTEMPORARY BUSHMEN

Mathias Guenther

Source: K. P. Köpping (ed.), *The Games of Gods and Men*, Berlin: LIT, 1997, pp. 203–29.

"Jesso Kreste – he is a man who gives me great difficulty" was the caveat of more than a few of the Bushmen with whom I talked about this figure. It was the opening or concluding line of numerous comments or narratives, reflecting both the confusion and the beguilement of so many farm Bushmen about this new supernatural being. Those with recent and lasting connections to the mission church at Dekar in the Ghanzi District of Botswana where I conducted field work, the "mission Bushmen" who attended catechism classes and regular Sunday church service, presented, more or less coherently, the basic Christian "party line", within the range of variation that can probably be deemed standard for most of the Christian rank-and-file. Moreover, in their view the trickster //Gauwa was equivalent to Satan (the former being less unequivocally evil), and the distinction between //Gauwa/Satan and Jesus Christ was clearly drawn. Those with tenuous ties to the new religion linked Jesso Kreste to //Gauwa and, if questioned about Satan, and being aware of this figure (not all Bushmen were), would either say that Satan is a different figure – another evil //Gauwa, or an evil spirit or ghost – or they would conflate Satan with //Gauwa and, taking the point to its logical, if heretical, conclusion, with Jesso Kreste! As is to be expected, such notions were of the deepest concern to the Calvinist evangelist and in his sermons he felt occasionally called upon to address himself to the problem of Satan's palpable presence within the minds of people and the midst of the congregation.

Some of the farm Bushmen with whom I talked about this new supernatural figure had woven it seamlessly into their religious world view and I heard story tellers present a myth featuring Jesso Kreste as a sterling Bushman *hua*, a genuine story of the old people, albeit one, that could, at times "give him difficulty". An example is the following narrative which I obtained from the Nharo man //Ose, an old trance dancer; its features and figures—the healing //Gauwa, Jesso Kreste and the People of the Early Race, Addam and Effa—were things he had himself seen, in a dream.

> The people who were there in the beginning were two Bushmen, Addam and Effa. They were a man and a woman and they lived each of them in a big termite hill. They stood in a row, the woman's was about as far from the man's ant hill as !Khuma//ka's hut from here [approx. 80 metres]. His hill was standing here. Sometimes he visited her, sometimes she visited him.
>
> You cannot see them, they just stayed inside their ant hill huts. But we, the dancers, we are able to see them, if we follow a plan. Dancers are very fortunate to be able to see them and they see them only rarely. After a long time the woman and the man will come out of their hills and they only come to us (the dancers).
>
> There are arrows in these houses. They are at the front of the hill-houses, on the threshold. And Jesso Kreste, he is the one who will come and take them to the *//gauwani*, who will take them to the dancers [when they come to their place in trance]. But when Jesso Kreste comes to take arrows from Addam and Effa he will not take them from out of their hands. He will find them just outside their hills, in bundles. He will take these bundles of arrows and will give them to his servants (the *//gauwani*). And we (the doctors) will take these arrows from Jesso Kreste's servants. . . .
>
> The people who stayed in the ant hills were just like that. No one can see them; they have no land, they just stay in their hills. And when we (the doctors) ask the *//gauwani* for arrows they, in turn, will act as Jesso Kreste, who will take them from the two people.
>
> This is the story I heard about Addam and Effa. . . . It is a story that is giving me difficulty.
>
> (Guenther 1989: 46)

This narrative, as well as an explanatory comment added by the narrator[1], reveal the creative way in which new concepts are integrated with old ones. The mediating, providential role of Jesus Christ serves the dancers who, in entering the Trickster-God's realm as spirits to obtain the healing arrows with which to treat the sick back in the villages, will no longer have to confront the trickster's spirit servants (the *//gauwani*) directly. This they were previously required to do, at their gravest peril, before the arrival of Jesso Kreste on the supernatural scene. Like their master //Gauwa, the trickster god, the *//gauwani* are capriciously dangerous and the encounter with either //Gauwa or any of his servants could cost the shaman his life. Jesso Kreste, a //Gauwa himself, but one serene, passive and strongly committed to healing, is far less dangerous.

Like the Ghanzi farm Bushmen at Dekar, the Zhu/'hoan (or !Kung) at Tshum!kwi (or Tshumkwe) across in Namibia have had contact with Christianity, for about the same length of time (Budack 1980, Volkman 1982:9, 46–49, Gordon 1992:177–79). As in Ghanzi, this contact has been more or less tenuous and sporadic and it seems that the variability and vagueness of Christian beliefs is similar to what it is in Ghanzi. Examples of partially syncretistic Christian notions among the *Zhu/'hoansi* are an admiration for Eve as the discoverer of veld foods and scepticism about Mary's immaculate conception. Jesus Christ is held to have had three wives. (ibid.:9)

Let us listen in on a Sunday sermon delivered at the Dutch Reformed mission church by the Afrikaner missionary, Dominie Swanepoel. Taking his text from John 3:1–27, about Jesus and the Samaritan woman, he delivers the following homily:

> Jesus and his people had travelled far and came to the well. Jesus sat alone. But he had no cup to get water. While he waited, a woman came from the village to get water. Jesus asked her for water. She said, 'I can't give you water, you're Jewish'. But Jesus had looked closely at the woman. Before Jesus asked for water he looked deep into her heart. He saw that she was a bad woman. 'You must help this woman.' So he spoke with her, saying, 'Go call your husband.' 'I have no husband,' she replied. 'I know', said Jesus. 'You have five men. You take a man to help you, and fight with him, then take another. People abuse you. People make you grieve.' Jesus doesn't want to give us just food and clothes and water. Jesus says, 'You know who God is? You can ask for anything. God can give it to you. He can help you.' Jesus said, 'I am God. I am God's son.'
>
> (J. Marshall 1982; Volkman 1982: 46)

Commenting on the sermon at the end of the service, the Zhu/'hoan woman N!ai makes the following remarks:

> Now really! Those two at the water hole had never even met before. How can a woman go down in a water hole with a perfect stranger calling himself "God's son!" It would have been very bad. Her husband would have punished her for being alone with such a man. That man was fooling her.
>
> (J. Marshall 1982, Volkman 1982: 48)

N!ai has evidently failed to grasp the moral intentions and mystical nature of Jesus. She appears to mistake solicitousness for solicitation and Jesus claiming to be God's son as enticing sweet-talk, holding as its goal not spiritual salvation, but carnal seduction. 'That man was fooling her', indeed, "that man" was acting towards the Samaritan woman very much as the Trickster would have, had he been there in Jesus's place. Like Jesus, the trickster has several wives and, as a "man who likes the women", he is forever on a search for yet another amorous conquest.

The above are two examples of creative conflation of the Christian Jesus Christ with the Bushman trickster. It appears that in the process of *Götterdämmerung* that is settling on the supernatural landscape of the Kalahari Bushmen, the Trickster does not readily abandon the field to his rival. He stays put, and instead of being pushed away and obliterated by his new rival, he blends his identity with Jesus Christ. According to Alan Barnard (1992: 263) the christianized Khoe Khoe (who are the Bushmens' pastoralist ethnic cousins) notice parallels between their trickster-god Heitsi-aibib and Christ, indeed, they may, in their commentary about one of his many exploits, refer to him explicitly as "unser Jesus der alten Zeit" ("our Jesus of olden times", Schmidt 1980: 241)[2]

After presenting a thumb-nail sketch[3] of the Bushman trickster, I will adress myself to two main questions, one ethnological, the other theological: What is the degree of correspondence of the Bushman trickster with Jesus Christ? Does the Bushmen's redefinition of Christ reveal elements that are indeed inherent in this figure, or the religion based on it?

The Bushman trickster

The central and most prominent figure on the myhtological landscape of the Khoisan peoples of southern Africa is the trickster and veld god //Gauwa. Known under a number of different names (Pisamboro, Heiseb, Pate, =Gao!na or Kaoxa, //Kaggen, Jackal and others), he appears in as many or more guises amongst the various Khoisan groups. This variety and multiplicity is a reflection of the heterogenity that characterizes Bushman belief in general (Guenther 1979). Like tricksters everywhere, //Gauwa is inherently and pervasively ambiguous: he is of the earth (the veld) and the sky (heaven, the Bushmen's netherworld); he walks laterally across the ground, or the lower regions of the sky (which he traverses, spider-like, on invisble fibres stretched above the ground) and flies vertically, heavenward. He is a being associated with and responsible for life – the hunt and health – and he brings death. He roams about in the mythological past as well as the historical present. His gender is most commonly male; however, he can also assume a female guise. His moral deportment may be upright (as he is capable of perfroming caring and beneficent acts) but usually it is coarsely amoral: gluttony and lechery are his prime shortcomings. He craves meat, fat and honey, both literally and metaphorically, as these three most cherished of food substances are cognates for sex in Bushman symbolism. The Bushmen describe him as "a man who likes the women" – of all ages, from maidens to matrons, including his own daughter-in-law and his own mother whom he seduces or rapes. Lust and gluttony may combine in his relationship to his wife: deeming her to be "meat" – a delectable game antelope – he, or his kin, may kill, butcher and eat her. Another fault is his penchant for malicious pranks, accompanied with boastful jeering and *Schadenfreude*.

He confounds ontological categories, as he is either human nor animal, or a bizarre, humanoid or therianthropic distortion of either. "That man", //Gauwa, along with his! Kung and /Xam counterpart =Gao!na (Marshall 1962: 228, 233–38, Biesele 1993: 180–81) and /Kaggen, is also a god who is capable of eliciting numinous sentiments in the people. As divinity he is linked to certain vital affairs of the living, such as hunting, healing and passage ritual. The veld-god was a "Master of Animals" who either protected game animals from hunters, or led a hunter towards whom he was well disposed to his prey. His healing role, as master of medicines and custodian of healing arrows in the context of the curing trance dance, is seen in //Ose's narrative at the beginning of the paper[4]. He is present at initiation rites; he jealously guards girls during menarche and keeps away human rivals. As *//Gauwassa*, his female guise, he is present when young men are instructed by their elders during male initiation.

Through "some sense of logical necessity" (Marshall 1962: 228) – perhaps, because both beings are unpredictable and morally ambiguous, bringing both game and health, as well as dearth, death and disease to humankind – the Bushmen merge the two trickster personas. Yet, having merged these two opposite beings – vulgar, deceitful prankster the one, protector of animals and dispenser of medicines and guardian of rules at initiation, the other – and "insisted . . . that they are one and the same" (Marshall 1962:233), the Bushmen also differentiate between them. They approach the God from the "religious perspective" (*à la* Geertz 1966: 26–28) and they laugh and scoff at the Trickster during story telling sessions, deriding him for all his foolish and uncouth outrages. As shown by Lorna Marshall (1962: 233–35) with respect to the !Kung trickster-god =Gao!na, this merging of two opposite supernatural figures creates no small measure of confusion in the minds of the Bushmen whose thinking about this central figure of their belief struck her as "vague and inconsistent" in a number of ways.

It is only among the Christianized Bushmen, who have been introduced to a dualistic notion of divinity that merges //Gauwa with the wholly and unequivocally evil figure of Satan, that the two godly beings become compartmentalized, morally and mystically. Yet the old ambivalence about the traditional trickster-god lingers on, in the feelings of even some of the most committed converts to the new religion. This is evident in a statement of the old farm Bushman Gaishe, a recent convert at the mission and the evangelist's church interpreter:

> The oldest people did not separate these two men; they did not say this one is good and this one is not good. Now we are told that

//Gauwa is bad and only N!eri and his son Jesso Kreste are good. But we think that //Gauwa is not so bad; he is, after all, under N!eri's control. And some things they do together; for example, to punish a bad person. N!eri will let //Gauwa have him.

Jesso Kreste, the trickster of farm Bushman myth and belief

The figure here profiled is that of Jesso Kreste not Jesus Christ; it is derived from the notions on this central figure of Christian religion held by those Bushmen who have appropriated the figure and have folded it into their traditional beliefs. Their statements are frequently presented with the claim that Jesso Kreste is someone the old, old people have also known and believed in, that he is "definitely a Bushman person". Notwithstanding this claim, he is, nevertheless, a new religious element, one about which there is evidently a good deal of confusion as the knowledge people have about him is often second- third- or fourth-hand. Thus, the accounts I received were widely varied. The degree of syncretism, or of recognizability of Christian features, ranged from high to low; the former included many of the "mission Bushmen", the latter "farm Bushmen" such as //Ose, whose narrative was presented above. Many of the accounts I obtained had gone though a process of rethinking, casting the new supernatural figure in the terms of an informant's own personal beliefs. As a consequence of this process of redefinition and cultural and individual tailoring, Jesus Christ is to many farm Bushmen Jesso Kreste, the latest addition to the culture's gallery of Gauwa trickster figures.

In appearance, this Jesso Kreste looks different from //Gauwa in any of his other guises. He is fully human and not misshapen: a tall, thin person with a white face and beard. His abode is //Gauwa's realm, the "good place" in heaven, where he lives as one of a number of other //Gauwas, along with the souls of dead people. He lives on his own (although according to some accounts he may have several wives), in a dwelling that is either a two-storey "European house", or a tall termite hill. Most of his time is spent sleeping on a large "European bed"; sometimes he rouses himself to walk about and to perform a miracle or two. Because of his largely somnolent state, trance dancers are unable to summon him to the dance fire; instead, they will have to go to him themselves, as spirits in trance. It is also easy, and happens frequently, for //Gauwa, in one of his ill-intentioned moods, to steal healing arrows from Jesso Kreste. This will deprive trance dancers of one of their means of curing. Of all of the *//gauwani*, he is the one easiest to be tricked.

Jesso Kreste's domain, the "good place" in heaven, is described as a "European place". It looks not unlike Ghanzi town, the district capital, with all of the amenities of modern life – houses, trucks, stores, school, hospital – at the exclusive disposal of Bushmen[5]. The "bad place" is a burnt stretch of veld, with half-dilapidated grass huts that look abandoned and small.

Scattered throughout are ember-lit, smouldering fires (the sky's faint stars), except for one blazing fire in the centre, in which bad people are burned. Wretched-looking, shivering people skulk around the huts and cower by the fires, some of them munching on flies, the principal food item available to the people at the "bad place". The entrance to both places is guarded each by two //Gauwas.

We thus see Jesso Kreste within an extensively acculturated supernatural setting wherein he plays a passive role. This reflects the ancillary and peripheral nature of this new //Gauwa within the Bushman belief system.

Moving from a description of physical traits of Jesso Kreste to metaphysical ones, we note that, like //Gauwa, Jesso Kreste is the son of God. His divine nature enables him to perform miracles, such as walking on water, feeding multitudes with just a small amount of bread and water and healing or resurrecting people who are sick or who have died. While //Gauwa has also had such powers, the concept of miracle, as a discrete and deliberate display of supernatural power, is new within Bushman mystical culture. The term that has been coined is *aressa*; its meaning was explained to me as "making a thing that was never made before". The Bushmen look at Jesso Kreste the miracle worker with some ambivalence: "he makes you believe a thing that is not", "he turns things around and makes them different from how they normally are". To one informant *aressa* is a "bad thing", akin to harming someone with witchcraft, "the sort of thing //Gauwa might do to a person when he wants to kill him". Miracles are thus an addition to the trickster's bag of tricks; they are a species of deceit and another technique to bring about "topsy-turvydom", albeit with ends that are, all in all, beneficient.

A number of farm Bushmen are aware of the three central elements of Christology, the passion, resurrection and ascension of Christ. Most of those "in the know" will also tell the story in recognizably Christian form. Others have not grasped this aspect of Jesus Christ and it is not part of their concept of Jesso Kreste. However, when bringing up this element in discussions and briefing informants on it, the story resonated with their own view of the //Gauwa-Jesso Kreste. They could make sense of it in the context of that view. Being beaten, torn apart and killed is one of the plights also of the trickster, which he has suffered many times over, whenever one of his misdeeds backfired on him. And in the process of his own suffering and death, he may, unintentionally, bring boon to mankind. Moreover, after dying, he "resurrects" himself again, springing back to life. Similarly, regarding his ascension, an informant likened it to //Gauwa's power of flying up the sky, back to his place in heaven, or to his father, the Creator God. The next time he is summoned, by a dancer in the act of curing an afflicted fellow human, he will descend as well to be in the village amongst humans again, to bring to them healing medicines. Or, he will come down to the veld, to help an animal evade a hunter or a hunter to kill an animal. The ascension element is part also of the Kungs' beliefs about the trickster: after his time on the veld was over – as the trickster-protagonist-he ascended the sky and became divine (Biesele 1993: 22). Thus, the basic plot elements and story line of the passion, Jesus being scorned, scourged and killed, resurrecting himself and ascending to, and descending from, heaven – are appreciated in a different mythological context, by persons who are outside the Christian fold and unaware of the theological and spiritual significance, to Christians, of Golgotha, Easter and Pentecost.

In a number of ways Jesso Kreste deviates from the trickster protagonist. Jesso Kreste is more closely linked to the divinity-trickster than to the veld trickster; thus, while, perhaps, he "likes the women" – and may even be married to several of his own – and while Bushmen may see an element of trickery and deceit in his miracles, he is not a prankster and vulgarian, but sedate and serene (as well as somewhat tired, unlike the restlessly active protagonist of the stories). Also, his ritual role does not go beyond healing; while baptism is held to be a ritual equivalent to male initiation rites, he is not a presence at their performance. Moreover, he is neither a protector of animals nor a helper of hunters. He is never anything but human in his guise and not associated with any animal; the Bushmen seem unaware of the allegorical identification of Jesus Christ with the dove or the lamb.

The more religiously acculturated a Bushman is, the longer this list of divergent traits gets, and the more Jesso Kreste converges with Jesus Christ. The link to //Gauwa of old gets broken; instead, the trickster-god is merged with the new saviour's antithesis, Satan. The ambiguity of Jesso Kreste, and the emotional ambivalence farm Bushmen feel towards this trickster being in whom good and evil converge gives way to clarity and unequivocation. Jesus Christ, like his divine father, is wholly good and nothing but good, to Christianized Bushmen.

These tend to look with shocked embarrassment, or derisive laughter, at any Bushman who talks about Jesus Christ in the trickster idiom. Such talk is protestingly dismissed as "lies of the old people", perpetrated by benighted, leather-clad, *kauka* ("backward") veld Bushman-bumpkins. Do the *gaba* ("modern") Bushmen, however, "protest too much"? Is this merger of Jesus Christ with the trickster based on nothing more than superficial, spurious and specious traits? Is it a gross distortion and misunderstanding of Jesus Christ, an egregious Christian *faux pas*, necessarily so that it is cast in terms of a vastly different system of belief? Or have the veld Bushmen recognized traits in the Christian Saviour that are indeed inherent in this figure but which have gone unnoticed or unacknowledged in the religion founded by and on him? And for what reasons?

In playing around with these latter questions in the concluding section of the paper, as an anthropologist, I enter unfamiliar waters. In the eyes of theologians, I am now doubtless the fool who rushes in where angels dare not tread. My excuse for nevertheless forging ahead is the theme of this conference, and the protagonist of my paper; both allow one a certain degree of *Narrenfreiheit*. I thus offer my remarks in that spirit, not so much as a definitive exercise of scholarship but as a ludic exploit of *scurrilitas*.

Jesus Christ as trickster

Jesus Christ shares a number of significant ontological traits with the trickster by virtue of both figures holding the symbolic-structural status of mediator. Jesus Christ as God-incarnate, and Trickster as semidivine, both mediate between such fundamental polarities of religion and existence as human-divine, body-spirit, profane-sacred, earth-heaven, contingent-eternal, life-death. Deriving from their mediating state, both are restless and peripatetic and both are positioned at the spatial or social margins of the domain they inhabit, be it the remote veld and the lower caelial regions or the lowly social status, due to humble, or even illegitimate (viz. Thiering 1992) birth. Both are transformers of the cultural, social and religious order, a role that is reinforced in the case of the historical Jesus, by his imputed role as political agitator and anti-Roman revolutionary (Brandon 1967 and 1968).

Healing the sick and resurrecting the dead (including himself), powers shared by both mediating beings, both derive from their dual nature. As healers their supernatural make-up provides both figures with the capacity to transcend the frailties and limitations of the body and to restore to it wholeness and well-being by means of potent mystical healing powers, while their human nature conveys to them a direct, existential understanding of the pain that afflicts the body. Moreover, in the case of the veld god, through his association with nature, he has access to its regenerative and restorative forces, such as medicinal plant and animal substances. Apart from healing, both figures are also *Heilbringer*, providential supernatural facilitators who bring boon and salvation to humankind. While this function is much less prominent in the Bushman trickster, and tricksters generally, than in Jesus Christ, it is nevertheless part of the latter's role as culture hero.

In both cases the body, manifesting each figure's human, earthy and worldly aspect, is a prominent feature[6]. Its needs, functions, and lusts, and the exuviae that come forth from its orifices, are embellished elements of the Bushman trickster (as of all tricksters and "the mortification of the flesh", the body's pains through torture, dismemberment and death, are themes common to both the trickster and Jesus Christ. For all his spirituality, the "*body* of Christ" is a palpable symbolic and ritual presence in Christianity. It is manifested in the sacrament of communion, when this body is eaten and then its blood drunk, and in the countless religious paintings that depict Jesus naked, at birth, suckling lustily at Mary's breast, and at death, on the cross or in Mary's lap.

The miraculous power that enables both figures to heal allows them to overcome death, through resurrection. The ascent and descent from heaven of both figures (albeit under different mystical and mythological circumstances) is the shuttling back and forth, between binary poles, of all mediators.

In view of all of these shared traits, are we justified, then, in characterizing Jesus Christ as a trickster, as do some Ghanzi Bushmen? The very question might seem blasphemous to most Christians in the context of the christological and theological doctrines of mainstream Christianity (Apte 1985:232). Indeed, even the very possibility of Christ's being able to laugh (and thereby revealing humanness), which was posed as a theological question by the medieval ecclesiastic Methodus of Philippi, is already troubling to some Christians (Cormier 1977:X, 10–13). Others asserts that while he may not ever have laughed (but only smiled [Cormier 1977:12:]), Jesus did employ humour – subtly so, by means of irony, incongruity and double-meaning – in his words and actions (Webster 1960; cited in Apte 1985: 232). And, moving from the son to the father, here, too, "the very possibility of God laughing is already blasphemy" (Zucker 1967:316), to the insiders of the nomos, the Christian ruling order. If the mere question is already blasphemous to the insiders, the affirmative answer of the Bushman outsiders must seem heresy-writ-large. Yet, one can understand why such would be their answer; the common attributes of these two mediating figures are numerous and significant. Jesus Christ would thus seem to hold the potential for filling the trickster's shoes. While one or another theologian might recognize this potential, for instance Harvey Cox (1969: 139–54) who contends that Jesus Christ was "something of a holy fool" (see also Miller 1969: 140–41), Christianity does not permit this potential to be realized, however, for reasons of doctrine and religious style and sentiment. These are opposed, deeply and irreconcilably, to the trickster's anti-structural constitution.

It is manifested in many ways. The trickster is characterized as the "personification of ambivalence" by one writer (Diamond 1972: xiii), and as the embodiment of self-contradiction and the "spirit of disorder, the enemy of boundaries" by another (Kerényi 1972: 185). The trickster is the ultimate "marginal man" who "accepts rejection and rejects acceptance" (Zucker 1967: 313) and is contemptuous of social order and status, which he turns on their heads. As for society's culture and its institutions, he is both its destroyer and the creative "culture hero" (Apte 1985: 230–31). As shape-shifter and mingler of categories, deceiver, vulgarian and violator of norms, he reveals the "hidden truths" of disorder underneath order (Koepping 1985: 213). In addition to the inherent disorder within the apparent order, what the trickster reveals as well, as an equally unsettling truth, is the relativity and finiteness of order, what Zucker (1967: 315) calls the "paradox of order". The antics and ambiguities of the trickster lead one to realize that beyond the nomos, the sacred order and reality within which each person has his place, there lie "the infinite possibilities of the outside" (Zucker 1967: 315, also see Turner 1967: 93–111; 1974: 231–71 and 255). To reach this realization is to have challenged the claim to absoluteness and infinite validity of the accepted order. The "spirit of disorder" can thus also become an "enabler", "whose actions, good or bad, bring certain ideas and actions into the field of possibility" (Toelken 1969: 221; cited in Basso 1987: 365).

Like rituals of rebellion and the transition phase of passage rites (Gluckman 1954, 1965), the trickster "affirms by denying" (Zucker 1967: 317). Like ritual, he plays out the dialectic between structure and anti-structure, order and disorder, nomos and chaos, certainty and uncertainty, rhetoric and anti-rhetoric, that reveal, ultimately, the oscillating complementarity between society and communitas. As shown by Gluckman (1954 and 1965) and Turner (1969), such instances of reversal or communitas also lead to a renewed recognition, as well as reaffirmation, of order and structure, as that which "is being broken down is always implicit there, for the very act of deconstruction reconstructs" (Babcock 1978: 99, speaking about the *picaro*, a literary cousin of the trickster). Moreover, as with the realization of the relativism of order discussed above, new possibilities once again open up for society in its ordered state, analogous to playing the next hand in a game of cards, after having shuffled the deck.

Moving from social-structural to psychological-personal considerations, these instances of anti-structure also provide emotional benefit to members of society who may cumulatively harbour resentment towards the restrictive rules of the social order. As the ultimate "out person, whose activities are outlawish, out-landish, outrageous, out-of-bounds and out of order, [and to whom] no borders are sacrosanct" (Hynes and Steele 1980: 3), the trickster is an effective steam-valve for people when they are in the process of telling, or being told, of the trickster's antic exploits. The experience provides catharsis, "the purging of the soul from its antimomal tendencies" (Zucker 1967: 312).

Official Christianity gives little leeway to the force of communitas within its ritual and myths, however. As for the protagonist of this paper, "tricksters and their foolishness lie somewhat fallow within mainstream Christianity and are often suppressed as they are developed within popular Christianity", according to the religious scholars William Hynes and Thomas Steele (1980: 17), in an insightful paper on the subject of the trickster figure in folk Christianity. As shown by the Jesuit theologian Hugo Rahner, Plato's admonition to the "truly spiritual man", that God "is worthy of being taken with blessed seriousness" (Rahner 1965: 38) and Luke's (6: 25) exhortation "Woe upon you who laugh now, you shall mourn and weep", have both been taken to heart by members of the Christian fold. It has led Christians into soul-searching on the question as to whether they may "go on merrily playing when a stern and strict choice has to be made for eternity" (Rahner 1965: 92). Paul, too, put a damper on mirth and risibility in his church when he enjoined Christians to refrain from "ribaldry" (*morologia*), "smartness of talk" (*eutrapelia*) and, above all, "the chatter of fools" (*scurrilitas*—the vice of the *scurra*, "the clown, the eternally jovial windbag" (Rahner 1965: 96).

The reasons for the dour earnestness of mainstream Christianity are manifold and beyond the scope of this paper. Presumably they stem from the stoicism and rationalism, the dualism, asceticism, austerity, puritanism and world denial that are hallmark features of Christian theology and Christian religious deportment, especially so during the Protestant era, when "mirth, play and festivity came in for . . . scathing criticism" (Cox 1970: 4). Moreover, as pointed out by one theologian, the great stress in Christology is on the "tragedy of the crucifixion", so much so that "a stranger coming to our culture, coming to the Gospels without preparation, might be excused for thinking of them as the story of Christ's passion, with introductory passages added" (Trueblood 1964: 19). Given this ardently serious portent surrounding the ideational and emotional core to Christology and Christianity, it is to be expected that mirth and laughter are conspicuously absent from the comportment both of Jesus Christ and his Christian fold.

Thus, since the Enlightenment, the communitas-style religious festivals known as the Feast of Fools (*festum stultorum*), which was celebrated throughout the Middle Ages in a variety of forms, has become progressively and pervasively suppressed by the mainstream Church (Flögel 1989: 432–34; Zucker 1967:313–14; Cox 1970:3–6). It had became increasingly anti-authoritarian, lampooning the clerical establishment with such features as the *epicopus puerorum* (children's bishop), the *fatuorum papam* (fool's pope), and a parody of the mass that consisted of bringing a braying ass into the church, to worship this incarnation of the Lord of Disorder, in the form of braying by both priest and congregation. In medieval times these liminal festivals were tolerated, and even participated in by the ecclesiastical leaders (Flögel 1789:432–34). Indeed, according to the 18th-century historian Friedrich Flögel (1789: 441–57), the latter were so given to festive hilarity that they regularly took jesters into their services, to be entertained by them at all times with prankish hilarity. Prelatic fools were found at the courts of popes (ibid.:434–40), electors, cardinals, (arch)bishops and abbots. However, being an institution of power, with "little capacity for self-caricature and self-irony" (Cox 1969: 141), in the 13th century the church started to ban jesters from the domiciles of its prelates. That done, it began issuing prohibitions against the feast of fools. For several centuries these went unheeded by the rank-and-file; however, the festivals finally came to an end by the 16th and 17th centuries, the same time witches and wildmen were banished and branded, and burned, as heretics (Hynes and Steele 1980: 17). To this day "wild children" – such as appear on one's threshold in North America each October 31st at Halloween, in the guise of witches, ghosts and demons demanding treats and threatening "tricks" – are looked at askance by the fundamentalist Christian sector.

This austerity-bent and "law-and-order" course of mainstream Christianity increases the need for a steam valve and communitas-style ritual with which to invert and reassert the overly oppressive order. One way for Christians to "lighten up" is to induct a trickster figure into their religion. While such a step would be anathema to the church, according to Hynes and Steele (1980), it has nevertheless happened, albeit not within the *ecclesia*, the hallowed halls of the Great Tradition of Christianity. Instead, where we can find the trickster is within popular Christianity, especially the folklore of the Christian folk.

The scriptural character fastened on and "transfigured" to the trickster is not Jesus Christ, however. The levity and vulgarity that surround the trickster figure are at odds with the serenely pious beliefs and sentiments Christian folk anywhere hold about the central figure of their faith. Instead, the trickster figure is St. Peter, Jesus Christ's deputy and the rock on which he built his church, as well as his. As shown by Steele and Hynes (1980: 4–9), Simon Peter is also, in a number of significant ways, the symbolic inversion of his master. All this makes Peter a suitable metonymic and metaphoric trickster-candidate through whom to challenge, lampoon and invert the religious order. Hynes and Steele focus on this figure in the context of Yaqui and southwest and central American oral literature. San Pedro is seen to be a prominent protagonist in tales that are tricksteresque in bent. He is capricious, deceitful and vainglorious, avaricious, hedonistic and lewd. He violates taboos, shifts his shape, and attempts miracles. Accompanying him on his exploits on earth is Jesucristo, whom he forever tries to outwit and who acts as his foil, accentuating San Pedro's foibles and folly. Another arena for San Pedro antics is heaven, where he is cast in the liminal role as turnkey and keeper of the gates of Heaven. As such he is frequently duped by entrance seekers holding dubious moral credentials. Much the same figure is found in European folklore, in both fairy tales and folk, such as Grimm's *The Tailor in Heaven* and *Brother Lustig* (Grimm) and the jokes about St. Peter guarding the "Pearly Gates".

A second trickster figure that one finds in folk religion – one more in line with mainstream church teachings – is the Devil (Zucker 1967: 313–14). Unequivocally evil in the writings of theologians and teachings and preachings of priests, the official portraiture shows this dark figure of Christianity as tempter, negator, agent of evil, pain and death. These are the dark and destructive sides also of the trickster; indeed, as shown by early English church sculptures that depict cloven-footed, demonic figures wearing the fool's cap, the conflation of trickster/fool and devil may be quite explicit (Billington 1984: 3). However, outside the official church the representations of the devil can be a good deal more equivocal (Russell 1984: 62–91, 129–33), especially in folklore, in such fairy tales as Grimm's "The Devil with the Three Golden Hairs", "The Peasant and the Devil", "The Devil's Sooty Brother". The folkloric devil is seen to be a full-fledged trickster, very much the anti-structural Lord of Disorder, ambiguous on every score (Russell 1984: 71), including the moral one (as he is capable of good and generous deeds, creating ambivalence).

In addition to these two principal mechanisms for introducing the trickster into popular Christianity, one can think of at least two other ways whereby folklore has drafted trickster figures into religious lore. One of them is to draw such figures not from the hallowed domain of scriptures but from the more worldly domain of church history. An especially rich source are the annals and legends of hagiography. These report on a number of saints who were well-rounded trickster figures, namely the "Fools for Christ's Sake" who roamed the natural and urban landscape of early Eastern Orthodox Christianity (Syrkin 1982). Most prominent amongst them was the canonized "holy fool" Symeon of Emesa of the sixth century; Marcus and Thomas and the ninth-century Andrew were others, and, after the movement had spread to Russia, the notoriety of the Christ-Fool Vasilij Blazennyi was such as to spook as elevated a member of the ruling class as Czar Ivan IV, "the Terrible" (Syrkin ibid.:159). Like tricksters, the Fools for Christ's Sake flouted rules of decency; for example, they relieved themselves in public, walked around naked, entered a woman's bath, danced with harlots – chastely, the hagiographers point out, and without lust. They conducted their every action with foolishness and buffoonery, antagonized people with pranks, lied, performed miracles such as turning wine into vinegar, curing the sick or resurrecting the dead. In Symeon's case, one of the dead to be resurrected was himself, whereupon, like Christ, he ascended to heaven. Unlike tricksters, however, the actions of Christ's fools were deliberate and their motivation was unequivocally good. There was method to their madness, according to the hagiographers, as their aim, despite appearances to the contrary, was the salvation of the souls of people. As suggested by Syrkin (ibid.:157), their antics are a literal and naive heeding of Paul's definition of the apostles' calling: "We are fools for Christ's sake" (I Corinthians 4:10). As for Symeon, he is treated by Syrkin (ibid.:168) as an earthy (in)version of Christ, his opposite in action and deportment, yet like him of pious and holy intent. He brings salvation "down to earth", imbuing it with the "details of everyday, mundane life" (such as gluttony, drinking, playing games, dancing, visiting inns). According to Syrkin (ibid.:158–9), elements of this tradition of asceticism can also be found in the western Christianity, especially Francis of Assisi and his followers, all of whom Francis referred to as *joculates domini* ("jesters of the Lord"). While abstaining from the moral excesses of their Eastern counterparts, they displayed divine folly and *laetitia spiritualis* (spiritual joy) by transgressing certain social and clerical rules, attracting, and rejoicing in abuse and insults, loving inanimate and animate nature, treating animals like humans and preaching to the birds (ibid p. 158–59).

A second trickster-prototype that folklore and legend drew from history is the earthy, irreverent, yokelish buffoon-cleric. Such figures are seen to occupy the lowest rank in the church hierarchy; they are country priests or monks, of humble origin, "natural louts in a cassock" (Welsford 1935: 202). The best-known folkloric figure is Friar Tuck of Sherwood Forest. Other, more classically tricksteresque figures, were the historical Florentian Piovano Arlotto (Welsford p.43, Flögel 1789: 477–87) and the legendary German

"Wigand von Theben, Pfaffe von Kalenberg" (Welsford p.42–43) – who chalked up such outrages as bathing naked in the river before the eyes of the shocked Duchess, being driven through the countryside in a manure cart, and playing "incredibly coarse" tricks on his congregation.

A more surreptitious folkloric mechanism for inverting and lampooning the Church is to co-opt a mundane trickster who operates in the secular world and to tag religious themes of liminality and inversion, satire and blasphemy onto this figure. A case in point is the German Till Eulenspiegel, *alias* Howleglass, his name in English folklore (Welsford 1935: 44–47)[7] Among his dupes, the rich and powerful – from greedy and conceited bakers, tailors and burghers to university rectors, dukes and the king of Denmark – were his favourite marks, along with priests and abbots. His acts of blasphemy were "too coarse for repetition here" (Welsford ibid.:44). He was baptized three times (twice in dirty water) and at his death he jeered at the Holy Spirit, claiming that just as it informs humankind so he will inform it after his death. He was buried standing up.

Thus, notwithstanding the order-and-structure agenda of Christianity, the trickster has found his way also into this religion (as into so many others), in forms that are more or less subversive of the church. He is one of the key triggers for communitas and liminality within mainstream Christianity. As suggested by Hynes and Steele (1980: 17), one of the "official" ways whereby Christianity addresses itself to the troubling anti-structural, unruly forces that threaten to undermine the nomos, is to posit the actions and will of God to "lie above all rationality". Such a notion, however, is, so Hynes and Steele (1980: 17), "largely unsuccessful" in Christianity, as "ultimately . . . the stoic rationality surrounding the God of mainstream Christianity proves too deeply rooted to be dislodged". With its emphasis on the Divine Word, or Reason, as the ultimate ground and being of all that there is, little scope is provided within the Great Tradition of Christianity for communitas. Order and disorder have been separated and equated with goodness and evil; with respect to this pair of ontological and moral opposites, Christians commit themselves, exclusively and austerely, to only the one set.

As shown by Victor Turner (1969: 94–203), liminal figures – from Saint Benedict and Francis of Assisi, through Teresa of Avila, the Wesleys and Quakers to Tolstoy – and communitas-style movements – the sects and cults they and others have founded – have forever broken out of mainstream Christianity, in the course of its two-thousand year history. Many and varied were and are these figures and movements: from mendicant or flagellant beggars roaming the rural and urban landscape in medieval Europe – one of whose modern counterparts might be the "Bikers for Christ" – to "Charismatics" and "Holy Rollers", "Peyotists" and "Pentecostalists" who chant and dance and who trip out and "speak in tongues", issuing forth unintelligible utterances. We see "spriritualists" calling forth the beings from the preternatural world and "faith healers" and "holistic healers" of every description, using the full range of shamanic healing techniques. There are venal, hustling "tele-evangelists" and itinerant "revivalists", some of them deceitful, avaricious and carnal. And speaking of carnal, we come across the "Children of God" who proclaim, and evidently lustily practice, "free love", sending nubile emissaries – the "Hookers for Jesus", out into the streets for some "flirty fishing" – "eff-eff'ing" – by means of which to seduce and lure new recruits into the "Family of Love" (Rudolph 1993: 32). On the opposite side, the side of virtue, we find the unworldly "Fools for Christ" and "Jesters of the Lord" who turn tricks of a more innocent kind, intended to save, not tempt, souls. More than a few of the leaders and followers of these liminal movements are "out of touch with reality" – quixotic, unstable, demented – occasionally deeming themselves divine messengers or even incarnations of Christ: from the historical-legendary St. Francis who talked to the animals and the sun and moon, and Catherine of Siena and Joanne of Arc, each with her visions, voices, trances and ecstasy, to today's incestuous and polygynous Moses David (father and leader of the "Children of God") and the sex-crazed "savage Messiah" Rock Thériault roaming the woodland wilderness of Quebec and Ontario (Kaihla & Laver 1993).

Jointly and mystically, these disparate and disassembled figures could be seen to constitute the body of the anti-structural church. We might christen this anti-church *Ecclesia Ludens*, in opposition to the *Ecclesia Sancta*, her saintly sister. And just as the latter is declared to be the "true bride of Christ", so we could regard her wayward sister as one of Trickster's more favoured hussies.

Notes

1 Healing arrows (*/xobe*, not *k"au*, regular hunting arrows) are filled with *tso* medicine [healing potency, activated by dancers in trance]. They are tiny, about one-third the size of a match stick, and if they are combined with the *n//atse//xaba* plant by the doctor, they will look like the thorns of this plant. They are all over the inside of Addam and Effa's ant hills and are used by these two people, just like we use household utensils, kettles, pots or cups. They are bundled up, and bundles of them are placed outside their hills, to be collected by Jessu Kriste. They just give them as gifts to him, to give to the //gauwani, to help the people. They make them so that they may be given as presents to the //gauwani. The women's arrows, from Effa's hut, are given to women, who learn to dance from the men and who give to the women these arrows which they receive from the //gauwani. (Guenther 1989: 45) In this commentary Eve's role provides an explanation on how women can be effective as trance healers. They were so quite rarely in the past; however, as a result of increasing existential stress and the great increase in the incidence of disease amongst farm Bushmen, coupled with the virtual loss of the women's economic role as gatherers, women now have both more motivation and more time to turn to healing themselves (Guenther 1975/76, 1976; Lee 1984; 15, 113–15).

2 Much the same happened amongst the Winnebago, where the trickster Hare merged with Christ, such that some Indians felt they had no need for Jesus Christ as they already had Hare (Henderson 1964: 104–5).

3 Descriptions and discussions of the Bushman trickster figure can be found in Bleek, W. 1864, Schmidt 1977/78; Hewitt 1986; Guenther 1986: 219–25, and Biesele 1993: 103–15.
4 See Guenther (1986, chapter 5) for more details on the ritual role of the Nharo trickster god.
5 The depiction of the netherworld in such European-technological, "cargo cult-ish" terms reflects the state of economic depression and "relative deprivation" of the farm Bushmen who live within a society that is dominated economically and politically by the white and black settlers and is rife with inter-ethnic tension. (See Guenther 1976, 1986)
6 I was alerted to this parallel by my colleague Peter Eglin.
7 This trickster esque figure has also found its way into Khoisan oral tradition (Schmidt 1993:150–54). In its pioneer trekboer context in southern Africa the place of the duped burgher has been taken by the *baas* (151–54). The Devil-trickster, too, is part of this store of syncretic, acculturated Khoekhoe oral literature (134–50).

Bibliographic references

Apte, M. L.
1985 *Humour and Laughter – An Anthropological Approach.* Ithaca: Cornell University Press.

Babcock, B.
1978 *The Reversible World.* Ihaca: Cornell University Press.

Barnard, A.
1992 "Hunters and Herders of Southern Africa", *Cambridge Studies in Social and Cultural Anthropology.* Cambridge: Cambridge University Press.

Basso, E. B.
1987 *In Favour of Deceit – A Study of Tricksters in an Amazonian Society.* Tucson: The University of Arizona Press.

Biesele, M.
1976 "Aspects of !Kung Folklore", in, R. B. Lee and I. De Vore, (eds). *Kalahari Hunter-Gatherers*, pp. 302–24. Cambridge, MA: Harvard University Press.
1993 *Women Like Meat – The Folklore and Foraging Ideology of the Kalahari Ju/'hoan.* Johannesburg: Witwatersrand University Press.

Billington, S.
1984 *A Social History of the Fool.* Sussex: The Harvester Press.

Bleek, W. H. I.
1864 *Reynard the Fox in South Africa.* London: Trübener & Co.

Brandon, S. G. F.
1967 *Jesus and the Zealots.* Manchester University Press.
1968 *The Trial of Jesus of Nazareth.* New York: Stein & Day.

Budack, K.
1980 "Vom Völkerhass zur Nächstenliebe. Die Missionare und die San", Part 18 of 'Die Völker Südwestafrikas' *Allgemeine Zeitung*, Windhoek, September 26th.

Cormier, H.
1977 *The Humour of Jesus.* New York: Alba House.

Cox, H.
1970 *The Feast of Fools: A Theological Essay on Festivity and Fantasy.* New York: Harper & Row.

Diamond, S.
1972 *Introductory Essay: Job and the Trickster*, in P. Radin *The Trickster*, pp. xi–xxv, New York: Schocken Books.
Flögel, K. F.
1789 *Geschichte des Hofnarren*, Liegaitz & Leipzig: David Siegert. (Facsimile reprint, Hildesheim: Georg Olms Verlag, 1977)
Geertz, C.
1966 "Religion as a Cultural System", in M. Banton (ed.) *Anthropological Approaches to the Study of Religion*, (A.S.A. Monograph 3). Pp. 1–46. London: Tavistock Publications.
Gluckman, M.
1954 *Rituals of Rebellion in South-East Africa*. Manchester University Press.
1965 *Custom and Conflict in Africa*. Oxford: Blackwell.
Gordon, R.
1992 *The Bushman Myth The Making of a Namibian Underclass*. Boulder: Westview Press.
Guenther, M.
1975/76 "The San Trance Dance: Ritual and Revitalization among the Farm Bushmen of the Ghanzi District, Republic of Botswana", *Journal of the South West African Scientific Society*, 30:45–53.
1976 "From Hunters to Squatters: Social and Cultural Change among the Ghanzi Farm Bushmen", R. B. Lee and I. De Vore, (eds.) *Kalahari Hunter-Gatherers*, pp. 120–33. Cambridge, MA: Harvard University Press.
1986 *The Nharo Bushmen of Botswana*. (Quellen zur Khoisan-Forschung 3). Hamburg: Helmut Buske Verlag.
1989 *Bushman Folktales Oral Traditions of the Nharo of Botswana and the /Xam of the Cape*, Stuttgart: Franz Steiner Verlag Wiesbaden.
"Tricksters, Trancers, Foragers: Structure and Anti-Structure", in *Bushman Religion*.
Henderson, J. L.
1964 "Ancient Myths and Modern Man", in C. G. Jung (ed.), *Man and his Symbols*, pp. 95–158. New York: Laurel.
Hynes, W. J. & T. J. Steele
1980 "St.Peter: Apostle Transfigured into Trickster", Paper presented at the American Academy of Religion Annual Conference, Dallas, Texas. November.
Kaihla, P. & R. Laver
1993 *Savage Messiah: The Shocking Story of Cult Leader Rock Thériault and the Women who Loved Him*. Toronto: Doubleday Canada.
Kerényi, K.
1972 "The Trickster in Relation to Greek Mythology"; in P. Radin, *The Trickster*, p. 171–91. New York: Schocken Books.
Koepping, K.-P.
1985 "Absurdity and Hidden Truth: Cunning Intelligence and Grotesque Body Images as Manifestations of the Trickster", *History of Religions*, 25:191–214.
Lee, R. B.
1984 *The Dobe !Kung*. New York: Holt, Rinehart and Winston.

Marshall, J.
1982 "N!ai: The Story of a !Kung Woman", (film) Watertown, Mass.: Documentary Educational Resources.
Marshall, L.
1962 "!Kung Bushman Religion", *Africa*, 12:221–51.
Miller, S.
1967 "The Clown in Contemporary Art", *Theology Today*, 24:318–28.
Rahner, H.
1967 *Man at Play*. New York: Herder & Herder.
Rudolph, B.
1993 "Family of Fear", *Time*, September 13:32.
Russell, J. B.
1984 *Lucifer – The Devil in the Middle Ages*. Ithaca: University Press.
Schmidt, S.
1977/78 "Der Trickster der Khoisan-Volkserzählungen als Regenkämpfer", *Journal of the South West African Scientific Society*, 31:69–93.
Syrian, A. Y.
1982 "On the Behavior of the Fool for Christ's Sake", *History of Religions*, 22: 150–71.
Thiering, B.
1992 *Jesus and the Riddle of the Dead Sea Scrolls*. San Francisco: Harper.
Toelken, B.
1969 "The Pretty Language of Yellowman: Genre, Mode, and Texture in Navaho Coyote Narratives", *Genre*, 2: 211–35.
Trueblood, E.
1964 *The Humor of Christ*. New York: Farrar & Rinehart.
Turner, V.
1967 "Betwixt and Between: The Liminal Period in Rites de Passage", in his *The Forest of Symbols*, pp. 93–111. Ithaca: Cornell University Press.
1969 *The Ritual Process*. Chicago: Aldine.
1974 "Passages, Margins and Poverty: Religious Symbols of Communitas", in his *Drama, Fields and Metaphors*, pp. 231–71. Ithaca: Cornell University Press, pp. 231–71.
Volkman, T.
1982 *The San in Transition Vol. 1: A Guide to N!ai, the Story of a !Kung Woman*, Boston: Cultural Survival.
Webster, G.
1960 *Laughter in the Bible*. St. Louis: Bethany.
Welsford, E.
1935 *The Fool: His Social and Literary History*. New York: Farrar & Rinehart.
Zucker W.
1967 "The Clown as the Lord of Disorder", Theology Today, 24:306–17.

70

CONVERSION TO PROTESTANTISM AMONG URBAN IMMIGRANTS IN TAIWAN

Hsing-Kuang Chao

Source: *Sociology of Religion*, 67(2) (2006), 193–204.

Since the 1970s, Christianity in Taiwan has had little growth, while conventional religions, such as Buddhism, Daoism, and the folk religions have increased their adherents. However, some Christian churches are growing. For example, the Bread of Life Christian Church, established in the 1950s and based in Taipei City, has grown from one local congregation to 131 congregations around the world.[1] A few congregations of Presbyterian and Baptist denominations are also growing. These congregations not only attract transfer members from other Christian churches, they also gain converts from non-Christian backgrounds. These growing churches are located in urban areas or adjacent areas of industrial parks. What distinguishes these growing congregations?

Until recently, most studies of religious conversion have been done in the Western world, especially in North America, where Christianity is the mainstream religion. In Chinese societies, Christianity is not the majority religion, rather, in Taiwan the religious market is dominated by folk religions, Taoism, and Buddhism. Are the dynamics of the conversion process in Taiwan the same as suggested by scholars in the Western world?

Christian conversion in Taiwan

Although Western Christianity has promoted modern medicine, secondary and higher education, and social welfare in many Chinese societies, and thus has earned very high prestige, Christian churches continue to have difficulty recruiting new members from these societies. Christianity is still regarded as a foreign or Western religion. Tensions exist between Christian doctrines and rituals and Chinese traditional values and cultural practices. Conversion to Christianity commonly results in the violation of norms relating to family life and negatively impacts the intimate relationships of family members. For example, while filial duty is the central value of Chinese society, with ancestor worship being one of the most important filial duties as well as the mechanism that unites family members, ancestor worship is prohibited by Christian churches in Taiwan (Chao 1996:460).[2] Moreover in the rural areas of Taiwan, participating in the fair held at the site of a temple and donating to the temple are considered duties of all villagers, but Christian churches commonly forbid Christians to fulfill these duties. Converts, then, are often regarded as deviants by family members and friends. Despite the long-lasting tensions between local religious traditions and Christianity, however, conversions to Christianity occur frequently.

Multiple concepts and theories have been introduced to explain the conversion process (e.g. Lofland 1978; Stark and Bainbridge 1985; Greil and Rudy 1984; Snow and Machalek 1983; Richardson 1985; Dawson 1990; Bader and Demaris 1996). Stark and Finke (2000:118–119) indicated that attachments lie at the heart of conversion, and that conversion therefore tends to proceed along social networks formed by interpersonal bonds. This is especially so for immigrants. When immigrants change their residence, they are free from the original social bonds but also lose the social support that was provided by the original social networks. Conceivably, immigrants may pay a lower cost when they decide to change religion and participate in a new religious organization that is different from their traditional faith (Cavendish, Welch and Leege 1998; Stump 1984).

Stark and Finke (2000:118–119) also emphasize the importance of cultural continuity. If people have been socialized into a religion, they will attempt to conserve their religious capital in making subsequent religious choices. Hexham and Poewe (1997:43–46) argued that the Catholic Church converted the heathen English to Catholicism because it both remained distinct and absorbed local cultural traits. The accommodation of a world religion to a folk religion of a local culture reduces the cost of joining the world religion. A flexible theological stand, therefore, may be very important to a church, if converts are to be gained.

Several sociological studies on conversion to Christianity among overseas Chinese have supported the importance of interpersonal attachments and religious continuity in the conversion process. For example, Fenggang Yang's research on the Chinese Gospel Church in the Houston area (Yang 2000:186) revealed that interpersonal attachments of Chinese immigrants to church members in cell groups proved to be a highly effective method to promote conversion. In another study, Yang (1998:253) found that allowing converts to conserve their traditional culture by emphasizing the compatibility of Confucianism and conservative Protestantism, was one of the key elements for involving Chinese immigrants in the Christian church. Because most Chinese regard Confucianism not as religion but as a traditional philosophy of life, evangelical Chinese Christians can retain Confucian moral values without falling into a stigmatized syncretism. This allows the Chinese churches to retain cherished Confucian values about family and ascetic ethics and still incorporate Christianity's teaching on the supernatural.

Other studies of conversion to religions movements in Taiwan found that the mechanisms to convert people into new religious movements were the same as those in the Western world. In my study (Chao 2000) of conversion to a new Buddhist cult, the Suma Ching Hai International Association (SCHIA), which attracted many followers from Buddhism, Great Dao, and other folk religions in a very short period, I found that reducing tension with the conventional religious culture while maintaining some uniqueness was very important. The leader of SCHIA proclaims that "the Quan Yin Method"[3] is the best meditation practice, while she also allows her followers to keep their original religious faith and worship their gods as they wish. Many converts indicated that religious experiences, such as healing, meeting family members or the Master Suma Ching Hai in a dream, and resolving personal problems by the practice of the Quan Yin Method, influenced their religious choice.

Lin (2003) studied another new religious group and discovered that people were introduced to the meditation group by their relatives and close friends. The group members testified about the benefits of meditation to the prospects and invited them to participate in the meditation practice, but they did not tell the prospects that the meditation practice is a part of a new religion. Most prospects accepted the invitation and participated in the meditation practice because they expected that the meditation would alleviate stress, cure chronic disease, and improve psychological and physical health. Lin (2003:557) emphasized that the meditation practice reduces the tension between the new religion and conventional religions.

In short, the existing studies of religious conversion in the West and Taiwan show three important elements: personal bonds, cultural continuity, and religious experience. Institutional factors are important as well, for the churches that offer appealing religious services are likely to grow. Therefore, to study Christian conversion in Taiwan we should attend to the importance of personal networks and cultural continuity. Personal networks may bring people into contact with the church and develop affective ties with church members. Cultural continuity means that prospective converts are likely to favor those churches that provide a foundation to retain their conventional religious culture. In Taiwan, given the widespread of Buddhism, Daoism, and folk religion, paranormal or extraordinary experiences are a major part of the cultural continuity. In other words, whether or not the individuals who are brought to the Christian church do convert may be dependent, to a large extent, upon whether or not they experience something special that is in line with traditional religious practices.

Data and method

In order to explore the pattern of conversion among urban immigrants, two churches, Pan-Tin Presbyterian Church (PTP) and Tunghai Bread of Life Christian Church (TBL), were selected as the study sites. They are affiliated with different denominations and hold different theological stands. PTP is a congregation of the Presbyterian Church in Taiwan, the oldest denomination in Taiwan that adopts a moderate theological stand toward social issues. TBL is affiliated with the Taipei Bread of Life Christian Church, which has been strongly influenced by the Third Wave Charismatic Movement. Both churches are located in the western edge of Taichung, the third largest city in Taiwan. But their immediate neighborhoods are different. The PTP is surrounded by farmhouses, and the TBL is located in a business area.

Both Pan-Tin Presbyterian Church and Tunghai Bread of Life Christian Church are middle-size Christian churches in Taiwan, with about two hundred and fifty members and visitors involved in the Sunday service of each church weekly. In Taiwan, about 60% of Christian churches are small, with less than 100 members attending Sunday services, and less than 5% of Taiwanese Christian churches have more than 300 members participating in Sunday services.

Each year between 2000 and 2003, more than 10 percent of Sunday service participants were baptized in PTP, and more than 20 percent of Sunday service participants were baptized in TBL. With the pastors' assistance, the author gathered a list of converts and invited them to be involved in this study. In order to reduce the effect of the churches' religious socialization, we invited only those converts who had been baptized less than two years to participate in this study.

The data were collected mainly through in-depth interviews, participant observation, and document analysis. Between September 2001 and June 2003, the author and his research assistants frequently visited the two churches for long-term observation. Thirty-nine converts were interviewed, twenty-one from PTP and eighteen from TBL. All interviewees were immigrants who moved to Taichung city less than five years earlier. We also interviewed seven lay leaders and two senior pastors regarding church characteristics and strategies to convert new members. Church publications, such as the church's annual report, and other materials such as the pastor's evangelist publications were collected for document analysis.

The profile of the churches

The PTP was founded in 1982. It is located on the western edge of the Taichung Industrial Park because the church leaders hoped that the development of the Park would attract a massive population flow into this area and that the congregation would recruit many Christian as well as non-Christian immigrants. The PTP has attracted many Taiwanese-speaking Presbyterian immigrants from southern Taiwan. Most of the members hold high school or junior college diplomas and are workers at the Taichung Industrial park.

Pastor Chuang, who was brought up in a folk religious family, has been the pastor since 1982. When he was a teenager, his family was bothered by demonic spirits. After they failed to gain help from conventional religions, a friend of the family's brought his family to a Christian church to seek help. Because the Christian church helped the family to solve the problem, all family members converted to Christianity and he later attended a Presbyterian seminary. Pastor Chuang's personal religious experiences in fasting, exorcism, and healing have become the focal point of PTP since he took the pastorship.

Although the Presbyterian Church in Taiwan discourages local congregations from practicing charismatic signs and wonders, Pastor Chuang does preach about the power of fasting, exorcism, and instant healing. He also encourages church elders to participate in exorcism and healing rituals. Based on his spiritual experiences, he insists that all spiritual problems and difficulties of everyday life are caused by demons of conventional religions and converting to Christianity is the only way to free people from the demons' control. Such freedom requires fasting and exorcism.

To reach non-Christians, the PTP established a community service center in the early 1990s. The center has provided many different programs, such as a cooking club and an English camp, to attract women and children. Pastor Chuang and his wife are responsible for taking care of new visitors. They make phone calls to people who have participated in the church's activities and visit them at their homes.

The TBL was established by Pastor Lin in 1997. The TBL church is located on the eastern edge of Taichung Industrial Park near Tunghai University. Pastor Lin said that he expected the church would attract many participants from the industrial park and the university. Although Pastor Lin was brought up in a folk religious setting, he converted to Christianity when he was in junior high school. His Christian faith was fostered by the Navigators Taiwan, a conservative outreach ministry, when he studied at Tunghai University. He trained and served as a part-time co-worker in the Navigators Taiwan for several years. After he read the famous Korean Pastor Cho's church growth monograph and visited the Faith Community Baptist Church in Singapore, he decided to leave the Navigators Taiwan to establish a church that would adopt both Faith Community Baptist Church's cell church model and the practice of charismatic signs and wonders. Compared with the PTP, most of the TBL members are better educated. They either serve as faculty/staff members in surrounding universities, work in the business field, or are the white-collar staff at the Taichung Industrial Park.

All church members in the TBL are asked to participate in a cell group. The group leaders are responsible for taking care of group members and participating in a Bible study workshop led by Pastor Lin during the week. All group members are encouraged to share their faith, spiritual experiences, happiness and needs and to pray for each other during the weekday group gathering in the group leader's residence. If any member's problem cannot be solved in the cell group, the group leader will ask for assistance from Pastor Lin. Practicing glossolalia, exorcism, and instant healing is very common in church gatherings at TBL. Pastor Lin insists that glossolalia, exorcism, healing, and worship music are the gifts of the Holy Spirit for those who suffer from different problems and needs. He does not want to get involved in arguments regarding what is the correct theological stand. The church's goals are to meet people's immediate needs with the gifts of the Holy Spirit and convert them to Christianity.

In sum, the TBL and the PTP share some common characteristics: First, both proclaim that their faith regarding the supreme authority of God and Jesus is not compatible with conventional beliefs. Second, they are, in Dean Kelly's (1986) term, strict churches. Both congregations encourage members, especially lay leaders, to show high commitment to the church's goals and beliefs, and a willingness to suffer and sacrifice for them. Third, both churches emphasize the importance of the work of the Holy Spirit, including exorcism and instant healing, in everyday Christian life. Fourth, they tend to adopt a realistic or practical perspective on Christian faith. Rather than dogmatic expositions, they strongly focus on charismatic practices to meet their members' needs in everyday life. This allows new members to retain their conventional religious concept that gods are responsible for whatever people need, and still accept Christianity's teachings on the supernatural (Stark and Finke 2000:124).

The TBL and the PTP are different in three ways. First, the TBL is a charismatic church while the PTP discourages members from practicing glossolalia in church gatherings although it practices exorcism and spiritual healing. Second, TBL uses its cell groups as the major mechanism for recruiting people into the church while the PTP is a Presbyterian congregation and the pastor is responsible for the spiritual needs of members and visitors. Third, the formal education of TBL members is overall higher.

The PTP conversion process

Among the twenty-one interviewees from the PTP, only one interviewee came to the church without preexisting links to the people in the church. Seven converts were brought into contact with the PTP by friends, six by relatives, three by colleagues, another three by church staff, and one by a neighbor. Five of the twenty-one interviewees were college students. They had regularly participated in church activities, including Sunday services and the college fellowship group "Fish Mission," and developed interpersonal attachments with college peers and lay leaders in the PTP. Other interviewees irregularly participated in the church's activities, mostly Sunday services, but had very few opportunities to intensively interact with church members before they converted to Christianity; however, all of them maintained intensive relations with Pastor Chuang, his wife, or other church staff.

The data show that those who developed affective bonds both with Pastor Chuang and with other members were more easily converted than those who only interacted with Pastor Chuang or another church staff. Those in the later category took, on average, two more years to be converted. In contrast, seven of eight interviewees who converted within six months after they were brought in developed close relationships with Rev. Chuang, his wife, and other church members.

All interviewees appreciated the psychological comfort, emotional support, and acceptance from church members. Four interviewees reported that the most important acts of support from the church members were financial, including providing a job, a residence, or financial aid. Another two interviewees most appreciated Rev. Chuang's help with family matters, such as funeral affairs. About half of the interviewees (nine out of twenty-one) claimed that they experienced charisma before they converted to Christianity. Some expected to have charismatic experiences as a condition to convert, while others had these experiences unexpectedly. Having mystical experiences was the key factor promoting conversion among these prospects. Eight of nine interviewees who had charismatic experiences—notably healing and exorcism—interacted with Pastor Chuang closely.

The TBL conversion process

At TBL, all eighteen interviewees were brought into contact with the church through preexisting social networks. Thirteen of them especially appreciated the emotional support received from cell group members. Fourteen of the eighteen interviewees developed new interpersonal attachments with cell group members soon after they were brought into contact with the church. They intensively interacted with the cell group leader and the member who brought them to participate in the church.

Most prospects did not intensively interact with church staff or Pastor Lin before converting to Christianity. However, if the cell group leader could not meet the prospect's needs through psychological comfort, emotional support, or material aid, they were referred to Rev. Lin for spiritual support.

Nine interviewees claimed that they experienced charisma, including glossolalia, exorcism, or healing, before converting to Christianity. Twelve of them converted less than a half-year after they were brought into contact with the church. For the few who took more than one year to convert to Christianity having charismatic experiences was not significant, rather the psychological comfort and emotional support provided by the cell group was what attracted them to the church.

The congregations compared

The interviews showed that no one converted to either congregation because of the moral teaching or doctrine regarding eternal life. The most crucial factors that persuaded them to join and to stay in the congregations were, first, receiving emotional support, including acceptance, encouragement, and sympathetic prayer from church members and, second, having charismatic experiences.

About a half of the interviewees from the PTP and more than half of the interviewees from the TBL indicated that they experienced charisma before they converted to Christianity. Many interviewees from the TBL emphasized that they could practice glossolalia or prophecy or had the experiences of exorcism and healing, but most of the PTP members' charismatic experiences tended to be physical and psychological healing after practicing fasting. No interviewee from the PTP mentioned that she or he could practice glossolalia or prophecy.

Why did members of two churches experience different charisma? It is clear that religious socialization in the churches plays a significant role in fostering the different experiences. In PTP, Pastor Chuang was the only church leader who was able to practice charisma, but he never practiced glossolalia. On the other hand, TBL cell group leaders and Pastor Lin practiced glossolalia, but only Pastor Lin and a few core leaders performed exorcism and healing ritual for members.

The conversion process in the TBL was on average shorter than in the PTP. The TBL is a cell group church. A prospect would be involved in a cell group as soon as he or she was brought into contact with the TBL. If the prospect stayed in the cell group for a period of time, he or she would intensively interact with other group members and receive various forms of social support from the interpersonal attachments. In contrast to the TBL, the PTP is a local congregation of the Presbyterian Church, and the pastor, not the church members, plays the major role in taking care of visitors. Although the PTP has a few fellowship groups, such as a seniors club and a couples club, these groups exist for the well being of members rather than for the visitor's benefit. Most prospects in the PTP participated in church activities only occasionally. The lack of small groups in which prospects may develop interpersonal attachments in the church extends the conversion process in the PTP.

Discussion

The Taiwanese have a very practical approach to religion. Kuo's research (2001) on Taiwanese religiosity indicates that people participate in religious practices to gain worldly rewards regardless of from which god or spirit these originate. A very famous Chinese historian and diplomat, Mon-Lin Chung, wrote a story in a book entitled *Hsi-Chao* (Western Wave) regarding the perception of Christianity and Jesus among Chinese rural farmers. In the story, a missionary tells the farmers that Jesus is the greatest God and would save their souls from hell. A farmer asks the missionary to bring Jesus to his house and install him on his ancestral table, so that he could worship Jesus together with other gods. The missionary replies that Jesus is the only one true God and one cannot worship Him with any idol at the same time because the Bible tells us "worship no God but me." The farmer decides not to worship Jesus because he believes that Jesus is only one of the gods and that if people worship more gods they would earn more blessings.

Although some scholars (e.g. Chen 1995) expect that the traditional and highly magically oriented conventional religions in Taiwan may give way with modernity, other researchers (Chiu 1997; Kuo 2001) have found that major religious perceptions among most Taiwanese have not changed. For most Taiwanese, their attitude toward religion is still pragmatic and utilitarian. People utilize and manipulate the supernatural in exchange for miracles and rewards that may satisfy their daily needs regardless of what gods or spirits are involved. Religious doctrine itself is not important.

Based on Protestant tradition, many Taiwanese Protestant churches are dedicated to dogmatic expositions and strongly focus on a literal understanding of the Bible, but a scholar in history and folk religions (Sung 1993:194) claims that the failure to accommodate conventional religious culture has resulted in the lack of growth by the Presbyterian and other Christian churches since the 1970s.

In our study, the two churches have adopted a very flexible theological stand and a practical strategy to convert people. Pastor Lin indicates that the major mission of the TBL is to meet people's needs. He thinks that people in the urban area need psychological comfort, spiritual support, and especially, the gifts of the Holy Spirit. His vision is to build a large church to attract as many people as possible, and he does not care about theological stands. Pastor Chuang of the Presbyterian church also has a dream to build a temple that can accommodate at least ten thousand people. Although Pastor Chuang was trained in a Presbyterian seminary, his strong folk religious background has led him to value exorcism and spiritual healing, and these practices have been important in attracting people to PTP.

However, we have also observed that the accommodation of Christian values to the conventional religious culture is not unlimited. In order to convert people as true Christians, the two churches ask all converts to participate in a public baptism ceremony and give testimony during the baptism ritual. More importantly, all the converts are asked to remove their family altar or ancestor table by themselves or along with church leaders. Without these types of significant differences from conventional faiths, the Christian church would lack a basis for successful conversion (Stark 1987:16).

Summary and conclusion

Why do urban immigrants convert to Christianity, which is still a minority religion in Taiwan? These immigrants do not seem to be searching for ultimate meaning or everlasting life but are attracted to Christian churches that meet their needs for social support and emotional comfort through the attachments formed in churches, and that provide the rewards that come from having charismatic experiences. Urban immigrants join a Christian church to solve personal difficulties experienced during their settlement process. Understandably a newcomer who participates in a cell group church and intensively interacts with different group members tends to convert more quickly than the prospect who is involved with only one or a few members of the church staff.

About half of the converts in this study indicated that charismatic experiences were the crucial factor leading to their decision to convert. Such experiences satisfied their immediate needs and provided cultural continuity with their religious past. As indicated by the other papers in this issue, charismatic experiences seem to be less important among Chinese immigrants to the United States. This is a topic that requires further research.

This study suggests that the adaptation of Protestant tradition, including dogmatic expositions and the emphasis on a literal understanding of the Bible, to the conventional religious culture, which emphasizes the provision of ways to gain immediate rewards, should become the major strategy for attracting converts in Taiwan. If Protestant churches adapt their religious culture to the conventional religions, which emphasize gaining practical benefits, prospective members are likely to remain and eventually convert to Christianity.

We do not conclude that Christian doctrines, especially the moral teachings, play no role in the conversion process among Taiwanese urban immigrants. We plan to continue our research in order to examine the conversion pattern at churches affiliated with mainline denominations that emphasize the importance of dogmatic expositions to find out if their dogma is an attractive feature of these churches.

Notes

1 Among the 131 local congregations, 52 congregations are located on the island of Taiwan, and the other 79 congregations are located overseas.

2 The author conducted survey research in 1996. Findings revealed that more than 60 percent of respondents who were non-Christian did not want to convert to Protestantism because Protestant churches prohibit ancestor worship.

3 The Quan Yin Method is the most important meditation practices of the Suma Ching Hai International Association. Master Ching Hai insists that her followers must directly learn the Quan Yin Method from her.

References

Bader, C. and A. Demaris. 1996. A test of the Stark-Bainbridge theory of affiliation with religious cults and sects. *Journal for the Scientific Study of Religion* 35:285–303.

Cavendish, J., M. Welch and D. Leege. 1998. Social network theory and predictors of religiosity for black and white Catholics: Evidence of a "black sacred cosmos"? *Journal for the Scientific Study of Religion* 37(3):397–410.

Chao, H-K. 1996. hau jen yu chi tu chiao tiao cha yen chiu tai wan pu fen (A report of the survey research on Chinese and Christian). In *Church Chi tu chiao yu tai wan (Christian church and Taiwan)*, edited by C.-P. Lin, 457–477. Taipei: Yu chou Kuang Publisher.

——. 1997. The religious market change and the transformation of a Taiwanese immigrant Christian church in Los Angeles. A paper read at the annual meeting of the Society for the Scientific Study of Religion, San Diego, CA.

——. 2000. The seekers of the immediate enlightenment: The three dimensions of conversion. A paper read at the annual meeting of the Society for the Scientific Study of Religion, Houston, TX.

——. 2004. Tai wan chiao hei tseng chang ti she hei hsueh yen chiu: hsin hsing tzung chiao fa chan kuan tien chu tan (Sociological perspective of church growth in Taiwan: An application of the theory of new religious movements). In *Chi tu Chiao yen chiu lun wen chi (Essays on Christian studies)*, edited by the Graduate Institute of Religious Studies, Tung Hai University, 1–17. Taichung: Tung Hai University.

Chen, H. 1995. The development of Taiwanese folk religion, 1683–1945. Ph.D. dissertation, Department of Sociology, University of Washington.

Chiu, H-Y. 1997. Tai wan min chung ti tzung chiao hsin yang yu tzung chiao tai to (Religious faith and religious attitudes among Taiwanese). In *Tai wan tzung chiao pien chien ti she hei cheng chih fen hsi (The influences of socio-politic factors on religious change in Taiwan)*, 1–40. Taipei: Wu-Nan Publisher.

Dawson, L. 1990. Self-affirmation, freedom, and rationality: Theoretically elaborating "active" conversion. *Journal for the Scientific Study of Religion* 29:141–163.

Greil, A. L. and D. R. Rudy. 1984. What have we learned from process models of conversion? An examination of ten cases studies. *Sociological focus* (Oct.):305–323.

Hexham, I. and K. Poewe. 1997. *New religions as global cultures: Making the human sacred.* Boulder, CO.: Westview Press.

Kao, W. P. 2001. Chiu ho hsin ti tzung chiao hsing (Old or new religiosity?). A paper read at the Conference of Religion and Social Change. Institute of Sociology Academia Sinica, Taipei.

Kelley, D. M. [1972] 1986. *Why conservative churches are growing: A study in sociology of religion with a new preface for the Rose edition.* Macon, GA: Mercer University Press.

——. 1978. Comment: Why conservative churches are still growing. *Journal for the Scientific Study of Religion* (Spring):1–9.

Lin, P. H. 2003. Kai Hsin Kuo Cheng Chung Ti Hsin Nien Chuan Huan Mei Chieh Ye Tzu O Shui Fu (Media of faith transformation and self-conviction in the conversion process). In *Hsin Yang I Shih Yu She Hei lun wen chi (Essays on faith, ritual and society)*, edited by Institute of Ethnology, Academia Sinica, 547–581. Taipei: Institute of Ethnology, Academia Sinica.

Lofland, J. 1978. Becoming a world-saver revisited. In *Conversion careers*, edited by J. Richardson, 10–23. Beverly Hills, CA: Sage.

Lofland, J. and R. Stark. 1965. Becoming a world-saver: A theory of conversion to a deviant perspective. *American Sociological Review* 30:863–874.

McKinney, W. and D. R. Hoge. 1983. Community and congregational factors in the growth and decline of Protestant churches. *Journal for the Scientific Study of Religion* 22:51–66.

Perrin, R. D. and A. L. Mauss. 1991. Saints and seekers: Sources of recruitment to the Vineyard Christian Fellowship. *Review of Religious research* (December): 97–111.

Poloma, M. M. and B. F. Pendleton. 1989. Religious experiences, evangelism, and institutional growth within the Assemblies of God. *Journal for the Scientific Study of Religion* 28:415–431.

Richardson, J. T. 1978. *Conversion careers: In and out of the new religions*. Beverly Hills, CA: Sage.

——. 1985 The active vs. passive convert: Paradigm conflict in conversion/ recruitment research. *Journal for the Scientific Study of Religion* 24:119–136.

Snow, D. A. and C. L. Phillips. 1980. The Lofland-Stark conversion model: Critical assessment. *Social Problems* 27:430–447.

Snow, D. A. and R. Machalek. 1984. The sociology of conversion. *Annual Review of Sociology* 10:167–190.

Stark, R. 1987. How new religions succeed: A theoretical model. In *The future of new religious movements*, edited by D. G. Bromley and P. E. Hammond, 11–29. Macon, GA: Mercer University Press.

Stark, R. and W. S. Bainbridge. 1985. *The future of religion: Secularization, revival and cult formation*. Berkeley, CA: University of California Press.

Stark, R. and R. Finke. 2000. *Acts of faith: Explaining the human side of religion*. Berkeley, CA: University of California Press.

Stump, R. W. 1984. Regional migration and religious commitment in the United States. *Journal for the Scientific Study of Religion* 23:292–303.

Sung, K-Y. 1993. *Tzung Chiao yu she hei (Religion and society)*. Taipei: Tung Ta Publisher.

Taylor, B. 1976. Conversion and cognition: An area for empirical study in the micro-sociology of religious knowledge. *Social Compass* 23:5–22.

Yang, F. 1998. Chinese conversion to evangelical Christianity. *Sociology of Religion* 58:237–58.

——. 2000. Chinese gospel church: The sinicization of Christianity. In *Religion and the new immigrants*, edited by H. R. Ebaugh and J. Saltzman Chafetz, 180–195. Walnut Creek, CA: AltaMira Press.

71

CHRISTIANITY AS A NEW RELIGION

Charisma, minor founders, and indigenous movements

Mark R. Mullins

Source: M. R. Mullins, S. Susumu and P. L. Swanson (eds), *Religion and Society in Modern Japan*, Fremont, CA: Asian Humanities Press, 1993, pp. 257–72.

Japanese history provides rich data for the study of the transplantation and indigenization of religions. This process can be documented and analyzed with reference to several religious traditions in vastly different sociohistorical circumstances. The Buddhist tradition was introduced to Japan via China and Korea from the late sixth century, Roman Catholic Christianity was transplanted in the sixteenth century, and various Protestant denominations began missionary efforts from the latter half of the nineteenth century after Japan reopened its doors to the West.

Considerable attention has been given to the study of early Protestant missionary efforts and the subsequent transplantation of churches from Europe and North America. By contrast, comparatively little is known regarding the many indigenous and independent movements that broke away from the mission churches. The reference to Christianity as a New Religion in the title of this paper is not because it is a foreign-born religion and a relatively recent arrival to Japan. Rather, "newness" is related primarily to the fact that indigenous Christian movements broke away from the mission churches and resemble New Religions in so many respects. These movements have charismatic founders and involve significant innovations in beliefs, rituals, and social organization. In this sense, therefore, these Christian-related movements may be viewed as "New Religions" in the Japanese context.

Church-sect theory and the study of indigenization

Over the course of a century scores of Protestant mission organizations from Europe and North America established churches in Japan. During this same period nativistic reactions to these imported expressions of Christianity eventually led to the creation of a number of movements or sects organizationally independent of the mission churches. Japanese scholars refer to many of these movements as Christian-related New Religions, and several such groups were included in the massive reference work on New Religions published in 1990.[1] These groups, however, do not fit easily into typologies of Japanese New Religions because of their indebtedness to the established Christian traditions. For this reason, in fact, SHIMAZONO (1992: 72) recently suggested that a separate typology was needed to adequately deal with Christian-related New Religions in Japan.

Adapting church-sect theory, Figure 1 provides a comparative typological framework for understanding Christian religious organizations in Japan according to three criteria: basic orientation, self-definition, and degree of indigenization. This typology is hardly intended to provide a definitive statement, but it should clarify in a new way the complex relationship between imported and indigenous religions. Readers will note that some groups included in this figure are often regarded as heretical by established or dominant churches. They are included here because this typology is based on an interpretative sociology of religion, rather than theological criteria, and priority is given to the actors' definition of the situation. As BERGER and

Self-Definition (Claims to Legitimacy)	Degree of Change Indigenous ←→ Non-Indigenous Self-support, self-control, self-propagation	
	Native-Oriented	Foreign-Oriented
Monopolistic (Sectarian)	Spirit of Jesus Church Original Gospel	Mormons Jehovah's Witnesses Baptist International Mission
Pluralistic (Denominational)	Non-Church (Mukyōkai) Christ Heart Church The Way	United Church of Christ Roman Catholic Church Anglican Church Lutheran Church* Baptist Church* Reformed Church

* There are a number of Lutheran and Baptist churches in Japan that represent various European (German, Norwegian, Finnish) and North American traditions.

Figure 1 Typology of indigenization.

KELLNER (1981: 40) explain, sociological concepts "must relate to the typifications that are already operative in the situation being studied." Therefore, groups that define themselves in Christian terms or in continuity with the Christian tradition are also included in this typology.

First of all, it is necessary to distinguish indigenous movements from the imported denominations and independent evangelical churches in terms of their basic orientation or dominant reference group. The basic orientation of a Christian religious body in Japan tends to be either "foreign-oriented" or "native-oriented." Transplanted religious organizations, including the Anglican Church, Roman Catholic Church, Lutheran denominations, and the United Church of Christ (the largest Protestant religious body in Japan that incorporates Methodist, Reformed, Presbyterian, and Congregational churches) are still "foreign-oriented" in many respects and therefore located at the non-indigenous end of the continuum. These denominations still receive foreign missionaries and their understanding of theological orthodoxy and models for church polity and organization are taken primarily from Western churches.[2] Similarly, there are scores of independent evangelical groups in Japan whose dominant reference group tends to be American evangelicalism. While these independent groups are indigenous in terms of the standard criteria of self-government, self-support, and self-propagation, their "foreign-orientation" is still apparent in their literature, tracts, and theology, which is largely "translated" materials from North America.

Indigenous movements, on the other hand, are "native-oriented" and do not measure their perception of religious truth by the standards of orthodoxy defined by Western theology or ancient church councils. According to most indigenous movements, God's self-revelation did not end with the canon of the Christian Scriptures. God continues to reveal deeper truths to those who are open to the ongoing work of the Holy Spirit. While some of these movements operate with the closed canon (the Non-Church movement, for example), many share a common belief that God continues to reveal new truths hidden from or as yet ungrasped by Western churches. Most of these groups produce their own literature, including monthly or quarterly magazines, editions of the Bible (sometimes specially edited versions), and collections of the founder's writings and lectures. If not revealing radically new truths, indigenous movements at least share in common the conviction that God is calling them to develop Japanese cultural expressions of the Christian faith that are at least as legitimate as the national churches and denominational forms that have emerged over centuries in Europe and North America.

Although indigenous movements share many common features, they can be distinguished in terms of their self-understanding and claims to legitimacy. Religious organizations can be distinguished by whether they claim to be "uniquely legitimate," thus denying the legitimacy claims of other groups, or "collegially legitimate," thus accepting the claims of other groups. Several movements, for example, are placed in the denominational category (for want of a better term) because they make only modest claims for themselves.[3] The Non-Church movement (Mukyōkai), the Way (Dōkai), and Christ Heart Church (Kirisuto Shinshū Kyōdan), for example, only claim to be Japanese expressions of Christianity, not the exclusive path to salvation.

Two groups are placed in the category of indigenous sect because of their tendency to emphasize exclusive truth claims. The Spirit of Jesus Church (Iesu no Mitama Kyōkai) and the Original Gospel (Genshi Fukuin, sometimes referred to as Makuya or the Tabernacle movement), for example, both regard Western churches and Christian traditions as inadequate and distortions of New Testament Christianity. While some of the publications produced by Makuya (including the writings of the founder, Teshima Ikurō) seem rather collegial and inclusive, both groups claim to have recovered authentic Christianity before it was corrupted by Hellenistic culture. This movement has cultivated "ecumenical relations" with many Jewish organizations in an effort to recover the Hebrew roots of Christianity. It continues to sponsor annual pilgrimages to Israel and sends leaders to study Hebrew on a kibbutz, but it has maintained a sectarian stance toward other Christian churches.

Social background to the rise of indigenous movements

It has been noted in many different contexts that foreign missionaries often fail to distinguish their national culture from the religious faith they seek to transplant. Protestant missionaries to Japan have been no exception. Transplanting the faith has usually included denominational distinctives and loyalties, church polity, forms of leadership, and church architecture, all born in very different socio-cultural situations. Summarizing this tendency in the early period of Protestant mission to Japan, Kitagawa (1961: 40–41) explains that:

> More often than not, European and American missionaries attempted to Westernize as well as Christianize the Japanese people and culture. Japanese converts were made to feel, consciously or unconsciously, that to decide for Christ also implied the total surrender of their souls to the missionaries. The task of evangelism was interpreted by most missionaries as transplanting *in toto* the church in the West on Japanese soil, including the ugly features of denominationalism—an unhappy assumption, indeed.

After Japanese converts were introduced to the Scriptures and went on to pursue serious theological study, many realized that it was possible to distinguish the Christian faith and biblical tradition from the theology, church polity, and cultural values of American and European missionaries.

As native leaders gained a more critical understanding of the Christian tradition and became aware of the significant differences in doctrine and practice among the mission churches, they began to assert more confidently their own ideas as equals of their missionary teachers. The fact that numerous denominations were competing for converts on Japanese soil (each with their own doctrinal peculiarities and forms of government) indicated to many native leaders that there might be room for Japanese interpretations and cultural expressions of Christianity. Missionaries, however, found it difficult to receive instruction from their Japanese disciples. UCHIMURA Kanzō (1916: 233), the founder of Mukyōkai (Non-Church) and one of the most articulate critics of the mission churches, expressed the sentiments of many Japanese Christians in the following passage:

> Missionaries come to us to patronize us, to exercise lordship over us, in a word, to "convert" us; *not* to become our equals and friends, certainly not to become our servants and wash our feet. . . . We believe that the Gospel of Christ is the power of God unto salvation to every one that believeth; but unless through God's grace we save ourselves, we shall not be saved—certainly not by foreign churches and missionaries.[4] [Emphasis in the original]

It is important to recognize that indigenous Christian movements were not merely the result of personality conflicts and power struggles with foreign missionaries. By the late Meiji period the social climate had become decidedly anti-Western and nationalistic, after an earlier phase of worshipping everything Western (*seiyō sūhai*). In his study of attitudes toward modernization in Japan, Marius JANSEN (1965: 5) notes that "the responses of representative and leading Japanese were necessarily conditioned by the climate of opinion within which they moved." This statement is equally valid with respect to Japanese Christian leaders active during this period. The establishment of State Shinto and revival of Confucianism, on the one hand, were accompanied by parallel developments among Japanese Christians. Many Christians exchanged the displacement theology of the missionaries for a fulfillment theology in an effort to recover and legitimate the cultural riches of native traditions. The approach of missionaries came to be regarded by many indigenous leaders as "smelling of butter" (*batākusai*) or "smelling of the West" (*seiyōkusai*) This identification of Christianity with the West had become a stumbling block to propagation and many leaders became convinced that "Japanization" or "de-Westernization" was the only way forward. Independent indigenous movements became the most extreme examples of this process. While nationalism and conflict with missionaries were important "precipitating factors" that clarify the "timing" of these movements, we must consider other factors to explain their "content."

The enabling factor: imported and native religious elements

In referring to indigenous Christian movements as New Religions I do not intend to suggest that they are created exnihilo. New Religions do not appear out of thin air: they draw on "vital elements of the religious heritage" (Earhart 1989: 236). Consequently, we must give attention to this "enabling factor" in the development of New Religions. In the Japanese context, New Religions draw from a vast reservoir of beliefs and practices related to ancestors, the spirit world, Buddhist, Shinto, and Confucian traditions. Similarly, the charismatic founders of Christian movements may have unusual insights and be creative individuals, but they do not start from scratch

MINOR FOUNDER	MOVEMENT	DOMINANT WESTERN INFLUENCES	DOMINANT NATIVE INFLUENCES
Uchimura Kanzō (1861–1930)	Non-Church (1901)	William S. Clark, Professor and lay Christian, Sapporo Agricultural College, Amherst	Confucianism, Bushidō
Matsumura Kaiseki (1859–1939)	Church of Japan (1907), The Way (1912)	James Ballagh, Dutch Reformed Church, Yokohama Band, New Theology, Darwinism	Neo-Confucianism (Yōmeigaku), Shinto
Kawai Shinsui (1867–1962)	Christ Heart Church (1927)	Tōhoku Gakuin College (German Reformed Church)	Confucianism, Buddhism, mountain asceticism, Kyōkenjutsu
Murai Jun (1897–1970)	Spirit of Jesus Church (1941)	Aoyama Gakuin College (Methodism), True Jesus Church, Taiwan, Unitarian Pentecostalism	Folk religious traditions and the ancestor cult
Teshima Ikuro (1910–1970)	Original Gospel or Tabernacle of Christ (1948)	Zionism, Jewish Traditions	Uchimura Kanzō and Non-Church principles, folk religious traditions, mountain asceticism
Nakahara Masao (1948–)	Okinawa Christian Evangelical Center (1977)	Plymouth Brethren Missionary influence, Dispensationalism	Okinawan shamanism

Figure 2 Selected minor founders and indigenous movements.

when organizing a new church or movement. They draw on the imported teachings, rituals, and organizational forms of the mission churches, as well as on various indigenous religious traditions. Native and exogenous elements are creatively adapted by minor founders and form the basis for new organizations. The religious experiences of these leaders and their unique combination of foreign and indigenous elements give rise to new formulations of belief-systems, new rituals and forms of religious practice, sometimes an enlarged canon, and even new forms of social organization.

Notwithstanding the popular myth of the homogeneous Japanese, it is necessary for us to recognize the cultural diversity of this receiving society in order to understand these new indigenous forms of Christianity. Religious diversity (folk religion, Shinto, Buddhist sects, Confucianism) and competing group loyalties (rival clans, social classes, and regions) provided the complex matrix for Japan's encounter with Christianity. The various reinterpretations of Christianity result from this complex interaction between imported foreign elements and diverse native traditions. Figure 2 highlights the dominant foreign and native influences on selected minor founders and movements.[5] Only through in-depth case studies will we be able to unravel and assess the actual impact of various religious traditions on founders and adherents. Here we have only briefly indicated that many different streams of foreign influence (reformed theology, pentecostalism, dispensationalism, unitarianism) have been mixed in unique ways with indigenous elements to produce new expressions of Christianity.

Minor founders, innovation, and charismatic authority

The anti-Western social climate, growing nationalism, and dissatisfaction of Japanese Christians with Western missionaries are important precipitating factors that illuminate the development of indigenous Christian movements. These factors alone, however, do not provide an adequate explanation for the birth of these movements. Like other Japanese New Religions, indigenous Christian movements represent much more than social crisis and "reaction" to imported Christianity. The break with Western mission churches and the creation of viable alternative forms required strong charismatic leaders. "The innovative decision of the founder," EARHART (1989: 236) points out, "cannot be completely subsumed by either social factors or the influence of prior religious factors." How are we to understand the charismatic leaders who play such a key role in the development of indigenous movements? WEBER (1964: 46) made no distinction between charismatic individuals who renewed an old religion and those who founded new religions, but subsumed both under the category of prophet. Werner STARK (1970: 84), however, drew attention to the need for another concept to deal with innovations within a religious tradition:

> In order to describe Paul of Tarsus correctly, we need some such concept as that of a minor founder. In Paul, we behold an archetype which was to be re-incarnated many times in the history of the Church. Behind him, there appear such figures as Benedict, Francis, Dominic, Bernard, Ignatius, Alphonso, and many others. They were all minor founders, revolutionaries and reformers and even reactionaries (goers back to the original) rolled into one, and certainly not routinizers in the sense of Kipling and Weber.

Although Stark's comments are limited to the role of minor founders in the history of European or Western Christianity, this category seems equally relevant to understanding the development of Christianity in non-Western contexts.

More recently, Anthony BLASI has drawn attention to the category of "minor founder" again in his study of early Christianity, *Making Charisma: The Social Construction of Paul's Public Image* (1991). Arguing that Paul was much more than a "routinizer" of the charisma of Jesus, BLASI (14–15) explains that he ". . . . was a 'minor founder,' a founder who resembles major founders in so far as he was an agent of change but who was more conservative than they insofar as he maintained a basic continuity with what had come before him. Paul did something new, but he did it within an already recognizable Christian subculture." Similarly, the charismatic leaders of indigenous Christian movements also create something new, but in recognizable continuity with an existing religious tradition. Minor founders in Japan departed from the religious traditions imported by foreign missionaries in significant ways, but at the same time passed the Christian heritage on to people in this new cultural context. Perhaps we could summarize by saying that a "minor founder" is a charismatic individual who gives birth to a new religious movement in an effort to address the needs of a new type of member, while at the same time conceptualizing the movement as an extension, elaboration, or fulfillment of an existing religious tradition.

From a sociological perspective, "charisma" and "charismatic authority" can only be understood in terms of the social relationship between a "leader" and "followers." Individuals can claim to have direct contact with God and to have received new revelations, but a movement will not be born if the new message does not meet the needs and aspirations of a significant audience. The message must have some appeal and followers must be convinced that these particular individuals have a special connection with the sacred. The break with an existing tradition, in this case with imported mission churches, requires a powerful figure whose personhood authenticates the claims. While founders and movements vary in the degree to which they reject existing traditions and introduce new elements, at the very least they claim to have direct access to the sacred and to have an independent basis of religious authority. UCHIMURA Kanzō (1920: 592), for example, one of the strongest advocates for an indigenous Christianity and founder of Mukyōkai, claimed:

> Japanese Christianity is not a Christianity peculiar to Japanese. **It is Christianity received by Japanese directly from God without any foreign intermediary; no more, no less.** In this sense, there is German Christianity, English Christianity, Scotch Christianity, American Christianity, etc; and in this sense, there will be, and already is, Japanese Christianity. "There is a spirit in man: and the inspiration of the Almighty giveth him understanding." The spirit of Japan inspired by the Almighty is Japanese Christianity. It is free, independent, original and productive, as true Christianity always is.
>
> No man was ever saved by other men's faith, and no nation will ever be saved by other nations' religion. Neither American Christianity nor Anglican faith, be it the best of the kind, will ever save Japan. Only Japanese Christianity will save Japan and the Japanese.
>
> (Emphasis mine)

The charismatic authority of minor founders is based on their convincing claims to direct contact with the sacred, sometimes additional revelations, and their persuasive personalities. It is also not uncommon to find claims of miraculous healings in the early stages of these movements. Matsumura, Kawai, Murai, Teshima, and Nakahara, for example, five of the six founders included in figure 2, each claimed to have either experienced personal healing or been used by God to heal others. During subsequent phases of the institutionalization process, the charismatic authority of these minor founders is reconfirmed and routinized. In some cases, the teachings and writings of the founder came to be viewed with equal or similar authority to the Bible. Even if religious groups distinguish in principle between the canon (Bible) and the founder's writings, in practice they tend to function with similar authority in the community. Religious services normally include readings from the Bible as well as numerous references to the founder's teachings, example, or quotations from his or her writings. Just as Christians normally view the Hebrew Bible and Jesus' interpretations of these ancient texts as "sacred," members of indigenous Christian movements tend to merge the Scriptures and their founder's interpretation.

These minor founders sometimes even become the object of veneration and special ritual respect. Kawai Shinsui, for example, the founder of Kirisuto Shinshū Kyōdan (Christ Heart Church) is paid ritual respect with bows to his photograph at the beginning and end of each service. His writings are also quoted as frequently as the Judeo-Christian scriptures. On a number of occasions I have even heard the deceased founder addressed in prayer ("Chichinaru Kamisama, Iesu Kirisuto, Kawai Shinsui Sensei" ["Father God, Jesus Christ, Kawai Shinsui . . ."]), as though he has become a part of the

Holy Trinity in the minds of some followers. This tendency to venerate minor founders has a long history, as NAKAMURA Hajime (1964: 454) explains with reference to Japanese Buddhism:

> One result of this absolute devotion to a specific person is that the faithful of the various Japanese sects are extreme in the veneration with which they acknowledge the founder of the sect and perform religious ceremonies around him as the nucleus. **One has absolute faith in the master as well as in the Buddha, without feeling that there is the slightest contradiction.** It is not that one pays less attention to the Buddha, but the idea is perhaps that a profound faith in the master and devotion to the Buddha have the same significance.
> [Emphasis mine]

In much the same way, members of Christ Heart Church appear to experience no cognitive conflict in "believing in Jesus Christ" and venerating the founder, Kawai Shinsui, who made the salvific significance of Christ real to them through his teaching and example.

What distinguishes indigenous Christian movements from other New Religions is the fact that minor founders link their new insights to the existing religious tradition. This can take the form of "fulfillment" or "restorationist" explanations. In fulfillment explanations, the teaching of these founders is understood as the additional truth Jesus promised his disciples ("when the Spirit comes he will guide you into all truth"). The new insight fulfills or even supersedes the understanding of Christianity found in the Western churches. In restorationist explanations, Western churches are viewed as degenerate, and indigenous movements assert that they are only recovering or restoring important truths once held by the early church. No matter how severely these movements are assessed or criticized by mission churches or the dominant orthodoxy, in one form or another each regards itself in continuity with the Christian religion or, at the very least, more fully expressing the teachings and intention of Jesus.

Future directions

The foregoing discussion can be regarded as no more than the preliminary spade work needed for constructing a more adequate understanding of indigenous Christianity. In concluding this essay, I would like to suggest areas for future study and comparative research.

First of all, we still need a basic inventory and documentation of indigenous Christian movements. There are at least six other movements I am aware of about which almost nothing is known. Case studies of these movements are needed before we can move on to more reliable generalizations regarding these types of movements in Japan. While each movement developed out of a particular set of circumstances (specific foreign influences, personality conflicts, and indigenous proclivities), comparative analysis of these groups will likely reveal a number of common features. Religious authority in major Buddhist sects in Japan, for example, is transmitted through father-son blood lineage.[6] To what extent have Christian movements adopted or adapted this traditional pattern of leadership succession? So far I have discovered a similar pattern in at least three movements. While not always passed from father to son, religious authority tends to stay in the family of the founder. In the Spirit of Jesus Church, authority was transferred to the founder's wife and, according to my informants, his daughter is in line to be the next bishop. Christ Heart Church is now in its third generation of leadership. The founder's authority was first transferred to his son and recently to his grandson. Matsumura Kaiseki and his wife were childless, but adopted a son to take over as head of The Way. The adopted son's wife, and then daughter, succeeded him as head (*kaichō*) of this religious body. It seems, therefore, that the imported organizational forms and authority structures (representative forms of government) are not readily adopted by Japanese if they have a choice. This is just one area that deserves additional consideration in future comparative studies.

The relationship between charismatic leadership, indigenization, and numerical growth also needs to be addressed. According to Robert Lee's *Stranger in the Land: A Study of the Church in Japan* (1967), the Westernness of Christianity is a major obstacle to numerical growth. Without indigenization, he argues, significant growth cannot be expected. All of the movements in figure 2 experienced significant growth at one time in their history, but today most are barely holding their own or are in a state of rapid decline. The current membership of these groups varies widely, but ranges from several hundred to twenty or thirty thousand.

Mukyōkai, for example, was estimated to have between fifty and one hundred thousand members in the late 1950s,[7] but two decades later Caldarola's study (1979) placed the membership at about 35,000. A follow-up study is needed, but my guess is that Mukyōkai has continued to experience decline since then. In the late 1970s, the Original Gospel consisted of close to 60,000 members, organized into some 500 home Bible-study groups around the country. In 1990, however, I was informed by a leader in the Tokyo office that there were only 150 groups meeting nationwide and approximately 25,000 subscribers to their magazine *Seimei no hikari* (Light of Life). The headquarters of the Spirit of Jesus Church reports that it has over 300 ministers, close to 200 churches, and a total membership of 420,000. The membership figure is clearly inflated and cannot be accepted at face value. This church practices baptism for the dead, more specifically baptism for the ancestors of living members. Some observers have been overheard suggesting rather cynically that this is guaranteed to be one of the fastest methods of church growth! Although still a generous figure, the active membership of 23,283 reported by church headquarters provides us with a more accurate picture of the actual strength of this movement. Christ Heart Church has declined to a membership of approximately 1,300 and adherents to The Way number less than 300 nationwide. Nakahara's Okinawa Christian Evangelical Center, the most recently organized group included in figure 2, is currently in a phase of rapid growth and has baptized over one thousand adherents in just over a decade.

A study of growth and decline patterns in these movements raises the question of whether groups can dig their own graves through "over-indigenization." Comparative studies of religious movements indicates that those maintaining a "medium level of tension" with the larger society are the ones that are growing. STARK (1987: 16) explains that a "movement must maintain a substantial sense of difference and considerable tension with the environment if it is to prosper. Without significant differences from the conventional faith(s) a movement lacks a basis for successful conversion." In the case of some indigenous Christian movements in Japan, they have become so indigenous that there is minimal tension and ineffective mobilization of members for recruitment activities. This is clearly the case with Christ Heart Church and The Way. While these two movements experienced significant growth under charismatic founders, the routinized indigenous forms have not provided an adequate foundation for long-term growth. It is also undeniable that the conservative Confucian character of movements organized decades ago appear rather austere to contemporary Japanese. "What will give one generation a sense of unifying tradition," YINGER (1970: 112) correctly notes, "may alienate parts of another generation who have been subjected to different social and cultural influences."

Finally, we need to consider the role and significance of indigenous Christian movements for the larger Japanese society. To what extent, in other words, do these movements represent significant social change? In his study of the New Religion Gedatsu-Kai, for example, EARHART (1989) discovered that in spite of the new elements introduced by the founder it was in many respects a revitalization movement of traditional Japanese religiosity, or a "return to the center." In fact, involvement in Gedatsu-kai leads to increased participation in traditional religious practices, such as worship before a *kamidana* (Shinto god shelf) and *butsudan* (Buddhist altar), and visits to the local Shinto shrine and to the family Buddhist parish temple. Similarly, HARDACRE's (1984) study of Reiyūkai Kyōdan revealed that it attempted to revitalize the traditional extended family (*ie*) and ancestor veneration, and that the role of women was largely confined to domestic and religious duties. Only a serious study of the teachings of indigenous Christian movements, an analysis of social relations, gender roles and status, and a survey of the actual practices of members will reveal whether they represent alternative cultural values and social roles, or in fact reinforce traditional Confucian ideals. We may also discover that many indigenous Christian movements represent primarily "a return to the center" rather than significant social change.

Notes

1 See Inoue Nobutaka, *et al.*, eds., *Shinshūkyō jiten* [Encyclopedia of the New Religions], Tokyo: Kōbundō, 1990. This indispensable volume contains over a thousand pages of information on New Religions in Japan.

2 See Reid (1991) for studies of indigenization within the United Church of Christ in Japan, Nishiyama (1985) on the Anglican Church, and Doerner (1977) on the Roman Catholic Church.

3 I have used the denominational category in order to emphasize the self-understanding of these groups, even though they lack the characteristics normally associated with a denomination in the West.

4 Uchimura's (1886: 159) pessimism regarding the prospects of Western Christianity was expressed as early as 1886, when he wrote: "Which of the nineteen different Christian denominations which are now engaged in evangelizing Japan is to gain the strongest foot-hold there? In our view,—and let us express this view with the most hearty sympathy toward the earnest endeavors of the missionaries of all the denominations—none of them. One reason is that mere transplanting of anything exotic is never known on Japanese soil. Be it a political, scientific, or social matter, before it can be acclimatized in Japan, it must pass through great modifications in the hands of the Japanese."

5 Several of the founders and movements in figure 2 have already been the focus of serious field research, Mullins (1990), Ikegami (1991), Caldarola (1979).

6 See Fujii (1986: 164) for a discussion of transmission of leadership and authority in Japanese Buddhist sects.

7 This is the estimate provided by Howes (1957: 125) and is based on attendance at Bible study meetings and lectures as well as subscriptions to Mukyōkai magazines.

Part 18

INTERNAL AND EXTERNAL STRUCTURES

72

THE HIDDEN SPHERE OF RELIGIOUS SEARCHES IN THE SOVIET UNION

Independent religious communities in Leningrad from the 1960s to the 1970s

Olga Tchepournaya

Source: *Sociology of Religion*, 64(3) (2003), 377–88.

This study deals with the independent religious communities that began their activity with the liberal reforms and antireligious policy of Nikita Khrushchev. The paper confines itself to the near-Orthodox independent religious communities that existed in Leningrad from the 1960s to the 1970s. A specific characteristic of those communities was their closeness to various kinds of Russian nationalistic groups and to the dissent movement.

Through an analysis of interviews with former participants in the religious communities, autobiographical texts and various documents, an attempt is made to reconstruct the significance of individual religious searches by the young intellectuals of Leningrad who took part in the religious communities, and their values and ideology during the 1960s and '70s. Criticism and disillusionment with communism preceded conversion of these soviet intellectuals to Orthodoxy. The specific context of atheistic government resulted not only in a particular combination of the elements of restored religious tradition, but also in special techniques of validation of their religious faith.

Introduction

This paper presents the results of research conducted for my Ph.D. into independent religious communities in Leningrad in the 1960s and 1970s. There are numerous sociological and historical studies of religion in the Soviet Union on the one hand, and of dissident movements on the other hand (Ellis 1986; Alecseeva 1992; Anderson 1994),[1] but none has concentrated on the religious seekership of soviet intellectuals. Left unstudied have been issues concerning individual conversions and opportunities to engage in a religious search under the conditions of an official anti-religious policy that limited the activity of religious institutions and the circulation of spiritual literature.

From the mid-1960s, with various interruptions from government agencies, there emerged a number of independent religious communities of soviet intellectuals with the aspiration of restoring religious traditions. These religious communities were independent of the government and emerged as the result of an ideological confrontation with official soviet policy. These organizations can be characterized by their principles of liberty, the equality of their participants, and the clandestine nature of their activity.

The main sources of information for my study were 14 structured interviews with former participants of the religious communities, and autobiographical texts, *samisdat* and *tamisdat*, collected from 1999 onwards.[2]

In the interviews I concentrated on the following areas: the biographies and histories of conversion of the interviewees; the organization of religious life in the Soviet Union; the origins and founding of the religious communities; experiences of participation in the communities; and the participants' relations with official ideology and government, religious institutions, and dissident groups. My analysis of the texts attempted to reconstruct the values and ideologies of the religious seekership of the young intellectuals of Leningrad who took part in the religious communities during the 1960s and '70s.

The first stage of my research showed that there were many different types of seekership, depending on how close the seeker had been to various religious confessions. I limited the scope of this part of the research by selecting only those independent religious communities that were close to the Russian Orthodox Church and had existed in Leningrad in the 1960s and '70s. A specific characteristic of these communities was that they were associated with Russian nationalism.

In this paper I shall discuss questions concerning the faith and religious searches of the participants in the independent religious communities. My approach is informed by the theories of William Bainbridge and Danièle Hervieu-Léger. Their interpretations of the processes of conversion and the validation of faith can help us to understand how young soviet intellectuals managed to seek out religious experiences in a situation in which there was an absence of religious freedom.

Terminology of research

1. "Independent religious communities" are defined as those groups that emerged as a result of individual religious searches and social and/or political protest. The groups were united by new sacral objects and rituals, and

common ways of validating their faith. They were characterized by new organizational structures, based on individual liberty of the participants.

2. "Integral space of information" (a concept coined by Alexander Daniel) means the appearance of a clandestine opposition in the Soviet Union in which dissidents and marginal members of the society had an opportunity to exchange information. This was one of the foundations for the formation of an opposition (Daniel 1998).

3. The notion of a "rupture of religious tradition" arises from Hervieu-Léger's definition of religion as the system of practices, symbols and ideology that constitute, develop and control a feeling of individual and collective belonging to particular beliefs. Religion consists of faith and tradition. The religious tradition reproduces itself through rituals, ceremonies, and religious literature (Hervieu-Léger 1999). The absence of freedom of religion, state regulation of participation in rituals and ceremonies, and the restricted circulation of religious texts lead to the rupture of religious tradition.

Historical context: the Orthodox Church in soviet years

From the start of the Soviet Republic, the Marxist idea of the withering away of religion had been instigated by the government. The repressions and persecutions of the most religious institutions had begun with the antireligious decrees in 1917, after which all religious confessions were separated from the state, their juridical rights were removed, and their educational activity was forbidden. The period of the 1930s is well known as a time of cruel repressions against the Russian Orthodox Church and other religious institutions, when large numbers of churches, cloisters and seminaries were closed and destroyed, and many of their clergy were imprisoned and executed.

During the Second World War, these repressions were halted but then reintroduced after 1953. Thus, the liberal reforms undertaken by the government of Nikita Khrushchev were combined with a new anti-religious policy. The idea of a speedier implementation of communism, proclaimed at the Twentieth Congress of the Communist Party of the Soviet Union in 1956, was a cause of this antireligious policy, because, according to the doctrine of Marxism-Leninism, religion could no longer survive. The most important legislative measures during the 1960s were the religious reforms of 1961, which had separated the priests from parishes and controlled the economic activities of religious institutions; and the 1962 Law, which controlled all religious rituals such as baptisms, marriages, and burial services. Besides this, the government continued to close and destroy churches, and antireligious propaganda was intensified. Then, during the 1970s, the antireligious policy became less aggressive and active, but it did not make much difference to the difficulties that the churches were facing.

The Council for Religious Affairs played the most important role in the anti-religious scene. This state institution was subordinated to the Supreme

Soviet of the USSR, and, in common with the KGB (the Committee of Governmental Security) controlled the emergence of new religious institutions, the activities of clergy, and both underground and official religious organizations. Their power consisted of two functions: the Council for Religious Affairs to order and direct; and the KGB to correct and punish.

This policy against religious institutions was not completely successful, and religiosity did not disappear from the Soviet Union, but it did weaken religious institutions by limiting their activities and making them dependent on the state. Most religious institutions lost credibility because of their compromises with the state. The result of all these factors was the interruption of religious tradition. Unlike the development of religiosity in Western European countries, where religious institutions (such as the Catholic Church) became weaker as a consequence of their compromise with modernity and internal development, the weakness of the Russian Orthodox Church was caused through the influence of the government. But it led to the same results: many young, well-educated adherents were dissatisfied; the situation stimulated them to become religious seekers, and led to the emergence of new religious movements in the USA and European countries (Hervieu-Léger 1999; Glock and Bellah 1976), and to the emergence of independent religious communities in the USSR. In the Soviet Union, the government controlled the number and structure of religious institutions, their activity and international contacts, and the distribution of literature. These conditions determined the development and characteristics of religious searches during the late-soviet period.

During the 1960s, this interest in religion in the USSR was combined with the emergence of political ideas concerning the reformation of the communist regime, but religious and political interests became separated in the 1970s because of the failure of the idea of building "communism with a human face" (in other words, overcoming Stalinism and building a communist society without state repression or ideological pressure). Almost all my respondents were educated in atheistic families, and the entire soviet educational system was atheistic, which is why among the most significant problems for the participants in the independent religious communes had been an absence of religious knowledge and the breakdown of a religious tradition.

The development of religious communities: getting over the interruption of the religious tradition

Studies of the dissident movement and the interviewees themselves distinguish between two periods: the sixties and seventies. The majority of researchers use the following time-spans for the epoch: the sixties cover the period from 1953 or '56 to 1968, and the seventies from 1968 to 1986 (Voronkov 1993; Levada 1998; Chuikina 1996). The main difference is that during the sixties intellectuals were mostly included in official attempts to reform the communist regime. There were no strict boundaries between official and oppositional cultural and political activities. By the end of the sixties, after the liberal reformation was struck down, the dissident movements became more active. Their participants moved from the official sphere to the marginal; poets and philosophers became stokers and lift operators. It was a period of consolidation of the dissident movement, when different groups came closer together in their opposition to the common enemy (Alecseeva 1992; Voronkov 1993). An integrated space for information was formed as a result of this trend, and it gave the dissident groups an opportunity to constitute common principles for their activities.

My interviews and the autobiographical material revealed the existence of 11 near-Orthodox independent religious communities in Leningrad. The two earliest appeared in the mid-sixties, three belong to the end of the sixties, and six emerged in the seventies.

The first religious communities of the 1960s were secret, closed groups; the number of participants is unknown; these communities did not intend to extend their activities. There are some characteristics that were common to all the dissident movements of the 1960s (Voronkov 1993; Vaissié 1999). Among the specific traits of these religious communities that I was able to identify was an absence of relations with the Orthodox Church and other religious institutions. This can be explained by a mistrust of priests on the one hand, and an unwillingness to run the risk of punishment on the other hand. In the historical context of the mid-sixties, when ideas of liberal reform were combined with an anti-religious policy, there were two possibilities for the development of religious seekership. The first way consisted of clandestine attempts to restore or innovate religious practices and rituals: "*. . . the liturgy, which was performed at the apartment of the progressive (in the contemporary meaning of this word) intellectuals, brothers Sergei and Vadim Tan'chiki. The brothers Tan'chiki played the roles of priests*" (memoirs of interviewee #7, 2000:99). The members of these religious communities were mostly artists and poets etc. The government watched over all such religious activities and treated the participants of these groups as mentally sick. The second way was to pursue potential political reform based on religious values and principles. These ideas were very close to nationalism. The majority of such groups appeared in Moscow, but the most significant — The All-Russian Social-Christian Union for the Liberation of the People — emerged in Leningrad. Members of that group were Masters and Doctoral students, or young professors (mostly in the humanities). It was a unique group not only because of its specific political program based on the ideas of N. Berdiaev — but also because it had organized safety measures: every new-comer had to present three references from older members of the community. Moreover, the community consisted of sections, and only the leader of these sections might have access to information about the program, organizers and activity of the community. Despite these precautionary measures, it was an

Table 1 Chronological list of independent religious communities.

Periods	*Names*	*Orientations and topics of searches*	*Reason for disappearance*
'Sixties	1. All-Russian Social-Christian Union for the Liberation of the People (VSHSON)	Political and religious	Imprisonment of participants
	2. Home Church of the brothers Tan'tchiki	Religious rituals	Forced psychiatric hospitalization of organizers
End of 1960s and beginning of 1970s	1. Group of S. Stratanovskii	Russian religious philosophies, literature and poetry	Merged with other religious groups
	2. Group of B. Ivanov	Russian religious philosophies	Merged with other groups
	3. Group of T. Goritcheva and B. Grois	European religious philosophies and theologies	Merged with other groups
'Seventies	1. Religious and Philosophical Seminar	European religious philosophies and theologies	Deportation or imprisonment of most active participants
	2. Poetry Seminar of V. Krivulin	Religious literature and poetry	Closed itself down
	3. Theological Seminar of K. Ivanov	Russian religious philosophies, modern theology and church tradition	Death of charismatic leader, closed itself down
	4. Religious and Philosophical Seminar of S. Grib	Religious philosophy, science, Orthodox tradition	Transformed into the Soloviev Society in the 1980s.
	5. "The Commune"	Russian religious philosophies and politics	Imprisonment of activists
	6. Educational Seminar of the Philosophy of E. Pazuhin	Russian religious philosophies and Church tradition	Closed itself down

informer who denounced the community to the KGB. Most of the active members were subsequently imprisoned as organizers of a plot to overthrow the communist regime.

The independent religious communities that appeared at the end of the sixties were still small, but they were more open. They were much more interested in having relations with the more liberal Orthodox priests and other unofficial religious groups, and they looked for sympathizers within circles of marginals and dissidents. These religious communities displayed a tendency to unite with each other, to become more open and to expand. They became involved in the production and consumption of dissident information. It was during this period that the foremost types of activities of religious communities and their organization were formed. The communities generally functioned as clandestine "home circles" or seminars. Their meetings took place on a regular basis (about once a week or twice a month) in the apartments of the organizers or activists; the participants discussed problems of faith, wrote reports on different religious topics (such as early Christianity, the writings of the Church Fathers, and a variety of different religious teachings). They defined the aims of their communities as religious education, the free discussion of religious questions and fraternity between their members. The development of near-Orthodox communities shows that their activists and participants were mainly men, unlike the Russian Orthodox Church itself, where the parishioners were mostly old women. It was not until the seventies that a community was organized by a woman, Tatiana Goricheva, who was also an activist in the only feminist group, "Maria," that existed in the Soviet Union.

In the seventies, interest in religion acquired more of a mass character. The largest and most representative communities of this period were the Religious and Philosophical Seminar of Gorichesva and Krivulin and a Seminar known as "The Commune." The former concentrated on western philosophy and theology; the latter was similarly inclined, but also focussed on the Orthodox concept of communion.

Samisdat reviews of independent religious communities appeared only from the beginning of the seventies, when a few small earlier groups united to form larger entities (see Table 1). The division of religious seekership into two general streams was a significant development during this period. The first stream turned to relations with the Orthodox Church, where the participants of the religious communities attempted to "professionalise" their belief, and to transform it into traditional religiosity. Others preferred to continue their searches in the area of western theology and religious philosophies.

> In 1974 I produced a report "Church faith and faith in the secular world." And this report aroused indignation from the readership. They saw these two things together, which were like another world. I affirmed that there are these two different kinds of faith and we

> have to choose between them. . . . That is the way in which my idea was so scandalous. However, it was clear that if we were to carry on, then there would be a schism. And actually our seminar began to divide within itself.
>
> (interview #5, 2000)

However, by the end of the seventies, tendencies towards a rapprochement with the Russian Orthodox Church developed. Simultaneously, the sphere of religious seekership and the quantity of participants had extended by the end of the '70s. At the beginning of the development of the religious communities all the members of a community knew each other. In the latest groups the situation changed: the leaders and activists of different communities associated, but within the communities many new and unknown participants were involved. These internal changes, accompanied by suppression by the government, resulted in the disappearance or restructuring of the independent religious communities in Leningrad.

Histories of conversion and validation of faith in the independent religious communities

In my interviews, the former participants of independent religious communities described how they converted to a faith and came to their religious community. I distinguished two possible paths for this process: one of these ways was for organizers and activists of communities, and the second was for ordinary participants.

After their conversion, the leaders of the religious communities were active not only in their search for new knowledge and experience within the religious sphere, but also in their search for supporters. The first small religious circles of young intellectuals consisted of such enthusiasts, who aspired to communicate with other believers. Those meetings brought them to an awareness of the necessity of organizing larger communities. Information and ideas were diffused into their circles of friends, and further participants were led into the communities by the leaders or activists. Some participants were interested in religion before they came there, others converted later. William Bainbridge notes that conversion is always related to inner contradictions, which stimulate individuals to start a religious search. Because of the limitations and restrictions of the religious sphere in the Soviet Union, all the young converts had shared the experience of seekership. They used accessible texts such as Russian religious philosophers and religious poetry from the beginning of the twentieth century. The existence of this shared, though limited, informational base facilitated the unification of the earliest groups.

Respondents mentioned different starting-points for their religious searches. For some, it could have been an aesthetic experience (connected with, for example, poetry, cinema, or the history of ancient or oriental culture);

for others it could have been participation in hippie or oriental underground movements. However, the start of their search was always accompanied by disillusionment with communism and the soviet reality.

> A passion for Christianity appeared at the end of the sixties. That happened after a final disillusionment with the idea of the possibility of socialism as a system, an ideology, or a way of lift. And religion became a way to escape the official ideology, a way to salvation. . . .
> (interview #5, 2000)

In other words, criticism and disillusionment with communism were common reasons for the deprivation experienced by these soviet intellectuals, and which preceded their conversion to Orthodoxy.

Why, we might ask, was it that all these different interests and religious beliefs came together to give birth to the independent religious communities? First, the communities allowed their participants to extend the sphere of their religious searches in a situation in which there was only a limited circulation of literature and in which religious institutions were severely weakened. Secondly, the religious communities constituted a specific context with an internal language and in which religious rituals could be performed. The participants could escape from the pressures and control of the state. Additionally, the religious communities gave their participants the opportunity to validate their faith.

The French sociologist of religion, Danièle Hervieu-Léger, suggests an analysis of ideal-types of validation of faith as a method in the study of individual religious searches. Validation of faith is a process of verification of a correspondence of individual faith with an authoritative equivalent that is seen as a form of religious self-identification in modern societies. Hervieu-Léger proposes five types of validation. (1) The *institutional* type is based on the authority of the religious institution. It is a traditional and conformist way of validating faith. (2) The *communal* type is based on a correspondence between individual faith and the religious teaching of the community; the notion of coherence is crucial for this type. (3) *Mutual* validation of faith is based on trust and the authority of one's neighbour. (4) *Auto-validation* of faith is a subjective confidence in one's own tightness. (5) The last type of validation of faith is *charismatic*. It is based on the authority and influence of a charismatic leader and may be combined with other types (Hervieu-Léger 1999:185–190). The advantage of this theoretical approach consists in the possibility it provides of analyzing any religious communities or movements, not merely Christian ones. Furthermore, it can take into account the modern processes of individualization and the privatization of religion.

The formation of independent religious communities from individual religious searches, even the necessity of searches for new adherents and supporters, shows that 'communal' and 'mutual' types of validation of faith were of primary significance for most participants in the Leningrad religious communities. In two of the communities of the seventies, there was a ‘charismatic’ leadership and type of validation of faith. One of respondents describes a very significant history of rupture between the leader of “The Commune” (a religious community of the seventies, see table 1) and a liberal Orthodox priest, Dmitrii Dudko. The reason for this conflict was the claim of the priest to control and direct the religious search and faith of the leader and the members of The Commune. Here, it was ‘auto-validation’ of faith that was typical for the leaden and active participants. For example, some members of The Commune and some Orthodox priests accused Eugenie Pashing (the organizer of the Educational Seminar of the Philosophy of E. Pazuhin) of heresy. This resulted in the dissolution of the community. It did not, however, shake Pasuchin’s faith as he continued to believe in the rightness of his position.

All the independent religious communities combined Hervieu-Léger’s types of validation along with another form of validation — that of faith through *texts*. Interviews and biographical materials show that reading the Bible, the texts of the Church Fathers, religious philosophers and theologians, and religious poetry, as well as the writing of religious essays and articles by members of religious communities were sacralized. It was not just a way to gain knowledge of the religious sphere and to overcome the disruption of Russia’s religious tradition; it was also a way to profess one’s faith. This specific role of texts in a religious search can be explained by the socio-historical conditions of the late soviet epoch: the weakness of the Russian Orthodox Church and difficulties in relationships with priests; the illegality and dangers of religious activity; and the very instability of the independent religious communities themselves. All these circumstances led to a sacralization of religious literature, which was considered a reliable and authoritative source for one’s religious search and as a medium for the validation of faith.

Another interesting result of the analysis of the validation of faith is that the tendency of the religious communities of the seventies to rapprochement with the Orthodox Church was not supported by an institutional type of validation of faith. Some members and leaders were inclined to this path, but most were not. This is one reason why the entry of the religious communities into the Orthodox Church occurred only at the individual level, not at the level of the groups themselves.

Conclusion

The analysis of my interviews shows that in the development of religious communities in the sixties and seventies there were two clear tendencies: one towards openness and expansion; and the other towards a rapprochement with the Orthodox Church. These were the only possible paths for a religious search under the suppression of the government. Using these strategies, the participants succeeded in overcoming the rupture of religious tradition, but the religious communities themselves eventually disappeared. As they became larger and more open to new adherents, they were no longer producing new concepts and goals. The independent religious communities, based on the liberty of their members and an openness without discipline and strict organization, could not exist for long. Moreover, the unification of two or more different communes frequently led to clashes between their charismatic leaders. Most former participants in the religious communities eventually located their lives within the religious sphere — an indication that a religious tradition was restored at least at the individual level. Some of them became adepts, priests or monks within the Orthodox Church; others became teachers of such subjects as the history of religion, or theology.

Structural opportunities for religious seekership were limited by the anti-religious policy of the government and the disruption of the religious tradition. These conditions resulted in the marginalization of all kinds of religious activities, and the closing of independent religious searches for dissident movements and a connection with the underground realm of the dissemination of literature. On the one hand, the necessity to get over the disruption of the religious tradition led to the study of traditional religious doctrine and limited the sphere of religious seekership — and the possibility of creating new religious doctrines in the communities. On the other hand, the experience of an individual religious search, and participation in independent religious communities made the entry to traditional religious institutions difficult. In these restricted circumstances, religious literature became the most relevant source not only for the restoration of a religious tradition, but also for the validation of faith. The use of texts by participants in the religious communities was a creative process. Through an analysis of the texts, published in *samisdat*, it can be argued that the participants and the leaders of the communities played a positive role in the restoration of a religious tradition and the activity of religious institutions during the late-soviet period — and later.

Notes

1 Dissident movements are those of people who participated in various activities, organizing the struggle against the Soviet State system. The basis of the dissident movement was an oppositional worldview that united people against governmental ideologies.

2 *Samisdat* are texts that were published Clandestinely and distributed by authors themselves. *Tamisdat* are texts secretly smuggled abroad and published there.

References

Alecseeva, L. 1992. *Istoria inakomysliya v SSSR*, Vilnus-Moskva.

Anderson, J. 1994. *Religion, state and politics in the Soviet Union and successor states*, Cambridge, New York, Melbourne: Cambridge University Press.

Bainbridge, W. S. 1997. *The sociology of religious movements*. New York and London: Routledge.
Casanova, J. 1994. *Public religions in the modern world*. Chicago and London: The University of Chicago Press.
Champion, F. 1995. Nouveau mouvement religieux et nouvelle religiosités mystique-ésotérique in *Religions et Société, Cahiers Français*, no. 273, October–December, 13–18.
Chuikina, S. 1996. Uchastie zhenchin v dissidentckom dvijenii. Sluchai Leningrada. in *Gendemoe izmerenie cotsial'noi i politicheskoi aktivnosti v perechodnyi period*. Pod red. A. Temkinoi i E. Zdravomyslovoi. Trudy CNSI, #4. St.Petersburg.
Daniel, A. 1998. Dissidentstvo: kultura, uskol'zauchaya ot opredelenia in Rossia/ *Russia Semidesyatye kak predmet istorii russkoi kul'tury*. Moskva-Veneciya.
Ellis, J. 1986. *The Russian Orthodox church: A contemporary history*. London: Croom Helm.
Clock, C. Y., and R. N. Bellah, eds. 1976. *The new religious consciousness*. Berkeley: University of California Press.
Hervieu-Léger, D. 1996. *Les identités religieuses en Europe*, éd. avec G. Davie, Paris: Flamarion.
——. 1999. *Le pèlerin et le converti. La religion en mouvement*. Paris: Flamarion.
Istoria. 2000. Istoria leningradskoi nepodtsenzurnoi literatury (History of Leningrad's oppositional literature) 1950–1980. S-Petersburg.
Levada, J. 1998. Rubezhi i ramki semidesiatych in *Neprikosnovennyi zapas*, No. 2: 72–78.
Pospelovskii, S. 1995. *Russkaya Pravoslavnaia Tserkov' v XX veke*. Moskva.
Vaissié, S. 1999. *Pour votre liberte et pour la notre. Le combat des dissidents de Russie*. Paris: Robert Laffont.
Voronkov, V. 1993. Die Piotestbewegung der "Sechziger"-Generation. Der widerstand gegen das sowjetische Regime 1956–1985 in *Osteuropa*, #10.
Zakonodatel'stvo. 1969. *Zakonodatel'stvo o religioznych kul'tach* (legislation on religious cults), Moskva.
Zdravomyslova, E. 1996. Prerequisites of civil society in Soviet Russia: "Saigon" as public sphere. In: *Civil Society in the European North: Concept and Context. Collection of Articles*, edited by E. Zdravomyslova and K. Heikkinen. CISR Working Papers, #3: 116–119. St.Petersburg.

73

AMERICAN EVANGELICALISM IN ZIMBABWE

Paul Gifford

Source: Paul Gifford, *Christianity and Hegemony*, New York: Berg, 1992, pp. 121–43.

From Rhodesia to Zimbabwe

Zimbabwe, formerly Rhodesia, was colonized by the British in the 1890s, and among those pioneers were Christian missionaries. The Christian churches can boast a proud record in health and education during the colonial years, but with some notable exceptions, like the Anglican, Cripps, and the Methodist, White, who articulated black grievances, the churches were not conscious of their role in the colonizing enterprise as a whole. An insight into this role is provided by the following comment of Cecil Rhodes himself to the parents of a Dutch Reformed missionary: "Your son among the natives is worth as much to me as a hundred of my policemen."[1]

When Britain began to dismantle its empire, white Rhodesians refused to bow to British pressure to accommodate African aspirations, and unilaterally declared independence from Britain in 1965.[2] Black resistance became open war in 1972, escalating until Prime Minister Ian Smith was forced to negotiate a settlement with black nationalists in 1979. During the years of this increasingly bloody war, the Smith government, controlling all the media, presented the struggle as a clash between Christian civilization and godless communism. Moreover, of all the nationalist leaders, it was Robert Mugabe in particular whom they painted as an archetypal Marxist thug. Hence the consternation of white Rhodesians when, in the internationally supervised elections marking Zimbabwe's independence (1980), Mugabe won an absolute majority in parliament.

The Jesuit-educated Mugabe is not opposed to Christianity; nor are the members of his Cabinet, most of whom are also products of missionary education. Some are quite active in their churches. Mugabe appointed the Methodist minister Canaan Banana as Zimbabwe's first (non-executive) president, the highest dignity in the country. Mugabe, Banana, and government ministers have frequently called on the churches to play their full part in creating the new Zimbabwe.[3]

The response of the mainline churches since independence has been hesitant and confused. Between 1965 and 1980, Rhodesia was ostracized by the international community, and the predominantly white-led churches in their isolation largely succumbed to government propaganda. The Anglican church seemed particularly susceptible, and some of its most prominent spokesmen frequently denounced the nationalists as communists and terrorists and urged support for Smith's "Christian government."[4] These pronouncements have been responsible for the Anglican church's low profile since independence. Rhodesia's United Methodist church was headed by Bishop Abel Muzorewa, who as a party to Smith's "Internal Settlement" in 1978 actually became prime minister of the short-lived country of Zimbabwe-Rhodesia in 1979. In this role he was seen as Smith's puppet and a traitor to the black cause, and his political party was all but annihilated in the 1980 elections. However, he continued in politics until 1985, while still head of the United Methodist church. His criticisms of the government in those years, coupled with counterallegations that he was implicated in dissident activity in Matabeleland, led to open conflict with the government and compromised the Methodist church, which has been particularly unsure of itself in the new Zimbabwe. Similarly, the first post-independence general secretary of the local council of churches (now called the Zimbabwe Christian Council) was closely linked to Bishop Muzorewa. This made the ZCC also appear in a rather ambiguous light, and prevented it from acting with any confidence or authority.[5]

The Roman Catholic church came out of the liberation war in rather better shape. Though in no sense developing anything like a liberation theology, one of the bishops publicly denounced Smith's government, publications of the Catholic Justice and Peace Commission drew international attention to abuses of Smith's security forces, and by the end of the war several priests and nuns on mission stations were openly on the side of the guerillas.[6] However, in the early years of independence, the Catholic bishops denounced abuses committed by government forces in combatting dissidents in Matabeland. Although privately he may have heeded the criticism, Mugabe's official reaction was one of furious repudiation. Speaking to the combined heads of religious denominations at Easter 1983, Mugabe took the opportunity to excoriate the Catholic bishops publicly. This experience chastened, even cowed, the Catholic authorities. Subsequent government allegations that it is the Catholic Justice and Peace Commission that has fed critical material to foreign bodies like Amnesty International have not made Catholic authorities any more confident in their public leadership.

For all these reasons, the mainline churches have since independence failed to provide notable public leadership, either singly or together. While cautiously feeling their way to a new relationship with a self-styled Marxist government, they have tended to retreat to ministering to their own flocks, administering their (often considerable) plant, or involving themselves in their own development projects.

If mainline churches have preserved a low profile since independence, the same years have witnessed the advent of a particularly confident evangelical revival. This evangelical sector of Christianity includes the older free churches, but comprises mainly fundamentalists, Pentecostals and new charismatic groups which promote a pietistic, otherworldly, personal, privatized Christianity, which is often dispensationalist and characteristically has American ties. For convenience we will consider these evangelicals under three headings: the transnationals, crusades, and local groups.

The religious transnationals

In the years since independence, all the major American religious transnationals have appeared on the Zimbabwean scene.[7] Campus Crusade was founded in California by the Presbyterian Bill Bright in 1951. The organization is dispensationalist, personal, privatized, sees the threat of communism everywhere, is associated with conservative causes within the United States, and tirelessly promotes American interests abroad. In Latin America, its adherents see themselves as the shock troops countering liberation theology. In Zimbabwe, Campus Crusade was established in 1979 as Life Ministries. By 1988 it had a full-time ministerial staff of ten, of whom six were U.S. expatriates. Most of these Americans have been trained at Campus Crusade's international headquarters in California. Its activities in Zimbabwe include university chaplaincy, the training of local pastors, and running seminars for senior government and business personnel at Lake Kariba, Fothergill Island, Nyanga, and other resorts.

Youth With a Mission (YWAM) was founded in the United States in 1960 by Loren Cunningham, and now has its headquarters in Hawaii. In 1985 it claimed to have 5,100 long-term missionaries and 190 permanent YWAM bases, and to send out 15,000 short-term missionaries, more than any other mission. It is Pentecostal, dispensationalist, and tends to see the United States as God's champion on earth. Although YWAM came to Rhodesia in the 1970s, it closed after a short period because of the war. After independence it was reestablished in 1981 by a local couple who had previously run their own ministry in Bulawayo. In 1987 YWAM had seven full-time workers in Harare (five white Zimbabweans, one South African, one North American) and six in Bulawayo (five black Zimbabweans and one North American). Its work has three thrusts. First, it is involved in evangelization, which includes helping local churches and founding churches where none existed before. Secondly, it trains would-be missionaries in its discipleship training school near Bulawayo. Thirdly, it engages in relief work, particularly along the Mozambique border. The number on short-term mission work varies; once a group of forty came for three weeks' concentrated evangelization. The advantage of such short-term work is that it can be done on a tourist visa.

The Full Gospel Businessmen's Fellowship International (FGBMFI) began in Los Angeles in 1952, founded by Demos Shakarian, a prominent California dairyman. It fosters a worldwide revival to prepare for the imminent return of Christ. It is Pentecostal, but is non-denominational and includes Catholic charismatics. President Reagan had close links with it; he claimed his ulcers were cured by FGBMFI members who prayed over him during his term as governor of California. Many prominent members of Reagan's administration belonged to it, as do many in authority in the United States military and in related industries. The FGBMFI began in Zimbabwe in 1983, founded by a South African group who controlled the Zimbabwean chapter until it became autonomous in 1985. By 1988 there were four Zimbabwean chapters in Harare, Bulawayo, Karoi and Gweru. The Harare chapter has about sixty members, of whom about 95 percent are white. Members are from a variety of professions and businesses, and most belong to local Pentecostal churches.

Jimmy Swaggart Ministries is based in Baton Rouge, Louisiana, and has been operating in Zimbabwe since January *1985*. In Zimbabwe there is no strictly evangelistic mission, merely an office for Jimmy Swaggart's Relief Ministries and Jimmy Swaggart Child Care International, which exist to channel aid rather than to proselytize. However, the office does distribute Swaggart's books, tapes, and videos; the videos have had regular screening on Zimbabwean television. The office had an aid budget in 1986 of Z $2,500,000 (approximately U.S. $1,500,000), most of which went to Mozambique and Mozambican refugees in Zimbabwe. All its activities in Zimbabwe are closely scrutinized by the Zimbabwe government, because of the suspicion that some of its activities may have been directed to helping Renamo rebels in Mozambique. These suspicions arose not just because of Swaggart's own well-publicized anticommunism, nor just because of the aid given to the Nicaraguan Contras by the American religious Right, nor just because Swaggart literature was discovered in 1985 at a captured Renamo base. They arose because in 1986 in Washington a spokesman for the pro-Renamo Mozambique Information Office stated that Jimmy Swaggart was providing aid through Assembly of God Churches in Renamo-held territory. Swaggart's aides would not comment on this claim. The Zimbabwe officials of Jimmy Swaggart Ministries insist that all such suspicions are groundless.

World Vision International grew out of American Evangelicalism at the height of the cold war, when conservative Evangelicalism was closely identified with anticommunism. Its anticommunism was still strong when World Vision began operations in Vietnam. Its seemingly limitless funds and large headquarters opposite the U.S. embassy emphasized its close links with the U.S. Agency for International Development; its willingness to report its activities to USAID led to charges of informing for the CIA. At the same time, it continually refused to join with other Vietnam aid agencies in protesting against human-rights violations or the maltreatment of refugees. Criticism of World Vision increased after attention was drawn to events in Salvadorean refugee camps for which World Vision was responsible. The publicity elicited a report from World Vision headquarters admitting some of the criticisms, but insisting that the abuses were the work of individuals in their employ, not the policy of World Vision itself.

World Vision came to Rhodesia from South Africa in 1969. In 1979 it severed its links with South Africa and became World Vision Zimbabwe. Since independence it has expanded greatly and in 1988 employed about fifty in its Harare office and another fifty in the field. This workforce comprises almost entirely black Zimbabweans, all of them evangelical Protestants. In 1986 its budget was Z $2,500,000 (approx. U.S. $1,500,000). It is involved in development, relief, and (the primary reason for all its activity) evangelism. As well as World Vision Zimbabwe, Zimbabwe hosts a separate branch of World Vision responsible for its activity in Mozambique.

Rhema Bible Church, although not in the same league as the transnational just mentioned, is an offshoot of Kenneth Hagin's Rhema Bible Church in Tulsa, Oklahoma. Kenneth Hagin is a prominent American media evangelist, best known for his prosperity gospel, that is, the insistence that health and wealth are signs of a true Christian. Rhema began in Zimbabwe in April 1982 with six people meeting in the pastor's home. By 1987 it had six hundred adults and 175 children attending its Sunday morning service, and three hundred adults attending its evening service. Of its adherents, about 20 percent are black. It boasts sixteen full-time employees, two bible schools, audio and videotape ministries, a prison ministry, a youth ministry (of 150), a hospital ministry, a radio ministry, and Compassion Ministries, its relief arm in Zimbabwe's four camps for Mozambican refugees. Rhema also sees itself called to work in the surrounding countries of central Africa. Rhema's Christianity is a faithful reflection of its parent body's: it is fundamentalist in Scripture, millennialist, stresses healing and tongues, practices discipling, and insists that health and prosperity are the right of every true Christian, so much so that poverty and illness disclose a deficient Christian life. Its U.S. ties are manifest. The founder and pastor of Rhema in Zimbabwe is a graduate of Gordon Lindsays's Christ for the Nations in Dallas. Rhema's two bible schools use a course devised in the United States by founder Kenneth Hagin. Rhema's Compassion Ministries have received considerable aid from Pat Robertson's Operation Blessing. Rhema's audio and videotape collections feature, along with some South African evangelists, almost all the major figures of American Evangelicalism – particularly Swaggart.

Crusades

Besides the above transnational which have established themselves in Zimbabwe, other organizations purveying the same kind of Christianity have visited the country. Preeminent among these is Christ for All Nations (CFAN). CFAN was founded in South Africa by a German Pentecostal, Reinhard Bonnke, who has taken his revival crusades all over the continent and as far afield as Scandinavia, the United States, and New Zealand. In 1986, to facilitate its access to all African countries, it moved its headquarters from Johannesburg to Frankfurt. CFAN conducted three revivals in Zimbabwe between 1980 and 1986. These were events of some importance, particularly the last, held in CFAN's new tent which, with seating for over 32,000 people, they claim is the biggest movable structure in the world. The third crusade in May 1986, which involved 130 local churches, was staged in conjunction with a "Fire Conference" which drew four thousand evangelical leaders from forty one African countries.

The Christianity of both crusade and conference was standard American Evangelicalism. This was obvious from the bookshop, where the material on sale comprised twelve titles by Jimmy Swaggart, eighteen by Kenneth Hagin, three by Ray McCauley (the founder of Rhema in South Africa, who flies both the South African and United States flags at his Johannesburg church), eleven by Kenneth and Gloria Copeland of Fort Worth, seven by Gordon Lindsay of Dallas, and three by John Osteen of Houston. Apart from these, and five titles by Elijah Maswanganyi of South Africa, there were only thirteen other miscellaneous titles on sale. The American connection became even clearer from the list of key speakers. Bonnke apart, the most important speakers at the crusade and conference were: Loren Cunningham of Hawaii, founder of YWAM; Ralph Mahoney of World Missionary Assistance Plan, California; Wayne Myers, now of Mexico; and both Copelands and Ray McCauley, whom I have just mentioned.[8]

Given that the revival was held in Zimbabwe, it was not surprising that overt displays of anticommunism were rare. The message was rather one of "hands-off" politics. However, it became evident soon afterwards that at least some of the speakers were hiding their full political agenda when Ralph Mahoney, on his return to the United States, published a blistering attack in his magazine on Zimbabwe, describing it as a communist tyranny, in contrast to South Africa, which he presented as an embattled democracy. He claimed Zimbabwe was characterized by corruption, mismanagement, police and military brutality, and anti-Americanism. By contrast, South Africa, as the only "viable prosperous capitalist country on the continent" deserved the West's support. Mahoney concluded: "May [Africa's] people find the reality of Jesus Christ . . . sufficient for their desperate needs." That plea to cling to Jesus alone and stay out of politics may seem a very apolitical message. In southern Africa, however, to stay out of politics is a decisive vote for the status quo, and thus this message is in fact a very political one.[9]

Explo '85 was a crusade of a similar kind. This satellite video conference was organized from the United States by Campus Crusade, and linked up audiences in fifty-four countries. The main speakers included Billy Graham and the California-based Argentinian Luis Palau, and during the four days of the event Campus Crusade's Bill Bright gave keynote addresses from (interestingly, given U.S. strategic interests) South Korea, the Philippines, West Berlin, and Mexico City. Campus Crusade in Zimbabwe organized the Zimbabwean end of this event at Harare's International Conference Centre, and fifty-nine local churches took part.

Maurice Cerullo, another California-based Latin American, conducted a "miracle crusade" at Rufaro stadium, Harare, in February 1985. Cerullo, with Luis Palau, was one of the founders of the Latin America Evangelical Fraternity (CONELA) set up in Panama in 1982 in opposition to the liberation- oriented Latin American Catholic Bishops Conference and the Latin American Council of Churches. Maurice Cerullo Ministries has an office in Harare which directs activities in ten sub-Saharan African countries. This office also offers a mass-circulation free correspondence Bible course in both Shona and English. In mid-1988, 1,847 were enrolled for the English course, 457 for the Shona.

Besides such mass crusades, there has been a steady stream of speakers promoting this Christianity to smaller and select audiences. For example, Ed Louis Cole of California conducted public seminars in international hotels in Harare and Bulawayo in mid-1988, and addressed various other audiences before going on to give similar seminars in South Africa. His Christianity was the normal American export, with perhaps a stronger than normal prosperity component. It should also be noted that in May 1988, when the Californian John Wimber visited South Africa with his message of healing and personal success, and his inattention to social structures, many evangelical churches in Zimbabwe organized transportation to his seminars in Johannesburg.[10]

Before leaving the subject of crusades, mention must be made of the multi-media *Carter Report*, staged at Harare's International Conference Centre over a period of two weeks beginning 21 May 1988. This event was preceded by an elaborate advertising campaign on television and the mass distribution of glossy leaflets. This promotion was as subtle as it was expensive; the nine thousand who queued for the first evening were not quite sure whether they would witness more than the mysteries of Near Eastern archaeology. Only after a few days did it become clear the the report was promoting Christianity; it needed a few more days to make clear that it was promoting Seventh-Day Adventism. Thus the Carter Report was different from all the ministries and crusades mentioned above, which all promoted one product, standard American Evangelicalism; this one ended up giving considerable importance to Seventh-Day Adventist emphases like sabbatarianism and a surprisingly virulent anti-Catholicism. However, this media event by J. J. Carter, a Texas-based Australian, in many important respects did reinforce the standard American revivalism with which we are concerned here, being scripturally fundamentalist (often bizarrely so), predicting an imminent return of Christ, and focusing purely on personal or "family" morality, with no concern for structural matters.[11]

Local ministries

Since independence there has been a mushrooming of small local ministries promoting American Evangelicalism. Although Zimbabwean, these ministries are closely linked with American organizations. For example, Harare's Northside Community Church in mid-1988 adopted a program of door-to-door evangelism called Evangelistic Explosion, using the techniques (and videos and literature) of Dr. C. Armstrong, its American creator. Different Zimbabwean ministries may often have links with the same U.S. organization. For example, it was mentioned above that the head of Zimbabwe's Rhema Bible Church studied with Gordon Lindsay's Christ for The Nations in Dallas. Another graduate of Lindsay's runs a ministry called Africa for Christ in Gweru (he gives an address in Dallas as well); this opened its own Bible college in 1987 with nine students. Also, an Harare organization called Global Literature Lifeline distributes a thoroughly fundamentalist Bible correspondence course which at any one time caters to 10,000 Zimbabweans. This body also publishes seven of Lindsay's publications, with some subsidy from Lindsay's organization, and distributes them with its own biblical material.

Zimbabwe's most notorious local ministry also has links with Lindsay. Shekinah Ministries, an offshoot of the White Assemblies of God Church at Chipinge on the Mozambican border, was discovered aiding the Renamo bandits in Mozambique in 1987. Shekinah had fully taken over the anti-communism of the American religious Right, and one of its Australian missionaries used to telephone government troop movements to the Renamo representative in Washington, for which he was sentenced to ten years in prison by a Mozambican court. Shekinah received aid from several U.S. evangelical bodies, among them Lindsay's Christ for the Nations, which provided money for a van in 1987.[12] Thus Christ for the Nations in Dallas has fairly close links with at least four independent ministries in Zimbabwe; or put the other way, there are at least four different Zimbabwean ministries propagating the Christianity associated with Christ for the Nations.

Significance

Zimbabwean churches, ministries, and revivals which promulgate this American evangelism are not only linked with organizations in the United

States, but are considerably interconnected among themselves. Consider Harare's Rhema Bible Church, discussed earlier. Rhema plants churches itself; by 1987, about twelve, some in the refugee camps. Rhema establishes them and gives them six months' finance and support. These churches are called simply "Christian" and are autonomous, but the brand of Christianity is, naturally enough, Rhema's. Rhema's pastors have close personal links with the (Wesleyan Holiness) King's Church and the (Pentecostal) Christian Life Centre. Rhema took a prominent part in the 1986 CFAN crusade. Rhema pastors teach at Bishop Guti's Africa Multination for Christ Institute, Zimbabwe's biggest Bible college. It has close links with Andrew Wutawanashe, pastor of the (black) Family of God church; much of the Christian literature used in the refugee camps was written by Wutawanashe. Rhema works closely with Zimbabwe's Africa Enterprise, a subsidiary of the South Africa-based organization founded by Michael Cassidy, a graduate of Fuller Theological Seminary, in Pasadena. At least one of Rhema's pastors works in Africa Enterprise's "Go Teams" (groups of three who witness in homes or at work), and in the refugee camps Rhema uses Africa Enterprise's "*Fox Fires*" (young Bible college students who operate in pairs in rural areas). The director for sub-Saharan Africa of Morris Cerullo World Evangelism attends Rhema. The director of Zimbabwe's Jimmy Swaggart Ministries was formerly Rhema's business manager; he still attends Rhema with two others from Swaggart's Harare office. Most important, Rhema educates many local Zimbabwean pastors, whose previous theological education may have been fairly rudimentary.

Rhema is run by three elders, its three pastors. Two of these, together with the pastor of Bulawayo's Christian center, comprise the three directors of the Africa Fellowship of Christian Ministers. This fellowship is for leaders in ministry, most of whom are pastors. It meets for two days every two months; in 1987 it had fifty paid members, but it can have up to 120 at these assemblies. The meeting in November 1987, attended by well over one hundred Zimbabwean pastors, was conducted by Ray McCauley, whom we met above at the CFAN crusade. The June 1988 meeting, on the topic of money, was addressed by Californian Ed Louis Cole, a proponent of the prosperity gospel. In these ways Rhema influences local pastors. (Note that both YWAM and Campus Crusade give a similar priority to the education of local pastors.)

These ministries and churches are also all linked to the same media producers. Zimbabwe, like so many third world countries, suffers from a lack of foreign exchange. Foreign currency reserves are allocated to essential imports, and religious literature is not classified as essential. The mainline churches have access to considerable funds overseas, but they use these funds for development projects and to maintain physical plant, such as schools and hospitals; they do not import modern theology, either popular or academic, to which they give a fairly low priority. Consequently it would be hard to find in Zimbabwe, outside the university bookshop, any work of modern theology. However, Harare's Word of Life bookshop is always well stocked with evangelical favorites like Bill Bright, Tim LaHaye, and Francis Schaeffer, because its supplies are donated by the American missionaries of the Evangelical Alliance Mission (TEAM), which owns the shop. Swaggart's literature is readily available as well, brought in by his local office, and Lindsay's booklets are published locally under licence. The result is that someone interested in Christian literature can find virtually nothing else but American Evangelicalism. As regards literature, this kind of Christianity has won by default. The victory is even more comprehensive in the field of audio and video cassettes.

Members of mainline churches have not remained unaffected by this evangelical growth. They are influenced by literature and tapes, and as directors of evangelical ministries are also increasingly invited to conduct services on evenings or weekends (often involving media presentations) for mainline church groups. This influence is increasing. In 1989 a group of fourteen churches combined in a "Down to Earth" outreach program in the affluent northern suburbs of Harare, a program involving house fellowship groups and culminating in a crusade "with evangelists from Zimbabwe and elsewhere." Behind the project was the fundamentalist Northside Community Church. The thirteen participating churches included, not surprisingly, the Church of the Nazarene, and Baptist and Pentecostal fellowships; more surprisingly, five Anglican and one Catholic parish participated. It is significant that the steering committee of eleven pastors included only two Anglicans and did not include the Catholic; the initiative came from the evangelical component, and the mainline churches followed.[13]

The level of awareness

Since independence, Zimbabwe has witnessed a remarkable evangelical revival. The Christianity of this revival is totally American. Most of its literature and its audio and video cassettes have come from the United States. Many of its ministers are American, and so is much of its funding. This funding is considerable, and (World Vision excepted) these evangelical bodies, unlike the mainline churches, spend little on development. Their funds go to evangelizing, or, when they go beyond that, to relief. There is nothing African about this Christianity. Inculturation is never mentioned. African culture is not to be Christianized; it is to be repudiated for a totally new existence in Christ.

The leaders of this revival are almost exclusively white, either Zimbabwean, South African, or American. This contrasts starkly with Zimbabwe's mainline churches, whose leadership is totally black. The directors of the transnationals discussed above (World Vision excepted) are white. The eleven-man (they are all male) steering committee of the Down to Earth program just mentioned is totally white. The planning committee of CFAN's 1986 Fire Conference contained twenty-one whites and one black. Its key speakers were all white, with one exception. Is it significant that elsewhere in independent Zimbabwe only the business sector is still dominated by whites?

This Christianity is not overtly anticommunist. Shekinah Ministries, as mentioned above, was proved to be aiding anticommunist Renamo forces in Mozambique. Thomas Schaaf, a member of Mission to Mozambique, an offshoot of Mutare's One Way Christian Centre, left Zimbabwe in 1985 to appear in Washington as a spokesman for Renamo. But they are exceptions. At first sight this Evangelicalism appears totally apolitical. It is privatized, personal, pietistic, and pays no attention to the social structures within which Christians operate, or refers to them only to insist that they do not matter; true Christianity can flourish under any system. By thus deflecting attention from any political structures, this revivalist Christianity is a decisive vote for the status quo. For this reason it is a very political Christianity.

The question naturally arises of what level of awareness this phenomenon is operating on. Is there, in the spread of this very political Christianity, a conscious strategy for political and cultural hegemony? If this book deals with the gray areas between intended and unintended political ramifications of Christian organizations, where does Zimbabwe fall in this zone? To what degree are the undoubted political effects of this Christianity consciously intended?

It must be said that there is no simple answer. The level of consciousness in this area cannot be compared to that in countries like South Africa, the Philippines, or those in Latin America, where there is an open split within Christianity. In South Africa, for example, one can hear Archbishop Tutu insisting that a true Christian must oppose the apartheid regime in the name of the Gospel; one can also hear evangelicals urging obedience to lawful authorities and resistance to communist subversives intent on overthrowing Christian civilization. Each side may denounce the other for betraying the Gospel. The clash is given prominence in the media. In these circumstances, it is obvious that Christianity assumes different and conflicting forms, which have dramatically opposed sociopolitical effects.

North of the Limpopo, however, the situation is entirely different. In nearly all of black Africa there is no comparable polarization within Christianity. There is little that could be called liberation theology against which any right-wing Christianity could appear in clear relief. Generally, anything presented as "Christian" will be accepted completely uncritically. Thus not only do Catholics attend Seventh-Day Adventist crusades, and Baptists attend Pentecostal revivals, in a way that would be impossible in the West; now Christians can be found espousing theologies which on the face of it could be called completely contradictory. Thus in most of Black Africa mainline church leaders with close links to the World Council of Churches (WCC) can be found endorsing the crusades of preachers who espouse a

Christianity that undermines everything the WCC stands for. This lack of theological awareness is perhaps the major reason for the unchallenged spread of this right-wing Christianity.

Zimbabwe's Christian Marching Church of Central Africa exemplifies much of this. This Marching Church is an independent church, founded in 1954, with perhaps five thousand members in 1990. In 1981 the bishop purchased a farm near Chegutu where he opened a Bible school. To run this complex, he invited an Englishman who had previously established Benson Idahosa's Bible school in Benin City, Nigeria. (Idahosa, with close links to Christ for the Nations of Dallas, was another main speaker at Bonnke's Fire Conference mentioned above.) The Englishman belongs to a Christian fellowship, part of Britain's House Church movement; he draws a continual stream of short-term assistants to teach in the Bible school from this fellowship, as well as from related groups in the United States. The more than thirty students in the Bible school, from various denominations, thus imbibe a fundamentalist, otherworldly, dispensationalist, miraculous kind of Christianity, though in this case one derived primarily from Britain, not the United States.

The bishop of the Marching Church is prominent in the ZCC, and on his farm operates several development and training programs, including a craft workshop for women, and dairy and poultry schemes where the Bible students are trained for self-sufficiency. One might think he would have more affinity with a WCC theology than the British House Church theology of his Bible school, but in fact he does not seem to see any difference, or at least gives it no importance. He simply takes assistance from wherever he can.

This seems to be true of all church leaders in Zimbabwe, those prominent in the ZCC as well. Their priority is obtaining foreign aid for development projects – and, cynics say, furthering their own bureaucracies, status, fundraising trips, and currency holdings overseas.

In comparison with this, theological reflection has no importance at all. Even those Zimbabwean church leaders who may say they are alarmed at the growth of right-wing Christianity do nothing to educate their followers on the issues involved, or make available theological material of a socially committed or intellectually defensible kind. In January 1990 Harare's Word of Life bookshop carried seven different multivolume sets of Bible studies; all were fundamentalist, and at least four contained the entire American evangelical agenda. Apart from these, there was probably not another Bible study series to be found in the country. The result is that any Christian wanting to study the Bible will be forced, through the lack of anything else, to use one of these seven. Thus this kind of Christianity spreads because of the lack of awareness and misplaced priorities of mainline leaders.

When one turns to the foreign missionaries propagating this kind of religion, the issue is still not simple. Certainly their Christianity upholds the present system and serves the interest of its current beneficiaries, but to what extent can one postulate a conscious promoting of this Christianity precisely for its sociopolitical effects? It is true that in an officially Marxist country like Zimbabwe, these missionaries would want to save as many souls as possible from atheistic communism and subsequent eternal damnation; they might even encourage voting for more capitalist parties in elections, for example. But for most this could be a consciously religious act, and in no sense dictated by political considerations. Their activity need in no way be qualitatively different from that of many (say) Catholic priests, whom one would not easily associate with the aims of Western hegemony, at least in the sense under discussion here.

The general lack of theological and sociological awareness and the absence of any open debate affect these missionaries too. Most of them come from an American subculture where God and the United States are virtually identified, as are Satan and the Soviet Union. This is their conditioning from birth, they meet few who would challenge it, and the Bible schools they attend are not calculated to encourage critical thought.

It would be hard to posit for many of these missionaries conscious goals of social and political control; these are concepts that come from the world of the social sciences, which almost by definition Bible college products have no knowledge of. Their factual knowledge is often as deficient as their theoretical consciousness. When the present author remarked to one of these missionaries, "Your God speaks with the same voice as the chairman of the IMF," he received the serious reply, "What is the IMF?" It is quite possible that the majority are perfectly sincere when they insist that their agenda is purely religious. Their religion has undeniable political effects, but for most these are not intended *as political*. Views which in others would have to be called political, in them (because of their background and education) can be entirely religious.

Nor should too much be read into the efforts of these missionaries to educate local pastors; as mentioned above, this often forms a large part of their strategy. Of course, the net result of this is that local pastors come to subscribe to the whole evangelical package, and entire local churches are taken into the American evangelical camp. But there is no need to see this as a conspiracy or as a conscious political ploy. The mainline conception of "church" leads the mainline churches to confine their efforts within their own denomination or to direct their attention to the unchurched. These evangelicals have a different notion of church; for them the church of true believers consists of all born-again Christians whatever their denomination. Their preoccupation with local churches and pastors is perfectly consistent with their understanding of "church," and need indicate nothing sinister. It is the mainline churches' lack of interest in these churches that has made the latter particularly vulnerable to this evangelical concern.

No doubt there are Christian missionaries who have a political as well as a religious agenda, or who are explicitly conscious of the political issues wrapped up in the religious. A good example is Ralph Mahoney. In a 1987 article he deplored developments in Zimbabwe: "The nation became the object of communist interest some fifteen years ago, resulting in a ten-year civil war. The war ended tragically when the leaders of Rhodesia were betrayed by U.S. Government State Department leaders. Other Western nations broke their promises as well, and the struggling white minority could not hold out against the betrayal. A Marxist (communist) government came to power and now rules the nation."

Mahoney is equally explicit on the significance of South Africa: "If we continue to swallow the communist propaganda and believe the simplistic thesis that Africa's complex problems will be solved by destroying the only viable, prosperous capitalist country on the continent, we shall see the greatest human tragedy in human history unfold before the year 2000. South Africa is under seige now by communists. And our Western nations abandoning [sic] the peoples of South Africa but in fact contributing to the downfall of this one prosperous stable democracy."

Obviously Mahoney considers enunciating and mobilizing for political goals to be part of his religious crusade, but it would grossly distort the picture of Zimbabwe to attribute this agenda to others. In fact, twelve leading evangelicals in Zimbabwe who had been involved with Mahoney in Bonnke's Fire Conference publicly rebuked him and demanded an apology for Zimbabwe. They denounced his politics while adhering to the same theology. Perhaps this belief that one can preserve the theology of Bonnke's Fire Conference but repudiate its political ramifications indjcates the lack of reflection in Zimbabwe on these issues.[14]

There remains the further question of outside manipulation of missionaries by parties with vested interests in a certain political order – manipulation by governments, intelligence agencies, business concerns and so on. Grace Halsell, for instance, has documented the decisions of both the Israeli government and the leaders of the American Jewish community to coopt American evangelicals in support of Israel.[15] Penny Lernoux has described the Banzer Plan, a Bolivian government ploy to use church factions for political interests.[16] Rhodesia itself furnishes a good example of an attempt to coopt the churches in its service. A confidential military "Directive for National Psychological Campaign" has the heading: "Target Group: Churches." Its obejective was spelled out clearly: to get Christians "to recognize the communist terrorist as the national enemy." It stated that the churches' "full support should be sought to bring about a quick end to the terrorist war and to promote the benefits of the [1976] proposals."[17] Such examples make one wary of the possibility of similar instances in Zimbabwe, but to date there is no hard evidence of such manipulation.

Growing awareness

Despite what has just been said, there are signs of a growing awareness of some of the issues involved here. It is interesting to note that these developments have been triggered by the government rather than the churches. The first step occurred in mid-1988, coinciding with the publication of a short treatment of the sociopolitical effects of American Evangelicalism in Zimbabwe.[18] It appears that this whole issue was discussed in cabinet, and the government, uneasy for some years, now decided to take firmer control in this area. Although reluctant to do anything which could be seen as curtailing freedom of religion, the government took immediate action in Zimbabwe's camps for Mozambican refugees, where groups like Jimmy Swaggart Ministries, World Vision, and Compassion Ministries were already working, and where similar groups were founding churches.

As the government recognized that such bodies may have a political as well as a religious agenda, it banned any new religious organizations from entering the camps. This ban was rather heavy-handed, and had the effect of excluding groups like the Catholic Maryknoll Sisters, whom no one could consider agents of right-wing subversion. The ban was eased after a time, though no foreigners are allowed to live in the camps even now.

This crisis had the effect of forcing the mainline churches involved in the camps to reflect on their activity. In Zimbabwe's eastern province, bordering Mozambique, ten different denominations formed a task force to ask the churches established in the camps what services they required from outside. The answers included more contact with communities outside the camps, training, and books. The task force was then disbanded, and the same ten churches constituted a pastoral committee to meet these needs. This has worked so well that the commissioner for refugees has decreed that all Christian groups wanting to work in the camps must operate through this body. This has effectively meant that extraneous evangelical activities have been curtailed; Christian influences within the camps are definitely mainline and no longer evangelical. The intent now is to introduce this system in the camps in Zimbabwe's other provinces.

Another consciousness-raising step, this time initiated by the churches, was a workshop in Harare in August 1989 on the subject of "Religion and Oppression: the misuse of religion for social, political and economic subjugation in eastern and southern Africa." This workshop, conducted by the Ecumenical Documentation and Information Centre of Eastern and Southern Africa (EDICESA), was attended by church leaders from the Christian councils of the twelve neighboring countries which make up EDICESA. The papers of South African participants in particular served to spread awareness of the issue to Christian leaders of the region. The proceedings of the workshop were published and given wide publicity.[19] In an extensive article in Zimbabwe's *Sunday Mail*, major church leaders, including the Anglican

Archbishop, the general secretary of the ZCC, and former President Banana, were asked for their comments on the threat posed to the region by right-wing Christian bodies.[20]

Two months after this workshop, a particularly well known evangelical, Rev. Peter Hammond of Front Line Fellowship, was captured by Mozambican soldiers on 24 October 1988 when he, a South African, and six American missionaries entered northern Mozambican Tete province. They were flown to Maputo, interrogated, then released on 30 October. This event was given wide publicity, for Hammond is a leader of an extreme fringe of South Africa's religious right, outspoken in his anti-communism, allegations of abuses in Angola and Mozambique, support for Renamo and the apartheid regime, and portrayal of the South African Defence Force (SADF) as a "missionary force."

In mid-November 1990, African churchmen gathered in Harare for the second assembly of the African Christian Peace Conference to discuss issues affecting justice and peace in Africa. Two government ministers and former President Banana addressed the meeting, and in their comments all dealt with liberation theology as distinct from oppressive religion. But it was President Mugabe's address, officially opening the conference in St Mary's Anglican Cathedral, which was given most prominence in the media.

Mugabe outlined the different sociopolitical effects of different kinds of Christianity. He called on churches to refuse to be used against progress and justice. He referred to Hammond and his other "missionaries funded by right-wing churches in America." He actually named Shekinah Ministries and Jimmy Swaggart Ministries as openly funding and supporting MNR bandits. "There are still many others who work among refugees and new settlements pretending that they are confronting communism with the Gospel. We condemn the activities of such organizations who, in the name of God, have been supporting the forces of darkness and reaction in southern Africa." He commended the role of churches in South Africa who have stood so boldly with the forces of liberation against apartheid.[21]

This publicity seems to be having some effect. One result of President Mugabe's address and his remarks distinguishing oppressive from liberating Christianity was to provoke the general secretary of the Zimbabwe Student Christian Movement to write an article in Harare's *Sunday Mail* calling on the government to ban new churches. He deplored the proliferating new churches, and called for a curb on "the regular influx of self-styled, anti-socialist, get-rich-quick imported evangelists who wish to turn Zimbabwe to a procapitalist God." He called on the ZCC to work with the government in banning these churches.[22] The significance of the article is that its author comes from this evangelical background himself. He admits that until he heard Mugabe's address at the African Peace Conference he had had no idea of the political role of these churches.

Thus, slowly, the sociopolitical role of American evangelical Christianity is coming to be acknowledged. However, the level of awareness is still remarkably low, and under these circumstances this evangelical Christianity is spreading rapidly. In the opinion of this author, its rapid growth owes more to this general lack of awareness than to any conscious strategy of hegemony on the part of its exponents.

Notes

1 Cited in P. Zachrisson, An *African Area in Change: Belingwe 1894–1946. A Study in Colonialism, Missionary Activity and African Response in Southern Rhodesia* (Gothenburg, 1978), p. 267.
2 In 1965 there were about 200,000 whites in Rhodesia out of a population of six million. By 1988 there were about 100,000 whites in Zimbabwe out of an estimated population of eight million.
3 C. F. Hallencreutz, "Ecumenical Challenges in Independent Zimbabwe: ZCC 1980–85," *Church and State in Zimbabwe*, eds., C. Hallencreutz and A. Moyo (Gweru, 1988), pp. 276–89.
4 M. Lapsley, *Neutrality or Co-option? Anglican Church and State from 1964 until the Independence of Zimbabwe*, (Gweru, 1986).
5 Hallencreutz, "Ecumenical Challenges," pp. 265–75.
6 See I. Linden, *The Catholic Church and the Struggle for Zimbabwe* (London, 1980).
7 For a fuller discussion of all these transnationals, both in general and within Zimbabwe, see P. Gifford, *The Religious Right in Southern Africa* (Harare, 1988).
8 For an analysis of Bonnke's Christianity, see P. Gifford, "'Africa Shall Be Saved.' An Appraisal of Reinhard Bonnke's Pan-African Crusade," *Journal of Religion in Africa* 17 (1987), pp. 63–92.
9 See Gifford, *Religious Right*, pp. 69–70.
10 Wimber is Professor of Church Growth at Fuller Theological Seminary, Pasadena, California. A good example of his Christianity is J. Wimber with K. Springer, *Power Evangelism: Signs and Wonders Today* (London, 1985).
11 Copies of all Carter's presentations are available from PO Box W19, Waterfalls, Harare, Zimbabwe.
12 For accounts of the trial of the Shekinah missionary, see *Sydney Morning Herald*, 28 March 1988, and *Bulletin* (Sydney), 12 April 1988.
13 *Northern News* (Harare), February–March 1989.
14 See Gifford, *Religious Right*, pp. 69–70.
15 G. Halsell, *Prophecy and Politics: Militant Evangelicals on the Road to Nuclear War*, (Westport, Conn., 1986), especially pp. 145–60.
16 P. Lernoux, *Cry of the People: The Struggle for Human Rights in Latin America: The Catholic Church in Conflict with U.S. Policy*, 2nd ed., (New York, 1982), pp. 142–47.
17 See Gifford, *Religious Right*, pp. 47–48.
18 Gifford, *Religious Right*, pp. 109–10.
19 The proceedings, *Religion and Oppression: the Misuse of Religion for Social, Political and Economic Subjugation in Eastern and Southern Africa* (Harare, 1989), are available from EDICESA, P.O. Box H 94, Hatfield, Harare, Zimbabwe.
20 P. Deketeke and C. Chitsaka, "Exposing Churches Which Serve Two Masters at Same Time," *Sunday Mail*, 15 October 1989.
21 See *Herald*, 16 November 1989.
22 F. Mpindu, *Sunday Mail*, 31 December 1989.

74

Excerpt from 'THE PERSISTENCE OF APOCALYPTICISM WITHIN A DENOMINATIONALIZING SECT

The apocalyptic fringe groups of Seventh-day Adventism'

Ronald Lawson

Source: Thomas Robbins and Susan Palmer (eds), *Millennium, Messiahs, and Mayhem: Contemporary Apocalyptic Movements*, London: Routledge, 1997, pp. 207–21, 225–6.

Introduction

The origins of Seventh-day Adventism were urgently apocalyptic. Its founders had all been disciples of William Miller, whose proclamation throughout the American Northeast that the Second Coming of Christ would occur on October 22, 1844, had spawned the "Millerite Movement." Although grief-stricken and humiliated by the "Great Disappointment," this segment of the movement continued to anticipate the imminent return of Jesus. Its leaders regarded this belief as so central to their faith that they enshrined it in the name they adopted: Seventh-day *Adventist*.

October 1994 marked the 150th anniversary of the failure of Miller's prophecy—and a further century and a half of preaching that Jesus would soon return. However, during this period American Adventism has been transformed: Adventists have grown in number, put down roots in the society, and experienced prosperity. This paper investigates the extent to which an urgent apocalypticism continues to be taught and believed within Adventism today.

Theoretical focus

This question is explored with the help of church-sect theory. Developed first in Europe (Troeltsch 1931 [1911]), this theory proved especially stimulating once Niebuhr applied it to the religious situation in the United States (1957 [1929]). The religious pluralism and absence of an established church here caused researchers to alter the theory's nomenclature, as they now compared *sects* with *denominations* rather than *churches*, and tested Niebuhr's claim that all *sects* would inevitably be transformed into *denominations* (Yinger 1957, 54). Eventually Stark and Bainbridge, responding to confusion caused by differences among researchers in the lists of characteristics used to define *sect* and *denomination*, put forward a single dimension, "the degree to which a religious group is in a *state of tension* with its surrounding sociocultural environment" (1985, 23). According to this definition, sects are in high tension with their environments while denominations have low tension (49–51).

Although research has shown that not all sects become denominations,[1] as generations pass most of those that survive and grow compromise with the world, thus reducing tension and moving toward denominational status (Wilson 1969 [1963], 371, 372). This usually occurs as they increase their participation in the wider society and as influential members experience upward mobility and then find that the tension between their religious group and society is inconsistent with their interests (Stark and Bainbridge 1985, 134, 99, 103). Since an urgent apocalyptic position anticipates "the end of the world"—the sudden destruction of society—a group holding such a position is, by definition, in high tension with its environment. However, intense apocalypticism is difficult to maintain: "The expectation that the world is to overturn through supernatural action is necessarily subject to repeated postponement" (Wilson 1973, 36).

As a religious group begins to move from *sect* toward *denomination*, its membership is likely to become more diverse. For example, Niebuhr realized that some members would become uneasy with change and compromise, and would hold fast to the traditional teachings, thus creating theological diversity within the ranks and risking, ultimately, a new sectarian schism (1957 [1929], 19–20, 54).

Research methods

This paper is a product of a large study of international Seventh-day Adventism, whose data include more than 3,000 in-depth interviews from fifty-four countries and questionnaires from interviewees (who are mostly church employees) and samples of college students and laity. It focuses on the North American Division of the Adventist Church (the United States and Canada), drawing on data from interviews, questionnaires, and books, periodicals, and tapes published by the official Adventist publishing houses, independent organizations of conservative and liberal Adventists, and "independent ministries" on the fringes of Adventism. It also utilizes data from four other relevant surveys of North American Adventists.

Apocalyptic urgency among early Adventists

William Miller had concluded from his study of the apocalyptic visions of the biblical books of Daniel and Revelation that "the time of the end" had begun in 1798 and that the Second Coming of Christ would occur in 1844 (Numbers and Butler 1987). Although he withdrew after the failure of his prediction and most of his followers dispersed, a small group reinterpreted the key prophecy: October 22, 1844, was the beginning of the pre-advent judgment in heaven and was the final date singled out by time prophecy; the return of Jesus would follow quickly. A young visionary, Ellen White, played an important role in confirming this interpretation. Since they initially held that with the beginning of judgment the "door of mercy" had been shut, they made no efforts to evangelize. Even after they came to believe that they were called to share their message with others, they avoided formal organization and foreign evangelism, believing that insufficient time remained.

Miller's prophecies had portrayed governments as wild beasts that hurt God's people. Adventists elaborated on these prophecies as they developed their eschatology further. They adopted a unique interpretation when some members were arrested for violating state "blue laws" following their adoption of the Saturday Sabbath: beginning in 1851, they denounced the American Republic, identifying it with the second beast of Revelation 13, which "had two horns like a lamb" and spoke "like a dragon." They saw the early days of the U.S., when it had adopted its Constitution and Bill of Rights, positively—as symbolized by the beast's lamb-like appearance, with the two horns representing the principles of political and religious freedom. But, pointing to slavery and to the religious intolerance they had experienced, they held that it had betrayed both principles—it was a dragon in lamb's clothing, and was destined to play a persecuting role in the world's final events (Morgan 1994, 238). That is, Adventist eschatology invoked tension with the state: it was highly sectarian at this point.

Extending the time

The new sect finally created a formal organization and chose a name for itself in the early 1860s. Having organized, Adventists then began to build institutions and, in 1874, they sent their first foreign missionary to Europe. Many more missionaries followed—and more institutions were built abroad. The building spree between 1860 and 1901 included 16 colleges and high schools, a medical school, 75 "sanitariums" or hospitals, 13 publishing houses, and 31 miscellaneous institutions (such as health food factories). Although these institutions were created in order to facilitate Adventists in their goals of spreading their "last warning message" and thereby ushering in Christ's kingdom, the result was gradual goal displacement: there was an inevitable tension between longer-term building and organizing and the urgency of their message.

Meanwhile, Ellen White had elaborated on Adventist eschatology, with special attention to the final events just before the Second Coming. The main players would be Satan[2] and his henchmen—the Roman Catholic Church,[3] "Apostate Protestantism,"[4] "Spiritualism,"[5] and the U.S. government. These would persecute God's "remnant"—the loyal Adventists—beginning in the United States:

> When Protestantism shall stretch her hand across the gulf to grasp the hand of the Roman power, when she shall reach over the abyss to clasp hands with spiritualism, when, under the influence of the threefold union, our country shall repudiate every principle of its Constitution as a Protestant and republican government . . . then we may know that the time has come for the marvelous working of Satan and that the end is near.
>
> (White 1885, 451)

White's eschatology was published in final form in 1888 in *The Great Controversy between Christ and Satan*. The details of the eschatology reflected the times in which White wrote—spiritualism was in vogue, and a Protestant establishment was trying to shore up its position by, among other things, introducing a "national Sunday law" that would protect and codify the state blue laws. Although White declared that "the final events" would be "rapid," her detailed list of future events created an impression that the end was somewhat more distant—especially when the national Sunday law failed to pass in both 1888 and 1889. Adventists had a part in this outcome—they had chosen to work against the fulfillment of their own sign of the eschaton.

The elaboration of Adventist eschatology had involved some reshaping, especially of their view of the United States. While they continued to identify America with the two-horned beast, it was no longer portrayed as already in the dragon phase, but as still lamb-like, and its demise was thus seen as less imminent. That is, the time believed to be remaining before the Second Coming of Christ was lengthening, and tension with the state was beginning to relax. Moreover, Ellen White now counseled rapprochement with civil authorities in order to facilitate missionary work, urging Adventists to help prolong the future of America "so the Adventist message could go forth and flourish" (Butler 1974, 193). Adventists thus found themselves in an anomalous situation where they wished to delay the end of the world in order to have greater opportunity to preach that it was at hand. Consequently, although their rehoned eschatology saw the passage of a national Sunday law as the culmination of the prophecy concerning the two-horned beast, and thus a sure signal that the end was at hand, they felt obliged by Ellen White's counsel to "extend the time" to respond boldly to this threat (Butler 1974, 196–198; Morgan 1994, 241–42). A flurry of political activity culminated in the creation of what became the Public Affairs and Religious Liberty Department within the General Conference,[6] which institutionalized the Adventist Church's role as a watchdog of the First Amendment.

During the following decades, Adventism continued to accommodate the state. It altered its stance on military service, pursued accreditation for its colleges, and accepted government aid for its schools and hospitals (Lawson 1996a, 1996b). In order to gain accreditation, it exposed its academics to graduate study at major universities, which inevitably made the content of their courses less sectarian, and thus also impacted their students. Meanwhile, accreditation prepared the way for widespread upward mobility among graduates of Adventist colleges (Lawson 1995).

Adventism also began to adjust to the religious economy. In the 1950s church leaders participated in a series of meetings with two well-known Evangelical scholars, Walter R. Martin and Donald Grey Barnhouse, who, in the process of writing a series of studies on Christian "cults," had begun researching Seventh-day Adventism. When Adventists published their answers to the Evangelicals' questions, it was revealed that they had denied three doctrines that had been widely held among them but were offensive to Evangelicals (QOD 1957). All were relevant to the specialness of Adventism and its endtime message.[7] Although some members expressed a sense of betrayal over the new formulation of belief, there was widespread relief when Martin's book declared that Adventists were not a cult but were "bretheren" of the Christian Evangelicals (Martin 1960).

Adventists were putting down roots in society and, in the process, becoming world-affirming. The apocalypse was less imminent. Adventist spokespersons sometimes recognized this explicitly. For example, when, during World War II, Supreme Court decisions strengthened religious liberty and Roosevelt included freedom of religion as one of his four basic freedoms, the editor of the official church paper commented that what Adventists had prophesied clearly lay further in the future (Editorial 1943). Seventh-day Adventism had become a denominationalizing sect.

Expectancy and delay

This does not mean that Adventists had abandoned their eschatology. They continued to believe that Jesus was returning soon and to look expectantly for signs of the fulfillment of Ellen White's whole eschatological scenario. Consequently, they remained prone to excitement whenever they found evidence that the return of the Lord might be near. Although the Adventist Church, as a corporate religious body, learned the lesson of 1844 and has never set or endorsed a date for the Second Coming, groups of Adventists have focused on particular dates for that event more than twenty times in the past 150 years (Paulien 1994, 24). Their attention was often drawn to these "signs of the times" by Adventist evangelists, for eschatology remained at the center of Adventist evangelism—it attracted crowds and gained conversions, especially during times of crisis. Adventist evangelists made much of both world wars, the great depression, the election of John F. Kennedy, the first Catholic, as president; the Cuban missile crisis; the first expedition to the moon;[8] the sexual revolution of the 1960s and rise of the gay movement; and the cold war.[9] The Adventist Church also used the expectation of the return of Jesus—and fear of not being ready—to maintain the commitment of its members and to control their behavior.

However, there was considerable burnout on the issue over time as the extended delay made its impact: it proved increasingly difficult to maintain a high level of expectation. Most Adventists settled into a state of chronic fretfulness about the Second Coming. While they have "held onto the Sabbath," members of the baby-boomer generation, in particular, "are frankly embarrassed by those wild, apocalyptic books on which this church was founded" (Fagal 1992, 3; Branson 1991, 2).

As Adventists have buried generations of forebears who believed that they would live to see Jesus return, they have tried to find reasons for the delay. Two main explanations have been put forward, each of which is associated with a response:

1. The delay has been caused because members' characters are not yet ready for translation. The response is to somehow attain fully sanctified lives (Douglass 1975). Interviewees who hold this position admitted that they experience a lot of stress, for most feel that they have not "arrived," and are therefore responsible for the delay—or in danger of being lost.
2. Since Jesus had stated that the gospel would be preached in all the world and then the end would come, the problem must be that Adventists have failed to complete this task. This is the explanation espoused most strongly by the administrators who address the issue. Their response has been to pour more energy and resources into evangelism and other forms of spreading the "Advent message."

The fragmenting of the Adventist apocalyptic

The data suggest that the doctrine of the Second Advent, as taught and believed within American Adventism today, is fragmenting:

(1) *Church administrators*. Church administrators deliver mixed messages. On the one hand, they make strong affirmations of the traditional doctrine. Adventism's creed, the list of twenty-seven "fundamental beliefs," passed at the 1980 General Conference Session with strong administrative backing,

continues the expectation that the return of Jesus will be soon. A book by the current president of the General Conference, published to coincide with the 150th anniversary of the Great Disappointment, notes that the unexpected delay is causing some to question, but affirms that "WE STILL BELIEVE!" (Folkenberg 1994, 9).

On the other hand, when an Adventist publishing house was sued by the Equal Employment Opportunity Commission because of its discrimination against women in salaries and promotions, the defense brief, which must have been written with the input and approval of church leaders, distanced present-day Adventism from its "earlier" anti-Catholicism as "nothing more" than a manifestation of an attitude common among conservative Protestant denominations in earlier decades "which has now been consigned to the historical trash heap so far as the Seventh-day Adventist Church is concerned" (Pacific Press Case 1975, 4). Was this mere opportunism, or a straw in the wind?

Adventist leaders preside over a strongly centralized, hierarchical organizational structure. Its institutions root it strongly in this world: for example, the finances of its massive U.S. hospital system dwarf the budget of the General Conference, and its hospitals are currently eagerly engaged in mergers with non-Adventist hospitals—sometimes with Catholic hospitals—in order to strengthen their positions.

(2) *Adventist evangelism.* Adventist evangelism—whether it adopts the form of blockbuster public meetings making full use of multimedia, "Revelation Seminars," magazines such as the *Signs of the Times*, "soul-winning" books, or television and radio programs—still focuses strongly on "endtime events." Adventist evangelists typically invoked the timeline prophecies to show that the "time of the end" began in 1798 and that 1844 was the last pinpointed date, which left the Second Coming as the next major event—and would then point to whatever current events seemed appropriate to suggest that the denouement was very near. However, many evangelists and writers have eagerly updated their eschatological content since the collapse of the Soviet empire in 1989, for they now claim to see a convergence of trends preparing the way for the fulfillment of Ellen White's predictions. These "trends" include the following: (i) papal influence has grown dramatically, coming to the fore in the role played by Pope John Paul II in the collapse of communism; (ii) the U.S., having emerged as the sole superpower, is finally in a position where it could, in alliance with the papacy, press the whole world into conformity with an attack on God's elect; (iii) the New Christian Right has emerged as a political force in the U.S. and has built an alliance with the Catholic Church over abortion and other social issues, and both are attacking church-state separation and receiving some cooperation in this from the Supreme Court; (iv) a resurgence of spiritualism is occurring in several guises—in the New Age movement and the widespread interest in "near-death experiences" and appearances of the Virgin Mary (Finley 1992a, 1992b; Moore 1992, 1995; Goldstein 1993, 1996).

Although the grim Adventist eschatological scenario is portrayed as close to culmination, it is still future for Adventist evangelists. With their unhindered access to meeting spaces, advertising, publishing, and the airwaves, their utilization of modern conveniences, and their satisfaction with the image that Adventism and its institutions project to society, they are clearly personally comfortable in America today.

(3) *Pastors.* Since Adventist evangelism emphasizes eschatology, converts are usually those attracted by this topic. However, when they join Adventist congregations, they find that their pastors typically give far less emphasis to eschatological subjects than the evangelists. When I asked 115 North American pastors what themes they stressed in their sermons, only 7 percent mentioned eschatological subjects as their prime theme.

These data should not be interpreted as suggesting that Adventist pastors in North America are ignoring the topic of the apocalypse. When 296 pastors responding to another survey were asked how many sermons they had preached over the preceding twelve months "where the Second Coming had been the sole subject," the median response was three (Rosado 1991).[10] More than half (50.3 percent) of 1,988 North American members included within a survey of the world membership of the Adventist Church sponsored by the General Conference reported hearing a sermon on "the Second Coming or last day events" "more than once" during the preceding year. On the other hand, only 23.8 percent had heard a sermon dealing with "the 2,300 years or other prophetic events"—topics that were likely to have been more urgent in tone (World Survey). That is, most of the pastors who choose to address the topic of the Second Coming in their sermons approach it as a doctrine, without a great deal of urgency.

When the responses of interviewees to a block of questions asking to what extent they agreed with statements rooted in Adventist eschatology were cross-tabulated with age, a sharp age break emerged. Those who had entered the ministry before the mid-1960s—when a seminary degree was not the norm and very few of the college religion teachers had doctorates—were much more likely to answer that they "strongly agree" or "agree" with these statements; on the other hand, those who had entered the ministry later were more prone to "disagree" or "strongly disagree." Since a seminary degree was the norm for the latter, they had been exposed to scholars with advanced degrees from the finest universities and also, increasingly, in the Adventist colleges during their baccalaureate programs. This interpretation is confirmed by cross-tabulations between "years of education" and the same block of eschatologically rooted statements: those with only sixteen years education tended to agree with the statements, while those with higher degrees tended to disagree. That is, the key to understanding the relatively low priority accorded to apocalyptic preaching by pastors lies in what is taught in the seminary and by the religion departments of Adventist colleges.

(4) *The seminary and departments of religion* in general avoid the traditional Adventist approach to eschatology. Several of the forty-nine such teachers interviewed mentioned that they would not teach a course on Daniel and Revelation or that no one was willing to do so. Interview excerpts illustrate the tone of these comments:

> The Second Advent is not now an important part of Adventist faith and life. . . . Daniel and Revelation has not been really important in Adventist scholarship during my career. There have always been courses on them, but the area has not been terribly important to the intellectual life of the church. We've had a collective subliminal awareness that traditional interpretations don't make a lot of sense. We have over-interpreted these pictures, which really say that there is a struggle between good and evil which God will win. We've tried to interpret each detail, to do left-brain analysis to what is really a right-brain piece of art.
>
> I preach the Second Coming, but differently—my emphasis is not on time, but on its influence on ethics. . . . I am having difficulty preaching the signs of the coming in the old way—they are ordinary historical events, so that every generation could see them in their time—so many periods expected His return. . . .
>
> My course, "Apocalyptic Studies," presents apocalyptics as a literary genre, as just another way of writing theology.

These attitudes are confirmed in seven recent books where theologians have addressed apocalyptic themes. The following quote is representative of them all:

> My purpose . . . is to highlight the text of the Bible rather than comment on the continuing swirl of current events. . . . The safest course is to understand the Bible's view of the end on its own terms, rather than expecting direct answers to the kinds of questions that only people in our day could have asked. Our Bible is the product of God speaking to people in another time and place. . . . The purpose of the Bible's teaching about the end is not to satisfy our curiosity about the future but to teach us how to live as we await the end. . . . When will the Son of Man come? There is nothing in the current scene that gives us the absolute certainty that the end is immediately before us—or a long time in the future.
>
> (Paulien 1994, 13, 34, 89, 159)

(5) *Laypersons.* In surveys of 785 church members and 1305 students at Adventist colleges, I asked to what extent they agreed with the statement "Christ will return in your lifetime." One-seventh (14.7 percent) of the

members and one-fifth (21.1 percent) of the students agreed strongly. More than three-fifths of the members and half the students answered "uncertain," which is theologically technically correct since Jesus said "no man knows the day. . . ." As expected, cross-tabulations showed converts to be significantly more urgently apocalyptic than members raised by Adventist parents.

A survey of more than 13,000 students in Adventist high schools found that 31.3 percent worried "very much" "about not being ready for Christ's return," and 21.3 percent "about not being faithful during the Time of Trouble." (Another 28.4 percent and 22.5 percent respectively worry "quite a bit.") Urgency engenders fear among this age group (Valuegenesis Study). When these same questions were asked in a survey targeted at 3,300 Hispanic students, the proportion admitting to being fearful proved to be higher still: 59.5 percent worried "very much" about not being ready for Christ's return and 45.1 percent about possibly proving unfaithful during the Time of Trouble (AVANCE Study). (Another 17.9 percent and 20.1 percent respectively worried "quite a bit.")

That is, while large majorities of laypersons show a belief in the doctrine of the Second Coming, urgent apocalypticism seems to be much less widespread, being concentrated among converts and, often fearfully, among younger students exposed to indoctrination in Adventist schools.

Movements on the fringes of Adventism

Urgently apocalyptic "independent ministries" on the fringes of Adventism have multiplied in recent years. Their growth is associated with the frustration of many converts who, having been attracted by the eschatological preaching of the Adventist evangelists, are disappointed to find far less of this in the churches they join after their baptisms. These ministries have so disturbed church leaders as a result of the flow of their outspoken literature around the globe and the perception that they are diverting considerable amounts of income from the denominational conduit, that the Annual Council of the church in 1991 voted to condemn them as "producing distrust and division that hinder the work of God" ("Perth Declaration" 1991, 7). In 1992 the North American Division of the church published a large book, *Issues: The Seventh-day Adventist Church and Certain Private Ministries*, laying out its grievances with some of the ministries as a warning to members. Like the early Christians, who continued to think of themselves as Jewish and therefore focused their evangelism on Jews—initially in Jerusalem, and then in the cities to which they had scattered—the leaders of these groups continue to identify with Adventism, even if they have been disfellowshipped, and to focus their efforts on reaching Adventists. (The best known of these ministries was David Koresh's Branch Davidians.)

The fringe apocalyptic ministries are much more urgent in their apocalypticism than most mainstream Adventists. They generally differ from the latter (who have themselves been shown to be very diverse on this issue) in at least one of two main ways. First, many of them are so impatient with the long delay in the Second Coming since 1844 that merely pointing to recent world events as new evidence that the general Adventist eschatological scenario is on track (as the leading evangelists have done) is unsatisfactory to them: they want more direct proof that these are the very last days and Jesus is about to come. To accomplish this they often develop some kind of timeline prophecy that focuses on the current period. Second, they often see the Adventist church leadership as so compromised with the "world" and the members as so "lukewarm" in their spirituality that the church is unready to receive Christ and as such is responsible for his delay. Some of them portray the official church as having shifted positions on beliefs and behavioral standards, so that it has obscured the "last warning message" bequeathed to it through Ellen White, and present their own group as the true "historic Adventists." When criticisms of church leadership are met, in turn, with charges of heresy and attempts to subject them to church discipline, the rancor escalates.

My analysis divides these urgently apocalyptic groups into five categories. The attempts to apply time prophecies to the present differ considerably from one category to another.

(1) *The 6,000 year umbrella time prophecy*. The argument here is that, according to Bishop Ussher's biblical chronology, the creation took place about 4004 B.C., so that the sixth millennium is closing. If each millennium is symbolized by one day, the seventh, or Sabbath, millennium—what the book of Revelation calls THE millennium—is about to open. Premillennialists believe that Christ returns before then.

One of the authors who falls into this category, G. Edward Reid, is an unusual case, for he is a lone writer rather than the head of a ministry, and he holds a departmental position at the headquarters of the Adventist North American Division. He submitted his book manuscript, which suggests that Christ will return by the year 2000, to the Review and Herald (R&H), an Adventist publishing house, but it was rejected because the editors saw it as too apocalyptic and irresponsible in its biblical interpretation. However, he was able to gain the support of the marketing staff, which is made up of old hands from the Adventist Book Centers (ABCs), one of the havens of Adventist fundamentalists. When he was able to raise money to self-publish the book, he arranged for the R&H job-printing division to print the book; this erroneously leaves the impression with many readers that it has the "imprimatur" of the publisher, especially since its marketing division signed up to distribute it through the ABCs and it carries, on the back cover, an endorsement from the chair of the religion department at Southern College, the most conservative of the Adventist colleges in the United States (Reid 1994).

A. Jan Marcussen is best known as the author of *National Sunday Law* (1983), a simplified rehash of the position put forward by Ellen White in the

Great Controversy, with no attempt to link it to current events. He has struck a chord among a segment of Adventists, for they have provided him with the funds to print and distribute 7.8 million copies of the book in nineteen languages since 1983. His newsletters attempt, with poor documentation, to show that the law is about to be enacted. He also puts forward other evidence that the end is upon us, and in his newsletter of mid-November 1995, he used the 6,000-year theory to cement his case, claiming that this period would culminate in 1996.

(2) *The Jubilee Cycle*. This approach takes the Levitical Jubilee year, based on seven "sabbatical years" for a total of forty-nine years, through seventy cycles—a symbolic number—and thus to our day. However, although the dates of some sabbatical years are known, there is disagreement about the dating of jubilee years in biblical times. Consequently, various proponents disagree about the ending of the seventieth cycle. An earlier group in the Pacific Northwest settled on the year 1987, and expected the Second Coming that year. The person best known for this timeline, Larry Wilson of Wake Up America Seminars, initially announced that the cycle ended in 1992, before settling on 1994. For him this is the beginning of the final period, during which the usual timeline prophecies, such as the 1,335 days of the book of Daniel, are applied as literal rather than symbolic (a day for a year) days. He expected the events accompanying the Great Tribulation to begin in 1994 or 1995, and that this would include a large asteroid hitting the earth. These events would culminate in the Second Coming of Jesus "around 1998" (Wilson 1994, 1). In a defensive "addendum" inserted in the fifth edition of his most widely circulated book after the close of 1995, he states that he does not regard the delay as a failure of his interpretation. He continues to preach and to publish—the number of copies of this book in circulation has passed 500,000 (Wilson 1994).

(3) *Applications of the timeline prophecies of Daniel and Revelation to the present*. This has been done by several ministries, usually as literal days. Some of them see this as a second (dual) fulfillment, others as the prime application. They look for clues in current events, and link them to the prophecies—a method that gives them a great deal of scope, and therefore also room for disagreement with one another. The best known of these is Charles Wheeling of Countdown Ministries in Alabama—perhaps because he has been active over a long period. He saw the Iran-Iraq War (beginning in 1980) as the harbinger of the Battle of Armageddon; more recently, he has found the Persian Gulf War in prophecy. He looks for an international crisis in the banking system, and is currently very interested in the actions and sayings of the pope. Because he rejects the earlier applications of the timeline prophecies, the year 1844 has no special significance for him. Even though this would seem to put him at odds with the writings of Ellen White, he has been extraordinarily active in publishing and distributing millions of copies of the *Great Controversy*—both in whole and in part—in many countries (Wheeling 1995).

(4) *The status of Jerusalem.* William Grothier of the Adventist Laymen's Foundation and Bible Prophecy Seminars, and editor of the monthly paper *Watchman, What of the Night?*, stands apart from the other ministries in his focus on the status of Jerusalem as a sign of the end of time.[13] He sees the unification of Jerusalem in 1967 as the "beginning of the end of time," and its appointment as capital of Israel in 1980 as the close of probation for nations—and also, because of its illegitimate changes in its doctrine, of that of the corporate Adventist Church; individuals have a little extra time, but that too is now petering out (Grothier 1995; 1994). In a switch, he focused his paper during 1995 on the aims of the papacy as given in recent encyclicals.

(5) *Those who "sigh and cry" over the apostasy of the Adventist Church.* Several prominent ministries—Hope International (publisher of *Our Firm Foundation*), the Hartland Institute (a college without accreditation and publisher of *The Last Generation*), Cherrystone Press (the personal vehicle of Dr. Ralph Larson), and Prophecy Countdown (a television and short-wave radio ministry) fall into this category. Their key complaint is about changes in Adventist doctrine, such as in the nature of Christ (from sinful—like ours—to sinless—like pre-fall Adam's) as a result of the Bible conferences with Evangelicals Martin and Barnhouse during the 1950s. Because these changes impact on Adventist eschatology (such as the belief that the final generation must overcome as Jesus overcame and stand perfect at the close of probation) and apostasy within the church was predicted by Ellen White, the latter is therefore seen as a clear sign that the end is imminent (Larson 1993, 180).

Although most of the ministries in this category may be counted as doctrinally orthodox, they have drawn much more fire from Adventist leadership than the other categories: the condemning book *Issues* was aimed directly at them—by name—by church leadership, and most of their leaders have been disfellowshipped since its publication in 1992. They have come under attack because their orthodoxy makes them more attractive to unsettled Adventists, they appear to attract considerable sums from their supporters that might otherwise have gone into denominational coffers, their criticism of the official church and its leadership is constant and uncompromising, and their influence is being felt among Adventists in the developing world because of the widespread distribution of their publications there. (Because it comes without cost to recipients there, the circulation of *Our Firm Foundation* is said to exceed that of the official church paper.)

[. . .]

Notes

1 Yinger, for example, introduced the concept of *established sect* (1946, 22–23).
2 The dragon of Revelation.

3 This interpretation was first made by European Protestant reformers.
4 By this White meant all the Protestant church organizations together with those members who failed to accept the Adventist message.
5 Since Adventists believed in "soul sleep"—that is, that the dead were dead until resurrected—any attempt to contact the dead was, by definition, of the devil.
6 Church headquarters.
7 These doctrines were that Christ was born with a sinful nature (this change disowned the bulwark of last-generation perfectionism), that the writings of Ellen White were free of error and equal to the Scriptures, and that Adventists alone comprised the biblical Remnant.
8 It was argued that surely God would step in to prevent sinful man's landing on a place without sin.
9 While Evangelicals generally saw the creation of the state of Israel as of cosmic significance, this was not part of Adventist eschatology.
10 This survey was introduced in a manner that was likely to encourage exaggerated reporting of attention to that topic.

References

Branson, Roy. 1991. "The Power of Apocalypse." *Spectrum* 21 (3): 2.

Butler, Jonathan. 1974. "Adventism and the American Experience." In *The Rise of Adventism: Religion and Society in Mid-Nineteenth-Century America*, edited by Edwin S. Gaustad. New York: Harper and Row.

Editorial. 1943. *Review and Herald*, July 22.

Fagal, William. 1992. "The New Awakening." *Adventists Affirm* 6 (1): 3–4.

Finley, Mark. 1992a. *Confidence Amid Chaos*. Boise: Pacific Press.

——. 1992b. "How Near is Near?" *Adventists Affirm* 6 (1): 12–24, 40.

Folkenberg, Robert S. 1994. *We Still Believe*. Boise: Pacific Press.

Goldstein, Clifford. 1996. *One Nation under God?* Boise: Pacific Press.

——. 1993. *Day of the Dragon*. Boise: Pacific Press.

Larson, Ralph. 1993. *Apostasy is the Issue*. Cherry Valley, CA: Cherrystone Press.

Lawson, Ronald. 1996. "Church and State at Home and Abroad: The Evolution of Seventh-day Adventist Relations with Governments." *Journal of the American Academy of Religion*. Forthcoming.

Martin, Walter. 1960. *The Truth about Seventh-day Adventism*. Grand Rapids, MI: Zondervan.

Moore, Marvin. 1995. *Armageddon: The Devil's Payday*. Boise: Pacific Press.

——. 1992. *The Crisis of the End Time*. Boise: Pacific Press.

Morgan, Douglas. 1994. "Adventism, Apocalyptic, and the Cause of Liberty." *Church History* 63 (June): 235–249.

Niebuhr, H. Richard. 1957 (1929). *The Social Sources of Denominationalism*. Cleveland: Meridian.

Numbers, Ronald L., and Jonathan M. Butler. 1987. *The Disappointed: Millerism and Millenarianism in the Nineteenth Century*. Bloomington: Indiana University Press.

Patterson, Gary. 1994. "The General Conference and the Branch Davidian Crisis." Talk at the New York Adventist Forum, June 11.

Paulien, Jon. 1994. *What the Bible Says about the End-Time*. Hagerstown, MD: Review and Herald.

"Perth Declaration." 1991. Minutes of Annual Council. *Adventist Review* 168 (45): 7.
QOD. 1957. *Seventh-day Adventists Answer Questions on Doctrine*. Washington, DC: Review and Herald.
Reid, G. Edward. 1994. *Even at the Door*. Self-published.
Rosado, Caleb. 1991. Data from a survey of pastors from five U.S. conferences.
——. 1993. "The Appeal of Cults." *Adventist Review* 170 (30): 16–20.
Stark, Rodney, and William Sims Bainbridge. 1985. *The Future of Religion*. Berkeley: University of California Press.
Troeltsch, Ernst. 1931 (1911). *The Social Teaching of the Christian Churches*, translated by Olive Wyon. New York: Macmillan.
Wheeling, Charles. 1995. "The Time has Come." Tapes of meetings recorded at Henderson, NC, November 3–4. Jemison, AL: Countdown Ministries.
White, Ellen. 1885. *Testimonies for the Church*, vol. 5. Oakland: Pacific Press.
——. 1888. *The Great Controversy between Christ and Satan*. Oakland: Pacific Press.
Wilson, Bryan R. 1969 (1963). "A Typology of Sects." In *Sociology of Religion*, edited by Roland Robertson. Baltimore: Penguin.
——. 1973. *Magic and the Millennium*. New York: Harper and Row.
Wilson, Larry. 1994. *Warning! Revelation is about to be Fulfilled*, fifth ed. Brushton, NY: Teach Services.
Yinger, J. M. 1946. *Religion in the Struggle for Power*. Durham, NC: Duke University Press.
——. 1957. *Religion, Society and the Individual*. New York: Macmillan.

75

NATIVE EVANGELISM IN CENTRAL MEXICO

Hugo G. Nutini

Source: *Ethnology*, 39(1) (2000), 39–54.

We know little about native evangelical sects[1] that have been established in these places during the past 70 years, especially since the late 1970s. Anthropologists occasionally mention them (see Aubrey 1974; Díaz de la Serna 1984; Gaxiola *et al.* 1984; Juárez Cerdi 1997; Zapata Novoa 1990), but provide scanty information on the nature and form of their evangelism, and the circumstances and conditions that led groups or individuals to reject Catholicism.

In the course of an ongoing investigation of Protestant evangelism in the Tlaxcala-Pueblan Valley and the Córdoba-Orizaba regions of Mexico (see Nutini n.d.; Nutini and Isaac 1974) I encountered five native evangelist sects, two in the former and three in the latter. Two of them were founded in 1936 and 1951; the other three were established within the past ten years. It is notable that the converts to these native evangelist sects all broke away from Catholicism for similar reasons. The main reasons consistently given for conversion to native evangelism are dissatisfaction with Catholic doctrine or practice, desire for more personal religious expression, greater freedom in organizing the congregation, the high cost of worship (particularly with rural folk), and disillusionment with the Catholic Church's lack of interest in the economic and social well-being of its members.

The aforementioned research indicates that there are no significant differences of motive for converting to native evangelism or Protestant evangelism. (Protestant evangelical sects differ significantly from one another doctrinally, of course, but they all have the same attraction for disenchanted Catholics desirous of some form of religious change. Converts may adduce idiosyncratic grounds for choosing Pentecostalism, Mormonism, or any other Protestant evangelist sect, but the reasons for conversion are basically the same.) Thus, native evangelism and Protestant evangelism, irrespective of doctrinal differences and modes of proselytism, are part of the same religious movement that is wresting souls from Catholicism.

Conversion is supported by the central doctrinal and pragmatic concerns that native and Protestant evangelism share: the Bible as the sole source of religious understanding and moral action; total rejection of the cult of the saints; emphasis on individual religious identity; lack of hierarchy in ritual and ceremony; administrative decentralization and democratic organization of the congregation; preaching as a core vehicle for religious experience; and the congregation as a source of social and psychological support. There are of course differences between native evangelist sects, just as there are differences between Protestant evangelical sects; those of the former depending largely on which Protestant group served as their model. Thus, native evangelical sects are in most respects extensions of Protestant evangelism, and whatever differences obtain between them are centered on reactions to local conditions and the need of dissatisfied Catholics to proceed on their own terms, though they are well aware they are emulating a Protestant model.

This article focuses on two native evangelical congregations in the Córdoba-Orizaba region: one of very recent inception, the other founded five decades ago. The aims of the presentation are threefold: 1) to describe the doctrinal configuration and organization of these congregations; 2) to ascertain their evangelical lineage and modifications; and 3) to compare them with respect to motivations for and modes of conversion. This exercise should illuminate a religious tide that is not well understood, and appears bound to spread under the increasing proselytism of Protestant evangelism in most countries of Latin America.

Amistad y Vida A. C. (Cristianos)

An association called *Amistad y Vida A. C. (Cristianos)* was founded eight years ago in the city of Córdoba, and within three years had an established congregation. The name translates as Friendship and Life Association, but its members call themselves *Cristianos* (Christians), and they are regionally known as such. The association was founded by a 52-year-old man from Ciudad Juárez, in the state of Chihuahua, who had been converted to Pentecostal ism when he was 35. In 1999 the sect had approximately 600 members in the cities of Córdoba and Fortin and their immediate environs. Due to active individual and collective proselytism, it has expanded to the cities of Orizaba and Huatusco. During the past two years the sect has proselytized in the nearby states of Puebla, Tlaxcala, and Oaxaca. Today it has about fifteen congregations and a total membership of more than 3,000.

Dissatisfied with several aspects of Pentecostalism, the founder decided to launch a new movement, and he is currently its "director," as he calls himself and is called by congregants. Significantly, this sect has the appearance of a group of dissident Catholics who have formed a civic association, as the name indicates. This was the original intent of the founder, evidenced by his eschewing having any religious title such as pastor or minister. Moreover, the fluid, nonhierarchical organization of the congregation also prompts wondering whether Cristianos is a sect or simply a religious association. The following description and analysis demonstrate that Cristianos is a sect because it entails a religious creed, an ensemble of rituals and ceremonies, and a moral code of behavior.

The rapid expansion of the movement in the region led to the emergence of local leaders around whom independent congregations were established. These leaders coalesced as the equivalent of pastors, although with the deliberate intent to avoid hierarchy the congregation calls them *oradores* (prayer leaders). The position of orador is little more than that of a prayer co-ordinator, for in the conduct of religious services and the administration of congregation affairs, male or female congregants can, and often do, function as oradores. There are few status differences between the director, oradores, and the congregation. The congregation regards the others as leaders and organizers but shows them no reverential behavior, and the relationship among all is characterized by friendship and fraternity. Of several dozen Protestant and native evangelical congregations with which I am acquainted, none approaches Cristianos in the egalitarian organization of the congregation.[2]

As elicited from the founder of the sect, who will remain anonymous, early in 1992 he began to gather several families in private residences in order to analyze the Bible. The immediate success of these reunions prompted the founder to train a cadre of men and women to function as oradores to lead Bible and prayer sessions of from ten to fifteen people throughout the week. By the beginning of 1993, the group had reached a membership of more than 150, and the founder decided that there should be a weekly service; at which point the group became a congregation. True to the founder's belief in a personal, simple Christianity, there was never any intention of building a temple, and the weekly service takes place in a rented venue or in an open field on the outskirts of the city. This became the model of the congregations that have subsequently been established in regional cities. While membership is occasionally drawn from nearby rural areas, the sect has a basically urban orientation.

The director emphatically asserted that a primary incentive to form a group was unhappiness with the Catholic Church in doctrinal matters; namely, the church's inability to address concerns about many aspects of Catholicism and its insistence on blind compliance with dogma. Thus, in characteristic Protestant evangelist fashion, the budding sect became, doctrinally and pragmatically, totally Bible-centered in its search for truth and guidance. When the founder and many congregants were asked to differentiate between Catholic dogma and absolute reliance on the Bible in the conduct of religious and social life, the stock, formulaic answer was that the Bible was the word of God while the church, since its beginnings, had perverted the content of the Bible for the benefit of hierarchical interests.[3] (Note that the dogmatic approach to religious experience is not denied, only that anything that is not stated in or implied by the Bible cannot be dogmatically asserted.)

Quite frequently, congregants would elaborate by stating that Catholics, by misinterpreting the Bible, worshiped false gods (evidently referring to the cult of the saints) and objects in the form of persons, and that they do not know the true nature of the deity, manifested in Jesus Christ, as being in the heart of each person. Most damning, they asserted that practicing Catholics go to church not out of conviction and love of God but purely out of habit and for self-serving reasons when tragedy strikes. The priest officiates the mass, attendants listen, but there is no communication between them; people go home and that ends the worship of God for the week. These are views expressed with consistent regularity by Cristianos in comparing what they did as practicing Catholics.[4]

Regarding the social-psychological profile of Cristianos, preliminary analysis of the data indicates that this sect attracts individuals with upwardly mobile aspirations, desirous of improving personal behavior, with a strong sense of leadership, independent, and responsive to challenging the established order. Cristianos generally are middle class, a few are working class, yet the most consistently verbalized pragmatic reasons for conversion were complaints about church bureaucracy (i.e., the paperwork involved with administering the sacraments, particularly marriage and baptism). Other criticisms were about the elitism of priests, who favor the affluent; their aloofness and inaccessibility to the poor; the fees they charge for religious services, which are occasionally more than the poor can afford; and the Catholic parish's disinterest in the parishioners' well-being. The most serious complaint, perhaps, was that the parish failed to meet one's expectations of a community; that the priest and the congregation cannot be counted on for guidance and support when parishioners have economic difficulties and personal problems. A middle-class, affluent informant poignantly encapsulates this sentiment as follows:

> Since I was a child I was a good Catholic. I complied with all my duties toward God, but I never felt that I was part of a community, dedicated not only to worship our creator, but also to help each other to be better human beings. This is the ideal that I always dreamed of and I found among the Cristianos.

As far as I can determine, all Cristianos were church members in good standing before conversion. So how can we interpret these doctrinal and pragmatic reasons for abandoning Catholicism for some version of evangelism? This is the key question for understanding the conversion of Catholics to evangelism. Based on the ongoing investigation of both native and Protestant evangelism, I suggest that the initial and primary reasons for conversion are pragmatic, as specified above, regardless of the proselytism that went on. Individuals convert because of dissatisfaction with Catholicism, and not because they must study the Bible as the only road to salvation and the good life, or the realization that they were worshiping false gods, or other doctrinal reasons presented to them by proselytizers. Once individuals have been converted and have sufficiently internalized the creed of an evangelical sect, with the fervor characteristic of all converts, the original reasons for conversion are still there but take subsidiary importance to doctrinal reasons: the latter, in a sense, become a rationalization of the former.

In the case of Cristianos, informants invariably asserted that, in retrospect, Catholic indifference and lack of communitarianism may have played a role, but deep down what really motivated them to convert was what they experienced in their newly found conception of religion: evangelism as a way of life, in communion with God, and without priestly constraints and interpretations. Imbued with the enthusiasm and exhilaration of having found a new and true understanding, Cristianos (most of them barely two or three years from having been practicing Catholics) almost to a man attribute conversion to the truth and goodness of the new faith, making everything else of secondary importance.

It should be noted that there are also idiosyncratic and particularistic reasons for conversion to native and Protestant evangelism. We have not yet interviewed many informants in depth, but we have ascertained that conversion often takes place because of immediate causes that have little to do with what converts object to in Catholicism and what they expect to find in evangelism. Various forms of social and personal crises are the most common idiosyncratic conditions leading to conversion. From what I know of sixteen cases of native and Protestant evangelical conversion, it seems that the fundamental motive was the belief that a change in religious orientation would positively resolve a crisis (which in turn and in a self-fulfilling manner becomes a powerful reinforcer of faith in evangelism). This is the case, for example, of two Cristianos who underwent conversion, one in the aftermath of an emotionally devastating divorce and the other after her father died, leaving all his property to a younger sibling. How generalized is this syndrome we do not yet know, but I have the strong suspicion that it is quite frequent, and must be considered as an important supplement to the doctrinal and pragmatic reasons mentioned above.[5]

The Cristianos' creed is a simple version of Pentecostalism, and reflects the former religious affiliation of the director. It is eminently practical and devoid of any theological elaboration, little more than a sacred text framing the conduct of an ensemble of people who believe in the virtue of elementary Christian living. Thus, in the course of conversion, the individual is instructed in five fundamental beliefs extrapolated from the New Testament: 1) the Trinity, but emphasizing the redemptive nature of Jesus

Christ as the guide to moral behavior; 2) the Bible (both the Old and New Testaments) as the only source of religious knowledge; 3) that God the Father, God the Son, and God the Holy Ghost are pure spirit, and worshiping them in physical representation is idolatry; 4) the spiritual and physical curative power of the Holy Ghost; and 5) that faith in Jesus Christ does not ensure salvation if it is not accompanied by good works and a righteous life.

There are subsidiary beliefs that are an extension of the fundamental beliefs or have a customary origin. Cristianos are Anabaptists, and baptism is by total immersion. It takes place after an individual has been thoroughly indoctrinated in the creed and pragmatic orientation of the sect. It is a rite of obedience; a reaffirmation to abide faithfully and fully committed to the word of God, because infant baptism does not count, or as the director puts it, "because baptism symbolizes the purification of the soul and the beginning of a new, healthy life." (This interpretation of baptism is greatly at variance with the conception of the sacrament in both mainstream Protestantism and Catholicism; essentially it stands for the sacrament of confirmation as it is practiced in most Christian denominations.) The only other sacrament Cristianos recognize is marriage; confirmation, the Eucharist, confession (penance), ordination, and extreme unction are abhorred and regarded as subterfuges for exploitation and control.

Marriage, on the other hand, is of great importance as a sacrament. Married converts do not go through a second ceremony, but place great emphasis on the institution and the family as focal points of attention in the Cristiano conception of a good and healthy life. Much of the indoctrination and preaching that takes place during the weekly assemblies is concerned with family values, ranging from the organization of the household to the socialization of children. In sporadic meetings throughout the week, when a dozen or so congregants get together in private homes, and in more formal talks for the entire congregation, topics such as sexuality, drug use, alcoholism, family life, the problems of adolescents, and courting before marriage (*noviazgo*) are addressed. Special meetings sometimes take place to deal with the immediate practical and spiritual problems of men, women, children, and young married couples. They are organized and conducted *pro bono* by the more educated members of the sect and supervised by the director. On these occasions the meaning of leading a virtuous life acquires direct didactic meaning for personal and group behavior.

Based on the teachings of the Bible, Cristianos must live according to principles that include the sanctity of matrimony (faithfulness of spouses, proper care of offspring, and a fiscally and physically well-organized household); abstention from "noxious substances" (drinking, smoking, and using drugs); and generating harmonious relations with those around you (*prójimo*). These precepts are based on a selfless adoration of God, and not on the rare entreaty of the deity when disaster or tragedy strikes. This is an exacting code of moral behavior, but all the respondents to questionnaires (45) and informants in open-ended interviews (twenty) asserted that it is largely realized, which observation confirms, and went on to contrast it with the perfunctory ethical behavior of Catholics. That Cristianos adhere to their strict behavioral code may be posited on the newness of the sect and the demographic homogeneity of its membership.

There is no established liturgy in the Sunday weekly assembly; rather, the service is a free-flowing meeting combining Bible reading and textual explanation, discussion of a topic previously agreed on (any of those mentioned above), singing, emotionally voiced praises and exaltations of the Lord, and personal testimonials about miracles attributed to the Holy Ghost or some positive change in a member's life. The service, which lasts about two hours, does have a certain order of presentation. It begins with singing and praising the Lord, followed by testimonials, then Bible reading, topical discussion, and ends with singing and testimonial demonstrations of faith. The service is conducted in an ambiance of manifest joy, intimacy, and exhilaration. Everyone is allowed to speak, praise the Lord, give testimony, express opinions, and ask questions. The observer gets the impression of an integrated congregation, socially and religiously highly motivated, and democratically organized. This generalization is based on observation of the original congregation founded by the director in the city of Córdoba, but there is sufficient information to suggest the same evaluation of all fifteen congregations of the sect.

One of the most effective means of ostensibly conveying the essential canon of Cristianos, the director stated, is to engage in various forms of community service. The congregation occasionally sponsors cultural events, such as shows for children in the public squares of Córdoba and Fortin, and rents meeting halls for lectures on married life, family problems, and sexual orientation for the young. These events have as an underlying theme the objective of persuading people to accept Jesus in their hearts, which will perhaps lead them into the sect. This is soft-sell proselytism, which the director and several members of the congregation refused to acknowledge, sophistically alleging that conversion was a matter of conviction once people realize that Cristianos had the true path to salvation.

The hands-on activism of Cristianos also includes a social-work dimension wherein members organize visits to jails, hospitals, asylums, and orphanages. They extend spiritual help, but do not overtly engage in proselytism. More significantly, they offer material help, particularly to jail inmates and orphans, by bringing then food, toys, and occasionally giving them money. Social welfare activities also include inducing and helping jail and asylum inmates to engage in some kind of craft production; Cristianos sell the finished products and return the proceeds to the inmates. These activities are voluntary and part of Cristianos' commitment to help those in need.

The investigation of Cristianos in Córdoba-Fortin suggests that the congregation, as a social and religious group, may be likened to an extended kinship unit or a *compadrazgo* (ritual kinship) network (Nutini 1984). The intimacy of interaction, the reciprocity and exchange, and the consciousness of being an integrated group are more akin to folk kinship than to the organization of a religious congregation. It is rather baffling how, in a very short period of existence, the congregation has developed such successful mechanisms of group cohesion that go far beyond its primary religious raison d'être. Material, psychological, and spiritual help is always available to those in need merely for the asking. Despite the fact that the sect's founding is so recent, testimonials of the curative manifestation of the Holy Ghost abound. At least twenty informants declared that since conversion their lives have been bettered not only spiritually but interpersonally and bodily: their married lives have improved, they have been cured of physical illness, and in one case a nearly blind man recovered his sight.

This is in stark contrast with the ethos of the Catholic parish in the Córdoba-Orizaba region. The consensus among Cristianos is that practicing Catholics do believe in salvation through good works, but in such a general way as to be ineffectual to the here and now. Catholicism, they say, is a convenient, easy religion (*cómoda*) that allows its practitioners to reach the kingdom of heaven despite smoking, drinking, and doing other injurious things to their bodies and doing very little to ameliorate the well-being of fellow coreligionists. Self-serving, perhaps, but to a man, Cristianos maintain that by closely following the dictates of the Bible they contract an obligation with themselves to do good work and help those in need that redounds in personal salvation as well as betterment of the community.

Despite their low-key approach to proselytizing, Cristianos have become quite visible in the Córdoba-Orizaba region, and their reputation for uprightness and commitment to good works has provoked the envy and ire of parish priests and many Catholics. The priests fear the conversion effectiveness of Cristianos more than the Protestant evangelical sects, which for several decades have proselytized in the region with modest gains. This concern is based on the fact that a group of Catholic dissidents, independent of Protestant evangelism, has been able to achieve what the church has been promoting for more than a decade; namely, the remaking of the parish into a socially active congregation.

La Luz del Mundo

La Luz del Mundo (The Light of the World) is a native Mexican movement founded in Guadalajara, Jalisco, in 1936, which by the late 1940s had established congregations in many rural and urban areas of northern Mexico. During the following four decades La Luz del Mundo had established congregations throughout Mexico and had expanded to Guatemala, Nicaragua, and several other countries of Central and South America. The first congregation in the Córdoba-Orizaba region was founded in 1974, and the one in Fortin, the focus of this article, two years later. Today the sect has approximately ten congregations in the region, and another 40 or so in central Veracruz.

The founder of the sect was Arón Joaquín, who is referred to as "the Apostle." Today, the Apostle is his son, Samuel Joaquín, who succeeded him when Arón died twenty years ago. The pastor of the Fortin congregation said the position was neither elected nor nominated. He went on to say that God appointed the original Apostle, and his son after him, by divine design; the "signal" (read proof) for these divine appointments was that the teachings and work of Arón and Samuel had led to such an astonishing growth of the new faith that this could only be interpreted as divine intervention. Indeed, La Luz del Mundo faithful believe that the Apostle is a representative of Jesus Christ on earth. This is not the view held by the pastors of a Pentecostal and a Seventh Day Adventist congregation in Orizaba. They stated that Arón and Samuel were very able politicians and organizers who had managed to dominate the assembly that governs La Luz del Mundo.

Unlike Cristianos, this institution is well organized, like other Protestant evangelical sects, and has a hierarchical configuration. The see of the sect is in Guadalajara, where the Apostle resides. He has a bureaucratic staff that has grown in proportion to the expansion of the sect. The major territorial subdivision is the jurisdiction, normally composed of about 50 congregations under the leadership of an "evangelist pastor." He is assisted by "evangelist deacons," who supervise local congregations, function as co-ordinators of intercongregation affairs, and keep the evangelist pastor informed of what transpires locally. The leader of each congregation is titled "minister pastor," and "evangelist workers" and "missionaries" complete the local hierarchy. The evangelist workers assist the minister pastor, and the missionaries are involved with proselytizing. An assembly, consisting of all jurisdictional pastors, meets twice a year in Guadalajara. *De jure* it is La Luz del Mundo's administrative and theological body; *de facto* it is dominated and controlled by the Apostle. The assembly is a kind of large privy council with ultimate authority on organizational and doctrinal matters. Its function is to legislate changes in doctrine, formulate strategies in proselytizing activities, regulate aid to jurisdictions, and so on. La Luz del Mundo has a competently managed organizational structure, which accounts for its rapid expansion; what are not yet clear are its sources of income, without which it would not have achieved such spectacular success. Whatever the case, at the top the sect has the appearance of a moderate theocracy centered on the Apostle. At the congregational level, however, it has a democratic organization that approaches the egalitarianism of Cristianos. The attitude of congregants to the pastor is not subservient, interaction between pastor and deacons and the congregation at large is fluid, and a genuine spirit of community prevails. This egalitarian ambiance of conviviality and informality, as in the case of Cristianos and most Protestant evangelist congregations, appears to be one of the most significant attractions for disenchanted Catholics.

Membership of the local congregation, at least in Mexico, averages about 300, according to the pastor of the Fortin congregation, which with some 400 members is significantly larger than the norm. There is no definitive information on the total membership of La Luz del Mundo today. If the information about the assembly, the number of congregations per jurisdiction, and the average congregation membership is correct, the total membership of the sect is about 1,125,000 (75 multiplied by 50 and 300, with more than two-thirds in Mexico, the rest in other Latin American countries as specified above, and some in the United States along the Mexican border).

In Fortin, one of the most salient characteristics of La Luz del Mundo is the residential pattern of the congregation, in that the households of its members are located around the physical structure of the temple. The idea goes back to the founder of the sect, who realized that residential propinquity was a protection against the discrimination and antagonism that the sect initially experienced. The idea caught on, and today about half of all congregations follow this pattern. The Fortin temple was constructed on the outskirts of town, where there was room for urban expansion, and as the congregation grew, converts and their families acquired house sites near each other. This was made possible by the foresight of the original pastor of the congregation who, with sect funds, was able to buy several acres of land that ultimately became part of the city. This is a most satisfactory arrangement, probably unique among native and Protestant evangelical sects, and particularly well suited to the Fortin congregation, which consists almost entirely of urban, working-class people. Otherwise, it should be noted, La Luz del Mundo converts are both lower-class urbanites and peasants, and only recently have efforts been made to proselytize among middle-class people.

The pastor and many members of La Luz del Mundo gave reasons for conversion quite similar to those of Cristianos, and predictably engaged in the kind of justifications described above. Despite class differences, members of both sects verbalized disenchantment with Catholicism in strikingly similar terms; viz., the lack of social warmth, the absence of any feeling of community, priestly elitism, and lack of support. Even the post hoc rationalization that the main motivating factors for conversion are the truths emanating from the Bible and that Catholics worship false gods are similarly verbalized by members of La Luz del Mundo. Clearly, members of La Luz del Mundo and Cristianos share a similar ethos and a basic creed ultimately derived from Protestant evangelist sects. Thus, to avoid repetition, the creed and ethos of La Luz del Mundo are best established by comparison with those of Cristianos.

Both sects are Trinitarians, with a strong emphasis on Jesus Christ, a literal interpretation of the Bible, and a total opposition to iconolatry; and are Anabaptists, who practice baptism by total immersion, recognize only marriage as a sacrament, and believe that faith in Jesus does not ensure salvation if it is not accompanied by good works. They differ on the following points. On the one hand, the symbolic and curative power of the Holy Ghost is absent in La Luz del Mundo, and its rituals and ceremonials do not exhibit the charismatic fervor of Cristianos religious services. On the other, the cult of La Luz del Mundo is centered exclusively on Jesus Christ as the pivot of salvation, and there is a more focused ritual and ceremonial complex that gives the creed a basically practical makeup, in contrast with the essentially expressive orientation of Cristianos.

The differences in ethos may be summarized as follows. First, regarding good works. La Luz del Mundo congregants believe that their duty is to help their own, and unlike Cristianos do not engage in community service. Second, La Luz del Mundo proselytism is more systematic and aggressive than that of Cristianos, as its congregants engage in door-to-door propagation of the faith and buttress it with written material, like all Protestant Evangelical sects. Third, the self-help within the congregation is mostly material, and there is little of the social and psychological support that characterizes Cristianos; a member may solicit and get support for building a house, but there is no emphasis on mutual help concerning personal or family problems. Fourth, La Luz del Mundo, like traditional evangelical sects, is concerned primarily with demanding adherence to a moral-religious code; hence, there is nothing like the serious concern of Cristianos with the social well-being of individual congregants, or with doing good work outside of the congregation. Fifth, all hierarchical positions in La Luz del Mundo (from Apostle to local missionaries) are exclusively occupied by males, in stark contrast with the male-female egalitarian-ism that in all domains obtains among Cristianos. Moreover, La Luz del Mundo faithful are essentially fundamentalists; they do not accept homosexuality, are adamantly opposed to abortion, and do not permit divorce, none of which is part of the liberal social ethos of Cristianos.

Because of residential propinquity, in addition to the main Sunday meeting, La Luz del Mundo religious services take place every day at 5 a.m., 9 a.m., and 6 p.m., and they may draw 80 or 90 men, women, and children. Depending on their working schedules, men and women attend one of these meetings two or three times a week. They are informal prayer gatherings conducted by the pastor assistants (evangelist workers) or men or women specially designated by the pastor. The Lord is praised in chant-like fashion by the entire gathering, and any individual has the right to stand up and chant the glory of Jesus; the service concludes by someone reciting a passage of the Bible from memory. The only participation of women in positions of ritual or ceremonial leadership is confined to these daily meetings.

The Sunday meeting, on the other hand, is extremely well attended and may occasionally draw the entire congregation. Although not strict, the liturgy of the Sunday service (the equivalent of the Catholic mass, as the pastor puts it) is more structured than that of Cristianos. It is called *La Oración* (the supplication or entreaty), and is conducted either by the pastor or one of his assistants. It begins with the *Reconciliación*, a communal prayer of thanks to the Lord, with the attendants on their knees, followed by silent prayers that last for several minutes. Then the attendants stand and ask the officiant to praise the glory of the Lord, which he does like a litany, with the audience as a chorus. This is followed by reading of a chapter of the Bible, and ends with a psalm sung by all attendants. The service concludes with an elaborate prayer for the Apostle and his family and less elaborate ones for the various members of the hierarchy. This illustrates the somewhat theocratic nature of La Luz del Mundo, a feature not present in Seventh Day Adventism, which the former resembles the most in creed and overall organization; rather, La Luz del Mundo is closer to Mormonism in its conception of hierarchy and leadership.

Other religious gatherings that take place in the temple and attached meeting hall include Sunday school from noon to 2 p.m. for both children and adults, and Bible study groups in the late afternoon throughout the week. The Sunday school is conducted by one of the assistant pastors, whereas the study groups are organized by groups of congregants. There is a great deal of instruction on leading a good and healthy life according to La Luz del Mundo morality, consisting mostly of being close to God, abstaining from drinking and smoking, and being helpful to fellow congregants. An emphasis on education and personal and household hygiene complements the temple-centered activities of the congregation. Literacy is a main concern, and if new converts cannot read and write, they are immediately assigned someone to teach them. There is significant concern with personal appearance and with keeping one's house and its vicinity clean and tidy, and the pastor or his assistants do not hesitate to counsel or admonish congregants when they are remiss. As a congregation, La Luz del Mundo exhibits a pronounced concern to present a proper public image as a model for emulation.

Collectively, La Luz del Mundo exhibits a significant degree of economic integration. The Fortin congregation is largely self-sufficient because it is more affluent than most, but if the congregation undertakes a project beyond its resources, help may be sought from other congregations within the jurisdiction (for example, labor for improvements of the temple or the attached meeting hall). Economic help is available from the Apostle's headquarters when needed; in fact, most congregations receive a small yearly subsidy. Individually, on the other hand, the congregation is a veritable economic corporation. The concept of help (*ayuda*) is always nonreciprocal labor exchange or outward donations in kind or cash among congregants when the need arises. It is well institutionalized, and individuals know at all times when and what to provide. In this respect, like Cristianos, La Luz del Mundo congregation has much in common with a folk community. In a context such as this, all religious services are free, and individuals are encouraged to take advantage of them.

Proselytizing is direct and intensive. Those missionaries and evangelist workers who have received training in preaching venture through the region two or three times a week to spread the gospel of La Luz del Mundo. Traveling in pairs, they go from door to door and occasionally preach in public places, particularly in rural communities. This may be hazardous, particularly in isolated villages, where missionaries have frequently been insulted, occasionally injured, and told never to come back. Women never engage in proselytizing, not because of the danger involved but because the sect forbids it.

La Luz del Mundo has also elicited the animosity of local priests and many Catholics, albeit not as many as Cristianos. Having had a longer trajectory in the region, and being more like a Protestant evangelical congregation, the sect is viewed with less concern and is considered to be easier to deal with than Cristianos. Nonetheless, its members have occasionally been harassed, and one priest wisely noted that "La Luz del Mundo, as a well-organized sect in the Protestant mold and with significant economic means at its disposal, is potentially more dangerous to the church than the idealistic and disorganized Cristianos." Although not yet investigated, it seems that the social-psychological profile of La Luz del Mundo converts is not significantly different from Cristiano converts.

Conclusions

The main purpose of this article is to highlight the increasing saliency of native evangelism, modeled after traditional Protestant evangelism. There are good reasons to believe that sects similar to the Cristianos and La Luz del Mundo are proliferating throughout rural and urban Mexico. This certainly is the case in the central part of the State of Veracruz, the Tlaxcala-Pueblan Valley, the Sierra de Puebla, the State of Morelos, Mexico City, and several regions in the State of Mexico. The remainder of this article assesses the prospects for this new brand of evangelism to increase in importance and challenge the predominance of Catholicism in Mexico.

The success of native evangelism, to judge by the two examples presented here and the sects I have identified in the Tlaxcala-Pueblan Valley, suggests that it not only constitutes a threat to Catholic hegemony but is also developing into a formidable adversary of Protestant evangelism. Protestants give the appearance of accepting their more recent rivals, but there is an undercurrent of hostility, especially toward the Cristianos, who are envied because the sect has successfully managed to proselytize among middle-class people, with whom, at least in the Córdoba-Orizaba region, sects such as the Pentecostals and Seventh Day Adventists have had little success. Basically, native evangelists are perceived by Protestant evangelists as newcomers who do not embody the true spirit of the Bible. The pressure on Catholicism is bound to increase as evangelicals become more numerous and powerful. My tentative assessment is that evangelists will manage to unite when their number and influence reach a point when disaffection with the church erupts into violence, as has already happened in several parts of Mexico, most notably in Chiapas during the past decade.

The two native evangelical sects described here have a similar creed and doctrine but show differences in ethos, organization, and pragmatic orientation. Cristianos, with an almost nihilist emphasis on egalitarianism, lack of hierarchical organization, and a pronounced liberalism, appeals mostly to idealists with a fairly secure middle-class material existence, who reject Catholic rigidity in a search for a meaningful religious experience and a return to an idealized traditional community. This is in sharp contrast to the appeal exerted by La Luz del Mundo among the disadvantaged, who accept a hierarchical and fundamentalist sect that provides for their material improvement.

The contrast between these two sects is most apparent when the structure of the congregation is compared. With rather minimal organization and soft-spoken proselytism, Cristianos achieved very rapid success because of the nature of the group of Catholics to whom it appeals. But the idealistic ethos of Cristianos does not bode well for the aim of the sect to expand. For this to happen, good organization and aggressive proselyting are a *conditio sine qua non*. A good example is Christianity itself, which became an expanding world religion only after adopting Roman religious and political organization, without which it would have remained an obscure sect. La Luz del Mundo has grown steadily and continuously for the same reason; i.e., an effective hierarchical organization. It already is a serious competitor of sects like the Mormons and Jehovah's Witnesses, which have had a much longer presence in Mexico. Thus, I think that Cristianos will remain a regional or folk sect of limited significance. Unless it is willing to change its organization and engage in more aggressive proselytizing (an unlikely prospect), Cristianos will not generate the potential for much further growth. By contrast, La Luz del Mundo will become a major evangelist sect, buttressed by its appeals to a wider sector of the population. In the contest for the souls of Catholics, nationalistic considerations may become increasingly important when made-in-Mexico sects, such as La Luz del Mundo, assume greater appeal than imported evangelical varieties.

The most significant factor that this research has so far yielded is the consistently uniform reasons given by converts to native and Protestant sects for rejecting Catholicism. The dissatisfaction with several aspects of Catholicism is likely to increase, as evidenced by the success of Cristianos to convert middle-class people. This brings us to the church's reaction to the spectacular success of Protestant and native evangelism during the past generation.

The antagonism against Protestant and native evangelism in the Córdoba-Orizaba region and the Tlaxcala-Pueblan Valley has so far remained latent and covert. But the appearance of tranquility is not likely to persist for long, as evangelists of all persuasions have become more active and assertive. So far, evangelists have maintained a low profile, but this is bound to change when they realize that the government is serious about enforcing freedom of religious expression. When this comes to pass, in my opinion the church will take a much tougher stance. While parish priests have hitherto tended to characterize evangelical success as a passing fad that will vanish in time, diocesan authorities take a more realistic position, and for the past decade or so have tried to institute minor social and religious changes to make Catholicism more attractive. Particularly in the diocese of Tlaxcala, the bishop has encouraged establishing local prayer groups without clerical leadership, revitalizing organizations such as *Acción Católica* (Catholic Action) for community development, and instructing priests to be more concerned with the material needs of their parish. Whether these measures have resulted in diminishing conversion has yet to be determined, but they illustrate the great concern of the Mexican church leadership with native and Protestant evangelism.

This article aims to call attention to the growth of native evangelism in Mexico and elsewhere in Latin America where Protestant evangelism has been present for generations. Its success is due not so much to its employment of similar methods of proselytizing, but because native evangelism is symptomatic of a momentous transformation that is likely to change the religious landscape of the continent dramatically. From this perspective, addressing the following questions is imperative: 1) Can the Catholic Church make the necessary doctrinal and programmatic changes to counteract Protestant and native evangelism without resorting to an outright religious war? 2) What are the different social and economic variables that configure the process of conversion to evangelism? Or why has no form of Protestantism made significant inroads among the solid middle class and superordinate sectors of society? 3) What is the probability that in a generation or so Catholicism may lose its dominance in Latin America? Or will the spectacular growth of evangelism be tempered by high dropout rates, an effective Catholic reaction, or other social and economic factors? 4) How is conversion from Catholicism to Protestant and native evangelism related to the fast growth of secularization that the folk sector of most Latin American populations has been undergoing for more than a generation? 5) What is the breaking point in the precarious and unstable coexistence currently characterizing Protestant and native evangelism and Catholicism at which latent hostilities will turn into organized persecution?

Notes

1 The term sect, as understood in this article, is a body of people subscribing to religious doctrines and practices different from those of an established church, or major denomination of a church, from which they have separated.

2 This extreme egalitarian organization of the congregation worries those closely associated with the director; they rightly see it as an organizational impediment to their expectations that Cristianos will grow into a widespread evangelical movement.
3 Not surprisingly, almost identical responses were elicited from pastors and members of about two dozen Jehovah's Witness, Seventh Day Adventist, Pentecostal, and Mormon congregations in the region studied. What Protestant evangelist sects take from the Bible in formulating their basic creeds varies; what remains invariant is that all religious experience originates in this sacred text.
4 This and subsequent information come from a twenty-item questionnaire administered to 45 Cristianos in the cities of Córdoba and Fortin during the summer of 1999.
5 This opinion is based on fourteen cases of crisis conversion to Pentecostalism, Mormonism, and Seventh Day Adventism. The circumstances are similar to the Cristianos cases, but the actual choice of evangelist sect may have to do with the kind of proselytism to which a person in crisis was exposed.

Bibliography

Aubrey, A. 1974. Una iglesia sin parroquias. México, D.F.

Baldwin, D. J. 1990. Protestants and the Mexican Revolution: Missionaries, Ministers, and Social Change. Urbana.

Bastian. J. P. 1983. Protestantismo y sociedad en México. México, D.F.

—— 1986. Breve historia del Protestantismo en América Latina. México, D.F.

—— 1990. El impacto regional de las sociedades religiosas no Católicas en México. Cristianismo y Sociedad 28(105):57–74.

Bowen, K. 1996. Evangelism and Apostasy: The Evolution and Impact of Evangelicals in Modern Mexico. Montreal.

Bridges, J. C. 1973. Expansión evangélica en México.

Deiros, P. A. (ed.) 1986. Los evangélicos y el poider político en América Latina. Grand Rapids.

De los Reyes, A. 1990. Historia de las Asambleas de Dios en México: Los pioneros. México, D.F.

Díaz de la Serna, C. 1984. El movimiento de la renovación carismática como un proceso de socialización adulta. México, D.F.

Garrand-Burnett, V. 1992. Protestantism in Latin America. Latin America Research Review 27(1):218–40.

Gaxiola *et al.* 1984. Iglesia y grupos religiosos en México. México, D.F.

Juárez Cerdi, E. 1997. Mi reino sí es de este mundo. Michoacán.

López Cortés, E. 1990. Pentecostalismo y milenarismo: La iglesia apostólica de la fe en Cristo Jesús. México, D.F.

Martin, D. 1990. Tongues of Fire: The Explosion of Protestantism in Latin America. London.

Metz, A. 1994. Protestantism in Mexico: Contemporary Contextual Developments. Journal of Church and Estate 36(1):57–78.

Nutini, H. G. 1984. Ritual Kinship: Ideological and Structural Integration of the Compadrazgo System in Rural Tlaxcala. Princeton.

—— n.d. Changes in the Stratification System in the Córdoba-Orizaba Region; 1940–1995.

Nutini, H. G., and B. L. Isaac. 1974. Los pueblos de habla Nahuatl de la región de Tlaxcala y Puebla. México, D.F.

Penton, M. J. 1985. Apocalypse Delayed: The History of the Jehovah's Witnesses. Toronto.

Stoll, D. 1990. Is Latin America Turning Protestant? The Politics of Evangelical Growth. Berkeley.

Willems, E. 1967. Followers of the New Faith: Cultural Change and the Rise of Protestantism in Brazil and Chile. Nashville.

Zapata Novoa, J. 1990. El mercado de las conciencias: Sectas y cultos en Monterrey. Monterrey, México.

Part 19

CROSS-NATIONAL PENTECOSTALISM PAST AND PRESENT

76

'HEATHENDOM' AND THE POWERS OF DARKNESS

On the role of the Devil in the preaching of the missionaries of the Norddeutsche Missionsgesellschaft in the nineteenth century and the contemporary African churches

Birgit Meyer

Source: originally published in *Trinity Journal of Church and Theology*, 7(1/2) (1997), 15–27; revised by author, 2010.

Travelers to Ghana will hardly be able to overlook that in Accra the Devil is omnipresent. Popular high-life songs such as "You Devil Go Away from Me!" come out of the loudspeakers in workshops and petrol stations. One can also read that cry on many T-shirts and car stickers. On posters and banners churches declare "War against Satan" and call for prayer meetings where demons—especially witches—will be destroyed and where the Holy Spirit, healing, and riches will be received. There even exists a popular allegorical song about a football match between the team of Jesus and that of Satan, which is of course won by the former.

The obsession with the Devil is not new, but can be traced back to the nineteenth century, when mission societies as the *Norddeutsche Missionsgesellschaft* (NMG) were active in order to convert the "heathens" to God. In this context the missionaries talked a lot about the Devil, whom they represented in their sermons as the head of the traditional gods. In this essay I shall first deal with the role of the image of Satan in the preaching of the missionaries and its reception by the first converts. Then I shall show which role this image plays currently in the *Evangelical Presbyterian Church* (EPC) and two churches which seceded from it, *Agbelengor* and the EPC 'of Ghana'.[1]

The missionaries' image of Satan

> Yes, if the heathens were merely unknowing, weak and frail people, if they felt their poverty and misery and longed for salvation; however, among them the Devil has had his unlimited kingdom for such a long time that they have become his slaves and have sunk into bestial and demonic conditions. One has to break chains to free them, one has to overcome Satan's bulwarks to save them from the government of darkness and transfer them into the realm of God's dear son.
> (*Monatsblatt der NMG* [MB] 1854: 3)

This quotation stems from a sermon delivered by the Pietist pastor Mallet on 12 November 1854 (MB 1854: 3) in Bremen at the sending of two missionaries to the Ewe. It is not merely an ill-founded insult, but rather an important and meaningful statement. Like the missionaries of other mission societies, those of the NMG exported their image of Satan to Africa and this had a great impact on Ewe Christianity.

The Pietist worldview was based on the dualism of God and Satan. While enlightened theologians following in the footsteps of Balthazar Bekker and Friedrich Schleiermacher[2] fought this dualism, regarding belief in the existence of the Devil as an outmoded superstition, the nineteenth-century Pietists among whom the Awakening gained momentum stuck to Luther's image of Satan[3] as a real creature able to take possession of people; Luther therefore retained the practice of exorcism. The best popularization of his image of Satan certainly is *the* Song of the Reformation: 'A Mighty Fortress Is Our God' [German: *Ein feste Burg ist unser Gott*], a hymn which has, of course, also been translated into Ewe (*Mawu nye mɔ̃ sese na mi*).

The dualism of God and the Devil appears also in the lithograph of *The Broad and the Narrow Path*, which could be found on the walls of many nineteenth-century Pietist households, including those of the missionaries.[4] Moreover they were familiar with Blumhardt's 'Healing of Gottliebin Dittus' —an account of the exorcism of evil spirits in which Blumhardt expresses his conviction that popular religion in Württemberg was dominated by the Devil and that his power had to be broken. He reported that in the course of his work with Gottliebin he realized 'that everything that had hitherto been reckoned under the most ridiculous popular superstition, stepped over from the world of fairy tales into reality' (1978 [1850]: 58; original in German, my translation). By regarding magic and witchcraft as really existing occult powers which had to be fought actively, he clearly departed from the image of the Devil held in modern Protestant theology. Many theologians had difficulties with his diabology: liberal enlightened theologians because they regarded it as superstitious, and Pietists because Blumhardt devoted too much attention to the Devil.[5] Although in Pietist circles the existence of Satan was not denied, paradoxically it should rarely be mentioned. Among lay believers, however, Blumhardt's account was extremely popular. The missionaries certainly knew it, since Blumhardt held close contacts with the mission house in Basel, where the NMG missionaries were trained. Ideas of devilish powers of magic and witchcraft came from Germany to Africa, non-Christian power in Africa not being denounced as superstitions but regarded as really existing occult powers.

Among the Ewe the missionaries clearly diabolized the indigenous religion:

> The great Apostle Paul has said in 1 Corinthians 8,4: Hence we know that an idol is nothing in the world, or in a better translation: that there is no idol in the world. He does not mean by this that what the heathens worship as gods has no existence, since according to 1 Corinthians 10,20 he himself considered the gods of the heathens to be demonic realities. And in Ephesians 6,12 he talks about lords and authorities, about the rulers of this world, who reign in the darkness of this world, and about evil spirits under heaven. There is an authority of darkness, an influence of diabolical powers. It is most pronounced among those who worship idols and who are thus subject to the direct control of darkness. *These are the heathens surrounding us, separated from God, but all the more bound to the Devil.*
> (MB 1864: 157; my emphasis)

Also for the missionaries, Ewe gods (*trɔ̃wo*) and spirits thus were real entities which were regarded as agents of the Devil. Non-believers were called *abosamtɔwo* (belonging to the Devil). The missionaries regarded Satan and his agents as powerful and able to make use of their diabolical powers efficiently. These dark forces manifested themselves through the 'heathen religion' in general and the activities of traditional priests and priestesses in particular. In accordance with their missionary calling they had to fight against Satan and his vassals and destroy the old Ewe religion. In order to achieve this, street sermons were held.

The Devil scored highly in the range of preaching topics. One missionary wrote the following extract about a street sermon at the market place of Anloga, a 'centre of fetishism, and linked to fetishism by the Devil himself as it were':

> I started with the mission order, Matthew 28,10–20, and explained to the people that we had come to them because of this order and that we had left our beautiful country, as well as our father, mother and family in order to work among them for the King of heaven, and that there were just two things: either the eternal glory through Jesus Christ, or, for the one who scorned and despised Jesus, there was no other thing than eternal damnation. I begged them to become reconciled with God through Christ, I depicted death to them with all its horrors and explained that death would lose its horrors as soon as one believed in Christ. *Then I finished with an attack on*

> *the fetish, contrasting the power of the Devil with the power of Christ, thereby comparing them.*
>
> (MB 1854: 193; my emphasis)

Many Ewe converts took over this missionary representation. But rather than turning away definitely from the satanic forces as was wished by the missionaries, many Christians remained under its spell. They experienced the relationship between Christianity and 'traditional religion' as hegemonic: the old gods and spirits were integrated as Christian demons into the Christian universe of discourse. They could not abandon them.

The condition for becoming a member of the congregation, who in most cases lived at a distance from the 'heathens' in the Christian village (*Kpo̱dzi*), was knowledge about the basic elements of Christian faith, an acceptable way of life and dissociation from all pagan practices. Admission into the congregation implied material, ideal, social, and spatial separation from the other inhabitants. What made the Ewe convert to Christianity? Beside the attraction of the Christians' material properties and the qualifications achievable in the mission schools and usable in colonial institutions, the contents of the Christian religion were also a reason for conversion. Missionaries' sermons about the Devil and his equation with the ghosts and Gods known so far had an especially strong appeal. That this equation was of great importance for the first Ewe Christians can be demonstrated by a well-documented example.

In 1890 the missionary Däuble examined sixteen men and women in order to find out whether they were ready to be baptized. This examination had been preceded by baptismal lessons given by the native pastor Mallet. Däuble interrogated each candidate separately about the reason for conversion and finally admitted five men and six women.

> Most of them gave the following reason: *The devil, that is the fetishes, the evil spirits and fetish priests* had troubled, deceived and ruined them, had killed their children or siblings or had not rescued them from death as promised. They had made the required sacrifices, but in vain, they had not got the help asked for. That is why they now came to God, whom they had left, in order to find redemption, peace, happiness and life; they would not like to die in the worship of idols as well. In former times they had not known anything about God and also nothing about sin, but now God had sent his Word to them and changed their minds, he had opened the door for them so that they could be saved.
>
> (MB 1890: 31; my emphasis)

These answers reveal a dissatisfaction with the religion adhered to so far and with the sacrifices brought in vain. This religion was now associated with the Devil, *Abosam*, and rejected. The Christian God was opposed to the Devil in a dualistic way. Although this dichotomization was in line with the missionaries' teachings, the missionary had certain objections:

> Many of them are much more occupied and driven by *the fear of the devil* than by the anguish of conscience over their own sin, and in some cases it was difficult to make clear to them *that not only the devil would ruin them*, but that everyone would be lost because of his personal sin. Moreover, I told them *that they may not attribute misery and suffering to the devil and evil spirits only*. After all, they themselves called the fetish priests liars and deceivers, and that is what they indeed were. Hence the things they made them believe were lies as well. If for instance, they said that they had to make sacrifices because otherwise the devil would kill their child, this was a lie. If the child then would die, and they made them believe that the devil had killed it, this was a lie. But I would believe that God had taken their children away in order to convince them of the deceit of the fetish worship and to draw them to Himself.
>
> (MB 1890: 31; my emphasis)

Through this critique we can get a glimpse of how the Ewe themselves understood their Christian faith. To them it meant protection from a power hostile to life. They related Satan with evil and God with good and it seems that they did not know a punishing God or a feeling of internal sinfulness. Still in 1903 the NMG missionary Spieth complained[6] that beside the 'still not yet fully erased belief in the existence of gods . . . especially the heathen conception of evil often has a lasting effect' (1903: 11). The heathen concept of evil became manifest in the fact that the sinners withdrew from their personal responsibility by attributing their faults to the Devil. 'This heathen way to excuse oneself, in the case of the Christians, appears in the fact *that they foist everything on the devil*. A fall, for example, is preferably described as a *deception by the devil*' (1903: 11; my emphasis), Spieth remarked.

The Devil was the link between the Christian and the pre-Christian religion: as *Abosam* he represented all *trɔ̃wo* and as the Devil he was God's counterpart. He integrated the gods known so far into the Ewe's Christian worldview. Thereby the pre-Christian religion became meaningful in the light of Christianity. Moreover it became an integrated, though negatively defined and transformed, part of it. As the Devil played such a crucial role in the missionaries' worldview, it is not astonishing that he did even more so in the Ewe's and that through him the pre-Christian religion became a building block of their Christian interpretations. The baptismal candidates seem to have perfectly grasped the central dichotomy of the missionaries' worldview continuously communicated to them and applied it to their own situation. Nevertheless the missionary Däuble remained unsatisfied, because the candidates' self-image was still too positive and missed an awareness of sin. Whereas the Ewe held evil powers under *Abosam* to be the causes of misfortune and misery, the missionaries explained this in the last instance by means of the badness of human beings, which drove them towards the Devil or invoked God's anger and punishment. It was the aim of Däuble's examination to find out how far the Ewe realized this, and he found that this hardly was the case. The candidates were thus not converted satisfactorily, but still remained attached to the old religion.

Däuble's critique illustrates that he had difficulties in grasping how the candidates themselves understood their new religion. That their ideas differed was evident, but how the Ewe Christians married new and old ideas remained obscure for the missionaries. Everything points to the fact that the Devil *Abosam* had a central position in the Ewe's Christian ideas. By conceptualizing the pre-Christian religion as diabolical they rendered it negative, but it nevertheless became a basic ingredient of Ewe Christianity. Although the missionaries themselves had demonized the pre-Christian Ewe religion, Däuble's reaction shows that their understanding of *Abosam*, which he regarded as a product of 'heathen' backwardness, went too far for him. The fact that the Ewe took the Devil too seriously may have caused some missionaries not to emphasize or even to deny the existence of the previously demonized Gods and spirits.

That the problem of pagan survivals connected to Christianity through *Abosam* remained common becomes clear from other sources. The Ewe teacher Theodor Sedode, who seemed to deny the existence of lesser deities, critically referred to the following superstitious conceptualization:

> When I once asserted in the baptismal lesson that there are no idols, one grey man looked at me astoundedly and replied: 'Surely there are idols, but the God of the Christians is more powerful than all of them.' *Likewise, the existence of sorcery, sorcery power, witches and all sorts of evil spirits is firmly believed in, which limits the Christian faith very much and makes superstition persist.* The best console themselves with the words: God is more powerful, and since I belong to God they cannot harm me.
>
> (Baeta and Sedode 1911: 16; my emphasis)

However, the continued belief in the existence of these entities was not all. To the dismay of the missionaries it happened relatively often that Christians 'backslid into heathendom,' because they sought refuge from old family gods and approved magical means—for a long time missionary medicine was in no way superior to traditional cures. For many Ewe Christians it was difficult to rely in case of sickness solely on the power of prayer; for exorcism in the footsteps of Blumhardt did not exist in the Ewe church. Since the Devil remained alive in the image of the old gods and spirits, Ewe Christians had something to fall back on in cases of crisis. They were confronted with the dilemma that the old gods were satanic yet much easier to reach through sacrifices and other rituals than the Christian God. Compared to Ewe religion the anti-ritualistic Pietism of the missionaries was not very practically oriented, and this has remained a problem until today.

I think that the obsession with demons above all stems from the fact that actual societal developments and the aspirations of the converts were out of tune. Although they wanted to leave behind traditional society (an aim which they in fact realized at least partially by moving to *Kpodzi*), they still were related to their 'heathen' family and traditional authorities economically, socially, and politically. Through the image of the Devil they had at their disposal a discourse through which they could reflect upon the negative aspects of traditional society. At the same time they could express their desire to return to it—after all, Christianity often was unable to solve existential problems. Through the image of the Devil they were able to approach the forbidden from a safe distance.

Current Ewe Christians' image of the Devil

In the EPC the absence of healing rituals remained a problem. In case of sickness many Christians could not help but consult traditional priests. Many adopted a stance described as *Mawu vide, dzo vide*—a little bit of God and a little bit of magic. Since church members did not want to return to the 'old' religion officially because they considered themselves 'civilized,' most of them visited the priests in secret. A tension existed between the experience of the power of the traditional gods and the inability or unwillingness of the Christian God to bring about health and wealth. It is exactly this tension which the Independent African Churches try to overcome: They strive to develop adequate means to overcome suffering and mishap in the framework of Christianity.

This striving formed the background of two secessions which occurred in the EPC: those of *Agbelengor* and the EPC 'of Ghana.' *Agbelengor* was originally a so-called *prayer group* within the EPC, and it emphasizes much more than the EPC the existence of both evil spirits and the Holy Spirit. In this group people were delivered from demons, family gods who wanted to possess them, or witchcraft.[7] Exorcism occurred by the laying on of hands in the name of the Holy Spirit. Since the EPC authorities then—in 1960—had severe problems with these practices the group seceded and founded a church of its own: *The Lord's Church*, or *Agbelengor*.

Today this church has spread all over the Volta Region and even to Accra. In the meantime, it came to regard itself as a Pentecostal church and therefore calls itself *The Lord's Pentecostal Church*. In the sermons there is much talk about the Devil and his demons. The religion of the ancestors is represented as *Devil-worship*. But whereas they could not have been conscious of the fact, all those who were born after the arrival of the first missionaries should know better. Under no condition should a Christian participate in family rituals in the course of which libation is poured to the ancestors and family gods are prayed to. Pouring libation—a practice which many EPC members regard as relatively harmless—may bring a person into the sphere of influence of Satan and harm him or her. This may even happen without a person being aware of the fact: a spirit may have taken possession of a person for a long time before it manifests itself through dreams or illness. This is preached in many Pentecostalist churches. Some even have a questionnaire through which all contacts which a person has with such powers are registered.

These churches propagate a very strict attitude towards 'traditional religion.' Far from regarding it as a complex of more or less harmless popular customs, they take them extremely seriously: old forces are even active if one is not aware of the fact. This emphasis on the danger imbued in traditional religion and on its continued influence on the unconscious is a characteristic feature of the Pentecostal churches. In contrast to mission churches such as the EPC, they claim that conversion to Christianity does not entail a linear transition of the boundary between 'heathendom' and Christianity; rather, this boundary has to be the place where the last fight between God and the Devil is to be fought. For this reason they are continuously occupied with the religion which they seek to leave behind.

But it does not remain at talking alone. Like many other Pentecostal churches this church has a *healing station* at Tokokoe near Ho, close to the Togo border. When I visited this station I was surprised to find out how many persons possessed by old gods and spirits were assembled there. While the congregation sang anti-satanist songs, row by row the afflicted were called to the front, where a preacher laid hands on them. If a person remained calm, this was regarded as a sign that the Holy Spirit did not meet any resistance when he entered the person. If, however, a person began to move, this was interpreted as a sign of demonic possession. The preacher would then shout: 'Come out! What's your name? *Do Go* [come out]! *Nko wo de* [what's your name?]?' until the spirit manifested itself through particular movement patterns.

Interestingly, it is possible to infer the identity of a spirit from the movements of a possessed person, because they are the same as those which the traditional priestesses perform during the trance-dances. We are thus confronted with a mirror image of 'traditional religion.' Once it is known which spirit has taken possession of a person, the person is separated from it symbolically: He or she is individualized. People say that the Devil works above all through blood ties while the Holy Spirit breaks them, for God individualizes. In this church I talked, for instance, to a young woman who was visited in her dreams by *Wuve*—the Peki state god who manifests itself as a man dressed in a black gown wearing a knife in his hand—who asked her to become his priestess. One of the spirits she wanted to be liberated from was this god. She wanted to live in Accra alone and have nothing to do with her 'heathen' family any longer.

Not only Satan himself, but all his specific appearances are taken seriously in this church and it tries to free people from the powers of darkness. How far this is successful, of course, begs the question. Often people keep returning with the same problem, explained by preachers as being because, once delivered, the person continued to live in the old context. A person who stays in the family house after deliverance from a family god—and often there is no other choice for financial and social reasons—according to the preachers is again exposed to the satanic influence and, once the zeal of prayer ceases, can easily be recaptured by these powers.

I talked to many members of this church about the reasons why they had become members. Especially, many elderly people had formerly been EPC members. They claimed that when they fell sick they could not find help in the EPC, whose authorities did not take demons particularly seriously. Many people told me that they had realized that their problems had been caused by witchcraft and other forces without them being aware of it. Since prayer and modern medicine failed to work, they had sought refuge in a Pentecostal church. They said that only in the new church had they experienced the power of prayer and that they regarded the EPC as powerless because the Holy Spirit was not called upon: 'There they don't know how to pray.'

Thus, here the old gods are regarded as really existing entities, while they are denounced as horrible at the same time. Here 'traditional religion' is identical with the realm of Satan. Therefore in these circles there is little appreciation for the reform attempts of the former Moderator of the EPC, Professor N. K. Dzobo, to Africanize Christianity.[8] In the view of the Pentecostalists, the Devil himself is brought into the church by appreciating and integrating traditional elements. Basically they thus reproduce the ideas of the missionaries which I sketched in the beginning.

Therefore it is no great surprise that the conflict between the *Bible Study and Prayer Fellowship* (BSPF), a Pentecostalist prayer group laying much emphasis on the Holy Spirit, and Professor Dzobo resulted in the foundation of the EPC 'of Ghana.' In this secession other matters played a role as well, but the image of the Devil certainly stood central in this conflict (see Meyer 1992). The BSPF countered Dzobo's Africanization by the Pentecostalization of the church. It is clear that these dissidents were much more educated than the members of *Agbelengor* who split away thirty years earlier. Nowadays the elite need not be ashamed of laying emphasis on the Holy Spirit, and the new dissidents are sufficiently self-assured to claim the name of the church, and thereby the missionary heritage. And it certainly is the case that they stand much closer to Blumhardt's practice of exorcism than many current missiologists and African theologians who focus on developmental aid and for whom the belief in the existence of the Devil is an outmoded superstition.

Clearly a historical line leads from Württemberg Pietism to the Pentecostal movement (see Lange 1979; Ruhbach 1989).

Also in the EPC 'of Ghana' there is continuously talk about the Devil and his agents. Here, too, traditional religion is totally diabolized. It is stressed that it is impossible to drive away Satan with Beelzebub, true deliverance from evil being possible only through the Holy Spirit. *Mawu vide, dzo vide* is regarded as a stance which can only lead into misery. The church is thus involved in a total war with Satan and his agents. It is considered wrong to keep silent about the realm of darkness, as happens in the EPC, for on the contrary, as one catechist of the EPC 'of Ghana' in Peki, trained in the EPC seminary in Peki, told me: 'When the knowledge of Jesus increases, then the knowledge of demons also increases.' This message is also communicated in the sermons and services. Especially in the services which take place before the *Deliverance-ritual*, people who have been liberated from evil spirits give testimony. Often they describe vividly their own experiences in the realm of darkness. Among other things, they recount that not only the old gods and spirits, but also new ones are the agents of Satan. They tell about the realm at the bottom of the ocean which is inhabited by mermaids—*Mami Water*—and from there luxury goods are spread over the earth whose owners become servants of the Devil, that is, people walking on the broad path of the world and succumbing to worldly temptations. Also there would be people who sacrifice a beloved family member in exchange for wealth, the theme of the Devil contract (see Meyer 1995b). Thus, there are all sorts of collective fantasies pertaining to the realm of Satan and his grip on the world. This sort of horror story is above all popular among the young members of the EPC 'of Ghana.'

The 'EPC of Ghana,' too, practices exorcism in the way described above. I have attended a great number of *Deliverance-meetings*, in whose course old gods and spirits such as witchcraft, but also new ones such as *Mami Water* were exorcised. However, Deliverance is not always successful. In Peki I got acquainted with a then seventeen-year-old girl who had formerly been a member of the EPC. In the night and in daydreams the spirit of her murdered uncle, a so-called *ametsiava*-spirit appeared to her.[9] She tried to be liberated from this spirit, because she preferred to finish secondary school rather than serve this spirit, but since neither *Agbelengor* nor the EPC 'of Ghana'—not to speak of the EPC—was able to achieve this, she eventually let herself be initiated as a priestess.

Most members of the EPC 'of Ghana,' of course, once belonged to the old EPC. Responding to my question why they had left the old church, they replied that only here had they understood the Bible and the power of the Holy Spirit. Moreover, they found that the church leaders would deal too easily with the old gods and spirits, because they did not want to deal with them, talking at best about Satan, but never about particular spirits. Of course also a number of pastors converted, for instance a pastor who had a conflict with the EPC authorities prior to the split because he had informed members of the congregation about his experiences with a witch, who had appeared to him and his wife in the night. The church order denounces the belief in the existence of these powers as unimportant. This pastor, however, regarded witches as important agents of Satan and did not wish to keep silent about their evil deeds but to fight them actively. Now he serves the EPC 'of Ghana.'

This example shows that already before the split belief in the existence of Satan and demons existed in the EPC. But this is still the case after the split, also among pastors. Dzobo's new theology was and is acceptable only for a small minority. The difference between the two churches is that in the old EPC there is no explicit talk about particular evil spirits and no institutionalized practice of exorcism. Although many EPC pastors do not deny the existence of Satan and associate him with 'traditional religion,' they think that the Devil does not deserve too much attention. They regard conversion to Christianity as a definitive turn away from diabolical powers which need not be repeated again and again. For many church members this is acceptable as long as they are well. However, if they fall into a crisis from which they cannot be liberated with the usual remedies, many of them eventually seek refuge in churches which exorcise in the name of the Holy Spirit.

I attribute the increasing obsession with demonic powers to the fact that many people are not able to separate themselves fully from so-called 'heathendom.' On the one hand, they indeed want to be modern Christians, that is, individualist and independent from their families; on the other hand actually they are very much linked to their families, especially in a difficult economic situation. Notions such as possession by a family god or witchcraft —also a power operating through blood ties—reflect this alliance. The Pentecostalist churches do indeed offer exorcism rituals through which people are liberated from these powers—they are, as stated above, individualized —yet this is a symbolic act which expresses the dependency on powers representing the family as much as the deliverance from them. While demonizing these powers, all powers associated with striving for wealth are represented as satanic. People who were shocked by their asocial egoistic striving and now seek a new morality also want to be delivered from these powers, without being able to dissociate themselves fully from the former.

Thus, the image of the Devil is a vehicle for the representation of what one wishes to leave behind without being fully able to do so. We may conclude that the Pentecostalist churches fully brought into practice Blumhardt's theology and ritual practice, which the missionaries failed to implement totally because they were reluctant to introduce the practice of exorcism. The mission church, by contrast, focused and still focuses above all on the final turn away from the Devil and refuses to talk about him too much. Here again we confront the paradoxical nineteenth-century Pietist concept of the Devil, which ascribes him a central place on the one hand, and tabooizes him as a topic of conversation on the other. While the Pentecostalist churches, just like Blumhardt, tend towards the first option, the EPC—while not denying the Devil's existence, tends towards the second.

Notes

1 First presented to the Theological Commission of the Evangelical Presbyterian Church on October 7, 1996, this summarizes my dissertation (Meyer 1995a), based on research in the archives of the NMG (Stab 7, 1025) and fifteen months fieldwork among the Ewe in Peki between 1988 and 1992, made possible through the assistance of the *Amsterdam School for Social Science Research*, the *Netherlands Foundation for the Advancement of Tropical Research* (WOTRO), the *Norddeutsche Mission*, the *E.P. Church*, and the inhabitants of Peki.

2 See Bekker's famous book *De betoverde weereld*, in which he denounced the belief in the existence of the Devil as a superstition (Bekker 1691), and Schleiermacher's *Der christliche Glaube* (1861 [1830]): 'the representation of the devil, as it developed among us, is so unviable one can expect nobody to be convinced of its truth' (1861: 209; my translation). As he considered the biblical texts dealing with the Devil and demons culturally determined, Satan and evil spirits being not demonic realities but images personifying the abstract force of evil, he believed Christianity should go beyond the dualist conception of God and the Devil, which attributed too much power to the latter, and concentrate on God and Jesus. Schleiermacher's position, that of modern Protestant theologians, demythologizes the Devil and demons and speaks about evil not in terms of a person (*der* Böse), but as an abstract force (*das* Böse) (Tavard 1981: 298ff.).

3 On Luther's image of Satan, see, for example, Brückner and Alsheimer (1974), Selge (1993).

4 For the meaning this image had for nineteenth-century Pietists, see Scharfe (1980, 1990).

5 On the debates about the deliverance of Gottliebin, see Schulz (1984).

6 Besides Westermann, also Spieth wrote ethnographic studies about the Ewe. With his books *Die Ewe-Stämme* (1906) and *Die Religion der Eweer in Süd-Togo* (1911) he became known outside mission circles.

7 Ewe connect witchcraft (*adze*) and jealousy. Many rich people fear being bewitched by a poorer envious family member. Such fear reflects an ethic focusing on the distribution of money and riches among members of the paternal extended family and condemning individual accumulation of wealth. Witchcraft accusations therefore indicate blockages in the family circulation of money and riches.

8 Dzobo's *Meleagbe* ("I am alive") theology strives to integrate the positive life-affirming aspects of "traditional religion" into Christianity. These religions are not mutually exclusive, but can rather be synthesized. See Dzobo (1988a, 1988b, 1992, n.d.).

9 An *ametsiava* is a person who died a violent death and manifests himself or herself as a spirit who wants to be worshipped by the living family members.

References

Baeta, Robert and Theodor Sedode (1911) *Reste heidnischer Anschauungen in den Christengemeinden Togos. Zwei Aufsätze von Lehrern der Norddeutschen Mission*, Bremen: Verlag der Norddeutschen Missionsgesellschaft.

Bekker, Balthasar (1691) *De betoverde weereld. Synde een grondig Onderzoek van 't gemeen Gevoelen aangaande de GEESTEN, deselver Aart en Vermogen, Bewind en Bedrijf: als ook 't gene de Menschen door derselver Kragt en Gemeenschap doen*, Amsterdam: Daniel van den Dalen.

Blumhardt, Johann Christoph (1978) *Die Krankheitsgeschichte der Gottliebin Dittus. Herausgegeben und eingeleitet von Gerhard Schäfer*, Mit einer Interpretation der Krankenheilung von Theodor Bovet, Göttingen: Vandenhoek & Ruprecht.

Brückner, Wolfgang and Rainer Alsheimer (1974) "Das Wirken des Teufels. Theologie und Sage im 16. Jahrhundert," in W. Brückner (eds.), *Volkserzählung und Reformation. Ein Handbuch zur Tradierung von Erzählstoffen und Erzählliteratur im Protestantismus*, Berlin: Erich Schmidt Verlag, pp. 394–418.

Dzobo, Noah K. (1988a) "Life: Central Ideas as Found in Biblical and Indigenous African Traditions," paper presented at the Second Theological Consultation, Bremen.

—— (1988b) "The Gospel and African Culture: Contemporary Issues Related to . . . ," paper presented at The Consultation on the Gospel and African Culture, Gaborone, Botswana, April 25–30, 1988.

—— (1992) "The Gospel and the Life Affirming Religious Culture of the Third World of Africa," paper presented at the International Consultation on Bilateral Dialogue, Princeton Theological Seminary, April 21–25, 1992.

—— (n.d.) "Introduction to Meleagbe Theology," unpublished manuscript.

Lange, Dieter (1979) *Eine Bewegung bricht sich Bahn. Die deutschen Gemeinschaften im ausgehenden 19. und beginnenden 20. Jahrhundert und ihre Stellung zu Kirche, Theologie und Pfingstbewegung*, Giessen: Brunnen Verlag; Dillenburg: Gnadenauer Verlag.

Meyer, Birgit (1992) "'If You Are a Devil You Are a Witch and, If You Are a Witch You Are a Devil.' The Integration of 'Pagan' Ideas into the Conceptual Universe of Ewe Christians in Southeastern Ghana," *Journal of Religion in Africa* 22(2): 98–132.

—— (1995a) *Translating the Devil. An African Appropriation of Pietist Protestantism. The Case of the Peki Ewe in Southeastern Ghana, 1847–1992*, Amsterdam: Universiteit van Amsterdam, Dissertation.

—— (1995b) "'Delivered from the Powers of Darkness.' Confessions about Satanic Riches in Christian Ghana," *Africa* 65(2): 236–55.

Ruhbach, Gerhard (1989) "Der Erweckung von 1905 und die Anfänge der Pfingstbewegung," *Pietismus und Neuzeit. Ein Jahrbuch zur Geschichte des neueren Protestantismus*, vol. 15: *Der Gemeinschaftsbewegung*, Göttingen: Vandenhoek & Ruprecht, pp. 84–94.

Scharfe, Martin (1980) *Die Religion des Volkes. Kleine Kultur- und Sozialgeschichte des Pietismus*, Gütersloh: Gütersloher Verlag.

—— (1990) "Zwei-Wege-Bilder. Volkskundliche Aspekte evangelischer Bilderfrömmigkeit," *Blätter für württembergische Kirchengeschichte* 90: 123–44.

Schleiermacher, Friedrich (1861) *Der christliche Glaube nach den Grundsätzen der evangelischen Kirche*, 5th ed., vol. 1, Berlin: Georg Reimer.

Schulz, Michael T. (1984) *Johann Christoph Blumhardt. Leben-Theologie-Verkündigung*, Göttingen: Vandenhoek & Ruprecht.

Selge, Kurt Victor (1993) "Luther und die Macht des Bösen," in C. Colpe and W. Schmidt-Biggemann (eds.) *Das Böse. Eine historische Phänomenologie des Unerklärlichen*, Frankfurt am Main: Suhrkamp, pp. 165–86.
Spieth, Jacob (1903) *Das Sühnebedürfnis der Heiden im Ewelande*, Bremen: Verlag der Norddeutschen Missionsgesellschaft.
Tavard, Georges (1981) "Dämonen. Kirchengeschichtlich," in G. Krause and G. Müller (eds.) *Theologische Realenzyklopedie*, vol. 7, Berlin and New York: Walter de Gruyter, pp. 286–300.

77

THE TRANSNATIONALISATION OF BRAZILIAN PENTECOSTALISM

The Universal Church of the Kingdom of God

Paul Freston

Source: A. Corten and R. Marshall-Frantani (eds), *Between Babel and Pentecost: Transnational Pentecostalism in Africa and Latin America*, London: Hurst & Co., 2001, pp. 196–215.

The process by which the Universal Church of the Kingdom of God (UCKG or UC) has expanded to over fifty countries is an important example of a key religious change of the late twentieth century: the transformation of Pentecostalism into a global religion and the shift in its centre (of numerical growth and missionary initiative) to the Third World.[1]

The globalisation of Pentecostalism

The study of Pentecostalism helps overcome the parochialism of certain perspectives on religion in an era of globalisation. We must take into account what has actually happened to Christianity in recent decades: recession in Europe and stagnation in the US, countered by the expansion of Protestantism in Latin America and of many forms of Christianity in Africa and the Far East. But Beyer's *Religion and Globalization*,[2] for example, has nothing on this Christian (largely Pentecostal) growth in the Third World. Even globalisation theorists who discuss religion, such as Robertson[3] and Waters,[4] have nothing on it. The constitution of a global Pentecostalism[5] is often ignored by academia because it has occurred independently of religious initiatives from the developed West.

This global Pentecostalism is culturally polycentric.[6] The history of Christianity is of serial expansion, in contrast to Islam's progressive expansion.[7] Whereas the latter spreads from a constant heartland, Christianity suffers periodic shifts in its demographic and geographical centre. Advances beyond its periphery are accompanied by decline in the old heartlands. The result is constant interaction with new cultures. In 1900, more than 80 per cent of professing Christians lived in Europe or North America; currently, about 60 per cent live in Africa, Asia, Latin America or the Pacifier.[8]

According to Waters, a globalised world would have a single society and culture, probably not harmoniously integrated, and with high multi-centricity.[9] Pentecostalism's foundation document, the Biblical narrative regarding the descent of the Holy Spirit on the day of Pentecost, in which each person in the cosmopolitan crowd heard 'the wonders of God in their own tongue', is the basis for its current polycentric globalisation. In fact, without much numerical impact, Pentecostalism set out from Los Angeles in 1906 and quickly reached the four corners of the earth through missionary and immigrant networks which intersected with the starting-points in American popular Protestantism. Born amongst the poor, blacks and women, on the underside of American society, Pentecostalism was exported at virtually no cost, often by non-Americans. It is this popular, counter-establishment Western Christianity which has become one of the most globalised religious phenomena. After considerable growth in recent decades, usually autonomously, in Latin America, Africa and East Asia, this Third World Pentecostalism now expands to other countries of the same continents and to the First World. In line with globalisation theories regarding the complexity of global cultural flows,[10] globalised Pentecostalism is characterised by 'a multisource diffusion of parallel developments'.[11] The British diaspora and Anglo-Saxon missions responsible for much worldwide expansion of Protestantism since the eighteenth century have now been overtaken by other diasporas (African, Caribbean, Latin-American, Chinese and Korean) and by other missions.

While many religions are becoming globalised, the scale of Pentecostalism is different. Pentecostal expansion often follows diasporas (Africans in Europe; Latinos in the US). Frequently, diaspora churches serve a broader clientele than at home, following categories imposed by the receiving society: Africans in general join Nigerian churches in England; Hispanics in general join Puerto Rican churches in the US.

There is also a missionary effort transcending diasporas. Little is known about the missionary movement of the new mass Third World Protestantism. While it can reflect tendencies in secular labour markets (cheap labour for Western-controlled missionary enterprises), it is mostly better studied as an autonomous Third World social movement. In 1993 the World Evangelical Fellowship estimated 40,000 Protestant missionaries from Third World countries, compared with 88,000 from the traditional missionary-sending centres. Soon the former may be the majority.

Latin America accounts for much of this. Pentecostal churches expand within Latin America and among US Hispanics. Brazilian missions, with a long tradition among the historical churches, are now mainly Pentecostal. A 1994 Protestant publication talked of 800 Brazilian missionaries abroad. In 1997 a newsmagazine spoke of 1,700.[12] The Assemblies of God, God is Love and the Christian Congregation are at the forefront. But the Brazilian church with the greatest foreign presence is the Universal Church of the Kingdom of God. We shall look at the UCKG's expansion in general, before concentrating on two case-studies: Portugal and England.

The global expansion of the UCKG

The Igreja Universal do Reino de Deus was founded in 1977 in a poor suburb of Rio de Janeiro by Edir Macedo, a former state lottery employee. I have examined the characteristics of this church elsewhere;[13] here, I mention only aspects relevant for understanding its global expansion.

Brazil has the second largest community of practising Protestants in the world, and the largest community of Pentecostals. So it is no surprise that the UCKG has expanded abroad; what surprises is the speed and extent of this expansion. The missionary vision is typical of many Brazilian churches, but the capacity to make this vision a reality has to do with a unique combination of elements. According to a survey in Rio,[14] the social composition of the UCKG is lower even than that of most Pentecostal churches. While 45% of the population earn under two minimum salaries, and 58% of Protestants, the UCKG rate is 63%. Only 21% of the population has four years or less of schooling, versus 39% of Protestants and 50% of UCKG members. Whites are 60% of the population, 49% of Protestants and only 40% in the UCKG. This grassroots base is linked with institutional power due to hierarchical organisation, political strength (seventeen members of Congress), financial wealth and media empire (daily newspaper, thirty radio stations and the third largest television network).

While seeing itself as heir to the Evangelical tradition, the UCKG also has links with traditional Brazilian religiosity. In the phrase of one leader, 'We do not follow a European or American Evangelical tradition; we start from the religious practice of the people'. As a result, in the opinion of the president of the Brazilian Evangelical Association, the UCKG is a new syncretic religion which mixes 'Evangelical teachings, precepts of the medieval Catholic Church and Afro-Amerindian elements'.[15] But it is also (thanks to constant methodological innovation facilitated by centralised control) a bricolage of practices from diverse sources, well adapted to times of globalisation.

One opinion poll found the UCKG had the lowest approval rating of the principal Brazilian institutions: only 17%, even lower than Congress.[16] Among Protestants, however, it is not so rejected. Another survey showed 32% of Pentecostals in São Paulo (versus 8% of the general population) saw positive aspects in the UCKG.[17] Even so, its image is worse than that of other denominations.[18] This negative image follows the UCKG abroad. However, the situation in each country has to be explained not by the church's image in Brazil but by the way this information is used by local protagonists with their own agendas.

The UCKG invests heavily in foreign expansion. In 1995, twelve of the twenty-two members of its World Episcopal Council were located abroad. Since it had 2,100 churches in Brazil and only 225 elsewhere, the bishops abroad looked after a much lower number of churches. Another indication is the care taken when starting work in new countries. A commission investigates the probabilities of success, studies relevant laws, devises the legal constitution of the church, evaluates the most appropriate discourse and the best locations for churches, besides carrying out rental or purchase of buildings.[19]

From data in UCKG publications and the secular media, I present a reconstruction of its worldwide expansion. Founded in 1977, the UCKG crossed Brazil's frontiers in 1985 when it opened in Paraguay.[20] Expansion was slow until 1990, reaching only the US, Argentina and Portugal. Perhaps unfruitful beginnings in the US, plus investment in the purchase of Brazil's TV Record network in 1989, limited foreign expansion in the 1980s. But in the 1990s the rhythm increased. By 1993, it is said to have reached various countries of Latin America (Colombia, Venezuela, Uruguay, Chile, Mexico, Puerto Rico, Honduras, Guatemala, Panama), Africa (South Africa, Angola, Mozambique, Botswana, Cape Verde, Guinea-Bissau) and Europe (France, Spain, Holland, Italy). By 1995, it is reported to have spread further: to the Dominican Republic, Nicaragua and El Salvador; Nigeria, Kenya, Malawi and Congo; England and Luxembourg; Japan and the Philippines.[21] Leaflets issued by the UCKG-England claim even quicker recent expansion: a late 1995 version talks of over forty countries; the mid-1997 version mentions over seventy countries. On the other hand, a TV Record documentary broadcast in October 1997 lists only forty-five countries, of which fourteen are in Latin America, thirteen in Africa, eleven in Europe, four in Asia and three in North America and the Anglophone Caribbean.[22] From subsequent church publications, it seems that by late 1998 the UCKG was present in at least fifty-two countries outside Brazil.[23]

In 1995 the number of churches abroad was estimated at 221, distributed as follows: Portugal fifty-two, Argentina twenty-two, US seventeen, South Africa seventeen, Mexico eleven, Paraguay nine Colombia seven, Mozambique seven, Philippines seven, Canada seven, other countries five or fewer. The continental totals were: Latin America seventy-five, Europe sixty-three, Africa fifty-two, North America twenty-four, Asia seven.[24] Later sources (especially the *Folha Universal*) suggest that by late 1998 there were at least 500 churches. The continental percentages may not have changed greatly.

Three cultural blocs account for over 90% of UCKG churches abroad: the Latin American bloc, including Hispanics in the US; the Portuguese-speaking bloc; and the African bloc. Some remaining countries may also fall into these categories. The Swiss churches were started by Portuguese immigrants.[25] The French work began with Portuguese, and seems to have continued amongst blacks.[26] In Holland, it started amongst Portuguese-speaking immigrants, mainly from Cape Verde. The services in Dutch added subsequently seem to attract largely immigrants from Surinam.[27] The Japanese work seems to be amongst the Nippo-Brazilian immigrants. Thus, the Lusophone, Latin American and African worlds, with which the Brazilian homeland of the UCKG has cultural or linguistic links, provide the vast majority of the worldwide membership.[28] The non-Iberian white world, Asia and the politically inaccessible Middle East remain a challenge.

This does not mean the UCKG is incapable of the cultural adaptation (or, in Eastern Europe and Asia, the political negotiations) necessary for such challenges. In February 1997 the first church in Russia opened. In June it started daily services in Moscow's Progress Theatre.[29] Although the theatre rental was later rescinded by the city council, the church acquired its own headquarters and a daily radio programme. Faced with restrictive new laws for religious organisations, the UCKG joined with eight other churches to form the Russian Alliance of Pentecostal Evangelical Faith, which in March 1998 achieved full government recognition. Thus, the incipient UCKG could function on a par with Russian groups established since the early years of the century. In achieving the support of such groups the church's financial capacity and international presence were key: the UCKG took the president of the Alliance to observe its work in Portugal.[30] If it gets round restrictions on religious pluralism, the church may find greater space in Eastern Europe than in Asia or among the majority populations of the developed West. But the only other Eastern European country attempted thus far is Romania,[31] whose Latin-based language makes communication easier for Brazilian pastors.

The trajectory in the US confirms difficulties in crossing cultural frontiers. In 1986 an American pastor handed over a church in Manhattan to Edir Macedo and acted as his sponsor with the American authorities.[32] The following year, the UC began a cable TV programme. Today, it has over twenty churches, including a theatre in Los Angeles, a newspaper with a circulation of 100,000 and a television production studio.[33] But this story hides a basic change of strategy. Initially, services and programmes were in English. The church stagnated. A fascinating article, written in 1991 by a UCKG pastor, reflects the dilemma.

> Up to now, the [UCKG] is the reflection of a peculiar society . . . permeated by the belief and fear of the spirits and, consequently, exorcism is the most frequent practice. [. . .] We will have to see how [it] adapts to cultures in which people do not have the same fear of spirits. [. . .] Making converts in New York is not as easy as in Brazil. The people . . . think they do not need the help of anybody, much less someone from Brazil.[34]

The solution, however, was a change of public; this avoided the question of cultural adaptation. Television programmes and services switched to Spanish, and the Hispanic population then made growth possible.

According to recent UCKG statistics, its greatest success is in Portuguese-speaking Mozambique (thirty churches),[35] Colombia (forty-seven churches),[36] Argentina, South Africa and Portugal. In all these countries, stress has been laid on social work as a means of gaining the sympathy of the population and sometimes of overcoming political opposition to the church's presence.

South Africa may now rival Portugal as the strongest UC outside Brazil, and is said to cover the financial losses from all other UCKG churches in Africa. The first church opened there amongst Portuguese-speakers in 1992, but the transition to Soweto and to English was made by 1993.[37] In 1998, it filled Ellis Park rugby stadium for a ceremony which included 'dances and joyful songs of praise, mostly in African languages'.[38] By that time, it claimed 115 churches and 200 South African pastors, presumably all black.[39] South African pastors are also used as missionaries throughout Africa, as well as in Jamaica, England and the US. (The last-named country may be related to an attempt to break into the African-American world; in 1997 the UCKG claimed a church in Brooklyn catering for that community.)[40] However, Brazilian pastors also enjoy success. At the church in Pietermaritzburg, frequented by blacks and occasionally a few poor Afrikaners, services are in a mixture of English and Zulu, but what impresses the blacks is the facility with which the white Brazilian pastors adapt culturally. 'These whites are blacks', they say, in a tribute to the UCKG's missionary methods which may presage success all over sub-Saharan Africa.

Success in South Africa may also be related to the moment of the country, in which newly-created expectations begin to be frustrated and new religious groups proliferate. The UCKG can appeal both to the disappointed as well as to those who need moral reinforcement to take advantage of the new opportunities.

Another success story is Argentina, where in 1997 the UC had forty-six churches.[41] But Latin America is not always receptive. In Chile, after six years' activities and despite having gained legal status, it was subjected in late 1997 to government pressures. Visas were denied to Brazilian pastors, on the basis of suspicions of irregular financing, a suspicion apparently communicated to Chilean authorities by elements within the Brazilian police. Despite lukewarm support from the Brazilian consulate, the UCKG's strength in the Brazilian congress ensured a satisfactory solution.[42] In Peru, it had to resort to using another name: the Comunidad Cristiana del Espíritu Santo.

This is not the first time the UC has faced a legal embargo, usually provoked by local opponents' use of the church's negative image in Brazil. Nor is it the first time it has got round the problem by using a different name. The tactic has been used in the North-East of Brazil, in Spain, in Italy and in Oporto. In Colombia and Mexico it is called Oración Fuerte al Espíritu

Santo. Another tactic is to make agreements with already existing churches abroad (US, Japan) to make it bureaucratically easier to get started. As in Brazil, the UCKG abroad is characterised by creativity. We shall see examples in our two case studies from Europe.

The UCKG in Portugal: a Luso-Brazilian church?

The Universal Church began in Portugal in December 1989. By 1997, it claimed sixty-two churches: twenty-one in Greater Lisbon, ten in Greater Oporto, twelve in the South, thirteen in the Centre, a mere four in the very Catholic North and two in Madeira.[43] The following year, it was talking of eighty-five churches.[44] The official publication, *Tribuna Universal*, claimed a circulation of 50,000 in 1997. In 1995, the UCKG had programmes on twenty-three radio stations, six of which belonged to the church,[45] and a daily TV programme. There is great emphasis on social work: distribution of food and clothing, work with drug addicts, an old people's home and an orphanage. In this way, the church seeks the legitimacy denied it by important social sectors.

The UCKG's public is 'middle-aged women, maids, young people of all ethnic origins and retired people of both sexes'.[46] The *Tribuna Universal*[47] has an article about ageing which shows awareness of a possible clientele: 'An early exit from the job market is a relatively new phenomenon in Portugal, but may increase due to Portugal's entry into the European Community . . . The population between fifty and sixty-five is on unstable ground, since the trend is to reduce social rights.'

In a country where all Protestant churches (except Maná, a Pentecostal church of Portuguese origin) are small and stagnant, the attraction of the UCKG may have to do with the moment of entry into the EU and the abrupt development it has brought, on the one hand bringing opportunities for those who know how to take advantage of them, and on the other hand bringing anguish to those who feel left behind or whose traditional lifestyle is threatened. This creates an opening for the prosperity gospel which the UCKG preaches, as well as new social space for non-Catholic groups.

Although most UCKG leaders in Portugal are Brazilian, there is growing participation of Portuguese. But the church makes no effort to hide its origin. Critics in the media say it speaks 'the language of the Brazilian soap operas' so popular in Portugal.[48] The church itself proudly admits to what it calls a 'reverse "colonisation-evangelisation"'. Members assimilate the Brazilian way of speaking; in the prayers, 'everyone cries out to the Lord in "Brazilian".'[49] Pastors lead the way in this Brazilianisation; one of them, after leading a whole service in 'Brazilian', found it necessary to tell me he was in fact Portuguese to explain why he still longed to see what the UCKG was like in Brazil.

If the church in Portugal uses Brazilianisms it is because it knows they produce dividends. A church which plans its international expansion so well would not commit such an elementary error in Christian mission theory if it were prejudicial. Although there is anti-Brazilian feeling in sectors of Portuguese society, especially the middle class and sectors of the media and intelligentsia, the lower class is attracted to aspects of Brazilian culture. A partial Brazilianisation could be a form of resistance by those less favoured by European integration.

As in Brazil, the UCKG invests heavily in the media, taking 'advantage of what was left of an undignified national radio licencing process, [acquiring through intermediaries] radios with financial problems which needed an injection of capital'.[50] But television was more problematic. The church managed to get programmes on SIC and on the satellite channel Eutelsat (to reach emigrant Portuguese in Europe). But in 1995, it was legally prohibited from using Portuguese television.

At the same time as the saint-kicking episode in Brazil (in which a UCKG bishop, in a live TV programme, kicked an image of Our Lady of Aparecida, patron saint of Brazil, to show it could not answer prayers), similar problems occurred in Portugal. Similar in the sense of a resistance from important social sectors which showed the UC had too blatantly crossed the invisible frontiers that still mark the social and political space of Protestant groups in both countries. Kicking the patron saint on her national holiday, and attempting to buy the Coliseu theatre in Oporto, were overly daring steps for which the UCKG did not yet have the necessary support.

The Portuguese media had been calling for the authorities to react. '[The UC] has infiltrated our daily life, importing new expressions, strange rites . . . a truly multinational business . . . [whose growth] could go as far as political power. A route paved with much money and obscure twists, to which authorities and civil society reacted with apparent indifference until the Coliseu "affair".'[51]

The language is similar to that used by some Brazilian media: the comparison with the economic as a way of delegitimising the religious; the sinister phrases ('infiltrated', 'strange rites', 'obscure twists'); the encouragement of state intervention.

Some organs of the Brazilian press are no different. *O Globo,* which belongs to the media group most concerned about the media power of the UCKG, describes thus (November 1995) an incident in northern Portugal:

> Teenagers destroyed a UCKG church. [. . .] After breaking everything, they painted on the floor words such as 'demon'. [. . .] Only the members were spared. [. . .] The 'bishop' João Luís threatens to hold a new service tomorrow morning in what is left of the building. [. . .] Everything happened after the evangelicals decided to use the York Cinema in a shopping mall. [. . .] The shopkeepers accused the sect's followers, without proof, of committing various thefts in the commercial area.

Probably the church's clientele looked more like the 'dangerous classes' than the usual clientele of the mall. The article attributes the cause of the disorders to a decision by the Evangelicals (the UCKG), and not to an orchestrated action by shopkeepers for economic reasons, and describes the bishop's decision to hold another service the next day in the ruins of the church, despite the physical risk, not as courageous but as a 'threat'.

Another Brazilian newspaper describes an incident in Portugal in language which creates greater identification with the UCKG: the church members 'heard xenophobic slogans which told Brazilians and the Universal Church to go back to Brazil'.[52] In late 1995, churches in three towns were attacked: Matosinhos, Venda Nova and Póvoa de Varzim. In reply, the UCKG circulated a note in English: *Inquisition in Portugal*. The message is clear: the Portugal which desires to be modern and European cannot allow such restrictions on freedom of religion.

Another UCKG initiative met with legal resistence: the founding of a political party. In Brazil, its participation in elections has been through a range of secular parties, so why create a party of its own in Portugal? Within the Protestant world, it would be a means for exercising hegemony. Outside, it would be a way of getting round exclusion in the party system and achieving (in the medium run) a certain bargaining power for conquering social and political space. In Brazil, the electoral system encourages parties to offer space for Protestant candidates, and allows these candidates to get elected on their own electoral strength. In Portugal, the pre-determined party lists prevent candidates from minority groups getting elected solely with the votes they bring to the slate. It would be necessary first to show the UCKG's electoral strength, and then bargain with some traditional party disposed to open a slot.

Creating the party was hard. The name would be Evangelical Party, an invitation to pan-Protestant electoral collaboration and a reply to the UC's exclusion from the Evangelical Alliance. Later, the name Social Christian Party was attempted. Registration was denied because the constitution does not permit religious parties. Soon afterwards, registration was achieved, with the name of Party of the People (Partido da Gente).

It was said the UC hoped to elect ten candidates to parliament in October 1995, with votes from all Protestants. But it is unlikely the hierarchy had such high hopes. Even to get a sizeable proportion of votes from UC members would be an achievement in a country with a solid party system. In fact, they received very few votes and elected no one. The UCKG's strong parliamentary presence in Brazil has yet to be replicated anywhere abroad.

The church has also faced battles within the Protestant community. At the time of the attacks on its buildings, the Portuguese Council of Christian Churches, consisting of historical denominations, repudiated the attacks but claimed to understand their motivation: 'We believe there is an expression of rage on the part of many who feel cheated'. However, the greatest clash has been with another representative entity, the Evangelical Alliance of Portugal (AEP).

In 1992 the UCKG applied to join the AEP, hoping for some of the respectability enjoyed by older Protestant sectors, and for allies in its battles. However, the report of an AEP commission, dated 1993, concludes that the UCKG's body of doctrines 'is very close to the doctrinal principles of the AEP, but its "guiding ideas" . . . as well as some of its practices, put it outside the traditional universe of the Portuguese evangelical churches'. There were said to be four main deficiencies. The UCKG has a 'rigid hierarchy with unipersonal discretionary powers'. Leaders are immune from evaluation, 'on the grounds they are "commanded" directly by God . . . in dreams, visions and through the Bible'. The UCKG uses 'magical-sacramental methods in the relationship between the "human" and the "divine", the "material" and the "spiritual"', such as red roses for health, yellow roses for prosperity, white roses for sentimental questions and photographs anointed with holy oils. Lastly, it does not emphasise 'fundamental doctrines of the Gospel, but its "guiding ideas", some of which are heretical'.

The list of heretical ideas includes the following: 'All evils . . . are of demonic origin'; 'healing is a right acquired through Christ'; 'pastors have the gift of healing . . . regardless of the faith of the sick person'; 'complete deliverance [from demonic oppression] is only possible through participation in the church; no-one is blessed at home'; 'baptism by immersion is an indispensable condition for all blessings'; 'through participation in Holy Communion . . . the participant enjoys the physical health Christ enjoyed'; 'all men are children of God . . . [disregards the problem of original sin]'; 'money is the lifeblood of the church'; 'tithing is fundamental for physical, spiritual and financial life'. Parts of this list are surprising, in light of UCKG practice elsewhere. It usually speaks against dreams and visions,[53] and is not known for a sacramentalist theology. Others seem to be phrases heard in sermons, and could be exegeted in a more orthodox way. Some criticisms could be applied to churches, or sectors of them, which belong to the AEP.

As for the 'magical-sacramental methods', the AEP here echoes Evangelical criticisms of the UCKG in Brazil. The UCKG does indeed break with the symbolic poverty of Brazilian Protestantism. But there do seem to be limits; although it makes ample use of symbols, there is no use of images in worship. Previous Pentecostalism had democratised the word through speaking in tongues and prophecies; the UCKG, however, breaks dependence on the word, making ample use of sight, touch and gesture. Soon after the AEP's refusal of the UCKG, an article by Bishop Macedo entitled 'Idolatry and Symbolism: the Difference' commented: 'Many Evangelical brothers have criticised us for our free distribution of roses, anointed handkerchiefs, consecrated oil etc.' But the Bible, he says, is full of symbols. Jesus also used physical elements such as clay to awaken faith, and the apostle Paul did miracles through his personal objects.[54]

It is possible the AEP's refusal of the UC had to do with wariness of the hegemonic force it would represent in the small and static Portuguese Evangelical world. The UC showed its displeasure by opening a rival entity, the Federation of Evangelical Churches of Portugal, literally right across the road from the headquarters of the AEP.

An AEP bulletin[55] throws light on the UC's possible concern with representative entities at the current stage of relations between Evangelicals and Portuguese society. It talks of conversations between the AEP and the government, intended to lead to official recognition of the Evangelical community through its representative organs, with the same rights enjoyed by the Catholic Church. It also talks of a commission with representatives of all confessions, including the Catholics, presided over by the president of the AEP, which is petitioning for the implementation of a law which grants religious groups daily access to public television.

Portugal, thus far, is the only country outside Brazil where the UCKG has achieved national visibility. It also seems to be the foreign country which supplies the most pastors. Perhaps the decision to open a church there in 1989 marked a new strategy after relatively fruitless effort in the US. Portugal would become the beach-head for international expansion, and not only amongst Lusophone communities, as we shall see in the case of England.

The UCKG in England: a black church?

England represents a very different religious field. In Portugal the UC is an unsettling force in a weak Protestantism in a traditionally Catholic country: a Protestantism dominated by churches of foreign origin and with little tradition of autochthonous churches. In England, on the other hand, the UC does not mean much in a traditionally Protestant but now secularised country, with a Protestant state church and a plethora of free churches. Although ethnic churches are growing, there is no tradition of success among the native white population by foreign churches, especially from outside the English-speaking world. What the two countries do have in common, besides membership in the EU, is the presence of immigrants from the former colonies.

The UCKG began in England in June 1995, with a small church in the London neighbourhood of Brixton. In October of that year, it bought the Rainbow Theatre in Finsbury Park for $4 million, having previously attempted to purchase the Brixton Academy for $6.4 million. Shortly afterwards, it opened a church in the second largest city, Birmingham. In March 1996, the 1,500 seats in the Rainbow were filled for the visit of Bishop Macedo. In the next month, publication of *The Sower* magazine began. By mid-1997, the English UC had its own bishop, Renato Cardoso, son-in-law of Macedo. In late 1998 the UC claimed four churches and three 'nuclei' (smaller centres with fewer services), and had the family as its main emphasis, in line with the Labour government's professed concern for the strengthening of family life.[56]

The initial strategy had been to begin in grand style at the Brixton Academy, a famous concert hall. A secret bid had been leaked to the press, causing local opposition and intervention by the borough council. But the result was not wholly negative. The unknown UCKG was in the main newspapers. Although the media made some use of Brazilian anti-UCKG material, the tone was moderate, more of curiosity than concern. The Brixton Academy was not the English equivalent of the Coliseu in Portugal or the saint-kicking in Brazil, since the purchase was disallowed on cultural grounds. In England, with its liberal and Protestant tradition, there was no controversy about the very existence of the church, much less any destruction of buildings.

The Rainbow Theatre, which the UC acquired later, is in a mixed area: Indians, Pakistanis, Greeks, Irish, blacks and white English intermingle in the rather run-down streets. But the Brixton Academy shows the strategy with which the UC arrived. Brixton is the most famous black district of London. The small UC church functioning there is frequented almost exclusively by blacks, although the pastors in 1996 were Portuguese whites. Even at the Rainbow, 90% of the public is black. The UCKG in England has made the black community its main target and thus comes close to the category of 'Afro-Caribbean church' in the English religious world.

Talking about Peruvian Pentecostals in New Jersey, Vásquez says that Peruvian identity is dissolved in that of 'Hispanics' or 'Latinos' imposed by American society.[57] Similarly, immigrants (and their descendants) from Jamaica, Barbados, Nigeria or Ghana are redefined by British society as 'blacks'. At most, they are divided into 'West Indians' and 'Africans'.

In the religious field, many blacks are in churches classified as Afro-Caribbean. To understand the implications of this strategy for the UCKG, we need to know something of the English religious world.

Although the 'Celtic fringe' of Britain (Wales, Scotland and Northern Ireland) has higher figures, only 9% of the population of England frequent a church.[58] The theologically liberal churches are declining and the Evangelical ones growing. There is increasing Protestant fragmentation, with many new charismatic groups. In Anglicanism, the Evangelical wing has grown (from 10% of the clergy and 15% of the laity in 1950, to 50% of the clergy and 35% of the laity in 1987). But Evangelicals in general are middle class, and much of their limited presence among the lower class is due to Pentecostals. The latter represent only 4% of British Protestantism, although they are the fastest growing segment in the 1990s.

In 1990 42% of British Pentecostals were in Afro-Caribbean churches. Caribbean immigration since the 1950s and African since the 1970s led to separate churches, often after frustrated attempts at integration into white churches. The Afro-Caribbean field is very polarised. On the whole, Caribbeans and Africans do not go to the same churches.

The 1990s are a moment of crisis for the black churches. On the one hand, their spiritual values are increasingly recognised as important for British Christianity. Together with the growing importance of evangelicalism comes the growing importance of blacks within Evangelicalism, symbolised in 1996 by the election of a black Pentecostal as head of the Evangelical Alliance. On the other hand, the churches are affected by the drama of 'naturalisation': the younger generation, born in the country, is impatient with old traditions and in search of its own identity. Another factor is that almost half the young people of Caribbean origin marry non-blacks. In this context, the UCKG (with its exotic origin, message of success and self-respect, attempt to integrate the poor of all colours, and its predominantly white leadership) can offer a halfway house between a traditional Afro-Caribbean and a white church.

While the UC deliberately started out amongst blacks, the church shows awareness of the dangers. The black community should be a beach-head, not a prison. The trap of becoming an Afro-Caribbean church haunts the UC's activities.

On the one hand, blacks are cultivated as the initial target and subsequent mainstay of the membership. The main Jamaican newspaper in London was used to announce the initial activities, at first with the testimony and photo of a black Brazilian, then, with a West Indian from London, and finally with four blacks from London (two West Indians and two Africans). The first issue of *The Sower* (April 1996) has the testimony of a black South African ('I tried doctors, witchdoctors, inyangas and sangomas'). The next issue declares: 'The devil has said in your mind "You can't do it! You are poor, you don't have knowledge, you are black, you have no rights to receive".' In July 1997 there is the testimony of a black couple from Birmingham: 'When on holiday in Jamaica, some friends introduced us to . . . 'spiritualists'. But they really practised Obeah . . . 150 pounds for a blood bath [with the] blood of pigeons'. The testimony of a sterile Nigerian woman attacks the African 'spiritual' churches in London: 'There, my problems only became worse'. An advertisement for the Universal Classics shop stresses the availability of 'African designs'.

All this is reflected in the services: in Brixton, an almost totally black church; at the Rainbow, 90% black, perhaps two thirds Caribbean and one third West African. As in Brazil, the young man from the street can enter a UC service without feeling out of place, but one sees the influence of Caribbean ecclesiastical culture in the suits of the middle-aged men and the elegant hats of the women. At certain moments, especially the more joyful songs, the service suddenly looks typically Caribbean, except for the white Brazilian pastors. In the exorcisms, voodoo, obeah and West African divinities are mentioned. Occasionally, the possessed talk in African languages and are exhorted by the pastor, amidst applause, to 'speak a language I can understand; speak English'.

On the other hand, the UC seems aware of the danger of getting trapped in the 'black church' category, and tries to ensure the black community is a door into Britain and not its final destination. The first issue of *The Sower* has a testimony of a white Brazilian; the second issue, of an Indian from New York; a later issue, of an Indian from London ('my parents were strict Hindus'). Articles against Islam also show concern for the largest ethnic minority, the Asians. The evolving concern to move beyond the black community can be seen in publicity leaflets. One version has four testimonies: two of Africans, one of a West Indian and one of a white. A later version alters the proportions: one African, one West Indian and two whites.

An analysis of *The Sower* reveals other tactics for the English context. One is the attack on Islam: 'The symbols, traditions and rituals . . . come from a pre-Islamic Arabian pagan deity'; 'the true essence of Islam [is] a form of cultural imperialism'. In a Protestant context, another tactic more common than in Brazil is intra-Protestant polemic. The first issue says the magazine will warn against false teachings. The Evangelical church has turned into an 'improved Catholic church'. Just as 'Catholic' and 'Christian' are mutually exclusive in UC language in Brazil, so it seems are 'Anglican' and 'Christian' in England.[59] Leaders, movements and trends in the international evangelical world are attacked: Billy Graham 'teaches Catholics are just another Christian denomination'; the AD 2000 Movement 'preaches more than one gospel'; and the Toronto Blessing[60] is the target of several articles which attribute it to Satan. But anti-Catholic polemic continues, despite being attenuated in contemporary British evangelicalism: 'Evangelicals and Catholics together? Not the true evangelicals'; 'Roman Catholic Church charged with aiding in murders [during the Argentine military regime]'.

A publicity leaflet begins with a declaration of faith which places the UCKG within orthodox Christianity ('one God, eternally existing in three persons'), within Protestantism ('two ordinances – baptism in water and the Lord's Supper'; 'sanctification as a progressive work of grace'), within Evangelicalism ('the Scriptures in their original writings as fully inspired'; 'the substitutionary sacrifice' of Christ) and within Pentecostalism ('baptism of the Holy Spirit'; 'divine healing as an integral part of the gospel'). It affirms eschatology as the dynamo of the church ('the last chance to receive salvation' before the Second Coming – a greater emphasis now than in the early UC). As in Portugal, social work is stressed: 'faith without deeds is dead . . . orphanages, homes for the elderly, hunger relief campaigns, free medical assistance, blood donation, schools, reintegration of the homeless . . .'.

At a morning service in August 1997 at the Rainbow, Bishop Macedo himself led half the service. He conducted it in the usual UC oscillating rhythm, alternating loud music and fervent prayer with moments of calm and concentration. Following the usual emphasis for Sundays, and also Macedo's own recent stress on greater spiritual formation, he prayed: 'O Lord, more than heating or prosperity, give these people salvation'. The singing mixed traditional and recent English choruses with translations of Brazilian Evangelical songs. (In the afternoon service, a translation was sung of the famous UC song used after exorcisms: 'out, out, out'.)

On the same afternoon there was the annual Day of Decision service, with 1,500 people packing out the Rainbow. Surprisingly, Macedo did not appear; even in the morning, his appearance had been discreet and unannounced. In the afternoon service, the rhythm was very different, with exorcism predominating. The pastor called upon the evil in people's lives to appear: 'come out, manifest'. Initially, he invoked evil in general, later specifying voodoo, *oxóssi, candomblé* and other names which appeared to be West African religious entities. Africans were a majority amongst the exorcised.

The UC as a black church (in Britain) is in the tradition of the African Independent Churches.

> 'Many African Christians believe the [missionary] church is not interested in daily misfortunes, illness, encounter with evil and witchcraft. [. . .] The need is for a power beyond that of the spirits, diviners and sorcerers. The alleged syncretism in African Christianity is not so much a sign of a lack of Christian commitment as an expression of the fact that Christianity has not been made to respond fully to culturally-based religious aspirations. But in the independent churches, there is an open invitation to bring fears and anxieties about witches, sorcerers, bad luck, poverty and illness'.[61]

If the UC is based initially in the black community, the pastorate is based on Brazilian-Portuguese collaboration. Except for a few black English unpaid assistants, all the leadership is Luso-Brazilian. Portuguese, of course, can work anywhere in the European Union. In England, and much of Europe, the UCKG is a Luso-Brazilian church. It may already constitute the largest Protestant missionary effort ever to come out of Portugal.

Conclusion: global perspectives of the Universal Church

In the Introduction, we viewed Pentecostalism as a globalised and culturally polycentric faith. The combination is important. As Smith says, new traditions must connect with vernacular styles: 'It is one thing to be able to package imagery and diffuse it [but] quite another to ensure [the] power to move . . . populations . . . The meanings of even the most universal of imagery for a particular population derive as much from the historical experiences and social status of that group as from the intentions of purveyors.'[62]

A contemporary African theologian asks whether 'the modern Western world, in Christian recession but with increasing interest in the occult, [is so] impervious to the experiences of Christian transcendence recorded in the South?'.[63] Mass adoption of Christianity in Africa, he suggests, might have global relevance. The same might be asked of Brazilian Pentecostalism. Certainly, in ethnic, cultural and economic terms, Brazil is a bridge between Europe and Africa and its churches might have a bridging role for the Third World minorities at the heart of the developed West.

The UCKG is not only tuned in to global registers; it is also a most Brazilian religion. It appears to see itself as a Latin American Protestant reformation, that is, a Protestantism attuned to the religious traditions of the continent. In response to accusations of syncretism, it replies that one can be Evangelical and still use popular religious traditions as a starting point.

At the same time, the UCKG is in the tradition of Christian expansion in the European Dark Ages and in twentieth century Africa: of an encounter of the 'powers'. The UCKG is not free floating; as an Evangelical and Pentecostal church, it has to sustain this identity by plausibly justifying its actions for a sufficient number of Christians. Analysing the UC as a business can produce insights but is ultimately reductionist, because its whole economic empire is functional for its religious mission and cannot be explained in purely pragmatic terms. The problem it faces in many countries is that a certain image arrives together with the church itself. The negative image then predominates among elites before the UC can build a popular base and a political counter-force. In a country with long traditions of pluralism and religious freedom such as Britain, this is not serious. But it can be in countries like Portugal with a monolithic religious tradition and recent democratisation. Even so, membership of the EU reinforces democratisation and should guarantee UC survival there. In Eastern Europe the UC could have a large field, but it faces difficulties not only from slow economic reform (given the UC ideology of self-employment as the route to success) but from lack of a pluralist tradition and from legal restrictions on religious freedom.

The UC uses Third World communities as an entry into the First World. Portugal is the exception, since the church there is basically amongst the native population, aided by linguistic and cultural affinity and perhaps by Portugal's still precarious 'Europeanness'. Thus far, the UC's international expansion has depended on some or all of the following factors: cultural affinities (Luso, Latin, African); religious pluralism and freedom; poor immigrants; and populations of Christian background (Latin-American, Caribbean, African, Portuguese, Russian). It is not yet clear whether the church will be successful among non-Christianised peoples, above all in Asia.[64]

In 1991 Manuel Silva said we should have to see 'how the [UC] adapts to new cultures in which people do not have the same fear of spirits . . . but, following Jacques Ellul's ideas, they may find that new demons are lurking in the big cities of the world and in other cultures'.[65] At that time, the UCKG replied by opting for the Hispanics and forgetting the Anglo-Americans. It has also not had success in the African American community, replete with churches and a developed awareness of cultural difference, and unlikely to welcome a church led by white Brazilians who would be classified as Hispanics. But in Britain it was easier to penetrate the black community, which is more recent, smaller, with fewer cultural resources, divided between West Indians and Africans and between immigrants and local born, and where the tradition of separate churches is new and still regretted by many. In addition, the UCKG leaders do not fit easily into any common ethnic category in British society.

The UC may be unique because, unlike other Third World Pentecostal groups, it has the political power and economic strength to guarantee some visibility even in the developed world. In current Protestantism, only South Korea could play a similar role. But Korea lacks the ethnic, cultural and linguistic links with other countries such as Brazil has with Europe, the Americas and Africa. In this respect, it is significant that the UCKG's presence in Asia is limited effectively to the Philippines and the Nippo-Brazilians in Japan. By the late 1990s, Asia was viewed by the church as its next great challenge;[66] it will certainly be the greatest test yet of the Universal Church's ability to live up to its name in contexts which are both non-Christian and have few cultural affinities with the Brazilian cauldron in which it emerged.

Notes

1 This chapter is based on fieldwork in Portugal, Britain and Brazil. A less up-to-date version in Portuguese is forthcoming (1999) in the journal *Lusotopie*.
2 Peter Beyer, *Religion and Globalization*, London: Sage, 1994.
3 Roland Robertson, *Globalization*, London: Sage, 1992.
4 Malcolm Waters, *Globalization*, London: Routledge, 1995.
5 The Pentecostal-charismatic wing accounted for 6 per cent of worldwide Christianity in 1970, and is currently estimated at 25 per cent (see Peter Brierley, *Changing Churches*, London: Christian Research, 1996).
6 The struggle for a 'culturally polycentric Christianity' is regarded by Cox as the heart of the discord between Leonardo Boff and the Vatican (see Harvey Cox, *The Silencing of Leonardo Boff*, Oak Park, IL: Meyer-Stone, 1988).
7 Andrew Walls, 'Christianity in the Non-Western World: A Study in the Serial Nature of Christian Expansion', *Studies in World Christianity*, vol. 1, no. 1, 1995, pp. 1–25.
8 Andrew Walls, 'The Western Discovery of Non-Western Christian Art' in Diana Wood (ed.), *The Church and the Arts*, Oxford: Blackwell, 1992, p. 571.
9 Waters, *Globalization*, p. 3.
10 Mike Featherstone, 'An Introduction' in Featherstone (ed.), *Global Culture*, London: Sage, 1990, p. 10.
11 Irving Hexham and Karla Poewe, 'Charismatic Churches in South Africa: A Critique of Criticisms and Problems of Bias' in Karla Poewe (ed.), *Charismatic Christianity as a Global Culture*, Columbia, SC: University of South Carolina Press, 1994, p. 61.
12 *Veja*, 23 April 1997.
13 Paul Freston, 'Breve História do Pentecostalismo Brasileiro: 3. A Igreja Universal do Reino de Deus' in A. Antoniazzi *et al.*, *Nem Anjos Nem Demônios*, Petrópolis: Vozes, 1994, pp. 131–59; 'Pentecostalism in Brazil: A Brief History',

Religion, no. 25, 1995, pp. 119–33; 'The Protestant Eruption into Modern Brazilian Polities', *Journal of Contemporary Religion*, vol. 11, no. 2 (May 1996), pp. 147–68; '"Neo-Pentecostalism" in Brazil', *Archives de Sciences Sociales des Religions*, no. 105 (Jan.–Mar. 1999).

14 ISER, *Novo Nascimento*, Rio de Janeiro, 1996, p. 10.

15 *Folha de São Paulo*, 7 Jan. 1996 and 10 Sept. 1995.

16 *Jornaldo Brasil*, 26 May 1996.

17 *Folha de São Paulo*, 14 Jan. 1996.

18 ISER, *Novo Nascimento*, p. 46.

19 *Veja*, 19 April 1995 and 23 April 1997.

20 The *Folha Universal* (the UCKG weekly newspaper in Brazil) of 21 Dec. 1997 affirms that the church started in the US in 1980. This may be a misprint, since Manuel Silva, 'A Brazilian Church Comes to New York', *Pneuma*, vol. 13, no. 2 (Fall 1991), pp. 161–5, seemingly referring to the same events, talks of 1986, and the TV Record documentary mentioned below suggests the church's first foreign undertaking was in Paraguay.

21 *Veja*, 19 April 1995; *Folha de São Paulo*, 17 April 1995.

22 The countries were listed in the following order: Russia, Jamaica, Angola, Guinea-Bissau, Ivory Coast, Kenya, Malawi, Mozambique, Nigeria, South Africa, Tanzania, Uganda, Zambia, Zimbabwe, Cape Verde, India, Israel, Japan, Philippines, Dominican Republic, El Salvador, Guatemala, Honduras, Nicaragua, Puerto Rico, England, France, Germany, Holland, Italy, Luxemburg, Portugal, Spain, Switzerland, Canada, Mexico, the USA, Argentina, Bolivia, Chile, Colombia, Ecuador, Paraguay, Peru, Belgium. Several countries missing from this list are on lists published by the secular media, either by journalistic error or because the work there was discontinued, or even because the church forgot to include them in the documentary: Uruguay, Venezuela, Panama, Congo, Senegal, Botswana.

23 In the *Folha Universal* from late 1997 to Nov. 1998 we see reference to new countries (Romania, Lesotho, Madagascar and Ethiopia), besides confirmation of Venezuela and Uruguay.

24 *Veja*, 19 Apr. 1995.

25 Programme on *TV Record*, 21 Aug. 1998.

26 Programme on *TV Record*, 4 July 1998.

27 In a programme on Holland (*Rede Família*, 15 Nov. 1998), the only white Dutch person to give a testimony was married to a woman from Cape Verde.

28 Although outside these blocs, even Italy (Latin and Catholic heritage) and the Philippines (Catholicism and Spanish colonisation) are culturally close.

29 *The Sower*, July 1997.

30 *Folha Universal*, 10 May 1998.

31 Programme on *TV Record*, 22 Aug. 1998.

32 Silva, 'Brazilian Church'.

33 *O Estado de São Paulo*, 18 Sept. 1995; *Folha de São Paulo*, 17 Sept. 1995; *IstoÉ*, 14 Dec. 1994.

34 Silva, 'Brazilian Church'.

35 *Folha Universal*, 18 Oct. 1998.

36 *Folha Universal*, 13 Sept. 1998.

37 *IstoÉ*, 14 Dec 1994; Ronaldo Didini in *Veja*, 23 Apr. 1997; *Folha Universal*, 14 Dec. 1997.

38 *Folha Universal*, 11 Oct. 1998.

39 At Ellis Park, thirty-five new pastors were consecrated. From the names, twenty-two of these were Brazilian or Portuguese and thirteen were black South Africans, but none were South African whites (*Folha Universal*, 11 Oct. 1997).

40 *Folha Universal*, 21 Dec. 1997.
41 Programme on *TV Record*, 15 Aug. 1998.
42 *Folha Universal*, 14 Dec. 1997 and 17 May 1998.
43 *Tribuna Universal*, 10 Dec. 1997.
44 Programme on *TV Record*, 6 June 1998.
45 Five were in other names, due to legislation prohibiting groups from owning more than one station and 30% of another (*IstoÉ*, 14 Dec. 1994).
46 *Público* (Lisbon), 2 Aug. 1995.
47 7 July 1996.
48 *Público*, 27 Aug. 1995.
49 *Plenitude*, Sept. 1997, p. 38.
50 *Público*, 27 Aug. 1995.
51 *Ibid.*
52 *Folha de São Paulo*, 13 Nov. 1995.
53 The second number of the UC magazine in England gives 'ten reasons why we shouldn't believe in dreams' (*The Sower*, May 1996).
54 *Folha Universal*, 13 Mar. 1994.
55 *A Voz da Aliança*, Jan.–Mar. 1996.
56 *Folha Universal*, 23 Aug. 1998.
57 Manuel Vásquez, 'Transnationalization and Religious Practices among Peruvian Christians in Paterson, NJ', paper presented at XX Congress of the Latin American Studies Association, 1997.
58 Data on the British religious field are from Christopher Sinclair, 'Evangelical Belief in Contemporary England', *Archives de Sciences Sociales des Religions*, no. 82 (April–June 1993), pp. 169–81, Brierley, *Changing Churches*, and various editions of the *UK Christian Handbook*.
59 *The Sower*, 4 Apr. 1996, pp. 2, 5, 6, 7; May 1996, p. 19.
60 The Toronto Blessing, an ultra-charismatic phenomenon characterised by faintings and animal sounds, has influenced many British churches.
61 Allan Anderson, 'Pentecostal Pneumatology and African Power Concepts: Continuity or Change?', *Missionalia*, vol. 19, no. 1 (April 1990), pp. 67, 71f.
62 Anthony Smith, 'Towards a Global Culture?' in Featherstone, *Global Culture*, p. 179.
63 Kwame Bediako, *Christianity in Africa*, Edinburgh University Press, 1995, p. 166.
64 The UC opened a church in India in 1996, and claimed 200 members a year later. Its radio programme had been banned (*Folha Universal*, 20 July 1997).
65 The reference to the French sociologist Ellul, author of *The New Demons* (1973), is noteworthy.
66 *Folha Universal*, 21 Feb. 1999.

Bibliography

Anderson, Allan, 'Pentecostal Pneumatology and African Power Concepts: Continuity or Change?', *Missionalia*, vol. 19, no. 1 (April 1990), pp. 65–74.

Bediako, Kwame, *Christianity in Africa*, Edinburgh University Press, 1995.

Beyer, Peter, *Religion and Globalization*, London: Sage, 1994.

Brierley, Peter, *Changing Churches*, London: Christian Research, 1996.

Cox, Harvey, *The Silencing of Leonardo Boff*, Oak Park, IL: Meyer-Stone, 1988.

Featherstone, Mike, 'An Introduction' in Mike Featherstone (ed.), *Global Culture*, London: Sage, 1990, pp. 1–13.

Freston, Paul, 'Breve História do Pentecostalismo Brasileiro: 3. A Igreja Universal do Reino de Deus' in A. Antoniazzi *et al.* (eds), *Nem Anjos Nem Demônios: Interpretações Sociológicas do Pentecostalismo*, Petrópolis: Vozes, 1994, pp 131–59.
——, 'Pentecostalism in Brazil: A Brief History', *Religion*, no. 25, 1995, pp. 119–33.
——, "The Protestant Eruption into Modern Brazilian Polities', *Journal of Contemporary Religion*, vol. 11, no. 2 (May 1996), pp. 147–68.
——, ' "Neo-Pentecostalism" in Brazil: Problems of Definition and the Struggle for Hegemony', *Archives de Sciences Sociales des Religions*, no. 105 (Jan.–Mar. 1999).
Hexham, Irving, and Karla Poewe, 'Charismatic Churches in South Africa: A Critique of Criticisms and Problems of Bias' in Karla Poewe (ed.), *Charismatic Christianity as a Global Culture*, Columbia, SC: University of South Carolina Press, 1994, pp. 50–69.
ISER (Instituto de Estudos da Religião), *Novo Nascimento: Os Evangélicos em Casa, na Igreja e na Político*, Rio de Janeiro, 1996.
Robertson, Roland, *Globalization*, London: Sage, 1992.
Silva, Manuel, 'A Brazilian Church Comes to New York', *Pneuma*, vol. 13, no 2 (Fall 1991), pp. 161–5.
Sinclair, Christopher, 'Evangelical Belief in Contemporary England', *Archives de Sciences Sociales des Religions*, no. 82 (April–June 1993), pp. 169–81.
Smith, Anthony, 'Towards a Global Culture?' in Mike Featherstone (ed.), *Global Culture*, London: Sage, 1990, pp. 171–91.
Vásquez, Manuel, 'Transnationalization and Religious Practices among Peruvian Christians in Paterson. NJ', paper presented at the XX Congress of the Latin American Studies Association, 1997.
Walls, Andrew, 'The Western Discovery of Non-Western Christian Art' in Diana Wood (ed.), *The Church and the Arts*, Oxford: Blackwell, 1992, pp. 571–85.
——, 'Christianity in the Non-Western World: A Study in the Serial Nature of Christian expansion', *Studies in World Christianity*, vol. 1, no. 1, 1995, pp. 1–25.
Waters, Malcolm, *Globalization*, London: Routledge, 1995.

78

CERTAIN KNOWLEDGE

The encounter of global fundamentalism and local Christianity in urban south India

Lional Caplan

Source: Wendy James (ed.), *The Pursuit of Certainty: Religions and Cultural Formations*, London: Routledge, 1995, pp. 92–110.

Introduction[1]

There can be few narratives which convey so starkly the impact of global on local forms of knowledge as those relating the history of Western Christian missions to peoples of the non-Western world. The shape of Christianity in south India today – and more particularly of urban Protestantism, with which I am especially concerned in this chapter[2] – reflects 'indigenous' accommodations to Euro-American theologies and mission strategies in the course of Western colonial and post-colonial domination. Thus a rigid distinction between local and global in this context is difficult to sustain, since what began as an import from the West evolved over many years into an Indian Christian synthesis, a species of *local* religion.[3] But if globalization is not a recent phenomenon, its contemporary character differs perceptibly from that obtaining in the past. In south India, as elsewhere, the most rapidly expanding form of contemporary mission Christianity is fundamentalist Protestantism[4] – a term which, for my present purposes, embraces evangelical and Pentecostal religiosities.[5] Originating mainly in North America, where such forms of Christianity have taken firm root since the Second World War and especially during the past quarter of a century, they are being exported around the globe by US-led and -financed missions and para-church organizations, challenging the religious cultures which had previously evolved under the aegis of the historic churches. This chapter examines the encounter between these two kinds of religiosity.[6]

One way to approach this 'cultural struggle' is to regard it as an opposition between 'faith' and 'certitude'. Towler has recently suggested that faith, which he deems the characteristic cognitive style of 'conventional' Protestantism, implies 'a continuous act of aspiration'. It demands awareness of the 'inherently complex and problematical character of the events and experiences demanding explanation'; doubt is therefore an intrinsic part of faith. By contrast, 'sectarian religion' – and here he would probably include varieties of fundamentalism – is characterized by certitude (Towler 1984). A spate of recent analyses of fundamentalist approaches to religious phenomena similarly identifies as a crucial feature the insistence on privileged access to absolute truth. '[Fundamentalists] are convinced that their purchase on the truth is, like the truth itself, complete and absolute, unqualified by partial understanding or error' (Deiros 1991: 169). Their need to consider scripture inerrant and to 'subscribe to a fixed and rigid creed' renders them, in Ostow's view, 'reluctant to tolerate doubt, uncertainty and ambiguity' (1990: 101; see also Marty and Appleby 1991; Lawrence 1990; Averill 1989).[7]

In Madras city, the capital of Tamil Nadu state in south India and the locus of my study, this new and aggressively promoted form of global Christianity has, during the past two decades, come increasingly to challenge one variety of Protestant religiosity and reinforce another. Indeed, the notion of a solidary corpus of local religious knowledge confronting or encountering an alien cultural flow is much too simplistic for it masks, among other things, a profound discrepancy of religiosities within the Indian Protestant community of Madras. The dominant sector (both lay and ecclesiastical) has for some time been committed to theological liberalism, social 'activism' and a collaborative approach to non-Christian religions – the ingredients of 'faith'. The majority of ordinary Protestants, by contrast, eschew such tendencies, retaining strong beliefs in the centrality of worship and the total veracity of the Bible, alongside attachment to everyday knowledge about misfortune which they share with the non-Christians among whom they live. In this chapter I consider how the fundamentalists encounter these opposed religious proclivities. I first examine the contexts in which their certainties are asserted; second, identify those aspects of fundamentalist belief and behaviour which accord with local knowledges and finally consider how Madras Protestants assess and respond to these new global religiosities.

Protestant Madras

Christians in Madras were estimated to number 237,000 in 1981 or just under 7.5 per cent of the city's population.[8] There are reputed to be more churches in Madras than in any other south Asian city (Hedlund 1986). Within the Christian fold Protestants are a minority, comprising perhaps 30–35 per cent of the total, or some 80,000 people. Cities like Madras were never included in the 'comity' arrangments obtaining among Protestant missionaries, whereby each Society focused its efforts on specific areas and refrained from entering the 'territory' of another. As a result the missionaries of numerous organizations were active in the city.[9] Nonetheless, conversions among the resident population of Madras were never very numerous and missionaries frequently complained of the difficulties and frustrations attending their work in this large urban centre.

Protestant numbers only expanded as a result of migration from various parts of south India by those already professing Christianity. The principal Protestant migrations occurred in response to infrastructural growth and economic developments in the metropolitan region during the second and third quarters of the twentieth century and especially following independence. A minority, who had been able to take full advantage of educational opportunities in mission schools and colleges, began to fill some of the senior positions which had previously been monopolized by Europeans in the large commercial, industrial, educational and administrative organizations of the Raj.

These new Protestant elites also entered the churches which had previously been reserved for Europeans, occupied the pews the latter had vacated, continued to worship in English and assumed lay control of ecclesiastical structures created with the formation in 1947 of the ecumenical Protestant Church of South India (CSI).[10] The CSI – which federated the Presbyterian, Congregational, Methodist and Anglican churches in south India[11] – is the largest Protestant church in India and contains the biggest non-Catholic following in Madras, with nearly half the city's Protestants in its membership. The CSI leadership, as well as the community's Westernized elites, many of whom serve the church in various secular capacities, have a strong commitment to the social gospel. This is a direct legacy of the dominant liberal theological emphasis within Euro-American missionary circles which gained the ascendancy in the early part of the twentieth century and especially as independence approached. In the context of contemporary south India the social gospel means a concern for economic development and the alleviation of hardship. The CSI is involved in a host of programmes to improve environmental conditions and better the life-chances of those most in need. These various welfare schemes are meant to benefit the poor irrespective of religious affiliation.

One obvious corollary of this kind of intense engagement with the 'world' is that religions other than Christianity, and relationships with non-Christians, are conceived in a positive light. Protestant leaders of the CSI and other major denominational churches acknowledge the 'spirituality' in Hinduism and other religions.[12] Among other things, Protestant leaders of mainline churches like the CSI tend to eschew the negative attitudes and aggressive evangelism which characterized the early missionary approach to Indians of other persuasions. This may be partly to avoid offending the sensitivities of both government and militant Hindu organizations but it also emerges from an outlook which seeks to communicate the values of Christianity through example rather than exhortation. Ecumenical sentiments are frequently heard from the pulpits of elite congregations and are widely shared by well-to-do, cosmopolitan Protestants who are regularly engaged in welfare and development activities as part of their commitment to the social gospel.

Popular religiosities

The vast majority of Protestants – those outside the small power bloc – are indifferent to or at best weakly committed to the social gospel. Norman (1979: 6) has suggested that 'everywhere in the Third World' we find a tendency for sophisticated elites who comprise the church's leadership to 'superimpose the liberal and radical political idealism . . . of the developed world upon the diffused religiosity around them' (*ibid.*). For most ordinary Protestants in Madras this 'diffused religiosity' suggests, for one thing, a sharing with non-Christians of popular ideas and practices concerning the causes of and remedies for affliction. In a study of 'intermingling patterns of culture' among Protestant groups in south India conducted in 1953, Diehl found that despite a century and a half of missionary influence Christians still revered a range of (non-Christian) ritual specialists (magicians, soothsayers, 'god-dancers', fortune-tellers, 'persons inspired by the gods', etc.). People 'are apt to show confidence in [these] professionals who offer their services . . . at times of unexpected crises'. He concluded that it was 'not so much the person exercising this practice as the conceptual outlook behind it that has a hold on people' (Diehl 1965: 135–6). Twenty years later when I conducted fieldwork in Madras I also found that the majority of non-elites, like the Hindus among whom they live and work, continued to attribute many if not most kinds of everyday misfortune (joblessness, illness, unhappy marriages, disobedient children, examination failures, etc.) to either sorcery (*suniyam*), the capricious acts of evil spirits (*pey*), or other kinds of mystical agents (Caplan 1987b). In the (English) words of an Anglo-Indian: 'When something goes wrong people here in Madras think, "Ah, this one's been conjured, or that one's been pilled"'.

At the same time, the religious proclivities of most Protestants include an attachment to the pietism bequeathed them by the early missionaries, who insisted on the centrality of the Bible and worship in Christian life. Protestant families still identify the observance of Sabbath, daily prayers at home and belief that the Bible is God's literal truth as the core of their religious convictions. The persons who most persistently articulate this view today are the lay preachers, who emerge from the same neighbourhoods and social backgrounds as the majority of Protestants and share their conservative outlooks. While lay preachers are sometimes criticized by clergymen and church leaders for their lack of originality and anti-intellectualism, they express the religious predilections of most church members in the CSI's Tamil congregations, who welcome the Bible-based sermons they preach – calling for simple devotion, warning of the dangers of sin and promising individual salvation.

Both aspects of popular religiosity, however, have been effectively demoted in the course of the twentieth century. The Euro-American missionaries, like their successors in the Indian church hierarchy, by and large refuse(d) to countenance indigenous ideas about misfortune. Thomas (1982) has traced the gradual decline in magical practices and beliefs in England during the seventeenth century. By the era of Protestant expansion throughout the non-Western world these beliefs had all but disappeared from orthodox religion (see Wilson 1973: 71–82), so that the missionaries who arrived in India had been trained in a post-Reformation atmosphere which disparaged thaumaturgical solutions. I was often told by people who had been educated or worked in Christian establishments before independence that the missionaries never spoke about such matters, except to dismiss them as nonsense, or to laugh them away. In the words of one fundamentalist critic, 'The church has many Saduccees – those who deny all that's miraculous and supernatural' (Stanley 1991: 134). In brief, then, Protestants looked in vain to their missionaries and their indigenous clergy for a satisfactory response to their traditional explanations of adversity. Cosmopolitan Protestant elites reinforced ecclesiatical derogation of popular beliefs by dismissing them as the 'superstitions' of simple and uneducated co-religionists.

Further, that aspect of popular religiosity which invoked a simple, conservative approach to Christian belief and practice – the legacy of early missionaries – had by the early part of the twentieth century also been demoted. It was, as I have indicated, overtaken by a theology of liberalism and the social gospel espoused by a confident, modernist and increasingly developmentoriented ecclesiastical hierarchy, supported by a rising middle class. The mass of ordinary Christians, denied the authenticity of their own religious outlooks by the dominant segment within the church and community, are precisely those most attracted to and by recent fundamentalist ideologies which have transformed the Christian 'scene' in Madras.

Global fundamentalism

Fundamentalism in Madras cannot be fully understood simply in the context of historical developments within the Indian Christian fold or even the wider political setting of south India. The post-Second World War Protestant mission field has been transformed as the USA's global economic dominance, its anti-Soviet crusade and the rise of the New Right combined to encourage a reawakening of fundamentalist Christianity. To evolutionism and modernism, which had been the bugbears of fundamentalism from the earliest days, was added the threat of communism, the definition of which soon came to include any government intervention in social arrangements, or any hint of political (as well as religious) liberalism (Barr 1977: 109).[13]

This North American world-view has been systematically exported to all parts of the globe as fundamentalists have become increasingly wealthy and influential at home. By 1986 well over half the 38,000 US personnel in Protestant missions overseas – with a total operating budget of over $500 million – were associated with fundamentalist organizations (see Wilson and Siewert 1986). Ammerman suggests that fundamentalists tended to see 'American military and economic might as guarantors of their ability to evangelize the world' (1991: 40). In the 1970s and 1980s numerous USA-based missions and para-church organizations with a conservative fundamentalist outlook established branches in many areas of Asia, including south India, where they created links with local Christian groups and imported their communications skills, refined in domestic contexts, to these new international settings. It was evidence of how, with their commodification, religions in the USA were expanding their markets (Appiah 1991: 344).[14]

In Madras, foreign missions based mainly in the USA provide financial and other forms of support for most of the large and successful fundamentalist congregations. These missions also seek out independent groups which show signs of expansion, to offer them association and assistance. Many of the latter succumb, although a few choose to retain their autonomy. One well-known evangelist with branches in several parts of Tamil Nadu state has been approached on numerous occasions but has so far resisted any 'takeover' attempts. However, many small sectarian groups with ambitions to grow, or evangelists convinced they have been specially chosen by God, frequently seek to attach themselves to such missions. One explained: 'I know I am called to blow the trumpet for the Lord. . . . So I affiliated to the . . . whose moorings are in the USA.' Some members of elite CSI congregations and the church's lay leadership find such foreign ties threatening: a prominent member of the church acknowledged that '[T]here is a lot of money on and in fundamentalism . . . everywhere you look there is some American fundamentalist group offering money to someone to set up something here.' Some missions do not confine themselves to assisting only fundamentalist organizations.[15] They occasionally offer clergy from mainline churches like the CSI the opportunity to undergo specialist training in their theological colleges abroad, or arrange speaking tours in the USA for senior ecclesiastical figures. In these and other ways they seek to influence the 'modernist' churches to adopt a more sympathetic attitude to fundamentalist doctrine and practice.

Promoting fundamentalism

Foreign evangelists provide models for the many local charismatic figures who claim to have been chosen to do 'God's work'. The preaching skills, modes of self-presentation and performance techniques of the former are known to and emulated by the latter, despite not having access to the same kinds of sophisticated technologies.[16] The most important occasions on which fundamentalist doctrines are promoted are the 'Crusades' – open meetings extending over several evenings – which are organized by fundamentalist organizations and usually attract many hundreds and even thousands of spectators. Crusades are carefully structured, following patterns developed abroad. 'Big time evangelism', according to Marsden, regards the winning of converts as a science and has developed increasingly sophisticated techniques of persuasion (1987: 242–3).

Crusades feature entertainment by gospel singers, nowadays using modern electronic instruments and complex (usually Japanese-made) sound systems; 'messages' by locally popular personalities; and, to crown the evening, the appearance of the star evangelist, who, in presenting the 'Word of God', might use lighting and microphone techniques borrowed from the latest pop singers. These events are advertised by leaflets distributed at all Madras churches, and on the city's ubiquitous wall posters. When I was most recently in Madras in late 1991–early 1992 there were at least a dozen such Crusades being promoted simultaneously by poster and street banner.[17] Frequently the star attractions are foreigners, who tend to come to Madras in the pleasantly temperate winter months and link up with one or more fundamentalist groups who make the detailed arrangements for the visit.

Most local evangelists operate within a neighbourhood context, visiting homes and preaching to a range of small independent prayer groups. Some establish and lead their own fellowships to which persons from different denominations and sects (or none, for they sometimes attract Hindus) in the vicinity affiliate on an informal basis. I first heard about Sister Rachel's assembly when I was visiting members of a CSI congregation situated in a densely populated part of the city inhabited mainly by small artisans and secure but low-paid employees of industrial and public concerns. My host, a third-generation Christian and regular churchgoer, mentioned how several members of his immediate family, though staunch CSI supporters, often attended a nearby assembly run (in their own home) by a couple who welcomed all those who came for help and comfort.

On the two occasions I was present there were perhaps a dozen adults, mainly women (several of whom I recognized as members of the CSI congregation), and as many children in the room. Sister Rachel, a quiet, serious woman, led them in singing and prayers – mainly personal requests for boons – and then offered a lengthy Bible reading and exegesis. Finally, she called for 'testimonies'. The women who stood up to testify spoke not only or even predominantly of their own problems but of those relating to their close kin. They referred to a variety of challenges and difficulties overcome within the family – employment found, examinations passed, surgery undergone without ill-effects, a good marriage arranged, an illness healed and so on. These successes were all attributed to the prayers offered and fasts undergone by Sister Rachel, who, they attested, was being 'used mightily by God'. After the testimonies, when most of the people had left, she invited a few women to meet her individually in another room to discuss their problems. Her husband occasionally takes the service but acknowledges that only his wife has the requisite gifts which give her the 'power' to transform people's lives in the way we heard.

One CSI congregant who was among the women present when I attended the assembly later told me:

> Our pastor is a good man who serves God in his way but he has too many members to worry about so he can't listen to our individual problems. Anyway, he is only the bishop's employee and doesn't have the power of someone like Sister Rachel, who is especially chosen by God to do His work.

Though the activities of such evangelists are restricted to local areas and tiny fallowings, they tend to emulate (and frequently criticize) the performance styles of the more popular figures. If they achieve extra-neighbourhood reputations, they might be invited to share the platforms of the more famous evangelists, possibly of those from the West. Eventually, they may hope to achieve sufficient fame to attract large audiences on their own. (At that point they would probably begin to preach in English and have a Tamil translator.) The most popular indigenous evangelists are known and travel throughout south India and to other parts of Asia, where the local Tamil communities organize Crusades. Several have now established organizations to handle their business and travel arrangements, reply to the countless letters asking for help and advice, and promote the records and tapes of their songs and sermons, which are broadcast on commercial radio stations beamed to south India.[18] The most successful evangelist in south India has upwards of 100 employees to run his many enterprises, which include, in addition to the above, a 'Prayer Tower' (where, for a fee, daily prayers are offered during the first years of an individual's life); weekly open sessions, where families can meet counsellors to request special prayers and watch videos of the evangelist; a 'degree'-giving Institute of Evangelism; and (still in the planning stages) a medical college.

Like famous fundamentalist preachers in the USA, these local evangelists represent themselves to their publics by means of narratives which draw heavily on the imagery of death/destruction and rebirth (see Ostow 1990: 106). Their autobiographies, which become public knowledge through print and by word of mouth, contrast their lives before and after their transformation from nominal to true Christian, from doubter to believer. They portray themselves, in the period prior to 'conversion', as on the brink of spiritual and/or physical death. They speak and write of bodies 'full of sores and pain', scholastic failure and unemployment, association with unsavoury people, sin-filled lives (smoking, drinking, cinema-going, wearing jewellery, political activity), being on the verge of suicide and, in at least one case, taking poison and being pronounced dead.

The evangelists' first encounter with Jesus is invariably dramatic and assumes a Biblical quality. Luminous hands lift them up to heaven, as in the case of a well-known female preacher, whose biography goes on to report how she:

> heard a voice saying 'My child, my child, my child.' I looked up and the sky opened and I saw a person hanging from a cross. Like Jacob, I met God in a vision. He said 'I have selected you for my work.'

For others, like a popular evangelist who admits to having once been a political activist in the Dravidian movement, the encounter with Jesus is prefigured by a blinding flash of light:

> There was a bright light which blinded my eyes and I felt a hand grasping mine and pulling me upwards into the heavens. I heard a voice saying 'My son, I have forgiven you all your sins.' I knew my conversion was like Paul's the Apostle.

They hear God's voice speaking to them, see His finger pointing to an open Bible, or meet him face to face in a vision. 'I felt the presence of another being in the room. . . . He was the most wonderful person I had ever seen. He told me he was Jesus and we talked for three hours.'[19] The biography of one North American preacher who rose to prominence in the 1940s relates how his conversion came when he was visited by 'an angel bathed in light'. Such books were familiar to several evangelists in Madras and undoubtedly influenced how they chose to represent themselves (see Lindsay 1950; Lanternari 1976: 329). The creation of these local texts and the imagery they promote can therefore be seen as reflecting increasing tendencies towards what Deiros refers to as market-oriented evangelism (1991: 164).

Charismatic fundamentalism

These preachers constantly reiterate the messages of fundamentalist Christianity. They inveigh against the 'coldness' of worship in the traditional churches and the absence of 'strong', i.e. evangelistic, sermons. They attack the clergy for their failure to provide spiritual leadership. They blame the ecclesiastical hierarchy for having allowed the 'cancer' of modernism to sweep through south India, into the Christian colleges, schools and churches (see Daniel 1980: 89–90). The social gospel favoured by the church and community leadership is derided for, among other things, neglecting the quest for individual salvation. Protestant theological institutes and the religious intellectuals who dominate them, are especially vilified for teaching their students (the future clergy) that the Bible contains truths but not the Word of God. In contrast, the fundamentalists insist on the total veracity of the

Bible and reject the notion of competing interpretations. They promote once again the simple 'Christian virtues': in the words of one, 'the body is a temple of God and must not be defiled by smoking, drinking, adultery or fornication'. In short, the new fundamentalists have revived the message of certainty brought by the early missionaries but subsequently overtaken by the social gospel of 'faith', with its acknowledgement of alternative truths.

Fundamentalist evangelists, therefore, advocate views about the nature of Christianity which readily accord with those of ordinary Protestants in Madras. Even more importantly, the majority of these preachers are in tune with popular beliefs about the aetiology and character of misfortune and, furthermore, offer a means of deliverance from it. This requires a word about the Pentecostal leanings of most such figures. Although the first Pentecostal missionaries came to south India in 1908, soon after the 1906 Los Angeles revival which signalled the birth of the 'tongues' movement, as it is sometimes known, it grew slowly and haphazardly in these early years (see George 1975; Sara 1990).[20] It was only after 1960, with the 'charismatic revival' in the USA – most of the major 'televangelists' in North America are Pentecostals – that its impact was felt around the world; it is now widely recognized as the third largest 'force' in Christendom (Goodman 1988: 52).

The success of Pentecostalism in the non-Western world is often attributed to its reaffirmation of local knowledges about the 'supernatural' causes of affliction. In cultures with strong beliefs about the efficacy of mystical agents, writes Wilson, 'the appeal of any missionary denomination which includes thaumaturgical elements should be precisely these, rather than other features of its teachings, activities or organization' (1973: 121). Similarly, Anderson argues that where possession and ecstasy are culturally normal, 'Pentecostalism is fully normal and healthy' (1979: 15). Even the Fuller Seminary in California, one of the most respected theological institutes in the USA, dominated since its founding after the Second World War by fundamentalists and 'progressive' evangelicals, introduced a new course in the 1980s on 'Signs, Wonders and Church Growth', 'on the assumption that much of church growth around the world was associated with charismatic signs' (Marsden 1987: 292).

Far from rejecting popular theodicies, Pentecostals in Madras are wholly in tune with them. During one visit to a neighbourhood evangelist I was told:

> The most common causes of troubles in people's lives are evil spirits (*pey*) and the work of sorcerers (*suniakaran*). The *pey* possess people [on their own or at the behest of sorcerers] and bring calamities and failures, misunderstandings in the home and especially illnesses. If a sorcerer sends an evil spirit he is probably being paid by someone who is angry [with the victim]. People go on seeing doctors to cure their diseases but they don't get better. You have to get rid of the spirit first and only then the person will improve.

> Sometimes sorcerers use magical substances to harm their victims. Once a young woman was brought here and they said she was ready to be married but whenever boys came to see her they ran away. Her relatives couldn't understand it because she was fair and beautiful. So I prayed and asked for God's power and I soon found out that it was the girl's own aunt who was responsible. The woman depended on her niece and didn't want her to get married, so she had paid a sorcerer to put some paste on the girl's face to make her look like like an old hag when boys came to see her.

These kinds of popular belief are shared with Hindus and others outside the Protestant fold. But they are Christianized, by identifying the sources of affliction – evil spirits, sorcerers, etc. – as the servants of Satan. For the first time in the experience of Madras Protestants, then, there is a Christian rationale for and response to such traditionally recognized symptoms of evil in the world. Moreover, these fundamentalists are unanimous in characterizing the lesser deities of non-Christian religions as part of the Satanic pantheon. Just as the early Christians made demons of the gods of Greece and Rome, the Pentecostals relegate Hindu divinities to a similar status (see Russell 1977: 58). While the more popular preachers are somewhat circumspect in expressing such views, because of the growing sensitivity of militant Hindu organizations such as the Rastriya Swayam Sevak Sangh (RSS), neighbourhood evangelists, away from the public glare, continue to offer such unecumenical opinions. (Indeed, Catholics fare little better in the demonology of the average Pentecostal preacher.) Even the CSI's somewhat feeble attempts to 'indigenize' its ritual is seen by some fundamentalists as a concession to Hinduism, a compromise with devil worship. 'There can be no fellowship between light and darkness,' I was told.[21] Such views are especially disapproved of by the orthodox Protestant churches, which continuously seek dialogue and accommodation with Hindu organizations.

Pentecostal evangelists not only acknowledge the reality of evil spirits and other malign agents in the everyday lives of those whom they attempt to persuade but seek to demonstrate their power to overcome these forces. They therefore put the greatest doctrinal stress on the significance of the Holy Spirit in the Christian trinity and identify for special attention its powers or 'gifts' – as set out in Paul's First Letter to the Corinthians (I Cor. XII: 4–11).[22] While all those who receive baptism in the Holy Spirit may obtain one or more of these gifts, only those specially chosen by God – the charismatics – are granted the majority of, if not all, the boons. One Pentecostal leader related how he had come by his charisms:

> After I accepted Jesus, God would talk to me, as you and I are talking now. Then I was filled with the power of the Holy Spirit and got the gift of tongues. After that, God began to give me many

> gifts without my asking: about ten gifts he has given me. The latest is prophecy.

Some claim gifts not on Paul's list, such as the abilities to identify members of an audience who are afflicted in some way, to nullify the effects of sorcery or witchcraft, even to bless and curse in the name of God.

The most important charism is that of healing, for it is on the extent of this power that most charismatics base their claim to be 'used mightily by God' and it is on their ability to heal that their reputations ultimately depend. The most prominent charismatic figure in Madras speaks of being anointed with the Holy Spirit in order to be used 'for the comforting of the sorrowful and for the healing of the sick in body'. The public appearances of the more popular Pentecostal preachers are almost invariably represented as 'divine healing Crusades'. One wall poster, announcing the meetings of a US evangelist, advertised him as the 'World-renowned Outstanding Healing Gift Minister. Millions Receive Healing all over the World. The Blind See, the Deaf Hear and the Lame Walk'.[23] One CSI clergyman, critical of these activities, commented that 'healing has become big business here. At the rate these healers are healing, there shouldn't be one unhealthy person left in Madras.'

One 'Good News' Crusade I attended, which featured an American charismatic well known to local audiences, was held over a period of seven nights on a huge area of beach used for various kinds of public performance. On the evening I was present there was an audience of some 10,000 people, according to the stewards. After several choirs and soloists had sung gospel songs and a brief speech had been made by the head of the organizing committee (which included members of numerous sectarian groups as well as representatives of several independent fundamentalist-leaning fellowships), the star evangelist arrived with a large entourage, several of whom preached to the crowd briefly, with one also reminding them that the evangelist's latest cassettes and pamphlets were available at the stalls situated around the grounds. As it grew dark and the lights came on, he took the stage. As he moved around with a portable microphone, tossing it from one hand to the other, throwing his arms and legs about, his Tamil translator moved with him, duplicating his every gesture. The emphasis throughout the hour-long 'message' was that a miracle was about to occur in everyone's life. 'I am expecting a miracle, a great miracle. You will see proof of the living God tonight.' The Evangelist continuously referred to Jesus' healing miracles and called on those who needed healing to raise their hands (nearly everyone in the vast audience did so). He then proceeded to admonish the evil spirits which brought each illness and commanded them to leave 'in the name of Jesus'. The excitement of such an occasion invariably produces some dramatic results and the evangelist's media team were on hand to record on tape, film and video the 'testimonies' of people who claimed to have been delivered of their particular problems. A group of specially trained assistants was, as usual, also available to counsel those who had, as a consequence of their experience, decided to accept Christ as their personal saviour.

Assessing charismatics

Pentecostals have experienced the fastest recent growth of any Christian group in south India and one report suggests that by 1986 they were the third major 'tradition' in Madras, exceeded only by the Roman Catholic and CSI churches (Hedlund 1986). Nonetheless, Pentecostal and other fundamentalist groups still attract a comparatively small proportion of the Christian population to their ranks. Most people retain their attachments to the institutional churches, because, it is said, they feel bound by sentiment to the churches of their parents, prefer to celebrate their marriages there, wish to have burial rights in their cemeteries, or because it is still considered somewhat disreputable to join a sectarian group outright.

But if most Protestants remain anchored in the historic churches, fundamentalist views and practices have increasingly become part of their religious culture. Most Protestants outside the tiny elite attend many of the large Crusades which take place in Madras each year and in this way become familiar with fundamentalist discourses. Apart from the drama and entertainment value (the music is almost always lively), they appreciate the oratorical skills and 'strong messages' of the evangelists, which speak to and reinforce their own knowledges about both the basic truths of Christianity and the aetiology of affliction. A few members of the historic churches have been persuaded to the extent of taking 'second baptism' and participating fully, if secretly, in the rites of one or other fundamentalist fellowship. Some attach themselves for a time to a sectarian leader in the hope that his or her charismatic intervention will cure an illness, deal with the effects of sorcery, or be instrumental in obtaining a much needed job. Many more attend the regular prayer meetings of neighbourhood evangelists to 'be in the presence' of the Holy Spirit, as well as to hear the 'Word of God' and savour the 'warmth' of worship said to be so lacking in their own churches. Pastors of (non-elite) CSI congregations often complain that after Sunday services in their own churches, 'everyone' goes to the Pentecostals. According to one: 'I can name at least fifty members of my congregation who come for the 7:30am Eucharist service, go home for breakfast and by 10am are at the Pentecostal assembly.'

Even so, they are by no means invariably persuaded by the charismatic claims of the evangelists. The latter are judged, sometimes harshly, by ordinary people who can (and do) withdraw their support at any time. A preacher's large following, his or her thriving organization, or a substantial prayer hall, usually built with donations from individuals who have personally experienced the evangelist's gifts, or with the help of foreign sponsors, are visible evidence of divine and human favour. However, preachers who are deemed to have become too self-seeking, or to have forgotten that they are God's servants and not the other way round, can quickly forfeit the trust of ordinary people. There are several failed charismatics who serve as apt illustrations of how once-popular evangelists can fall short of their ministry and lose their fallowings. Assessments are also based on the success of the charismatics in granting supplicants' wishes. The evidence for their powers is available for everyone to see and hear, since, as I have noted above, those who have been the beneficiaries of these charisms publicly 'witness' to the gifts of the evangelists. Ordinary people are often accused by the latter of being fickle but, as befits the growing commodification of religion, they 'shop around' for the latest spiritual 'products', sometimes discarding the old. During the intervals between each of my visits to Madras (see note 2), it became clear that some earlier favourites had lost popularity and new stars had arisen.

But it is not only the public which judges them; they assess one another as well. Local charismatics are intensely competitive and their evaluations of one another are rarely generous (though I have never heard a foreign preacher criticized). They frequently attribute stubborn 'symptoms' in their clients to the incompetence of healers who 'treated' the victims of mystical attack before them and underline the near fatal consequences of putting oneself in the hands of a less gifted or, worse still, 'false' healer. They are especially caustic about other charismatics known to have health problems, for this is clear evidence that they are unable to heal themselves, let alone others. I have heard at least one well-known evangelist attacked for continuing to hold down a job since, his critics asserted, 'You can't do God's work part-time.' The lesser figures also accuse the more popular ones of abandoning the 'true gospel' so as to curry favour with a wider public.

This constant sniping among local healers, like the fickleness of the public's loyalty to particular individuals, paradoxically attests to a vigorous, even buoyant charismatic scene in Madras. Thomas' (1982: 771) argument that in seventeenth-century England the 'epistemological demand for certain knowledge' based on demonstration ultimately eroded the status of magical beliefs would not be readily applicable to the south Indian situation I have described. Failure to demonstrate healing power may diminish public confidence in particular preachers, but not in the certainty of local knowledge which these charismatics reinforce.

Conclusion

The recent effervescence of fundamentalist forms of Christianity in urban south India represents a striking instance of how international power realignments shape and transform the processes of globalization. Fundamentalist knowledge has been generated within the USA metropolitan setting, promoted abroad through US finance, personnel and technologies and authenticated largely by US dominance. The link between North American power and its global cultural products should seem too obvious to need stating, yet Said has recently felt compelled to draw attention to the considerable 'swathe' the USA now cuts through the rest of the world and the 'almost total absence' in writings by literary theorists, historians and anthropologists of 'any reference to American imperial intervention as a factor affecting the theoretical discussion' (1989: 214). Just as the 'success' of eighteenth- and nineteenth-century Protestant missions outside the West cannot be understood apart from the 'old colonial' contexts in which they took root, any understanding of contemporary fundamentalist influences must consider the religio-cultural implications of this 'new colonial' situation. To avoid the 'circumstances of global power' is to invite the kinds of critique directed at so much postmodernist writing (Harvey 1980: 117).

The increasing pre-eminence of fundamentalist Christianity in urban south India (as elsewhere) can be read as a reassertion of religious certainty and exclusivity against the established churches' admissions of doubt, accommodation and ecumenism, ingredients of the social gospel which has been ascendant within the Protestant church and missions for the better part of a century. The earlier Protestant missionaries had offered their converts the certainties of denominational paths – albeit competing certainties – and a guarantee that Hinduism was the road to perdition; certainties backed, it should be said, by the power of the colonial state. In time, however, the emerging Protestant middle class rejected denominational verities and the church itself, along with the community's elites, turned towards a religion of 'faith'. With independence, such an official Protestant stance enabled the church to survive in an increasingly self-conscious 'Hindu' environment.

The great majority of ordinary Protestants continued to favour a religious culture comprised of two distinctive (and in certain senses conflicting) sets of beliefs and practices. One, the legacy of their early missionaries, stressed a simple, pietistic and Bible-centred approach to Christian life and worship. The other constituted a species of popular knowledge about misfortune through which they (along with the non-Christians amongst whom they lived) understood the world of adversity around them. Both kinds of certainty were effectively denied by the church hierarchy, as by urban Protestant elites. The confidence of most Protestants in the veracity of such knowledge helps to explain, on the one hand, its persistence in the face of marginalization and, on the other, the success of global (especially Pentecostalist) fundamentalism in the past few decades. The ideologies purveyed by the foreign evangelists and their local counterparts accord with and give credence to these local certainties.

The advance of fundamentalist forms of Christianity in south India might therefore be understood both as the certainty of global power located within the metropolitan centre and as a meeting of global and local religious verities. The duality, however, can only be heuristic; for, as we have seen, global knowledge (that of the early missionaries) became part of local

Protestantism, while one aspect of popular religiosity (ideas about mystical agency) was incorporated (if instrumentally) in the epistemology of global fundamentalism.

What I remain uncertain about is the different statuses of the certainties encountering one another. Lambek (in Chapter 11 of this volume) suggests we might look to Bakhtin for a useful distinction between the certainty of authoritative discourse that is externally imposed and the certainty of internally persuasive discourse. We can tentatively characterize the discourses of early Euro-American missionaries and content porary US fundamentalists as *explicit* credos from without, while popular explanations of misfortune would count as *implicit* forms of certainty. But this would be to essentialize these knowledges which are, in practice, constantly reformulated and, as Bakhtin notes, in dialogic interrelationship (1981: 341–2). Moreover, in the urban south Indian context the authoritative discourses of Western religious ideologues have in the past been and continue in the present to become internally persuasive for large sections of the local Protestant community. At that point they are transformed from global to local certainties.

Attention to global–local interchanges raises questions about the view long held in south Asian studies that we can only make sense of 'minority' world religions by situating them primarily in the Hindu context (see Dumont 1970: 205–11). Such an approach attributes little relevance to transnational politico-religious currents; or, as one critic puts it, 'foreign influence is submerged in an all-pervasive Indian sump' (Stirrat 1992: 196). In his own study of Catholicism in Sri Lanka, Stirrat acknowledges the importance of indigenous Sri Lankan forces but insists on the need to take account of 'the wider world of the Catholic Church' (*ibid.*). Making a not dissimilar point, Werbner (in Chapter 6 of this volume) suggests that there are crucial aspects of Sufism which transcend specific cultural environments. Thus an interest in processes of globalization requires us to keep both parts of the equation in our sights. As anthropologists, our focus almost inevitably falls on the 'vernacular' (James and Johnson 1988), on the subaltern communities and localities which respond to (even resist) invasive cultural forces (Hannerz 1992: 35). But 'globalization' is not a monolithic process, with similar outcomes in every instance. The situation I have discussed in this chapter demonstrates aspects of local mediation, homogenization and creolization of cultures but also reveals the inexorable spread of Western religious ideologies. One certain knowledge is that the encounter we are attempting to understand is not an equal one.

Notes

1 I am indebted to Wendy James for her stimulating pre-conference notes circulated to participants in the Section on 'Religious and Cultural Certainties' at the ASA Decennial Conference in July 1993 and for subsequent editorial advice.

Thanks are also due to Pat Caplan for helpful comments on an earlier draft of this chapter.

2 I have followed developments in Madras for nearly twenty years, conducting fieldwork there in 1974–5, 1981–2 and 1991–2. The most recent visit of approximately four months was made possible by an award from the Nuffield Foundation and a supplementary grant from the British Academy, to whom I express my gratitude.

3 Lambek (in Chapter 11 of this volume) makes the point that the 'local' culture he observed in 1975 was a product of much earlier, mainly Islamic, influences which had reached Mayotte.

4 The notion of 'fundamentalism' has acquired some extremely negative connotations of late and clearly should only be employed as a comparative, analytic term with the utmost caution (see Caplan 1987a). The term does, however, have a respectable ancestry in the context of twentieth-century Protestant history and it is for this reason that I feel justified in using it without constant resort to inverted commas.

5 Although there are some significant theological distinctions among fundamentalists, evangelicals and Pentecostals, there are also important similarities (see Wilcox 1992). Deiros (1991) conflates these terms in his discussion of Latin American fundamentalism, while Anderson argues that Pentecostalism should be regarded as part of the fundamentalist movement (1979: 6).

6 The specific political contexts in which Western religious ideologies are purveyed and understood have been transformed since (and by) India's independence. Whereas until well into the twentieth century Christian missionaries benefited from official protection if not active state support, the post-independence era saw successive governments curtailing missionary numbers and activities. At the same time, Indian Christians have come to regard themselves as a vulnerable minority in a population increasingly jealous of its 'Hindu' character.

7 Shamsul (in Chapter 5 of this volume) suggests a not dissimilar divide among Malaysian university students. On the one side are those associated with the radical *dakwah* revivalist movement, who insist on the certainty of Islamic 'revealed knowledge' and on the other are those who, through commitment to unrevealed (human) knowledge gained from social sciences, tend to affiliate to the moderate wing of *dakwah*.

8 Some two-thirds of Indian Christians reside in the four southern states of Kerala, Andhra Pradesh, Karnataka and Tamil Nadu. They form the largest minority in the latter, with a population in 1981 of approximately 2.8 million or just under 6 per cent of the state's total.

9 The first Protestant mission in south India was a Lutheran station established in the first decade of the eighteenth century in the Danish territory of Tranquebar on the Coromandel coast. The first mission in Madras city was set up in 1726.

10 The CSI was formed in part because the missionaries realized the folly of perpetuating their denominational distinctions in the Indian context. Increasing interdenominational co-operation in the health and education fields and the emerging Indian nationalist movement, further encouraged ecumenical thinking. But its realization was at least as much due to an emerging Indian Christian middle class which could not tolerate rigid denominational barriers in the course of economic and social advancement (see Caplan 1980).

11 Baptists and Lutherans were the only two major Protestant denominations which remained outside the union.

12 As Marsden points out, the suggestion that God reveals himself in non-Christian religions can have 'profound implications for missionary programs' (1980: 167).

13 In the USA of late the association between fundamentalism and right-wing politics has become explicit (see Wilcox 1992). Deiros, writing about the 'phenomenal'

expansion of fundamentalist groups in Latin America, suggests that the link between this growth, the US (Republican) administration's political offensive and support for right-wing regimes is 'forged of ideology, history and world-view, not of conspiracy' (1991: 176–7).

14 Such forms of Christianity have not only been exported outside the West of course. Coleman has studied a Swedish sect which has been heavily influenced by US fundamentalism (1991).

15 Some of the more 'progressive' fundamentalists are ready to engage with and thereby influence modernist churches, which contradicts the general tendency towards separatism among such organizations. Thus Billy Graham has often been attacked by other fundamentalist groups for co-operating with non-fundamentalist churches, as has Jerry Falwall of the 'Moral Majority' for his readiness to make common cause with unbelievers (see Ammerman 1991: 46)

16 Deiros notes how in Latin America local evangelists 'consciously imitate US counterparts' (1991: 164).

17 For the first time in 1992 I noticed one such Crusade being advertised on a huge billboard of the kind which normally only announces a new film. The US evangelist's face appeared between the giant cut-out figures of several Tamil movie stars in Ramboesque poses.

18 Since they cannot broadcast on state radio in India, these evangelists buy time on such stations as Radio Ceylon and Radio Seychelles. There are, as yet, no televangelists in south India.

19 The US evangelist Pat Robertson was said to 'scandalize' Biblicist fundamentalists of the Falwell ('Moral Majority') type because of his reports of conversations with God (Averill 1989: 115).

20 Anderson reports that scores of Pentecostal missionaries went abroad in the early years of the twentieth century convinced that with their facility for 'speaking in tongues' they would have the miraculous ability to preach the gospel in the languages of the natives. He reports widespread disillusion when they discovered that glossolalia meant something quite different (1979: 139).

21 The staid Fuller Seminary in California was 'chagrined' at the advice given by one member of staff to Christians who happened to visit 'pagan' temples on their travels in foreign lands: they would be well advised, he suggested, to 'exorcise their homes from demons' who might have 'attached themselves to persons or luggage' (Marsden 1987: 294).

22 These are prophecy, tongues, healing, faith, interpretation, discernment, wisdom, miracles and knowledge.

23 This excerpt from Matthew XI: 5 is frequently quoted in the advertisements of fundamentalist evangelists. Leaflets promoting the appearance of Morris Cerullo, 'the World Famous International Evangelist', at the Royal Albert Hall in London in 1992, announced his 'Great Miracle Crusade – Salvation – Healing – Miracles' and ended with 'The Blind See, the Deaf Hear, the Lame Walk'.

24 Anderson notes that Pentecostal healing prayers almost always include a commandment to the 'deaf spirit', the 'cancer demon', etc. to come out in the name of Jesus (1979: 95).

References

Ammerman, N. T. (1991) 'North American Protestant fundamentalism', pp. 1–65, in M. E. Marty and R. S. Appleby (eds) *Fundamentalisms Observed*, Chicago: University of Chicago Press.

Anderson, R. M. (1979) *Vision of the Disinherited: the making of American Pentecostalism*, New York: Oxford University Press.

Appiah, K. A. (1991) 'Is the post- in postmodernism the post- in postcolonial?' *Critical Inquiry*, 17: 336–57.

Averill, L. J. (1989) *Religious Right, Religious Wrong: a critique of the fundamentalist phenomenon*, New York: Pilgrim Press.

Bakhtin, M. M. (1981) *The Dialogic Imagination*, M. Holguist (ed.), trans. C. Emerson and M. Holquist, Austin, TX: University of Texas Press.

Barr, J. (1977) *Fundamentalism*, London: SCM Press.

Caplan, L. (1980) 'Class and Christianity in south India: indigenous responses to western denominationalism', *Modern Asian Studies*, 14: 645–71.

—— (1987a) 'Introduction', pp. 1–24, in L. Caplan (ed.) *Studies in Religious Fundamentalism*, London: Macmillan.

—— (1987b) *Class and Culture in Urban India: fundamentalism in a Christian community*, Oxford: Clarendon Press.

Coleman, S. (1991) 'Faith which conquers the world: Swedish fundamentalism and the globalization of culture', *Ethnos*, 56: 6–18.

Daniel, J. (1980) *Another Daniel*, Madras: The Laymen's Evangelical Fellowship.

Deiros, P. A. (1991) 'Protestant fundamentalism in Latin America', pp. 142–96, in M. E. Marty and R. S. Appleby (eds) *Fundamentalisms Observed*, Chicago: Chicago University Press.

Diehl, C. G. (1965) *Church and Shrine: intermingling patterns of culture in the life of some Christian groups in south India*, Uppsala: Hakan Ohlssons Boktryckeri.

Dumont, L. (1970) *Homo Hierarchicus: the caste system and its implications*, trans. Mark Sainsbury, Chicago: University of Chicago Press.

George, T. C. (1975) 'The growth of Pentecostal churches in south India', MA thesis in Missiology, Fuller Seminary, Pasadena, CA.

Goodman, F. D. (1988) *How about Demons? Possession and exorcism in the modern world*, Bloomington, IN: Indiana University Press.

Hannerz, U. (1992) 'The global ecumene as a network of networks', pp. 34–58, in A. Kuper (ed.) *Conceptualizing Society*, London: Routledge.

Harvey, D. (1980) *The Condition of Postmodernity: an enquiry into the origins of cultural change*, Oxford: Basil Blackwell.

Hedlund, R. E. (1986) 'Church planting in selected Indian cities', unpublished seminar paper. Church Growth Research Centre, Madras.

James, W. and D. H. Johnson (eds) (1988) *Vernacular Christianity: Essays in the Social Anthropology of Religion, Presented to Godfrey Lienhardt* (JASO Occasional Papers no. 7), Oxford and New York: JASO/Lilian Barber Press.

Lanternari, V. (1976) 'Dreams as charismatic significants: their bearing on the rise of new religious movements', pp. 321–35, in A. Bharati (ed.) *The Realm of the Extra-human: ideas and actions*, The Hague: Mouton.

Lawrence, B. B. (1990) *Defenders of God: the fundamentalist revolt against the modern age*, London: I.B. Taurus.

Lindsay, G. (in collaboration with W. Branham) (1950) *William Branham: a man sent from God*, Jeffersonville, IN: William Branham.

Marsden, G. (1980) *Fundamentalism and American Culture: the shaping of twentieth-century evangelicalism 1870–1925*, New York: Oxford University Press.

—— (1987) *Reforming Fundamentalism: Fuller Seminary and the new evangelicalism*, Grand Rapids, MI: William B. Eerdmans.

Marty, M. E. and R. S. Appleby (eds) (1991) *Fundamentalisms Observed*, Chicago: University of Chicago Press.

Norman, E. (1979) *Christianity and the World Order*, Oxford: Oxford University Press.

Ostow, M. (1990) 'The fundamentalist phenomenon: a psychological perspective', pp. 99–125, in N. Cohen (ed.) *The Fundamentalist Phenomenon: a view from within: a response from without*. Grand Rapids, MI: William B. Eerdmans.

Russell, J. B. (1977) *The Devil: perceptions of evil from antiquity to primitive Christianity*, Ithaca, NY: Cornell University Press.

Said, E. (1989) 'Representing the colonized: anthropology's interlocutors'. *Critical Inquiry*, 15: 205–25.

Sara, K. O. (1990) 'A Critical Evaluation of the Indian Pentecostal Church of God – its origin and development in Kerala', MA thesis, Serampore University.

Stanley, R. (1991) 'Signs and Wonders', *India Church Growth Quarterly*, 13: 133–7.

Stirrat, R. L. (1992) *Power and Religiosity in a Post-Colonial Setting: Sinhala Catholics in contemporary Sri Lanka*, Cambridge: Cambridge University Press.

Thomas, K. (1982) [1971] *Religion and the Decline of Magic*, Harmondsworth: Penguin Books.

Towler, R. (1984) *The Need for Certainty: a sociological study of conventional religion*, London: Routledge and Kegan Paul.

Wilcox, C. (1992) *God's Warriors: the Christian Right in twentieth-century America*, Baltimore, MD: Johns Hopkins University Press.

Wilson, B. (1973) *Magic and the Millennium*, London: Paladin.

Wilson, S. and J. Siewert (eds) (1986) *Mission Handbook: North American Protestant ministries overseas*, Monrovia, CA: Missions Advanced Research and Communication Center.

79

JOANA'S STORY

Syncretism at the actor's level

André Droogers

Source: S. Greenfield and A. Droogers (eds), *Reinventing Religions: Syncretism and Transformation in Africa and the Americas*, Lanham, MD: Rowman and Littlefield, 2001, pp. 145–62.

Introduction

Syncretism usually is looked at from the supra-individual level. Either the religions from which elements are selected or the religion that is the result of such a syncretic process is at the center of analysis. Even though anthropologists are in the habit of giving due attention to "real people doing real things," rarely do informants speak directly to the reader. The discourse remains almost always on the structural level. Yet if the triangle of signification developed in chapter 1 makes some sense, it would seem useful to pay attention to the way actors deal with structures and how their way of interpreting events and positioning themselves is related to this process. Such a micro-anthropological approach might make visible how an individual engaged in the syncretic process constructs his or her identity, making an effective and strategic use of the repertoires or religious beliefs and other schemas that are available in his or her social environment.

In this chapter such an effort is undertaken. The main character is Joana (not her real name), a Brazilian woman, at the time of the fieldwork in her forties and living in the greater Porto Alegre metropolitan region. Part of her life history is described and analyzed. Taped conversations with her took place in 1990 and 1995, as part of my research on the religiosity of people who do not consider themselves members of a religious institution.

To Joana, the years between 1990 and 1995 had been particularly turbulent. As I will show, her religious beliefs helped her to survive the consequences of a failed marriage with a violent man and the tragic end of a harmonious but impossible relationship with another man. In marshalling all the resources available to her, she showed herself to be doing what anthropologists think of as "syncretizing," without knowing the term. Her case also shows how religion and its mixing may empower a woman when she is confronted by the disadvantages of gender differences. This is not a form of power that necessarily enables her to influence other people's behavior. The prime beneficiary of the syncretic empowerment seems to be Joana herself, because she found a way to manage her life and to survive a deep crisis. Though her problem was partly that there was a difference of power between genders, and her husband exercised his power over her in a violent manner, her form of empowerment did not lead him to change his behavior but gave her the power to live her own life.[1]

I present her story as she told it. No effort was made to verify the events with other people. What use did Joana make of the religious resources she has come into contact with in the course of her life? What are her views on what it is to be a woman, a man (in the south of Brazil where she lived)? The two aspects of power that were mentioned above will be examined in the context of gender and religion: How did Joana manage to survive and to (re)organize her life? And what role did her religious experience play in this syncretic process of empowerment?

An interesting characteristic of Joana's story is that she belongs to the category of persons who do not participate in institutionalized forms of religion. Yet her repertoire of religious models comes to a large degree from institutionalized religion. To facilitate our understanding of the contrast between an actor's free use of repertoires and the institutional aspect of religion, a distinction might be made among three dimensions of institutionalized religion: (a) the internal, (b) the external (both predominantly social structural, but always with a signification aspect) and (c) the supernatural (predominantly cultural or symbolic, but often with a social structural aspect). The social relations existing in the internal and external dimensions are subject to cultural meaning-making. The beliefs concerning God, gods, spirits and saints, on the other hand, imply relations—modeled after the social structure—between them and believers: God is the Father/Mother, etc.

The relations between the opposite categories in each dimension are in fact power relations. Internally, religious specialists and lay people dispute their spheres of influence. Often gender is an essential part of this dimension, as for example when religious specialists are exclusively or predominantly male. Externally all the believers are related in some way to society where a certain religious view may be dominant, perhaps theirs, just as a particular gender definition may predominate. Alternative views and definitions may occur. Supernaturally speaking, power is also present in the relationship between believers and sacred entities, and here too gender notions may be of influence as when God, gods or spirits are explicitely viewed as male or female.

The three dimensions should be viewed in connection with each other. In each concrete case, one should expect idiosyncrasies as a consequence of the particular link or absence of linkage among dimensions. This may include contradictions among dimensions, since it is improbable that the three dimensions will ever be in total harmony and consistency. What is affirmed at one point can be contradicted in another situation. Thus the supernatural dimension has much weight, especially in official ideal versions of religions. Yet, in practice the supernatural dimension may at times be ignored as in the internal dimension—principles being amended under the influence of practice.

An advantage of this inter-dimensional approach is that the usual debate between mechanistic and subjectivist approaches may be avoided. Structure and agency both receive due attention, because the relationships between actors, including supernatural ones, are taken into account. Besides, a focus on the supernatural dimension will help to avoid a one-sided reductionist view on religion, as if the social structural mechanisms explain everything. Important as these latter may be, they cannot be taken as the only factor in the process of religious production, and it seems worthwhile to consider cultural structural processes as well.

Since the focus in this chapter is on one actor, a few remarks should be made with regard to the relationship between agency and structure. Actors can be shown to interpret events and phenomena, appealing to a repertoire of meanings available in structures, both symbolic and social in nature. As was shown in figure 1.1 in chapter 1, signification praxis can be represented within the triangle of signification, connecting events, structures and actors. When events or phenomena cannot be interpreted by an appeal to the available social and symbolic structures, structural changes will occur and new meanings will be added to these structures. On the other hand, events and phenomena are partly formed under the influence of social and symbolic structures. It is within this triangle that actors construct their identity with regard to gender as well as religion.

This may be stated in a different way in terms of the connectionist approach developed recently within cognitive anthropology.[2] The central question in cognitive anthropology is how knowledge is organized culturally. Connectionism takes its name from the connections that are assumed to exist between parallel archives of knowledge in the human mind. Thanks to these connections, these archives can be consulted simultaneously, as it were paradigmatically, just as the conductor of an orchestra, within a split second, in one summarizing view, consults the scores of the different instruments. This approach contrasts with the usual view that people organize their knowledge in the same manner as when they speak or write: i.e., according to so-called sentential logic. One might also call this a syntagmatic approach, just as when a listener to a CD with orchestral music selectively hears the main theme only and is able to sing or whistle along. Now, if people, as was suggested above through the triangle of signification, consult social and symbolic structures in their meaning-making process, they are appealing, in a simultaneous manner, to different but connected archives. Once they reach a conclusion in the paradigmatic manner, they will formulate this in the easier observable syntagmatic manner of sentential logic.

The term "schema" often is used instead of archive. D'Andrade defines schema as "the organization of cognitive elements into an abstract mental object capable of being held in working memory with default values or open slots which can be variously filled in with appropriate specifics."[3] The open slots remind one not only of a computer, but also of an empty bureaucratic form that must be filled in in terms of a concrete case. Religion is packed with schemas that help people to organize and interpret their experience. Again, these schemas are not as eternal as the gods that populate them are said to be: people adapt schemas to their experience, just as their schemas act as constraints on their behavior. Each new situation obliges a person to make a rapid and simultaneous consultation of the available schemas that fit the situation—usually a routine procedure; but if the schemas do not fit the situation or simply have been forgotten, new schemas will be developed, perhaps after some degree of confusion and chaos.

Power, in its aspect of influence on behavior, has the tendency to slow down this process, because it depends in its exercise on the constancy of certain schemas, imposed on the actors that are being influenced. Those in power therefore prefer the verbalized sentential logic over the—to them, risky—connectionist "let a thousand flowers flourish" practice. The politicians do not like subversives. The clergy generally do not like the heretics. Similarly, concrete gender situations can be interpreted and managed with the help of a number of more abstract schemas with regard to maleness and femaleness. Schemas are subject to change, according to changes in the signification process. Changing views on gender refer to alterations in current schemas.

There is one more characteristic of the concept of schema that is worth mentioning. D'Andrade distinguishes among three classes of schemas, organized hierarchically.[4] The first class of schemas is that of the master motives, containing a person's most general goals, acting rather autonomously in instigating behavior (e.g., love, security, play, providing for oneself). Below this is the class of more intermediate goals that help in the realization of the master motives. D'Andrade gives the examples of a job and marriage. The lowest class is that of the schemas that depend on the preceding classes for their motivation. These schemas are often part of daily routine. Thus, if the master motive of marriage is love, marriage in turn motivates the writing of a love letter or the purchase of a bouquet. Behavior is understood by D'Andrade to be the result of hierarchically organized sets of goal-schemas.[5] The motivational force of schemas diminishes according to the hierarchy of the three classes. Each person defines his or her own hierarchy.

Armed conceptually, I turn now to Joana's story.

Joana's story

Joana's case illustrates how religion can be a source of power for a woman. When I first met her, in 1990, Joana gave me the impression of being a happy and balanced person. She had been married for almost twenty years. Her husband was employed as a salesman in an international technical firm and spent much of his free time, especially on weekends, performing regional folk music on local stages. The couple had two daughters, then aged seventeen and nine. Joana was a successful professional. With two years of higher education—interrupted by her marriage—she had worked as a secretary and was now teaching a foreign language to children in a commercial language school.

After being introduced to her in 1990 by her brother-in-law, I queried Joana as to what religion meant to her. Perhaps because it was our first contact, she did not tell me at the time about the trouble she already was having with her husband. She also did not speak about the relationship she had with another man.

When we met again in 1995, her situation was radically different. She had gone through years of deep trouble and in the course of our conversation it became clear that in 1990 life had not been as happy and equilibrated as she had presented it. In what follows I will quote mainly from the 1995 interview. Reference will be made to the earlier interview, however, to show the ongoing process of meaning-making.

Between 1990 and 1995 Joana's marriage had ended. The facts are rapidly told. While working as a musician at places where drinks were on the house, her husband had gradually come to drink too much. As a consequence he lost his regular job as a salesman. The family lost friends. At home he became violent to the point of once, shortly before the interview, trying to kill Joana with a butcher's knife while she was ill in bed. She escaped, as she puts it, by a miracle. She then left him and moved with her daughters to another apartment. Her husband then went to Argentina to work as a musician.

In telling me what happened, Joana refers constantly to her religious convictions.

> Many things happened, including a break-up of the family . . . because my husband is a very difficult person. And thanks to my faith, my conviction that God exists, that someone exists who protects us, I am talking with you today. . . . His latest attack was meant to kill me. It was really very difficult.
>
> He is an alcoholic. He is someone who doesn't have faith in anything. He believes only in himself. He doesn't understand that he needs treatment, that he must have faith in something, that he has to salvage the good things and channel them in a productive manner. . . . For me this was very difficult because I am a very

> objective person. I have a strong will. I have an ideal in life which is my mission: to obtain security for my daughters . . . to make a harmonious home for them. And all this was falling apart.
>
> My daughters also have much faith. None of us regularly attends an institutional religion . . . but we never lose contact with God, from where we get our strength, from where strength really comes. . . . You can see that from their and my faith I always succeed in winding up on my feet. . . . I felt as if I were in a deep dark hole from which I was unable to get out. . . . I was unable to rest, I couldn't eat . . . because he always was making trouble, breaking things, threatening us verbally and sometimes physically.

Joana explained that she always confided in her husband, took care of him, devoted her life to him. She was shocked when he started to behave aggressively. She said that she had always believed that when one married it was for life. As she explained, she felt that she had only one card to play because at the time she thought marriage is for eternity. Therefore she was desperate when things began to go wrong. She concluded, "in a very cold manner," that life is a game in which one may win or lose. She emphasized, however, that one need not idly accept things when they start to go wrong. One must have faith.

> Only somebody who has a very great faith is able to live through such a situation. So thanks to my faith, I knew that God would never leave me alone, that he was waiting for an opportunity, that he would give me a chance to get out of this, to breathe anew as a human being deserves to.

Yet at the height of the crisis her daughters had suggested that God did not exist, because if he did he would not permit these things to happen. Why, they asked, do good people have to suffer so? Joana answered them:

> Only God can answer this for us. We do not have the right to judge what he does. He knows why he is doing these things. One day, [however, we will realize that] all we are going through will enable us to grow and have a marvelous future. Then we will understand why these things happen. Everything in life is a lesson. . . . One should be a warrior and fight the adversities of life. So I think my faith, and my desire to understand what happened, to want to be part of a whole, helped me to be able to talk with you today.

Joana recognizes the role her husband's free will played in destroying him, even though God is the source of this free will. "He [her husband] likes this [the life he leads], so you have to let him live it, isn't that so? It is the free will that God has given him, the right to choose what he wants." Joana is proud, however, to have reacted in time to save herself, after a period in which she took him to a psychotherapist and to Alcoholics Anonymous. When nothing changed she decided that it was time to save herself and her daughters. She believes that she did enough for him and that her conscience is clear.

Joana went on to discuss her belief in guardian angels. She told me about her religious experience as a child, when she was a member of the Assembly of God, a Pentecostal church in which her father, a former Kardecist-Spiritist, was a pastor for some time. She spoke lovingly about her father, telling me, for example, how he always welcomed guests at his table and made hospitality a central value in his house, even though the family scarcely had enough for itself. Her mother was from a Lutheran family. Joana's interest in angels came from neither Pentecostalism nor Lutheranism. "They believed that only God exists and nothing else, no mentor, no guide, it was always God." In 1995, angels had become popular commercially in Brazil and elsewhere. Shops carried statues of them in their windows and sold books about them. With one exception, however, all the books were translations of North American publications.

> . . . a year ago, I got one of those angels as a present. I still keep it in my bedroom. . . . It is not the image that gives me strength. But it makes me feel good when I come into the room, I see the little face of that little angel, . . . and it gives me a kind of strength.

Joana then spoke about God:

> I always talked with God. It was not that I used "ready-made" prayers. . . . I open my heart to him, because I know that he sees everything. I know that better than anyone else God sees everything, he knows all that happens, and why one exists, because I think nothing happens by chance. With me it is like this: I am not an adept of any religion. However, I believe very much in the supreme being, who knows why things happen.

In 1990 Joana did not talk about angels, but the statements she made about the Catholic saints were similar to what she would say five years later about them. The reason why she wanted to be baptized in the Catholic church at the age of eighteen, despite her Pentecostal upbringing, was that she was fascinated by the saints whom she found to be beautiful. As a former Protestant she added that she was aware that the saints in the church were only images before whom she refused to kneel and ask for things. "You don't bargain with God," she insisted. "You may make a request, but then you will have to wait. If you deserve what you ask for, you will get it. I asked a lot from God, and he has helped me and has given me strength." Yet she has her favorite saints, such as St. George and St. Theresa, both of whom, she said, have helped her.

Nevertheless, she does not consider herself to be a typical Catholic and has her difficulties with the institution, its dogmas and especially with its claim to having the absolute truth. "All religions are true, not only the Roman one." Yet she now considers herself to be a Catholic, but of her own making. She refers to Christ and St. Peter as the bringers of the Catholic faith. Yet her view is that faith is much more general and in the end a matter of conscience.

> A person's heart is the church of God. God first came into my heart and then I went to the religion. God always was my friend, the best friend I have. . . . I think the best judgment, the best God we have, is our conscience. We all have faith.

In the 1990 interview Joana was very critical of what she considered to be the commercial activities in the Catholic church, such as baptism and burial being given only after payment. She compares the richness of the church with one of her earliest experiences with religion, when a priest teaching religious education in her class at a public school said that all the rich children would burn in hell. Joana says she then decided not to take part in church life.

Joana referred to a very un-Catholic element in her religious beliefs in our 1995 conversation: reincarnation. "I believe in other lives, and in lives already lived." She linked this to the idea that what a person experiences and suffers from in this life is a consequence of what she or he has done in a previous life. By suffering now you pay, as it were, for what you have done in the past. She used this notion to explain her husband's violence and believes that by now she has fully paid her debt from a former life because "not even Christ would accept what he did to me." The fact that she escaped from his attempt to kill her as by a miracle gives a special meaning to the idea that her life has been saved and that a new phase definitely has begun. She compared herself to a Phoenix risen from the ashes. Yet she still lives with the trauma of her past and almost every night she dreams that she is fleeing from her husband. She says that her prayers are her therapy and when her daughters have nightmares in which their father appears she advises them to pray and to ask God for protection and to take these traumas away.

In 1990 Joana referred to the Kardecist-Spiritist belief in reincarnation when she told me that early in her marriage she had given birth to two still-born babies. She still was grieving for them at the time. Her eldest sister, though not a Kardecist, had told her that she in fact was privileged because God used her womb so that "these spirits of light" could come into her body and move on again.

This helped her overcome the loss of the two children. Treatment by a Kardecist therapist later on helped her with a problem of persistent headaches.

Joana also told me about her eldest daughter who suffered from a pain in the leg and who in a dream saw herself being operated on by the spirit of a young doctor who had recently died in a traffic accident in the town where they live. The girl identified herself increasingly with Kardecism. She has intuition, Joana observed, but is afraid to become a medium herself.

In 1993 Joana participated in a Bahai group for about six months, but withdrew because she did not wish to assume the leadership role she was offered. Also, she did not agree with some of the central ideas of Bahai belief, despite finding that faith in general and its prayers in particular beautiful. She had trouble, for example, accepting the belief that Christ, like many other enlightened persons, was merely a "sun ray" from God and that Bahaullah was "almost more divine than God himself." To her Christ is a marvelous figure. Even if he is not the son of God, to her he should be "because he fought, he sacrificed himself for the ideal he had, for the appreciation he had of human beings, for his simplicity and his abnegation."

Talking about these experiences Joana concluded that organized religion always exaggerates and distorts. Its obligations deny free will: "One should see God as a good thing, not as a being that is going to punish us." She prefers to pray by herself, which does not preclude the possibility that now and then she may attend a religious session and enjoy it, be it Bahai or Kardecist-Spiritist or other. "Sometimes I enter a Catholic church when there is nobody there and I pray. It does me good, and it gives me a delicious peace. I feel really better."

Her youngest daughter remained within the Bahai group and even went to international meetings. Eventually, however, she also left, although she did not abandon the faith itself. Joana tells how, at the time she herself was involved with the Bahais, she first attempted to live apart from her husband. The members of the group helped her. The way her youngest daughter, who still identifies as a Bahai, lived through the events, also had religious overtones. The girl had promised to pray a certain number of prayers to Bahaullah in whom she "has very great faith." Though she has distanced herself from the Bahais, Joana says that she supports her daughter's participation: "It is good to have such faith." After Joana escaped the assault by her husband, her daughter pledged to pray to Bahaullah for nine consecutive days in payment of the *promessa* (vow) she had made. Making a vow, usually to a saint, and fulfilling it when one has received what one has asked for are very common in popular Catholicism. This practice had been adopted and incorporated by her daughter as part of her Bahai faith.

Joana has discovered other sources of strength. She saw a movie about the life of Tina Turner and learned to her surprise that the famous singer had lived through situations similar to what she experienced. One of her daughters then gave her the book the movie was based on. She identified with Turner even more as she read it. She learned from it, she said, not to hold on too long to things that bother you, be it work, or a marriage.

"I think this is what I am doing, allowing myself to have a bit of happiness in my way," she added.

"Thanks to the good God," Joana sees her relationship with her daughters as being harmonious and even a form of sisterhood (the Portuguese word for sisterhood, *irmandade*, also is used to refer to a religious order).

Towards the end of the 1995 interview, when she was talking about her belief in reincarnation and in memories from previous lives, Joana offered an example. She spoke about a platonic relationship she had had for eight years with an older man who was not married. It ended with his death in 1993. The relationship according to Joana was characterized by great affection. "I had a very good friend. He was somebody like . . . if I were not married at the time, he would have been the ideal person that I always wanted in my life." It was a case of love on both sides. Yet, they did not get involved sexually because "he understood my situation . . . that I would never want to do something I believed was wrong. I would not feel good about it."

Joana told her husband about the relationship and he did not object to it. She would not leave him for this man. Although they continued to see each other socially, Joana would never visit him at his apartment.

They first met when Joana took a job as a secretary in an office where he was employed. No one else seemed to like him, which made her wonder why she did. "To me he was the sweetest person you can imagine." She was almost certain that she had met him previously somewhere and had been fond of him. Thinking about it, she remembered having dreamt about him when she was a girl. The dream took place in a castle with beautiful lawns surrounding it. The two were together, a couple obviously in love. "It was something very real to me, I even felt his body at my side. He cared for me and liked me." The conclusion she reached was that they had been lovers in a former life who had met again in this one.

Shortly before his death he had telephoned her asking her to come to his apartment. Joana still remembers the exact date. She refused, however, telling him: "You know I will always love you, but I cannot visit you." He countered that some day when she would decide to visit him, it would be too late. Her reaction was to ask whether this was a threat, "that on the day that I would be free, you would not want me anymore?" Two weeks later when she called him at his office, the secretary said that she could not speak with him. Joana felt guilty believing that it was because she had refused to come to his place. She then was transferred to the secretary's boss who told her that her friend had died on the day she had last spoken with him. The official cause of his death was an aneurysm.

Joana felt that she had been robbed.

> My God, why this? I live with a very difficult person who tortures me. I am not ashamed of what I thought then: Why did he die and not

> my husband? Why does somebody die who is good and productive in life. But today I understand that I can't control life. It just happens. It is fate that one has to accept and that happens. It passes, it passed. No other way. Because of what happened, I believe in my previous lives. This immense causality . . .

Joana's presentation of this episode in her life emphasized the contradiction that whereas her friend always was kind and caring with her, to others he was thought of as being nasty and imposing and was not liked because of it. The only explanation she could come up with came from a dream that, she said, may have been a brief rememberance of a former life. "I really expect, and I say this sincerely, that we will have another life together . . . [although] an enormous emptiness remained here. It has marked me." Joana added that one day she read the phrase, "God who made the shoulders also made crosses." She concluded that God knows the size of a person's shoulders and thus also that of the cross the person is able to carry. "And also till when you have to carry it. I think the most difficult part I have finished carrying. I put it down already. It's over." At times she thinks that he is not dead, that one day he will call her and tell her it was all a joke. On the day of our interview, Joana reported having seen someone on a passing bus who could have been his twin. The man had lifted his sunglasses and looked at her. "But of course, it was not him. If it had been, he would have gotten off the bus at the next stop. So it wasn't him. But I was really upset."

Discussion

Joana's story enables us to examine how one Brazilian woman creatively mobilized pieces from several of the religious belief systems in her culture to find meaning and understanding in a time of personal crisis. It shows syncretism in the making and reveals the process of syncretizing. It also offers us insight into some of the power processes that occur in the construction of gender identities in a religious context. The case is not necessarily representative at the societal level, although it represents a process that may be occurring on a much wider scale. It may be that the Brazilian cultural context is optimal for the combination of ideas and practices that would seem incompatible in other settings.[6] The events in Joana's married life forced her to find meaning in what had happened to her. With every new event she was obliged to construct her own triangle of signification, drawing on a score of schemas in her repertoire, as it was accumulated and adapted in the course of her life. Strikingly, the schemas she used, including her views on gender, are basically, though not exclusively (Tina Turner!), religious in nature. In maneuvering her triangles of signification she managed to survive, defending herself and her two daughters. The vocabulary she used expressed her struggle and directly referred to power and strength (*força*).

In the course of her life, Joana has become acquainted with a number of religious worldviews. Some of these she knew from her own experience, whereas others were known to her through discussions with friends and relatives. Thus she had learned about Kardecist-Spiritism indirectly and assimilated it through discussions with her sister. Direct participation does not seem to be a precondition for the adoption of ideas. Seen from the perspective of institutionalized religion, some of these views are considered mutually exclusive, but this did not impede Joana from picking and choosing and using them as she liked. Her decision not to actively participate in a religious group put her in what might be thought of as the informal sector of religion. One might say that she did not have a religion, but was very religious. The experiences she has had with a variety of religions in the course of her life have led her to avoid participation. Yet she understands and knows these religions, in their internal and external dimensions, and especially in their supernatural dimension. The way in which she constructs her religious identity is an indirect criticism of rule-directed formal institutionalized religion, which she considers *bitolada*: narrow, limited, short-sighted. The use she made during our conversations of parallel schemas (in connectionist terms) from different religions put her nearer to the paradigmatic comparative pole (the conductor's view of the scores) than to that of syntagmatic sentential logic (the single theme whistled by the listener), which she in fact condemned as dogmatic and too narrow. Her independent position has made it possible for her to apply such a syncretic approach.

Thus, indirectly, the elements she took from different religious sources made her case in a certain way representative of more than one institutionalized religion, though mainly at the symbolic level, more than at the social structural level, which she generally avoided. What she experienced was relevant only to her, yet it was clearly grounded in the repertories of the Brazilian social and cultural context, even though she made her own selection. The Afro-Brazilian religions were virtually absent from her discourse. In 1990 she had talked about Umbanda, saying that she liked "the vivid colors, the music that is theirs," but that she thought of it as a pagan religion. She was not attracted to it, "not even a little bit."

It is the syncretic climate of Brazilian society, it appears,[7] that enabled Joana to construct her religious and gender identity in the way she did. The Brazilian minimal credo seems to be: A person should have faith, it does not matter which one.[8] Joana showed us how in a creative manner the relative freedom of agency (the subjectivist pole) can be combined with structural constraints (the mechanistic pole) in the construction of identity in the course of life's events. She consciously used her freedom to be religious without having to join a religious group, and thus distanced herself from institutionalized settings. When the Bahai group wanted her to take a leadership role, she refused and in the end dissociated herself from the group. On the other hand, she very much depended for her repertoire of religious ideas and meanings on the institutionalized religions she had been in contact with throughout her life. In this process of cultural praxis not only her religious but also her gender identity—and that of her husband!—is very much at stake, primarily because of the failure of their marriage.

When we take a closer look at the cultural repertories of meanings she used, a striking diversity of schemas presents itself.[9] It is striking in comparison with the efforts by most of the institutionalized religions to protect their boundaries and thereby their identities. It is less striking when understood from the viewpoint of the individual actor, as a way of being religious.

At the top of the hierarchy of schemas, a dynamic and heterogeneous concept of God is present as a source of help but also of trial. To Joana He is very much a master motive. The idea is even that He kills her friend and lets her husband live on. Therefore there is also some doubt about the existence of God as a moral and just being as He is conceived of in the Judeo-Christian tradition. It is not clear whether God is outside or inside the person (in the form of moral conscience), or both. God is also the source of the human free will, which Joana mentions as one of the explanations for her suffering. Simultaneously she refers to an inevitable destiny in life.

Christ plays a different role, at the intermediate level of the hierarchy of schemas, because he is a means to a goal of the highest level. To Joana he is an example of perfection, *uma pessoa maravilhosa* (a marvelous person) representing struggle, sacrifice, an ideal, valorizing human beings, simplicity, abnegation, all master motives that to her make him the Son of God, despite what the Bahai faith maintains. Though the difference of opinion led her to leave the Bahai group, Christ is not important to her in her struggle for life. Nor is his mother, the Virgin, who, although she was mentioned in the 1990 interview, was not included in the 1995 conversation.

In a more abstract way faith (*fé*) is an important ingredient, representing optimism and confidence and as such is another master motive. Joana referred to her ex-husband as somebody without faith. Faith is important, as she told her daughter, and it is more important to have faith than to have a specific faith. In this way elements from a variety of religions could be combined in her own faith.

Whereas God seemed to occupy a central place when interpretation of events was needed, this did not exclude an appeal to other schemas for the explanation of affliction. A prominent role was given to the Kardecist belief in reincarnation, which also appeared high in Joana's hierarchy of schemas. To her it explained the death of her still-born babies and also suggested to her that the suffering she endured in her marriage was seen as a form of debt payment carried over from a former life. On the other hand, her belief in reincarnation justified and legitimated her love for her friend and the hope or even certainty that they would be together in the future.

Another source that provided Joana with strength, though more on the intermediate level of schemas, was that of the guardian angel. The image not only made her think of the protection they give, but of their childlike innocence which represented a master motive to her. Next to the angels, also at this intermediate level, certain Catholic saints were a help.

Though the details are not clear from the interview, the Bahai group aided Joana when she first attempted to leave her husband. In offering assistance they also were part of the intermediate level, contributing to a higher goal schema (happiness) through practical third level schemas such as direct counseling.

Clairvoyance, also as an accepted intermediate level schema, provided a way of legitimating and explaining events such as her friend's allusion to his early death. Though not quoted in the fragments above, Joana told me that both she and her daughter have predicted certain events. In the days before her husband attacked her, for example, her daughter had complained that she felt something terrible was going to happen.

Besides these religious schemas, there are secular ones that Joana refers to. At the intermediate level her job provided a source of strength and self-respect. Also at the intermediate level, when trying to explain her husband's alcoholism, she relied on psychotherapy to emphasize his limitation of affect (a master motive) as a reason. Yet when asked whether she herself received treatment, her answer was that her therapy is prayer, thus returning to the intermediate level of the religious field.

It is also striking that certain metaphors were helpful as intermediate schemas. Struggle was a meaningful concept to her and to her daughters. Joana also compared life to a game of cards, in which we have to play the hand we are dealt. When speaking of her relationship with her daughters, sisterhood was mentioned as a source of strength. Phoenix raising from the ashes was the metaphor she used to describe—what she called—her resurrection, again a religious image. There are certain Portuguese words that Joana used to point to situations of bliss: *maravilhoso* (marvelous), *harmonia* (harmony), *lindo* (beautiful), *gostoso* (delicious).

Indirectly, and occasionally directly, Joana presented gender roles in an ideal marriage as parts of a master motive. Her fondness for her father suggests that his behavior was the model of masculinity to her. When she described her critical attitude towards marriage candidates, it is clear that she had certain criteria, and when speaking of her ideal view of a home she mentioned some of these master motives: love, dedication, fidelity, respect. Marriage, for her, comes from God and must be eternal. In a negative sense, her husband's behavior also defined a gender role. In her friend Joana found what was lacking in her husband. In times of crisis, she had to choose between alternative schemas of the intermediate and low level that competed for preference: must she stay with her husband or seek a divorce? Is she to help her husband and believe his promises, or should she leave him? Is she to be faithful to him, or will she opt for a life with her friend? Should she have sex with him or should she abstain, even from visiting him?

Joana claimed to take strength from religion and therefore obtained from it the power to survive. As she put it, "I am now strong enough to put this to an end." Though in a male-dominated society it can be considered as normal for women to accept the alcoholism of their husbands—a common low-level schema in Brazil—Joana refused. As she told her story her moral and personal power, nourished by the master motives of the highest level, was in strong contrast with the physical force of the intermediate and low levels that her faithless ex-husband used against her. Her relationship with her friend is described as sweet (*doce*) and therefore corresponding to a high level gender schema. Yet people did not like him, which suggested that in his relationships with them he applied his own intermediate and low level power schemas. To Joana, the superiority of the sweetness schema was a convincing argument for her love, despite or even because of the fact that he was not amiable to others.

Referring to the two aspects of power we may ask: Is Joana's power of the kind that is capable of influencing other people's behavior? This is not clear from her story. Since her participation in formal bureaucratic structures was minimal—she would not even join religious groups—with the possible exception of her work, she lacked frameworks within which to influence other people.

With regard to her personal relationships, she was not able to modify her husband's attitude or behavior, even though she tried. It seems probable that the training she gave to her daughters, together with the "sisterhood" they shared when the family was in trouble, was a way of influencing them. Her friend respected her, even though in the end he invited her to come to his apartment. Apart from these examples Joana did not seem to have power as a behavior-influencing factor.

Is the power she has then more an illustration of the second aspect of power, survival in life? Her discourse puts a much stronger emphasis on the way she used her relationships with God, angels and saints to obtain power to survive, than on efforts to influence people. The power that Joana has, then, is her strength to survive, as when she escaped from death at the hands of her husband.

Conclusion

Joana's story was presented for the purpose of examining the syncretic process at the level of the actor. The analytical focus was on relationships among gender, power and religion. Questions were asked with regard to Joana's use of religious resources, her views on gender issues and her ways of exercising power, both as a capacity to influence people and to survive.

From Joana's story a case can be made for defining power not only as the capacity to influence other people's behavior, but also to organize one's life. Though she expresses herself more in terms of strength (*força*) than of power (*poder*), the way she endured the events of her life certainly may be considered empowerment. The most important source of this empowerment, although she did not participate in organized religion and therefore lacked the support of a group, was her "religiosity," which she constructed from a wide variety of religious ideas and practices available in her culture. Since religion, more than any other aspect of—in this case Brazilian—culture, offers answers to questions about life and death, it may come as no surprise that the survival aspect of power has a strong religious component. To a woman, gender is often the primal area where power processes take place. Joana's life phase between interviews was marked by the failure of her marriage. The way she talked about this experience clearly shows her way of living her religiosity and also her views on gender.

The analysis of Joana's story also shows the relevance of a praxis approach and of schema theory. Her account of the events and her interpretation of her life made clear that cultural and social structures, agency and structure, formal and informal behavior, public and private domains should be studied together in a dialectical manner, in an effort to understand how the extremes touch each other and are linked. Schema theory proved to be a useful tool in this regard because it helped us to understand how Joana, as an actor, had her own way of managing the schemas available to her, as she found them in Brazilian cultural and social structures. She did this by defining their importance, rejecting some (Assemblies of God, Umbanda) selecting others (God, reincarnation) and by applying them in her own way in the process of interpreting the events that characterized her life. Though this personal hierarchy of schemas was not consistent nor fully formulated at all times, it helped her to make sense of her life and—to a lesser extent—to influence the people nearest to her.

Notes

1 I am grateful to Els Jacobs and Marjo de Theije for their insights with regard to power and gender. The first draft of this chapter was read as a paper during a symposium they organized during the BRASA meeting in Cambridge in September 1996. My co-editor was kind enough to help me polish that paper to a publishable article.

2 See Maurice Bloch, "Language, Anthropology and Cognitive Science," *Man* 26 (1991), no. 2: 183–198; Roy D'Andrade, *The Development of Cognitive Anthropology* (Cambridge: Cambridge University Press, 1995), 138–149; Naomi Quinn and Claudia Strauss, "A Cognitive/Cultural Anthropology," in *Assessing Cultural Anthropology*, Robert Borofsky, ed. (New York: McGraw-Hill, 1994), 284–300; Claudia Strauss and Naomi Quinn, *A Cognitive Theory of Cultural Meaning* (Cambridge: Cambridge University Press, 1997).

3 D'Andrade, *The Development*, 179.

4 D'Andrade, *The Development*, 232.

5 D'Andrade, *The Development*, 233.

6 See chapter 3 by Greenfield for elaboration of this point.

7 André Droogers, "Syncretism, Power, Play," in *Syncretism and the Commerce of Symbols*, Göran Aijmer, ed. (Gothenburg: IASSA, 1995), 38–59; André Droogers, "Identity, religious pluralism and ritual in Brazil: Umbanda and Pentecostalism," in *Pluralism and Identity: Studies in Ritual Behaviour*, Jan Platvoet and Karel van der Toorn, eds. (Leiden: Brill), 91–113.

8 André Droogers, "A religiosidade mínima brasileira," *Religião e Sociedade* 14 (1987), no. 2: 62–86.

9 Katherine Ewing, "The Illusion of Wholeness: Culture, Self, and the Experience of Inconsistency," *Ethos* 18 (1990), no. 3: 251–279.

WORLD CHRISTIANITY

Critical Concepts in Religious Studies

Other titles in this series

Available

Buddhism
Edited and with a new introduction by Paul Williams
8-volume set

Paganism
Edited and with a new introduction by Barbara Jane Davy
3-volume set

Women and Religion
Edited and with a new introduction by Pamela Klassen
4-volume set

Women and Christianity
Edited and with a new introduction by Kwok Pui Lan
4-volume set

Religion and Politics
Edited and with a new introduction by Jeffrey Haynes
4-volume set

Religion and Human Rights
Edited and with a new introduction by Nazila Ghanea
4-volume set

Psychology of Religion
Edited and with a new introduction by Justin L. Barrett
4-volume set

Forthcoming

Spirituality
Edited and with a new introduction by Paul Heelas
4-volume set

Anthropology of Religion
Edited and with a new introduction by Phillips Stevens Jr.
4-volume set

Religion and Science
Edited and with a new introduction by
Sara Fletcher Harding and Nancy Morvillo
4-volume set

Religion and Globalization
Edited and with a new introduction by Veronique Altglas
4-volume set

Religion and the Environment
Edited and with a new introduction by Roger Gottlieb
4-volume set

WORLD CHRISTIANITY

Critical Concepts in Religious Studies

Edited by
Elizabeth Koepping

Volume I

Routledge
Taylor & Francis Group
LONDON AND NEW YORK

First published 2011
by Routledge
2 Park Square, Milton Park, Abingdon, OX14 4RN

Simultaneously published in the USA and Canada
by Routledge
270 Madison Avenue, New York, NY 10016

Routledge is an imprint of the Taylor & Francis Group, an informa business

Typeset in Times NR MT by Graphicraft Limited, Hong Kong
Printed and bound in Great Britain by MPG Books Group, UK

British Library Cataloguing in Publication Data
A catalogue record for this book is available from the British Library

Library of Congress Cataloging-in-Publication Data
World Christianity : critical concepts in religious studies / edited by Elizabeth Koepping.
p. cm.
Includes bibliographical references and index.
ISBN 978-0-415-46827-5 (set) – ISBN 978-0-415-47291-3 (1) –
ISBN 978-0-415-47290-6 (2) – ISBN 978-0-415-47289-0 (3) –
ISBN 978-0-415-47288-3 (4) 1. Christianity.
I. Koepping, Elizabeth.
BR121.3.W67 2010
270.09–dc22
2010006472

ISBN 978-0-415-46827-5 (Set)
ISBN 978-0-415-47291-3 (Volume I)

Publisher's Note

References within each chapter are as they appear in the original complete work.

CONTENTS

Acknowledgements xvii
Chronological table of reprinted articles and chapters xxi

General introduction 1

VOLUME I

Introduction to Volume I 23

PART 1
Context and content 33

1 **Excerpt from 'Nature is to culture as praying is to suing: legal pluralism in an American suburb'** 35
CAROL J. GREENHOUSE

2 **From pagan to Christian priesthood** 44
DAVE PASSI

3 **Liturgical adaptation** 48
P. ABEGA

4 **Excerpt from 'Beliefs of Catholics in Asia'** 57
EDMUND CHIA

PART 2
Foundations: the Bible as agreed text 67

5 **Excerpt from 'The Bible and colonialism in the global context'** 69
PUI-LAN KWOK

6 Excerpt from 'Polarity or partnership? Retelling the story of Martha and Mary from Asian Women's perspective' 79
RANJINI REBERA

7 *Han*-laden women: Korean 'comfort women' and women in Judges 19–21 85
YANI YOO

8 Excerpt from 'Hermeneutical drama on the colonial stage: liminal space and creativity in Colenso's *Commentary on Romans*' 94
JONATHAN A. DRAPER

9 Challenging the Christian monopoly on the Bible: an aspect of the encounter between Christianity and Malegasy traditional religion in contemporary Madagascar 112
GEORGES RAZAFINDRAKOTO AND KNUT HOLTER

PART 3
The early church in the Eastern Mediterranean 121

10 Ritual 123
WAYNE A. MEEKS

11 Office charisma in early Christian Ephesus 153
ANTHONY J. BLASI

12 A complete history of early Christianity: taking the 'heretics' seriously 165
MAJELLA FRANZMANN

PART 4
Early Christian expansion: from Tunis to China 179

13 Christianity and local culture in Late Roman Africa 181
PETER BROWN

14 Excerpt from 'Mountain Constantines: the Christianization of Aksum and Iberia' 198
CHRISTOPHER HAAS

15 Excerpt from 'Thomas Christians and the Thomas tradition' 213
ROBERT FRYKENBERG

16 **Ch'ing-Tsing: Nestorian Tablet: eulogizing the propagation of the illustrious religion in China, with a preface** 227
COMPOSED BY A PRIEST OF THE SYRIAC CHURCH, 781 AD

17 **Paganism in the Greek world at the end of Antiquity: the case of rural Anatolia and Greece** 233
FRANK R. TROMBLEY

PART 5
Consolidation on five continents 255

18 **Rural people, the Church in Kongo and the Afroamerican diaspora (1491–1750)** 257
JOHN K. THORNTON

19 **'The best thus far discovered': the Japanese in the letters of Francisco Xavier** 268
ROBERT RICHMOND ELLIS

20 **Misreading and its creativity in Sino-Western cultural communication at the end of the Ming Dynasty** 280
SUN SHANGYANG

21 **Crossing gender boundaries: Tupi and European women in the eyes of Claude d'Abbeville** 295
LAURA FISHMAN

PART 6
Elite assumptions and lay agency 309

22 **The significance of the manuscript** 311
ANTONIO-MA ROSALES

23 **Wu Li (1632–1718) and the first Chinese Christian poetry** 328
JONATHAN CHAVES

24 **'*Come vero prencipe Catolico*': the Capuchins and the rulers of Soyo in the late seventeenth century** 348
RICHARD GRAY

25 **Bounded identities: women and religion in colonial Brazil, 1550–1750** 367
CAROLE A. MYSCOFSKI

26 Excerpt from 'The church at Nanrantsouak: Sébastien Râle, S.J., and the Wabanaki of Maine's Kennebec River' 379
WILLIAM A. CLARK, SJ

27 Excerpt from '"A dangerous zeal": Catholic missions to slaves in the French Antilles, 1635–1800' 394
SUE PEABODY

28 Excerpt from 'A Lübeck prophet in local and Lutheran context' 409
JÜRGEN BEYER

PART 7
Inter-continental Enlightenment? 423

29 Christian Virgins in eighteenth-century Sichuan 425
ROBERT E. ENTENMANN

30 Excerpt from 'Conversations in Tarangambadi: caring for the self in early eighteenth century South India' 441
EUGENE F. IRSCHICK

31 Conversion, identity, and the Indian missionary 470
KEELY MCCARTHY

VOLUME II

Acknowledgements ix

Introduction to Volume II 1

PART 8
Nation, state and person in nineteenth-century World Christianity 11

32 The Parsis of Bombay and Christian conversion, 1839–1845 13
JESSE S. PALSETIA

33 Cultivation, Christianity and colonialism: towards a new African genesis 28
JOHN L. COMAROFF AND JEAN COMAROFF

34 Catholics in protest: lower-caste Christianity in early colonial Madras 51
APARNA BALACHANDRAN

35 Excerpt from 'Christianity without civilization: Anglican sources for an alternative nineteenth-century mission methodology' 65
SARA H. SOHMER

PART 9
Gender, education and conversion 79

36 Missionary maternalism: gendered images of the Holy Spirit Sisters (SSpS) in colonial New Guinea 81
NANCY LUTKEHAUS

37 Young converts: Christian missions, gender and youth in Onitsha, Nigeria 1880–1929 95
MISTY L. BASTIAN

38 Excerpt from 'Devils, familiars and Spaniards: spheres of power and the supernatural in the world of Seberina Candelaria and her village in early 19th century Philippines' 117
GREG BANKOFF

PART 10
Religion, ethnicity and the nation 135

39 Conversion by affiliation: the history of the Karo Batak Protestant Church 137
RITA SMITH KIPP

40 The making of an ethnic collectivity: Irish Catholic immigrants in nineteenth-century Christchurch 160
LYNDON A. FRASER

41 The limits of religious ascription: baptized Tatars and the revision of 'apostasy,' 1840s–1905 179
PAUL W. WERTH

42 Religion and modernization in 19th century Greece 201
NIKOS KOKOSALAKIS

PART 11
Local agents of mission 223

43 Indians and the breakdown of the Spanish mission system in California 225
GEORGE HARWOOD PHILLIPS

44 Hidden but real: the vital contribution of Biblewomen to the rapid growth of Korean Protestantism, 1892–1945 237
CHRISTINE SUNGJIN CHANG

45 Kimbanguism and the question of syncretism in Zaïre 253
WYATT MACGAFFEY

PART 12
Roman Catholic fields of engagement with Pentecostals 271

46 Excerpt from 'In the absence of priests: young women as apostles to the poor, Chile 1922–1932' 273
GERTRUDE M. YEAGER

47 Reinterpreting Chilean Pentecostalism 285
JUAN SEPULVEDA

48 Glossolalia and possession among Pentecostal groups of the Mezzogiorno 307
MARIA PIA DI BELLA

PART 13
Negotiating religious and political competition 321

49 The Lord of Heaven versus Jesus Christ: Christian sectarian violence in late-nineteenth-century South China 323
JOSEPH TSE-HEI LEE

50 Revolutionary anticlericalism and hegemonic processes in an Andalusian town, August 1936 340
RICHARD MADDOX

51 Orthodox mission in tropical Africa 368
STEPHEN HAYES

52 **The spirit and the scapular: Pentecostal and Catholic interactions in Northern Nyanga District, Zimbabwe in the 1950s and early 1960s** 383
DAVID J. MAXWELL

VOLUME III

Acknowledgements ix

Introduction to Volume III 1

PART 14
Living texts 11

53 **Coptic cultural nationalism** 13
S. S. HASAN

54 **Ritual, history and identity in Goa** 21
ALEXANDER HENN

55 **Fellowship in contemporary religion and ethics: report on oral enquiry into beliefs of village people in Catholic diocese of Zhouzi** 38
YOU XILIN AND CHEN LIANGUO

56 **The imitation of Christ in Bicol, Philippines** 61
FENELLA CANNELL

PART 15
Discerning theology in context 81

57 **The status of Christian women in Kerala** 83
SUSAN VISVANATHAN

58 **Contested masculine spaces in Greek Orthodoxy** 94
ELENI SOTIRIU

59 **Gender and change in an African immigrant church: an anthropologist and a (former) prophetess reflect** 106
DEIDRE HELEN CRUMBLEY AND
GLORIA MALAKE CLINE-SMYTHE

60 **Excerpt form 'Faith, fashion and family: religion, aesthetics, identity and social organization in Strasbourg'** 127
ATWOOD D. GAINES

61 **The feminization and professionalization of ordained ministry within the Mâ'ohi Protestant church in French Polynesia** 149
GWENDOLINE MALOGNE-FER

PART 16
Relating to place 163

62 **Experiencing spirit: religious processes of interaction and unification in Aboriginal Australia** 165
FIONA MAGOWAN

63 **Excerpt from 'Religion as resistance in Jamaican peasant life: the Baptist Church, Revival worldview and Rastafari Movement'** 181
JEAN BESSON

64 **Structural obstacles to grassroots pastoral practice: the case of a base community in urban Brazil** 195
MANUEL A. VÁSQUEZ

65 **Inuit Pentecostal and evangelical movements in the Canadian Eastern Arctic: the case of the healing the land rituals developed by the Canada Awakening Ministries** 212
FRÉDÉRIC LAUGRAND AND JARICH OOSTEN

66 **'Culture' as a tool and an obstacle: missionary encounters in post-Soviet Kyrgyzstan** 230
MATHIJS PELKMANS

67 **The Faith-healers of the Assemblies of God in Burkina Faso: taking responsibility for diseases related to 'living together'** 253
PIERRE-JOSEPH LAURENT

PART 17
Texts biblical and local 273

68 The fundamentals of fertility: cosmology and conversion in a southwestern Nigerian Town 275
ELISHA P. RENNE

69 Jesus Christ as trickster in the religion of contemporary Bushmen 298
MATHIAS GUENTHER

70 Conversion to Protestantism among urban immigrants in Taiwan 317
HSING-KUANG CHAO

71 Christianity as a new religion: charisma, minor founders, and indigenous movements 329
MARK R. MULLINS

PART 18
Internal and external structures 343

72 The hidden sphere of religious searches in the Soviet Union: independent religious communities in Leningrad from the 1960s to the 1970s 345
OLGA TCHEPOURNAYA

73 American evangelicalism in Zimbabwe 357
PAUL GIFFORD

74 Excerpt from 'The persistence of apocalypticism within a denominationalizing sect: the apocalyptic fringe groups of Seventh-day Adventism 374
RONALD LAWSON

75 Native evangelism in Central Mexico 389
HUGO G. NUTINI

PART 19
Cross-national Pentecostalism past and present 407

76 'Heathendom' and the powers of darkness: on the role of the Devil in the preaching of the missionaries of the Norddeutsche Missionsgesellschaft in the nineteenth century and the contemporary African churches 409
BIRGIT MEYER

77 The transnationalisation of Brazilian Pentecostalism: the Universal Church of the Kingdom of God 423
PAUL FRESTON

78 Certain knowledge: the encounter of global fundamentalism and local Christianity in urban south India 443
LIONAL CAPLAN

79 Joana's story: syncretism at the actor's level 463
ANDRÉ DROOGERS

VOLUME IV

Acknowledgements ix

Introduction to Volume IV 1

PART 20
Clothed for glory: dress for Christians 11

80 Excerpt from 'Nakedness and clothing in early encounters between Aboriginal people of Central Australia, missionaries and anthropologists' 13
PEGGY BROCK

81 To honor her head: hats as a symbol of women's position in three evangelical churches in Edinburgh, Scotland 25
RUTH BORKER

PART 21
Church within walls 43

82 The immediacy of eternity: time and transformation in a Roman Catholic convent 45
REBECCA J. LESTER

83 Women living between the church and the state: a case study of Catholic women religious in contemporary rural China 68
LI WENWEN

PART 22
Church beyond walls: the performance of pilgrimage 85

84 Excerpt from 'Pilgrimage and patronage in Brazil: a paradigm for social relations and religious diversity' 87
SIDNEY M. GREENFIELD AND ANTONIO MOURÃO CAVALCANTE

85 Division and demolition at the tomb of a beloved saint: the evolving character of an Orthodox Christian pilgrim centre in India 104
ALEX GATH

86 Performing pilgrimage: Walsingham and the ritual construction of irony 121
SIMON COLEMAN AND JOHN ELSNER

87 Persistent peregrination: from Sun Dance to Catholic pilgrimage among Canadian Prairie Indians 140
ALAN MORINIS

88 Bernard Mizeki: missionary saints and the creation of Christian communities 154
DANA L. ROBERT

89 Excerpt from 'John Wesley slept here: American shrines and American Methodists' 169
THOMAS A. TWEED

PART 23
Performing Christianity 179

90 Catholic hymns of Michigan Indians 181
GERTRUDE PROKOSCH KURATH

91 Uduk faith in a five-note scale: mission music and the spread of the Gospel 191
WENDY JAMES

92 Excerpt from '"Almost persuaded now to believe": Gospel songs in New Zealand evangelical theology and practice' 207
BRYAN D. GILLING

93 **Women as religious and political praise singers within African institutions: the case of the CCAP Blantyre Synod and political parties in Malawi** **224**
CLARA HENDERSON AND LISA GILMAN

94 **Excerpt from 'Dalit theology in Tamil Christian folk music: a transformative liturgy by James Theophilus Appavoo'** **242**
ZOE C. SHERINIAN

95 **Syncretic objects: material culture of syncretism among the Paiwan Catholics, Taiwan** **262**
CHANG-KWO TAN

96 **Introduction to *Christianity in Indian Dance Forms*** **280**
FRANCIS PETER BARBOZA

PART 24
Issues for Christianity in the twenty-first century **295**

97 **Beyond Christendom: Protestant–Catholic distinctions in coming global Christianity** **297**
D. PAUL SULLINS

98 **Religion and the awakening of indigenous people in Latin America** **316**
CRISTIÁN PARKER GUMUCIO

99 **Half a century of African Christian theologies: elements of the emerging agenda for the twenty-first century** **332**
TINYIKO SAM MALULEKE

Index 354

ACKNOWLEDGEMENTS

The first thanks must go to those fifteen authors who allowed me to edit their texts, as the result enabled more readings to be included and a broader sweep of Christianity across the world presented. Nancy Lutkehaus, Birgit Meyer, Jesse Palsetia, Dana Robert and Li Wenwen deserve special thanks for revising their own text. Adrian Bird and Jackie Larm, graduate students of New College, helped with the mechanics of collating: Patrick Ntawuyamara did sterling work on the scanner.

During the twelve months of intensive work on it, colleagues in the School of Divinity at Edinburgh University patiently listened to my endless snippets of past and present Christian practice: Hans Barstad, Cecelia Clegg, Jane Dawson, Paul Foster, Paul Parvis and especially Caroline Blyth read and commented on various introductory segments. Freya Koepping critically read all my texts and Olga Koepping translated one reading: Lisa Williams has been a helpful editor. My many post-graduate students in the Centre for the Study of World Christianity put up with slower than usual responses to their work and contributed in various ways to the completion of these readers: my thanks are due to all.

The publishers would like to thank the following for permission to reprint their material:

Carol J. Greenhouse for permission to reprint Carol J. Greenhouse, excerpt from 'Nature is to Culture as Praying is to Suing: Legal Pluralism in an American Suburb', *Journal of Legal Pluralism*, 1982, 21, 21–29.

Garry Trompf for permission to reprint Dave Passi, 'From Pagan to Christian Priesthood', in G. W. Trompf (ed.), *The Gospel is Not Western: Black Theologies from the South-West Pacific* (Orbis, 1987), pp. 45–48.

Japan Mission Journal for permission to reprint Edmund Chia, excerpt from 'Beliefs of Catholics in Asia', *Japan Mission Journal*, 2002, 56, 3, 173–181.

Kwok Pui-lan for permission to reprint Kwok Pui-lan, excerpt from 'The Bible and Colonialism in the Global Context', *Theology & Life*, 2007, 30, 218–237.

Yani Yoo for permission to reprint Yani Yoo, '*Han*-Laden Women: Korean "Comfort Women" and Women in Judges 19–21', *Semeia*, 1997, 78, 37–46.

Journal of Theology for Southern Africa for permission to reprint Jonathan A. Draper, excerpt from 'Hermeneutical Drama on the Colonial Stage: Liminal Space and Creativity in Colenso's *Commentary on Romans*', *Journal of Theology for Southern Africa*, 1999, 103, 13–32.

Georges Razafindrakoto and Knut Holter for permission to reprint Georges Razafindrakoto and Knut Holter, 'Challenging the Christian Monopoly on the Bible: An Aspect of the Encounter between Christianity and Malegasy Traditional Religion in Contemporary Madagascar', in K. Koschorke and J. H. Schørring (eds), *African Identities and World Christianity in the Twentieth Century: Proceedings of the Third International Munich-Freising Conference on the History of Christianity in the Non-Western World* (September 15–17, 2004), (Harrassowitz Verlag, 2005), pp. 141–148.

Yale University Press for permission to reprint Wayne A. Meeks, 'Ritual', in *The First Urban Christians: The Social World of the Apostle Paul* (Yale University Press, 1983), pp. 140–163.

Oxford University Press for permission to reprint Anthony J. Blasi, 'Office Charisma in Early Christian Ephesus', *Sociology of Religion*, 1995, 56, 3, 245–255.

Wiley-Blackwell for permission to reprint Majella Franzmann, 'A Complete History of Early Christianity: Taking the "Heretics" Seriously', *Journal of Religious History*, 2005, 29, 2, 117–128.

The Johns Hopkins University Press for permission to reprint Christopher Haas, excerpt from 'Mountain Constantines: The Christianization of Aksum and Iberia', *Journal of Late Antiquity*, 2008, 1, 1, 101–126 © 2008 by the Johns Hopkins University Press.

Oxford University Press for permission to reprint Robert Frykenberg, excerpt from 'Thomas Christians and the Thomas Tradition', in *Christianity in India* (Oxford University Press, 2008), pp. 102–115.

Cambridge University Press for permission to reprint Frank R. Trombley, 'Paganism in the Greek World at the End of Antiquity: The Case of Rural Anatolia and Greece', *Harvard Theological Review*, 1985, 78, 4, 327–352. © The President and Fellows of Harvard College, published by Cambridge University Press.

John K. Thornton for permission to reprint John K. Thornton, 'Rural People, the Church in Kongo and the Afroamerican Diaspora (1491–1750)', in Klaus Koschorke (ed.), *Transcontinental Links in the History of Non-Western Christianity*, Vol. 6 (Harrassowitz Verlag, 2002), 33–44.

The University of Pennsylvania Press for permission to reprint Robert Richmond Ellis, '"The Best Thus Far Discovered": The Japanese in the Letters of Francisco Xavier', *Hispanic Review*, 2003, 71, 2, 155–169.

Michigan State University Press for permission to reprint Laura Fishman, 'Crossing Gender Boundaries: Tupi and European Women in the Eyes of Claude d'Abbeville', *French Colonial History*, 2003, 4, 81–98.

The University of the Philippines Press for permission to reprint Antonio-Ma Rosales, 'The Significance of the Manuscript', in *A Study of a 16th Century Tagalog Manuscript on the Ten Commandments: Its Significance and Implications* (University of the Philippines Press, 1984), pp. 68–80.

The American Oriental Society for permission to reprint Jonathan Chaves, 'Wu Li (1632–1718) and the First Chinese Christian Poetry', *Journal of the American Oriental Society*, 2002, 122, 3, 506–519.

Edinburgh University Press for permission to reprint Richard Gray, '*Come vero Prencipe Catolico*: The Capuchins and the Rulers of Soyo in the Late Seventeenth Century', *Africa: Journal of the International African Institute*, 1983, 53, 3, 39–54. www.evppublishing.com

Elsevier for permission to reprint Carole A. Myscofski, 'Bounded Identities: Women and Religion in Colonial Brazil, 1550–1750', *Religion*, 1998, 28, 329–337, Copyright Elsevier, 1998.

The Catholic University of America Press, Washington, DC, USA, for permission to reprint William A. Clark, excerpt from 'The Church at Nanrantsouak: Sébastien Râle, S.J., and the Wabanaki of Maine's Kennebec River', *Catholic Historical Review*, 2006, 92, 3, 225–226, 231–240, 245–251. © *The Catholic Historical Review*.

Duke University Press for permission to reprint Sue Peabody, excerpt from '"A Dangerous Zeal": Catholic Missions to Slaves in the French Antilles, 1635–1800', *French Historical Studies*, 2002, 25, 1, 55–63, 66–72. Copyright, 2002, the Society of French Historical Studies, All rights reserved. Published by Duke University Press.

Palgrave Macmillan for permission to reprint Jürgen Beyer, excerpt from 'A Lübeck Prophet in Local and Lutheran Context', in Bob Scribner and T. Johnson (eds), *Popular Religion in Germany and Central Europe, 1400–1800* (Macmillan, 1996), pp. 166–177, 180–182.

Duke University Press for permission to reprint Eugene F. Irschick, excerpt from 'Conversations in Tarangambadi: Caring for the Self in Early Eighteenth Century South India', *Comparative Studies of South Asia, Africa and the Middle East*, 2003, 23, 1&2, 254–270. Copyright, 2003, *Comparative Studies of South Asia, Africa and the Middle East*. All rights reserved. Published by Duke University Press.

The University of North Carolina Press for permission to reprint Keely McCarthy, 'Conversion, Identity, and the Indian Missionary', *Early American Literature*, 2001, 36, 3, 353–369. Copyright © 2001 by the University of North Carolina Department of English. www.uncpress-unc.edu.

Disclaimer

Chronological table of reprinted articles and chapters

Date	*Author*	*Article/Chapter*	*Source*	*Vol.*	*Chap.*
1917	Composed by a priest of the Syriac Church, 781 AD	Ch'ing-Tsing: Nestorian Tablet: eulogizing the propagation of the illustrious religion in China, with a preface, composed by a priest of the Syriac Church, 781 AD	Charles F. Horne (ed.), *The Sacred Books and Early Literature of the East*, vol. XII: *Medieval China*, New York: Parke, Austin and Lipscomb	I	16
1957	Gertrude Prokosch Kurath	Catholic hymns of Michigan Indians	*Anthropological Quarterly*, 30:2, 31–44	IV	90
1968	Peter Brown	Christianity and local culture in Late Roman Africa	*Journal of Roman Studies*, 58:1&2, 85–95	I	13
1974	George Harwood Phillips	Indians and the breakdown of the Spanish mission system in California	*Ethnohistory*, 21:4, 291–302	II	43
1978	Ruth Borker	To honor her head: hats as a symbol of women's position in three evangelical churches in Edinburgh, Scotland	Judith Hoch-Smith and Anita Spring (eds), *Women in Ritual and Symbolic Roles*, New York: Plenum Press, pp. 55–73	IV	81
1979	P. Abega	Liturgical adaptation	Edward Fashole-Luke (ed.), *Christianity in Independent Africa*, London: Collings, pp. 597–605	I	3
1982	Carol J. Greenhouse	Excerpt from 'Nature is to culture as praying is to suing: legal pluralism in an American suburb'	*Journal of Legal Pluralism*, 20, 21–9	I	1
1983	Richard Gray	'*Come vero prencipe Catolico*': the Capuchins and the rulers of Soyo in the late seventeenth century	*Africa: Journal of the International African Institute*, 53:3, 39–54	I	24
1983	Wayne A. Meeks	Ritual	Wayne A. Meeks, *The First Urban Christians: The Social World of the Apostle Paul*, New Haven, CT: Yale University Press, pp. 140–63	I	10

Chronological table continued

Date	*Author*	*Article/Chapter*	*Source*	*Vol.*	*Chap.*
1984	Antonio-Ma Rosales	The significance of the manuscript	Antonio-Ma Rosales, *A Study of a 16th Century Tagalog Manuscript on the Ten Commandments: Its Significance and Implications*, Quezon City: University of the Philippines Press, pp. 68–80	I	22
1985	Atwood D. Gaines	Excerpt from 'Faith, fashion and family: religion, aesthetics, identity and social organization in Strasbourg'	*Anthropological Quarterly*, 58:2, 47–62	III	60
1985	Frank R. Trombley	Paganism in the Greek world at the end of Antiquity: the case of rural Anatolia and Greece	*Harvard Theological Review*, 78:4, 327–52	I	17
1987	Nikos Kokosalakis	Religion and modernization in 19th century Greece	*Social Compass*, 34:2–3, 223–41	II	42
1987	Dave Passi	From pagan to Christian priesthood	G. W. Trompf (ed.), *The Gospel Is Not Western: Black Theologies from the South-West Pacific*, Maryknoll, NY: Orbis, pp. 45–8	I	2
1988	Maria Pia di Bella	Glossolalia and possession among Pentecostal groups of the Mezzogiorno	*Annales, ESC*, 4: 897–907; translated by Olga Koepping	II	48
1988	Wendy James	Uduk faith in a five-note scale: mission music and the spread of the Gospel	Wendy James and Douglas H. Johnson (eds), *Vernacular Christianity: Essays in the Social Anthropology of Religion Presented to Godfrey Lienhardt*, JASO Occasional Papers, pp. 131–45	IV	91
1991	Francis Peter Barboza	Introduction to *Christianity in Indian Dance Forms*	Francis Peter Barboza, *Christianity in Indian Dance Forms*, Delhi: Sri Satguru, pp. 1–7, 214–16	IV	96
1992	Paul Gifford	American evangelicalism in Zimbabwe	Paul Gifford, *Christianity and Hegemony*, New York: Berg, pp. 121–43	III	73

1992	Alan Morinis	Persistent peregrination: from Sun Dance to Catholic pilgrimage among Canadian Prairie Indians	Alan Morinis (ed.), *Sacred Journeys: The Anthropology of Pilgrimage*, Contributions to the Study of Anthropology, 7, New York: Greenwood Press, pp. 101–13	IV	87
1993	Mark R. Mullins	Christianity as a new religion: charisma, minor founders, and indigenous movements	M. R. Mullins, S. Susumu and P. L. Swanson (eds), *Religion and Society in Modern Japan*, Fremont, CA: Asian Humanities Press, pp. 257–72	III	71
1994	Wyatt MacGaffey	Kimbanguism and the question of syncretism in Zaïre	W. E. A. van Beek, Th.E. Blakely and D. L. Thomson (eds), *Religion in Africa: Experience and Expression*, London: James Currey; Portsmouth, NH: Heinemann, pp. 241–56	II	45
1994	Sara H. Sohmer	Excerpt from 'Christianity without civilization: Anglican sources for an alternative nineteenth-century mission methodology'	*Journal of Religious History*, 18:2, 174–8, 180–1, 185–8, 195–7	II	35
1995	Anthony J. Blasi	Office charisma in early Christian Ephesus	*Sociology of Religion*, 56:3, 245–55	I	11
1995	Fenella Cannell	Imitation of Christ in Bicol, Philippines	*Journal of Royal Anthropological Institute*, 1: 377–94	III	56
1995	Lional Caplan	Certain knowledge: the encounter of global fundamentalism and local Christianity in urban south India	Wendy James (ed.), *The Pursuit of Certainty: Religious and Cultural Formulations*, London: Routledge, pp. 92–110	III	78
1995	Bryan D. Gilling	Excerpt from '"Almost persuaded now to believe": Gospel songs in New Zealand evangelical theology and practice'	*Journal of Religious History*, 19:1, 92–110	IV	92
1995	Rita Smith Kipp	Conversion by affiliation: the history of the Karo Batak Protestant Church	*American Ethnologist*, 22:4, 868–82	II	39
1995	Richard Maddox	Revolutionary anticlericalism and hegemonic processes in an Andalusian town, August 1936	*American Ethnologist*, 22:1, 125–43	II	50

Chronological table continued

Date	*Author*	*Article/Chapter*	*Source*	*Vol.*	*Chap.*
1995	Jean Besson	Excerpt from 'Religion as resistance in Jamaican peasant life: the Baptist Church, Revival worldview and Rastafari Movement'	Originally published in Barry Chevannes (ed.), *Rastafari and Other African-Caribbean Worldviews*, London: Macmillan; Chapel Hill, NC: Rutgers University Press, pp. 47–63; revised by author, 2009	III	63
1996	Jürgen Beyer	Excerpt from 'A Lübeck prophet in local and Lutheran context'	Bob Scribner and T. Johnson (eds), *Popular Religion in Germany and Central Europe, 1400–1800*, London: Macmillan, pp. 166–77, 180–2	I	28
1996	Robert E. Entenmann	Christian Virgins in eighteenth-century Sichuan	Daniel H. Bays (ed.), *Christianity in China: From the Eighteenth Century to the Present*, Stanford, CA: Stanford University Press, pp. 180–93	I	29
1996	Lyndon A. Fraser	The making of an ethnic collectivity: Irish Catholic immigrants in nineteenth-century Christchurch	*Journal of Religious History*, 20:2, 210–27	II	40
1996	Stephen Hayes	Orthodox mission in tropical Africa	*Missionalia*, 24: 383–98	II	51
1996	Juan Sepulveda	Reinterpreting Chilean Pentecostalism	*Social Compass*, 43:3, 299–318	II	47
1997	Mathias Guenther	Jesus Christ as trickster in the religion of contemporary Bushmen	K. P. Köpping (ed.), *The Games of Gods and Men*, Berlin: LIT, pp. 203–29	III	69
1997	Ronald Lawson	Excerpt from 'The persistence of apocalypticism within a denominationalizing sect: the apocalyptic fringe groups of Seventh-day Adventism	Thomas Robbins and Susan Palmer (eds), *Millennium, Messiahs, and Mayhem: Contemporary Apocalyptic Movements*, London: Routledge, pp. 207–21, 225–6	III	74
1997	Tinyiko Sam Maluleke	Half a century of African Christian theologies: elements of the emerging agenda for the twenty-first century	*Journal of Theology for Southern Africa*, 99: 4–23	IV	99

1997	David J. Maxwell	The spirit and the scapular: Pentecostal and Catholic interactions in Northern Nyanga District, Zimbabwe in the 1950s and early 1960s	*Journal of Southern African Studies*, 23:2, 283–300	II	52
1997	Birgit Meyer	'Heathendom' and the powers of darkness: on the role of the Devil in the preaching of the missionaries of the Norddeutsche Missionsgesellschaft in the nineteenth century and the contemporary African churches	Originally published in *Trinity Journal of Church and Theology*, 7:1–2, 15–27; revised by author, 2010	III	76
1997	Ranjini Rebera	Excerpt from 'Polarity or partnership? Retelling the story of Martha and Mary from Asian Women's perspective'	*Semeia*, 78: 93–4, 101–7	I	6
1997	Manuel A. Vásquez	Structural obstacles to grassroots pastoral practice: the case of a base community in urban Brazil	*Sociology of Religion*, 58:1, 53–68	III	64
1997	Yani Yoo	*Han*-laden women: Korean 'comfort women' and women in Judges 19–21	*Semeia*, 78: 37–46	I	7
1998	Simon Coleman and John Elsner	Performing pilgrimage: Walsingham and the ritual construction of irony	Felicia Hughes-Freeland (ed.), *Ritual, Performance, Media*, London: Routledge, pp. 46–65	IV	86
1998	Carole A. Myscofski	Bounded identities: women and religion in colonial Brazil, 1550–1750	*Religion*, 28: 329–37	I	25
1999	Greg Bankoff	Excerpt from 'Devils, familiars and Spaniards: spheres of power and the supernatural in the world of Seberina Candelaria and her village in early 19th century Philippines'	*Journal of Social History*, 33:1, 37–55	II	38
1999	Jonathan A. Draper	Excerpt from 'Hermeneutical drama on the colonial stage: liminal space and creativity in Colenso's *Commentary on Romans*'	*Journal of Theology for Southern Africa*, 103: 13–32	I	8

Chronological table continued

Date	*Author*	*Article/Chapter*	*Source*	*Vol.*	*Chap.*
1999	Nancy Lutkehaus	Missionary maternalism: gendered images of the Holy Spirit Sisters (SSpS) in colonial New Guinea	Originally published in Mary Huber Taylor and Nancy Lutkehaus (eds), *Gendered Missions: Women and Men in Missionary Discourse and Practice*, Ann Arbor, MI: University of Michigan Press, pp. 207–35; revised by author, 2009	II	36
2000	Aparna Balachandran	Catholics in protest: lower-caste Christianity in early colonial Madras	*Studies in History*, (N.S.) 16:2, 241–53	II	34
2000	Misty L. Bastian	Young converts: Christian missions, gender and youth in Onitsha, Nigeria 1880–1929	*Anthropological Quarterly*, 73:3, 145–58	II	37
2000	John L. Comaroff and Jean Comaroff	Cultivation, Christianity and colonialism: towards a new African genesis	J. De Gruchy (ed.), *The London Missionary Society in Southern Africa*, Ohio University Press, pp. 55–72	II	33
2000	Alex Gath	Division and demolition at the tomb of a beloved saint: the evolving character of an Orthodox Christian pilgrim centre in India	*Culture and Religion*, 1:2, 171–87	IV	85
2000	Joseph Tse-Hei Lee	The Lord of Heaven versus Jesus Christ: Christian sectarian violence in late-nineteenth-century South China	*positions*, 8:1, 77–99	II	49
2000	Hugo G. Nutini	Native evangelism in Central Mexico	*Ethnology*, 39:1, 39–54	III	75
2000	Thomas A. Tweed	Excerpt from 'John Wesley slept here: American shrines and American Methodists'	*NUMEN*, 47: 41–2, 45–7, 51–4, 61–4, 66	IV	89
2000	Paul W. Werth	The limits of religious ascription: baptized Tatars and the revision of 'apostasy,' 1840s–1905	*Russian Review*, 59:4, 493–511	II	41

2001	André Droogers	Joana's story: syncretism at the actor's level	S. Greenfield and A. Droogers (eds), *Reinventing Religions: Syncretism and Transformation in Africa and the Americas*, Lanham, MD: Rowman and Littlefield, pp. 145–62	III	79
2001	Paul Freston	The transnationalisation of Brazilian Pentecostalism: the Universal Church of the Kingdom of God	A. Corten and R. Marshall-Fratani (eds), *Between Babel and Pentecost: Transnational Pentecostalism in Africa and Latin America*, London: Hurst & Co., pp. 196–215	III	77
2001	Pierre-Joseph Laurent	The Faith-healers of the Assemblies of God in Burkina Faso: taking responsibility for diseases related to 'living together'	*Social Compass*, 48:3, 333–51	III	67
2001	Keely McCarthy	Conversion, identity, and the Indian missionary	*Early American Literature*, 36:3, 353–69	I	31
2002	Jonathan Chaves	Wu Li (1632–1718) and the first Chinese Christian poetry	*Journal of the American Oriental Society*, 122:3, 506–19	I	23
2002	Edmund Chia	Excerpt from 'Beliefs of Catholics in Asia'	*Japan Mission Journal*, 56:3, 173–81	I	4
2002	Cristián Parker Gumucio	Religion and the awakening of indigenous people in Latin America	*Social Compass*, 49:1, 67–81	IV	98
2002	Sue Peabody	Excerpt from '"A dangerous zeal": Catholic missions to slaves in the French Antilles, 1635–1800'	*French Historical Studies*, 25:1, 55–63, 66–72	I	27
2002	Elisha P. Renne	The fundamentals of fertility: cosmology and conversion in a southwestern Nigerian Town	*Journal of the Royal Anthropological Institute*, (N.S.) 8: 551–69	III	68
2002	Zoe C. Sherinian	Excerpt from 'Dalit theology in Tamil Christian folk music: a transformative liturgy by James Theophilus Appavoo'	Selva Raj and Corinne Dempsey (eds), *Popular Christianity in India: Riting Between the Lines*, SUNY Series in Hindu Studies, New York: State University of New York Press, pp. 233–53	IV	94
2002	Chang-Kwo Tan	Syncretic objects: material culture of syncretism among the Paiwan Catholics, Taiwan	*Journal of Material Culture*, 7:2, 167–87	IV	95

Chronological table continued

Date	*Author*	*Article/Chapter*	*Source*	*Vol.*	*Chap.*
2002	John K. Thornton	Rural people, the Church in Kongo and the Afroamerican diaspora (1491–1750)	Klaus Koschorke (ed.), *Transcontinental Links in the History of Non-Western Christianity*, vol. 6, Wiesbaden: Harrassowitz Verlag, pp. 33–44	I	18
2002	Susan Visvanathan	The status of Christian women in Kerala	Arvind Sharma (ed.), *Women in Indian Religions*, Oxford: Oxford University Press, pp. 189–200	III	57
2003	Robert Richmond Ellis	'The best thus far discovered': the Japanese in the letters of Francisco Xavier	*Hispanic Review*, 71:2, 155–69	I	19
2003	Laura Fishman	Crossing gender boundaries: Tupi and European women in the eyes of Claude d'Abbeville	*French Colonial History*, 4: 81–98	I	21
2003	S. S. Hasan	Coptic cultural nationalism	S. S. Hasan, *Christians versus Muslims in modern Egypt: the century-long struggle for Coptic equality*, Oxford: Oxford University Press, pp. 201–8	III	53
2003	Eugene F. Irschick	Excerpt from 'Conversations in Tarangambadi: caring for the self in early eighteenth century South India'	*Comparative Studies of South Asia, Africa and the Middle East*, 23:1&2, 254–70	I	30
2003	Rebecca J. Lester	The immediacy of eternity: time and transformation in a Roman Catholic convent	*Religion*, 33: 201–19	IV	82
2003	Olga Tchepournaya	The hidden sphere of religious searches in the Soviet Union: independent religious communities in Leningrad from the 1960s to the 1970s	*Sociology of Religion*, 64:3, 377–88	III	72

2003	Li Wenwen	Women living between the church and the state: a case study of Catholic women religious in contemporary rural China	Originally published in Peter Ng and Wu Xiaoxin (eds), *Christianity and Chinese Society and Culture: The First International Young Scholars Symposium*, Hong Kong: Chinese University of Hong Kong, pp. 359–84; translated and revised by author, 2009	IV	83
2004	Clara Henderson and Lisa Gilman	Women as religious and political praise singers within African institutions: the case of the CCAP Blantyre Synod and political parties in Malawi	*Women and Music*, 8: 22–40	IV	93
2004	Eleni Sotiriu	Contested masculine spaces in Greek Orthodoxy	*Social Compass*, 51:4, 499–510	III	58
2005	Majella Franzmann	A complete history of early Christianity: taking the 'heretics' seriously	*Journal of Religious History*, 29:2, 117–28	I	12
2005	Fiona Magowan	Experiencing spirit: religious processes of interaction and unification in Aboriginal Australia	Peggy Brock (ed.), *Indigenous Peoples and Religious Change*, Leiden, Netherlands: Brill, pp. 157–75	III	62
2005	Georges Razafindrakoto and Knut Holter	Challenging the Christian monopoly on the Bible: an aspect of the encounter between Christianity and Malegasy traditional religion in contemporary Madagascar	K. Koschorke and J. H. Schørring (eds), *African Identities and World Christianity in the Twentieth Century: Proceedings of the Third International Munich–Freising Conference on the History of Christianity in the Non-Western World* (September 15–17, 2004), Wiesbaden: Harrassowitz Verlag, pp. 141–8	I	9
2005	Dana L. Robert	Bernard Mizeki: missionary saints and the creation of Christian communities	Originally published in *Yale Divinity School Library Occasional Publication No. 19*, New Haven, CT: Yale Divinity School Library; revised by author, 2009	IV	88
2006	Hsing-Kuang Chao	Conversion to Protestantism among urban immigrants in Taiwan	*Sociology of Religion*, 67:2, 193–204	III	70
2006	William A. Clark, SJ	Excerpt from 'The church at Nanrantsouak: Sébastien Râle, S.J., and the Wabanaki of Maine's Kennebec River'	*Catholic Historical Review*, 92:3, 225–6, 231–40, 245–51	I	26

Chronological table continued

Date	*Author*	*Article/Chapter*	*Source*	*Vol.*	*Chap.*
2006	Sidney M. Greenfield and Antonio Mourão Cavalcante	Excerpt from 'Pilgrimage and patronage in Brazil: a paradigm for social relations and religious diversity'	*Luso-Brazilian Review*, 43:2, 63–89	IV	84
2006	Jesse S. Palsetia	The Parsis of Bombay and Christian conversion, 1839–1845	Originally published in *Journal of the American Academy of Religion*, 74:3, 615–45; revised by author, 2009	II	32
2006	Sun Shangyang	Misreading and its creativity in Sino-Western cultural communication at the end of the Ming Dynasty	Yang Huilin and Daniel H. N. Yeung (eds), *Sino-Christian Studies in China*, Cambridge: Cambridge Scholars Press, pp. 2–16	I	20
2006	D. Paul Sullins	Beyond Christendom: Protestant–Catholic distinctions in coming global Christianity	*Religion*, 36: 197–213	IV	97
2007	Peggy Brock	Excerpt from 'Nakedness and clothing in early encounters between Aboriginal people of Central Australia, missionaries and anthropologists'	*Journal of Colonialism and Colonial History*, 8:1, 1–11	IV	80
2007	Deidre Helen Crumbley and Gloria Malake Cline-Smythe	Gender and change in an African immigrant church: an anthropologist and a (former) prophetess reflect	Jacob K. Olupona and Regina Gemignani (eds), *African Immigrant Religions in America*, New York: New York University Press, pp. 158–81	III	59
2007	Pui-lan Kwok	Excerpt from 'The Bible and colonialism in the global context'	*Theology & Life*, 30: 218–31, 37	I	5
2007	Frédéric Laugrand and Jarich Oosten	Inuit Pentecostal and evangelical movements in the Canadian Eastern Arctic: the case of the healing the land rituals developed by the Canada Awakening Ministries	Originally published in *Numen* 54: 229–69; revised by authors, 2009	III	65

2007	Mathijs Pelkmans	'Culture' as a tool and an obstacle: missionary encounters in post-Soviet Kyrgyzstan	*Journal of the Royal Anthropological Institute*, (N.S.) 13, 881–99	III	66
2007	You Xilin and Chen Lianguo	Fellowship in contemporary religion and ethics: report on oral enquiry into beliefs of village people in Catholic diocese of Zhouzi	*China Study Journal* (Spring/Summer): 68–84	III	55
2007	Gertrude M. Yeager	Excerpt from 'In the absence of priests: young women as apostles to the poor, Chile 1922–1932'	Originally published in *The Americas*, 64:2, 207–42	II	46
2008	Christine Sungjin Chang	Hidden but real: the vital contribution of Biblewomen to the rapid growth of Korean Protestantism, 1892–1945	*Women's Historical Review*, 17:4, 575–95	II	44
2008	Robert Frykenberg	Excerpt from 'Thomas Christians and the Thomas tradition'	Robert Frykenberg, *Christianity in India*, Oxford: Oxford University Press, pp. 102–15	I	15
2008	Christopher Haas	Excerpt from 'Mountain Constantines: the Christianization of Aksum and Iberia'	*Journal of Late Antiquity*, 1:1, 102–26	I	14
2008	Alexander Henn	Ritual, history and identity in Goa	Alexander Henn and Klaus-Peter Köpping (eds) *Rituals in an Unstable World: Contingency, Hybridity, Embodiment*, Frankfurt: Peter Lang, pp. 205–24	III	54
2008	Gwendoline Malogne-Fer	The feminization and professionalization of ordained ministry within the Mâ'ohi Protestant church in French Polynesia	I. Jones, J. Wootton and K. Thorpe (eds), *Women and Ordination in the Christian Churches: International Perspectives*, New York: T&T Clark, a Continuum imprint, pp. 177–88	III	61

GENERAL INTRODUCTION

Christianity is currently the most widespread world religion and the one with which the greatest number of people identify: it has long spanned the globe. Quickly developing from a rather ethnically based assemblage in Palestine around 40 CE, it was helped along by being adopted as the state religion of the Roman Empire in 380 CE. In common with other universal religions, Christianity's theology, organization, practice and history are actually embodied in, affected by and affect locality, being both universal *and* parochial. Yet even a specific locality, practice and organization are not a unified arena of thought and action, but rather a fuzzy-edged multiple context, whose perspectives on the Christian text represent or derive from varied ethnicities, ideologies and events, and from gender, class and caste differences. Geertz's comment on the near-futility of identifying the breaks and continuities in defining 'a culture' is relevant here: 'the view of culture, a culture, this culture, as a consensus on fundamentals – shared conceptions, shared feelings, shared values – seems hardly viable . . . : it is the faults and fissures that seem to mark out the landscape of collective selfhood.'[1]

So might we also regard so-called 'world religion' labels such as Buddhism, Hinduism, Islam and Christianity: broad generalizations covering complex and contested texts and contexts. There is thus not one Christianity but rather legion Christianities, legion theologies, legion practices, yet the sheer power and theological clout carried by some clusters of churches, but not others, may belie equality between them. Moreover, internal variations may be regarded by religious and social elites as inadequate, syncretic or plain wrong. There can, in other words, be tension between the universal divinely given Word and the local words in which it is uttered,[2] and between theologies constructed by what EuroAmerica sees as the true core, with its world wide web of heirs, and those of vastly more numerous yet locally embedded thinkers and practitioners, uninterested in or ignored by the big players.[3] This was arguably ever so.

These four volumes of readings put two millennia of World Christianity in context by drawing on perspectives from history, theology, ecclesiology, sociology and anthropology. The first three volumes present material from all the continents, organized not divisively by region, which all too easily essentializes structures and privileges elites, but rather moving holistically from the first to the twenty-first century, adding regions and traditions in due order.

Swiftly weaving through world arenas of contested historical processes of amity and enmity, negotiation and conversion, apathy and agency, the final volume concentrates on the performance of Christian faith throughout the world.[4]

There are two prime reasons for this historically ordered thematic approach. First, it seems more fitting for a tradition which, to give some examples, saw a Lutheran missionary in South India in 1710 keeping up a regular correspondence in Latin with the Puritan Coton Mather in New England via Hamburg and London; the Persian Orthodox Bishop Raumun Sauma going from China to Rome and Bordeaux in the thirteenth century, Roman Catholic Mexican priests sent to the Philippines and African Christians (unwillingly) to the Americas in the sixteenth century; and the last one hundred and fifty years of Pentecostalism taking off simultaneously in four continents.[5]

Second, starting 'at the beginning' and adding areas as we go may curtail the tendency to take EuroAmerica as the yardstick, as if the 'point of gravity for Christianity'[6] really did first move southwards only in the late twentieth century. As I suggested above, power and validation were broadly speaking Eurocentred in the last three centuries, and tend still to be, whatever the state of gravity. Two-thirds of World Christians now live in Africa, Asia and Latin America rather than EuroAmerica and its outliers: in 900 CE, there were more Christians east of the Bosphorus than west. Plus ça change!

During the first millennium, Christianity was present in the entire world then known to travellers and writers: Northern Africa, southern and parts of central and western Europe, Arabia, India, central Asia and China. Almost all northern Europe[7], South and central America were encompassed in the following five hundred years, the final three hundred years seeing total coverage. Which specific theological views were established in what location varied according not only to the socio-political context of the period, the transmitters and the receiving religions and social ideologies, but also the evolving theology, orthodoxies interchanging with heresies, fashions and personnel. The Syrian Orthodox church's theology in India, for example, is specific to that area not only because it is Orthodox, and arguably captured by caste, but because it was established long before the doctrinally important fourth and fifth century Councils of Nicaea and Chalcedon. It is clearly necessary to be aware of the *historical* context in which each reading is embedded; the *social* context in general and in particular; the particular *ecclesial* structure involved; and the general and specific *theology*: in short, when, where and who, which and what.

These four planks, which will be discussed below, form the loom-frame of these volumes. The long weft threads of power, agency, syncretism, gender, ethnicity and identity, contextualization, conversion and transmission run throughout the texts: crucial points relating to each are outlined below in this General introduction. These are woven with the warp threads of topic, time and place, descriptions thickening as time and the density and breadth of sources increase. Each volume sets out the historical context and crucial weft links, followed by a discussion of issues linking each cluster of chapters and brief comment on each chapter.

Christianity in these volumes may appear in unexpected guises and versions, and no north–south or secular–religious dichotomies make sense on the ground. Illiteracy cannot be equated with gullibility, nor book-learning with doctrinal purity; belief in Christ as saviour may be more an addition to a person's identity as Christian than integral to it; and the inherent dangers of power and its abuse run through this institution, just as through every other institution or gathering of people.

Below, I shall set out basic approaches to the topic and the four essential planks of theology, sociology, ecclesiology and history which make up the loom, and then set the long warp threads – such as power, syncretism, context, conversion – which stretch through these volumes. These two steps form the essential basis onto which the many readings on World Christianity can be woven in an intelligible and indeed intelligent manner. Once this second stage is complete, I shall briefly set out just how all these various elements work together by looking at this particular tradition on the ground, pointing out just how fine-tuned the questions must be before any assumptions, much less conclusions, are made.

Commonalities in the study of religion

It is not my brief here to describe the theological positions of all Christian groups: thick as these volumes are, so much important material on interesting topics and great writers has already been sifted out. What is necessary, however, is to give a working 'basic theology' for readers from religious studies and social sciences, including those with specific faith positions and those without, and then call on 'basic sociology' to furnish another crucial tool. 'Basic ecclesiology', giving the gist of the main churches, and a segment on the place of history complete the four planks for the loom on which the 'Christian cloth' can be woven.

Gadamer's general caution that 'Researchers need to free themselves through reflection from that which otherwise and unbeknownst oppresses us'[8] is as relevant in the study of religion for the believer in this or in another tradition as it is for the agnostic and the atheist. Its value lies in the need both for a dispassionate reception of material and for hearing the viewpoint – agnostic, believer, atheist – of those writing the texts where this speaks to the content or critique. Evidence of failure to do this is provided by earlier anthropologists bracketing off Christian aspects in many research settings, an omission which led to an irretrievable loss of material. Such opposition to missions on the assumption (certainly not without varying degrees of validity) that Christianity destroyed or at least altered earlier ways was all the odder given anthropologists' frequent dependence on missions for shelter, initial contacts and language.[9] The work of anthropologists is beginning to approach Christianity in a less apologetic or antagonistic manner, thus taking seriously the oft-stated intention to see the world from others' viewpoint, not a researcher's often egocentric 'relativism'.

Given the focus on just one religion, taking the category 'religion' apart would be redundant. Alerting readers to the many Christianities past and present is not. Before going into historical, ecclesiological, theological and sociological approaches, a few general points are therefore in order. Two recurrent and related issues appear to be universally relevant to what anthropologists, sociologists, religious studies and indeed liturgical practitioners and adherents link to religion.

The first concern is: what is (after) death? Do the visible living and the less visible dead only relate sequentially, any interaction being restricted to the next life and place, or is the link unbroken by death, communions of saints and phalanxes of caring friends continuing to be part of the living? Total separation may well be assumed in post-Enlightenment thought and is indeed all too often assumed to be *the* Christian view. This is not the case either theologically or ecclesially[10] despite social scientists, along with much EuroAmerican Christianity, often assuming that the so-called natural and supernatural are universal categories. In early Christianity, and indeed in many current Christianities, the divide is largely absent.[11]

The second and linked concern is: what is evil, especially that which steals life in untimely fashion;[12] why do evil or bad things happen especially to 'good' people; and how is wholeness restored. Christians, but by no means all, may say that problems result from the innate sinfulness, especially the selfishness and greed, of all humans. This was linked by St Paul (CE 50–60) to separation from God after Adam and Eve sinned, later elaborated by St Augustine (CE 354–430) into the doctrine of Original Sin and guilt borne by all. This view is regularly revised, refined and reoriented – and as regularly rejected by a proportion of the faithful even in those churches holding it. Scholars of any ilk are attuned to the fact that all systems of thought and practice have an ideal which contrasts with the real – yet do tend to leap on such gaps in religions as improper, as if dissent and dissembling are more significant in the field of religion than in other areas of life.

There is normally a link between the two concerns of death and the vicissitudes of life. If joining God as Ultimate in some way at death, or at least avoiding "a bad end", is a salvific hope, then daily life and its choices – related to joys and sorrows, good or bad outcomes – may well be lived with that end in mind. In contexts where there is a degree of fit between the legal system and the underlying or overt theology, a wish not to court hell after death may coincide with that to avoid prison on earth. Adherents who may wish for the possibility of a good death (or orient life choices away from a bad one) and those merely enculturated within a socio-legal context influenced by that faith position may each make similar choices, albeit for different reasons.

Aggregations of people in specific times and places commonly face these and other imponderables by prescribing a particular relationship to the Ultimate/Other/God and proscribing alternate utterances and acts, if necessary through trials for heresy,[13] expulsion, denigration: what silent adherents actually think remains untapped. At other times and places, religious authorities may lack the legal powers of the particular polity to insist on one way, may have no wish to control the outward practice of individuals or, faced with already established alternative religious orientations, must rely on influence, witness and negotiation, together with grudging or positive acceptance of other ways.

The first approach is often assumed to be exclusivist, for, taking one Christian stream, if only faith in Christ is salvific, other versions are logically excluded for the spiritual health of all. Yet we must be careful here, for a decision for unanimity may be less for salvific than socio-political and ethnic reasons. The core concern may be as much that '(proper) Greeks are Orthodox' or 'proper Spaniards are Roman Catholic' as that 'all Greeks or Spaniards are saved.' Likewise, a plurality of religions does not necessarily mean all ways are seen as valid (though it well might) within that plurality. It will, however, involve some degree of social accommodation. Institutional expression of exclusivity, however, must always be questioned. The vocal may well have exclusive views, but ordinary people may reckon their neighbours' faith differently, the need and the wish to 'get on' pushing ideological exclusivity into the background. This is especially the case for rural people expecting to live with their neighbours for life,[14] and for the sceptic in every place. These questions cannot be dealt with further here, but do come up in the readings.

Following on from that last point, and picking up on Geertz and the futility of boundary-making, it is important to emphasize the fact that while Christianity and its denominations may be described in terms of doctrines, written and/or performed texts, and delineated in such a way that one is clearly different from another and from other faiths, this may not be the case at the level of praxis or of deep-structural assumptions about the world which go beyond the visual and verbal expression. At that deeper level, unspoken assumptions in a region may act as an umbrella for *all* religious traditions there. Seeing the world as antagonistic; regarding unbalanced exchange as dangerous; assuming sexual activity in general may kill men and 'improper' activity will damage fertility of crops and women: such knowledge may well be common to, and seen as common by, people practising ostensibly different faiths. Attending rituals across the spectrum; shifting for healing from one to another and back; keeping what outsiders or liturgical functionaries define as double or triple religions' discourses but a local sees merely as the proper and wise way of living there; shifting membership to another church are all the everyday stuff of lives, not that which must be explained.

Basic theological plank

All the material in these readings looks at people and contexts identifying with or not explicitly rejecting the ethical system expressed by Christianity and the social systems embedded in it. At the broadest, we are including people who identify more with Christianity than any other religion, and thus people for whom Christmas is a major point in the year, whether for beach holidays, skiing trips, gift exchange, special food or the annual church visit. The 'reasonably interested' Christian and the deeply committed adherent will also see Christmas as the first of the two major festivals of God as Son, the second being Easter, and the third major festival, Pentecost, for God as Holy Spirit. These three aspects or representations of God are formalized as the Trinity. Those identifying as Christians revere and worship one God existing before time (as do Jews and Muslims), Christians assert that God was briefly manifested as or incarnated in his Son Jesus Christ, born of Mary and filiated to her carpenter husband Joseph, his exact status being the focus of Christology as developed by the early Church Fathers. After Jesus's crucifixion on behalf of, and to expiate the sins of, all people, followed by his resurrection after three days and ascension to heaven in around 30 CE as described in the Gospels, Christian believers have understood God to be universally present and immanent in the Holy Spirit stressed in Pentecostal worship.

An achieved or ascribed member accepts God, and is accepted by God, with varying consciousness and understanding. This is usually marked or effected by adult or infant Baptism in the name of the Trinity, or Jesus alone, with water and often oil. Another common core ritual is the sharing of bread and wine (or locally agreed alternatives) by members after consecration by the liturgical leader, in memory or re-presentation of the body and blood of Jesus, through whom salvation comes after death: some traditions and individuals stress "this wond" salvation. The forgiveness of sins by God, commonly pronounced by a liturgical leader and mediated by Christ for all through his sacrificial death, is a crucial element. This does not slickly ignore the offence, whether one of commission or omission. Rather does it invalidate both revenge and unending self-loathing for the confessing penitent, who is reconciled with and loved by God, and encouraged in love and justice to further reconciliation with the neighbour, forming the basics of Christian ethics.

The balance between faith and works varies. Roman Catholics, for example, have often been simplistically held up as 'works only', the believer contributing to his own salvation. Lutherans, on the other hand, have been characterized as 'faith only', in which the believer could contribute nothing at all towards her salvation. Yet a more balanced view is that the wish to act in neighbourly love and quiet charity (works) for others, often asserted to be a crucial Christian marker, emanates from the gift of grace through faith. The neighbour for a believing Christian includes all people, liked or disliked, known and unknown, epitomized by the widely known Good Samaritan parable. Such a horizontal universalism was not always acceptable to central or local authority, nor does it fit easily with the demands of family or clan. War and systemic inequality within and between groups suggests adhering to this even in principle, let alone practice, has had its difficulties for clergy and laity alike. All believers are equal before God, irrespective of ethnicity, gender or rank, though, again, potentially disruptive demands prove easier to hear than to follow. Dissent movements tend to home in on at least one of the above issues.

Believers are expected to minister to each other as well as to be ministered to by leaders trained specifically for the job or (more rarely) chosen by the group without further training. Reasons for the latter variation would be where a direct call from God is judged sufficient; where group leadership is collective; or where the status of the chosen one – be that king's or pope's son in medieval Europe or a chief's son in the initial conversion of Iceland in 1000 CE – was sufficient qualification. The main work of such leaders is to teach, preach and celebrate between two and seven sacraments. Initial leaders chosen by Jesus were male apostles. Those leaders chosen by or working with Paul, a post-Jesus convert whose writing laid the crucial foundation for the church as a viable organization, were male and female, women like Phoebe and Junia appearing in his letters as equals. The redoubtable Hilda, Abbess of Whitby, who organized a Synod there in 657, was a woman of Episcopal status in charge of male and female religious houses. Female liturgical leadership faded away until the late twentieth century, but overall male leadership within clearly gendered churches is still the norm.[15]

Given that the message of the New Testament, and the salvific figure of Christ in God are said to be for all people rather than an ethnically specific tradition, adherents should be ready to go out and pass on the faith (from Matthew) or witness to it (Luke) both in their immediate surroundings and in more distant places. This, variously interpreted, lies at the basis of the early church described in the mission journeys of Paul from around 45 CE, and of the subsequent spread of Christianity, which has already been noted. The performance of the faith is the subject of Volume Four.

Basic sociological plank

The inter-disciplinary nature of these volumes, makes it necessary to set out some of the social science issues which influenced the choice of readings. A selection of literature enables readers to gain a more thorough understanding of certain points.[16] However, in order that this introduction itself furnishes readers with the basic intellectual wherewithal to get the most out of the readings, I shall briefly survey some basic points making up the sociological plank for this work's loom.

Power

One common and perfectly valid approach to power, as in Max Weber, is that power (*Macht*) is the probability that A can get B to do what A wills, whatever B wants and indeed whether or not the exercise of A's power is legitimate, that is, authorized by the institutional context in which that power is exercised, be that the state, the school, the church. This is essentially 'power over', which is rather often seen as domination and therefore negative – which can seem a little naïve. Authority (*Herrschaft*) legitimates power. A priest may be seen as having the power through God to forgive sins and consecrate bread and wine, and, provided s/he holds a current licence from the particular church, is authorized to do so. A disbarred or laicized minister has no authority but may still retain power. A local congregation may cease to accept a person as their legitimate religious leader on social, political, theological or moral grounds, despite a higher authority retaining him. Such a minister would be effectively powerless, an impasse usually resolved rather dramatically by one or the other party departing. Less obvious straining under the power of a leader may be the formation of cliques and murmuring circuits, patient waiting until the present pain has passed or, if alternatives are available, moving to another group.

As Stephen Lukes, among others, explains, the most refined use of power is that which is so internalized that those affected by it do not even consider opposing it. That is, the question is less how power is exercised, but how the need for its *overt* exercise is avoided by securing compliance through subordinates' automatic consent. This is Lukes's three-dimension power, and it is clearly linked to the Gramscian view of hegemonic power exerted by state and other authorities to 'embrace' the under-group, the dominated, so that they do not recognize the control, and fail to perceive what would otherwise be – for Gramsci – their best interests. Whether or not people are willing, or even wish to be, dominated; do not realize they are; are tactical strategic actors in a state of silent resistance; or live under compliance while pursuing personal agendas by manoeuvring among obstacles[17] – or variations and amalgams thereof – is a matter for sociological argument. Here it is sufficient to suggest that people negotiate within the constraints they perceive and those they have so internalized they do not perceive, using what agency, power and room for manoeuvre their context, particular status and interests afford.[18]

Christians voluntarily accept the ritual power of liturgical leaders, even if not of a specific leader, if that assists the intention underlying their church involvement. A believer might reasonably be assumed to accept the organizational hierarchy which usually exists, very few, the Society of Friends being one, managing to survive long term without any hierarchy at all. This does not mean the exercise of power within churches is unproblematic,[19] yet nor does it mean there must always be a problem. Power exists, and is a crucial thread throughout these readings. Clearly the illegitimate exercise of power in a church, as in any institution, has deleterious effects. Any institution which presumes that merely because its intentions are 'good' the downside of power will be absent risks continual abuses of power.[20]

Overt and covert conflict and contest involved in the exercise or avoidance of power crucially underpin many of the readings. If we take the 'public transcript' as signifying private consent without further examination, we may fail to grasp the internal dissent involved in a 'sudden' decision of an entire segment of a church to join another denomination. Individuals may observe what they see as an improper or at least unreasonable exercise of power in a church and do nothing about it if they see no alternative[21] – nor may they necessarily find such behaviour especially intolerable if the perceived nature of external power is that, unlike local power, objection is futile. Asking a woman some years ago what she thought of a new Malaysian law regarding financial provision for engaged women, she answered: 'What sort of daft question is that! It's a government law, it's *paksa* – force – and you don't reflect on force.' Yet that does not mean that the church in that village is not reflected on critically – but nor does it mean that reflection on it, even very critical, will lead to change. If irritation, resentment and apathy outweigh salvific and social benefits for enough (important) villagers, change may eventually ensue.

Representation

Speaking or writing about others necessarily means acting 'on their behalf'. Any institution does this in the name of the members, effectively disenfranchizing them, for to present all views of all people always would be impossible. However, this process is fraught with the danger of misrepresentation. Public representations endowed with public meaning, to use Sperber's term,[22] held as ordered action, ritual and doctrine in the church context, would need to be related to the corresponding private mental representations of individuals, held as a memory (personal and familial), a belief (which may not relate closely to that held at the institutional level) and an intention (for belonging or going along to church).

Misrepresenting, assuming private intentions reflect public representations and the parts echo the whole, is almost inevitable. This can be unwitting when an anthropologist, or indeed a priest, assumes all being written of agree with the sentiments of the majority, the vocal minority or the writer's coterie. It may be intentional, or structurally inbuilt. A priest may represent the people in their prayer to God and also to bishop, moderator or president: s/he may also represent Christ during the Eucharist. The one figure is thus the *Vertreter* – the representative, legitimately speaking for others, on their behalf, according to the theology of the particular denomination. But as representative of the collectivity beneath, s/he also acts as, or performs as, the *Darsteller* – the re-presenter, setting forth and demonstrating what we can perhaps call almost the assumed content, the world-view, of the collectivity. The danger of misrepresenting lies in that doubling of roles. As the sociologist Spivak put it, 'there is rarely an identity of interests between representer and representative. The event of representation as *Vertretung*, on behalf of the other, behaves like *Darstellung*, setting out of the other on behalf of the representative'.[23] It is in this potential context of 'speaking for' in social and literary life and text that we find the link between representation and power. Caution, even scepticism, is therefore always advisable.

Conversion

Whether achieved through a big bang or evolution,[24] religious conversion is commonly seen as a 'fully conscious break with a person's former ways through self-determination and passionate inner struggle'.[25] This view leaves those whose conversion to a new religious identity is not accompanied by such efforts and effects in a classificatory limbo. The apparent problem concerns less the inadequacy of the converts or of their conversion than an understanding which assumes those identifying with a specific religion relate to the 'official faith and belief' aspect as well as the social attitudes and perhaps the rites of passage. People may well combine both.

The sociologist of religion Rambo has suggested that anthropology is perhaps best placed to offer both meticulous contextualizing of conversion events and processes over time and a reasonably dispassionate analysis.[26] Both are important. The implication of conversion being a process is that the conversion event, if there is one, is but one point amid what may (but need not) be a slow and unpredictable unfolding in which there will be a lag between institutional or personal change and any psycho-social adjustment there might be.[27] A synchronic glimpse misses much. The decision to change or add to that identity may be a consequence of marriage, or part of a search for educational opportunity, employment or recognition as a full citizen of whichever polity – neighbourhood or nation – is relevant to the person converting. It may also reorient the individual mind to the immanent, transcendent or refracted Other in an immediately spiritually stirring experience or, more imperceptibly, over a long period, even a lifetime.

Long-term field research can both access the meaning of the process and, if conversion is seen as a breach, shed light on the meaning and significance of the tradition in a particular time and context. This is especially relevant in colonial or neo-colonial discussion about conversion contexts, when 'the poor' are assumed to be unable to act of their own volition in adopting the new faith (whether or not they intend to leave the old one, which is always a moot point) but are assumed to have been beguiled, paid, pressured. Certainly these things happen: but they cannot be assumed. Moreover, such views imply that conversion by an elite person is done for 'right reasons', for they have the intelligence and dispassion to make such a judgement, whereas the poor are too stupid to decide for themselves. Such an assumption is unacceptable.

Contextualization

Arguably, Christianity has always contextualized itself as it fitted into new spaces after Pentecost 30 CE, translating meaning and text, negotiating a space to talk, a place to be, with nomads, villagers and townspeople in both the short and the long term. This is inevitable. But in bringing a church from one spot to another, what the bringer takes as 'core essentials of the faith' are all too likely to be, or to include, *already* contextualized versions revised in a quite different milieu. The Anglican mission to Korea from 1890, for example, though building its first church in totally Korean style, insisted on the liturgy being an exact translation, orally and visually, of that then pertaining in London. Superficial contextualization – language use, the wearing of shoes in buildings or not, ritual change[28] and some accommodation to local hierarchical patterns – is the most studied issue and the one most easily available. These are certainly important anthropologically and indeed theologically (the complexities, occasional successes and frequent failures of which cannot be explored here), and recur throughout the readings.[29]

Language is particularly interesting. Where the incomer's language is used, for example, full belonging may be restricted to a particular class which over time (often in but not restricted to colonial periods) privileges access for church-goers to any benefits in education and therefore employment which the church brought: whether such privileging was intentional or not must be ascertained in each case. Even where one of many local languages is chosen, that group of native speakers is privileged above others, and may alter the internal power dynamics between groups, especially where differently estimated churches choose different languages. Bible translation, however, may be crucial to retaining or reviving a language. The fillip given to written Welsh during the Reformation churches is a case in point. Williams's comment that 'the services [the translators] rendered in laying the modern foundation of religion, language, literature and national awareness in Wales was Epoch-making' can be echoed by many peoples over the centuries until the present day.[30]

There are many examples of contextualization which directly conflict with the theological and biblical texts. Sometimes a practice which appears 'correctly localized' looks different to an insider. In Tonga, for example, the pew for the king is set at the same level as the pulpit, far above the people, and in giving him Communion the high status word is used for 'eat' and 'drink,'[31] ordinary people getting the everyday word. Such replication of hierarchy may seem theologically questionable, though it was done regularly in Europe from Constantine's time. The wearing of local dress in church for preachers would surely be applauded as good: how value judgements, ignorant or informed, thrive! In Tonga, when the pastor wears a locally made pandanus sarong, the specific weaving style indicates his social (not clerical) status, which is improper. A breakaway Methodist church which demanded all ministers wear trousers if preaching to avoid this status marker was making a theological statement which an outsider all too easily misreads as a Eurocentric imitation.

Contextualization of Christianity is often shorthand for what the 'ethnic other' other does elsewhere. Given its ubiquity, and given that more articles in these volumes deal with Christianity in Asia, Africa, Latin America than in EuroAmerica, let me briefly exemplify ordinary everyday contextualized Christianity in 2009 Middle America as heard in a Baptist sermon.[32] The 1776 constitution of that country aims for the life, liberty and *happiness* of its people. This, our happiness and the success of all our right-thinking enterprises, was the overall tenor of the sermon, the preacher clutching a closed Bible throughout. It was also the clear comment of the one secular writer referred to, who 'thanked our God and Father for his provision of happiness for all his children'.[33] It was not a Baptist sermon as in Myanmar, which would be tightly biblically based and conceptually linked to endurance, suffering and salvation, but rather a person-centred success-oriented feel-good approach to Jesus as King-Emperor in which 'knowing your context' meant, or seems to mean, fulfilling one's own obligations as father, and realizing our full potential as people.

Certainly there is tension, if not plain conflict, in every ideological system, whatever the intention: this was no exception. And there have been problems with externally driven contextualization, or with the failure to realize that all systems change in their own time. A Christian church in India which accepts caste is fully contextualized in opposition to the Christian, though not the local, text, as were segregated churches in South Africa or America. The introduction of Vedanta-based practices in mid-twentieth-century India by local and foreign priests brought a system which included the Laws of Manu into a church 80 per cent of whose members are *dalit*, and thus oppressed by those very laws. Contextual issues for Christians of Muslim background in those Muslim countries where conversion out of that faith is prohibited may lead to a change in burial practice formerly held sacrosanct. At death, all officially Muslim corpses will be given a Muslim burial, and so all those privately belonging to Muslim-background Christian churches develop a very specific theological attitude to the body after death which minimizes the importance of faith-relevant funeral rites.

Syncretism

In social sciences, syncretism is usually seen as the unconscious and spontaneous interweaving and merging of religious traditions. Put simply, it 'involves the combination of diverse traditions in the area of religion',[34] with the recognition that all such traditions should be regarded as syncretic. It is a description of what normally occurs, not an evaluation of the theological appropriateness of such occurrences. Syncretic processes are inevitable, for whether ideas travel horizontally between and within groups or vertically, ordinary thinkers, commentators and those with special interests communicate with each other and, where relevant, with potential followers, including sceptics. Communication must utilize a ritual and verbal language with associated concepts which can readily, or at least adequately, be appropriated. Doctrinal amnesia helpfully elides such origins, for, as Droogers says. 'Once a religion is established and religious founders have completed its codification, these syncretic origins are often forgotten'. He had earlier defined syncretism as 'religious interpenetration, either taken for granted or subject to debate'. This does rather essentialize religions, unless referring to the formal versions, for 'penetrated' implies discrete units. As I implied above, 'religions' on the ground tend to be discrete more in theory than practice.

Within theological discourse, syncretism tends to be negatively judged, as a pollution of the pure text. Yet this suggests a naïve view of cultures (and faiths) as closed boxes rather than unbounded hybrid constellations sparkling with contested alternatives and variations used by 'bricolaging' individuals and groups according to their particular social status and perceived context. Where not rejected outright for impurity, syncretism is not infrequently used by theologians to slam what is not understood. Naturally this is more readily noticed when looking at systems and patterns other than one's own, 'my sophisticated multiple discourses' too easily being 'your deviant or simple syncretism'. In the face of worldwide multiple belonging there are moves within the theology and missiology of some traditions to acknowledge multiple belonging as not being illegitimate,[35] or even as unavoidably normal.

In a context where one group, a powerful group exercising authority, is able to make decisions about the orthodoxy of another clearly power is the core issue, just as it is when the group in authority decides to tolerate variation, the act of toleration being itself one of power, for it assumes the possibility of refusing to tolerate or withdrawing what only passed for acceptance. It is normal that actual people's belief systems include elements from other systems which the person may not so identify or indeed keep secret, and which do not necessarily become an issue for the institution. What can easily be called syncretism can also be seen as the perfectly normal exercising of agency – but such agency applied in Brazilian *favellas*, African townships or Indian *dalit* villages is more commonly denigrated as syncretism.

Secularization

Secularization is assumed, again as an ideological not evidenced statement, to be relevant to 'modern western society' and its echoes. While it is certainly advanced in Europe[36] it may be useful to reflect more carefully. A context where all residents are ineluctably part of the local socio-cultural system, including what, when otherwise excised, is called religion, is not a secularized system. However, as soon as opting out of that totality for another system is allowed to some residents, the splitting of the whole into optional choices of action (private thought always being possible) enables secularization. I have already referred to the secularizing potential in medieval European blasphemy in Europe. Early nineteenth-century Catholicism in France was clearly uninteresting to a majority at that time, Orléans in 1820 seeing just 20 per cent take Easter Communion (the crucial obligation of membership) and in nearby Loiret just 2 per cent of adult males communicating at Easter in 1852.[37]

Even an explicit separation between religion and the state has to be examined carefully. A majority of American Presidents have been Episcopalian; flags deck both Capitol and chancel; a proposed translation of the anthem brought the newspaper riposte that 'the flag and the national anthem are sacred and should never be altered'; and the assistance given to the independence-seeking Philippines by America in 1898 (which resulted in it colonizing that country) was given in the name of the 'Bible, the Cross and the Flag'. The way France separates church and state is rather different, no symbols whatsoever of any faith tradition being allowed on government property. '*Notre Patrimoine ici*' may indeed substitute for '*Notre père qui est en ciel*' – but a 'secular' worship of the state does differ from the harnessing of religion by the state.

Basic ecclesiology plank

The six main streams of worldwide Christianity set out in these readings are: Roman Catholicism, Greek, Russian, Syrian and African Orthodoxy, Episcopal Protestantism (largely Anglican and Lutheran), Evangelical Protestantism, Pentecostalism and locally originating Christianities in each continent. Even those with common liturgies, doctrines and mobile personnel are in no way 'the same' in each manifestation, and readers should be constantly alert to think beyond overt titles and obvious content in readings to what is actually the local practice at the specific time to which a paper refers. Moreover, as I have made clear above, the capacity of individuals to ignore boundaries and rules and go to any church, or indeed to totally other traditions, for their salvific or social comfort should perhaps be assumed as the norm, exceptions being just that, exceptional. Presbyterians' collectively murmured individual prayers in Korea, for example, appear closer to Pentecostal than to Scottish or Dutch forms of Calvinism, their dawn prayers derive more from local Buddhist practice and, though outlawed by ministers, visits by local Christians to local shamans for healing are not unknown.[38]

This is an appropriate point to comment briefly on mission and missionaries, so often linked, or even intellectually restricted, to EuroAmerican peddling of the faith. This is an inadequate assumption and one which does an injustice to all those people in and from all continents who work and worked as Bible women, colporteurs, mission leaders and helpers both within their own country and overseas: to take one simple example, late nineteenth-century Tamil Lutherans from South India were crucial to that church's work in the then Tanganyika.[39] Whatever readers' views on mission, this is an important point – remembering Gadamer – to bear in mind. It is of course possible to see in various times and places both that such local workers willingly shared or colluded in a Gramscian embrace and also that they worked willingly for the faith which burned in their hearts. The most quickly spread mission and ministry movement in Asia, especially China and points on that journey including Tibet and the northern side of the Himalayas, was the Church of the East, from the second to ninth century and lasting (outwith India) to the fourteenth century.[40] The current century's core mission-sending countries are, first, the USA, followed closely by Korea and then India within its own borders. Internal mission in China is also increasing quickly.

Mission in earlier Orthodox and Roman Catholic churches (the two split finally in 1054) was on the whole slow and flexible, each worker being very much dependent on his own survival skills amid isolation. Recent mission movements depend on continual home ties and communication, which often means continual home control. Between these two ends lies the push to Asia, Africa and Latin America by Roman Catholic Spanish and Portuguese, for whom religion and the state were inseparable, soon followed by various broadly Protestant groups, as well as less-Iberian Roman Catholics, linked to several European countries and later to America. The intertwining or indeed at times opposition between colonial government and missionary movement will be referred to in the Introductions to Volumes I and II, just as will their collusion. Suffice it to say here that not all colonial governments supported missionaries, and not all missionaries supported colonialism, from Korean Bible workers opposing Japanese colonization to Las Casas opposing the violence of the Spanish Empire. Christianity does have a case to answer, and at some times and places that case is serious: but the issue is in no way simple. Christians may see themselves as obliged to acquaint others with their faith, and it may have been the underlying intention of some countries and missions at certain periods to convert all to one church by force, but that does not obtain in all times and contexts. Seventeenth-century Jesuits in Goa, India, were determined to convert all to their faith or expel them: twenty-first-century Jesuits in India are more likely to be sanctioned by the Vatican for accepting other faiths as equally valid ways to the divine.[41]

Basic historical plank

The final plank is history. Given its crucial place in the organizing of the first three volumes, it is necessary to highlight some issues: given that historical processes are discussed in the Introduction to each volume, comment here will be brief. The historian Frankiel notes two approaches in World Christianity: those stressing continuity between pre-Christian and Christian cultures and those focusing on esoteric forms.[42] One could add those more often within the faith may find continuity for particular reasons, just as the outsider may headline the esoteric: but then unreflected upon inclinations and intentions plague us all. Her note on discontinuity, though, is important, for too often continuity is assumed because ritual or texts, even a name, fit a seemingly continuous narrative. Jesus was a healer. Many modern churches, particularly the Pentecostally inclined (which can include most churches in an area) in parts of Africa, East and South East Asia, stress healing more than churches in EuroAmerica, but the split is in no way absolute. Frankiel continues: 'If an evangelical Christian from the year 1800 were to witness the faith-healings of 21st century Pentecostal churches, he would almost certainly declare that, despite Christian language and symbolism, this was not authentic Christianity'. From the third century to the mid-nineteenth, the sick were prayed for privately, but not prayed over for healing.

The believer's argument might be: 'We are reviving what was lost over the years, so ours is the authentic version,' and it is easy for the researcher or reader unversed in theology or church history to be persuaded by such internal validations. The theologian Williams extends Frankiel's line: 'a contemporary arguing that primitive Christianity is fundamentally at one with modern feminism may be failing to reflect on how apparently similar formulations or policies across the centuries may draw on radically different sources'.[43] A final comment from him nicely rounds off this setting out of the four planks supporting these readers, for it applies widely:

> Good historical writing constructs that sense of who we are by a real engagement with the strangeness of the past, that establishes my or our identity now as bound up with a range of things that are not obvious to the world we think we inhabit . . . Bad history is anything which refuses this difficulty and enlargement, whether by giving us a version of the past that is just the present in fancy dress or by dismissing the past as a wholly foreign country.[44]

The threads at work: commonalities in the study of World Christianity

I have set out the four planks making up the loom which enables the weaving of World Christian presence and significance over the last two thousand years, and given the long thematic threads, such as contextualization and syncretism, which will bear the burden of regional and processual infilling in these four volumes of readings. To guide the reader who wishes to use the texts in a discerning manner, let me pick out crucial points to bear in mind when reading unfamiliar and, equally, familiar material. This starts with a raft of questions, followed by a contextualized discussion.

Questions to set the scene

How Christianity is and has been perceived and received all over the world clearly depends on many factors, which may change over time. A cursory check-list would include: precisely who purveyed exactly what version of the faith and when; what was and is its relation to state and local powers in each region and period; who in terms of ethnicity, class or caste initially and perhaps eventually and currently accepted it in that community, region or nation; how its offerings compare with or complement what is locally on offer. In some contexts, ranging from the '*cuius regio*' of Europe to early and modern Latin America, issues of conversion would be relevant: was it done for whole categories of people by the ruler's or leader's or incomer's fiat; what conversion was done on a person-to-person basis and whom did such individuals represent. Where the faith came from one country or segment thereof to another, were the more obvious agents of conversion, the teachers, preachers and bible-distributors, of local or regional origin or from totally outside local rankings, or were they lay immigrants who brought and spread their faith with them by teaching neighbours over the fence or by marriage. Other points would include: was or is Christian uptake mostly rural or urban, and which denominations were where; is it the only faith, or one of a plurality; is it or has it been a crucial purveyor of formal education and if so for which category of student; is being Christian, or a certain version of Christian, part of the class system such that church allegiance may change as class ranks are climbed. Attending church in rural Georgia, USA, may be part of a rural lawyer's demonstration of probity and reliability as well as, or independent of, personal belief: that action may contribute to maintaining church–power links – just as the same action in Soviet-time Georgia could be an anti-elite statement. Attending a certain church prior to applying for a school or university run by that church may, though need not, relate to the need for a liturgical leader's reference: it may also be an act of hope or, indeed, of faith.

What to look for: specificity of context

The above gives the starting point for clarity, but more is necessary. The next area of enquiry relates to a particular Christianity's elimination of or integration with the locally understood visible and less visible world over time in one place. This includes a clear grasp of local religious traditions: the locally restricted – including African Traditional religion and parallels across the world – and the more universal, including Confucianism, Daoism, Shinto, Islam, Hinduism, Sikhism, Judaism and Buddhism, with all their regional and temporal variations, schisms and linkages. From there we would need to move to an analysis of the more obviously 'theological and philosophical' issues, such as the nature of the person, ethics, the source of evil, and the relation between local and ultimate spiritual forces at both superficial and deep-structure level.

The particularity of context is important, and is too often skimmed over or ignored as 'others' are seen with simplistic uniformity. To assume only Wahabi, or more generally Sunni, Islam will be relevant to understanding Islam in Indonesia, the Philippines and much of India will not be useful, as those regions were heavily influenced by Sufism, as was Islam in West Africa. Christianity in those areas is therefore also likely to be influenced directly both by Sufism and also by local reactions to and conflicts with Wahabism. Thai Buddhist women cannot be ordained monks in Thailand, but must go to equally Theravadan Sri Lanka for an ordination which is barely accepted in Thailand. As with Sufi or Wahabi, so too the Theravada tradition has to be unpacked, for it too influences the way Thais (and Burmese) of Buddhist background (less so the minority hill-tribe people) are Christian. While other issues also apply, Thai Anglican women cannot be ordained priests: Sri Lankan women are. Careful attention to the fissures and fractions in *all* contexts is therefore vital.

Who defines Christian identity: processes of power

If a Christian tradition is established, another potentially important issue, as with other universal traditions, are the criteria used to define the 'proper' 'unadulterated' 'pure' version. Who has the power to define an acceptably Orthodox, Roman Catholic, Anglican, Lutheran, Protestant, Pentecostal or any other performance of faith? Who can understand the layered meaning behind what seem 'obvious' intentions? Thomas Aquinas's view that 'the goal of an action decides what sort of an action it is, worthy of praise or blame', might seem to offer some assistance. Yet this assumes that a person enculturated in one context can understand the goals of another without making any effort to learn by asking, seeing, observing and reflecting; a slow job indeed. Moreover, unless observers realize their intention in doing an action may be different from that of other actors, they may not realize there is any need to learn that there may indeed be a gulf between their own and others' understanding of action and intention. Without this, there will be scant chance that what one Christian seems to be doing is actually what the observer assumes.

This does not matter if the decision maker has no control over the other, no influence on the other being accepted as Christian. Indeed it may seem obvious who is a 'proper Christian' – one sharing 'core' beliefs as defined by the viewer. Yet what is performed – attendance at church, for example – can be seen, but that bears no necessary relation to what is believed.[45] Who is a 'pure' Christian becomes rather a tricky issue, as heterodoxy may be present in any person. But if one category decides, and the decision matters to one identifying as Christian, fully accepted membership can be important. Let me clarify this. It is possible to buy tickets for an ordinary football or baseball match on the open market, so formally acknowledged club membership may be unimportant, especially for people who, while they are fans, are not that fussed if they get to the game or not. But for particular games, a Cup Final or the Rose Bowl, tickets may be for members only. Then it matters who is counted in or excluded, and, however regular the attendance or strong the identification, the club will exclude non-members. The decision in that case is straightforward: if the annual dues were paid, the supplicant is a member; if not, they will be excluded from that particular benefit. With Christianity (to take just this religion), the equivalent to the Cup Final ticket may be being given the Eucharist, feeling (fairly) secure about salvation, however understood, being able to marry or (often more important) be buried by the church. Similar to the slightly disappointed peripheral fan who is happy to watch the game on TV, the person identifying as Christian who is not deeply bothered about any of those markers may not mind much about potential exclusion.

Criteria for exclusion may be very much local, even if explained as theological. If all those in a local Christian community with locally appointed and accredited liturgical leaders agree that, for example, taking the Eucharist and going to a local non-Christian ritual, or drinking alcohol, or having two spouses at the same time or a second after marrying the first in church are fully compatible, then there will be little gap between a multiple-religionist's, serial monogamist's or polygynist's felt Christian identity and the church's acceptance of that identity. If there are no authorized external ties, as with certain churches in all countries, there may be few accreditation problems. A somewhat similar outcome between locality and inclusion for quite different reasons occurs in a context such as a nation-based parish system still obtaining in England, where all resident in the parish have the right to be buried by the local state church representative, without either ever attending church or paying dues. This pattern is now unusual.

If, however, as is more often the case, a local congregation is part of a wider system of presbyteries, dioceses, assemblies, with bishops, presidents, senior pastors, superintendents or other supra-local designated leaders, then rules for membership may mean that some who identify themselves as Christian will be not so regarded by the gatekeepers. This may have social effects in contexts where to be Christian is to be socially normal; it will have practical effects, in that those whose membership is contested may be excluded from performing or being the recipient of rituals; and it may be felt to have salvific outcomes.

The cloth of World Christianity

This brief outline has shown something of the way social scientists can look critically at Christianity from approaches combining, and taking seriously, anthropology, theology, history and ecclesiology. As noted at the outset, the volumes are organized thus. Volume I, after setting the scene in first-century Palestine, moves from early China to the end of the first major Roman Catholic swing across the Americas, South and East Asia, North, South East and South West Africa and the rise of Protestantism across the world. The second takes that spread to the 1960s, after Vatican II, the founding of the World Council of Churches and the start of the explosive growth of post-colonial Christianity, and the third presents contemporary material picking up more firmly of these four initial planks of theology, sociology, history and ecclesiology. The final volumes dances, sings, contemplates, prays and walks its way towards the twenty-first century.

Notes

1 C. Geertz, *Available Light*, Princeton: Princeton University Press, 2000, p. 250.

2 The inculturated Gospel becomes part of the 'deep structure' of being of a worshipping community. See Gittins in 'Beyond Liturgical Inculturation', *Irish Theological Quarterly*, 2004. See also 'Behold the Pig of God', A. Tofaeono, in *Pacific Journal of Theology* 33, 2005.

3 A. McGrath's *Christianity: An Introduction*, Oxford: Oxford University Press, 2006, has a chapter on World Christianity, but the next chapter, 'Christian Practice' is almost entirely EuroAmerican. Such parochialism occurs elsewhere: 'Asia', in Lee's excellent *The Trinity in Asian Perspective*, Nashville: Abingdon, 1996, is Chinese.

4 Texts on world and regional Christianity are legion: *Oxford History of Christianity*, ed. J. McManners, Oxford: Oxford University Press, 1992; *World History of Christianity*, ed. A. Hastings, Grand Rapids, MI: Eerdmans, 1999; E. Isichei, *History of Christianity in Africa*, London, 1995: O. Kalu, *African Christianity: An African Story*, Pretoria, 2005: K. Koschorke, F. Ludwig and M. Delgado (eds), *A History of Christianity in Asia, Africa and Latin America*, Grand Rapids, MI: Eerdmans, 2007; *The Church in Latin America 1492–1992*, E. Dussel, Maryknoll, NY: Orbis, 1992; the eight-volume *Cambridge History of Christianity*, 2009, and the seven volumes by K. Latourette, *A History of the Expansion of Christianity*, Grand Rapids, MI: Eerdmans, 1976; L. Sanneh, *Whose Religion is Christianity*. See also mission historians: R. Frykenberg, B. Stanley, D. Robert; sociologist: T. Ranger.

5 Ernst Benz, 'Ecumenical Relations between Boston Puritanism and German Pietism', *Harvard Theological Review* 54/3, 1961; *Mission to Asia: Narratives and Letters of the Franciscan Missionaries in Mongolia and China in the 13th and 14th Centuries*, ed. C. Dawson; S. O'Brien, 'A Transatlantic Community of Saints: The Great Awakening and the First Evangelical Network, 1735–55', *The American Historical Review* 91/4, 1968.

6 See P. Jenkins, *The Next Christendom: The Coming of Global Christianity*, Oxford: Oxford University Press, 2007, which assumes it was not global earlier, and others.
7 See Orri Vesteinsson's *Conversion of Iceland*, Oxford: Oxford University Press, 2000 and *The Cross Goes North*, ed. M. Carver, York: Medieval Press, 2003.
8 H.-G. Gadamer, in J. Habermas, D. Henrich and J. Taubes (eds) *Hermeneutik und Ideologiekritik*, Frankfurt: Suhrkamp, 1971, p. 296.
9 See Stipe *et al.*, 'Anthropologists versus Missionaries', *Current Anthropology* 21, 1980; S. van der Geest and J. Kirby, 'The Absence of the Missionary in African Ethnography', *African Studies Review* 35/3, 1992; J. Robbins, 'Belief, Time and the Anthropology of Christianity', *Current Anthropology* 48/1, 2007; J. Clifford, *Person and Myth: Maurice Leenhardt in the Melanesian World*, Durham, NC: Duke University Press; A. Orta, 'Metaculture, Missionaries and the Politics of Locality', *Ethnology* 37/2, 1998.
10 See 'On the Need for Nice Ancestors', in *Food, Friends and Funerals*, E. Koepping, Berlin: Lit, 2007.
11 See B. Saler 'Supernatural as a Western Category', *Ethos* 5/1, 1977.
12 See D. Parkin's introduction to his edited *The Anthropology of Evil*, Oxford: Blackwell, 1985.
13 Blasphemous utterances may be a sign of 'decadence or secular critical thinking', but they were not usually prosecuted: see G. Schwerhoff, 'Horror Crime or Bad Habit: Blasphemy in Premodern Europe 1200–1650', in *Journal of Religious History* 32/4, 2008.
14 Wesley Arajah, *Not Without my Neighbour*, Geneva: WCC, 1999.
15 J. Manville, 'The Gendered Organisation of an Australian Anglican Parish', *Sociology of Religion* 58/1, 1997; D. Gaitskell, 'African Bible Women in Transvaal Methodism', *Journal of Religion in Africa* 30, 2000.
16 S. Lukes, *Power, a Radical View*, Basingstoke: Palgrave, 2005; *Syncretism in Religion, a Reader*, ed. A. Leopold and J. Jensen, London: Equinox, 2004; S. Sykes, *Power and Christian Theology*, London: Continuum, 2006; J. Scott, *Domination and the Arts of Resistance*, New Haven, CT: Yale, 1990; R. Shaw and C. Stewart, *Syncretism/Anti-Syncretism*, London: Routledge, 1994; A. Droogers, 'The Power Dimensions of the Christian Community', *Religion* 33, 2003.
17 D. Tilly, 'Domination, Resistance, Compliance', *Sociological Forum* 6/3, 1991.
18 See P. Brown, *Authority and the Sacred*, Cambridge: Cambridge University Press, 1995, for a nuanced discussion of power.
19 See S. Sykes, *Power and Christian Theology*, London: Continuum, 2006.
20 The theologian W. Wink writes: 'With some thrilling exceptions, the churches of the world have never yet decided that domination is wrong.' *When the Powers Fall*, Minneapolis: Fortress, 1998, p. 11.
21 If alternative churches are unavailable (rural regions and areas of sparse Christian presence) lay power can be constrained; as with doctors or schools, alternatives empower users.
22 D. Sperber, 'Interpreting and Explaining Cultural Representations', in G. Pálsson, *Boundaries: Understanding and Interpreting Anthropological Discourse*, Oxford: Berg, 1993.
23 Gayatri Chakravorty Spivak, 'Can the Subaltern Speak?', in *Marxism and the Interpretation of Culture*, 1988, p. 276.
24 The 'paradigmatic' conversion of Paul was both event and process; see R. Peace, *Conversion in the New Testament: Paul and the Twelve*, Grand Rapids, MI: Eerdmans, 1999, p. 25.
25 Schmidt in D. Wulff, *Psychology of Religion*, New York: John Wiley, 1991, p. 497.

26 L. Rambo, 'Anthropology and the Study of Conversion', in A. Buckser and S. Glazier, *The Anthropology of Religious Conversion*, Lanham, MD: Rowman and Littlefield, 2003. See also R. Hefner, *Conversion to Christianity*, Berkeley: University of California, 1993.
27 See D. Hollan, 'Pockets Full of Mistakes: The Personal Consequences of Religious Change in a Toradja Community', *Oceania* 58/4, 1988, pp. 275–89.
28 See T. Asad, *Genealogies of Religion: Discipline and Reasons of Power in Christianity and Islam*, London: Johns Hopkins, 1993; C. Bell, *Ritual*, Oxford: Oxford University Press, 1997.
29 *Christian Worship Worldwide*, ed. C. Farhadian, Grand Rapids, MI: Eerdmans, 2007; R. Schreiter, *Constructing Local Theologies*, Maryknoll, NY: Orbis, 1985; P. Hiebart, *Transforming World Views*, Grand Rapids, MI: Baker, 2008.
30 Glanmor Williams, *The Welsh and Their Religion: Historical Essays*, Cardiff: University of Wales Press, 1991, p. 158.
31 See H. Nieumeitolu, 'The State of the Gospel in Tonga: The State and the Gospel in Tonga', unpublished PhD diss., Edinburgh, 2007.
32 This one sermon may have been atypical for that preacher, though I am told it was not.
33 S. Covey, *The Eighth Habit of Highly Successful People*, New York: Simon and Schuster, 2004, p. iii. His earlier *7 Habits* also asserts, 'your life is carefully designed by you,' and 'think with an abundance mentality: believe there is plenty for everyone': both are cultural, not Christian norms.
34 Shaw and Stewart Syncretism/Anti-Syncretism, London: Routledge, 1994, p. 7.
35 See C. Corneille (ed.) *Many Mansions*, Maryknoll, NY: Orbis, 2004.
36 See G. Davie, *Europe, the Exceptional Case*, London: Darton, Longman and Todd, 2002; S. Bruce, 'The Persuasive World View: Religion in Pre-modern Britain', *British Journal of Sociology* 48/4, 1997.
37 M. Phayer, *Sexual Liberation and Religion in 19th Century France*, London: Croom Helm, 1977.
38 T. Lee, 'Indigenised Practices in Korean Evangelicalism', in R. Buswell, *Religions of South Korea*, Princeton: Princeton University Press, 2007.
39 D. Jeyaraj, in K. Koschorke, *Transcontinental Links in Non-Western Christianity*, Wiesbaden: Harrassowitz, 2002.
40 See A. Atiya, *History of Eastern Christianity*, Notre Dame, IN: University of Notre Dame Press, 1967.
41 J. Dupuis, long-serving Jesuit priest in India, whose *Towards a Christian Theology of Religious Pluralism*, Maryknoll: Orbis, 2001, led to his silencing by Ratzinger.
42 T. Frankiel, 'The Cross-cultural Study of Christianity: An Historian's View', *Religion* 33, 2003.
43 R. Williams, *Why Study the Past*, Grand Rapids, MI: Eerdmans, 2005.
44 Ibid., p. 24.
45 See A. Nesti, 'What Do Believers Believe? Catholicism in Poggibonsi', *Social Compass* 49/1, 2002.

INTRODUCTION TO VOLUME I

Part 1: Context and content

The idea that Christianity is a universally agreed single religion concerned with the sacred as distinct from the secular, in which belief, identity and praxis form one coherent whole which inevitably conflicts with others ways of relating to the visible and less visible world, has already been dealt with and to an extent demolished in the General introduction to these volumes. The context in which people live and relate to others increasingly includes people of varied views and traditions, augmented by information from diverse sources. While this has been the case, and that worldwide, far more often than beliefs in the ideological 'purity' of an unchanging past might suggest, we do certainly need to examine assumptions about the content of 'Christian belief and practice'. This is the more necessary the greater the familiarity readers feel with this particular tradition. These first four pieces therefore lay out crucial threads, the weft of these volumes.

Aspects of Christian theology are expected to exert some influence on daily life for church members and affiliates, but less, or enen not at all, within realms defined as secular. The tie between Christian ideology and law in the EuroAmerican world may seem more a matter of history and philosophy than current thought: but it exists. Greenhouse's article (Chapter 1), based on her fieldwork near Atlanta, deals with the way Baptist theology affects legal practice in a small town in a manner reminiscent of those many systems (including seventeenth-century New England) in which the visible and less visible world form part of a unified cosmological system. Recourse to law indicates a failure of faith for that segment of the town which is Baptist.

The second text picks up a point which will recur throughout these volumes. Conversion to Christianity may occur in contexts of strong encouragement if not force, and may include outright rejection by the convert (or forbidding by the converter) of former or alternative traditions. This need not be the case. A useful perspective may be to assume a convert achieves their Christian identity with as much or as little agency as an ascribed Christian maintains that identity. Passi, an Anglican priest on those islands linking Cape York and New Guinea, respects the ways of his forebears. Some readers may find his notion that Christianity is the 'fulfilment' of tradition (Chapter 2) diminishes the latter. Yet such views, much discussed in nineteenth-century

India by both Farquahar and Slater, are part of Passi's own negotiation of the systems within which he lives, and demand to be so treated.

Picking up from Passi, Abega, a Roman Catholic priest in Cameroun, discusses liturgical farces and the eventual integration of Beti thought into church life, replacing the nonsensical or offensive introduced practices which found priests 'sniffing' an assumedly smelly Christ or singing not 'you are good' but (a slight tonal difference) 'you are a cudgel' (Chapter 3)! The integration, however, was and is not without problem, which may recall the issue of power raised in the General introduction. Just as who decides who is Christian, who decides what contextualizing is acceptable and what 'sinful truck with the devil' is crucial.

The final piece (Chapter 4), again by a priest, discusses actual belief of Catholics in Asia. Discussing two theologians writing on 'Asia', Chia asks: 'Do [they] know anything about what the ordinary lay Catholic on the pews of Asian churches – not just lay theologians – believes?' He shows through a survey just how diverse is that belief and in general how different from official doctrine, especially regarding other religions.

Part 2: Foundations: the Bible as agreed text

The one text crucial to all Christian traditions is the Holy Bible, and especially The New Testament. The Old Testament (Hebrew Bible) was written between 500 and 150 BCE, the New Testament in Greek from around 50 CE to 120 CE. Literalists assert the entire text is not only inspired but also given by God: all accept that it was transcribed by men from varied ethnic and status backgrounds to describe events, mythical and actual, to advise, order, encourage or admonish. In common with other ritual and canonical texts, 'The Bible' is often assumed to have existed as it is 'from the beginning': this is not the case. Which books would actually be included in The New Testament was a contested point settled in the western church after 367, Athanasius opting for 27, for 'in these alone the teaching of godliness is proclaimed'.[1] A little later the Syrian Orthodox church (already established in South India) decreed only twenty-two books sacred, a further nine being later added by Ethiopian Orthodox.

Recital of the Bible in Latin Greek or Syriac by a priest was usual in the first three centuries of Christian history, literacy being more for government, prelates and public order than personal piety. Orthodox Bibles and liturgies in everyday Armenian, Coptic, and Georgian were used from the fourth century onwards. Such vernacular translations 'owed much to the desire among these groups for cultural definition and distinction (religious and ethnic). Centralised authorities tend to promote a single unifying language, while those affirming local or group identity often use language to signal independent traditions and histories'.[2] This increased with the self-contained regional churches in the Caliphate period.

Parts of the Bible were translated into many European vernaculars by the thirteenth century, though not Czech or English. The vernacular version was only fully and readily available across Europe in or just after the Reformation, finally enabling all believers to understand it.[3] Catholic missions translated more liturgy and catechisms: Protestants translated Bibles, initially in segments in the earlier European tradition, before or more usually after a mission began. The 1879 Ross Bible in Korean preceded the 1884 mission, while that in Tamil by Ziegenbalg appeared first in 1715, nine years after his arrival: Massachusetts converts had their first Bible in 1665. Translation into languages, dialects and patois continues.

Textual interpretation usually favoured the doctrinal view of a church and the socio-political context of the particular gatekeepers, blatantly with race in the case of the South African Dutch Reform church and certain pre-civil rights American groups. Critical faculties of listeners meant not every verse or idea would have been accepted, scepticism being an option not restricted to the literate. Not without objection, modern biblical criticism has grown rapidly over the last forty years from its nineteenth-century German roots. Increasingly important exegesis from ethnic, caste, class or gender perspectives reflects societal changes as does a move back to literalism.

The survey article on post-colonial biblical interpretation in Africa and Asia by Kwok (Chapter 5) and the dissection of specific texts, one New Testament and one Old, by Rebera (Chapter 6) and Yoo (Chapter 7) indicate the way such approaches challenge the status quo. Draper's discussion of Colenso's much-contested reflections on the text as translated by and taught to mid-nineteenth-century Zulu (Chapter 8) should caution us against assuming that only modernity opens eyes. Churches use an open Bible as the source of learning and salvation, but this is not its only use. As Razafindrakoto and Holter make clear in the final text (Chapter 9), it can be a source of political power and, when hung over a cradle, a powerful protection.

In short, and in common with other written or performed texts, the number of books in the Bible is not uniform, nor are interpretations, and nor is the use made of it by members, affiliates or opponents.

Part 3: The early church in the Eastern Mediterranean

Having set out core issues in the approach to Christianity and to the Bible in both the General introduction and the first two parts of this volume, we now need to examine the initial foundation and organization of this new religious movement, as is proper when approaching any sociological phenomenon. Gender in this period was discussed in the introduction, and so these papers address other basics which were followed, opposed or transformed, together with equally durable tensions, all of which become evident to varying degrees wherever the church spread from its initial Mediterranean enclave.

First, the ritual practices of these early Christians are set out by Meeks (Chapter 10), using the New Testament Epistles and the writing of Pliny, Hippolytus, Tacitus and Suetonius as well as modern anthropology. In using early sources only, Meeks successfully sets aside the many additions to what initially were two straightforward rituals, initiating a person into the group through the cleansing rebirth of water and sharing a meal pregnant with symbolic meaning for all participants. These rituals apart (and the latter has not always survived), the regular meeting was for teaching, singing, praying, interpreting, advising and even admonishing, all of which had the aim of building up each linked church community. Baptism moved the adept from the world to the fellowship of Christ through separation, transition and re-incorporation: the central agapé meal, recollecting the Body and Blood and being of Christ, reiterated the communion of all. However, the equality given in Christ within the group of slave and free, women and men, clashed with the inequality of the outside. The ensuing religious–civic tension remained until the Emperor Constantine became Christian after 312 CE: by the end of that century state hierarchy sidelined Galatian equality.

Blasi (Chapter 11) discusses the social organization of the early motley group of followers spread after the mission journeys of Paul and others across the Levant and along the coasts and cities of present-day western Turkey and Greece to southern Italy. He uses Weberian terms in arguing that had the charisma of Jesus and those early disciples not been routinized, the fledgling church could not have survived. 'Office charisma' achieved compliance from the public. He argues that given the lack of legal and, one might add, agreed doctrine and textual codes in the early years, and lacking charismatic leaders of the calibre of the initial founders of the movement, formally agreed offices and appointed office-holders become even more important.

These two discussions of ritual and organization – the theological and practical content of the meetings and the bishop–presbyter–deacon organization of churches – may leave the reader with the view that everything in the Christian garden was quickly clear. That might seem the case in hindsight: ritual practice, ecclesial order and the biblical canon more or less set by the fourth century, and separate churches linked by mission journeys and letters of individuals with supra-local authority or at least clout.

Franzmann, however, turns this upside down in 'Taking the "heretics" seriously' (Chapter 12). A myriad of groups after Jesus's death vied for precedence and, over the years, one major cluster gained power thanks to some deals with the Roman state, a power it then used to eliminate dissent.[4] Until recent text discoveries at Nag Hammadi from the late 1940s, heretics got a bad press, with no possibility of alternative reading, much less rehabilitation. Gnostics, Frantzmann insists, deserve a clearer place in Christian history and theology. Humphrey and Laidlaw make rather a similar point concerning the anthropology of ritual: 'Why should anthropologists listen only to the winners in the contest [of ritual interpretation?]'.[5] However difficult, religious studies should certainly attempt to do that – for which a grasp of the basics of Christian theology and early practice is essential.

Part 4: Early Christian expansion: from Tunis to China

Before the Roman Empire adopted Christianity in Rome and (with varying determination) its outlying provinces, Christianity was an established minority faith in Armenia (the first Christian country), in Georgia, in Ethiopia–Eritrea, in Southern India, with an even earlier start in present-day Pakistan, and across the North African coastal plain. By the sixth century, China had Christian churches and communities. Christianity, within five hundred years of the 120 CE New Testament text completion, was thus a 'World Religion' and, then as now, the most widespread. And just as now, it was also polycentred from Tunis to Khanbalik in China and legion points between, northern Europe taking another thousand years to complete its conversion.

The readings in this part each illustrate one direction of this swift expansion. While both Brown and Haas discuss North Africa, Brown (Chapter 13) has an interest in the church practicalities which recur in these volumes: how did Augustine teach, how did he Latinize the institution, how did he negotiate different ethnicities, set up training for bright lads,[6] cobble together a local anthropology with inadequate language skills? How, having decided where salvation lay, did he fight opposition defined (as Franzmann pointed out) as heresy, the only solution for which was (for him logically acceptable) forced conversion? Haas takes a rather more political-organizational approach, discussing the way kings and other leaders related to and used this new faith to their own advantage (Chapter 14). His approach to conversion, which was discussed in the General introduction and will reappear throughout these volumes, is careful, considering the available alternatives and the strategies employed in the Eritrean and Georgian Christian kingdoms of Aksum and Iberia.

Frykenberg, in his monumental text on Indian Christianity, highlights the place of the Syrian Orthodox Christians there, starting with the apostle Thomas (Chapter 15), assumed to have come in 52 CE, or at least to have given his name to largely endogamous Christians, well established at the highest levels of that caste society and integrated in the political and economic structures of Kerela and Tamil Nadu. Their centre was, and still is, Syria, all South Indian bishops being consecrated in the Cathedral of Damascus. Their continued existence is arguably the longest continuous *community* presence outside the Mediterranean and Near East.[7]

The text of the Syriac tablet found in China in 1634 (Chapter 16) shows us yet another way of approaching this early expansion, for it sets out the basics of the faith as understood and taught in China by priests, travellers and teachers from the Church of the East, sometimes referred to incorrectly as Nestorians. The movement east, intensifying after religio-political clashes at the various Councils to settle doctrine called from Nicea (325 CE) onwards, was one option for the losers who given the changing times may have been winners the next time round had they the patience and political support to sit tight. The tablet's text, Orthodox with a Chinese slant, attests to the intellectual vibrancy of the faith, somewhat faded by the time of its demise in late fourteenth century China.

The final text (Chapter 17) takes us back to the eastern Mediterranean, where Trombley carefully shows the very slow manner in which Christianity actually became embedded in that region, virtually part of the 'heartland' of the New Testament. From soldier-monks combing the countryside and converting the laggards, to tenth-century peasants still maintaining their old ways alongside or instead of the new, he illustrates the continual negotiation and resistance involved the world over when ways of seeing the visible and less visible expressed in the daily round of ordinary people change or are changed.

Part 5: Consolidation on five continents

The polycentred Christianity of 900 CE was very different from the Christian expansion to five continents after 1491, with its hierarchical and usually Rome-based theology, liturgy and practice. Whatever the short- and long-term ecclesial effects of the Spanish and Portuguese colonial powers given by the pope to Iberian kings, the link between Empire and Catholicism was set, rather resembling the *cuis regio, eius religio* of contemporary Europe, where religious and national identity merged under a divine sovereign. The Reformation growth of Protestantism quickly changed the European but less swiftly the overseas landscape. The Counter-Reformation did affect and perhaps constrict the process of Roman Catholic mission, which was also much influenced by Iberian attitudes to Muslims in India, the Philippines and elsewhere after their 1492 expulsion from Spain.

The mission 'home base' was a Europe of writing paper, printing presses allowing speedy distribution of catechisms, and faster ships transporting letters and controllers to distant congregations, as the Jesuit mission in China found to its cost.[8] Issues of cultural negotiation, or contextualizing, became rather sharper – or the greater use of paper affords a wider spread of sources. The articles in this block recount and critique contemporary views on the 'depth' of conversion; the interplay between missionaries' own enculturation and their grasp of other ways; their position, whether foreign or local born, as cultural bricoleur; the way parishes in Africa or Brazil actually worked; and the way local people utilized the church to achieve emancipation or deal with other colonizing powers. In short, we come more clearly to power, agency, contextualizing and the mutual negotiation of the self and the other. No place was isolated: priests moved around; ecclesial rules for Mexico applied to the Philippines; Danish or Portuguese moved their slaves from Africa to India, other Africans going to the Caribbean and South America; and squabbles between religious orders were played out globally.

Thornton (Chapter 18) sets out a core yardstick often used for Christianity beyond EuroAmerica – but not within, and it is worth noting. Kongolese, Christian from 1491, held that Jesus born of Mary died on the cross and was resurrected, but were uninterested in either the Virgin Birth or salvation as more than protection. His response to the question whether this was sufficiently divergent for their faith to be doubted is that the same yardstick be used for all. The Jesuit Francis Xavier's time in Japan, from 1549, was unsuccessful in terms of conversion rates, the increase later that century coming both with a mission policy including thorough language and cultural learning for the missionary *and* a Japanese wish to utilize this new system of thought. But Ellis notes Xavier's link to another recurrent theme (Chapter 19): Japan represents the Other through whom he discovers his own inner self. It may be worth reflecting on the contested similarities between anthropologists and missionaries from this example. Sun (Chapter 20) discusses the misreading of the Others' text by the Jesuit Ricci and, in his view, the impact that had both on the process of mission there but also the development of the European Enlightenment, Leibnitz suggesting that 'Chinese missionaries be sent from China to teach us [Europeans] deism'. As Sun makes clear, the significance is less who was right, but rather that reciprocal (mis)understanding becomes part of a constructive transmission, interpretation and application both across and within differing contexts.

This was also the case with the Capucin priest Abbeville. Fishman (Chapter 21) discusses his attitude to Tupi Brazilian women, his chastizing of French women with Tupi virtues such as amity and modesty, and the taking up of these stories by European literati such as Rousseau, again largely to French women's detriment. She discusses his admittedly biased material, agreeing with anthropologists that it is nevertheless of great value.

Part 6: Elite assumptions and lay agency

How and what congregations were taught, and how converts or commoners engaged with churches as part of their earthly survival, is the concern of these six articles. While incoming power and local agency are variably evident in all the readings, the first three discuss the teaching of foreign clergy and the second the ways in which congregations utilized them. Power and agency, control and resistance, culture and representation: such pairs relate to any context, whether unearthing underclass resistance,[9] assuming the absence of agency among the colonized[10] or decrying the conversion of the lower orders.

First, the top-down view. Rosales's Spanish Franciscan priest, Oliver, described late sixteenth-century Filipino lowland life in his teaching of the Ten Commandments in the early Filipino church (Chapter 22). He skilfully used key Tagalog concepts such as debt and repayment, loyalty and patronage in his nuanced explanations. He and others learnt from Mexican priestly disasters and refrained from destroying idols, preferring reason and time. Jesuits in China such as Ruggiero also used local imagery for religions poetry, much as Chinese Buddhists did, though, as Chaves (Chapter 23) elegantly shows, the Christian attempt was vastly improved when the cultivated poet and artist Wu Li entered the order. Gray's paper on the Capuchins in Kongo (Chapter 24) indicates how a church in Africa was run, showing tensions between Portuguese or Spanish Catholic and Dutch Protestant missions which were echoed elsewhere. Internal stresses were clear between the foreign Capuchins and some local Catholic priests: another common tale. The Soyo (Kongo) Church and state were closely linked under the actively Catholic king, leading nobles, as in Europe of the time, being church leaders. Canon law began to affect Kongo marriage rules much as they were affecting Christians in Europe at that time. Women in colonial Brazil, as in Europe, were divided by prelates and the wider society into the worthy – elite or commoner – and the wanton. As Myscofski makes clear (Chapter 25), 'worthiness' related as much to 'fit' with local mores as the successful imposing of alternatives. All women had agency – but the Brazilian elite women remained jural minors for both priest and spouse. Not so for mixed-race, slave or Indian women, for whom 'worthiness' rules and expectations were expected to apply as much or as little as for their class peers in Europe.

Second, the common people had power too, as the remaining papers on Indians of Maine, slaves in the Antilles and urban peasants in northern Germany show. Indeed, the greater the elite's internal dissension the greater was the lay power. The French Jesuit Râle arrived in Quebec in 1690, learnt Wabanaki and translated the liturgy. Faith apart, Clark sees the converts' maintenance of an internalized Catholicism against the encroaching Puritan English as part of defending their land and life-way against foreign occupation (Chapter 26). Slaves in the French Antilles, not infrequently owned by Capuchins and Jesuits, chose to convert: those in Senegal earlier had not taken that path. One reason Peabody gives is that instruction was in French or Creole, essential for communicating with owners, and conversion could again be seen as (though not necessarily limited to) surviving enforced life-change (Chapter 27).

Christian daily life all five continents shared many similarities, which is not surprising given that Goa, Kongo and Mexico had a thorough Christian arrangement before interior Latvia and Estonia were fully accepted as Christian in 1525. Opposing the church and its representatives was also a general 'World Christianity feature' in all continents. Beyer shows in his discussion of a 1629 poor Lutheran Lübeck prophet (Chapter 28) that a German pastor and town council could be utilized by the subaltern, in this case a poor man wisely speaking through a prophet rather than the traditional but by then abhorred Catholic saint. Amid Lübeck's war famine and disease, he spoke for the common people, to cajole and even to criticize the church.

Part 7: Inter-continental Enlightenment

The final readings, all from the eighteenth century though each rooted in earlier events, are drawn from China, India and North America. All touch on issues which are still important in World Christianity studies. The intellectual and religious changes of seventeenth-century Europe were developing into the Enlightenment. The divinity of western European monarchs began to dwindle after the 1649 execution of one, the upheavals of the French Revolution and the ensuing wars, most becoming politically useful symbols ruling more by earthly acquiescence than heavenly ascription. Protestants were beginning overseas mission work separate from the 'caring for expatriates only' chaplaincies typical of earlier Danish, Dutch and British colonial practice which protected commercial projects such as the VOC – a company with Dutch state backing – or the more independent East India Company of London. Protestants had different views of conversion, the individual, education and the Bible from Roman Catholics, whose expansion declined or ceased with the demise of the Iberian Empire and the difficulties of France, the latter's mission in India being especially weakened.

These readings each touch on a critical issue: the training and initiating of ritual specialists, a lack of which had hastened the demise of the church in Central Asia in the first millennium. Christianity in the so-called 'Age of Discovery' had been disseminated by people rather many of whom assumed only they, purveyors of European culture, could represent God adequately, the few ordained locals (other than to an extent in China and Japan) being a scorned drop in the ocean. When the Rites Controversy led to most foreign priests leaving China after 1745, a handful of locals and expatriates were left to maintain the church there. Some local priests were trained, but it was the Chinese Virgins who taught girls, baptized the sick and evangelized. Their importance, however, did not stop male priests controlling and even constraining them, a point both Entenmann here (Chapter 29) and Tiedemann elsewhere[11] make clear, as does Li in Volume IV (Chapter 83).

Irschik's paper on the Lutherans in Tamil Nadu shows a new congregation pattern (Chapter 30). Begun by the German Pietists Ziegenbalg and Plütschau in 1708 in the Danish port of Tarangambadi (or Tranquebar), Lutherans insisted each conversion was between an individual and God, whose inspired Word, not created liturgy, each convert must know. Converts therefore needed to be educated in local languages and developed in the faith by local pastors, the first of whom was ordained in 1729. While all mission involves a 'conversation' between clergy and laity, in the enclosed space of an isolated mission in which the missionary has little if any 'back-stage' private space, both missionized and missioner change – a point brought up most sharply by the French Protestant missionary and anthropologist Leenhardt, who, when asked how many converts he had made in thirty years, replied 'one', meaning himself.[12] Ziegenbalg's difficulties with the Halle mission, summed up as 'we sent you to convert the heathen not introduce heathen ideas to Europe in your writing about their gods', typify a rather common problem which, again, is not entirely of the past.

Finally, McCarthy (Chapter 31) presents a Mohegan Indian missionary to his own people, who wrote his own story, observing the racism which saw a contradiction between his Christian and Indian identities, still an issue in Christianity, and the lower regard for his evangelism than that of a white person, a continued issue and arguably still present in slightly different guise. Yet Occam did not convert to 'mimic and resist' but because he believed – and, as McCarthy points out, belief and commitment are as integral to the study of conversion as a convert's rational negotiation of worlds.

Notes

1 B. Ehrman, *Lost Christianities*, Oxford: Oxford University Press, 2003, p. 230.
2 *In the Beginning: Bibles before the Year 1000*, ed. Michelle P. Brown, Washington, DC: Smithsonian Institution, 2006.
3 See *Church and Culture in Seventeenth Century France*, H. Phillips, Cambridge: Cambridge University Press, 1997, for the effect of Protestantism on linguistic and literacy skills of Languedoc peasantry.
4 Elaine Pagels, *The Gnostic Gospels*, 1980, and *Adam Eve and the Serpent*, 1988, back up Franzmann's approach.
5 C. Humphrey and J. Laidlaw, *The Archetypal Actions of Ritual*, Oxford: Clarendon, 1994, p. 246.
6 See also R. Lane-Fox, 'Literacy and Power in Early Christianity', in *Literacy and Power in the Ancient World*, ed. A. Bowman and G. Woolf, Cambridge: Cambridge University Press, 1994.
7 S. Bayly, *Saints Goddesses and Kings*, Cambridge: Cambridge University Press, 1989, outlines Syrian Orthodox life in South India.
8 A. Ross, *A Vision Betrayed: Jesuits in China and Japan, 1542–1742*, Edinburgh: Edinburgh University Press, 1994.
9 J. C. Scott, *Weapons of the Weak: Everyday Forms of Peasant Resistance*, New Haven, CT: Yale University Press, 1985.
10 F. Fanon, *Wretched of the Earth*, London: Penguin, 1964.
11 R. Tiedemann, 'Controlling the Virgins: Female Propagation of the Faith and the Catholic Hierarchy in China', *Women's Historical Review* 17:4, 2008.
12 J. Clifford, 'Field-Work, Reciprocity and the Making of Ethnographic Texts: The Example of Maurice Leenhardt', *Man* 15/3, 1980.

Part 1

CONTEXT AND CONTENT

1

Excerpt from 'NATURE IS TO CULTURE AS PRAYING IS TO SUING

Legal pluralism in an American suburb'[1]

Carol J. Greenhouse

Source: *Journal of Legal Pluralism*, 20 (1982), 21–9.

[. . .]
In terms of the cultural choices involved, court use is not a simple matter of alternatives. Before a person can sue, he must have not only a legally justiciable issue and a legal forum, but also a personal conceptualization of conflict that is adversarial in structure and remedial in orientation. This article focuses on an ideology of conflict that renders all conflict "non-justiciable," i.e., on a group that does not permit its members any overt remedial actions, but which nevertheless manages to survive in secular society. The ethnographic data derive from a suburban community in the United States. The people who are the focus of the study reported here do not consider that they lack access to justice, but their concept of justice specifically excludes recourse to law. In the conclusion, the implications of the findings for the study of litigation and non-litigation in their social-cultural contexts are explored.

History, ideology, and court use in an American town

The town which this paper considers is slightly over two square miles in area, with a population of 4,000 (U.S. Census, 1970) in a county whose residents number about 100,000. The population of the town is exceptionally homogeneous: it is white (98 percent in 1970), educated, earning an average yearly family income of over $12,000, and living in privately owned housing.

The county court sits in the center of town in a Victorian courthouse on Main Street. It is divided into an inferior court and a superior court, each of which handles both civil and criminal complaints. A retired judge sits once a week in special sessions to hear divorce cases. All other cases are heard by one of two other judges. The county has several justices of the peace, who invariably refer their cases to the inferior court after an initial hearing and a processing fee. The court personnel are well-known and well-liked among the long-term residents; the courthouse is centrally located and is frequently visited for conversation in addition to official business. The court clerks are members of old families, and the judges' families, although considered "newcomers" by the long-term residents, have lived in the town for about sixty years.

The general pattern of court use in this town appears to be simple enough. Virtually no one who is part of the established population (four or more generations of residence) uses the courts. The civil court is, however, crowded with cases, primarily involving businesses and/or individual "newcomers."[2] This general pattern is not surprising in and of itself, since many Americans never consult a lawyer during their lives (Curran and Spalding, 1974:79), let alone litigate. Whatever interest there is in this pattern is in the fact that it is the newcomers who are the constituents of the court, and not the long-term established residents. The relational distance hypothesis would suggest that people who are involved in face-to-face relationships of some depth and extent prefer and have available less formal, more private, and more perfect remedies than the court offers. Newcomers, having fewer inhibitions or alternatives deriving from their social ties, use the court more freely.

But a single hypothesis cannot account for the two types of non-litigants in the town. These subgroups' membership overlap only marginally: (1) The first group uses the court as an integral part of its adversarial strategies, which take place outside the courts. These people are not court-users, but they are certainly law-users, threatening litigation as a prod toward compliance. This group consists of a network of long-term residents and/or prominent local businessmen and their families. (2) The second group uses neither the court nor the law. It consists of devout Baptists, who comprise the town's oldest Baptist congregation, a group of about 1,500. In demographic and socio-economic terms, the two groups are very similar. In terms of their legal ideologies, they are not. In terms of legal ideology, the first group of non-litigants is continuous with litigants, but the Baptists are discontinuous with both of the other two groups. For the non-Baptists, access to justice moans access to lawyers. They express both a preference for "getting along" and distaste for the loss of privacy that a lawsuit represents to them. Their view of the court *as an institution* is not a negative one; they *prefer* other remedies when circumstances permit, which they usually do. For the Baptists, on the other hand, access to justice means access to God.

As the town's Baptists explained their faith to me, their ideology proscribes litigation and, in fact, any attempts at redress apart from unilateral forgiveness or prayer. They cite the New Testament: Romans 13:18–19 exhorts Christians to "avenge not yourselves . . . : for it is written vengeance is mine, I will repay, saith the Lord." The town's Baptists interpret this passage as prohibiting remedial initiatives involving any third party but Jesus. To act otherwise is sacrilege, a failure of faith. Furthermore, the Bible preaches forgiveness, sacrifice, and a community built on love. By these things, Christians can distinguish themselves from non-Christians: ". . . Love one another: . . . By this shall all men know that ye are my disciples" (John 13:34–35). Finally, the Baptists' concern with spreading their faith ("witnessing") to non-Baptists inspires them to lead "lives of good witness," i.e., exemplary lives that will attract non-Baptists to the church. These three factors: proscription of secular justice, the ideal of Christian community, and evangelism, justify avoidance of the courts and all other agents of secular law, e.g., lawyers, for purposes of interpersonal disputing. Baptists view the court itself as a profane institution, needed only by non-believers and the unfaithful. Their rejection of the court applies equally to the roles of plaintiff and defendant. They explain that the Bible is quite explicit on the matter of threatened lawsuits (Matthew 6:40): "And if any man will sue thee at the law, and take away thy coat, let him have thy cloak also." Thus, in the local ideology, a devout Baptist settles out of court quickly and fully any demands made against him.

The local Baptists' view of the court does not preclude their suffering from grievances, only from resolving them at law. They do not segregate themselves from the non-Baptist community, and their range of problems is no different from that of other groups. They live in town, and many of them commute daily to jobs in Atlanta. The potential for victimization is obvious; the town's Baptists often refer to themselves as persecuted—but they also note that the moral triumph is theirs.

The remedies that the Baptists do allow themselves are of three sorts: 1) unilateral (avoidance and prayer), 2) bilateral (apology, joking, and prayer with another person), and 3) trilateral (gossip, counseling, and mediation). These three categories apply to distinct social fields within the town. The Baptist concept of community precludes avoidance within the church congregation; avoidance applies only to outsiders. Avoidance is generally glossed as unilateral forgiveness, but such forgiveness does not take place face-to-face. Bilateral and trilateral remedies apply within the church and to an intermediate group known as "prospects," that is, candidates for conversion. The distinction between insiders (including prospects) and outsiders is, for local Baptists, an absolute one. Acceptance of Christ is the crucial index of the Baptists' world: it separates Baptists from the secular and (therefore) profane world. Local Baptists do not accept other Christian sects as authentic; to be a non-Baptist is to be a non-Christian.

Importantly, then, Baptist Christianity implies a social organization of conflict resolution. Because non-Baptists do not belong to the community of God, Baptists believe them to be dangerous, unpredictable, moved by self-interest—in general, only partly socialized. Although actual relations between Baptists and non-Baptists are routine and cordial, they are constrained by distrust on the part of the Baptists. Baptists expect conflict from non-Baptists, and so seek to avoid them. In practice, they cannot avoid them entirely, since, as I have said, they live lives that are thoroughly enmeshed in the non-Baptists' world. Their avoidance is mental only, i.e., an inner aversion. What is important is that Baptists *define* non-Baptists as the source and embodiment of conflict. By corollary, within their church community, Baptists exclude the possibility of conflict. Disputes are quickly and generally interpreted as a spiritual lapse: the offender is redefined as an outsider to the church social community by virtue of his having caused trouble. Troublemakers are by definition (or by redefinition) outsiders, and vice versa. Disagreements and minor disputes are handled verbally and, significantly, are not defined as conflict by the participants. Within the church community, harmony exists by definition, and verbal remedies (gossip, prayer, joking, and so forth) are referred to simply as "speech." So, conflict and Christianity follow the same boundary, Christians on the one side, conflict on the other.

Because Baptists locate their expectation of conflict not in situations, or in rules of behavior, but in social structure (Baptists/non-Baptists), their concept of conflict is not defined in terms of time and space. Baptists do not conceptualize or discuss conflict in terms of *cases*, but in terms of *salvation*, i.e., acceptance of and by Christ. Harmony and love are immanent in Christians; conflict is immanent in non-Christians. Cases and the adversary model of conflict are entirely extraneous to their concept of conflict. Since the distinction between conflict and harmony does not pertain to behavioral rules, but to professed identification with a sacred ideology, the secular courts and the law in general are completely irrelevant as remedial tools. The only remedy for conflict, in the Baptists' eyes, is salvation.

Several questions emerge out of this discussion: First, are there no circumstances under which Baptists use the legal apparatus of the town; i.e., how well does their ideology account for their actual behavior? Second, why is the Baptist/non-Baptist distinction so salient in this community? Third, why is the boundary between the different groups in the town conceptualized by the Baptists in terms of use of law? Finally, does any of this matter to the other people of the town? The answers to these questions are interrelated.

First, to my knowledge, Baptists do not use legal agencies to press personal claims in the context of disputes, although, as noted above, this absence of litigation is difficult to evaluate given the general American pattern of court use. Baptists do pay taxes, write wills, own real estate, call the police to investigate burglaries, register their marriages with the state, and so on. I have no contemporary evidence that would suggest that Baptists' aversion to the law extends beyond trouble in interpersonal relationships. Thus, in their own dealings with Baptists, non-Baptists do encounter them in the legal settings that are associated with the life cycle and to some extent with business. They are less likely to enter into the Baptists' circle of social relations from which adversarial conflict and the law are excluded. Non-Baptists, therefore, are unlikely to find the Baptists' professed law-aversion credible, since they do not appreciate what the differences between these two settings mean in Baptist terms.

This raises the second question, i.e., why the Baptist/non-Baptist distinction is so salient in this community. It is certainly an important distinction to the people themselves. The local Baptists, for example, lump non-Baptists together as unsaved, and use an array of metaphors for them that merges non-believers with "city folk," businessmen, the wealthy, newcomers, and the power elite, although these groups are in actuality not coterminous, nor even exclusively non-Baptist. For non-Baptists, religious identity has less importance than it does among the Baptists, but the Baptists are referred to as a conspicuous social group in terms ranging from jokingly derisive to overtly hostile. It is clear from conversations, public prayer, and church services, that local Baptists believe themselves to be victims of social prejudice. And although so far as I could observe this is not the case, their belief is important in itself. Finally, this group of Baptists, unlike the South's Baptists in general, do not participate in civic affairs, except, I believe, by voting. They do not run for office nor publicly support political candidates. The local Baptists, then, do not match the image of Southern Baptists in general: they do not enjoy the same cultural hegemony by any means. Why not?

Genealogies, old maps, lists of deacons, church registries, diaries, letters, land records, and other sources suggest that the Baptists' sense of isolation has to do with the history of the town at least as much as with contemporary religious values. The town's first settlers were Baptists, establishing a church only three years after the territory was ceded by the Indians in 1821. The early settlers were poor farmers sparsely scattered over what was to become the town and then the county in the 1840s. By then, the town was encircled by two "rings" of farms: the more central consisted of large plantations, and the more peripheral of small farms and small manufacturers, e.g., of jugs and millstones. In 1849, the Methodists established a church, and it quickly became the church of the gentry: county officeholders, doctors, lawyers, merchants, bankers, and the wealthiest farmers all appear on its first registry. The Presbyterians were a small minority on the outskirts of town, dominated by one large and solidary landowning family.

The history of local Baptists, then, is, to some extent, the history of the local small farmers. The small farmers of the county rose and fell twice before the ultimate collapse of small farming in the 1950s and 1960s. During the period just after the Civil War, farmers with small holdings were relatively advantaged in comparison with the large plantation owners, since land lost much of its value, while manufacturing provided a cushion against loss. Land sales records for this period suggest that farmers on the periphery were able to buy portions of the former plantations, improving their economic condition, if not their social position, considerably. During the Depression of the

1930s, small farmers again were able to hold onto their land, and as the suburbs and, later the highway, extended to this area after World War II, their less profitable farms were the first to be sold for development as real estate.

Even so, while this brief glimpse of their history helps account for the composition of the membership of the Baptist church, their conviction that they are disadvantaged, and even their somewhat ascetic values, it does not explain why the Baptists' ideology of law does not extend to reject other institutions associated with the power elite—their business, their credit, and their fashions. Put another way, why is it that the court and the law, for local Baptists, are the relevant emblems of religious identity and tradition? Why not, as among the Amish, for example, agriculture and, negatively, television, current dress styles, and business (Hostetler, 1963)?

Some further history helps answer the last question. At the period when the county was being formed, two major conflicts divided the Baptist church in the united States and the South. The first was the issue of slavery: the Southern Baptists formed a separate convention in 1845 over the slavery question. Soon afterward, the Southern Baptists divided over the issue of missions (essentially a question of church expenditures for benevolent associations). The Southern Baptists were officially pro-mission, but a sizable minority—fearing that some "benevolent associations" might be abolitionist groups—was vehemently opposed, and seceded from the Southern Baptist Convention. These national and regional issues had a major impact on local Baptists. By their sect's identification with slavery, the Baptist church became identified with the state's aristocratic planters, but the aristocrats were only a small minority in this county. Most of the county's voters were in what was then the Clarke party—a populist coalition that was the eager mouthpiece of Andrew Jackson. The county voted for secession in 1861 (fifteen years after the period we are discussing), but on states' rights grounds, not slavery. So, on the slavery question, the local Baptist church became isolated by the contradiction between its sectarian aristocratic associations and its local small-farmer constituency.

Simultaneously, the missions question divided the local church so severely that by 1847 few members remained. During the decade before secession, the church had to rebuild itself or fail. It managed to revive in this era of intense political strife by preaching against politics altogether. Withdrawal from politics and from political institutions was a strategy for religious institutional survival and credibility. Why withdraw from the courts? The judgeships were the first "plums" of any new administration—they were the most important of a new governor's political appointments. The anti-politics strategy was successful in the mid-1800s during the county's early years of strife and it remains effective today, when other conflicts (integration, zoning, and planning, for example) threaten the community. The church today is burgeoning with over 2,300 members, and a growing budget and physical plant.[3]

Few townpeople I met were aware of the early history of the Baptist church in the town, and none—even at the Baptist church—had any interest in such things, except as odd bits of unrelated knowledge. For the Baptists, scripture is an adequate idiom in which to express their position in the town and their behavior in relation to the court and to conflict. The modern Baptists in town merge city people with newcomers, the rich, the wealthy, and the damned because these are all symbols of the profane world in which Baptists refuse to participate and by opposition to which they define themselves. The histories of the Methodist and Presbyterian churches—whose members today comprise the group of non-litigants who are not law-averse—did not take the same course as that of the Baptists. These churches were never so deeply threatened by political conflict. Thus, the answer to the third question—why legal ideology follows religious lines—lies in the relationship of this particular community to the local, regional, and national issues that have shaped its history.

The final question was whether and why the situation of legal pluralism in this town matters to the people who live there. Clearly, it matters to the Baptists. A person's orientation toward conflict and the law is determined by his orientation toward God, and to a believer this makes all other considerations redundant. To the non-Baptists, though, whose preference for out-of-court settlements is entirely secular, legal pluralism has a different significance. While they know of the Baptists' aversion to using the courts and lawyers, they do not accept the Baptists' explanation of it because it is in terms of a conception of order that non-Baptists do not share. Where Baptists see the world as divided into the saved and the unsaved, non-Baptists see multiple competing social groups. Where Baptists see Jesus as replacing the secular system, the other groups see Jesus as validating the secular system. Where the Baptists see contradiction between heaven and earth, the non-Baptists see authentication. Where the Baptists withdraw to pray, the non-Baptists assume they are forming a cabal. The role of the "moral majority" in the last presidential election was repugnant to the local Baptists as the very antithesis of their ethic; to the non-Baptists, the activities of the moral majority merely confirmed their suspicions that Baptists use their religion to suit their own political ends. When local Baptists and non-Baptists happen to differ over public matters, as in a particularly bitter recent episode involving the destruction of historic buildings to expand the church's parking facilities, factions divide along religious lines that reiterate endlessly. The non-Baptists' consciousness of legal pluralism in their community is in terms of the competition that they feel divides their community. They perceive the Baptists as a large anti-progressive group, held in thrall by a spellbinding preacher (he is in fact effective, but not the hypnotic hellfire sort), which, as the church grows, threatens to obstruct the development of the county. For the non-Baptists, this last is the central political preoccupation.

IV. Conclusions

The Baptists in the community described above adhere to an ideology which in three major respects differs from the assumptions of the anthropological literature on dispute settlement and law generally, discussed at the beginning of this paper. First, their ideology cuts them off from all judicial resources, and they are also precluded from all forms of overt disputing. This is a double problem of containment and effacement of conflict. In effect, Baptists limit their definition of their jural community to a domain in which conflict is not acceptable. God, solves this problem for them, in that he is believed to create and fill a normative vacuum simultaneously.

Second, Baptists do not conceptualize conflict in terms of cases, but in terms of social structure. Conflict is not a question of rules or interests but entirely a question of an individual's spiritual state. Adversarial modes of processing conflict, then, are not appropriate, nor is a remedial system that is oriented towards redress. The local Baptists classify the components of their community's social structure in a way that draws the limits of culture short of the limits of society. Their perception of the unsaved as unsocialized refers specifically to what Baptists see as their untamed individuality, untrammeled self-interest, and senseless passion for material things. The Baptists' view of human nature is just that: natural, with precisely the connotation that opposes it to culture. Jesus not only saves, he civilizes. Without Jesus, human law is doomed to fail; with Jesus, human law is superfluous.

Third, Baptists do not accept that human authority has any place in private relationships. They resist both human judges and any secularly-based differentiation of their congregation. Wealth, education, power—none of these matter. Authoritative resolution of disputes is rejected so as to protect relationships from the extension of authority into the relationships themselves. Disputing creates winners and losers, and that is intolerable to a group committed to the equality of its members.

[. . .]

Notes

'My concerns in this long-ago essay were to connect one community's religious idioms about law to specifics of place and local history; while the description of local Baptists should have given more attention to varieties of belief and practice, the account of the church's place in the cross-currents of local history remains relevant to my understanding of the town' (Author's note, December 2008).

1 The ethnographic research that is the basis of part III of this article began in 1973 and ended in 1975, with a brief visit of a few weeks in 1980. With one exception which is noted in the text, the town reported is that of 1973–1975.

Field work was funded by a training grant from the National Institute of Mental Health to Harvard University's Department of Anthropology.

2 The term "newcomer" might mean anyone whose family settled in town in this century. One judge is considered a newcomer, although his parents moved to

town just after the first World War. Currently, most judicial personnel are well-respected newcomers.

3 Increasing religious participation is not in competition with secular society, but is a function and facilitator of it, now as then. In the same way that the church destructures (or *re*structures) conflict, it depoliticizes secular life for its congregants by encouraging a devaluation of earthly rewards. Thus, if Baptist workers are upwardly mobile, they express their success in terms of a widening opportunity for service, not in terms of effective competition or increased personal income.

Bibliography

CURRAN, Barbara A., and SPALDING, Francis O. (1974). *The Legal Needs of the Public*. Chicago: American Bar Foundation.

HOSTETLER, J. A. (1963). *Amish Society*. Baltimore: Johns Hopkins.

2

FROM PAGAN TO CHRISTIAN PRIESTHOOD

Dave Passi

Source: G. W. Trompf (ed.), *The Gospel Is Not Western: Black Theologies from the South-West Pacific*, Maryknoll, NY: Orbis, 1987, pp. 45–8.

My ancestors worshipped a god, Malo,[1] an idol you could see, feel, touch. When the missionaries came to the Torres Strait Islands, my grandfather was a priest of Malo's cult. Yet he was one of the first converts to Christianity.[2] He saw that the Anglican Church was a fulfillment of the old cult; because of his vision I also see the church as fulfillment. It came to fulfill, not to destroy. I see the old cult much as the Old Testament; the New Testament, the church's book, shows the element of grace, which never came into our traditional religion. That element fills to the full extent the traditions of our islands.

The role of priest, as held by my grandfather, was hereditary. It had been held by his father before him. He sat in authority as his fathers had, and those who passed in front of him would have to crawl on their knees and keep their head lower than his head. The priests (*zogoga*) were immensely powerful. A priest possessed special spiritual powers, for example, the gift of sleepwalking (*modu*). By *modu*, the priest could secretly cut the ropes of enemy boats and send them away by the current or he could tighten the ropes of his own people's boats for safety. When his people fished, he would recite the right prayers—the preserved sacred psalms of worship—and these would lead to a good catch or protect those fishing if sharks attacked.

I remember too that my grandfather, when he was very old, foretold the time of his death. "Come here, grandson," he called to my eldest brother. "I have heard what people are saying, so I want you to take me out [to prepare for the funeral]." When my brother told him at night he was ready to do as he was asked, grandfather said: "No, not yet, the rain will not come yet . . . but about this time of night . . . the rain will come." It so happened at the time he died. Before passing away, he promised his son: "Whatever is bad, I will not pass on to you." This was part of the custom of passing down hereditary power. Such things may appear to some as superstitions, but they are not. It would be an insult for the persons who accept these customs to hear them called superstitions. It is sad that these traditions have almost been lost and it is fortunate that some know about them and can pass them on.

My grandfather gave up his old role in the cult to become a Christian. He gave up his authority and all the power that made him who he was, and he became a Christian. I do not really know why, I do not fully understand it, although I see that the power of God was there in his decision to leave everything belonging to him behind and go to work under a Melanesian mission worker.

The London Mission Society (LMS) sent the original missionaries (1871) but they did not impress my grandfather much, even though he did become Christian. Some years later (1915), when the Church of England assumed responsibility for the islands, he accepted the new ways more completely. He saw the Anglican preaching and practice as the fulfillment of the old cult. He asked himself why the LMS had required so many of the old rituals to be discontinued; especially since ritual forms—all the actions he was so used to in the past—had such a great significance for him. As he saw it, the Anglican liturgy and the ritualistic approach of Anglicanism were the fulfillment of the old cult. I do not believe any European influenced him in this; it was his own judgment. He was used to rituals for different times and circumstances, what I would call "opportunistic" worship.

I will give some examples to show why he and others after him made these connections. One simple one has to do with bowing in reverence. My grandfather was used to bowing reverently before Malo. It was a true tradition, for this bowing was to be done before or among the elders, out of respect for people who were civilized. On becoming Christian, my grandfather would bow on entering the church and walk bowed over until he had taken his seat. To explain to missionaries and others who asked him about this, he would reply: "Your God is the true God, yet you do not revere Malo" (that is, the same God who was now worshipped under a different name).

A more complicated example has to do with the initiation of priests in the old cult and the ordination of priests in the Anglican Church. Traditionally, because the office of priest was hereditary, the sons, who were candidates, would lie prostrate, one in a certain category lying on top of one in another, surrounded by warriors, while the sacred drums were played. The belief behind this part of the ceremony was that the god Malo would come when the candidates had "arrived" like this. He would come down and stretch his legs three times over the candidates as they lay there together and fill them with his powers. The god went through and over them. Something like this persists in Anglican ordination. As an ordinand, I had to lie flat. The people in the congregation stood up when they saw me like that, and even though the actual ordination really comes when the bishop says a prayer over the candidate, our people saw the Malo tradition in the prostration and thus a special fulfillment in Anglicanism.

What of God? In Christianity it is hard to pinpoint God; in tradition it was easy. God was there to feel and touch and had a special place in the mountains. To the islanders the god Malo's nature, existence, and name were quickly perceived. When we think back, our minds could conceive and grasp nothing greater than Malo. Malo was the greatest thing existing on the earth, so reverence and special care with regard to Malo came into traditional life in many and varied ways.

Missionaries and even I myself at this point in time have to hunt for the continuance of this traditional sense reverence; it can easily be missed since all sorts of other things come into the picture today. Traditional activities connected with the church today, for example, seem to concern money—often an exchange of money (as at a marriage or funeral). We do not find any hint of Malo in the mountains nor do we have any of the special sacred ropes related to his cult. Still I am sure traditional reverence is to be found. It may be hard for an outsider to discover it. One day a person may come across a spiritual place and be stunned into a whisper; yet the next day he or she might just wander through the same place, cutting the bush without any care. Reverence is hard to pin down because it serves a purpose in the head at varying times.

Like the traditional cult, the Anglican liturgy has a definite structure and is an important, constant reminder of reverence. Sometimes the feeling arises that the parts of this liturgy are so robust that they can be handled casually. I believe liturgy is crucial to getting across the idea of awe and reverence, qualities that are disappearing and need to be brought back to life in the Torres Strait.

We should not forget the institutional side of things. The unity of eight different tribes depended on Malo, who was central and whose high priest presided in each of these tribes. What would have happened if there had been no institutions? If there had been no centrality of religion, our society—in a very small world of some five or six miles square—would have lost out to the enemies. Thus the importance of centrality is expressed in my tradition and has directed my own and my people's choice of the Christian model appropriate for us (the Anglican Church government being hierarchical). Mind you, the *zogoga* priests were different from Anglican ones! For the most part, they were not so holy, and in performing ceremonies they were not themselves, not themselves at all, but were taken over by the power of the god (who enabled them to sleepwalk).

Other institutions once existed that do not have an equivalent in the Anglican Church—and ought not to have. I am thinking of sorcery, in which the name of Malo was used and is still evoked today. I am told that people still get a stone and talk to it, saying the magical words "*Malo, omi.*" If they hit an enemy with this stone, he or she surely will die. Sometimes the sorcerer or sorceress and the victim fight with stones and the former usually wins. If after a stone fight the intended victim walks off, the sorcerer or sorceress can still talk to a stone and simply throw it in the air just to make the *noise* of the spell. As soon as victims hear this noise, they forget everything and they know it is time to die. Many people today, of course, will tell you that this is not true, but I have it on my grandfather's authority. We should not have this side to religion in the church, since the church is to preach grace and love.

Other aspects of the old cult may also appear undesirable, but observed in a certain way they are valuable. These concern discipline or law, for there were certain rules, regulations, and wise sayings of Malo that served to hold my people together. For example, it was extremely important—as it is today—that if anything, such as a coconut leaf, falls to the ground, to the earth, it must be left to rot there. I know a place where a large branch has fallen and it remains across the path, about waist high. It is not to be removed and people either go under or jump over it. What is the meaning of all this? It is a reminder about trespassing and theft. Malo (as shown by these falling objects) keeps his own boundaries; so the young learn that we must not walk on other people's land or trespass their boundaries or steal what belongs to other people.

Another example of discipline from the old days: As part of the worship in the high priest's cult the warriors would walk in two lines on the beach near a certain village. This dance-walk was to be performed in such a way that anybody coming after them would think that only two people had walked there, since those following the leaders were to tread exactly where the leaders had trod. The walkers had to be disciplined. So perfectly was this part of the ritual to be followed, in fact, that if a warrior put one foot outside the track, he would be killed straightaway. This was a hard discipline. Now when I think about how my people think, I appreciate that there are certain aspects of Anglicanism—church law, the set order of doing things—that appeal to them and to their need for definition and regulation in their lives.

These are some of the ways in which I see Christianity as a fulfillment of my people's tradition. Things my grandfather did before me were certainly important to our people; he compared the old rituals and practices to see how well Christian forms would fit them. I have simply carried on his work, trying to compare. When I consider my church's relation to tradition, I find that they fit together very well.

Notes

1 Some writers refer to this god incorrectly as Malu.

2 For the missionary Impact on the Torres Strait see N. Goodall, A History of the London Missionary Society 1895–1945 (London, 1954), pp. 420ff.; cf. G. Peel, Isles of the Torres Straits (Sydney, 1947), chaps. 10–12.

3

LITURGICAL ADAPTATION

P. Abega

Source: Edward Fashole-Luke (ed.), *Christianity in Independent Africa*, London: Collings, 1979, pp. 597–605.

This chapter merely provides some historical evidence on which later historians can build to trace the itinerary of the progress of Christianity in Africa. It deals with the experiment in liturgical adaptation in the parish of St Paul de Ndzon-Melen, in the southern suburbs of the town of Yaoundé, the capital of the United Republic of Cameroun. We will sketch in the historical background to this experiment, and will examine the Biblical foundations on which any authentic Christian experience must rest. The cultural model for this experiment will be presented in the third section. The description of the new liturgical rite will take up the fourth section, and in conclusion we shall attempt to show what are the fruits we expect from it for an authentic Christian life on African soil.

Historical background

We are all aware of the conditions in which our peoples were Christianized: through ignorance, dishonesty or scorn for the African, to whom they refused the status of a man, an adult, the missionaries acted as if the Black man was a *tabula rasa*, a grown up child, who had lived in a historical and cultural void. One could therefore instil into him any gesture or any symbolism one desired, with no fear of the consequences, no traumas, no regrettable confusion. In illustration of this, we should mention a gesture that was particularly offensive to us: the kissing of the cross or the altar. In fact among the Beti the cultural category of the kiss does not exist. But it was at all costs necessary to get the people to adopt it. To translate this idea, use was made of the Beti word for 'sniff', *nyumulu.* Now in Beti one only 'sniffs' something, if one wants to find out whether it is getting high. In this case how can one 'sniff' Christ? Did he smell bad? Who cannot see the stupidity of introducing a gesture completely foreign to the mentality of the people?

Nevertheless our people began to 'sniff' Christ without much grasp of the symbolic category underlying the gesture. And even now many of our colleagues in the priesthood 'sniff' the altar, without asking themselves what this gesture might mean. We could recite a long list of such examples, but that is not the object of this paper. This example merely illustrates the discomfort that a certain kind of Christianity inspired in the more thoughtful amongst us. The year which can be called the turning point was 1958, the year in which, newly armed with the baccalaureate, we entered the major seminary. That year we began to say out loud what many people were saying in a whisper, for fear of excommunication. And it was in 1958, at the major seminary of Otélé, that attempts at liturgical adaptation began seriously.

Religious singing was the first field of exploration. The lack of adaptation was here particularly evident. Most of the languages of South Cameroun are tone languages. The art of overlaying these languages with prefabricated Western melodies had the effect of completely upsetting the language, resulting in meaningless phrases, or even comical absurdities that rob prayer of its seriousness. An example: In Ewondo there are four homographic words in pairs. The first on a low tone and the second on a high tone give the following sequence: *O ne m'ben yéné ma ngó*, (you are good have pity on me). In the other sequence we have the first on a high tone and the second on a low tone and this gives: *O ne m'bén yéné ma ngo*, (you are a cudgel look at me poor sheathfish). Thus instead of the prayer of the first sequence, in the second formula we ask God to knock us senseless, since he is a cudgel and we are a fish. And it is the second meaning which prevails with the overlaid Western melody.

When it was decided to begin to restore order to the situation, Latin was still the obligatory language sung at mass. The first change was to sing Latin to African tunes as in the mass called 'the mass of the canoers'. The attempt to adapt some psalms to Camerounian tunes proved catastrophic. It was necessary to take a very dangerous step at a time when Rome still forbade the introduction of modern languages into the liturgy, and sing the psalms of the breviary in the Camerounian languages to Camerounian tunes.

This did not happen without encountering a great deal of resistance. I remember an amusing occasion when the parish priest stopped the seminarists in the middle of mass; when questioned by the seminarists after the mass, he replied: 'I cannot understand either the words or the music; it is nothing but shouting, there's no piety in it.' Yet the enthusiasm aroused at a popular level by these songs ought to have made him more circumspect. The movement, once launched, could only spread further.

One of our colleagues in the priesthood, Abbé Pie-Claude Ngumu, has made it his life's work. His task has been not only to enlarge the movement that had been begun, but to deepen it and make it ever more authentic. He was ordained in 1960, and made curate of the parish of St Luke at Tala. There he started a church choir, and since he possessed musical talent as a composer, he experimented with new songs for this choir. At this period he had the good fortune to arrange the enthronement of Archbishop Jean Zoa, the first Camerounian Archbishop of Yaoundé, in the cathedral of Yaoundé. This event will long be remembered in the annals of the country for its originality, its authenticity and its magnitude.

After he was made curate at the Cathedral of Yaoundé, Abbé Ngumu founded the famous choir of the *Maîtrise de la croix d'ébène* at Yaoundé. This choir represented the Cameroun at the first Festival of Negro Arts at Dakar in April 1966. There it carried off the first prize for African religious song.

But the great turning point in this experiment occurred in 1968, when Abbé Pie-Claude Ngumu was made founding priest of the parish of St Paul of Ndzon-Melen with a mission to experiment with a new liturgy. It was granted to the author of these lines to participate in the creation of this new liturgy. Relieved from my duties as Latin teacher at the minor seminary of Mvolyé, I was made a curate to assist Abbé Pie-Claude Ngumu in the Ndzon-Melen parish in 1969. It was at our suggestion that he decided to introduce the dance as a necessary adjunct to our music. Our melodies are always rhythmic; while they are being played, those present have the greatest difficulty in stopping themselves from beating time with head, finger, or foot. So then we asked why this movement that people had so much difficulty in restraining should not be given free rein. Yielding to our requests in this matter was the starting point of that liturgy that has been so much talked about, the liturgy that is the pride of the Cameroun, and certainly marks an epoch in the history of the church. Since it was launched, this experiment has met with a varied reception: for some it constitutes an attempt to paganize Christianity; for others it is one of the finest achievements of post-conciliar Catholic Christianity. Since then, Canadian, French and Belgian television services have filmed it for themselves. It surprised everyone by its originality at the festival of Algiers. We could go on for ever listing individual favourable reactions. We will confine ourselves to quoting that of Alioune Diop who admitted, after being present at this mass, that he had communed in the great cry of Africa, acclaiming the Lord, beyond the Beti words which he did not understand. But to remove any taint of paganization of the church, let us look at the Biblical foundations for such a procedure.

The theological and Biblical foundations of this indigenization

The great mystery to reflect upon here is the mystery of the Incarnation. Coming from the right hand of the Father, 'the Word of God was made flesh'. Henceforth there exists in the person of Jesus the indissoluble union of two halves: on the one hand the Word of God sharing with the Father the absolute, the unalterable, the universal; on the other hand the Son of Man destined to become universal, assuming through the ages the differing faces of mankind at all times and all places. At the historical level this man bears the face of a Jew, an Aramean—a face both historical and contingent, and an exemplar.

This face of the Jew almost concealed the true intentions of God in his saving action. Indeed from the very first Council of Jerusalem the question was raised as to whether every man had to become a Jew to have access to God's salvation. In the apostolic college there were many who fell into this heresy; they demanded circumcision, an essentially Jewish rite, as a condition of entry into God's new people.

But at every vital moment in the history of his people, God raises up the providential man, to keep the first aim in view. That man was the apostle Paul. This Jew, who had at first been so Jewish that he had persecuted the Church of Christ because he thought it anti-Jewish, this man who had received his revelation not from men, but directly from Christ, this man, I say, was the first to stand up and oppose this Judaization of the Christian from every people and from every age. And this means, in concrete terms, that though Christ is unchanging in his aspect as Word of God, his face as a Jew, on the other hand, must act as a pattern for all the faces Christ is called upon to assume in becoming incarnate in every people.

But how can this incarnation of Christ in every people take place? Christ remains present in his church through those means of contact which we call the sacraments, the means whereby he continues to place himself within the reach of men of all times and all places. Now if we go back to the source of the sacraments and observe them at their origin, Christ, who instituted them, did not fix the form of any sacrament. He did not say how any one of them was to be carried out. All the sacraments are instituted in principle. 'This is my body, this is my blood, do it in remembrance of me.' How? Nothing is said. For us, that means that Christ intended that each people should develop each sacrament with the gestures that spoke for it. So that although each people partakes of catholicity in its adherence to the principle, the way in which it carries out this principle in its life is, in essence, particular, and that is true of all the sacraments.

This incarnation, moreover, does not happen exclusively at the level of the sacraments; it also happens at the level of the perception of the message. The Gospel can be compared to a great musical instrument with a wide and varied range. On this instrument each people is invited to play, in its own register, a hymn of praise to the Eternal.

These ideas are confirmed by the apocalyptic vision of the final scene in Heaven. There Saint John shows us all the peoples of the earth gathered around the Lamb praising God, each in his own tongue, his own liturgy. These people come from everywhere. They are performing a miracle that is the reverse of the one at Pentecost. At Pentecost, the apostles were speaking one language, but those present heard them in their various languages. Around the Lamb of God each people speaks its own language, but the Divine listener hears only one and the same hymn of praise.

In short, since Vatican II, the church understands that it is one in diversity. It understands that catholicity, universality does not in any way mean uniformity. It understands that God's enormous riches have been shared out among the peoples; that we must not reject any of these riches. On the contrary we must set up *omnia in Christo.*

The basic cultural model

Therefore drawing on Beti sources, we had recourse to the traditional Beti assembly in our efforts to reorganize the Catholic mass. What form does this assembly take? The assembly (etógán, ekóán) is called by any member of the tribe who has a problem; this problem may be particular or general. Whatever this may be, this meeting is always informal at the time it is convened, that is to say that there is no fixed agenda. The members making up the assembly are informed then and there of the subject of discussion. And it is the member who has convened the assembly who informs the assembly about the matter in question, either in person, or through an intermediary he has designated. When everyone has understood the subject, they deliberate so that each can express his point of view. For those who have had the good fortune to take part in such meetings, it is a real pleasure to listen to these oratorical contests, where the arguments for or against a particular suggestion come into conflict. It is a true passage of arms, with proverbs flying back and forth like bursts of gunfire aimed at each member of the assembly. When all those wishing to make a contribution have expressed their point of view, the Ndzo rises to sum up the discussion, and proposes the solution or solutions decided upon. The people agree by various acclamations.

Then the convener gives a meal to the whole assembly. This meal has a two-fold significance. It signifies gratitude towards those who answered yes to his call for an assembly; he tries in this way to repay them for the trouble they have gone to on his behalf. The second dimension of this meal is one of communion. Indeed, communion at the family table is an outward sign of the communion of hearts over the proposed solutions. After this meal the members separate and return to their own homes. In short, the assembly comprises two parts: the shared word, and the equally shared meal. This two-fold communion in the word and in the meal also constitute the two dimensions of the traditional Catholic mass.

The presentation of the new mass

The traditional Catholic mass does indeed comprise the two dimensions of communion mentioned above, but it still troubled us in many respects. On the one hand, at the beginning of the mass, one recited many prayers without first knowing why one had been called together by God. Then the sentiments expressed are somewhat ill-assorted. A sentiment like that of praise can be found in the *Gloria*, the *Sanctus*, and in the various eucharistic prayers. Repentance for sin is found in the *confiteor*, *misereatur*, *Kyrie*, *Gloria*, some prayers from the canon, *Agnus Dei* etc. Lastly and most importantly this mass shows up a dichotomy in the manner of participation, the officiating priest on the one hand, and the congregation on the other. The Ndzon-Melen mass tries to remedy these deficiencies. The Melen liturgy conforms to a very logical, coherent internal structure, as we hope to make clear in the following brief description.

First the Melen liturgy has the intention of being a true action of the people of God, as is suggested by the etymology of the word *Leitourgia*. Through the choir of the choristers the people are closely associated with the action of the priest. When the priest presents the Gospel at the appointed place, the choir escorts him there with singing and dancing. When he has finished consecrating the bread, the choir runs up to join with him in acclaiming the Lord who has arrived in the midst of his people. Finally it is the same choir that guides the multitude of the faithful in making the required movements, and it is the choir which carries the people's offerings to the altar. In short, henceforth the dichotomy between priest and congregation is ended; actions carried out beside the people are no more. Everything is accomplished by the people, with them and in the midst of them. Here is a description of what happens.

The service begins with the acclamation of the book, out of which the word of God they are to share together will be taken. While the ministers are dressing, the balafons strike up the song and the people dance. The president brings the incense and censes the book. Then the cross is placed at the head of the procession, while the president takes the book, comes out first, and shows it to the congregation, who acclaim it with a splendid acclamation. The procession sets off with the deacon or master of ceremonies carrying the open book that the president has handed to him. He walks in the middle, behind the president, and from time to time one of the servers censes the book during the procession. When they arrive at the appointed place, the celebrant enthrones the book and all the ministers take their places.

After the enthronement of the book, comes the proclamation of the word. Leaving out all the introductory prayers, the commentator gives a short introductory talk to the congregation to herald the mystery of the day. The people sit down and listen to the three readings, interspersed with the coda of a tune played quietly by the instruments during the reading. This ends with the solemn proclamation of the Gospel and the final song meditation takes us right into the word of the one who has called together his assembly. Then comes the homily, a sermon in the form of a dialogue between the congregation and the celebrant. After bringing to birth the truth of the day, with the maieutics of Socrates, the celebrant concludes this concerted activity with various recommendations.

Then there rises up, like a hymn of acclamation and assent, the song of the Credo (*m'ayébo*). During the singing the crowd bring their offerings to the designated place: money, plaintains, sweet bananas, groundnuts, yams, macabo, sugar canes, vegetables of all kind, eggs, chickens, kids etc . . . in short, everything that the Lord found good at the creation or which is the fruit of man's industry for his further development. At the end of the Credo those who are called reflect upon their conduct, reveal their intentions to the Lord both as individuals and as a community. A hymn of supplication has taken the place of the *Kyrie* (kud a bía ngól). Finally the celebrant concludes the whole of this first part by the prayer of the day (Collect). As can be seen, prayer forms a kind of conclusion to the activity as a whole, not an introduction as in the traditional mass.

The second part follows immediately: the preparation of the communion meal. The choir goes in a dancing movement to collect the offerings of the people to carry them to the altar. This procession of the offerings is one of the most moving parts of this celebration. The people, clapping their hands and bearing their offerings to the Lord's altar in all their brilliant colours, gives one momentarily the illusion of participating in a celestial liturgy. The priest blesses the offerings one by one as they are presented to him, and the choir carries them back to a specially prepared place round the altar. While the choir is going back to its place, still dancing, the priest arranges the eucharistic elements on the altar. With no other transition, he formulates the invocation over the offerings and strikes up the great hymn of the action of grace (Preface). At the singing of the *Sanctus* four to six young girls come around the altar at a dancing pace, like the ten virgins who had gone forth to await the arrival of the bridegroom. Then comes the consecration of the bread and the wine. These two actions are accompanied by shouts of ovation (ayangá) and applause (kób) from the crowd. At once several other members of the choir run forward to join the young girls, and with the entire crowd of people sing the hymn of praise. In this new liturgy, the *Gloria* has become a song of welcome, bursting with joy, from a people happy to receive at last their Emmanuel. After this song of praise, the choir dances back to its place. The canon continues until the singing of the *Pater noster*, sung by the whole congregation, which is followed by the prayer after the *Pater.* Then a last pause to own oneself a sinner and call upon the Lamb of God to bring us his peace. After the prayer asking for peace, the faithful greet each other by shaking hands.

Then follows the communion meal in which all are invited to participate, if not materially at least spiritually. It goes without saying that an exhortation to come and make one's communion would be superfluous, since in the traditional communion meal, it is taken for granted that one should take part in it. During the communion the people sing the Lord's blessings.

After the communion meal and the purification of the sacred vessels, the people of God dance to a song about the active power of Grace; and the whole of this part of the ceremony ends with the last prayer of the people. After this prayer the priest blesses the congregation, and gives them leave to depart. During the dismissal, the choir performs a last song, reflecting upon the work of Grace made effective in the course of the mass. Thus ends the great liturgy of Ndzon-Melen. It may last two hours or even three, and people never tire of remaining standing in order to be a part of this august assembly. In short, we have here a liturgy for and together with God's people.

By way of a conclusion

The Ndzon-Melen liturgy is a step in the direction of what is called the indigenization of Christianity, an expression popularized by the Catholic bishops at the time of their most recent symposium in Rome. What in concrete terms is meant by this expression?

We outlined above a preliminary approach to the question: Christ wishes to make himself the universal man, so that he can be reached by man, wherever he comes from, and thus be able to lay before him the message of salvation in the light of his own concepts. But what are the benefits of indigenization for someone who has accepted Christ's message?

Firstly indigenization puts an end to that dichotomy which a certain type of evangelization creates in any man: a life which can be called Christian, and another natural, profane life, as it were, separate from Christ. In Africa this dichotomy has not been seen, as it has elsewhere, in terms of a juxtaposition, but in terms of opposition and conflict. It is assumed that, since the missionaries regarded our traditional religion and our symbolic cultural arsenal as the work of the Devil, every time that the African reverts to curative or divinatory practices etc., he does what is fundamentally evil in the eyes of the Christianity he has been taught. But nevertheless his whole being continues to be influenced subconsciously by traditional rituals. Therefore there is a perpetual conflict between the human values instituted by our ancestors for the well-being of our society, and this Christian vision instituted by the era of the missionaries. Here we could quote the opposition between Christian marriage and traditional marriage; and the equally clear-cut opposition between the Catholic priest and the traditional priest who is called a sorcerer. Our aim is to take what is worthwhile from these traditional rites and characters, and integrate them into Christianity. By doing this we hope to overcome the conflict instituted in the past between traditional African people and Christ. We hope to overcome the dichotomy between the Christian and profane life, and recreate the unity of the person who has been baptized, who must be wholly Christian and wholly at home in his society. Christ will in this way create a twofold authenticity. We shall be authentically Christian and sons of God, and authentically men of our different lands in the image of the Son of God, who is authentically Son of God, and Son of Man.

The second benefit we anticipate is the Future of the Universal. When God creates man in his own image, he does not give all his attributes to every individual; he distributes them to each man according to his possibilities and his design (cf. the parable of the talents). When God creates societies, he creates them in the image of divine society. Without making more divine societies, he endows each society with certain values different from those of other societies. When each people eventually brings to Christ the values granted to it by the Creator, the uniting of these values will then be able to recreate on this earth the manifold, complex countenance of God. That is what some of us call the Universal. God alone is a universal factor. The other universal is gestating, gradually coming to birth wherever the various peoples of the world learn to contribute their different values to the common good and create a single value which will be the very image of God. This will only happen if everyone accepts the foundation of everything in Christ.

4

Excerpt from 'BELIEFS OF CATHOLICS IN ASIA'

Edmund Chia

Source: *Japan Mission Journal*, 56(3) (2002), 173–81.

1. *Dominus Iesus* and the *sensus fidelium*

The Vatican *Declaration Dominus Iesus*, released by the Congregation for the Doctrine of the Faith (CDF) in September 2000, became the most "talked about" Vatican document in recent Church history. A significant criticism of the document is that it does not resonate well with the ground realities of the Church's relations with persons of other religions. In an article written for an issue of an Indian theological journal specifically dedicated to *Dominus Iesus*, American theologian Paul Knitter even suggests that, "I find that there are many Catholics who are painfully struggling with the traditional teachings that Jesus is the one and only savior of all other people. In view of their encounter with the depth of religious experience in their non-Christian friends, many Catholics, both Asian and American, find it difficult to continue insisting, to these other religious friends and to themselves, that a saving experience of God must come only through Jesus and find its fulfillment only in him and his church."[1] A fellow American Richard McBrien in his article also advanced the thesis that among the Asian theologians there is the possibility that some may have erred: "In two or three cases, theologians may have gone too far in collapsing any meaningful distinction between Jesus of Nazareth as the Christ of faith and other so-called 'Christ figures'."[2]

[. . .] Had McBrien met enough Asians to come to that conclusion? Has he read enough Asian books – not only those available in the West, but also those by Asian publishers – to surmise that only very few Asians have problems with Jesus' uniqueness? On the other hand, how Knitter has arrived at his own conclusion that McBrien is probably wrong? Does he have any data to substantiate his claims that "many" Catholics in Asia find it difficult to profess Jesus as the one and only savior? Does he know anything about what the ordinary lay Catholic on the pews of Asian churches – not just Asian theologians – believe?

These questions, asked of McBrien and Knitter, could also be posed to everyone else writing on Asian theology. Few, if not none, of the Asian theologians actually have any data to substantiate their hypotheses. At best, theologians project their personal theological orientations onto their Catholic brothers and sisters and suggest it to be the *sensus fidelium* of the People of God in Asia. This "false consensus bias" influences much of the theological writings of Asia, especially when one attempts to speak on behalf of the Church in Asia. Moreover, many Asian theologians do not have too much contact with the Church and Christians living in other Asian countries other than their own. In fact, it is not surprising to find more Asian theologians who have visited and/or lived in European and American cities as compared to those who have done the same in another Asian city. Consequently, when the Indian theologian speaks of "Asian theology" s/he is in fact speaking from her/his own experience of India rather than of Asia as a whole. Likewise, when a Taiwanese theologian claims something to be "not in harmony with Asian beliefs," chances are that s/he has never ever been to Manila, Delhi, or Jakarta but has often visited Paris, New York, or Rome. In a way, theirs is really a comparison between the West and their experience of their own particular country rather than the West and Asia as a whole.

An empirical survey

It is in view of this absence of data that an empirical survey was conducted to get a feel of the *sensus fidelium* of the Asian Church on the issues raised by *Dominus Iesus.* A questionnaire survey was sent out by means of email to persons from all across Asia. Between January and March 2002, a total of 394 responses were received from nearly twenty countries, from as far West as Pakistan, India and Sri Lanka to as far East as Indonesia and the Philippines to as far North as Japan, Korea and even Mongolia and China. [. . .]

From the results of the survey, a few observations can be made. [. . .]. Contrary to the presuppositions and demands of *Dominus Iesus*, this significant proportion of Asian Catholics do not believe that either Jesus, the Church or Christianity is the sole, unique or normative repository of truth. It is important to be reminded that these same respondents also affirm the basic beliefs which *Dominus Iesus* postulates, except that they reject some of the more extreme and exclusive assertions, especially those which seem to question the integrity and authenticity of the other religions.

Thus, if *Dominus Iesus* were to be re-written for Asia, it would probably not begin – as does *DI*, 1 – with the mission mandate: "Go into the whole world and proclaim the Gospel to every creature. He who believes and is baptized will be saved; he who does not believe will be condemned"

(Mk 16: 15–16). Instead, it would probably begin with: "Stop judging, that you will not be judged" (Mt 7: 1) or "Do to others whatever you would have them do to you" (Mt 7: 12). Such is the respect Asian Catholics have for their neighbors of other faiths and such is the respect they expect others to have for them in their belief of Jesus, the Church and Christianity.

Another observation is that a very small percentage of the respondent sample affirmed the more exclusivistic assertions of *Dominus Iesus.* Specifically, only 17% of the 394 respondents affirm that God's revelation is given only in Jesus and not in the other religions, 50% affirm that Jesus is the only savior and that there can be no other savior figures, 12% affirm that the other religions are not means of salvation, 35% affirm that the other religions are deficient as compared to those in the Church who have the fullness of the means of salvation, 22% affirm that the Bible is the only Word of God and that other scriptures are not God's Word, 30% affirm that Christianity is the only true religion and 20% affirm that it is not within God's plan to have many religions. In other words, in very general terms, only about 20–25% of Asian Catholics would subscribe to the very exclusivistic aspects advanced by *Dominus Iesus*, which do not acknowledge that truth can also be found in other religions.

It cannot be glossed over that a significant 50% of the respondent sample affirm the assertion that Jesus is indeed the one and only savior for all of humankind. To be exact, it was 49.7% as 196 out of the total of 394 respondents affirm this theological doctrine. On the other hand, 198 (50.3%) did not affirm the doctrine. This, however, does not mean they reject the doctrine. Out of this 50.3%, about half or 25% affirm the possibility of other savior figures while the other half are undecided on the issue. The finding is significant as it is primarily this issue of the possibility of other saviors, which has been most sensitive and controversial. That 25% of the respondents were unable to declare their position on the issue is also significant. To be sure, the theory of the plurality of saviors remains ambiguous and is not as definitive as *Dominus Iesus* has made it out to be. The *sensus fidelium* of the People of God of Asia certainly reveals that. Moreover, even *Dominus Iesus* is not as definitive as it seems. In fact, article 14 of the document invites the Church "to explore if and in what way the historical figures and positive elements of [the other] religions may fall within the divine plan of salvation" (*DI*, 14). The findings of the research, therefore, call to question the very strong reprimands – such as "it must be firmly believed" or "it is contrary to the faith" – which *Dominus Iesus* employs. To be sure, the issues are far from firm and final. Moreover, if the *sensus fidelium* does net correspond to these doctrinal positions, no matter how insistent the Vatican is about them, such beliefs cannot be forced upon the People of God, especially in Asia, where Christians experience other religions everyday of their lives.

In summary, therefore, one can say that amongst Asian Catholics responding, more than 90% believe in the basic tenets of the Christian faith.

Amongst these, about 40–50% also display a theological openness to other religions while only half that number, or 20–25%, harbor theological positions which exclude the viability of the other religions.

The respondents speak

One very important statistic is that only 84% of the respondents agree that the Church is a means of salvation. Given that more than 90% of the sample are believing Christians, one would have expected many more of the respondents to affirm this fundamental tenet of the Christian faith, viz. that salvation comes through the Church. After all, isn't that why one is baptized into the Church? On the other hand, it would be presumptuous to imagine all Catholics are aware of this point of catechesis. A comment by an undergraduate respondent captures this well: "I'm guilty of not remembering much from my catechism, so I don't really understand the full significance of baptism. I guess it is a very important thing – after all, it's a sacrament – but I'm not sure about this." While this lack of knowledge may be few and far between, others who do understand the significance of the Church and baptism raise questions about the authenticity of the institutional Church, thus clouding their own ecclesiological understandings about the Church in relation to salvation. "Yes, the Church is a way of being and supporting each other and is a means of salvation. However, the Church as an institution is failing I feel to be a true follower of Christ. It has wealth, yet keeps asking for donations. It has fallen sick, since ancient days, from power, wealth, control, ambition, pride, selfishness, and self-righteousness," remarks a young woman who works at management level for a non-profit women's organization. Thus, if only 84% – and not much more – of the sample affirm the Church as a means of salvation, it could be because of a variety of reasons, ranging from plain ignorance as to what the theological assertion implies to a sincere conviction that the Church is forfeiting its rightful role as a means of salvation.

However, on the question of whether the Church is "necessary" for salvation, the majority of Asian Catholics seem quite clear on the matter as only 36% of the respondents insists the Church is necessary. Most of these responses probably did not take into account the subtlety expressed in *Dominus Iesus* which continues to insist that the Church is "necessary" even if it grants that salvation is also possible for "those who are not formally and visibly members of the Church" (*DI*, 20). With or without this subtle qualification in *Dominus Iesus*, Asian Catholics, on account of their lived experience, are generally convinced that baptism is not necessary, just as they feel the Church is not necessary. A self-employed woman from Singapore expressed this conviction thus: "Our God is a kind God and would he neglect those who for some reasons were not baptized? Like my mum who was a very kind soul and passed away without being baptized because no one brought the knowledge and faith to her. But I believe she is now happy with God in eternity." Another respondent, a Malaysian journalist, expressed similar convictions but in question form: "What about Encik Mokhtar, the Muslim man working for the conservation of the Belum Valley forests, because he as a human person is a steward of creation? What about the strong presence of God's spirit in his actions and words? Is he excluded from salvation just because he is not baptized? [Encik Mokhtar is just one example of a real person. I mention it here because I saw Christ-likeness in his ways and actions and speech on a recent research trip up to the forest]." Perhaps this issue of the necessity of the Church for salvation, in the context of religious pluralism, is best captured by the response of a bishop, who asserted: "The Church is necessary for salvation in the sense that it is a Sign as well as a witness to the invitation for the salvation of all. If one does not recognize this Sign, or does not want to accept the invitation, then it usually means that the person has found some other way meaningful to him/her. Therefore, I do not think it is necessary for every person to be baptized. But it is necessary for each person to find some Sign or direction in his/her life. As a Christian, I must continue to give witness to the Sign which I think is the correct and true one"

This brings the discussion to whether Christianity is indeed the true religion or if Jesus is the fullness of God's revelation or if Christians have the fullness of the means of salvation. The statistics showed that 91% of the respondents affirm Christianity as a true religion, 72% affirm the assertion that Jesus is the fullness of God's revelation and that 62% affirm the assertion that, indeed, Christians have the fullness of the means of salvation. The responses, however, have to be looked at in view of the fact that a great proportion of these respondents – as discussed earlier – had also affirmed the truth of other religions, the possibility of other revelations, and the efficacy of other religions as means of salvation. For those who operate from an exclusive and dialectical either-or philosophical mindset, such a position may seem contradictory and thus untenable. However, for Asians who generally operate from a mutually inclusive both-and mindset of complementarity, it is all too common for such display of openness to and acknowledgment of two different and perhaps contradictory truths. The comments of a student from Japan captures this spirit well: "For me, Jesus is my only savior. But I am not sure about others. If there are people who have their own savior, I think we should all respect their faith." Others see this openness as an existential and pragmatic matter. A respondent who works as an administrative assistant described it such: "We are all brought up in a multiracial country. It is our duty to respect one another regardless of religion. Whether it is the fullness of the means of salvation or not. This question makes me feel uncomfortable . . . Sorry . . . If you let others see this, hmmm, you gonna start a fight . . . Ten Commandments: Love your neighbor as you love yourself!" Ignoring the fact that this last quote of "love for neighbor" is not really part of the Ten Commandments, the message is clear – our lived reality demands we respect each other's ultimate commitments, even if we ourselves sincerely believe in our own unique Christian commitment that Jesus is indeed God's revelation and our savior. A general manager of a finance company in Indonesia expressed similar sentiments: "I feel very lucky and proud to be a Catholic because according to me Catholicism is the correct and true religion. But it should be noted that other than the Catholic religion, all humankind can be saved too." Yet another respondent, a retired teacher from Malaysia, reconciled this seemingly contradictory dilemma thus: "I'm sure of my own religion and so I follow my religion. Maybe other religions can be true too and I hope other people can be saved by their religion. If there are different roads to go to Kuala Lumpur, I prefer to go the way I'm sure of instead of trying some other ways that I may end up getting lost." Others expressed similar sentiments of openness to other religions but with a certain bias towards that which they themselves adhere to. A pastoral counselor had this to say: "Personally I am biased that the revelation of Jesus seems more wholesome than most others, but again by no means the totality. A bit like the Rolls Royce of automobiles. Most cars can take you to the same destination but some others are more lovely, comfortable and wonderful to ride in."

[. . .] These last comments beg further discussion, especially in connection with *Dominus Iesus*' caution on the "mentality of indifferentism 'characterized by a religious relativism which leads to the belief that one religion is as good as another' " (*DI*, 22). In fact, in response to the question if other religions could also be means of salvation, the respondent of the last comment also said: "Why not? I believe in one thing but why should everyone be made to believe what I believe?" These comments, it must be reminded, have to be taken in light of the fact that the respondents have also acknowledged the definitiveness of Jesus' revelation and his salvific role for all of humanity. Thus, in no way does it suggest the theological position taken lacks rootedness, as it would if it were relativistic and subjectivistic. In fact, the same respondent further declared: "Personally, I would not want to belong to any other religion, but if one is already of another, I can't see why it is less good if the person is not of deviant character." A Filipino teacher expressed rather similar sentiments, but from a hypothetical perspective: "Had I been born to a family where Islam is the known true religion, or Buddhism, I would adhere to it as I do adhere to Christianity as my family's religion." Another respondent, a Religious Brother of an indigenous tribe living on the Borneo island, had this to share about his own personal life: "I grew up with my Muslim relatives and friends and therefore I have no problem accepting Islam. Each and every person is different and God's revelation also varies from one person to another. I think everyone has a right to choose a belief system that suits his/her uniqueness." Another respondent, a young female TV producer, advises: "To each his own. I believe if it works for you and makes you a better person, that's cool."

On the other hand, of course, there are those who, like *Dominus Iesus*, reject such "relativist" theories. One respondent, who works as a Management Support Officer, asserts: "The other religions are man-made religions which may teach their followers to be good, but ours is the true religion where our God comes down to mankind to live as one of us, to show us the way and to die in order to save us. No other religion can boast of this and that He rose again, which proves His divinity." Another, a General Project Manager of two Industrial Estates and a Freelance Architect, shared similar sentiments: "Not because I am a Catholic, but as far as I know there's no quote nor word in any other religion which guarantees people salvation. It's only Jesus Christ who taught and guaranteed our salvation." Another respondent, a Religious retired from active high-school teaching, suggested why the relativist theory could be problematic: "There could not be more than one savior as that would imply different teachings and paths of salvation. Since truth can only be one and so there can be only one religion that is the true religion." Yet another respondent, a young priest from the Mekong valley, personalized this affirmation of faith. When asked if Christianity is the true religion, he responded: "Yes, I certainly believe. If I do not believe it why can I totally give my whole life to God and for God." Others rejected the relativist hypothesis by appealing to hypothetical situations, as for example, the response of a young woman who was an Electronic Publisher before but is now a homemaker: "If we believe that truth is revealed in other religions, then we might as well say that salvation and truth can be via the other religions. When that happens we might as well worship other gods and forget about 'I believe in one God.' And when you believe in other religions you might as well believe and practice the things condoned by the other religions – If they teach the principles of Christianity [believe in one God, love thy neighbor, forgiveness, thou shall not kill, etc.] then Yes. However, if they teach these and then something else contradictory, then No." [. . .]

Discussion on the survey

A final area which needs to be discussed is the feedback received on the survey itself. To be sure, many of the respondents expressed surprise at a survey of the present nature. This is in part because academic surveys are not as common a feature in Asian cultures as they are in the West. Moreover, surveys which deal with religious questions are even more atypical. [. . .]

A few wrote back to request for more time to work on the survey, saying something to the effect that "I want to reflect carefully on the questions because I think they will help me to work through my beliefs." One person said she was making photocopies of the survey and would request her parish priest to distribute it to all the parish-council members, for "it will be good for them to do." On the basis of some of these feedback, it looked as if the survey had become more than a statistical instrument to measure Asian Catholics' beliefs as it had also taken on the function of a formation tool. [. . .]

If many of the respondents were unfamiliar with the nature of the questions asked, they found the questions truly interesting. A Religious Sister from the Mekong Valley had this to say: "May I not answer the questionnaire. It's very catching. My superior in the house told me in a joking manner she is afraid she might lose her faith while reflecting on the questions asked!" A few more messages, which expressed similar sentiments, were equally friendly. Other friendly messages also advocated caution as, for example, one message which read: "This could be controversial so brace yourself for some negative feedback by some well meaning Catholics." Two messages, however, were particularly pointed. The first, which had responded to the questions half-way, had this to say: "I don't like to answer your questions anymore. If you like to know more, it is better you ask the bishops, especially those who have doctorate degrees. Please excuse me if I am too rude." The second, with a similarly angry tone, was even more direct in his challenge to me: "To Edmund. I come straight to the point. Why are you doing this survey? Why is it necessary for you to do this survey? Why are you targeting Catholics? Who authorized you with those questions in your so-called survey? Are you trying to doubt the Catholics' faith, or create confusion? What's your objective?"

As can be seen from the preceding comments, the questionnaire was not only thought provoking but viewed with a certain degree of suspicion as well, in view of the questions, which seemed to have hit at the core of the Christian's being. In fact, the questions seemed to have caused much tension as they questioned the respondent's faith, especially in relation to her/his lived reality of religious pluralism. Of course, one way to deal with such tension is to block out the lived reality and act as if persons of other religions did not exist. Another way is to simply relegate them to the "unsaved" and be contend that Christianity is the superior and only true religion. The sincere seeker, however, will find such strategies of dealing with the tension untenable and could end up being even more confused and vulnerable. An emotive comment from one respondent captures this sense of vulnerability well: "I believe that only Christianity is for me, and it is different from the rest in a special way. However, I feel uncomfortable in saying my religion is the best, simply because that would imply that the other religions are not good and doing something wrong. That is difficult to say because a lot of religions preach goodness, and it is difficult to say goodness is wrong, just because it is of a different religion. Yet, I also am torn by the fact I've learnt all the time in Sunday School that Christianity is the true religion. It is true, but does it necessarily mean that others are not? What is religion anyway? Common beliefs? Ultimate truths? Argghh . . . this is confusing." Another response, which expressed a similar dialectical tension, had this to say: "This is what I believe, although deep in my heart wish this is not 100% right, so more people can be saved from hell."

Conclusion

These last two comments seem to indicate that there are some Asian Catholics who have to struggle with their contextual reality of the experience of truth and beauty in the other religions, which is then juxtaposed against their catechism, which insists that these are not from God. It is as if their experience and heart seem to be perceiving reality one way while their knowledge and head suggest otherwise. This is probably what Paul Knitter was referring to when he said many Catholics are "painfully struggling" with the dichotomy between the teachings of their faith as against their day-to-day experience of very positive relations with persons of other religions. This struggle adheres as the catechism and theological formation imparted in most Asian seminaries and Sunday Schools continue to be those that are borrowed from the West, where the phenomenon of religious pluralism is absent or ignored. Hence, it comes as no surprise that the masses, the grassroots, are in the main indoctrinated with theologies which are alien to their contextual experience and which do not resonate with their lived realities. [. . .]

On the theological and cognitive levels they might articulate theologies which assert the superiority of Catholicism, but on the affective and experiential levels, they might be convinced that this could not be. In other words, if there are only a few Asians who can dogmatically pronounce the possibility of other saviors and the truth of other religions, there are many who actually feel and experience such a reality from the depths of their being even if they may not be able to intellectually assert that conviction.

References

1 Richard McBrien, "'Finding' Christ in Other Religions," *National Catholic Reporter*, (22 December 2000).

2 *Ibid.*

Part 2

FOUNDATIONS: THE BIBLE AS AGREED TEXT

5

Excerpt from 'THE BIBLE AND COLONIALISM IN THE GLOBAL CONTEXT'

*Pui-lan Kwok**

Source: *Theology & Life*, 30 (2007), 218–31, 37.

[. . .] In "Signs Taken for Wonder," Bhabha begins by telling the story that under a grove of trees outside Delhi in May 1817, an Indian catechist Anund Messeh found about five hundred people debating spiritedly about a Hindi version of the Bible. They insisted that the Bible was a gift from God to them, and not a book about the religion of the European Sahibs. They said they would be baptized, but would defer it until next year, and they would not partake of the Eucharist because they were vegetarians and the English ate meat. For Bhabha, this example illustrates what he has called "the ruse of recognition," a recognition that both mimicked and mocked colonial power at the same time.[12] He writes:

> The colonial presence is always ambivalent, split between its appearance as original and authoritative and its articulation as repetition and difference. It is a disjunction produced within the act of enunciation as a specifically colonial articulation of those two disproportionate sites of colonial discourse and power: the colonial scene as the invention of historicity, mastery, mimesis or as the "other scene" of *Entstellung*, displacement, fantasy, psychic defence, and an "open" textuality.[13]

Bbabha's discussion of ambivalence, mimicry, hybridity, and difference in this widely quoted and much debated essay has challenged the rigid binarism of the colonizer and the colonized, and created the "in-between" space where the agency of the indigenous can be articulated and subversion imagined. In this way, an important change of perspective occurs, which goes beyond "the noisy command of colonialist authority or the silent repression of native traditions" to look at the interstices where the discursive conditions of dominance are turned into grounds of intervention.[14]

Bbabha's theoretical insights offer an interpretive framework to examine the issues of biblical authority and translation in the colonial context. One of Bhabha's favorite quotes from a missionary concerns how the Indians did not treat the Bible as a Holy Book as the early missionaries had expected. In a land where the Vedas had been circulated for millennia in the oral form, a disheartened missionary reported that the arrival of the written Bible aroused such curiosity that people gladly received it, not for reading the contents, but for using it as waste or wrapping paper, or barter in the market.[15] Similar non-recognition or misrecognition occurred in cultures in which the idea of a book that was supposed to contain the Word of God would seem foreign to many people. For example, Vincent Wimbush maintains that the encounter of Africans with the Bible had been problematic, for "cultures steeped in oral traditions generally find the concept of religion and religious power circumscribed by a book at first frightful and absurd, thereafter, certainly awesome and fascinating."[16] Among the Tamils in Sri Lanka, the Bible was regarded by some as a magical object which could ward off evil and bring good luck. Scripture portions were used as a talisman or amulet, and even carefully suspended from the roof near a sick person.[17] These examples from various cultural backgrounds demonstrated poignantly that the notion of "sacred scripture" was not universally held, and a monologic inscription of the authority of Bible could not be easily assumed and registered across the chasm of cultural and religious differences.

If the Bible has signified for the missionaries an authority of colonial Christianity, it also opened a specific space for the articulation of hybridity, thus allowing the Indians to construct a counterhegemonic discourse. A concrete example of hybridity was the translation of the English Bible into the indigenous languages and dialects. For Bhabha, "the process of translation is the opening up of another contentious political and cultural site at the heart of colonial representation."[18] The translation of the Bible into the vernacular loosened missionaries' control of meaning, and allowed for creative negotiation with indigenous idioms, languages, and systems of thought. For whether the missionaries have opted for a stricter principle of "formal correspondence" or a more flexible principle of "dynamic equivalence," the Bible, rooted in its Mediterranean cultures, could not be translated into another tongue without much ingenuity. The missionaries had to consult native experts frequently on matters from correct pronunciation to finding appropriate words to translate the foreign terms. The assertion of native agency, in the roles of language teachers, translators, compilers, and editors, was unacknowledged in missionary reports and the names of native collaborators deemed insignificant. But the contribution of native Christians was indispensable, for without their help and partnership, the translation projects would not have been brought to fruition.

Translation is a meaning-construction process, which involves intimate knowledge of the style, rhetoric, figuration, local color, and other specificities of the languages one translates.[19] In *Illuminations*, Walter Benjamin laments, "all translation is only a somewhat provisional way of coming to terms with the foreignness of languages."[20] In China, the interminable question of how to render the Hebrew and Greek terms *Elohim* and *Theos*, or *God* into the Chinese language had created a conundrum since the seventeenth century, first among the Catholic missionaries, and then among the Protestants. The translation of the Greek term *logos* in the first chapter of the Gospel of John is another case in point. The Chinese Bible translates *logos* by the word *dao*, a heavy-laden word with complex connotations of philosophical and religious meanings in Daoism. The use of the term *dao* recasts and transposes the Hellenistic religious concept into Chinese idiom and religious background. In Australia, *logos* has been translated as "dreaming" in the Pitjantatjara language, spoken by an Aboriginal community in the central desert. This translation would be shocking for those who do not know the background of the Aboriginal religious worldview, but according to Roland Boer, dreaming "designates a form of religious mapping, an ideological construction whereby the universe is rendered understandable in religious terms."[21] Are the Aboriginals and the Chinese reading the same Bible, if the former interpret *logos* as dreaming and the latter as *dao*? Bhabha, with his characteristic embrace of ambivalence, reiterates: "Here the word of divine authority is deeply flawed by the assertion of the indigenous sign, and in the very practice of domination the language of the master becomes hybrid – neither one thing nor the other."[22]

Although Bhabha's theoretical contribution in demystifying the fantasy of the total dominance of colonial power is widely acknowledged, his strong articulation of a linguistic turn in cultural studies, and specifically his emphasis on the instability of colonial discourse, and on intertextuality and translation has irked some of his critics. Scholars with a Marxist bent have charged that Bhabha has reduced the political and social effects of colonialism to the level of enunciation, discourse, and textuality, as if by deconstructing the signifying process and the reiteration of linguistic and cultural difference, the problems of colonialism would be ameliorated.[23] His concept of hybridity has been much dissected and debated by scholars in different disciplines. Bhabha has intended to use the concept to destabilize the binarism of the colonizer and the colonized and a static and homogenous notion of culture, so that a multiple and polymorphous subjectivity, a heterogeneous community, and a mutable social and cultural formation can be articulated. But as Benita Parry asserts, the overemphasis on hybridity and difference would call into question the possibility of forming a community of resistance and would make it impossible to articulate political conflicts and struggles in antagonistic terms to mobilize people to fight against oppression.[24] In the field of biblical studies, Boer contends that the notion of hybridity can be misleading because "it is not that Christianity has a core whose Scriptures' meanings may be transmitted, or whose doctrines and texts may be subverted in the colonial relation."[25] Christianity, for Boer, is essentially syncretistic, which is constantly changing and metamorphosing into new forms which are distinct from earlier forms.

While Bhabha interprets translation as repetition and hybridity, Lamin Sanneh, a scholar of world mission born in Gambia, has examined the wider cultural transformation brought by the translation of the Bible into African vernacular languages. In his book *Translating the Message*, Sanneh argues that the missionary movement, when viewed through the vernacular paradigm, has revitalized African languages and cultures: "Missionary adoption of the vernacular, therefore, was tantamount to adopting indigenous cultural criteria for the message, a piece of radical indigenization far greater than the standard portrayal of mission as Western cultural imperialism."[26] While the colonial officials insisted on imposing the language of the colonizers because of their belief in the deficiency of indigenous languages, Sanneh argues that some missionaries demonstrated a regard for the local cultures and believed that the vernacular Bibles could help ushering in the kingdom of God. Although Sanneh does not intend to defend the role of missionaries in colonialism, he nevertheless claims that the missionaries did not always act according to the interests of the colonial government. For example, David Livingstone, one of the best-known missionaries in Africa, defended and safeguarded indigenous heritage, though he was also caught in the paradoxical role of providing modern schools and introducing "civilization" to the "primitive" Africans. For Livingstone, the Christian message could be expressed in the African vernacular because Europe had no monopoly of the truth (108–9). Sanneh praises the missionaries for their efforts in linguistic studies and for their cultural projects of compilation of grammars, lexicons, and instituting orthographies and vernacular alphabets as helping to set the standard for anthropology, linguistics, music, law and other fields (206). William Carey, for instance, established a language center and a printing press at Serampore in India, which subsequently produced religious materials in forty-four languages and dialects. Carey's linguistic research contributed to the renaissance of Bengali prose literature, Sanneh argues, which instilled pride and confidence in the people and over time shielded the people against "the unstated logic of colonial overlordship" (102).

Contending that the vernacular project has played a crucial role in the renewal and revitalization of African cultures, Sanneh describes how the vernacular Bibles have preserved the African names for God and their religious worldviews that depended on it:

> It began to dawn on the African populations that the missionary adoption of the vernacular categories for Scriptures was in effect a written sanction for the indigenous religious vocation. The God of the ancestors was accordingly assimilated into the Yahweh of ancient Israel and "the God and Father of our Lord Jesus Christ" (159–60).

In his later work *Encountering the West*, Sanneh further elaborates on the effects of the vernacular project on literacy in the mother tongue and the promotion of nationalistic sentiment of the African people. While some anthropologists, notably Jack Goody, questions the benefits of introducing the writing system to oral cultures,[27] Sanneh expresses no such caution: "through the vernacular channel Africans entered an immense stage of human consciousness in which the printed word and native diction combined in elucidating the encounter not just with the brave new world of the West but with ancient forms that always told God's far from certain mindfulness for the race and tribe."[28] The reinvigoration of African cultures and languages contributed to a sense of peoplehood, because it reinforced the notion of ethnicity based on shared cultural and linguistic characteristics. For Sanneh, the vernacular movement paved the way for the formation of cultural identity, the assertion of nation boundaries, and prepared the Africans to critique colonial rule and the doctrine of white racial supremacy and to take their place in the world of modern nations.[29]

Sanneh's glowing review of the missionaries' vernacular project and its positive impact on culture is debatable as scholars who have studied the details of the inscription process hold the opposite view. In *Contracting Colonialism*, Vicente Raphael chastised translation as integral to conversion, which helped to secure colonial conquest and the colonization of the mind. Writing from the context of the Philippines, Raphael documents how the Spanish missionaries subscribed to the belief of a hierarchy of languages and treated Tagalog as inferior, which had to be subjected to the explanatory rules and grammars of Latin. In creating a written system for Tagalog, the missionaries standardized the pronunciation, syntax, and lexicon of Tagalog according to the rules of Latin, mediated through their Castilian vernacular, and in this way alienated Tagalog from the native speakers:

> The linguistic machinery of Tagalog is thus made to refer to an origin and destination beyond its community of native speakers – to God's Word as it is expressed in the discourse of Spanish Catholicism and in relation to the grammatical grid of Latin. It is as if Tagalog were alienated from the Tagalogs by the missionary-translator, who, after endowing it with a grammar and lexicon in his *arte*, gave it back to them in the form of prayers, sermons, and confessionals.[30]

In a typical Orientalist fashion, the missionaries assumed the position of authorities, who could speak for and represent Tagalog better than the Tagalogs themselves. They dismissed the native written language *babbayin* as totally inadequate and failing to encode the proper pronunciation and superimposed the romanized script, while retaining the Latin or Castilian forms for key Christian terms, such as *Dios*, *Virgen*, *Espíritu Santo*, *Cruz*, *Doctrina Cristiana*, and so forth.[31] But much to the chagrin of the missionaries, Tagalog could not be unequivocally reinstated in Spanish-Christian terms, Raphael declares, as some aspects of the vernacular would invariably escape missionary inscription. While Sanneh stresses the translatability of the Christian message, Raphael insists that it is the untranslatability of some aspects of Tagalog and the misapprehension of the concepts such as spirit, repentance, master, slave, obedience and submission that protected the people from the overdominating power of linguistic hierarchy and colonial control.

The divergent positions of Raphael and Sanneh highlights the complexities in evaluating the nexus of translation of the Bible, vernacular literacy, and colonialism. Raphael approaches translation more or less as a proselytizing strategy, based on cultural imperialism of the missionaries. Sanneh, on the other hand, has other interests in mind when he argues mission as translation. By placing Africa at the center of his study, a continent that accounts for 522 out of the 1808 languages into which the Bible has been translated, Sanneh hopes to highlight the multiplicity of the Christian tradition. His aim is to advance a pluralistic model of Christianity by underscoring the translatability of the Christian message to mitigate the overdominance of its Western form. In reading his works, however, one needs to ask, Is it too delimiting to look at mission through the lenses of translation? And is it appropriate to delineate the missionary impact on culture as if it were a domain largely separable from the economic, political, and military domination?

Seen from a broader perspective, Sanneh's argument that literacy and the written medium paved the way for the development of nationalism applies only to the educated elites but not the subalterns.[32] He is certainly correct that education and literacy opened a space for the subjectivity and agency of the elites, especially for those trained in mission schools and colleges, who served in the colonial bureaucracy and later assumed important roles in national independence. What was left out, however, were the vast majority whose opportunity for social advancement was limited because of their lack of access to education and because of the high premium hitherto attached to literacy. And neither Raphael nor Sanneh takes into consideration the gender dimension in the politics of translation. Mary John Mananzan claims that precolonial Filipino society was more egalitarian and inclusive of the two sexes, but this communal society was changed by the imposition of the colonial system and the Catholic Church's discrimination against women.[33] Raphael does not investigate whether the change from orality to a written language had affected the social structures of the Tagalog society.

Sanneh, for his part, has been taken to task by African feminist theologians who ostensibly demonstrate the colonizing and gendering effects of biblical translation. Dora Mbuwayesango contests Sanneh's argument that scriptural translation helped Africans to preserve their names for God, for she chastises this practice as colonizing the African religious systems. For example, while the Shona term *Mwari* is a spirit without gender and sexuality, its use to translate *God* casts it in human form, associated with predominantly male metaphors.[34] The same problem surfaces in the translation of *God* by *Modimo* in the Setswana Bible, as Gomang Seratwa Ntloedibe-Kuswani attests.[35] By ignoring the indigenous religious system, these biblical translations coopted the African deities as if they were the names for the God of Abraham, Sarah, and Moses, and not of their African ancestors. Furthermore, they give the erroneous impression that the activities of these deities can be understood through the Bible, and since the native myths and stories are circulated through the oral medium, they are considered less authoritative than the missionary writings. These feminist theologians bring into sharp relief the question of whether biblical translation reinscribes both colonialist and patriarchal biases. While male scholars claim that the translation of the Bible into the vernacular promotes nationalism or a sense of peoplehood, just as the translation of the Bible into English and German had apparently done so in an earlier period, these feminist theologians challenge a monolithic definition of "nation" and "people," if these terms do not include women.

The relationship between the Bible and the subaltern has only been recently studied by scholars who pay attention to class and gender difference. In recovering native agency in negotiating the meaning of the Bible, scholars have often left out the roles played by women, especially the Bible women, who brought the Bible to the illiterate women. Most of the early Bible women received some training from the female missionaries and they might also be graduates of mission schools. Often as the only literate or semi-literate women in their communities, they performed the important roles as community organizers, counselors, and teachers. They would visit women in their homes to teach them how to read and write, narrate stories from the Bible, and sell them some Bible portions and Christian Primers. In her study of the work of Bible women in the Basel Mission in India, Mrinalini Sebastian employs the term "transaction" to describe the exchange between the listeners and speakers of the stories of the Bible. She cites this fascinating report of the experience of two Bible women in a Mopla houschold, narrated by the missionary who was in charge of the Bible women:

> Why the devil, why Judas Iscariot have been created, these are questions, which greatly perplex them. Michal and Julia, two of our

> Bible-women often visit also the houses of Moplas and are startled at the curious ideas prevailing among their women. That Christ is in heaven and will come again to judge the quick and dead, they will not object to, but they will not admit that He died on the cross. "It is the devil that has been crucified," they will say; "Isa Nabi went to heaven without dying. He was a good man, but you abuse Him by your stories. Mary, too, is in heaven, there she sews and sews day and night in order to make her wedding-dress. But as often as she has done with it and shakes it out in order to fold it up, it tears asunder and she must begin anew. But finally she will succeed, then Isa Nabi will appear. . . . . . ." People who relish this kind of rubbish will find it naturally difficult to appreciate the plain and chaste truths of the unadulterated Gospel.[36]

We would never know the stories about Jesus and Mary that Michal and Julia had told these Mopla women and how the two responded to their imaginative reconstruction of biblical stories. Sebastian comments on the transaction process: "In contrast to the tendency of the writer of this report to fix the truth of the 'unadulterated Gospel,' the accommodating story of the Mopla women, makes conversation possible, even when dissent is not withheld."[37] Sebastian's careful combing through the missionary records and her concrete case study show that the subalterns were not passive listeners, but active participants in selecting what biblical stories to believe in and what stories to deconstruct or retell.

While previous discussion on the Bible and colonialism focused primarily on translation, literacy, and textual formation and interpretation, several recent works have elevated the discussion to a new level as they look at the Bible through broader cultural lenses. These crucial texts include *Bible in Modern China: The Literary and Intellectual Impact* (1999); *The Bible in Africa: Transactions, Trajectories, and Trends* (2000); *African Americans and the Bible: Sacred Texts and Social Textures* (2000); *The Bible and the Third World: Precolonial, Colonial and Postcolonial Encounters* (2001); and the two *Semeia* volumes, one presents fresh data on the Bible in Australia and the Pacific (2001) and the other on "The Bible in Asian America" (2002).[38] The publication of these volumes on the encounter of the Bible with the Third World, indigenous peoples, and racial minority groups in America provides a wealth of new information, signaling a maturation of scholarship on the Bible in these communities.

[. . .]

The above discussion of the Bible in colonial discourse, translation and literacy, the Bible and the subaltern, Aboriginal agency, and newer researches on sacred text and social texture points to the fact that the Bible is indeed a double-edged sword – it has been used as an instrument by the colonizers and has been seized upon by some to fashion a rhetoric against colonial domination and by others to create a rich language world. The relation between the Bible and colonialism will remain controversial and contested, depending on the standpoint of the researcher and the nexuses of issues he or she has choosen to focus on. As part of the civilizing mission, the introduction of the Bible created the same paradoxical effect as the introduction of Western science to "modernize" the colonized world. As Gyan Prakash points out, the claim by Western scientific narratives that science is universal implies that it cannot be limited by Western approaches and rules out the participation of the natives. When science "went native" in nineteenth-century India, that is, when the Indians recovered scientific knowledge in their own traditions, the assumed superority of Western science was undermined.[52] Similarly, when the Bible "went native," its claim to be a universal Gospel opened the floodgate for the native people to reclaim their religious knowledge and spiritual values and challenge colonial authority. It is ironical that the Bible as icon of Western civilization has unexpectedly prepared the way for decolonization.

Notes

12 Homi Bhabha, "Signs Taken for Wonder: Questions of Ambivalence and Authority under a tree outside Delhi, May 1817" in *The Location of Culture* (London: Routledge, 1994), 115.
13 Ibid., 107–8.
14 Ibid., 112.
15 Ibid., 92, 122.
16 Vincent Wimbush, "Reading Texts through Worlds, Worlds through Texts" in *Semeia* 62 (1993), 131.
17 Sugirtharajah, 159. In Nigeria, the Bible was also treated as a magical object to ward off evil spirits, see Justin S. Ukpong, "Popular Readings of the Bible in Africa and Implications for Academic Readings" in Gerald O. West and Musa W. Dube ed., *The Bible in Africa: Transactions, Trajectories and Trends* (Atlanta: Society of Biblical Literature, 2000), 587.
18 Bhabha, 33.
19 See Gayatri Chakravorty Spivak, "The Politics of Translation" in *Outside the Teaching Machine* (New York: Routledge, 1993), 179–200.
20 Walter Benjamin, Hanna Arendt ed., *Illuminations* (New York: Schocken Books, 1969), 75.
21 Roland Boer, *Last Stop Before Antarctica: The Bible and Postcolonialism in Australia* (Sheffield: Sheffield Academic Press, 2001), 173.
22 Bhabha, 33.
23 Arif Dirlik, "The Postcolonial Aura: Third World Criticism in the Age of Global Capitalism" in Anne McClintock, Aamir Mufti, and Ella Shohat ed., *Dangerous Liaisons: Gender, Nation, and Postcolonial Perspectives* (Minneapolis: University of Minnesota Press, 1997), 501–28; Aijaz Ahmad, *In Theory: Classes, Nations, Literatures* (New York: Verso, 1992).
24 Benita Parry, "Signs of Our Times: Discussion of Homi Bhabha's The Location of Culture" in *Third Text* 28/29 (1994), 15.
25 Boer, 164.

26 Lamin Sanneh, *Translating the Message: The Missionary Impact on Culture* (Maryknoll: Orbis Books, 1989), 3. Hereafter page references will be given in parentheses in the text.

27 Jack Goody, *The Logic of Writing and the Organization of Society* (Cambridge: Cambridge University Press, 1986).

28 Lamin Sanneh, *Encountering the West: Christianity and the Global Cultural Process* (Maryknoll: Orbis Books, 1993), 86.

29 Ibid., 75.

30 Vicente L. Raphael, *Contracting Colonialism: Translation and Conversion in Tagalog Society under Early Spanish Rule* (Durham: Duke University Press, 1993), 38.

31 Ibid., 29.

32 For the comparison between the interaction of the Bible with the elites and subalterns, I benefit from the discussion of science as it affects Indian elites and subalterns by Gyan Prakash in *Another Reason: Science and the Imagination of Modern India* (Princeton: Princeton University Press, 1999), 34–46.

33 Mary John Mananzan, "The Filipino Woman: Before and After the Spanish Conquest of the Philippines" in Mary John Mananzan ed., *Essays on Women* (Manila: Institute of Women's Studies, 1991), 6–35.

34 Dora R. Mbuwayesango, "How Local Divine Powers Were Suppressed: A Case of Mwari of the Shona" in Musa W. Dube ed., *Other Ways of Reading: African Women and the Bible* (Atlanta: Society of Biblical Literature, 2001), 63–77.

35 Gomang Seratwa Ntloedibe-Kuswani, "Translating the Divine: The Case of Modimo in the Setswana Bible" in ibid., 78–97.

36 Mrinalini Sebastian, "Reading Archives from a Postcolonial Feminist Perspective: 'Native' Bible Women and the Missionary Ideal" in *Journal of Feminist Studies in Religion* 19(1) (2003), 22.

37 Ibid.

38 Eber, Wan, and Walf, eds., *Bible in Modern China*; West and Dube, eds., *The Bible in Africa*; Vincent L. Wimbush, ed., *African Americans and the Bible: Sacred Texts and Social Textures* (New York: Continuum, 2000); Sugirtharajah, *The Bible and the Third World*; Roland Boer, ed., "A Vanishing Mediator? The Presence/Absence of the Bible in Postcolonialism" in *Semeia* 88 (2001); and Tat-siong Benny Liew, ed., "The Bible in Asian America" in *Semeia* 90/91 (2002).

52 Prakash, 49–85.

6

Excerpt from 'POLARITY OR PARTNERSHIP? Retelling the story of Martha and Mary from Asian women's perspective'

Ranjini Rebera

Source: *Semeia*, 78 (1997), 93–4, 101–7.

Introduction

> There is a story from a very conservative little village in Asia that goes like this: There once lived two sisters and a brother, whose parents had died. None of them was married, but the house they lived in was owned by the oldest of the three—a sister. As is the custom in South Asia she was the mother-figure in the home. She ran the home, made many of the decisions for the family, and was very protective of her younger sister and very supportive of her only brother. Because she was the owner of the house and property, she also had considerable status in the village community. She was considered to be a woman of means, as well as the real head of the family, though her brother was the figurative head of the family. In recent times this little family had become friends with another man. He traveled to many villages as a teacher and would make it a point to stop and visit this family whenever he passed through their village. At this point in our story, it appears that he was coming to dinner with the two sisters. Their brother was away from home and the two sisters were planning to entertain him to dinner.

The storyteller paused for response and reactions from the audience.

The first time I heard a similar introduction to a study of Luke 10:38–42 was at a South Asian Women's Leadership training workshop in Lahore, Pakistan. The storyteller and study leader was Christine Amjad Ali, a New Testament scholar from Pakistan. The responses she elicited from participants as she told this story, making pauses at significant points, reflected insights framed within South Asian culture and tradition (Amjad Ali: 144–46). Those responses included the following comments:

- "Single women would never invite an unmarried man into their home."
- "A single man would never accept an invitation to an unchaperoned dinner with unmarried sisters."
- "The women in the neighborhood would have a great deal to say to the sisters."
- "A good elder sister would never involve her younger sister in such a situation. It would reflect on her reputation."
- "Why did the brother not do something about the matter? What about his responsibility for his two sisters?"

[. . .]

> *V. 40: "But Martha was distracted by her many tasks; so she came to him and asked, 'Lord, do you not care that my sister has left me to do all the work by myself? Tell her then to help me.'"*

Asian women are sometimes puzzled by this verse. It does not quite fit the accepted behavior codes between two sisters and an unrelated male. It becomes doubly puzzling for South Asian women when they equate Jesus to the pastor or priest in the local church. For them it would be unthinkable to air any family disagreement in such a public manner. A workshop participant from Bangladesh made the observation that should she have any complaints about her sister she *may* see her pastor privately and ask for advice on how to deal with a "lazy" sister. Her first preference would be to go to another woman in the family circle rather than to a male outsider. What was more difficult to accept was the offering of hospitality combined with a complaint about behavior and then expecting the honored guest to arbitrate in the matter!

A further observation related to Mary's silence in the face of Martha's words was that in Asian culture it was most probable that the younger sister would not challenge her older sister in the presence of an outsider. She would remain silent and perhaps challenge her sister at a more private time. Manisha Roy, in examining the many relationships between family and kinship networks, writes of the daughter-mother relationship that the daughter "must respect and obey her mother and mother-figures (paternal aunts, older classificatory siblings) while listening to what they instruct her about her future life" (156; see also Rebera, 1995b:43–60, 77–95). Martha as the mother-figure in the family would fit the role of "older classificatory sibling," and, given that role, Mary would hesitate to be disrespectful towards her older sister. Hence Mary's silence.

> *Vv. 41–42: "But the Lord answered her, 'Martha, Martha, you are worried and distracted by many things; there is need of only one thing. Mary has chosen the better part, which will not be taken away from her.'"*

The encounter between Jesus and the two sisters climaxes with Jesus' words to Martha that are traditionally interpreted to favor Mary's stance of contemplative discipleship as being of a higher category than Martha's which was reflected in "fretting and fussing about so many things" (NEB). Jesus' response has been used to validate women's participation in the church as one of silence and women's spirituality as derived from an unquestioning dependence on Christ.

The difficulty in reconstructing this verse from a feminist perspective is reflected in the many articles and chapters written by feminist scholars about this encounter. Jesus' use of the words "chosen the better part" has challenged feminist scholars in the rereading of this text. An important factor in the understanding of these words has been the need to eliminate the polarization of women's ministries that has been caused by male-centered theology based on these verses.

A role-play of this pericope by a group of Indian women led to significant insights. Once again the sisters had been portrayed as being in a close sibling relationship. Both Martha and Mary were portrayed as disciples-in-training. This factor gave each sister the independent right to seek approval from their *guru*, Jesus. Therefore, when Jesus responded to Martha he was not seen as pitting one sister against the other, but as supporting Mary in her choice with what was best for her. He was accepting of Mary's desire to be different in her apprenticeship. He was also seen as understanding of Martha's "mother-figure" concern for the welfare of her younger sister. Martha's worry and distraction were connected to the reputation of the younger sister. Christine Amjad Ali observed, "Perhaps we think that Jesus was walking around with a halo on his head and that everyone would know that he was the wonderful Son of God! But he did not. He was an ordinary Asian man in an Asian country who was a good friend to these two sisters and their brother" (144). Jesus' response was seen as an assurance that being apprenticed to him was "a better thing" than following the traditional dictates of society that often confined and limited women in public and private roles.

In South Asian culture for a woman to remain unmarried after the age of twenty years is often a reflection of an inadequacy on the part of the woman as well as her parents. In the case of two unmarried sisters, with no parent in evidence, this would be an even greater burden. To break such societal barriers and to become a *sishya* to an unmarried male is to compound the negative attitudes extended to such a family. In the discussion that followed this role-play, many drew attention to the role of unmarried women in ministry in India. In the Protestant churches they are viewed as being "different" from women who are wives and mothers. Single women in ministry are often pitied as being unable to fulfill their obligations as a woman, which is to marry and have children. In a rapidly developing technological India, singleness among women is growing. The right to choose marriage and/or a profession is becoming a visible phenomenon in urban, middle-class India. Therefore, the issue of the status of single women is becoming a focus for discussion and debate. Viewing these verses from the perspective of single women, choosing to build their own journeys in their own manner, and reading Jesus' response as a validation of that right, adds weight to the argument that the right of choice is not a gender-based prerogative but a human right.

Partnership not polarity

The focus in all the retellings I have participated in has been on the two sisters as the central figures in the story, rather than on Jesus or his response to Martha's words. This emphasis falls easily into the structure of chapter 10 as it deals with the choice of men and women to be disciples, how this choice is exercised, and the sending out of the seventy in pairs. The re-telling of this pericope from an Asian perspective is imperative if Asian church women are to be released from androcentric interpretations that continue to polarize women, define women's ministry, and hold us captive within kyriarchal traditions. Gao Ying from China writes:

> In traditional Chinese biblical interpretation, women are led to believe that they should try to be Christians like Mary but not Martha. But here the analysis shows that the Chinese church also needs "Marthas" to peform administrative affairs. As a matter of fact there are many "Marthas" today in the Chinese church who are making contributions to the church's ministry.
>
> (60)

Chung Sook Ja from Korea claims:

> Many Korean male pastors understand Martha as a woman who was involved in many activities outside of her church, and Mary as a woman who dedicated herself to work in her own church. They emphasize that, because Martha's attitude was not welcomed by Jesus, church women should not be active in many things outside of their churches and should, rather, work in their local churches.
>
> (1993:19)

The Asian feminist perspectives presented here are by no means the norm in Asia. They are a part of a branch of feminist scholarship that is still in its infancy. They are indicative of the struggle for Asian scholarship to establish its own genre in the field of biblical scholarship. For Asian women retelling biblical texts from our own realities has great significance.

- It places the culture of biblical women side by side with the culture of Asian women. This enables us to see the similarities between socio-cultural attitudes and expectations of women as they existed in Hebrew society and in Asia today. It moves us away from the written text to the exploration of those realities that are common to women in both settings. Once we begin our search for meaning from this position, we see the events and characters in the Bible as persons we can relate to, rather than as events that are used to be prescriptive regarding our attitudes and behavior as Christian women.
- Episodes such as the Martha and Mary pericope assist in reclaiming Asian traditions that have been lost through influences from outside the region. Concepts of discipleship that expressed an accepted role for women in Asian religious practice can be reintroduced to add deeper meaning to the claims of women for a discipleship of equals in a kyriarchal church. Such a process moves Mary from the foot of the pulpit to the position of an equal.
- Such study moves the focus from polarizing women in the church to one of partnership. It eradicates the "Martha-or-Mary" stereotype and replaces it with understandings of "Martha—the disciple" and "Mary—the disciple" working in partnership with each other and with Jesus. This concept is developed further by Chung Sook Ja of Korea who explores Jesus' partnership with Mary and Martha as "Women becoming Disciples for Partnership," claiming:

> I want to develop women's liberation into the action in community by interpreting this story as an example of Jesus' new community in partnership. Jesus' declaration about "the most important part" should be understood from the perspective of partnership. For Jesus the role distinction was not a big issue, but the broken partnership between Mary and Martha was.
>
> (1992:251)

- For a patriarchal Asian church to hear the voice of women as initiators for change, we have to re-open doors that closed or were half-closed when Euro-centered education became accepted as the only vehicle for learning and research. Communication processes rooted in the culture of the people need to be used as a significant vehicle for initiating such change.
- In cultures where women's identity continues to be derived from our relationship to a male figure, be it a father, husband, brother, uncle, or male priest, it becomes an urgent task to release women from such a loss of identity. It is through the reclaiming of our identity as Asian women who are different from each other, as Martha and Mary were different, that we can claim the right to be equal in all aspects of discipleship and the right to be equal partners within the community of faith.

References

Amjad Ali, Christine

1995 "Role Models for the New Community: Mary and Martha." Pp. 143–47 in *Affirming Difference, Celebrating Wholeness: A Partnership of Equals.* Ed. Ranjini Rebera. Hong Kong: Christian Conference of Asia.

Chung Sook Ja

1992 "Bible Study from the Perspective of Korean Feminist Theology." Ph.D. diss., San Francisco Theological Seminary.

1993 "Women's Discipleship for Partnership." *In God's Image* 12.1:18–20.

Gao Yin

1994 "Martha and Mary's Relationship with Jesus from a Feminist Perspective." *In God's Image* 13.1:60–63.

Rebera, Ranjini, ed.

1995b *Affirming Difference, Celebrating Wholeness: A Partnership of Equals.* Hong Kong: Christian Conference of Asia.

Roy, Manisha

1993 *Bengali Women.* Chicago: University of Chicago Press.

7

HAN-LADEN WOMEN

Korean "comfort women" and women in Judges 19–21

Yani Yoo

Source: *Semeia*, 78 (1997), 37–46.

I. Introduction

This essay concerns how a reader of the Bible can understand the issue of the so-called military comfort women (*Jongun Wianbu* or *Jungshindae* in Korean), a distorted term for Korean women who were forced to give sexual service to Japanese soldiers during the colonization of Korea by Japan (1910–1945). Approximately 200,000 Korean women, or 80% of the entire Asian "comfort women" population, were conscripted by deceit or abduction. This hard fact was concealed until the early 1990s. The issue was publicized through the efforts of many women and attained special attention at the women's conference of the United Nations in Beijing in 1995. The Beijing conference requested that the Japanese government fully compensate the victims.

The story in Judges 19–21 is the biblical text with which we can best make an analogy with the "comfort women" issue. While "comfort women" have the twentieth-century Asian setting, the biblical women are found in the eleventh-century BCE Canaanite setting. Many hermeneutical questions and suspicions arise. What relationship exists between the women in Judges 19–21 and "comfort women"? Why do we bring a contemporary reality to the Bible which was shaped as a religious canon a long time ago? What would the Bible say about the issue of "comfort women"? We do not intend to give answers to these questions, but to demonstrate how the "comfort women" story can be illuminated through the biblical story and vice versa. We will first deal with the issue of "comfort women" and analyze the biblical story in Judges 19–21. Then we will try to connect the feelings of these victimized women in terms of *han*, a Korean word for wounded heart, as a hermeneutical clue.

II. Confluence of "comfort women" and women in Judges 19–21

A. Korean "comfort women": historical overview[1]

According to Prof. Chung-Ok Yun, both Korean women and men had been used as a labor force by Japan since 1910 when Korea became its colony. In the early stage, Korean women went to Osaka, Japan, to work in the factories there. When they arrived they found out that in most cases their duty was to prostitute themselves for Korean men who were laborers. In this way, the women were forced into prostitution for Korean men at first and then to Japanese men later. The Sino-Japanese war in 1937 resulted in the conscription of 1,150,000 Korean men into forced labor and the Nanking rape of the same year caused the draft of 200,000 Korean women into systemized sexual slavery. In August 1944 Japan officially decreed "The Labor Decree of Women *Jungshin*" and justified "The Service Corps of Women Patriots" and "The Service Corps of Women Laborers," which had already existed.

As survivors testify, the women taken were placed in two categories. The first group of women were Labor *Jungshindae* who were not involved in forced sexual service and worked in munitions or textile factories in Taeku and Pusan in Korea, Shizuoka Numazu, and Matsubara Matsuzo in Japan. The second category concerns us. They were the military "comfort women" who were forced into sexual slavery in Teinchin, Manchuria, Peking, and Shanghai in China, La Paul Island, Singapore, the South Pacific Islands, Saipan Island, and in less well-known places.

Most "comfort women" were confined to small rooms about the size of a double bed and were not allowed to leave except for time for the basic needs. They were raped by dozens of soldiers every day of their confinement. If a woman escaped and was captured, she was brutally tortured. One victim still has a scar on her back from the torture of a hot iron.

As of January 1992, 181 witnesses reported to the Korean Council for the Women Drafted for Sexual Service by Japan: 94 Labor *Jungshindae*, 55 military "comfort women," and 32 unclassified. "Unclassified" comprises reports by the families, relatives, and neighbors of those who did not return.

Where, then, are the rest? First, the Japanese military eliminated evidence about military "comfort women" by shooting, burying alive, and abandoning these women in order to conceal what Japan did to them. Second, it is reported that many "comfort women" committed suicide. Some men witnesses who were returning from the draft in the same ship saw "comfort women" throw themselves into the sea even as the ship neared

Korea. Third, some women who could not return settled in foreign countries. Fourth, it is assumed that there must be many among survivors who remain unidentified. We need to point out that Korean patriarchal culture prompted the survivors to commit suicide, discouraged them from coming back to their home country, and made them remain silent over fifty years.

B. Women in Judges 19–21

The biblical story has been studied from many angles. Among others, Stuart Lasine's suggestion interests us: the narrative here intends to reveal the "ludicrous and topsy-turvy nature of the world" (37). But my thesis goes further: through the descriptions of an unnamed woman's gruesome death and the massacre of other women, the story invites the reader to witness and denounce the human evil against fellow human beings, especially women. Through a close reading of the narrative we will pursue this thesis.

Two scenes of hospitality are at work in chapter 19: the Levite's father-in-law's hospitality to the Levite at Bethlehem in Judah and then an old man's hospitality in Gibeah. In the first scene, three main characters are called the Levite/his son-in-law, his concubine[2]/young woman, and his father-in-law/her father or the young woman's father, respectively. Though at a glance these relational terms appear randomly, they are deliberately used to divide the characters into two parties: (1) the Levite and (2) his father-in-law and the woman. The "woman's father" is twice (19:4, 9) in apposition with "his father-in-law," emphasizing the existence of two invisible parties. The frequent occurrences of "her father's house" and "the young woman's father" indicate intimacy between the woman and her father. The Levite is isolated and weakened in the following ways and thus makes a weaker party.

First, the man does not belong to the place where he lodges now. The place is called "*her* father's house" (19:2, 3), not "*his* father-in-law's house." Second, the man is totally voiceless, in contrast to his talkative father-in-law. Third, he is controlled by the host, his father-in-law (Jones-Warsaw: 175, n. 2; Yee: 164). The host successfully makes him stay longer. Fourth, the Levite gets even with his concubine. During his stay at "her father's house," the narrator never calls him "the Levite" which indicates a higher social status, nor the woman "*his concubine.*" Only on the departure day, the expression "his concubine" reappears (19:9) and it functions as a literary device to foreshadow her powerless destiny.

If the father-in-law and his son-in-law are put in oppositional relationship, how should we understand the father-in-law's hospitality? The hospitality is extraordinarily bountiful and it looks to be intentional rather than simply customary. Although the two men eat and drink together at the same table, they seem to conceive different thoughts. While the Levite wants to go back to his house with his concubine, his father-in-law makes him stay longer. The father's good treatment of his son-in-law may be understood as a protective measure for his daughter,[3] reflecting the father's wish for his son-in-law: be nice to her. Though the space does not allow to introduce individual cases of "comfort women," when we remember them, the father's behavior here resembles Korean parents' desperate attempts to hide and save their daughters from being caught by the Japanese soldiers.

Tension and threat are escalating as the narrative unfolds. In the second hospitality scene, the Levite and his company are taken in by an old man at Gibeah. Their rest is interrupted by the men of the city who ask to bring out the Levite to have intercourse with him. The old man offers, "Here are my virgin daughter and his concubine. . . . Ravish them and do whatever you want to them. But against this man do not do such a vile thing" (Judg 19:23). When the mob would not listen to him the Levite turns over his concubine to them. At last, she is gang-raped by the mob through the night. Next morning the Levite finds her lying at the door of the house, with her hands on the threshold. The painful picture of her hands on the threshold invites the reader to witness the unspeakable violence against a powerless human being. Her body is dismembered into twelve pieces by her husband. As Phyllis Trible puts it, "Of all the characters in scripture, she is the least. . . . Captured, betrayed, raped, tortured, murdered, dismembered, and scattered —this woman is the most sinned against" (80–81).

Overwhelming violence does not stop there. The Israelite alliance asks the Benjaminites to hand over the men of Gibeah to put them to death. As the Benjaminites refuse, a war between the Benjaminites and the alliance breaks out. Chapter 20 describes the war in detail. The Benjaminites lose the war: all women are destroyed (cf. 21:16) and only 600 men survive. Chapter 21 concerns how to get wives for the 600 men. The alliance chooses to kill all the inhabitants of Jabesh-gilead except for 400 virgins. To get 200 more women, the alliance has the Benjaminite men kidnap young women at the Shiloh festival, just as the Levite handed his concubine over to the Benjaminites before in Gibeah. Trible (83) points out rightly that the rape of one woman became the mass rape of 600 and the concubine's incident is used to justify the expansion of violence against women.

The absurdities of the story are found in various ways. First, the characters are thoroughly nameless. In the Bible it is quite unusual for this kind of long narrative not to have a named character. Rather, only an insignificant figure, Phinehas, is named (20:28). Second, the actions of the characters are inconsistent, illogical, and anti-social. The Levite who comes to bring his concubine back and to "speak tenderly to the heart" (19:3) surrenders her to the mob and dismembers her body, and lies to the Israelite assembly about the incident. The old man in Gibeah offers to the mob not only his unmarried daughter, but also his guest's concubine without even consulting with him. The mob at first wants the Levite, but they end up raping the woman. The alliance is eagerly engaged in the war and seems to forget what originally mattered. Third, the subsequent stories are not closely related. The story line flows from the concubine's death to the actual war and to finding brides. At first, the brutal death of the concubine looks like a direct cause of the war. But as soon as the war begins, the incident is never again mentioned. In fact, at the end of the story in chapter 21 the conclusion of the war has nothing to do with the seemingly original cause of the war. That is, as chapters 19 and 20 are related, so chapters 20 and 21 are related, but chapters 19 and 21 are not related.

All these absurdities and ironies serve to signify the implied intention of the story, which condemns violence against women. Although the narrative includes male victims, it is more plausible to contend that the narrative primarily aims to stress victimization of women. The case becomes clearer when we consider the vivid and detailed description of the appalling death of the Levite's concubine.

How, then, does the biblical story illuminate the "comfort women" story and vice versa? The two stories expose a typical relationship between women and war. The following observations are discerned from the confluence of the two.

1. Women were nameless and thus demeaned. "Comfort women" lost their names from the moment of their being taken and were called by numbers like 1, 2, 3. They were sometimes called by an insulting nickname, *Sen-pee*; *Sen*, a derogatory name in Japanese for *Choson*, the former name for Korea, and *Pee*, probably hard pronunciation for "p" in "prostitution" in English. Not to mention the anonymity of the Benjaminite women, women of Jabesh-gilead, and women at the Shiloh festival, the namelessness of the Levite's wife, a main figure of the story, is a way of silencing and demeaning her.

2. Women were treated as "things" which have genitals. The Japanese arrested women who were not married. What most "comfort women" had to do was to "service" the Japanese soldiers until the women's sexual organs were swollen, torn and bleeding. In the treatment of women at Jabesh-gilead the yardstick for choosing women to keep alive or to kill was virginity. Those "women who have lain with men" were massacred. The other women were made brides of the Benjaminites.

3. Women were victims of state-organized rape and extravagant violence. The violence in both cases was systematic and collective. Although Japan insists that "comfort stations" were privately run, documents, witnesses, and ex-officers whose consciences are burdened keep coming up. In the biblical story, killing, kidnapping, and rape (through forced marriage) of women were ordered by the alliance. These state- and alliance-organized rapes constitute genocide. The massive rape of Korean women reveals Japanese intention of defiling Korean women and thus destroying their power to reproduce Korean children. The Israelite alliance destroyed the Benjaminite men, women, and children altogether except 600 men. The tribe was about to disappear. These are parallel examples of attempted genocide.

4. Women were victims of wars which were derived from tribal/national and male conflicts/interests. It is redundant to say the "comfort women" system was a result of wars which interested Japanese imperialists. In the biblical story the exact cause of the war was in question. At first, the abuse of the Levite's concubine looks like the direct cause of the war. But we need to note that the narrative reflects conflict among tribes in the formative period of early Israel.[4] Once the war broke out, neither the incident of the concubine was mentioned again, nor did the resolution or conclusion of the war have anything to do with her. Thus, the Levite's concubine was a victim of tribal conflicts which had already been going on.

5. Women were gifts and scapegoats. "Comfort women" were official gifts from the Japanese Emperor to "comfort" the soldiers who were "patriotically fighting for their country to liberate Asian peoples." "Comfort women" were on the list of military supplies and were shipped with the munitions. Similarly, the Levite handed over his concubine to the mob of the town to save himself. She was a dispensable commodity, used to solve an annoyance between males. Women of Jabesh-gilead and Shiloh can be considered as gifts to the Benjaminite soldiers although the narrative disguises this reality with the concern about the extinction of the tribe.

6. Victimized women were forgotten with no comfort. To the women who were used to "comfort" men or to resolve conflict between males there is no comfort. Far from apology and compensation from the Japanese government and understanding and support from Korean people, "comfort women" have been kept secret in modern history. The women in Judges 19–21 have been neglected in the long history of biblical interpretations and sermons. Only recently feminist scholars started giving new light to the story.

C. Han: a hermeneutical clue[5]

I believe that a Korean word, *han*, is the most appropriate psychological term to make a connection between "comfort women" and women in Judges 19–21. Although the Koreans commonly call themselves the people of *han*, it is *Minjung* theologians[6] in the 1970s that first utilized the term in theology. *Han* is understood as "the suppressed, amassed and condensed experience of oppression caused by mischief or misfortunes so that it forms a kind of 'lump' in one's spirit" (Suh: 65). Or, it is "a sense of unresolved resentment against injustice suffered, a sense of helplessness because of the overwhelming odds against, a feeling of total abandonment . . . , a feeling of acute pain and sorrow in one's guts and bowels making the whole body writhe and wiggle, and an obstinate urge to take 'revenge' and to right the wrong all these constitute."[7]

I venture to say that *han* represents almost exclusively women's feelings, even though the definitions of theologians and psychiatrists do not attribute a specific gender connotation to the term. While the term can still be applied to men, few idioms about *han* are related to them. There are expressions in

Korean like "a woman who has so much *han* inside," "*han* laden woman," and "if a woman conceives *han*, even in the midst of Summer it congeals to frost." There is no such saying about men's *han*.

What about, then, the *han* of comfort women and biblical women? "Comfort women" have been forced to be silent for fifty years. Several brave "comfort women" (they are now called "*Jungshindae* grandmas") started speaking out. Their first utterances were "we have so much *han* in our deepest hearts" and "we have lived lives which were filled with *han*."

Women in Judges 19–21 can also be called "women who have so much *han* inside." First, the unnamed woman in Judges 19 was a concubine, a secondary wife, who had limited rights (Steinberg: 15–17). Second, she was turned over by her husband to the gangs to be raped, an unbearable betrayal. The betrayal is shockingly intensified by the husband's cutting up of her body into twelve pieces. It means double contamination against her body and thus double *han*. Third, she was gang-raped through the night. In the patriarchal culture which teaches women to keep their chastity as their life, gang-rape denotes multiple killings over one woman. Fourth, she was never properly buried, nor consoled. As Korean folk tales tell, her soul would be restlessly wandering until it is consoled. Fifth, innumerable women in Judges 20 and 21 were targeted and destroy. All women of Jabesh-gilead except 400 women were murdered because of the fault of the men of their city (not attending the assembly). All the women who ever slept with men (the Bible does not say how it was figured out) were killed; the 400 women of Jabesh-gilead who never "knew" men were taken and became wives of strangers, that is, were raped; 200 young women at the Shiloh festival were also taken and raped. All these women have become souls who are wandering between the world beyond and this world with absolute despair and solitude until they are consoled.

The biblical women and "comfort women" are victims of imperialism, militarism, racism, and patriarchy. The biblical women truly are the "comfort women" who were kidnapped without having a clue what would happen to them and were humiliated in confined environments. Like present day "comfort women," the biblical women are our sisters who are still raped and battered today. As Trible (87) claims, "to take to heart this ancient story is to confess its present reality."

III. Conclusion: toward the resolution of *han*

The resolution of *han* depends on the consolation of the *han*-laden women. I believe that the task of *han*-resolution of the biblical women can only begin from our repentance for ignoring them, to new and more appropriate interpretations of their stories, as exemplified in the work of Trible and other feminist scholars, in new sermons, in specific rituals, and in ways which will become apparent.

The resolution of the *han* of "comfort women" can also begin from our repentance for neglecting them. War criminals must be found and punished. Although the Japanese government finally accepted their crime recently after its long denial, they still neglect the responsibility of compensation for the victims.

In the Fall of 1992, a twenty-six-year-old Korean woman named Kum-i Yun was murdered by an American soldier in a city of Korea. She was found dead in a room filled with much chemical detergent used as an attempt to conceal criminal evidence. She had been mutilated, a broken Coca-Cola bottle in her vagina, twelve inches of an umbrella stick in her anus, and bruises all over her body. What the Israelites shouted at the news of the dismembered concubine in the ancient day becomes our cry today: "Has this ever happened since the day the Israelites came up from the land of Egypt until this day?" (Judg 19:30). We say, "Yes, and it must stop!"

As long as women are being victimized like Ms. Yun, women of today cannot be satisfied by only reinterpreting the Bible, correcting the history, and receiving reparation. Although our repentance and attempt not to forget the past aim to let it happen never again, our enemy is much stronger than us. The deep-seated diseases like militarism, imperialism, and patriarchy are all over in the world and our sisters are still suffering from them. Our attempt to resolve *han* must continue and so must our fights to prevent all evil powers from causing *han.* The biblical story and the story of Korean "comfort women" compel us to work together with women around the world to end violence against women. Only then will the spirit of *han* recede from the world and the spirit of peace and justice prevail.

Notes

1 The historical overview on "comfort women" relies on *Jungshindae Issue Materials I* and *Jungshindae Issue Materials II* published by Korean Council for the Women Drafted for Sexual Service by Japan.

2 Mieke Bal insists that the term, *pilegesh*, should be translated as "wife" instead of its common translation, "concubine" (83–86). But we will use the term concubine because it is more fitting than 'wife' to the narrative mood and intention.

3 Jones-Warsaw (175) suggests that the father was probably seeking some assurances of his daughter's safety. Fewell and Gunn (133) wonder if the father intentionally delays his son-in-law because he was hesitant to send his daughter back to possible mistreatment.

4 Niditch (107) points out that the woman functions as a catalyst for war to solve conflicts between men.

5 For extensive studies on *han*, see Lee and Park.

6 *Minjung* theology of Korea is compatible with liberation theology of Latin America. Although *Minjung* theologians tend to avoid giving an exact definition of 'Minjung,' it roughly means 'mass of people in oppressive situation.'

7 This is Hyun Young Hak's definition and is requoted from Chung (42).

Works consulted

Bal, Mieke

1988 *Death & Dissymmetry: The Politics of Coherence in the Book of Judges.* Chicago: University of Chicago Press.

Chung, Hyun Kyung

1990 *Struggle to Be the Sun Again.* Maryknoll, NY: Orbis.

Fewell, Danna Nolan and David M. Gunn

1993 *Gender, Power, & Promise: The Subject of the Bible's First Story.* Nashville: Abingdon.

Jones-Warsaw, Koala

1993 "Toward a Womanist Hermeneutic: A Reading of Judges 19–21." Pp. 172–86 in *A Feminist Companion to Judges.* Ed. A. Brenner. Sheffield: Sheffield Academic.

Korean Council for the Women Drafted for Sexual Service by Japan

1992a *Jungshindae Issue Materials I.* Seoul.

1992b *Jungshindae Issue Materials II.* Seoul.

Lasine, Stuart

1984 "Guest and Host in Judges 19: Lot's Hospitality in an Inverted World." *JSOT* 29:37–59.

Lee, Jae Hoon

1994 *The Exploration of the Inner Wounds—Han.* Atlanta: Scholars.

Niditch, Susan

1993 *War in the Hebrew Bible: A Study in the Ethics of Violence.* New York: Oxford University Press.

Park, Andrew Sung

1993 *The Wounded Heart of God: The Asian Concept of Han and the Christian Doctrine of Sin.* Nashville: Abingdon.

Steinberg, Naomi

1993 *Kinship and Marriage in Genesis: A Household Economics Perspective.* Minneapolis: Fortress.

Suh, Nam Dong

1981 "Toward a Theology of Han." Pp. 51–66 in *Minjung Theology: People as the Subject of History.* Ed. Yong Bock Kim. Singapore: CTC-CCA.

Trible, Phyllis

1984 *Texts of Terror: Literary-Feminist Readings of Biblical Narratives.* Philadelphia: Fortress.

Yee, Gale A.

1995 "Ideological Criticism: Judges 17–21 and the Dismembered Body." Pp. 146–70 in *Judges and Method: New Approaches in Biblical Studies.* Ed. Gale A. Yee. Minneapolis: Fortress.

8

Excerpt from 'HERMENEUTICAL DRAMA ON THE COLONIAL STAGE

Liminal space and creativity in Colenso's *Commentary on Romans*'[1]

Jonathan A. Draper

Source: *Journal of Theology for Southern Africa*, 103 (1999), 13–32.

Missionaries, the Bible and colonial hegemony

It has become a commonplace of our modern African perspective that missionaries were the vanguard and agents of colonialism, knowingly or unknowingly. Unknowingly, by a species of false consciousness, because the gospel was embedded in an undifferentiated way in European culture so that it inculcated the hegemony of empire and because the missions stimulated a dependence on, and often supplied, European goods and services which created a capitalist economy with all that entailed in terms of labour and land. Knowingly, in their relationships with and dependence on the protection of the imperial authority, and often by advocating vociferously the extension of colonial administration over communities among whom they were working.

While there is no doubt that the missionaries played all these roles to a greater or lesser extent, it is also important to realize that the Africans themselves were not mere pawns in a game played by others, but were also agents in an ongoing process, knowingly or unknowingly. Unknowingly, because their acceptance or non-acceptance of the gospel was made in terms of their own implicit theologies and cultural categories, which constantly slipped through the fingers of their missionary mentors, and because their use of European goods and services was part of a complex web of intra-African relationships and goals. Knowingly, in that from the outset they injected aspects of resistance into the discourse with the missionaries and because their discourse and relationships were often conscious attempts to control and manipulate the new sources of power with which they were confronted. The modern liberation movements were the culmination of a long process of resistance and renewal.

In other words, the history of missions and of the reception of the Bible must be seen as a dialectical process, an unequal one in many respects to be sure, but nevertheless a more intricate, contested and mutual process than has usually been recognized. This has been aptly characterized by Jean and John Comaroff in their study of the mission among the Tswana people, which this paper explores, as a "long conversation":

> In the long conversation to which this gave rise—a conversation full of arguments of words and images—many of the signifiers of the colonizing culture became unfixed. They were seized by the Africans and, sometimes refashioned, put to symbolic and practical ends previously unforeseen, certainly unintended. Conversely, some of the ways of the Africans interpolated themselves, again detached and transformed, into the habitus of the missionaries. Here, then, was a process in which signifiers were set afloat, fought over, and recaptured on both sides of the colonial encounter.[2]

Bishop John William Colenso's *Commentary on St Paul's Epistle to the Romans newly translated and explained from a missionary point of view*, which was published at his mission station at Ekukhanyeni near Pietermaritzburg in 1861, is an illuminating early example of this conversation and will be the subject of this study. The book caused a storm of controversy and was the key evidence produced in his trial and delation as a heretic in 1863 by an ecclesiastical court convened by the Metropolitan of the Anglican Church in South Africa, Bishop Robert Gray in Cape Town. This commentary, together with his *Commentary on the Pentateuch* published in four volumes from 1862–1863, caused shock waves also in England and led to the convening of the first worldwide conference of the Anglican Church, the Lambeth Conference of 1868, which has since become a regular and central part of international Anglican identity.

Jean and John Comaroff develop a particularly helpful model of the relationship between *hegemony* as the power of the taken-for-granted world view which is shared by particular communities and controls human behaviour unseen, and *ideology* as the conscious and contested "effort to control the cultural terms in which the world is ordered and, within it, power legitimized"[3]. The relationship between hegemony and ideology is fluid, unstable and constantly shifting:

> Hegemony, we suggest, exists in reciprocal interdependence with ideology; it is that part of a dominant worldview which has been

naturalized and, having hidden itself in orthodoxy, no more appears as ideology at all. Inversely, the ideologies of the subordinate may give expression to discordant but hitherto voiceless experience of contradictions that a prevailing hegemony can no longer conceal.[4]

Most significantly, for our purposes, the Comaroffs argue that there is always a gap between hegemony and ideology, a liminal space, out of which forms of resistance and new consciousness may emerge:[5]

> Between the conscious and the unconscious lies the most critical domain of all for historical anthropology and especially for the analysis of colonialism and resistance. It is the realm of partial recognition, of inchoate awareness, of ambiguous perception, and, sometimes, of creative tension that liminal space of human experience in which people discern acts and facts but cannot or do not order them into narrative descriptions or even into articulate conceptions of the world: in which signs and events are observed, but in a hazy, translucent light; in which individuals or groups know that something is happening to them but find it difficult to put their fingers on quite what it is. It is from this realm, we suggest, that silent signifiers and unmarked practices may rise to the level of explicit consciousness, of ideological assertion, and become the subject of overt political and social contestation—or from which they may recede into the hegemonic, to languish there unremarked for the time being.[6]

The missionaries came from an England in accute intellectual and social crisis arising out of the related phenomena of the Enlightenment and industrial capitalism, so that the (contested) area of ideology was proportionately large in comparison with the (silent and uncontested) area of hegemony. The collision of their European culture with African culture thus provided a rich vein for potential exploration.

Colenso learnt Zulu by long and arduous conversations with Zulu converts at his mission, particularly William Ngidi, whom he characterizes as having "the reasoning powers of mature age".[7] He compiled a Zulu dictionary, a Zulu grammar and translated much of the Bible (including Romans), as well as many other secular works, into Zulu. His work on the Zulu language continues to be recognized by linguists in the field.[8] This Zulu conversation was not a superficial or one-sided exchange, but fundamentally challenged important aspects of the missionary's own received world view, as he wrote in *Romans*:

> Such questions as these have been brought again and again before my mind in the intimate converse which I have had, as a Missionary, with Christian converts and Heathens. To teach the truths of our

> holy religion to intelligent adult natives, who have the simplicity of children, but withal the earnestness and thoughtfulness of men,—to whom these things are new and startling, whose minds are not prepared by long familiarity to acquiesce in, if not to receive, them, —is a sifting process for the opinions of any teacher, who feels the deep moral obligation of answering truly, and faithfully, and unreservedly, his fellow-man, looking up to him for light and guidance, and asking, 'Are you sure of this?' 'Do you believe this?' 'Do you really believe that?'.[9]

Colenso highlights the same dilemma he faced in honest conversation with Ngidi in his *Commentary on the Pentateuch*:[10] "I dared not, as a servant of the God of Truth, urge my brother man to believe that, which I did not myself believe, which I knew to be untrue."[11]

For Colenso, crucial areas of British hegemony (what is "self-evidently true") were breaking down under the impact of the African experience, and this in the situation where important gaps in the ideology of post-Enlightenment, industrial Britain were emerging among the educated elite he represented. His *Commentary on Romans* is a valuable source of insight into the hermeneutical and cultural issues which came into play in this meeting of Africa and Europe, particularly since the nature and authority of the Bible was one of the focal points of conflict.

The Comaroffs suggest that both missionaries and the colonized Africans should be understood as actors in a two-sided drama, and that the context of both parties should be explored before any attempt is made to delineate their interaction. This is the procedure we shall follow here, albeit briefly.

Bishop John William Colenso (1814–1883)

The Nonconformist missionaries of the Comaroffs' study were largely drawn from upwardly mobile men from the newly industrialized areas, poorly educated and socially marginalized: "persons caught between the rich and the poor, either indeterminate in their class affiliation or struggling hard to make their way over the invisible boundary into the bourgeoisie".[12] They enacted their marginalization in the mission field by moving beyond the boundaries of colonial administration. They were subsequently caught between and manipulated by both the colonial authorities and by the African authorities. Their response to the Tswana people was pragmatic, reactive and unreflective, assuming that simply proclaiming the Word found in the Bible and teaching cleanliness and industry would evangelize the natives. Their assumption was that African languages were simple "folk languages" not difficult for advanced (European) people to grasp and utilize, so that their translations were "a hybrid creation born of the colonial encounter itself".[13] Colenso presents a profile with marked differences.

Much has been written about Colenso already,[14] and there is no need to elaborate overly here. Colenso was born into a lower middle-class family, his father being a civil servant of sorts (mineral agent for the Duchy of Cornwall) and owning an interest in a tin mine. By the time Colenso was sixteen, however, the flooding of the mine had led to a financial ruin of the family, his mother had died and he himself was forced to do menial work to help provide for his siblings. At this age he switched from the Nonconformism in which he was raised and chose to seek ordination in the state Church of England. Colenso went up to St. John's College, Cambridge, worked his way through his undergraduate years as a Clerical Sizar and was elected a Fellow of the College. His intellectual acumen and energy were quickly recognized, especially in Mathematics for which he wrote a well regarded series of school text books. The poverty of his own family led to an accumulation of debt, compounded by a disastrous fire to a property he had purchased. He fell in love with and married a woman from a respectable upper middle class London family and took a parish in order to enable himself to marry, according to the current practice. However, he was only able to marry because benefactors cleared his debt. Thus Colenso was upwardly mobile but socially and economically marginal to the upper middle class to which he now belonged.

His marriage, however, introduced him to a new intellectual circle in which the influence of the philosopher-poet Samuel Taylor Coleridge was strongly felt, as Colenso became personally acquainted to varying degrees with some of the most innovative thinkers of his age, in particular Frederick Denison Maurice (1805–1872, liberal theologian and Christian Socialist), Arthur Penrhyn Stanley (1815–1881, church historian at Oxford and Broad Churchman), Julius Charles Hare (1795–1855, liberal theologian and Broad Churchman), Thomas Carlyle (historian, moralist and philosopher), Charles Kingsley (1819–1875, novelist, theologian and Christian Socialist), and Benjamin Jowett (1817–1893, classicist and biblical commentator). His obvious abilities and growing circle of influential friends led to his nomination as Bishop of Natal, and he was consecrated in 1853.

F. D. Maurice was particularly influential on the young Colenso, with his denial of the doctrines of total depravity, a predestined saved elite and eternal punishment. His brand of Christian universalism emphasized the presence of God in all human beings and human community, God's work in nature and in history. Conversely, Maurice emphasized human solidarity and responsibility for the realization of the Kingdom of God on earth, which developed into his espousal of socialism.[15]

Colenso, like Maurice, emerged from Calvinist roots and he found these ideas liberative. He was to have a somewhat checkered relationship with this influential circle in England,[16] but it meant that he began his work in the mission field with an insecure but significant foothold in an elite which was constantly challenging the received ideas and practices of European society.

The ideas of geologist Sir Charles Lyell and scientists like Charles Darwin were familiar and much debated here, as were the challenges of German theologians and Biblical scholars.[17] Colenso himself not only read Lyell, who rejected the Biblical account of creation on the basis of the age of the earth, but summarized his ideas for his Zulu students in his *First lessons in science* published at Ekukhanyeni in 1861, at the very time he was working on *Romans*.

In the language of the Comaroffs, this circle with which Colenso felt affinity was engaged in bringing these matters out of the silence of hegemony into the contested field of ideological discourse. When Colenso, with his earnest and open study of Zulu language and custom, encountered the African world-view, this meant that he and his Zulu dialogue partners found themselves in the interstices between hegemonic silence and ideological repetitions in which "human beings often seek new ways to test out and give voice to their evolving perceptions of, and dispositions toward, the world".[18] It would be too much to claim that Colenso's *Epistle to the Romans* expresses an emerging implicit Zulu consciousness, and yet we may hear echoes of their questions and modes of resistance to missionary discourse in Colenso's answers in the contrapuntal way discussed by Edward Said.[19]

Zulu converts of Ekukhanyeni

The Nonconformist missionaries among the Tswana envisaged a complete separation of church and state, sacred and secular, which was embedded in the *laissez faire* capitalism of the era. They strove to convert individuals to a spiritual kingdom, while maintaining, even bolstering and protecting, the traditional 'secular' authority of the chiefs. Such a position conflicted with the holistic African world view, in which religion was embedded in society and the power of the chief was undergirded and proclaimed by his control over rain-making ceremonies. As a result, their early converts were themselves marginals and their conversion seemingly superficial.[20]

The difference between this scenario and Colenso's approach should not be exaggerated, yet it is important to note that Colenso began with the central concept of the universal brotherhood of man and Fatherhood of God (using the terminology of the time),[21] and within that the Christian family rather than the conversion of the individual. This is the origin of his opposition to breaking up polygamous marriages, which he stated already in his *Ten weeks in Natal* (1855), and on which he wrote an eloquent treatise.[22] He obtained the services of William Ngidi, a convert from the American mission, and spent more than two years becoming fluent in Zulu language and culture by constant conversation. His first and most important missionary venture was the establishment in 1856 of a Boy's Institution at his station at Ekukhanyeni, which was targetted at the sons of chiefs.

Among the many young Zulu men who were to play significant roles in later years in Zulu culture and resistance, was Mkhungo, son of King

Mpande by his favourite wife Monase and brother of Mbulazi. Mbulazi was the leader of the faction defeated by Cetshwayo, his half brother, and killed in the battle. Colenso took an active interest in the whole affair, visiting both Cetshwayo and Mpande at their respective kraals, and toyed with the idea of installing Mkhungo as king. In the end Colenso realized the danger and foolishness of such intervention and supported Cetshwayo and his successors.

Colenso not only spent endless hours translating and writing text books for his school and discussing them, but gave his pupils their own voices in his revolutionary publication in Zulu and English together of *Three native accounts of the visit of the Bishop of Natal in September and October, 1859, to Umpande, king of the Zulus.*[23] In other words, unlike the first Tswana converts, these Zulu converts were not social marginals. Indeed they continued to play important roles in Zulu society after the demise of the Boy's Institution itself. Magema Magwaza Fuze, son of Matomela chief of the Ngcobo people, was trained as a printing compositor. Fuze was the person who alerted Colenso to Shepstone's duplicity in the case of Langalibalele in 1874, and it is a tribute to their relationship that Colenso trusted him above Shepstone.[24] Fuze and Ngidi refused to be intimidated in the face of stiff interrogation by the magistrate hearing the affair, and signed as witnesses to a petition for clemency for Langalibalele.[25] The three repeated their work of legal defence of the rights of the Zulu against the colonial authorities in the case of Matshana in 1875.[26] Fuze proved well able to continue printing texts of the Bible on the press at Ekukhanyeni on his own, while Colenso was long absent in England, writing him letters to keep him informed of his work.[27] He was to write the first book in Zulu by a Zulu person, *Abantu Abamnyama lapa Bavela Ngakona.*[28] Ndiyane was the son of a headman from Maqonqo (Table Mountain) and became a teacher at the school in 1859 (leaving because of 'sexual misconduct' in 1861). William Ngidi of the Ntete had left Zululand in 1840 (after the Battle of Blood River and the murder of Dingaan), was baptized in 1855 by American Missionaries and played a key role in Colenso's mission. He was able to act as Colenso's trusted emissary and advisor in negotiations with both Cetshwayo and Mpande. He was a man of standing in Zulu society, whose father Mapepesi and lineage were well known to King Mpande as a valiant warrior, independently of Colenso. Indeed, the king related the story of the murder of Mapepesi as one of treachery and land theft, which he would have prevented if he had been there, though one must make allowances for rhetorical exaggeration.

Just as the Britain from which Bishop Colenso came was a society in crisis and in the throes of transition, so Zulu society was in a state of crisis and transition. The rule of Chaka had created a new Zulu hegemony over a part of the eastern seaboard of Southern Africa, which reached into the interior, creating considerable movement and dislocation of peoples.[29] [. . .] William Ngidi closes his account with a praise poem expressing something of the crisis:

> Yes, indeed, my brothers, the weapons of war should be beaten into ploughs for cultivating the ground, and war-shields be sewed into garments of clothing, and peace be proclaimed, on the north and on the south, and on both sides, through the Father of our Lord Jesus Christ, Unkulunkulu, who ever liveth, and all evil become peace, I mean become goodness.[30]

It is no accident that Colenso becomes preoccupied with the fate of the departed in his commentary, as we shall see. The role of kinship and the ancestors is a central question for Zulu society and the concept of eternal damnation of those ancestors who had never heard the gospel, or even who refused to hear it, would make Christianity incomprehensibly cruel. In a time when death was so omnipresent, this was no mere idle theological question. In Colenso's arguments in Western categories, we may hear the questions and problems of his African dialogue partners.

Colenso's Commentary on the Epistle to the Romans

Translation

Colenso's Romans is significant in a number of respects, but perhaps in none more than that he worked simultaneously with the Greek and Zulu text, even though he wrote in English. His translation of the text from Greek, which he provides in English, also served his translation of Romans into Zulu following his usual careful practice of detailed discussion with William Ngidi and others about both text and meaning.[31] His fluency in Greek from a sound Classical training at Cambridge allowed him conceptually to bypass his nineteenth century English Authorized Version conditioning and allowed new possible meanings to emerge, which might be more congenial to the Zulu environment in which he worked. Colenso frequently underpins his interpretation with reference to the meaning of a Greek word or its grammatical form or even to textual evidence. [. . .]

Context of the text

Colenso undertook his commentary fully aware of the new historical critical methodology emerging in Germany. One of the key hermeneutical moves Colenso makes is to see Romans as addressed to Jews and not Gentile Christians, i.e. there was no Christian church there separate from the synagogue and the Jewish believers held on to their former Jewish identity. This means that the purpose of the letter is to overcome Jewish prejudices against Gentiles and their own sense of superiority and privilege. In terms of its implications for his interpretation, Colenso identifies the Jewish believers to whom Paul was writing with the Christian British people of his own day. They were those who relied on their inherited possession of the faith and wished to exclude the heathen Zulu from eternal life and consign them to eternal damnation. They were the ones who wished to impose customs and laws other than the gospel as a condition of salvation, for example the terminating of their polygamous marriages and families before baptism. Their demand for the "faith" of an individualistic conversion experience as a legal requirement for salvation represented a new kind of works. On the other hand, the "Greeks" or Gentiles represent for Colenso the heathen Zulu among whom he was working. [. . .]

Outline of the commentary

Colenso identifies the "*key-words*" for interpreting Romans in 1:16: "for the power of God it [the Gospel of Christ] is unto salvation to every one that believeth, both to Jew first and Greek".[32] He sees this as addressing three Jewish prejudices: belief in favoured status and rights to enter the kingdom through race; refusal to accept the complete equality of the meanest Gentile, and a trust in the Law and rites and ceremonies. Since his hermeneutical key identifies Jew here as Briton and Greek as Zulu, the implication is that salvation is to everyone, both Briton first and Zulu, without any distinction of race or favour.

The qualification "to everyone that believeth" might seem to undermine this universality. Not so for Colenso, for God continues to reveal himself, not just in the Bible but also in reason and experience, so that the heathen Zulu continually experiences both the grace and the wrath of God in the same way the English person does. This comes to the level of conscious enjoyment with conversion to Christianity, but is not confined to the "saved". He is able to point to the sense of the present passive verb *apokaluptetai* found parallel in 1:17 and 18, rejecting the Authorized Version's "is revealed", which implies a completed act, for "is being revealed", which implies a continuing process.[33] In this rendering he is quite justified, since the present tense normally presents an action going on at the time of writing.

The implications of this bold statement are drawn in 1:20. Since God is revealed in nature, all human beings have a duty to fear, love, trust and obey God; but while all are therefore without excuse as a general rule, this does not apply to every individual concretely in the same way. Children, imbeciles and heathen could not with justice be abandoned to eternal punishment by God for what they could not know. People can only be judged on the basis of their own behaviour, inasmuch as they did or did not respond to the Light in the measure it was revealed to them. Many Christians are put to shame in their behaviour by the heathen:

> Probably their worst sins of murder and uncleanness are not more essentially abominable in God's sight than the slanderous talk, and

> malicious acts, and dishonest practices, and self-indulgent, selfish lives, of many Christians, whom He alone can judge, who knows the secrets of all hearts, and the share of His goods committed unto each-and not we.[34]

There is a difference between wilful sin and ignorance and we are not authorized to judge between them. Zulu people are capable of great virtue: brave, kind, just and generous; they are also capable of killing others on suspicion of being *umtakati.* But then English people burnt witches in sincere belief that they were doing God's will. So a Zulu chief who abuses his cultural power for his own ends for vengeance or greed, is in a different position from one who obeys Zulu custom in the belief that s/he is doing good. We do not suffer for Adam's sin but for our own: "But the Apostle teaches, what the Bible everywhere teaches, and our own hearts teach also, that the essence of moral guilt consists in the commission of acts of *conscious wilful sin,* whether sin of negligence or sin of presumption".[35]

This being the case, Britons have no right to pronounce on the moral guilt or otherwise of the heathen any more than on the Jew. Indeed, Colenso regards the Zulu as alienated descendants of Abraham who have gradually sunk into ignorance from their ancestry as sons/grandsons of Abraham through Esau or Ishmael.[36] Yet they still are monotheists like these Semitic ancestors, he argues, and correctly so it seems, though there are some ambiguities.[37]

Just as the Jews were entrusted with the Law and the prophets, but were unfaithful, so Christians today were entrusted with the Old and New Testaments and the sacraments. This is their only advantage, not in some exclusive possession of salvation, as Colenso comments on 3:2:

> All his [Paul's] language may be well applied to those unfaithful Christians, who bring dishonour on the Name of God among the heathen in the present day, and whom the heathen himself, though unbaptised, and ignorant of the name of Christ and the letter of Christianity, yet keeping the law of truth and right, according to his light, shall one day judge. For instance, it might be asked, 'If you say the heathen may be saved without the knowledge of the Gospel, what advantage, then, hath the Christian, or what profit is there in Christian Baptism?' And a similar answer might be given: 'Much, in every way: in the very first place, because to them are entrusted the Holy Scriptures, the books of the New Testament as well as the Old?' And to this we might go on to add, 'To them are given the means of grace, and the hope of glory.'[38]

Here again, the Jews of the Epistle become the British of Colenso's *Romans.* This raises the question of the nature of sin: surely the heathen are under original sin, having inherited the Fall of Adam, whereas the British can claim through baptism to have been redeemed from sin (implicitly from birth, since the British are baptized as babies!). Not so says Colenso. Paul does not say, "For all have sinned, and come short of the glory of God" as the Authorized Version translates it. Instead, the aorist (hēmarton) implies a single completed individual act and is best translated by the English present, "For all sin, and come short of the glory of God".[39] Sin is not inherited but is a matter of individual human responsibility, a product of human fallibility by which all indeed do sin. According to 3:21–26, God's dealing with Israel was intended to put right this situation, as the Law and prophets indicate, but this was misunderstood. Now, however, the work of Christ has made all human beings righteous, without any distinctions at all:

> But now it is revealed that this gift of righteousness is meant for all, that all are being made righteous, (the Greek present, implying their continuing state of righteousness), all men everywhere, though many more may not yet have heard them, and so may have little or no present enjoyment of their Father's Love.

The Apostle's words in this verse most probably mean this, because he afterwards (v.15–19) fully and explicitly states that the justification spoken of here extends to *all*, to those who have never heard the name of Christ, and who cannot have exercised a living faith in Christ, as well as to Christians. It is *certain* that, in this latter passage, he is speaking of the whole human race.

And even in heathen men, who have never heard the Gospel, and cannot "believe" in the full sense of the word, there is a faith in the Living Word, which speaks within them, there is a living obedience to the law of truth and love, which they find written upon their hearts by the finger of God, which is akin to the true living faith of a Christian, and to which is granted a kindred feeling, a measure of enjoyment, even in this life, of the gift of righteousness, a sense of gladness and freedom in the consciousness of at-one-ment with the Right and the True, a share of the Peace of God's children, "which passes all understanding".[40]

This universal and objective atonement achieved by Christ is experienced in an attenuated way by those who have never heard the Gospel by their experience of nature and its bounty. Nevertheless, only Christians are able to know the "shewing forth of (*endeixin*, not 'declare' as in the AV) His righteousness" (3:24) fully and explicitly through faith in Christ, which is God's purpose and not some kind of punitive retribution exacted from the human Jesus as a punishment for Adam.

Human culpability is limited by the extent of their knowledge of what they are doing, so that heathen cannot be held to break the Law until they know it and understand it, and however we find Zulu customs, they are not culpable until they truly know the alternative way (4:15):

> And so, too, among the ignorant heathen, many things are practised, which, however offensive in the eyes of a white man and a Christian, are not transgressions of God's known Law, and are not reckoned as sins in the sight of Him, who searcheth the hearts and judgeth righteously the children of men, until that Law is brought home to them, brought home to their hearts and consciences by the teaching of His own Good Spirit, not merely reiterated in their ears, with the voice of authority, by the lips of a Missionary, laying down the law to them, often with most obscure and defective utterance, in some difficult native tongue, upon matters of the deepest personal and social interest. Among the reproofs that will be passed 'in that day,' are there none that will justly belong to us, Christians and Missionaries, for the harsh, uncharitable, judgments, which we have passed in our arrogant self-confidence upon our heathen fellow-men?[41]

Thus Colenso interprets "Made righteous then out of faith, we have peace with God through our Lord Jesus Christ" (5:1) to refer to the objective existence of the gift of salvation for all. Any insistence on prior belief for it to become effective is instituting a new form of works. The sin of Adam could not have led, in a literal way, to the origin of organic death in the species, since scientific discoveries, and especially geology, show that death existed in the world before the origin of the species. Paul may or may not have believed in this primitive myth, but we have no right to expect him to know our modern scientific data or to have any insight impossible in his day. In any case, the Bible is not infallible as Word in this sense, but is a vehicle for the Word:

> It is possible that St. Paul entertained this notion himself, namely, of *all* death having come into the world by sin. For we have no reason to expect scientific knowledge of any kind, beyond that of the people of his age, in a Scripture writer. It is not in this way, by securing an historian, or prophet, or evangelist, or apostle, from all errors of detail in matters either of science or of fact, that the power of the Divine Spirit is exhibited in Scripture. The 'spirit and the life,' which breathes throughout the Holy Book, that which speaks to the heart, and touches the main springs of being in a man, that which teaches him what is pure and true and loving, and gives him living bread to feed upon in the secrets of his own spiritual consciousness, this is the work of God's Spirit, these are the 'words which the Holy Ghost teacheth,' not a mere historical narrative, or a table of genealogies, or a statement of scientific facts, cosmological, geological, astronomical, or any other, in all which matters the books of the Holy Scriptures must be tested by the ordinary rules, which critical sagacity would apply to any other human compositions.[42]

The language of death and life, sin and justification, must be taken as figurative and not literal.

From 5:15 Colenso is now able to draw the logical conclusion that since, *all* in "as in Adam all died" clearly refers to all human beings regardless, then *all* in "so also in Christ shall all be made alive" also refers to all human beings regardless. This salvation is objectively achieved for all as a free gift, whether a human being knows it or not. But this objective salvation of all human beings needs to be experienced subjectively for its full benefit to be realized, even if this is not in the conventional Christian manner:

> Whenever the 'unrighteousness' of any Jew, Christian, or Heathen, 'is forgiven, and his sin covered,' whenever he feels any measure of the peace of God's children, in the faithful discharge of any duty, or in forsaking any path of evil,—whenever there is brought home to his heart in any way the message of God's Fatherly Love by means of any one of Earth's ten thousand voices,—then he hears, as it were, a fresh declaration of righteousness, he may know that he is recognised again as a child of God's House.[43]

This experience is what Paul calls new life, as all share in the life of the Body of Christ. This is how Colenso interprets Paul's reference to baptism in Romans 6. The signs of this new life are objectively displayed in the sacraments of Eucharist and baptism, which do not depend on the subjective state in which we come to them. They are signs not only to believers but to all human beings, whether they know they are benefiting or not. This has been called very subjective, but in reality it is the reverse. Colenso could rejoice in taking a service in the Zulu liturgy he had translated already by 1856 among the bones of the "Bloody way" north of the Tugela,[44] or at the royal kraal of Mpande where his young men officiated, "our dear boys have been the first to publish the Word of Life among the Zulus".[45] The sign is effective corporately rather than individually; it is not dependent on understanding or participation to be experienced as a reassurance and blessing.[46]

Colenso comes now to the well known anthropological passage in Romans 7:21: "I find the law to me, willing to do what is beautiful, that evil is present to me." The Zulu, just like Jew and Christian, has a struggle between good and evil in his/her life:

> And if, in spite of this, the pious heathen has given his heart to do the good, and refused to do the evil, it was only because he had a strength supplied to him, from a source which he knew not. In his flesh, indeed, though he knew it not, there was no good thing; but in his Lord, unknown, perhaps by Name to him as yet, but by whom he was known, there was Life from which the life of his spirit came.[47]

This double nature of man is known in Zulu cultures, so that there is no essential anthropological difference between the Zulu person and the European person. This is critical because a number of anthropologists were openly questioning whether missions to the heathen were desirable or even possible, since these indigenous people were innately inferior products of evolution who would gradually die out in the face of the more advanced civilizations. Colenso faced this very question in his Lecture to the Marylebone Literary Society in 1865.[48] In his dialogue with his Zulu converts, Colenso had found that Zulu people have a strongly developed conscience, which for him was evidence of the presence of the divine Spirit in them, the "higher powers which raise us above the mere brute animal".[49] Outward differences of race and colour mean nothing if the Zulu person manifests the two essential human characteristics, namely reason and human affection.

This ethical sense is expressed particularly in the concept of *uNembeza*, which Colenso makes the focal point of his recognition of the objective redeeming work of Christ among the heathen:

> Among the Zulus there is a distinct recognition of the double nature of man. They speak of the *uGovana*, which prompts him to steal and lie, commit murder and adultery, and the *uNembeza*, which 'bids him,' as a native would say, 'leave all that.'[50]

This is nothing less than the divine Spirit of Romans 8:16, which is present in all human beings who do not quench it by evil doing. Indeed, the "Sons of God" of 8:19 refers to the whole human race, all of whom are groaning for liberation and will indeed all eventually be liberated to eternal life.[51] Colenso correctly identified *uNembeza* as the central moral principal of Zulu culture. It is related to the legitimate anger derived from *uMvelingqangi* aimed at "sustaining order and a good life," and so motivates ethical conduct, whereas *uGovana* refers to destructive immoral anger which leads to wrongdoing.[52] Colenso held onto this Zulu understanding vigorously, both in his preaching to the heathen, whom he enjoined to follow the *uNembeza* within them,[53] and in his defence of the human dignity, equality and rights of the Zulu people before European racists who would deny it.[54]

In the light of the objective nature of the atonement wrought by Christ and in the light of the nature of the moral struggle experienced by all human beings, Christian or heathen, Colenso is led to interpret the "groaning" of "all the creature" as it waits for the "freedom of the glory of the children of God" as a denial of endless punishment. We have already seen that this may be in part attributed to the questions posed by his Zulu converts concerning the position of the *amaDlozi* (living dead or ancestors). However, it also represents a final adoption of the position advocated by F. D. Maurice, which he had equivocated about earlier. The confrontation with Zulu culture impacted at a point where the cultural hegemony of his own society had emerged into the sphere of contestation. This produced the "liminal space" which calls forth some of the most sustained argumentation in his whole commentary.[55] It also pushes him to question the authority of the very text he is interpreting and in doing so clarifies for him what is most fundamental to his humanity, namely reason and conscience/love:

> Whatever contradicts that Law, whether it be the word of man, or the dictum of a Church, or the supposed teaching of Holy Scripture, cannot, ought not to, be a Law for him. . . . But no seeming authority of the Church or Scripture ought to persuade a man to believe anything, which contradicts that moral law, that sense of righteousness, and purity, and truth, and love, which God's own finger has written upon his heart. The voice of that inner witness is closer to him than any that can reach him from without, and ought to reign supreme in his whole being. The Light, in which he there sees light, the Voice which he hears, is the Light of the Divine Word, is the Voice of his Lord. We may be certain, then, that any interpretation of Scripture, which contradicts that sense of right which God Himself, our Father, has given us, to be a witness for His own perfect excellencies, must be set aside, as having no right to crush down, as with an iron heel, into silence the indignant remonstrance of our whole spiritual being.[56]

Endless punishment is immoral and incompatible with Divine goodness and is ruled out, especially since it would allow special privilege to the Briton and a cruel injustice to the Zulu who have never heard the gospel.

> And it is often so stated as to involve the multitudes of ignorant, untaught, heathen, the great mass of humankind, in the same horrible doom of never-ending despair, making this beautiful and blessed world the very shambles, as it were, of Almighty Vengeance, while some few individuals, called by the name of Christians, but living comfortably all the while, notwithstanding their professed belief that myriads of their fellow men are, every moment, passing into perdition, will, by some special act of Divine favour, be so fortunate as to be excepted from it. I need hardly say that the whole Epistle to the Romans is one of the strongest possible protests against such a notion.[57]

Instead, Colenso takes Paul's words in 8:28 to apply generally to humanity, "all things work together for good, being called according to a purpose" Salvation cannot depend "idly" on the accident of birth.[58]

With regard to Romans 9–11, Colenso perceptively describes it as "the language of prophecy", by which he means that it should be taken figuratively and not literally.[59] There is actually no favouritism in God's judgment for anyone. In accordance with his hermeneutical key, he points to the applicability of the disobedience of Israel to the behaviour of the British:

> All will be judged according to their works, and according to the Light vouchsafed to them. With reference to the Light, which we, Christians of England, have received, it might be said, in like manner, 'England has God loved, and Africa has He hated.' Yet not all English Christians are children of the Light, nor are all African heathens children of Satan, but those, who have received most, shall have most required of them.[60] [. . .]

Conclusion

Colenso set out on his missionary task convinced of the duty of the "enlightened Briton" and the benefits of "her standard of victory waving in triumph on many a shore";[61] indeed his first enthusiastic friendship in the Colony was with that unscrupulous agent of empire, Theophilus Shepstone, but he ended up isolated and ridiculed by his countrymen and in a somewhat "treasonous" alliance with the exiled Cetshwayo against the machinations of both empire and the wily Shepstone.[62] His Commentary on Romans provides a fascinating insight into the beginning of the "long conversation" between British missionaries and Zulu converts, which fundamentally altered the consciousness of both parties.

Colenso can be seen at one level as a representative of the emerging Enlightenment Biblical hermeneutics beginning to affect Britain from Germany. Yet this could not explain the storm which greeted his work, which many even more radical critics escaped. It was his status as a Colonial Bishop, with all that entailed in terms of legitimating empire both by the silence of European hegemony and the discourse of imperial ideology, which made his "defection" so unforgivable. [. . .]

Notes

1 *Bishop John William Colenso, Commentary on Romans.* New Ed with commentary, J. A. Draper, Pietermaritzburg: Cluster, 2003.

2 Jean Comaroff and John *Of revelation and revolution*, vol. 1 *Christianity colonialism and consciousness in South Africa* (Chicago: University of Chicago Press, 1991) 17–18.

3 Comaroff & Comaroff, *Of revelation and revolution*, 24.

4 Comaroff & Comaroff, *Of revelation and revolution*, 25.

5 This liminal space seems akin to what Victor Turner finds in the ritual process and calls "anti-structure", open to experimentation, creativity and play. Perhaps one might also note that Turner sees in this liminal space the potential for the emergence of what he calls *communitas*, a discovery of that fundamental human community or ubuntu, which is usually controlled or suppressed by social

structures. See Victor Turner, *The ritual process structure and anti-structure* (Ithaca: Cornell University Press, 1969) 94–165. Here indeed there may have been the possibility for a genuine discovery of their mutual otherness and possible community by missionary and convert.

6 Comaroff & Comaroff, *Of revelation and revolution*, 29.

7 John William Colenso, *The Pentateuch and Book of Joshua critically examined* (London, 1862–1963) viii.

8 C. M. Doke, "Bantu language pioneers of the Nineteenth Century", *Bantu Studies* 14 (1940) 234–235, C. M. Doke and D. T. Cole, *Contributions to the history of bantu linguistics* (Johannesburg, 1961) 45, cf. J. Guy, *The heretic a study of the life of John William Colenso 1814–1883* (Pietermaritzburg: University of Natal Press, 1983) 65–67.

9 John William Colenso, *St. Paul's Epistle to the Romans newly translated and explained from a missionary point of view* (Ekukhanyeni: Mission Press, 1861) 199.

10 John William Colenso, *The Pentateuch and Book of Joshua*, vi–viii.

11 The questions themselves represent the injection of resistance generated in the "hidden transcript" of the colonized into the "official transcript" of the missionary, in the terminology of James Scott, *Domination and the arts of resistance hidden transcripts* (New Haven: Yale University Press, 1990).

12 Comaroff & Comaroff. *Of revelation and revolution*, 85.

13 Comaroff & Comaroff, *Of revelation and revolution*, 218.

14 G. W. Cox, *The life of John William Colenso, D. D. Bishop of Natal* (London, 1888); B. B. Burnett, "The mission work of the first Anglican Bishop of Natal, the Rt. Reverend J. W. Colenso, between 1852–1873". Unpublished MA Dissertation, Rhodes University, 1947, A. O. J. Cockshutt, *Anglican attitudes* (London, 1959), P. Hinchliff, *John William Colenso, Bishop of Natal* (London: Nelson, 1964), G. W. Warwick, "The contribution of Bishop Colenso to Biblical criticism", Unpublished MA Thesis of the University of Natal, Pietermaritzburg, 1966.

15 Cf. Hinchliff, *John William Colenso*, 32–42, Guy, *The heretic*, 24–30.

16 He came close to espousing Maurice's rejection of damnation in his *Village sermons* of 1854, but retreated in the face of public criticism. Maurice, in his turn, was to publicly condemn Colenso for his radical universalism and critical Biblical scholarship. At a meeting of the two in 1862, Maurice admonished Colenso to retract his books and resign his see Guy, *The heretic*, 116–117.

17 A. R. Vidler, *The church in an age of revolution*, 2nd ed (Harmondsworth: Penguin, 1971) 112–133.

18 Comaroff & Comaroff, *Of revelation and revolution*, 30.

19 Edward W. Said, *Culture and imperialism* (London: Vintage, 1994). Impressively documented by Hlonipha Mokoena, D. Phil, Cape Town 2005. See also P. la Hausse de Lalouviere, 2000.

20 Comaroff & Comaroff, *Of revelation and revolution*, 252–255.

21 Colenso, *St. Paul's Epistle to the Romans*, 74, *Bringing forth light five tracts on Bishop Colenso's Zulu mission*, ed. R. Edgecombe, Killie Campbell Africana Library Reprint Series 4 (Pietermaritzburg: University of Natal Press, 1982) 213.

22 Colenso, *Ten Weeks in Natal* (London: Macmillan, 1855).

23 Magema Fuze, Ndiyane Magwaza and William Ngidi, *Three native accounts of the visit of the Bishop of Natal in September and October, 1859, to Umpande, King of the Zulus, with explanatory notes and a literal translation, and a glossary of all the Zulu words employed in the same designed for the use of students of the Zulu language* (Ekukhanyeni: Mission Press, 1860) 163–195. The English translation is reprinted (with notes by R. Edgecombe) in Colenso, *Bringing forth light*, 161–203.

24 Guy, *The heretic*, 207–208.
25 Guy, *The heretic*, 210–211.
26 Guy, *The heretic*, 244–245.
27 Colenso, *Bringing forth light*, 225–227.
28 Published in 1922, also translated into English as *The black people and whence they came* in 1979.
29 The origins and character of the *mfecane/difaqane* is a matter of some dispute, but most historians acknowledge some connection of this phenomenon with the rise of the Zulu kingdom.
30 Berglund, *Zulu thought-patterns*, 193.
31 Colenso, *Bringing forth light*, 228.
32 Colenso, *St. Paul's Epistle to the Romans*, 9. The translation cited is Colenso's, unless otherwise stated.
33 Colenso, *St. Paul's Epistle to the Romans*, 14–15, 17–19.
34 Colenso, *St. Paul's Epistle to the Romans*, 24.
35 Colenso, *St. Paul's Epistle to the Romans*, 28–32, esp. 31.
36 Colenso, *St. Paul's Epistle to the Romans*, 34–35, cf. 215. The exact origin of this hypothesis I have failed to ascertain.
37 Berglund, *Zulu thought-patterns*, 43, points out that there is a distinction between *ukukhonza* (worship proper), which is due only to *uMvelingqangi*, and *ukuthetha* (reverence), which is due to the *amadlozi* (shades) in ritual celebrations. However, there are ambiguities, relating to *iNkosikazi yaseZulwini* (the Heavenly Queen) and perhaps also *Nomkhubulwana* (the Maiden) if she is a separate entity. Cf. Berglund, *Zulu thought-patterns*, 63–74.
38 Colenso, St. Paul's Epistle, 53.
39 Colenso, St. Paul's Epistle, 61–62.
40 Berglund, *Zulu thought-patterns*, 62–64.
41 Colenso, St. Paul's Epistle, 84.
42 Colenso, St. Paul's Epistle, 99–100.
43 Colenso, St. Paul's Epistle, 103.
44 Colenso, *Bringing forth light*, 67.
45 Colenso, *Bringing forth light*, 109.
46 Colenso, *St. Paul's Epistle to the Romans*, 115–9.
47 Colenso, *St. Paul's Epistle to the Romans*, 152.
48 Colenso, *Bringing forth light*, 205–206.
49 Colenso, *Bringing forth light*, 210.
50 Colenso, *St. Paul's Epistle to the Romans*, 156.
51 Colenso, *St. Paul's Epistle to the Romans*, 173.
52 Berglund, *Zulu thought-patterns*, 255–256.
53 Colenso, *Bringing forth light*, 86.
54 Colenso, *Bringing forth light*, 215–221.
55 Colenso, *Bringing forth light*, 215–221.
56 Colenso, *Bringing forth light*, 175–201.
57 Colenso, *Bringing forth light*, 190–191.
58 Colenso, *Bringing forth light*, 207.
59 Colenso, *Bringing forth light*, 215.
60 Colenso, *Bringing forth light*, 215.
61 R. Edgecombe, "Introduction", *Bringing forth light*, xiv.
62 Guy, *The heretic*, 332–349.

9

CHALLENGING THE CHRISTIAN MONOPOLY ON THE BIBLE

An aspect of the encounter between Christianity and Malegasy traditional religion in contemporary Madagascar

Georges Razafindrakoto and Knut Holter

Source: K. Koschorke and J. H. Schørring (eds), *African Identities and World Christianity in the Twentieth Century: Proceedings of the Third International Munich-Freising Conference on the History of Christianity in the Non-Western World* (September 15–17, 2004), Wiesbaden: Harrassowite Verlag, 2005, pp. 141–8.

Introduction

It is often recognised that the Bible plays a central role in the Western mission movement of the last couple of centuries. One thing is that the movement grew out of a new interpretation of the Bible,[1] another that wherever the missionaries came, they considered it important to translate the Bible, so that the word of God could be read and heard in the vernacular languages.

Traditionally, the interpretation of the Bible and the definition of its proper use in church and society was a monopoly of the church establishment. The Western missionaries, of course, had the educational and institutional power of defining how the Bible should be used and read. And soon their models of handling the Bible were to be echoed by local church leaderships. Nevertheless, the Bible was eventually also to be used and read outside the control of the church establishment. The mission policy of establishing schools and making bibles available in vernacular languages inevitably lead to a gradual democratisation of the power of handling the Bible.

This phenomenon can not least be observed in Africa. One thing, and well known, is the role of the interpretation of the Bible – for example with regard to the question of polygamy or the relationship to traditional religious rituals[2] – in the rapid growth of the so-called African Initiated Churches.[3] Another thing, and less known, but not less interesting, is the role of the interpretation of the Bible within segments of more traditional African religion. In the interface between Christianity and African traditional religion, aspects of influence obviously have been going in both directions, and scholars today are increasingly acknowledging that the reception of the Bible in Africa is not necessarily linked to a reception of Christianity as such.[4]

This interface between Christianity and African traditional religion is not only something of the past. It is an ongoing process, whose many facets – such as for example the role of the Bible – can still be seen and analysed. This article will exemplify this process, by discussing how and why the Bible – eventually and perhaps even surprisingly – is being used amongst some Merina traditionalists in Madagascar. The article is based on field research made by Georges Razafindrakoto in 2001, for a M.Phil. thesis supervised by Prof Knut Holter.[5] A total number of 21 traditionalists were interviewed; 10 traditio-practitioners (cultic leaders) and 11 followers (members of a cultic group), belonging to eight geographical contexts within the traditional heartland of the Merina in Madagascar. The practices and interpretations offered by these traditionalists can obviously not be considered representative of Merina traditionalism as such. Still, the glimpses that are to be presented in this article may serve to illustrate the process of interaction between Christianity and Merina traditional religion.

The article will first, very briefly, survey the religious context – in Merina – of the use of the Bible outside the realms of the church. Then, the use of the Bible is seen from two perspectives; first a presentational "how", and then a more critical "why". Finally follows a brief word of conclusion.

Religious context: Merina traditional religion versus Christianity

Madagascar is often called a continent in miniature.[6] Geographically the island belongs to Africa, whereas it demographically forms a bridge between Africa and Asia. Madagascar has more or less eighteen ethnic groups, whose backgrounds can be traced partly to the African continent, but partly also to Southeast Asia. Central, in many aspects of the word, is the Merina ethnic group, whose ancestors came from Indonesia, probably in the seventh century C.E, and who now inhabits the central plateau of the island.[7]

The traditional religion of the Merina is centred around the creator god – Zanahary ("the one who created", also called Andriamanitra ("the fragrant king") – and the ancestors. Zanahary cannot be approached directly, and the position between god and followers is therefore occupied by the ancestors.[8] The relationship with the ancestors is especially expressed in certain burial rites, and the ancestors are called upon as intermediary agents, conveying human requests to Zanahary and relaying his response back.

Merina traditional religion is kept up by cultic leaders – men and women – who act on behalf of a community or a group of followers. In the following these leaders are called "traditio-practitioners" rather than priests, as their responsibilities include a broader spectrum of functions, such as priest, diviner, healer, seer, and astrologer.

The first Protestant missionaries – British with a Reformed background – came to Madagascar in 1818. Later on, Norwegian Lutherans and French Catholics made important contributions to the christianisation of the island, and then not least of the Merina. Today around half of the Malagasy population belong to a Christian church, and the percentage is considerably higher in the traditional heartland of the Merina.[9] An important exponent of the strong church growth are the various revival movements, which especially are found within the Protestant churches.

The relationship between the Christian churches and traditional religion has been – at least on a surface level – rather hostile. Church leaders have warned against paganism and syncretism, and traditionalists have warned against the religion of the foreigners, neglecting traditions and ancestors. Below this surface level, however, there are obvious aspects of interaction. Merina traditional religion is increasingly open to aspects of Christianity, and Malagasy Christianity – both Protestant (e.g. aspects of its revival movements) and Roman Catholic (e.g. aspects of its christianisation of traditional burial rites) – shows signs of being influenced by traditional religion.

Bible translation was considered an urgent task for the early British missionaries, and a complete Bible was published as early as in 1835.[10] The missionaries were actually asked by King Radama I (1810–1828) to develop a written language, and the Bible was the first book to be published in Madagascar. Even today, the Bible remains the most popular book in Madagascar, amongst Christians, for obvious reasons, but also amongst some Merina traditionalists. And it is this latter group and their use of the Bible which will be discussed in the following pages.

How is the Bible used?

In an article attempting to map African biblical interpretation, Gerald O. West distinguishes between an *open* Bible, that is the Bible interpreted as a text, and a *closed* Bible, that is the Bible interpreted as a sacred object.[11] This distinction is helpful also with regard to Merina traditio-practitioners' use of the Bible.

The Bible as a closed book

The expression "closed book" is used to describe the phenomenon that the Bible may be used as a magical item. In this case it is the Bible as a book, and not some particular biblical text, which is considered important. The

Bible is here taken as a sacred object, and as such it is an instrument of power, which may be used for various purposes.

One example illustrates how the Bible may be used for cultic purification. Cultic purity holds an essential place in traditional Merina religion, as Zanahary as well as the ancestral spirits are holy. Accordingly, all utensils used for cultic activity – such as candles, incense, holy water in containers, horns for charms, bottles for traditional medicine, plates and bowls for blood from sacrifice, etc. – are to be purified daily. An informant (follower) describes how this is done in traditional contexts. The traditio-practitioner first washes her hands with water and soap, then she says a prayer and carefully washes each of the utensils, and finally she sprinkles it all, saying *masina* ("holy") three times, before placing the utensils on the shrine-table. When the Bible is introduced into this ritual, it is made part of the completing of the purification. The traditio-practitioner takes each of the utensils and lets them hang for a brief moment above the Bible. Being asked, the traditio-practitioner says that so is done because the Bible universally is believed to be holy. In other words, the Bible has, as a holy book, power to cleanse the cultic utensils from various sorts of impurity.

A second example illustrates how the Bible may be used for healing. Traditionally, healing has been a central part of the responsibility of the traditio-practitioners, and Merina traditionalists therefore tend to go to them instead of going to medical doctors. The traditio-practitioners are said to perform their healing partly by knowledge – not least about medicinal plants – and personal experience, but partly also by help of the ancestral spirits possessing them. When the Bible is introduced here, it is mainly to add power to the traditional aspects of the healing process. An informant (traditio-practitioner) describes how he invokes Zanahary and his possessor spirit, praying them to show mercy and to help the patient to recover. Then he prepares the traditional medicine and gives it to the patient, explaining how it is to be taken. However, before the patient leaves, this traditio-practitioner takes the Bible and places it on the region of the body where the patient feels pain. So is done, he argues, because the Bible, as a holy book, contains a divine power that increases the healing process. And further, the traditio-practitioner argues, it is the spirit that possesses him that allows him to use the Bible for this purpose.

A third example illustrates how the Bible may be used for protection. The Merina society has traditionally been characterised by fear of witchcraft or evil spirits. Not only are death and various kinds of diseases – of persons as well as cattle – supposed to be caused by evil spirits that are manipulated by witches, but so are also nature phenomena such as lightning and hail. In consequence, therefore, people tend to go to the traditio-practitioners seeking protection. An informant (traditio-practitioner) describes how people permanently feel threatened by visible and invisible enemies, and therefore use all means to protect themselves and their cattle and business. He describes three kinds of charms; one is charms against witchcraft, another is charms against hail, and a third is charms used to call back the soul of a sick person. When the Bible is introduced here, it is, again, based on the assumption that it contains divine power. An informant (traditio-practitioner) tells how she advises people who are tormented by nightmares to put the Bible under the pillow, because the evil spirit becomes powerless when it comes across a sacred object. She also advises people to touch the Bible when witches are terrorising them. In consequence, those who plan to return to their home late in the evening are advised to keep small bibles in their pocket, to be touched in case of witches.

The Bible as an open book

The expression "open book" is used to describe the phenomenon that the Bible is being read and interpreted into a certain context. In this case it is certain biblical texts which are considered important. The biblical texts are taken as messages from Zanahary, and they are being read and used for seemingly relevant purposes.

One example is that some Merina traditio-practitioners have started to read the Bible publicly. The traditio-practitioners have traditionally been illiterate, but due to the general growth in national education they now have an average educational background. An informant (traditio-practitioner) describes how he gathers his followers every last Saturday of the month, partly to strengthen the fellowship amongst them, but partly also to organise a devotion to praise Zanahary and the ancestors. The devotion consists of three parts; (i) an invocation of Zanahary and the ancestors, followed by a long prayer of intercession, (ii) a reading of texts from the Bible, and (iii) a sharing of joy and experiences. The reading of the Bible follows patterns from church services: first the Old Testament and then the New Testament. However, the informant admits that he prefers the Old Testament, not least because it apparently is closer to life as it is experienced by his followers. An important example here is the set of sacrifice regulations found in Leviticus, which to some extent is parallel to traditional Merina sacrifice regulations. Another example is found in the many parallels between Merina and Old Testament proverbs.

A second example is that the Bible is being used as a reference book for morals. One of the traditional obligations of the traditio-practitioners is to give moral advice to their followers. And amongst those traditio-practitioners who have started to use the Bible in their services, one can see a clear tendency of using it as a general source for moral instruction. A few examples can illustrate this. One example concerns the fear of God. An informant (traditio-practitioner) describes how the traditio-practitioners encounter people whose trust in God has weakened, and how biblical texts are used to face this challenge. A favourite text is Genesis 1:1 ("In the beginning God created heaven and earth"), another is Psalm 14:1 ("The fool says in his heart: There is no God"). Another example concerns the respect for parents and other authorities. An informant (traditio-practitioner) tells how Exodus 20:12 ("Honour your father and mother") can be used, as the Decalogue is universal and not only for Jews and Christians. And he also points out Proverbs 13:1 ("A wise son heeds to his father's instruction") as a relevant text. A third example concerns marriage. An informant (traditio-practitioner) describes how couples come to her for marriage counselling, and she points out two texts from Genesis 2 as central in that respect. One is v. 18 ("It is not good for the man to be alone") and the other is v. 22 ("The Lord God made a woman from the rib he had taken out of the man"). These two biblical texts she knows by heart, she says, and she uses them to point out three important aspects of marriage; its sacredness, the importance of love, and a suitable behaviour.

Why is the Bible used?

In an attempt at describing why the Bible is introduced and used in certain Merina traditionalist contexts, a distinction will be made between an *inside* (emic) perspective, where reasons given by Merina traditionalists themselves are presented, and an *outside* (etic) perspective, where a more critical perspective is voiced.

Inside perspective

From an inside perspective, it should be observed that the Merina informants acknowledge the peculiarity of making use of the Bible in a traditionalist context. Still, it is said that many traditionalists find the Bible very attractive, as it is universally acknowledged as a holy book, and that Christians have no right to be exclusive owners and users of this book. An informant (traditio-practitioner) claims that the Bible is a universal book, and she also points out Old Testament examples of God speaking to and making use of non-Israelites, such as Balaam (Numbers 22–24) and Cyrus (Isaiah 45). From this follows, she argues, that God is free to reveal himself in Christian as well as in Merina traditional contexts.

Another informant (traditio-practitioner) argues that the Bible actually is part of the Merina heritage. As pointed out previously, the Bible was the first book to be published in the Merina language. The translation of the Bible provided the skill of writing for the Merina people. At the same time, however, the Merina people made their language available for the Bible, and an essential part of the material used by the missionaries for the translation work was taken from Merina traditional religion.

Outside perspective

From an outside perspective it seems that the key concept in the Merina traditionalists' use of the Bible is the question of legitimacy. In a sum, the function of the use of the Bible seems to be a legitimising of Merina traditional religion. In a context where traditional religion has been, and still is, heavily attacked by Christians, some traditionalists have decided to counter this with the help of the central Christian icon, the Bible. Two informants (traditio-practitioners), who work together, defend their use of the Bible by comparing it to the scorpion. In the scorpion's tail, they argue, there is not only the poisonous sting, but also a natural antidote. The same is the case with the Bible, they claim. The Bible is poisonous and may even be mortal to Merina traditional religion. But at the same time the power of the Bible may be used as an antidote to protect Merina traditional religion from eradication.

The translation of the Bible into Malagasy, back in the early 19th century, took place in a context where the Christian translators constituted a religious minority versus the vast majority of the Merina traditionalists. In order to contextualise the biblical message and make it understandable for potential Merina converts, the translators deliberately made use of a religious terminology that was typical of Merina traditional religion. Today, the situation is completely different. The Christians have become the majority amongst the Merina, and it is the new minority, the Merina traditionalists, who in a way reclaim a set of terminology and concepts that used to belong to them alone. They reclaim this set, and they use the biblical associations now attached to it, to legitimise their own traditional religion.

One example concerns the name of God. Traditio-practitioners argue that the fact that the Bible translators used traditional Merina names for God, reflects that they actually acknowledged that the Merina tradition and the Bible talk about the same God. This is then used to legitimise a plurality of devotional expressions, leaving a room also for Merina traditionalism. An informant (traditio-practitioner) argues that it is the same God, and that Christians and Merina traditionalists are allowed to worship him in different ways. Christians think they are called to worship him in churches, he argues, and may do so according to his will. Likewise, however, traditionalists think it is better to worship him in sacred places, and they may also do so, again according to his will.

Another example is the pointing out of similarities between Levitical and Merina traditional sacrificial regulations and practices. An informant (traditio-practitioner) argues that it is the traditionalists – and not the Christians – who are loyal to the sacrificial regulations in Leviticus. The Christians claim to be following the Bible, but in practice they do not. The Merina traditionalists, on the other hand, follow Levitical sacrificial regulations; not only with regard to form, but even with regard to content, for example as they prefer sheep and bulls. The Bible, accordingly, is used to legitimise the cultic regulations and practice of Merina traditionalism. And the same informant goes on saying that if the Christians really want to eradicate Merina traditional sacrificial practices, they should first delete the very same sacrificial regulations from the Bible!

Conclusion

This paper has outlined how some Merina traditionalists make use of the Bible in their religious practices, and it has been argued that the function of their use of the Bible is to legitimise Merina traditional religion against the growing Christian majority. The various cases exemplify that the church has no monopoly on the use and interpretation of the Bible, as the reception of the Bible is not necessarily identical with the reception of Christianity. Rather, it seems that the Bible – closed or open – tends to live its own life amongst the Merina.

Notes

1 The most important example is probably W. Carey, *An Enquiry into the Obligations of Christians, to Use Means for the Conversion of the Heathens* (Leicester 1792; facsimile edition, London 1934).
2 Cf. the contribution by Adrian Hermann in this volume.
3 For case studies related to African Initiated Churches in Nigeria and South Africa, respectively, see D. T. Adamo, *Reading and Interpreting the Bible in African Indigenous Churches* (Eugene 2001); D. C. van Zyl, "In Africa Theology is not Thought Out but Danced Out. On the Theological Significance of Old Testament Symbolism and Rituals in the African Zionist Churches" (*Old Testament Essays* 8, 1995, 425–438).
4 For a brief discussion, with examples from African and African American experiences, cf. G. O. West, "Mapping African Biblical Interpretation", in: G. O. West/M. W. Dube (Eds.), *The Bible in Africa.* Transactions, Trajectories and Trends (Leiden 2000, 29–53), 36f.
5 Cf. G. A. Razafindrakoto, *Using the Bible in Traditional Merina Religion.* A Case Study of How and Why the Bible is Used by Traditio-Practitioners Amongst the Merina (Thesis for the M.Phil. Degree in Theology, School of Mission and Theology, Stavanger 2002).
6 For brief surveys, cf. J. Mack, *Madagascar.* Island of the Ancestors (London 1986); F. Ramiandrisoa, *Atlas historique du peuplement de Madagascar* (Antananarivo 1975); P. Verin, *Madagascar* (Paris 1990).
7 Cf. O. C. Dahl, Migration from Kalimantan to Madagascar (Oslo 1991), 121.
8 For introductory surveys, cf. M. Bloch, *Placing the Dead.* Tombs, Ancestral Villages, and Kinship Organisations in Madagascar (Seminar Studies in Anthropology 1, London 1971); L. Molet, *La conception Malgache du monde du surnaturel et de l'homme en Imerina* (Paris 1979); A. De Padou Rahajarizafy, *Filosofia Malagasy* (Fianarantsoa 1970).

9 For an introductory survey, cf. D. RALIBERA *ET AL.* (Eds.), *Madagascar et le christianisme* (Histoire oecuménique, Paris 1993); for statistics, cf. D. B. BARRETT *ET AL.* (Eds.), *World Christian Encyclopedia.* A Comparative Survey of Churches and Religions in the Modern World. Vol. 1 (Oxford [2]2001), 466–469.
10 Cf. L. MUNTHE, *La Bible à Madagascar.* Les deux premières traductions du Nouveau Testament malgache (Oslo 1969).
11 Cf. WEST, "Mapping" 48–49.

Part 3

THE EARLY CHURCH IN THE EASTERN MEDITERRANEAN

10

RITUAL

Wayne A. Meeks

Source: Wayne A. Meeks, *The First Urban Christians: The Social World of the Apostle Paul*, New Haven, CT: Yale University Press, 1983, pp. 140–63.

Was early Christianity a religion? Not at all, declares E. A. Judge. To first-century observers,

> the talkative, passionate and sometimes quarrelsome circles that met to read Paul's letters over their evening meal in private houses, or the pre-dawn conclaves of ethical rigorists that alarmed Pliny, were a disconcerting novelty. Without temple, cult statue or ritual, they lacked the time-honoured and reassuring routine of sacrifice that would have been necessary to link them with religion.[1]

To use religion as a model for describing early Christian groups would amount, in Judge's view, to "mislocating them under . . . an unhistorical rubric."[2] This is a useful warning, especially given the array of visible forms by which cults in the Roman Empire publicly displayed themselves. Ramsay MacMullen has assembled examples of these forms in the first chapter of his recent book on paganism. Not only did the first-century Christians lack shrines, temples, cult statues, and sacrifices; they staged no public festivals, dances, musical performances, pilgrimages, and as far as we know they set up no inscriptions.[3]

Christianity's difference from other cults should not be exaggerated, however. Judge's assertion that the early Christian communities were "without . . . ritual" is manifestly false. Not only does Pliny describe some of their rituals to Trajan, but it is surely ingenuous to describe the Christians of sixty years earlier as meeting merely "to read Paul's letters over their evening meal," as if their meeting and that meal had not been set about with ritual from the beginning. In fact Pliny did not think of Christianity as "conclaves of ethical rigorists," but as "a perverse, uncontrolled superstition."[4] It is hard to see why not only Pliny, but also Tacitus and Suetonius[5] would apply the term *superstitio* to an ethical debating society that had no ritual.[6] One uses such a term to characterize someone else's rituals that one does not like. If they had not been "perverse and uncontrolled" or, as Judge puts it, "a disconcerting novelty," they could have been called *religio.*

The early Christian movement also fits reasonably well under the rubric of religion as described by some modern social scientists. The anthropologist Melford E. Spiro, for example, defines religion as "an institution consisting of culturally patterned interaction with culturally postulated superhuman beings."[7] That the Pauline Christians believed in superhuman beings can hardly be doubted; we shall examine some of those beliefs more closely in the next chapter. For Spiro, interactions with those beings include both ritual behavior and moral behavior, behavior believed to be in accord with the "will or desire of supernatural beings or powers."[8] Pauline groups exhibited both. In the previous chapter we discussed some of the ways in which the groups shaped and regulated behavior to accord with what they took to be "the will or desire of" God and Christ. Here we shall examine what we can see of their ritual system.

A large and growing number of social scientists construe ritual as a form of communication. It does not just include certain patterns of language; it is itself a kind of speech. To interpret ritual is, "in effect, trying to discover the rules of grammar and syntax of an unknown language."[9]

Many of the scholars who adopt this perspective would say that ritual communicates the fundamental beliefs and values of a society or a group. Ritual is often said to be symbolic action, representing what the society holds to be of primary importance, or indeed the very structure of the society. There are a number of problems with this view, however, not least of which is the difficulty of clearly distinguishing between representation in the mind of the actor and in the mind of the external observer.[10] If it is the latter case, this definition does not distinguish ritual from other social behavior. Moreover, the observer's deductions are likely to be circular, as Jack Goody has pointed out:

> For it can be said, in an important sense, that all social action [and not just magicoreligious behavior] is "expressive" or "symbolic" of the social structure, because the more general concept is simply an abstraction from the more specific. It is not, however, "expressive" in the way many sociologists implicitly assume, that is, it does not express major principles of social behaviour. Indeed such an approach simply involves the reification of an organizing abstraction into a causal factor.[11]

For Emile Durkheim, who with Robertson Smith initiated the modern discussion of ritual, the relation of ritual to language was more intrinsic. Ritual did not merely encode ideas that could be expressed otherwise; rather, it *created* the essential categories of human thought. For Durkheim, ritual solved the Kantian problem of the origin of the necessary concepts. "Ritual and religion did publicly," says Ernest Gellner, "what the Kantian transcendental ego did only behind the impassable iron curtain of the noumenal."[12] Thus Mary Douglas, one of the most imaginative of Durkheimian anthropologists, treats "ritual forms, like speech forms, as transmitters of culture," but insists that they create as well as reflect social reality. She adds: "Ritual is more to society than words are to thought. For it is very possible to know something and then find words for it. But it is impossible to have social relations without symbolic acts."[13] Other communications-oriented students of ritual take a similar position with more or less important variations. Berger and Luckmann, for example, describe "the social construction of reality," and Clifford Geertz proposes that "sacred symbols" serve to synthesize "world view" and "ethos" of a community.[14]

There are a number of problems with the Durkheimian perspective. For Durkheim, ritual was able to do its work only by perpetrating a benign fraud. The actor in a rite spoke of "God" or "the gods," but Durkheim knew that he really meant "society." Nevertheless, Durkheim's followers preserve an insight often forgotten in modern interpretations of myth and ritual: ritual does not only or primarily convey information. It does something. If we are to think of ritual as a kind of speech, then perhaps we ought to think preeminently of the kind that J. L. Austin called "performative."[15] The appropriate question, as we undertake to describe the rituals mentioned in the Pauline letters, is "What do they *do*?"

Minor rituals

The obvious starting point for our search might seem to be the two great ritual complexes, baptism and the Lord's Supper, which were of self-evident importance in the earliest Christian communities. However, the very fact that these ceremonies continued to be central to Christian worship in subsequent centuries caused them to accrete increasingly complex actions and meanings. That accretion makes it difficult to divest these rituals of the accumulated "theology of the sacraments" and to avoid an anachronism in performing the needed act of historical imagination. When the Christians of the Pauline mission baptized converts and gathered for common meals in memory of Jesus, they framed these special occasions with a very fluid and rapidly developing system of small ritualized actions. By these gestures, formulas, and patterns of speaking they discovered and expressed their identity as "brothers and sisters in Christ," "the assembly of God," "the holy and elect," "the body of Christ," and so on. Unfortunately no written description of these little rites survives, but we do find clues about a number of them in the letters. These clues may help to correct our perspective on the larger, more familiar sacraments.

Coming together

The regular meeting of a group at a familiar time and place itself becomes a ritual, in the broad sense of the word we have adopted. And the meeting begets rituals to define and accent its activities, to signal its beginning and end, to separate friendly milling around and gossip from more serious business, to call attention to the leaders' authoritative utterances.

"When you come together" is a clause that Paul uses several times in his correspondence with the Corinthian saints. The verb *synerchesthai*, quite simply "to come together," occurs in 1 Cor. 11:17, 18, 20, 33, 34—all referring to meetings "to eat the Lord's Supper" (for Paul's chiding negative in vs. 20 shows that that was supposed to be the purpose of the meetings)—and in 14:23, 26. Two phrases underline the commonality of the meeting: *en ekklēsia* (in *synerchomenōn hymōn en ekklēsia*) in 11:18 and *epi to auto* (in *synerchomenōn . . . epi to auto*) in 11:20. Given that these phrases are combined in 14:23, the regulations set forth there for spirit-possessed communication when "the whole *ekklēsia*" gathers probably also refer to occasions at which the common meal is the central ritual. Paul uses the alternative verb, *synagein*, "to gather," which is fairly frequent in Acts, only at 1 Cor. 5:4, where a solemn assembly is ordered for the purpose of expelling a member who has violated the sexual taboos (discussed above, chapter 4).

The earliest extant letter specifies that the letter is to be read "to all the brothers" (1 Thess. 5:27). In the Letter to Colossae, Paul's surrogate takes for granted the reading of this letter in the assembly, and gives instructions that it also be read in Laodicea, and the Laodicean letter in Colossae (Col. 4:16). The form of all the Pauline letters assumes that they will be read at a regular gathering of the *ekklēsia*,[16] but not necessarily to all the groups of a given city at once. Galatians affords the special instance of addressees belonging to a wider area than one city, and the plural in the address makes it plain that several assemblies are expected to receive the letter, either in multiple copies or in successive meetings as Paul's messenger takes it from one place to the next. It may also be that in some cities the letters were read successively in individual household assemblies rather than to "the whole assembly" gathered in a place like Gaius's house in Corinth. The *ekklēsia* that meets in Nympha's house in Laodicea (Col. 4:15) is probably not the entirety of the *Laodikeōn ekklēsia* (vs. 16), nor is the meeting in the house of Philemon and Apphia the only such in Colossae (Philem. 2). So also in Rome there are several household assemblies (Rom. 16), and we cannot be sure whether there was one common meeting place for all of them. The practice doubtless depended on the practical problem of finding adequate room for a citywide assembly in a given place.[17] Gaius's contribution was important enough to be singled out in the remark identifying him (Rom. 16:23); it was probably unusual at this early date.

How often did the groups meet? We do not know. By Pliny's time the Christians in Bithynia were meeting weekly, on a "set day" (*stato die*).[18] Around 150, Justin confirms that that day was Sunday.[19] Acts 20:7 and Ignatius, Magnesians 9:1 provide earlier evidence. We might guess that the gatherings for common meals would have been weekly from the beginning, the Christian "family" following the example of Jewish sabbath observance, but no text confirms this surmise. A weekly rhythm to the life of the congregation and the ascription of some importance to Sunday are suggested by Paul's directive to the Corinthians and the Galatians about the collection for the Jerusalem poor: "The first day of every week, let each of you set aside privately and save up whatever his prosperity permits, so there need be no collections when I come" (1 Cor. 16:2). However, since the directive is for "each one" to set aside money at home (*par' heautō*), it offers no proof that the assembly was also on "the first day of every week."

In the Ekklēsia

What happened in the assemblies? The closest thing we have in the letters to outright description is the series of admonitions in 1 Corinthians 11 and 14. Some of the actions mentioned there are confirmed for other places by mention in other letters. "When you assemble," writes Paul, "each has a psalm, a teaching, a revelation, a tongue, an interpretation" (14:26). As Barrett remarks, "Church meetings in Corinth can scarcely have suffered from dullness."[20] Let us begin with the psalm. There are a number of clues that chanting and singing were normal parts of the Christian meetings. Both Col. 3:16f. and the parallel text, Eph. 5:18–20—both probably adapting traditional language—speak of "psalms, hymns, and spiritual odes." There is not much use trying to distinguish among the three synonyms, although some ancient and modern commentators have tried. Gregory of Nyssa, for example, thought of psalms as accompanied by instruments.[21] The psalms may have included some from the biblical psalter, which was very important in early Christian interpretation and apologetic; but the fact that all three are seen as manifesting in the singers the presence of the Spirit or the *logos* of Christ (Col. 3:16) indicates that most were probably original Christian compositions or adaptations. The likelihood that many of them followed Jewish models is confirmed by some fragments sifted from the letters. As Lightfoot observed, "Psalmody and hymnody were highly developed in the religious services of the Jews at this time."[22] To his references to Philo we may now add the important evidence from Qumran, including the "Hymns" or "Thanksgivings" scroll from Cave 1.[23] This does not exclude general Hellenistic influence as well, for hymns to and about the deities were prominent in cults of all sorts, and sometimes the forms were not altogether different from the Jewish ones.[24]

Perhaps we even have some examples of those psalms, hymns, and spiritual odes. It is widely agreed that Paul quoted one in Phil. 2:6–11, which originally would have sounded something like this:

> [Give thanks to Christ,]
> who being in the form of God
> did not count it his good luck
>   to be equal to God,
> but emptied himself,
> taking the form of a slave,
> taking human likeness
>   and found in shape a man,
> he humbled himself
>   and was obedient to the point of death.
> That is the reason God has raised him on high
> and given him the name
>   higher than any name,
>   that in the name of Jesus
>   "every knee should bend,"
>   of earthly and heavenly and chthonic beings,
>   "and every tongue confess":
>   "The Lord is Jesus Christ"
>   —to the glory of God the Father.

Analysts of the Pauline letter style have identifed a great many other "hymns" or "confessional poems" or fragments thereof, including Col. 1:15–20, Eph. 1:3–14, and 1 Tim. 3:16. Not all are equally convincing. In its present form Eph. 1:3–14, for example, like 2 Cor. 1:3–7, is a literary "blessing" that belongs to formal epistolary style, but it probably also incorporates elements of liturgical blessings used at baptism. That is not the same as a hymn, however.[25] It is also disappointing that the enormous diligence and ingenuity displayed by many exegetes to restore the "original" strophes, stichoi, and meter of these liturgical fragments have almost never resulted in agreement between any two scholars. It is fair to infer that a large subjective factor is involved. We may also wonder whether the chants of the early Christians were necessarily any more regular than the present form of these putative fragments. If they had been as precisely balanced and metrically true as some of the reconstructions, then we would have to suppose that the letter writers who edited them into their present misshape were tone deaf indeed. More likely, the "spiritual" chants were composed freely according to sense-lines, rhythmic but not precisely scannable. They probably followed a few common patterns and used stereotyped turns of phrase (including scriptural lines, as in Phil. 2:11, as well as Christian formulas). In that case they would not have been exactly the same on any two occasions.

There is one surprising detail in the verses just quoted from Colossians and Ephesians. Although the singing is addressed to "the Lord" (Eph. 5:19) or to "God" (Col. 3:16), it is also the means for "speaking to one another" (Ephesians) or, more specifically, for "teaching and admonishing one another" (Colossians). That community-oriented function is consistent with the reason for Paul's preference for prophecy in clear speech to glossolalia: the glossolalist speaks only to God; the prophet, to human beings (1 Cor. 14:2f.). The test is whether speech in the assembly "builds up" the *ekklēsia* (vss. 3–5); that is the summary rule Paul applies in the verse we started with, 1 Cor. 14:26: "Let all [psalm, teaching, revelation, tongue, interpretation] be for upbuilding [*oikodomē*]." Here is a candid statement of the social function that Paul and his associates see for the distinctive sorts of singing and speaking that take place in the spirit-filled meetings. By chanting psalms, hymns, and odes to God (or to the Lord), among other things the congregation also "taught" and "admonished" themselves and "built up" the community. One large role of ritual speech and music is thus to promote group cohesion, as we emphasized in chapter 2. *Oikodomē* is more than social cohesion, however.[26] It involves, by "teaching and admonition," the formation of the community's ethos. By the images of the group's special language, the poetic reiteration of statements and metaphors of fundamental beliefs, reinforced by musical rhythms and charged with the high emotional level induced by cumulative interaction in the meetings, the group's peculiar "knowledge" grows. With it, attitudes and dispositions take form; the kinds of behavior "worthy of the way you received Christ" are learned.

"Instruction" and "admonition" in Col. 3:16 are functions of the whole congregation—by means of their singing or chanting. Elsewhere, too, the letters appeal to the addressees to "admonish" or "exhort" one another (as in 1 Thess. 4:18; 5:11, 14; 1 Cor. 14:31; Rom. 15:14). That does not mean that these functions were not led by individuals or performed by individuals on behalf of the congregation. "Each one" could offer "a psalm, a teaching," and so on. Instruction, exhortation, and consolation were especially to be expected from prophets (1 Cor. 14:3, 19), but admonition is also a function of the local leaders who "labor" and "protect/preside" (1 Thess. 5:12). These are individual *charismata* (1 Cor. 12:8–10, 28–30; Rom. 12:8), but given to the "one body"; so Paul wants them understood, and so his disciples who wrote Colossians and Ephesians construed them.

Historians of liturgy commonly assume that the Christian meetings included, from the beginning, the reading and exposition of scripture—that is, of what the second-century church would begin to call the Old Testament. The primary reason for that assumption is the supposed example of the Jewish synagogue. We must be careful, however, not to explain one unknown quantity in terms of another, equally unknown. The fact is that extant descriptions of synagogue worship and orders for it are from the New Testament itself or from much later sources. Only by means of small allusions in the writings of Philo and Josephus and a few other writers, and by more or less plausible deductions from the style of these and of other Jewish literature is it possible to guess what synagogue liturgies in the first century may have included.[27] That scripture texts were read and homilies were based on them seems very credible indeed, but details are quite uncertain. Is there anything in the Pauline letters themselves that suggests that reading and exposition of scripture took place in the Christian assemblies—perhaps as part of the activity indicated by "instruction," "teaching," "admonition," "consolation," "words of wisdom," "words of knowledge"? There is nothing explicit. However, the rich allusions to and arguments from scripture that Paul sometimes includes in his letters, a practice also visible in the work of his disciple in, say, Eph. 2:11–22; 4:8–12; 5:21–33, presuppose *some* means for learning both text and traditions of interpretation. Regular readings and homilies in the assemblies are the most plausible.

Besides exposition of scripture, preaching in the assemblies must have included other things, preeminently statements about Jesus Christ, and inferences, appeals, warnings, and the like, connected logically or rhetorically with those statements. Examining some of the recurrent patterns of language in the Pauline corpus and in other early Christian letters, Rudolf Bultmann and, more systematically, Nils Dahl have suggested that several reproduce typical rhetoric of preachers. Dahl describes five such patterns. The "revelation pattern" says that what the Christians now know (about Christ) is "a secret, hidden for ages," "but now revealed" to the elect. The "soteriological contrast pattern" sets the preconversion life of the Christians ("Once you were . . .") against their new status, which they must live up to ("but now you are . . ."). The "conformity pattern" is hortatory: "Just as the Lord forgave you, so also you [ought to forgive one another]." The "teleological pattern" permits a broad range of implications to be drawn from christological statements, as in 2 Cor. 8:9: "You know the grace of our Lord Jesus Christ, that, rich as he was, he became poor for your sakes, that you might be enriched by his poverty [and therefore ought to be ready to send money to the poor in Jerusalem]." Finally, there is the simple introduction of exhortations or advice by "I appeal to you by the name of the Lord Jesus," or ". . . in the Lord," or the like.[28] Some of these had wider application than preaching. They could also shape formulas that are liturgical in a narrower sense, like the doxology added in most manuscripts to one of the last chapters of Romans.[29]

Moreover, we may assume that the paraenetic sections of the Pauline letters are fairly close to the sort of exhortations that would have been made orally in the regular meetings. Given that the letters include not only specifically Christian forms but also many of the topics, forms of argument, and figures common to popular rhetoric, oral exhortation doubtless used them, too. Joining the meeting in Gaius's overcrowded dining room, we might have heard, along with reminders of our life before baptism and our new life now, revelations of "words of the Lord," prophecies about things to come, admonitions to love each other as Christ loved us, as well as discourses on the topos "on marriage," or "on brotherly love." We would have been urged to exercise body and mind for the great contest of life, pressing on to the goal, not fearing the pain or the difficulties, which would prove our character. The Christian prophets and exhorters did not speak only novelties, a "Holy Ghost language." The uninstructed outsider (*idiōtēs*) who came in off the street to hear this kind of preaching would not think he was hearing the gibberish of some frenzy, but nevertheless he would find something strange, perhaps numinous about it (1 Cor. 14:23–25). What was odd was just the blend of the familiar and the novel.

Of course the assemblies included prayer. How formal was it? The fact that one could pray either "by tongue" or "rationally" ("with the mind," 1 Cor. 14:13–15) suggests some mixture of the spontaneous and the customary—though further reflection may show that the line between rational and spiritual prayer is not identical to the dichotomy between formal and formless (see further below). The best-known form of Jewish prayer is of the style, "Blessed art thou, Lord our God, King of the Universe [or other suitable epithets], who doest . . . [or, "because thou has done . . ."]. This is the style of the standard daily prayer that is among the oldest parts of the synagogue liturgy, the Tefillah ("*the* Prayer"). That the early Pauline groups adapted this pattern of prayer is suggested by numerous echoes in epistolary forms, some of which we have already noticed, such as "Blessed be the God and Father of our Lord Jesus Christ, the Father of mercies and God of all consolation, who consoles us in our every affliction . . ." (2 Cor. 1:3f.). The third-person formulation in lieu of the second-person in fact accords with an older prayer style, but its appearance in the letters is dictated by the epistolary situation. In worship the Christians may well have said, "Blessed are you, God and Father of our Lord Jesus, . . ."[30]

A great many other small forms, "acclamations," "doxologies," and the like that are embedded in the letters also probably reflect the common language of prayer: "Thanks be to God who gives us the victory through our Lord Jesus Christ" (1 Cor. 15:57; cf. Rom. 7:25; 2 Cor. 2:14; further adapted, Rom. 6:17; 2 Cor. 8:16; 9:15); "God . . . to whom be glory for ever and ever. Amen" (Gal. 1:5; Rom. 11:36; 16:27; more elaborate, Eph. 3:21; still in use, 2 Tim. 4:18; elaborated 1 Tim. 1:17). The "amen" that follows the doxology in many instances was also liturgical, following a Jewish pattern (1 Cor. 14:16) of congregational response to a prayer.[31]

The formula "in the Name of Jesus" or similar phrases must also have punctuated Christian worship very frequently, because the admonition about congregational singing in Col. 3:17 concludes, "And everything you do, in word or in deed, (do it) all in the name of the Lord Jesus, giving thanks to God the Father through him" (see also Eph. 5:20). Indeed, early Christians including Paul adapted from Joel 3:5 the phrase "every one who calls on the name of the Lord," understanding "Lord" to mean "our Lord Jesus Christ"

(1 Cor. 1:2 and often). Moreover, the "hymn" that Paul quotes in Phil. 2:6–11 pictures a heavenly enthronement of Christ in which, at the signal "in the Name of Jesus," everyone kneels. Those doing obeisance in the mythic picture are superhuman powers; we would probably not go far wrong to imagine that the Philippian Christians were accustomed, on hearing the same formula at some point in their worship, probably in connection with baptism,[32] to bend *their* knees and confess, "The Lord is Jesus Christ." What is done on earth is confirmed in heaven—or, rather, the reverse.

We have been talking about "forms," "rites," "customs or practices of a formal kind."[33] Yet one of the most vivid (and noisiest) activities in the Pauline assemblies was glossolalia—at least that was the case in Corinth, and the source used by the author of Acts for his Pentecost story probably presupposes a widespread phenomenon in the early churches. Surely glossolalia and ritual are polar opposites? Paul certainly saw a dangerous tension between the extravagance of speaking in tongues at Corinth and the rational behavior he preferred—between uncontrolled enthusiasm and "decency and order." We would form a seriously distorted picture of these meetings, however, if we were to assume that glossolalia and other manifestations of spirit possession were formless, while ritual behavior was pure form. Neither is true. The formal procedure, the known pattern, was the framework within which the individual Christian more or less spontaneously sang "his" psalm or prayed "his" prayer. Anyone who has attended modern-day services of the free church traditions will know how large a proportion of supposedly spontaneous prayer consists of endlessly repeated linguistic patterns.

Moreover, even the extreme form of antistructural behavior, glossolalia, has also its forms and occasions, some of them very specific and rigid, as is evident from the discoveries of Felicitas Goodman, mentioned in the previous chapter. Not only does glossolalia in modern groups occur at predictable times in the service, framed by rather clearly defined ritual procedures; there are also quite specific verbal formulas and physical actions that to some extent channel and limit the ecstatic behavior. In adepts, there are even "trigger words" that can induce or terminate the trance.[34] Paul, at least, thought the same was true at Corinth, for he gives explicit directions about the number of glossolalists who are to be permitted to speak and clearly expects that the *charisma* can be controlled within the framework of the other ritual procedures we have been describing. Thus we are led to a conclusion that at first might have seemed paradoxical: that such exotic and presumably spontaneous behavior as speaking in tongues was also ritual. It occurred within the framework of the assembly, performed by persons who were expected to do it. It happened at predictable times, accompanied by distinctive bodily movements, perhaps introduced and followed by characteristic phrases in natural language. It did what rituals do: it stimulated feelings of group solidarity (except, as at Corinth, for those nonspeakers made to feel excluded); it increased the prestige of individuals, thus creating or underlining roles, and marked the occasion as one of solemnity (in the older sense, not the now common one of being dull and humorless).

A number of other hints of ritual are to be found in the letters, but it is impossible to be sure what their contexts may have been. Were there formulas for beginning and ending a meeting? In 1 Cor. 5:4 the Corinthians are told what to do when they "gather in the name of the Lord Jesus," a formula we have met in other contexts. Does that mean that this formula is pronounced in some suitable sentence to call the assembly to order? Again, we know that the use of the Shema ("Hear O Israel, the Lord our God is one Lord . . . ," Deut. 6:4f.) had a prominent place early in the synagogue liturgy. Is familiarity with it through a similar use in the Christian gatherings presupposed by Paul's pointed allusions in 1 Thess. 1:9 and Rom. 3:30? A "holy kiss," is mentioned in the conclusions of four of Paul's letters and also in 1 Peter (1 Thess. 5:26; Rom. 16:16; 1 Cor. 16:20; 2 Cor. 13:12; 1 Pet. 5:14). Was it a ritual marking the end of a meeting? Or did it, as in some later liturgies, mark the transition to the Supper? The same sort of question often arises about the *anathema* against anyone who "does not love the Lord" and the Aramaic prayer, *marana tha*, of 1 Cor. 16:22. To these questions we find no definitive answers.

We have found a wide range of little actions and verbal formulas and references to larger, more general activities that occurred, it seems, with fair regularity in the Pauline communities. Although most of our evidence comes from a few passing references, particularly in the Corinthian correspondence, we are safe in assuming that many if not all of these were common. The earliest of the letters reassures us that this was so, for it speaks already of instruction, admonition, prayer, thanksgiving, prophesying and perhaps other "ecstatic" demonstrations (the *pneuma* is not to be "quenched"), the holy kiss, and the reading of the apostolic letter (1 Thess. 5:12–27); and it ends, as a meeting might, with a benediction (vs. 28). We discover a very free, charismatic order, but an order nonetheless: there are customary forms. These assemblies, marked by these forms, were also the setting for the two major ritual complexes, baptism and the Lord's Supper.

Baptism: ritual of initiation

Exactly what did Paul do and say when he baptized the household of Stephanas? To what symbolic action do he and the author of Colossians refer when they speak of "being buried with [Christ] in baptism"? Nowhere in the letters do we find a straightforward description of the ritual. The people to whom Paul and his disciples were writing knew what the procedure was; it was the implications of the event that the leaders had to interpret and reinterpret. Consequently, we are fairly well supplied with interpretations of baptism, with examples of what it meant in at least one sense, or what Paul and his co-workers wanted it to mean. Yet we have to rely on inference to answer the simplest questions about what happened, and we will remain ignorant, however clever our detection, of many details that might, if we knew them, alter our total picture of the ritual. Nevertheless it is neither impossible nor useless to sort out what we *do* know and can with fair probability infer about Pauline baptism, along the lines that an ethnographer might use to describe initiation into some modern sect.

Our task is made easier by the efforts of a number of scholars in this century to detect, by stylistic analysis, formulas quoted or paraphrased by the letter writers.[35] We have already noticed a number of these forms and observed in passing that several of them probably were at home in the baptismal ritual. We shall now examine them more systematically.

The center of the ritual, as the terms *baptizein* and *baptisma* indicate, was simply a water bath. In one of Paul's reminders, the conversion of Corinthian Christians from their former life of vice is summarized thus: "But you were washed, you were made holy, you were justified in [or, by] the name of our Lord Jesus Christ and in [or, by] the Spirit of our God" (1 Cor. 6:11). The fact that baptism could be construed as a symbolic burial with Christ (Rom. 6:4; Col. 2:12) suggests a complete immersion in water. That was the case with the normal Jewish rite of purification, the *t^ebilah*, which was probably, at whatever distance, the primary antecedent of Christian baptism. The first full description of the Christian rite, in Hippolytus's *Apostolic Tradition*, which probably represents Roman practice at the end of the second century, attests a threefold immersion.[36] However, the little manual of church order called the Didache ("Teaching of the Twelve Apostles"), which may represent traditions as much as a century older than Hippolytus, probably in Syria, provides for pouring water thrice over the head, in case sufficient water for immersion is not at hand (7:3). Most of the artistic depictions of baptism, in Roman catacombs and sarcophagi of the third and succeeding centuries, show the candidate (usually depicted as a child) standing in water, with the officiant pouring water over his head. The earliest identifiable Christian meetinghouse discovered by archaeologists, at Dura-Europos on the Euphrates, contained a basin that would hardly suffice for immersion.[37] Perhaps the Pauline groups, too, had to adjust symbolism to physical necessity.

Where *did* they baptize? In the "living water" of a stream? That was what the Didache preferred, no doubt on the model of some of the biblical prescriptions for purification.[38] Most often, however, the Levitical rules mention only "water," without specifying "living water," and by the time of Christianity's beginnings Pharisaic sages seem already to have invented the *mikveh*, an immersion pool deemed pure if it had adequate dimensions and the prescribed construction even though its water was still.[39] Yet we cannot very well imagine the synagogue officers in an eastern city admitting to their mikveh one of Paul's groups of uncircumcised gentiles, chanting about a messiah equal to God, crucified, resurrected, and reigning in heaven. It is only slightly less fantastic to picture them taking over a room in a public bath.[40] And even a Gaius or an Erastus is not likely to have had a private bath. The river seems our best guess, or else a tub and a bowl.

The Christian converts were baptized naked. Analogy with the Jewish rites might suggest that; it is explicit in the Roman practice described by Hippolytus and indicated in all the early portrayals of baptism in Christian art. What confirms the fact for the Pauline groups is the variety of metaphorical allusions to taking off and putting on clothing that we find in those parts of the letters that refer to baptism. Those allusions are of two sorts, as we shall see: the mythical notion of taking off the body, the "old human," and putting on instead Christ, the "new human"; and the rather common ethical figure of taking off bad habits and putting on virtuous ones. The convergence of both types in the baptismal reminders of Pauline paraenesis is most easily accounted for on the assumption that the candidates from the beginning took off their clothes to be baptized and put them back on afterward, and that these natural actions were given metaphorical significance.[41]

Anointing, which would play a significant role in later baptismal liturgies,[42] is mentioned in the Pauline corpus only once, 2 Cor. 1:21. The context, which hearkens back to the conversion of the Corinthian Christians, suggests that it was connected already with baptism.[43] The gift of the Holy Spirit, mentioned in the same passage and frequently elsewhere, was also associated with baptism, but there is nothing in the letters to indicate how this gift was symbolized. We have seen that some of the *pneumatikoi* at Corinth took glossolalia to be the sign par excellence of possession of (or by) the Spirit, and that belief was still known when Acts was written (10:44–46). We can scarcely believe that every convert on emerging from the water of baptism fell into a trance and spoke in tongues, however, if for no other reason than that it would then be hard to understand either the divisions over the practice at Corinth or Paul's arguments in trying to bring it under control. The Acts passage just cited suggests an alternative sign, for the Cornelius household were both "speaking in tongues" and "extolling God" (RSV)—more precisely, "magnifying [*megalynōn*] God." That is, they were shouting out the kind of acclamation found also in pagan contexts, "Great [*megas*] is God!"[44] The response in the Pauline groups may have been simpler: Gal. 4:6 and Rom. 8:15f. suggest that the newly baptized person shouted out the Aramaic word *Abba* ("Father"), and that this was understood as the Spirit speaking through him, at the same time indicating his adoption as "child of God."

Whether in the Pauline communities there was a formal creed, or confession of faith, at baptism is debated. Baptism is the most likely setting for the simple confession mentioned by Paul in Rom. 10:9, "The Lord is Jesus!" (*kyrios Iēsous*). That corresponds, as we saw above, to the acclamation of the exalted Jesus by cosmic powers, depicted in the hymn quoted in Phil. 2:10f. Such a declaration was at least one referent of early Christian interpretation of the Joel passage, "Everyone who calls upon the name of the Lord will be saved" (as, for example, in Rom. 10:13); Paul's biographer still associates this with baptism in his description of Paul's conversion (Acts 22:16). Furthermore, the connection with Phil. 2:10f. suggests that baptism was the *Sitz im Leben* for this and similar poems or canticles that depict Jesus' descent or humiliation followed by cosmic exaltation. "Singing to Christ as to a god," which Pliny discovered the Christians of Bithynia doing at their dawn meetings for (initiatory?) oaths, may thus have been the practice sixty years earlier among Christians of Asia and Macedonia.[45]

So far we have examined clues from the Pauline and deutero-Pauline letters for what the congregations concretely did when they initiated new members. Some of these may become a little clearer when we turn to the ways in which the letters *interpret* baptism. Before taking up those applications of baptismal motifs, however, let us consider what it may have meant to the participants that their initiatory ritual was a rite of cleansing. It was not preceded by a washing; baptism *was* a washing.

The significance of this fact begins to emerge when we compare baptism with activities that both ancient and modern observers have regarded as its closest analogies, the Jewish immersion of proselytes and the initiations into pagan mysteries. In the mysteries, some ceremony of washing or sprinkling often prepared candidates for admission to the mysteries proper. In the Eleusinian mysteries, for example, there was an official in charge of such rites, called a *hydranos.* A marble relief from the fourth century B.C. depicts a goddess, probably Persephone, in this role, pouring water from a phial over a young, nude figure; it cannot fail to remind us of the earliest pictures of Christian baptism, six centuries later.[46] These lustrations, and perhaps also bathing in the river Ilissos, were among the preparatory rites of the Lesser Mysteries held at Agrai, which were as a whole a preparatory purification for the Greater Mysteries held later in the year at Eleusis.[47] On the second day of the latter (16 Boedromion), the cry went up, "To the sea, O Mystai!" whereupon the whole company, each initiate and his pig, bathed, and later the pigs were sacrificed. But all this took place in Athens, three days before the great procession to Eleusis. It was all public and well known, no part of the secret *teletē.*[48] Similarly the initiate of Isis first received a washing, then fasted for ten days before the initiation proper.[49] One had to be pure before entering a sacred space and time.

The same was true of the water rites of Judaism, which in ancient Israel were closely associated with the temple and cult. The extension and democratization of the concept of purity and the means for attaining and restoring it were part of the religious revolution of the Pharisees. To a remarkable degree they seem to have transformed the notion of the sacred by associating it, and the cleanness that represented it, with the group that keeps itself pure and loyal to the commandments—not just in temple precincts at festival time, but daily in the home, in the midst of the unclean world. The immersion pool was one of the innovations of that revised conception of purity and its uses.[50] Yet among the Pharisees there is implied, so far as I can see, no permanent transition from the impure world into the pure community. The line between is constantly in flux; purity must be continually reestablished in response to voluntary or involuntary actions of the member of the sect, or to accidents that befall him. Thus the boundary between the sect and the world is wavering and porous, and the Pharisee does not, accordingly, represent his sect as the only "real" Israel, nor does the immersion in the mikveh become an initiation. Even the immersion required of proselytes is only a special case of the ordinary purifications and not an initiation in itself, despite the attempts of some scholars to make it the direct antecedent of Christian baptism.[51]

By making the cleansing rite alone bear the whole function of initiation, and by making initiation the decisive point of entry into an exclusive community, the Christian groups created something new. For them the bath becomes a permanent threshold between the "clean" group and the "dirty" world, between those who have been initiated and everyone who has not. It is that obvious sense of the rite separating pure from impure on which Paul trades in his admonitions of 1 Cor. 5–6, which we examined in the previous chapter. There he takes as self-evident that pure/impure can be a metaphor for moral/immoral, and thus he can shift to the figure "cleanse out the leaven," like a Jewish family before Passover, to command the removal of a sexual deviant from the group. It is plausible that the Corinthian Christians, or some of them, had understood the rules they had learned and that Paul had earlier written to them to mean that they should avoid contamination by the polluting world, but that the group's own purity was impregnable. Paul tries to reverse that understanding (1 Cor. 5:9–13). The world is impure, but this is not their concern; what is polluting is internal misbehavior. They are not to try to withdraw from the world. To be sure, to sue one another in pagan courts is an appalling transgression of the boundaries, but what is really polluting is that their suits imply a desire to cheat one's "brother," which is behavior typical of what they were, as outsiders, before "you were washed, you were made holy, you were justified . . ." (6:1–11). That allusion to baptism, as we saw, led Paul's argument back to concern with sexual matters, now in terms of the purity of the individual body: united with Christ as if (spiritually) in marriage, the body (like the community: 3:16) is a "temple of the Holy Spirit within you" (6:12–20). As we shall see, those motifs also are closely connected with baptism. Paul's argument depends on common recognition that baptism draws a line between the unwashed world and the washed Christians, and that "clean" is a metaphor for "behaving properly." In the second century, the Church would further emphasize the height of the threshold between outside and inside by a dramatic series of exorcisms leading up to baptism,[52] but there is no evidence for such a procedure in the Pauline communities.

Allusions to baptism occur principally in passages in which Paul tries to correct misunderstandings or to argue on the basis of a common starting point, as in the passage just mentioned and in Rom. 6; 8:12–17; Gal. 3:26–4:6; 1 Cor. 1–4; 12, and in the paraenetic reminders that make up most of Colossians and Ephesians. Paraenetic reminders are appeals to recall what happened when the addressees first became Christians, both the ritual of baptism and the instruction that accompanied it, and to behave in ways appropriate to that memory.[53] These passages have often been analyzed for their ideational content and for their parallels, connections, and possible antecedents in the history of religions. Our purpose is different; we are trying to see what baptism did for ordinary Christians, disregarding the question of where its elements may have come from and even the profounder theological beliefs that Paul and some of the other leaders associated with it, unless we can be sure those were integral to the common understanding. I shall begin by listing the most prominent motifs and then try to determine some of their interrelationships in the pattern of ritual action.

Foremost among the motifs that Paul takes for granted, known not only to members of groups he founded but also to the Christians in Rome, is the image of dying and rising with Christ. This is expressed not only in the language of analogy ("As Christ was raised from the dead . . . so also we . . .") but also in the language of participation ("We have been baptized into his death . . . ," Rom. 6:3f.), as well as by verbs compounded in *syn–*, "with" (Rom. 6:4, 8; Col. 2:12f.; Eph. 2:5f.). A variation of this theme is that the stare of the convert prior to his baptism is itself death; baptism is a death of death, the beginning of life (Col. 2:13; Eph. 2:1,5).

Were death and rising mimed somehow in the ritual? In liturgies of the later church, sometimes the usual posture of prayer, standing with arms raised and palms forward, was taken to represent crucifixion,[54] but there is no hint of anything similar in the Pauline literature. Attempts to find in Paul's reference to the "stigmata of Jesus" he carried (Gal. 6:17) evidence for signing or even tattooing with the cross at baptism have not been convincing. Descent into the water obviously did not mime Jesus' death, but it could be construed as "being buried with Christ" (Rom. 6:4; Col. 2:12), and rising from the water could very well signify "being raised with Christ" (Col. 2:12; 3:1; Eph. 2:6). For death itself, some other action would have to be found; the Pauline Christians found it in the removal of clothing before entering the water. That became "taking off the body" or "the old human." Reclothing afterward could then represent the new life of resurrection.

The clothing imagery comprises an elaborate complex of metaphors. What is "taken off" is variously construed as "the old human," "the body of flesh," and the vices associated therewith. This "removal of the body of flesh" is "the circumcision of Christ," that is, the Christian equivalent of Jewish circumcision of proselytes (Col. 2:11). What is "put on" is Christ himself, as "the new human," who is "being renewed . . . according to the image of his creator" (Col. 3:10). Characteristic of the "new human" is unity, the end of the opposed sets of roles that typified the "old human": Jew/Greek, slave/free, male/female (Gal. 3:28; 1 Cor. 12:13; Col. 3:1 of.; cf. Ignatius, Eph. 6:8). There are patent in this language numerous allusions to the biblical account of the creation of man and to expansions of that account in Jewish lore. Among the latter was a reading of Gen. 1:27 as the creation of an original androgynous human in the image of God, then divided (Gen. 2:21f.) into male and female halves. Moreover, the "garments of skin" made for the fallen couple by God were nothing else than the physical bodies, necessary to replace the "garments of light" (a pun in Hebrew) which had been the "image of God." In view of these elements, baptism suggests a restoration of paradisiac motifs: the lost unity, the lost image, the lost glory.[55] The paraenetic reminders of baptism in the letters blend these mythical motifs with a more commonplace use of clothing imagery that appears frequently in the rhetoric of Hellenistic moralists, including Hellenistic Jewish writers and later Christian writers, both orthodox and gnostic. They admonish the readers to take off vices and to put on virtues in their place.

There is some evidence, principally in Ephesians, that the baptized and now reclothed person was next "enthroned with Christ in the heavenly places."[56] We can perhaps imagine how that could have been mimed, but the texts tell us nothing more.[57] Perhaps this element was present in the baptismal practice of Pauline communities from an early date, for the polemic of Paul in 1 Cor. 15 and his sarcasm in 1 Cor. 4:8 can be understood as opposing a too-enthusiastic appropriation of just such a notion. If the poems celebrating the exaltation of the Lord who had descended from heaven (Phil. 2:6–11; cf. Col. 1:15–20) were chanted at this point in the service, as I suggested above, a symbolic elevation of the believer at the same time would be fitting.

Like the unseen powers mentioned in the poem, the novice most likely then proclaimed, "The Lord is Jesus!" This confession would appropriately signify the change of dominion he had now undergone, from the world ruled by demonic powers, the "elements of the world," to the realm in which "the living God" and his Christ reign. From his new Lord he received certain gifts: the Spirit, adoption as God's child, power. He responded with the cry, "Abba! Father!"

It is immediately apparent that a great many of these motifs sort themselves out as pairs of opposites:

death, dying	life, rising
descending	ascending
burial	enthronement
old *anthrōpos*, body of flesh	new *anthrōpos*, body of Christ
oppositions	unity
taking off	putting on
vices	virtues
idols, demons, rulers of this world	living God, Christ Jesus as Lord

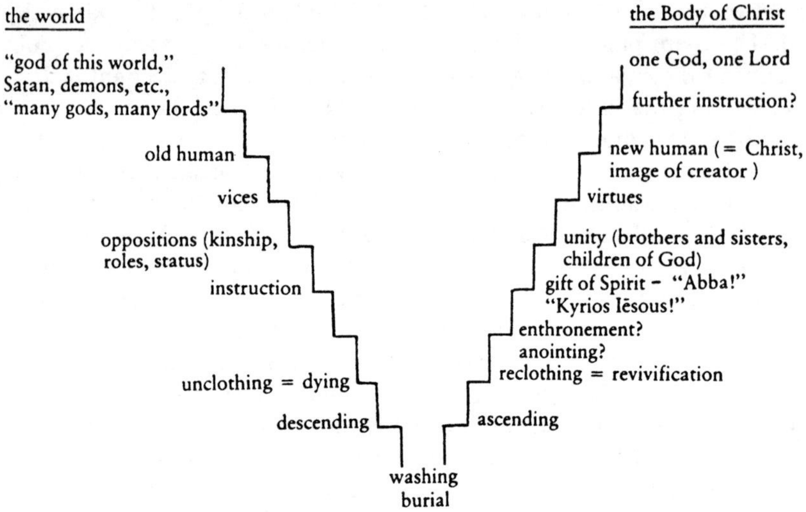

Figure 1

Furthermore, if we array these opposites according to the temporal stages of the ritual, the result is two nearly symmetrical movements. The first, characterized by descending action, climaxes with the "burial" in the water; it signifies the separation of the baptizand from the outside world. The second, a rising action, marks the integration of the baptized into another world, the sect on one plane, the heavenly reality on another. Figure 1 shows the verbal and conceptual progression.

This progression corresponds to the phases of every initiation or rite of passage: separation, transition, and reaggregation.[58] Nudity, symbolic death, rebirth as a child, abolition of distinctions of role and status—all are typical of the transitional or liminal phase in initiations. The most common picture of rites of passage, however, is abstracted from ceremonies that mark transition from one status to another within a small, homogeneous society: from child to man, from elder to chief. Baptism in early Christianity was different from that, different from, say, confirmation or first communion in an Irish Catholic parish, because the group which the initiate enters does not entirely share the same symbolic universe as the society from which he came. It sees itself, as a whole, distinct from "the world" even though, as we have seen at several points, the actual boundary between the two was more ambiguous than that simple statement would suggest. Victor Turner's extension of the concept of liminality to include an "anti-structural" component in more complex social situations, including the condition of marginal groups within complex societies, helps us to relate the early Christian rites to the theory of ritual.

The difference is apparent in the figure 1, in which some liminal elements had to be placed, not at the perigee of the parabola, but high on the "reaggregation" side. It is said of the body of Christ itself that "here there is neither Jew nor Greek, slave nor free, no male and female." The *ekklēsia* itself, not just the initiates during the period of their induction, is supposed to be marked by sacredness, homogeneity, unity, love, equality, humility, and so on—as Turner would say, by *communitas.* However, we have seen abundant evidence (chapters 3 and 4, above) that the Pauline groups suffered some tension between this mode of socialization, which opposes the normal structures of the macrosociety, and the old structures. The latter are not completely escapable, for the Christians continue to live in the city and to interact with its institutions, and besides, they still carry some of its structures in their minds and in the houses where they meet. Thus in the paraenesis of the later letters of the Pauline school, Colossians and Ephesians, reminders of the new "antiworldly" relations introduced in baptism stand alongside admonitions for proper behavior in hierarchically structured roles: husbands/wives, fathers/children, masters/slaves. These tensions also invade the meetings for the Lord's Supper.

The Lord's Supper: ritual of solidarity

The Pauline letters yield much less information about the other major ritual of early Christianity, the *kyriakon deipnon* (1 Cor. 11:20). The only explicit references to it are in 1 Cor. 11:17–34 and 10:14–22, and there it is easier to see the social implications that Paul is advocating than it is the ordinary social process of the ritual. He does, however, quote a sacred formula used in the celebration,[59] which differs slightly from the versions found in the later synoptic Gospels, and his polemic against aspects of the Corinthian practice permits some inferences about the usual procedure and understanding. First of all, the basic act is the eating of a common meal, at which it is possible that "one goes hungry, another is drunk" (1 Cor. 11:21). It is "the table of the Lord" (10:21). Festive meals were a common feature of the life of voluntary associations of all sorts, and the Christians' Supper was still understood in this way by Pliny, who early in the second century in Bithynia forbade such meals, in accordance with Trajan's ban against clubs (*Ep.* 10.97.7). A dining room was also "a distinctive and ubiquitous feature of cult centers" in antiquity, and invitations to dine "at the couch of Helios, Great Sarapis," or the like were a familiar part of urban social life.[60] For Christians to meet at intervals for such a meal with their Lord Jesus would not seem out of the ordinary.

In the second place, the ritual action imitates the meal of Jesus with his disciples "on the night in which he was betrayed" (11:23). The rite focuses on two moments: the breaking and distribution of bread at the beginning of the meal, accompanied by thanksgiving and a formulaic saying, "This is my body, which is for you; do this as my memorial"; and the passing of the cup of wine after the meal, with a parallel formula, "This cup is the new covenant in my blood; do this, as often as you drink, as my memorial" (11:24f.).[61]

The repeated injunction, "Do this as my memorial" (not found in the version of Mark and Matthew), shows that in the Pauline and even pre-Pauline tradition the celebration is understood as a cultic commemoration of Jesus. Most pointedly, it is a re-presentation of his death, as Paul's added comment in verse 26 underscores. This concept, too, would have been quite familiar in the environment of the early Christian groups, for, as Bo Reicke says, "The connection of the concept *anamnēsis* ['memorial'] with death is quite typical for people in antiquity."[62] It was also typical that a meal by the family, friends, or fellow burial-club members of the deceased would be the means of commemoration.[63] However, to understand the specific function of the memorial of Jesus it is perhaps most relevant to observe that it repeats under different imagery one of the central motifs of baptism. That is, the repeated sacrament of the Supper re-presents this central content of the initiatory ritual. Both rituals keep in the minds of the believers the fundamental story of the Lord's death. Beginning with this pre-Pauline (Antiochene?) tradition, the motif of commemoration would dominate the way the Eucharist was understood at least into the third century.[64]

Third, the formula contains an allusion to the vicarious meaning of the death in the expression "my body which is for you." This recalls similar expressions in many of the compact, formulaic sentences found in the letters, which are often thought to reproduce early Christian creedal summaries or preaching slogans.[65]

Fourth, there is an eschatological element: "until he comes." To be sure, that phrase belongs to a comment that Paul adds to the tradition, but some connection with Jesus' eschatological coming is found in all versions of the early Eucharistic tradition, though in varied verbal formulations. The Aramaic phrase that Paul quotes in the closing of this letter, *marana tha* (16:22), very likely also belongs to the setting of the Lord's Supper, as it does in the Didache (10:6).

Paul cites the Eucharistic traditions only in order to address certain conflicts which have arisen in the Corinthian congregation. In an illuminating way, Gerd Theissen has undertaken to reconstruct the social conditions underlying the disturbances rebuked by Paul in 1 Cor. 11:17–34 and to analyze Paul's "social intention" in his interpretation of the Supper in that passage.[66] I have already adopted much of Theissen's construction, with a few criticisms, in chapter 2. It may be helpful to recall here the main outline. The divisions in the group (11:18) are primarily between rich and poor. The wealthier members of the church are hosts of the gatherings and probably provide the food for all. Quite in accord with the expectations in many ancient clubs and with the practice often followed at banquets when dependents of a patron were invited, the hosts provide both greater quantity and better quality of food and drink to their social equals than to participants of lower status. The conflict was thus between "different standards of behavior," between "status-specific expectations and the norms of a community of love."[67] Paul's response, Theissen suggests, is a compromise, which asks that the wealthy have their private meal (*idion deipnon*) at home, so that in the Lord's Supper (*kyriakon deipnon*) the norm of equality can prevail. At the same time, Paul sets the social tensions into a larger symbolic universe by making them part of an "eschatological drama." The sacrament is "a zone under taboo, in which violation of norms has as its consequence incalculable disaster."[68] Paul underlines this notion by blaming sickness and deaths which have occurred in the community on such violations (11:30). Paul's social intention in all this is that revealed in 10:16: the transformation of a multiplicity of individuals into a unity.[69] Another way to put this would be to say that the *communitas* experienced in baptism, in which divisions of role and status are replaced by the unity of brothers and sisters in the new human, ought to be visible, in Paul's intention, in the Supper.

For Paul and his co-workers, the corollary of unity in the body of Christ is strict exclusion from all other religious connections. That is, group solidarity entails strong boundaries. Consequently Paul uses traditional language from the Supper ritual,[70] which speaks of the bread as "communion of the body of Christ" and the "cup of blessing" as "communion of the body of Christ," to warn that any participation in pagan cultic meals would be idolatry. The single loaf used in the ritual symbolizes the unity of Christ and of the believer with Christ and, consequently, the unity of the community in its participation in Christ (10:17). Just as in 6:12–20 Paul argues that union with the body of Christ excludes union with a prostitute, so here he insists that the unity presented in the Supper is exclusive. "You cannot drink the cup of the Lord and the cup of demons; you cannot share the table of the Lord and the table of demons" (10:21). It is this exclusivity of cult that was perhaps the strangest characteristic of Christianity, as of Judaism, in the eyes of the ordinary pagan. In this context, the ritual of the Lord's Supper entails for Paul a picture of the world that can be diagrammed as in Figure 2.

Thus, Paul uses the symbolism of the Supper ritual not only to enhance the internal coherence, unity, and equality of the Christian group, but also to protect its boundaries vis-à-vis other kinds of cultic association.

It must be stressed, however, that this symbolism of exclusivity is only one dimension of the complicated argument in 1 Cor. 8–10 about "meat offered to idols." While the passage just discussed absolutely excludes as idolatrous any participation in a pagan cultic meal, Paul is also at pains to show that nonsymbolic eating of pagan-butchered meat is a matter of indifference (10:25–27). It is only when the meat is deliberately made a symbol—whether through a public location, in an *eidōleion* (8:10), by uninformed belief of the "weak" Christians that idols are real (8:10; cf. vs. 7), or by a

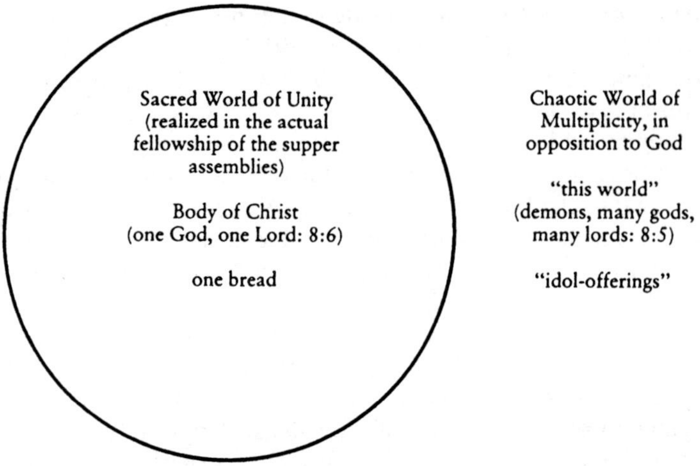

Figure 2

statement deliberately calling attention to the religious (sacrifical) character of the meat (10:28)—that it is forbidden for the Christian. To this extent Paul shares and approves the desacralizing *gnōsis* of the "strong" Christians at Corinth, by confirming the right and freedom of Christians to participate in the macrosociety so long as that participation does not upset the internal harmony and development of the Christian community. The complexity of Paul's interpretation implies that the intrinsic symbolism of the ritual is malleable; it is patient of multiple interpretations.

The unity symbolized by the Lord's Supper, I have suggested, can be seen as a reminder or re-presentation of the liminal transcendence of societal oppositions that was declared in baptism. Now it is commonly asserted that this baptismal unity and egalitarianism is "merely sacramental," that is, as a purely symbolic leveling it signifies an ideal state, perhaps a future eschatological state, but has no effect upon actual social roles.[71] Indeed, that is the way rites of passage ordinarily work in situations in which the boundaries of the religious association are more or less coterminous with the society. The temporary suspension of hierarchical classifications in the liminal period only reinforces their power in the ordinary world into which the initiate is then reintegrated. However, in the case of a group that maintains a strong identity distinct from the larger society, some aspects of liminality may linger in its daily life. The early Pauline communities were understandably not all of one mind about the implications of being, after baptism, all brothers and sisters in the one body.

For Paul, it was a matter of intense concern that at least one of the typical instances of reunification declared in the "baptismal reunification formula"[72] should have concrete social consequences. That there was now no distinction between Jew and gentile was for him (and for his learned disciple who wrote Ephesians) the most dramatic expression of the justification enacted by God through Christ Jesus. When, therefore, Cephas, Barnabas, and the other Jewish Christians at Antioch were persuaded to stop sharing the common meals with uncircumcised Christians, it was not merely a purely spiritual unity in the ritual meal that was at stake, but also the social unity of the church.[73] This unity points to the life of the "new human" now to be manifested in the life of the congregations and, in God's future, in the world. It is expressed in the ritual meal and perhaps also in other meals, for Gal. 2:12 does not restrict its reference to the Lord's Supper.

Yet the result was an ambiguous situation, and the letters reveal some confusion about the implications of the symbols of unity, not only in the practice of the Pauline groups, but even in Paul's own mind. Thus he may say that the slave at conversion has become "the Lord's freedman" and the "free person Christ's slave" (1 Cor. 7:22) and can ask Philemon to receive his runaway back, "no longer as a slave, but more than a slave, a beloved brother" (Philem. 16), but he nowhere urges Philemon or other owners to free their slaves. And the authors of the later letters in his name quote Christianized household rules that require slaves strictly to obey their masters. On the other hand, women do exercise some social roles in the Pauline missionary activity and congregational life that are equivalent to those of men, and Paul himself stresses equivalence of rights and duties in marriage (1 Cor. 7). Still, he objects to *symbolic* disregard for sexual differences in the dress of male and female prophets (1 Cor. 11:2–16). The relation between the symbolic reality presented in the rituals and everyday reality, both in the inner life of the group and in interaction with the larger society, remained an area of controversy and ambiguity. And, of course, this ambiguity remains at the heart of our own hermeneutical perplexity when we try to understand what rituals do for people.

Unknown and controverted rituals

We have squeezed about all the information we can from the quotations and allusions in the literature. Yet we surmise that the Pauline Christians used still other ceremonies of which we know virtually nothing. We know, for example, that some of them died during the span of time covered by the letters, and we know that funeral rituals were of enormous importance to people in Greek and Roman society. A great many of the clubs we have mentioned were formed primarily to assure the associates a decent burial and memorial. We can be certain that the congregations Paul founded provided equivalent services for their members, but, apart from one utterly enigmatic remark, the letters say nothing at all about what was done for those who, as they said, "had fallen asleep." Probably the Christians buried their dead in the same places and in the same fashion as their neighbors. Those who could afford it probably erected inscriptions recalling high points of the deceased's life, indicating significant titles of status or profession, and giving the dates—but if they did, either the inscriptions remain lost or there was nothing overtly Christian about them to distinguish them from the others that have been found. The commonest memorial rite was a meal in honor of the departed, often around a table-shaped stone in the cemetery, on several specific anniversaries of the day of death. In later centuries this practice was common among Christians as among pagans—the first clear evidence is in Tertullian.[74] Nothing would seem more natural than for the Christians of Paul's groups, for whom common meals were already so important, to hold funeral meals for deceased brothers as well—either separately, or as part of the Lord's Supper, which was already an *anamnēsis* of the Lord's death. Yet there is not a word about such meals, not even in the consolation that Paul offers the Thessalonian Christians (1 Thess. 4:13–18), where we might have expected it. Perhaps the customs were too well known to mention. Paradoxically, the one practice that is mentioned, in 1 Cor. 15:29, is mystifying to us. Paul is arguing with the *pneumatikoi* at Corinth that resurrection does not mean only spiritual exaltation now, but a real, future resurrection of the dead body. "Otherwise," he asks, "what are they doing who are baptized for the dead? If the dead are not raised at all, why are they baptized on their behalf?" What *are* they doing? The Corinthians presumably knew, but we do not, despite interesting speculations without end.

The Pauline Christians also got married. And if a widow decided to remarry (although Paul preferred that she remain single), she should do so "only in the Lord" (1 Cor. 7:39). Presumably this means that she ought to marry a fellow Christian, and presumably the same rule would apply also to persons not previously married. But did "in the Lord" also imply a Christian ceremony? We do not know.

Besides the regular gatherings of the Christians, which probably but not certainly occurred weekly, did they also observe an annual calendar of seasons or any special festivals? Some Jewish Christians did, and both the missionaries who tried to reform the Pauline churches of Galatia and the syncretistic cult that developed among the Christians in Colossae tried to introduce the celebration of "days and months and seasons and years" (Gal. 4:10; Col. 2:16: "festival or new moon or sabbath"). Paul resisted this innovation vigorously and so did his disciple, the author of Colossians. Yet some commentators have found in 1 Cor. 5:6–8 and 16:8 reason to believe that Paul himself and his churches celebrated both a Christianized Passover and Pentecost (*Shabuoth*).[75] That is a far from necessary conclusion, however.

Acts and the Pauline letters provide only tantalizing glimpses of the rituals practiced by the Pauline groups, but those glimpses are enough for us to see that they had adopted or created a rich variety of ceremonial forms. There is a striking mix of the free and the customary, familiar and novel, simple and complex, in what we can see of their meetings. The *idiōtēs* or unbeliever, entering one of these meetings, might have thought them a bit odd, but he would have recognized them as a cultic community of some kind. Whether he called them a dangerous superstition or a strange religion would depend on personal sympathy or lack of it.

Notes

1 Judge 1980*b*, 212.
2 Ibid.
3 MacMullen 1981, 1–48, with abundant documentation, pp. 141–67.
4 *Ep.* 10.96.8: "Nihil aliud inveni quam superstitionem pravam, immodicam."
5 Tacitus *Ann.* 15.44.3; Suetonius *Nero* 16.3.
6 Celsus, who had made a more thorough investigation of the subject toward the end of the century, accused the Christians not of having no rites, but of performing them in secret (Origen C. *Cels.* 1.3). Morton Smith has argued that the Christians were not only labeled superstitious by outsiders, but often accused of practicing magic (1978, 1980).
7 Spiro 1966, 96.
8 Ibid., 97.
9 Leach 1968, 524.
10 See the classic discussion of "manifest" and "latent" functions in Merton 1967, 73–138.
11 Goody 1961, 157.
12 Durkheim 1912, 22; Gellner 1962, 119f.
13 Douglas 1973, 42, 78.
14 Berger–Luckmann 1966; Geertz 1957, 1966.
15 Austin 1975.
16 This is implicit in the opening formulas of the letters.
17 Cf. MacMullen's remarks about difficulty finding space for a large dinner party (1981, 36).
18 *Ep.* 10.96.7.
19 *1 Apol.* 67.
20 Barrett 1968, 327.
21 Dibelius–Greeven 1953 and Lohse 1968 are typical of those who see no clear distinction.
22 Lightfoot 1879, 225, citing Philo's report of hymns of thanksgiving in Alexandria for deliverance from a pogrom (*Flacc.* 121–24).
23 1QH. See Vermes 1978, 56–65, and the further literature cited there.
24 See MacMullen 1981, 15–24. Dibelius–Greeven 1953 *ad loc.* call attention to Epictetus *Diss.* 1.15–21, who declares that anyone who recognizes the pervasiveness of providence ought constantly to express thanks, even while digging and plowing and eating, by "a hymn to God."
25 Dahl 1951.
26 Vielhauer 1939.
27 The reconstruction, by the learned Protestant pastor Paul Billerbeck, of "a synagogue service in the time of Jesus," published posthumously without references to sources (1964), illustrates the danger. It draws together evidence from rabbinic literature of a wide range of dates and provenances, all later than the New Testament, without any clear principle of selection or attention to the problems of redaction or history of tradition. For a more careful discussion, see Schürer 1973–, 2:447–54.

28 Dahl 1954; cf. Bultmann 1948–53, 1:105f.
29 Rom. 16:25–27; see Gamble 1977.
30 On the *b^e^rakah*, Audet 1958.
31 Schlier 1933.
32 See later in this chapter.
33 *Oxford English Dictionary* s.v. "rite."
34 Goodman 1972.
35 Braumann 1962 undertook to recover the major motifs in the baptismal liturgy presupposed by Paul, but his exegesis is superficial. Schille 1952, 1962 has many imaginative suggestions but no way of testing them. For a good review of the latter, see Dahl 1955. Dinkler 1962*a* provides excellent general surveys.
36 Hippolytus *Trad. apost.* 21; text in Botte 1963, 48–50.
37 See Kraeling 1967.
38 Lev. 14:51f.; 15:13; Num. 19:17; and elsewhere.
39 Neusner 1977, 57f., 83–87. I am by no means equating the function of the *t^e^bilah* as a whole with Christian baptism, although the former most likely provided a number of the fundamental procedures for the latter. Neusner's note on p. 87 is apposite: ". . . the Mishnaic conception of the immersion-pool bears no relationship to baptism for the removal of sins. . . ."
40 Perhaps not completely unthinkable, though: the priests of Isis at Cenchreae made use of "the nearest bath" (*ad proximas balneas*) for "the customary ablution" of an initiate, according to Apuleius *Met.* 11.23. Acts 8:36; 16:13–15, 33 imply that any available water could serve.
41 It soon occurred to someone that it would be more appropriate to have the baptized put on new, white garments after immersion. See Klijn 1954 and J. Z. Smith 1965 (with extensive literature). But nothing in the Pauline texts requires us to suppose that that practice was already in use.
42 Already quite elaborate in Hippolytus *Trad. apost.* 21.
43 Lampe 1967*b*, 61f.
44 Acts 19:28, of Artemis; see the examples cited by Epictetus, cited above, n. 28; Aelius Aristides *Sacr. serm.* 2.7,21 (of Asklepius); Minucius Felix *Octav.* 18.11.
45 There is room for doubt whether the "oath" mentioned by Pliny referred to baptism, but most interpreters have taken it to, for rather good reasons. See, e.g., Nock 1924*a*; R. M. Grant 1948, 56.
46 Mylonas 1961, 194 and fig. 70; Kerényi 1967, fig. 14.
47 Clement Alex. *Strom.* 4.3.1, cited by Mylonas 1961, 241.
48 Mylonas 1961, 224–85.
49 Apuleius *Met.* 11.23; not to mention the sevenfold washing that Lucius was inspired to undertake before praying to the goddess, while still an ass (11.1).
50 Neusner 1977; cf. idem 1973*a*.
51 Notably Moore 1927, 1:323–53; 3:n. 102; Rowley 1940; Jeremias 1949; Dix 1937, xl; Cullmann 1948, 9, 56, and passim. Criticism: Dahl 1955; Michaelis 1951. It is true that in the late compilation of rules about proselytes, Gerim 2.4, *t^e^bilah* is treated as one of the indispensable procedures through which a proselyte "enters the covenant," along with circumcision. It has been argued, on the basis of certain statements by Philo, *QE* 2.2, *Virt.* 175–86; remarks by Epictetus, *Diss.* 2.9.19–21; and the debate between R. Eliezer and R. Joshua in the *baraita* of b Yeb. 46a, that (male) proselytes were sometimes received by baptism alone, without circumcision. I think in each case that overinterprets what the texts say or, in the case of the Greek sources, do *not* say. Space does not permit me to argue the issue here.
52 Hippolytus *Trad. apost.* 20.

53 See Dahl 1947.
54 E.g., Odes Sol. 27; Tertullian *De orat.* 14; Minucius Felix *Octav.* 29.8.
55 Much of the evidence is collected in Meeks 1974.
56 Eph. 2:4–7; cf. 1:3 and Col. 1:5,12; 2:12,20; 3:1–4.
57 For later examples, see the wide-ranging remarks of Widengren 1968; on Mandaean ceremonies of "raising up" that may reflect influence from Syrian Christian rites, see Segelberg 1958, 66f., 89–91. Coronation with wreaths was important in certain Syrian, Armenian, Coptic, and Ethiopic Christian baptismal rites, according to Bernard 1912, 45f.
58 Van Gennep 1909; V. Turner 1969, 94–130.
59 Barrett's skepticism on this point (1968, 264) seems excessive.
60 MacMullen 1981, 36–42 (quotation from p. 36). Broneer 1973, 33–46, describes two interesting subterranean facilities, each with two dining rooms containing altogether eleven couches, under the theater and the Poseidon temple at Isthmia. Dennis Smith 1980 has collected a great deal of evidence of this sort. On the possible influence of club meals on early Christian practice, see Reicke 1951*a*, 320–38.
61 Trans. Barrett 1968 *ad loc.*
62 Reicke 1951*a*, 257. He backs this statement by citing inscriptions from the imperial age, e.g., one from Nicaea in which a certain Aurelius leaves money to the village of the Racelians, "for them to make my memorial".
63 Reicke 1951*a*, 257–64; later Christian meals for the dead, 101–49; antecedents in paganism and Judaism, 104–18. Although Reicke thinks the cult of the dead "fundamentally foreign" to "normal Judaism," he admits that there is a good bit of evidence for Jewish memorial meals (263, 104–18).
64 Dahl 1947, 21f., and the literature cited in his n. 49.
65 E.g., Rom. 5:6,8; 14:15; 1 Cor. 15:3; 2 Cor. 5:15, 21; Gal. 1:4; 2:20; 3:13; Eph. 5:2,25.
66 Theissen 1974*b*.
67 Ibid., 309.
68 Ibid., 312.
69 Ibid., 313f.
70 Käsemann 1947, 12f.
71 This view has been forcefully expressed by, among others, Ste. Croix 1975, 19f.
72 Meeks 1974, 180–83.
73 Dahl 1977, 109f.
74 *De monog.* 10; *De cor.* 3; Reicke 1951, 120–31. Mart. Polyc. 18:3 shows that at least for martyrs the practice was known earlier.
75 See Jeremias 1954, 900–904, and further literature cited there.

List of abbreviations

EvT	Evangelische Theologie
HR	History of Religions
HTR	*Harvard Theological Review*
IESS	International Encyclopedia of the Social Sciences
*RGG*³	*Religion in Geschichte und Gegenwart*, 3d ed.
TDNT	Theological Dictionary of the New Testament
TZ	Theologische Zeitschrift
ZNW	*Zeitschrift für die neutestamentliche Wissenschaft*

Bibliography of secondary works cited

Audet, J. P. 1958. "Esquisse historique du genre littéraire de la 'bénédiction' juive et de l' 'eucharistie' chrétienne." *RB* 65:371–99.

Austin, J. L. 1975. *How to Do Things with Words.* Edited by J. O. Urmson and Marina Sbisà. 2d ed. Cambridge, Mass.: Harvard University Press.

Barrett, Charles Kingsley. 1968. *A Commentary on the First Epistle to the Corinthians.* Harper/Black New Testament Commentaries. London: Black; New York: Harper & Row.

Berger, Peter L., and Luckmann, Thomas. 1966. *The Social Construction of Reality: A Treatise in the Sociology of Knowledge.* Garden City, N.Y.: Doubleday.

Bernard, J. H. 1912. *The Odes of Solomon.* Texts and Studies, vol. 8, pt. 3. Cambridge: At the University Press.

Billerbeck, Paul. 1964. "Ein Synagogengottesdienst in Jesu Tagen." *ZNW* 55:143–61.

Botte, Bernard. 1963. *La Tradition apostolique de Saint Hippolyte: Essai de reconstruction.* Liturgiewissenschaftliche Quellen und Forschungen, 39. Münster: Aschendorff.

Braumann, Georg. 1962. *Vorpaulinische christliche Taufverkündigung bei Paulus.* Beiträge zur Wissenschaft vom Alten und Neuen Testament, 82. Stuttgart: Kohlhammer.

Broneer, Oscar, ed. 1973. *Isthmia.* Vol. 2: *Topography and Architecture.* Princeton: American School of Classical Studies, Athens.

Bultmann, Rudolf K. 1948–53. *Theologie des Neuen Testaments.* 2 vols. Neue theologische Grundrisse. Tübingen: Mohr (Siebeck). References are to the translation by Kendrick Grobel, *Theology of the New Testament.* 2 vols. New York: Scribner's, 1951–55.

Dahl, Nils Alstrup. 1976. "Form-critical Observations on Early Christian Preaching." In *Jesus in the Memory of the Early Church.* Minneapolis: Augsburg, 1976, pp. 30–36.

——. 1955. "The Origin of Baptism." In *Interpretationes ad Vetus Testamentum Pertinentes Sigmundo Mowinckel Septuagenario Missae*, ed. Nils A. Dahl and A. S. Kapelrud, pp. 36–52. Oslo: Land og Kirke.

——. 1977. *Studies in Paul: Theology for the Early Christian Mission.* Minneapolis: Augsburg.

Dibelius, Martin, and Greeven, Heinrich. 1953. *An die Kolosser, Epheser, an Philemon.* 3d ed. Handbuch zum Neuen Testament, 12. Tübingen: Mohr (Siebeck).

Douglas, Mary. 1973. *Natural Symbols: Explorations in Cosmology.* 2d ed. London: Barrie & Jenkins.

Durkheim, Emile. 1912. *Les Formes élémentaires de la vie religieuse: Le Système totémique en Australie.* Paris: Alcan. References are to the translation by J. W. Swain, *The Elementary Forms of the Religious Life.* 1915. Reprint. New York: Free Press, 1965.

Geertz, Clifford. 1957. "Ethos, World View, and the Analysis of Sacred Symbols." *Antioch Review* 17:421–37. Reprinted in Geertz 1973, 126–41.

——. 1973. *The Interpretation of Cultures: Selected Essays.* New York: Basic Books.

Gellner, Ernest. 1962. "Concepts and Society." In *Transactions of the Fifth World Congress of Sociology* 1:153–83. References are to the reprint in *Sociological*

Theory and Philosophical Analysis, ed. Dorothy Emmet and Alasdair MacIntyre, pp. 115–49. London and New York: Macmillan, 1970.
Gennep, Arnold van. 1909. *Les Rites de passage: Étude systématique des rites de la porte. . . .* Paris: Nourry. Translated by M. B. Vizedom and G. L. Caffee, *The Rites of Passage*. London: Routledge and Kegan Paul; Chicago: University of Chicago Press, 1960.
Goodman, Felicitas D. 1972. *Speaking in Tongues: A Cross-Cultural Study of Glossolalia*. Chicago and London: University of Chicago Press.
Goodspeed, Edgar J. 1950. "Gaius Titius Justus." *JBL* 69:382–83.
Goody, Jack. 1961. "Religion and Ritual: The Definitional Problem." *British Journal of Sociology* 12:142–64.
Grant, Robert M. 1948. *After the New Testament: Studies in Early Christian Literature and Theology*. Philadelphia: Fortress, 1967, pp. 55–56.
Jeremias, Joachim. 1949. "Proselytentaufe und NT." *TZ* 5:418–28.
——. 1954. "πάσχα." *TWNT* 5:895–903. References are to the translation in *TDNT* 5 (1967):896–904.
Kerényi, C. [Károly]. 1967. *Eleusis: Archetypal Image of Mother and Daughter*. Reprint. New York: Schocken, 1977.
Käsemann, Ernst. 1947. "Anliegen und Eigenart der paulinischen Abendmahlslehre." *EvT* 7:263–83. References are to the reprint in *Exegetische Versuche und Besinnungen*, vol. 2, pp. 11–34. 3d ed. Göttingen: Vandenhoeck & Ruprecht, 1964.
Klijn, A. F. J. 1954. "An Early Christian Baptismal Liturgy." In *Charis kai Sophia: Festschrift Karl Heinrich Rengstorf*, ed. Ulrich Luck, pp. 216–28. Leiden: Brill.
Kraeling, Carl H. 1967. *The Christian Building. The Excavations at Dura-Europos: Final Reports*, vol. 8, pt. 2. New Haven and London: Yale University Press.
Lampe, G. W. H. 1967*b*. *The Seal of the Spirit: A Study in the Doctrine of Baptism and Confirmation in the New Testament and the Fathers.* 2d ed. London: S.P.C.K.
Leach, Edmund. 1968. "Ritual." *IESS*, vol. 13, pp. 520–26.
MacMullen, Ramsay. 1981. *Paganism in the Roman Empire*. New Haven and London: Yale University Press.
Merton, Robert K. 1967. *Social Theory and Social Structure: Five Essays, Old and New*. New York: Free Press.
Mylonas, George F. 1961. *Eleusis and the Eleusinian Mysteries*. Princeton: Princeton University Press.
Neusner, Jacob. 1977. *A History of the Mishnaic Law of Purities*. Studies in Judaism in Late Antiquity 6. Part 22: *The Mishnaic System of Uncleanness*. Leiden: Brill.
Ste. Croix, G. E. M. de. 1975. "Early Christian Attitudes to Property and Slavery." In *Church, Society, and Politics*, ed. Derek Baker, pp. 1–38. Studies in Church History, 12. Oxford: Blackwell.
Schille, Gottfried. 1952. "Liturgisches Gut im Epheserbrief." D. Theol. dissertation, Göttingen.
Schürer, Emil. 1973–. *The History of the Jewish People in the Age of Jesus Christ (175 B.C.–A.D. 135)*. Edited and revised by Geza Vermes, Fergus Millar, and Matthew Black. Edinburgh: Clark. 2 vols. to date.
Smith, Dennis E. 1980. "Social Obligation in the Context of Communal Meals: A Study of the Christian Meal in 1 Corinthians in Comparison with Graeco-Roman Communal Meals." Th.D. dissertation, Harvard University.
Smith, Jonathan Z. 1965. "The Garments of Shame." *HR* 5:224–30.

Spiro, Melford E. 1966. "Religion: Problems of Definition and Explanation." In *Anthropological Approaches to the Study of Religion*, ed. Michael Banton, pp. 85–126. Association of Social Anthropologists Monographs, 3. London: Tavistock.

Theissen, Gerd. 1974*b*. "Soziale Integration und sakramentales Handeln: Eine Analyse von 1 Cor. XI 17–34." *NovT* 24:179–205. References are to the reprint in Theissen 1979, 290–317.

——. 1979. *Studien zur Soziologie des Urchristentums.* Wissenschaftliche Untersuchungen zum Neuen Testament, 19. Tübingen: Mohr (Siebeck).

Turner, Victor. 1964. "Betwixt and Between: The Liminal Period in *Rites de Passage.*" In *Proceedings of the American Ethnological Society, 1964.* References are to the reprint in idem, ed., *The Forest of Symbols: Aspects of Ndembu Ritual.* Ithaca, N.Y.: Cornell University Press, 1977, pp. 93–111.

Vermes, Geza. 1978. *The Dead Sea Scrolls: Qumran in Perspective.* Cleveland: Collins-World.

Vielhauer, Philipp. 1939. "*Oikodomē:* Das Bild vom Bau in der christlichen Literatur vom Neuen Testament bis Clemens Alexandrinus." D. Theol. dissertation, Heidelberg. References are to the reprint in *Oikodome: Aufsätze zum Neuen Testament*, ed. Günter Klein, vol. 2, pp. 1–168. Theologische Bücherei, 65. Munich: Kaiser.

Widengren, Geo. 1968. "Heavenly Enthronement and Baptism: Studies in Mandaean Baptism." In *Religions in Antiquity: Essays in Memory of Erwin Ramsdell Goodenough*, ed. Jacob Neusner, pp. 551–89. Studies in the History of Religion, 14. Leiden: Brill.

11

OFFICE CHARISMA IN EARLY CHRISTIAN EPHESUS

Anthony J. Blasi

Source: *Sociology of Religion*, 56(3) (1995), 245–55.

In his description of office charisma, Max Weber (1978:1139–1141) speaks of the reversal of "genuine charisma" into its opposite; originally the holder of charisma would be "ennobled by virtue of his own actions" (1978:1139) and a personal following, but with office charisma legitimacy comes by virtue of inheritance or a ritualized acquisition of the office, irrespective of the personal or "genuine charisma" of the individual (Weber 1978:1139–1141). The incumbent of an office that is the locus of charisma, in contrast to the personal charisma of the holder of that office, follows procedures that tend toward the kind of authority that Weber (1978:217–218) terms "legal," wherein rules follow the logic of instrumental reason, where an abstract system of law that may be applied to cases develops, where holders of authority are themselves subject to an impersonal order, where members of an organization obey the law *as members*, and where members obey their superior not because of the latter's person but because of the order that those superiors represent. I say "tend toward," since Weber's depiction is that of a pure type rather than any real case.

Office charisma is important in the continuation of religious entities beyond the time of their founding figures and in the maintenance of formal religious organizations. Apart from peculiarly religious phenomena, office charisma is vital in business organizations that survive their founding entrepreneurs and in political organizations that survive their founding revolutionaries. In the modern governmental world, office charisma is essential to the effectiveness of non-political, civil service offices. In democracies, where a large sector of the public prefers governance by someone other than the politician who ends up holding office, it is office charisma that is needed in order to obtain from that part of the public a general compliance with the legislated will of the government.

In the modern world, office charisma in religious organizations sometimes assumes a wider significance when legitimacy has not been established in secular contexts. For example, with the establishment of more or less artificial states in the Middle East in the wake of colonial administrations, theocracy as a form of political legitimation in effect substitutes religious office charisma for its political counterpart. It may well be a transitional form of legitimation, comparable to the era of the "divine right of kings" and their established religions in post-feudal European history. A similar transitional role for religious office charisma may be seen in the histories of education, medicine, and retirement facilities, with religious sponsorship of schools, hospitals, and homes for the elderly.

The purpose of the present study is to examine an instance in which office charisma emerged in order to bring to light some of the key factors that are involved. The intent, therefore, is to elaborate Weber's model, not "test" it; we want to see why personal charisma would reverse itself into its opposite, and under what conditions the personal charisma of Jesus of Nazareth, diffuse as it was after his execution, would reverse itself into the office charisma of early bishops, deacons, and presbyters. The instance in question is the development of such church offices in early Ephesian Christianity. Our "data" for a given moment in time are derived from a literary source — the letter of Ignatius of Antioch to the Ephesian Christians — and leading up to the time of that letter the data include background information contained in the texts of the New Testament. Because organizational developments may occur differently in different places, our focus on one community, Ephesus, will hopefully simplify matters. Consequently, information emanating from other locales will be relevant as historical information that impinged on Ephesus as elements of the Christians' heritage, their prior cultural history. Ephesus had been a Christian community for quite some time when Ignatius wrote to the Christians there; a number of references to the Ephesian Christians are to be found in the New Testament.

Ignatius of Antioch

Early in the second century C.E., during the reign of the Roman Emperor Trajan (98–117), a Christian bishop from Antioch was arrested in Syria and sent under guard to Rome for execution. Rather than follow a route through the Asia Minor city of Ephesus, a major Christian center, as well as through Tralles and Magnesia, the entourage took a northern route through Philadelphia to Smyrna. The churches that had been bypassed, including Ephesus, sent delegations to meet Ignatius in Smyrna — evidently as a show of support. A number of letters from Ignatius to these and other churches have been preserved, including one written from Smyrna to the Ephesian Christians (Holmes 1992:129–135). Our focus is on this letter.

One of the interesting features of Ignatius' letter to the Ephesians is the fact that he refers to their bishop, Onesimus, their deacon, Burrhus, and to Christian patterns of internal governance in general. For example:

> For Jesus Christ, our inseparable life, is the mind of the Father, just as the bishops appointed throughout the world are in the mind of Christ.
>
> Thus it is proper for you to act together in harmony with the mind of the bishop, as you are in fact doing. For your presbytery, which is worthy of its name and worthy of God, is attuned to the bishops as strings to a lyre (Ig. Eph. 3–4, translation in *Apostolic Fathers*; numbers refer to paragraphs in the Greek).

It appears that some of the Christians had not remained in communion with the bishops: Ignatius warns that those not "in the sanctuary" with the bishop lack the bread of God (Ig. Eph. 4.2). He also refers to certain people "with evil doctrine" whom the Ephesians resisted (9.1). In order to interpret this information in the light of development processes in organizations, it is necessary to examine some of the models of governance that appeared earlier in Christian history. Specifically, we need to know what was meant by *presbyter* and *presbytery*, by *bishop*, and by *deacon.* We also need to know what contexts may have been associated with such terms and offices:

Aspects of early Christian governance

The sociology of early Christianity, as distinct from a sociology of the Palestinian Jesus movement, focuses on the new religious movement that formed around the posthumous charisma of Jesus (see, e.g., Blasi 1986, 1988, 1991). Looking at the phenomenon as a new religious movement sidesteps the issue of whether the church/sect typology applies at all to early Christianity; movements allow for the presence within them of diverse social movement organizations, some of which may be more sect-like and some more denomination-like; a perfect "church" form (Weber 1978:1164–1169), of course, would be impossible in the pluralistic context of the Roman empire. In the contemporary sociology of early Christianity, Harry W. Eberts (1994) has been engaged in remarkably informative research on differing patterns of governance among different, ethnically identifiable groupings of Christians. Closely examining the terms used in the New Testament to refer to groupings of Christians, Eberts notes that there were three groups — Disciples, Apostles, and Brothers — and that the Disciples experienced a split that gave rise to a fourth group, the Hellenists. The Disciples were governed by the Twelve, the Hellenists by the Seven, the Apostles by the Assembly, and the Brothers by the Presbyters. He observes that the clientele of the Disciples consisted of members of diaspora synagogues, that of the Hellenists consisted of Greek-speaking Jews and proselytes, that of the Apostles consisted of godfearers (Gentiles partially participating in Jewish life) in diaspora synagogues, and that of the Brothers consisted of members of Judean synagogues. This pattern was soon disrupted by "terminating events" that Eberts identifies for each grouping, between the years 31 and 65. Since Ignatius was writing decades later we could only expect to find traces of this quasi-ethnic pattern of groupings reflected in his letter to the Ephesians but we can learn from Eberts to take the terms used for Christian groupings and their respective offices seriously, and to be wary of the editorial purposes of some New Testament authors, especially the author of Luke/Acts, of seeing the history of the early Christians as one rather than many stories.

Bishop — episkopos

We have observed that Ignatius, himself a bishop, identifies Onesimus of Ephesus as a bishop. The term that translators render as "bishop" is *episkopos*, literally, "overseer." If we take Paul's Letter to the Philippians to be an authentic letter of Paul of Tarsus (Collins 1988:15), then by far the earliest reference to bishops in the New Testament is the address section of that letter, where Paul directs his communication to, among others, bishops in Philippi (Phil. 1.1). The office of bishop would appear, then, in a Gentile church founded by Paul (see Acts 16), and it would occur in the plural in one community.

The term also appears in the Acts of the Apostles, in an emotional scene in which Paul, on his way to Jerusalem (and eventually to Rome where he was martyred), stops in Miletus and sends for the presbyters of Ephesus, who come out to Miletus for his farewell address. The address includes this sentence: "Take care of yourselves and all the flock, in which the Holy Spirit has placed you as bishops to shepherd God's church . . ." (Acts 20.28).[1] Such a speech, following the authorial practice of the time, would have been a composition of the author of Acts, "Luke," rather than the person depicted as speaking, Paul (see Aune 1987:124–128). It seems to equate presbyters and bishops, but in no other place in Acts do these terms appear to be interchangeable. Acts appears to use several sources for the legends it reports, yet the term bishop does not appear in the source material, but rather only in this dramatized episode. In fact, associating the Pauline tradition of Gentile churches (which had bishops) with the presence of presbyters in Ephesus seems to be a point of the composition.

In general, Acts presents Paul as a major figure, a founding personage, of the Christian churches in Asia Minor and Greece. Judging from his letters Paul had been a controversial figure in his own day, and the narrative in Acts relating Paul's taking up a relief collection for the Jerusalem Christians implies that the latter would not even accept such a gift from the churches Paul had founded. In such a context Acts appears as a work of advocacy calling for a wider acceptance of the Pauline tradition and presenting the earlier hostility toward Paul as an outgrowth of an argument over Torah observance (especially, circumcision), an argument that no longer concerned a live issue at the time that Acts was being written. Establishing an equivalency between the presbyters, whom Paul knew in Ephesus, and bishops, who were to be found in the Gentile churches, would be an aspect of the author's argument that Paul's Gentile Christianity should be accepted as equivalent to the Christianity coming from a more Jewish environment.

The effort to gain acceptance for Paul and even to have him endowed with considerable posthumous charisma succeeded (Blasi 1991). One of the effects of this effort was the composition of a body of letters in Paul's name — a typical way of honoring a personage from the past in ancient times as well as of maintaining authorial anonymity (Meade 1986; Collins 1988:75–86). One of the resultant deutero-pauline letters, First Timothy, lists moral qualities that the author thought a bishop should have (1 Tim. 3.2). Another such letter, Titus, uses the term *bishop* interchangeably with *presbyter* (Tit. 1.7), much in the manner of Acts 20.28. Both of these letters tend to associate the Pauline charisma with the office of bishop.[2]

The evidence is limited, but the foregoing review of it leads us to believe that the office of bishop was more recent than that of presbyter, apostle, the Twelve, or the Seven, which appear in earliest Christianity in Jerusalem. There seemed to be a felt need on the part of the authors of Acts, First Timothy, and Titus to buoy up the authority of the office by associating it with the charisma of Paul, and similarly to gain wider acceptance for Paul among Christians who already accepted the institution of the presbytery.

Deacon — diakonos

Ignatius speaks of Burrhus of Ephesus as a deacon of the Ephesian church. The word used in Greek is *diakonos*, literally "waiter" (as at a banquet; see Gal. 2.17) and "messenger." It seems to identify a person with a serving function rather than a condition of being born into slavery, which would be indicated by another expression, *doulos*, or of being taken into slavery in war, which would be indicated by *andrapodon*. In the New Testament the use of *diakonos* to refer to a Christian church office occurs in the Pauline and deutero-pauline literature.[3] In the Corinthian correspondence, written in Ephesus, Paul refers to himself not only as an apostle but also as a deacon (1 Cor. 3.54, 2 Cor. 3.6, 6.4). In a controversy passage he refers to his opponents within the Christian church as false apostles who disguise themselves as deacons of righteousness (i.e., servants of God; 2 Cor. 11.15) and makes a point of breaking the flow of his rhetoric in order to avoid referring to advocates of Gentile Christians observing Torah prescriptions as deacons of Christ (2 Cor. 11.23). The letter to the Philippians (1.1) is addressed to bishops and deacons. Interestingly, Romans 16.1 refers to a Christian woman, Phoebe of Cenchreae, with the masculine noun, deacon (accusative form: *diakonon*). All of this tells us that the Pauline Gentile churches had male and female officials called deacons from a very early point in time in Christian history.

While the Acts of the Apostles associated presbyters with the office of bishop, as noted above, it does not refer to deacons. Rather it is in the deutero-pauline letters, seemingly influenced by Acts, that the term appears again. The Letter to the Ephesians and the Letter to the Colossians imitate Paul's style by having "Paul" identify himself as a deacon (Eph. 3.7, Col. 1.23 and 1.25); they also identify someone named Tychicus as a deacon (Eph. 6.21, Col. 4.7). Colossians 1.7 speaks of Epaphras as a fellow deacon of Paul. More significantly, First Timothy lists the desired moral qualifications for deacons and makes a point of identifying them as different persons from women, contrary to the earlier practice of Paul. Specifically, the letter says a deacon should be a husband of one wife (1 Tim. 3.8–13). It also says a good servant of Christ (*diakonos Christou*) would put the letter's instructions before the Brothers (1 Tim. 4.6); it should be recalled that a Christian grouping in Jerusalem had been called the Brothers, and we cannot exclude the possibility that First Timothy was directed to a church that identified itself with the earlier Judean grouping. The whole passage reflects an effort to impose a reticence over women at banquets (a presence having negative moral connotations in Hellenistic culture) on the whole of Christianity, including Jewish Christians (see Corley 1993).

Presbyter and presbytery — presbuteros and presbuterion

Presbuteros is the comparative of *presbus*, "old man;" hence it translates as "elder" and as one having greater dignity or power. *Presbuterion* refers to a council of such persons. In the synoptic gospels and in most instances in the Acts of the Apostles the terms refer to a grouping of Jewish leaders in Jerusalem. Since about 300 B.C.E. religious and civil authority in Jerusalem had been intermittently in the hands of a high priest together with a council of elders (Sanhedrin), equivalent to senates or *gerousia* elsewhere in the region. The Christian grouping in Jerusalem known as the Brothers similarly had leaders called presbyters (see Acts 11.30); Acts often refers to these Christian presbyters in Jerusalem, sometimes pairing the reference with mentions of "apostles" (Acts 15.2, 15.4, 15.6, 15.22, 15.23, 16.4, 21.18). Early in his missionary career, when he was associated with a church at Antioch and working together with Barnabas, Paul was appointing presbyters in churches in eastern Asia Minor (Acts 14.23). Later, in Miletus when he was ready to leave for Jerusalem, Paul called together the presbyters of the Ephesian church for his farewell address (Acts 20.17). Because we cannot be certain of the historicity of this event, and because there were non-pauline as well as Pauline Christians in Ephesus (see, e.g., Acts 18.24–19.7), we cannot conclude that there were presbyters in the churches that Paul had founded independently. In fact, there are no references to presbyters to be found in the authentic Pauline letters, which generally reflect situations in Paul's independent, Gentile churches.

First Timothy, a pseudonymous letter addressed to a companion of Paul who is identified as a Jewish Christian in Acts — Jewish descent through his mother (Acts 16.1), circumcised (Acts 16.3) — speaks of the hands of the *presbyterion* having been laid on Timothy when his gifts came to him through prophecies (1 Tim. 4.14). It also says presbyters who rule well, especially by their preaching and teaching, should be honored (1 Tim. 5.17) and that any accusations against presbyters require two witnesses (5.19). The latter, of course, is a matter of due process in Jewish tradition. A similar work, the Letter to Titus, speaks of "Titus" appointing presbyters in every town (Titus 1.5) — reminiscent of Acts 14.23. These deutero-pauline letters thus lead us to believe that their churches, continuous in some way with the Brothers of Jerusalem, had presbyters who acted collectively in Christian ritual, and who preached and taught. The Letter to the Hebrews also speaks of presbyters witnessing to the faith (Heb. 11.2), and the Letter of James speaks of presbyters praying over the sick and anointing them with oil (James 5.14). In First Peter the author identifies himself as a presbyter addressing presbyters; he exhorts the latter to tend to the flock and not be domineering. He also exhorts the younger people to be subject to the presbyters (1 Pet. 5.15).

A presbyter also appears in the New Testament as the author of the Second and Third Letters of John. In fact, the author simply identifies himself as "the presbyter." The two letters may be instances of a presbyter "preaching and teaching." And the Revelation of John seems to reflect a collective ritual function of presbyters; the author reports visions of twenty-four presbyters worshipping in heaven (Rev. 4.4, 4.10, 5.6, 5.8, 5.11, 5.14, 7.11, 11.16, 14.3, 19.4) with one presbyter occasionally speaking (Rev. 5.5, 7.13).

Summary

We have traced the background in early Christianity of three kinds of leadership office, as made evident in New Testament word usage. We selected the three because Ignatius of Antioch found it meaningful to write the Christians of one community, Ephesus, about them at one point in time, in the early second century C.E. *Bishops* had appeared in the plural in one Pauline church, Philippi, in the mid fifties. Later works — the Acts of the Apostles, First Timothy, and Titus — equate bishops with presbyters, seemingly in an effort to establish some continuity between the Pauline Gentile churches and the more Jewish ones. *Deacons*, including female deacons, had similarly appeared in the Pauline context. Only male deacons appear in the deutero-pauline contexts some time later (Colossians, Ephesians, First Timothy, Titus). *Presbyters*, however, appear to have been present in the community of the

Brothers in Jerusalem and in the early mission churches founded by Paul and Barnabas, before Paul had set out independently to found his own Gentile churches — all this according to legends reported in the Acts of the Apostles. In one redactional passage (as opposed to source material) in Acts, however, the author endeavors to equate presbyters with bishops. Presbyters are known in some of the Johannine literature, which is generally associated with Ephesus and its hinterland, and in First Timothy and Titus they are said to preach, teach, and as a collectivity engage in ritual. In short, there is a Pauline Gentile pattern of bishops and deacons, a Jewish pattern of presbyters, and evidence of bridging the two patterns in a redactive passage in the Acts of the Apostles and in two "pastoral" deutero-pauline letters — first Timothy and Titus.

Ignatius' points on governance for the Ephesians

At the time Ignatius was writing his letter to the Ephesians, there had been a variety of ways that the Christian churches governed themselves. Ignatius himself and the Ephesians under Bishop Onesimus came out of the tradition of Paul of Tarsus; Ignatius speaks of himself and the Ephesians as fellow initiates (*summustai*) of Paul (Ig. Eph. 12). When speaking only of his Ephesian addressees and not of himself, he says that they were in an "understanding" or "agreement" with the Apostles; apostle is an office that was held by Paul and others in the Gentile Pauline mission, and as a named grouping the Apostles were the Christian community to which Paul had belonged early in his career as a Christian. So Bishop Ignatius speaking as a Pauline Christian is addressing the Ephesian Christians, led by Bishop Onesimus, who traced their heritage (and perhaps their organization) back to not only Paul but to an understanding with the Apostles. This understanding may reflect either an outgrowth from Paul's earlier career, when he had belonged to the Apostles, or an accommodation between a Gentile Pauline church and the Apostles. In either case, it is the heritage of the Apostles that did not have a tradition of bishops as a form of governance. We need to distinguish between locations in and near Palestine, where the Apostles were a local grouping near the home territory of Jesus of Nazareth, and more remote locations where an apostle had been a missionary who had founded churches and had left Gentile bishops in charge of them. It seems that the Apostles, having less hierarchy because of not having been founded by a personage from abroad, would have some difficulty accepting the authority of bishops when traveling into western Asia Minor and Greece; similarly Apostles would be reluctant to recognize bishops as authoritative when Christians from the latter areas traveled to the Apostles' home territory (presumably the situation that occasioned the presence of a bishop, Ignatius, in Antioch).

If Ignatius, in encouraging unity among the Ephesian Christians under Bishop Onesimus, seems to be consolidating a merger of two traditions (that of Paul and the Apostles, and that of the apostle Paul) that had already taken place, he also seems to be encouraging a merger with another Christian grouping, the Disciples. Ignatius himself had been trying to gain acceptance to the Disciples; he says that he was hoping his impending martyrdom would enable him to become a Disciple (Ig. Eph. 1). Decades before hand the Disciples had been a Christian grouping in Jerusalem that had been governed by the Twelve and an assembly (Acts 6.2). Their missions were undertaken in and near Palestine (Acts 8). At some point in time there had been an overlap between the Twelve and the Apostles (Acts 6.6), but most of the legends contained in Acts refer to the Disciples as a separate grouping, having Peter and John as their major personages. At one point Paul ministered to Disciples in Antioch (Acts 14.19–23).[4] Ignatius was not alone in trying to join the Disciples; he speaks as one just beginning to undertake becoming a Disciple and as one addressing fellow students (Ig. Eph. 3).[5] Of course if the Disciples were to engage in a merger or some other kind of association with the Gentile Pauline Christians, it would be helpful if they could deal with a responsible leadership (e.g., bishops) who could speak for the Gentile Pauline Christians.

It is difficult to ascertain the leadership structure of the Disciples after the Twelve had been disbanded in Jerusalem in 43 C.E. They may well have had councils of presbyters, as did the Apostles and the churches founded by Paul in his earlier missionary career. It will be recalled that both the Jewish community in Jerusalem and the Jewish Christian Brothers there had presbyters, and that presbyters were known of in at least some churches associated with some of the Johannine works. Councils of presbyters seem to have been a very common form of governance. The association of different Christian groupings with one another in the time of Ignatius appears to have resulted in the appearance of the episcopal and the presbyterial forms of governance together. We have already seen some of the New Testament works equating bishops and presbyters, but this turns out to be a facile linguistic endeavor. The historical reality, as opposed to a literary ideal, appears to have found one bishop and a presbytery together in a church: Ignatius praises the Ephesian church of Bishop Onesimus for being ordered in one subordination under one bishop and one presbytery (Ig. Eph. 2). Moreover, he would have the bishops and presbyteries sharing in a consensus. He says:

> For Jesus Christ, our life without division, is the Father's will (*gnome*), as the bishops who are installed throughout the boundaries are in the will (*gnome*) of Jesus Christ (Ig. Eph. 3).

And he goes on to praise the Ephesians' presbyters for being in harmony with the will (*gnome*) of the bishop (Ig. Eph. 4). He also pointedly calk for a unity with the bishop and the whole church:

> Do not be misled: If anyone is not inside the sanctuary, he comes short of the bread of God. For if one and a second prayer have such great strength, how much more is that of the bishop and the whole church (Ig. Eph. 5).

Toward the end of the letter Ignatius encourages the Ephesian Christians to gather together so that they would obey the bishop and the presbytery with an undisturbed mind (Ig. Eph. 20).

Conclusion

How should we interpret these historical data? What are their implications for office charisma? I would propose that first a unifying impetus, such as one that would tend to centralize authority in structures such as a composite of bishop and presbytery, would be occasioned by external relations. In the case of the Christians of the time of Ignatius and Onesimus, official Roman persecution appears to have provided a salient external relation. There is no evidence that the Romans distinguished among the Christian groupings — Disciples, Apostles, Brethren, and so forth. Rather they dealt with the Christians as one grouping, and it therefore became helpful and perhaps even imperative for the Christians to react as one grouping. We might refer to this kind of event as a *group/environment transaction*, and as a type it would stand in contrast to a situation created by a "divide and conquer" stratagem.

Second, I would suggest that efforts of subgroupings within an identity group (such as Disciples, Apostles, etc. within Christianity) to deal with each other (e.g., efforts to establish understandings, associations, mergers) help consolidate the position of whatever office may be in place, because each group needs to enable other groups to deal with a responsible party who can speak for it. We might refer to this kind of event as a *subgroup/subgroup transaction.*

Third, I would suggest that office charisma comes not only from a primary personage whose charisma has been "routinized" (e.g., that of Jesus of Nazareth) and not only from a second founder's charisma (e.g., that of Paul of Tarsus) but also from intervening forms that mediate between the personal charisma figures of the past and the beholders of charisma in a present. Ignatius, for example, did not abandon either the bishop-and-deacon structure of the Gentile mission or the presbytery structure of the older Christian homeland, but rather sought a unifying consensus that would be emergent in an association between both kinds of structure. We might refer to this as *historical retention.*

Fourth, I would suggest that effective office charisma inheres in the manifest purposes of organizations. For Ignatius, for example, the purpose at hand was worship; those not united to the bishop and presbytery as a whole entity were not in the sanctuary and fell short of the "bread of God." Claims to office charisma that would not be inhering in the groupings' purposes would probably be disregarded.

Consequently we can speak of an elaboration of the office charisma model, which had been formulated by Max Weber. Office charisma is enhanced by group/environment transactions, even when the character of the transactions is hostile (as was the case with persecution); it may be undermined by a policy of malign neglect or perhaps by a policy of divide and conquer. Office charisma is enhanced by subgroup/subgroup transactions; it would be undermined by a propensity of each group to carve out separate isolable spheres of activity for themselves. Office charisma is enhanced by the historical retention of recent forms that have mediated the founding charisma; it would be undermined by efforts to abandon the ways of the recent past and simply "restore" a form from the more remote past. Finally, office charisma is enhanced by inhering in activities in which group members engage as members of the group; it would be undermined by being separated from such activities or overmuch identified with matters that do not pertain directly to the purposes members have for participating in the group.

The uses made by Ignatius of the differing kinds of Christian leadership office in his hortatory letter to the Ephesians do not enable us to speak of a pure type of legal authority as described by Weber (1978:217–218). Specifically, we have no evidence of an abstract body of church law for this early point in Christian history. Indeed, neither the Roman state nor the scattered Jewish leadership had yet developed systematic legal systems. This, of course, can only have the ironic effect of making offices and their holders, in the absence of a personage endowed with personal charisma, more important, not less so; people who have little by way of a code to live by need leaders.

Notes

1 My translation, from the *Nestle-Aland Novum Testamentum Graece.* Published translations often obscure relevant features of the Greek in the course of rendering the texts in smoothly-flowing modern languages. Consequently I often supply my own translations in order to retain something from the original that may be important historically but not particularly significant in terms of the devotional or liturgical purposes that Bible publishers have in mind.

2 The term *episkopos* also appears in 1 Pet. 2.25, where God (or Christ) is said to be the overseer of souls.

3 In the gospels it refers to a lowly state that Jesus encourages the Twelve to assume in order to be first in the kingdom (Mk. 9.35 and 10.43, with parallels at Mt. 20.26 and Lk. 22.27). Mt. 23.11 makes a similar point with the word with respect to Scribes and Pharisees. It simply refers to servants at Mt. 22.13 and in Jn. 2. One can only speculate about these usages reflecting church offices; it may well be that the name of the church office presupposed these and similar sayings traditions.

4 Acts 14.28 also speaks of Disciples in Antioch.

5 *nun gar archen echo tou matheteuesthai kai proslalo humin hos sundidaskalitais mou.*

References

Apostolic Fathers. 1992. Greek texts and English translations of their writings, 2nd ed. Translation by J. B. Lightfood and J. R. Farmer. Grand Rapids, MI: Baker Book House.

Nestle-Aland Novum Testamentum Graece. 1979. Edited by K. Aland, M. Black, C. M. Martini, B. M. Metzger, and A. Wikgren. Stuttgart: Deutsche Bibelstiftung.

Aune, D. E. 1987. *The New Testament in its literary environment*. Philadelphia, PA: Westminster.

Blasi, A. J. 1986. Role structures in the early hellenistic church. *Sociological Analysis* 47:226–248.

——. 1988. *Early Christianity as a social movement*. Bern and New York: Peter Lang.

——. 1991. *Making charisma: The social construction of Paul's public image*. New Brunswick, NJ: Transaction.

Collins, R. F. 1988. *Letters that Paul did not write: The Epistle to the Hebrews and the Pauline Pseudepigrapha*. Wilmington, DE: Michael Glazier.

Corley, K. E. 1993. *Private women, public morals: Social conflict in the synoptic tradition*. Peabody, MA: Hendrickson.

Eberts, H. W., Jr. 1994. Pluralism and ethnicity in early Christian mission. Paper presented at the 1994 Sociology of Early Christianity Workshop, Toronto.

Holmes, M. W. 1992. The letter of Ignatius, Bishop of Antioch. In *The Apostolic Fathers*, 2nd ed. Translation by J. B. Lightfood and J. R. Farmer. Grand Rapids, MI: Baker Book House.

Meade, D. G. 1986. *Pseudonymity and canon: An investigation into the relationship of authorship and authority in Jewish and earliest Christian tradition*. Grand Rapids, MI: William B. Eerdmans.

Weber, M. 1978. *Economy and society. An outline of interpretive sociology*. Vol. 1, edited by G. Roth and C. Wittich. Berkeley: University of California Press.

12

A COMPLETE HISTORY OF EARLY CHRISTIANITY

Taking the "heretics" seriously[1]

Majella Franzmann

Source: *Journal of Religious History*, 29(2) (2005), 117–28.

The heterodox have been treated unfairly within the histories of mainstream Christian tradition, whether by their ecclesiastical opponents or by recent and current scholarship. This article outlines the place of Christian Gnostic belief and practices in the processes of self-definition and institutionalization that took place within the early history of Christianity and makes a plea to reinstate the "heretics" to their rightful place in any academic discussion of the history and beliefs of Christianity.

The early history of most of the world's great founder religions is a murky affair. There are usually few, if any, records from the earliest days that survive without some elaboration and additional material, and the attempt to untangle the real events in any certain historical sense is enormously difficult, if not impossible. The passing on of stories of founders and early founding groups gathered about them and the detail of the revelation event that precedes the "career" of most founders go together with survival for any new religious movement in the early years. The movement must first deal with the crisis of the death of the founder, and then usually other crises in quick succession until some stability is found, generally not until well after the first few generations of believers. By the time records of the life of the founder and his revelation appear in written form, early crises have already permanently shaped and altered those records. Thus the "orthodox" texts which purport to record the life and words of the "founder"[2] and the early history of Christianity provide evidence of internal squabbles and external pressures

— including internal clashes between different cultural groups (e.g., Acts 6:1–6), resistance from those opposed to movement beyond the religious boundaries of the founding community (e.g., Acts 15:1–29), early challenges to leadership or spiritual authority (e.g. Gal. 2:11–14; Jn 3:22–30), and external persecution (e.g., Mk 13:9–13; Acts 12:1–4).

With the second generation of believers, what was originally the Jesus movement within Judaism began to settle down within its various social and political environments and began the process of becoming a religion in its own right, as groups negotiated a place for themselves in both the religious and socio-political worlds. As the movement settled, and indeed to help it settle, groups became more or less concerned for organizational matters in relation to praxis and belief. Inevitably, as a religious movement moves from stories and simple sayings or statements of belief to more complex doctrines, the potential for disagreement among members and larger groupings increases. As more rules are made about behaviour and ritual, further room for disagreement arises. Rules are as much about defining what is left out as much as what should be kept in, and at this stage of settling down and increasing institutionalism, various Christian groups became more concerned about who was a member and who was not a member. At this stage, the labels of orthodoxy and heterodoxy become important for the purposes of making a clear distinction between groups.[3]

Orthodoxy and heterodoxy are terms applied to groups relative to where one stands. Thus Christian groups later identified as mainstream, labelled Christian Gnostic groups as heretical, and Christian Gnostic groups in turn labelled heretical those who had so labelled them.[4] Finding appropriate terms to cover the variety of these early Christian groups is difficult for any historian. The terms "mainstream" or "orthodox" can be used of one group, or a cluster of early Christian groups, only in retrospect, and even then the terms are somewhat misleading, since the group/s cannot be clearly delineated with any surety in those early years. Scholars who presume to do so are simply believing the rhetoric of the winners that "things were always thus from the beginning."

No straight line of development flows from the originating vision or foundation group through to what later becomes the mainstream group. A more realistic picture for early Christianity should show an originating vision that gave rise to multiple groups with multiple responses to the vision in behaviour and belief. As these multiple groups developed, and the lines were drawn increasingly clearly between the various responses, some groups compromised with others and merged (e.g., Petrine and Johannine churches), and some groups did not compromise.

Eventually within early Christianity, a cluster of groups managed to gain the upper hand in the internal and external struggles, partly through political alliance with the Roman state and the resulting social status that flowed from such an alliance. They became the bearers of Christian orthodoxy, the title of "orthodox" or "mainstream" as much about political and social success as about right belief. Having gained a position of supremacy, it was an easy step to use political power to persecute those in opposition. A good example of such supremacy in political, social and religious terms is provided by the "orthodox" bishop, Athanasius of Alexandria, who apparently could call on military troops when necessary to deal with opponents.[5] As Roger Bagnall writes in relation to him, he "made himself a symbol of embattled orthodoxy by casting his vicissitudes in terms of theological divisions."[6]

Standing against this large Christian group gaining increasing political power and social status, the "heretics" of the third and particularly the fourth centuries CE were excluded from those considered orthodox and were vilified and physically abused. Those opposed to, or not aligned with, the orthodox "winners" had no chance of fair treatment in the subsequent record of history. As Bagnall comments further:

> The perennial tendency to apply theological categories to disagreements over political power within the church only exacerbates the unreliability of ancient literature as a witness to contemporary realities.[7]

Christian Gnostic groups, as the major cluster of groups categorized as heretics within the histories of early Christianity, provide a good example of those who could not expect fair treatment.[8] Prior to the discoveries of the Nag Hammadi material, little was known of them at first hand, scholars needing to rely on information from early Christian apologists of the mainstream group such as Irenaeus, Tertullian, Clement of Alexandria, Origen, Eusebius, and Epiphanius of Salamis. From these writers come the names and characteristics of various Gnostic groups, and sometimes the writers include a snippet from Gnostic writings.

A distinct disadvantage lies in having to depend on the apologists for information, since the nature of such writings is to describe opponents in some derogatory way, to construct them as the despised "other." On the simplest level one finds ridicule. For example, the Gnostic founder Mani and his followers, the Manichaeans, are ridiculed as maniacs, by a not-so-subtle play in Greek on the name of Mani (from the Greek *μανία* meaning madness, frenzy, or mania).[9] Most notably, Augustine denigrates his former coreligionists in his famous anti-Manichaean treatizes, constructing dialogues between himself and an inept Manichaean opponent, whose opposing statements he so easily counteracts or ridicules from the point of view of his own orthodox understanding.[10]

As expected, a great deal of slander appears against the heretics, a favourite theme being the supposed sexual exploitation of women followers by various Gnostic teachers. From such accusations, it seems a short step towards real demonization of Gnostic groups.[11] One of the most malicious of the apologists is the church father, Epiphanius who describes various Gnostic cultic rites, in one of which human semen and menstrual blood are used in a kind of eucharist (Panarion 26.4–5).[12] It seems the Gnostics themselves were aware of these denunciations, for one finds similar denunciations in their works. The *Pistis Sophia*, Book IV, chapter 147, for example, reports that Jesus calls this the "sin (that) surpasses every sin and every iniquity." Those who commit such a sin will be condemned to the outer darkness.[13] Worst of all from Epiphanius is the denunciation of Gnostic groups who use dismembered aborted fetuses as matter for the eucharist (Panarion 26.5). Most scholars would agree that Epiphanius has allowed his imagination free rein here, indulging in pornographic writings for his own and others' titillation. This scenario of eating fetuses is a quite common theme through history, typical of the worst type of religious sectarian polemic.

By deliberately provoking their stronger opponents, the Gnostics did not help their cause as minority groups in this tussle for the label of orthodoxy. As mainstream apologists held up Gnostics for ridicule, Christian Gnostics in turn held up various teachings and praxis of other Christian groups for ridicule. The writer of the Gospel of Philip, for example, ridicules the teaching that the Virgin Mary conceived Jesus by the power of the Holy Spirit (55.23–27), in stating that no woman can impregnate another, a statement clearly influenced by the feminine gender of the original Aramaic word for Spirit, רוח (rûaḥ). The same gospel states that the Gnostic undergoes baptism with insight, while baptism by other Christian groups is worthless (64.22–31).[14] However, while parts of the canonical gospels might have come under criticism by Christian Gnostics, nevertheless they still frequently used parts of the canonical gospels to support their own theological positions.[15]

Turning to the Gnostic writings for information about themselves reveals a very complex picture of many different groups with diverse mythologies or theologies and organization. However some degree of commonality can be identified within that diversity: the belief that matter, the world and human flesh, are evil or at best fatally flawed; that humans inhabit a dualistic universe, divided between light/goodness/the spirit and darkness/evil/matter; that believers are basically spiritual people who have been awakened to their inner insight, literally *gnosis* (hence the name "Gnostics"); and that believers are essentially strangers in the physical world (or "passers by"; Nag Hammadi Gospel of Thomas Log. 42),[16] trapped here in their human flesh,[17] awaiting their return to their place of origin in the world of light where the ineffable God or Father of Light exists, their salvation assured by the gift of insight which all equally possess.[18]

Just like its orthodox counterpart, Christian Gnosticism exhibits elements of its roots in Aramaic Judaism, Christian Gnostic texts reworking Jewish primary texts like the creation myths of Genesis, but diverging from orthodox Judaism by taking a negative attitude to the Jewish creator God. If the world is evil, then its creator must be evil. The Jewish creator God is presented as the Demiurge, the evil and ignorant creator, who together with dark cosmic powers under his command, the archons, creates an evil or flawed world and the first human beings.[19] This theme of the evil nature of creation and matter in general underpins the strong dualism running through the Gnostic writings: heaven over against earth, light against darkness, spirit against matter, the mind or spirit against the body.

The Christian Gnostics' particular understanding of the world and their place in it affects what they find valuable and worth celebrating and theologizing about in the life of Jesus of Nazareth. Gnostic dissatisfaction with a world that is ugly and a flesh that is repugnant and a prison for the spirit produces a view of a saviour who can show them a way out of this ugliness by awakening the beauty and purity of the insight within them, and who can promise a place of purity after their escape from this physical world. The Gnostic Saviour, Jesus, does not come to the world to exorcise its evil or forgive sins, or to die for the sin of the world, but to awaken the Gnostics to the insight that they already possess, prepare the way and bring them home to the heavenly world of light.[20] In receiving insight, the Gnostics experience equality and union with him.[21] There is a lack of focus on strict hierarchies in this idea of equality with the Saviour. The Nag Hammadi Apocryphon of James goes so far as to imply that the Gnostic may even become better than Jesus. In this text, Jesus tells believers to become better than himself (6.19), to hasten to be saved and, if possible, to arrive even before him (7.10–15), for thus the Father will love them (7.15–16).[22]

That Gnostics emphasize Jesus as a saviour and revealer does not itself divide mainstream Christians from Gnostic Christians. Rather, the difference lies in the interpretation of what kind of saviour Jesus is and how he came to be in the world in order to carry out the revelation. In some cases, the differences in interpretation are not at all clear. An example of this can be found in a comparison of the Nag Hammadi Gospel of Truth and the New Testament Gospel of John. The Gospel of Truth describes itself as follows:

> The gospel of truth is a joy for those who have received from the Father of truth the gift of knowing him, through the power of the Word . . . the one who is the thought and the mind of the Father . . . the one who is addressed as the Saviour . . . This is the gospel of the one who is searched for, which was revealed to those who are perfect through the mercies of the Father — the hidden mystery, Jesus, the Christ. Through it he enlightened those who were in darkness. Out of oblivion he enlightened them, he showed (them) a way. And the way is the truth which he taught them.
>
> (16.31–38; 18.11–21)[23]

The Gospel of John 1:5 also presents this theme of the Word of God and relates the activity of the Word to the themes of light and darkness: "The light shines in the darkness, and the darkness did not overcome it." The concept of Jesus as a way which is the truth for believers is also found in Jn 14:6: "I am the way, and the truth, and the life. No one comes to the Father except through me."

Thus both the Gospel of Truth and the Gospel of John represent Jesus as the Word that came forth from the Father to bring light in the darkness, and as the truth and the way out of the darkness to the Father. The passages illustrate the difficulty, in some aspects at least, in separating Gnostic Christian ideas of Jesus from mainstream Christian ideas of Jesus, although it is easier to understand in this case since the Gospel of John stands on the very (theological) edge of the mainstream tradition.

Other Gnostic ideas of Jesus clearly differ from mainstream ideas. Most importantly perhaps, the view of the nature of Jesus and how he manages to come into the human world separates the mainstream Christian groups from Christian Gnostic groups. If, as the Gnostics say, the world and the flesh are evil or fatally flawed, and act as prisons for the Gnostic spirit, then the heavenly revealer cannot allow himself to be caught and imprisoned in the flesh. The more human-like the form that he chooses, the more he immerses himself in the world of the flesh, the more he will be in danger from the dark powers that rule there. Though the Gnostic texts themselves do not completely agree on an understanding of the nature of Jesus, generally, the idea of Jesus the Saviour having a real human birth in real human flesh and later a real death is abhorrent to all Gnostics.[24]

As with the concept of Jesus as Saviour, so with the ritual practices of the Gnostic and mainstream groups. While both groups practise many rituals of the same name and type, among them baptism and the eucharist, the difference between them lies in their interpretation rather than in the naming or carrying out of that ritual activity. The Gnostics do not accept a Saviour with real physical flesh, and yet the Gospel of Philip speaks of the eucharist as the flesh and blood of Jesus. However, the same gospel also states that Jesus' flesh is the Logos and his blood is the Holy Spirit (57.6–7). Thus, at least for this Gnostic gospel, the flesh and blood of Jesus in the eucharist is spiritual flesh and blood.

Again, for a system that cannot accept a real death for Jesus, baptism cannot be interpreted, as it is in the mainstream tradition, as a means of bringing the believer into association with the death and resurrection of the Saviour as Paul writes in Rom 6:3–4:

> You have been taught that when we were baptised in Christ Jesus we were baptised in his death; in other words, when we were baptised we went into the tomb with him and joined him in death, so that as Christ was raised from the dead by the Father's glory, we too might live a new life.

In what seems a deliberate denial of this teaching, the Gospel of Philip 77.7–12 states that Jesus emptied the baptismal waters of death so that the believer would not go down into death when entering the water.

Not surprisingly, a religion that emphasizes salvation through individual insight, the equality of all believers, and a view of the world and the flesh as evil, also has little concern for hierarchical structures in the community. Ingvild Gilhus notes the spin-off from these ideas into Gnostic opposition to existing social structures and the Gnostic practice of status reversal within their own ranks.[25] The lack of concern for hierarchy follows through to a lack of structured ritual. The church father, Tertullian, later himself branded a heretic when he joined the Montanists, tends a little to hyperbole when attacking Gnostics on both points:

> To begin with, it is doubtful who is a catechumen, and who a believer; they have all access alike, they hear alike, they pray alike . . . Simplicity they will have to consist in the overthrow of discipline, attention to which on our part they call brotherly . . . All are puffed up, all offer you knowledge . . . The very women of these heretics, how wanton they are! For they are bold enough to teach, to dispute, to enact exorcisms, to undertake cures — it may be even to baptize . . . Nowhere is promotion easier than in the camp of the rebels, where the mere fact of being there is a foremost service. And so it comes to pass that today one man is their bishop, tomorrow another; today he is a deacon who tomorrow is a reader; today he is a presbyter who tomorrow is a layman.
>
> (Praescr. 41)[26]

Any new religious group attempting to establish itself and settle down in the world has to set up the processes by which authority functions in the group. Tertullian's disgust with the lack of structure and ritual formality in Gnostic groups, the presence of women in what is a man's job, goes deep to the heart of the uneasy relations between his group and the Gnostic groups he knew. Tertullian is not just concerned for orthodox reflections on the founder. How a group stays together and its orthopraxis are as important as orthodoxy. However, prior to the strong push to institutionalization in early Christianity, a flexibility similar to that practised by the Gnostics is evident, especially in Paul's writings about the Church as the spiritual organism of the body of Christ, in which all members bring a variety of spiritual gifts to build up that body, and in which no distinction of race or class or gender distinguishes one from another. In his letter to the Galatians, he writes:

> All baptised in Christ, you have all clothed yourself in Christ, and there is no more distinction between Jew and Greek, slave and free, male and female, but all of you are one in Christ Jesus
>
> (Gal. 3:28).

And again, in his first letter to the Corinthians he states:

> Just as a human body, though it is made up of many parts, is a single unit because all these parts, though many make one body, so it is with Christ. In the one Spirit we were all baptised, Jews as well as Greeks, slaves as well as citizens, and one Spirit was given to us all to drink.
>
> (1 Cor. 12:13)

How quickly this teaching of Paul was forgotten in the institutionalization phase that followed, and how easily Tertullian let that basic Pauline Christology slip from view when considering the Gnostics and their flexible community that strove for the equality of all.

Gnostic groups too, in general, were not interested in compromise or alliances. They were interested in personal spiritual power, and their overriding goal was to escape from the world of material darkness in which they were strangers. A model was at hand that could compel them to act in this way. The canonical (but marginally orthodox) Gospel of John presents sayings from Jesus to his disciples concerning "the world" which hates him and them, a world to which they do not belong; rather they belong to another world and kingdom entirely (Jn 15:18–19; 18:36). In similar vein the canonical First Letter of John states that the world is to be equated with "the desire of the flesh, the desire of the eyes, the pride in riches," which are in opposition to the Father (1 Jn 2:15–16). Here are passages that would strengthen any resolve to put aside the things of the world, to shun worldly power and alliances. Here is compelling teaching for those, such as the Gnostics, who did not wish to deal and compromise with those they considered to be aligned with the powers of darkness in this world or with those who were ignorant of the truth. In the end, the Gnostics were hunted down by these opponents, went underground, or fled farther to the east of the Roman empire.[27]

Much unites but also much divides the interpretation of Jesus in mainstream and Gnostic groups and the spin-off from that into ritual and organization. The problem then for a fair hearing for the Gnostics and an honest historical view of earliest Christianity is that the effort of any religious group towards self-definition and the clear statement of identity occurs most intensely in those times of institutionalization when the focus is on what divides rather than unites groups, when the processes of defining and maintaining orthodoxy and orthopraxis are almost an obsession. Also at this stage any groups that are not in step with the mainstream group, for spiritual, dogmatic, social or political reasons, are labelled most strongly as heretics and most severely persecuted. In one sense, the real problem for the Gnostics was that they simply existed in the wrong place at the wrong time. By their very nature, groups that follow ideologies of personal salvation, such as the Gnostics, inevitably threaten the processes of institutionalization, when groups try hard to form a strong and well-defined religious identity. Gnostic emphasis on the spiritual power within the individual directly conflicts with a process that aims to place ultimate spiritual power in those at the top of a strict hierarchy.[28]

While Kurt Rudolph presents Gnostic groups culturally and geographically as marginal in the Graeco-Roman world — he describes Gnosticism as "a Hellenistic garment over an oriental-Jewish body," a politically and culturally marginal movement on the borderline between the East and Rome[29] — Ingvild Gilhus presents them in sociological terms as equally marginal. In her words, borrowing from the twentieth century social anthropologist Victor Turner, they are "permanent liminal groups,"[30] that is they are groups who exist constantly in an in-between state. They exist in the in-between of the physical world, because they have been separated from their heavenly homeland but have not yet returned to that land of light.[31] In this liminal state, the Gnostic receives *gnosis* (insight) and experiences *communitas*, a community of "equal individuals under the authority of the elders or the instructors."[32] But cultural or spiritual marginal status does not mean that these groups necessarily functioned only as small isolated groups on the edge of society, thereby deserving the kind of minority status they are frequently given within early Christian histories. If they had not shown reasonable success in gaining members, sometimes by "poaching" from opposing Christian groups,[33] the mainstream group would not have found them such a threat and taken such measures to overcome them.

That the threat was real is evident in the vehemence of the attack against the Gnostics by their orthodox contemporaries. However, the unfair treatment dealt to the heretics by their earliest opponents continues in contemporary scholarship. When theologians and church historians describe what was happening in those early centuries, they do not give the heterodox views of the Saviour any credence as part of the total Christian picture. The so-called heretics show up as little more than shadowy figures who lurk in the wings, rather than as people who have their own place on the stage of Christian history. Certainly no appreciation is demonstrated that heretics may actually have had a valid spiritual life centred on Jesus.

As one cluster of groups within early Christianity, Gnostic Christians have something to offer towards the total picture of early Christian belief and praxis, no matter how they are later judged by their opponents. The Gnostic view of the founder, for example, should be taken seriously in any study of early Christologies. Each Christian group presents their interpretation of the founder out of reflection on traditions and key scriptures handed down to them; each relies on their ongoing experience of Jesus to guide what they are saying and writing about him. Similar processes of reflection and interpretation operate in each group, and the sum of these reflections adds up to a total picture of what Christians, Gnostic or otherwise, thought about their Saviour in these early centuries.

Scholars must take seriously that heretics believed in their experiences of the heavenly Jesus and knew something of him from those experiences, just as orthodox groups believed in their own experiences of the risen Jesus and reflected on those experiences in subsequent generations. Yet, studies of Jesus still focus on canonical works, still treat the canonical gospels as the only real source for any kind of valid information about Jesus, as if these writings are historically guaranteed, rather than just one among many attempts at theological reflection from insiders about who this Jesus was. Moreover many scholars appear to know very little about the breadth of material available about Jesus, not just in New Testament apocrypha, but also in the so-called heretical works.[34] That the Christian churches today do not look at Jesus outside of canonical works is understandable. They want to protect their followers from hearing about the heresies and perhaps being led astray. But it is inexcusable for historians to limit the field of valid enquiry. While some of these scholars may belong to Christian churches or even may be religious professionals within these churches, within the scholarly world they are expected to be proper historians or exegetes.

Thus the first problem for study of the heretics may well be a scholar's personal belief. Every undergraduate student knows the problem or the opportunity that a personal believing stance can be for studying religious phenomena. They know that often the most difficult area for study is their own tradition, if they have one. The issue is not new, of course, and for anyone who studies hermeneutics, the idea that the self of the researcher intrudes in, or is actually the catalyst to, interpretation is self-evident. The old claims for the objectivity of academic study have long since been superceded by a strong awareness of the necessity to reflect upon the prejudices and presuppositions that influence even the very questions brought to research, let alone how conclusions and judgements about research are formed. However, the great debates about theory and method often pass by the work of day-to-day engagement with material.

Why is it so difficult for some scholars to take the Gnostics seriously as early Christian groups, including them in their own hermeneutics about Jesus? Apart from the issue of personal faith mentioned above, historians themselves may be influenced by their primary sources, by those who write history. It is a truism that official history is written by the winners, and stars the winners only. The history of Christianity reads as a long list of those religious professionals who either won in the debates over major doctrinal issues, or managed to consolidate positions of power through political alliance. History focuses on them as the ones who define and maintain orthodoxy. On the other hand, heretics are relegated to the edge of the histories; they are the opponents, the losers. Where they figure at all in the histories, they are fair game for ridicule or vilification.

When scholars accept the winners' view of Christianity as the whole story, or the only authentic story, they disregard not only the ordinary believer who very rarely appears of any importance in the process, but also disregard the so-called heretics. In a similar way up to the recent past, scholars often ignored anything non-Western in the history of Christianity. While there is some attempt now to unearth the early history of Christianity in countries like China or Africa, there is not the same impetus to add the heretics to their rightful place in the histories. It is difficult to believe that, as recently as 1990, the New Testament scholar Robert Grant could write:

> In spite of the exciting and valuable Gnostic documents recovered from Nag Hammadi in Egypt, the basic starting point for the study of the Gnostics has to lie in the earliest criticisms by Christians who wrote against heretics.[35]

Scholars believe the rhetoric, the propaganda of the winners that they have read for so long. They believe the history from the mainstream Christian group which holds only the canonical scriptures and their interpretation of them as the true basis of what historically a Christian and Christianity meant so that all other early systems or alternate systems must be judged in their light. Why should the paradigm of one Christian group be axiomatic for the history and analysis of the entire movement?

To allow minority heretical groups a voice that overwhelms the voice of the orthodox would present a similar lack of balance as pertains currently. But the heretics must be allowed a place and must be considered in any accurate historical presentation of Christianity. The Gnostics belong as much to the history of early Christianity as any so-called orthodox group. The spotlight on centre stage in the history of Christianity must be shared by all groups who have contributed to that history, heterodox or otherwise.

Notes

1 This article contains some material that has been reworked from my professorial inaugural lecture, M. Franzmann, *Heretics and Hermeneutics: Taking the Gnostic Jesus Seriously*, The 2001 Inaugural Public Lecture Series (Armidale: Publications Office, University of New England, 2002).

2 The term "founder" may only be used very loosely of Jesus of Nazareth, as Douglas Pratt, *Religion: A First Encounter* (Auckland: Longman Paul, 1993), 43, indicates within a comparison of the activity of the founders, Muhammad, the Buddha Gotama, and Jesus of Nazareth: "The religion of Christianity emerged also after the death of the pivotal figure whose concern, arguably, was not so much to start a new faith as to fulfil, reform, and remake that which was already there. It may be contended that it was people like St Paul who actually 'founded' Christianity, although, undeniably, it is Jesus the Christ who is the *founder figure* in this case."

3 For general theory on the formation, development of identity, and survival of groups, see, for example, D. W. Johnson and F. P. Johnson, *Joining Together: Group Theory and Group Skills*, 4th ed. (Boston: Allyn and Bacon, 1991); and T. Douglas, *Survival in Groups: the Basics of Group Membership* (Buckingham, PA: Open University Press, 1995). In relation to religious groups, see K. A. Roberts,

Religion in Sociological Perspective, 2nd ed. (Belmont, CA: Wadsworth Publishing Company, 1990), esp. ch. 7: "Emergence and Viability of Religious Movements: Charisma and Its Routinization," 147–64; see also R. Stark, "How New Religions Succeed: A Theoretical Model," in *The Future of New Religious Movements*, ed. D. G. Bromley and P. E. Hammond (Macon, GA: Mercer University Press, 1987), 11–29.

4 The term "heretic" or "heresy" is derived from the Greek word αἵρεσις, which means "a choice," taking by preference one thing rather than another. As used by religious groups, especially Christians, the term has come to be associated with groups or individuals who allegedly make a wrong choice or a bad choice, usually with reference to some aspect of belief. Over against heretics are the orthodox, who have allegedly made the right choice about what to believe.

5 Edwin A. Judge and Stuart R. Pickering, "Papyrus Documentation of Church and Community in Egypt to the Mid-Fourth Century," *Jahrbuch für Antike und Christentum* 20, (1977): 47–71, include a letter addressed to a leader of the Meletian community in Egypt, documenting the maltreatment of Meletians in Alexandria by the supporters of Athanasius, which included the use of military troops (57).

6 R. S. Bagnall, *Egypt in Late Antiquity* (Princeton, NJ: Princeton University Press, 1993), 303–304.

7 Bagnall, *Egypt in Late Antiquity*, 305.

8 There is much disagreement among scholars about what the terms "Gnostic" and "Gnosticism" mean. Although the debate has been going on for quite some time, especially since the international conference on Gnosticism in Messina in 1966, most people researching in the area continue to use the traditional terms. The latest label suggested by Michael Williams of "biblical demiurgical traditions," instead of "Gnosticism" understandably has been found to be too unwieldy; M. Williams, *Rethinking "Gnosticism": An Argument for Dismantling a Dubious Category* (Princeton: Princeton University Press, 1996), 51–3.

9 See the helpful summary of this ridicule from various writers in S. N. C. Lieu, *Manichaeism in the Later Roman Empire and Medieval China*, 2nd ed., Wissenschaftliche Untersuchungen zum Neuen Testament 63 (Tübingen: Mohr [Siebeck], 1992), 136.

10 R. Jolivet and M. Jourjon, *Oeuvres de Saint Augustin 17: Six traités antimanichéens*, 2nd series (Paris: Desclée de Brouwer, 1961).

11 For an overview of the accusations made by a variety of heresiologists, see K. Rudolph, *Gnosis: The Nature and History of Gnosticism* (New York: HarperSan Francisco, 1987), 9–25.

12 K. Holl, ed., *Epiphanius: Ancoratus und Panarion Haer. 1–33*, Die griechischen christlichen Schriftsteller der ersten Jahrhunderte 25 (Berlin: Akademie Verlag, 1915).

13 C. Schmidt, ed., *Pistis Sophia*, Nag Hammadi Studies 9 (Leiden: Brill, 1978).

14 B. Layton, ed. and W. W. Isenberg, trans., "The Gospel According to Philip," *Nag Hammadi Codex II, 2–7 together with XIII, 2*, Brit. Lib. Or. 4926(1), and P. Oxy. 1, 654, 655*, ed. B. Layton, Vol. 1, Nag Hammadi Studies 20 (Leiden: E. J. Brill, 1989), 142–215.

15 On the use of canonical Christian scripture in the Nag Hammadi texts, see C. A. Evans, R. L. Webb, R. A. Wiebe, eds, *Nag Hammadi Texts and the Bible: a Synopsis and Index* (Leiden/New York: E. J. Brill, 1993). The canonical gospels are also well used by Manichaeans. The Gospel of Matthew, for example, is well documented in major texts like the Manichaean Psalm Book; see the index in C. R. C. Allberry, *A Manichaean Psalm-Book. Part II*, Manichaean Manuscripts in the Chester Beatty Collection, Vol. 2 (Stuttgart: W. Kohlhammer, 1938), 47*–48*.

16 B. Layton, ed. and T. O. Lambdin, trans., "The Gospel According to Thomas," in *Nag Hammadi Codex II, 2–7 together with XIII, 2*, Brit. Lib. Or. 4926(1), and P. Oxy. 1, 654, 655*, ed. B. Layton, Vol. 1, Nag Hammadi Studies 20 (Leiden: E. J. Brill, 1989), 52–93.

17 The Nag Hammadi text *Interpretation of Knowledge* 6.28–29 speaks of the spirit trapped in nets of flesh; E. H. Pagels and J. D. Turner, "NHC XI,1: The Interpretation of Knowledge," in *Nag Hammadi Codices XI, XII, XIII*, Nag Hammadi Studies 28, ed. C. W. Hedrick, (Leiden: E. J. Brill, 1990), 21–88.

18 For a detailed overview, see Rudolph, *Gnosis*, 53–272.

19 On the Jewish creator god as Demiurge, see for example, the Nag Hammadi texts, Epistle of Peter to Philip 135.8–136.5, M. W. Meyer and F. Wisse, "NHC VIII,2: *Letter of Peter to Philip*", in *Nag Hammadi Codex VIII*, Nag Hammadi Studies 31, ed. J. H. Sieber (Leiden: E. J. Brill, 1991), 227–51; see also the Second Apocalypse of James 58.2–6, C. Hedrick, "NHC V,4: The (Second) Apocalypse of James," *Nag Hammadi Codices V,2–5 and VI with Papyrus Berolinensis 8502,1 and 4*, Nag Hammadi Studies 11, ed. D. M. Parrott (Leiden: E. J. Brill, 1979), 105–49; and the Gospel of Philip 75.2–11 in Layton and Isenberg, *Nag Hammadi Codex II, 2–7*, 142–215.

20 For extensive studies of the Gnostic Jesus, see M. Franzmann, *Jesus in the Nag Hammadi Writings* (Edinburgh: T&T Clark, 1996); and M. Franzmann, *Jesus in the Manichaean Writings* (Edinburgh: T&T Clark, 2003).

21 As Burton Mack, "Lord of the Logia: Savior or Sage?," in *Gospel Origins and Christian Beginnings: In Honor of James M. Robinson*, ed. J. E. Goehring *et al.*, Forum Fascicles 1 (Sonoma, CA: Polebridge, 1990), 3–18, esp. 11, writes concerning the Gospel of Thomas: Jesus is a supernatural revealer whose appearance in the world brought enlightenment to his true disciples. Enlightenment is understood as knowledge of one's self as belonging to an other-worldly order of divine origin and self-sufficiency. Thus the boundary erodes between Jesus as revealer figure and his true disciples as enlightened ones.

22 F. E. Williams, "The Apocryphon of James: I,2: 1.1–16.30," *Nag Hammadi Codex I (The Jung Codex). Introductions, Texts, Translations, Indices*, Nag Hammadi Studies 22, ed. H. W. Attridge (Leiden: E. J. Brill, 1985), 13–53.

23 M. L. Peel, "The Gospel of Truth: I,4: 43.25–50.18," *Nag Hammadi Codex I (The Jung Codex). Introductions, Texts, Translations, Indices*, Nag Hammadi Studies 22, ed. H. W. Attridge (Leiden: E. J. Brill, 1985), 137–215.

24 For a detailed study of the nature of the Nag Hammadi Jesus, see Franzmann, *Jesus in the Nag Hammadi Writings*, 71–98.

25 I. S. Gilhus, "Gnosticism — A Study in Liminal Symbolism," *Numen* 31 (1984): 106–28, esp. 119.

26 Tertullian, "The Prescription Against Heretics," in *Ante-Nicene Fathers*, Vol. 3, rev. ed., ed. A. Roberts and J. Donaldson (Peabody, MA: Hendrickson Publishers, 1994), 243–267, esp. 263.

27 The largest Gnostic group to come under persecution from the fourth century onwards was Manichaeism. For the history of its movement east, see Lieu, *Manichaeism*, 106–15, 192–304, passim.

28 For a more thorough outline of these processes, see M. Douglas, *How Institutions Think* (Syracuse, NY: Syracuse University Press, 1986).

29 K. Rudolph, "Zur Soziologie, soziologischen 'Verortung' und Rolle der Gnosis in der Spätantike," in *Studien zum Menschenbild in Gnosis und Manichäismus*, ed. P. Nagel, Wissentschaftliche Beiträge, Martin-Luther-Universität, Halle-Wittenberg 39 (K 5) (Halle [Saale], 1979), 19–29, esp. 25 (my translation).

30 Gilhus, "Gnosticism," 106–28. Gilhus draws principally on Victor Turner's outline of the three phases of *rites de passage* as separation, *limen* (margin), and aggregation.

31 *Contra* Gilhus. While I accept Gilhus's basic outline and identification of key elements of Gnostic liminality, I disagree with her identification of the Gnostic's liminal stage as separation from the world prior to entrance into the heavenly region or fullness of salvation.

32 Gilhus, "Gnosticism," 119.

33 See, for example, Irenaeus's problem with the heretic Marcus who lures away to his own group both men and women members of Irenaeus's community; Irenaeus, "Against Heresies," in *Ante-Nicene Fathers*, Vol. 1, rev. ed., ed. A. Roberts and J. Donaldson (Peabody, MA: Hendrickson Publishers, 1994), 309–578, esp. 334–336.

34 See my overview of the problem in Franzmann, *Jesus in the Nag Hammadi Writings*, 1–23.

35 R. M. Grant, *Jesus after the Gospels: The Christ of the Second Century* (London: SCM Press, 1990), 41.

Part 4

EARLY CHRISTIAN EXPANSION: FROM TUNIS TO CHINA

13

CHRISTIANITY AND LOCAL CULTURE IN LATE ROMAN AFRICA

Peter Brown

Source: *Journal of Roman Studies*, 58(1&2) (1968), 85–95.

I

The task of this paper is, in part, an invidious one: for I shall have to begin by looking a gift-horse in the mouth. I shall have to question a group of opinions that link the rise of Christianity in Africa with a resurgence of the local culture of the area. This resurgence, it is said, explains not only the rapid collapse of Roman rule at the time of the Vandal invasion of 429, but the disappearance of Roman civilisation and of Christianity itself in Africa in the early Middle Ages.[1]

Discussion of this suggestion, however, tends to be jeopardised from the start because claims for the honour of being the resurgent local culture of Late Roman Africa have been enthusiastically advanced on behalf of *two* distinct and mutually-exclusive local cultures, associated with the *two* native languages—with Punic, on the one hand, and with 'Libyan' (which is often described by a convenient if perilous anachronism as 'Berber'), on the other. What is more, these claims have been advanced by two equally distinct groups of scholars, handling different evidence. The evidence for the survival of Punic—or, so as not to prejudge the issue, of a *lingua Punica*—is literary: Augustine of Hippo[2] and Procopius[3] are the sole authorities for the period. The evidence for 'Berber,' by contrast, is largely confined to the interpretation of Libyan inscription[4] and of traces of unchanging habits of worship and craftsmanship allegedly betrayed in the remains of the Christian Churches of Central Numidia.[5]

The rival claimants, therefore, overlap neither in area nor in subject matter. If Punic survived in Late Roman Africa, it survived in a limited area, in the traditional areas of Carthaginian settlement, in certain Punicised towns of Numidia, and, perhaps, in the countryside, as an ill-defined fringe of 'Punicised' Libyan *patois*, for which some evidence had been adduced in Tripolitania.[6] The area of known Libyan inscriptions does not coincide with this; still less do the modern islands of Berber speech. These are associated with the High Plains of Numidia and the mountainous hinterland of the coast. So little do these areas overlap, indeed, that Dr. Frend and Dr. Courtois[7] have argued that the *lingua Punica* to which Augustine refers (when he writes in Thagaste and Hippo) is not even 'Punic', but the entirely non-Semitic Libyan dialect of Numidia: an educated Latin, Augustine merely used 'Punic' as the undifferentiated, Latin term for *any* native language in Africa, much as the modern European tends to lump together Berber- and Arabic-speakers as 'Arabs'.

But this difference between 'Berber' and 'Punic' is not a difference only in location. Different areas of experience are involved, documented by different kinds of evidence. Those who invoke 'Punic' are, often, historians of religious ideas. Their argument is almost exclusively linguistic: it turns on the survival of a language and of ideas associated with a language. Such ideas are plainly difficult to delimit: they are not necessarily peculiar to a region or a class; they are, rather, vehicles for the spread and assimilation of religious propaganda. S. Gsell,[8] followed by E. F. Gautier,[9] for instance, fastened on references to Punic as evidence for the survival of the ancient Carthaginian culture of Africa, and, so, as evidence of the vitality of the specifically Semitic bedrock of North African life. With the language, so they argued, went a body of distinctive religious ideas that remained radically different from those of classical Roman paganism, and akin to those of the Jews and the Arabs. Recently, Marcel Simon has ascribed the remarkable success of Judaism in North Africa, and the emergence of the more rigidly Judaistic traits in African popular Christianity, to the survival of Punic as a spoken language, closely related to Hebrew, and its adoption, as a language of culture, by the Berbers of the hinterland.[10] The success of Christianity, in the third century, has been explained by a similar kinship of ideas.[11] And, throughout, it has been assumed that Islam trumped Jews and Christians alike, in bringing a Semitic religion and a Semitic language to a Punic population.

Those who look to 'Berber' claim to be more firmly rooted: they have been archaeologists and sociologists. The greatest single impetus to Dr. Frend's *Donatist Church* was the discovery of an extraordinary number of Christian churches in Southern Numidia, marked by distinctive features of native craftsmanship and, apparently, maintaining local traditions of cult-practice that stretch from prehistoric times to the sub-Islamic pieties of the modern Berbers. From the churches recorded by Berthier in his *Vestiges du christianisme antique* of 1943, Dr. Frend moved to the society of S. Numidia as a whole, in the Late Roman period, and the role of religion in this society.[12] His *Donatist Church* is suffused with the same enthusiasm for what is local, for what is continuous, for what is associated with an immemorial ethnic group such as the Berbers, that has inspired many studies of the village-life and the religious eccentricities of the present-day Maghreb. Faced by Dr. Frend's perspective, indeed, the ancient historian and the theologian cannot buck the issue by limiting themselves to sifting the evidence he presents for his interpretation of the rise of Donatism in Numidia: if they wish to challenge him, they must be prepared to take part in a debate on the factors operative in the history of North Africa, in which the pre-historian, the historian of Medieval Islam and the sociologist of modern Algeria have each got something important to contribute.[13]

Where the protagonists of both 'Punic' and 'Berber' seem to agree, however, is in their interpretation of the manner in which a resurgence of local cultures impinged on the social and political life of Roman Africa in the fourth and fifth centuries, and in the crucial rôle of Christianity as providing the vehicle for this resurgence.

Very briefly, the expansion of Christianity in Africa in the third century, and the permanent division of the Christian Church between Catholics and Donatists, after 311, coincided with the weakening of the hold of the Romanized classes of the towns on the under-Romanized countryside. Donatism allied itself with the resurgent culture of the country-districts of Numidia, and of the lower classes of the towns: Catholicism, with the Romanized upper-classes—the great landowners and the civic notables. As the support of the Emperors identified Catholicism with the interests of the central government in Africa, so opposition to the Catholic Church became the focus of social and political grievances. The notorious Circumcellions, the wandering monks of Donatism, were implicated in peasants' revolts that shook the Roman agrarian system of Numidia in the 340's, and threatened to do so throughout the century. The Donatist hierarchy, also, supported the usurpations of Moorish chieftains, such as Firmus and Gildo. Nor was Africa alone in this. With the exception of Gaul, it is said, the resurgence of local cultures in the Late Roman Empire is associated with the rise of Christianity: in Egypt and Syria, possibly (say some) in Africa, it produced a vernacular literature.[14] In all these provinces, the rise of great local churches, often divided from the established church of the Roman Empire by trifling theological differences, provided an expression for an active or passive rejection of Greco–Roman culture, and so paved the way for an alternative to the Roman Empire in the form of Islam.

So compact a summary inevitably fails to do justice to the seminal quality of a book such as Dr. Frend's *Donatist Church.* But it is in this form that Dr. Frend's suggestions have often been repeated by many scholars—and repeated with a certitude and comprehensiveness which noticeably increases with the distance between the retailer and his contact with the evidence for the social and religious life of Late Roman Africa. Even the most learned of us have learnt to tread the straight and narrow path between right and wrong on this issue: when the author of a most valuable article says that

'Cause-and-effect connexions, beyond absolute demonstration, but fairly clear, can be drawn between Coptic and Gnosticism, Punic and Donatism',[15] I feel that this is an academically impeccable way of saying, in the words of the poet:

'O let us never, never doubt,
What nobody is sure about.'

Leaving aside the total lack of epigraphic evidence for the survival of either Punic or Libyan as significant languages in the fourth century,[16] the literary evidence for the rôle of local feeling, still more of social and political motivation, in the Donatist controversy is exceedingly fragile. It has not survived the sober gaze of Professor Jones, in the *Journal of Theological Studies* of 1959;[17] I have often had occasion to dissent;[18] and Dr. Emil Tengström has now meticulously dismantled many vital links in the chain of evidence, assembled by Dr. Frend and others, for the social and political aims of Donatism.[19]

The questions posed by Dr. Frend and by other advocates of the role of a resurgence of local culture in the religious life of Late Roman Africa are more important than the highly debatable answers they have given to such questions. It is myopic merely to answer these answers. For the questions raised have wider implications. What is at stake is not only the relation between Christianity and local cultures in North Africa, but the relation between Christianity and classical civilisation as a whole in the Latin West in the Late Roman and early medieval periods.

II

Let us look again at the 21 passages in which Augustine speaks of the *lingua Punica.* Two passages refer to words and constructions that are plainly Semitic;[20] but one passage makes it clear that Augustine, by himself, was not able to judge the precise meaning of a word.[21] Five passages refer to the *lingua Punica* in the dealings of the bishop with the countryside around Hippo.[22] It is a language which a bishop, Catholic and Donatist alike, would only make contact with through an interpreter. This *lingua Punica* is featureless: the passages do not reveal a specific language. What they do reveal, however, is a linguistic situation: in and around Hippo, we are dealing with a largely bi-lingual society, where a farmer, for instance, will interpret into Latin a conversation he has just had in Punic.[23] The remaining references occur largely in Augustine's sermons: they are comments on the meaning of untranslated Hebrew words in the Bible, such as mammon, Edom, Messias, through an appeal to Punic.[24] These comments are too easily dismissed as merely academic. Yet, I would suggest that they tell us something which the other passages do not: for they cast light on the motives of Augustine in referring to Punic, on what he wished to achieve, and, so, on his views on the position of the *lingua Punica* in the culture of the African church.

First, we must remember Augustine's intellectual equipment. His own schooling in Latin had done little to help him master any language, even his own, from the grammar, the syntax, the accidence, in the manner of modern linguistics. What he had always learnt was to fasten on words: 'One read Vergil, not as one might look out from a vantage point over a vast landscape, but as one might admire a necklace of pearls, passing them through one's fingers, examining one after the other.'[25] We are well on the way to the *Etymologies* of Isidore of Seville: understanding a language or a culture means grasping the meaning of isolated words. Punic, therefore, usually comes to Augustine like the signposts of a foreign country: single *nomina Punica*, which he invariably handles in isolation.[26]

To this educational trait, we must add Augustine's distinctive mystique of language. He believed that the common usage of words often reflected a providential design to establish more firmly in men's minds certain profound truths. Frequently applied to Latin in his theological treatises, this habit of the *grammaticus* has led him to be acclaimed as a forerunner of linguistic philosophy.[27] Applied to Punic, it takes on a more romantic turn.

In one passage, concerning the spoken language of the countryfolk of Hippo, we come across a clue to the attitude of Augustine and its possible roots. When he was still a priest in Hippo, his bishop, Valerius, had overheard countryfolk using the word 'salus' in conversation: *salus*, he was told, meant 'Three' (compare the Hebrew, *shalosh*). The information intrigued Valerius and Augustine: for every time a Punic speaker said *salus* in Latin, meaning 'Salvation', he was also saying *salus*—Three—in Punic; and so he was being reminded, by the mysterious providence of language, of the relation between Salvation and the Trinity.[28]

He was also told that these countryfolk called themselves *Chenani*. This, he thought, was a mis-pronunciation for *Cananaei*: they had come, in the distant past, from the Land of Canaan. Marcel Simon has drawn attention to the importance of this idea. The myth that the inhabitants of North Africa were either relatives of the Hebrew people, or near-neighbours, was an old Jewish tradition that appears in the *Book of Jubilees*. It had played a part in conciliating the Jewish communities of North Africa to the local inhabitants;[29] one suspects that in this passage, and in his many appeals to the Punic equivalent of Hebrew words, Augustine has stepped into the shoes of the *rabbis*[30]—he has deliberately placed the population of his diocese in the penumbra of the Chosen People.

It is this perspective that determines Augustine's attitude to the *lingua Punica*. It is a learned perspective: like the Latin origin of the Rumanian nation, even when believed, it casts its pattern upon ethnic realities from a dizzy height. A similar 'imaginative nationalism' led Donatists to claim Simon of Cyrene as a fellow-*Afer*,[31] and American senators to invoke the Emperor Septimius

Severus and Saint Augustine in favour of the Negro cause. As with many such 'imaginative nationalisms', it served a good purpose: as with the debate on whether Bulgarian or Serbian was most akin to the Macedonian dialect in the late nineteenth century, philology was a prelude to annexation. The *Chenani* of Hippo are Canaanites precisely because they reminded Augustine of the Canaanite woman of the Gospels: she had come to ask Christ for *Salus*—for health. Though not a member of the Chosen People, the Canaanite woman could claim to be a close relative; and, like the countryfolk of Hippo, the divine providence had prepared her to link the idea of Salvation—*salus*—with her word for Three. But there is no doubt, in this story, as to who would be the source of salvation among the Canaanites of Hippo—the Catholic bishop of the town; and no question whatsoever that, when they came to the point, they would ask for it in good Latin—for the *Salus* of Catholic baptism.[32]

This anecdote shows clearly the direction in which Augustine wished the linguistic currents of his diocese to run, at a time when, as a priest and a star-preacher, he was more directly concerned than at any other period of his life with the problems of evangelisation and reform by the spoken word.[33] The *lingua Punica* has a privileged place in his mind: but only as a step towards full Latinity—in this incident, as in his sermons, 'Punic' hovers in the wings of a Latin culture.

For I would suggest that there was only one 'language of culture' in Late Roman Africa—that was Latin; that the particular form of Christianity in the Later Empire, Catholic and Donatist alike, demanded a 'language of culture'; and, so, that the rapid Christianisation of Numidia involved, not a resurgence of any regional culture, but the creation of a Latin—or sub-Latin—religious culture on an unprecedented scale.[34] The problems posed by the creation of a popular Latin culture are far more solidly documented in the literature of African Christianity than are the fleeting references to a *lingua Punica.*

First of all, we must envisage a missionary situation. The greatest weakness of any view that sees, in the division between Catholic and Donatist, the opening of a fissure between classes or races, is that it ignores the fluidity of the situation up to the age of Augustine. Numidia was not Christianized suddenly: most leading Donatists of the fourth century were converts direct from paganism.[35] At the end of the fourth century, Donatist and Catholic groups still faced each other on either side of a wide, neutral zone of pagans yet to be converted.[36] It is a situation which modern experience of Christian missions has shown to be more conducive to zeal than to mutual tolerance.

Now one of the distinctive features of Christianity in the ancient world as a whole, and in Africa in particular, is that it was a Religion of the Book. Like Judaism, the Christianity of the African clergy was a Law—a *lex*.[37] The bishop's authority stemmed from his preservation of his Law, and his professional activity consisted in expounding it.[38] This Law was, quite concretely, the *codex* of the Holy Scriptures. The fact that some Catholic bishops had handed on these *codices* to be burnt, during the Great Persecution of 304, branded their party, forever, as 'the *traditores*', the 'handers-over' of the Holy Books 'to alter one word of which must be accounted the greatest sacrilege'.[39] 'You come with edicts of Emperors', the Donatist primate of Carthage told the Catholics: 'we hold nothing in our hands but volumes of the Scriptures'.[40] The *panache* of this remark is deeply revealing. It was as a Religion of the Book that the Christians of Africa thought they had been persecuted; it was as a Religion of the Book that the Donatists thought they had been betrayed; and it was as a Religion of the Book that Christianity spread into the countryside of Africa.

For, outside the educated upper-classes, the struggle between Christianity and paganism was not just a conflict of two religions: it was a conflict of two different cultures, associated with two different types of religion. Paganism, in the Roman world, like the religion of any primitive society, was inextricably embedded in the local language: the Lycaonians, in the *Acts of the Apostles*, acclaimed Paul and Barnabas as gods, Λυκαονιστί.[41] The earliest vernaculars in the Roman Empire are *pagan* vernaculars, and the revival of one language, in the third century, that of Phrygian, was a *pagan* revival.[42] Even the most imposing paganism in the Late Antique world, the Zoroastrianism of Sassanian Persia, remained largely pre-literate. It was enshrined in murmured prayers, passed on by word of mouth. Only in the sixth and seventh centuries were the Zoroastrian holy books written down, to save the traditional faith from the inroads of two literate religions, Christianity and Islam.[43]

To abandon paganism was to change one's culture: it was to forget the formulae and liturgies of one's ancient tongue, and to expose oneself to the uniformity of a written book. The situation was not very different from what can now be observed, for instance, in the paganism of New Guinea: 'To understand Tangu, to think the way they do, is to think in their language. The axioms and ideas contained within Tangu sorcery beliefs and activities are best expressed in the Tangu language, which itself expresses the way in which Tangu think about themselves and the world outside . . . by teaching pidgin English, and more recently English, the (Christian) mission hopes to draw Tangu out of the confines of their language' (K. O. L. Burridge, *Mambu: a Melanesian Millennium*, 1960, 70–71). Thus to participate fully in Late Roman Christianity, as a clergyman or a monk, inevitably involved suffering the fate which Irish legend ascribed to a convert of St. Patrick: 'He baptised him and handed him the A.B.C. . . .'[44]

This Latin was more than a 'popular' Latin: it was a Latin that invited literacy—it had the simplicity and uniformity of an ideological language. It had emerged, in the towns of the third century, as amazingly homogeneous: far from betraying an 'African temperament', the Christian Latin of

Carthage was uniform with that of Rome; that of an educated Christian, uniform with that of a simple deacon.[45] This 'clerical language, with its solemn dignity, cold-blooded anger and misuse of Biblical words to interpret and criticise contemporary affairs',[46] remains common to both sides of the Donatist controversy. In the vast correspondence of Augustine, it is possible to recognize at a glance the open-letters which he wrote to his Donatist opponents: they are all in the 'professional' Latin of the African church.[47]

Behind Augustine's vast output in Hippo, we can sense the pressure of the need to extend this religious literacy as widely as possible. The recruitment of the clergy on both sides; the introduction of the monastic life by Augustine and his friends; the consequent growth of a piety based on the *Lectio Divina*—all these changes of the late fourth century placed more and more weight on the Latin language.[48] The Latin of the Scriptures might disgust the educated pagan: but many members of the Christian clergy first learnt to read and write in this Latin,[49] such as the elderly colleague of Augustine who had 'grown up in a farm and had little book-learning'.[50] Augustine would adapt his style to such people: they were his *fratres in eloquio latino inerudití*.[51]

The *sermo humilis*—the 'humble style'—of Augustine's sermons was far more than an exercise in inverted snobbery: it is part of an attempt to enable a bilingual society to participate in an exclusively Latin religious culture, gravitating around a Latin holy text.[52] Augustine's method of allegorical exegesis even betrays this pressure: for his approach to the Scriptures involved moving backwards and forwards throughout the whole length of the Bible in each sermon. By piling half-verse on half-verse, from Genesis to St. Paul and back again, *via* the Psalms, the bishop would create a whole skeleton of verbal echoes, well suited to introducing large areas of the text to an audience used to memorizing by ear. And, like the inspired schoolmaster that he remained, Augustine could hold the whole congregation together, with the hope that those in the back, who had heard the Passion according to St. Matthew for the first time,[53] might, one day, join the *cognoscenti* in the front, who knew why the prophets used the past tense to speak of future events, or why there were 13 Apostles and only 12 thrones.[54]

And there is no greater spur to taking an interest in a sacred text than the fact that the experts so patently disagree about it. Ever singe the time of Cyprian, controversy had taken the form of bundles of citations—*testimonia*.[55] When Augustine took over the church of his Donatist opponents, he covered its walls with posters of such *testimonia* in support of his case;[56] and Donatist pamphlets are no different.[57] By the end of the fourth century, it would have been as difficult for a Christian citizen of Hippo, Donatist or Catholic, *not* to know why the Ark of Noah was tarred inside and out,[58] what the navel of the Beloved in the *Song of Songs* stood for,[59] who was the 'strong woman' of the Book of Proverbs,[60] and why she spun wool for her husband,[61] as it would be for us *not* to recognize Mr. Wilson or

President Johnson in a newspaper cartoon. Where the Bible ended, the popular song took over: Augustine wrote one such—the *Psalmus abecedarius*, '*The A.B.C. against the Donatists*', 'to reach the attention of the humblest masses and of the ignorant and obscure, and to fasten in their memories as much as we can'.[62]

The African church never lacked controversy. The arrival of the Vandals in 429 meant the arrival of yet another group of ecclesiastical opponents—the Vandals being Arian heretics—who, again, were bilingual: speaking Gothic, their language of ecclesiastical culture was almost certainly Latin.[63] Once again, the armoury of Latin controversy was trundled out: the *testimonia*,[64] and the popular song—an 'A.B.C. against the Arians'.[65]

This is true of the third missionary group in Africa. Manichaean propaganda reached all classes:[66] it was current in the villages of Numidia,[67] as well as among the intelligentsia of Carthage;[68] among humble artisans,[69] as among great landowners.[70] While in Egypt Manichaean literature passed, almost immediately, into Coptic, in Africa it remained exclusively Latin.[71]

The Christian culture of Africa, therefore, was exclusively Latin. How many people did it affect? This problem cannot be solved by quantitative analysis: one cannot place those, for instance, who chose to be buried in Latin as one mass, against the untold millions who, apparently, did not.[72] We are dealing with a bilingual population. The issue, therefore, is one of direction. Which way did the cat jump? In which way did Christianity alter the balance in this bilingual situation?[73]

One feature should be stressed. The effect of religious movements is not always to group themselves around the existing contours of class and culture: it is part of their appeal that they do by-pass such divisions. This is particularly true of the fourth century: in Africa, religion became a *carrière ouverte aux talents.* The leader of the Western Manichaean movement, Faustus of Milevis, was one such autodidact: a poor man's son, 'I found at once,' Augustine wrote of him, 'that the man was not learned in any of the liberal sciences save literature, and not especially learned in that. He had read some of Cicero's speeches and a very few books of Seneca, some of the poets and such writings of his own sect as had been written in Latin. . . .'[74] His religion had gained him an *entrée* into Latin culture.

Christianity, indeed, had joined hands with that other agent of social mobility in Africa—the teaching profession. In 320, a Moor, the grandson of one of the rude cavalrymen of the Emperor's *comitatus*, had settled down in Cirta as a 'professor of Roman letters'.[75] The process continued throughout the fourth century: looking through the personnel of the Donatist Church[76] and reading the sermons of African preachers,[77] one wonders whether, for the one bishop who might have entered the Church, in Gaul or Italy, as a spectacular *avatar* of the local senatorial magnate, there were not a score of minor clergy, in Africa, whose careers and outlook reincarnated the *grammaticus* and the small-town lawyer.

Beyond the few who actually became literate through religion, there were the listeners.[78] Christian preaching and Christian controversy—religious debates being a star-attraction in African towns of the fourth century[79]—would have had an effect similar to that of the wireless in many multilingual societies: its constant broadcasts would have tipped the balance in favour of the uniform language of culture. In Hippo, in the early fifth century, the works of Cicero were not available;[80] but the Latin of the Psalms had become popular songs,[81] and the Latin of the Bible so familiar that it, and not the Latin of the classics, was considered 'good' Latin.[82]

III

This, I would suggest, was the cultural function of the rise of Christianity in Late Roman Africa: far from fostering native tradition, it widened the franchise of the Latin language. Nowhere is this more true than in Numidia, where the Donatist Church was strongest. For it is highly questionable to isolate Numidia as being any more 'rural' than the other provinces of Late Roman Africa: and to persist in describing Numidian Donatism as a distinctively 'rural' religion is to misunderstand the role of the towns in the Late Roman period. The vigour of these towns should not be underestimated.[83] If there is a conflict of social groups in fourth-century Numidia, it is not between 'town' and 'country' but, perhaps, between two layers of the aristocracies of the towns. The 'traditional' local aristocracy of *curiales* and *grammatici* tended to be either pagan or Donatist, while the 'new' aristocracy of *honorati*, as dependents on Imperial patronage, followed their masters into Catholicism.[84] The Donatist Church of Numidia was a church of 'great churches',[85] that is, of huge, urban basilicas, dedicated, as that of Timgad, to praising the Donatist bishop, in Latin.[86] The Latin slogans on altars, on the graves of martyrs, the Latin Biblical citations around baptisteries and above the lintels of country-churches are the shadow of this new, confident Latin culture of the Christian Church.[87] The Donatist bishops, their clergy, and their followers had gained, by their conversion to Christianity, a culture which they shared with the rest of the Latin world, and, having gained it in Latin, they not unnaturally claimed to be right, in Latin. To treat Donatism as a manifestation of 'African separatism' blunts its challenge. It does scant justice to the roots of the Donatist ideology in the common culture of Latin Christianity.[88] For the historian of the religious divisions of the Christian Church, such a view can be an easy way out: it resembles the judgement of the Yugo-slav court which dismissed *The New Class* of Milovan Djilas as a manifestation of 'Montenegrin separatism'; it is a convenient way of drawing the sting of a challenge couched in terms of a universal body of doctrine, common to both sides, and so guaranteed to hurt—whether this is the 'true' Socialism of Djilas, or the 'true' Church of a Donatist. The atmosphere of Christianized Africa is not that of a region drifting out of the Roman world:

it is a doctrinaire and cocksure belief that what was good for Numidia was good for the Roman Empire: 'What has been done in Africa,' wrote one, 'must appear in the whole world.'[89] Tyconius was more right than he could have dreamed. For his commentary on the *Apocalypse* filtered into the Catholic tradition under the blessing of Augustine: it was vital to early medieval exegesis.[90] If the Spanish manuscript illuminations, from which the Christ in Majesty of the Romanesque tympanum derives, owe anything to the Tyconian commentary of Beatus of Liebana, then the traveller to Moissac may still see, on the great porch, a distant echo of the ecclesiological rancours of a fourth-century Donatist.[91]

There is, indeed, one facet of the rise of Christianity in Roman society, as of the rôle of religious movements in any society, which has not been stressed as strongly as it deserves. It is generally assumed, by most students of Donatism, that the function of Christianity was to provide an ideological expression for pre-existing tensions: that religion can act as the vehicle of social grievances, that it can strengthen the solidarity of submerged groups. What is overlooked is the rôle of religion as a mediator: how a religious movement, such as Christianity, can make the culture of an élite available to a wider audience, how its appeal lies partly in its ability to enable people to participate in something different from their ordinary existence. Yet a look at the sermons which African bishops preached on great occasions should convince us of this—they are glorious displays of rhetoric, the Latin language of the towns parading in its Sunday best.[92]

Perhaps the debate on the rôle of local culture in Late Roman Africa has been tied too closely to the problem of the rise of the Donatist Church. There is one point which this hypnosis with the superbly-documented age of Augustine tends to miss. The history of African Christianity remains well-known to us, to the mid-seventh century at least. In all this period, from 430 to 698, there is not one mention of the *lingua Punica*.[93]

I should like to end by asking why this should be so.

My reason is, briefly, that it was no longer necessary. The late fourth and early fifth centuries was a period of crisis: it marks the peak of missionary activity in Numidia, and the peak of competition between Donatists and Catholics. To save a Donatist from eternal damnation it was necessary to talk to him even in the *lingua Punica*.[94] But, with the forcible elimination of the Donatist clergy, after 411, the peasantry could settle down to the normal perils of under-evangelization, perils less spectacular than evangelization by the wrong side.

Also, there was no time. In 430, Roman rule collapsed in Numidia; by the end of the century, the Vandals had as good as abandoned the province for the Carthaginian coastline. The Donatist 'holy city' of Timgad had been pillaged by mountain-tribes from the Aures and the Hodna. Throughout the sixth century, Numidia was overshadowed by their 'Moorish' kingdoms.[95] In the fourth century, these mountaineers had been beneath religion.[96] They had regarded the Donatist controversy with the same indifference as the Highland clans of the seventeenth century had regarded the literate rancours of the Lowland Scots. We can glimpse what had happened by the end of the sixth century: Gregory the Great found to his surprise that Catholic bishops of Numidia had been collaborating with their Donatist colleagues.[97] The reason is not difficult to understand: faced by the resurgence of what Dr. Courtois has called *l'Afrique oublieé*, the Forgotten Africa of the mountains and the deserts, these two groups of Latin professionals had decided that the devil they knew was better than the devil they did not know. It is a sign of the future: the Christian has already become isolated as the *Roumi*, the man of Roman faith and Roman culture, in an alien world.

The Christian Latin culture of the West was the culture of men in a hurry: the missionary had to expand, the scholar had to preserve.[98] Like the Romans of Africa in the fifth and sixth centuries, who had hastily converted the classical monuments of their towns into fortresses, these men used what was to hand—the Latin language. By contrast, vernacular cultures grew up in the East under very different conditions. Far from reflecting any conscious desire to remove the yoke of Rome, these local cultures assumed its continued existence: in the fourth, fifth and sixth centuries, they could grow up peaceably, among the placid subjects of a world well policed by the two great empires of Byzantium and Persia. At exactly the time when, in the Byzantine Empire, Greek philosophy and medicine were passing quietly into Syriac, and Syriac imagery, in turn, was colouring the hymns and liturgy of the Byzantine Church, the Latin civilization of Africa had left no alternative but barbarism. We meet a cultivated African, Donatus, throwing in the towel:

> violentias barbararum gentium imminere conspiciens . . . ferme cum septuaginta monachis copiosisque librorum codicibus navali vehiculo in Hispaniam commeavit.[99]

We are left with the old problem, that has exercised historians of the classical tradition and of the growth of the Papacy: there *is* some connection between Christianity and the survival of Roman civilization in the west. The possibility that there had existed, in Late Roman Africa, a powerful Christian Church, hostile to the Roman towns, rooted in the native cultural traditions of the countryside, had seemed, for a moment, to offer an alternative to that view. I do not think that there is an alternative. Christianity won, in the West, as elsewhere in the Roman world, because it won the battle for the towns:[100] it absorbed their culture, it transmitted this culture, on its own terms, to those who had not enjoyed it to such an extent, or, rather, to those who would not have enjoyed it on such easy terms in the social and cultural conditions of the Later Empire.[101] (There may be a direct connection, in the Late Roman period, between the narrowing of Latin culture in its pagan form—its 'aristocratisation'—and its widening—its 'democratisation'—in its Christian form. For the Christian Church had the best of both worlds: its urban structure and the recruitment of its bishops would constantly transmit the culture of an élite to large congregations, as Augustine, in Hippo, would spell out the sheltered mysticism of Plotinus in simple Latin.)

There is always a social and cultural history yet to be written, of the terms on which Christianity won this victory in the Roman towns: it would aim, above all, to explain the gradual realisation, throughout the fourth century, of that most breath-taking of all intellectual sleights of hand—the solemn identification, by Christian apologists from Origen and Lactantius onwards, of Christianity with *true* Greco-Roman culture, and the great tradition of Greco–Roman religion with all that was barbaric, un-Roman, not *évolué*.

We have seen how this happened in one area of the Latin culture of Africa. Whether we think it was worth happening, depends on whether we take Roman civilisation, in its Late Roman form, for granted as an unquestioned good thing. One may doubt it: Christianity gained respectability at the high cost of adopting a town-dweller's assumptions on the passivity of the country-side, and by committing itself, disastrously, to a town-dweller's contempt of the barbarian.[102] In Africa, it paid the heavy price of gradual extinction. Elsewhere in Western Europe it survived. Perhaps the price was not paid until later. The failure of so many Western missions, from the inner erosion of the great Jesuit venture in China to the rise of nationalism in the *Tiers Monde* is, perhaps, the delayed payment for the Christian victories of the fourth and fifth centuries.

Notes

1 For a discussion of the literature on this problem, see P. R. L. Brown, 'Religious Dissent in the Later Roman Empire: the case of North Africa', *History* XLVI, 1961, 83–101.
2 Collected and commented by W. M. Green 'Augustine's Use of Punic', *Semitic and Oriental Studies presented to W. Popper* (Univ. of California Publications in Semitic Philology, XI), 1951, 179–90: see inf. pp. 87–9.
3 Procopius, *de bello Vandalico* II, 10.
4 See esp. J. B. Chabot, *Recueil des inscriptions libyques* (1940–1);
5 See esp. W. H. C. Frend, The Revival of Berber Art', *Antiquity* XVI (1942), 342–52.
6 G. Levi della Vida, 'Sulle iscrizioni "Latinolibiche" della Tripolitania', *Oriens Antiquus* II (1960), 65–94, and 'Frustuli neo-punici tripolitani', *Acc. Lincei, Rend. sci. mor. stor. e filol.* ser. 8, XVIII (1966), 463–82.
7 W. H. C. Frend, 'A Note on the Berber background in the life of Augustine,' *Journal of Theological Studies* XLIII, 1942, 188–91.
8 S. Gsell, *Histoire ancienne de l'Afrique du Nord* IV, 1918 (1929 [3]), 179 and 496–8; VI, 1928 (1929 [2]), 108–13, VII, 1928 (1930 [2]), 107–8.
9 E. F. Gautier, *Le Passé de l'Afrique du Nord. Les siècles obscurs*, 1942, 134–57.
10 Marcel Simon, 'Le judaïsme berbère dans l'Afrique ancienne,' *Revue d'histoire et de philosophie religieuses* XXVI, 1946 (= *Recherches d'histoire Judée-Chrétienne*,

1962, 30–87) and 'Punique ou berbère?', *Annuaire de l'Institut de Philologie et d'Histoire Orientales et Slaves* XIII, 1955 (= *Recherches* . . . 88–100).

11 W. H. C. Frend, *Martyrdom and Persecution in the Early Church*, 1964, esp. p. 332.

12 A. Berthier, *Les Vestiges du Christianisme antique dans la Numidie centrale*, 1943, esp. 220–4, and Frend, *Donatist Church*, esp. 52–9.

13 Frend, *Donatist Church*, p. xvi: 'Is Donatism part of a continuous native tradition as fundamentally unchanged as the Berbers in the outline of their daily life?' Compare E. Dermenghen, *Le culte des saints dans l'Islam maghrébin*, 1954 and G. Drague, *Esquisse d'histoire religieuse du Maroc*, 1951; but, for a shrewd criticism of this tendency to concentrate on the local, continuous peculiarities of religious life in the Maghreb, to the exclusion of its wider context, namely, the interaction of this life with the orthodox culture of the towns, see J. Berque, 'Cent vingt-cinq ans de sociologie maghrébine,' *Annales* XI, 1956, 296–324.

14 R. MacMullen, 'Provincial Languages . . . ,' (above, n. 1) 14.

15 R. MacMullen, 'A note on *Sermo humilis*,' *Journal of Theological Studies*, n.s. XVII, 1966, 108–12, at p. 109.

16 Picard, 'Pertinax . . . ,' 57–8, displays equal scepticism on both Punic and Libyan; MacMullen, 'Provincial Languages . . . ,' 12–13, dismisses Libyan and retains Punic with some hesitation.

17 A. H. M. Jones, 'Were the ancient heresies national or social movements in disguise?', *Journal of Theological Studies*, n.s. X, 2, 1959, 280–295.

18 Brown, 'Religious Dissent . . .' (above, n. 1) esp. 91–5; see also Brown, 'Religious Coercion in the Later Roman Empire: the case of North Africa,' *History* XLVIII, 1963, 283–305, at 293–7, and *Augustine of Hippo: A Biography*, 1967, at 217 and 227–30.

19 E. Tengström, *Donatisten und Katholiken: soziale, wirtschaftliche und politische Aspekte einer nordafrikanischen Kirchenspaltung* (Studia Graeca et Latina Gothoburgensia XVIII, 1964).

20 *Ep. ad Rom. incoh. expos.* 13.

21 *de magistro* XIII, 44.

22 *Ep. ad Rom. incoh. expos.* 13; *Ep.* 66, 2; *Ep.* 108, 14; *Ep.* 209, 3; *de haeres.* 87.

23 *Ep. ad Rom. incoh. expos.* 13.

24 *Loc. in Hept. I*, ad Gen. I, 24.

25 H. I. Marrou, *S. Augustin et la fin de la culture antique*, 1938, p. 25.

26 e.g. *Ep.* 17, 2.

27 Marrou, op. cit. (n. 25), p. 16 and '*Retractatio*', 1949, p. 676.

28 *Ep. ad Rom. incoh. expos.* 13.

29 Simon, 'Le judaïsme berbère' (= *Recherches* . . . pp. 39–42) and A. Chouraqui, *Les Juifs de l'Afrique du Nord*, 1952, pp. 14–19.

30 Jerome, *Liber hebraicarum quaestionum in Genesim*, ad Gen. XXXVI, 24 (*P.L.* 23, 993B–994A) refers to an appeal to Punic *apud Hebraeos.*

31 *Serm.* 46, 41.

32 'Baptism' was spoken of by such *Punici Christiani* as *Salus: de pecc. mer. et rem.* I, XXIV, 34.

33 Brown, *Augustine of Hippo*, 138–42; 206–7 and 235–6.

34 The important distinction between a spoken *patois* and a 'language of culture', introduced by Simon, 'Punique ou berbère?' (*Recherches* . . . 95–6) in favour of Punic, seems to me to favour only Latin: see Picard, 'Pertinax . . . ,' 58, n. 2, on the meagre quality of Punic inscriptions.

35 Bishop Marculus: *Passio Marculi* (*P.L.* 8, 760); while Vitellius Afer—Gennadius, *de script eccles.* 4 (*P.L.* 58, 1063)—wrote '*against the pagans*'.

36 *de catech. rud.* xxv, 48. Simultaneous attacks on rural shrines by Catholics and Donatist Circumcellions: *Serm.* 62, 13.
37 W. H. C. Frend, 'A Note on the Great Persecution in the West', *Studies in Church History* ii, 1965, ed. C. J. Cuming, 146–8, and Brown, *Augustine of Hippo* 217.
38 Brown, *Augustine of Hippo* 259–63.
39 *Acta Saturnini* 18 (*P.L.* 8, 701B).
40 Augustine, *Ad Don. post Coll.* i, 31.
41 *Acts of the Apostles* 14, ii.
42 E.g. W. M. Ramsey, 'The Tekmoreian Guest-Friends', *Journal of Hellenic Studies* xxxii, 1912, 151–70.
43 J. Tavadia, 'Zur Pflege des iranischen Schrifttums', *Zeitschr. deutsch. morgenländ. Gesell.* 98, 1944, 337.
44 This has been clearly seen and brilliantly expressed by H. I. Marrou, *Histoire de l'Éducation dans l'Antiquité*, 1955^3, 418–21 (the citation appears on p. 439).
45 Christine Mohrmann, 'Les origines de la latinité chrétienne à Rome', *Études sur le latin des chrétiens* iii, 1965, 67–126.
46 A. Harnack, *History of Dogma* (Dover Books, 1961), v, 25.
47 Christine Mohrmann, 'S. Augustin écrivain', *Recherches augustiniennes* i, 1958, 43–66, at p. 65.
48 See, in general, Marrou, *Histoire de l'Éducation . . .* , 439–40. The situation would be similar to that in which Augustine found himself on becoming a priest in Hippo in 391: his bishop Valerius, as a Greek, was handicapped by lack of a Latin education—Possidius, *Vita Augustini* v, 3.
49 See Rémi Crespin, *Ministère et Sainteté: pastorale du clergé et solution de la crise donatiste dans la vie et la doctrine de S. Augustin*, 1965, 116–17. This shows that the clergy was not recruited from classes that would have been literate.
50 Possidius, *Vita* xxvii, 10.
51 *Retract.* ii, 29 on the *de agone christiano*. It is important to note that, though written in simple Latin, the ideas in this book are far from being those of 'popular' African Christianity: see Brown, *Augustine of Hippo* 245.
52 See esp. R. MacMullen, 'A note on *Sermo humilis*,' *Journal of Theological Studies*, n.s. xvii, 1966, 108–12.
53 *Sum.* 232, 1.
54 *Enarr. in Ps.* 49, 9; *Serm.* 249, 3.
55 *Testimoniorum ad Quirinum libri iii* (*C.S.E.L.* iii, 35–184).
56 *Retract.* ii, 27; cf. Possidius, *Indiculus*, 'De testimoniis Scripturarum contra Donatistas et idola'.
57 See esp. J.-P. Brisson, *Autonomisme et christianisme dans l'Afrique romaine*, 1958, 145–9.
58 *Ep. ad cath.* v, 9.
59 Optatus of Milevis, *de schism. Don.* ii, 8.
60 *Serm.* 37, 2.
61 *Serm.* 37, 17.
62 *Retract.* i, 20.
63 Victor Vitensis, *Historia Persecutions Vandalicae* ii, xviii, 53.
64 E.g. *Florilegia Biblica Africana saec.* v, ed. B. Schwank, Corpus Christianorum, ser. lat. 90, 1961.
65 By Fulgentius of Ruspe; ed. Lambot, *Revue bénédictine* xlviii, 1936, 231–4.
66 On the composition of the Manichaean movement in Africa, see Brown, *Augustine of Hippo* 54–5.
67 *Ep.* 64, 3.
68 *de util. cred.* xiv, 32.

69 The names given in the abjuration of a Manichee: *P.L.* 42, 518.
70 E.g. Romanianus, patron of Augustine: *C. Acad.* II, iii, 8.
71 See, most recently, T. Save-Söderbergh, *Studies in the Coptic Manichaean Psalmbook*, 1949.
72 As by Chr. Courtois, *Les Vandales et l'Afrique*, 1955, p. 128; his remarks on the quality of the Latin of the inscriptions are more cogent.
73 Cf. C. Jullian, *Histoire de la Gaule* VIII, 310, on the rôle of the Church in finally Latinising the Gallic countryside.
74 Augustine, *Conf.* v, vi, II, and *Contra Faustum* v, 5.
75 *Gesta apud Zenophilum, C.S.E.L.* XXVI, 185.
76 See esp. P. Monceaux, *Histoire littéraire de l'Afrique chrétienne* VI, 1922.
77 J. Leclercq, 'Prédication et rhétorique au temps de S. Augustin', *Revue bénédictine* 67, 1947, 117–31, at pp. 129–30.
78 Augustine, *Enarr. in Ps.* 121, 8: 'nos simus codex ipsorum'.
79 E.g. Augustine's debate with a Manichee in a packed bath-house: *C. Fort.* I and Possidius, *Vita* VI, 2. The crowd gathering in a debate with a Donatist bishop: *Ep.* 44.
80 *Ep.* 118, II, 9.
81 *Enarr. in Ps.* 132, I.
82 *de doct. christ.* II, xiv, 21.
83 P. A. Février, 'Toujours le Donatisme: à quand l'Afrique?', *Rivista di storia e letteratura religiosa* II, 2 (1966), 228–40, esp. 234 f.
84 See the evidence ingeniously discussed by T. Kotula, *Zgromadzenia prowincjonalne w rzymskiej Afryce w epoce późnego Cesarstwa* (1965).
85 *Enarr. in Ps.* 21, 26.
86 Brown, 'Religious Dissent . . .', (above n. 1) 92.
87 On the repercussions of establishing a bishop in such villages, see Brown, 'Religious Dissent . . .', 95.
88 An oversight handsomely remedied by W. H. C. Frend, *Martyrdom and Persecution in the Early Church*, 1964. See Brown, *Augustine of Hippo* 212–25.
89 T. Hahn, *Tyconius-Studien*, 1900, p. 85.
90 Gerald Bonner, *Saint Bede in the tradition of Western Apocalyptic Commentary* (Jarrow Lecture, 1966).
91 H. Schlunk, 'Observaciones en torno al problema de la miniatura visigoda', *Archivo Español de Arte* 71, 1945, 241–64, at pp. 262 f.
92 See the example in J. Leclerq, 'Prédication et rhétorique au temps de S. Augustin', *Revue bénédictine* 67, 1947, at pp. 121–5.
93 The following recent work provide some indication of the prosperity and Latin civilisation of Africa after 430: H. I. Marrou, 'Épitaphe chrétienne d'Hippone à réminiscences virgiliennes', *Libyca* I, 1953, 215–90.
94 *Epp.* 66, 2 and 209, 3. In the last case, there is no evidence that Augustine's final choice for bishop of Fussala did speak the *lingua Punica*: it was plainly an accomplishment that could be dispensed with.
95 Chr. Courtois, *Les Vandales et l'Afrique* 315, n. 7 (on Timgad) and 325–38 (map on p. 334).
96 Hence Augustine's accusation that the Donatist bishops had supported the Moorish usurper Firmus: *Ep.* 87, 10. This accusation is made only to a bishop of Caesarea in Mauretania. Seeing that this town had been sacked by Firmus, and that the Christian bishop had had to appeal to the Emperor to save the town from paying taxes after the disaster (Symmachus, *Ep.* I, 64), Augustine's accusation is in deliberate bad taste. His handling of many incidents in Donatism would repay re-consideration in this light: see Brown, *Augustine of Hippo* 228–30.

97 The incident has been admirably studied by R. A. Markus, 'Donatism: the Last Phase', *Studies in Church History* I, ed. C. W. Dugmore and Charles Duggan, 1964, 118–26. This article, and the author's 'Religious Dissent in North Africa in the Byzantine Period', *Studies in Church History* III, ed. C. J. Cuming, 1966, 140–9, show how much of general importance for our understanding of the evolution and fundamental characteristics of African Christianity can be gained from careful study of the events of the late sixth century.

98 '. . . il faut faire vite': Fontaine, *Isidore de Séville* . . . II, 884.

99 Ildefonsus of Toledo, *de vir. ill.* 4 (*P.L.* 96 200 c).

100 This is not to deny the interest of the survey of W. H. C. Frend, 'The Winning of the Countryside', *Journal of Ecclesiastical History* XVIII, 1967, 1–14.

101 On the 'aristocratisation' of culture see, for instance, R. MacMullen, 'Roman Bureaucratese', *Traditio* XVIII, 1962, 367 f.

102 See Brown, 'The Later Roman Empire,' *Economic History Review* 2 ser., XX, 1967, at pp. 331–3, and 'Approaches to the Religious Crisis of the Third Century', *English Historical Review*, LXXXIII (1968), at pp. 542 ff.

14

Excerpt from 'MOUNTAIN CONSTANTINES
The Christianization of Aksum and Iberia'[1]

Christopher Haas

Source: *Journal of Late Antiquity*, 1(1) (2008), 101–26.

In September of 324, after his victory at Chrysopolis over his erstwhile imperial colleague, Licinius, the emperor Constantine could look out over the battlefield with the satisfaction that he now was the sole ruler of the Roman world. Ever since his public adherence to the Christian God in October of 312, Constantine had been moving slowly but steadily toward more overt expressions of favor toward Christianity through his avid patronage of the Church and his studied neglect of the ancient rites. For nearly eight years after his conversion in 312, Constantine's coinage continued to depict pagan deities like Mars and Jupiter, and the Christian emperor was styled "Companion of the Unconquerable Sun" until 322.[2] Christian symbols made only a gradual appearance. This cautious attitude toward religion on the coins can be ascribed to Constantine's anxiety to court the loyalty of the principal recipients of the coins—the army, still largely pagan. After Chrysopolis, such caution seems to have been abandoned and Constantine came into his own as a Christian emperor. Constantinople was founded, the Council of Nicaea was convoked, and Palestine was marked out as a Holy Land by lavish imperial churches. Constantine also reformed the coinage in 324, issuing coins of new weight. His victory banner, the *labarum*, bearing the monogram of Christ was displayed on relief sculpture, statuary, and over the gates of the palace.

The initial Christianization

Far from imperial Rome, a thriving kingdom located south of the Roman frontier likewise was undergoing momentous changes. The kings of Aksum, in the highlands of modern Ethiopia and Eritrea, had been issuing gold coins ever since the time of king Endubis in the late third century. Aksum was the only kingdom in ancient sub-Saharan Africa to mint coins, and one of four contemporary kingdoms in the world to issue gold coins, a testimony of Aksum's wealth, power, and role in international trade. In approximately the same year as Chrysopolis, the Aksumite king Ezana I made a significant change in the iconography of his coins.[3] Previously, Aksumite kings were shown proudly wearing a diadem while overhead there was a solar disc within a crescent moon, representing the Aksumite gods for the sun and moon, or Mahrem, the warrior-god whom the kings took as their special patron. Ezana abruptly replaced this traditional religious iconography with a new symbol, the Cross, which remained prominent on Aksumite coinage until its end in the seventh century. One of Ezana's near successors in the mid-fourth century went further and depicted a large cross that nearly filled up the reverse of his coins. This prominence given to the Cross predates any analogous depiction on Roman coinage.[4]

Despite Eusebius of Caesarea's vision of a coextensive church and empire, by the fourth century, Christianity was spreading rapidly beyond the imperial frontiers, due largely to the active patronage of monarchs who predated or were contemporary with Constantine's own conversion to Christianity.[5] The Syriac kingdom of Osrhoëne, focused on its main urban center of Edessa, probably was the first to embrace the new religion, perhaps as early as the reign of king Abgar VIII in the third century.[6] Situated near the Euphrates, astride the principal caravan route between the Roman and Sassanian empires, Edessa served as a vital conduit for Christianity into the Persian east. The church flourished within Sassanian Mesopotamia until Constantine's ill-considered letter to Shapur II, in which he recommended Christianity to the *shahan'shah* and voiced his concern for Shapur's Christian subjects.[7] Henceforth, Christians suffered repeated persecution within the Persian realm, although they continued as one of the Persian Empire's most significant religious minorities.[8] Christianity followed trade routes down the Red Sea, and indeed, strong evidence suggests that Christian communities were established along the Kerala coast in south India as early as the first or second centuries. Christianity also took root in the Caucasian regions of Colchis, Iberia, and Armenia, where king Tiridates IV converted to Christianity perhaps as much as a full decade before the Battle of the Milvian Bridge in 312.[9]

It is vital in all these instances to distinguish carefully among the various stages within the process of Christianization. In some cases, we can speak only of the presence of small numbers of foreign-born Christians, usually through trade, diplomacy, or as the enslaved victims of barbarian *razzias*. Occasionally we hear of individual bishops making periodic pastoral forays beyond the imperial borders, such as Ulfilas among the Goths of the lower Danube beginning ca. 340. More common is the missionary-bishop who secures the patronage of a local ruler, such as Patrick with the Irish chieftains in the mid-fifth century; Augustine of Canterbury with king Ethelbert of Kent in the years after 597 CE; and, shortly thereafter, the Nestorian bishop Alopen, who was warmly received by the T'ang emperor Taizong in 635.[10] It is a big step, however, between the introduction of Christianity and its establishment with a formal church structure of bishops and synods, as well as its adoption by a broad cross-section of society, including the ruling elite of king and nobility.

Christianization is a notoriously difficult process to trace, especially because many of the sources used by scholars date from eras sometimes centuries removed from the actual events. Moreover, the narrative of conversion often is closely linked to the formation of ethnic or national identity, and care must be taken not to follow blindly much later sources that deliberately archaize in order to promote a particular agenda. These methodological difficulties have bedeviled students of Christianization, but at the same time, they have spurred scholars to develop an array of models intended to elucidate Christianization in a variety of cultures.[11]

A comparative approach can offer a useful methodology for exploring the contours of Christianization.[12] This is especially true for those who see Christianization as just one specific type, among many, of large-scale religious transformations.[13] Cultural anthropologists over the past two decades have employed a comparative methodology in order to highlight the particularities of religious conversion in many different cultural settings.[14] At the same time, comparative analysis also has become more common in late antique studies, facilitated by the field's expansion to regions well beyond the confines of the Mediterranean.[15] Likewise, the extension of Late Antiquity's chronological limits by some scholars to include the Umayyad caliphate has enriched our understanding of both early Byzantine and early Islamic cultures.[16]

The model proposed in this study for understanding the dynamics of Christianization during Late Antiquity emerges through a comparative analysis of the kingdoms of Aksum and Iberia, two kingdoms whose rulers embraced Christianity in the early fourth century. For each of these states, the interplay between monarchical power and religious policy often has been examined in light of the complexities of particular local developments, which gradually are becoming clearer by ongoing archaeological and textual studies. A comparative approach, however, also can illuminate the process of cultural transformation occurring in these kingdoms separated by nearly two thousand miles. Although neither kingdom served as a principal buffer state between the major empires of Rome and Sassanian Persia, they guarded vital access routes for trade and migration in the Caucasus region and near the Red Sea. Consequently, they hardly can be considered peripheral to the major theater of war in the region of the upper Euphrates, the center of what Garth Fowden has identified as the "Mountain Arena."[17] Both Aksum and Iberia were factors in the competitive diplomacy of the Roman and

Sassanian Empires, and on occasion became major players in proxy wars between the two empires.[18]

When the monarchs of these mountain kingdoms adopted Christianity, the new religion of the Roman emperor, they made a cultural choice with profound international implications. As we shall see, however, neither king Mirian III of Iberia nor king Ezana I of Aksum embraced Christianity as the result of Roman diplomatic initiatives. Indeed, in each case, the Roman emperor responded late to the changed religious preferences of the local monarchs. Moreover, their espousal of Christianity should not be considered as equivalent to the conversion of the two kingdoms. Instead, the royal conversion stood as but one phase, though an admittedly crucial one, in a remarkably similar process of Christianization in Aksum and in Iberia. In both cases, this was a multi-phased process that took centuries to complete.[19]

For western readers, probably the most familiar link between these two kingdoms is provided by the church historian Rufinus of Aquileia. Sometime in 402 or 403, Rufinus produced an abridged Latin translation of Eusebius' *Ecclesiastical History* and continued the narrative in two additional books down to the death of the emperor Theodosius I in 395. Embedded in his long description of Constantine's reign in book 10, Rufinus provides back-to-back narratives of the evangelization of Aksum and Iberia. He begins with the story of Aedesius and Frumentius, two Christian youths from the city of Tyre who were shipwrecked along the Red Sea coast and sold into slavery, probably near Adulis, Aksum's chief port. Their native talent and Greek education came to the notice of the local king (possibly Ella Amida or Ousanas) who made Aedesius his cupbearer and Frumentius the master of his correspondence and accounts. They became indispensable servants, and after the death of the king and his testamentary manumission of the youths, his widowed queen asked them to stay on and administer the kingdom during thc minority of her young son, Ezana. They agreed, and largely under the direction of Frumentius, Christian merchants were granted privileges and places of worship. Once the young king reached his majority, Aedesius and Frumentius returned to the Roman world. Frumentius went to Alexandria, where he reported to bishop Athanasius the favor accorded to Christianity by the new king and the need for a formal mission with a bishop and priests. Recognizing this tremendous opportunity, Athanasius appointed the obvious man for the job, Frumentius, as the bishop. Frumentius then returned to the kingdom where, as Rufinus puts it, "many barbarians were converted" and where "from that time on, there came into existence a Christian people."[20]

Rufinus joins this narrative with his account of the conversion of Iberia by saying, "It was at this time, too, that the Iberians who dwell in the region of Pontus accepted the Word of God and faith in the kingdom to come." He goes on to tell of an unnamed slave girl, a Roman captive whose modesty and ascetic practices impressed her Iberian owners. When the prayers of the young captive led to the healing of a sick child, the Iberian queen, who was suffering from a grave illness, went to the ascetic's hut and asked for prayers. The queen was healed immediately, and the young captive converted the queen to Christ. The king initially was resistant to his wife's new religion until he, too, encountered a miracle one day while hunting. He had been riding through the woods when he suddenly was enshrouded by a threatening darkness. He called upon Christ, his wife's new God, and daylight returned, allowing him to return to safety. At the urging of the young Christian slave, the king laid the foundations of a church to commemorate his new faith. The church was completed, but only after the young woman's prayers miraculously overcame obstacles that had hindered the church's construction. Thereupon, the king requested that Constantine send clergy to help establish the faith in Iberia.[21] [. . .]

Both kingdoms possessed a pre-Christian religious substratum that included, if not clearly established Jewish communities, at least an indigenous receptivity to ideas and practices within the currents of Jewish life in the Mediterranean. Setting aside the traditions enshrined in the *Kebra Nagast* about the queen of Sheba and Solomon, and their son Menelik and the coming of the Ark of the Covenant to Aksum, there is much in the Aksumite religious background that echoes Judaism.[22] Abstention from pork appears to be a pre-Christian practice, and concepts about sacral kingship and ritual purity also reflect this influence.[23] Although there is considerable debate about the precise origins of the Falashas, Ethiopia's ancient Jewish community, there is a consensus that strong Semitic influences from South Arabia, if not outright Jewish migration, helped to create this community prior to the introduction of Christianity. An Aksumite inscription of uncertain date, for example, attests east through Iberia.[24] Jewish burials are attested from Urbnisi, in the western region of the Mtkvari River corridor.[25] In addition, two late antique epitaphs of Jews come from the necropolis at Samtavro in Mtskheta, the political center of Iberia.[26] These epitaphs, as well as formulae possibly attributable to Jewish graves, suggest that the entire southern part of the Samtavro necropolis was given over to Jewish burials.[27] It may be significant that this section is adjacent to the portion of the necropolis reserved for Iberian royal burials, perhaps suggesting that the Jewish community, a community of resident foreigners, came under the patronage of the monarchy.[28] [. . .]

These connections of both kingdoms with Mediterranean Judaism should be seen as part of a larger background of cross-cultural contacts that become pronounced in the centuries leading up to the period of Christianization. In both cases, we should note the vital role played by international trade in facilitating cultural exchange through the presence of foreign merchants, as well as foreign-born skilled craftsmen who plied their trade under wealthy indigenous patrons. This is a common dynamic that occurred in regions as diverse as south India, where Syrian merchants brought Judaism and Christianity, and in central Asian cities along the Silk Road, where Sogdian merchants spread Manichaeism, Judaism, and Christianity.[29] Before long, trade opened many doors to Islam near the Indian Ocean and southeast Asia.

In Aksum, Rufinus' account speaks explicitly of Christian merchants from the Mediterranean who were sought out by Frumentius and accorded royal patronage, including aid in the construction of churches.[30] There had long been a close connection between Mediterranean craftsmen and the two kingdoms. Die-cutters from Alexandria appear to have helped initiate Aksumite coinage. Burials from the vicinity of both capitals indicate that the upper classes of Aksum and Iberia developed a taste for Mediterranean luxury goods, including glass goblets and plates of gold and silver. This is especially noteworthy for Aksum, because it was well removed from the kingdom's main entrepôt at the port of Adulis. Trade between Aksum and the eastern empire was given such a prominent place in relations between the two kingdoms that its disruption by the ruler of Himyar in the early sixth century is stated by Malalas to be the reason for Justinian's request that Kaleb I intervene militarily across the Red Sea. Given the volume of trade, it is probable that foreign merchants and craftsmen brought not only their wares, but their gods as well.[31]

Despite the emphasis placed on royal conversions in the literary traditions of Aksum and Iberia, the question arises whether the local monarchs initiated the Christianization of their kingdoms or whether, instead, there were indigenous Christians prior to the conversion of the king. It would be useful to know the number and social position of these indigenous Christians, for these factors might allow us to gauge the significance of the royal conversions. Do we have what has been called a "top-down model of conversion" or does the monarch participate in, and eventually come to lead, a process that had been going on in his kingdom, much as Constantine did in Rome? [. . .]

The assertion of royal priority in matters of religion strengthened the hands of the monarchs in dealing with the local lords. Even if, as in the case of Iberia, the king was a relative latecomer to Christianity, he quickly became the new religion's chief promoter. In both kingdoms, an important stage in this process is the construction of the kingdom's principal church in the capital through the lavish bestowal of royal patronage. These buildings served as more than just churches. They also housed the most holy relics of the kingdom, relics that connected the capital with the holiness of Jerusalem. Ezana and his successors built the magnificent cathedral of Aksum, Maryam Tseyon, (or "St. Mary of Zion"), which also was known as the Gabaza Aksum, that is, "the holy place of Aksum." Its holiness derived from the Ark of the Covenant, believed to have been brought to Aksum by Solomon's son, Menelik. The splendor of this structure was extolled to Muhammad by two of his wives who had dwelt in Aksum during the 620's after the Hijra. Meanwhile, in the Iberian capital of Mtskheta, Mirian III was directed by St. Nino to build a church that was given the name Svetiskhoveli, or "the life-giving pillar," from a miraculous central pier of the church that was only set in place through the saint's prayers. Aside from the pillar, Svetiskhoveli's most sacred relic was the Robe of Christ. The Ark of the Covenant and the Robe of Christ became the talismans of the two kingdoms, relics too sacred to display, which radiated holiness from the new cathedral church in the capital out through the rest of the kingdom. Thus, in each case, the capital was transformed into a sacred center, and remained a pilgrimage site long after the political center had moved elsewhere, from Aksum to Lalibela, and from Mtskheta to Tbilisi.[32]

The Christianization of the countryside

Despite royal enthusiasm for the new religion, and its adoption within court circles, Christianity took root slowly in the rural districts of the two kingdoms.[33] This comes as no surprise, especially because the countryside was evangelized in a patchwork fashion even in some Roman territories, such as Syria, Palestine and central Italy, that had long possessed active Christian communities.[34] Augustine, John Chrysostom, and Maximus of Turin call attention to the persistence of polytheism on the rural estates of their wealthy parishioners.[35] In a passage perhaps more noteworthy for its hyperbole than for its numerical precision, John of Ephesus claimed that he could still find (by his count) 80,000 pagans to baptize in the backcountry of Caria, Lydia, and Phrygia in the mid-sixth century.[36] Indeed, it has been suggested that a principal reason for the lack of missionary work beyond the imperial frontiers was that Roman bishops were too occupied evangelizing country districts in their own dioceses. Pagan sanctuaries and high places dotted the countryside of Aksum and Iberia. The tenacity of these traditional belief systems can be seen in the archaeological record of the fourth and fifth centuries. Royal dictates alone could not sway the rural population.

The first steps in the Christianization of the Iberian and Aksumite countryside occurred in the late fifth and early sixth centuries, through the efforts of small bands of foreign-born monks, in both cases from Syriac-speaking regions. They arrived in each kingdom as disciples of one leading ascetic, and they eventually dispersed throughout the kingdoms to evangelize, work miracles, and establish monasteries. Within a generation, indigenous monastic traditions took root, and facilitated the spread of Christianity into the more peripheral regions of both kingdoms. In each of the ecclesiastical traditions, the monks are venerated collectively: in Ethiopia, they are known as the Nine Saints; in Georgia, as the Thirteen Syrian Fathers. They also are venerated individually, most often in connection with a church or monastery founded during their lifetime. It usually is assumed that these Syrian monks were refugees from the persecutions initiated by Byzantine emperors against those who did not subscribe to the creed of the Council of Chalcedon in 451. As a consequence, they are viewed as Monophysite dissidents who fled from

Syria looking for a more congenial theological climate.[37] This interpretation probably holds true for the Aksumite Nine Saints, for the Aksumite church closely followed the theological stance of its hierarchical leader, the Alexandrian patriarch. Nearly the entire Egyptian (or Coptic) church stoutly supported the cause of patriarch Dioscorus, the "Militant Father" who was exiled after Chalcedon. As a consequence, the fifth-century Aksumite church followed Alexandria into schism, and the Ethiopian church remains non-Chalcedonian to this day. There is, however, no clear evidence for Monophysite leanings among the Iberian Thirteen Syrian Fathers. It is just as likely that a combined missionary and ascetic impulse sent them to Iberia, the same motivation that inspired St. Patrick and St. Columbanus. Perhaps an even better comparison would be the ministry of St. Severinus in fifth-century Noricum (modern Austria), who is portrayed by his biographer as monk from eastern lands sent by God to care for the inhabitants of a distant province.[38]

The Nine Saints arrived in Aksum during the reign of Ella Amidas (c. 475–486), and according to their *gedle* (acts), they stayed at court for nearly twelve years.[39] Admittedly, the *gedle* of the Nine Saints constitute a problematic set of source material. The traditions concerning them seem to have taken shape during the Zagwe dynasty in the ninth and tenth centuries, and only took a definitive form after the beginning of the Solomonic dynasty in 1270. In places, the *gedle* are heavily mythologized, but there is enough material in them consistent with archaeological material and with what is otherwise known about the Aksumite kingdom, to suspect that the basic narrative goes back to Late Antiquity.[40]

Under the leadership of Ze-Mikael, known as Aregawi ("the Elder"), most of the Nine Saints dispersed throughout the Aksumite kingdom and devoted the rest of their careers to converting the countryside and introducing monasticism. Two of them, Pentelewon and Liqanos, stayed on at Aksum, settling on two hills near the city that previously had been the sites of pagan temples.[41] These two Greek-speaking ascetics served as spiritual directors to the king and to his advisers. Pentelewon, as holy man and intercessor for the Aksumite court, functioned in much the same fashion as his near contemporary, Daniel the Stylite, who advised the emperor Anastasius (491–518) from his pillar in the suburbs of Constantinople.[42] The other saints settled on hilltops and at prominent crossroads, scattered strategically on either side of the main Aksum-Adulis corridor, in what today is Eritrea and the Ethiopian province of Tigray.[43] In almost every case, the new ascetic settlements were accompanied by the occupation of an earlier pagan site. These pagan sites were not all destroyed, but as at Yeha, Christianized by employing much of the earlier Sabaean pagan sanctuary as the foundation for a new church, today one of the oldest in Ethiopia.[44] The most venerated of the Nine Saints, Aregawi, established the renowned monastery of Debre Damo, situated atop a steep mesa (or *amba*), accessible only by a rope let down a

55-foot cliffside.[45] Like the other monastic foundations of the Nine Saints, Debre Damo appears to have been occupied prior to the fifth century. The Nine Saints converted their new hermitages with very little opposition from the local pagan inhabitants, owing not only to their reputation for holiness and miraculous deeds, but also to explicit support from the Aksumite king, who occasionally made high-profile visitations to the monasteries.

Sometime in the 530s or 540s, a Syriac ascetic later known as John of Zedazeni arrived at Mtskheta with twelve monastic co-laborers.[46] Like the Aksumite Nine Saints, these ascetics first presented themselves to the monarch and to the ecclesiastical authorities. Once they received the blessing of the Catholicos (the Christian patriarch of Georgia),[47] however, none of these monks remained long in the capital, and unlike Sts. Pentelewon and Liqanos, they did not even settle in the capital's suburbs. John was the closest to Mtskheta, but it took a strenuous day's climb to reach his dwelling at the top of a peak commanding a view of the Mtkvari and Aragvi river valleys—the heart of the Iberian kingdom. He chose his retreat because Mt. Zedazeni was the site of a prominent pagan sanctuary. He reportedly demolished the temple, and became renowned among the country people for his ability to cure illnesses, cast out demons, and even tame the wild bears that roamed in great numbers on Mt. Zedazeni.[48]

John's disciples fanned out across Iberia, following his example of asceticism, miracle working, and evangelization. They settled throughout the Mtkvari valley, from Urbnisi to Garedji (today near the border of Azerbaijan). Four of them even crossed the steep ridge of the Gomboris Kedi into the Alazani River valley, thereby spreading the work of the Syrian Fathers into the modern Georgian region of Kakheti. David of Garedji first dwelt on a mountainside overlooking the newly inaugurated political capital of Tbilisi, and functioned in the now-familiar role of the Syriac holy man, working miracles and arbitrating in local disputes. He then retired to a semi-arid desert in southeastern Kakheti, and replicated in distant Iberia the austerities of the Syrian desert.[49] All together, the Thirteen Syrian Fathers established some sixteen monasteries and other churches, many of whose sixth-century foundations still can be observed today.[50]

John's disciples fanned out across Iberia, following his example of asceticism, miracle working, and evangelization. They settled throughout the Mtkvari valley, from Urbnisi to Garedji (today near the border of Azerbaijan). Four of them even crossed the steep ridge of the Gomboris Kedi into the Alazani River valley, thereby spreading the work of the Syrian Fathers into the modern Georgian region of Kakheti. David of Garedji first dwelt on a mountainside overlooking the newly inaugurated political capital of Tbilisi, and functioned in the now-familiar role of the Syriac holy man, working miracles and arbitrating in local disputes. He then retired to a semi-arid desert in southeastern Kakheti, and replicated in distant Iberia the austerities of the Syrian desert. All together, the Thirteen Syrian Fathers established some sixteen monasteries and other churches, many of whose sixth-century foundations still can be observed today. [. . .]

Christianity and culture

Following the reigns of two strong monarchs, and the introduction of monasticism with its resultant evangelization of the countryside, comes the final stage in this initial Christianization of the two kingdoms. Both Aksum and Iberia experienced a great creative outburst of cultural energy that transformed their traditional cultures and endowed them with a rich representational language with which to articulate their new faith. In both kingdoms, however, this cultural dynamism coincided with a period of rapidly waning political fortunes: after the death of Kaleb, Aksum soon lost its hard-won possessions in South Arabia and fell into economic decline, whereas in Iberia, the monarchy suffered from dynastic disputes until a much weakened kingship was abolished ca. 580 by the *shahan'shah* Khusro I.

In the case of Iberia and Aksum, therefore, Late Antiquity witnessed a flowering of cultures outside of the Greco-Roman mainstream, and the catalyst for a dynamic cultural explosion in these two kingdoms was the adoption of Christianity as the medium for the native elite to patronize artists and architects, and for churchmen to express their devotion. Both cultures saw the rapid development of literature, as newly refined alphabets facilitated first the translation of east Roman liturgical and biblical texts, and then the composition of local saints' lives and martyr acts. Under Kaleb's son and eventual successor, Gabra Maskel (ca. 558–588), the Aksumite priest Yared combined Syriac motifs with indigenous Ge'ez hymnody and thereby composed the nucleus of the *Deggwa*, the main corpus of Ge`ez antiphons. In Iberia, prayer books, monastic *typica*, and *troparion* hymns in honor of the saints were composed in Georgian by the beginning of the sixth century.[51] The single greatest expression of the new face of Iberian culture, however, was in stone. During the course of the sixth century, Iberian architects moved beyond mere adaptations of Byzantine church architecture to develop a soaring architectural style that remains distinctive.[52] In both kingdoms, book illumination, iconography, and church decoration saw the beginnings of a rich tradition in this same period.[53]

In the middle years of the sixth century, a much-traveled former merchant from Alexandria retired to monastic life. He then drew up a curious geographical work that contained his valuable observations of life along the trade routes as well as his own bizarre cosmological theories harmonizing the world with the design of the Mosaic Tabernacle. Cosmas Indicopleustes, in his *Christian Topography*, noted with enthusiasm that dozens of foreign kingdoms had embraced Christianity, and that they contained "no limit to the number of churches with bishops and very large communities of Christian people, as well as many martyrs, and monks also living as hermits."[54]

Cosmas understood very well that Christianization was multiform in its full expression. Aksum stood high on his list of Christian states, a list that also included the kingdoms of the Caucasus.

As we have seen, the initial process of Christianization in Aksum and Iberia took at least two centuries to complete. Christianization followed a remarkably similar course in the two kingdoms, and passed through several distinct phases:

1 Preexistent monotheistic ideas, coupled with an established Jewish community;
2 Early contact with Christianity through trade and the presence of Christian merchants, craftsmen, and diplomats;
3 Conversion of the royal house through the efforts of foreign-born Christians;
4 Importation of an ecclesiastical hierarchy in response to royal conversion;
5 Christianity as a tool of the monarch to promote centralization;
6 Construction of a church in the capital housing a particularly sacred relic;
7 Establishment of Christianity beyond the capital by a group of foreign monastics, supported by the local monarchy;
8 Vigorous promotion of Christianity by a strong monarch; and
9 Elaboration of distinct local patterns of Christianity and Christian culture.

Naturally, it would be useful to discern the reasons for such close parallels. Was their similarity only a function of their peripheral status to the principal empires of Late Antiquity? Or does their similarity amount to a model of Christianization that could be applied elsewhere? It may be especially instructive to see if this model applies to the emerging Christian monarchies of central and northern Europe in the early Medieval period. If it proves to be more widely applicable, it may be possible to go a step further and apply the model to the larger empires of Late Antiquity. This, in turn, may provide some structural clues as to why Christianization succeeded in Rome under Constantine and his successors, while Yazdgard I (399–420) failed to take the crucial royal decision for Christianization in Persia.[55] It even may help to explain the initial success of Christianity at the court of the T'ang emperor Taizong (626–649), and Christianity's eventual decline in China some three centuries later.[56]

Although larger imperial states obviously possessed their own distinctive dynamics in the relation between religion and empire, the "mountain Constantines" in the much smaller kingdoms of Aksum and Iberia clearly made bold choices of their own in religious policy that initiated the cultural transformation of their late antique kingdoms, and perhaps can provide models for understanding similar transformations in other smaller players in the late antique world.

Notes

1 The following individuals generously shared with me their suggestions and assistance: Niko Chocheli, Nika Vacheishvili, David and Lauren Ninoshvili, Mary Chkhartishvili, Peter Brown, and Walter Kaegi.

2 P. Bruun, "The Disappearance of Sol from the Coins of Constantine," *Arctos* n.s. 2 (1958), 15–37; Idem, "The Christian Signs on the Coins of Constantine," *Arctos*, n.s. 3 (1962), 5–35; A. H. M. Jones, *Constantine and the Conversion of Europe* (London, 1949), 83–87;

3 The nomenclature of the Aksumite kings in this period is rather tangled. For a discussion, see T. T. Mekouria, "Christian Aksum" in G. Moktar, ed., *UNESCO General History of Africa*, vol. 2, *Ancient Civilization of Africa* (London, 1981), pp. 401–420 at 406–407.

4 S. C. Munro-Hay, "Axumite Coinage" in R. Grierson, ed., *African Zion: The Sacred Art of Ethiopia* (New Haven/London, 1993), 101–116 at 109–110.

5 R. Fletcher, *The Barbarian Conversion* (New York, 1997); P. Brown, *The Rise of Western Christendom*, 2nd ed. (Oxford, 2002); S. H. Moffett, *A History of Christianity in Asia, Vol. 1: Beginnings to 1500*, 2nd rev. ed. (New York, 1998); Ralph W. Mathisen, "Barbarian Bishops and the Churches 'in barbaricis gentibus' during Late Antiquity," *Speculum* 72 (1997) 664–697.

6 J. B. Segal, *Edessa, the Blessed City* (Oxford, 1970), 70; A. N. Palmer, "King Abgar of Edessa, Eusebius and Constantine," in H. Bakker, ed., *The Sacred Centre as the Focus of Political Interest* (Gronigen, 1992), 3–29.

7 Theodoret, *Hist.eccl.* 1.24.

8 S. P. Brock, "Christians in the Sassanian Empire: A Case of Divided Loyalties," in S. Mews, ed., *Religion and National Identity, Studies in Church History*, vol. 18 (London, 1982), 1–19.

9 Although some recent commentators have placed Tiridates' conversion closer to 314: C. S. Lightfoot, "Armenia and the Eastern Marches," in A. Bowman, Averil Cameron, P. Garnsey, eds., *The Cambridge Ancient History: Volume 12, The Crisis of Empire, AD 193–337* (Cambridge, 2005), 481–497 at 487.

10 For Christianity in seventh century China, see P. Y. Saeki, *The Nestorian Documents and Relics in China*, 2nd ed. (Tokyo, 1951); Moffett, *A History of Christianity in Asia*, vol. 1.287–323;

11 For useful discussions of conversion models in a Mediterranean context, see H. A. Drake, "Models of Christian Expansion," in W. V. Harris, ed., *The Spread of Christianity in the First Four Centuries: Essays in Explanation*, Columbia Studies in the Classical Tradition 27 (New York, 2005), 1–13.

12 A methodology employed at length in William Tabbernee, ed., *Early Christianity in Contexts* (Grand Rapids, MI, forthcoming).

13 L. R. Rambo, *Understanding Religious Conversion* (New Haven, 1993), 97–101; Idem, "Theories of Conversion," *Social Compass* 46.3 (1999), 259–271.

14 R. W. Hefner, ed., *Conversion to Christianity: Historical and Anthropological Perspectives on a Great Transformation* (Berkeley/Los Angeles, 1991).

15 For an effective use of the comparative method beyond the imperial frontiers, see J. Howard-Johnston, "The Two Great Powers in Late Antiquity: A Comparison," in Averil Cameron, ed., *The Byzantine and Early Islamic Near East. III: States, Resources and Armies* (Princeton, 1995), 157–226.

16 As expressions of this trend, see B. Caseau, "Sacred Landscapes," in G. Bowersock, P. Brown.

17 G. Fowden, *Empire to Commonwealth* (Princeton, 1993), 15–19.

18 G. Greatrex, "Byzantium and the East in the Sixth Century," in M. Maas, ed., *The Cambridge Companion to the Age of Justinian* (Cambridge, 2005), 496–497,

501–502; Z. Rubin, "Byzantium and Southern Arabia," in D. H. French, C. S. Lightfoot, eds., *The Eastern Frontier of the Roman Empire* (Oxford, 1989), 383–420.

19 Comparative studies of Christianization, with some attention to theoretical considerations, may be found in J. Muldoon, ed., *Varieties of Religious Conversion in the Middle Ages* (Gainesville, FL, 1997); P. Urbańczyk, ed., *Early Christianity in Central and East Europe* (Warsaw, 1997); L. von Padberg, *Die Christianisierung Europas im Mittelalter* (Stuttgart, 1998); G. Armstrong, I. N. Wood, eds., *Christianizing Peoples and Converting Individuals*, International Medieval Research VII (Turnhout, 2000).

20 Rufinus, *Hist.eccl.* 10.9–10; also Sozomen, *Hist.eccl.* 2.24, Socrates, *Hist.eccl.* 1.19; Theoderet, *Hist.eccl.* 1.22,

21 Rufinus, *Hist.eccl.* 10.11; also Theodoret, *Hist.eccl.* 1.23.

22 Solomon, the Queen of Ethiopia, and the birth of Menelik: *Kebra Nagast* 24–32, Wallis Budge, tr., *The Queen of Sheba and Her Only Son Menyelek (I) Being the Book of the Glory of Kings, Kebra Nagast* (Oxford, 1922), 21–39.

23 The unusual absence of pig bones in Aksumite sites seems to indicate a dietary choice not made on the basis of food supply, but from an ideological imperative.

24 Josephus, *Ap.* 1. 22.

25 T. Mgaloblishvili, I. Gagoshidze, "The Jewish Diaspora and Early Christianity in Georgia," in T. Mgaloblishvili, ed., *Ancient Christianity in the Caucasus* (Surrey, 1998), 39–58 at 49–50.

26 *Mtskheta*, vol. 3, 207. A useful survey of the literary sources concerning the Jewish community of Mtskheta may be found in C. B. Lerner, *The Wellspring of Georgian Historiography: the Early Medieval Historical Chronicle, The Conversion of Kartli, and the Life of St. Nino* (London, 2003), 60–66.

27 The epigraphic corpus may be found in N. Babalikashvili, "O pamjatnikx evreiskoj epigrafiki iz Mckheta," *Macne* 6 (1970), 271–288. For discussion of the Samtavro necropolis, see M. Ivashchenko, "Samtavroijskie pogrebenija pervyx trex vekov nashej ery," *Mtskheta* 1 (1980), 189–215.

28 T. Mgaloblishvili, "The Jewish Diaspora and Early Christianity," 51–52.

29 For India, see S. Neill, *A History of Christianity in India, Vol. 1: Beginnings to A.D. 1707* (Cambridge, 1984); A. M. Mudadan, "The Indian Church and the East Syrian Church," *Indian Church History Review* 6. 1 (1972), 23–42. For this process in Central Asia, see R. Folz, *Religions of the Silk Road: Overland Trade and Cultural Exchange from Antiquity to the Fifteenth Century* (New York, 1999).

30 Rufinus *Hist.eccl.* 10.9, ". . . he (Frumentius) gave them extensive rights, which he urged them to use, to build places of assembly in each location, in which they might gather for prayer in the Roman manner. Not only that, but he himself did far more along these lines than anyone else, and in this way encouraged the others, invited them with his support and favors, made available whatever was suitable, furnished sites for buildings, and everything else that was necessary, and bent every effort to see that the seed of Christianity should grow up there," (trans. Amidon). For trade between Rome and Aksum, see Eusebius, *VConst.* 4.71; *CTh* 12.12.2 (356 CE). Malalas, *Chron.* p.43, also mentions Roman traders in Axum circa 500 CE.

31 On Aksumite trade, see G. Connah, *African Civilizations: An Archaeological Perspective*, 2nd ed. (Cambridge, 2001), 103–107.

32 On this link between sacredness and political centralization, see the useful collection of articles in H. Bakker, ed., *The Sacred Centre as the Focus of Political Interest* (Gronignen, 1992).

33 In the Aksumite kingdom, one indicator of this gradual process of Christianization is a shift away from pagan decorative elements on pottery and metalwork: A. Manzo, "Skeuomorphism in Aksumite Pottery? Remarks on the Origins and Meanings of Some Ceramic Types," *Aethiopica* 6 (2003), 7–46.
34 Theodoret, *Hist.ecct.* 16,17; Marc.Diac. *VPorphyrii*; Greg.Mag. *Ep.* 3.59, 8.18.
35 Joh.Chrysos. *Homil. in Act.* 18.4; Aug. *Enarr.in psalm. LIV* 13, *Ep.* 58.1; Max.Taurin. *Serm.* 91.107.
36 John Eph. *Lives of the Eastern Saints* 47, E. W. Brooks, ed., tr., *PO* 18.681. See also W. H. C. Frend, "The Winning of the Countryside," *Journal of Ecclesiastical History* 18.1 (1967), 1–14; K. Harl, "Sacrifice and Pagan Belief in Fifth- and Sixth- Century Byzantium," *Past and Present* 128 (1990), 7–27; F. Trombley, *Hellenic Religion and Christianization*, 2 vols. (Leiden, 1993–94), 2;52–133; Fletcher, *Barbarian Conversion*, 34–65.
37 D. M. Lang, *Lives and Legends of the Georgian Saints*, 2nd rev. ed. (London, 1956), 81–83; Rapp, *Studies in Medieval Georgian Historiography*, 321.
38 Eugippius V *Severini* 1.1.
39 On the Nine Saints, see C. Conti Rossini, *Storia d'Etiopia* (Bergamo, 1928), 156–163; Hable-Sellassie, *Ancient and Medieval Ethiopian History*, 115–121; E. A. W. Budge, *The Book of the Saints of the Ethiopian Church* (Cambridge, 1928), 1.116–118, 155, 198, 299–300; 2.205; 3.688, 944; 4.1009–1010.
40 Munro-Hay, *Aksum*, 14, 207–208; Hable-Sellassie, *Ancient and Medieval Ethiopian History*, 115–121.
41 *Deutsche Aksum-Expedition* 4.1–2. The hills today are known as Debre Pentelewon and Debre Qonasel; Munro-Hay, *Ethiopia, the Unknown Land*, 333–335.
42 *Life of Daniel the Stylite* 65, in E. Dawes, N. H. Baynes, eds., *Three Byzantine Saints* (London, 1948).
43 Another large group of foreign-born monks, known as the Sadqan (the "Righteous Men"), settled to the south and east of Aksum. They met with much stiffer resistance, and many of them perished as a result of fierce local persecutions: see C. Conti Rossini, *Ricordo di un soggiorno in Eritrea* (Asmara, 1902); Hable-Sellassie, *Ancient and Medieval Ethiopian History*, 115, 125–126.
44 F. Anfray, "Fouilles de Yeha," *Annales d'Ethiopie* 9 (1972), 45–64; Hable-Sellassie, *Ancient and Medieval Ethtoptan History*, 117–118.
45 Phillipson, *Ancient Ethiopia*, 128–131.
46 On the Thirteen Syrian Fathers, see K. S. Kekelidze, "On the Arrival of the Syrian Missionaries in Kartli," *Etyudy* 1 (1956), 19–50; D. M. Lang, *The Georgians, Ancient Peoples and Places* (New York, 1966), 156–157.
47 For the rank of Catholicos, see Mathisen, "Barbarian Bishops," 665–6.
48 *K'art'lis C'xovreba*, 208–209 (interpolation 10 in Thomson, *Rewriting Caucasian History*, 363–364).
49 *Life of David of Garesja*, in Lang, *Lives and Legends of the Georgian Saints*, 83–93; *K'art'lis C'xovreba*, 209–210 (interpolation 10 in Thomson, *Rewriting Caucasian History*, 364–365).
50 G. N. Chubinashvili, *Architecture in Kakheti* (Tbilisi, 1959); Idem, "On the Initial Forms of Christian Churches," in Mgaloblishvili, *Ancient Christianity in the Caucasus*, 185–195, at 194; T. Mgaloblishvili, "Introduction," in Mgaloblishvili, *Ancient Christianity in the Caucasus*, 3–14, at 10.
51 Rayfield, *Literature of Georgia*, 9–12.
52 V. Beridzé, "L'architecture religieuse géorgienne des IVe–VIIe siècles," *Bedi Kartlisa* 36 (1978), 25–42.

53 M. E. Heldman, "The Heritage of Late Antiquity," in Grierson, *African Zion*, 117–119; H. Machavariani, "The Art of Georgian Manuscripts," in Soltes, *National Treasures of Georgia*, 117–121.

54 Cosmas Indicopleustes, *Christianike Topographia* 3.179 (J. W. McCrindle, tr.), 120; text in W. Wolska-Conus, *Cosmas Indicopleustes, La topographie chrétienne*, 3 vols. (Paris, 1968).

55 The favor extended to Christians in the early portion of his reign earned for Yazdgard the epithet, "the sinner" (*athīm*) from the *magi*: J. P. Asmussen, "Christians in Iran," in E. Yarshater, ed., *The Cambridge History of Iran*, vol.3 pt.2, *The Seleucid, Parthian and Sasanian Periods* (Cambridge, 1983), 924–48, at 939–941; A. Christensen, *L'Iran sous les Sassanides* (Copenhagen, 1936), 264–268.

56 A. F. Wright, "T'ang Tai-Tsung and Buddhism," in A. F. Wright, D. Twitchett, eds., *Perspectives on the T'ang* (New Haven, 1973), 2–263; N. Standaert, ed., *Handbook of Christianity in China, Vol. 1: 635–1800, Handbuch der Orientalistik* 4.15.1 (Leiden, 2001), 1–43.

15

Excerpt from 'THOMAS CHRISTIANS AND THE THOMAS TRADITION'

Robert Frykenberg

Source: Robert Frykenberg, *Christianity in India*, Oxford: Oxford University Press, 2008, pp. 102–15.

[. . .]

The Church of the East

Traders, settlers, and refugees came from the West to the shores of India. They came individually or in groups, in fits and starts, over many centuries. Commercial relations between the Indian and Roman worlds increased after the rediscovery, during the first century, of seasonal winds (monsoons) that predictably and steadily blew ships across the Arabian Sea to India during certain months of each year and then just as predictably and steadily blew them back across the same sea to the shores of Africa and Arabia. In both Strabo's *Geography*[16] and the *Periplus of the Erythraean Sea* (*c.* AD 47),[17] by an unknown mariner writing about the time of Thomas, we learn that fleets of ships with up to seven sails and 300 tons in size moved back and forth across this sea. Roman Peace (*Pax Romana*) helped to bring increasing traffic and prosperity to the littoral fringes of the Indian Ocean.[18] Romans themselves, we know from archaeological findings in South India, built colonies along the shorelines of India; and Indians themselves moved into the market-places of Egypt where Greeks and Arabs, Jews and Syrians, Armenians and Persians benefited. Sanskrit and Tamil epics mention *Yavana* (Greek) ships laden with glass, gold, and horses, which returned with gems, ivory, pepper, exotic animals and birds, especially peacocks. Greek workmen were used to build Chola palaces.[19] One tradition, as already shown above, even transfers the substance of the *Acts of Thomas* legend from the Indo-Bactrian to a Chola monarch of Madurai. Thus, whatever historicity the story and tradition of Thomas may or may not possess, historical evidence confirms that comparable events did happen during the time of Thomas and that these occurred at the same times and in the same places. Thus, it is entirely plausible to conclude that such events might have involved the Apostle Thomas himself.

Hints of early Christian presence in India are found in writings which date only a century or two later than AD 73, the date of Thomas's death, as this has been preserved in local traditions of Thomas Christians. From Alexandria, the citadel of early Christian learning, a Jewish-Christian scholarly convert named Pantaenus, who had been mentor to Clement and Origen, determined 'to preach Christ to the Brahmans and philosophers'.[20] According to Eusebius, he went as far as India 'and found that Matthew's gospel had arrived before him and was in the hands of some there who had come to know Christ'. Whether this 'India' was the same, or even the real, India to which Pantaenus went cannot be determined; however, 'Brahmans' mentioned by Jerome could hardly have come from anywhere but India. Moreover, Jewish communities such as the ancient Beni Israel, dating themselves back to the first Exile, had already long been settled along the shores of western India; and more Jews arrived after the destruction of Jerusalem in AD 70, with yet another wave following them in the year 136. Thus, there can be no reason to doubt that Christian and Jewish communities were already settled along the shores of the subcontinent by the second century. Muslim communities arose along the same coasts only 400 years later.

Evidence of links between Christians in Parthian Persia and Christians of Edessa (now Urfa in modern Turkey) is strong. Due to the religious pluralism of Parthian rulers, Christians were able to organize a religious community and to become an important minority within the Persian Empire. This community seems to have consisted mainly of middle-class, mercantile and professional families whose members were well off. They became known for their skills and occupied prominent positions of trust in medicine, science, and government. As already mentioned, Edessa, the capital of a tiny principality known as Osrhoene, was so tightly squeezed between the empires of Rome and Parthia that it was often under pressure from one power or the other. Even so, it became a leading centre of Christian culture. Its language, the Aramaic dialect known as Syriac, became the literary and liturgical language for all 'Eastern' (Assyrian, Babylonian, Chaldean, or Persian) Christians. Its theological schools and scholars became famous. Among them was Addai, or Tatian (b. 150), whose polemic against Greek cultural dominance over Christian institutions and whose *Diatessaron* or Harmony of the Four Gospels, while condemned in the West, long remained the only Gospel available to Christians and churches of the East. During the reign of Abgar VIII (AD 177–212), Christians of Edessa and Persia became caught up in theological controversies with the West. One of these was over the date of Easter. When Romans conquered Edessa in AD 216, Christians of Mesopotamia and

Persia, once again caught in the middle between the two empires, became increasingly suspect. Adeshir, founder of the Sassanian dynasty (in 226) and restorer of Zoroastrian religious dominance, had hardly reconquered Edessa and Syria in 258 when he captured the Roman Emperor Valerian. Zoroastrian priests (*mobeds*) then mounted fierce and deadly campaigns against Christians within Sassanian domains. Calamity struck Christians of the East again over a century later. On Good Friday, 17 April AD 341, at Seleucia-Ctesiphon, the capital twin cities bestriding the Tigris, Shapur II put to death the Catholicos, Simon Bar Sabbae, and over a hundred prominent Christian leaders within his realm. Many years of martyrdom and suffering followed.

Following the promulgation of Yezdgerd's Edict of Toleration in AD 410, an event in the East that can perhaps be compared to the Edict of Constantine eight-five years earlier in the West, the Persian Church enjoyed a limited time of restoration and comparative tranquillity. This reached its zenith under the ecclesiastical rule of Catholicos Isaac, 'Grand Metropolitan and Head of All Bishops'. But, during the previous century, theological disputes with Christians of the West had produced a deepening rift with Eastern Christians. After the creeds of 325 and 381 ended the Arian controversy by declaring that Christ was 'one in essence with the Father', Christological disagreements between Cyril (Bishop of Alexandria) and Nestorius (Bishop of Constantinople) remained unsettled. More seriously, theologians at Edessa, (Assyria, Chaldea, and Persia) and throughout the Sassanid Empire beyond the boundaries of Byzantium, refused to view Mary as *Theotokos* or 'Mother of God'. Thus, after 422, especially after the Council of Ephesus in 431, ties with the West became weaker. The Patriarchate of Babylon or 'The Church of the East', during times when free from persecution, continued to hold increasing and unchallenged sway among Christians of Persia and India. The Council of Chalcedon in AD 451, for all practical purposes, finally ended such disputes in the West. But debates in the East continued, seriously undermining and weakening the inner strength of Eastern Christian communities, especially those that lay beyond the reach of Byzantium—in Persia and beyond.

Just one century before many Eastern Christians fell beneath the shadow of *dar-ul-Islam*, an Indian Christian traveller from Alexandria visited the Island of Socotra and the West coast of India. In his *Christian Topography* (*c.* AD 535), Cosmas Indikopleustes described Syrian Christian bishops and communities that he found along the coasts of India and Sri Lanka. By then wars between Sassanid and the Eastern Roman rulers of Byzantium had begun to bring more waves of refugees to India; moreover, severe political pressures within Persia prompted a further severance of Christian bonds between East and West. By then also, the Patriarch of Babylon (or Chaldea) had long claimed ecclesiastical authority over Malabar Christians.

The Roman Catholic epithet for these Christians, as for most Christians of the East, was 'Nestorian'. This term, applied by Western Christians to all Christians of India at the end of the sixth century, was much more a matter of ecclesiastical and geographical distinction than it was a term applied to any theological, or 'diophysite', doctrine, or of rituals related thereto. Meanwhile, even as missionary ventures across Asia and into China continued to grow, doing so well into the thirteenth century, Muslim expansion (632–42) effectively cut off the East from Byzantium and the West, doing so more effectively than any previous event. A drastic and diminishing communication thereafter closed off occasions for theological or ecclesiastical conciliation between East and West.

The question of why Christianity disappeared in so much of Persia, as also from many parts of Arabia, and vanished so completely, remains largely unanswered. At least two possible factors have been suggested as having played an important part in this disappearance. First, in various forms of Syrian and Persian Christianity—stemming from Antioch and Babylon, as from Edessa—language was allowed to become a barrier between clerical leadership and ordinary believers. The language of the Church, Syriac (a form of Aramaic), became the exclusive preserve of the learned and literate, the only vehicle through which the Gospel, biblical literature, theological learning, and liturgy was transmitted from one generation to the next. In Persia and other lands to the east of Mesopotamia, Syriac was not the tongue of the common people. Efforts made to translate some Scripture, sermons, and religious discourses, especially hymns, into Pahlavi, were not effective; and, for the most part, the language of the Church remained alien and could not be understood by the majority of those Christians who were not learned or not literate. Persian elites, as also elites in various parts of India, held a great affection for the beauty of their language. The failure of Christians to use Persian for purposes of faith and worship, doctrine, and scholarship left an enormous void of residual ignorance, a gulf which could not easily be bridged. The same situation seems to have been replicated among Christians in India.[21]

Second, institutions of Christianity in the East became increasingly, if not predominantly, monastic in character and celibate in normative social behaviour. As a consequence, very little is known about the daily life of the ordinary Christian believer, either in Persia or in other eastern lands. While extraordinary missionary efforts and ventures were undertaken, carrying the Gospel to China and India, if not to islands beyond, both the faith and the faithful became increasingly isolated and relegated to the elite few. Strict celibacy was equated with spirituality: some even suggested that celibacy might be mandatory for gaining eternal salvation. The great Persian saint and scholar Aphrates had written as early as the fourth century that Christians had become divided into two groups: the 'Offspring of the Covenant' (*Bar Qiyama*) and the 'Penitents'. Those dedicated to an ascetic and celibate life could be baptized while those who were not so inclined were sometimes denied baptism.[22] This virtually Manichaean separation between the tiny elite and the masses, between those dwelling in the Light and those consigned to living in Darkness, coming at a time when the Church faced a strong and hostile state religion that inflicted persecutions over long periods of time, greatly weakened the Christian community and left it vulnerable. And while the bar between marriage and baptism did not last, the strict rules of the Bar Qiyama continued to be upheld—with celibacy, prolonged periods of fasting and prayer, vows of poverty, simplicity of food and garb, ceaseless study, and silence. Such world renouncing was not attractive to Zoroastrians. Such ways were viewed as a blasphemy against life itself. Ironically, with the coming of Islam, both Christians and Zoroastrians were driven out of Persia. Sunni Islam, at least initially, was averse to asceticism and elitism alike, striving to obliterate all distinctions between the religious and not so religious, between specialists and ordinary people. Armenian Christians, coming from the homelands and strongholds to the north and west, managed to maintain a more clear and distinct identity within Islamic lands than some other Christians. From their homeland, this striving and thriving Christian community did well within the Islamicates of the East in the centuries which followed.[23]

The waves of refugees

From an Indian perspective, arrivals of successive waves of Christians on the western shores of India, taking place at various times over centuries, either as refugees and settlers and traders, can be documented. Such waves can be dated by looking at royal grants of lands and privileges which Christians received. These grants, duly certified as deeds or documents, were inscribed on copper plates, stone slabs, and/or palm leaf (*cadjan*). These were later embellished and reinforced by oral traditions.

One such tradition indicates that, as early as AD 293, a great persecution occurred within the Chola kingdom ('Cholamandalam' along the east coast). Seventy-six families fled to Malabar and settled among Christians of Quilon. Some of these then came under the influence of a Tamil Shaiva (presumably *bhakti*) teacher who some felt possessed extraordinary powers. Disputes also arose over religious rites, such as smearing ashes on one's forehead and venerating the five products of the cow. Apparently, considering what cannot be found in early sources, virtually no formal church structures existed that could help to provide doctrinal discipline or ecclesiastical control. Such institutional authority, when found, seems to have come from the Church of the East in Sassanian Persia.

Solid historical evidence of formal church life in India, albeit tenuous, dates from the year AD 345. In recent years, a combination of rigorous textual analysis of oral traditions, consisting of folklore within ancient immigration songs, such as the *Purātanappāṭṭukal* and *Kēralōpatti*, with intensive archaeological, historical, and textual research into fresh resources in Mesopotamia (what is now Iraq), has enabled Jacob Kollaparambil to come up with arguments that tend to set at naught the prejudices and scepticism of some earlier Eurocentric work by such scholars as Alphonse Mingana.[24] These tend to confirm the view that, three years after the beginning of the Great Persian Persecution that stretched from 340 to 401 and just one year after the martyrdom of Catholicos Simon Bar Sabbae, already mentioned above, a community of 'East Syrian' or 'Babylonian' Jewish Christians landed on the Malabar coast. This community consisted of seventy-two 'royal' families from seven clans (or septs), numbering some 400 persons. It was led by a Jewish Christian merchant banker named Thomman Kinnān (Thomas Kināyi) and a bishop (*metran*) named Uraha Mar Yausef (Joseph). These leaders, together with four pastors (*katthanars*) and many deacons, came to India under the authority of the Catholicos of the East in Seleucia-Ctesiphon. As was later to be sung about in the *Nallōrōṛōśilam*, 'He [Thomas] went to Ezra [or Yezra] and obtained Blessing [*Anugraham*]' before embarking. This migration was also celebrated in another song, the Kottayam *Valiyapalli*. Within strophe four of this song, Malankara Nazranis continue to sing the words:

> For great devotion he started / With delight from the country of Uz
> On that day Kinayi Thomma / With seventy-two families.[25]

Other texts indicate that the decision to migrate to Malabar might perhaps have come during a meeting between Joseph, Thomas, and the Catholicos that was held in Jerusalem and that, prior to the embarkation of the community, Thomas had been sent on a reconnaissance mission.

That Thomas was cordially welcomed by the Emperor of Kerala, the Cheraman Perumal, and that the new community received special grants and privileges that were formally certified and engraved on copper plates, specifying exactly what tracts of land were to be occupied by the Christian settlers and what prerogatives of status they were to enjoy, seem beyond doubt. The copper plates themselves, as title deeds, documented the presence of these highly cultivated and gifted newcomers.[26] They were allotted lands by 'extending *ells* measured by an elephant, each being equal to the length of ten palms'.[27] The newly occupied lands were very similar to the alluvial black soil and marshy fields that had been left behind in Uruk (Uruha). These lands were located in the delta of the Periya River, not far from the Chemkal estuary on one side or from the city of Kodungallur (Kurumaklur, Cranganore, which was the same as Muziris of ancient times) on the other. In later times, the settlers would move southward, settling on lands bordering black paddy fields east of the Vembanadam backwater lagoons. The places of settlement—Udayamperur, Kottayam, Kaduthuruthy, and Kallissery, as also Brahmangalam (Karippadam), Kallara, Neendur, Kaipuzha, Mannar, Kuttoor, and Veliyanad—are places in the region where the majority of

'Southists' can still be found. Privileges enjoyed by the Christian immigrants alone included wearing of golden flowers in their hair during weddings, riding on royal elephants or palanquins, use of royal parasols, playing seven kinds of musical instruments, sitting upon carpets, erecting pavilions (*pandals*), use of sandalwood paste, and even allowing their women to whistle with a finger in the mouth as was done by other royal women. Such privileges were allowed only to those who were descended from kings: these Jewish Christians claimed direct descent from the lineage of David.[28]

The year of this arrival was 345. It is embedded in line thirteen of the immigration song, *Mūvaroruvanṭ Kalpanayāle.* It is found in the Malayalam word *sōvāla* and is an alphabetical chronogram that means '345'.[29] Whatever the case, the local attraction for this elite community of Jewish Christians, henceforth called Malankara Nazaranis, lay in their energetic and enterprising aptitude for doing business. Those who had once prospered in Mesopotamia prospered in India, and were seen as generating local prosperity wherever they settled; their presence was courted and coveted by local rulers. Hardly a decade after the arrival of Thomas Kināyi, Theophilus the Indian, actually a native of the Maldive Islands, was sent on a mission to southern Arabia, Ethiopia, Sri Lanka, and India by the Roman Emperor Constantius. The historian who wrote of this mission, an Arian by the name of Philostorgius, was described in the *Bibliotheca* of Photius. In this work, he expressed disgust at the way Christians of India worshipped, in violation of the 'Apostolic Constitutions' of fourth-century Syria which required that 'all people should *stand* in perfect stillness' whenever the Gospel was read in public.[30] Indian Christians remained 'in a sitting position and did other things that were repugnant to divine law'.[31] Some critical scholars, such as Alphonse Mingana, T. K. Joseph, and A. E. Medlycott, have felt that, at the very least, this document serves to show that congregations of faithful Christians then resident in India worshipped God in the name of Christ and read the Gospel regularly under the ministry of local pastors. This, quite clearly, was a culturally indigenous community in that this was not only culturally parochial in form but also well integrated into local cultures of India. It was also a community very much out of touch with the Graeco-Roman world.[32] Theophilus claimed that he had remedied the repugnant behaviour of Indian Christians so as to confirm 'the dogma of the Church'. Mingana, in his commentary, indicates that the Christians found by Theophilus in India may have been akin to Christians of Socotra and that they 'made use of the Syriac language in their church services'.[33]

As also already mentioned, references to the Christians of Malabar and Sri Lanka were made by 'Cosmas the India Traveller' (Cosmas Indikopleustes). This merchant or monk from Alexandria also recorded what he had found on voyages of exploration in his *Christian Topography* (from the Greek: *Topographia Christiana*, circa 535–6):

> The church, far from being destroyed, is multiplying, the whole world filled with the doctrine of Christ, and the Gospel is being proclaimed in the whole world. This I have seen with my own eyes in many places, and have heard narrated by others . . . Even in the Island of Taprobane [Sri Lanka] in Inner India, where also the Indian sea is, there is a church of Christians, clergy and believers . . . The same is true in the place called Male [Malabar], where the pepper grows, and the place called Kaliana, and there is a bishop appointed from Persia.
> (Book III, ch. 64)

> This is a Great Island in the ocean situated in the Indian Sea. By the Indians it is called Silendipa, among the Greeks Taprobane. There the jacinth stone is found. It lies beyond the country where the pepper grows . . . The same island has a church of Persian Christians who are resident in that country, and a priest sent from Persia, and a deacon, and all that is required for conducting the worship of the church. The natives and their kings are [quite another kind of people, pagan, or heathen (from ἀλλόφυλοι)].
> (Book XI, ch. 130)[34]

The refugees from *dar-al-Islam*

Meanwhile, to the west of India, the gap generated by steady processes of alienation—between the Church of the East and Churches of the West, both Catholic and Orthodox—continued to widen. This became an almost unbridgeable chasm after the year 632, with the rise and expansion of Islam. Regimes claiming submission to *dar-al-Islam* provoked spasmodic waves of Christian refugees fleeing from persecution across the Arabian Sea. Copper-plate inscriptions (*ollas* or *sasanams*) indicate that these newcomers also were highly esteemed for the wealth that they generated.[35] One set of late eighth-century copper plates (*ollas* or *sasanams*) in Quilon indicates that a grant was given by a king named Veera Raghavan Chakravarti to a leading (Christian) merchant of Kodungallur (Cranganore, or ancient Muziris) named Iravi Kortthan (perhaps *Katthanar*, meaning 'pastor' or 'priest'). Another set of copper plates (*ollas* or *sasanams*), known as the *Tarisapalli* (Persian Christian) plates of Quilon, is still preserved in Thiruvalla and in Kottayam.[36] This shows that extensive privileges, in land holdings and high status, were bestowed in the time of Perumal Sthani Ravi Gupta. These were given by the subordinate Ayyan Adikkal, Raja Rama of Venadu, to Marwan Saphir Isho (Sabr'isho), lauding him as 'Restorer of the City' (*nagaram*). These privileges, in the year 825 and confirmed again by Sthani Ravi, the Ayyan of Venād in 849 and 880, acknowledged the aristocratic status and perquisites of the *Tarisapalli* (Persian Christian community) in relation to members of the no less noble status of *Anjunānnam* (Jewish trade guilds) and the *Mānigrāmmam* (members of trade guilds, many of whom were also Christians or Jews)—all of whom were co-holders of power within the *nagaram*.[37] Lands granted were demarcated in the traditional manner, 'by letting a female elephant roam free' to mark the territory that was desired.[38] Autonomous authority, known as the 'seventy-two privileges', included the enjoyment of full local self-government, armed self-protection by a militia of 600 Christian warriors, exemption from corvée labour, custody of weights and measures, special bride-price privileges, and right to receive hereditary services from various lower-level communities, such as crop cultivators (*vellalars*), oil-producers (*vaniyars*), washermen (*vannars*), toddy-tappers (*ilavars*), artisans and carpenters (*tachars*), and menials. Even Christians from polluting castes were to be allowed to enter the Quilon fortress.[39]

During these same years, records of the *Anglo-Saxon Chronicle* for 883 contain the astonishing words: 'The same year Sigehelm and Aethelstan took to Rome, and also to St Thomas and St Bartholomew in India, the alms that the [King] Alfred had promised to send thither.'[40] How knowledge could have reached pre-1066 Conquest England is an intriguing question about which one can only speculate. Perhaps some late version of the *Acts of Thomas* that had somehow become linked to Gregory of Tours (*c.* CE 590) might have reached the pious and upright ruler across the Channel. In light of other known merchant or pilgrim adventurers who travelled incredibly long distances during those centuries, such an event is not implausible.[41]

Some critics have questioned whether the concept 'India' as it is found in these early sources is really the same as the India that we know. They see it as an indefinite or vague geographical expression that has also been applied to Abyssinia (or Ethiopia), eastern Arabia, or Persia, and that it cannot be definitively identified with what we know as 'India'. Europeans, after all, were 'ignorant' about India in those days, especially after Islam had thrown up a barrier between India and the West. Such critiques often betray an ignorance of the history of those times. Arabs and Greeks, as well as Syrian Christians, had long maintained active contacts with India, both by land and sea. Muziris, close to what later became known as Cranganore and in proximity to Malankara, had remained a thriving entrepôt of overseas commerce, both in the west (Africa and Persia) and with the seaports further to the east.[42]

Quite clearly, in processes that stretched over a course of more than a thousand years, if not longer, different Christian communities evolved within what was a highly segmented society in Malabar. From the outset, these seem to have been, for the most part, an aristocratic and indigenous elite. Hindu in culture, Christian in faith, and Persian or Syrian (Orthodox) in doctrine, ecclesiology, and ritual, these Christians, at least some of whom were a compact Jewish Christian community, gradually evolved into what constituted a complex of high-caste communities whose occupational position, ritual purity, and social ranking, as merchant traders and merchant warriors—sometimes even as local rulers—became ever more firmly fixed and well grounded. Within a Brahmanically framed social order (*varnāshramadharma*) of a 'four-class' or 'four-colour' (*chaturvarniya*) system, most Thomas Christians seem to have been categorized as falling somewhere between the Kshatriya and Vaishya strata of castes. Christian cultures—not all being of the same caste (*jāti*) or lineage (*vamsha*)—were far from uniform in quality and texture. Yet all Christians possessed features which were distinctly native to the land, or 'Hindu' in the original sense of that term.

In time, Jewish Christians of the most exclusive communities descended from settlers who accompanied Knayil Thomma (*Kanāyi*) became known as 'Southists' (*Tekkumbhāgar*). With their claims to royal descent and purer blood, traced back to King David, they more carefully preserved their own lineages and more strictly avoided ritual pollution. They distinguished between themselves and 'Northists' (*Vatakkumbhāgar*). The 'Northists', on the other hand, claimed direct descent from the very oldest Christians of the country, those who had been won to Christ by the Apostle Thomas himself. They had already long inhabited northern parts of Kodungallur. They had been there even before various waves of newcomers had arrived from the Babylonian or Mesopotamian provinces of Sassanian Persia. Conflicts between these two endogamous wings of the Thomas Christian community, on matters both small and large, became chronic. Nevertheless, both groups constructed churches in close proximity to each other in such places as Kaduthuruthi and Kottayam.[43]

'Southists' in particular, if not other Thomas Christians, shared a world of common culture and inhabited a common space with other high-born peoples (castes or *jātis*). Their men wore tonsures, with shaven heads having tufts of hair comparable to tonsures worn by certain monks in the West. As Malankara Nazaranis, their positions seem to have paralleled those of the Nayars—in the nature of special relations with Brahmans and with each other. Their places of dwelling were referred to as *tharavād* and their rituals for removing pollution, their uses of *ghee* and *ghur*, and their ways of handling food and drink and utensils, were very similar. Even in matters of interdining and intermarriage, as also in disposal of pollution connected to dead bodies (*pulakuli*), rituals of Nayars and these Thomas (or Syrian) Christians became linked. A new husband, for example, tied a *thāli* around his bride's neck (albeit with a cross attached to it), and performed a very similar kind of traditional ceremonial for investiture of the 'marriage cloth'. Even in the celebration of *Onam* and *Vishu*, at harvest and new year festivals, elite communities functioned within a common cultural framework.

Indeed, as wealthy merchant bankers and traders whose transactions and travels called for armed protection by skilled warriors, the same kind of training in martial sciences (*kalāri-pāyat*) was given to boys of both Nayar and Christian communities. Training in such disciplines, commencing when boys were aged 8 and continuing until they were 25, was given by *guru* fencing masters known as *panikkars.* According to the *Villiarvattom Pāna*, the power of Malankara Nazaranis who scattered along the Malabar coast reached so far that, at one time, they were able to form their own 'little kingdom'. This realm, stretching intermittently north and south along the coast, with its capital at Mahadevapattanam ('Port of the Great God', sometimes spelled Mogoderpatnam) on the island of Chennamangalam, seems later to have moved to Udayamperur so as to avoid Arab depredations. Udayamperur, with its Great Church as a central place of worship, had been constructed, according to Thomas Christian tradition, by the Villiarvattam Raja circa 510. This 'little kingdom' seems to have survived until well after the coming of the Portuguese in 1498. Only after receiving what, in their view, turned out to be duplicitous or insincere promises of help in their perpetual struggles to defend themselves from Arabs, did the Malankara Christians finally see themselves betrayed and then partially conquered by the Raja of Cochin. Even so, the fact remains that these Thomas Christian forces, as such, were never completely subdued by force of arms.

Conclusion

Canonical belief in the significance of the arrival and survival of Thomas Christians from ancient times onwards is extremely important for understanding the entire history of Christianity in India. While much data has been uncovered and while there may yet be more that is continuously being sifted, the historicity of apostolic origins rests upon conjectural or uncertain evidence. Yet, large measures of circumstantial and corroborative evidences are such that the plausibility, if not possibility, of historicity cannot be entirely or lightly dismissed. An attempt has been made, within these pages, to show that, along with all other histories of India from ancient times to the present, what starts as a tiny and thin trickle of traditions was increasingly reinforced by more and more concrete and durable kinds of architectural, epigraphic, and numismatic data and that this stream, increasingly strengthened by oral traditions and literary texts, becomes broader and broader until, like the mingling convergences of the numerous branches of the Ganga and the Brahmaputra that criss-cross and diverge in the bewildering variety of streams to form that labyrinthine maze known as the Sundarbans, they merge into an ocean of probabilities.

The tradition that Thomas the Apostle came and worked and died in India is as old and as deeply rooted in India as many of the earliest Christian traditions. That this tradition is accepted as canonical cannot be denied. While, despite manifold, parallel, and venerable sources, there is not enough evidence to compel unqualified acceptance, neither are there sufficient grounds, due to the rich array of extremely complex and difficult strands of circumstantial evidence, to dismiss outright or disprove the historicity of this tradition. Some accretions of evidence cannot be accepted as having any claim to historical validity. But other elements, some of much earlier origin, handed down through known writers going back to patristic and apostolic times, are reliable. Fanciful legends of later centuries that cluster around these earlier elements do not nullify or even weaken the core of the original tradition. An impartial study of understandings drawn from this tradition can be viewed on the same level as many of the generally accepted facts about ancient India and about ancient Christianity elsewhere.

Thus, it seems certain that there were well-established communities of Christians in South India no later than the third and fourth centuries, and perhaps much earlier. That at least some communities were of foreign origin and that they were led by pastors and bishops that used Syriac as their language of learning and liturgy is also clear. That these immigrant newcomers settled in proximity to pre-existing Christian communities is no less clear. Some of the Christians from the earliest times not only became identified with the imperial Perumals of Malabar (aka Kerala) but also with Pandiyan and Chola kingdoms, and especially with the Pallava regime centred near Mylapore (Mailapur). That these earliest Christians tried to spread their faith to the non-Christians among whom they lived is not at all clear. But, in light of facts known and not known, millions of Thomas Christians remain certain that their founder was none other than the Apostle himself. For them, this is an established article of faith—a part of their own canon from which there can be no deviation.

Thus, as we shall see in the chapters that follow, from what occurred in later centuries, Thomas Christians continued to represent the earliest and strongest expressions of indigenous Christianity to be found anywhere in the continent. Both in ideological and in institutional forms, these Christians gradually became separated by historical circumstances into more and more distinct communities, all of which continued to thrive. Each of these separate Thomas Christian communities continues to lay claim to being inheritors of the apostolic tradition of St Thomas as the historic basis, both for their origins and for their doctrinal and ecclesiastical authority.

Notes

16 *The Geography of Strabo*, trans. H. C. Hamilton and W. Falconer, 3 vols. (London: H. G. Bohn, 1854–7).

17 *The Periplus of the Erythraean Sea & Ptolemy on Ancient Geography of India*, ed. Sudhakar Chattopadhyaya (Calcutta: Praja, 1980). While this informs us that the monsoon was discovered by a Greek named Hippalus, few doubt that knowledge of seasonal winds was of much greater antiquity. One of many treatments of ancient Greek texts, a historical geography of India in the context of *Geographike* by Claudius Ptolemaeus, a Greek scholar, and *Periplus Maris Erythraei*, 1st-century anonymous travelogue.

18 E. H. Warmington, *Commerce between the Roman Empire and India* (Cambridge: Cambridge University Press, 1928).

19 Arikamedu, for example, was a Roman station regularly guarded by two cohorts of troops: cf. R. C. Mortimer Wheeler *et al.*, *Ancient India* (July 1945). About its

expense Pliny complained. Such well-known classics of ancient Tamil as the *Silapppadikaram*, *Manimekhalai*, and *Pattinippalai*, not to mention *Puranas*, also mention *Yavana* (Greek) soldiers, etc.

20 Jerome, taken from James Noll Ogilvie, *The Apostles of India* (London: Baird Lecture, 1915) (taken from 'Eusebius: V.10.1').

21 Of course, some may argue, language barriers also prevailed elsewhere, as in Latin Christianity and in Islam among non-Arabic speakers. When Celtic, Anglo-Saxon, Germanic, Nordic rulers converted to Christianity, family members who entered the clergy strengthened bonds with the laity, as also for revered *mullahs* within *dar-ul-Islam*. In the East, where unconverted rulers were influenced by learned non-Christian priesthoods, Christian belief among ordinary Christians could have destructive consequences.

22 Arthur Vööbus, *Celibacy, A Requirement for Admission to Baptism in the Early Syrian Church* (Stockholm: Estonian Theological Society in Exile, 1951). Aphrates, in this respect, may have reflected, in some measure, the Zoroastrianism from which he had been converted.

23 A footnote to these events was recorded in far-off England where, for the year AD 883, the *Anglo-Saxon Chronicle* reported on the conveying of 'alms that the king vowed to send thither, and to India to St. Thomas and St. Bartholomew'. Some quibble over what was meant by 'India' but we know that other long journeys of that nature occurred, in both directions.

24 Syriac documents, translated by Alphonse Mingana, indicate that it was the Catholicos of Babylon who sent 'Thomas of Kināyi' (alias 'Thomas of Kana' or 'Thomas of Jerusalem') and Bishop Joseph on this mission. Mingana, *The Early Spread of Christianity in India*; T. K. Joseph, *Malabar Christians and their Ancient Documents* (Trivandrum: Popular Press, 1929). Both Joseph and Kollaparambil, while not disputing Mingana's translations, take issue with his interpretations.

25 Jacob Kollaparambil, *The Babylonian Origin of the Southists among the St. Thomas Christians* (Rome: Pont. Institutum Studiorum Orientalium, 1992), 23, quote from J. Vellian, *Purātanappāṭṭukal* (Kottayam, 1985), 5 and C. Choondal, *Christian Folk Songs* (Trichur: Kerala Folklore Academy, 1983).

26 The original two sets of plates mysteriously vanished not long after being shown to Alexis de Menezes, Archbishop of Goa, in 1599. Copies, with exact descriptions of fine metal plates one and a half palms long and four fingers broad, inscribed on both sides, and bound by thick wire, in archaic forms of Syriac, Kufic Arabic, and Malayalam ('Chaldean, Malabar, and Arabic') and translations, give a clear sense of what the original contained. See Joseph, *Malabar Christians*, 3–7, 32–4; and A. Mathias Mundadan, *The Arrival of the Portuguese in India and the Thomas Christians under Mar Jacob, 1498–1552* (Bangalore: Dharmaram College, 1967), 170–3.

27 Mundadan, *The Arrival of the Portuguese in India*, 170.

28 Ibid. 172. There is not a shred of evidence, from these sources, that these were Ebionites.

29 Kollaparambil, *Babylonian Origin*, 89–98: 'III. The Year of the Southists' Immigration'.

30 Samuel H. Moffatt, *The History of Christianity in Asia* (New York: Harper Collins, 1992), 267.

31 *History of the Church by Sozomen and Philostorgius* (London: Henry G. Bohn [Bonn's Ecclesiastical Library, 1855), 445. *The Ecclesiastical History of Sozomen: Comprising a History of the Church from A.D. 324 to A.D. 440. Translated from the Greek with a memoir of the author.* Also, *Epitome of the Ecclesiastical History of Philostorgius compiled by Photius, Patriarch of Constantinople*, trans. Edward Walford.

32 Mingana, *Early Spread of Christianity*, 26–7; Joseph, *Malabar Christians*, 2; Medlycott, A. E., *India and the Apostle Thomas, an Inquiry, with a Critical Analysis of the Acta Thomae* (London: David Nutt, 1905) 186–202, 186–7.

33 Mingana, *Early Spread of Christianity*, 27. Brown, *The Indian Christians of St. Thomas*, 68; and Moffatt, *History of Christianity in Asia*, 267. Brown, Leslie, *The Indian Christians of St. Thomas: An Account of the Ancient Syrian Church of Malabar* (Cambridge: Cambridge University Press, 1982 [originally 1956]).

34 J. W. McGrindle, *Christian Topography of Cosmas Indicopleustes* (London: Hakluyt Society, 1907), 118–29; and/or *The Christian Topography of Cosmas Indicopleustes*, trans. and ed. O. E. Winstedt (Cambridge: Cambridge University Press, 1909). Also quoted, with commentary, by Stephen Neill, *A History of Christianity in India: Beginnings to 1707* (Cambridge: Cambridge University Press, 1984), 36–7; Mingana, *Early Spread of Christianity*, 30–1; Joseph, *Malabar Christians*, 1–2; S. G. Pothan, *Syrian Christians of Kerala* (Bombay: Asia Publishing House, 1963), 27.

35 See photocopies and hand drawings of these two sets in S. G. Pothan, *The Syrian Christians of Kerala* (Bombay: Asia Publishing House, 1963), between pp. 32 and 33, with translations in appendices I and II, pp. 102–5.

36 *Travancore Archaeological Reports, Series II* (Trivandrum: Government Press, 1920), 75–80. The first set of plates was issued in the fifth regnal year of Sthani Ravi, or the year 849.

37 Mundadan, *The Arrival of the Portuguese in India*, 166–9.

38 Brown, *The Indian Christians of St. Thomas*, 75.

39 Joseph, *Malabar Christians*, 33–7. Also see Mundadan, *The Arrival of the Portuguese in India*, 166–9; Brown, *The Indian Christians of St. Thomas*, 74–5.

40 *The Anglo-Saxon Chronicles*, trans. and ed. Anne Savage (New York: St Martin's/Marek, 1983), 97.

41 Neill, *A History of Christianity in India*, 44.

42 P. J. Thomas, 'Was the Apostle Thomas in South India?', in Hosten (ed.), *Antiquities from San Thomé and Mylapore*, p. x.

43 Kollaparambil, *Babylonian Origin*. Of course, this interpretation is only one of several descriptive explanations for distinctions between the two communities.

16

CH'ING-TSING: NESTORIAN TABLET

Eulogizing the propagation of the illustrious religion in China, with a preface

Composed by a priest of the Syriac Church, 781 AD

Source: Charles F. Horne (ed.), *The Sacred Books and Early Literative of the East*, Vol. XII: *Medieval China*, New York: Parke, Austin and Lipscomb, 1917.

[. . .]

"Behold the unchangeably true and invisible, who existed through all eternity without origin; the far-seeing perfect intelligence, whose mysterious existence is everlasting; operating on primordial substance he created the universe, being more excellent than all holy intelligences, inasmuch as he is the source of all that is honorable. This is our eternal true lord God, triune and mysterious in substance. He appointed the cross as the means for determining the four cardinal points, he moved the original spirit, and produced the two principles of nature; the somber void was changed, and heaven and earth were opened out; the sun and moon revolved, and day and night commenced; having perfected all inferior objects, he then made the first man; upon him he bestowed an excellent disposition, giving him in charge the government of all created beings; man, acting out the original principles of his nature, was pure and unostentatious; his unsullied and expansite mind was free from the least inordinate desire; until Satan introduced the seeds of falsehood, to deteriorate his purity of principle; the opening thus commenced in his virtue gradually enlarged, and by this crevice in his nature was obscured and rendered vicious; hence three hundred and sixty-five sects followed each other in continuous track, inventing every species of doctrinal complexity; while some pointed to material objects as the source of their faith, others reduced all to vacancy, even to the annihilation of the two primeval principles, some sought to call down blessings by prayers and supplications, while others by an assumption of excellence held themselves up as superior to their fellows; their intellects and thoughts continually wavering, their minds and affections incessantly on the move, they never obtained their vast desires, but being exhausted and distressed they revolved in their own heated atmosphere; till by an accumulation of obscurity they lost their path, and after long groping in darkness they were unable to return. Thereupon, our Trinity being divided in nature, the illustrious and honorable Messiah, veiling his true dignity, appeared in the world as a man; angelic powers promulgated the glad tidings, a virgin gave birth to the Holy One in Syria; a bright star announced the felicitous event, and Persians observing the splendor came to present tribute; the ancient dispensation, as declared by the twenty-four holy men [the writers of the Old Testament], was then fulfilled, and he laid down great principles for the government of families and kingdoms; he established the new religion of the silent operation of the pure spirit of the Triune; he rendered virtue subservient to direct faith; he fixed the extent of the eight boundaries, thus completing the truth and freeing it from dross; he opened the gate of the three constant principles, introducing life and destroying death; he suspended the bright sun to invade the chambers of darkness, and the falsehoods of the devil were thereupon defeated; he set in motion the vessel of mercy by which to ascend to the bright mansions, whereupon rational beings were then released, having thus completed the manifestation of his power, in clear day he ascended to his true station.

Twenty-seven sacred books [the number in the New Testament] have been left, which disseminate intelligence by unfolding the original transforming principles. By the rule for admission, it is the custom to apply the water of baptism, to wash away all superficial show and to cleanse and purify the neophytes. As a seal, they hold the cross, whose influence is reflected in every direction, uniting all without distinction. As they strike the wood, the fame of their benevolence is diffused abroad; worshiping toward the east, they hasten on the way to life and glory; they preserve the beard to symbolize their outward actions, they shave the crown to indicate the absence of inward affections; they do not keep slaves, but put noble and mean all on an equality; they do not amass wealth, but cast all their property into the common stock; they fast, in order to perfect themselves by self-inspection; they submit to restraints, in order to strengthen themselves by silent watchfulness; seven times a day they have worship and praise for the benefit of the living and the dead; once in seven days they sacrifice, to cleanse the heart and return to purity.

It is difficult to find a name to express the excellence of the true and unchangeable doctrine; but as its meritorious operations are manifestly displayed, by accommodation it is named the Illustrious Religion. Now without holy men, principles cannot become expanded; without principles, holy men cannot become magnified; but with holy men and right principles, united as the two parts of a signet, the world becomes civilized and enlightened.

In the time of the accomplished Emperor Tai-tsung, the illustrious and magnificent founder of the dynasty, among the enlightened and holy men who arrived was the most-virtuous Olopun, from the country of Syria. Observing the azure clouds, he bore the true sacred books; beholding the direction of the winds, he braved difficulties and dangers. In the year of our Lord 635 he arrived at Chang-an; the Emperor sent his Prime Minister, Duke Fang Hiuen-ling; who, carrying the official staff to the west border, conducted his guest into the interior; the sacred books were translated in the imperial library, the sovereign investigated the subject in his private apartments; when becoming deeply impressed with the rectitude and truth of the religion, he gave special orders for its dissemination.

In the seventh month of the year A.D. 638 the following imperial proclamation was issued:

> Right principles have no invariable name, holy men have no invariable station; instruction is established in accordance with the locality, with the object of benefiting the people at large. The greatly virtuous Olopun, of the kingdom of Syria, has brought his sacred books and images from that distant part, and has presented them at our chief capital. Having examined the principles of this religion, we find them to be purely excellent and natural; investigating its originating source, we find it has taken its rise from the establishment of important truths; its ritual is free from perplexing expressions, its principles will survive when the framework is forgot; it is beneficial to all creatures; it is advantageous to mankind. Let it be published throughout the Empire, and let the proper authority build a Syrian church in the capital in the I-ning May, which shall be governed by twenty-one priests. When the virtue of the Chau Dynasty declined, the rider on the azure ox ascended to the west; the principles of the great Tang becoming resplendent, the Illustrious breezes have come to fan the East.

Orders were then issued to the authorities to have a true portrait of the Emperor taken; when it was transferred to the wall of the church, the dazzling splendor of the celestial visage irradiated the Illustrious portals. The sacred traces emitted a felicitous influence, and shed a perpetual splendor over the holy precincts. According to the Illustrated Memoir of the Western Regions, and the historical books of the Han and Wei dynasties, the kingdom of Syria reaches south to the Coral Sea; on the north it joins the Gem Mountains; on the west it extends toward the borders of the immortals and the flowery forests; on the east it lies open to the violent winds and tideless waters. The country produces fire-proof cloth, life-restoring incense, bright moon-pearls, and night-luster gems. Brigands and robbers are unknown, but the people enjoy happiness and peace. None but Illustrious laws prevail; none but the virtuous are raised to sovereign power. The land is broad and ample, and its literary productions are perspicuous and clear.

The Emperor Kau-tsung respectfully succeeded his ancestor, and was still more beneficent toward the institution of truth. In every province he caused Illustrious churches to be erected, and ratified the honor conferred upon Olopun, making him the great conservator of doctrine for the preservation of the State. While this doctrine pervaded every channel, the State became enriched and tranquillity abounded. Every city was full of churches, and the royal family enjoyed luster and happiness. In the year A.D. 699 the Buddhists, gaining power, raised their voices in the eastern metropolis; in the year A.D. 713, some low fellows excited ridicule and spread slanders in the western capital. At that time there was the chief priest Lohan, the greatly virtuous Kie-leih, and others of noble estate from the golden regions, lofty-minded priests, having abandoned all worldly interests; who unitedly maintained the grand principles and preserved them entire to the end. The high-principled Emperor Hiuen-tsung caused the Prince of Ning and others, five princes in all, personally to visit the felicitous edifice; he established the place of worship; he restored the consecrated timbers which had been temporarily thrown down; and re-erected the sacred stones which for a time had been desecrated.

In A.D. 742 orders were given to the great general Kau Lih-sz', to send the five sacred portraits and have them placed in the church, and a gift of a hundred pieces of silk accompanied these pictures of intelligence. Although the dragon's beard was then remote, their bows and swords were still within reach; while the solar horns sent forth their rays, and celestial visages seemed close at hand. In A.D. 744 the priest Kih-ho, in the kingdom of Syria, looking toward the star [of China], was attracted by its transforming influence, and observing the sun [*i.e.*, the Emperor], came to pay court to the most honorable. The Emperor commanded the priest Lo-han, the priest Pu-lun, and others, seven in all, together with the greatly virtuous Kih-ho, to perform a service of merit in the Hing-king palace. Thereupon the Emperor composed mottoes for the sides of the church, and the tablets were graced with the royal inscriptions; the accumulated gems emitted their effulgence, while their sparkling brightness vied with the ruby clouds; the transcripts of intelligence suspended in the void shot forth their rays as reflected by the sun; the bountiful gifts exceeded the height of the southern hills; the bedewing favors were deep as the eastern sea. Nothing is beyond the range of the right principle, and what is permissible may be identified; nothing is beyond the power of the holy man, and that which is practicable may be related.

The accomplished and enlightened Emperor Suh-tsung rebuilt the Illustrious churches in Ling-wu and four other places; great benefits were conferred, and felicity began to increase; great munificence was displayed, and the imperial State became established. The accomplished and military

Emperor Tai-tsung magnified the sacred succession, and honored the latent principle of nature; always, on the incarnation-day, he bestowed celestial incense, and ordered the performance of a service of merit; he distributed of the imperial viands, in order to shed a glory on the Illustrious Congregation. Heaven is munificent in the dissemination of blessings, whereby the benefits of life are extended; the holy man embodies the original principle of virtue, whence he is able to counteract noxious influences.

Our sacred and sage-like, accomplished and military Emperor Kien-chung appointed the eight branches of government, according to which he advanced or degraded the intelligent and dull; he opened up the nine categories, by means of which he renovated the Illustrious decrees; his transforming influence pervaded the most abstruse principles, while openness of heart distinguished his devotions. Thus, by correct and enlarged purity of principle, and undeviating consistency in sympathy with others; by extended commiseration rescuing multitudes from misery, while disseminating blessings on all around, the cultivation of our doctrine gained a grand basis, and by gradual advances its influence was diffused. If the winds and rains are seasonable, the world will be at rest; men will be guided by principle, inferior objects will be pure; the living will be at ease, and the dead will rejoice; the thoughts will produce their appropriate response, the affections will be free, and the eyes will be sincere; such is the laudable condition which we of the Illustrious Religion are laboring to attain.

Our great benefactor, the Imperially conferred purple-gown priest, I-sz', titular Great Statesman of the Banqueting-house, Associated Secondary Military Cornmissioner for the Northern Region, and Examination-palace Overseer, was naturally mild and graciously disposed; his mind susceptible of sound doctrine, he was diligent in the performance; from the distant city of Rajagriha, he came to visit China; his principles more lofty than those of the three dynasties, his practise was perfect in every department; at first he applied himself to duties pertaining to the palace, eventually his name was inscribed on the military roll. When the Duke Koh Tsz'-i, Secondary Minister of State and Prince of Fan-yang, at first conducted the military in the northern region, the Emperor Suh-tsung made him (I-sz') his attendant on his travels; although he was a private chamberlain, he assumed no distinction on the march; he was as claws and teeth to the duke, and in rousing the military he was as ears and eyes; he distributed the wealth conferred upon him, not accumulating treasure for his private use; he made offerings of the jewelry which had been given by imperial favor, he spread out a golden carpet for devotion; now he repaired the old churches, anon he increased the number of religious establishments; he honored and decorated the various edifices, till they resembled the plumage of the pheasant in its flight; moreover, practising the discipline of the Illustrious Religion, he distributed his riches in deeds of benevolence; every year he assembled those in the sacred office from four churches, and respectfully engaged them for fifty days in purification and preparation; the naked came and were clothed; the sick were attended to and restored; the dead were buried in repose; even among the most pure and self-denying of the Buddhists, such excellence was never heard of; the white-clad members of the Illustrious Congregation, now considering these men, have desired to engrave a broad tablet, in order to set forth a eulogy of their magnanimous deeds. [. . .]

17

PAGANISM IN THE GREEK WORLD AT THE END OF ANTIQUITY

The case of rural Anatolia and Greece*

Frank R. Trombley

Source: *Harvard Theological Review*, 78(4) (1985), 327–52.

I propose to discuss what might be called the "mechanics of conversion" in the countryside of the sixth-century later Roman Empire. This process consisted fundamentally in implanting monasteries in districts where few villages had been Christianized, or where the population was nominally Christian but so badly instructed that earlier pagan cult practices persisted.[1] There is considerable evidence for rural conditions in the hagiographic lives of monks and in the ecclesiastical histories of this period.[2] One of the principal difficulties in this sort of study is the geographic distribution of the sources. Hagiographic texts are, in effect, local histories, largely confined to the environs of the monastery. Thus, we are reasonably well informed about western Asia Minor and Galatia in the sixth century, for which sources like this exist, but hardly know anything about paganism in Greece until the tenth century, when monasteries finally began to appear in rural districts.

It should be borne in mind as well that paganism survived elsewhere in the eastern Mediterranean world, but in provinces which were only superficially hellenized. Thus, there were pagan Syrian villages near Qalat Simān between Antioch and Beroia-Aleppo[3] where the monastery of Symeon Stylites the Younger lay, and in Egypt Coptic villagers and diviners continued the cults of the Nile River gods down through the eighth century.[4] I have here concentrated on the evidence for the ethnically Greek sections of the empire, preeminently western Asia Minor and the Peloponnese.

A section of the *Codex Justinianus* dating from after 472 CE makes specific reference to the survival of rural paganism and to efforts at its eradication:

> If any unholy and defiled pagan (*hellēn*) does not make himself manifest, whether living here or in the countryside (*chōra*), and run to the churches with his household, that is to say wives and children, let him submit to the aforesaid penalties, let the fisc confiscate their property, and let them be given over to exile.[5]

Another clause provides for the immediate baptism of the young children of recently converted pagans, prior to their instruction in the ecclesiastical canons and scripture, in order to assure their "genuine conversion" (γνησία μετανοία).[6] This part of the law sought to prevent their acculturation by partially catechized and not yet baptized parents. References to sixth-century rural temples and pagan local cultures are rare. Procopius mentions the conversion of temples dedicated to Artemis and Iphigenia at Komana in his own time.[7] It is unclear whether the priesthood and cult attested by Strabo, which had sacred lands 2 *schoini* (= 60 stadia) in circuit and a colonate numbering 6000 cultivators, lasted until this time.[8] The situation in western Asia Minor is much clearer thanks to the pen of John of Ephesus.

John, the Syrian Monophysite bishop of Ephesus, describes his own missionary work in western Asia Minor in his *Ecclesiastical History*.[9] Nicknamed "the idol-breaker" and "over the pagans" (*'al-ḥanephē*), he began the work of converting the pagans in the civil provinces of Asia, Caria, Lydia, and Phrygia around the year 540.[10] John claimed to have redeemed "many thousands" of persons from "the error of idol-worship" in the rugged mountains of Caria near the city of Tralles. He indicates that "a great and renowned idol-temple of the pagans" stood in that district, called Dareira in the Syriac text.[11] The temple in question appears to have been that of the Isodromian Mother in the Mesogeis massif near Tralles mentioned in Strabo's *Geography* (9.5.19). The *-eira* ending of the locality's name recurs frequently in Lydian toponyms.[12] The "old men" of the place told John that at one time 1500 smaller temples lay under its jurisdiction, and that its priests had educated the people in customary law (νόμος).[13] John indicates that the entire district was pagan in religion, and, based on his account, it appears that Dareira had a well organized local culture.

Under a provision of the Theodosian Code pagan temples reverted to the imperial fisc after being closed.[14] John of Ephesus, with the approval of the government and contrary to the common practice of converting temples into churches, ordered this temple to be razed. He then supervised the construction of a new monastery on the same spot, which received extensive subsidies from the emperor Justinian (527–65). Three separate imperial rescripts confirmed the jurisdiction of the monastery at Dareira over the fourteen churches and seven monasteries also constructed in that district.[15] William Mitchell Ramsay remarked long ago that "such a Christian ecclesiastical establishment took the place of the ancient Anatolian *hieron* as a center of social and municipal life."[16] A sixth-century inscription from

Alexandria Troas indicates that former temple lands were at times organized under the administration of a monastery: "On behalf of the vow of the villages and people of St. Tryphon, and all those who make offerings in it, and all their households."[17] The name of the monastery's saint—in this case St. Tryphon—replaced the earlier invocation of the god or goddess.[18]

None of this is new. John of Ephesus's account is consistent with known evidence about temple conversions in the fourth through sixth centuries.[19] Critics have, however, doubted that a large pagan population could have existed anywhere in western Asia Minor as late as 542, and, perhaps more convincingly, have felt that his final figure of 80,000 conversions in the course of a year or two was simply fantastic.[20] Yet the painstaking collection of information from scattered sources demonstrates the plausibility of this story.

John of Ephesus wrote another work entitled *The Lives of the Eastern Saints*, which reports not only some additional details about the conversion of western Asia Minor, but suggests a chronology as well.[21] The biographical sketches in this work refer to ecclesiastical personnel who assisted John in Asia, many of them Syrians. In a section dated 565/6, the author notes that the "thirty years" since he first went to Constantinople were spent "on account of the conversion from the error of paganism of the districts of Asia," during which time 80,000 persons were baptized, and 98 churches and twelve monasteries were built.[22] The thirty years were roughly 536–66.[23] John was already in western Asia in 542 when consecrated bishop, and had probably begun the mission some years before.[24] The conversion of 80,000 pagans seems a less formidable task if considered over a thirty-year period. Let us average these figures for the sake of argument. The result comes to about 2700 converts, 3.3 churches, and well under one monastery per year. We know that the typical sixth-century Anatolian village had a population of 250–700 persons.[25] A large village might number 1000 persons.[26] The figure of 80,000 can in view of these estimates be said to represent 100 or so unchristianized villages, or an average of 25 per province. This conjecture is somewhat confirmed by a comparison of the number of churches built to the number of converts: 98 churches and twelve monasteries for 80,000 persons is proportional to one institution per 720 persons, the mean size of an Anatolian village. The remarkable convergence of these figures, all drawn from different sources, suggests that John is here speaking of rural churches, built in large and medium-sized villages, and monastic foundations in the midst of small hamlets (χωρία), all of them built at a rate of 3.6 per year to serve the 3.3 villages annually converted.

The task of breaking down the cultural ethos of rural paganism was a painstaking and much protracted business.[27] John's earliest collaborator was Deuterius, the Monophysite metropolitan of Caria.[28] Many eastern clerics and monks joined him later in the campaign. Kashish, the Monophysite bishop of Chios, arrived to help him in 556 at the latest.[29] Leontius the Presbyter, who collaborated with Kashish, did so before 558, as internal evidence from the text suggests.[30] Other persons, like a certain Abraham, "worked in Asia for many years."[31] These fragmentary data suggest that the serviceable manpower at John's disposal increased with time. John's assistants complained at times of the "high rugged mountains" and "tiring nature of the country,"[32] where villages and temples often lay isolated in high valleys and flock tenders roamed from place to place.

John of Ephesus notes in his *Ecclesiastical History* that the expense of constructing churches and monasteries was raised in part by grants from the emperor Justinian, in part from a tax laid on the newly converted villages.[33] The latter surcharge brings no surprise, nor does the imperial contribution, inasmuch as that emperor is commemorated in the inscriptions and in Procopius's work the *Aedificia* as "fond of building," (φιλόκτιστος).[34] To these sources of funds must be added a third hitherto unnoticed source mentioned by John in the *Lives of the Eastern Saints*. He had a friend and collaborator named Theodore, a court official who held the rank of *praepositus sacri cubiculi*, or Grand Chamberlain, a position of very great influence and honor, since its holder enjoyed direct access to the emperor and set the agenda for court business.[35] Theodore reportedly gave John a *kentenarion*, that is, a sum equal to 100 pounds of gold or 7200 *nomismata*, to be "sent to the regions of Asia."[36] This money was almost certainly used for the construction and furnishment of churches. These were probably small basilicas and single-aisled churches with apses.[37] We may conjecture that artisans were at times hired to cut some fine capitals and ambos, and to improvise some fine mosaics.[38] The play of sunlight on white marble and richly colored mosaics was thought to provide a necessary emotional element to the conversion of the rustic pagan, whose animistic world view must have weakened but slowly in his rough surroundings.

John of Ephesus mentions the western Anatolian cults in the second part of his *Ecclesiastical History* only briefly:

> In the year 542 the kindness of God visited Asia, Caria, Lydia, and Phrygia, thanks to the zeal of the victorious Justinian and by the activity of his humble servant [John of Asia] . . . When God opened the minds of [the pagans] and made them know the truth, he aided us in destroying their temples, in overturning their idols, in eradicating the sacrifices which were offered everywhere, in smashing their altars defiled by the blood of sacrifices offered to pagan gods (*aux démons*), and in cutting down the numerous trees which they worshipped, and so they became estranged from all the errors of their forefathers. The saving sign of the cross was implanted everywhere amongst them, and churches of God were founded in every place.[39]

In *The Lives of the Eastern Saints* he recalls that the four deacons, Abraham, Kyriakos, Barhadbshabba, and Sergius, were "strengthened to abolish paganism, overthrow idolatry, uproot altars, destroy temples (ναοί) and cut down trees."[40] These statements are consistent with those of fifth- and sixth-century Greek texts dealing with the Anatolian countryside and with other regions of the Mediterranean basin as well.[41] There are many attested cases of temple conversions, the destruction of sacred trees and groves, and the suppression of rural shamans. Let us consider some of the more striking texts.

The fifth-century life of St. Hypatius describes his missionary work in Phrygia and Bithynia. Of the latter province the hagiographer notes:

> [Hypatius] had zeal for God and converted many places in Bithynia from the error of idol-worship. If he heard that there was a tree or some other such [cult object] which persons worshipped, he went there at once taking along his disciples the monks, cut it down, and burned it. Thus they became Christians in part.[42]

This text confirms the surmise of Johannes Geffcken that the monks were the "shock troops" of Christianization.[43] The rustics became Christians "in part": not all of them were converted, nor did their daily customs change that radically. Sacred trees are reported in the sixth century as well. In Lycia, the men of the village of Plakoma complained of an ancient cypress tree, eighty feet tall and seven feet in diameter, "in which there dwells the spirit of an unclean idol; it harms men and the tilled lands."[44] Nicholas, the hegumen of the local monastery of Hagia Sion, ordered the men of the village to cut down the tree. When they refused, the task fell to the monk himself. Louis Robert cites this text to prove that the cult of Artemis Eleuthera survived into the sixth century.[45] The fear which the villagers expressed of the idol (ξοάνον) suggests that an unconverted idol temple existed within their memory, and that demonic powers were ascribed to its deity by the recent converts, as they learnt in Psalm 95: 4–5: "The gods of the pagans are demons." Sacred groves are mentioned as well. In the mid-sixth century the monk Theodore of Sykeon in Galatia inspected a site, probably a sacred grove, where Artemis was thought to appear:

> He heard about a place which was about eight miles away called Arkea, which was impossible for anyone to approach because of the popular clamor that Artemis lived there with many demons and harmed people unto death. Astonished at this rumor, he ran to that place . . . and spent the entire afternoon in the places believed to be sacred to Artemis. [But nothing happened.][46]

The accuracy of this typology shows that the memory of the Artemis cult lingered in this district. Artemis' epiphany in the afternoon, holding court in a grove with a group of lesser deities, is attested in the life of

St. Symphorianus of Augustodunum in third-century Gaul, another region affected by Celtic cultural forms.[47] Sacred groves are seemingly attested in northern Syria as well.[48]

Memories of the old cults seem to have been fed by rustic shamans, who claimed to be able to predict the future and find lost objects. Hypatius is reputed to have conversed with such a man, who asserted that revelations came to him at night, after he had told the person seeking guidance to sacrifice a cow, a sheep, or a bird at the idol temple; "angels" sometimes made direct revelations to him, he claimed.[49] Our author adds that he was an "old man" (*γέρων*), a term often used for monks.[50] It will be recalled that John of Ephesus's men destroyed many rural temples and altars. Until that time, abandoned temples—such as the shrine of Apollo Klarios at Colophon[51]—littered the Anatolian countryside, and a person bent on sacrificing could usually slip in at night and perform rites, all this notwithstanding the fourth-century Constantinian legislation and the subsequent laws against sacrifice collected in the fifth-century Theodosian Code.[52] The "old men" who told John of Ephesus about the history of the idol temple at Dareira may well have been priests of the sort described here. A local diviner is reported in the life of Theodore of Sykeon. The man reputedly had the power to dispatch spirits and bring down clouds of locusts on his clients' enemies, for a fee it would seem. He owned magic books—this in a Galatian village—and had not yet been baptized—this in the mid-sixth century.[53]

John of Ephesus's subordinates held clerical ranks from deacon all the way up to bishop, but all had previously been monks. Most of them were Syrians, but there were also Armenians and Iranian Aramaeans as well.[54] Their effectiveness in converting western Asia Minor may have been hindered to some extent by a lack of familiarity with the local dialects. There is absolutely no epigraphic evidence for the survival of the Phrygian language beyond the fourth century CE.[55] The prevailing language was the local Greek dialect, barbarous to Atticized ears and equally strange to the Syrian monks, who learned Greek as a second language in their provincial schools, in the marketplace, and in the Christian scriptures.[56] The difficulties and slow progress which they made have been noted. Other sources suggest that the most successful converters of pagans were monks who, in youth, had a stake in the village economy, knew the rudiments of agriculture, spoke the local *koinē*, had friends and relatives in the community, and understood the yearnings which lay behind the local cults. The case of fifth-century Phrygia, prior to its Christianization, is illustrated in the life of St. Hypatius:

> There were not even one or two [monks] in Phrygia at that time, not even one or two here and there, and if a church existed somewhere the clerics were indifferent because of the country. . . . When the population heard about Hypatius and were amazed that such a man came from their country, they all became Christians, little by little.[57]

An analysis of the lives of St. Nicholas of Hagia Sion and of St. Theodore of Sykeon shows that this was often accomplished by the monks' taking over some of the functions of the rustic shaman, but only after Christianizing the rite (*Ritenchristianisierung*). It is generally recognized by students of early Anatolian religion that pre-Christian and even pre-Greek aetiologies and customs are passed on through the hagiographic lives under consideration here.[58] Only a person who knew local culture thoroughly could accomplish conversions through these means.

Nicholas was born in the Lycian countryside in the early sixth century, became a monk in youth, and joined the monastery at Hagia Sion.[59] R. M. Harrison's survey of the Lycian hinterland has tentatively identified the site of this monastery in the hamlet of Karabel.[60] There are no traces of ecclesiastical buildings anywhere in rural Lycia dated earlier than the sixth century.[61] It seems quite improbable, considering the similar case of western Asia Minor, that the Lycian countryside became widely Christianized until after the rural churches and monasteries were built and staffed.

The existence of a cult centered on a sacred cypress tree has already been mentioned. Nicholas's biographer also mentions an "ancient spring" (ἀρχαία πηγή) which caused the farmers of the village of Arnabandea anxiety after a woman was supposed to have been cast in it by a spirit dwelling in it. The spring's waters had become turbulent and muddy, and men and animals feared to drink from it.[62] Sacred springs, often enclosed in temple precincts, abounded in rural Anatolia.[63] This site, too, seems to have been a cult center prior to the arrival of the monks, for the villagers refer to Nicholas's ability to "free the sacred site at the spring" (τὸ ἱερὸν εἰς ἁγιασμὸν ἠλευθερώσας) from the spirit or pagan god.[64] Previous catechization had convinced the people that the old gods were harmful demons. Nicholas arrived at the spring, but a lacuna in the text hides from us the immediate sequel.[65] The people seem not to have overcome their fear, however, because later on Nicholas was persuaded to divine for "hidden water" (ὕδωρ κεκρυμμένον) near the village.[66] The Anatolian shamans claimed to have power over geological and meteorological phenomena. Nicholas took care, however, to perform the service with a gospel book (μεγαλεῖον) and an array of crosses at hand.[67] On another occasion, Nicholas was challenged by the *deuterarios* of the monastery when he dismissed the stonemasons who were cutting marble for the apse of a basilica because of a planned pilgrimage to Palestine. Nicholas replied to him: "The stone obeys me" (ἐμοὶ ὑπακούει ὁ λίθος).[68] Some other cases of the adoption of shamanistic practices to the needs of the recently Christianized villages will be seen in the life of Theodore of Sykeon.

The pagan sacrifice, banned once again by the Justinianic law of 529, lay deep in the ethos of rural village life.[69] Whatever its cultic significance, it functioned as the symbol and instrument of the community's solidarity. Nicholas and the monks of Hagia Sion made a remarkable concession to their recently converted congregations by sponsoring sacrifices which used Christian cult formulae and were held at rural chapels. Thirteen such incidents are reported in the life of St. Nicholas.[70] I quote from one of the more complete descriptions:

> The clerics from Plenios came in a procession with the Christ-beloved people with crosses and met Nicholas at the chapel of St. George. He followed them from there with seven calves. After they went into the chapel . . . he slaughtered (literally, "sacrificed") the seven calves. The crowds assembled and two hundred couches were laid. [Nicholas] also brought one hundred measures of wine and forty *modii* of wheat. All ate and were filled, and gave thanks to God who gave grace to his servant Nicholas. Left over were sixty measures of wine, 100 loaves of bread, and four measures of oil.[71]

Although the example of the Israelite king David was cited as the basis for these acts, the details given here fit the typology of the pagan sacrifice.[72] The sacrifice (*θυσία*) survived in Turkish popular religion until Ottoman times as the *kurban*, and is attested as late as 1570, when the *dermatikon* or priest's share was apportioned in the ancient Hellenic manner.[73]

The adaptation of Christianity to the older pagan culture occurred also in Galatia. Theodore of Sykeon, hegumen of a prominent local monastery near Ankyra, flourished in the late sixth and early seventh centuries (ob. 613).[74] The existence here of a grove sacred to Artemis and of a pagan shaman has already been noticed. Peter Brown's article on the holy man in late antiquity omits reference to the local monk as supplanter of the rural diviner, and as one who proved that the "magic" of the new religion was superior to that of the old cults.[75] For example, Theodore is reputed to have broken the grip of the aforementioned pagan diviner named Theodotos Kourappos over a village near the monastery. Kourappos in the end confessed that his powers were inferior, burned his magic books, loosed the spells he had cast on persons, animals, and buildings, and submitted to baptism.[76]

Theodore of Sykeon was born in the countryside and remained there all his life, except for visits to Constantinople and Palestine, and his brief tenure as bishop of Anastasiopolis, a provincial town of Galatia Prote.[77] He knew the superstitions of the rustics, and they attributed great powers to him.[78] On one occasion, when some workmen shifted a large stone atop a quarry and it rolled downhill toward an apple tree, Theodore is said to have grieved for the tree, and to have ordered the stone to turn aside. The hagiographer adds: "At once, like an intelligent person (*ὡς ἄνθρωπος συνετός*), it inclined away from its attack on the tree."[79] Steeped in primitive animism, the Galatians ascribed an "attack" to the stone, and mastery over its movements to the monk. A very striking case is recorded in connection with hailstorms:

> In the village of Reake a wild cloud periodically attacked the land, and would cast hail upon the vines when they were ripe. . . . Theodore led a procession around the vineyards and fields, and having made a prayer, he stuck four crosses of wood into the ground at opposite ends of the boundary (ἐκ τετράντου).[80]

Here we have a "wild cloud" (νέφος ἄγριον) which "attacks" the fields. Nilsson mentions the use of *horoi* in the configuration of "magic circles" to protect fields in pre-Christian Greek lands.[81] The respective practices seem to be identical and dictated by rustic common sense. On another occasion Theodore inserted a cross into the bank of the Sangaris river which was undermining the arable land of the monastery at Sykeon, and ordered it to change its bed.[82] Such practices predated the Christian religion and the monks who supervised the new congregations.

The central plateau of Anatolia was at best marginal agricultural country. Rainfall varied from year to year, and droughts were common.[83] Theodore is reputed many times to have directed rain-bearing clouds to parched fields.[84] This, too, was a common practice among the pre-Christian shamans known as *nephodioktai* or "cloud-drivers."[85]

There is much else of significance for the present discussion in the life of Theodore of Sykeon, but I shall limit my remarks to the above. It suffices here to say that the pre-Christian ethos remained quite strong in the rural and mountainous districts of Anatolia. The life of Theodore mentions the settlement of many solitary monks in the upland districts of Galatia.[86] The experience of the monastic catechists must have been quite similar throughout the sixth century, wherever they went.

We have yet to describe the precise methods used to Christianize villages. A sixth-century text, the life of Abraham the solitary, offers some important details about this process.[87] The village of Taenia lay near Lampsacus in northwestern Anatolia and was regarded as a "large village" (κώμη μεγάλη καὶ πολυάνθρωπος), having more than 1000 inhabitants.[88] Sacrifice and idol-worship were practiced there, and an unclosed temple still stood.[89] The bishop of Lampsacus had sent numerous presbyters and deacons to convert the place, but without success.[90] He then called upon Abraham, a local solitary monk. Abraham entered the village, endured considerable physical abuse, and in a year's time converted the population of Taenia, while teaching them the ecclesiastical canons and scriptures.[91] The village was deemed "converted," and the bishop of Lampsacus thereupon furnished regular clergy.[92] Pagan and Christian, however, must have continued to live side by side for some time. One is reminded of the island of Philae in Egypt, where Christian bishops and a pagan priesthood led their communities side by side for about 150 years, until 537.[93] The life of Abraham does not, unfortunately, indicate that churches were built, or whether the temple was closed, dismantled, or converted into a church. It is significant that a large number of the new clergy was selected from the recently converted congregation of Taenia, whose members had been Christians no longer than a year.[94] It would not be surprising if certain types of *Ritenchristianisierung* arose under these conditions.

There remain to be considered briefly some fragments of evidence which attest to the survival of cult and the Christianization of rite in the seventh through the tenth centuries.

The Canons of the Quinisextum Council, held at Constantinople in 691–692, indicate the survival of pagan cult practices at that time.[95] Most of the forbidden behavior reflects a continuation of sixth-century practices. For example, the Sixty-first Canon condemned diviners of various types.[96] Among these were the so-called *nephodioktai* or "cloud-drivers" mentioned in the fourth-century pseudo-Justin, who reputedly "drive clouds wherever they wish by certain invocations to cast hail and immoderate rainfall."[97] in the competition between Christian and pagan in the countryside, monks like Theodore of Sykeon had in effect become rural "rainmakers," but the older sort who used pagan invocations still found employment in the late seventh century.

The Sixty-first Canon also condemned "animal leaders." This seemingly innocuous practice belonged to the pagan subculture, as a text from the chronicle of Theophanes the Confessor shows:

> In 544 a certain man named Andrew appeared from the land of Italy, wandering from village to village and having with him a yellow dog, which was blind and performed wonders upon command. While he stood in the agora with a crowd round about, the man was given small rings of gold, silver and iron which he concealed from the dog. He set them in the ground, heaped it into a mound, and bade the dog perform. It took and gave each person his own ring. The dog similarly delivered by name the coins of different emperors which had been mixed together. While a crowd of men and women stood by, the dog indicated upon being asked which women were pregnant, and which men were fornicators and adulterers, miserly and generous. And it told all with truth, wherefore they said: "It has the spirit of Python."[98]

The Canon also condemned the purveyors of amulets.[99] Theodore of Sykeon is reported a century earlier to have hurried to the village of Apokoumis where the people lay sick from the foul meat they had boiled in a cauldron and eaten. Upon his prayer, all recovered except one of the headmen. His brother had not awaited the prayer of the monk, but ran instead to a woman who performed invocations and made amulets. The man is reputed to have died as soon as the device was attached to him.[100] Want of space prevents a more full analysis of the Quinisextan Canons here.

Pagan cult practices are attested in the eighth century as well. The cult of Kybele seems to have persisted in Caria, one of the provinces evangelized by John of Ephesus. Following a description of the cult of Kybele, Cosmas of Jerusalem reports: "Certain irrational pagans in the mountains of Caria practice self-castration even until the present day, as the story goes, gripped by this ancient custom."[101] Pagan diviners continued to ply their trade in the towns of the empire, as when the Arabs raided Pergamum in 717:

> When Maslama [the emir] reached Pergamum, he besieged it and took it by the permission of God. . . . By the admonitions of a certain sorcerer (*magos*), the citizens brought a pregnant woman and killed her. After taking the fetus and boiling it in a cauldron in a sacrifice abominable to God, all who wished to wage war dipped in the cuffs of the right hand. Because of this they were delivered to the enemy.[102]

The chronicler makes no mention of the bishop of Pergamum, who must have argued heatedly with the citizens (οἱ τῆς πόλεως) about their intended act. This report was undoubtedly published to discourage desperate resort to magic when towns came under siege—as often happened in seventh- and eighth-century Anatolia.[103] The ninth-century life of St. Ioannikios mentions a rural seer (μαγομάντις) named Gourias, a non-Greek, non-Christian name, who practiced poisoning and magic arts (μαγικὰ ἔργα). The man lived in the country-side of the Thrakesion theme.[104] There is, finally, a tenth-century case of *Ritenchristianisierung* from Caria. The life of Paul the Younger of Mt. Latros describes it thus:

> A drought and generally severe shortage of water gripped Miletus. Certain like-minded men, not less than forty of them, assembled from different villages, formed a procession, and went up to the peak of the mountain with hymns beloved to God. This peak was not only very high, but very difficult to climb. An extremely large stone lies on the peak. This stone was called sacred from of old.[105]

Many miracles were thought to occur through the agency of the stone. Hermann Usener has pointed out that stone fetishes were common in pre-Greek Anatolia.[106] The cult of this particular stone seems to have lasted through all phases of religious transformation in western Asia Minor.[107] The hagiographer also mentions a very ancient iron cross which stood on the peaks beside the stone.[108] It is conceivable—but hardly proveable—that this cross was set in place by John of Ephesus's monks four centuries earlier. Since then the cult formulae had become Christian, but the practices still bore a striking resemblance to their pagan predecessors.

The evidence so far cited has immense significance for rural Greece between the sixth and tenth centuries, particularly for the Peloponnese. There is no sound evidence for the establishment of monasteries on mainland

Greece before the ninth century. When they were founded, monasteries were usually put in the coastlands, in places like Aegina, lower Phocis, and Thessalonica, to name a few.[109] It is unlikely that the rustics were largely converted without the steady catechetical work so abundantly attested for western Asia Minor. Greek urban religious life had strong ties to the local and rural temples. This allegiance was transferred to the basilicas as more citizens became Christian.[110] It should be borne in mind in this connection that the cities of the later Roman Empire often had substantial pagan populations even at the end of the sixth century. John of Ephesus, our best witness, reports large numbers of pagans in eastern cities like Edessa, Antioch, Baalbek, and Ḥarrān.[111] The last-mentioned town was largely pagan at the time of the Arab conquest, as al-Balādhurī reports, and even beyond.[112] *The Miracles of John and Cyrus*, an untranslated text full of information about the crypto-pagans of Alexandria, dates from the early seventh century, and papyri attest the survival of the Nile River cults in the eighth century.[113] Based on analogous evidence like this and what is known about Anatolia, we should not err in supposing that pagans continued to live in Athens and other towns of Greece well past the beginning of the Slavic *Landnahme* in the late sixth century, and that the countryside had its share of ethnically Greek pagans whose devotion to the chthonic deities had changed little since antiquity.

The temple complex at Lykosoura in Arcadia furnishes a case in point. It housed the cults of the chthonic Demeter, Despoina, Artemis, and Anytos. A single-aisled Christian basilica of sixth-century date was erected there. It served, perhaps, as the locus for a competing martyr cult and for a *prosmonarios*, an ecclesiastic who oversaw the temenos now dismantled and watched for the practitioners of proscribed cults.[114] The Appendix to the eighth-century *Ekloga* of Leo III, a simplified law code then in use, observes: "Let apostates who make sacrifices and temples be denounced by every person. If they had become Christians from pagans, and had been baptized, they shall be executed."[115] It would not be surprising if such behavior persisted at Lykosoura during the troubled period of the Slavic *Landnahme* in the Peloponnese. It is but a short jump from this time into the ninth century, when the inhabitants of Maina were converted to Christianity during the reign of the Byzantine emperor Basil I (869–86).

Our source for this event, the *De administrando imperio* of the emperor Constantine VII Porphyrogenitus, is quite clear in its main points: the citizens of Maina were not Slavs but descendants of the ancient Greeks, they were called *hellēnes* by the local inhabitants, and they claimed to have been idolators in ancient times.[116] Another section of this text has been overlooked. It states: "They have paid an agreed sum of four hundred *nomismata* [as their tax assessment] since ancient times." It would seem that the imperial administration had always remained in touch with Maina and that the series of tax registers dating back to the sixth century remained unbroken, or was known to be unbroken, in the ninth century. The government, anxious to keep its tenuous grip on the coastlands of Greece, made no demands on the people of Maina in the area of cult, and defended them against the Slavic tribes as long as the required tax monies were paid.[117]

The ninth-century court historian Joseph Genesios mentions the existence of pagan cult practices on the Spartan plain, while describing the voyage of a naval unit commanded by a certain Adrian, who was sailing to Sicily to raise the Arab siege of Syracuse:

> Having reached the Peloponnese, he put in at the harbor called Hierax and was hindered there by a very bad wind for fifty days. . . . A certain citizen approached and gave him the bad news that . . . Syracuse had been taken. . . . Adrian investigated the source of the rumor, and received this answer: "In the district of Helos there is a plain about eight miles off. On that evening certain shepherds approached and said that Syracuse had been taken, based on the account of visiting demons which were themselves present at the city."
>
> Adrian did not believe this, but hoped to get fuller information. With this in mind he reached the district delimited to the shepherds where the spirits of the air dwelt. The spirits replied to a certain shepherd that their abode had been in Syracuse, that they fed on residual Christian blood, that they knew Adrian was investigating events, and that they fully knew his name and official rank. Adrian did not believe this, but still took the day-old news into account. After fifteen days, the rumors reckoned to be false were revealed to be true by persons coming from Syracuse.
>
> Such knowledge by the indigenous spirits, or rather their knowledge of events completed, has persisted among the people of the same district until the reign of the most pious emperor Leo VI.[118]

There is not the slightest suggestion here that the shepherds were Slavs. If so, one might have hoped for references to interpreters. It was difficult to Christianize herdsmen, as I have repeatedly stressed, because of their migratory habits. Monks would have had, literally, to follow them around the countryside to ensure that the shepherds avoided acts of divination, particularly during the summer, which the flocks spent in the high pastures.

Let us consider next the life of Nikon the Metanoïte, who died in 998.[119] Nikon made periodic catechetical tours through the southern Peloponnese, and seems to have converted many half-Christian and pagan villages.[120] Archaeological evidence confirms that the church maintained an institutional presence on the Spartan plain during the Byzantine "Dark Age." An impost block from a church, dated to the seventh or eighth century, was discovered near Sparta, and is noted in Demetrios Pallas' *Monuments paléochrétiens de*

Grèce.[121] This presence had become quite thin by Nikon's day. One section of his hagiographic life reports:

> He departed from Argos, then went on from Sparta. He next reached the land of the Dorians, built two churches there, proclaimed repentance to all, and went on to Maina. He crossed over from there to Kalamas. He arrived in Arcadia next, after coming from Korone, Methone, and Mesyne, which the inhabitants called Bourkanon. He went through the remaining village-towns and led limitless multitudes to conversion.[122]

Among other things, this text indicates the position of Maina as being somewhere on the Spartan plain east of the Taygetos range, since Nikon "crossed over from there to Kalamas." It appears that the "land of the Dorians" encompassed the flatlands which run southwest to the point where the Taygetos meets the sea. This district had a few churches in the late tenth century,[123] but these structures hardly met the needs of the rural population, inasmuch as two new ones had to be built. There is not the slightest suggestion that monasteries existed anywhere in the southern Peloponnese at this time. The situation described here supports the view that this stretch of country remained missionary country throughout the tenth century.

I wish, in conclusion, to cite a text which, so far as I know, has not been cited in connection with the study of late paganism in Greece. It stands in the life of George the Hagiorite, one of a series of Athonite monastic biographies composed in Georgian during the eleventh century. The text in question refers to pagan Bulgars, but strongly suggests that their cult site had been in use since antiquity. I quote from the Latin translation of the text:

> There is among the villages of the Holy Mountain a certain village called Livadia, whose site is somewhat back from the sea in an empty desert between terrible mountain saddles, where in my opinion none of the holy men [of Athos] ever lived. The Bulgars called Slavs settled there long ago—men who are stupid and brutelike. . . . In this village, from the earliest times until our own age, there survived an effigy made of marble (*ex marmore*), the figure of a woman. This the stupid men worshipped, saying: "Rain and all good things come from it. . . ." George was moved by mercy, but bore their destructive habit badly when he saw those men, the worshippers of the idol, when they went up to it in such great impiety. Once, when he set out for Constantinople and passed through the said village, some men approached him and said: "If you wish to prosper in all your affairs, ask the goddess that she would help you with the emperor." The holy man said: "Oh, really! Go and show her to me. For such

> good news I thank you much!" And so the men led the holy man to their ridiculous and lifeless goddess, at which he gazed and told them: "Let me go away alone and consider her." At dawn on the next day he ordered an iron hammer and set out, himself the old man with the *oikonomos* and two other companions. When he approached the place he drew the sign of the cross in front of him and began to recite the gospel according to John: "In the beginning was the Word" and the rest. Those men said to him: "Woe to you! You contemplate your own death." The old man smiled, and like a strong warrior, armed with the cross of Christ, he rushed quickly at the effigy and began to smash it with the hammer and broke it into little pieces.[124]

The amusing nature of this text should not distract us from the basic issues which it raises. Athos had been a monastic enclave for some 50–100 years by the time of this incident, since ca. 964, yet a pagan cult center lay within the perimeter of the Holy Mountain.[125] It was prior to this a rough, rocky place of habitation to perhaps a small number of heremitic ascetics. Its Bulgaro-Slav rural population was certainly isolated from developments in the Bulgar Kingdom, of which the Christianization began in 864 with the baptism of Boris I (852–89). In the end it was a Georgian, not a Greek, who went up into the crags and peaks to smash the idol. Perhaps the Georgians were better mountaineers than the Greeks. Perhaps, as a well traveled Iberian, George knew something of the Bulgar dialect, which the Greeks ignored.[126] It is conceivable, as well, that the Greeks simply lived in accommodation with the pagans, because such practices still existed in the Greek countryside and were generally tolerated. There are, for the present, no firm answers to these questions.

The action of George the Hagiorite emphasizes once again the importance of the role of monks in eliminating pagan cult centers. It took a man of conviction to brave high mountains in order to perform such tasks, and few had such determination even among the monks. The effigy of the goddess was of great antiquity. Cut from marble, it had stood there "since the earliest times."[127] It is to be doubted that there could have been a mistake about the antiquity of the statue. There is no record, so far as I know, of middle Byzantine marble statuary in Greece. Many ancient statues stood in the public squares of Byzantine towns, and the pedimental sculptures of some pagan temples still stood in place.[128] Although direct proof of continuity of cult is lacking at Livadia, it is a plausible hypothesis that the Bulgars took over this cult from the Greeks. Since the Bulgars did not settle in the Balkan peninsula in great numbers until after 679,[129] we should infer that the Greek cult persisted until at least the end of the seventh century, but probably longer, inasmuch as the Bulgar settlement of the southern fringes of the Balkans took considerably longer, probably until the ninth or tenth century.[130]

The foregoing analysis suggests that the monks who Christianized the countryside in the fifth and sixth centuries found the rural ethos intractable in some localities. The process was itself a protracted one which began with the foundation of small churches, chapels, and monasteries, and advanced by the reorganization of the agricultural communities' cultural life. This was achieved not so much by the eradication of the old practices as by the Christianization of cultural forms. The barriers to this were in great part cultural and linguistic, in part economic. Catechists who understood the rustic ethos were always in demand. John of Ephesus's importation of Syrians to western Asia Minor is striking proof of a manpower shortage in this sphere. The sixth century was marked by the considerable infusion of men and money into the Mediterranean hinterlands.[131] This trend must be regarded as an important conditioning factor in the transformation of the old cults, but not in any case the determining one. The hagiographic texts suggest that the geniality and forbearance of the monastic catechists often carried decisive weight in this process of transition.

Notes

* This article is the revised text of a paper delivered in the Modern Greek Studies Panel at the Conference of the American Philological Association, Cincinnati, 30 December 1983.

1 This problem is barely alluded to in Johannes Geffcken, *The Last Days of Greco-Roman Paganism* (trans. Sabine MacCormack; New York: Elsevier North-Holland, 1978), the only thoroughgoing study of the decline of Hellenic paganism.

2 The tendency is to rehabilitate hagiographic texts as sources. See, e.g., Stephen Mitchell, "The Life of Saint Theodotus of Ancyra," *Anatolian Studies* 32 (1982) 92–113. For the use of hagiography to reconstruct rural social and economic life, see Frank R. Trombley, "Monastic Foundations in Sixth-century Anatolia and Their Role in the Social and Economic Life of the Countryside," *GOTR* 30 (1985) 45–59.

3 Paul van den Ven, ed., *La Vie ancienne de S. Syméon stylite le jeune* (Brussels: Societé des Bollandistes, 1962). Some examples: a pagan from the village of Apate near Antioch whom Symeon urged to reject Aphrodite and all idols (1. 130–31); pagan shepherds in the countryside (1. 163); the pagan village Poulion which had a sacred grove (1. 166); a rural wedding at a pagan village (1. 168–69); and dangers popularly attributed to "ancient" (and presumably pagan) tombs at the village of Kalinea (1. 201).

4 Roger Rémondon, "L'Égypte et la suprème résistance au Christianisme (V^e^–VIIe siècles)," *Bulletin de l'Institut Français d'Archéologie, Cairo* 51 (1952) 63–78.

5 *CJ* I 11.10.3 in P. Krueger, ed., *Corpus Iuris Civilis* (Berlin: Weidmann, 1929) 2. 64.

6 *CJ* I 11.10.5.

7 Procopius *Wars* I 17.11–12.

8 Strabo 12.3.32.

9 John of Ephesus, *Historic Ecclesiastica; Pars Tertia* (= *Hist. Eccl.*; CSCO 105, 106; Paris, 1934–35).

10 Ibid., 2.45.
11 Ibid., 3.36.
12 E. Honigmann, "Geographica: L'histoire ecclésiastique de Jean d'Ephèse," *Byzantion* 14 (1939) 620–21.
13 John of Ephesus *Hist. Eccl.* 3.36.
14 *CT* 16.10.25 in T. Mommsen, ed., *Theodosiani Libri XVI cum Constitutionibus Sirmondianis* (Berlin: Weidmann, 1905) 905. Cf. Garth Fowden, "Bishops and Temples in the Eastern Roman Empire A.D. 320–435," *JTS* n.s. 29 (1978) 53ff.
15 John of Ephesus *Hist. Eccl.* 3.36.
16 William M. Ramsay, "The Orthodox Church in the Byzantine Empire," idem, *Luke the Physician and Other Studies* (London: Hodder & Stoughton, 1908) 153.
17 Henri Grégoire, *Recueil des inscriptions grecques chrétiens d'Asie mineure* (Paris: Laroux, 1922) 4.
18 Michael Rostovtzeff, *Studien zur Geschichte des römischen Kolonates* (Berlin/Leipzig: Teubner, 1910) 287–88 and 288 n. 1.
19 There is an urgent need to update the list of converted temples given in Friedrich Deichmann's article, "Frühchristliche Kirchen in antiken Heiligtümern," *Jahrbuch des Deutschen Archäologischen Instituts* 54 (1939) 105–36.
20 Cf. the cautious approach of I. Engelhardt, *Mission und Politik in Byzanz* (Munich: Institut für Byzantinstik und Neugriechische Philologie der Universität, 1974) 12–22a.
21 John of Ephesus, "Lives of the Eastern Saints," *Patrologia Orientalis* 17 (1923) 1–307; 18 (1924) 511–698; 19 (1926) 152–285. This series hereinafter cited as *PatOr*.
22 John of Ephesus *PatOr* 18. 681.
23 Ibid.
24 Ibid., 680–61.
25 Some statistical data are forthcoming for the sizes of villages in sixth-century Lycia in the life of Nicholas of Hagia Sion (BHG 1347): *Hagios Nikolaos: Der heilige Nikolaos in der griechischen Kirche* 1 (Leipzig: Teubner, 1913) 1–55. The work force of the village of Arneae (*εἰς ὅλην τὴν κόμην*) which assisted stonemasons in quarrying numbered no less than 75 (ibid., 33, lines 12–14). Assuming the ratio of the work force and total population of the village to be about 1 to 3 1/2 (allowing for infant mortality, periodic outbreaks of the bubonic plague, etc.), one gets a figure of 262 persons.
26 The Metaphrastean recension of a sixth-century life Abram the Solitary suggests this figure. The village of Taenia near Lampsacus is characterized as "a large and populous village" (*κώμη . . . μεγάλη καὶ πολυάνθρωπος*) PG 115, 52A. The hagiographer indicates that a large number of the villagers was converted, about 1000 persons (*περί που χιλίους τὸν ἀριθμὸν ὑπάρχοντας*), ibid., 60A. For the date see Rochow, "Religiöse Strömungen," 239.
27 See the rather dated observations of William M. Ramsay, "The Permanence of Religion at the Holy Places in Western Asia," in idem, *Pauline and Other Studies in Early Christian History* (3d ed.; London: Hodder & Stoughton, 1906) 163–88.
28 John of Ephesus *Hist. Eccl.* 2.44.
29 Kashish settled on Chios no later than 553, and crossed over shortly thereafter to assist John in Asia; *PatOr* 19. 162 n. 1 and 163.
30 *PatOr* 18. 646.
31 Ibid., 650.
32 This is clearly implied in John of Ephesus *PatOr* 18. 659. See below, n. 125.
33 F. Nau, "Analyse de la second partie inédite de l'Histoire ecclésiastique de Jean d'Asie," *Revue de l'Orient Chrétien* 2 (1897) 482.

34 Ἰουστινιανοῦ αὐτοκράτορος [το]ῦ φιλοκτίστου. Inscr. no. 1: Ihor Ševčenko, "The Early Period of the Sinai Monastery in Light of Its Inscriptions," *Dumbarton Oaks Papers* 20 (1966) 262.
35 John of Ephesus *PatOr* 19. 200–203. Jones, *LRE* 567–70.
36 John of Ephesus *PatOr* 19. 204.
37 For architectural examples of a rural monastic basilica (ante 462) and a small three-apsed basilica (Justinianic or earlier) possibly built within a temple enclosure, see, Arthur C. Headlam, *Ecclesiastical Sites in Isauria (Cilicia Trachea)* (London: Macmillan, 1893).
38 Ibid. Building materials were at times reused from abandoned temples.
39 See n. 33.
40 John of Ephesus, *PatOr* 18. 659.
41 Stephen McKenna, *Paganism and Pagan Survivals in Spain up to the Fall of the Visigothic Kingdom* (Washington, DC: Catholic University of America Press, 1938) 104 and 129.
42 Callinicus of Rufinianae, *De Vita S. Hypatii Liber* [BHG 760] (Seminarii Philologorum Bonnensis Sodales; Leipzig: Teubner, 1895) 8.
43 Geffcken, *Greco-Roman Paganism*, 170.
44 *Hagios Nikolaos* (ed. Anrich), 13–15.
45 Louis Robert, "Villes et monnaies de Lycie," *Hellenica* 10 (1955) 197–99.
46 *Vie de Théodore de Sykéôn* (trans. and ed. A.-J. Festugière; Brussels: Societé des Bollandistes, 1970) 1. 13–14. Cf. Festugière's note, ibid., 2. 179.
47 "Passio S. Symphoriani Martyris," *Acta Primorum Martyrum*, (ed., T. Ruinart; Amsterdam: Wetsten, 1713) 82. Symphorianus lived in the town of Augustodunum during the reign of Aurelian (270–275).
48 *Vie de Syméon*, 166. See note 3 above.
49 *Vita S. Hypatii*, 90–91. Cf. the condemnation of angel-worship by the Thirty-fifth Canon of the Synod of Laodicea (saec. IV): "Christians are forbidden to abide in the church of God, and depart, and summon angels, and make assemblies. If anyone is found in this secret idolatry, let him be anathema." G. A. Rhalles and W. Potles, *Syntagma tōn theiōn kai hierōn kanonōn* (Athens: Chartophylakos, 1853) 3. 201.
50 Cf. John Moschus, *Pratum Spirituale*, PG 87. 2851–3112, passim, for frequent references.
51 See note 38 above.
52 *CT* XVI.10. For a detailed commentary, see, *The Theodosian Code and Novels and the Sirmondian Constitutions* (trans., C. Pharr *et al.*; Princeton, 1952) 472–76.
53 Books of this genre were still common in the sixth-century cities. E.g., the pagan trials conducted by the imperial judge Amantius at Antioch ca. 554–58 turned up books, idols, and service vessels; *Vie de Syméon* 1. 143.
54 The four deacons Abraham, Kyriakos, Barhadbshabba, and Sergios—more typically of the lower cleric ranks—were, respectively, a Syrian, a Greek or Armenian from Maiferkat-Martyropolis, an Aramaeo-Persian, and an Aramean from the village of Ar'a Rabtha in Ingilene; *PatOr* 18. 658–59.
55 For a recent summary of the hellenization of Phrygia, see Speros Vryonis, *The Decline of Medieval Hellenism in Asia Minor and the Process of Islamization from the Eleventh through Fifteenth Century* (Berkeley/Los Angeles: University of California Press, 1971) 45–49.
56 John of Ephesus relates that a certain Elijah and Theodore began their careers as traders operating between Sasanid Persia and their hometown Amida, and later settled in Melitene to practice eleemosynarian activities. In all these places

the *koinē* was Greek or Syriac (*PatOr* 18. 576–79). Nothing is in fact known about the linguistic skills of John of Ephesus's catechists named in n. 54 above. Their piety must in any case have exceeded their knowledge of the local *koinē*.

57 *Vita S. Hypatii*, 8.

58 E. Kirsten, "Artemis von Ephesos und Eleuthera von Myra mit Seitblick auf St. Nicolaus und auf Commagene," in S. Sahin *et al.*, eds., *Studien zur Religion und Kultur Kleinasiens: Festschrift für Karl Dörner* (Leiden: Brill, 1978) 465.

59 Anrich, *Hagios Nikolaos*, 4, lines 2–3 and p. 7.

60 R. M. Harrison, "Churches and Chapels of Central Lycia," *Anatolian Studies* 13 (1963) 117–51.

61 Ibid., 148–51.

62 Anrich, *Hagios Nikolaos*, 16–17.

63 A temple complex built at a spring is attested for Laodikea Kombusta (present-day Ladik) in Phrygia. The spring or ἁγιασμός was channeled into a rectangular cement tank. The shrine was subsequently converted into a Christian building, probably a church. A fourth-century inscription records the extensive building program of a certain bishop Eugenius.

64 Anrich, *Hagios Nikolaos*, 17, line 2.

65 Anrich suggests a possible sequel by quoting a different text, ibid., 17–18 n. 2.

66 Ibid., 19, lines 7–9ff.

67 Ibid., 20, lines 3–4.

68 Ibid., 33, lines 7–8.

69 *CJ* I 11.9.4.

70 Anrich, *Hagios Nikolaos*, 42–45.

71 Ibid., 55–56.

72 Ibid., 55, lines 16–18.

73 Speros Vryonis, "Religious Changes and Patterns in the Balkans, 14th–16th Centuries," in H. Birnbaum and S. Vryonis, eds., *Aspects of the Balkans* (The Hague/Paris: Mouton, 1972) 174.

74 See above, n. 46. Cf. Trombley, "Monastic Foundations," 45–51.

75 Peter Brown, "The Rise and Function of the Holy Man in Late Antiquity," *JRomS* 61 (1971) 80–101.

76 Festugière, *Vie de Théodore*, 1. 34. All citations hereinafter are from the first volume of this work.

77 M. Lequien, *Oriens Christianus* (Paris, 1740) 1. 485–86. The relevance of the life of Theodore to questions of ecclesiastical land management has been little more than noted in passing. See Jones, *LRE*, 903, 916; G. E. M. de Ste. Croix, *The Class Struggle in the Ancient Greek World* (Cornell: Cornell University Press, 1981) 225–26, 496.

78 Cf. the Anatolian superstition about evil spirits which manifested themselves as "black dogs" (Festugière, *Vie de Théodore*, 85, 126).

79 Ibid., 47–48.

80 Ibid., 45.

81 Martin P. Nilsson, *Geschichte der griechischen Religion* (Munich: Beck, 1967) 1. 113–14.

82 Festugière, *Vie de Théodore*, 40–41. See also 46, 111, and 113.

83 Still useful is the work of Max Cary, *The Geographic Background of Greek and Roman History* (Oxford, 1949).

84 Festugière, *Vie de Théodore*, 12. The ritual was performed before the apse of a rural chapel. When Theodore made the pilgrimage to Jerusalem, it was the Galatians in his entourage who asserted his capacity to summon a rain-bearing cloud from the west (44).

85 See below, notes 96 and 97.
86 Festugière, *Vie de Théodore*, 43.
87 *Vita S. Abramii*, PG 115. 44B–77A.
88 Ibid., 52A.
89 Ibid., 56A.
90 Ibid., 52B.
91 Ibid., 60A.
92 Ibid.
93 A dedicatory inscription of Smetchem the protostolist stands in the temple of Isis at Philae, bearing the date 20 December 452 CE. Also present is the inscription of Damonikos, Count of the *limes* of the Thebaid, who repaired the wall at Philae (dated 11–12 December 449 or 468). The latter inscription mentions the bishop Abba Daniel, who was undoubtedly the prelate of the place, which was an episcopal see as early as 362 (Le Quien, *Oriens Christianus* 2. 613–14).
94 *Vita S. Abramii*, 60D.
95 For the text of the Canons, see: Rhalles and Potles, *Syntagma* (Athens, 1852) 2. 295–554.
96 Rhalles and Potles, *Syntagma*, 2. 442–43.
97 Ps. Justin, *Quaestiones et Responsiones ad Orthodoxos*, PG 6. 1277C–D.
98 Theophanes the Confessor, *Chronographia* (ed. C. de Boor; Leipzig: Teubner, 1883) 1. 224.
99 See note 96 for citation. For some examples of amulets, see: Campbell Bonner, "Two Studies in Syncretistic Amulets," *Proceedings of the American Philosophical Society* 85 (1942) 466–71.
100 Festugière, *Vie de Théodore*, 113.
101 Kosmas of Jerusalem, *Scholia in Gregorii Nazianzeni Carmina*, PG 38. 502.
102 Theophanes, *Chronographia*, 390–91. Bury conjectures that the *magos* in question here was one of the hekatontarchs or centurions mentioned in the Sixty-first Canon of the Quinisextum. Jones, *LRE* 2 (1889) 398. For this form of divination, see, Eusebius *Hist. eccl.* 8.14.5.
103 The most convenient summary of the Arab raids is still E. W. Brooks, "The Successors of Heraclius to 717," *Cambridge Medieval History* (1913) 2. 391–417. Cf. the translations of al Tabari and other early Arabic texts in idem, "The Arabs in Asia Minor (641–750), from Arabic Sources," *JHS* 8 (1898) 182ff.
104 *Vita S. Ioannicii, ActaSS, Nov. IV*, 395a–396c. For the development of ascetic practices among pagan holy men, hermitism, pilgrimage, and their movement to the country-side in the fifth century and after, see Geffcken, *Greco-Roman Paganism*, 240–41. The Gourias incident fits this typology.
105 *Vita S. Pauli Iunioris in Monte Latro* (BHG 1474) *AnBoll* 11 (1892) 53–54.
106 Hermann Usener, "Übersehenes," *KS* 4 (Leipzig/Berlin: Teubner, 1913) 198.
107 See above, nn. 16, 27.
108 *Vita S. Pauli Iunioris*, 55. At other times crosses were cut on temple walls or cult effigies. Cf. the inscription at Philae: "The Cross + conquered. May it always conquer! +++" (Bernand, *Inscriptions de Philae*, no. 201, pp. 256–67).
109 Athanasia housed and supported monks at Aegina (ante ca. 860), and eventually established a monastery for women (*ActaSS, Aug. III*, p. 170d–e [BHG 180]).
110 This problem still awaits definitive study.
111 Rochow, "Religiöse Strömungen," 231–42; idem, "Die Heidenprozesse unter den Kaisern Tiberios II Konstantinos und Maurikios," in F. Winckelmann, ed., *Studien zum 7. Jahrhundert in Byzanz* (Berlin: Akademie-Verlag, 1976) 120–30.
112 The emir ʿIyadh ibn Ghamn accepted separate capitulations from the Christian and pagan (*al-Harnānīyah*) factions of Ḥarrān. Al-Balādhurī, *The Origins of the*

Islamic State . . . The Kitāb Futūḥ al-Buldān (New York: Columbia University Press, 1916) 272–73.

113 Ibid., 241–42.

114 I have myself visited the site and viewed the objects in the Lykosoura Museum, including coin finds from the reign of Tiberius Constantine (578–82). The erection of a chapel (εὐκτήριον) and staffing it with a *prosmonarios* is attested at the sacred spring of Khonai. Christian and pagan alike continued to frequent the site. A converted pagan erected the structure. This aspect of the story appears to be accurate, despite other mythological elements found in this text. F. Nau, "Le miracle de Saint Michel à Colosses," *PatOr* 4. 542–62 (BHG 1282).

115 *Ecloga Leonis et Constantini cum Appendice*, Appendix 4.20 (ed. A. C. Monferratus; Athens: Fratrum Perri, 1889) 66–67.

116 Constantine Porphyrogenitus, *De administrando imperio* (ed. G. Moravcsik; trans. R. Jenkins; Washington, DC: Dumbarton Oaks, 1967) 236.

117 This thesis has never been put forward. Cf. A. Bon, *Le Peloponnèse jusqu'au 1204* (Paris: Presses Universitaires de France, 1951). It is consistent with the toleration shown the neo-Manichaean Paulician sect in Phrygia and Lycaonia, and later in Armenia, down to the end of the reign of Nicephorus I (803–11).

118 *Iosephi Genesii Regum Libri Quattuor* (ed. A. Lesmueller-Werner and I. Thun; Berlin: De Gruyter, 1978) 82–83.

119 *Vita Niconis* in S. P. Lambros, ed., *Neos Hellēnomnēmōn* 3 (1906) 131–222, 256 (BHG 1366).

120 The function of the *periodeutes* is set forth in the Fifty-seventh Canon of the Council of Laodicea (saec. IV). Cf. the glosses of Balsamon *et al.* in Rhalles and Potles, *Syntagma* 3 (Athens, 1853) 222–24. It is uncertain whether Nikon held this rank officially.

121 D. Pallas, *Les monuments paléochrétiens de Grèce découverts de 1951 à 1973* (Rome: Pontificio Istituto di archeologia Cristiana, 1977) 194–95.

122 *Vita Niconis*, 161.

123 Bon, *Le Peloponnèse byzantin*, 69–70.

124 For a Latin translation of the Georgian text see P. Peeters, "Histoires monastiques georgiennes," *AnBoll* 36/37 (1917–19) 104–5.

125 The earliest Athonite chrysobulls date from ca. 964 in the reign of Nicephorus II Phocas (963–69), and refer to the Lavra of St. Athanasius. Franz Dölger, *Regesten der Kaiserurkunden des oströmischen Reiches von 565 1453* (Munich/ Berlin: Oldenbourg, 1924) 1. 90–91, 95 (Tzimisces). The Lavra of the Georgians at Athos was not founded until after the death of George the Hagiorite. Peeters, "Histoires monastiques," 71–72.

126 Bulgars settled in the vicinity of Hierissos between 913–27 according to an Athonite document. Cf. the discussion of the scholarship in Rochow, "Religiöse Strömungen," 250 n. 2.

127 Franz Dölger has analyzed this text as evidence for a supposed Slavic or proto-Bulgar cult (ibid.). To my mind, this misses the point.

128 Among the marble objects found at Athos thus far are columns, sarcophagi, funerary steles, and a statue of Attis of Roman date, the last-named having been observed in 1914 in the Vatopedi Library by Charles Avezou (ibid., 39–40). See the *Parastaseis syntomoi chronikai* in T. Praeger, ed., *Scriptores Originum Constantinopolis* (Leipzig: Teubner, 1901), which mentions many statues of pagan gods in Constantinople. The origin of these spolia is not always given. Some examples are a Zeus preserved in the Hippodrome (71, lines 7–9) and a Perseus and Andromeda in the Constantiana baths (72, lines 13–15). A statue (στήλη) of Artemis also stood in the Hippodrome (70, lines 11–12),

as well as idols (εἴδωλα) taken from Rome (59, lines 14–16). The survival of statuary in provincial towns is less well attested.

129 Theophanes, *Chronographia*, 356, lines 18–19.

130 See above, n. 126.

131 Trombley, "Monastic Foundations," 58–59. Cf. the general observations of Oswyn Murray, review article, "Ramsay MacMullen, *Enemies of the Roman Order*," *JRomS* 59 (1969) 264–65.

Part 5

CONSOLIDATION ON FIVE CONTINENTS

18

RURAL PEOPLE, THE CHURCH IN KONGO AND THE AFROAMERICAN DIASPORA (1491–1750)

John K. Thornton

Source: Klaus Koschorke (ed.), *Transcontinental Links in the History of Non-Western Christianity*, vol. 6, Wiesbaden: Harrassowitz Verlag, 2002, pp. 33–44.

In a letter addressed to the Governor General of Angola on July 6, 1803, the king of Kongo wrote: "By His infinite mercy and the grace of God, I the King of Congo Dom Garcia Fifth, Catholic King . . ." a rather standard set of formulae in use in Kongo for over three centuries.[1] In announcing himself as a Catholic King Garcia was announcing once again what has always been a controversial issue for students of African history, that is, to what extent was Kongo really a Christian country. Many scholars have argued that Christianity was taken on as a political ploy, designed to win friends in Europe and influence trade. Anne Hilton, one of the foremost of these scholars frequently contends that political issues were more on the agenda than real religious change in her influential history of Kongo.[2] Against this, Richard Gray has argued that Christianity took real religious root and became an undeniable background to Kongolese thought.[3]

By far the most common approach to Christianity in Kongo is to argue that it was essentially a royal cult. Both David Birmingham,[4] and Anne Hilton have argued that Christianity hardly took hold in rural areas. The lack of Christianity in rural areas was something of a secret that the Kongo elite tried to guard against outside knowledge. When Capuchin missionaries came to Kongo after 1645 they discovered the rural religious life that put a strain on their relations with the court.[5]

Surprisingly, one of the strongest supports for some sort of Christian identity among the rural people of Kongo comes from the Diaspora. There it is revealed that common people in Kongo did have a remarkable sense of a Christian identity, and not just the elite, for they were rarely enslaved and transported. In 1754, priests in Brazil were summoned to learn that a certain Pedro Congo, a slave unlikely to be of elite origin, was conducting some sort of religious services in a "synagogue". Upon questioning, Pedro revealed that he had been teaching "Christian doctrine" and that the people who had come to learn were slaves from "Mina" or the Slave Coast.[6] At about the same time, Moravian missionaries in Saint John (Virgin Islands) noted that Kongolese slaves greeted all newly arrived slaves from the slave ships, and gave them a sort of "country baptism" by dipping their fingers in water and then sprinkling the person to be baptized in the face, then making the sign of the cross three times, and singing in their language, then putting salt both in their mouth and on their heads, which he believed they had learned from priests or other black people in their own country. Then they gave the newly baptized five or six blows, for the sins they had committed in Guinea and from that point forward they watched out for them as a sort of spiritual protector.[7] A number of other scattered reports from priests and other observers across the Americas reveal that Kongolese in America were proud of being Christians, as they were in Africa. They were even prepared to serve as informal missionaries to spread that Faith to slaves of other nations.[8]

In fact, determining if rural Kongolese were "truly Christian" is a matter of considerable theological significance and weight. It requires a definition of Christianity that is non-sectarian yet objective. In today's world, for example, some in mainstream churches in the United States have serious doubts about the true Christianity of Jehovah's Witnesses, or the Church of Jesus Christ of Latter Day Saints. Many evangelical Christians in the United States argue without blinking that the Catholic Church is not Christian. The problem is more compounded in Africa, where one might debate, in today's world, the Christian sincerity of many independent churches in central and southern Africa.

What are the core doctrines of Christianity, without which one may not be considered Christian, even if one professes to be? How does one determine if they are being met in a particular society at a particular time? How much does sin equal apostasy – for example, does the keeping of multiple wives equal sinful behavior or does it mark the polygamist as a non-Christian, even though in Kongo, typically only one wife would actually be married and the others might be held simply as "concubines", a practice common enough in Europe at the time.

Often the standard in Kongo seems to be the degree to which the pre-existing religious apparatus was overthrown and replaced by one from Europe.[9] One might describe this as a missionary goal, and especially one framed in the colonial period. Even missionaries were not always inclined to accept it. The Jesuit Mateus Cardoso went so far in 1624 as to maintain that "originally they did not worship idols, nor temples where they adored and venerated them, they only knew God, and they adored him as the author of all good, who they call Zambianpungo . . ."[10] Under these circumstances, exactly what parts of the pre-existing Kongolese religion needed overthrowing, and which did not? In this period the Church itself often wondered about these matters, in both China and India there were radical compromises with pre-existing traditions.

Scholarship has tended to be very priest-centered in its appreciation of religious life. Christianity, in this view, could not exist independent of the clergy, and if the clergy were not providing constant supervision and correction everywhere, the country would soon lapse back into its pre-existing situation.[11] Such a viewpoint is understandable for Catholic interpretations, for without the sacraments, which could only be given by priests, one could not be saved. Even here, however, a person might be Christian in belief and suffer from a lack of clergy, as for example, the Irish did for long periods, and even the Portuguese in the first years after the restoration of 1640. Priests, recognizing the good will that people showed the religion, even if their practice did not meet standards, tended to put the blame on lack of instruction, or in other words, lack of sufficient regular priests. Capuchins, upon their arrival in Kongo, presented the lack of clergy as the most charitable explanation for what they felt was a lack of Christianity on the part of the bulk of the Kongolese population. While this is unashamedly a plea for more clergy and an expanded role for them, it also assumes that only under clerical direction could religious life develop. Beyond that, it is a sectarian view, not only of Catholics, but specifically of clergy. Historians of religion should recognize this and examine religious life more impartially.

A great deal of what we know about Kongo's religious life was written by regular clergy, like the Capuchins. They were not the only people to write of Kongolese Christianity, of course, but they immersed themselves in the religious life of the country and understanding or changing it was one of their primary goals. Prior to 1645, clerical visitors mentioned rural life and Christianity only in passing, while the Capuchins, banned by circumstances and rivalries with the secular clergy to the rural areas, could describe it in full detail. Scholars have tended to take the writing of the regulars more or less as given and assume that they are unbiased reflections of reality.

In fact, regular clergy were not without bias on this issue. Quite apart from purely theological issues, as cited above, regular clergy were regularly seeking to expand their own role in the country, and often to do so at the expense of established secular clergy.[12] In such contests, the regulars wrote and left behind much more than the seculars did, and the result is that modern historians have been left with their virtually uncontested viewpoint. Thus the harsh denunciations of irregular life that Capuchins wrote concerning Kongo's secular clergy shortly after they arrived in the country, need to be read with at least some consideration of these issues. Regulars had an interest from time to time in proclaiming the religion of the country defective, and thus continuing their role in it. Citing violations of Christian custom would be one way to assure their European patrons that their presence was still needed, even urgently.

Likewise, regular clergy often had an aggressive attitude towards civil authorities, quick to perceive any thwarting of their ambitions for complete control of their sphere of interest. When Diogo I (1545–1561) refused to allow Jesuit priests the freedom they wished to control religious life in Kongo, they were quick to denounce him, not just as a political meddler in ecclesiastical affairs, but as an apostate.[13] Capuchin accounts of Garcia II, who occasionally accused them of acting as Spanish spies, or of aiding members of the court who were his enemies, was subject to similar denunciations.[14]

This paper will seek to understand the growth and development of rural Christianity in Kongo, understanding its relationship to that of the capital and of the foreign missionaries, and taking as its starting point the remarkable facts alluded to above. Somehow, Kongolese in rural districts managed to adopt a self-identification as Catholics, including knowing at least the form of the sacrament of baptism, and were prepared to carry this to foreign lands when fate made them slaves.

From the very beginning the kings of Kongo sought to evangelize the rural areas as well as the rich and powerful. The four priests who came in 1491, having finished baptizing the people of the court went, as they were ordered, to "the unknown places, some here and some there, diligently seeking to reveal to the whole world our faith and the name of Christ." In this task they would be assisted by whatever Kongolese were already knowledgeable of the Faith.[15] This pattern of lay evangelization supplementing whatever could be done by the clergy was to the standard pattern for the conversion and education of the rural people in Christianity.

During the reign of the first Christian king, João I Nzinga Nkuwu, the ecclesiastical organization was haphazard, and it was not until the reign of his son and successor, Afonso I (1509–1542) that the Church can be said to have been truly established in Kongo. Afonso's first task was to understand the religion theologically, and to create a Kongo centered understanding of the new Faith. This task, which occupied many years, employed Afonso, a number of Portuguese priests, and an intellectual group of Kongolese elites working and studying in both Kongo and Portugal to achieve.[16] In addition to the theological issues, Afonso also provided the Church with an institutional infrastructure, royal financing and legal presence everywhere in the country. If the goal of this project was to evangelize the elite, it was spectacularly successful, for the elite was firmly attached to Christianity from that point onward.

A simple proof comes from a legal inquest conducted a few years after Afonso's death. Afonso's son, and successor Pedro I (1542–1545) was overthrown in a coup by his grandson Diogo I, and the unfortunate Pedro took sanctuary in a church in Mbanza Kongo. Remarkably enough, Diogo honored the right of sanctuary and did not immediately arrest his dangerous predecessor, who in fact used the asylum to plot to overthrow his rival again. In their plots, Pedro and his associates swore Christian oaths, and sought to obtain Papal support for their plans. Diogo for his part tried to get other nobles to swear similar oaths of support for him and his family and against the supporters of Pedro.[17] None of these actions were simply show to win European favor, for they were entirely domestic affairs, and they reflect the level of commitment of the elite to Christianity by the middle of the 16th century.

Afonso also laid plans for the evangelization of the whole country. In a letter of 1526, for example, Afonso outlined an ambitious plan for building regional churches, and a structure that would require at least 50 priests to carry out.[18] He hoped that his son Henrique, as the first bishop in Kongo, would be able to ordain clergy and that Kongo would become more self-sufficient in this capacity. Unfortunately, that did not come to pass. Henrique, who returned after his ordination as a bishop in 1521 was frequently sick and unable to carry out his functions to the degree his father hoped, and died in 1531.[19] After his death, the epsicopal position[20] was vacant and in 1534 Kongo was placed under the authority of the bishop of São Tomé. Bishops never managed to ordain or provide enough clergy for the full sacramental apparatus of the Catholic Church to be offered by priests. Gaspar Cão, one of the bishops (served from 1556–1565), was pointedly accused of his shortcomings on this score, and his defense revealed that even under the best of circumstances relatively few Kongolese were ordained in the 1550s.[21] This arrangement, and most other ones that followed, even after the elevation of Kongo to an Episcopal see in 1596, did not serve the interest of Kongo developing a formal ecclesiastical structure with a bishop ordaining as many clergy as needed to carry out its functions. A survey of 1600 revealed the presence in the whole of Kongo of some 12 churches, typically located in the major provincial capitals, each with a curate. Such curates would have little power to do more than visit their regions once a year, hardly enough to provide the sort of ratio of priests per capita that would be needed for full control by ordained clergy.[22] Portugal, under whose patronage bishops with control over Kongo fell, never cooperated in the project, used the office for political purposes, and thus thwarted the development of a systematic parochial system with a permanent self-replacing priesthood.[23]

In spite of the absence of this formal structure, it would seem that many of Afonso's plans for evangelization were met. This is strongly supported by the reports of the first Jesuit priests to visit Kongo in 1548. In August 1548, shortly after their arrival at Mbanza Kongo, the country's capital, Jorge Vaz, one of the Jesuits, took a missionary tour in the densely populated valleys that lay just beyond the mountain on which the city was built. He triumphantly reported the performance of 2,700 baptisms in a short period of time. He catechized the adults who had not received any religious instruction, and for this task he had the use of "a local man [*hum homem da terra*] who knows our language" and served as catechist. Since he baptized people of advanced age, and gave them their catechism (all in the space of 23 days), the visit reflects the relatively limited education provided to people even within a few kilometers of the capital, but also the potential for lay catechists to work the region.[24]

The point is more telling when one considers that a few years later, after the Jesuits became involved in the dispute with Diogo over jurisdiction and more mundane political matters, they decided to exact a higher standard for baptism. After this point, in 1555, Jesuits would baptize no one unless they were fully instructed, suggesting that they were no longer comfortable with the level of Christian knowledge in the country, but also that they were finding fault now as much because of the disputes as their sudden discovery of discrepancies.[25]

Afonso had probably been able to carry out his remarkable evangelization of the country with so few clergy through the development of a strong lay organization. In his plan for the church, Afonso already noted the possibility of using lay teachers and catechists to carry out educational functions. This organization must have had better success than the more ambitious one to use clergy. The strength of the lay organization is further demonstrated by the success of "chapel boys" in carrying the Faith beyond the borders of Kongo during the reign of Diogo I. In a memorial written shortly after Diogo's death, Sebastião Souto, a priest in the court, noted that Diogo had sent these chapel boys to a wide variety of countries to the north, south and east of Kongo, winning the first elite converts.[26] While not ordained missionary priests, clearly Diogo had enough faith in them to trust them to spread the Faith, and no doubt they were even more secure in their functions within Kongo.

These chapel boys were drawn from the educated nobility, some would eventually go on to be ordained as the few Kongolese priests, most others would end up in political careers. D. João, a Kongolese priest who met the Carmelites in Mbumbe in 1583, for example, was a nephew of King Alavro II of Kongo, and one of his relatives was the ruler of Nsundi. He had been educated in his youth in Portugal (and hence could speak Portuguese with near native proficiency), and was a priest of the Evangile, no doubt so ordained in Portugal.[27] While João had gone on to be ordained as a priest, a great many others did not, most served as assistants to secular clergy, or simply conducted lessons sponsored by senior relatives who held political positions, or served the various regulars as assistants and catechists whenever they went on missions.

The activities of the lay church are not well documented through most of the later 16th and early 17th centuries, but the results were obvious enough. When Carmelite priests traveled in the rural areas in the 1580s, and then when Capuchins again worked more intensively in these areas after 1645, they found a remarkable knowledge of Christianity. In some areas, priests found people who had not seen a priest in many years, and yet they flocked to the priests, singing hymns. They were surprised to see how many possessed basic knowledge of the rudiments of the faith in spite of their relatively limited contact with the establishment of the church.[28]

The Capuchins, who reported these details, were quick to point out how many "superstitions" the people possessed, and how unorthodox their faith was in particular. This element of their writing has often been taken to show that they revealed a low level of adherence to the Christian faith. Indeed, the "war" that Capuchins waged against traditional *nganga* or priests, overshadows entirely the other notes concerning the positive aspects of their knowledge, evidence that there was a regular aspect of training that was not entirely pre-Christian throughout the country.[29]

If one accepts this distinction of a positive acceptance of Christianity, that is one that values core Christian theological ideas, against a negative acceptance, which is one that rejects existing ideas and practices, then the status of the rural church can look quite different. Allowing that a reasonable positive statement of Christian beliefs might be found in knowing the Apostles' Creed, as it was printed in the Kikongo catechism of 1624, one might be better able to judge the state of Christianity. Although this was not the first catechism for Kongo (there was one printed in 1557, but it is not extant), it probably reflects the basic need for a teaching tool, as well as providing texts and explanations for the prayers that formed the basis for teaching.[30] No doubt oral teaching to a largely illiterate population required memorization of such prayers as well as an explanation.

The teaching of basic prayers such as the Hail Mary and Hail Holy Queen (Salve Regina), as well as the Apostles' Creed undoubtedly formed virtually the whole of the education work of the lay religious network. In this context, a good many priests noted that people could understand the Creed, though in Kongo, as everywhere, there were those who did not. Such a statement affirms the uniqueness of God, the role of Jesus as a savior, and the existence of the Holy Spirit. It does not explicitly prohibit any behavior, for example, polygamy or even the worship of idols. The full catechism does, of course, go into more details, though interestingly enough, because the Kikongo catechism of 1624, the one in use until the last years of the 19th century, was simply a translation a text made from Portuguese, it did not address any of the behaviors that Kongolese did which the formal church disapproved of.

It is interesting and instructive to consider this in contrasting the development of Christianity in Kongo with that of the Kimbundu speaking areas to the south. In Angola, where the Portuguese took over political control, conversion to Christianity was often linked to submission to the Portuguese colonial government. Similarly, the Portuguese tended to keep clergy for their own use, and devoted little time to missionary work. Beyond that they never developed a lay educational community along the lines of Kongo. It is not surprising then, that even in the 18th century, when missionaries were very few, the rural people of Angola were not regarded as being as good Christians as those of Kongo. It is also interesting that the Kimbundu catechism, developed around 1626, but only published in 1642 was written for the population of Angola and does specifically prohibit a number of local religious customs.[31]

It is probably safe to say that for purposes of this population recognizing Jesus' role as savior is central to Christian theology. In Kikongo "savior" was *mukangi*, derived from the verb *kukanga*, meaning to save or rescue.[32] It might be used in the phrase "through the sign of the holy cross God delivers us from our enemies" or *kuna nima a kisinsu kia santa Cruz kutukangila e Nfumu etu Zambi a Mpungu etu kwa ambeni etu*."[33] A related word, *lukangu* was used in the Creed to mean to forgive, as in "the forgiveness of sins" *lukangu lua masumu*.[34] Thus, the concept of savior has as much to do with help at any time as taking one up to Heaven, an important point, since a number of priests complained that Kongolese did not understand the Afterlife in what they thought of as the correct way. In Kongo the dead remained imminent in the areas around their tombs, helping or punishing their descendants as the situation warranted, while in Christian theology of course, the dead went off to other places, remote from this earth and had no influence upon the living. This was something that even the Jesuits of 1548 noted, as well as Capuchins visiting later, and it was probably a fixed element of local belief that never yielded very well to specific Christian teaching.

But this did not interfere with Jesus' role as savior, nor with that of his mother, whose title in Kikongo, *musundi* Maria, did not mean virgin, but rather "excellent one" or "extraordinary one", thus bypassing the theological knot of virgin birth. The Kongolese version of the Nicene Creed only has Jesus "born of the Virgin Mary" (a very straightforward *wawutilu kwa Musundi Maria*, with no special significance), and even where it explains, in the section devoted to explanation of the articles of the Faith, where the Portuguese model holds that Jesus was "born of the Virgin Mary while she remained always a virgin" the Kikongo completely avoids it by writing "*awutilu kwa Musundi Maria, asiidi o yandi mene ya mene Musundi*", which in Kikongo means literally, "he was born of the Excellent Mary, while she remained always an excellent one".[35] Stripped of the mystery of the virgin birth, Mary was nevertheless the object of considerable attention, as mother of Jesus, as an intercessor and protector, much as Jesus himself was.

Viewing these linguistic matters make it clear that some elements that Catholic theologians would hold dear were lacking in the rural conception of Christianity – there was no virgin birth, and salvation was little more than spiritual protection. But at the same time, these people surely did understand that Jesus was born of Mary and did walk the earth at one time. After his death he was resurrected and now serves as a spiritual guide and protector for Kongolese and anyone else who follows his cult. Is this sufficiently divergent from Christianity to be considered outside of Christian thought?

When one considers the long development of Christianity, beginning with the difficult question of the historical Jesus, to the transformation of his teaching by Paul and then through the debates of the early church as described in Irenaeus or the Gnostic gospels, to the merging with Roman and then with Germanic spiritual ideas, who is to say that a further new merger is not as Christian? It is probably true that "world religions" succeed because they blend and shape into local traditions as much as they force people in the areas into which they are carried to change completely their own views. It seems appropriate to use the same criteria in judging the religion of rural Kongo.

It was this unorthodox, yet well understood Christianity that Kongolese brought to the New World, and perhaps, like Pedro Congo or the informal catechists of Saint John's introduced to their fellow slaves in America. Hein Vanhee and Terry Rey, each in different ways, have sought to demonstrate how the role of Kongolese as Christians and as "bush teachers" may have done a great deal to shape the vision of Christianity that developed in post Revolutionary Haiti, when like Kongo, the ordained clergy had abandoned it.[36] The Haitian model is perhaps unique in the Americas, for in other places the hand of slavery or European and European-American dominance channeled whatever informal models developed from the interaction of Kongolese and other Africans into a more orthodox mode. At the same time, the Haitian model provides us with a unique glimpse into what may have gone on for a long time in the rural plantations, urban slums and other places where somehow African slaves merged their own ideas of the Other World with Christianity, perhaps with the help of Kongolese teachers.

Notes

1 Published in *Arquivos de Angola* 2nd series 19, 1962, 56.

2 A. Hilton, *The Kingdom of Kongo* (Oxford 1985); see for example pp. 60–65 dealing with Afonso I. While not entirely ruling out religious sincerity, she clearly casts his adherence to the cult in terms of the political advantages to be gained by it.

3 R. Gray, "Come Vero Principe Catolico: The Capuchins and the Rulers of Soyo in the Late Seventeenth Century" (*Africa* 53, 1983, 39–54).

4 A position taken by D. Birmingham in his review of Kongo Christianity in "Central Africa from Cameroon to the Zambezi," in: R. Gray (Ed.), *The Cambridge History of Africa.* Vol. 4 (Cambridge 1975), 332.

5 Hilton, *Kingdom of Kongo* 184–187.

6 Arquivo Nacional de Torre do Tombo, Inquisição de Lisboa, Processos, no. 16001.

7 C. G. A. Oldendorp, *Historie der caribischen Inseln Sanct Thomas, Sanct Crux und Sanct jan.* Kommentierte Edition des Originalmanuskriptes, Pt. 1, hrsg. von G. Meier/S. Palmié/P. Stein/H. Ulbricht (Dresden 2000), 741–742.

8 Other examples are gathered in J. Thornton, "On the Trail of Voodoo: African Christianity in Africa and the Americas" (*The Americas* 44, 1988, 464–466).

9 This is the standard that Gray uses, and still argues that the people of Soyo at least, and at least in the late 17th century met even this standard.

10 M. CARDOSO, "História do reino do Congo, cap. 3, fol. 3", in: A. BRÁSIO (ED.), *Monumenta Missionaria Africana/África ocidental* Vol. 5 (Ser. II, Lisbon 1969).
11 The most serious and careful approach to this attitude is found in A. HASTINGS, *The Church in Africa, 1450–1950* (Oxford 1994), 79–118.
12 For an exploration of this rivalry with many published documents, see L. JADIN, "Le Clergé séculier et les Capuchins au Congo et d'Angola aux XVIe et XVIIe siècles, conflits de jurisdiction, 1700–1725" (*Bulletin, Institute Historique Belge de Rome* 36, 1964, 185–483).
13 For a detailed study of the role of religious and political rivalries in the creation of our historical sources, see J. THORNTON, "Early Kongo-Portuguese Relations: A New Interpretation" (*History in Africa* 8, 1981, 183–202), for the Jesuit situation, see pp. 195–196.
14 For example, Biblioteca Nacional de Madrid, MS 3533, Antonio de Teruel, "Descripcion Narrativade la misión seráfica de los padres capuchinos en el reyno de Congo," (1664) pp. 122–128; Biblioteca Estense, Modena, MS Italicus 1380, α N.9.7, Giuseppe Monari da Modena, "Viaggio al Congo," (1726) pp. 472–476 (but actually reproducing a chronicle written by the prefect in the mid-17th century, Giacinto Brugiotti da Vetralla).
15 Rui de Pina, Untitled report on Mission to Kongo, 1492, fol. 99vb, reproduced in: C. M. RADULET, *O Cronista Rui de Pina e a "Relação do Reino do Congo".* Manuscrito inédito do "Códice Riccardiano 1910" (Lisbon 1992).
16 For a more detailed study of this project see J. THORNTON, "Perspectives on African Christianity", in: V. HYATT/R. NETTLEFORD (Eds.), *Race, Discourse, and the Origins of the Americas:* A New World View (Washington, DC 1995, 173–176).
17 The inquest, held in 1550, survives in Portugal, where a copy was sent to support the extradition of one of the plotters who had taken refuge in São Tomé, in: A. BRÁSIO (Ed.), *Monumenta Missionaria Africana.* Vol. 2 (Ser I, Lisbon 1953), 248–262.
18 Afonso I to João III, March 18, 1526, in: A. BRÁSIO (Ed.), *Monumenta Missionaria Africana.* Vol. 1 (Ser I, Lisbon 1955), 460–462.
19 For a good biography see F. BONTINCK, "Ndoadididiki Ne-Kinu a Mubemba, premier evêque Congo" (*Revue Africaine de Théologie* 3, 1979, 149–169).
20 Henrique had served as an apostolic vicar, and was technically the bishop not of Kongo, but of the vacant seat of Utica in Muslim occupied North Africa. Since Kongo was not yet an Episcopal see, there was no guarantee of succession.
21 Sentence of Cardinal Henrique in favor of the Bishop of São Tomé, 14 March 1571, in: A. BRÁSIO (Ed.), *Monumenta Missionaria Africana.* Vol. 3 (Ser I, Lisbon 1953), 11–12. 17.
22 Survey of churches and revenues in Congo, 1600, in: A. BRÁSIO (Ed.), *Monumenta Missionaria Africana.* Vol. 5 (Ser I, Lisbon 1955), 4.
23 See J. THORNTON, "The Development of an African Catholic Church in the Kingdom of Kongo, 1491–1750" (*Journal of African History* 25, 1984, 147–167).
24 Jorge Vaz to Simão Rodrigues, August 1, 1548, in: A. BRÁSIO (Ed.), *Monumenta Missionaria Africana.* Vol. 15 (Ser I, Lisbon 1988), 151–152.
25 For fuller details see THORNTON, *African Catholic Church* 149–150.
26 Sebastião Souto to Portugal, c. 1561, in: A. BRÁSIO (Ed.), *Monumenta Missionaria Africana.* Vol. 2 (Ser I, Lisbon 1953), 477–480.
27 Account of Diogo de Santissimo Sacramento, 1548, in: A. BRÁSIO (Ed.), *Monumenta Missionaria Africana.* Vol. 4 (Ser I, Lisbon 1954), 362–363.
28 For more documentation on this aspect of the church, see J. THORNTON, "Demography and History in the Kingdom of Kongo, 1550–1750" (*Journal of African History* 18, 1977, 511–515).

29 Thornton, *African Catholic Church* 157–159.
30 *Doutrina Christãa* (originally published in Lisbon 1569 by Marcos Jorge, with a Kikongo translation in 1624).
31 Gentio de Angola sufficientment instruido (Lisbon 1642).
32 Note that these forms of the verb, containing the infinitive marker *ku-* are 17th century forms, modern Kikongo no longer employs an infinitive marker (though Kimbundu does).
33 *Doutrina Christãa* I, 1. (I have modernized the spelling but not the grammar of the Kikongo sentence, hence the verb uses the archaic *ku-* infinitive marker). The verb *utukangila* means literally "he-us-saves" in which the ending *-ila* is used for action of one person on behalf of another.
34 Doutrina Christãa VI, 1.
35 Doutrina Cristãa VIII, 1.
36 H. Vanhee, "Central African popular Christianity and the making of Haitian Vodou Religion", in: L. M. Heywood (Ed.), *Central Africans and Cultural Transformations in the American Diaspora* (Cambridge 2002, 243–264); T. Rey, "Kongolese Catholic Influences on Haitian Popular Catholicism: A Sociohistorical Exploration", in: L. M. Heywood (Ed.), *Central Africans and Cultural Transformations in the American Diaspora* (Cambridge 2002, 265–288).

19

"THE BEST THUS FAR DISCOVERED"

The Japanese in the letters of Francisco Xavier

Robert Richmond Ellis

Source: *Hispanic Review*, 71(2) (2003), 155–69.

On August 15, 1549, Francisco Xavier, along with two other Spanish Jesuits, three Japanese converts, and two servants, arrived in the harbor of Kagoshima on the Japanese island of Kyūshū. Thus, he launched a brief period of missionary activity that climaxed in 1597 with the crucifixion of six Spanish Franciscans and twenty Japanese Christians, and ended in the early seventeenth century with the expulsion of all foreign missionaries and the closure of Japan to the West. Xavier, revered in western Christendom as the "Apostle of the Indies and Japan," was one of the first European observers of Japanese life.[1] In a series of letters to his co-religionists in India and Europe he recounts his journey to Japan, providing the early modern West with a window onto Marco Polo's fabled Zipangu while documenting for posterity the process through which Europe gradually asserted itself over the non-European world. In fact these letters reveal as much about mid-sixteenth-century Europe, in the throes of religious reformation and imperialist expansion, as about Japan itself. Yet they are also a kind of autobiography in which Xavier not only chronicles his extraordinary experiences but attempts to fashion a personal identity through and in opposition to what in subsequent Western discourse would become the very limit—both geographical and conceptual—of the Orient.

In his letters Xavier balances his discussion of Christianity by presenting the theological questions and doubts raised by his Japanese audiences. However, he denounces Buddhist monasticism with a zealousness exceptional even in a churchman of the Counter Reformation. In his judgment the *bonzes* (Buddhist monks) are avaricious, parasitical, and hypocritical. What is more, they are sexually profligate: some have relations with nuns, who regularly induce abortions, and most are practicing sodomites. Yet even though Xavier inveighs against Japanese religion and morality, he expresses great admiration for the Japanese people as a whole, enthusiastically declaring that they are "la mejor que hasta aguora está descubierta."[2] Xavier claims the Japanese exceed all non-Europeans through their goodness, honor, and politeness, and also because they are a "gemte bramqua" [white people] (letter 96, 277) and as such naturally predisposed to Christian conversion.[3] By defining the Japanese as inherently superior, he implicitly establishes himself, and by extension Europe, as the ultimate arbiter of human worth. But in so doing he also validates indigenous Japanese culture, which for the most part remained intact despite his dreams of conversion and the economic and military designs of the West until well into the nineteenth century.

Xavier was a prodigious traveler, even for his age, but not a prolific writer. Born in 1506 in what was then a Basque-speaking region of Navarre,[4] he journeyed across Europe to Paris, where he studied theology with Iñigo de Loyola; then to Rome to participate in the foundation of the Jesuit order; and finally to Lisbon, to spearhead the Portuguese evangelization of the East Indies. From there, he made his way as a missionary to Africa, India, the Spice Islands, and Japan, reaching the easternmost point of his peregrinations at the Japanese imperial capital of Kyōto. While in Japan, he wrote five letters in which he detailed his experiences and comments on Japanese life. Although the letters were addressed to the Portuguese mission in Goa, India, they were written mostly in Spanish, probably because Xavier's secretary at the time knew only that language.[5] Several more letters dating from before and after Xavier's Japanese sojourn also contain important information about Japan. They were written in either Spanish or Portuguese.[6] A total of 137 letters still remain from Xavier's entire correspondence. This constitutes his literary legacy, though according to Ignacio Elizalde, Xavier possibly composed several poems and dramas.[7] As Elizalde further demonstrates, Xavier wrote in a plain, unadorned Spanish, comparable in its simplicity to the spontaneous style of Teresa de Jesús, albeit even more imperfect than hers because of his long absence from Spain and his constant exposure to other languages (47–48).[8] In contrast to Teresa and other writers within Spain, Xavier influenced Spanish literature not through his own writing but the example he set in life, which became the subject of much Golden Age drama and poetry. Moreover, he may also have influenced traditional Japanese storytelling by having native Japanese minstrels incorporate Christian narratives into their ballads to help in the propagation of Christianity. As Leandro Tormo Sanz and Catalina Villanueva Bilar remark, after the Jesuits arrived in Japan, European elements began appearing in Japanese folklore, most likely as a result of what they regard as a cultural *mestizaje* of native Japanese bards (567–68).

Xavier was assisted in his missionary activities in Japan by a Japanese convert, Angirō (baptized Paulo de Santa Fe), whom he first met in Malacca in December 1547. Angirō had killed a man in Japan and fled with the Portuguese trader Jorge Álvares for the express purpose of joining Xavier and converting to Christianity. Angirō recalls his initial encounter with Xavier in a subsequent letter to Loyola (itself the earliest known text written by a Japanese in a European language):[9] "de la primera vista quedé muy edeficado y deseié de amor de le servir y nunqua dél me apartar" (Izawa 318). Xavier, however, was also edified by Angirō, whose tales of his homeland, coupled with his own personal qualities (Xavier was most impressed by Angirō's intellectual curiosity), instilled in him a yearning to visit Japan. Once there, Angirō was Xavier's linguistic and cultural mediator.[10] Angirō's ability to translate Christian doctrine from Portuguese into Japanese was nevertheless limited. He had only a rudimentary knowledge of Portuguese and, as a member of the samurai class, was unfamiliar with Japanese religious vocabulary and unable to read the Chinese script in which Japanese Buddhist theology was written. His translation of the Catholic catechism was thus flawed, and consequently Xavier often found himself unable to present a coherent Christian message to the Japanese people. As Urs App argues, the Japanese may actually have regarded Xavier, who hailed most recently from India, as the representative of another Buddhist sect rather than an entirely new religion (221). According to App, Angirō depicted Buddhism to Xavier in Christian terms, leading him initially to wonder if at some earlier time Christianity had reached Japan. He likewise portrayed Christianity to the Japanese in Buddhist terms, thereby creating an illusion of religious similarity, even though a conflict of religious ideologies was ultimately inevitable.[11]

Angirō's family and friends quickly converted to Christianity, but during Xavier's nearly two-and-a-half year stay in Kyūshū and western Honshū, the number of converts remained relatively small, and Christian teachings were continually contested. As Xavier explains, many Japanese had difficulty with the concept of God as universal creator, since this led inevitably to the vexed question of evil in the world. Even if God, as Xavier insisted, did not create evil, he created beings capable of evil, and from the Japanese perspective he was at least indirectly responsible not only for sin itself but also for its end result: hell. For many of Xavier's potential converts, the notion of an eternal hell undermined the image of a beneficent God. But more important, it threatened to subvert their cultural identity. Through the prayers of the *bonzes*, the Japanese traditionally believed that the souls of their ancestors could be rescued from hell. In affirming Christian doctrine (and most certainly in an effort to break the power of the *bonzes*), Xavier, like Virgil in Dante's *Inferno*, imparted the bitter lesson that the damned are in hell as a consequence of their own free choices and hence, despite our inclination to pity them, must be irrevocably left behind: "Muytos chorão os mortos . . . Eu lhes digo que nenhum remedio tem" [Many weep for the dead . . . I tell them that there is no remedy) (letter 96, 276).[12] According to the new religion, the living must forget the dead and focus on their freedom to do good in the here and now. What they will gain (in addition to salvation) is a heightened sense of individual worth. But they will also lose something of the past that binds them together as a people. In fact to be "born again" as a Christian in sixteenth-century Japan, with its long-established cult of ancestors, meant to be reborn less Japanese and as such primed for even greater Western incursions than Xavier himself ever imagined.

In attempting to justify Christianity, Xavier does not challenge Buddhism on theological grounds (nor does he distinguish between Buddhist and Shintoist aspects of Japanese religion),[13] but instead attacks the *bonzes.* As he explains, Japanese Buddhist sects all profess five fundamental commandments prohibiting murder, robbery, fornication, lying, and drinking alcohol. The *bonzes*, however, claim that most people are unable to uphold these precepts on a regular basis. They therefore offer to obey them on behalf of the people and through prayer and religious observance expiate their sins (as well as those of the damned in hell), provided, Xavier caustically notes, they receive material and monetary remuneration. Xavier is actually less judgmental about the native religion itself than what he ostensibly perceives as an economic exploitation of the people by the *bonzes*:

> Eles numqua fazem esmola, mas querem que todos lhas fação a eles. Tem abitos, modos e maneiras pera tirar dinheiro das gentes, os quaes deixo de sprever por evitar proluxidade. [They never give alms, but want everyone to give alms to them. They have customs, methods, and ways of squeezing money out of the people, which I shall not enumerate in order to avoid prolixity.] (letter 96, 258)

Xavier implies that the *bonzes* regard hell as if it were purgatory. His charge that they extort money for the remittance of the souls of the damned is nevertheless striking insofar as it echoes, at times almost verbatim, the diatribes of sixteenth-century Protestants against the sale of indulgences.[14] Xavier in fact seems to use contemporary attacks against Catholicism as a means of discrediting Buddhism and validating his own religion in the eyes of the Japanese.

Xavier deplores the *bonzes* even more for what he deems their moral laxity. Whereas Álvares remarks merely in passing and without judgment that they engage in sodomy,[15] Xavier takes their "sin against nature" as a decisive reason that traditional Japanese religion must be discarded.[16] Spaniards during the period of imperialist expansion often imputed the practice of sodomy to alien peoples in an attempt to justify conquest on moral grounds.[17] Xavier, whose aim is conversion rather than conquest, limits the charge to his religious rivals, unaware that they themselves had a tradition of condemning clerical carnality (Faure 209). He thus declares: "Tienen estos bonzos en sus monesterios muchos mininos, hijos de hidalgos, a los quales enseñan a leer y escribir, y con éstos cometen sus maldades" (letter 90, 188). Xavier does not denounce these relationships specifically as pederastic since from his perspective all acts of sodomy are mortal sins and as such equally evil regardless of the age of the participants. Yet as he reveals, homoerotic relations in pre-modern Japan typically crossed generational lines, and Buddhist monasteries were a locus of homoerotic activity. In fact, a whole genre of love tales of monks and their young charges (known as *chigo monogatari* [acolyte stories]) flourished during the fifteenth and sixteenth centuries.

Male homoeroticism was present not only in monastic life but also in the social organization of the samurai.[18] Xavier uses the term *hidalgo* to denote a samurai (a figure he clearly admires, perhaps because of Angirō)[19] since both maintain a rigorous code of honor despite the fact they are often poor. As Xavier observes, samurai never marry below their social class, even if in so doing they might raise their economic status, "de manera que más estiman la honra que las riquezas" (letter 90, 186). What Xavier does not notice, or perhaps ignores as irrelevant to his specific goal of conversion, is that the kind of sexual relations the samurai allow between their sons and the *bonzes* are integral to their own military ethos. During the late sixteenth and early seventeenth centuries, male homoeroticism, which came to be designated in popular Japanese discourse as *shudō* (the way of youths),[20] was increasingly identified with samurai rather than Buddhist monks. As Gregory M. Pflugfelder argues, *shudō* bonds between samurai were thought to foster the skills and values of honorable warriors. Through them, younger samurai developed military prowess and acquired the demeanor and attitude befitting their role, whereas older samurai continually endeavored to prove themselves worthy of emulation. According to Pflugfelder, *shudō* was therefore "believed to have a mutually ennobling effect" (71).

Xavier, in opposition to Japanese custom, uses the Christian conception of sodomy to create a distinction between a good people (including samurai) and a pernicious clergy. He alleges that the Japanese despise the sexual life of the *bonzes* but through force of habit have come to tolerate it: "aunque a todos paresca mal, no to estrañan" (letter 90, 188). The *bonzes* themselves are unmoved by the moral reprobation of the Jesuits: "todo to que [les] dezimos les cae en gracia . . . se ríen y no tienen ninguna vergüença de oyr reprehensiones de pecado tan feo" (letter 90, 188). But the people respond more strongly:

> quamdo hiamos pelas ruas, herão os meninos e outra gemte que nos perseguia, fazemdo escameo de nós, dizemdo: . . . «Estes são os que deffemdem o pecado da sodomia», por ser muito geral amtre eles. [When we went through the streets, children and other people would pursue us, ridiculing us and saying, "these are the ones who prohibit the sin of sodomy," because it is very common among them.] (letter 96, 261)

Sodomy, Xavier insists, is a common practice precisely because of the influence of the *bonzes*:

> Ho povo asy ho faz tomando deles exemplo, dizemdo que, se os bomzos ho fazem tambem ho farão eles. [The people thus do it, taking from them example, saying that if the bonzes do it, they will do it as well.] (letter 96, 268)

Xavier's comments are thus clearly contradictory, unless we are to understand that the "people" (and here he seems actually to overstate the case) regularly engage in practices they simultaneously accept and abhor. What he refuses to acknowledge is that the sexual life of the *bonzes* might mirror, rather than dictate, the mores of the society at large.[21]

This emphasis on sexual irregularity is crucial to Xavier's overall project. When the old religion is replaced by the new, not only will the sin of sodomy disappear but a natural order will be restored in consonance with the Christian doctrine of creation. Sodomy in the theological context of Xavier's writing is sinful because it is a gratuitous act breaking a natural chain of cause and effect that derives from God. In this rigid framework, the notion of God as First Cause is incompatible with any sexual act not specifically intended for reproduction. The Japanese conception of sexuality differs from the European in part, Xavier implies, because they do not believe in a Creator. In their world-view, nature and human beings in fact have no ultimate origin.

> Os japões nas lemdas de suas ceitas não tem nenhum conhecimento . . . da criação do mundo, do sol, lua, estrelas, ceo, terra e mar, e asy de todas as outras coussas, Parece-lhes a eles que aquilo nam teve primcipio. (letter 96, 264)
>
> [The Japanese, in the doctrines of their sects, have no knowledge . . . of the creation of the world, of the sun, moon, stars, sky, earth, and sea, and of all other things. It seems to them that all that has no beginning.]

Xavier regards this perspective as gravely dangerous: with no grounding in a First Cause, the world would collapse into sexual bedlam and chaos. Yet the open-ended vision of reality that provokes in him such anxiety also allows for a greater expression of sexual diversity, even if in premodern Japanese society the conditions of sexual life were clearly delimited.[22]

By witnessing what he perceived to be the evils of Japan, Xavier was transformed both personally and spiritually. In a letter to Loyola he writes:

> Jamás podrya escrybir to mucho que debo a los de Japón, pues Dyos nuestro Señor, por respeto dellos, me dyó mucho conocymiento de

> mis infynitas maldades; porque, estando fuera de mí, no conoscy muchos males que abya en my, hasta que me vy en los trabajos y pelygros de Japón.
>
> (letter 97, 287)

Though Xavier makes clear what he most abominates in the Japanese (religious doubt, clerical corruption, and concupiscence), he does not specify the evils he comes to acknowledge in himself. But he does shed light on the nature of his relationship to the Japanese. Japan, according to this passage, represents the Other through whom he discovers his own inner self. He confronts this self not when alone or in a state of introspection but when he stands outside of himself and his culture in a foreign land. At first he identifies with the Japanese he encounters since they seem to possess many of the attributes he most values as a European. But when they reveal to him other ways of being human, he recognizes his own potential difference as well. Rather than accept this difference, he chooses to distance himself from it. This entails a withdrawal not simply from an external Other but from the Other already within him.

The culminating moment of Xavier's visit to Japan occurred in Kyōto, at the court of the emperor. Xavier hoped to receive from him permission to preach throughout the realm and possibly also to convert him. But he and his companions failed even to gain an audience ("Nom pudemos falar com ele" [We were unable to speak with him] [letter 96, 262]) and were turned away from the palace gate. As a matter of fact, this was of little consequence since at this point in Japanese history the emperor held no real power, and afterwards Xavier petitioned the support of powerful feudal lords.[23] Yet the image of him standing at the entrance of the imperial household empty-handed (a gift was normally required for admission, and he had nothing to offer) suggests not only a temporary setback but, in a sense, the beginning of the end of his long odyssey. According to his testimony, Kyōto, the historical and cultural center of Japan, was a place of waste and destruction after years of civil war, and the emperor, the quintessence of the Japanese nation, was silent and invisible. If Japan, as Xavier has shown, is a mirror of the self, then the truth it imparts to him at this moment is his own existential emptiness. As he left Kyōto, he reportedly uttered the words of the 113th Psalm, "In exitu Israel de Aegypto" [When Israel exited Egypt] (Schurhammer 213), as if it were his own salvation he now sought rather than that of the Japanese people. Though his promised land was not of this world, his geographic course would henceforth lead westward, away from a land "aparejada para todo género de pecados" (letter 97, 290), away from the chaos of a world unordered by God, and, in the final analysis, away from the terror of nothingness.

The letters of Xavier nonetheless reveal a tension present in much orientalist discourse between a process of identification and differentiation. Initially,

Xavier discerns in the Japanese—beginning with Angirō in Malacca[24]—a similarity with Europeans, and in many passages of his letters seems eager to highlight cultural commonalities. He also invokes race by claiming that the Japanese are white.[25] In the sixteenth century the racial identity of East Asians had not been fixed in Western ideology and race as an epistemological category had not been grounded in biology.[26] Xavier largely disregards eye-shape, the primary physical characteristic that subsequent Europeans would use to establish Asian difference,[27] and takes skin-color as a sign of cultural equivalence between Japanese and Europeans. Yet this is in fact racism, albeit in nascent form, since whiteness is implicitly equated with cultural superiority. Xavier is so convinced of the preeminence of the Japanese over all other non-Christians that he confidently reports that "entre todas las tyerras descubyertas destas partes, sola la gente de Japón está para en ella se perpetuar la chrystyandad" (letter 97, 291). Ironically, of course, Christianity in the long run made fewer inroads in Japan than in any other East Asian country.

Yet even if the Japanese are like him (from the Christian perspective they too, after all, are endowed with immortal souls), they are also profoundly different, or rather must continually be posited as such if he is to maintain his ideal self. In ontological terms, this self remains ungrounded, appearing only insofar as it is differentiated from the non-Christian in the initial phases of proselytization. When the non-Christian accepts conversion, difference is erased and new converts are sought in an endless cycle of identity-formation. If, however, the non-Christian refuses conversion and remains obstinately different, then the act of self-affirmation that informs the missionary project (despite all the apparent self-sacrifice) short-circuits. This is the plight of Xavier. Virtually alone in an alien milieu, he must either assume as his own the Other's difference or retreat, as he eventually does, and resume his project elsewhere. Japan in his letters is thus not a site of Christian or Western self fashioning but instead a sign of the impossibility of any permanent self-identification, whether as Christian, Western, or merely human.[28]

Needless to say, Japan's reaction to Xavier and the West was motivated by more concrete concerns than these. Japanese rulers became increasingly hostile to Christian missionary activity in the late sixteenth century, especially after the arrival of the Franciscan friars whose presence they regarded as a prelude to conquest by Spanish forces poised menacingly in the Philippines. Fear of the Spanish to a large degree prompted the Japanese to close their doors to the West in the seventeenth century.[29] But Xavier, to his credit, never favored military conquest and discouraged the Spanish from even approaching Japan. In what is perhaps the noblest passage of his entire correspondence (letter 108, 356–57), he ostensibly attempts to alert the Spanish to potential disaster. Yet in so doing he not only prevents a clash between Spanish and Portuguese but also surreptitiously safeguards Japan from onslaught by Spain. The Spanish, who at the tune referred to the

Japanese archipelago as the Islas Platarias,[30] dreamed of finding silver deposits exceeding in wealth even the riches of the Andes. As Agostinho de Azevedo wrote of Japan: "Estas são as Platárias por que os Castelhanos sempre sospirão" [these are the Silver Isles, which the Spanish have always craved] (Schurhammer 549n15). But as Xavier cunningly remarks (revealing only the half truth of his orientalist vision), the seas surrounding them are treacherous, the people are vicious and warlike, and the land is sterile and barren. He exhorts his fellow Jesuit, Simón Rodríguez, to communicate these warnings to the rulers of Castile and Emperor Carlos V himself and to dissuade them from sending an armada of "discovery" to Japan's shores. Xavier's writing, despite his own dreams of spiritual conquest, thus belies the facile efforts of many later historians to subsume Christian missionary activity within larger imperialist schemes even if, in the final analysis, the Cross often did render non-Europeans more vulnerable to the sword.

Notes

1 The first Europeans to reach Japan's shores were Portuguese traders, who arrived in either 1542 or 1543 (Boxer v: 15–18). One of these was Jorge Álvares. Xavier had Álvares record his observations of Japanese geography and society and sent them to Europe for publication. This was the earliest account of Japan to gain wide circulation in the West. It is reproduced by Izawa (240–57).

2 Schurhammer and Wicki, letter 90, 186. Unless otherwise indicated, all citations are from this source. Letter numbers and pages are indicated in parentheses. All translations are mine.

3 Contemporary Japanese-American activists speak of the United States's "racist love" of Japanese Americans, which posits them as a "model minority." This attitude aligns Japanese-Americans with whites, thereby erasing cultural differences while simultaneously maintaining them in a position of alterity.

4 "Xavier" is in fact the Basque name of the castle where he was born. It means "new house" (Brodrick 330n1).

5 The letters from Japan, numbered 90–94 in the Schurhammer-Wicki series, were all written in Kagoshima on 5 November 1549. Letters 90–93 are in Spanish. The last three paragraphs of letter 93 are in Portuguese. Letter 94 is in Portuguese, with a postscript in Spanish.

6 I also cite from letters 96 and 97 (Cochin, 29 January 1552) and letter 108 (Goa, April 1552). Letters 96 and 108 are in Portuguese and letter 97 is in Spanish.

7 A sonnet historically attributed to Xavier, *No me mueve, mi Dios*, was probably the work of an anonymous Jesuit. For a discussion of this text, see Elizalde (59–105).

8 I know of no similar studies of Xavier's influence on Portuguese writing.

9 Angirō's letter is reproduced by Izawa (314–20).

10 It is not clear from the letters why Angirō was able to return to Japan without facing retribution for his earlier crime.

11 App, who writes two articles on Xavier's discussion of Japan both prior to and during his visit, highlights Xavier's ignorance of Japanese Buddhism. Ross, in contrast, argues that Xavier's effort to translate Christian doctrine into Japanese reveals a belief that "becoming a Christian was not to be linked inextricably to becoming Portuguese" (28). Ross thus sees Xavier as an early practitioner of the adaptive missionary style of the Jesuits in East Asia.

12 Xavier in fact wavers on the question of the fate of the dead, and attempts to assuage the anguish of the Japanese by informing them that God's law is inscribed in the hearts of all humans, including pagans (letter 96, 267). But he does not, as claimed by subsequent Catholic apologists (e.g. Brodrick 263 and Schurhammer 235–36n101), actually affirm that the pagan ancestors of the Japanese might be saved.

13 Didier argues that Xavier is disconcerted by the diversity of Japanese Buddhist sects and blind to Shinto, since in his own native culture (Counter-Reformation Europe and post-Reconquest Spain) differing religious traditions could not coexist (18).

14 Martin Luther, in a similar vein, states in his 27th thesis: "There is no divine authority for preaching that the soul flies out of purgatory immediately the money clinks in the bottom of the chest" (Dillenberger 493).

15 Álvares writes that the *bonzes* "vsan la sodomia con los muchachos q enseñan y esto no es abominable autre ellos en general" (Izawa 253).

16 For further examples of how the Jesuits used sodomy to disparage Buddhism, see Cooper 46, 47, 315, 318, 319, and 322.

17 The sixteenth-century Spaniard Juan Ginés de Sepúlveda invoked sodomy as a reason for war against the Native Americans (I: 57). [. . .] Europeans were so inclined to impute sodomy to their enemies that Xavier's testimony by itself is not a reliable gauge of the extent of homoerotic practice among Japanese Buddhist clergy (209).

18 For representations of samurai homoeroticism in premodern Japanese writing, see the tales of the sixteenth-century author Ihara Saikaku translated by Schalow. [. . .]

19 Xavier's respect for the samurai is often explained by their ostensible similarity to the Spanish *hidalgos.* Didier, for instance, claims that because of the samurai Xavier felt completely at home in Japan (19). Xavier, however, never explicitly compares Japan and Spain.

20 *Shudō* is a contraction of *wakashudō (wakashu*=adolescent-male and *dō*=way). As Pflugfelder points out, not only is the erotic object male but, as in most traditional Japanese discourses, the erotic subject is male as well.

21 Cabezas recognizes the larger scope of homoerotic activity in sixteenth-century Japan, but replicates the negative stance of Xavier when he writes that "*la sodomía era rampante* entre los bonzos y los samurais" (49; emphasis added). [. . .]

22 Though male-male sexual expression was accepted in Japanese religious and military orders, male-male sexual relations were never an alternative to heterosexual marriage, and female-female sexual relations were largely ignored. As Pflugfelder points out, the primary kinship metaphor of *shudō* was in fact brotherhood, not marriage (41).

23 The strategy of the Jesuit missionaries was to convert the leaders of a nation first, and through them the people. Brodrick argues that when Xavier realized that the Japanese emperor was powerless and the country had no supreme authority figure, he began to turn his attention away from Japan toward China in the hope of converting the Chinese emperor and through him spreading Christianity in East Asia (219).

24 After Xavier's departure Angirō again fled Japan, perhaps to avoid persecution by Buddhist clergy, and became a pirate in the China seas.

25 Pero Díez, a Galician from Monterrey, Mexico, whose recollections form the basis of the earliest written account of the Portuguese "discovery" of Japan, describes the Japanese as a "gente . . . blanca é barbada" (Izawa 235).

26 Spain in the early modern period had already developed a proto-racism through the concept of *limpieza de sangre*, which located Semitic difference not merely in religious practice but in the body itself. Xavier makes a point of noting that there were no Jews or Moors in Japan.

27 Elsewhere Xavier remarks that though the Chinese have "ojos muy pequeños" (letter 97, 291), they too are a "genta blanca."

28 As App insightfully suggests, the whole question of sameness and difference is complicated by mutual misunderstanding. To the extent that the Japanese interpreted Christianity as an avatar of Buddhism, difference appeared to them "in the guise of the same" (242). App argues that Xavier realized this at the end of his Japanese sojourn and therefore believed his entire mission had failed.

29 Japan also took an aggressive stance towards Spain. Prior to the "Closed Country" policy of the seventeenth century, the Japanese for the first time in their history considered large-scale foreign conquest. The military leader Hideyoshi even attempted to make the Spanish governor of the Philippines recognize him as suzerain.

30 The Islas Platarias (also known as the Isla Rica de la Plata) were not always identified with Japan, and as Knauth points out, continued to haunt the European imagination long after Japan was known to the West (197).

Works cited

App, Urs. "St. Francis Xavier's Discovery of Japanese Buddhism: A Chapter in the European Discovery of Buddhism (Part 1: Before the Arrival in Japan, 1547–1549)." *The Eastern Buddhist* (New Series) 30 (1997): 53–78.

——. "St. Francis Xavier's Discovery of Japanese Buddhism: A Chapter in the European Discovery of Buddhism (Part 2: From Kagoshima to Yamaguchi, 1549–1551)." *The Eastern Buddhist* (New Series) 30 (1997): 214–44.

Boxer, C. R. *Portuguese Merchants and Missionaries in Feudal Japan, 1543–1640.* London: Valorium, 1986.

Brodrick, James. *Saint Francis Xavier (1506–1552).* Garden City: Image Books, 1957.

Cabezas, Antonio. *El siglo ibérico del Japón: La presencia hispanoportuguesa en Japón (1543–1643).* Valladolid: U de Valladolid, 1994.

Cooper, Michael, ed. *They Came to Japan: An Anthology of European Reports on Japan, 1543–1640.* Berkeley: U of California P, 1965.

Didier, Hugues. "Des «hidalgos» à l'autre bout de la terre?" *Corps Ecrit* 17 (1986): 11–19.

Dillenberger, John, ed. *Martin Luther: Selections from His Writings.* Garden City: Anchor Books, 1961.

Elizalde, Ignacio. *San Francisco Xavier en la literatura española.* Madrid: Consejo Superior de Investigaciones Científicas, 1961.

Faure, Bernard. *The Red Thread: Buddhist Approaches to Sexuality.* Princeton: Princeton UP, 1998.

Izawa, Minoru, ed. *El padre maestre Francisco Xavier en el Japón.* Tōkyō: Sociedad Latino-Americana, 1969.

Knauth, Lothar. *Confrontación transpacífica: El Japón y el Nuevo Mundo hispánico, 1542–1639.* México, DF: U Nacional Autónoma de México, 1972.

Las Casas, Bartolomé de. *Historia de las Indias.* Ed. Guillermo Piña Contreras. Vol. III. Hollywood: Ediciones del Continente, 1985.

Leupp, Gary P. *Male Colors: The Construction of Homosexuality in Tokugawa Japan.* Berkeley: U of California P, 1995.

Pflugfelder, Gregory M. *Cartographies of Desire: Male-Male Sexuality in Japanese Discourse, 1600–1950.* Berkeley: U of California P, 1999.

Ross, Andrew C. *A Vision Betrayed: The Jesuits in Japan and China, 1542–1742.* Maryknoll: Orbis, 1994.

Saikaku, Ihara. *The Great Mirror of Male Love.* Trans. Paul Gordon Schalow. Stanford: Stanford UP, 1990.

Schalow, Paul Gordon. "Kūkai and the Tradition of Male Love in Japanese Buddhism." In *Buddhism, Sexuality, and Gender.* Ed. José Ignacio Cabezón. Albany: SUNY P, 1992. 215–30.

Schurhammer, Georg. *Japan and China, 1549–1552.* Vol. 4 of *Francis Xavier: His Life, His Times.* Trans. M. Joseph Costelloe. 4 vols. Rome: The Jesuit Historical Institute, 1982.

Schurhammer, Georg, and Josef Wicki, eds. *Epistolae S. Francisci Xaverii Aliaque Eius Scripta.* 2 vols. Rome: Apud *Monumenta Historica Societatis Iesu*, 1945.

Sepúlveda, Juan Ginés de. *Democrates segundo, o De las justas causas de la guerra contra los indios.* Trans. and ed. Ángel Losada. 2 vols. Madrid: Consejo Superior de Investigaciones Científicas, 1951.

Tormo Sanz, Leandro, and Catalina Villanueva Bilar. "El juglar japonés de San Francisco Javier." In *La juglaresca. Actas del 1er congreso internacional sobre la juglaresca.* Ed. Manuel Criado de Val. Madrid: EDI-6, 1986. 557–68.

Watanabe, Tsuneo, and Jun'ichi Iwata. *The Love of the Samurai: A Thousand Years of Japanese Homosexuality.* Trans. D. R. Roberts. London: GMP, 1989.

20

MISREADING AND ITS CREATIVITY IN SINO-WESTERN CULTURAL COMMUNICATION AT THE END OF THE MING DYNASTY

Sun Shangyang

Source: Yang Huilin and Daniel H. N. Yeung (eds), *Sino-Christian Studies in China*, Cambridge: Cambridge Scholars Press, 2006, pp. 2–16.

The contemporary American literary critic Harold Bloom holds that the history of poetry is the "history of misreading each other's poetry by the strong poets for the purpose of broadening their imaginary horizon", and that this kind of "misreading" more or less involves a certain creativity.[1] Yet, his discussion is still largely limited to misreading within one linguistic background. If we accept the philosophical idea that "language is the home of existence", we can safely say that there are as many manners of existence as there are languages and this will necessarily lead to cultural diversity. The essence of cultural communication is exactly the encounter of various languages and the manners of existence they encounter. The two parties involved in the communication are already prepossessed by the languages, the manners of existence or the cultural traditions, into which they are born. Human historical existence determines that its understanding cannot possibly be isolated from history or tradition. Consequently, no interpretation, either of "the other" or of cultural canons, can really start from scratch. Instead, pre-conception, or pre-understanding, is an inescapable historical fact, which constitutes the premise for all new interpretations. When the subject carries his/her "pre-understanding" into the home of existence of "the other", the first thing he might do, probably, is to misread "the other" by presuming a common ground between them. The ways of misreading may vary from person to person. Yet, it is almost certain that the depth and width of communication is in direct proportion to the extent of misreading.

A signal illustration is the Chinese misreading of Indian Buddhism and the resultant Zenism, or Chinese Buddhism, and the profound influence they exert on the native culture. Nevertheless, in this article, I limit my discussion to the misreading taking placing in Chinese-Western Cultural communication during the 16th and the 17th centuries. Hopefully, this study can shed some light on this issue.

Western missionaries' misinterpretation of Confucianism

The first substantial dialogue between Chinese and Western cultures took place at the end of the Ming Dynasty. Mediated by western missionaries and Chinese scholar-officials, it yielded admirable results. The single work by Matteo Ricci, entitled *History of the Introduction of Christianity in China*, or *The Journal of Matteo Ricci*, "exerted a stronger influence than any other 17th century historical work in such fields as literature, science, philosophy and religion. It introduced Confucius to Europe . . . It opened up a new world and revealed a new people . . ."[2] Similarly, according to Liang Qichao, the famous Chinese reformist, the benefits that the Chinese derived from the dialogue could not be over-stressed. When tracing the causes of these positive effects, we cannot leave unmentioned the policy of approaching Confucianism adopted by missionaries like Ricci.

From their experiences in China at the end of the Ming Dynasty, the missionaries came to see that military forces could not help in their "domesticating" of China. Instead, they could achieve their "spiritual hunting" only by inculcating Christian doctrines in a peaceful manner. More than this, Ricci came to the recognition that, only by enlisting the sympathy of the domineering scholar-officials, in other words, by adopting the upper-class strategy, could they "domesticate" China. For this purpose, he made friends with a large number of scholars, dressed like them, saluted in their manner, and pored over Confucian canons. Meanwhile, he sought a reconciliation between Christian and Confucian doctrines, and strove to formulate a system of Christian teaching and a missionary policy, which would be accepted by Chinese scholar-officials without incurring objections from Europe.

Ancestor-worship had long been a practice in Confucian culture. To facilitate his preaching, Ricci deliberately misinterpreted this custom. According to him, this rite was not a religious ritual. He introduced and commented on it this way:

> For all Chinese people, whether an emperor or a subject, the single most important event, according to Confucian teaching, is to

> offer sacrifice to ancestors at a certain time in the year . . . They believe the ancestors would eat the offerings, or have any use for them. They just do not know other ways they can show their love and gratitude to the ancestors. We were told that the rules were laid down not for the sake of the dead, but for the living. In other words, they set up a good example to encourage descendants and ignorant people to show filial piety to their parents . . . Anyway, they do not deify the dead, nor plead or pray for anything. Therefore, their practice has nothing to do with idol worship. Nor can it be called superstition.[3]

The meaning of Ricci's comments on ancestor-worship could be interpreted on two levels. First, ancestor-worship helped to sustain the moral principle of filial piety. Second, from the Christian point of view, ancestor-worship was not the same as idol-worship, hence did not need to be rejected as a heretic ritual.

From the historical point of view, the tradition of ancestor-worship in China cannot be simplified in the way Ricci did. As a rite, it has undergone a gradual development and a series of changes. It is proven by archeological discoveries that ancestor-worship played an important role in the Yin dynasty and that its gradual approximating of and merging with the previous deity-worship practices helped to set up the paradigm for later Chinese religion, in which ancestor-worship overweighed deity-worship.

During the Yin dynasty, ancestor-worship was still more or less a religious ritual. This resulted from the Yin people's deep conviction that their tribe was consigned by the Celestial Emperor to rule the human world, and the earthly kingdom was exactly the manifestation of the will of the Celestial Emperor. In their view, the Celestial Emperor had no direct contact with the lowly masses; thus, the latter's pleading could not reach the former. Therefore, it was only through their representative, the royal family and with the help of its ancestors, that the entreaties of the ordinary people could be heard. The ancestors were worshipped because it was believed that they had the power either to bless or to curse.

Owing to the stress on secular moral teaching, or, "the impact of the humanistic spirit", the end of the Zhou dynasty witnessed a change in worship practices. They began to shift toward secularized ethical ideas, such as "tracing to the source, returning to the seed" and "taking care to keep in mind the origin, and the people will stick to their virtuous nature". A signal illustration is a work entitled *On Rites* by Xun Zi, an ancient philosopher. Fundamentally an atheist, Xun Zi rejected the theological connotation of the concept of "heaven", and denied that "rite" was a "heaven-ordained order". As an alternative, he proposed "rite used to nurture affection" and "rite used to encourage gentility" as an explanation of the origin and function of "rite". Xun Zi commented on the rite of sacrifice this way:

> To sacrifice is to express the feeling of missing and love.
>
> . . .
>
> To be thoroughly faithful and respectful, impeccably polite and polished – who is capable of these except sages? Sages understand it, scholars practice it; officials reinforce it; and then masses will adopt it as a custom. To the learned, it is the human way. To the unlettered, it is a religious practice.[4]

This quotation shows the moral orientation of Xun Zi's interpretation of rite and ritual (including ancestor-worship). The religious sense was superseded by the secular moral concepts, such as loyalty and piety. It was proved by reliable evidence that Ricci's sound knowledge of Confucian canons, especially Xun Zi's work, enabled him to draw upon Confucian ideas in explaining the rite of ancestor-worship. As a result, there were remarkable similarities between Ricci's and Xun Zi's interpretations. Yet, even in his adoption of Xun Zi's ideas, misinterpretation was not totally absent. Xun Zi still recognized the rite of sacrifice as representing the human way to the learned and a religious practice to the unlettered, two strains of rite and custom in ancestor-worship, which characterized the different practices of the upper class and the people. Xun Zi noticed the religious, or superstitious, coloring of ancestor-worship among the folk people. Ricci, however, paid no attention to the original religious meaning of ancestor-worship, neither did he try to differentiate ancestor-worship as a rite and as a religious practice; perhaps he even deliberately ignored it. Instead, his reading of ancestor-worship in Confucian culture was exclusively moral-oriented. This strategy, frequently employed by Ricci, included two aspects. On the one hand, he started from the presumption of a common ground, and tried to reconcile the elements in Confucianism and cardinal Christian doctrines, which were seemingly similar, yet fundamentally different. On the other hand, he took great pains to dissolve the religious or heretical meaning of Confucian thoughts, concepts, customs and rites, which were incompatible with Christianity and undoubtedly religious or superstitious. Ricci intended to convince the Europeans that the Chinese rite was acceptable to Christianity. Only through this strategy could Ricci win support and sympathy from the religious headquarters of the European Catholic Church. The same strategy also enabled him to appeal to the Chinese mentality, and to avoid a complete rejection of western learning, which could have stemmed from the cultural clash.

The ancient Roman philosopher Lucretius held that nothing could come into being if atoms made no deviation, hence no collision, while traversing across vast space according to the gravity principle. In his *The Anxiety of Influence*, Bloom used this idea as a metaphor for his theory and treated deviation as a type of misreading. What I want to point out here is that if Ricci's misinterpretation of ancestor-worship in China stems from his lack of pertinent knowledge, his version of the Confucian "heaven" and the

"Sovereign on High" is none other than a deliberate distortion of the original meaning. Ricci quoted profusely the *Five Canons* about the Celestial Emperor to support his notions, such as: "Our God is exactly the same as the Celestial Emperor in the ancient canons" and "God and the Celestial Emperor differ only in their names". In order to prove the supremacy of God, or "the Celestial Emperor", he even criticized Zhu Xi's authoritative work *The Annotated Version of the Four Books.* In the *Golden Mean*, one of the *Four Books*, Confucius was cited as saying, "we offer sacrifice to heaven and earth in order to serve the Celestial Emperor". Zhu Xi noted, "The Celestial Empress was omitted for the sake of brevity". Ricci argued against him, saying, "In my opinion, Confucius undoubtedly meant the Celestial Emperor as an inseparable unity. Brevity was not the reason". Yet, according to Ricci, Zhu's note did not make any sense. He also interpreted "Heaven" in Confucian canons as God, because "heaven is the greatest", implying the one and only supreme Lord.[5]

By voluntarily appealing to the scholar-officials' adoration for antiquity, and by extolling and christianizing "the Celestial Emperor" in Confucian canons, Ricci hoped to lead them to God. Nevertheless, the Confucian "Celestial Emperor" is essentially different from God. It is true that deity-worship is the oldest religion in China. "This supreme deity was named 'heaven' in the Xia dynasty and the 'Celestial Emperor' in the Yin dynasty. The highly civilized Zhou people started to combine the two into the 'Heavenly Celestial Emperor' ". As recorded in the explication of the cracks in the oracle bones, the deity, whom the Yin people named the "Celestial Emperor" or "Emperor", was in charge of natural phenomena, and the dispensation of bliss and punishment in the human world. The religious overtone of deity-worship is remarkable. Nevertheless, essential differences exist between the Celestial Emperor, or deity, and the supreme Christian God. The Celestial Emperor was neither hypostasized as a creator of the world nor personified as a flesh-and-blood savior.[6] Ricci had no interest in discerning these original differences, but simply borrowed the title of "Celestial Emperor" (which was familiar to the scholar-officials), and wished to waken the scholars' fancy for their old religion. By establishing the affinities between the scholars and the ancients, Ricci hoped to promote their understanding of and belief in Catholicism, which was "just the same" (in fact, only superficially similar) as the old religion.

Ricci's affirmation and praise of Confucianism were based on his misreading. In his view, no other peoples made fewer mistakes in ancient times than the Chinese; there was no essential difference between Confucianism and Christianity. Although they had lost the ancient religious tradition, the Chinese led an honest, faithful life, guided by Confucian teachings and the natural law, or reason. Chinese ancestor-worship was not idol-worship. On the contrary, it contributed a lot to the ethical life. Ricci's conception of Confucianism had two consequences. Firstly, it sowed the seed for the later

"Disputation on Rite and Ritual", the central issue of which was the two terms ("the Celestial Emperor" and "God") and the Western attitude toward the Chinese rite. The quarrel between the European Catholic Church and the missionaries lasted more than a century. Secondly, Ricci's conception paved the way for creative misreading and the adoption of Chinese thought during the European Enlightenment.

According to the interpretation of missionaries like Ricci, the Chinese people never had a share in the bliss of the Gospels. In other words, they had not the least idea about Christian Revelation. Yet, they formulated a healthy moral system, which contributed to their matchless statecraft and advanced culture. The fact proved that "it is not impossible to create a society made up of atheists exclusively". In other words, society could develop without religion. This conclusion was drawn by Pierre Bayle (1647–1706), the last metaphysicist of the 17th century and the first philosopher of the 18th century, in his renowned work *Historical and Critical Dictionary*. Obviously, he had used China as an example, and drawn on the information introduced to the West by the missionaries, in order to debase religion and to extol reason. By so doing, he pioneered the Enlightenment movement.

The German philosopher, Leibniz (1646–1716) took the side of Longobardi, another missionary whose conception of Confucianism was essentially different from that of Ricci's, and believed that all Chinese were atheists. Later, owing to his close contact with missionaries, such as Joachim Bouvet and C. F. Grimaldi, he shifted to Ricci's side, accepted his theory of Chinese culture, and became a Chinese culture champion who enjoyed the most profound knowledge of Confucianism among his European contemporaries. He praised Confucius as the king of Chinese philosophy, and was convinced that the Chinese people worshipped reason, hence were deists, and that their deism enabled them to become the most virtuous people. Compared to the Chinese, what the Europeans had achieved in practical philosophy, including their life ethics and statecraft, was too piteously insignificant. In his opinion, the reason-oriented moral system of the Chinese was a prescription for man's sin. He even proposed "to have missionaries sent from China to teach us (Europeans) the application and practice of deism".[7]

Leibniz's theory of Chinese culture was further developed by his disciple Woolf. He replaced Leibniz's "the good" with "the true" as the criterion in evaluating and extolling Chinese culture. He observed, "the real foundation of philosophy is what agrees with the natural human reason. Anything against it is falsehood, and cannot be regarded as the real foundation" and "what contains the basis is true. Otherwise, it is false. This touchstone testifies the greatest truth in Chinese philosophy". Woolf sang high praise for the Chinese people's dependence on their own reason, rather than a deity's revelation. This attitude, he said, enabled the Chinese people to "act not out of habitude, or fear of the master, but completely out of their free will", therefore, "the action of the Chinese people implies an absolute power, which is drastically diminished in the action of us Europeans!"[8]

Objectively speaking, Leibniz, Woolf and some other Enlightenment thinkers exaggerated and imagined a lot in their eulogizing of Chinese culture and social conditions. Their picture of China was undoubtedly shaped by people like Ricci, who provided them with an inaccurate description of the reality of Chinese life through their misreading of Chinese cultural canons. The Enlightener's affirmation and evaluation of Chinese philosophy and culture may not be accurate, it may even be completely wrong. Yet it was through misreading and idealizing China that they extolled human nature, reason, and human rights. It is proven by historical facts that Confucius was once adopted by the Enlighteners as their patron god, and his ideas as a powerful weapon against Medieval religion. From this, we can conclude that, no matter what the original intention of the mediators might be, the communication between two essentially different cultures will inevitably transcend that intention and lead to their own constructive transmission, interpretation and application on a larger scale. What the Jesuit missionaries introduced to the Westerners were undoubtedly ideological bits and pieces from Chinese feudal culture. Yet, for the rising bourgeoisie and their Enlightenment movement, these bits and pieces became their reason-charged spiritual support. This fact demonstrates that the objective result of mutual interpretation and adoption of two qualitatively different cultures is unpredictable, so long as the two parties start with their respective needs and carry it on with sensitive creativity. More often than not, it can help the birth of a new age and accelerate the development of a new ideology.

Scholar-officials' interpretation and adoption of Catholicism

It was not until the early 17th century, that is, nearly twenty years after the arrival of Western missionaries, that some influential scholar-officials became receptive to Catholicism, apart from engaging in adopting, studying and spreading Western science. It was recorded in "An Introduction to Italy" in *The History of the Ming Dynasty* that the missionaries in China "were esteemed and solicited by officials of all ranks. Nevertheless, as Ye Xianggao, the head of the Cabinet, observed, "Those who had a real belief in Catholicism and could really see through the business of life counted no more than a handful".[9] Among them were Xu Guangqi, Li Zhizao, Sun Yuanhua, Wang Zheng and Yang Tingjun. Owing to their decisive influence, Xu, Li and Yang were known among the Jesuits and Chinese converts as "Three Pillars in Catholicism". In this article, I want to use Xu Guangqi as an example to illustrate how their prepossession by the Chinese traditional culture influenced the scholar-officials' misreading and adopting of Catholicism.

By the time of the 16th and the 17th centuries, it was not easy to find in Chinese ideological tradition an equivalent for the Western "religion".

Scholar-officials often cherished the cultural legacy created and handed down by saints and philosophers as "teachings" and "codes". These concepts were extremely inclusive. Xu Guangqi was no exception in adopting and employing them. In his view, "teaching" and "codes" included the usually ignored physics as well as metaphysics. In his *Ke Tong Wen Suan Zhi Xu* (1614), he wrote: "In our country, the Yellow Emperor started the subject of arithmetic, in order to cooperate with Rong Cheng, the calendarist. The subject was already full-fledged by the Zhou dynasty. Scholars had to sit in a test in this subject before they were able to obtain official posts. Those who mastered the Confucian Six Arts could enter the hall and take the high seat. If arithmetic were omitted, the Confucian teaching would be destroyed". Obviously, the Six Arts in the Confucian teaching did not exclude arithmetic. The inclusive nature of "teachings" and "codes" rendered them comparable to what we call "nature" today. Xu Guangqi made great efforts to restore arithmetic to its position in the "holy learning and orthodox strain". By exalting science, which was very much neglected in the Ming dynasty, he hoped to advance the transmission and application of the fruits of western science, which he believed and loved deeply. Yet, when he and some other scholar-officials identified Catholicism with the Western religion, which was introduced into China by people like Ricci, along with western science, they offered a misinterpretation based on the common-ground-presumption. Because of this, a French scholar criticized the belief of Xu and his followers as a "hodgepodge" of religion and science and technology, rather than pure Catholicism. Nevertheless, if we recognise the influence exerted by the traditional concept of "teachings" on the mental habit of the scholars, we will see this criticism is totally unreasonable. Because of his misinterpretation, Xu Guangqi went on to divide Catholicism into three categories: "Roughly speaking, his (Ricci's) theory falls into three categories. The foremost includes self-refinement and devotion to God. The next involves tracing the internal workings of every phenomenon to the utmost. Following this is the treatment of concrete objects".[10] In other words, Catholicism included morals and religion, which are concerned with self-refinement and devotion to God, and philosophy and science, which deal with the internal workings of the Chinese scholars to assimilate and adopt Western learning on the basis of their native concepts, such as "teachings" and "codes". This misinterpretation spared Xu the trouble of coining new terms, such as "pure religion". The common-ground-presumption was also responsible for his misinterpreting the Catholic doctrine, "serving God through self-abnegation". "We (Xu and Ricci) used to peruse the miscellaneous as well as significant points. Surprisingly, however, among such a large number of remarks, we did not find a single one which went against the principle of loyalty and piety, or did harm to moral life". His interpreting Catholicism in terms of Confucian teachings was immediately attacked as a corrupt reading and also an abuse of the religion. At the same time, his interpretation struck one as an apology for Catholicism.

In addition, Xu Guangqi voluntarily adopted Ricci's misreading of the "Celestial Emperor" in Chinese canons. According to Longobardi, Xu was clearly aware of the difference between God and the Celestial Emperor. "He believed firmly that neither the ancient nor the contemporary Chinese people had any idea about God. Yet, since the priests identified God with the Celestial Emperor out of good intention, the ordinary people had no right to object. What's more, since the title had survived, he concluded that it was rewarding for us to transfer the attributes of God to the 'Celestial Emperor'. As for the soul, he believed that the Chinese people's knowledge of it was far from enough".[11] Xu's voluntary misreading was meaningful in two ways. To say the least, it reflected his intellectual and spiritual need for Catholicism. Besides, it signified his prudence in selecting an appropriate approach to Catholicism, which was later so frequently attacked by orthodox scholar-officials.

As a self-claimed skeptic, Xu directed his doubts and criticism against traditional Chinese culture, for two reasons. Firstly, he was deeply convinced that Catholicism could settle his ultimate concern, help him "see through the business of life", and to reassure him of "the salvation of his body and soul". Secondly, Ricci had given an exaggerated depiction of "the thirty-odd Western Catholic countries" as "an Elysium" ruled by universal sympathy, consideration and peace for thousands of years. Xu sought to find or to establish a universally valid moral system that could encourage people "to pursue the good to the perfect, to eliminate the evil to the last". According to him, the Catholic moral system enjoyed a universal validity because Westerners believed in a creator-savior God, who dispensed reward and retribution with so much justice that his power "overwhelmed people", whose religious emotion of awe could not but "flow from the bottom of their hearts". Contrary to Catholicism, Chinese traditional moral philosophy lacked universal validity. Xu Guangqi argued as follows:

> Emperors and kings since the ancient time have practiced rewarding and retribution. Saints have engaged themselves in evaluation. They spare no efforts in regularizing people with the good and keeping them from the evil. Yet punishment and rewards can change only the external, and not the internal. As Sima Qian observed, the untimely death of Yan Hui the good man, and the longevity of Dao Du the evil man made people doubt the inevitability of justice. Therefore, the more the rulers keep on guard, the wilder deception runs. Once one law is laid down, a hundred evils find loopholes. The ruler aspires to rule wisely, but his resources fail him . . . How can all people be led to do good? The only remedy lies in Catholicism brought in by Western missionaries.[12]

In Xu's opinion, Chinese moral reason was no longer satisfactory or self-sufficient. The optimistic belief in the moral inclination to the good gave place to the reverence of an absolutely just God. The moral-oriented "royal dispensation of justice and the saintly engagement in evaluation" was no longer unconditionally effective. According to him, "sincere belief, faithful action", or the absolutely unfeigned moral intention and action, could only come from an external, supreme deity (God) who could inspire the religious awe. This notion represented Xu's voluntary shift from the secular to the religious moral, and from the internal transcending to the external transcending. Xu believed that this shift could "redeem Confucianism and repel Buddhism", or "improve the human reign" and "recuperate Buddhism".

Xu Guangqi's bold critique of Chinese traditional culture blended with the wave of critical thinking at the end of the Ming dynasty. He started his criticism by comparing and reflecting on the tripartite Chinese traditional culture (including Confucianism, Buddhism and Taoism) and the Western medieval religious moral, together with its function and effects as advocated by missionaries. He believed that he had found a satisfactory moral system in Catholicism. Yet all this was based on his personal experience. He based his examination of the Catholic influences and function on Ricci's imagined Western Elysium. The approach determined that his argument about the universal validity of Catholicism was nothing but a misinterpretation. Yet, this very misinterpretation deepened his comparative research of Chinese and Western philosophies, broadened his imaginary horizon, and separated him from the orthodox scholar-officials who inclined to the illusion that the Cathayan civilization was the best, and that what applied to China also applied to the world. The misinterpretation led him to imagine that there was a western world which enjoyed a more advanced culture and stronger power, and that the Middle Empire of China, which was deteriorating both economically and culturally, must modestly learn from the Western world, or "consult with them in modesty", so that "their achievements accumulated through three thousand years will fall into our hands instantly".[13] Only in this way could China catch up with the West. For this purpose, Xu advocated the strategy of "overtaking through communication", which meant that China must communicate with the West both in culture and science, in order to overtake the latter. This competitive sense was very valuable. Le Wenshen once observed, "The old-fashioned Chinese culturalists have no sense of competition", because "competition is the essence of nationalism".[14] Indeed, only when people gave up the illusion of an all-inclusive Cathayan civilization, could the competition sense be introduced into the scientific or ideological-cultural creative activities, and on the basis of differentiation, that is. In this aspect, Xu Guangqi was a worthy forerunner. Nevertheless, his competitive sense, as well as some concrete strategies, did not arouse particular interest in the ideological world in the Ming and Qing dynasties. Only when the Middle Empire was brought to face an even more powerful Western world, which posed a threat to its very existence, did Xu's idea resurface and assert its life force in various ways in modern patriotic movements.

Differentiating and the resultant interruption in creation

The misreading of Chinese and Western cultures by Ricci and Xu Guangqi undoubtedly provided a chance for the creative communication between China and the West. In this sense, "misreading is healthy from the historical point of view". In a particular historical period, however, misreading, to an individual, could be "a violation against continuity, because it contradicts the sole authority which recognizes nothing but itself".[15] In the case of Ricci and Xu Guangqi, this authority was Catholicism of the "holy learning and orthodox strain" of Chinese Confucianism. Consequently, we should not be surprised when their misreading met with criticism from the Jesuits and the Chinese scholars and monks.

During Ricci's activity in China, some Jesuits were already showing their dissatisfaction with his preaching strategy. After his death, missionaries were continually sent to China from the Dominican order, the Franciscan order and the Capuchin order. More and more people took issue with the "Riccian Rules", accusing Ricci of identifying the Celestial Emperor with God, humoring ancestor-worship and adoring Confucius. His most radical opponents included Longobardi and Didaco de Pantoja. They stressed the qualitative differences between God and the Celestial Emperor in Confucian canons, and warned against confusion. The Chinese people's "sacrificing to ancestors is a heretic ritual. The converts must not practice it, lest our holy religion should be contaminated".[16] The missionaries' discriminatory insistence and uncompromising attitude gave rise to a disputation of rite and ritual, which lasted a whole century, until even the Roman Pope and the Emperor Kang Xi of the Qing dynasty became involved. Pope Clemens VI decreed in 1704 that Chinese believers must not adore Confucius or worship their ancestors. In 1705, the Pope's special missionary, Carlo de Tournon, was dispatched to China and was granted an interview with the Emperor. Upon realizing that de Tournon's mission was to get rid of "Riccian rules", the Emperor promptly announced, "From now on, anybody who disobeys the Riccian rules shall be expelled from China". Those who abided by the rules and received a certificate for doing so were allowed to stay in China. In 1720, another missionary, Jean Ambroise Mezzabarba, was sent to China to demand again the suspension of the Riccian Rules. As a reaction against the Pope's uncompromising attitude, the Emperor Kang Xi ordered a complete ban of Western religion. The peaceful communication between China and the West met with a man-made interruption.

Prior to this, at the end of the Ming dynasty, an anti-West wave was already brewing among the orthodox scholar-officials and Buddhist monks. In 1616, Shen Que, a second-rate official of the Department of Rites in Nanjing, pleaded to the Emperor Wan Li thrice, suggesting that churches be pulled down and that missionaries be expelled. He also alluded to Xu Guangqi and others who helped Western missionaries. In 1639 and 1643, *The Collection for Expelling the Devil (Po Xie Ji)* and *The Collection for Shunning the Devil (Pi Xie Ji)* were published, which included pamphlets written by scholar-officials and monks who were bent on attacking western learning. The strategies they employed fell into two categories. The first was to exaggerate the limitless danger of preaching in China. The second was to discriminate, or to deepen the gap, between the two cultures in order to demonstrate that the introduction of Catholicism, an entirely different ideology, would lead to "the corruption of China by the alien countries", and to the replacement of the Emperor's brilliant civilization by the barbarian "devilish doctrine".

The anti-Catholic scholar-officials knew clearly that their most powerful weapon for warding off Western influence consisted in deepening the gap. The reason was that, by fighting against the exotic teaching, which was incompatible with "the holy learning and orthodox strain", they could win the public's sympathy and support.

By the time of the Ming dynasty, a human-centered moral system had been established in Confucian China. In this system, emphasis was put on faithful, honest living and self-cultivating, which would naturally lead to moral perfection. The central theme of *The Great Learning*, one of the *Four Books*, was captured in the observation that "from the emperor to the commoner, all are engaged in self-refinement, with no exception". Contrary to this, the religious morality advocated by Catholicism was based on the belief in God. The preoccupation with the Divine Justice on Judgment Day prevented the believers from acting against God's will. Ricci, and the scholar-officials who adopted Catholicism, like Xu Guangqi and Yang Tingjun, all attempted to prove that the Catholic moral system was objective, universally valid, and hence the best. Yet, to some anti-Catholic scholar-officials, religious morality itself encouraged the pursuit of bliss in the hereafter at the expense of virtue cultivation. Its premise lay in an immoral motive, that is, pleading for future bliss by "bootlicking" God. Xu Dashou commented in this respect as follows:

> Is there any other way of achieving bliss besides cultivating the virtue? In addition, the good and the evil in their conception are just the opposite to those of our saints. Lord Yu devoted himself to rites and self-cultivation. Should his good deeds come to nothing simply because he would not flatter the Celestial Emperor? If momentary bootlicking could wipe off the life-long sin, the Celestial Emperor was surely thousands of times more selfish than ordinary people.[17]

Quite the opposite, people like Chen Houguang were unreservedly confident in the self-sufficiency of the Confucian moral system. They believed sincerely that the need for a universally valid moral system could be satisfied without recourse to a transcendental personified deity. Their suggestion was "to apply the physical to the metaphysical, to help oneself rather than to plead for help".[18]

The anti-Catholic scholar-officials held that the saint's teachings were concerned only with the human world, and that the meaning of life consisted in nothing else but "the brisk vigor" and the perfection of virtue. They had no use for either bliss or punishment after death. Catholicism, on the contrary, urged people to spite the human world for the sake of eternal joy in the hereafter. Therefore, it was a violation and betrayal of life. Huang Zhen was skeptical to the Catholics' attempt to obtain final redemption and spiritual exaltation through self-inflicted corporeal punishment, as manifested in "shackling themselves without committing any crime, and beating their chests, begging for deliverance without doing anything wrong". To him, this practice was more frenzied and grotesque than religiously meaningful. Besides, it divested life of all its "brisk vigor", and hence was completely contradictory to the Chinese Saints' preoccupation with simple, decent enjoyment.[19]

These scholar-officials' rejection of Catholicism on account of its incompatibility with Chinese Confucianism was provoked by their sense of crisis, which was aggravated by their sensitivity. Since the Catholics spited the human world, held in contempt this life and devoted all their interest and attention to God and Paradise, any attempt to adopt and spread their religion would inevitably lead to deviation from the social hierarchy and custom in this World. The result would be "the upsetting of the moral order". It was true that Ricci did borrow some kernel Confucian concepts, such as "benevolence" and "piety". Yet he christianized the originally human-centered, secular sense of the Confucian moral system. In his *Tentative Analysis of the Art of Argument*, Chen Houguang criticized this christianizing attempt saying, "Ricci worships God as the greatest father of all people and the sole emperor in the universe. By praying to God day and night, one dismisses his father as being too trivial to be loved, and the emperor as being too secular to be respected . . . He also said that the benevolent should love God, which is totally against Confucius' teaching that the benevolent is humane and his only concern is to respect the father . . . Now, once God becomes the master, the son is no longer inferior to the father, nor is the subject inferior to the emperor. This surely contradicts the moral order . . ."[20]

The Confucian moral system and the feudal social structure in China were the enlargement of the family structure and the family members' interrelationship. This fact determined the former's dual nature, that is, the rigid hierarchy combined with a blood-based affinity. This nature necessarily led to the concept of Confucian earthliness, that is, those regulated by the Confucian moral rules could live nowhere else except in the secular world. The supreme power in this world was represented by the emperor and the father. Consequently, loyalty to the former and piety to the latter came as the first in the list of the Five Moral Rules. By contrast, the very First Commandment of Catholicism demands people's undivided devotion to God. It urges them to submit themselves as subjects to an external "altruistic other" and offer to him their reverence. Were this religion implemented, the heavenly command would inevitably clash with secular duty. Chen Houguang interpreted Catholicism as a deviation from the moral order "under the cover of devotion to God". This argument revealed the root of the clash.

In contrast to Chen, Xu Dashou stressed the great dangers brought upon the "Three Principles and Five Rules" by Catholicism, for the former advocated orderly hierarchy, while the latter championed equality of all people before God. Xu generalized the dangers as "the upsetting of the moral order". His objection was based exactly on the opposition between the Confucian moral system, which was based on kindred affinity, and religious egalitarianism, which was God-centered.

Anti-Catholic scholar-officials also discriminated between the different conceptions of human nature and "heaven" in Confucianism and Christianity. Their arguments were often so perspicuous and pertinent that "the western scholars found themselves tongue-tied". The late Ming anti-Catholic scholar-officials' exclusive mentality was pushed to an extreme by people like Yang Guangxian at the beginning of the Qing dynasty. At the same time, the missionaries insisted on a discriminative policy. Owing to these two reasons, a complete religion ban was actually enacted during the reign of the Emperor Yong Zhen. A feasible channel of Sino-Western cultural communication in a peaceful, fair manner was thus brought to an end. This interruption cost China the good chance of overtaking the West through competition and communication, which was what Xu Guangqi had dreamed about. This fact serves as a negative example, showing that if we differentiate between two civilizations so as to stubbornly reject an alien cultural legacy, we will lose the chance for mutual understanding and creative communication. On the other hand, voluntary communication and creative understanding based on a less than accurate understanding, or the misreading, of a foreign culture will prove beneficial to both sides. In any case, giving up communication and dialogue means self-isolation and hostility, which will lead to social and cultural retardation.

Before concluding, one more point needs to be clarified, that is, we must guard against universalizing the notion of "creative misreading". Misreading is not absolutely rewarding. This is the lesson we should draw from the disastrous results brought on to Chinese society and culture by the groundless misreading of Marxism during the years of ideological chaos. In this article, I only point our attention to a historical fact. It is not my intention to draw a universal rule or principle from a particular phenomenon in a particular time.

Notes

1 Harold Bloom, *The Anxiety of Influence*, translated by Xu Wenbo (Beijing: Sanlian, 1992), 3.
2 See the Preface to *The Journals of Matteo Ricci* (Beijing: Zhonghua, 1990), 651.

3 *The Complete Works of Matteo Ricci*, edited by Fu Ren University, 1st ed. (Guangqi, 1986), 85.
4 Chen Mengjia, *A Survey of Oracle Bones at Yin Relic* (Beijing: Zhonghua, 1988), 561.
5 *The True Meaning of the Lord of Heaven*, edited by Matteo Ricci (Taipei-Paris-HongKong: St. Louis UP., 1985), 122–126.
6 Ding Shan, *Collection of Chinese Ancient Religious Myths: Emperor and the Celestial Emperor* (Shanghai: Shanghai Wenyi, 1988), 62.
7 *German Thinkers on China* (Nanjing: Jiangsu People, 1989), 9.
8 Ibid., 32–34.
9 Ye Xianggao, "Introduction to a Tentative Reading of the Ten Commandments in Christianity", in *CangXia Yu Cao*, Vol. 5.
10 Xu Guangqi, "Twenty-Five Suggestions", in *Supplementary to the Works of Mr. Xu Wengding*, Vol. 1.*
11 Longobardo, "An Account of the Empire of China", in *A Collection of Voyages and Travels*, Vol. 1 (London: 1774), 168.
12 *The Series of the Documents on the Introduction of Catholicism to the East: Papers on the Disputation*, Vol. 1, 2nd ed. (Students Bookstore, 1986), 15.
13 Ibid., 10.
14 Le Wenshen, *Liang Qichao and Modern Chinese Ideology* (Chengdu: Sichuan People 1986), 148.
15 Ibid, 89.
16 Fan Guoliang, *A Sketch of the Introduction of Christianity in Yanjing*, Vol. 2 (Beijing: Beijing Jiu-Shi-Tang, 1905), 46.
17 Xu Dashou, *A Collection for Expelling the Devil*, Vol. 4.*
18 Ibid., Vol. 5.
19 Ibid., Vol. 3.
20 Ibid, Vol. 5.
* In the ancient Chinese books, there is no page number, only volume number.

21

CROSSING GENDER BOUNDARIES

Tupi and European women in the eyes of Claude d'Abbeville

Laura Fishman

Source: *French Colonial History*, 4 (2003), 81–98.

When Europeans traveled across the Atlantic to America, the borders they crossed were more than geographic. Their encounters with native inhabitants presented Europeans with societies whose political, economic, social, and religious structures were far different from those which were accepted as the norm. The volume of scholarship dedicated to analyzing the complexities of the interaction between Native Americans and Europeans continues to expand. More recently, greater attention is being paid to the importance of concepts of gender in the colonizing process.[1] Gender is a key factor in the structuring of all human societies, but because gender constructs are so deeply embedded, they often go unrecognized. Encounters with individuals or societies whose concepts of gender differ from our own can provoke strong reactions. Do we expand the borders of our own gender definitions, to recognize that what we had believed to be "natural" patterns of male/female activities and relationships are really cultural and historical constructs? Or are gender boundaries so tightly drawn that tampering with them threatens not only the integrity of the individual, but the very fabric of our social structure? These issues, though perhaps not always clearly articulated, were of concern to Europeans engaged in colonizing activities throughout the globe. To help clarify them, this paper will focus on the ways in which matters of gender were addressed by the French Capuchin missionary Claude d'Abbeville, who worked with the Tupinamba (or Tupi) natives of Maranhão in northeastern Brazil in the early seventeenth century.[2]

In 1612, three ships embarked from France, headed for Maranhão. The colonial venture in which they were involved had been initiated by Henri IV in 1604. Then, in 1610, Marie de Medici, regent for Louis XIII, had granted a royal charter to Daniel de la Touche, *sieur* de La Ravardière, who had established a colonial company. The monarchy had also granted authorization to the Capuchin order to accompany the expedition.[3] The Capuchins, a reformed order of the Franciscans, had been founded by the Italian Matteo de Bascio (1495–1552) and recognized by the papacy in 1528. Their work epitomized the spirit of religious renewal and spiritual activism characteristic of the Catholic Reformation. The Capuchin dedication to these goals was largely expressed through a vigorous campaign of overseas missionary activity, which was international in scope. Historians, in fact, have considered the Capuchins second only to the Jesuits in the range of their accomplishments.[4]

When Claude d'Abbeville arrived at Maranhão, he prayed, erected a cross, and reported in his initial letters that the hospitable welcome accorded the French by the Tupi was an indication that these natives would cooperate readily with him in carrying out his Christian mission.[5] Abbeville's full account of his experiences, *Histoire de la Mission des Peres Capucins en l'Isle de Maragnan et terres circonvoisines ou est traicte des singularitez admirables et des Meurs merveilleuses des Indiens habitans de ce pais*, was published in Paris in 1614.[6] In it, he provided a lengthy narrative of his own activities, together with detailed descriptions of the natives, their character traits, and the central elements of their social organization and culture.

Tupi society presented Abbeville with many "*singularitez et meurs merveilleuses.*" In particular, the appearance, behavior, and activities of native women were clearly very different from those of European females, and Abbeville was quite interested in exploring and explaining these contrasts. The great interest that he, and so many other Europeans, displayed in recording these details testifies to the central role of gender in the structure of societies. Indeed, European assessment of Native American societies was shaped in a significant way by the colonists' reactions to the gender constructs which they encountered in the New World.

For missionaries like Abbeville, the ideals of the Catholic Reformation were of central significance in establishing definitions of appropriate gendered behavior. Many European women firmly espoused the values of the Catholic Reformation, and they were inspired by the vitality of its message to pursue lives dedicated to religion. Yet, a path of worldly spiritual activism was denied to women. The decrees of the Council of Trent insisted on enclosure: female religious had to express their devotion within the walls of the cloister. To be sure, many women who took religious vows found ways to interpret papal strictures so as to broaden their range of activities. It is also true that nuns traveled to established overseas colonies where they were permitted to instruct girls within their convents. Nevertheless, official Church doctrines confined the spiritual dedication of women to the cloister. Most of all, decrees issued at the Council of Trent denied women any apostolic role.[7]

Missionary work of this era was seen as the province of men. It was believed socially and morally inappropriate, as well as physically dangerous, for women to engage in missionary activity. Underlying these attitudes were strong contemporary cultural assumptions that maintained that the most respected activities and vital work of society must be performed by men. Women, although by no means excluded from religious activity, were denied clerical roles on a par with men.

When transposed to a colonial environment, these attitudes about appropriate gender rules and roles raise important questions. To what degree did their assumptions about gender distort Europeans' perception of native women? Can we learn anything about the status of women in non-Western societies from the accounts Europeans wrote? Considering Abbeville specifically, how did gender constructs affect his definition of his mission and the strategies he employed to attain his goals? What impact did Christianity have on the lives of Tupi women, and was this change positive or negative?

Feminist scholarship in anthropological and ethno-historical research initially created a model of Native American women that emphasized their favorable status and autonomy. Female natives were portrayed as respected, productive, and powerful; they were not subject to male authority, and they controlled their own sexuality. This research served as a valuable corrective to traditional anthropological theories, which had been created by men and thus mirrored Western male concepts of gender. Feminist scholars also held that early accounts written by men minimized, when they did not neglect, the activities of native women.[8] The work of Eleanor Burke Leacock was seminal in developing the feminist approach. Drawing much inspiration from Marxist theories, notably Friedrich Engels' *The Origin of the Family, Private Property, and the State*, Leacock portrayed the Montagnais-Naskapi of eastern Canada as an egalitarian society, where women enjoyed high social status and personal autonormy.[9] Later feminist scholarship expanded Leacock's model by emphasizing the economic productivity of native women in diverse cultures, their central role in decision-making, and the subsequent deterioration of females' status that accompanied the process of colonization. The work of Christian missionaries, according to this interpretation, furthered the establishment of European gender concepts by imposing patriarchal structures on native societies. The research of Judith K. Brown on the Iroquois, Karen Anderson on the Montagnais and the Hurons, and Carol Devens on the native tribes of New France and the Great Lakes region elaborated this view.[10]

Does the work of Claude d'Abbeville confirm the ideas of this feminist scholarship? The evidence is mixed. His account does not depict an egalitarian society in which native women enjoyed a status equal to that of men. Tupi society appears to be male-dominated. Unraveling the layers of methodological, epistemological, and interpretive issues is a complex process. Should Abbeville's observations be discredited because they were distorted by his preconceived notions of gender? It may be that he was unable to recognize a more active and vital female presence among the Tupi because such a society was outside his realm of experience and expectations. As a missionary, moreover, Abbeville's goal was to convert the Tupi to Christianity, and it was essential for him to believe that this is feasible. Native values and behavior regarding sex roles that were contrary to Christian definitions presented major obstacles to his objective, so perhaps Abbeville preferred to deny native gender patterns. On the other hand, perhaps the early feminist model exaggerated the favorable status of native females out of an eagerness to document the experiences of women whose patterns of life differed so much from those common in Western societies. If so, then Native American women who enjoyed power and autonomy may have been presented as proof that patriarchy and male dominance are neither natural nor universal.

More recent scholarship that integrates a feminist perspective into its analysis of the colonizing process shows a change in orientation that parallels a new approach discernible in research dealing with colonialism in general. The focus now is less on exploitation and domination than on various levels of interaction between colonizers and native people. While not denying that the roles and status of Native American women were different from those of European females, more recent scholarship acknowledges that New World societies were far from egalitarian. Native peoples are no longer idealized as pure and simple creatures of nature, nor are they pitied as passive victims of a brutal onslaught. Rather, a growing respect for the integrity and complexity of New World societies has emerged, along with a fuller recognition of the intelligence and assertiveness of the natives, women as well as men. Earlier feminist scholarship, as discussed above, stressed the importance of matrilineal and matrilocal social structures. But even in societies where these forms were absent, native women were able to assert themselves in a variety of ways. They traded, negotiated, cooperated, and fought with Europeans. Sexual relationships between native women and European men provided opportunities for the development of new social, economic, and kinship networks. Native peoples thus sought to obtain whatever advantages they possibly could within the context of a challenging new reality.[11]

The status of Native American women in their aboriginal condition may never be determined with certainty. The natives were not literate, and ethnocentrism, to some degree at least, penetrates European narratives. The diversity and complexity of native kinship structures, in particular, challenged the analytical abilities of outside observers. Contact with colonists altered the reality of native life and impacted on the structures of native societies from the outset. The written accounts therefore record what Europeans saw and experienced while interacting with the natives. They cannot absolutely bear witness to the conditions of native life prior to contact. It is also important to emphasize the diversity that characterized Native American life. Numerous distinct societies were present, and they were dynamic, not static. The various cultural groups interacted with one another, as well as with Europeans. Thus, colonial experiences varied and were dependent upon many factors, including specific native contexts. General descriptions of the status of native women and men must be articulated with caution.[12]

When Claude d'Abbeville arrived at Maranhão in 1612, the Tupinamba had already experienced brutality at the hands of the Portuguese. Warfare had occurred, especially during the period from 1557 to 1572, when the colonial rulers of the regions of Bahia and Rio de Janeiro had begun an intense effort to enslave the natives. As a result, many Tupi had migrated north to Maranhão. Abbeville reported that he received a warm and hospitable welcome from the natives. The missionary interpreted this behavior as an indication of the natives' willingness to embrace Christianity. More likely, the Tupi were displaying an eagerness to form an alliance with the French in order to have a powerful European nation assist them in their efforts to resist the Portuguese. In order to attain this end, some measure of cooperation with the French on the part of the Tupi was necessary. Abbeville is aware of this motive as well, acknowledging that the Tupi needed military assistance and were also eager to obtain European trade goods.[13]

Warfare was one of the central and defining elements of Tupi culture. Feuding between villages was frequent and intense. This violent and brutal characteristic of Tupi life should not be underestimated. It is perhaps best exemplified in the treatment of prisoners of war, which was guided by precise ritual procedures culminating in cannibalism.[14] Abbeville regarded the fierceness of Tupi warfare, and the ritual cannibalism associated with it, as one of the greatest obstacles to Christian conversion. His descriptions of these native practices included their impact on women. Female prisoners of war were given to men to serve as their slaves, but they were also regarded as wives. Should such a woman engage in adultery, she would be put to death, and her body would be dismembered. Abbeville asserted that ". . . such cruelty is abominable to God," even though the natives explained to him that they killed such offenders to serve as an example to others.[15]

Male prisoners were surprisingly well treated, at least initially. Considered slaves, they were nevertheless given a good deal to eat, and they also received a Tupi woman as a sexual partner. Abbeville regarded the latter practice as particularly "strange." Eventually, the Tupi exacted vengeance by killing their enemy prisoners, then cooking and eating their flesh. Abbeville described this ceremony in great detail, commenting that the "greatest cruelty and inhumanity" was displayed when the Tupi also killed and ate any children that might have been fathered by the prisoner during his stay among them.[16] The institutions of Christianity and French law would, the missionary boasted, end all these practices, and might be perceived as ameliorating the lives of those Tupinamba women who were either held as slaves or married to prisoners. Abbeville claimed that the natives, if commanded by French officials, would modify their customs and put their enemies to an "ordinary death," rather than killing them in such a cruel fashion.[17]

The fact that warfare was an integral element of Tupi society elevated the position of men. Militaristic societies are male-dominant, as men perform the most vital activity.[18] Abbeville's account does, in fact, focus on Tupi men. They emerge from the pages of his narrative as more prominent and powerful. The village chief, or headman, appears as an experienced elder who had served as a "valiant captain." He had earned his status and esteem through great exploits in war, having killed many enemies. His authority was far from absolute, but he was greatly respected, and his advice was often followed. Oratorical ability was valued as well.[19] Abbeville gave no indication that Tupi women were involved in the leadership of the village. They do not appear as vocal participants who influenced decisions made by the council of elders. However, he represented Tupi women as active participants in the elaborate rituals that surrounded the treatment, execution, and consumption of the prisoners of war. Abbeville described these ceremonies in detail. A celebration of singing, dancing, jumping, and drinking continued for two to three days. Women were thus full participants in one of the most vital public rituals in Tupi culture.[20] Other sources indicate that Tupi women were also responsible for greeting the prisoner upon his arrival at their village, guarding the hut in which he stayed, and leading him to his execution with a special rope around his neck.[21]

Preparations for the important festival surrounding the execution of prisoners were elaborate, and this work was entirely performed by women. Tupi females were responsible for preparing large quantities of food and drink, both for their own households and also for ceremonial purposes. Here, their contribution to their societies was of the greatest importance. European colonists all concurred that Native American women were productive, hard-working, and performed numerous tasks which were essential to the survival of their people.[22] Abbeville expressed surprise at the level of intensity and also the diversity of tasks which characterized the work of native women. He observed that even in old age, women "never cease to work at what they are accustomed to do." Abbeville did comment that older men also continued to work at difficult tasks. However, it was Tupinamba women whom he described as being "usually more occupied than the men," since it was their sole responsibility to take care of the household, plant gardens, and "prepare everything necessary for food."[23] It is worth noting that since he wrote, the productivity of women, and the vital economic role of their labor in sustaining their societies, has been increasingly recognized by scholars in their analyses of native cultures.[24]

Yet despite this acknowledgement of the industriousness of native women, Abbeville's ultimate assessment of Tupi society was that it was unproductive, because the natives were "perpetually lazy" and did not "care to work very much." Always the optimist, the missionary interpreted this aspect of native life in a positive way, idealizing a people as happy, joyous, and content due to their lack of concern for material possessions.[25] In this respect, Abbeville resembled other colonists who applied contemporary European standards of labor which incorporated dominant definitions of gender. Work performed by women, although recorded in detail, was undervalued or even denied in the final assessment of native society. Thus, Abbeville did not see the crucial and necessary work performed by Tupinamba women as an indication of the significant role of women in their society; rather, that labor served to enhance the image of native men as unproductive and idle. Abbeville's European reaction to the productivity of native females also reinforced the assessment of native men as dominant and in control, because the women were often portrayed as overworked and oppressed.[26]

Claude d'Abbeville ultimately evaluated Tupi society in terms of what native men did or did not do. And one of the most striking things that they did do was to marry numerous wives. Abbeville's discussion of the native practice of polygamy—or, more exactly, polygyny—is insightful as well as detailed. He knew that if Christian conversion was to take hold, then this practice had to end as monogamous marriage was introduced. The communal family structure of the natives would be altered as well. Abbeville asserted that the Tupi were "not all capable of receiving baptism, especially those married in the native fashion." As a missionary, he was adamant on this point: "God wishes man to be content with one wife," and those who agreed to be baptized had to accept this precept.[27] Abbeville, however, strove to understand the reason behind the institution of polygyny, and he wanted his reader to comprehend it as well. Hence he stressed that polygyny served a social rather than a sexual function for Tupi men. Having multiple wives was a sign of a man's status. Village leaders therefore married many women in order to demonstrate their esteem, satisfying their egos, not their lust.[28]

This missionary's measured analysis of Tupi marriage practices may have been influenced by his reading of the Old Testament. Polygyny was a common practice among the ancient Israelites, and the Bible makes many positive references to it. A prime motive for polygynous marriage was to enhance the likelihood of producing male offspring, as sons were highly valued. And, like the Tupi, the men of ancient Israel regarded multiple wives as an indication of prominent economic and social status.[29] But Abbeville also made an effort to understand polygyny from a female point of view. He commented that since the Tupi were frequently engaged in brutal warfare, there was an insufficient number of men to allow each woman her own individual husband. He also commented that polygyny enabled women to share the household work and horticultural labor, which, as earlier noted, was arduous and time-consuming.[30]

The switch from polygyny to monogamy thus might have had a deleterious effect on native women; but Abbeville did not believe that female Tupi constituted any greater obstacle to his mission than men, nor did he present them as exhibiting any greater hostility toward conversion. He reported that native mothers "... cherish their children tenderly, yet are willing to part with them so that they may be instructed." Significantly, the missionary emphasized the importance of working with youngsters. Because they were not yet married, Christian marriage, as well as conversion, could be more readily imposed upon them.[31]

As Abbeville's discussion of polygyny continued, his surprising empathy for Tupi women was transformed into a critique of contemporary European females and an affirmation of the necessity of male control. He did not depict the communal structure of Tupi households as egalitarian. One wife was regarded as the principal one, as she was loved the best by her husband and, therefore, she could command the other wives. Abbeville expressed astonishment that all the women "... live in peace, without envy, jealousy, or riots." He attributed this behavior not to the wise leadership and direction of the principal wife, but to that of the husband, whom all the wives obeyed.[32] He then commented that the Tupinamba "... live in amity amidst their paganism," and thus serve as "... a good lesson for many Catholic families who received the light of faith and sacrament of marriage yet cannot live together in peace ... without quarrel, discord, and division."[33] The implication was that women were responsible for this lack of domestic tranquillity, as it was the Tupi females whom Abbeville praised for living in harmony. In his depiction, they subjected themselves to male authority, whereas he chided European women for not conforming to societal ideals of appropriate female conduct.[34]

Abbeville's discussion of motherhood in Tupi society exhibited the same characteristics as his comments on Tupi marriage. Praise of the natives ultimately served as a means to denigrate Europeans, women in particular. Misogynist tendencies of this era, emanating from both the secular and the religious spheres, doubtless influenced his judgment. Abbeville expressed great admiration for native women in their role as mothers. He appeared pleased to observe infants and young children allowed to grow without the restrictions of swaddling and tight clothing. He asserted that mothers loved their children deeply and never abandoned them; children were always in the company of their mother. He admired the strength of native women, who rested for only two or three days after childbirth. He was especially impressed with the dedication of Tupi mothers, evidenced by their nursing their own babies. His picture of virtuous conduct, however, was apparently created to chide Europeans for their moral laxness. Women bore the brunt of his chastisement, as he faulted them for their lack of patience, evidenced by the fact that they gave their babies out to be nursed. In direct contrast to the Tupi, European mothers appeared unfit, since they did not provide their babies with adequate love and attention. But Abbeville's adulation of native women was carried to an absurd rhetorical extreme when he reported that women who were eighty and even one hundred years of age were still able to bear and nurse children.[35]

A modern reader might expect a Catholic missionary of this era to express revulsion or horror at the nudity of the natives, especially of women. But Abbeville did not. Nor did he portray female Tupi as promiscuous or lewd, maintaining that they were ". . . modest and restrained in their nudity, with no movement, word, or action to offend."[36] This attitude initially surprises the reader, since it seems to have contradicted prevalent early modern European attitudes regarding female sexuality. Women were considered inherently more sexual than men, driven by physical desires that they were unable to control; women were typically viewed as "sexually insatiable."[37] But the reader soon encounters a familiar pattern, as the defense of Tupi women is used once again to chide European females, ". . . whose artificial devices, unrestrained simperings, and new inventions . . . cause more mortal sins and ruin more souls than do the Indian women with their brutal and odious nudity."[38] Abbeville clearly was no defender of nudity, for he proudly related how one native woman arrived naked at a baptismal ceremony and immediately ran to cover herself, realizing that her condition was "indecent and shameful."[39] Thus, he characterized nudity, like polygyny, as a cultural practice which must end if Christian conversion was to occur. Still, he was optimistic that he would obtain the desired results, because he viewed the natives as inherently good. Harsh condemnation of Tupi women as lascivious would only cause him to despair of ever attaining his goal.

Abbeville did not portray Tupinamba women as exhibiting sexual license or autonomy. In this regard, his discussion contradicted a stereotype that associated non-Western, "primitive" women with promiscuous conduct. But Abbeville's assessment also raises questions about feminist anthropologists' claim that native females enjoyed considerable control over their own sexuality.[40] The complexity of native kinship structure and marriage practices probably eluded European observers to a large degree. This fact probably explains why Abbeville made some contradictory observations in his account, reporting in one passage that divorce was easily obtainable, involving only mutual consent, yet at another point relating that a woman could not end her marriage without her husband's permission.[41] In any event, the critical factor in determining the degree of sexual independence experienced by a Tupi woman appears to have been the status of the man with whom she was interacting. Thus, Tupi society hardly appears, in his account, as egalitarian.

The sexual conduct of women married, or promised in marriage, to tribal chiefs or other powerful men was restricted. Premarital and extramarital sexual relations were prohibited. Most likely, it was these marriages that required the husband's consent for divorce to occur. In any case, young women were not given the opportunity to select their spouses; rather, family permission was necessary. Marriage patterns were clearly defined and were primarily matrilocal. Union with a maternal uncle was most highly preferred: it was considered ideal, that is, for a female to marry her mother's brother. If, for some reason, such a union could not occur, a young woman might marry someone from another kinship group. This man would reside with his wife's relatives, and was obligated to serve and work for them. Therefore, daughters were highly valued, because it meant that a family could acquire additional status and resources through the services of multiple sons-in-law. However, matrilocality did not apply if the young woman married a chief or other tribal leader. In this case, she moved into her husband's household, and he provided her family with gifts and favors in exchange.[42]

Abbeville thus depicted the sexual activity of Tupi females as constrained, especially in relations with males of high status. Standards of sexual conduct were clearly different from those in Europe, but the natives did define acceptable and unacceptable behavior. Therefore, Abbeville asserted, French men must refrain from sex with Tupi women, as this would create hostility by violating native standards of acceptable conduct. Strict regulation of sexual activity figured prominently in this missionary's program. French men were forbidden to commit adultery with native wives, and sexual relations with unmarried females were likewise prohibited. Abbeville believed that French men would ". . . not only ruin their souls by such sin," but would destroy the colony as well. His insistence on these regulations, and the addition of his personal commentary indicate that interracial sex between French men and native women was indeed occurring. Abbeville viewed such activity as a threat to the stability of the colony, as well as being offensive to his moral sensibilities.[43] His goals and interests were, however, at odds with those of non-clerical colonists. Nor did he view sexual relations between French men and native women as a means to promote amity between the two societies. Instead, he considered such activity a disruptive force, as the French were likely to violate circumscribed codes of conduct. Abbeville might not approve of native standards, but he also believed that changes must not be harshly imposed.

As might be expected of a Counter-Reformation missionary, Abbeville blamed the Devil for the existence of offensive native customs.[44] Belief in the power of witches and the existence of the Devil was certainly a reality for the Capuchin and his colleagues. Witchcraft trials and executions were underway in contemporary Europe, of course, and the overwhelming majority of the victims of the European witch-hunt were female.[45] Abbeville undoubtedly was cognizant of the hunt, yet interestingly, he did not single out native women as practitioners of witchcraft. Rather, he described the native "*pagé*" or sorcerer, who communicated with the Devil and other evil spirits. Each village had several *pagés*, who were greatly esteemed and honored, and were believed to have the ability to cure sickness. Abbeville reported that almost all the *pagés* were the principal elders of the villages. He also referred to a native man revered as a prophet, and whom the Tupi believed had descended from the sky.[46]

Thus, Abbeville denied a crucial role to native women; but by the same token, he also spared them—perhaps surprisingly—from bearing the onus of responsibility for all the evil practices of the Tupinamba. By blaming the Devil, and not the natives themselves, for the existence of cruelty and brutality, Abbeville created a scenario in which missionary work was more likely to succeed. Once Christianity and French law were established, he boasted, and "servitude to the Devil" had ended, the Tupi would experience "regeneration through baptism"[47] The only obstacle he perceived was external to the society, and evangelism could overcome it. He saw nothing inherent in Tupi culture or character powerful enough to prevent his vision from becoming a reality. Neither did he depict native women in a negative way. He did not perceive them as presenting any specific obstacles to conversion, and he complacently believed that the introduction of Christianity, French law, and European gender concepts would uplift the lives of the natives, both men and women.

The amelioration of the lives of women has been a dominant theme in the history of contact between Western and non-Western societies, and it has persisted into the post-colonial era. Native women are typically portrayed as brutalized and oppressed, and Western societies often appear eager to champion their cause (although concomitantly ignoring injustices experienced by women within their own cultures). The essential role of gender in structuring colonized societies—like all human societies—is clear, as colonizers work to replace native patterns of marriage, work, and sexual activity with those which they believe to be civilized.

Claude d'Abbeville observed and recorded patterns of gendered behavior that challenged many contemporary European assumptions about human relationships and social structure. But this experience by no means persuaded him to question or expand gender boundaries. Tupinamba women emerge from his account as productive and valued members of their society, playing active roles in many important public rituals and ceremonies. Yet, Abbeville ultimately emphasized and valued the dominance and control of Tupi men. Was this indeed an accurate assessment of native culture? Or did he focus on the role of native men because this was consistent with contemporary European practices and expectations, which placed men in positions of status and authority? Were Tupinamba women subservient, modest, and submissive? Or is this portrait a distortion reported by a zealous missionary, eager to minimize any obstacles that might hinder the introduction of French law, culture, and religion? Tupi women may not have lived in an egalitarian society, experiencing sexual autonomy and political authority. Yet their productive, reproductive, and ritual roles accorded them a certain measure of recognition and respect within their culture, and presented future generations of historians, if not colonial Europeans, with evidence of the rich variety of gender constructs.

Notes

1 An important collection of essays is *Negotiators of Change: Historical Perspectives on Native American Women*, ed. Nancy Shoemaker (New York: Routledge, 1995). [. . .] See also *Women and the Colonial Gaze*, ed. Tamara L. Hunt and Micheline R. Lessard (New York: Palgrave, 2002). This collection, which contains my essay "French Views of Native American Women in the Early Modern Era: The Tupinamba of Brazil," examines the crucial role of gender in colonial encounters in Asia, Africa, and Europe, in addition to those in the Americas.

2 Claude d'Abbeville, born Clément Foullon, was one of four missionaries who left France in 1612. He remained in Brazil to establish and organize the mission, then returned to France after several months in order to solicit additional support and financial assistance. He died in Paris in 1632, never having returned to Brazil. See *Nouvelle Biographie Générale*, 46 vols. (Paris: Firmin Didot, 1853–66), 9–10:695.

3 John Hemming, *Red Gold: The Conquest of the Brazilian Indians, 1500–1700* (Cambridge, Mass.: Harvard University Press, 1978), is a comprehensive account of European colonial activity in Brazil.

4 See H. Outram Evennett, *The Spirit of the Counter Reformation* (Cambridge: Cambridge University Press, 1968), 14, 27.

5 These letters, dated 20 August 1612, were published as *L'Arrivee des peres capucins en l'Inde Nouvelle, appellée Maraguon, avec la reception que leur ont faict les Sauvages de ce pays, & la conversion d'icieux à nostre Saincte Foye* (Paris: Jean Nigaut, 1613).

6 Claude D'Abbeville, *Histoire de la Mission des Peres Capucins en l'Isle de Maragnan et terres circonvoisines ou est traicte des singularitez admirables et des Meurs merveilleuses des Indiens habitans de ce pais* (Paris: François Huby, 1614). All translations by author.

7 Merry E. Wiesner, *Women and Gender in Early Modern Europe*, 2d ed. (Cambridge: Cambridge University Press, 2000), 231ff. Claire Walker, "Combining Martha and Mary: Gender and Work in Seventeenth-Century English Cloisters," *Sixteenth Century Journal* 30 (1999): 397–418, notes that women in English cloisters established in France and the Low Countries experienced the Catholic Reformation's "gendering of spiritual labor," which insisted on strict enclosure for women and reserved missionary work for men. Financial difficulties did compel many of these nuns to engage in various forms of economic activity, but the prime means through which they could express their activism was prayer. That women religious did find ways to pursue active social roles is demonstrated by Elizabeth Rapley, *The Dévotes: Women and Church in Seventeenth-Century France* (Montreal and Kingston: McGill-Queens University Press, 1990).

8 For a discussion of male bias in anthropology, see the introduction to *Women and Colonization: Anthropological Perspectives*, ed. Mona Etienne and Eleanor Burke Leacock (New York: Praeger, 1980).

9 Leacock, *Myths of Male Dominance* (New York: Monthly Review Press, 1981), and "Montagnais Women and the Jesuit Program for Colonization," in *Women and Colonization*, 25–42.

10 Judith K. Brown, "Iroquois Women: An Ethnohistoric Note," in *Toward an Anthropology of Women*, ed. Rayna R. Reiter (New York: Monthly Review Press, 1975), 235–51.

11 See Susan Sleeper-Smith, "Women, Kin, and Catholicism: New Perspectives on the Fur Trade," *Ethnohistory* 57 (2000): 423–53.

12 For a discussion of epistemological issues and methodological problems that affect this research, see James Axtell, *Natives and Newcomers: The Cultural Origins of North America* (New York: Oxford University Press, 2001).

Despite these problems, an important anthropologist has attested to the value of much of this travel literature, including the work of Abbeville and his colleague Yves d'Evreux; see Alfred Métraux, "Les Précurseurs de l'éthnologie en France du XVIe au XVIIIe siècle," *Cahiers d'histoire mondiale* 7 (1963): 721–38.

13 Abbeville, 103f.

14 John M. Monteiro, "Tupinamba," in *Encyclopedia of Latin American History and Culture*, 5 vols. (New York: Scribner, 1996), 5:283.

15 Abbeville, 172ff.

16 Ibid., 283, 290ff.

17 Ibid., 296.

18 For an examination of the rise of patriarchy within militaristic societies, see Barbara S. Lesko, "Women of Ancient Egypt and Western Asia," in *Becoming Visible: Women in European History*, ed. Renate Bridenthal, Susan Mosher Stuard, and Merry E. Wiesner, 3d ed. (Boston: Houghton Mifflin, 1988), 32–42.

19 Abbeville, 329

20 Ibid., 290ff. Participation of native women in the rituals surrounding the torture and execution of prisoners was not unique to the Tupinamba.

21 Alfred Métraux, "The Tupinamba," in *Handbook of South American Indians*, 7 vols., ed. Julian H. Steward (Washington, D.C.: United States Government Printing Office, 1946–59), 3:120ff.

22 Sixteenth-century French travelers to Rio de Janeiro also provided testimony to the industriousness of Tupinamba women; see Jean de Léry, *Histoire d'un voyage Faict en la Terre du Brésil*, ed. Paul Gaffarel, 2 vols. (Paris: Lemerre, 1880), 1:141, 143, 148, 155; 2:35, 87, 96–99; André Thevet, *The New Found Worlde, or Antarctike*, trans. Thomas Hacket (London: H. Bynneman for T. Hacket, 1568), 60, 65.

23 Abbeville, 266, 309.

24 This is one of the central themes of the introduction and essays in *Women and Colonization.* See also Judith K. Brown, "Iroquois Women: An Ethnohistoric Note," in *Toward an Anthropology of Women*, 235–51, and Lucy Eldersveld Murphy, "Autonomy and the Economic Roles of Indian Women of the Fox-Wisconsin River Region, 1763–1832," in *Negotiators of Change*; Sleeper-Smith, "Women, Kin, and Catholicism."

25 Abbeville, 297ff., 313. Portrayals of the natives as carefree are quite common in travel literature of this era.

26 The overworked Indian woman and the lazy Indian man were prime components of negative English interpretations of native North Americans. See David D. Smits, "The 'Squaw Drudge': A Prime Index of Savagism," *Ethnohistory* 29 (1982): 281–306. Leacock, *Myths of Male Dominance*, 45, notes that the Jesuits often viewed hard-working Montagnais women as "slaves."

27 Abbeville, 125f.

28 Ibid., 279.

29 See the entry on "Marriage" in *The Interpreter's Dictionary of the Bible: An Illustrated Encyclopedia*, 4 vols. (New York: Abingdon Press, 1962), 3:278–83.

30 Abbeville, 279.

31 Ibid., 92f., 106f., 125f.

32 Ibid., 279f.

33 Ibid., 280f. Many French travel writers of the early modern era praised aspects of Native American life and culture to comment on certain moral flaws of

contemporary European society; see Gilbert Chinard, *L'Exotisme américain dans la littérature française au XVIe siècle* (Paris: Hachette, 1911).

34 Natalie Zemon Davis, "Women on Top," in *Society and Culture in Early Modern France* (Stanford, Calif.: Stanford University Press, 1975), 124–28, discusses the growth of political and social measures aimed at subjecting women to male authority in order to control their supposed unruly and disorderly nature.

35 Abbeville, 281f., 266. Geoffroy Atkinson, *Les Relations de Voyages du XVIIe Siècle et L'Évolution des Idées* (Paris: Droz, 1924), asserts that travelers to the New World who reported about native mothers nursing their own babies greatly influenced the thought of social critics in eighteenth-century France, notably Jean-Jacques Rousseau, who encouraged European women to adopt this practice. See also G. Pire, "Jean-Jacques Rousseau et les Relations de Voyages," *Revue d'histoire littéraire de la France* 56 (1956): 355–58.

36 Abbeville, 271.

37 Wiesner, *Women and Gender*, 57.

38 Abbeville, 271.

39 Ibid., 102, 128.

40 For studies that stress the egalitarian nature of gender relationships and the sexual autonomy of native women, see Leacock, *Myths of Male Dominance*, 32–35, 45–49; idem, "Montagnais Women," 25–42; Carol Devens, "Separate Confrontations: Gender as a Factor in Indian Adaptation to European Colonization in New France," *American Quarterly* 38 (1986): 461–80.

41 Abbeville, 278ff.

42 Ibid. Métraux, "The Tupinamba," 112ff., provides additional information.

43 Abbeville, 165ff.

44 Abbeville, "Epistre," n.p. See also 127, 295, 324f.

45 Among the vast literature on this topic, see E. William Monter, *Witchcraft in France and Switzerland: The Borderlands During the Reformation* (Ithaca, N.Y.: Cornell University Press, 1976).

46 Abbeville, 324ff., 77ff.

47 Ibid., 86.

Part 6

ELITE ASSUMPTIONS AND LAY AGENCY

22

THE SIGNIFICANCE OF THE MANUSCRIPT

Antonio-Ma Rosales

Source: Antonio Ma Rosales, *A Study of a 16th Century Tagalog Manuscript on the Ten Commandments: Its Significance and Implications*, Quezon City: University of the Philippines Press, 1984, pp. 68–80.

This chapter deals with the significance of the manuscript, and its importance from the point of view of the life and institutions of the early Filipinos, the work of evangelization and the theologico-moral concepts it contains.

Certain repetition of key ideas and considerations and their respective quotes could not be avoided entirely, either because their repetition would help in the better understanding of a point being made, or they could be considered and analyzed from another aspect. For instance, how the awareness of the extent in which idolatry influenced the natives contributes to the understanding of their psychology and local institutions, the method and approach used by Oliver, and the theologico-moral concepts taught to them.

I. Ethnological significance

The manuscript presents and describes many aspects of the Filipino way of life during the early years of Spanish occupation. With a richness in and an abundance of detail, Oliver paints a picture of the society of that period. Thus, the manuscript is not just a catechetical or moral treatise; it is also a record of early native customs, institutions and practices. In connection with this I intend to present Oliver's understanding of the way of life of the natives as revealed in their religion and the institutions of slavery and the family. His awareness of these aspects reveals his insight into their psychology.

A. The way of life of the natives

Through Oliver's descriptions one can reconstruct important aspects of early Filipino society. Thus, although many other histories and reports of the period also supply us with facts on the same subject, his personal touch and the context in which he presents the same facts give his work a unique character.

1. The local religion

Oliver's picture of the cultic life of the natives is vivid and rich in details. The importance of this area in their life is evident from the fact that they practiced an animistic religion. It seems that from the orientation of the explanations and the methodology used he was considerably aware of this, and therefore, has suited his approach to this situation.

He mentions, and attacks, the following objects of worship: the *anito*, the Devil, *Lacan Balingasay, Laca Pati, May Lupa*, the moon, the skies, man himself (i.e., anybody raised to the status of anito), the sea, and the *(Bathala) Maykapal.* Among the religious practices he brings up are the following: the natives consult the anito when they are sick or suffering; they pay for the services of the *catolonan*, the nauve minister of cult, to offer sacrifice and officiate at their celebrations; they make promises when something happens to them; and they make sacrifices to the idols of the fields that the rice may grow.

Most historians and reporters also mention these and even more facts about the ancient native religion. What is singular about Oliver's text is that his is the only place where the idol Lacan Balingasay is mentioned.

> . . . That king of old, named Ocohias, fell from his house which was very high. So, he sent his slave to the great Anito, named Beelzebub (which here would be Lacan Balingasay) to ask what would happen to him, whether he would die . . .

The note which refers to this idol under the First Commandment in Chapter 3 gives other details and explanations concerning his probable identity which are not necessary to repeat here. We must underline the fact, however, that the mention of this idol is Oliver's contribution to the study of the ancient deities of the early Filipinos. From the importance Oliver gives to him—he is the only idol mentioned in connection with a Bible story where he is described explicitly as a great and important idol like Beelzebub—he shows the role played by this idol in the religious practices of the natives.

2. The slave institution

One of the main characteristics of an animistic religion is its fatalistic view of life. This attitude is based on the fact that fundamentally man has no control at all of his life, his activities, his fate; everything is under the control, whims and dispositions of the many gods and spirits who rule his world. Since he has no control of anything, man abandons himself to his fate.

Whatever happens is the will of the gods. It is his lot in life about which he cannot do anything except bear with it or enjoy it, depending on its nature.

An area where this fatalism is manifested is in the institution of slavery. Its nature and sociological connotations have already been treated in the preceding chapters. The fatalism that characterized the religion, helped in the taking root of the practice of slavery and favored its development within the culture. Since whatever happens is the will of the deities, the factors that resulted in enslavement, such as non-payment of debts, inheritance of the condition, punishment for criminals and prisoners of war, etc. were accepted resignedly. Even if the society offers opportunities by which a slave could buy back his freedom, the conditions were such that the situation was better left as it was.

Much information on the slave institution is found in the manuscript. The master distributes the jobs among the slaves who must obey all orders under punishment of whipping. The master also divides the week as to when the slaves will work for him and when for themselves. If they are lazy and irresponsible, he tricks them into working more, that they may be better off. While they must seriously respect the master for what they owe him, the latter is bound "to instruct his whole household how to believe and to obey the commandments of the Lord God. [He must] make them pray daily and make them go to church also . . ." If he shirks from the responsibility of looking after the moral and spiritual welfare of his subjects, he will answer for it before the Lord and will share in their condemnation if they will be punished. Therefore, he must correct them if he sees them doing wrong. The influence of this on evangelization is treated in the section on the missiological significance.

3. Family life

The animistic religion also manifested itself in the family life and relationships of the natives. Ancestor worship is one of the principal expressions of an animistic religion. This consisted in the worship of a departed member of the family who has been raised to the status of a minor god, deity, or spirit. The natives offer sacrifice to him and ask his protection and blessing for their lives, activities and endeavors. It is this possibility that their parents and elders would one day be a member of the local pantheon that could have constituted a motive for the young to render them an obedience which was practically unconditional and almost absolute. Thus, by showing them this obedience the young assure for themselves the future protection and blessing of their parents and elders should they one day become gods. Children in the culture depended on the parents, who considered themselves responsible for their offspring so long as they remained in their household, no matter what their ages were.

There were children who mistreated their parents and elders by not giving them the respect due to them, and even neglecting to help them in their material needs as Oliver seems to imply in his description of what true respect for parents consists. On the other hand, Oliver was also aware of parents who did not fulfill their responsibility by bringing up their children in a way contrary to Christian formation, or who did not correct them when they saw them doing wrong. Oliver firmly reminds them that they would be punished if their children would be condemned. Other aspects of this point are discussed in the next main division of this chapter, which deals with man and his relationships.

4. Other aspects of native life

Oliver gives information not only about the local religion and the social class divisions, but also about other aspects and details of the life and living conditions of the natives and their surroundings. There are indications in the manuscript that most of the people engaged in agriculture. In fact his criticism of their religion includes references to the superstitious practices involved in this area. Some others engaged in commerce or trade. Some were even potters. People with responsibilities in the community were the chief, the local priestess called the catolonan, and the judge.

The homes of the natives are also described in the manuscript. They are mostly made of light materials, with simple stairs, removable and somewhat easily breakable, which Oliver compared to the ten commandments. He also mentions the *pusali*, the space under the section of the house that is used for washing and bathing.

Among the animals he mentions are the following: the *May Lupa* or crow, which the natives considered sacred; the *Vsa* or deer, the *Anvang* or carabao, the pig, the goat and the cat. He also compares the rich robbing the poor to the big fishes gobbling up the smaller ones. The plants he mentions are the *Itmo* or betel leaf, the rice, the *Talang* and the *Santol*, two common trees, as well as the ordinary grass. The means of transportation used by the natives are the *bangca* or boat with outriggers and usually a small sail, and the *Dauong*, a much larger boat, which he used to describe the ark used by Noah in the flood. The weapons for inflicting injury or killing mentioned are the *Yvà*, a long knife much like a sword, the *panà* or bow and arrow, as well as poison, and the *gauay*, a kind of witchcraft. The punishments inflicted on guilty parties are whipping, hanging, mutilation, or simply a punishment in kind depending on the offense.

Oliver's keen observation and surprising attention to detail and common life experiences can best be appreciated in the many examples and images he used. It was already mentioned how he compared the commandments to the stairs of a native home. Confronting the idols with God who created everything, he asks, "Can the pot compare with the potter who made it?"

The images of a pregnant woman whose time to deliver had arrived and a man carrying a heavy load illustrate God's patience running out; a violent flood illustrates his anger. His being filled up to overflowing with regard to his bearing with man's sinfulness is compared to the overflow of the contents of a device used to measure quantity. The Seventh Commandment is compared to an unused path, being covered with grass since nobody wants to use it. Woman as God's gift to man is like a precious ring given by a king to a commoner. The example of the big fishes eating up the smaller ones has already been mentioned. He even compares himself to a hunter who sees many deer before him and in his desire to catch all ends up with none. The person who enjoys gossip and evil talk about others is likened to a pig that likes to wallow in the mud. The man who believes others to be like him, deceives himself in the same way that a man sailing from the shore gets the impression it is the land that is moving away. Man's heart is the field he must cultivate on Sundays. Being tempted to sin against sex is like being presented with some delicious rice which one is not supposed to partake of. Thus, with the illustrations and images Oliver uses, the reader can get a fairly good idea of how the early Filipinos lived, and probably even have an insight into their psychology and behavior as well.

B. The psychology of the natives

Oliver's awareness of the natives' way of life gave him an insight into their ways of behaving. He claims, for instance, that the natives excuse themselves easily when they do wrong. The reason behind this can be found in the way they viewed the material world. An understanding of this fundamental concept is essential to the comprehension and appreciation of the native mentality and the various aspects of the way in which they viewed reality. They lived in a world inhabited by good and bad spirits. Because of the presence and continuous activity of these spirits that are in constant interaction with man, he is not in control of anything. Rather, it is he who is under the control, the whim and the mercy of the same spirits. This point has already been mentioned elsewhere in this study, so that there is no need to do it again here, but it is useful to underline that, if something happens, whether good or ill, it is not man who brings it about but the action and influence of the spirits. Thus, man excuses himself from any personal responsibility. Therefore, God manifested in the commandments, clearly and precisely, an expression of his will, so that man will no longer excuse himself in his sinning by claiming ignorance of what God wills and desires.

Oliver's awareness of the natives' way of thinking or reasoning is revealed in the way he has put the introduction to the Fifth Commandment:

> You are pleased everytime you hear in church this fifth commandment of God which says, do not kill your fellowmen. Do you not say to yourselves, "If I obey the other commandments of God as this one, what can the Lord God say to me? Would I not be a really good person then? Because, have I killed anyone?"

It is to this way of thinking and reasoning that he often appealed to, for example, when he tried to convince them to leave their evil and erroneous ways, or to accept his instructions. A somewhat long but pertinent paragraph under the Sixth Commandment typically exemplifies this aspect:

> So, everytime man commits adultery, the Devil benefits by gaining his soul. He also enslaves the soul of the one who commits impurity. Is that a small benefit of the Devil from your evil deed? Would man enjoy an activity if somebody else benefited from it? My children, what kind of madness is this that you have? Why do you let the Devil enslave your souls and permit him to drag them to Hell where your enemies are? To let your souls catch fire and burn there in the flames? Where is your reason? Suppose some delicious rice were set before you and you wanted to eat it, but if someone told you, even if he were a confirmed liar, that you should not eat it because it is poisoned, would you eat it anyway? Would you not be afraid to die? Would you not throw it away even if it looked delicious? Even if the warning that it was poisoned were not true? Well then, the Lord God warns you not to commit impurity, not to do evil things.

Oliver's insight into the native psychology comes through quite strongly in the way in which he formulates certain questions which are emotionally charged, because they incorporate attitudes and values which the natives held in high regard. There are many examples of this in the manuscript. For instance,

> . . . Could you be unfaithful to the Lord God? Could you make a fool of him? Do you not owe him anything? Does he not treat you like his sons? Did he not die on the Cross out of mercy for you? Were not your bodies, your souls and everything you have not given to you out of his mercy for you? Why do you not obey his will then?

A brief examination of the concepts used in this series of questions will make Oliver's approach more understandable. He brings in the notion of being "unfaithful." Undoubtedly this strikes a chord in the heart of a people that is closely knit and dependent on each other for their survival within the tribal unit. To be unfaithful to the Lord God is like being unfaithful to the tribal chief who is responsible for the group. It implies lack of community spirit, "walang pakikisama." Due to this dependence the natives owe their chiefs many things, from their livelihood to defense from attacks of other tribes. To forget these favors is a great sign of ingratitude and insensitivity. In fact, one of the greatest insults that could be made to a native is to call him "walang utang na loob," that is, one who has no sense of indebtedness or gratitude, an ingrate, in the worst sense of the word.

To treat someone like one's own is something for which the beneficiary cannot be thankful enough, particularly if the treatment comes from the chief himself. Finally, Oliver brings in the supreme sacrifice of Jesus Christ who gave his life for man. The image of someone offering his life for another is an expression of great love and altruism which everyone could understand. Thus, the emotions evoked by Oliver's questions proceed from fundamental concepts and values held in high regard by his listeners.

Oliver also mentions other qualities and modes of behavior, but they are of a more general nature. He notes, for instance, that the rich and powerful take advantage of the poor and weak in the same way the big fishes eat up the smaller ones. When people have many things to choose from, they do not know which one to pick and try to have everything, often ending up with empty hands. He also presented his version of the universal saying, "A thief believes everyone is a thief." We shall now see how Oliver's knowledge of the native institutions and psychology helped determine the content, method and approaches to be used in evangelization.

II. Missiological significance

Even more than just a treatise on the life and institutions of a people on the crossroads of two civilizations, the manuscript is also an example of how a missionary from one culture adapted a theologico-moral treatise to a particular group of listeners belonging to another. Oliver adjusted and adapted himself, his method and the content of his instruction to his listeners and the circumstances and situations he encountered.

A. The missionary and his method

Juan de Oliver's life and qualities as a man and as a friar-missionary have already been described and treated in Chapter 2. In this section I intend to present Oliver's talents and abilities as a teacher and a catechist. These aspects can be seen best in relation to the method he used in his work.

As already mentioned, particularly in Chapter 3, the methods of evangelization used in the Philippines were patterned after the ones used in Mexico. We know that Oliver spent a time there, albeit short, before proceeding to the Philippines. Being an intelligent man, endowed with a keen sense of observation and attention to details, he must have taken note of the methods then being used by his confreres in their work. Then, the four months or so needed to cross the Pacific could have given him the opportunity to reflect on his observations.

Thus, some of the failures of the first years of evangelization in Mexico were avoided in the Philippines. An example to illustrate this point can be taken from Oliver's attitudes and methods vis-à-vis the worship of idols. During the first years of evangelization, the missionaries in Mexico thought that the best way to uproot idolatry was to destroy statues, temples, ancient writings, in short, everything that would remind the natives of their pagan past. Years later, it was realized that the procedure was wrong. The missionaries did not know the psychology and mentality of the natives, for it was claimed that one of the good ways to know a people is through their religion. So, the next generation of missionaries changed tactics altogether. The destructive methods of the earlier years were substituted with more humane, more comprehensive techniques. The natives were to be converted from paganism through the use of arguments and reasoning. This was the situation in Mexico when the first Franciscans for the Philippines made their stop-over there in 1577. This was also what Oliver found there in 1581.

There is evidence of this method in Oliver's approach to the situation of idolatry he found in Balayan. Nowhere does he suggest the destruction of the idols and images, nor does he even imply the burning down of their shrines or the chopping down of their sacred trees. Nowhere does he instigate the converts to hunt down and exterminate their local priestesses and witch doctors. Rather, what he seems to be particularly concerned about was to show the natives their lack of good sense and discernment in the worship of worthless objects, powerless and mere creatures of the one true God, who alone deserves man's worship and adoration. He brings in arguments, comparisons, images and stories to support his affirmations.

Oliver often proceeds from what the people are and have. He bases his arguments on their appreciation of certain values and attitudes like respect, the sense of community, or indebtedness, fidelity, family cohesiveness. He appeals to their own moral sense.

> Since even just to threaten to bring harm on another is already sinful before God, how much more if the person were really harmed? Would that not be a sin at all? You know well which of the two is the greater sin. Even if you asked a child, could it not think similarly?
>
> Gentlemen, take as an example what you yourselves say, that a gentleman is ashamed to report an untruth . . . If it is an offense to an honourable person to ask him to witness to a lie, how much more would it not be a sin to the Lord God?
>
> . . . Suppose an evil man breaks into your house, for he wants to have sex with your wife or husband, or perhaps steal your gold. However, he was not able to carry out his intention, because there was something that deterred him . . . But if you knew he had bad intentions, would you not be angry with him because he is evil?

He makes quite effective use of questions, asked one after the other, as shown in the long citation of VI.E. The following is another typical example, ending with an affirmation of the teaching he wants to put across.

> For indeed, which servant would not be whipped by his master if he were disobedient? Would it not be foolish for a man to disobey the command of his Lord God? Which creature of God does not follow his will? Since the heavens were commanded by God to move, would they stop even for an instant? Has the sea gone beyond the limits set by God for it? It is man alone, therefore, who is disobedient and disrespectful, although he alone possesses reason which was also given to him by God, and has been favored beyond all the rest.

Together with his effective use of questions to bring out his arguments and to lead his listeners to the teaching he wants them to understand and accept, Oliver also uses dialogue effectively for a more dramatic effect. He uses this technique not only to add variety to his presentation of the subject, or to put it in a concrete situation, but also to make his affirmations appear as coming not from himself but from somebody else. A very typical example of this is the dialogue between the father and the son who were both punished in hell for having enriched themselves unjustly. The effect achieved by the interchange of regrets, accusations and curses is quite impressive. He also employed dialogue effectively in the stories from the Bible. His use of questions, dialogue, the second person, and the imperative mood, is an indication of his open, direct and conversational style. His narratives aim at realism, relevance and concreteness.

> But is there a place for hanging in Hell? Of course, there is. Would that very hot fire burning there without end not be a place for hanging? Can what we have here on earth be worse than what is there?

Mention has already been made of the examples he gave, the pictures described, the comparisons made and the images used: their realism, concreteness, conciseness and appropriateness. He used words that appealed to the senses. "He (God) covered it (Mount Sinai) with clouds, sent down lightning and thunder, that everything was burning." The following text suggests immediacy and presents the growing intensity of the images.

> The water of the River will not flow unless there is sufficient water and is confined with dikes. But if there is too much water because of a heavy rainfall and the water level has risen, the dikes are no longer able to hold in the waters. The wood of which the dikes are made is slowly eroded, and everything is carried away by the current, for the waters churn-up violently.

One can picture the surging, hostile crowd, for instance, at the capture of Jesus or the trial of Susanna. One can almost smell the pig wallowing in the mud. His always vivid description of hell is a challenge to the imagination. Picture the father and the son in hell: "When they died, God placed them both in Hell, in a deep and narrow pit, full of fire, where they bite each other, claw at each other like cats, curse and shout evil things at each other." One can feel and smell the burning flesh in the following text:

> . . . Each time you are tempted by the Devil to commit impurity, reflect first whether you will be able to bear with the fire in Hell. Dare to put your hand over a fire first, and if you can not suffer your hand to be burnt the whole day or for many days, would you be able to support that of Hell? To burn forever?

Oliver used various means to prove a point. The preceding paragraphs contain examples of the kind of arguments he often used. As already mentioned, he also brings in arguments based on the people's sense of natural morality and appreciation of human values or their emotions. Arguments based on nature are also resorted to in certain places, particularly in the explanation of the First Commandment. These types of arguments have already been mentioned and examples given earlier in this chapter, or are easily found in the manuscript.

Another approach which Oliver considerably employed is the one in which he regards his listeners as "children." Addressing the natives as his children produced certain psychological effects: it gave the missionary considerable motivation to work and show his real concern for and paternal interest in the natives' welfare, and it gave the listeners a sense of security and a feeling of being accepted. This attitude logically explains Oliver's visual and concrete approach to the explanations of the commandments. Though adults in age, his listeners were children in the faith and therefore, it was considered necessary to instruct them in the style used. Without taking from Oliver the credit for his concrete and vivid presentation of his material, his inventiveness and effective use of stories and other aids and techniques, it must be noted that the missionaries in Mexico used the same approach in relating to the natives.

B. The audience

The consideration of his listeners as children in the faith was also based on the fact that they had been baptized. There is only one reference to this in the manuscript. There are also other references which implied it, suggesting man being a child of God, for instance, that he forced man, whom he considers his son, to attend to his spiritual welfare out of mercy for him. He is the "true Father of us all," who will treat us like his sons and will bless us in heaven if we are obedient and respectful. This is also implied in Oliver's explanation of the duties of Christians on Sundays, as well as from the fact that the *Doctrina*, of which the Decalogue is an integral part, is intended for the instruction of new Christians.

An even more interesting detail in the manuscript is its being directed apparently to the rich and the ruling class or the nobility of the place. This is evident from the examples Oliver uses and the situations he presents. He addresses them, for instance, as "Guinoo," that is, "sir" or "gentleman," underlining their respectability as nobles. He also mentions their obligations to promote the spiritual and moral welfare of their subjects. He also addresses them directly: "What if you were not revered by your slave . . . The same ideas are implied in phrases like "the master who has slaves . . ." It has already been pointed out also that most of the sins mentioned from the Fifth to the Eighth Commandments probably belonged to them as well, in as much as it is often the rich and the powerful who have more opportunities and possibilities for committing them.

> . . . Man has become too evil; too many are committing adultery, everyone is burning with sexual passion and is evil in his heart towards the Lord God. Impurity has become man's favorite activity, and is engaged in without shame or fear.
>
> And yet although many behave this way in stealing the properties of others, it is particularly the master and above all, the rich people who do this, for they love Gold and want to possess the gold of others . . . that they may enslave their fellowmen.

The examples he uses show situations easily identifiable with the ruling class, as also, for instance, the father and son punished in hell for their theft and oppression, the already mentioned master-servant relationships, the story of Ocohias, and that of Joseph of Egypt, whom he deliberately referred to as "maharlica," the native term for a person of the nobility, and the mention of Christ's words about how difficult it is for the rich to enter Heaven.

This consideration makes an important point understandable. It is Oliver's comparing God to the master or the rich man: "The relationship between the master and the slave is similar to that between God and man." Places where he insists on obedience and submission have already been mentioned elsewhere.

This procedure would not be particularly surprising if one bore in mind that the same was used in Mexico. By converting the chief and the ruling class first, it was believed that the common people would follow suit. Then, it must also be noted that Oliver did not just cater to the rich and their interests. Though he accepted and appreciated their role in evangelization and used this knowledge effectively, he was also fearless in denouncing them.

Thus, although the master probably no longer engaged in downright killing, he must nevertheless avoid quarreling, keeping grudges, cursing others, uttering bad words in anger as well as saying evil words. Every evil threat he made on others will lead to his condemnation; if he wished to trap someone, he himself would fall into it. These might not refer specifically or exclusively to the masters or the rich, but it was they who usually had motives and occasions for doing them. Oliver probably had them in mind also when he threatened with eternal damnation "those who arrange the occasion so that they could commit adultery in their house."

Concerning their business affairs Oliver did strongly protest against their excessive greed for profit and gold, their habit of cheating their partners or people they were doing business with, as well as their usurious practices which often resulted in the enslavement of their debtors.

C. *The content of the instruction*

The content of the Decalogue as explained in the manuscript presents an incomplete view of Christianity and the Christian life. Many important points seem to have been left out. The section on the theological significance of the manuscript treats this aspect in greater detail. Thus, only some general notions about the content are given here and some of the ideas stressed by our missionary.

1. Summary of the content

Oliver's deep awareness of the native psychology and way of life determined not only his method but the content of his instruction as well.

> The general title is immediately followed by an extensive introduction to the commandments (pp. 272, 272v, 273), where Oliver brings up the need for and limitations to the create world. He cites the master-slave relationship as an example in the assigning of jobs and in the absolute obedience to be given by the slaves. The commandments were given so that man would have a guide in his life. He mentions the disobedience of Adam and the punishment it brought upon himself and the rest of mankind. He describes the lightning-and-thunder circumstances of the giving of the Commandments on Mt. Sinai, and compares them to the detachable and easily breakable stairs of the local houses. These stairs were given by God that man might be able to go up to Heaven, his true home. He underlines the need to obey all the Commandments, for to break one is to break all, as the example of the Hebrews showed. They were punished, even though they disobeyed only one of the commandments in worshipping the Golden Calf.
>
> The first commandment, *Ybiguin mo ang Dios, lalo sa lahat*, i.e., "Love God above all things," (pp. 273, 273v, 274), mentions the

divinities worshipped by the natives. These were the Anito, the spirit of the ancestors, which he identified with the evil person in hell, the Devil, Lacan Balingãsay, Laca Pati, May Lupa, the moon, the skies, man himself, the sea, and the Bathala Maykapal. Among the religious practices were: the consultation of the Anito in times of sickness or suffering, the paying for the services of the Catolonan, the making of promises in times of need, and the offering of sacrifice to the idols of the fields to assure the growth of the rice. Oliver refutes their beliefs and practices with strong affirmations of the power of the one true God. He tells the story of Ocohias and the sacrifice he ordered to be offered to Beelzebub and how God punished him and his men for this idolatrous practice. He stresses the need to love God alone and be faithful to him, giving the example of the priests who have left all things to give themselves completely to the Lord.

The second commandment, *Houag cang magpahamac manumpa sa ñgalan nang Dios*, i.e., "Do not dare to swear in the name of God," (pp. 274, 274v) points out the need to respect the name of God in the same way that the natives respect the names of their chiefs and elders, because he is the source of all holiness and every truthful speech. He also mentions that in truthful matters it is praiseworthy to swear to God.

The third commandment, *Mangĩlin ca cun Domingo, at cun Fiesta*, i.e., "Abstain from work on Sundays, and feasts," (pp. 274v, 275, 275v) illustrates that just as the masters and slaves divide the week between themselves, so God has also divided the week between himself and man. Oliver mentions specific activities to be done on Sundays: go to church, pray, listen to religious instructions. Man's heart is the field God wants him to work in on Sundays. He introduces a little casuistry concerning the kind of work that can be done on Sundays. He also mentions an interesting observation that God somehow "tricks" us so that we may attend to our spiritual welfare through this commandment because we would not do it by ourselves. He tells the story of the man who gathered firewood on the Sabbath and was sentenced by Moses and Aaron to be stoned to death.

The fourth commandment, *Ygalang mo ang iyong Ama at ang iyong Yna*, i.e., "Respect (honor) your Father, and your Mother," (pp. 275v, 276, 276v) brings up different relationships: authority (leaders, judges, priests) and subjects, parents and children (which he illustrates with two stories from the Bible: Noe and his sons for the duty of the children to respect their parents, and Heli and his sons for the duty of parents toward their children), masters and slaves, and husband and wife (which he illustrates with the story of the creation of Eve). A special point underlined is that Eve was given by God to Adam to save him from loneliness, and that she forms one body with him. Oliver develops the husband-wife relationship further with affirmations concerning the permanence and indissolubility of marriage. An interesting note mentioned in this commandment is Oliver's criticism of a kind of obedience practiced by the children, which he considered a treachery, of no value, and not practiced in Spain.

The fifth commandment, *Hovag cang matay nang capova mo tavo*, i.e., "Do not kill your fellowman,", (pp. 276v, 277, 277v, 278), stresses the extension of the meaning to hating, insulting, having bad intentions, keeping grudges, cursing, uttering of bad words in anger, and to every evil word to another. He mentions the different ways by which the natives caused death or harm to others: through weapons, poison and witchcraft. He brings in the story of Aman and Mordecai from the book of Esther. However, an even more interesting teaching he proposes here is non-violence and passive resistance to those who want to do us evil, the patient bearing of injustices, leaving to God the privilege of making revenge. As a final touch, he deals briefly but succinctly with the evils and seriousness of abortion, deliberately provoked whether by the woman herself or with the help of others.

The sixth commandment, *Hovag cang maquiapid sa di mo asava*, i.e., "Do not have sex with someone who is not your husband or wife," (pp. 278v, 279, 279v, 280), is one of the more vivid explanations and covers practically three full pages. Oliver brings in the story of the Flood to show how displeasing sexual offenses are to the Lord, and affirms the eventual—even imminent—destruction of the world by fire. He deplores the sexual customs and what he consideres sexual excesses of the natives. He deals with adultery, fornication, incest, masturbation, pederasty, and implicitly, perhaps homosexuality, as well as the seducing of others. His big issues, however, are adultery and fornication, and here he brings in the story of Joseph of Egypt and his resistance to the instigations of the wife of Putiphar. He also points out the main role played by the Devil in sins of sex, and that it is he who ultimately profits from such sins. He also mentions internal sins of sex which seem out of place, because he deals with them again in the ninth commandment. Interesting is his exhortation to respect the body and its specific organs, not using them for illicit sex. He concludes with a threat of God's impending anger on mankind, using the dramatic image of torrential rains and the consequent floods.

The seventh commandment, *Hovag cang magnacao*, i.e., "Do not steal," (pp. 280, 280v, 281), mentions the injustices practiced by the natives in their trade relationships: avarice and lust for gold, usury, cheating and deception, and again, the Devil's role as teacher of these. He cites the words of Christ about how few among the rich would enter Heaven, and the example of the elderly Tobias in the book of Tobit, who did not want to receive stolen property, and ending with a rather dramatic story about a local father and son who were punished in hell because of their theft.

The eighth commandment, *Hovag cang magbintang sa capova mo tauo, at houag ca namang magsinonĝaling*, i.e., "Do not accuse another falsely, and do not tell lies," (pp. 281, 281v, 282v), enumerates the three topics and sins against the commandment, each illustrated by a corresponding story: the false accusation of another is illustrated with the story of Susanna from the book of Daniel, which he described and dramatized at great length, using up almost a whole page in the process. An interesting detail in his version is the use of local trees, under which the two old men were when they saw Susanna, instead of the ones mentioned in the Bible. The second sin is the reporting of the faults of another, which he illustrates with the episode of Miriam, who was afflicted with leprosy for having made up stories about her brother, Moses. The third sin he mentions refers to the unfounded and false suspicion of others, illustrating this with an episode from the life of Bernard of Quintavalle, the first companion of St. Francis of Assisi, who was rewarded in Heaven with two bright eyes, because he never saw evil in others, nor suspected anyone of it.

The ninth commandment, *Hovag cang magnasa sa di mo asava*, i.e., "Do not desire one who is not your husband or wife," and the tenth, *Hovag mo namang pagnasaan ang ari nang capoua tauo*, i.e., "Do not desire the property of your fellowman," are treated together almost in passing, for the two commandments are explained in three short paragraphs, two for the ninth and one for the tenth, the entire explanation of both commandments hardly filling a page (pp. 282v, 283). Here the author simply stresses the sinful nature of evil thoughts, desires and intentions, whether directed to the husband or wife of another, or to his property. Though he brings in no stories or illustrations, his treatment is concretely situated and practical.

2. *Brief explanation of the content*

The summary of the content just presented reveals the concept of a God who is ever on the alert to punish transgressors, threatening the unstable and the unfaithful, demanding absolute submission and fidelity. Such a concept seemed necessary as an initial step to impress upon the newly converted Christian his obligation to remain faithful. The fear induced by such pedagogy would help assure the natives' permanence in the faith. In spite of it, however, there were still cases of some Christians returning to their pagan practices, as Oliver seems to hint in his explanation of the First

Commandment when he asks: "Christians, you who have been baptized, why do you despise God? Why do you turn your backs on him who created you?"

Oliver's zeal in uprooting idolatry on one hand and affirming the belief and worship of the true God on the other is understandable, because he realized that it was not just a question of idols, images and certain ceremonies, but that the animistic religion pervaded the lives of the natives to the core. Therefore, he insists, they ought to have absolute allegiance to the one true God and respect for his name.

He also stresses Sunday Mass, because it was the only day when Christians and new converts can receive instructions. If he would not emphasize this obligation, it would have been taken lightly, and backsliding to idolatry would follow soon after. Thus, on Sundays the natives were to occupy themselves with prayers, hear a complete Mass and listen to the instructions and sermon during the service.

Fear underlies man's submission, obedience and fidelity to God. In such an atmosphere where one is overwhelmed, so to say, by such a powerful and demanding God, Jesus Christ can find little place, and man himself is considered as a submissive creature, passive and without initiative, forced to obey God's commands out of fear of punishment and eternal damnation. It is not, however, the motive for being faithful to God and obedient to his commands only. It is also the motive for living a moral life. Oliver has been very emphatic and repetitious in pointing out that sins will be punished severely. The frequent mention of the Devil as principal torturer, and Hell as the terrible place of torment with horrible types of torture, contributed to the implantation of fear in his audience.

His treatment of marriage is brief but important. He underlines the equality between man and wife, for they are one body. Thus, he stresses the unity of marriage and affirms its indissolubility, explicitly stating that the bond remains until the death of one of the members. Oliver, however, did not simply affirm these fundamental teachings about Christian marriage. He also equally affirmed that the husband and wife are to love and respect each other. Woman, in fact, was given by God himself to man to be his companion, to save him from loneliness.

Oliver seems considerably clear in describing the specificity of sinful actions. Whether he is affirming the gravity of sins of thought and desire, or getting involved in some casuistry, the transgressions he considers gravely sinful are those which sight undermine the building up of the budding Christian community. Perhaps this explains his very strong stand against idolatry, as we have already mentioned. This same understanding motive also explains apparently his forceful denunciation of sins against sexuality, particularly those that are related to the family: adultery and incest. The primitive condition of the moral awareness of the people needed a specific, definite and detailed enumeration of sins and some casuistry which would be practical to them.

On the positive side of the picture, Oliver proposes respect as the basis of a sane and harmonious relationship in the society. Whether the respect is explicit, as the respect for God's name or for one's parents and elders, or just implicit as the respect for life (in the condemnation of abortion and murder), or the property of others (in the condemnation of theft and injustice in commerce and business), or the good name of one's fellowmen (in the condemnation of tale-bearing, murmuring and other sins of the Eighth Commandment), the underlying motive is God's command and will. This topic of respect is treated in greater detail in the section on man and his relationships.

23

WU LI (1632–1718) AND THE FIRST CHINESE CHRISTIAN POETRY[1]

Jonathan Chaves

Source: *Journal of the American Oriental Society*, 122(3) (2002), 506–19.

1.

It is well known that Jesuit missionaries in China quickly grasped the significance of learning and scholarship for the Chinese literati, and themselves made every effort to master the classical texts upon which Confucian education was based. One of these books was the *Shih ching* 詩經, or *Book of Songs*, an anthology of some 300 poems dating as far back as c. 1000 B.C., but compiled into a book ca. 600 B.C. Partly as a result of the inclusion of this material among the classical texts that had to be mastered to succeed in the civil service examinations, poetry came to occupy the preeminent position in the hierarchy of literary prestige. And this included the ability to write one's own original poetry, called for as well in the examinations. The writing of poetry also played a key role in social gatherings among the scholar-officials of China. Poetry was, in fact, a foundation stone of Chinese culture, and the Jesuit missionaries came to be fully aware of this fact.

Perhaps the first of them to envision the creation of a Chinese Christian poetry, which could help to bolster the prestige of Christianity itself among the educated elite of China, was Michele Ruggieri, S. J. (1543–1607), as recently demonstrated by Albert Chan, S. J. in an important study.[2] The poems attributed to him, however, were almost certainly written with the extensive help of Chinese collaborators. As Chan states, "It would have been impossible for him to write poems without help from some Chinese scholars."[3] The resulting poems remain curiosities of historical interest, but possess little literary value.

Chinese converts among the literati class would have helped Ruggieri, and would soon try themselves to produce a type of poetry which they must have realized had only one precedent in literary history: the creation of a Chinese Buddhist poetry in the late Han and Six Dynasties periods (second century through the sixth century), following upon the introduction of Buddhism from India and Central Asia in the first century A.D. Similar problems were encountered: new technical terms for which there were no real Chinese equivalents, names of human or divine personages in strange languages, and the languages themselves—Sanskrit or Latin—in which the source materials were written. The predictable result in the case of Buddhist poetry was the production of much virtual doggerel, doctrinally effective but of little or no aesthetic value. And yet some poets, such as the semilegendary Han Shan 寒山 (?fl. early 9th century) had found ways to write superb poetry that drew extensively upon Buddhist terminology and ideas. Perhaps something of the same achievement could be hoped for in the case of Christianity as well.

One of the most distinguished of all literati converts, the famed Hsü Kuang-ch'i 徐光啟 (1562–1633), has left a body of writings that includes eight poems.[4] Ad Dudink has argued persuasively that only five of these are authentic;[5] these are tetrasyllabic poems of the type known in Chinese as *tsan* 贊 (also 讚) or "eulogies" (see below). They cover such themes as the Ten Commandments, the Eight Beatitudes, the Fourteen Works of Mercy, and the Seven Cardinal Virtues Overcoming the Deadly Sins. They may be described as journeyman work, clearly intended for a purely didactic purpose. Hsü was by no means a poet of significance.

D. E. Mungello has called attention to a series of thirty-eight "inscriptions in Eulogy of the Sage Teaching" 聖教贊銘 by a certain Chang Hsing-yao 張星曜 (1633–1715), composed to accompany a series of paintings—unfortunately no longer extant—in a church at Hangchou (Hangzhou).[6] Mungello translates one of them, dedicated to St. Peter. Like the tetrasyllabic poems of Hsü Kuang-ch'i, these poems, in form, content, and tone, are strongly reminiscent of the *tsan* written for centuries to accompany paintings of Confucian, Taoist, and especially Buddhist figures. For example, the great Sung-dynasty literatus, Su Shih 蘇軾 (or Tung-p'o 東坡) (1037–1101) wrote a series of *tsan* to accompany eighteen paintings of Buddhist arhats (perfected monks) by the monk-painter Ch'an-yüeh 禪月.[7] The Chang Hsing-yao poems are stylistically extremely close to the Su Shih examples.

Still more ambitiously, the literati convert Li Tsu-po 李祖白—who helped to write and edit the book, *T'ien-hsüeh ch'uan-kai* 天學傳概 (Transmitted Summation of the Heavenly Learning) which called down the wrath of scholar-official Yang Kuang-hsien on the Chinese Christians, leading to Li's execution in 1665—produced a long poem in the classic *shih* 詩 format entitled "Ta tao hsing" 大道行, or "Ballad of the Great Way," in which he attempted to give a poetic history of Christianity, including its advent in China, and Li's own baptism in 1622. This poem, dated to 1658, has only recently been discovered by Ad Dudink in a seventeenth-century MS of Chinese Christian texts entitled *T'ien-hsüeh chi-chieh* 天學集解, "Collected

Explanations of the Heavenly Learning," deposited at St. Petersburg, Russia, where it arrived in 1827.[8] In this poem, Li begins by referring to the Supreme God—"The True Sovereign transcendently beyond all names and images!/ Self-established, eternally existent, cut off from origin or ending"—and then goes on to describe the creation of the universe. He narrates the coming to China of Matteo Ricci, S. J. (1552–1610), his own conversion, and the work of his teacher and priest, Adam Schall von Bell, S. J. (1592–1666) in helping to "establish the calendar."

The poem is an indication of how ambitious the enterprise of crafting a Chinese Christian poetry had become by the time that Wu Li was a young man—twenty-eight years old when Li Tsu-po wrote his "Ballad of the Great Way." And yet it remains clear that until Wu Li, there had been no major figure, already a significant poet in his own right, who succeeded in crafting a sizable body of Chinese Christian poetry, aesthetically and theologically successful.

2.

Wu Li 吳歷 is a familiar figure to students of Chinese painting. He is one of the so-called "Six Orthodox Masters" of early Ch'ing-dynasty painting. Works by him are now on display in some of the world's great museums, including in this country alone The Metropolitan Museum of Art in New York, The Cleveland Museum of Art, and The Freer Gallery of Asian Art in Washington, D.C., to name only three (see figs 1 and 4 for examples). His entry into the Society of Jesus in 1682, and his ordination as one of China's first Catholic priests in 1688, are well known, although the actual date of his baptism remains unclear.[9]

It has recently been demonstrated by Noël Golvers that Wu Li served as the catechist of François de Rougemont, S. J. (1624–76), a major Belgian (or Southern Netherlands—born in Maastricht) missionary known to several important literati of the day; Golvers argues most convincingly that Wu Li "appears to have prepared his spiritual life in the 1670's in the immediate company of de Rougemont as one of his catechists," and that "in or about 1671 . . . Wu Li was a Christian."[10]

That de Rougemont himself was seriously interested in employing poetry for the purpose of inculcating Christianity in the Chinese is indicated by his involvement in the publication of a collection entitled *Cantiones Rusticae*, or "Rustic Songs." In an entry in his Account Book, dating from shortly after March 18, 1676, he records, "Imprimendis Cantionibus Rusticis: 0–0–6–6", which is translated by Golvers, "For printing (my) Country Songs: 0.060 tael."[11] Golvers cites a statement by Hsü Yün-hsi in 1938 to the effect that these poems are extant, and entitled *Ts'ai-ch'a ko* 採茶歌 or "Tea-Gathering Songs." Golvers further speculates, following Ad Dudink, that these may in turn correspond to a set of unattributed poems currently found in a MS in the Bodleian Library in Oxford, MS Chin.d.51, one of the manuscripts collected by the noted sinologue, Alexander Wylie (1815–87). They prove to be one item in the collection entitled *Sheng-chiao shih-tz'u ko-fu* (romanticized by Wylie as *Shíng keaou she szê k'o foo*) 聖教詩詞歌賦, "Poems and Songs of the Holy Teaching." Wylie further describes the contents thus: ". . . [A] collection of stanzas, reflections, etc., on various points connected with the Christian religion."[12]

The actual MS has been examined by Ad Dudink, who suggests the possible link with de Rougemont,[13] and more recently by myself (in microfilm). It is a "grabbag" of Christian texts, not all of them poetry, but certainly including the set of "Tea-Gathering Songs," seven-character-per-line quatrains organized according to the twelve months, with a thirteenth poem for the intercalary month placed at the end. David Helliwell of the Department of Oriental Books at the Bodleian, opines that this text is one of those which Wylie had copied, rather than an original late Ming or early Ch'ing MS.[14]

In any case, the poems in question demonstrate that the compiler or author, whether de Rougemont with his assistants or someone else, was not only interested in using classical poetry to reach the literati, but was also attempting to forge a *folk* Christian poetry that would help reach out to a larger audience.[15] For there can be no doubt that these poems are stylistically consistent with authentic folk material of the sort collected in the 1920s and after by pioneering folklorists such as Ku Chiehkang 顧頡剛 (1893–1980) and his colleagues, especially the folksongs of the Hakka 客家 people, and from the Kuangtung and Fukien regions in general. The poems open with a line descriptive of a stage in the cultivation of the tea plant, and then go on to make a point about Christian theology or history. As an example, we may take the poem about the Fourth Month:

四月採茶茶葉香, 亞當夫婦太無良. 順魔食果方敢命, 百苦人身遺孽長.

In the Fourth Month, we gather tea, the tea-leaves now so fragrant!
Adam and his wife, Oh, how lacking in goodness were they!
They obeyed the Devil, ate the fruit, and thus dared risk their fate;
A hundred sorrows they evilly bequeathed to future generations.

Poems of this type were originally associated with courtship, and often had erotic implications. One of the Hakka love-songs published by Niu-lang 牛郎 ("Oxherd") in 1957, for example, reads as follows:[16]

飲過妹茶領妹情, 茶杯照影影照人. 連茶連影吞落肚, 一生難忘妹人情.

I've drunk down all your tea, my girl, and understood your feelings—
The teacup reflects your image, and your image reflects yourself!
Tea and image, I swallow them both, right down to my belly;
All life long I'll never forget your feelings for me, my girl!

Also characteristic of a certain mode of Chinese folksong is the passage through the months, reminiscent of the medieval European theme of the Occupations of the Months, often linked in China with references to various flowers and plants. In one such series from eastern Fukien, for example, the twelfth month is represented by this eight-character line (based on a seven-character structure, expanded to accommodate the double numeral for the name of the twelfth month):[17]

十貳月茶花滿山紅

In the twelfth month, the tea blossoms fill the mountain, red!

It is clear that de Rougemont, if he was indeed the author or compiler of the poems in question, would have had his sights set beyond the limited world of the literati. One wonders if the Jesuit missionaries went so far as to arrange for musical performances of such poems, complete with danced vignettes and stylized gestures, as would have been the case with the original folksongs, often used to accompany courtship and other rituals.[18] Given their well-known interest in theatre, opera, etc. this may well have been the case.

It is also of interest to note that the appropriation of secular folk forms for religious purposes probably had already been practiced for centuries by the Buddhists. Wang Ch'iu-kuei points out that Buddhist funerary rites throughout China make use of "morality songs (*ch'uan-shan ko* 傳善歌) in the form of 12-month flower-names."[19] Thus de Rougemont may well have felt a need to "compete" with the Buddhists in this arena.

3.

The Bodleian MS which contains what may be de Rougemont's Chinese folk-style poems also bears witness to what appears to be an extraordinary attempt by Jesuits to appropriate for evangelical purposes a mode of poetic *criticism* practiced in China, in which poems are written to describe and speculate upon archaeological objects. Such poems were particularly important in the Northern Sung dynasty in the circle of poet Mei Yao-ch'en 梅堯臣 (1002–60) and his associates, including the collector of antiquities—and himself a fine poet—Liu Ch'ang 劉敞 (1019–68).[20] On one occasion in 1052, for example, Mei and several friends were visiting this distinguished antiquary when he brought out two ancient coins in his collection, and asked them to guess the dates of these objects. Mei couched his response in the form of a poem,[21] and Liu wrote one as well. It is characteristic of these poems that the writers derive from the objects inspiration for Confucian meditations on history and contemporary policy, as Mei does when he expresses the hope that an ancient bronze crossbow trigger will be used as a model to construct new weapons and might help to stave off border incursions by the Tanguts and Khitans: "Don't let our border troops keep dying off like flies!"[22]

The Bodleian MS presents a long poem of this type entitled, "T'ieh shih-tzu ko" 鐵十字歌, "Song of the Iron Cross-Shaped Object," by a certain Liu Sung 劉嵩. This turns out to be a once-famous poet—his personal name correctly written 崧, and his dates 1321–81. Liu was well enough respected to be represented by no less than fifty poems—a very high number—in the prestigious and influential anthology, *Ming-shih tsung* 明詩綜 (Compendium of Ming-dynasty Poetry) edited by a major scholar, Chu I-tsun 朱彝尊 (1629–1709).[23] The Library of Congress possesses a Wan-li (1573–1620) period edition of Liu's poetry entitled *Liu Ch'a-weng hsien-sheng shih hsüan* 劉槎翁先生詩選 (A Selection of Poems by Mr. Liu Ch'a-weng [Liu Sung]) which, despite its name, is a multivolume, fairly comprehensive collection. It contains a number of long poems on archaeological objects, but not this particular poem. (There must therefore be some question as to the authenticity of the poem.)

In any case, the poem describes, and speculates on the function of, a huge (the examples described by Gaillard[24] are six-feet or so long) iron object shaped like the character *shih* 十—in other words, cross-shaped. We learn that it was discovered along the banks of a river in Lu-ling, Kiangsi, and that it might have been an anchor for rafts, or perhaps a prophylactic device to suppress or exorcise evil water demons. Liu further records that it bears an inscription of the Ch'ih-wu 赤烏 period, or 238–50, but this he questions.

Jesuit missionaries did not hesitate to take the object in question—which was still available for observation—as evidence of the early transmission of Christianity to Clina. Fr. Michael Boim, S. J. (1612–59), for example, writes as follows in a letter quoted by Athanasius Kircher, S. J. (1602–80) in his widely read *China Illustrata* (1667):[25]

> Beside a riverbank in Kiamsy [Kiangsi] Province an iron cross weighing about 3,000 pounds has been found. The inscription on the cross says it was erected in the Chinese era which began in 239 A.D. [*sic*]. Therefore, faithful Christians and preachers must have been among the southern Chinese almost 1415 years ago. . . .

(We might note that if the Liu Sung poem had been forged by, or at the behest of, the Jesuits, we would expect the inscription to have been *accepted* in the poem, as it is accepted by Boim, because this would have constituted key evidence for the early appearance of Christianity in China on the Jesuit theory that the object was a cross. This would seem to argue for the *authenticity* of the poem, at least.)

The poem attributed to Liu Sung is followed in the MS by a commentary by Hsü Kuang-ch'i, dated 1627 (and thus predating the Boim letter) and entitled *T'ieh shih-tzu ko hsün-i* 鐵十字歌訓義, "Explaining the Meaning of the Song on the Iron Cross-Shaped Object," which rebuts the poet's suggestions, and asserts that the object that puzzled the poet must in fact have been

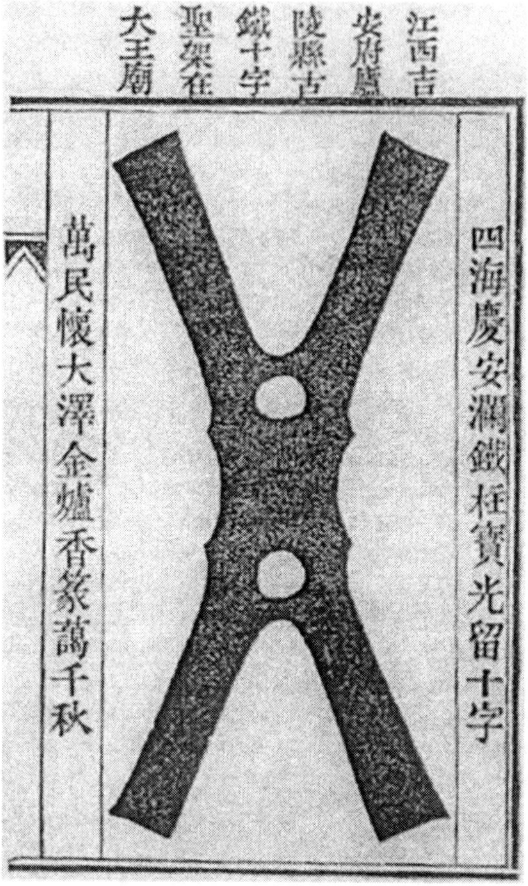

Figure 1 The "iron cross" as depicted in a woodcut from Joseph-Anna-Marie de Mailla, S. J. (1669–1748), *Sheng-shih ch'u-jao* 盛世芻蕘 ("Grass and Weeds from the Flourishing Age"), from Louis Gaillard, S. J., *Croix et swastika en Chine* (Shanghai, 1893), fig. 188.

a crucifix, thus representing early evidence of Christianity in China. This in turn is followed by a colophon of 1642 by Jesuit missionary Francesco Brancati, S. J. (1607–80), praising Hsü for his analysis. Paul Pelliot (1878–1945), however, questioned the authenticity even of the Hsü commentary.[26]

And yet the object in question—or objects, as there were apparently three of them discovered (it remains unclear whether Hsü, Boim, or Brancati *saw* the actual examples, while Gaillard certainly did)—as represented in a woodcut published by Fr. Joseph-Anna-Marie de Mailla (1669–1748) in a Chinese text (see Figure 1) clearly cannot be a crucifix. It is X-shaped, for one thing, and although St. Andrew's cross is X-shaped, it seems most unlikely that the object was meant for this. Instead, Louis Gaillard, S. J., who undertook and published in 1893 by far the most thorough study of the whole matter,[27] is certainly correct in speculating tentatively that the objects were intended for use as mooring devices for ferries, anchors (one of "Liu Sung's" theories), bases of support for undetermined objects, or some other purely secular use.

At any rate, while the attempt by the Jesuits to take the "crosses" as evidence of an early Christian presence in China seems, alas, merely willful,[28] it does bear witness to the high degree of sophistication in literati learning achieved by the men who were evangelizing such Chinese scholars as Wu Li.

4.

Wu Li's poetry has gone largely unnoticed, although the distinguished anthologist of Ch'ing-dynasty poetry, Teng Chih-ch'eng 鄧之誠 included several of his poems, together with a lengthy analytical essay, in his important two-volume anthology, *Ch'ing-shih chi-shih ch'u-pien* 清詩紀事初編 (Recording Matters Pertaining to Ch'ing Poetry—First Edition),[29] and Albert Chan, S. J., writing in the *New Catholic Encyclopedia* (1967),[30] has stated that "his poems are graceful and limpid, especially those of his later years, which couch Catholic thought in exquisite style; he was perhaps the first in China to find a poetic vehicle for Christian doctrine."

Wu Li's teacher in poetry was none other than Ch'ien Ch'ien-i 錢謙益 (1582–1664), one of the leading scholars of the day. In a preface he composed for an early collection of Wu Li's poetry, Ch'ien wrote that Wu "is not only good at painting; he is exceptionally skillful at poetry. The thought [in his poems] is pure and the style ancient. . . ."[31] Wu also associated, during the years 1670–71, with probably the leading and most influential circle of poets in China, that centering around Wang Shih-chen 王士禎 (1634–1711) in the capital, Peking. Among these men, the most exciting recent development was the rediscovery of the previously denigrated poetry of the Sung dynasty (960–1279), epitomized in the publication of a magisterial collectanea of anthologies of Sung poetry, the *Sung shih ch'ao* 宋詩鈔 (Texts of Sung-Dynasty Poetry), edited by Wu Chih-chen 吳之振 (1640–1717) and others. It was circulating in the Wang Shih-chen circle at precisely the moment that Wu Li was associating with them.

In general, the relative realism and simplicity of tone of Sung poetry were attractive to these poets, as well as the openness of Sung poetics to new, even bizarre, subject matter. At the same time, Sung poets were masters of a discursive, almost prose-like style suitable for putting forth ideas in verse. All of these characteristics were seen by Wang and his followers as providing salutary inspiration for correcting what they considered to be the decadence of poetic style inherited from the late Ming.

At the same time, there was an increasing interest in exploring the potential of other poetic genres beside the *shih*, most notably the *tz'u* 詞, or "lyric," and the *ch'ü* 曲, or "aria" (originally the sung portions of Chinese plays). These two types, actually very similar to each other, allowed the use of lines of differing lengths, whereas the *shih* has the same number of characters per line throughout the poem (usually five or seven). Wu Li would write some of his most striking Christian poetry in the *ch'ü* form.

The increasing interest in prose-like poetic diction, but also in relatively "popular" forms such as the "lyric" and the "aria," derived from a desire to use poetry to help bring about a revival of Confucian orthodoxy, something championed, for example, by Wu Li's teacher in Confucian thought, Ch'en Hu 陳瑚 (1613–75). Ch'en himself expressed a wish to write arias about "righteous scholars and loyal ministers" for a certain singer whose performance he admired.[32] This was because Ch'en Hu and his associates, such as Lu Shih-i 陸世儀 (1611–72), were part of a movement to seek in a revived Confucianism what Frederic Wakeman describes as "an antidote . . . to moral relativism."[33] These Confucian thinkers and teachers presided over a circle of students, including Wu Li, among whom there was a remarkable degree of questioning in the wake of the collapse of the Ming dynasty in 1644, and even what may be termed spiritual turmoil. Among the kinds of questions debated among them was the relationship between the term "Heaven" (*t'ien* 天) and the term "Lord on High" (*shang-ti* 上帝), both of which are found in the *Shih ching* and other Confucian classics. Ch'en Hu follows in the tradition of the famous Neo-Confucian thinker, Chu Hsi 朱熹 (1130–1200) when he argues that " 'Lord' is precisely 'heaven.' It is not that beyond heaven there exists a so-called 'Lord.' The ten thousand things are rooted in heaven. . . ."[34]

One of Ch'en Hu's pupils—and thus a fellow-student of Wu Li's—as well as a relative of Ch'ien Ch'ien-i's, Ch'ü Yu-chung 瞿有仲, actually turned some of this remarkable spiritual searching into poetic form, a particularly dramatic example of how poetry was being used to present and orchestrate the biggest questions confronted by mankind. This poem, entitled "Chün-t'ien yüeh" 鈞天樂 ("Music of Harmonious Heaven") describes a visit to the court of "Yellow Heaven" by the poet, who presents a petition to the celestial emperor—apparently one of a series of cyclical cosmic rulers—in which he complains of Heaven's unfeeling silence in the face of human suffering throughout history. The poet offers as a solution this suggestion:

> Why not establish a single lord for all of heaven and earth?
> Why not establish a single people for all of heaven and earth?

But Yellow Heaven ignores his plea, and simply continues his mindless feasting.[35]

Any account of the Chinese reception of Christianity that ignores such evidence of real philosophical questioning as this will run the risk of missing the most important point of all: that certain thinkers in China were, in the latter part of the seventeenth century, actually fantasizing about an orderly cosmos ruled by a single immutable lord, precisely the reality claimed by the opening sentence of the Nicene Creed.

Such an atmosphere of dissatisfaction quite naturally gave rise to frequent acts of conversion in the circle of Ch'en Hu and Lu Shih-i—and beyond, of course. Most of these were from Confucianism to Buddhism, but conversions from Taoism to Buddhism, or from Confucianism to Buddhism and then back again, are also described.[36] Given the fact that Wu Li found himself in the midst of this fury of conversion activity, his decision to convert to something seems less surprising. But why Christianity? The action is puzzling to begin with, because it runs counter to the conventional wisdom to the effect that the later seventeenth century was a time of decline in literati conversions to Christianity.

One attempt to explain Wu Li's conversion was made in 1987 by art historian Lin Xiaoping, who presented Wu's act as a rebellion "away from the constraints of the Confucian Five Relations towards a more genuine humanity."[37] He strives to establish that Wu was inspired by the Aristotelian aesthetics of Aquinas to pay closer attention to actual nature in his painting. In fact, the whole question of possible Western influence on Wu Li's painting is vexed. Lin finds it, but most scholars, myself included, see no sign at all that Wu's compositional and other elements derive from anything other than indigenous Chinese traditions. In any case, while Wu Li was undoubtedly moved to reject aspects of Neo-Confucianism, these would certainly not have included the Five Relationships; more likely, as certain of his poems reveal, they would have been points of ontology and cosmology. And if anything in the *Summa Theologica*—which was being translated into Chinese at the time—would have inspired Wu Li, it would have been precisely the Christian doctrine therein; the Aristotelian aspects would have been of secondary importance for him, especially as Chinese aesthetic theory as early as the Six Dynasties period (220–589) provided ample sanction for a mimesis-like concept of copying from nature.

Willard J. Peterson, in discussing the conversions of the "three pillars of the Chinese church," sensitively points out that "the minds and hearts of [these men] would not be fully accessible even if one could subject them to all sorts of prying interrogations. Available resources do not provide sufficient evidence to analyze any profound religious experience they may have undergone."[38] But Wu Li's religious poems and recorded sayings do serve as a source for some understanding of his theological interests and do hint at a "profound religious experience" beginning in intellectual, moral and spiritual dissatisfaction, and culminating in conversion.

Wu Li agreed with the general tendency among the scholar-officials with whom he associated to deplore moral decay and the burgeoning of what they saw as decadent cults, as well as to reject Buddhism. His views on both scores are succinctly put forth in a single poetic couplet dating from 1690:[39]

I'm delighted to see an official extirpating error;
absolutely no monk's-robes knock at my gate.

The first of these lines, as Ch'en Yüan has noted,[40] alludes to measures taken in 1685 by the provincial governor of Suchou, T'ang Pin 湯斌 (1627–87), to suppress "decadent shrines" and religious practices in that area, including various forms of shamanism and night-time gatherings of cult followers. T'ang destroyed the clay and wooden images in the shrines and set up in their place an image of Kuan Yü 關羽.[41]

Wu's statement in the second half of the couplet that he receives no Buddhist monks as visitors represents a change from the 1660s and early '70s, when one of Wu's closest friends was the Buddhist monk Mo-jung 默容 (d. 1672).[42]

But Wu went beyond his Confucian colleagues in rejecting aspects of Confucianism itself. In general it may be said that he upheld the Confucian moral order while questioning the cults of certain deities—or apotheosized human heroes, such as Kuan Yü—within Confucianism itself, as well as (Neo-)Confucian ontology or metaphysics. The Kuan Yü so admired by T'ang Pin Wu castigates as follows: "This man clearly openly sold the legitimacy of the Han dynasty to others. He is not worthy to be considered a 'Sage' [*sheng* 聖, the word used for 'Saint' in Chinese Christian writings]."[43]

More significantly, Wu Li set out to distinguish the Christian doctrine of the Trinity from confusion with an apparently similar conception in Confucian thought, and by implication to reject the idea of the One self-evolving into the Many which underpins virtually all Chinese (indeed, all "pagan") thought. This he does in the eleventh of possibly his most important group of religious poems, the twelve entitled *Singing of the Source and Course of Holy Church* 誦聖教源流,[44] In translation, the poem reads as follows:

"The Supreme Ultimate contains three—"
  muddled words indeed!
In fact, they start with primal energy
  to speak of original chaos.
From books of the past, we learned of old
  of sincerity, wisdom and goodness;
the Mysterious meaning now we understand
  of Father, Son and Holy Spirit.
The Persons distinct: close at hand, consider
  the flame within the mirror;
the Essence is whole: far off, please note
  the wheel that graces the sky.
The Holy Name has been revealed,
  His authority conferred;
throughout the world in this human realm
  the sound of the teaching supreme!

The first line is based on a passage in the "*Monograph on Pitchpipes and Calendrical Affairs*" 律曆志 in the *Han shu* 漢書 (official history of the Han dynasty):[45] "The primal energy of the Supreme Ultimate contains three as one. . . ." (*T'ai-chi yüan-ch'i han san wei* 太極元氣函三為一). Wu Li in his poem intends to distinguish the Christian idea (or rather, revelation) of God as these distinct persons sharing one essence from the idea of a primal unity self-evolving into the multiplicity of the variegated universe.

Wu, as we have seen, would have been introduced to Christianity by Chinese converts and by the Jesuits he himself encountered, primarily François de Rougemont, whose catechist he was, and Philippe Couplet, S. J. (1623–93). It was Couplet who invited Wu to accompany him to Rome in 1681, along with four other Chinese converts, although Wu was only to travel as far as Macau in the end, apparently as a consequence of a decision by the newly appointed Jesuit vice-provincial in China, Giandomenico Gabiani, that Wu was too old to take the trip.[46]

5.

Wu Li's poetry can be divided into four broad groupings:

1) "Conventional" *shih* poems virtually indistinguishable from similar poems by other writers past and present, but demonstrating a generally "neo-Sung" style.
2) What might be considered a transitional group of thirty quatrains in seven-character metre on life in Macau Christian themes are touched upon in the context of a broad portrait of the customs and festivals of the mostly Portuguese community.
3) *Shih* poems fully devoted to Christian themes.
4) *Ch'ü* poems on Christian themes.

Wu Li's Macau sequence[47] (see fig. 3 for the holograph) may well be the first poems in Chinese literature to describe Western customs in some detail on the basis of direct observation. Macau since the mid-sixteenth century had functioned as a sort of quasi-official trading post for the Portuguese; by 1635, when Antonio Bocarro wrote his detailed account of Macau (without actually having been there),[48] the population consisted of some 850 Portuguese families with "on the average about six slaves capable of bearing arms, amongst whom the majority and the best are negroes and such like," and a comparable number of "native families, including Chinese Christians." Wu Li, like Bocarro, noted the presence in Macau both of black slaves and of non-Han Chinese such as the Tanka boat people. The third poem in the sequence, together with Wu's own note to it, serves as a good example of Wu's interest in capturing a realistic "sense of place" and in introducing details of local and Portuguese custom (the frying of fish in olive oil):

Yellow sand, white-washed houses: here the black men live;
willows at the gates like sedge, still not sparse in autumn.
Midnight's when the Tanka come and make their harbor here;
fasting kitchens for noonday meals have plenty of fresh fish.

[Poet's note:] the blacks by custom admire a deep black color as beautiful; a pale black they consider ugly. There are two varieties of fish: shad and *liu* fish. They are fried in Western olive oil, and then eaten for the forty-day lenten fast.

Wu also describes in detail aspects of specifically religious life in Macau, including the practice popular in all Mediterranean and Iberian Christian societies of holding processions dedicated to certain saints through the streets of the town. His fourth poem was inspired by such a procession in honor of St. Francis Xavier 1506–52):

Holding candles, burning high,
  they welcome the great saint;
banners, pennants flap in wind,
  cannon roar like thunder.
On all sides streets are spread with grass,
  green like tapestry:
pedestrians are not allowed to trample it to dust.

[Poet's note:] when St. Francis Xavier emerges in procession, the streets are covered with flowers and grass to show reverence. The streets are called "Awe of Majesty, Love of Virtue."

The realism of these poems, their straightforwardness of diction, and their openness to unprecedented subject matter are all characteristics of Sung poetry and of the Sung-influenced Individualist movement in late-Ming (Kung-an) and early-Ch'ing letters.

Of Wu Li's third type of poetry, *shih* poems on religious themes, the "Song of the Fisherman" (*Yü-fu yin* 漁父吟)[49] is a particularly good example. Wu Li did write conventional "fisherman" poems on hermit-fishermen; one of these, inscribed on a hanging scroll of 1675,[50] itself provides an interesting variation on the theme:

My hermit's life, entirely passed within a single boat!
I ask the world for nothing, I only love pure calm.
I cast far off through rivers and lakes
  so I can read in peace,
yet ears and eyes still feel hemmed in
  by all these verdant mountains.

The hermit-fisherman's desire for tranquility is so great that he feels "hemmed in" even by the green mountains. It is almost as if he cannot find "rest in Nature," to use a phrase from George Herbert's (1593–1633) poem, "The Pulley."[51] The fisherman of "Song of the Fisherman," however, has friends who find rest in the "God of Nature" (Herbert):

From patching rips in tattered nets
  his eyes have gotten blurred;
he scours the river, does not disdain
  the tiniest fish and shrimp.
Selecting the freshest, he has supplied
  the feasts of sovereigns;
all four limbs exhausted now,
  dare he refuse the work?
Spreading nets he gets confused
  by water just like sky;
song lingering, still drunk, approaches
  dragons as they sleep.
Now hair and whiskers are all white,
  his face has aged with time;
he's startled by the wind and waves
  and fears an early autumn.
Some friends of his have changed their job:
  they now are fishers of men;
he hears, compared to fishing fish
  this task is tougher still.
Of late he finds the Heavenly Learning
  has come into the city:
to customers now happily add families that fast.

The allusions here to Matthew 4:19–21 are evident.

"Singing of the Source and Course of Holy Church," as we have seen, represents the culmination of Wu Li's theological *shih* poetry. The eleventh poem in this sequence has already been discussed; the second is also of particular interest, especially in light of Jacques Gernet's claim that "the seventeenth-century Chinese Christians never make any allusion to Jesus in their writings."[52] Wu in this poem orchestrates the theme of the Cross as a ladder to Heaven:

Before the firmament was ever formed,
  or any foundation laid,
high there hovered the Judge of the World,
  prepared for the last days!

This single man from his five wounds
  poured every drop of blood;
a myriad nations gave their hearts
  to the wonder of the Cross!
The heavenly gates now have a ladder
  leading to their peace;
demonic sprits lack any art
  to insinuate deception.
Take up the burden, joyfully
  fall in behind Jesus,
Look up with reverence towards the top of that mountain,
  follow His every step.

Heavenly ladders had, in fact, been mentioned in early Chinese literature. The *locus classicus* would be lines 35–36 of the poem "Shang shih" 傷詩, "Distressed by These Times" (as translated by David Hawkes) in the "Chiu ssu" 九思 ("Nine Longings") section—dating from the second century A.D.—of the *Ch'u tz'u* 楚詞 ("Songs of Ch'u") anthology: "Then, ascending heaven's ladder [*t'ien t'i* 天梯], I mounted the northern sky,/Climbed the jade terrace of the King of Heaven."[53] That ladders as images of divine ascent are widely disseminated is, in fact, well known, and the motif has been fully studied by Mircea Eliade in connection with shamanist usage.[54] The Christian image, of course, is rooted in Genesis 28:12–13, the episode of Jacob's ladder; as early as the second century, St. Irenaeus, Bishop of Lyons, was interpreting this ladder as a foreshadowing of the Cross.[55] It might also be noted that a ladder is frequently depicted in art as one of the Instruments of the Passion, and one such representation must have been seen many times by Wu Li, as it graced the superb façade of the Church of São Paulo in Macau,[56] built early in the seventeenth century.

6.

Wu Li's boldest experiment was the writing of suites of *ch'ü* poems on Christian themes.[57] The idea of adopting the popular "aria" form to serious subject matter, as we have seen, may have been stimulated by the interest of members of both the Ch'en Hu and Wang Shih-chen circles in using the *ch'ü* to convey such Confucian principles as filial piety and loyalty. Another possible influence may have been the remarkable "Sorrow of Ten Thousand Ages" (Wan-ku ch'ou 萬古愁), a suite of arias by Kuei Chuang 歸莊 (1613–73)[58] beginning with the creation of P'an-ku and sweeping over the whole of Chinese history (something in the manner of Ch'ü Yu-chung's poem discussed above, which may itself have been influenced by Kuei Chuang) to culminate in the fall of Nanking in 1645.

At the same time, as we have seen, the Jesuit missionaries themselves produced poems or songs (probably with ample help from Chinese converts —see below) and also encouraged literati converts to write Christian poems or songs in popular forms, including authentically "folk" forms such as the "Tea-Gathering Songs." Thus there would have been a remarkable convergence of interest in using popular forms to promulgate serious teachings between the missionaries and the Confucian scholars of the day.

Golvers quite correctly points out that "it is very probable that Chinese (Christian) *litterati* [*sic*] were involved in [a] polishing process,"[59] given that, as in the case of Ruggieri, it is most unlikely that any of the missionaries commanded sufficiently excellent Chinese to write such material without some mode of collaboration with literati converts. These may well have been the "*censores litterati*" referred to by de Rougemont in his Account Book as having been treated by him to "breakfast and an honorable luncheon."[60] Missionaries also, of course, worked closely with native craftsmen trained to copy Christian prints and the like, but in the case of poetry a more complex problem is involved, as such texts would have to be written in perfect Chinese, fully in harmony with the various regulations governing Chinese verse genres, and would undoubtedly require literati involvement. Determining the extent and nature of such collaboration will require further research in this area.

Conversely, in the case of writings by converts, it is known, as Golvers puts it, that "A Chinese convert, who had composed a Christian book, was ordered to present it to a father for revision and further diffusion, for fear that some heterodox elements might slip in."[61] Thus such poems as Wu Li's would at least have been checked for their theological orthodoxy.

Wu Li's *ch'ü* arias deal with such subjects as the Mass (there are detailed descriptions of the movements and gestures of the officiating priest); Christ's life and Passion; praise of the Virgin; and overviews of God's entire economy. One poem from the suite, "Music of Harmonious Heaven in Reverent Thanks to the Lord of Heaven" (Ching hsieh t'ien-chu chün-t'ien yüeh 敬謝天主鈞天樂)—a title which assimilates to the Christian heaven the "Harmonious Heaven" of an anecdote in the Taoist classic, *Lieh Tzu* 列子 (? 3rd cent. A.D.)[62] also used in Ch'ü Yu-chung's previously discussed poem—combines the Incarnation with the Presentation in the Temple:

"To the Tune, *Hsi ch'ien ying* 喜遷鶯"

Late in Han
God's son came down from Heaven
to save the people
and turn us towards the good.
His grace goes wide!

Taking flesh through the virginity
  of the Holy Mother,
    in a stable He was born.
Joseph too came to present Him in the temple:
there to offer praise was
Simeon.
They say He can
save our souls from their destructiveness
and sweep away the devil's wantonness.

Perhaps most remarkable of all is the suite of poems entitled "Moses Admonishes the People—Musical Stanzas," which bears the subtitle, "When Moses was done with his final testament, he continued in song and admonished the people, saying . . ." It is difficult to conceive of any more bizarre phenomenon in literary history than an imaginary oration by Moses intoned in classical Chinese, and yet that is what Wu Li gives us in these poems. In one of them, Moses reminds the people that there is only one Lord of Heaven—the very proposal put before Yellow Heaven in desperation and in vain by Ch'ü Yu-chung), describes for them the land of Canaan which he himself will never enter, and berates them for rebelling against God:

This wilderness!
If only you, His people,
  acknowledge one Lord of Heaven—
there is no second one!—
the Lord of Heaven will confer
  that rich and fertile land
to care for and to cultivate.

That land is luxuriant, fruitful, impossible to match!
The five grains profusely grow,
  there are no weeds and tares;
and it is even richer
in tender kid, fine wine.
Milk and honey, meat and oil there do overflow!
The Lord of Heaven loves you as His children:
who could foresee that you, once full and sated,
  would act like animals,
kicking, biting back!
—forgetting His great gift.

In striving towards the full prophetic voice in Chinese poetry, Wu Li is perhaps attempting the impossible. Is this a fascinating but ultimately failed experiment lacking either precedent or later influence? Or is it a major achievement that throws new light on the potential creativity of later Chinese poetry?

Notes

1 For a fuller presentation of certain aspects of this subject, see my book, *Singing of the Source: Nature and God in the Poetry of the Chinese Painter Wu Li* (Honolulu: Univ. of Hawaii Press, 1993).
2 Albert Chan, S. J., "Michele Ruggieri, S. J. and His Chinese Poems," *Monumenta Serica* 41 (1993): 129–76.
3 Compare also the comments of Noël Golvers on "the participation of some Chinese *litterati* [*sic*] . . . in this [Jesuit] publication program" in seventeenth-century China. Golvers, *François de Rougemont, S. J., Missionary in Ch'ang-shu* (*Chiang-nan*) (Louvain: Leuven Univ. Press, 1999), 485.
4 For the Chinese texts with English translations of all eight, see Wang Hsiao-ch'ao 王曉朝, *Chi-tu chiao yü ti-kuo wen-hua* 基督教與帝國文化 (Peking: Tung-fang ch'u-pan-she, 1997), 149–62.
5 Ad Dudink, "The Image of Xu Guangqi as Author of Christian Texts," in *Statecraft and Intellectual Renewal in Late Ming China: The Cross-Cultural Synthesis of Xu Guangqi* [Hsü Kuang-ch'i], ed. Catherine Jami *et al.* (Leiden: Brill, 2001), 134–44, esp. 134.
6 Mungello, *The Forgotten Christians of Hangzhou* (Honolulu: Univ. of Hawaii Press, 1994), 5, 48, 113–14, 179–82. I am grateful to Prof. Mungello for sending me photocopies of these poems.
7 *Tung-p'o hsü chi* 東坡續集 (in *Tung-p'o ch'i chi* 東坡七集, Ssu-pu pai-yao ed.), 10.5a–6b.
8 Adrian Dudink, "The Rediscovery of a Seventeenth-Century Collection of Chinese Christian Texts: the Manuscript *Tianxue jijie*," *Sino-Western Cultural Relations Journal* 15 (1993): 13.
9 For a good general introduction to Wu's life, see Eugene Feifel, trans., Ch'ien Yüan 陳垣, "Wu Yü-shan [Wu Li]—In Commemoration of the 250th Anniversary of his Ordination to the Priesthood in the Society of Jesus," *Monumenta Serica* 3 (1938), pp. 130–70.
10 Golvers, 437, 415–16. For de Rougemont's links to the literati, see Chaves, *Singing of the Source*, 44–46.
11 Golvers, 454–55.
12 Alexander Wylie, *Notes on Chinese Literature: With Introductory Remarks on the Progressive Advancement of the Art; and a List of Translations from the Chinese into Various European Languages* (Shanghai: Presbyterian Mission Press, 1867), 180.
13 Personal communication.
14 Personal communication.
15 This would appear to be consistent with a point recently made by Fr. Gianni Criveller in his book, *Preaching Christ in Late Ming China: The Jesuits' Presentation of Christ from Matteo Ricci to Giulio Aleni* (Taipei and Brescia: Taipei Ricci Institute, in collaboration with Fondazione Civiltà Bresciana, 1997).
16 Niu-lang, *Love Songs of the Hakka in Kwangtung*, in *Min-su ts'ung-shu* 民俗叢書, vol. 133, ed. Peking University Society for Chinese Folklore (1957; rpt. Taipei: Orient Cultural Service), 50.
17 Lou Tzu-k'uang 婁子匡, ed., *Folksongs of Eastern Fuchien*, in *Chung-shan Ta-hsüeh min-su ts'ung-shu* 中山大學民俗叢書, vol. 8 (1929; rpt. Taipei, 1970), 60–61.

18 For more on the performance aspect of such material, see Charles Hartman, "Stomping Songs: Word and Image," *Chinese Literature: Essays, Articles, Reviews* 17 (1995): 1–50, esp. 8–9.
19 Personal communication.
20 For this, see Jonathan Chaves, *Mei Yao-ch'en and the Development of Early Sung Poetry* (New York: Columbia Univ. Press, 1976), 199–218.
21 Ibid., 210–11.
22 Ibid., 213–14.
23 *Ming-shih tsung*, 2 vols. (Taipei: Shih-chieh shu-chü, 1962), 1: 4.1a ff.
24 See n. 27 below.
25 Charles Van Tuyl, trans., *China Illustrata . . . by Athanasius Kircher, S. J.* (Bloomington: Indiana Univ. Research Institute for Inner Asian Studies, 1987), 8.
26 Cited in Dudink, "The Image of Xu Guangqi . . . ," 124 n. 81.
27 Louis Gaillard, S. J., *Croix et Swastika en Chine* (Shanghai Imprimerie de la Mission Catholique, 1893), 218–74, including complete Chinese texts.
28 A similar conclusion is reached by Erik Zürcher, "Jesuit Accommodation and the Chinese Cultural Imperative," in *The Chinese Rites Controversy: Its History and Meaning*, ed. D. E. Mungello, Nettetal: Steyler Verlag, 1994), 55. He sees the use of the iron "cross" as an example of employing "archaeological objects [to provide] the foreign doctrine with its native roots and with a pedigree reaching back to primeval times: Christian counterparts to the Buddhist 'relics of Asoka.' "
29 Teng Chih-ch'eng, *Ch'ing-shih chi-shih ch'u-pien* (1965; rpt. Shanghai: Ku-chi ch'u-pan-she, 1984), 1: 85–86.
30 *New Catholic Encyclopedia* (New York: McGraw Hill, 1967), vol. 14, p. 1046.
31 Chaves, *Singing of the Source*, 6.
32 Ibid., 15–16.
33 Frederic Wakeman, Jr., *The Great Enterprise* (Berkeley and Los Angeles: Univ. of California Press, 1985), 1093–94.
34 For all of this, see Chaves, *Singing of the Source*, 17ff.
35 Ibid., 20ff.
36 Ibid., 30ff.
37 Lin Xiaoping, "Wu Li's Religious Belief and *A Lake in Spring*," *Archives of Asian Art* 40 (1987): 29. See also idem, *Wu Li: His Life, His Paintings* (Lanham, Md.: University Press of America, 2001), as well as Chaves, *Singing of the Source*, 35–36.
38 Peterson, "Why Did They Become Christians?—Yang T'ing-yün, Li Chih-tsao, and Hsü Kuang-ch'i," in *East Meets West: The Jesuits in China*, 1582–1773, ed. Charles E. Ronan, S. J. and Bonnie B. C. Oh (Chicago: Loyola Univ. Press, 1988), 129.
39 Fang Hao, ed., "Wu Yü-shan hsien-sheng 'San-yü chi' chiao-shih" 吳漁山先生三餘集校釋 in Chou K'ang-hsieh, op.cit., 88.
40 Ch'en Yüan, *Nien-p'u* 年譜 (chronology) of Wu Li, in Chou K'ang-hsieh, 17.
41 T'ang Pin, *T'ang Tzu i-shu* 湯子遺書 (ed. of 1870), *Chiang-nan kung-tu* 江南公牘, 9.38b–39a.
42 For Wu Li's relationship with Mo-jung, see Ch'en Yüan, "Wu Yü-shan chih Ch'an-yu" 吳漁山之禪友, in *Ch'en Yüan shih-hsüeh lun-chu hsüan* 陳垣史學論著選 (Shanghai: Jenmin ch'u-pan-she, 1981), 405–8.
43 Li Ti, S. J. 李杕, ed., *Mo-ching ji* 墨井集 (Shanghai: Zikawei Press, 1909), 5.76b. This rare book is the only complete collection of Wu Li's writings. The copy I consulted is in the East Asian Library at Washington University, St. Louis.
44 Ibid., 3.61a.
45 *Han shu* (Peking: Chung-hua shu-chü, 1962), 21A.964.

46 For this, see Chaves, *Singing of the Source*, 194n., and Theodore Nicholas Foss, "The European Sojourn of Philippe Couplet and Michael Shen Fuzong, 1683–1692," in *Philippe Couplet, S. J. (1623–1693): The Man Who Brought China to Europe*, ed. Jerome Heyndrickx (Nettetal: Steyler Verlag, 1990), 121–42.
47 Fang Hao, ed., "Wu Yü-shan hsien-sheng 'San-pa ji' chiao-shih" 吳漁山先生三巴集校釋, in Chou K'ang-hsieh, 103–16; see also Wang Tsung-yen's 汪宗衍 further annotations to these poems in Chou K'ang-hsieh, 141–46.
48 C. R. Boxer, "Macao Three Hundred Years Ago, as Described by Antonio Bocarro in 1635," *T'ien Hsia Monthly*, 6.4 (April, 1938): 281–316.
49 Fang Hao, ed., ". . . San-yü chi 三餘集 . . . ," in Chou K'ang-hsieh, 102.
50 Tomioka Masutarō 富岡益郎, *Shi-Ō Go Un* 四王吳惲 (Osaka: Hakubundō, 1919), plate 32.
51 John N. Wall, Jr., ed., *George Herbert: The Country Parson, the Temple* (New York: Paulist Pess, 1981), 284–85.
52 Jacques Gernet, *China and the Christian Impact: A Conflict of Cultures*, tr. Janet Lloyd (Cambridge: Cambridge Univ. Press, 1982), 223.
53 *Ch'u-tz'u pu-chu* 楚詞補注 (Ssu-pu pei-yao ed.) 17.12b; tr. David Hawkes, *The Songs of the South* (Harmondsworth, Middlesex: Penguin Books, 1985), 315.
54 Mircea Eliade, *Shamanism: Archaic Techniques of Ecstasy* tr. Willard R. Trask (Princeton: Princeton Univ. Press, 1964), 487–94.
55 Joseph P. Smith, S. J., trans., *St. Irenaeus: Proof of the Apostolic Preaching* (New York: Newman Press, 1952), 77.
56 The most comprehensive study of this church will be found in Gonçalo Couceiro, *A Igreja de S. Paulo* (Lisbon: Livros Horizonte, 1997); see illustrations on pp. 121, 134 et passim.
57 Fang Hao, ed., "Wu Yü-shan hsien-sheng 'T'ien-yüeh cheng-yin p'u' chiao-shih," 天樂正音譜校釋, in Chou K'ang-hsieh, 69–84. For the poems translated below, see pp. 73 and 81.
58 *Kuei Chuang chi* 歸莊集 (Shanghai: Ku-chi ch'u-pan-she, 1984), 157–61. Kuei Chuang was a painter as well; for this, see Jonathan Chaves, *The Chinese Painter as Poet* (New York: China Institute Gallery, 2000), 71–72.
59 Golvers, 444.
60 Ibid. and p. 98.
61 Ibid., 441.
62 Chaves, *Singing of the Source*, 25.

24

COME VERO PRENCIPE CATOLICO

The Capuchins and the rulers of Soyo in the late seventeenth century[1]

Richard Gray

Source: *Africa: Journal of the International African Institute*, 53(3) (1983), 39–54.

Students of Europe's contact with Africa have long regarded the Christian missions in the ancient kingdom of Kongo as a peculiarly potent symbol. For some the conversion and subsequent reign of Afonso I in the first half of the sixteenth century were a momentary aberration, a false dawn quickly to be obscured by the realities of the exploitation associated with mercantile capitalism and the horrors of the Atlantic slave trade. For others, the story of these missions has merely served to illustrate the continuing inviolability of indigenous traditions. Kongo society, it is argued, accepted only a thin veneer of Christianity, while its basic cosmology, practices and beliefs remained unchanged.

> Christianity affected only a slim minority. For the majority of the people of the Kongo, its ceremonies, its symbolism, its churches, and its clergy were less pretexts for belief than occasions for imitation. It left a lasting impression only where it managed to become associated with traditional usages. In trying to reach the people, it became an instrument of syncretism . . . Alongside a Christianity which was weakly established and in constant danger, the traditional religious pluralism and the syncretic cults oriented the religious life of the people of the Kongo from the sixteenth century on' (Balandier, 1968: 254–5).

These interpretations share a common assumption. Faced with what seems to be the virtual extinction of Christianity in the area by the mid-nineteenth century, scholars have assumed that the early missionary impact was fleeting and superficial, and that these missions met with insuperable difficulties or proceeded on false principles which inevitably involved them in failure. Yet the early influence of Christianity in Kongo cannot be usefully discussed without taking into account the fact that its impact varied enormously over time and space. At the capital, Mbanza Kongo or San Salvador, the role of Christian missionaries was very different in the reigns of Afonso I, or Garcia II (1641–61), or Pedro IV (1696–1718), while in the various regions of the kingdom there were even greater differences. If we take our standpoint in the late seventeenth century and consider carefully the evidence for that period, we are confronted in Soyo, a powerful, dominant region at that moment, not with failure but with an extraordinary depth and extent of Christian influence. Several factors distinguished Soyo from the rest of Kongo, yet so striking is the picture of Soyo's commitment to Christianity at this period that one is forced to reconsider the whole direction of religious change that was occurring at that moment. And, in doing so, one has to begin to reassess some of the previous interpretations of this major episode of Christian evangelism in Africa.

The emergence of Soyo

Soyo (Sogno, Sohio) was distinguished from the rest of the kingdom of Kongo by its natural resources, its geographical location and its historical development in the sixteenth and seventeenth centuries. According to a Capuchin from Pavia, Soyo was as large as the seventeenth-century state of Milan.[2] It stretched along the Atlantic coast northwards from the River Mbridge to the mouth of the Zaire and inland along the southern bank of this vast estuary. It was a sandy, relatively infertile area, whose principal natural product was salt obtained on the sea-coast (Cavazzi, 1687: 4), but from the end of the fifteenth century it was no longer a backwater. Its economic and strategic importance was suddenly transformed. The port of Mpinda, a few miles within the Zaire estuary, provided the natural gateway for trade and contacts with the Portuguese, and the capital of Soyo, Mbanza Soyo, was established some three miles in the interior behind Mpinda. By the seventeenth century the ruler of Soyo was asserting a degree of independence which at times culminated in active revolt against the king of Kongo. This insubordination was assisted by the existence of the Nfinda Ngula, a large, forested wilderness which separated Soyo from Kongo (Thornton, 1979: 41), but of even greater importance was the growth of trade with the Dutch.

After the Portuguese settlement in Luanda in the 1570s, the main commercial route of the *pombeiros* (trading agents of the Portuguese) between the Pool, San Salvador and Luanda ran overland by-passing Soyo, but with the arrival of Dutch traders in the coastal kingdoms north of the Zaire

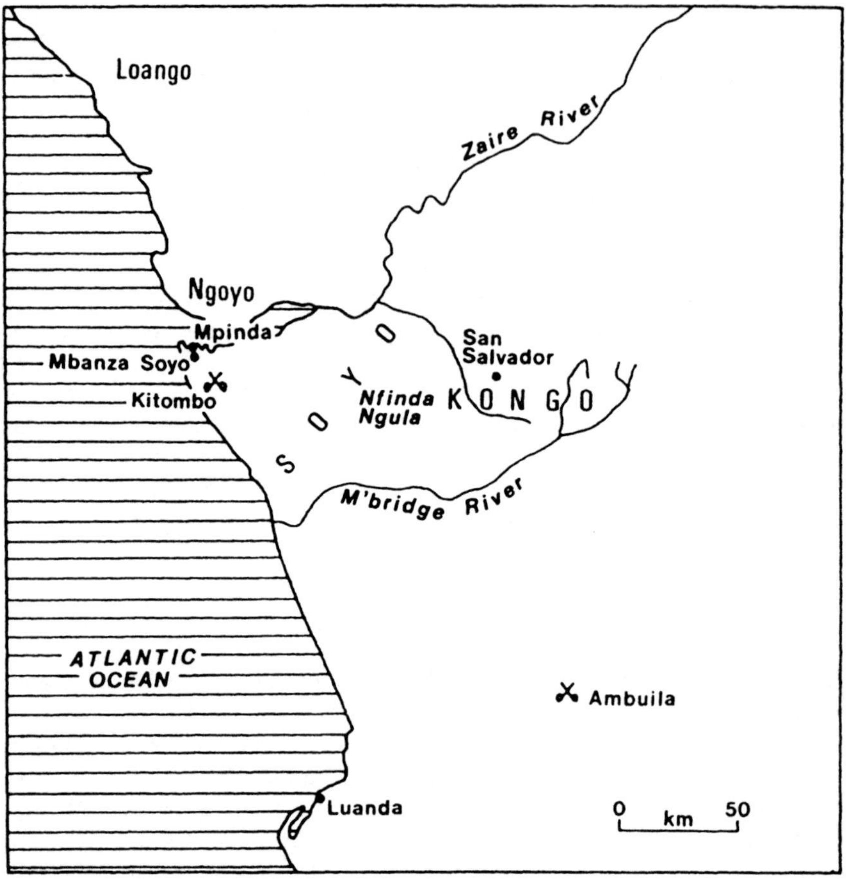

Soyo in the late seventeenth century.

and in the Zaire estuary in the 1590s, the fortunes of Soyo rapidly expanded. Unlike the Portuguese, the Dutch were willing to exchange firearms and ammunition for ivory, copper and slaves (Wilson, 1978: 140–9). In the 1630s the army of Soyo defeated that of the king of Kongo on several occasions (Dapper, 1670: 565–6) and Soyo became a haven for defeated, dissident factions from San Salvador (Thornton, 1979: 131), but it was only in the last third of the seventeenth century that Soyo emerged as a dominant power in the Kongo kingdom.

In 1665 the Portuguese advancing from Luanda defeated the Kongo army, killing the king and many of his nobility at the battle of Ambuila. Only a few months later the ruler of Soyo seized his opportunity to ransack San Salvador and place his protege on the Kongo throne, an intervention which was repeated in 1669. The following year the Portuguese governor in Luanda sent an army to invade and humble the upstart Soyo. After an initial defeat, however, the forces of Soyo rallied and, with Dutch armaments, smashed the Portuguese at Kitombo in October 1670, killing the Portuguese commander and taking many captives and much booty. It was a decisive victory. Not until the nineteenth century were the Portuguese again able to invade Kongo (*ibid.*: 193). Yet Mbanza Soyo was never able to take the place of San Salvador: it never provided the central focus for the whole kingdom of Kongo, nor did its rulers ever attain the luxury, power and life-style previously enjoyed by the powerful Kongo kings. There is nothing in the late seventeenth-century descriptions of Soyo to match the magnificence of Garcia II's reception of the Dutch envoys in 1642 (Dapper, 1670: 561–2). But by the 1680s Soyo was definitely thought to be the key to peace and prosperity throughout Kongo: its rulers were reported to be 'very powerful' and 'greatly feared' by the prominent people in Kongo.[3]

The missionary records of the late seventeenth century give the impression that in Soyo local power was concentrated on the ruler and his court at Mbanza Soyo. The principal office holders were the ruler's close kinsmen, and if news of his illness became public a succession crisis could be feared. The ruler could appoint and dismiss the governors (*mani*) of dependent towns and villages at will, and after one serious armed dispute with the captain-general of his army, in which the Capuchins acted as mediators, he took care to demote his opponents (Merolla, 1692: 154, 236–48). In so far as these sources provide an insight into the political structure and organization of Soyo in this period, they corroborate MacGaffey's opinion that 'the precolonial Kongo chief was much like the "Big Man" of Melanesia . . . a successful competitor in an unstable political system' in which, however, favourable conditions (as in late seventeenth-century Soyo) could for a period produce 'centralized, hierarchical and relatively stable regimes', while in the exercise of such power the existence of a centre was 'much more important' than clear territorial boundaries (MacGaffey, 1970: 263).

The Capuchins' advantages in Soyo

The Capuchins in Soyo were therefore probably correct in concentrating their efforts at Mbanza Soyo, and as the power of the rulers of Soyo increased so was the commitment of Soyo to Christianity extended and intensified. When the first Capuchin missionaries arrived at Mpinda in 1645 Soyo was already in their eyes a Catholic country. They were welcomed amidst scenes of great enthusiasm by the populace and ruler. A Dutch sea-captain attempted to prevent their landing, but Soyo, together with rest of Kongo as exemplified by Garcia II (Wilson, 1978: 304–5), showed little or no sympathy for Calvinist doctrines, however much the ruler and people of Soyo profited from Dutch commercial contacts. Hundreds of people brought their children and youths to be baptized, and the Capuchins throughout the seventeenth century did not hesitate to distinguish sharply Soyo and Kongo from their northern 'pagan' neighbours.

As the missionaries subsequently attempted to enforce the precepts of canon law they soon encountered in Soyo, as in the rest of the Kongo kingdom, widespread opposition. In Soyo, however, the Capuchins enjoyed peculiar advantages. In the first place, they were able to establish and maintain a continuous presence at Mbanza Soyo. Death and disease took a steady toll of the missionaries who arrived after 1645, and the arrival of reinforcements was sporadic after the first few years, so that elsewhere in Kongo, outside San Salvador, it was rare for any provincial centre to have a resident missionary for more than a few years at a time, particularly after the 1650s. But in Mbanza Soyo there were always one or two Capuchin priests, ably assisted by a brother, one of whom, Leonardo da Nardo, through prolonged service obtained a deep knowledge of the people and their language (Cavazzi, 1687: VII, 123, 856).

Even more important than this uninterrupted ministry, however, was the fact that in Soyo the Capuchins had no rivals. When the Capuchin missionaries arrived at San Salvador, there were several secular priests, of both Kongo and of mixed race. With many of these local priests the Capuchins were involved in bitter disputes over ecclesiastical jurisdiction. Inevitably this rivalry weakened their influence both with the king and other laity (Jadin, 1964; Wilson, 1978). In Soyo, however, the Capuchins were the sole, unchallenged providers of Catholic sacraments, save for a few months in 1673–74 when Flemish Franciscans and a Kongolese priest briefly intruded into their monopoly (Jadin, 1966).

The diplomatic role of the Capuchins

Throughout the seventeenth century the Capuchins in Soyo, as in Kongo, derived some of their influence from the particular position they occupied in the wider diplomatic world. They had been sent to Kongo by Pope Urban VIII in response to repeated overtures from the kings of Kongo who had long been attempting to establish a direct contact with Rome. The kings wanted to receive missionaries who would be independent of the Portuguese *padroado*, and it was no coincidence that the Sacred Congregation of Propaganda Fide selected the Capuchins for this task as theirs was the Order most closely identified with this new, powerful Curial organ, by which the Vatican hoped to assert its influence over Catholic missionary activity. The first parties of Spanish, Flemish and Italian Capuchins had slipped into Mpinda while the Dutch had temporarily occupied Luanda. After the reconquest of Luanda in 1648 the Portuguese Crown was prepared to continue to admit Italian Capuchins to this mission-field provided that they were not Spanish subjects and that they passed through Lisbon and Luanda. In Kongo the Capuchins became something of a diplomatic liability for Garcia II after 1648

(Wilson, 1978: 321–3), but the rulers of Soyo continued to appreciate the diplomatic benefits which could be drawn from these contacts with the missionaries from Rome.

Although the Portuguese in Luanda were defeated in their attempt to conquer Soyo in 1670, they still remained an ominous, hostile force, and the ruler of Soyo requested the pope to intervene on his behalf. As a result the papal nuncio elicited from the king of Portugal an admission that the ruler of Soyo was an independent prince. The nuncio also received an assurance from the king that the hostility of the governor of Luanda towards Soyo did not reflect the policy of Lisbon.[4] Firearms and artillery obtained from Dutch traders were undoubtedly the principal external factor in insuring the survival of an independent Soyo, and, as will be seen, the rulers of Soyo thoroughly appreciated the crucial importance of maintaining access to these weapons. It is also clear, however, that the rulers were anxious not to become entirely dependent on the Dutch. The links with papal diplomacy provided Soyo with an independent access, however tenuous and slight, to the world of European diplomacy, and this brought distinct, if intangible, advantages.

The Capuchins also played a major role in the protracted negotiations which eventually led to a re-establishment of relations between Soyo and the Portuguese. As early as 1685 the vice-prefect of the mission could report that the ruler of Soyo, '*Come vero Prencipe Catolico*', was prepared for the church to take a major part in this critical diplomacy.[5] While patiently assisting the Portuguese to strengthen their contacts with Soyo, the Capuchins steadfastly supported the ruler in his refusal to permit the Portuguese to establish a fort at the strategic port of Mpinda. They seem to have accomplished this task with at least a touch of that skill and charity which enabled members of their order to play similar roles in the diplomacy of seventeenth-century Europe,[6] and for more than a decade the Capuchins were intimately involved in the execution of Soyo's foreign policy (Jadin, 1970: 387–9).

The Capuchins and the Soyo authorities

The influence of the Capuchins in Soyo, however, was not solely, or even principally, due to their undoubted political and diplomatic value to the state. Far more fundamentally they possessed a basic, ritual significance. They were welcomed and respected as Christian priests who made accessible what were increasingly recognized as sacraments of salvation by Soyo's rulers and their subjects. As in any example of profound and extensive interaction between an African polity and Christian missionary activity, points of congruence were found between the new religion and the local social structures. In the Kongo kingdom as a whole the Capuchins occupied an ambivalent position. In most of the kingdom the points of congruence fluctuated and were unstable. At times, particularly for the first three years of their mission, the Capuchins saw themselves, and were seen by the ruler and people of Kongo, as allied to the king and his local representatives; at other times, especially when they later came into open conflict with Garcia II, they assumed some of the attributes of radical revolutionaries, seeking to take salvation to the poor, the marginal and the oppressed, or at least they were seen as the opponents of hostile and 'oppressive' rulers (Wilson, 1978: 328–35). In Soyo, although elements of tension between rulers and missionaries remained, as one might expect if evangelism preserved its potential prophetic challenge, the Capuchins were far more closely and continuously identified with the establishment, and in its turn, the ruling institution at the centre of Soyo became far more thoroughly Christianized than was the case with the government centred on San Salvador in the seventeenth century.

Most of the principal public rituals in Soyo were becoming centred around the Christian calendar by the late seventeenth century. The festivals of Easter, Christmas, Pentecost and All Souls had become major occasions, uniting ruler and subjects in colourful, enthusiastic displays of worship and rejoicing. On such occasions the ruler attended Mass splendidly arrayed in the white robes of the Order of Christ. Even on weekdays (for he normally attended church at least three times a week, either for Mass or the Rosary) he came specially attired, wearing on his breast a cross of solid gold, holding his rods of office and borne aloft in a hammock. He was accompanied by a crowd of attendants, who carried his velvet-covered chair, his faldstool, carpet and cushion, and he was preceded by musicians sounding trumpets, double-bells and other instruments. During Mass, before the reading of the Gospel, one of his pages was given a lighted torch, and at the end of the Gospel the missal was brought to him to kiss. At the end of Mass he came forward to the altar to receive benediction and accompanied the priest into the sacristy (Merolla, 1692: 169–75).

Besides these regular occasions for regal splendour and royal ritual participation two saints' days had become of great local political significance. As in Kongo every governor (*mani*) or headman of the towns and major villages of Soyo was obliged to present himself at Mbanza Soyo accompanied 'by all his people' to hear Mass and to render obedience to the ruler on the feast of St James on 25 July. At a great ceremony held outside the Capuchins' church, the ruler, after receiving a blessing from the priest, executed two war dances. Then, seated on his throne in the shade of a magnificent tree, he watched while each official, from the captain-general down to the village headmen, first received a blessing from the priest and then executed a war dance, bringing also a symbol of the tribute which they were each obliged to offer the ruler. These ceremonies went on for a fortnight, during which time the missionaries were kept busy dispensing the sacraments of marriage, penance and baptism, Fra Girolamo da Sorrento baptizing 272 people in one day alone (Merolla, 1692: 156–8; Jadin, 1970: 448–52). This ancient and well-established festival became matched in Soyo by the feast of St Luke on 18 October, at which the crushing defeat of the Portuguese in 1670 was commemorated with suitable devotion and pride in a crowded and joyous procession (Cuvelier 1953: 58). At Mbanza Soyo two of the town's six churches were particularly associated with rulers: one contained the tombs of the rulers and another was the royal chapel (Merolla, 1692: 168). By January 1702 the 'Gram Principe de Sonho' had acquired an official seal: the symbolism consisted solely of a cross.[7]

Christian rituals and symbols thus provided an impressive component of the court's pomp and splendour. In these circumstances the excommunication of the ruler became, as will be seen, a matter of considerable political concern. But the alliance between missionary and ruler was by no means limited to their joint participation at Mass. It included an important element of legitimation by the spiritual powers, who were intimately concerned with the public ratification of the ruler's accession. MacGaffey remarks how the candidate chief in Kongo 'had to submit to inspection by his peers to ensure that his spirit was appropriate to the role' (1970a: 30), and Fra Girolamo describes how, after the election of a ruler by nine electors, the missionary was immediately informed. If the choice 'had fallen on a worthy individual, the priest approved it and announced it publicly in church to the populace, otherwise the election would be null and void' (Merolla, 1692: 153). The consent and ritual support of the missionaries was sought at other crucial occasions: before declaring war the ruler obtained the approval of the superior of the mission, and as his army went out to fight it was fortified by Christian rites (*ibid.*: 119; Jadin, 1970: 457). On his side the ruler sent gifts of food to the missionaries and he allocated land to the slaves and servants of the mission when they married (Merolla, 1692: 156).

The rulers of Soyo may well have had greater need than the kings of Kongo for the political support and legitimation provided by Christian rituals. They seem to have lacked a well-established, indigenous tradition of legitimacy. Dapper's reference in his description of mid-seventeenth century Soyo to the fact that the area was divided among many chieftaincies who usually enjoyed independence but who by that time 'lived under another sovereign power' (Dapper, 1670: 544), forcibly suggests the upstart nature of the Soyo ruling establishment as known to the Capuchins. Its fortunes in the seventeenth century largely rested, as we have seen, on a series of successful rebellions against San Salvador, followed by the eventual destruction of this once-powerful capital. The measure of legitimation bestowed by the new religion may well, therefore, have been highly valued for political reasons by the rulers of Soyo.

The mission's disciplining of the ruling elite

Until one can gain a clearer view of the rise of the ruling dynasty in Soyo, this aspect of the political significance of Christianity as the source of ritual legitimation must remain somewhat speculative. But it is already abundantly clear that by the last quarter of the seventeenth century the mission had come to occupy a central role in the training, formation and even selection of Soyo's ruling elite. By that time the principal officials gained their education and training during a period of highly disciplined, committed and privileged service in the work of the mission.

The creation of a nucleus of disciplined, committed Christians went back to the early days of the Capuchin mission. Cavazzi describes their bold, 'inspired' decision to create congregations or confraternities (brotherhoods) for lay men and women in San Salvador and Mbanza Soyo, as 'a stupendous act' taken in the face 'of all human reason' (Cavazzi, 1687: III, 45, 342–3). The rules of these confraternities insisted that each member should hear Mass daily if at all possible; should make confession and communicate every first and third Sunday in the month taking part in public discipline; should fast every Saturday; should conduct prayers morning and evening and teach their families Christian doctrine; should shun dances and persuade 'concubines' to marry (Piazza, 1973: 54–6; Buenaventura de Carrocera, 1946–47: 123–4). Originally these confraternities were open to all, *Plebei e Nobili*, provided that they were of good reputation. In their early days, at least, they seem to have performed some of the functions of a purification or witchcraft-eradication cult: after the sermon 'many would lie prostrate on the ground' voluntarily and publicly confessing their failings (Cavazzi, 1687: III, 45, 342–3). Gradually membership of these confraternities became a prerequisite for high office in Soyo. Already in the early 1660s it was customary for judicial officials to be selected from members of the confraternities,[8] and in 1674 it was reported that the ruler of Soyo was normally selected from among the Confraternity of St Francis (Jadin 1966: 290).

At the head of this Christian elite were the interpreters or *Maestri della Chiesa.* Eight or ten in number, these men of 'noble' birth were, by the end of the seventeenth century, 'not only the most cultured in the Land, but also in good part relatives of the Prince' (Zucchelli, 1712: 138). Since few of the Capuchins in late seventeenth-century Soyo had sufficient command of the vernacular, the main task of these interpreters was to assist the missionaries in hearing confessions, and like the priests the interpreters operated under a seal of secrecy. The mission was thus incorporating into its structure the deep desires for purification spontaneously expressed in the early behaviour of members of the confraternities, and by the last quarter of the seventeenth century hand-picked scions of the Soyo rulers, and of the Barreto da Silva patrilineage in particular, were intimately collaborating in this routinization of piety. The interpreters also prepared the altars and taught 'the people the way of Salvation' (*ibid.*). In return for these services they were relieved of military service, paid no taxes, enjoyed benefit of clergy in legal cases and were buried with the missionaries. By the 1680s several of the principal officers of the court had served as interpreters, as had the two rulers elected in the 1690s (*ibid.*: 141–2).

This training, together with membership of the confraternities and the obligations which this involved of observing a strict Christian discipline, added an inner, spiritual dimension to the alliance and relationship of missionaries and ruler. It was not simply a question of political necessity or convenient ritual legitimation. Again Cavazzi enables us to catch a glimpse of an early stage in this process. Soon after the formation of the confraternities in the 1640s the ruler of Soyo became suspicious of the activities of these groups and began personally to attend their meetings. In this way he himself became exposed to the detailed teachings of the Capuchins and, under their influence, he repented and decided publicly to adopt Christian marriage (Cavazzi, 1687: III, 47, 346–7). In the relatively scanty evidence which is available it is difficult to trace this thread of inner conviction and to evaluate its influence on the relationship between the missionaries and the rulers; but, as will be seen, it occasionally surfaced, and the early training and service as interpreters and teachers undoubtedly brought missionaries and elite together in an intimate bond of what many of those involved would regard as deep Christian fellowship.

The test-case of Christian marriage

The depth and extent of Christian penetration into Soyo life and culture was, for the Capuchins, measured by their fortunes in two major areas of confrontation. The first was Christian marriage, as laid down by the Council of Trent. The evidence available suggests that here, somewhat unexpectedly, their efforts at imposing ecclesiastical discipline were being marked with increasing and substantial success. Membership of the Christian elite, the confraternities and the interpreters and teachers, naturally involved an acceptance of canon law marriage. The Capuchins went on to use this example of the ruling elite, together with its political power, to extend this discipline to increasing numbers of the ruler's subjects and dependants. On one occasion, about 1687, when the ruler had been excommunicated, he was ordered as penance to persuade three hundred of his subjects to adopt holy matrimony. In the event four hundred were presented, and a further six hundred immediately followed their example (Merolla, 1692: 227–34). By that time it was accepted that all the *mani*, the governors and headmen of major towns and villages, should be 'legitimately married' or be deprived of their office 'lest they should set bad examples to the common people' (*ibid.*: 149).

Later, at the height of the delicate diplomatic negotiations with the Portuguese, the missionaries decided to launch a further offensive on the matrimonial front. Wishing to train and place teachers in every district to instruct the people and prepare them for Christian marriage, the missionaries gathered the ruler, the electors, the war captains and all the elders into their church, where they pointed out to these leaders the responsibility they had before God towards their subjects, whose 'souls were being lost by their negligence'. To this appeal the Capuchins added the threat that, if these orders were not promulgated, they would leave and go to other more fruitful fields. Touched probably both by the threat and the appeal the ruler and his counsellors swore that they wished to live as good Christians, and immediately promulgated the necessary orders. The missionaries and teachers, in company with the ruler or one of the elders, then went out to search for those whom they regarded as living in 'concubinage', and in 1689 in Mbanza Soyo alone more than a thousand marriages were celebrated. Three years later the missionaries in Soyo confidently expected that, with the help of a zealous new ruler, Giovanni Barreto da Silva, 'soon everyone would be married'.[9]

These expectations were widely over-optimistic, and the missionaries in general failed totally to appreciate the nature and values of African marriage. Yet the evidence suggests that the principles enunciated in canon law were beginning to become as much respected in Soyo as they were in parts of contemporary Europe, where, as in Soyo, practice often failed to match principle. In the remoter parts of rural Catholic Europe in the eighteenth century, probably a majority of the villagers still lived together without being married according to canon law (Chadwick, 1981: 149), so it would hardly have been surprising if among the masses in Soyo the new rules of marriage were often more honoured in the breach than in the observance. Nevertheless the degree to which the missionaries were able to exert pressure towards an acceptance of canon law marriage is an extraordinary sign of the extent of their influence on the ruling elite and on the lives of at least those people of Soyo who lived within easy reach of Mbanza Soyo.

The interaction of Christianity and indigenous religion

For the missionaries the other touchstone of Soyo Christianity was the question of the continuing attachment of the people to the shrines, charms and other elements of their religion. The Capuchins' approach was one of straightforward confrontation. Encountering the literate civilizations of Asia some seventeenth-century missionaries had begun to appreciate the necessity of attempting to enter into a dialogue with alien cultures; in tropical Africa, recognition of the values of African institutions and beliefs was to prove far more elusive. Identifying most African rituals as the works of the devil the Capuchins generally demanded total renunciation. If a nominal Christian continued impenitently to officiate over these rituals they considered it perfectly just that he or she should be exiled into slavery across the Atlantic (Merolla, 1692: 106). The missionaries assumed that conflict between the new and old religions was inevitable and total. The evidence suggests that some Soyo converts may have agreed with them, and that a few of these were prepared, at least in private, to accept wholeheartedly a radical break with customary beliefs and practices.

While Andrea da Pavia was in Soyo a general assembly of the people was called 'with the consent and intervention of the Prince'. The question for debate was whether they 'wished to observe the laws of God or their superstitious ceremonies'. The reply was given that 'they firmly believed in God and in everything that was taught them, but that they also believed in their ceremonies and vain observances'. Afterwards many came in private to protest against what had been said in public, and these alone were admitted to the sacraments.[10] Besides these committed members of the elite and populace, another group of people who were almost totally identified with the Capuchins were the slaves of the mission, who maintained the hostel, served as medical aids in the hospital (*ibid.*: 399), and accompanied by the missionaries on their visitations. Shortly after his arrival in Soyo Fra Girolamo found that the slaves of the mission did not hesitate to lay hold of a hostile *nganga*, having no fear of his supernatural powers because they themselves wore medals 'given to them by us as preservatives against sorcery' (*ibid.*: 105).

The hostile *nganga* represented the other extreme of the religious spectrum in Soyo. When Cavazzi visited the area in 1663 he found that there was still a determined resistance against the Christian ruler and his wife. A church had been burnt in Soyo, a hostile charm had been placed against the ruler's wife and guards were mounted in the churches to prevent 'some superstitious Christians' from digging up and transporting corpses 'into the bush to the graves of their ancestors' (Cavazzi, 1687: VII, 123, 856; Wilson, 1978: 343–4). By the 1680s, however, the *nganga* in Soyo were very much on the defensive. Fra Girolamo and his confrères led attacks on hidden shrines and the impression is given that traditional ritual experts carried on their practices only at considerable risk to themselves, though, significantly enough, when the missionary and ruler were in dispute over the slave trade, 'the magicians and sorcerers' sought to exacerbate the situation (Merolla, 1692: 209).

In between these two extremes of Soyo religious commitment there was, as the reply of the ruler and the general assembly to Fra Andrea indicated, a whole range of people for whom the concept of religious conflict was minimal or even absent. They believed in God and 'everything that was taught them', but they also held to their own rituals. For them the new faith was part of a religious spectrum in which they continued to find relevance in many of the old beliefs and practices. Shortly before Fra Girolamo arrived in Soyo the ruler, Antonio I Barreto da Silva, had administered an oath to many of his subjects, some of whom however were able to stage a public protest against this act during Fra Girolamo's first sermon (*ibid.*: 89–93). Antonio I repented that evening, and this eclectic attitude to religion did not generally involve the ruler and people of Soyo in deliberate syncretism, in a conscious attempt to take elements of Christianity and create a new and distinct amalgam of beliefs. In the first decade of the eighteenth century such an attempt did emerge in Kongo around the young, prophetic figure of Dona Beatrice and the Antonine movement, but the people of Soyo, save in the remote south, were hostile to emissaries of this syncretistic sect (Cuvelier 1953: 159, 171, 228). In Soyo the interaction between religious beliefs was less dramatic, the process of change being gradual and cumulative.

The situation in Soyo in the late seventeenth century seems to have borne a striking resemblance to that of Kongo in the second half of the twentieth century where as reported by Janzen and MacGaffey, 'very few people think of themselves as non-Christian and "conversion" is no longer an issue' (1974: 16). In such a situation most individuals were not continually confronted with stark religious alternatives. There was a large middle ground of 'ambivalent flexibility', and across this religious spectrum there was a process of 'complex interaction and adaptation' (*ibid.*: 4, 17). The problem for a historian faced with such a situation is to identify the broad direction of change in religious thought and practice. Of course Christianity was, in Balandier's phrase, 'associated with traditional usages', but the crucial question is whether Christianity was being absorbed into an unchanged cosmology, 'a system of thought that remains African and traditional rather than European and Christian' (*ibid.*: 3), or whether the new religion, through its sacraments, liturgy, discipline and literacy, possessed sources of strength which enabled it over time to exert a cumulative impact.

The evidence for late seventeenth-century Soyo suggests, as we have already seen, that among the ruling elite something of this cumulative influence can be clearly discerned. In this narrow compass Soyo Christians were constantly being confronted with the challenges presented by the new religion, and many of them were gaining new insights into its implications. For the populace at large the evidence is much less abundant. Here a distinction must be drawn between the situation in Mbanza Soyo with its immediate neighbourhood, and the more distant areas of the region. The influence of the Capuchins was definitely concentrated on the capital. Because of the rains and the pattern of agricultural activity the visits of the missionaries to distant rural areas were restricted to the months from May to September (Jadin, 1966: 292), and even then they could undertake such visits only if there was another priest who could stay behind to maintain the mission at Mbanza Soyo. On their relatively infrequent visits they encountered in rural Soyo an almost universal enthusiasm for baptism, whereas resistance to this rite was encountered in some areas of Kongo. The popularity of baptism indicates a readiness of the majority to accept at least a nominal Christian identification, a move which in the minds of the missionaries exposed these adherents to the dictates of canon law. Baptism by itself could, however, have been readily absorbed by most recipients into an unchanged, folk cosmology. The jubilant acceptance of the rite even in the remoter parts of Soyo may therefore merely have testified to the absence of open hostility to Christian missionaries and their elite assistants.

Confessions, however, would seem to be another matter. The rite was by no means a formality: the investigations were often searching and prolonged, while absolution was withheld if the confessor was not convinced that penitence was sincere. Many Capuchin missionaries would have agreed with Fra Giovanni da Romano in regarding the confessional as the principal means of evangelism and of deepening the hold of Christian beliefs and discipline.[11] Like baptism, confession could be seen as essentially a rite of purification and as such highly congruent to Kongo religious practice. Unlike baptism, however, it must have been, at least in most cases, an ordeal not lightly entered upon. Willingness to submit to confession could be a good indication of popular attitudes. When Fra Girolamo visited Kitombo more than a decade after the battle with the Portuguese there he found that some people had not confessed since then on account of 'the great provocation' (Merolla, 1692: 127). Among the many hundreds of confessions heard annually by the Capuchins in Soyo some, especially in the outer rural districts, may have been fleeting encounters with little permanent effects, but the readiness of many of the people of Soyo to present themselves for this sacrament, even walking five or six days to do so (*ibid.*: 135), would seem to indicate an increasingly wide and deep commitment to the new religion.

Even in folk rituals, a new significance was becoming apparent. The ancestors, for instance, were beginning to be seen as synonymous with the holy souls of Catholic tradition. Fra Andrea da Pavia reported how, after his arrival in Soyo in 1688, he went to bed as usual on the eve of All Souls but was roused almost immediately by many people singing at the top of their voices. Informed by the mission's slaves that this was merely the normal devotions for the dead, he joined the torch-lit processions which visited the churches in the town and also the cemeteries where the graves were illuminated by many candles. 'Everyone was chanting prayers in their language', and Fra Andrea went on to assist them with great enthusiasm. Two hours before daybreak he sounded the church bells, sang the office, celebrated Mass and then led out another procession to the graves where he intoned the responses for the dead. The whole night passed in this manner for sleep was quite impossible. The next day, when all the ceremonies had finished, everyone came with their baskets 'each offering alms for the dead', so that the mission distributed ten tons of fruit and other gifts (Jadin, 1970: 440–1). The sacrifices for the ancestors had become alms for the church's poor; yet, it will be recalled, at the time of Cavazzi's visit only a generation earlier the ruler of Soyo had had to place guards to prevent the re-burial of Christians in ancestral cemeteries.

Fra Andrea also glimpsed something of the anguish and dilemma of the majority of Soyo Christians as, faced with the Capuchins' rigid missiology, they attempted to explore and appropriate for themselves these new religious horizons. When he reported to the Congregation of Propaganda Fide the response of the general assembly called to debate 'superstitious ceremonies' (see above), he went on to ask 'if in some respects they could be excused, for in their ceremonies they do not make an explicit, or implicit, pact with the Devil, but have a simple faith, from which one tries to raise them as much as one can'.[12] His question raised an issue of fundamental missiological significance. His assessment of Soyo rituals in this passage, if not in all his writings, showed far more understanding than that exhibited by most of his confreres, at least in their published works. As he said this was no Devil worship. Indeed he seems to have begun to grasp the fact that their beliefs and rituals represented not only a basic acceptance of supernatural powers but also a continuous attempt to summon their assistance in the constant conflict with evil, however that might be defined. Fra Andrea's final phrase might even imply that he was perhaps ready to take the first vital step towards a recognition of the positive, fundamental values in Soyo religion.

His report was submitted to the Cardinals of Propaganda Fide on 6 April 1693 by Cardinal Gaspare Carpegna, a great canon lawyer. Carpegna was to be an assiduous participant in the Congregation appointed in 1704 to consider the momentous issue of Chinese rites which involved similar missiological problems, so it is interesting to note that a decade earlier he was fairly sympathetic to the problems raised by Fra Andrea. While insisting that 'superstitions' should be combated through the confessional, Carpegna went on to suggest that certain sacred rites such as Benediction could be introduced to take the place of 'superstitions'.[13] The path towards adaptation was not wholly closed, and it might have developed had these Soyo Christians been permitted to foster their own Catholic priesthood. A Capuchin did later advocate the construction of a seminary (Jadin, 1964: 443–4), but in Soyo the highest post in the church effectively open to local people remained that of interpreter.

The mission, the rulers and the slave trade

This lack of an indigenous priesthood seriously hampered any prospect of a fruitful theological dialogue, and undoubtedly jeopardized the future development of Christianity in Soyo. A more immediate cause of grave tension between the Capuchins and the rulers of Soyo arose from the Atlantic slave trade, which provoked a continued and deepening crisis in the relations of church and state. Acting on a mistaken interpretation of instructions from Propaganda Fide (Gray, forthcoming), the Capuchins condemned the sale of baptized slaves to English or other heretical traders. Fra Girolamo twice excommunicated Antonio I, although he himself recognized the dangers of employing this drastic sanction (Merolla, 1692: 220). Some of his successors seem almost to have gloried in their power of interference and their ability to humiliate publicly the rulers of Soyo (Zucchelli, 1712: 160–73). Despite the bitter resentment that these theocratic pretensions must have aroused, Antonio II sent a cool, humble petition to Propaganda Fide. Written on 4 October 1701 his letter appealed over the heads of the Capuchins to what he hoped would prove an impartial authority. To the Capuchin insistence that he sold slaves only to the Portuguese or to those Protestants who traded with Catholic ports the ruler pointed out that the Portuguese would provide him with neither powder nor arms necessary 'for our defence against our enemies', and that Protestants trading with Catholic ports were but few in number. Antonio II failed, however, to mention that the trade also supplied him and his court with valued luxury imports, and that strategical considerations were not his sole motive. He, like European Christians involved in the trade, was ensnared in an immense structure of evil. Instead he stressed the necessity of preserving 'my Principality and the peace of my People', and he asked permission to conduct this trade without danger of excommunication for 'I am a Catholic Prince and desire the accomplishment of my salvation'.[14]

The interior, reflective beliefs of individuals are almost totally excluded from the records. Yet as one reads how Antonio II served the mission in his youth rising to the rank of interpreter, and how, despite his sharp disagreements with the Capuchins over the slave trade, he continued 'faithfully to promote the apostolate' (Cuvelier, 1953: 180, 289), one is prepared to accept, not as a mere phrase penned by a secretary well-trained in ecclesiastical correspondence but as an expression of a deeply held conviction, the claim that he was 'a Catholic Prince' and that he desired 'the accomplishment of [his] salvation'.

Conclusion

The records of the late seventeenth century do not therefore depict Christianity in Soyo as affecting 'only a slim minority' or as being 'weakly established': the judgement of contemporaries might rather have been that it was vigorous, expanding and in some respects almost arrogantly triumphant. One can perceive the ruling institution becomingly increasingly dependent on legitimation by recognized Christian ritual experts; an elite, trained and recruited through exposure to an extremely rigorous religious discipline; a gradual imposition of radically new practices concerning marriage, and the main public festivals becoming centred around the Christian calendar, with the Mass as perhaps the principal ritual focus in Soyo life. One can see Christianity and canon law as features distinguishing Soyo from its northern neighbours. One can even begin to glimpse something of the difficulties and anguish in which the people of Soyo were involved as they explored the implications of this Christian identity, while remaining subject to the jurisdiction of aliens who understood but a small part of this tension and conflict.

In such a situation the cumulative weight of a literate, universal tradition was considerable. The process of religious interaction was dynamic, though its direction could change. Christianity was then, and has ever been, 'in constant danger' (Balandier, 1968: 255), whether in long-established Christian territories, such as seventeenth-century Italy or France, or on the distant frontiers of overseas missions. Some grounds for deep anxiety had already appeared in Soyo. There was the ominous reluctance to raise an indigenous priesthood. Most obviously there were the tensions arising out of the slave trade, with both European and African Christians enmeshed in the system. With a terrible irony, missionaries and rulers were quarrelling to the point of repeated excommunications over an aspect of this evil whose importance was already, in the considered judgement of the Holy Office as handed down in 1686, paling into insignificance compared with the violation of human rights which the whole system involved (Gray, 1981: 37–9). Here indeed the Christian community in Soyo appears as a frail and fragile vessel to confront the greed and cruelty of several continents orchestrated by Europe. The dangers to the Faith were manifold, and these few decades in the late seventeenth century may have constituted for Soyo the deepest point of identification with Christendom. At some subsequent period the impetus slackened, the direction of religious change appears to have altered. One should not, however, allow this later story to determine our assessment of what was happening in the seventeenth century. Church historians should not fall, any more than others, into the trap of Whig interpretations; rather they should recall Ranke's dictum that every generation is equidistant from eternity. The meaning and message of salvation has ever to be discovered anew.

Notes

1 The research on which this article is in part based was undertaken with the help of an award from the British Academy. I am most grateful to Fathers Joseph Metzler OMI and Isidoro de Villapadierna OFM Cap., archivists respectively of Propaganda Fide and the Capuchin Generalate, for their advice and many acts of kindness. I would also like to thank for their comments and criticisms those who attended a conference at the School of Oriental and African Studies at which an earlier version was discussed, and those, especially Professor J. D. Y. Peel, who have read subsequent drafts. The following abbreviations are used for citations of documents from the archives of Propaganda Fide:
   SOCG Scritture originate riferite nelle Congregazioni generali.
   SC Africa Scritture riferite nei Congressi. Series Africa, Angola, Congo, etc.

2 SOCG 514, f.471, 'Compendiosa relatione . . . data da me F. Andrea da Pavia' considered on 6 April 1693.

3 SC Africa I, f.573v, Giuseppe Maria da Busseto to Prefect, 4 April 1685.

4 SC Africa I, f.365–6, Nuncio to Prefect, Lisbon, 3 May 1677.

5 SC Africa I, f.573v, Giuseppe Maria da Busseto to Prefect, 4 April 1685.

6 I refer not so much to the well-known abilities of Joseph de Paris, the 'Grey Eminence', but to the skills and achievements of other Capuchins such as Innocenzo da Caltagirone, Marco d'Aviano and Giacinto da Casale Monferrato. See Mariano d'Alatri (ed.) 1980.

7 SC Africa III, f.298v, Antonio Barreto de Silva to Prefect, Sonho, 17 January 1702.

8 SOCG 250, f.428v, Crisostomo da Genova's report, 10 January 1665, referring to conditions prior to his departure from Angola in July 1663.

9 SC Africa II, f.314–15 and 573v, Angelo Francesco da Milano to Prefect, Luanda, 4 March 1690 and 15 April 1692.
10 SOCG 514, f.471v, 'Compendiosa relatione . . .'.
11 Giovanni Belotti da Romano, 'Avvertimenti salutevoli . . .' f.287. Mss in Biblioteca Radini-Tedeschi, Bergamo.
12 SOCG 514, f.471v, 'Compendiosa relatione . . .'.
13 SOCG 514, f.472–472v, Comments by Cardinal Carpegna.
14 SC Africa III, f.288–288v, Antonio Barreto de Silva to Cardinals of Propaganda Fide, Sonho, 4 October 1701: '. . . ser eu Principe Catholico, e dezejar o acerto da minha salvação'.

References

Balandier, G. 1968. *Daily life in the Kingdom of Kongo from the sixteenth to the eighteenth century* (Eng. trans.), London: George Allen and Unwin.

Buenaventura de Carrocera, 1946–47. 'Dos relaciones inéditas sobre la Misión Capuchina del Congo', *Collectanea Franciscana* 16–7. 102–24.

Cavazzi, Giovanni Antonio da Montecuccolo. 1687. *Istorica descrizione de' tre' Regni Congo, Matamba, et Angola*, Bologna: Giacomo Monti.

Chadwick, O. 1981. *The Popes and European Revolution*, Oxford: Clarendon Press.

Cuvelier, J. 1953. *Relations sur le Congo du Père Laurent de Lucques (1700–1717)*, Brussels: Institut Royal Colonial Belge. Section des Sciences Morales et Politiques. Mémoires 32(2).

Dapper, O. 1670. *Beschreibung von Africa* (German trans.), Amsterdam: Jacob von Meurs.

Filesi, T. and Isidoro de Villapadierna. 1978. *La 'Missio Antiqua' dei Cappuccini nel Congo*, Rome: Istituto Storico Cappuccini.

Gray, R. 1981. 'The Vatican and the Atlantic slave trade', *History Today* 31 (March). 37–9.

——. forthcoming. 'Fra Girolamo Merolla da Sorrento, the Congregation of Propaganda Fide and the Atlantic slave trade', in M. Taddei (ed.) *La Conoscenza dell' Asia e dell' Africa in Italia nei secoli xviii e xix*, Naples: Istituto Universitario Orientale.

Jadin, L. 1964. 'Le clergé séculier et les Capucins du Congo et d'Angola aux xvie et xviie siècles', *Bulletin de l'Institut historique belge de Rome*, 36. 185–483.

——. 1966. 'Rivalités luso-néerlandaises au Sohio, Congo 1600–1675', *Bull. Inst. hist. belge de Rome*, 37. 137–360.

——. 1970. 'Andrea da Pavia au Congo, à Lisbonne, à Madère. Journal d'un missionaire capucin, 1685–1702', *Bull. Inst. hist. belge de Rome* 41. 375–592.

Janzen, J. M. and W. MacGaffey. 1974. *An Anthology of Kongo Religion*, Lawrence, Kansas: University of Kansas, Publications in Anthropology, 5.

MacGaffey, W. 1970. *Custom and Government in the Lower Congo*, Berkeley, Ca.: University of California Press.

——. 1970a. 'The Religious Commissions of the Bakongo', *Man* (N.S.) V(1). 27–38.

Mariano d'Alatri (ed.) 1980. *Santi e Santità nell' Ordine Cappuccino* I, Rome: Postulazione Generale dei Cappuccini.

Merolla, Girolamo da Sorrento. 1692. *Breve, e succinta relatione del viaggio nel Regno di Congo*, Naples: Francesco Mollo.

Piazza, C. 1973. *La Missione del Soyo (1713–1716) nella relazione inedita di Giuseppe da Modena OFM Cap.*, Rome: L'Italia Francescana.

Thornton, J. K. 1979. 'The Kingdom of Kongo in the Era of the Civil Wars, 1641–1718', University of California, Los Angeles, Ph.D. dissertation.

Wilson, A. 1978. 'The Kingdom of Kongo to the Mid Seventeenth Century', University of London, Ph.D. dissertation.

Zucchelli, Antonio da Gradisca. 1712. *Relazioni del viaggio, e Missione di Congo nell' Etiopia Inferiore Occidentale*, Venice: Bartolomeo Giavarina.

25

BOUNDED IDENTITIES

Women and religion in colonial Brazil, 1550–1750

Carole A. Myscofski

Source: *Religion*, 28 (1998), 329–37.

This article examines the creation of women's gender identity in the religious discourse of colonial Brazil and documents the creation of two separate norms—one for elite women and another for slave, lower-class, and mixed-race women. The Roman Catholic Church, closely linked with the Portuguese monarchic state and its colonial ambitions, transmitted both norms in religious guidebooks, missionary letters and sermons. This summary centers on the defining role for women in marriage, and indicates that the epoch of colonial Brazil is particularly important for feminist study. With the increasingly disparate perspectives on women from Late Antiquity, the Humanists, and Counter-Reformation theologians, this early modern era saw conflicted discourse concerning traditional gender roles.

This study emerges from my investigations of the construction of women's identity in the religious discourse of colonial Brazil. Roman Catholic mission plans, penitential handbooks, sermons on virtue and statements of women to the visiting Portuguese Inquisition reveal that the roles for women in the colony were complex and women's identity during this period in Brazilian history was not shaped by a single model for gender roles. This is particularly true when the subject is marriage—and that will be my focus here. Although the social norms of early modern Portuguese society in Brazil, under study here, repeatedly affirmed a central role for women so significant that its abrogation would surely bring social chaos, religious writers could not agree on its specific content. While the religious authorities agreed that women were distinctly different from men and saw marriage as the consummate purpose for women's existence, the emphases of their writings were not unified; the most striking differences appear when concern for maintenance of the class structure of society interrupts the religious discourse. Inevitably, it seems, the religious discourse that constructed gender in letters, sermons, laws and practices in this period in Brazilian history was not characterised by a single vision of wedded bliss to which all aspired (though few achieved), and women's identity was not shaped by a single model for gender roles. Instead, the religious discourse supported *two* dichotomies—between men and women, and between elite women and non-elite women.

This essay examines the discourse on marriage in order to discern the expectations for women and the feminine attitudes and behaviors deemed appropriate by religious writers in the first two colonial centuries. My discussion begins with a brief summary of the idealized elite role for women and statements from the writings of two religious authors supporting the elite ideal. The essay will continue with examples of women's responses to the expected roles and conclude with a summary of the contrasting gender role for non-elite women.

The ideal created for elite white women in colonial Brazil directed them to marriage, deemed natural for all and required for the elite.[1] Virginity before marriage was essential for political and family interests and the assurance of an untainted lineage; any sexual activity before marriage, even if she bore no child from it, excluded a noble girl from the best marriage prospects. Public rumors about her were perhaps even worse than her actions; she was expected to be invisible to public scrutiny, and guarded seclusion was recommended to fathers in order to prevent any damage to her reputation. Preservation of her honor, that is, the reputation of virginity, might be deemed a girl's only noteworthy accomplishment. Other virtues included beauty, nobility, wealth and youth—all intrinsic values; other inculcated attributes reinforced her self-effacement: discretion, shyness, modesty and prudence. Education in colonial Brazil was nominal for elite girls; she might learn to 'read, write, count, sew and embroider',[2] to aid in her oversight of a household. A girl's most important instruction was in simple prayer and basic Catholic doctrines; knowing her religious duties was essential not only for her own salvation but also for her guidance of future children.[3]

The parents of the girl contracted her marriage, arranging her dowry or marriage settlement as they selected for her a white, well-placed husband. An economic and social relationship rather than an affective bond, marriage was too important to be left to a girl's untrustworthy emotions. Girls might be married as young as twelve or thirteen, but fourteen was an appropriately mature age for marriage. Roman Catholic Church Council decrees emphasised the creation of a holy bond between the spouses, and required the bride's consent for marriage; before the priestly blessing, however, announcements of the upcoming wedding were posted to preclude incest or bigamy.

An elite married woman contributed only within the domestic sphere; her confinement within the house guaranteed not only her own fidelity but also the family honor. Besides perpetuating the patriarchal lineage and maintaining her honor, she kept the house in order and arranged meals and clothing for her husband, servants, slaves and later, children—her own and those of the extended household. Friendship between husband and wife was possible, but husbands were advised not to love their wives too much. Friendships with religious women or servants endangered her loyalty, and superficial attachments with peers were preferable. Docile and tractable, a virtuous wife was obedient to God and her husband, quiet, chaste and frugal; she might also cultivate personal charm, grace and some little artistic achievement. Without the strict guidance of a husband, however, women were more likely to be wild, garrulous, vain and profligate, especially in the purchase of cosmetics and clothing. Religious devotions enriched her spiritual life, and she might attend the ceremonies and festivals of local religious brotherhoods.

While a woman might be equal in religious achievement to her husband, the dangers to her virtue were grave. Adultery 'constituted an violation of the marital contract', a ' "theft" of honor'.[4] Law and tradition allowed her husband to kill her and her lover on suspicion of such betrayal. If her husband traveled, she stayed at a religious house—formally or informally constituted—to ensure her chastity. Her silent tolerance was presumed, however, for her husband's adultery and concubinage; she might even be expected to raise his children from such relationships. In her natural destiny as a mother, then, the *dona da casa* ('lady of the house') bore strong sons and few daughters, instructing them and all household dependents in religious doctrine and practice. Her care for her children should include breast-feeding, in order to transmit the stability and virtues of her lineage, as well as the oversight of their upbringing and, of course, strict protection for the girls.

Not surprisingly, this ideal for Brazilian elite women expounded by secular writers of the era was embraced by religious writers as well. During the late medieval and early modern periods in Portugal, the Roman Catholic Church collaborated with the imperial and colonial governments, supporting public policies and receiving, in return, considerable power in political, economic and legal spheres. This particular norm coincided with the Church's own interests in describing the human condition, and may be found repeated and justified in the writings of two noted religious authors from the sixteenth and seventeenth centuries, Martín de Azpilcueta Navarro and António Vieira.

Martín de Azpilcueta Navarro (1492[?]–1586) was a scholar at the University of Coimbra and educator of the first Jesuit missionaries to Brazil, including his nephew João Azpilcueta and the more renowned António da Nóbrega.[5] His confession guide, *Manual de confessores y Penitentes*, was among the first reflecting the doctrines that would be promulgated by Tridentine decrees.[6] In it, he bound women's lives to the preservation of chastity, but his concern for the primacy of religious conformity enforced women's submission to the sacrament of marriage. His confession guide, with its detailed lists of sins corresponding to the Biblical commandments and canonical laws, offers a necessarily dichotomized view of women. On the one hand Catholic doctrine insisted on individual autonomy and even women—possessed of free will and a conscience—must be capable of independent agency. On the other hand it persistently infantilized women by relegating them to the dominion of their fathers and husbands. This can be seen in the section on the fourth commandment (to honor one's parents), which begins by emphasising filial obedience. Once established in her marriage—a woman's proper place—her husband assumes responsibility for her behavior and her duty to obedience centers on him. Under the same commandment appear guidelines for the married relationship, with warnings that a woman sins grievously when she 'disobeys her husband notably', 'does not want what he wants', 'provokes him,' or 'despises to be subject to him'.[7] His authority is needed, Navarro explains, to 'command that she abandon her superfluous vanities and dishonest habits'.[8] If they cannot be thwarted, her vanity and even her pleasing attractiveness are only venial sins. Still, Catholic authority limits a husband's power over his wife—especially when it interferes with her religious practice or might lead her into sin. Thus, he could not prevent her from attending church or complying with commandments or canonical law or beat her 'excessively and cruelly', and she might disobey him if 'he wishes to be a vagabond'.[9]

Discussion of the marital relationship continues, as might be expected, under the sixth commandment (against adultery). Most warnings in that section are directed to men, preserving many traditional protections for women.[10] Discussions of the occasions for men to sin, however, range far beyond these two commandments, while women's lives—at least in this document—have no other sphere but marriage.

My second source, António Vieira (1608–97), was a controversial Jesuit missionary and author. Renowned as 'the greatest Portuguese and Brazilian preacher of the seventeenth century',[11] he gave his influential sermons in the royal chapel in Lisbon and the bishopric cathedral in Bahia. His writings also reveal the deep contradictions between the Catholic—nearly humanistic—doctrine of autonomy and the unrelenting struggle to exercise control over women. His statements on the place and value of women swing between exhortations on the centrality of religious commitment for the Christian soul and demands that women renounce their unfeminine independence; his actions as missionary supported the conversion of individual women—especially to the imperial civilisation he introduced.

His classically baroque sermons, especially the series on the Rosary, focus on proper piety; in them he calls women to religious devotion, but repeatedly castigates them as foolish, vulgar and prone to evil. His arguments reveal that virtue and vice in women are solely determined by their submission to marriage and to a husband's authority. In the 'Sermão Sétimo do Rosário', he contends that the women listed in Jesus' genealogy are notable only for their sexual infidelity. That sin, while found among men, is characteristic of women, and in women it is 'more offensive [and] more dangerous and pernicious'. Since their sole duty is to keep chaste before and in marriage, that single sin undoes the very nature of women, and 'encompasses all sins' they might commit.[12]

Even in the convent, a woman could escape neither her marital duty nor Vieira's criticism. In a sermon preached at the Convent of St Bernard, he reminded the nuns that they were 'wed to the Son of God' and so should forswear their natural inclination as 'daughters of Eve' to vanity. Those who admire themselves in mirrors are 'worse than idolators' since they have not only abandoned their religion but also their true spouse, and have put their own image before his.[13] Such a warning, cloaked in religious terms, might also serve for all women: their husbands must come first. And when Vieira considers the theme of spiritual blindness in another sermon, he turns his admonitions to men, advising each to end his wife's vanity and commence his daughters' seclusion from the public sphere.[14]

In the 'Sermão Décimo Sétimo do Rosário' he returns to this second theme, insisting that women 'must pray at home, and never outside of it'.[15] His biblical exegesis leads to the remarkable assertion that Eve encountered the beguiling snake outside the walls of Paradise, and had passed to her daughters an inclination to leave their own proper enclosures. The proper isolation of women would make them invisible to the public and their existence null, following God's plan:

> The Author of nature did not wish that woman be counted among the movables (i.e., the furniture). An edifice does not move from the place that it is put; and so should a woman be such a great friend of her house as if the woman and the house are the same thing.[16]

He argues that women's failure has again become a sin against fidelity in marriage, shifting the theme to focus on the single role that women may inhabit, that of submissive wife. Any activity beyond the domestic bounds—even attendance at religious devotions—is infidelity, for he contends that women feign religious piety as a pretext to go out to meet friends: it 'seems to be devotion but it is . . . licentiousness'.[17] Several years later in Lisbon, however, in the 'Sermão Vigésimo Segundo do Rosário', Vieira laments the privatisation of religion among elite women who preferred the Latin offices said at home over the vernacular rosary and had left church attendance to 'common women':

> Of old the greatest splendor in the churches . . . were the Portuguese ladies, when they came to worship God with their faces covered. They used to confess in the church, take communion in the church and hear the mass and sermon in the church. But what was once only permitted for extreme infirmity today is conceded for extreme vanity: the confessor must go to their houses [to] hear confessions there, say mass there, give communion there. You see whether it is more disrespectful for them to want God to go to their houses, or that they go to find Him. If the church (itself) could go there, they would have to wait till it does; but because the church cannot, they want the sacraments to go.[18]

These apparent contradictions in specific advice—stay home and pray but leave home to pray—may be reconciled if we recall that Vieira was not offering a detailed set of rules for women's lives, but was elaborating a single principle for the female gender. His repeated theme through all these writings was, again, the control of women through marital submission. This is presented clearly in the material above, even in the two contradictory passages: fidelity, whether to father, husband, God the Father or Padre Vieira, was the solitary virtue to which women must be dedicated.

Both religious writers directed their varied discussions to emphasize the need for control over women. For them, the proper woman was isolated within her marriage and household, and her activities, thoughts and sense of herself found their essential beginnings in her marital status; otherwise she defied God and man alike. Vieira found in women's essential nature a tendency to disturbance, chaos and sin owing to their inheritance from the sinful Eve. In so doing, he made their sin almost inevitable, their guilt undeniable and the need for religious control imperative. Navarro's text assigned sinfulness and guilt to men and women equally, but, as surely as Vieira, identified true womanhood with the role of the dutiful religious wife.

While we cannot know the responses of women to these authors, the records of the visiting Tribunal of the Portuguese Inquisition preserved statements of contemporary women's attitudes toward marriage. In Bahia in 1591, for example, Paula de Siqueira confessed to problems in her marriage. Siqueira had sought out a local woman who claimed to have had two husbands, both loving and 'tamed' by her powers, and from her learned magical words that would make a husband love his wife. Siqueira admitted that the magic had not improved her husband, and the Inquisitor ruled that she should be given 'spiritual penances' to mend her ways.[19] That same year, Antonia de Bairos, an elite woman in her seventies, told the Inquisitor that she had been exiled from Portugal for adultery on the testimony of her husband, and had subsequently entered a false marriage with a boat owner and fisherman in the colony. They had arranged false witnesses to swear to her first husband's death and were married with the license of the episcopal official. Having lived with the second husband for fifteen years, she fled the house fearful of 'the wounds and blows' that he dealt her, sought refuge in her local church, and confessed all to the pastor.[20] These two women, both of the elite classes, struggled with their husbands in conditions far from the idealized marriage of the era. Both had, however, clung to the possibility of amelioration for their inescapable condition. A different view comes from Pernambuco in 1594, when the wife of a carpenter offered evidence that her married life exceeded expectations and that her satisfaction led her into sin. Breatriz Martins confessed that she had committed heresy: she had asserted to friends visiting in her yard that the married state, 'made and ordained by God', was religiously superior to the orders of monks and nuns begun by mere humans. She explained further that she had learned this as a girl from a childhood instructor who had also taught her the wifely skills of cooking and washing.[21]

These three episodes reveal the continuing influence of the ideal directed to the elite European-descended women amidst the changing economic conditions of the colony and indicate that the social norms of Portugal might be subverted in Brazil. Still, as Brazil grew prosperous from its sugar cane industry and colonization expanded, the need for a regulated society was repeatedly articulated as a need for white women bound within the institution of marriage.[22] It is, in fact, this ideal that we find repeated by Brazilian historians through the early twentieth century and by English visitors to colonial and imperial Brazil as well. In their various accounts, the ideal is made real by addition of specific examples from the elite classes, and is often presented as the sole model for Brazilian womanhood. I would suggest, however, that the continuation of this ideal-turned-historical-fact served the purposes of historians and outsiders who wished to emphasise the (past) degeneracy of a society whose dominance was waning. The inclusion of evidence from the lives of slave, lower-class and mixed-race women changes the portrait that has been thus created and reveals the dichotomy I noted.

When we turn to consider women outside the elite group, we find little prose directed to Brazilindian, Africans and mixed-race women or to the Portuguese women of the lower classes in Brazil—no confession books offered advice on slave marriages, no sermons addressed the struggles of abandoned mothers. The ideals for elite white women certainly extended to them, such that they and the dominant class might use the preferred standard to enjoin cooperation or castigate failures. Still, within the colonial records there can be found expectations for a significantly different role, a role constructed by tradition, religion and law.

Girls outside of the elite group prepared themselves for marriage and for a working life. Virginity before marriage was valued among lower-strata white and mixed-race women, and was especially promoted by the missionaries among the converted Brazilindians: the Jesuit José de Anchieta reported with pride in 1554 that a recent Indian convert and his (unnamed) wife 'have taken care to keep their daughters virgins'.[23] Virginity was not, however, expected of most Brazilindian or African women; slave women were usually perceived as licentious and corrupting, and, when unsupervised or freed, tending toward prostitution. Among the lower classes, education might better be understood as training in domestic service. Rarely literate, a girl would instead be taught to spin, sew, cook and complete other household production tasks. Missionaries separated Brazilindian girls from boys for doctrinal instruction, thus depriving the former of the additional education in reading and writing provided to the latter; plans were made but never realized for 'virtuous women' to teach girls to sew and spin, so that they might marry converted youths.[24]

Following the emphatic decrees of the Council of Trent, marriage under a priest's blessing was preferred for aspirants to higher position in society, but was rarer among the lower classes. Women who had some white parentage, especially those whose parents had married, expected marriage with artisans, merchants, sailors and even small landholders. Marriage for slave women, whether native or African, was nearly impossible. Native Brazilindians were barred from marriage, often by the very missionaries who condemned their 'loose morals' and early colonists routinely disregarded the 'natural' marriages of native Brazilians when separating families in order to enslave the adults. Vieira himself denounced the practice of separating Brazilindian wives from their families to serve colonists, but later endorsed domestic service and slavery for Indian women, in tasks as wet-nurse, table-server, or maid for 'some poor [white] woman' who had no other servant. He stipulated that these 'exceptional cases' were only appropriate for older 'unattached' women, and that harvest work could be undertaken by some Indian women 'with their husbands'; otherwise, he warned, their salvation might be compromised.[25] African women, who made up fewer than forty percent of the slave population, had few opportunities to marry. Slaveholders preferred to prevent permanent relationships, especially those condoned by the church, so that they might sell individual slaves without legal or ecclesiastical reprisals. Colonial law inhibited marriages with its stipulation that free men took on the bondage of their wives. Furthermore, the Catholic Church itself made marriage more difficult for the lower-strata women, requiring publication of banns in the couple's home towns—nearly insuperable obstacle for African slaves—and fees for performing the ceremony.[26]

Rather than marriage, mixed-race women and native Brazilian women faced long- or short-term consensual unions, such as concubinage or cohabitation with single men (including priests), and clandestine or coercive sexual relationships with married men. The sexual exploitation of native Brazilian women was encouraged in several ways by the colonial system. For example, marriage could only be contracted if a woman were baptized, active in the church and understood Christian doctrine. White men of the upper strata forced enslaved women into concubinage, while poorer men, especially those who traveled frequently or had left wives in Portugal, might live 'as if married' with freed or biracial women apparently unhampered by resident priests and local church mandates.[27] Support for consensual rather than sacramental unions may be seen in the heretical claim repeated in Inquisition confessions that a man's sexual relations with an unmarried woman, especially an enslaved African or Brazilindian woman, was not a mortal sin.[28]

Women of the lower strata brought little property to a marriage, although the Brotherhood of the Misericórdia in Bahia set aside a small fund for the daughters of freed black women and 'unknown' fathers.[29] Once married, only the women of the sugar cane farming families might remain cloistered within the home; considered to be or aspiring to higher status, they avoided acquaintance with other women and men. Most poorer women prepared for an independent existence as innkeepers, bakers, 'shopkeepers, vendors, peddlers, . . . seamstresses or laundresses'.[30] Since the norms of the Brazilian slave society tied the upbringing of children to their mothers, these women might also expect to be single parents and heads of households; in the 1789 census of São Paulo, forty-six percent of the households were reported to be headed by women.[31] Their burden was increased by prevailing suspicions that fostered such Inquisition charges as witchcraft against a 'woman who has no husband' or homosexual sins against 'a single woman with children'.[32]

Religious devotions and church activities were deemed the province of women, even among the poorer women. Praised for their dedication to the Church, they might also find some solace there. Indeed, a sizable proportion of confessions and denunciations made by women to the Inquisition of the era was brought by those of the lower strata, and their statements suggest that they overcame the fear that that institution might provoke to call for justice for wrongs done by neighbors and husbands. Women of African descent found a unique welcome in the lay religious brotherhoods such as Our Lady of the Rosary in Salvador and Our Lady of Mercies in Minas Gerais. The Rosary brotherhood, usually established for enslaved men, admitted all blacks 'regardless of social position and sex, both free and slave'. Single as well as married women might be members, and several leadership positions were reserved for married women. In addition, '[f]emale members of the brotherhood played a vital and essential role in providing social services for brothers and their families stricken by sickness or poverty'.[33]

As can be seen, the expectations present in the gender role for women of the lower classes were not the same as those for elite women, but, I would contend, they still formed part of the same discourse expressing the concerns of the Luso-Brazilian governing classes. The elite ideal served to maintain the illusion of a unified society while dichotomising the ranks of women. At the same time, the barriers to marriage for poorer, biracial and enslaved women not only guaranteed the normative power held by the elites but also supported the priests' claim that such a depraved people required proper religious control. The reserve of unmarried and sexually available women was assured for the male-dominated colonizing enterprise that the Portuguese political and religious authorities planned.

The extent of the efforts to manipulate the gender role for women of the lower strata indicates, I argue, the growing power that the non-white, non-elite Brazilians were gaining in the colonial society. The repeated calls for control over women were in fact calls for renewed control in society articulated by those most observant of what they felt to be the dangers in the social reorganisation of the colony. While contemporary political authority borrowed the language of politics and government to discuss the roles of women, religious authors extolled the virtues of hierarchical religious dominion for the control of colonial society and personal life. Their insistence on sharp dichotomies between the sexes and complicity in the maintenance of class differences reinforced the dichotomous discourse that supported the power of the Portuguese crown over its colonists and the authority of the missionaries over Indian lives. The growing influence of humanism and the living examples of exceptional women (such as the queens of England and Spain) heightened the pressures that these writers might have felt and threatened the traditional concepts of authority in the government and church. Their responses, not surprisingly, were to re-establish economic and religious control by re-establishing their power—especially in power over women.

Notes

1 The sources consulted for this overview were Asunción Lavrin, 'Introduction: The Scenario, the Actors, and the Issues', in Asunción Lavrin (ed.), *Sexuality and Marriage in Colonial Latin America*, Lincoln, University of Nebraska Press 1989, pp. 1–43; Maria Beatriz Nizza da Silva, *Sistema de casamento no Brasil colonial*, Estudos brasileiros, vol 6, São Paulo, Editora da Universidade de São Paulo 1984; A. J. R. Russell-Wood, 'Women and Society in Colonial Brazil', *Journal of Latin American Studies* 9 (1977), pp. 1–34; Anna Maria Moog Rodrigues (ed.), *Moralistas do século XVIII*, Rio de Janeiro, Editora Documentário 1979; and Madre Maria Angela [Leda Maria Pereira Rodrigues], *A Instrução feminina em São Paulo, subsídios para sua história até a proclamação da Republica*, São Paulo, Faculdade de Filosofia 'Sedes Sapientiae' 1962.

2 José Joaquim da Cunha de Azeredo Coutinho, *Estatutos do Recolhimento de Nossa Senhora da Glória do lugar da Boa Vista de Pernambuco*, Lisbon, Typographia da Academia Real das Ciências 1798, p. 86, quoted in Maria Beatriz Nizza da Silva, *Cultura no Brasil colônia*, Petrópolis, Editora Vozes 1981, pp. 74–6.

3 The last years of the colonial period saw considerable changes: the statutes for a school for poor white girls declared that 'women need education equally' with men, since they are the partners of their husbands and 'First Teachers' of their children.

4 Angela Mendes de Almeida, *O Gosto do pecado: casamento e sexualidade nos manuais de confessores dos séculos XVI e XVII*, Rio de Janeiro, Rocco 1992, pp. 96–7.

5 Nóbrega received his baccalaureate from Navarro and corresponded with him from Brazil; the opinions of the senior Azpilcueta influenced Jesuit policies on catechizing Brazilindians. See Serafim Leite (ed), *Cartas dos primeiros jesuítas do Brasil*, São Paulo, Commissão do IV Centenário da Cidade de São Paulo 1956, I, pp. 132–45, 361.

6 Martin de Azpilcueta Navarro, *Manual de confessores y Penitentes, que contiene quase todas las dudas que en las confessiones suelen occurrir de los peccados, absoluciones, restituciones, censuras, & irregularidades*, Valladolid, Fernández de Cordova 1570.
7 Ibid., p. 137.
8 Ibid., p. 138.
9 Ibid., pp. 137, 138, 173.
10 Ibid., pp. 158–73.
11 Eduardo Hoornaert, *História da Igreja no Brasil*, 2 vols., *História Geral da Igreja na América Latina*, nos. 2 and 3, Petrópolis, Editora Vozes. 1977, I, p. 331.
12 António Vieira, *Sermões*, Gonçalo Alves (ed.), 5 vols, Porto, Lello & Irmão, Editores 1959, IV, pp. 43–50.
13 From the 'Sermão do Demónio Mudo, pregado no Convento de Odivelas, Religiosas do Patriarca S. Bernardo, no ano de 1661', ibid., I, pp. 328, 333.
14 'Sermão da Quinta Quarta-Feira da Quaresma, pregado na Misericórdia de Lisboa, no ano de 1669', ibid., II, p. 119.
15 Ibid., p. 414.
16 Ibid.
17 Ibid., p. 418.
18 Ibid., p. 153.
19 Heitor Furtado de Mendoça, *Primeira visitação do Santo Oficio às partes do Brasil: confissões da Bahia, 1591–1592*, Rio de Janeiro, F. Briguet, 1935, p. 50.
20 Ibid., pp. 66–7.
21 She was admonished by the Inquisitor that she should not discuss 'what she did not understand' and was sent to repeat her confession at the Jesuit monastery for her penance. Heitor Furtado de Mendoça, *Primeira visitação do Santo Officio às partes do Brasil: confissões de Pernambuco, 1594–1595*, José Antônio Gonsalves de Mello (ed.), Recife, Universidade Federal de Pernambuco 1970, p. 43.
22 Ilana Novinsky, in 'Heresia, mulher e sexualidade: algumas notas sobre o Nordeste Brasileiro nos séculos XVI e XVII', argues that the economic success of the colony also engaged the interest of the Portuguese Inquisition in establishing religious conformity and detecting hidden Jews. In Maria Cristina A. Bruschini and Fúlvia Rosemberg (eds), *Vivência: história, sexualidade e imagens femininas*, São Paulo, Livraria Brasiliense Editora, s.a. 1980, p. 229.
23 From Letter Four, 'Do José de Anchieta ao Ignacio de Loyola, September 1, 1544', in Hélio Abranches Viotti (ed.), *Cartas do Pe. José de Anchieta: Correspondência ativa e passiva*, 2nd ed, São Paulo, Edições Loyola 1984, p. 63.
24 Leite, *Cartas dos primeiros jesuítas*, III, pp. 37, 365, 514, 466.
25 Serafim Leite, *História da Companhia de Jesus no Brasil*, 10 vols., Lisbon, Livraria Portugália 1938–1950, IV, p. 121, quoted in Hoornaert, *História da Igreja*, I, p. 375.
26 Hoornaert, *História da Igreja*, vol 1, pp. 312–15; Donald Ramos, 'Marriage and the Family in Colonial Vila Rica', *Hispanic American Historical Review* 55: 2 (1975), pp. 209–21; and Stuart B. Schwartz, 'A população escrava na Bahia', in Iraci del Nero da Costa (ed.), *Brasil: história econômica e demográfica*, São Paulo, Instituto de Pesquisas Econômicas 1986, pp. 52–55.
27 C. R. Boxer, *The Golden Age of Brazil: 1695–1750*, Berkeley, University of California Press 1962, pp. 17–21. Ecclesiastical and colonial powers forbade concubinage and cohabitation, usually blaming immoral women, but the repetition of condemnations suggests that few heeded the laws.
28 This heretical statement about 'simple fornication' appears regularly among men's confessions and denunciations in the Inquisition records of the late 1500s and early 1600s.

29 A. J. R. Russell-Wood, *Fidalgos and Philanthropists: The Santa Casa da Misericórdia of Bahia, 1550–1755*, London, Macmillan 1968, pp. 192–3.
30 Susan A. Soeiro, 'The feminine orders in colonial Bahia, Brazil: economic, social and demographic implications, 1677–1800', in Asunción Lavrin (ed.), *Latin American Women: Historical Perspectives*, Westport, Connecticut, Greenwood Press 1978, p. 187.
31 Mary Lucy M. del Priori, 'O corpo feminino e o amor: um olhar (século XVIII, São Paulo)', in Maria Angela d'Incao (ed.), *Amor e família no Brasil*, São Paulo, Contexto 1989, pp. 33–4.
32 Heitor Furtado de Mendoça, 'Denunciações de Pernambuco 1593–1595', in Leonardo Duntas Silva (ed.), *Primeira Visitação Santo Officio às partes do Brasil: confissões e denunciações de Pernambuco 1593–1595*, São Paulo, n.p. 1929; facsimile ed. Recife, Fundação do Patrimônio Histórico e Artístico de Pernambuco 1984, pp. 24, 39, 108–10.
33 A. J. R. Russell-Wood, 'Black and Mulatto Brotherhoods in Colonial Brazil: A Study in Collective Behavior', *Hispanic American Historical Review* 54 (1974), pp. 580, 584.

26

Excerpt from 'THE CHURCH AT NANRANTSOUAK

Sébastien Râle, S.J., and the Wabanaki of Maine's Kennebec River'

William A. Clark, SJ

Source: *Catholic Historical Review*, 92(3) (2006), 225–6, 231–40, 245–51.

By the middle of the seventeenth century the Wabanaki[1]—the "People of the Dawn," occupying the territory from Lake Champlain eastward into what are now the Maritime Provinces of Canada—were a nation besieged. The devastation of six bloody wars with the English settlers along the Maine coast was still a quarter-century into the future, but a hundred years of increasing European economic pressure and fifty of direct European settlement on or near Wabanaki lands had taken their toll. Competing strategies for dealing with the Europeans, increasing dependence on their trade goods, the resulting rivalries and social dislocations, the ravages of previously unknown diseases, and the declining prestige of shamans apparently powerless in the face of all this had all contributed to a deep spiritual crisis among the Wabanaki.[2] Since 1611, the Kennebec band, living along the banks of the river that rises at Moosehead Lake in what is now northern Maine and empties into the Atlantic near the present town of Bath, had had at least passing contact with members of the Society of Jesus. The acquaintance grew into a serious religious encounter after the Kennebec Wabanaki allied themselves with Algonkian natives of the St. Lawrence valley in the 1640's, many of whom had already been Christianized by Jesuit missionary activity.[3] In 1646, the Wabanaki requested and were visited by their first "permanent" Jesuit missionary, Gabriel Druillettes, who instructed them through the winter and returned for nearly a year in 1650.

For the ensuing forty years, there was no resident missionary in the Kennebec valley. The Wabanaki seem to have nurtured their new-found faith, to the extent that they retained it, in their ongoing commercial contact with the French and St. Lawrence natives. During and after the first English war in 1675 ("King Philip's War") many of the Kennebecs migrated to mission villages built by the Jesuits near Quebec, while those who remained in Maine were visited by Jesuit travelers such as the brothers Jacques and Vincent Bigot.[4] But in the fall of 1693 or 1694, in the midst of the second English war ("King William's War"), a large group of Kennebecs was gathered into a Christian community at the village of Nanrantsouak in the middle of the Kennebec Valley by a Jesuit whose name is now permanently associated with the place and its people, Father Sébastien Râle.[5] [. . .]

[. . .]Râle's first employment upon his arrival at Quebec was in learning the Wabanaki language. In a letter to his brother, he points out that such learning could only be obtained through a close, sustained association with the Wabanaki themselves:

> I spent part of the day in their cabins, hearing them talk. I was obliged to give the utmost attention, in order to connect what they said, and to conjecture its meaning; sometimes I caught it exactly, but more often I was deceived,—because, not being accustomed to the trick of their guttural sounds, I repeated only half the word, and thereby gave them cause for laughter.[19]

In the beginning of 1691, Râle began compiling the fruits of these slow labors into a dictionary of the Wabanaki language, writing on the first of what became 550 pages, "1691: It is one year since I have been among the [*sauvages*]; I begin to put in order in the form of a dictionary the words that I learn."[20]

Because Râle was always in search of the *génie* of the language, he did not, despite his own epigraph, limit his dictionary to a mere list of words, but recorded whole phrases illustrative of their contextual uses and variations.

A patient perusal of these entries is extraordinarily suggestive of the sort of life he led among the Wabanaki. One can imagine him observing and participating in scenes of everyday life, catching a turn of phrase here and there, or carefully inquiring how to express a particular French thought. We can see the missionary here getting to know the people ("How old are you?") or learning about the family structure and relationships of those he was visiting ("I adopt him for my son.").[21] The amount of time he spent with the sick and the dying becomes evident in phrases such as, "Help me to get up"; or in a complete little discourse: "I am not benefiting anymore from the medicine that you gave me; it did me some good, but the sickness won't stop coming back"; or in the devastatingly eloquent illustration of the Wabanaki word for "both together": "If we could both die together, Jesus, that would be a great privilege."[22] By means of the dictionary, we can glimpse the priest listening to the intimacies of those seeking counsel or confessing their sins ("I love him with all my heart," and "I have jealous thoughts").[23] Perhaps at times Râle heard more than his European sensibilities allowed him to feel entirely comfortable with: in a subsection written almost entirely in Latin and entitled "*verba foeda*" ("indecent words"), he includes all the words for the sexual organs and for a variety of sex acts as well, using Latin circumlocutions to convey his meaning. One entry reads simply, "*pecco cum ea*" ("I sin with her").[24] Throughout the dictionary, of course, are also the words and phrases he would need to instruct the Wabanaki in the meaning and practice of their adopted religion: "prayer," "rosary," "you who are in heaven," "Mary preserved in her heart the words of her son," "I fight against the devil," and the beautifully simple instruction, "Take your hand and touch first your forehead, your stomach, and then your shoulders"—a lesson on making the sign of the cross.[25]

The significance of Râle's language work to the whole conduct of his mission can hardly be overestimated. As the Wabanaki historian Andrea Bear Nicholas observes, in an oral culture such as that of the Wabanaki the language embodies not only a particular means of creative self-expression but even the "unique view of reality, both past and present" which is the basis of cultural identity.[26] Râle's recorded observations indicate that, despite his inevitable ethnocentrism, he was able to notice and appreciate a variety of cultural features in those tribes with whom he spent time, from the quality speech of an Illinois chief to the tenderness of the Wabanaki toward their children.[27] His descriptions of some of the myths and customs of the partly-Christianized Illinois even seem to have been a bit too accepting for some of his countrymen: a comparison of certain original letters to an edited compilation of them that appeared in France around the time of his death suggests that the openness of the young Father Râle to cultural difference was somewhat greater than the norm for his fellow Frenchmen. For example, in one of the original letters we read:

> [The *Ottawas*] are very superstitious, and great tricksters (jongleurs). They are divided into three families from which they say they draw their origin, and in each family there are around 500 people. Some are of the family of Michabes, which means "Great Hare," . . .[28]

The corresponding passage in the version published in France (and subsequently used as the source for the esteemed *Jesuit Relations* English translation) adopts what may have been considered a more appropriately disapproving tone:

> [The *Outaouacks*] are very superstitious, and much attached to the juggleries of their charlatans. They assume for themselves an origin as senseless as it is ridiculous. They declare that they have come from

> three families, and each family is composed of five hundred persons. Some are of the family of *Michabou*, that is to say, of "the Great Hare."[29]

In relation to his own lifestyle, Râle's efforts to come to terms with native culture seem to have produced a variety of practical results. At times, he was unable to escape his own sensibilities. At others, he seems enraptured by the beauty and wisdom of native ways. Another of his stories illustrates this, as he describes the Wabanaki custom of eating a sort of stew from a bowl of bark:

> When I first arrived here I could not eat any of their food. They kept asking me, "Why are you not eating?" "Because," I answered them, "I am not accustomed to eating my meat without bread." "You will have to get over that," they answered, "it should not be difficult for a patriarich"(that is what they call those who are their teachers—it means "*patriarch*") "it should not be difficult to get over that since you know how to pray perfectly. It cannot be more difficult for you to surmount that than it is for us to accept and believe things we cannot see." So you see, we must not waver. We must live as they do, in order to win them over to Jesus Christ.[30]

Clearly, the transition from the France of Louis XIV to the Canadian woods was not an easy one. Looking past the ups and downs of thirty years toward the end of his life, however, Râle was able to give this succinct assessment of his success to his nephew: "As for what concerns me personally I assure you, that I see, that I hear, that I speak, only as a [*sauvage*]."[31]

Having passed through his initial period of linguistic and cultural training, Râle was recalled from the Illinois and assigned to the Kennebec mission, arriving at Nanrantsouak in the fall of 1694.[32] The village was located where the Sandy River flows into the Kennebec, in the present town of Madison, about thirty miles up the river from the then-abandoned English trading post at Cushnoc (Augusta). Previously, it does not seem to have been the primary village of the Kennebec Wabanaki, but the social devastations of war, famine, and emigration had so drained the Kennebec valley of its native population that Râle was able to gather in this one place, at least on a seasonal basis, most of the Wabanaki within reach of his mission.[33] (The actual numbers fluctuated; in 1714, Râle mentions "more than a hundred families," while at the time of his death in 1724, about two hundred persons were present in Nanrantsouak.[34]) In this way, out of a kind of necessity, the earlier concentration strategy of the Jesuits was merged with the later insertion strategy in the ministry of Sébastien Râle.

Despite being centered on this village, the Kennebec wabanaki remained highly mobile, because of the admixture of agriculture and hunting in their economy. After spring planting at Nanrantsouak, Râle would annually accompany the community to the coast in the summer, where they would live on seafood and wild fruit until harvest time. In the early winter, they would again "live better at the sea than during the summer" because of the seasonal abundance of water fowl. Around February, when the men "disperse[d] to hunt beavers and moose," Râle would return to the village with the women, children, and sick. On all these peregrinations, Râle would travel equipped for the Mass and sacraments, apparently at the insistence of the Wabanaki themselves.[35] In keeping with the practice of going where his villagers went, he is known to have been present for at least one peace conference between the Wabanaki and the English, and there is some evidence that he may also have accompanied at least one war party.[36]

Within the village, too, Râle was immersed in the ordinary life of the Kennebec band. He describes his involvement, apparently more than ceremonial, in marriage arrangements among members of the village.[37] Râle attended tribal councils and believed, "My advice always determines their decisions."[38] The curious interplay of intimacy and aloofness, of confident belonging and distant analysis, in Râle's descriptions of these activities continues also in the overtly religious sphere. The church, that is to say the Christian community, into which Râle organized this Wabanaki band relied heavily on the European order which Râle brought to his leadership of the sacraments and prayer. A succession of church buildings were erected and destroyed at Nanrantsouak over the course of Râle's career, each one decorated in large part by the missionary himself, who apparently had something of an artistic reputation. Of the last of these churches, the one that was burned on the day he died, he writes to his nephew that its furnishings "would be esteemed in our European churches."[39] In this aesthetically European building, the prayers and sacraments were held according to a nearly monastic schedule: Mass in the early morning (said, of course, in Latin), followed by catechism and an opportunity for confessions and counseling; vespers at sunset; frequent pious visits to the outlying chapels that were built on the paths to the river and the fields. Râle himself withdrew nightly, from vespers until Mass the following morning, so as to be able to continue his own regimen of prayer before and after rest.[40]

Within this imported order, Râle positioned the participation of his Wabanaki "flock." He writes that about forty young Wabanaki men (likely the majority of young men in the village), whom he designates "minor clergy," were trained by him and dressed in cassock and surplice as they would be in Europe, for participating in processions and serving at Mass, the Divine Office, and Benediction. Râle describes the processions as being attended by "crowds"; one can imagine the entire village turning out to see the odd spectacle of their sons and brothers arrayed in European finery.[41] For the participation of all the people in catechism lessons, vespers, and prayers during Mass, Râle prepared texts in the Wabanaki language. The project of translation was begun with the help of selected native speakers even before Râle had a clear grasp of the language: "I repeated to them in a clumsy manner some passages from the catechism, and they gave them to me again, with all the nicety of their language."[42]

Early in Râle's career, then, it is possible to see at least some participation of the Wabanaki themselves in shaping the presentation of the faith to their own people, and most interestingly Râle trusts them. The difference that such linguistic assistance could make to the substance of the teaching being given is illustrated by Râle himself in explaining the "indescribable force in the style and manner with which they express themselves":

> If I should ask you why God created you, you would answer me that it was for the purpose of knowing him, loving him, and serving him, and by this means to merit eternal glory. If I should put the same question to a [*sauvage*], he would answer thus, in the style of his own language: "The great Spirit has thought of us: 'Let them know me, let them love me, let them honor me, and let them obey me; for then I will make them enter my glorious happiness.'[43]

The language has a way of claiming the ideas of the faith for the Wabanaki; God here becomes much more the solicitous spirit of then-native myths than the aloof judge of stern catechism morality.[44] Perhaps the Wabanaki church was not an entirely European creature after all.

A somewhat more shrouded indication of genuine native influence in the church at Nanrantsouak is the presence of the outlying chapels mentioned previously. Râle provides few details about these buildings, but what he says is enough to raise some interesting questions and possibilities. To begin with, he uses different language to describe their origin. Having claimed "*j'y ai bâti une Église*"—"I have built a church there"—he writes of the chapels "*On a bâti deux Chapelles*"—"we" or "they have built," or "chapels have been built."[45] Who actually erected these buildings? One Catholic writer, trying to do justice to several conflicting pieces of evidence, suggests that it was the English Protestants, during one of the brief intervals of peace.[46] Râle's language leaves open the possibility that it was the Wabanaki themselves who built them. That possibility is reinforced by the discovery in the dictionary of several entries under "chapel": "Where will it be? What will the length of it be? Where will be the place for saying Mass? The altar must be in the east, and the door at the west."[47] However the buildings came to be, Râle provides us with two other tantalizing details of the way in which they were used. The Wabanaki, he writes, "never pass them without offering prayers therein." Further,

> there is a holy emulation among the women of the Village regarding the best decoration of the Chapel, of which they have care, when

> the Procession is to enter it; all that they have in the way of trinkets, pieces of silk or chintz, and other things of that sort—all are used for adornment.[48]

It seems, then, that although the chapels were clearly used for communal celebrations, they were also places where the Wabanaki felt free to pray in their own way, and places where their own aesthetic might also come into play. Thinking of the syncretistic tendencies often seen in other cross-cultural conversion situations, it is not difficult to imagine such chapels as places where the merging of Christian and native beliefs could be expressed in a somewhat more ample fashion, even if anything overtly shamanistic would never have escaped the priest's scrutiny.[49]

All in all, it is difficult to make an adequate assessment of the extent to which Râle was or wanted to be "inculturated," or the extent to which this was true of the Christianity he administered to the Kennebecs. The observation of Jean-Paul Wiest about Jesuits in China in the same era, that a failure to question themselves led to a failure to truly understand Chinese culture, clearly applies to Râle and his confreres in some ways.[50] They were early proponents of what Wiest calls the "frontier model" of mission, which, without relying on overt military conquest as the earlier "crusader model" did, nonetheless took for granted the superiority of Christian religion and European culture, and sought to extend the boundaries of the Christian world by more apparently spiritual means. On the other hand, it is difficult to believe that the kind of linguistic and day-to-day familiarity by which Râle lived with the Wabanaki over a period of thirty years would produce no adaptation in the missionary's way of thinking, in pastoral application if not in doctrinal formulation.

Unfortunately, as the story of the Kennebec church would eventually bear out, this cultural interplay was not being negotiated by the Wabanaki and their devoted missionary in isolation. The Jesuit's very presence in the village was a symbol of the fact that the Wabanaki were now forced to share their world with both the French and their English rivals. It was inevitable that their religious alliance with the French would be expected to carry through in distinctly non-religious ways as well. Undeniably, letters from the governing authorities in Quebec to Râle and many other fellow missionaries indicate their deep involvement in the territorial struggles of the time and the ongoing attempt to sway the Wabanaki toward the French and away from the English.[51] This does not, however, necessarily validate the standard English accusation that Râle was an *agent provocateur*. His favoring of the French cause in Wabanaki deliberations would have been a simple matter of survival for his mission. The English were not only a rival political power but also professed a "different religion." Laying aside considerations of French nationalism (which surely were present in some form), Râle's fundamental "given" for his work is that Catholicism is the true religion, which the

Wabanaki have embraced. From within this basic assumption—so unacceptable to the Puritans of old and to the new historians of today—his writing is entirely solicitous of the welfare of the Wabanaki. He defends their land rights and encourages their unity as a tribe. In his eyes, the Catholic religion has become a feature of the Wabanaki as a nation, just as it is of the French, and so he defends their right to practice it, which means defending his right to be with them, despite constant English objections. Discussing Wabanaki resistance to the constant temptation to abandon trade with distant Quebec for the convenience of the much nearer English settlements, he writes:

> they are hardly indifferent to their own interests, but their faith is infinitely dearer to them, and they believe that if they detach themselves from alliance with us, they will soon find themselves without a missionary, without sacraments, without the Sacrifice, almost without any religious service, and in serious danger of being plunged back into their previous unbelief.[52]

It may be that there is more of Râle than of the Wabanaki in these words, and yet they demonstrate very well the dynamic within which the Wabanaki expression of Christian faith was caught. Râle led a church that was born, lived, and died in the midst of a cultural conflagration. [. . .]

[. . .] The Wabanaki adopted Christianity in an attempt to maintain, or regain, their equilibrium as a people living on the land that they had always occupied. Until 1675, they seem to have had no clear sense of having been invaded, no strong reaction to being "crowded out" of their own land. Nonetheless, the appearance of the Europeans had already had profound internal effects in their communities, which they struggled to comprehend. Morrison outlines these, under rubrics such as disease, commercial and spiritual rivalries, and resulting tribal divisions (including in-fighting among the shamans).[71] The Wabanaki had come to live in a world of religious bewilderment and confusion that caused in them an almost panicked desire to find other solutions—a sort of "spiritual longing." As Morrison expresses it, "The Kennebecs' appeal for a priest came from a people who were pushed to the brink of physical and psychic survival."[72] This helps to explain the Christian zeal that Râle and others note in them;[73] but this zeal itself, unaccompanied as it was by similar conversion to European cultural values and practices, helps explain the chronic misunderstanding among the Wabanaki, the English, and the French.

A crucial fact in understanding the Wabanaki retention of their original communal identity is that they themselves sought out the teaching of the Jesuit missionaries who eventually came to them, after apparently being rebuffed in the first few contacts that they made with the French.[74] The Jesuits seemed to offer solutions to the many problems that the Wabanaki were encountering. At the same time, they seemed to exemplify the Wabanaki ideal of "the personal characteristics of socially constructive men of power" in a way which the shamans had ceased to do.[75] And while it may not be said of the French generally, individual Jesuit missionaries, at least, lacked the commercial interests of the English with which the Wabanaki had all too much contact. Thus one of the sachems described the Wabanaki attachment to Catholicism when urged by the English to send Râle packing:

> When you came here, you saw me a long time before the French governors, but neither your predecessors nor your ministers ever spoke to me of Prayer or of the Great Spirit. They saw my furs, my beaver and moose skins, and thought of these alone; this is what they looked for so eagerly; I was not able to furnish them enough, and when I brought many, I was their great friend, but only then. But one day my canoe missed the route; I lost my way, and wandered a long time at random, until at last I landed near Quebec, in a great village of the Algonquins, where the Black Robes were teaching. I had hardly arrived, when a Black Robe came to see me. I was loaded with furs, but the French Black Robe did not even bother to look at them. He spoke to me first of the Great Spirit, of heaven, of hell, and of the Prayer, which is the only way to reach heaven. I listened to him with pleasure, and I enjoyed his talks so much that I remained in that village a long time in order to hear him. In the end, the Prayer pleased me, and I besought him to instruct me; I asked for baptism, and received it. Afterward, I returned to my country, and recounted what had happened to me: they envied my happiness; they wanted to share it; they left to go find the Black Robe and ask him for baptism. Thus have the French acted toward me. If when you first saw me you had spoken to me of the Prayer, I would have had the misfortune of praying as you do, for I was not able to tell if your Prayer was good. Now, I tell you, I hold to the Prayer of the French; I accept it, and I will keep it until the world burns and comes to an end. Keep your workmen, your money, and your minister; I will speak of them no more. I will speak to the French governor, my father, and he will send me some.[76]

The story also demonstrates that despite their initiative, the conversion of the Kennebec Wabanaki was part of a wider process taking place among tribes with whom they had important contact. They were not, in fact, isolated, either in accepting the faith or in maintaining it during the time that they had no missionary, since before the coming of the Europeans they had always had bonds—of trade, language, and kinship—with the other peoples around them. These others faced the same great problems as the Wabanaki, and from them the Wabanaki first received the suggestion that "the Prayer" might hold the solutions. If we were to search for a "universal"—a cosmos of meaning and connection—into which to fit the phenomenon of the local Wabanaki church, this native web of relationships, values, and ways of living would be most appropriate for the role. It was this world that the Wabanaki who accepted Christianity were really trying to retain and reconstruct. Just as Europeans sought to draw the native peoples into the European cosmos, so the native peoples sought to fit the Europeans, and all the cataclysmic changes they had brought, into *their* cosmos. With the Puritans (and perhaps the French) we might today think of the Wabanaki as having become "*Roman* Catholics," but it is clear that "Rome" was not a meaningful or relevant concept in Nanrantsouak.

The heartiness with which the Wabanaki embraced the religion the Jesuits offered them suggests that it did for them what they needed it to do: it ordered the spiritual chaos that they were experiencing. It seems unlikely that it could have done this, however, if it had been experienced as entirely foreign at the outset. Rather, the ritual emphasis of Catholicism, its focus on moral social behavior, and its communitarian rather than individualist imagination greatly attracted the Wabanaki because these were elements of their traditional spiritual practice. "The religious alliance between the Abenaki and the French developed," says Morrison, "because their religious sensibilities were compatible."[77] So it is not surprising to hear the Wabanaki explain to the grumbling English traders at Cushnoc (Augusta), regarding Gabriel Druillettes, "We have adopted him for our comrade, we love him as the wisest of our captains, . . . and whoever assails him attacks all the Abenaquiois."[78] Similarly Râle, by his inculturation and long residence with them, became for the Wabanaki a bridge between the pre-contact and post-contact realities.

Telling details of precisely how the Wabanaki, in practice, fitted Christianity into their attempt to retain their traditional lifestyle and worldview are few and far between. Occasionally, however, a window opens in the European accounts that allows a glimpse of a deeper Wabanaki reality. Wabanaki women and children on the Penobscot River keep vigil for their warriors during the second conflict with the English (King William's War, 1689) by confessing and praying the rosary.[79] Father Druillettes listens to a chief, who feared for the souls of his sick children, explain how he tried to minister to them in the absence of the priest.[80] Father Râle marks the season of the tribe's annual move to the sea by referring to the feasts of Corpus Christi and Assumption, but his description of the pomp with which the former is celebrated suggests that such feasts quickly came to signify in the mind of the Wabanaki more than simply a point of Christian doctrine, with significant moments in the agricultural cycle being marked by them.[81] Included in matter-of-fact style in Râle's correspondence and in his dictionary are also notices of various other Wabanaki customs that surely had an unarticulated spiritual significance that the missionary never challenged: the custom of eating the food of someone who has just died, the "usual dances" at funerals, the killing of dogs for a war-feast.[82] In all of this, it is clear that the Wabanaki went on living their communal life, weaving their new religious practice into their ordinary traditional activities in a way that greatly strengthened both, secured the identification of church and community among them, and undoubtedly stiffened their resolve to defend themselves and their lands from English encroachments.

Given the general ethnocentrism of the Europeans, it is not surprising that the English were unable to recognize the Wabanaki initiative, both spiritual and political, in the resistance that they encountered increasingly from 1675 onward. The Wabanaki's spiritual renewal had been catalyzed by their contact with the French Jesuits, and so in the eyes of the English any trouble from their Wabanaki neighbors was simply a result of Jesuit agitation among the simple and easily misled natives. The several comments of Puritan churchmen on what they take to be Râle's distorted teaching to "his Indians" suggest now a Puritan failure to grasp the Wabanaki spiritual context within which Christian doctrine was heard and interpreted. Cotton Mather, the Puritan preacher most notorious for his support of the Salem witch trials, had an interview in 1696 with the Nanrantsouak chief Bomaseen, who was then being held for ransom in Boston, and reported that the Wabanaki had been taught

> that the Lord Jesus Christ was of the French nation; that His Mother, the Virgin Mary, was a French lady; that they were the English who had murdered Him; and, that whereas He rose from the dead, and went up to the Heavens, all that would recommend themselves unto His favour, must revenge His quarrel upon the English, as far as they can.[83]

Mather took these declarations at face value and denounced them to Bomaseen as "French poison," without ever, it seems, considering the possibility that they were a quite reasonable (though hardly orthodox) Wabanaki attempt to apply the Christian story to a very real circumstance in their own world. Nicholas speaks of narratives that

> blend myth and reality, the spirit world and the natural world, into a story that is at once captivating, haunting and instructive—an age-old technique of Native oral tradition that not only instructs, but reflects perfectly the reality of the Native world view.[84]

The likely application of such a technique can be discerned in other reports of Râle's instruction, such as the story, apparently stemming from reports of forest fires in Canada, that he predicted the destruction of the earth by fire in forty-nine days, or the account of the priest's dream of wrestling with the devil over the Wabanaki. Both of these were duly recorded (having been heard in translation from Wabanaki conversants) in the journal of Reverend Joseph Baxter, who conducted a short-lived Puritan ministry among the Wabanaki along the coast in 1717 and 1721.[85] "You will not find among Native People," Nicholas reminds us, "a Western preoccupation with separating dream from reality, the spiritual from the commonplace. All is real and all is truth."[86]

The Kennebec Wabanaki both became a church and remained a native community. In examining this phenomenon, we repeatedly encounter a religion that was fitted into the established way-of-life of a people who were yet being thrust into an unfamiliar role in an unfamiliar system, in the very land which they themselves grew increasingly anxious to preserve for its traditional meaning and uses. The Wabanaki do not seem to have imagined that they could rid themselves of the Europeans, nor did they express a desire to do so. They had become dependent on both the French and the English for European commodities for which previous generations of their people would have had no need. French Jesuit missionaries like Râle were now defining themselves by their lives with the Wabanaki, and the French authorities were relying on them to occupy their English rivals. The English, in their turn, tried hard to "pacify" the Indians—by treaty or by force—so as to keep the advantage of their trade and to continue uninterrupted the process of settlement on the eastern lands. As they were not isolated from other native tribes in their choice of Christianity, so the Wabanaki were not in a world apart from the Europeans either. They were enmeshed in the new system and they knew it; otherwise, adoption of Catholicism would have been out of the question. But they also knew what the Europeans seemed hardly to grasp—that they were a nation among nations just as the French or English were. The Wabanaki church was never simply a creature of French Catholicism or even of one zealous and devoted Jesuit missionary. For the Wabanaki, the Christian community was their very selves, their very identity, not because they had sold out to the Europeans but precisely because they were struggling not to sell out to them.

Notes

1 This is the now-preferred spelling of the native name once commonly rendered, and still frequently seen, as "Abenaki."

2 Kenneth M. Morrison, "The Mythological Sources of Abenaki Catholicism: A Case Study of the Social History of Power," *Religion*, 11 (1981), 235–263, and a later version of similar material in *idem, The Solidarity of Kin: Ethnohistory, Religious Studies, and the Algonkian-French Religious Encounter* (Albany, 2002) pp. 79–101, carefully consider the Wabanaki loss of confidence in their own traditional spiritual leaders.

3 Charles E. Nash, *The Indians of the Kennebec* ([1892]; reprinted, Hallowed, Maine, 1994), p. 16.

4 Ibid., p. 33. On early missionary activity in the Kennebec Valley, see Antonio Dragon, S. J., *Le Vrai Visage de Sébastien Râle* (Montreal, 1975), pp. 29–38.

5 *Nanrantsouak* is Râle's own transcription of a Wabanaki name, rendered by Englishmen as *Norridgewock* (or *Narridgeway*), now used by the town across the river from the site of the village.

[. . .]

19 "Letter from Father Sébastien Rasles, Missionary of the Society of Jesus in New France, to Monsieur his Brother," October 12, 1723, in Thwaites, *Jesuit Relations*, vol. 67, p. 143; for Râle's comment on the necessity of this strategy, see *ibid.*, p. 132. Morrison, *The Embattled Northeast*, p. 168, calls the personal contact that resulted from the decision of many to learn native language and live with the tribes the "crucial distinction between New France and New England."

20 Râle, Dictionary, p. 1. (Translation of the French dictionary entries is my own.) This manuscript, written in French and Wabanaki, was taken from Nanrantsouak during an English attempt to capture Râle in 1722.

21 *Ibid.*, pp. 11, 3.

22 *Ibid.*, pp. 11, 417, B37.

23 *Ibid.*, pp. 13, 293.

24 *Ibid.*, pp. 134.

25 *Ibid.*, pp. 414, 101, 113, 117, 119, 149.

26 Nicholas, "Wabanaki and French Relations," p. 16.

27 "Rasles to his Brother," in Thwaites, *Jesuit Relations*, vol. 67, pp. 162, 138.

28 "Letter of April 15, 1693," in Calvert, "Appendix," pp. 244–245 (addressed to a superior in France).

29 "Rasles to His Brother," in Thwaites, *Jesuit Relations*, vol. 67, p. 153.

30 "Letter of August 26, 1690," in Calvert, "Appendix," p. 237 (addressed to Râle's brother).

31 "Letter from Father Sébastien Rasles, Missionary of the Society of Jesus in New France, to Monsieur his Nephew," October 15, 1722, in Thwaites, *Jesuit Relations*, vol. 67, p. 93.

32 This date is sometimes given as 1693, due to some ambiguities in Râle's own reports.

33 Nash, *Indians of Kennebec*, p. 35, goes so far as to claim that Râle founded the village. Dragon, *Vrai Visage* pp. 51–52, gives a brief physical description of the village and makes it clear that its existence long predated Râle's arrival.

34 The larger number is mentioned in "Letter of August 17, 1714," in Calvert, "Appendix," p. 265 (addressed to Râle's brother). The smaller number is given in the account of Râle's death in "Letter from Father de la Chasse," in Thwaites, *Jesuit Relations*, vol. 67, p. 235, and is repeated in most of the secondary sources.

35 "Rasles to his Nephew" in Thwaites, *Jesuit Relations*, vol. 67, p. 93. Râle gives a fuller description of this migratory pattern to his brother in the "Letter of August 17, 1714," in Calvert, "Appendix," pp. 263–265.

36 "Rasles to his Brother," in Thwaites, *Jesuit Relations*, vol. 67, p. 199, and "Father Sébastien Râle, S.J.," *Catholic World*, p. 554.

37 Râle, Dictionary, p. 334.

38 "Rasles to his Nephew," in Thwaites, *Jesuit Relations*, vol. 67, p. 91.

39 *Ibid.*, p. 86.

40 *Ibid.*, pp. 87–93. "Letter of June 15, 1711," in Calvert, "Appendix," pp. 257–261, provides details of Masses and processions organized by Râle at the village of St. Francis Xavier near Quebec, where he and the Kennebecs sojourned from 1705 to 1711 during war with the English; *ibid.*, p. 261, he implies his intention to re-establish these practices in Nanrantsouak, to which he is returning.

41 "Rasles to his Nephew," in Thwaites, *Jesuit Relations*, vol. 67. p. 86; "Letter of June 15, 1711," in Calvert, "Appendix," p. 260.
42 "Rasles to his Brother," in Thwaites, *Jesuit Relations*, vol. 67, p. 145.
43 *Ibid.*
44 For discussion of the roles of *Gluskap*, who ordered the world, and *No-chi-gar-neh*, the spirit of the air, in the religious understanding of the Wabanaki, see Morrison, "Mythological Sources," p. 241, and *idem.*, *Solidarity of Kin*, pp. 82–86.
45 "Rasles to his Nephew," in Thwaites, *Jesuit Relations*, vol. 67, p. 86.
46 "Fr. Sébastien Rale, S.J.," *Catholic World*, p. 550.
47 Râle, Dictionary, p. 101.
48 "Rasles to his Nephew," in Thwaites, *Jesuit Relations*, vol. 67, p. 87.
49 Morrison, "Mythological Sources," p. 254, mentions the field chapels among other evidence that Catholic practice was well-suited to the native Wabanaki sense of the sacred dimension in all their ordinary activities. *Ibid.*, p. 236, he holds that "Abenaki Catholicism represents a syncretistic intensification of their ancient religious life," rather than a compartmentalization of the two belief systems.
50 Jean-Paul Wiest, "Bringing Christ to the Nations," *Catholic Historical Review* 83 (1997), 654–681.
51 Thwaites, *Jesuit Relations*, vol. 67, pp. 54–65, presents two such letters from Canadian authorities which were taken from Nanrantsouak in Râle's strongbox during the winter of 1722 by English raiders, and subsequently used as full proof of Râle's political employment.
52 "Rasles to his Nephew," Thwaites, *Jesuit Relations*, vol. 67, p. 95.
[. . .]
71 *Ibid.*, pp. 242–249. See also Morrison, *Solidarity of Kin*, pp. 86–93.
72 Morrison, "Mythological Sources," p. 244; *idem, Solidarity of Kin*, p. 88.
73 Morrison, "Mythological Sources," pp. 250–252, citing an account in Thwaites, *Jesuit Relations*, vol. 62, pp. 29–49, provides a description of the "considerable energy" behind Wabanaki Christian activities at the Quebec mission village of Sillery in the period just before Râle's Kennebec mission.
74 Nash, *Indians of Kennebec*, p. 15. See also Morrison, "Mythological Sources," p. 235. Nicholas, "Wabanaki and French Relations," p. 25, is careful to emphasize, however, that "Wabanakis did not seek out conversion in any significant numbers until hard-pressed by the unspeakable horrors of war, disease and starvation," brought on by European contact.
75 Morrison, "Mythological Sources," p. 249.
76 "Rasles to his Brother," in Thwaites *Jesuit Relations*, vol. 67, pp. 210–213 (translation adapted). See also "Fr. Sébastien Râle, S.J.," *Catholic World*, p. 549. Nash, *Indians of Kennebec*, pp. 15–17, provides historical details that corroborate the story as told here via a European impression of a Wabanaki storyteller's speech.
77 Morrison, "Mythological Sources," p. 248. Nicholas, "Wabanaki and French Relations," p. 25, has "no doubt that there are many points of comparison to be made," among them the "aim of communal well-being," but is much more circumspect about statements that seem to equate the two spiritualities.
78 Nash, *Indians of Kennebec*, p. 25.
79 Calloway, *Dawnland Encounter*, p. 144, quoting a letter of Fr. Pierre Thury of 1689.
80 Nash, *Indians of Kennebec*, p. 26. Morrison, "Mythological Sources," p. 237, notes as a characteristic of seventeenth-century Wabanaki community that "religious power was widely shared [but always] existed only for the people's welfare."
81 See "Rasles to his Brother," in Thwaites, *Jesuit Relations*, vol. 67, p. 215, for the annual migration, and *Ibid.*, p. 183, for the celebration of Corpus Christi.

82 Râle, Dictionary, p. 330; "Rasles to his Brother," in Thwaites, *Jesuit Relations*, vol. 67, pp. 183, 203.
83 Cotton Mather, *Decennium Luctuosum*, quoted in Charles M. Lincoln (ed.), *Narratives of the Indian Wars 1675–1699* (New York, 1913), p. 256.
84 Nicholas, "Wabanaki and French Relations," p. 14. Here she writes appreciatively of M. T. Kelly, *A Dream Like Mine* (1987).
85 Nason, *Journal of Several Visits*, pp. 8, 11.
86 Nicholas, "Wabanaki and French Relations," p. 14.

27

Excerpt from '"A DANGEROUS ZEAL" Catholic missions to slaves in the French Antilles, 1635–1800'

Sue Peabody

Source: *French Historical Studies*, 25(1) (2002), 55–63, 66–72.

The relationship between Catholic missionaries and Africans in the French Antilles has received little attention from outside the faithful for several reasons. Most North American scholarship on slavery and religion has focused on slaves' conversion to the Protestant sects that dominated British colonies and the United States.[2] Until recently the French colonies themselves have been marginalized within French national historiography; when they have been center stage, they are usually the focus of economic, political, and military studies that show scant interest in religious and cultural affairs.[3] Moreover, those who are sympathetic to the Catholic conversion enterprise do not have an especially happy story to tell. While the Catholic missions to Spanish and Portuguese America can point to widespread success with both indigenous peoples and African immigrants, the Carib Indians of the Antilles consistently and often violently rejected the efforts of French missionaries. And while the majority of African slaves and their descendants did embrace Catholicism in some of the French islands, such as Guadeloupe and Martinique, few had converted in France's largest and most populous and economically important colony, Saint-Domingue, before it claimed independence as Haiti in 1804. Thus, cultural historians have tended to focus on the emergence and importance of *Vaudou*, what Americans popularly call voodoo, and especially its role in the slave revolts of Saint-Domingue and the subsequent Haitian Revolution.[4]

Considerably less attention has been paid to slaves' appropriation, use, and transformation of Catholicism in the French colonies of the New World.[5] One factor is the scarcity of documents left by slaves themselves.[6]

Still, the documents left by missionaries, officials, colonists, and travelers trace the outlines of independent black activity within the Catholic Church. This study explores the efforts of the Catholic Church to convert African slaves and their descendants, the reasons enslaved and free blacks might have been receptive to this mission, and the crises of the second half of the eighteenth century that undermined the Church's effectiveness in converting the slave population, especially of Saint-Domingue.[7] I argue that the demographic revolution of the plantation complex, coupled with the rise of anticlericalism and the expulsion of the Jesuit order, made widespread conversion of slaves impossible in the late eighteenth century and may indirectly have influenced the unfolding of the Haitian Revolution.

The French effort to convert black Africans began not in the Caribbean but in French points of contact along the West African coast. As French trade in West Africa got under way, the Capuchin order attempted to establish missions in Guinea and Senegambia. There the missionaries found and described the three primary religious traditions of West Africa: the worship of local indigenous deities, Islam, and Catholicism. Father Alexis de Saint-Lô, for example, described some of the indigenous deities that varied from nation to nation, clan to clan, and even household to household.[8] He also found aspects of Islam, such as circumcision and the leadership of Muslim priests or *marabous*, and he found remnants of Portuguese Catholicism still being practiced in 1634, though without benefit of clergy for as many as thirty years.[9]

With the exception of a handful of Luso-African converts, however, and the legendary success of the Portuguese missions to the Kongo of central Africa, Catholicism made few inroads along the western coast of Africa.[10] The Capuchins were not successful in establishing a permanent African mission in areas of French contact. By 1639, they had abandoned their mission in Senegal because of the climate and its attendant hardships. English and Dutch merchants conspired with Africans against the friars and successfully undermined their mission to Whydah in 1644. Over the remainder of the seventeenth and the eighteenth centuries most of the French clergymen to arrive in West Africa were those associated with various slave-trading companies. Unlike the Portuguese missions to Kongo, which achieved remarkable success in the seventeenth century, French missions in West Africa achieved little sustained success before the nineteenth century.[11]

Meanwhile, on the other side of the Atlantic, the Capuchins and other religious orders turned their attention to the indigenous inhabitants of the smaller Caribbean islands that had avoided Spanish domination for over a century. Initial prospects here were likewise disheartening. In the first decade of the seventeenth century, twelve Spanish Dominican missionaries were martyred by Caribs on Guadeloupe. Sustained efforts to convert the Caribs did not really take off until the 1630s, after France, in competition with England and the Netherlands, set out to challenge the Spanish domination of the Caribbean waters by establishing permanent colonies. The first French colonists, under the patronage of Louis XIII's chief minister, Cardinal Richelieu, established settlements in Saint-Christophe in 1625, where the English gained a toehold at approximately the same time. From there, the French branched out first to the larger islands of Martinique, Guadeloupe, and Dominica in the 1630s and then to some of the smaller islands, such as Grenada, Saint-Barthélemy, Marie Galante, and Les Saintes. The Jesuits were the last major order to enter the French Caribbean, establishing a mission in Martinique in 1642.[12]

The Caribs were no more receptive to the gospel than were their West African counterparts, presumably because, like the French government, they saw the missionaries as a wedge that would ease French colonial penetration. Over the ensuing decades, representatives of the three primary orders (the Dominicans, Capuchins, and Jesuits)[13] and several lesser orders (the Carmelites and Augustinians) made repeated attempts to reach the souls of the Caribs, but they met with very little success. Prolonged warfare between Europeans and the Caribs culminated in the treaty of 1660 (negotiated by two priests) whereby the remaining six thousand Caribs retained sovereignty of Saint-Vincent and Dominica but formally relinquished control of the other islands.[14]

Meanwhile, the economic structure and the ethnic makeup of the French islands changed markedly during the middle decades of the seventeenth century. At the outset, European colonists' primary aims were the cultivation and trade of tobacco through the use of French indentured servants (*engagés*) and a small number of African and Amerindian slaves. In 1641, colonists began to cultivate sugar in Saint-Christophe, from which it soon spread to the other islands. Dutch planters and Portuguese Jews, expelled by the Portuguese in 1654 from the Dutch colony of Recife in Brazil, also migrated to the French colonies. Although Protestants were officially prohibited from settling in the French colonies by a royal decree of 1643, the Protestant population was not insignificant, especially in Guadeloupe.[15] The Dutch planters' capital, contacts, and knowledge of sugar production contributed to the revolutionary transformation of the islands' economies, resulting in a significant growth of the enslaved African population. A series of chartered companies attempted to supply the colonies with slaves from Africa, but their meager efforts were surpassed by privateering and illicit trade with the Dutch, English, and Spanish.[16]

The resistance of free Caribs to evangelism and the burgeoning number of African slaves led French missionaries to revise their strategy. Beginning in the middle of the seventeenth century, the Church turned to the enslaved population as the most promising pool of converts and eventually came to finance some of its missions to the French Antilles through slave labor. In the socially stratified societies of the seventeenth and early eighteenth centuries the church hierarchy saw no inconsistency in the promotion of slavery. In fact, until the late eighteenth century, few Europeans (or Africans, for that matter) opposed the institution of slavery *tout court*. Missionaries expected slaves and others to bear their station in life and enjoy their salvation in the hereafter. Slavery was justified as a means by which Africans and Amerindians would be brought into the fold.[17] For Catholic clergy, the primary concern was that slaves be allowed to live their lives consistent with Catholic teaching, not that they escape their condition as chattel.[18]

By the 1650s and 1660s, missionaries from various orders were holding catechism classes for both Amerindian and African slaves. Pierre Pelleprat, a Jesuit, gives one of the earliest descriptions of the methods used to convert Amerindians and Africans in 1655.

> We make use of every sort of means to win both [Indians and Africans] to God. Feast Days and Sundays we coach them separately, and because they are occupied with labor on workdays, we have drawn up cards that contain the principles of the faith from which they are read. We have even translated the Lord's Prayer, the Hail Mary, and the Apostle's Creed, the Ten Commandments, etc., into their languages for the same occasion; and we have arranged so that in most cases there is some French person designated to lead them in prayer mornings and evenings.[19]

At this early stage, the missionaries relied primarily on French catechists and made attempts to translate important elements of the creed into original African and Amerindian languages. The primary language of instruction, however, was a creolized French, described here again by Pelleprat: "We accommodate ourselves . . . to their manner of speaking which is ordinarily by the infinitive form of the verb, as for example: 'Me pray God; me go to Church; me no eat,' to mean 'I prayed to God; I went to Church; I haven't eaten anything.' And adding a word that marks the future or the past: 'Tomorrow me eat; yesterday me pray God,' and so on for the rest."[20] Similar methods were used by Dominican missionaries, although some attempted to learn the basics of some African languages to communicate with slaves.[21]

Over time, these missionary strategies had two important effects on the socialization of African and Amerindian slaves. The use of a common Creole language helped to forge a new identity based on slave status rather than individual ethnic identities. At the same time, the mass gatherings of slaves from many individual farms or plantations for instruction and worship created opportunities to socialize with others of the same status, facilitating communication over the region.[22]

Another feature of the Catholic missions, spearheaded by the Jesuits and probably based on their earlier successes with African slaves and freedmen in Portugal and Brazil, was the organization of urban colonial parishes along racial lines. One religious was given the title *curé des nègres* and entrusted with the sole responsibility for all black worshipers in his parish. By contrast, individual Dominican and Capuchin missionaries incorporated both blacks and whites in their ministry, though they generally held separate masses for the two populations. Eventually Dominicans and Capuchins would establish *curé des nègres* in the largest urban parishes. While it would be easy to read these distinctions simply as a result of the reinforcement of social hierarchies in a slave society, it should also be remembered that the slave populations did not, at the beginning, share the language or religion of the French. The *curés des nègres* were therefore taken up with efforts to communicate the tenets of the faith to a foreign population, while the other parish priests' duties were more like those of their counterparts in France.[23]

The most detailed account of missionary methods with slaves from this period is Jean Mongin's letter of May 1682 describing the Jesuit mission to slaves on Saint-Christophe.[24] Mongin was *curé des nègres* in Saint-Christophe in the 1680s. His twenty-thousand-word manuscript outlines his efforts to catechize, baptize, marry, and bury the twenty-five hundred slaves in his ministry. Mongin may have been exceptional in his zeal; his account is truly extraordinary for its methodical comprehensiveness. Yet his precision and tactics were not atypical for members of his order. Since their inception during the Catholic Reformation, the Jesuits had followed their founder, Ignatius Loyola, in regularizing and recording their missionary efforts. In addition to the published *Relations*, numerous manuscript letters circulated to inspire and instruct Jesuits in Europe and overseas.[25]

Mongin's first task upon arrival was to create a "catalog of souls," including the names of all the slaves in his district, along with the names of family members; whether they were married or living in sin; their race, place of birth, and approximate age; whether baptized, confessed, or communicated; and finally, "the levels of dedication and capacity for catechism."[26] Using this list, Mongin concentrated first on catechizing newly arrived adults to prepare them for baptism. To those who progressed, Mongin gave a present: an image, a medallion, or a rosary strung on a colorful ribbon.[27] Once baptized, slaves who confessed their sins and did appropriate penance could receive communion and marry other Christians. Mongin applied the remainder of his efforts to remedying the vices of those converts whose unrepented sins made them incapable of receiving communion.

Mongin, like other contemporaries, found that African slaves were eager to be baptized, wanting to go " 'up there' with the *BonDieu*, as they put it."[28] This receptivity to baptism is interesting, particularly given the missionaries' relative failure on the coast of West Africa. John Thornton has argued that one reason African slaves embraced Christianity in the New World is that many of them were Christians before they left Africa.[29] Thornton's argument may apply to slaves from the central African regions of Kongo and Angola, where the conversion of African royalty and nobility facilitated widespread conversion of the populace in the sixteenth and seventeenth centuries, yet these appear to be among the minority of slaves in the French West Indies before 1700 (see table 1).[30] Moreover, it is unlikely that many Christian Africans from Senegambia and Guinea were pressed into slavery by Europeans, because they often played important roles as trade intermediaries on the West African coast.[31]

[. . .]

[. . .] Most African slaves, however, were not Christian upon their arrival in the French colonies. What, then, made them so receptive to baptism? There are several approaches to answering this question. One can compare the religious ideas and practices of Africans and Europeans, looking for parallels that might ease the translation of one religious idiom into the other. For example, some scholars have pointed out similarities between African cosmologies and the Catholic world of saints and priests who intercede with God on behalf of individual supplicants. These similarities allowed Africans to maintain familiar beliefs and practices while adopting new sacred objects and figures from Catholicism. In the coercive context of slave society, such resonance also provided cover for African practices. Other scholars emphasize the revelatory dynamics in both religious traditions. Most important, the inclusiveness of both West African belief systems and Catholicism fostered a religious syncretism in which believers could simultaneously draw upon the spiritual powers, practices, and holy personnel in multiple spiritual traditions.[32]

Yet most West Africans did not embrace Catholicism in their homelands, forcing us to look beyond theology to the circumstances of the religious encounter. What else might the Catholic Church have offered African slaves that made conversion attractive? Religious instruction and worship offered opportunities to learn a common Creole language and customs, a way to communicate and interact with one's overseers and master, as well as the slaves in other language communities. Missionaries offered sacred and beautiful objects to those who advanced in their catechism. Moreover, conversion brought the potential for increased social standing in the eyes of the slaveholding class. One seventeenth-century observer felt that slaves were drawn to Catholicism because it made them the spiritual equals of their masters.

> One cannot tell of the joy and the consolation that these slaves receive to see themselves a little properly dressed [*un peu proprement habillez*] [on] feast days and Sundays, attending the same mass as their master, being treated with equality, and in the same manner by the priest to whom they go to confess, to not be distinguished from him at communion, to see those among them who die buried with the same ceremonies; and finally to see that the religion does not make any distinction of their persons with those who make masters of their liberty and persons.[33]

It is difficult to say whether slaves would have understood this spiritual egalitarianism in the same way as the enthusiastic French observer. Other material cues would have emphasized the social distance between master and slave, from dress to location in the sanctuary to the order for receiving communion.[34] Even if slaves did not equate baptism with "spiritual equality" with their masters, there is no doubt that conversion won them their masters' praise.

With time, peer pressure may have been a factor as well. As the slave population of the islands steadily increased, Jesuits and Dominicans began to use African converts to assist them in their evangelical work. Guillaume Moreau, Jesuit superior of the Guadeloupe mission from 1706 to 1710, describes how the missionaries used converted slaves to pressure newly arrived Africans of the same ethnicity to embrace Christianity. These Christian slaves

> teach [the new arrivals] their prayers, . . . take them to church and to catechism, make them attend mass, make them observe the ceremonies, and try to give them the most dedicated religion possible, often repeating to them that, having been brutes as they are, they have become children of God. So by dint of laying siege to them, telling them so by reason, by example, and by invitations, they persuade them to ask for baptism. So disposed, they bring them to the father who cares for the Negroes. He, having seen them, puts them in the hands of one of the Negro catechists who have the responsibility every Sunday and Feast Day of teaching [them] in church of the assiduity, the progress, and above all the conduct of those who are conferred to him.[35]

Jean-Baptiste Labat, a Dominican missionary who lived in the French Antilles from 1693 until 1705, adds that Creole Christian slaves refused to eat with newly arrived non-Christian Africans.[36] Once the majority of slaves of a plantation had converted, new arrivals may have sought Christianity as a way to join the community.

Likewise, planters on Saint-Christophe in 1682 were eager to have their slaves baptized. Mongin does not explain why planters embraced baptism for their slaves; though seventeenth-century piety should not be ruled out entirely, perhaps they felt that Christian slaves would be more docile and easy to control.[37] Christian doctrine could be used to encourage slaves' obedience and acceptance of the status quo. However, Christianity also holds that slaves' souls are equal to those of their masters before God, thus providing an alternative line of authority that could undercut the absolute secular power of the master over his or her slave. An example is the sacrament of marriage. Mongin notes that though planters were eager to have their slaves baptized, many resisted allowing their slaves to be married because "as soon as [the slaves] are married, . . . [the masters] cannot find buyers as easily or

. . . they cannot get rid of a slave who is not useful to them without depriving themselves of another who is." Mongin even took some masters to court to permit slaves to marry against their master's will. When Mongin introduced a waiting period between betrothal and marriage for slaves equivalent to the posting of banns in Europe, he encountered further resistance on the part of masters, since banns were rarely posted, even for whites, in the colonies.[38]

Mongin mentions other instances in which he acted as an advocate for slaves who were in conflict with whites. Once, as part of an effort to reform overseers who took advantage of their position to seduce or rape slave women, he threatened to withhold communion from a slave owner until she fired the errant overseer. On another occasion, he took a slave owner to court for murdering her slave. Mongin also acted as attorney for two slaves condemned to death and was successful in having their sentences commuted.[39]

One might expect that the missionaries' challenges to slaveholders' secular authority would have posed a threat to political powers in the island colonies. This threat seems to have been felt with regard to the Capuchin order, whose members were reputed to be greedy and prone to insubordination, their behavior inflammatory. Some of the Capuchins' conflicts touched on the issue of slavery. For example, in 1646, the Capuchins were expelled from Saint-Christophe because, according to one account, they preached the idea that once baptized, blacks could no longer be held as slaves, claiming, "It is an unworthy thing to use one's Christian brother as a slave."[40] In 1685 Capuchins wrote a letter to the Propaganda Fide in Rome requesting that slave owners be required to treat slaves humanely and justly.[41] Later, in 1705, the governor of Grenada complained to Jérome Pontchartrain, secretary of state for the marine, that the Capuchins were preaching that slave owners should feed their slaves meat, presumably because the slaves' meatless diet was contributing to their malnutrition and starvation. He hinted that he would like to replace the Capuchins with Jesuits,[42] who, at this stage, received almost unanimous praise from colonial administrators.[43]

Official resentment toward the Capuchins may have been based on the structural differences among the three orders. Capuchin, Dominican, and Jesuit missionaries all received royal pensions, which they supplemented with surplice fees. Unlike the Jesuits and Dominicans, however, Capuchins took the vow of poverty to limit their ownership of slaves to no more than a pair of domestic servants. By contrast, the Jesuits and Dominicans established large and successful slave plantations to finance their work.[44] The Capuchins were therefore necessarily more dependent on the royal pensions and the charity of colonists and thus perhaps more susceptible to charges of greed.[45] A second difference is that the Jesuits followed a top-down organizational structure, modeled on military command, whereas the Capuchin communities tended to be decentralized and quasi-democratic. The more disciplined Jesuit order seems to have appealed to colonial administrators.

Further evidence of the relationship between the Church and colonial administrators can be seen in the Code Noir of 1685, the first piece of royal legislation to address slavery in the French colonies.[46] Comprising some sixty articles, this edict sought to regulate master-slave relations in all of the French slaveholding colonies of the Caribbean. The law was originally drafted by the king's two top appointed officers to the Antilles, the governor-general and the intendant, in consultation with the most powerful colonists, at the behest of Louis XIV's minister of the marine, Jean-Baptiste Colbert.[47] One of the most striking features of the Code Noir is the centrality of Catholicism in the preamble and the first fourteen articles, which, among other things, required the baptism of all slaves and provided for their marriages and burials.[48] The Code Noir forbade the public exercise of any religion other than the Roman Catholic faith and held masters liable for any breach of this requirement by their slaves. It also prohibited masters from working their slaves on Sundays and holidays "in agriculture, the manufacture of sugar, or other works" under penalty of fine, punishment, and the confiscation of sugar. Likewise, slaves and free blacks were prohibited from holding markets on holy days, an indication of the growing presence of these markets in the colonial economies. Perhaps most remarkable was the ninth article, which levied heavy fines against free men who sired children with enslaved women. If the man was owner of the woman, the state was to confiscate both mother and child. However, if the man was unmarried and consented to marry the woman, both she and the child would be automatically manumitted and the child declared legitimate. Thus the law discouraged the sexual abuse of slave women and promoted interracial marriages, though it is difficult to say how often the law was followed in practice.[49] As a whole, the Code Noir reflected a generally cooperative relationship between the Church and political forces, both local and royal, where the worst abuses of individual greed were, theoretically, to be held in check by humanitarian paternalism.

By the end of the first decade of the eighteenth century, the division of parishes and missions among the various religious orders was pretty much established. The Jesuits had successfully edged the Capuchins out of the northern districts of Saint-Domingue—from Samana to Artibonite, including the vibrant commercial port of Cap Français—while the Dominicans served the districts to the south and west. The Jesuits also were responsible for all of the blacks of Guadeloupe, and the richest parishes of Martinique, including Fort Royal (the political capital of all the French West Indies until 1713, when Saint-Domingue split off).[50] The Dominicans had missions to blacks in Martinique as well as Saint-Domingue while the Capuchins also served blacks in Martinique and some of the smaller islands, including Grenada, Saint-Barthelemy, and Saint-Martin. The Carmelites' only sustained mission was on the small island of Marie Galante.

While the distribution of parish and missionary work among the various religious orders had been definitively established, ongoing rivalry between the orders, especially between the Jesuits and Dominicans, was quite apparent.[51] The Jesuits liked to portray themselves as especially zealous in their efforts to convert the African slaves, in contrast to the Dominicans, whose emphasis on theological scruples meant that fewer slaves were baptized.[52] The Dominicans responded to charges that they were inattentive to slaves by maintaining:

> In order to receive baptism, in addition to instruction, adults must have at least an imperfect contrition, called "attrition" of their sins. To have this sorrow, one must understand the goodness of God, the ugliness of sin, the sufferings that it exposes us to, and it takes time, assuredly, to make all this understood to people whose language we do not understand and who do not understand our own. Nevertheless, . . . it is wished that they be baptized as soon as they step off the boats. . . . If we refuse the sacraments to Negroes it is when they lead a disorderly life. For the rest, our missionaries do for them what they do for the others.[53]

The Dominican order, whose emphasis on learning and theology caused them, along with the Franciscans, to be chosen to conduct the tribunals of the Spanish Inquisition, gave its members a rather more exclusive notion of Christian doctrine than that of either the passionate Capuchin preachers, devoted to the Christian ideal of poverty, or the highly educated and zealous Society of Jesus, founded upon the ideal of apostolic labors in foreign lands.

Notes

2 Albert J. Raboteau, *Slave Religion: The "Invisible Institution" in the Antebellum South* (New York, 1978); Mary Turner, *Slaves and Missionaries: The Disintegration of Jamaican Slave Society, 1787–1834* (Urbana, Ill., 1982); Richard Price, *Alabi's World* (Baltimore, Md., 1985); Sylvia R. Frey and Betty Wood, *Come Shouting to Zion: African American Protestantism in the American South and British Caribbean to 1830* (Chapel Hill, N.C., 1998); and Jon Sensbach, *A Separate Canaan: The Making of an Afro-Moravian World in North Carolina, 1763–1840* (Chapel Hill, N.C., 1998).

3 On the French colonization of the Antilles, see Pierre Pluchon, *Histoire des Antilles et de la Guyane* (Toulouse, 1982); and Lucien-René Abenon, "La colonisation française en Amérique intertropicale," in *Les Français en Amérique: Histoire d'une colonisation*, ed. Lucien-René Abenon and John A. Dickinson (Lyon, 1993), 107–93.

4 On Haitian *Vaudou* during the French colonial period, see especially David Geggus, "Haitian *Vaudou* in the Eighteenth Century," *Jahrbuch für Geschichte von Staat, Wirtschaft, und Gesellschaft Lateinamerikas* 28 (1991): 21–51; and idem, "Marronage, *Vaudou*, and the Saint Domingue Slave Revolt of 1791," in *Proceedings of the Fifteenth Meeting of the French Colonial Historical Society*, ed. Patricia Galloway and Philip P. Boucher (Lanham, Md., 1992), 22–35. John Thornton's "On the Trail of Voodoo: African Christianity in Africa and the

Americas," *The Americas* 44 (1988): 261–78, is an interesting exception to this general trend. Thornton asserts that many of the "'syncretic' or 'mixed' cults of the New World can be traced to African Christianity" (262), that is, Christianity as adopted by Africans prior to their being transported to America as slaves. Thornton's research is based primarily on slaves in seventeenth-century Portuguese and Spanish America and may not have as much bearing on the French Antilles of the late eighteenth century.

5 On religion among French slaves, see Gabriel Debien, *Les esclaves aux Antilles françaises, XVIIe–XVIIIe siècles* (Fort-de-France, Martinique, 1974), 249–95; and Lucien Peytraud, *L'esclavage aux Antilles françaises avant 1789* (1897; rpt., Pointe-à-Pitre, Guadeloupe, 1973), 165–92, though these tend to blur the chronological trends by presenting a more thematic account. Charles Frostin, "Méthodologie missionnaire et sentiment religieux en Amérique française aux XVIIe et XVIIIe siècles: Le cas de Saint-Domingue," *Cahiers d'histoire* 24 (1979) James Latimer, *Foundations of the Christian Missions in the British, French, and Spanish West Indies*, vol. 1 (New York, 1984); Frostin, "Méthodologie missionnaire," 19–43; George Breathett, "Religious Protectionism and the Slave in Haiti," *Catholic Historical Review* 55 (1969–70): 26–39; idem, "The Jesuits in Colonial Haiti," *Historian* 24 (1962): 153–71.

6 While reading and writing skills were not illegal for slaves in the French colonies, there were no formal institutions that promoted slave literacy in the Antilles.

7 I have deliberately chosen to exclude from this article the results of my research on the religious history of blacks in French West Africa, Louisiana, and French Guiana, though these are important to the wider picture. In an assessment of the impact of French Catholicism on Africans in the diaspora, the Antilles are the logical place to begin. The sugar-producing islands of the Caribbean were France's most economically important overseas possessions and held the greatest concentration of Africans and their descendants in the French colonial empire.

8 Despite the great variation in local deities, certain features of West and Central African cosmology and worship are widespread, if not universal, giving a commonality to the region's religious outlook. These features include belief in a supreme deity who, compared with the lesser deities and ancestor-spirits, could be quite removed from the daily activities of the living. (Raboteau, *Slave Religion*, 5–16).

9 Alexis de Saint-Lô, *Relation du voyage du Cap-Verde* (Paris, 1637), 28–31, 62.

10 There is an extensive historiography of the African reception of Catholicism in Kongo. For a point of entry, see the many works by John Thornton, including, most recently, *The Kongolese Saint Anthony: Dona Beatrix Kimpa Vita and the Antonian Movement, 1684–1706* (Cambridge, 1998); and Wyatt MacGaffey, *Religion and Society in Central Africa: The BaKongo of Lower Zaire* (Chicago, 1986), esp. 191–216.

11 Vaumas, *L'éveil missionnaire*, 223–25. Henri Labouret and Paul Rivet, *Le royaume d'Arda et son évangélisation au XVIIe siècle* (Paris, 1929), 17.

12 In this article I have not addressed the multiple efforts by female religious orders to establish a presence in the French Caribbean. For example, the general census for 1687 lists thirteen *religieuses* along with some eighty-seven *religieux* (Adrien Dessalles, *Histoire générale des Antilles*, 5 vols. [Paris, 1847–48], 2:453).

13 French Dominicans are also sometimes referred to as "Jacobins," after their convent on the Rue Saint-Jacques in Paris.

14 The most lucid account of the Carib inhabitants' resistance to European domination is Philip Boucher, *Cannibal Encounters: Europeans and Island Caribs, 1492–1763* (Baltimore, Md., 1992).

15 The Huguenot population of Guadeloupe was 7.03 percent in 1671; see Gérard LaFleur, *Les Protestants aux Antilles français du Vent sous l'Ancien Régime* (Basse-Terre, Guadeloupe, 1988), 84.
16 Robert Louis Stein, *The French Slave Trade in the Eighteenth Century: An Old Regime Business* (Madison, Wis., 1979), 11–47.
17 While the Spanish monarchs preferred the *encomienda* system to the outright enslavement of Amerindians, other European nations, including France and Portugal, sanctioned their enslavement.
18 David Brion Davis, *The Problem of Slavery in Western Culture* (New York, 1966), 84–111, 197–222. Jacques Petit-Jean Roget includes some interesting examples of the missionaries' rationales for slavery in Martinique in his "La société d'habitation à la Martinique: Un demi-siècle de formation, 1635–1685," 2 vols. (Ph.D. diss., Université de Paris VII, 1978; reproduced by Université de Lille III, 1980), 2:1120–21. For a detailed discussion of Catholic and especially Jesuit attitudes toward slavery in Brazil, see also Dauril Alden, *The Making of an Enterprise: The Society of Jesus in Portugal, Its Empire, and Beyond, 1540–1750* (Palo Alto, Calif, 1996), 502–27.
19 Pierre Pelleprat, "Relations des missions des pères de la compagnie de Jésus dans les îles et dans la terre ferme de l'Amérique Méridionale" (Paris, 1655), reprinted in *Missions de Cayenne et de la Guyane française avec une carte géographique*, ed. M.-F. De Montézon (Paris, 1857–61), 50.
20 Pelleprat, "Relations des missions," 46–47.
21 Chevillard, *Desseins de son Eminence*, 142, 146. Du Tertre says that while parents generally retained their original African languages, most children born into slavery knew only French and "*bargouin*, which is used in the islands when speaking with the savages; it is a jargon of French, Spanish, English, and Dutch words" (*Histoire générate*, 2:511).
22 Guy Hazaël-Massieux, "Inculturation et langue de l'évangelisation aux Antilles," in *Cultures et sociétés Andes et Méso-Amérique: Mélanges en hommage à Pierre Duviols*, ed. Raquel Thiercelin, 2 vols. (Aix-en-Provence, 1991), 2:455–75. Sometime between the late seventeenth and mid-eighteenth centuries, missionaries created a Creole version of the Passion according to Saint John, reflecting an attempt to use music to reach the slaves. For an analysis of the Creole Passion, see Lambert Félix Prudent, "Pratiques langagières martiniquaises: Genèse et fonctionnement d'un système créole," 3 vols. (Ph.D. diss., Université de Rouen, 1993), 274–81.
23 For the Dominicans, see Du Tertre, *Histoire générate*, 2:504; Chevillard, *Desseins de son Eminence*; and Antoine Touron, "Guillaume Martel, missionnaire apostolique dans l'Amérique," in *Histoire des hommes illustres de l'ordre de St-Dominique*, 6 vols. (Paris, 1743–49), 6:587–639.
24 Jean Mongin, "Copie de la lettre du P. Jean Mongin, missionnaire de l'Amérique a une personne de condition du Languedoc écrite de l'île de Saint-Christophe au mois de mai 1682," as reprinted by Marcel Chatillon in *Bulletin de la société d'histoire de la Guadeloupe* 60–62 (1984): 86. My English translation of the Bibliothèque Municipale de Carcassonne manuscript version of Mongin's letter will soon be published electronically at www.amherst.edu/~aardoc.
25 For published letters, see the many editions published during the eighteenth and nineteenth centuries entitled *Lettres édifiantes et curieuses*.
26 Mongin, "Copie de la lettre," 82.
27 On the use of material rewards to foster Catholicism among slaves, see also Pelleprat, "Relations des missions," 51.
28 Ibid., 87. African slaves' enthusiasm for Christianity is echoed by the Dominican Du Tertre, *Histoire générale*, 1:468–70 and 2:503–5.

29 Thornton, "On the Trail of Voodoo."
30 Yet it is difficult to be certain.
31 It might further be objected that African Christians would not have been among those seeking baptism in the French slave colonies since, according to Catholic doctrine, the rite is supposed to be enjoyed only once in a lifetime. Yet there is evidence that some slaves sought multiple baptisms, perhaps understanding the rite as a purification, protective, or healing ritual, rather than an induction into an exclusive faith. Pierre-François-Xavier de Charlevoix, *Histoire de l'isle espagnole ou de S. Domingue: Ecrite particulièrement sur des mémoires manuscrits du P. Jean-Baptiste Le Pers, jésuite, missionnaire à Saint Domingue*, 2 vols. (Paris, 1730–31), 2:502.
32 John Thornton, "The Development of an African Catholic Church in the Kingdom of Kongo, 1491–1750" *Journal of African History* 25 (1984): 151–59; idem, *Africa and Africans in the Making of the Atlantic World, 1400–1800*, 2d ed. (Cambridge, Mass., 1998), 255; Wyatt MacGaffey, "Europeans on the Atlantic Coast of Africa," in *Implicit Understandings: Observing, Reporting, and Reflecting on the Encounters between Europeans and Other Peoples in the Early Modern Era*, ed. Stuart B. Schwartz (Cambridge, 1994), 254–61.
33 Jean Clodoré, *Relation de ce qui s'est passé dans les isles & terre-ferme de l'Amérique* (Paris, 1671), 48–49. I have translated *nègres* as "Negroes" throughout, though their meanings are not identical. *Nègre* frequently connotes slave status as well as racial difference. For a more thorough discussion of race and slave status in eighteenth-century French discourse, see Sue Peabody, *"There Are No Slaves in France": The Political Culture of Race and Slavery in the Ancien Régime* (New York, 1996), esp. chap. 4. See also the Jesuit Moreau, who writes, "Their slavery contributes to heightening this desire [for baptism] when they see that, being Christians, they are consoled and comforted by their fathers, loved by their masters, and almost equal to them before God" ("Mémoires concernant la mission," 73).
34 I have not found evidence regarding seating assignments in the church, though presumably the congregation was seated by rank, as in Europe, with the most important families in the front and slaves standing at the rear. By the end of the eighteenth century slaves and free people of color were required to stand together, apart from whites, in public and religious ceremonies (Ordonnance of 16 Oct. 1796, article 3, cited in Pierre Baude, *L'affranchissement des esclaves aux Antilles françaises, principalement à la Martinique du début de la colonisation à 1848* [Fort-de-France, Martinique, 1948], 58).
35 Moreau, "Mémoires concernant la mission," 72. The Dominican Labat also describes how the Christian plantation slaves used peer pressure and "one who is well instructed" to entice the newly arrived slaves to embrace Christianity. This teacher often stood as godfather or godmother during and after the slaves' baptism (*Nouveau voyage*, 2:398).
36 Labat, *Nouveau voyage*, 2:398.
37 Clodoré, *Relation*, 38–40. The seventeenth century has been identified as the "golden age of Christianization" in France (Jean Delumeau, *Catholicism between Luther and Voltaire: A New View of the Counter-Reformation* [London, 1977], 190; see also Emanuel Chill, "Religion and Mendicity in Seventeenth-Century France," *International Review of Social History* 7 [1962]: 400–425). On the piety of colonists in the Lesser Antilles, see Debien, *Esclaves aux Antilles françaises*, 251–52.
38 Mongin, "Copie de la lettre," 89–92; Arlette Gautier, *Les soeurs de Solitude: La condition féminine dans l'esclave aux Antilles du XVIIe au XIXe siècle* (Paris, 1985), 69.
39 Mongin, "Copie de la lettre," 113, 122–23.

40 Maurile de Saint Michel, *Voyage des Isles Camercanes en l'Amérique qui font partie des indes occidentales* (Mans, 1653), 80–81. However, Du Tertre's explanation for the Capuchins' expulsion makes no mention of slavery. Du Tertre faults a priest he identifies as Père Jerome, who publicly defended a colonist sentenced to death for intriguing against the governor (*Histoire générale*, 1:132, 297–98).

41 Arch. Prop. Acta 1685, fols. 35–37, cited in Janin, *Religion aux colonies*, 123. Janin cites another instance, undated, of Capuchin actions for slaves. Father Claude, the parish priest of Fort Saint-Pierre in Martinique, publicly opposed the execution of some slaves whom he considered innocent (the charges are not specified). When it came time to bury them, Claude had them dressed in red, as though they were martyrs (ibid.).

42 "Lettre de M. de Bouloc, gouverneur de la Grenade," published in *Annales des Antilles* 27 (1988–91): 66–67. One should not infer from these accounts that all Capuchins were champions of slaves' rights. In 1726 the slave André, a woodworker who came to be owned by Père Amboise, the curé of Cul-de-Sac, Guadeloupe, sued for his freedom on the grounds that he had already been manumitted by his previous owners. The Capuchins contested this lawsuit and, because the notarized act of manumission had not been authorized by the governor, André was confiscated and resold *au profit du roi.* A.N. Col., F 3 225, p. 291, cited in Lucien-René Abenon, *La Guadeloupe de 1671 à 1759: Etude politique, économique et sociale*, 2 vols. (Paris, 1987), 2:12.

43 See, for example, the 19 May 1685 report by the Marquis de Seignelay: "The majority of these religious (outside of the Jesuits who live an exemplary life and are a great help to this colony [Saint-Domingue]) either neglect their curial functions or live in perpetual conflict with one another" (Bibliothèque Nationale, Nouvelles Acquisitions Françaises [hereafter BN, NAF] 2610. p. 36, reproduced in Rennard, *Documents inédits*, 148–50). It should be noted that colonial officials were appointed by the crown and did not reflect colonists' attitudes. Indeed, George Breathett has found evidence of substantial opposition to all the religious orders by planters beginning in the middle of the seventeenth century ("Religious Protectionism," 28–31, 35–37).

44 For a thorough discussion of the financial situation of the religious orders, see Rennard, *Histoire religieuse*, 79–87, 157–69, 200–201.

45 For example, Governor Galifet of Saint-Domingue describes the Capuchins as "more greedy for silver than anyone in the world" (letter of 27 Dec. 1699, reprinted in Jan, *Congrégations religieuses*, 36–37).

46 "Code Noir, touchant la police des iles de l'Amérique" in M. L. E. Moreau de Saint-Méry, *Loix et constitutions des colonies françoises dous le vent*, 6 vols. (Paris, 1784–[1790]), 1:414–24. For extensive commentary on the Code Noir, see Louis Sala-Molins, *Le Code Noir ou le calvaire de Canaan* (Paris, 1987). Edward Long advocated the adoption of similar legislation for the English slave colonies and offered one of the few published English translations of the edict in his *History of Jamaica*, 3 vols. (1774; rpt., London, 1970), 3:921–34.

47 Vernon V. Palmer, "The Origins and Authors of the *Code Noir*," in *An Uncommon Experience: Law and Judicial Institutions in Louisiana, 1803–2003*, ed. Judith K. Schafer and Warren M. Billings (Lafayette, La., 1997), 331–59. Although the personnel filling these offices changed continually, Palmer's contention that the law emanated from colonial practices and concerns is well supported.

48 The Jesuits' influence on the final piece of legislation is evident in the first article, which makes no mention of slaves, but which bans all Jews from the islands. Palmer speculates that this article, which was not in the draft emanating from the colonial officials, was added in Paris in response to the Jesuits' 1682 report

protesting the Jews' alleged interference in Catholic missionary work ("Origins and Authors," 344–45).

49 Labat claimed to know only two white men who had married black women in all of the French islands (*Nouveau voyage*, 1:306). Léo Elisabeth, "The French Antilles," in *Neither Slave nor Free: The Freedmen of African Descent in the Slave Societies of the New World*, ed. David W. Cohen and Jack P. Greene (Baltimore, Md., 1972), 134–71, notes that by the 1720s, colonial officials were seeking to curb the growth of the free mulatto population through a variety of means (141–43). Published census records do not indicate what proportion of the enslaved population was mulatto.

50 Rennard *Histoire religieuse*, 187–92. The Martinique mission was the Jesuits' first. The missions to blacks of Basse Terre, Guadeloupe, dated from 1684.

51 The Dominican Du Tertre mounted a spirited defense of his order in the face of perceived slights by another author, Sieur Chaulmer, who, in his *Suite de nouveau monde chrétien,* "speaks of this new world, as though the Reverend Father Jesuits had been the only apostles and the only missionaries to it" (Du Tertre, *Histoire générate*, 4:360).

52 See, for example, Moreau, "Mémoires concernant la mission," 69–75.

53 Jean Vidaud to the Minister, 22 June 1713, reprinted in Rennard, *Documents inédits*, 167.

28

Excerpt from 'A LÜBECK PROPHET IN LOCAL AND LUTHERAN CONTEXT'

Jürgen Beyer

Source: Bob Scribner and T. Johnson (eds), *Popular Religion in Germany and Central Europe, 1400–1800*, London: Macmillan, 1996, pp. 166–77, 180–2.

On the evening of 10 April 1629, the Friday after Easter, the pastor at the cathedral church in Lübeck, Bernhard Blume, M.A., received an unexpected visitor at his home. One of his parishioners, David Frese, a humble citizen of Lübeck, had already called at four o'clock when the minister was out, but now he was finally able to tell of his experience at lunchtime. He had been on his way back from Grönau. On coming to the heath where the border between the territories of Lübeck and Sachsen-Lauenburg was located, near the white stone that had fallen down, he became full of fear and thought about returning when he heard somebody say, 'Listen, I want to tell you something!' Then he saw an old grey man, dressed in white, sitting on the fallen stone. Two white doves were perched on his right shoulder, and one on his left. All three doves where drenched all over, and tears were flowing from their eyes. The old man began to speak and asked why it was that the dead in Lübeck were not allowed to rest? The church of St George should remain standing. Enough sin had already been committed by tearing down another church earlier. On the contrary, every week two days of prayer should be celebrated at St George's; if this was not done, they would see what was going to befall them. This he should tell the pastors in Lübeck. Then the old man said: 'Go away now and do not look back!' Still very fearful, Frese walked away until he came to the Grönau toll-bar where he sat down for a while. Even while telling his story to the minister, he continued to be afraid. His heart was racing and he could neither eat nor drink.

Pastor Blume asked him if other people had requested him to put forward this account. David Frese replied that, on his life and as God was his judge, the event had taken place as recounted. His heart, however, already felt somewhat relieved, since he had delivered his message.

A short while after leaving Pastor Blume's house, he came back saying that he had forgotten one thing: the old man had said that a child had been born in this town to serve as a mirror for everyone, but that this had been obscured.[1]

Pastor Blume concluded his report about David Frese's statement by saying that the man was sound in mind and not intoxicated but simple and plain. Therefore there was no reason for suspecting fraud. Albert Reimarus, M.A., minister at the cathedral church, and Franciscus Greier were present during the interview.

The following day the entire clergy of Lübeck was assembled to discuss the case. They sent a letter to the town council, followed by Pastor Blume's report and a theological judgement on the case, concluding that the old man could not have been a messenger from God.[2]

Unfortunately, it is not possible to say anything about the reaction of the town council.[3]

Besides a few customary expressions in Latin, all the documents are written in High German. There is, however, one exception: on the two occasions when the old man is quoted in direct speech, the language switches to Low German.[4] Low German was doubtless the language spoken in the streets. It was probably still used to some degree in church services, but the administration had already used High German for a long time.[5] The ministers Blume and Reimarus were born in Lübeck and were therefore almost certainly native speakers of Low German.[6] Inserting a Low German quotation adds an authentic flavour to the account but this need not be more than a literary device.[7]

Nothing is known about David Frese's age, occupation, or his degree of literacy. His abode, however, 'in der Hartigsgruben in Hans Bueren gange' indicates a backyard dwelling.[8]

David Frese was a citizen (*Bürger*). Less than half the population had this status. In order to take up the civic rights (*Bürgerrecht*), applicants had to pay a certain amount of money (*Bürgergeld*) and to be at least twenty-five years old. The status of citizen was necessary to set up house or to employ staff. Even after an economic failure, a citizen would retain his civic rights. David Frese's status as citizen therefore does not tell us very much about his social standing. He was probably not povertystricken but it is quite unlikely that he belonged to the wealthy classes with influence in the town council.[9]

Lutheran popular prophets

What was this case about? David Frese's was not an isolated example; more than 150 similar cases are known from the Lutheran parts of early modern

Germany, and, beyond the scope of this book, more than 50 from Lutheran Scandinavia. The comparative material in this chapter will to some extent be taken from the larger hinterland of Lübeck, although prophets are known from a much wider area.

These prophets[10] seem to be an almost exclusively Lutheran phenomenon.[11] Medieval apparitions and apparitions in contemporary Catholic countries would be more likely to take the form of a saint appearing and urging the community to do penance and to erect a shrine in honour of the saint in question in order to avoid God's punishment.[12] This was one of the roots of the Lutheran prophets. After the Reformation, however, the tradition had to be adjusted to the new theological frame of reference if prophets were to have any success with ecclesiastical and secular authorities. They now operated within Lutheran definitions of repentance (see below), and saints were exchanged for angels, who were usually dressed in white.

A rather telling example is to be found in the records concerning the recatholicisation of the Upper Palatinate after 1620, when Catholic authorities took over and started the Counter-Reformation. For the remainder of the century there are numerous reports about the appearances of saints which led to the founding of shrines. However, from the whole period there are traces of only one popular prophet meeting an angel: this prophet was a Lutheran.[13]

Common to the Lutheran prophets was the fact that they received a supernatural revelation asking them to admonish their contemporaries to repent. Often, as in the case of David Frese, they were to inform the minister, who in turn was to preach the message to the congregation. At least until the Thirty Years' War, many pastors accepted the prophets' message as divine. The principal sin in the prophets' eyes was pride (often specified as luxuriousness in dress); other points of criticism were usury, avarice, or fornication. If people did not repent, God's punishment would arrive shortly; often this was described in the apocalyptic terms of plague, war, and famine (cf. Rev. 6: 1–8). The impending punishment was not specified in David Frese's account.

Almost all prophets can be called unlettered. Although a number of them were capable of reading and even writing, hardly any of them had received a formal (Latin) education. Only a fraction of them were nobles. Prophets were to be found in all occupations, in all age groups, in all types of settlements (from large cities such as Lübeck down to hamlets and the pastures of roaming shepherds), and among both sexes.

The stories about prophets were well known and – when related in pamphlets and sermons – standardised to a certain degree. It can be assumed that most people had heard about contemporary angelic apparitions. Regardless of whether one chooses to view an apparition story as genuinely divine, as a diabolic illusion, as a case of melancholy, or as fraud (the options available to contemporary theologians), tales about angelic apparitions enabled common people to speak out on local politics – and to be heard.[14]

With a view to explaining the background of a multitude of apparitions in early modern Germany and Scandinavia, I shall try to contextualise David Frese's case in the following pages.

Lübeck in April 1629

Several prophets made their appearance at a time of crisis, preaching under the conditions of plague, war, or famine.[15]

In 1629, times were not good in Lübeck. The Thirty Years' War had been going on for more than ten years. More troublesome for Lübeck, the Danish involvement in the war since 1625 had led to Catholic troops marching through Schleswig-Holstein right into Jutland. Troops of both sides had touched Lübeck's territory. Lübeck, although Lutheran, had maintained a neutral position during the war but was nevertheless severely handicapped by the fighting. Denmark had organised a blockade of the Trave, the river connecting Lübeck to the Baltic ocean. The general warfare had severely impeded normal trade. It goes without saying that this was very detrimental to the prosperity of a trading town like Lübeck. By the time of Duvid Frese's apparition, an end to this part of the war was drawing near. On 12 May 1629, peace was concluded in Lübeck between the emperor's and the Danish king's delegates.[16]

In April 1629, the world must have seemed out of joint to David Frese. Although negotiations were taking place in Lübeck, there was no guarantee that they would end by concluding peace. On the contrary, a contemporary pamphlet suggests that at the end of March the prospects for peace were meagre. It was only in the second half of April that the parties started to reach agreement.[17] Around the time of his apparition, an unusually large number of violent deaths were recorded in Lübeck.[18] Food prices were high.[19] Large numbers of refugees from the neighbouring territories had come to Lübeck, seeking a haven from the warfare at home.[20] The plague had last visited the city in 1625, leaving 7,000 Lübeckers dead.[21] In 1628, outbreaks of plague were reported from several towns in Schleswig-Holstein. In Hamburg, a town also crowded with refugees, the plague was continuing to ravage. In 1629, the plague came to Schleswig-Holstein again, though probably after April, reaching the town of Travemünde within Lübeck territory and even Lübeck itself.[22]

The war troubles made the town council push on with older plans to extend the city's fortifications. The church of St George was located in the area designated for the extension, quite close to one of the gates (*Mühlentor*). On approaching Lübeck from Grönau, one would pass this church. It was attached to a hospital catering for a number of lepers (*Seken*) and served by ministers of the nearby cathedral church. On 16 March 1629, Albert Reimarus (who was present when David Frese told his story to Pastor Blume) held the last sermon in the church. A short while later the destruction of the building was begun. On 20 March, the town council discussed what to do with the lepers inhabiting the hospital. It was resolved that the churchwardens should investigate where to find a place for them. Near the hospital, there was a cemetery used for the deceased inmates of the poorhouse and other poor folks. Because of the intended earthworks, this cemetery was to be moved. The corpses buried there were transferred to a new site further away from the town. The erection of a new church and a new hospital took some years, the new church being finally consecrated on 31 August 1646.[23]

The removal of a church, graveyard, and hospital was not a new occurrence in Lübeck. Already in 1622, the chapel of St Gertrude, a cemetery and the smallpox hospital outside one of the other gates (*Burgtor*) had had to give way for fortifications. Unlike the cemetery and the hospital, the chapel was not later re-established at another place. It is probably to this demolition that the old man was referring. In this case as well, the works had led to popular discontent ('wovon da das gemeine Volck sehr übel redete') and even members of the clergy had privately and publicly expressed negative opinions. This led the town council to instruct the clergy about the necessity and lawfulness of the new fortifications. After the works had started, the clergy were to persuade the parishioners of the usefulness of the measures.[24] The memory of this reprimand probably caused the clergy's cautious reaction in 1629.

By taking up the matter of the transfer of the corpses, David Frese was voicing a common concern. In their letter to the town council, the clergy related that the news about the apparition had spread quickly among the parishioners, who had expressed diverse views on it. It was to be feared that those who did not want to see their dead being moved would soon take up the issue and misinterpret ('mißdeuten') it. Although the clergy did not think there was any reason to stop the ongoing works, they nevertheless asked the town council to see that the workers transferring the corpses treated them with due reverence ('erbarlich vnd beschei-dentlich'), since an obvious discontent could be observed among the parishioners.[25]

In their judgement, the Lübeck clergy offered four possible interpretations of David Frese's apparition: (1) it could be a diabolic illusion leading to spiritual and maybe also to political troubles; (2) it could be a fraud organised by papists in order to tempt the congregation dangerously; (3) it could be the fantasy of someone whose dead were buried in the graveyard and who did not want to see them exhumed; (4) it could also have been arranged by those who wished to prevent the fortification works.

These four points seem very plausible, some more under contemporary circumstances, some even today. The first point was probably influenced by the memory of the disagreement in 1622 about the first chapel to be torn down. Furthermore, a standard argument in discussions about popular visions was that accepting them as divine would undermine the authority of the ordained clergy. The second point is not only commonplace, in that

Catholics could be suspected of anything evil, but recalls the fact that there were a few Catholics, even priests, resident in Lübeck. A year earlier the clergy had had some difficulties in preventing a former schoolmaster's conversion to Catholicism.[26] The third argument seems to be the most plausible, but then the apparition was also about the destruction of the church. Concerning the fourth point, the citizens were obliged to participate in the defence and to pay a special tax to finance the fortifications (*Grabengeld*).[27] Maybe the extensions were viewed by some as an unnecessary, or at least cumbersome work.

The spirits of the dead

David Frese saw the apparition on the Grönau heath. This uncultivated stretch of land might have had a reputation of being the abode of weird spirits.[28]

The clergy's judgement states quite correctly that there was no indication whether the old man should be taken for God, for a man, for a good or for an evil spirit, nor whether he was sent by God or by someone else.

According to the clergy, the doves 'are probably supposed to be the *manes* or souls whose corpses are resting in St George's cemetery. They are crying about the bad treatment of their bodies (*daß es ihren Leibern so vbel gehe*).' The theologians rejected this concept as an expression of paganism or papistry.

The apparition of souls from purgatory was indeed frequently recorded in Catholic countries. A Catholic author in 1618 reasoned that the tormented souls in hell were not allowed to leave their place of torture, whilst the rejoicing souls in heaven did not want to leave their blissful abode. Revenants were therefore a clear proof of the existence of purgatory.[29] In Lutheranism, with the rejection of purgatory, there was no possibility for souls to appear after death.

In the account of David Frese's apparition, no explanation was given for the three doves drenched with tears. There are possible associations with the Holy Trinity, in particular with the Holy Spirit. The clergy's interpretation could very well be nothing more than a learned construction, using the Roman concept of *manes*. On the other hand, three ministers had talked to David Frese, probably for much longer than a perusal of Pastor Blume's account would indicate, and they were also aware of the gossip in the streets. If the clergy's interpretation reflected popular notions we can here catch a glimpse of a much more varied world of spiritual beings than Lutheran orthodoxy would have accepted.

Apart from the Holy Trinity, all spirits active on earth could either be classed as good or as evil angels (i.e. devils). Good angels acted as guardian angels[30] and occasionally served as messengers (ἄγγελοι) to humans. All supernatural beings besides good angels were demonised even though they were not necessarily harmful in popular belief. Some of these beings survived underground until the nineteenth century, the age of collecting folklore from oral sources, for example the pixies, or Little People (*Unnerêrsche* or *Unterirdische*).[31] Very little is known about these characters' behaviour and function in early modern times. I shall restrict myself to two examples which do not match very well with nineteenth-century accounts.

In the 1570s, a girl from a Neumark village claimed to have been fed by the Little People for almost four years. She did not consume any ordinary food during this period. The Little People, however, were not only her benefactors but hurt her as well. When the girl was brought to town, she claimed that these country spirits had no power in an urban environment.[32]

In the 1730s, a woman in Lutheran Sweden was apparently communicating with several spirits. Of various kinds, these existed in great numbers within human beings. The number of vital spirits (*Lebensgeister*) increased with age. There were good ones and bad ones, and even spirits in-between which were not yet damned but were still hoping for salvation and were therefore more good than evil. These spirits had been created at the same time as the angels. At one point in the records, the woman seems to have suggested the existence of certain earth-spirits dwelling underground. She claimed to have divine authority to evoke in the name of God whatever vital spirits she wished from other people present, and not just evil spirits. She even claimed to be able to despatch one of her own vital spirits to absent persons in order to bring the vital spirit of someone else to her. She claimed that, in the presence of many people, this spirit clearly answered all her questions whenever she inquired about a person's condition and illness, the spirit speaking through her own throat without moving her tongue and lips.[33]

Comparable to a shaman, but in a Christian context, she could even send her spirits to God: 'One of the spirits assigned to her after intensive prayer goes to God, not leaving Him until its request (for an answer) is fulfilled. This takes about a day and a half.' A Pietist account reduced her range of spirits to a simple distinction between good and bad angels.[34]

This case raises the question of the role of the Lutheran pastors who wrote down the majority of the sources. To what degree were their reports pressed into the stereotypes of good and evil angels? An apparition story recounted by a Lutheran pastor might very well have covered up non-Christian concepts of the spiritual world or remnants or medieval practices. Some otherwise quite Lutheran angels, for example, still showed traits of the medieval apparition of saints in so far as they promised intercessory prayer.[35]

Returning to David Frese, it is difficult to say if the spirits of the dead (if the doves were such) were of a good or an evil nature. Being white in colour, they were probably meant to be good. Popular culture seems to have been rather unaware that Satan could transform himself into an angel of light (2 Cor.11:14).

It is very clear, though, that there was a desire to have the graves undisturbed. On the one hand, this is very understandable, especially if one's relatives were newly buried (as might have been the case with David Frese); on the other hand, there could be a connection with the hope for bodily resurrection on the Day of Judgement. This event was depicted graphically in prints and in church art, for example on the pulpit of the cathedral church in Lübeck.[36] The Easter Sermon, a few days before David Frese's apparition, might have mentioned it as well.

A few gravestones in Lübeck's churches request that the grave not be opened until the Day of Judgement.[37] This kind of inscription, however, is rather exceptional,[38] probably in part owing to the expense. The clergy's judgement on David Frese's case pointed out that almost all graves were disturbed anyway on the occasion of later burials, 'which would be difficult to change, due to the lack of space'.

Repentance

According to two Dominicans who spent four days in Lübeck on a secret papal mission in 1622, the Lübeckers adhered warmly to their Lutheran faith. Even weekday sermons were preached to overcrowded churches.[39]

The old man demanded that every week two days of prayer should be held at St George's. Public days of prayer were very common, being held both regularly and in times of crisis. They were usually decreed by the secular authorities. In Lübeck, they were held regularly on Tuesday and Thursday mornings, but apparently only in the major churches in town.[40]

What is repentance?[41] In Lutheranism, repentance no longer meant – as it had in medieval times – specific exercises of penance for example prayers, fasts and alms) for specific sins, but rather an inner conversion that should last one's whole life; i.e. man should constantly be aware of his sinful life and should live repentantly.

Divine punishment could be averted by showing repentance and by living in a manner agreeable to God.[42] The Lutheran prophets were true to official teaching on this point. By way of repentance one could gain influence over plague, war, and famine. The prophets offered the people a remedy for those threats over which they had no actual control.

Within the framework of the Lutheran theology of repentance, the prophets emphasised one thing: God's punishment would only be averted if *everyone* recognised their sins and repented. People (town, region, Christendom) were all collectively responsible before God. The good could no longer – as in the Middle Ages – do penance for other people's sins, but the evil people could bring calamities on the community from which the good would also suffer. The predicted horrors (such as plagues or earthquakes) were of such a nature that they did not strike individual sinners but whole communities.

The prophets' criticism of sin was modelled on the Ten Commandments and on Martin Luther's explanation of them in the *Shorter Catechism*, but the prophets attached special importance to the sin of pride. In their view pride manifested itself mainly in dress. This point of view was supported by the authorities issuing countless sumptuary edicts forbidding people to dress more richly than their order permitted.[43]

A proud person was neither open to teaching nor willing to convert. He either did not care about his salvation or felt sure about it and was therefore not open to the Lutheran concept of repentance.

Leaving the theological distinctions aside, what made days of prayer attractive for common people? Was it, on a very profane level, the fact that all work was forbidden? The Lübeck clergy feared that the townspeople would superstitiously attend the prayer services at St George's because they considered them to be in higher esteem with God ('für Gott höher vnd krafftiger geachtet'). The Lübeckers thought that the days of prayer 'will deliver the town from danger' ('die Stadt aus gefahr erretten werden').

Were these days of prayer meant as 'a kind of collective rite of exorcism' or would it 'be too easy to look at Keil's [a prophet in 1648] notion of penance – a notion that all one has to do is to show remorse in order for God to heap his blessings on the population – mechanically, or as a kind of magic'?[44]

From a theological point of view, it was not possible to obtain God's blessing *ex opere operato*:

> It is not enough to go to church every day and act like the Pharisees but we should change our life to the better. We shall not only sing the litany but arrange our conduct in such a way in the faith in Christ that the prayer might leave an impression with His Father ('daß das Gebet bey seinen [sic] Vater hafften möge').[45]

I would suggest that the majority of prophets (though not necessarily all of their followers) held the same view. They used the established institution of days of prayer in order to achieve their aim. Participation was compulsory. When the congregation was assembled, there was a chance of everyone becoming aware of his sins and repenting. The *collectivity* would show itself as repentant and thus urge God to end the present suffering and divert impending calamities.

Collective prayer in church was thought to be more powerful ('mit mehrer Krafft allgemeinen Gebeths') than individual prayer at home. This view was also expressed in a detailed edict of 27 March 1629, issued for the duchies of Schleswig and Holstein, admonishing the subjects to lead a Christian life. In general, it was not enough to show 'outward church-going, the external use of the sacraments, singing, prayer, etc.' if God's punishment was to be avoided.[46] Maybe David Frese had heard about this edict, which was valid in the immediate vicinity of Lübeck, and wished for similar action to be taken by the Lübeck town council. His message to the clergy was much more specific, though, asking for days of prayer to be held. There is no record of a Lübeck edict following David Frese's apparition. The preamble of a Lübeck edict issued in conjunction with the plague later in the year, however, stressed repentance as a remedy against the plague, together with God's mercy and sanitary measures – but this kind of statement was commonplace at the time.[47] [. . .]

* * *

Prophets as barometers of popular opinion

[. . .] There were several cases where the established cultural pattern of a Lutheran popular prophet was used for fraudulent purposes. At the end of the sixteenth century, a man in Dithmarschen made a living by acting as a penitential preacher.[66] Much more similar to David Frese, however, are cases where prophets tried to make a local political point.

In 1659, a cowherd in the Palatinate admitted to having invented his apparitions after noticing that angelic apparitions generally were being accepted benevolently. His aim was to scare the district officials (*Ampt-Leut*) who were oppressing the subjects – probably without the knowledge of their superiors – and force them to behave more mildly in the future.[67]

In the 1580s, a number of clergymen and members of the town council in Danzig openly showed Calvinist sympathies. This led to discontent among the parishioners. In 1587, pasquinades (*Dräuzedul, Paßquillen*) were posted in the town at night. The town council tried to quench this expression of discontent by promising 100 thaler for the name of a libeller. This curbed the libels to a degree, but not the popular discontent. The wife of a schoolmaster appeared in public, claimed to have had revelations, and warned the inhabitants against the Calvinists. She demanded to be heard by the town council, promising to reveal many miraculous things. When she was admitted, she talked against the Calvinists, and claimed to have seen one of the leaders of the clergy's Calvinist faction and some members of the town council burning in hell. This is rather early evidence of confessional identity at a popular level.[68]

Whether this was conscious fraud or not, Lutheran popular prophets can in many ways be used as indicators of popular beliefs and views, as in the way that David Frese's case can tell us something about the range of spiritual beings beyond the sharp theological divisions between demons and angels. By using the established cultural pattern of Lutheran popular prophets, ordinary people could speak out, and their words were recorded. In most cases, however, their message was mediated by the learned, normally by pastors.[69]

On the other hand, by using the established pattern, people acting as popular prophets had to fulfil the expectations of their listeners, for example by acting as spiritual advisors or living in an exemplary manner. People came hurrying from far away in order to profit – often financially – from their knowledge of and connection with divine power. Some prophets did not comment on local politics, but rather on the state of grace of individuals in the community. This cultural pattern was, after all, primarily determined by its religious content.[70]

Sometimes the prophets seemed to be more credible spiritual authorities than the ministers. This was probably due not merely to their bodily signs (ecstasy, fasts, muteness) but also to their language. They only spoke the vernacular and they were not capable of mixing it with Latin terms. Their performance could be much more vivid than that of ordinary preachers. It will suffice here to quote a report about a prophet in Stralsund in 1558/59, preaching 'with a terrible face, laughing [?] (*gry[ff]laggen*) and strange gestures, by shaking the head, clapping hands in lamentation, distortion of the whole body'.[71]

The prophets stood in an ambivalent relation to the ministers. They were dependent on the ministers' acceptance to a certain degree in order not to be proclaimed heretics. On the other hand they assumed some of the ministers' functions but without dissociating themselves from the clergy.

The prophets tried to lead their contemporaries to the Christian life which they themselves wanted to live. The prophets' activity suggests not only that laymen listened passively to the long sermons in church but that they also processed them actively. Theological reasoning was not only to be found in the clerical world. It concerned the prophets and their audiences as well, although the accentuation might differ; at any rate, common people's conceptions of the sacred were not restricted to magical beliefs. A magical world-view was certainly common, but at the time this did not exclude Christian belief. This applied to pastors as well.

The prophets offer fascinating insights into the interplay between learned theology and popular religion. Lutheran sermons not only contained biblical exegesis but drew just as much on collections of *exempla* and recent miracles in the neighbourhood in order to incite the listeners to repentance.[72] Pastors preached about prophets, whilst prophets retold the pastors' sermons, adapting them to their universe, and enabling us to look into it.

Abbreviations

AHL	Archiv der Hansestadt Lübeck
BKHL	Die Bau- und Kunstdenkmäler der (Freien und) Hansestadt Lübeck
BN	Bibliothèque Nationale, Paris
HAB	Herzog August Bibliothek, Wolfenbüttel
HDA	Handwörterbuch des deutschen Aberglaubens
MLGA	Mittheilungen des Vereins für Lübeckische Geschichte und Alterthumskunde
StBL	Stadtbibliothek, Lübeck
ZLGA	Zeitschrift des Vereins für Lübeckische Geschichte und Altert(h)umskunde

Notes

1 'Zu dem Ende, daß sich ein ieder daran spiegeln solle, aber es were verdungkelt worden'.

2 The only source for this apparition story is preserved in AHL, Geistl. Ministerium, Tomus IV (1628–1642) fols 83r–83v: letter from the clergy to the town council (11 April 1629); fols 84r–84v: report by Pastor Blume (10 April 1629); fols 85v–89r: theological judgement (misbound).

3 The town council enjoyed the services of three keepers of the minutes, who were on duty on different days of the week.

4 'Hore hir, Ich will die wat seggen – Gehe nu wegh vnd sehe di nicht vmb'. Given the liberal spelling conventions of the time, the differences from High German are very little.

5 W. Jannasch, *Geschichte des lutherischen Gottesdienstes in Lübeck. Von aen Anfängen der Reformation bis zum Ende des Niedersächsischen als gottesdienstlicher Sprache (1522–1633)* (Gotha, 1928) pp. 137–54;

6 Starck, *Lubeca Lutherano-Evangelica*, pp. 780–2 and 864–5. There seems to be no biographical information available about Franciscus Greier.

7 In Deecke's version (cf. n. 2), the Low German parts have been enlarged to comprise the old man's entire message.

8 The evidence of the parish registers is inconclusive. [. . .] On 10 August 1637, David Frese, *ein Boßman* (sailor) *in der Beckergrube in [Rüters]gange*, had a child baptised in yet another church (AHL, St Jacobi, Taufen 1636–41, p. 70). Although it is possible that all entries refer to the David Frese who had the apparition, there cannot be any certainty. None of the occupations mentioned, however, are very high on the social scale.

9 Cf. J. Asch, *Rat und Bürgerschaft in Lübeck, 1598–1669* (= Veröffentlichungen zur Geschichte der Hansestadt Lübeck, vol. 17) (Lübeck, 1961) pp. 18–20.

10 The word 'prophet' perhaps arouses association with Mohammed or the prophets of the Old Testament, but even contemporaries called some of these figures 'New Prophets'. See *Newe Prophetin. Von Schönebeche . . . Aus dem Latein ins Deutsche bracht, Durch M. Simonem Musœaejnium, Luchouianum . . .* (Eisleben: Petri, 1580).

11 A number of prophets made their appearance during the English Civil War but they belonged to sects and not to the state church. Only rarely did they claim to have angelic apparitions (P. Mack, 'The Prophet and Her Audience: Gender and Knowledge in The World Turned Upside Down', in G. Eley and W. Hunt (eds), *Reviving the English Revolution. Reflections and Elaborations on the Work of Christopher Hill* (London and New York, 1988) pp. 139–52).

12 W. A. Christian, *Apparitions in Late Medieval and Renaissance Spain* (Princeton, 1981).

13 The 1627 case of Anna Rumpfin at Amberg is to be found in Staatsarchiv Amberg, Subdelegierte Registratur, no. 217. I am grateful to Trevor Johnson for this reference.

14 A general study of Lutheran popular prophets in Germany, Scandinavia, and the Baltic states will be presented in my Ph.D. thesis. Some aspects have been treated in J. Beyer, 'Lutherske folkelige profeter som åndelige autoriteter', in B. P. McGuire (ed.), *Autoritet i Middelalderen* (Copenhagen, 1991) pp. 157–81. D. W. Sabean, 'A prophet in the Thirty Years' War: Penance as a social metaphor', in his *Power in the Blood. Popular Culture and Village Discourse in Early Modern Germany* (Cambridge, 1984) pp. 61–93.

15 For example, *Nova de Sibylla Marchica*, fol. A2r; H. F. Rørdam (ed.), 'Mestermanden i Viborg som Profet', *Kirkehistoriske Samlinger*, 6 (1867–8)

pp. 181–90, here p. 186 (the main document is in German, the prophet being a German soldier who stayed at Viborg after the war in Jutland was over. He worked as a hangman at the time of his apparitions in 1630.

16 For background reading on Lübeck see Graßmann 'Lübeck im 17. Jahrhundert'; W.-D. Hauschild, *Kirchengeschichte Lübecks* (Lübeck, 1981).

17 E. Wilmanns, *Der Lübecker Friede 1629* (diss. Bonn) (Bonn, 1904) pp. 37–48 and 64–70.

18 M. Sirckes, *Justitiæ et miseracordiæ dei temperamentum zwo Christliche Predigten Vom Krieg vnd Frieden /Für den Hochansehnlichen Königlichen Herrn Abgesandten / nach beschlossenen vnd publicirten Friede / auff dero Begehren zu Lübeck gehalten* . . . (Lübeck: Schmalhertz/Embß, 1629) p. 22.

19 C. Kuß, *Jahrbuch denkwürdiger Naturereignisse in den Herzogthümern Schleswig und Holstein* . . . , vol. 1 (Altona, 1825) p. 146 (for prices in neighbouring Schleswig-Holstein).

20 *Kurtzer Bericht / Wie man sich in werender Pestilentz . . . verhalten soll / Beneben der Taxa der Artzneyen / so auff der Apotheken verordnet . . . Mit angehengtem Eines Ehrbaren Raths Mandat vnd Verordnung auff diese Zeit gerichtet* (Lübeck: Jauchen S. Erben, 1629) fols B2^{v}–B3^{r} (BL); Weimann, *Der 30jährige Krieg*, pp. 16 and 41.

21 [K. v. Hövelen], *Der Kaiserl: Freien Reichs-Stadt Lübeck . . . Herrligkeit* . . . (Lübeck: Smalherzische Druckerey/Volk, 1666) p. 40.

22 Kuß, *Jahrbuch*, p. 142–5; [J. G.] Gallois, *Hamburgische Chronik* . . . vol. 3 (Hamburg, 1870) p. 65.

23 AHL, Ratsprotokolle bis 1813, I. Serie, 1629 (Friedr. Pöpping) fol. 57^{v}; [H. Lebermann], *Die Beglückte und Geschmückte Stadt Lübeck* . . . (Lübeck: Krüger, 1697) p. 29.

24 v. Hövelen, *Der Kaiserl: Reichs-Stadt*, p. 40; Starck, *Lubeca Lutherano-Evangelica*, pp. 606, 737 (quotation), and 774; W. Brehmer, 'Die Befestigungswerke Lübecks', pp. 413–4; *BKHL*, vol. 1, 1 (1939) p. 82. According to Brehmer, the town council promised in 1624 that the cemetery would not be touched; according to v. Hövelen, 'the new ditch was laid through the graveyard' in 1622.

25 'die weil nicht geringe Klagen vnd murren darüber gehöret werden' (the first draft had: '. . . darüber getrieben wirdt').

26 Graßmann, 'Lübeck im 17. Jahrhundert', p. 467.

27 Graßmann, 'Lübeck im 17. Jahrhundert', p. 448.

28 According to nineteenth-century folk-tales, it was a place to which evil spirits were fixed by a spell (Deecke, *Lübische Geschichten und Sagen*, pp. 178 and 393).

29 *Histoire remarovable d'vne femme decedee depvis cino ans en ca, laquelle est reuenuë trouuer son mary & parler à luy aux faux bourgs S. Marcel lez Paris* . . . (Paris: Alexandre, 1618) pp. 5–7 and 15–16.

30 I. Franck, *Mikaelidagens predikan* (= Bibliotheca theologiae practicae, vol. 31) (diss. Uppsala) (Lund, 1973) pp. 120–5.

31 For Lübeck, see Deecke, *Lübische Geschichten und Sagen*, pp. 174–6.

32 A. Angelus, *WiderNatur vnd Wunderbuch* . . . (Frankfurt a. M.: Collitz/Brachfeld, 1597) pp. 206–[210] (HAB); this case is dealt with by H. C. E. Midelfort, 'The Devil and the German People: Reflections on the Popularity of Demon Possession in Sixteenth-Century Germany', in S. Ozment (ed.), *Religion and Culture in the Renaissance and Reformation* (= Sixteenth-Century Essays and Studies, vol. 11) (Kirksville, 1989) pp. 99–119, here pp. 99–100. Two similar cases from Lutheran Iceland in 1638 are described by Gìsli Oddsson, 'De mirabilibus Islandiae', ed. by H. Hermannsson, *Islandica*, 10 (1917) pp. 31–84, here pp. 75–6.

33 C.-M. Edsman, *A Swedish Female Folk Healer from the Beginning of the 18th Century* (= Skrifter utg. av religionshistoriska institutionen i Uppsala (hum. fak.), vol. 4) (Uppsala, 1967) p. 85.
34 Edsman, *A Swedish Female Folk Healer*, p. 89; English translation by Edsman (p. 125).
35 O. Tschirch, 'Ein Niederlausitzer Geisterseher', *Niederlausitzer Mitteilungen*, 4 (1895) pp. 150–67, here pp. 159 and 166.
36 *BKHL*, vol. 3 (1919–20) p. 151.
37 F. Techen, 'Die Grabsteine der Lübeckischen Kirchen', *ZLGA*, 8 (1900) pp. 54–168.
38 Techen, 'Grabsteine des Doms', p. 57, n. 22; 'Grabsteine der Lüberckischen Kirchen', p. 59.
39 Wieselgren, 'Itinerarium Danicum'.
40 L. Schmidt, 'Kirchliche Buß- und Bettage', *TRE*, vol. 7 (1981) pp. 492–6.
41 The Greek *μετάνοια* is rendered into Latin as *pœnitentia* and into German as *Buße* but none of these languages allow for the English distinctions between *penance, penitence*, and *repentance*.
42 For an example from Lübeck, see M. Sirckes, *Justitiae et Miseracordiae*, p. 56.
43 For Lübeck see J. C. H. Dreyer, *Einleitung zur Kenntniß der . . . [Lübecker] . . . Verordnungen* . . . (Lübeck: Donatius, 1769) pp. 568–70.
44 Sabean, 'A prophet in the Thirty Years' War', pp. 69 and 91.
45 N. Heldvad, *Tractatus Physic[o]-theologicus, oder . . . Bedencken / von den Er[d]biebungen* . . . (Copenhagen, 1632) fols B2^{v}–B3^{r}.
46 Published by E. Pontoppidan, *Annales ecclesiæ Danicæ diplomatici oder . . . Kirchen-Historie Des Reichs Dännemarck*, vol. 3 (Copenhagen: Lynow, 1747) pp. 771–92, quotations pp. 789 and 772. Himself a Pietist, Pontoppidan very much approved of this earlier effort to improve church life.
66 F. C. Dahlmann (ed.), *Johann Adolfi's genannt Neocorus, Chronik des Landes Dithmarschen*, vol. 2 (Kiel, 1827) pp. 323 and 352.
67 B. Anhorn, *Magiologia Christliche Warnung für dem Aberglauben und Zauberey* . . . (Basel: Meyer, 1674) pp. 93–6 (BL). I owe this reference to Martin Gnann in Tübingen.
68 C. Hartknocb, *Preussische Kirchen-Historia* . . . (Frankfurt a. M., Leipzig, and Danzig: Beckenstein, 1686) pp. 720–52, esp. pp. 745–6.
69 Among the exceptions are: 'Hans Neuschels Leinwebers zu Hirschbergk Bericht an Herr Martinum Proserum . . . geschrieben den 10. Sept. Ao. 1632', *Wanderer im Riesengebirge* (March 1903) p. 35; Hans Engelbrecht (cf. H. Reller in *Neue deutsche Biographie*, vol. 4 (Berlin, 1959) p. 511); Johann Warner/Werner (cf. R. Haase, *Das Problem des Chiliasmus und der Dreißigjährige Krieg* (diss. Leipzig) (Leipzig, 1933) pp. 70–8).
70 Beyer, 'Lutherske folkelige profeter', pp. 173–9.
71 C. H. Tamms, *Peter Suleke, ein Religionsschwärmer des 16. Jahrhunderts* (Stralsund, 1837) p. 14.
72 A typical example is Alardus, *Zeichen vnd Wunder-Predigt*, see also W. Brückner, 'Protestantische Exempelsammlungen', in *Enzyklopädie des Märchens*, vol. 4 (Berlin and New York, 1982–4) pp. 604–9.

Part 7

INTER-CONTINENTAL ENLIGHTENMENT?

29

CHRISTIAN VIRGINS IN EIGHTEENTH-CENTURY SICHUAN

Robert E. Entenmann

Source: Daniel H. Bays (ed.), *Christianity in China: From the Eighteenth Century to the Present*, Stanford, CA: Stanford University Press, 1996, pp. 180–93.

The Institute of Christian Virgins, an order of Chinese Catholic women, originated among Chinese women, living with their families, who chose to lead lives of celibacy and religious dedication in eighteenth-century Sichuan. Individual Christian Virgins were organized into an order under missionary supervision in 1744. Thereafter the institute evolved from a loose and informal group comparable to contemplatives into one called to a mission of active evangelism. Its aspirations, however, conflicted with the traditional role of women both in the church and in Chinese society, and in 1784 the church imposed new rules upon the order and brought it more fully under church control.

The history of Christian Virgins in China must be considered in the context of eighteenth-century Chinese Catholicism. It was a difficult time for Chinese Catholics: in 1724 the Yongzheng emperor proscribed their religion, European missionaries were expelled from China or forced into hiding, Chinese Catholic communities were driven underground, and the church was weakened by apostasy as well as persecution. Over the course of the eighteenth century the number of Christians in China fell by a third.

In Sichuan, however, Catholicism flourished, particularly in the second half of the eighteenth century. The number of Catholics in the province grew tenfold from 1750 to 1800, despite the church's insecure and illegal existence. The frontier environment of Sichuan, populated mostly by recent settlers from Central and South China, proved hospitable for illegal and "heterodox" religions such as Catholicism and the White Lotus sect, which provided their members with a sense of community and belonging. Moreover, the governmental apparatus was weak, and officials were more concerned with the potentially seditious White Lotus religion than with Catholicism.

The success of the church in Sichuan can also be attributed in large part to the active role of its indigenous leadership. European missionaries were visible and vulnerable to persecution and expulsion. Moreover, although Sichuan was under the jurisdiction of the Société des Missions Étrangères de Paris after 1753, there were too few French priests to serve a rapidly growing Catholic population. The society's aim, moreover, was to create a Chinese clergy and to build a native church. Thirty-three Chinese priests served in Sichuan during the course of the eighteenth century.[1] By 1804 there were eighteen Chinese priests but only four French missionaries in the province.[2]

By the end of the century Sichuan had 40,000 Catholics dispersed over a province the size of France. Most lived in tight-knit communities, known as *chrétientés* or "christendoms" in the writings of French missionaries. A *chrétienté* was the community of Christians within a locale, usually a small minority of the population, but sometimes including all the inhabitants of a hamlet. Priests traveled constantly to visit these communities, but many Catholics saw a priest no more than once a year. In the absence of clergy, leadership in these communities devolved to lay leaders. A *chrétienté* would elect a lay leader of the congregation (*huizhang*), who was vested with authority by a priest. He would take responsibility for religious instruction and assume leadership over the *chrétienté* in the priest's absence, conducting worship services, preparing the sick for death, and reporting to the priest when he visited. Lay evangelism was conducted primarily by catechists, from whom some of the Chinese clergy was recruited.[3]

Among those most responsible for the vitality and growth of the church, however, were the Christian Virgins. These women undertook the duty of teaching girls, training catechumens for baptism, and baptizing dying infants. They also engaged in famine relief and medical care. They actively sought converts as well. Their most lasting contribution was undoubtedly as teachers in schools for girls.

Origins of the Christian Virgins

There may have been Catholic women in Sichuan dedicated to a life of celibacy and religious contemplation as early as the 1640s.[4] Few of the late-Ming Catholic community in Sichuan, however, survived the devastation visited upon the province during the Ming-Qing transition. In the decades that followed, a Chinese Catholic presence in Sichuan was reestablished through immigration and evangelism.

There is evidence suggesting lay celibacy among Catholics in Sichuan as early as the first years of the eighteenth century. In 1705 the French missionary Jean Basset accepted as catechumens two young widows who were determined never to remarry, despite pressure from their relatives.[5] A few men, including some catechists, also chose to live as celibates.[6]

One of the earliest Christian Virgins was Agnes Yang, a woman of Mingshan District in western Sichuan. As is true of most Chinese Catholics of her time, her Chinese name has not been recorded. Basset had at first refused to baptize her because she was engaged to marry a non-Christian, and Basset feared that she would not be able to observe her faith after her marriage. She then took a vow of chastity. "God who inspired her aim delivered her from the great encumbrance," reported the later French missionary Joachim Enjobert de Martiliat, "for the fiancé died within the year." This occurred before Basset left Sichuan in 1707. Martiliat visited her in 1733, when she was over 50.[7]

By the 1740s there were, according to Martiliat, eighteen or twenty such women living in seven different *chrétientés*. They all lived with their families rather than in a community. They were, Martiliat reported, targets of slanderous rumors and attacks. "Most have been sorely tried by the infidels, who, full of envy seeing such rare virtues flourishing among the Christians, arouse a thousand evil incidents to make them abandon their sacred vow or at least obscure their fame," he wrote. "But the grace of God has rendered their efforts vain, and their virtue is now so well known that the gentiles themselves have developed much veneration for them."[8]

Voluntary celibacy was regarded with great suspicion in China. One scholar notes that women who chose celibacy "were suspected of being vampires or harbouring nefarious designs, and they were often persecuted, both by the authorities and by the population."[9] Marriage was nearly universal for women, although poverty prevented many men from marrying.[10] Sichuan was for much of the eighteenth century a frontier society where men outnumbered women and where there were strong pressures on women to marry. Occasionally men even resorted to the practice of *kang-qiang*, or abducting unmarried women or widows and marrying them by force.[11]

The choice of a vocation of celibacy violated Chinese norms and occasionally led to friction within families. In 1748, for example, the Chinese priest Andreas Ly (Li Ande) reported that the patriarch of the Zhao family refused to recognize his sisters and granddaughters who had taken vows of celibacy as members of his family. He treated them "as strangers and as Buddhist nuns."[12]

In 1754 Clara Sun, a "virgin devoted to God" (*virgo Deo devota*), was arrested in a local persecution of Christians. Andreas Ly records her interrogation by the local magistrate.[13]

"What is your age?"

"Thirty-eight years."

"Why are you not married?"

"My father had me betrothed twice, but both of my fiancés died. In any case, I never really wanted to get married. If anyone sought to compel me, I would sooner die here in front of you in this court. Such a death would be greater to me than any happiness. If you want me to marry despite my wishes, you would be undertaking an impossible task."

"If you never get married, how will you live?"

"I have adopted my cousin's son; he will support me to the end of my days. My father, too, has reserved part of his land to be left to me."

"I order you to return to your home and marry."

"There is no way I can obey this order of yours."

Clara Sun was thrown into prison. She was released after her father promised to arrange a marriage for her, but she never did marry.[14]

Her determination never to wed, although presumably for religious reasons, parallels that of women in late Qing and Republican Guangdong who formed sisterhoods, rejected marriage, and took vows before a deity never to marry.[15] Non-Christian Chinese women also could choose a religious vocation as Buddhist nuns. In some cases rejection of marriage, either of the institution or of a particular potential husband, may have reinforced religious celibacy.

Christians were often suspected of sexual license, a charge often made against the White Lotus sectarians. Christians sometimes met at night to escape detection, and their assemblies included both sexes. A magistrate of Xintu interrogating Christians revealed the suspicions of the Catholics' neighbors. "They say that every day, morning and night, you pray to God, and men and women gather together; that at night, you keep in good order as long as the prayer lasts, then as soon as it is over, you extinguish all lights and engage in shameful and abominable crimes. Is that true?"[16]

Such suspicions extended even to those bound by a vow of celibacy, both priests and Christian Virgins. Martiliat reports in his diary accusations against the latter, as well as against missionaries and Chinese Catholics, for committing "infamies avec les femmes."[17] In his diary Andreas Ly recounted rumors about sexual improprieties committed in confession and wrote a letter to his colleagues warning them to avoid occasion for such suspicions.[18] In 1769 a French missionary, Jean-François Gleyo, was questioned by officials about the manner in which he instructed women.[19] During a tenancy dispute in 1755 an apostate accused his Catholic landlord of hiding six nubile virgins in his home to be given in marriage to rebels.[20]

Both Agnes Yang and Clara Sun had fiancés who had died, evidently not an uncommon circumstance among Christian women who later chose to take vows of celibacy. Both could have perhaps justified their celibacy in Confucian terms as devotion to their late fiancés, although they did not follow the customary practice of living with their would-be parents-in-law. Legally they were regarded as widows, even though their marriages had never been consummated.[21] Martiliat's account of Agnes Yang indicates that she enjoyed that status: "to the title of virgin she has added that of chaste widow, which is much respected in China. She has reached the age of 50, which makes her eligible according to Chinese law for a monument to women of her status, for which her father is now working."[22] Neither Clara Sun nor her interrogator seems to have thought that she might claim the status of widow, however. In any case she would have had difficulty claiming to be a chaste widow, having been twice betrothed.

It appears that in 1746 Martiliat released one woman from her vow of chastity and gave her permission to marry, possibly because violations of her vow threatened a scandal. It was said that she had used drugs obtained from a non-Christian doctor to terminate three pregnancies. In February 1747 she was married to a young man who on his wedding night discovered to his consternation that his bride was not a virgin. He sent her back to her father; his mother prevented him from repudiating her on the grounds that it would bring shame upon both families.[23]

The establishment of the Institute of Christian Virgins

The threat of such a scandal was one of the reasons that the European missionaries in Sichuan thought it necessary to regulate the lives of the Christian Virgins. The Dominican vicar apostolic of Sichuan, Luigi Maggi, began to formulate a set of regulations for them, based on rules established by Dominicans in Fujian for celibate women there.[24] Maggi died in 1744 before completing his task, and the project was continued by Martiliat, his successor as vicar apostolic in Sichuan. Martiliat dropped some rules that related specifically to Dominicans and added one regarding the frequency of sacraments.[25] He issued the regulations on All Saints' Day, 1744, and they continued in use into the twentieth century.[26]

Several of the regulations were designed to protect the Virgins' chastity and reputation. Christian Virgins were to live in their parents' houses, since there were no convents in Sichuan and unmarried women living together were suspected of being prostitutes. Moreover, Christian Virgins, unlike Buddhist nuns, did not shave their heads or wear distinctive clothing to indicate their religious vocation. They were not to go out without permission from their parents and the priest, and then only when accompanied by someone else. They were to avoid male relatives over the age of ten outside of their immediate families and maintain the strictest reserve with priests.

The Christian Virgins were to lead simple and austere lives. They were to wear simple clothing of black, white, or blue, and avoid ostentation in dress. They were to comport themselves with dignity; they were not to talk about "vain and useless things" but to confine themselves to pious matters. They were to worship separately from men, and were absolutely forbidden to take the role reserved to men in leading prayers. They were not to attend theatrical performances, eat dainty food, or drink alcohol except for medicinal reasons. Each day they were to recite the Apostle's Creed three times and the Lord's Prayer and Ave Maria each eighty-three times. Their time was regulated as well. Most of the day was to be spent in work "proper to women," such as weaving and preparing meals.

Martiliat declared that the Virgins were "entrusted to us," suggesting that they required the protection of male church authorities. This view accorded with Chinese attitudes, particularly the concept of the "three dependencies" (*sancong*) to which a woman was subordinated: to her father as a child, to her husband as a wife, and to her son as a widow.[27] Similarly the Christian Virgins were entrusted to both the priests (*shenfu* or "spiritual fathers") and their natural fathers, since they continued to live with their paternal families. They had no independent means of livelihood. Clara Sun, as we have seen, adopted a son to support her in her old age. In another case several decades later, a woman who had renounced an engagement to a non-Catholic and resolved to become a Christian Virgin was supported by her brother, who turned over to her and their mother land he had inherited from his father.[28]

The rules issued by Martiliat formally established the Institute of Christian Virgins. The institute was not a religious congregation but a loose organization of women united by common rule under the supervision of missionaries. The Christian Virgins took temporary vows of chastity and lived at home in lives of prayer and meditation. Twenty years later, in response to questions from the Sacred Congregation for the Propagation of the Faith, the vicar apostolic of Sichuan explained that "here there is no convent of nuns, but nevertheless, there are truly nuns here. They willingly stay with their parents, where they work with their hands for their livelihood. Nuns of this kind are bound only by a simple vow of chastity, and they make the vow in public before an altar."[29]

Martiliat's regulations were inspired in part by those for the women under Dominican supervision in Fujian, as well as similar orders outside of China. One model was the Daughters of Charity established in France in 1633 by St. Vincent de Paul, whose members take simple vows, renewed annually, and as their name indicates, do charitable work in society rather than remain in a cloister. Another was the Amantes de la Croix, founded in 1670 in Vietnam by Bishop Pierre Lambert de la Motte, a member of the Société des Missions Étrangères. Women of this order taught schools for girls; cared for sick women and children, both Christian and non-Christian; baptized infants in mortal danger; and were bound by strict regulations and vows of celibacy, poverty, and obedience. They lived in small communities, sometimes of only two women.[30]

In the years that followed, Martiliat brought the rules to celibate women he encountered in his pastoral visits to the scattered Christian communities of Sichuan.[31] "I gave them the regulations to sustain them and advance them on the path of perfection," he wrote. "The regulations must take the place of a director for them, for they are fortunate when they have the opportunity to see a missionary twice in one year. They all live with their families; it is not possible to cloister them in one house. Thus they are much exposed to temptation and dissipation, and it is for that reason that I wanted to bring them some remedy by means of the rules that I have prescribed for them."[32]

Moÿe's reorganization of the society

The transformation of the institute into an organization of women who went into the world to teach and evangelize occurred over three decades later. It was largely the initiative of Jean-Martin Moÿe, a French missionary who had founded the Sisters of Divine Providence of Portieux in Lorraine before coming to China in 1772.[33] Moÿe believed that women excelled men in piety, zeal, and prudence, as well as in their knowledge of religion. Unlike men, who according to Moÿe paid little attention to anything but commerce and the vanities of this world, women were the ideal servants of their faith.[34] Their lay evangelism became a main force in gaining new converts.

Moÿe recruited several women, married and single, to work for the church. Some were called to such service as an alternative to marriage or remarriage. One young woman of the prominent Christian Luo family of Chongqing, for example, had been betrothed to a non-Christian since childhood. Her father, in poor health, offered to secure her release from the engagement and dedicate her life to God. After making restitution to the fiancé, he regained his health and his daughter joined the Institute of Christian Virgins. Moÿe advised another woman, a young widow, not to remarry but to continue in her work in teaching prayers to other women.

In another case a girl of eleven or twelve joined the institute after recovering from illness. Moÿe had administered extreme unction; on the following day her mother carried the girl to mass in her arms so she could receive communion. The girl began to recover that evening. After learning to read and write she took vows as a Christian Virgin. Another missionary, Jean-François Gleyo, sent her to Suifu, where she instructed new converts and opened one of the two largest Catholic schools in Sichuan.[35]

The Christian Virgins of the late eighteenth century seem to have come from well-established Catholic families. Among them were two sisters of the Chinese priest Stephanus Tang Bairong and two aunts of another priest, Benedictus Sun.[36]

Married women as well served the church, although outside the institute. One of them, Monique Sen, was said to combine "a manly courage with the virtues proper to her sex." Her husband had been sent into exile during a local anti-Christian persecution in 1772. Monique and her sister Lucie traveled to proselytize until her husband returned from exile. Monique's aunt, Madeleine Ouen, was also active in spreading Catholicism.[37]

Moÿe was well aware of the reservations some had about this role for women. He justified it in part by pointing out that they were preaching only to other women. In a report to the Propaganda he wrote: "The Sacred Congregation may be astonished and take badly that in this country—

I do not speak of others—women are charged with preaching the Gospel; but there are none but do it with prudence and according to the rules of strictest propriety, for the hearers are all women, and one easily comes across pious, wise, and fervent women in China."[38]

In 1777 a drought, bringing crop failure, famine, and disease, struck eastern Sichuan. Moÿe recruited both married and single women to baptize dying children—*l'oeuvre angélique.* He provided the recruits with a minimal livelihood and some were supported by their families. Subsisting on little but cakes of maize, the women sought out sick or abandoned children to baptize them. Moÿe later reported to the Propaganda that 30,000 children were baptized in his district in 1778 and 1779. Nearly all of them, however, had been *in articulo mortis*, and nearly all soon died. Moÿe reported that a third of the district's population had perished from famine or disease, and that the Catholics had suffered losses to the same degree.

Officials in Chongqing had established a camp for refugees outside the city and arranged for the distribution of rice. Many of the refugees died; some children survived their parents for but a short time before dying of neglect. Catholic women from Chongqing, led by the wife of a wealthy merchant, went to the camp to distribute medicine. At first soldiers barred them from the camp, thinking that they had come to pilfer the relief grain, but admitted them after learning of the women's purpose. Women carried out important relief works during the famine, and Moÿe recognized that they were a valuable resource for the church.[39]

Two years later, in 1779, according to Moÿe's letter to a fellow missionary, Moÿe heard a voice saying "Habe magnum zelam ad educandam prolem" (have great zeal for educating youth).[40] Moÿe resolved to recruit Christian Virgins for the task of teaching in schools for girls and to reorganize the order according to the model of the Sisters of Divine Providence, considering them a branch of that congregation. He tried to win the support of his colleague Jean-François Gleyo, but Gleyo at first felt that the obstacles to the project were insurmountable. Later, however, Gleyo wrote to Moÿe telling him that he had changed his mind after seeing a vision of the Virgin Mary, who told Gleyo that the project was her work. Gleyo enthusiastically endorsed Moÿe's efforts, and proposed calling the women Virgins of the Congregation of the Holy Mother (Shengmuhui de guniang).[41]

Moÿe charged Christian Virgins with the task of instructing new converts and daughters of Christian families. He sent one of the most able of them, Françoise Jen, to Gleyo's district in western Sichuan. She had learned to read and had studied Christian doctrine in order to teach others. At the age of eighteen she had taken a vow of celibacy. Gleyo sent her to a Christian family and she established a school for girls in their house. Later, after the mother of her host family died, she moved to the neighboring *chrétienté* and established a school there. Another school was established near Fu Zhou by Monique Sen, a married woman, who often traveled from *chrétienté* to *chrétienté*, stopping for a few days at each one to teach children the essentials of their faith.

Jean-Martin Moÿe reshaped the Institute of Christian Virgins into essentially a new order. He and Gleyo also established a normal school under Françoise Jen to train Christian Virgins to be schoolmistresses. At that school Moÿe introduced new rules, fixed hours for prayer and instruction, and established regular exercises of piety to strengthen the "four pillars" on which the institute was to be built: simplicity, trust in providence, poverty, and charity.

Moÿe also won the initial approval of his superior, François Pottier, bishop of Agathapolis and vicar apostolic of Sichuan. Pottier asked Moÿe to send one of the Christian Virgins to him to establish a school in western Sichuan with the help of another missionary, Jean-Didier de Saint Martin. Moÿe eventually sent Françoise Jen to Pottier for that purpose.

The schools did not always operate smoothly. Despite the austerity of the Christian Virgins' lives, it cost the equivalent of about sixty francs a month to operate a school for a dozen or fifteen girls. Some parents refused to send their daughters to school for a variety of reasons: they did not see the point of educating girls or they wanted their daughters to stay at home and work. Some feared that their daughters would follow their teacher's example and choose a life of celibacy, which would require their families to continue supporting them. Some *chrétientés* were composed entirely of people too poor to support a teacher. A few schools met regularly, particularly those in major cities such as Chongqing and Suifu, but schools in small towns generally met irregularly because of fear of attracting attention.[42]

Tensions between the Church and the Institute

Despite his initial support, Pottier was soon expressing serious reservations about the new role of the Christian Virgins. In a report of September 1782, Pottier wrote that "although I have highly praised that institute, and although I have earnestly desired its success in the vicariate, I have discovered grave excesses in execution, which unless I deceive myself, will be avoided only with great difficulty."[43]

Pottier expressed his reservations in detail in a letter to Jean Steiner, director of the Société in Paris. Among the problems Pottier perceived was the young age at which some girls took vows of chastity, as young as eleven in one case. Pottier also feared that the Virgins were not adequately protected from threats to their virtue. The schools were established in private homes, but "the houses are not convents. The missionaries are not always there to watch what goes on, and relatives of both sexes come and go in the house." Moreover, despite their vow of chastity, the Virgins' dress did not distinguish them from other women, and there was always danger that someone might take advantage of them. In one case, Pottier reported, a Virgin was kidnapped by assailants but able to escape; in another case someone offered a house to a Virgin for use as a school with the intention of seducing her.

Another problem was that the Christian Virgins lacked assured sources of income and generally taught for free, relying on their neighbors' charity. "These Virgins have no dowry and cannot hope for one from their parents," Pottier complained, "for the goods go to the male children." Finally, Pottier objected that the Virgins read lessons and taught publicly, contrary to Chinese mores and the traditions of the church. "In many *chrétientés* they preside over communal prayer in assemblies including men; they read meditations in a loud voice and preach sometimes like a missionary. . . . I have discussed, criticized, and objected to a number of things in this establishment."

Pottier further reproached Moÿe for exceeding his powers in publicly receiving Virgins' vows of chastity, a power reserved to the bishop. Pottier also objected to anyone taking the vow before the age of 25, the standard age for such vows in Christian countries.[44] By that age, of course, nearly all Chinese women had been married for several years, so any woman taking a vow of chastity at 25 would have been long determined not to marry.[45]

Pottier's objections were supported by his coadjutor, Jean-Didier de Saint Martin. Nevertheless, Pottier was not willing to abolish the institute without advice from Rome. He wrote to the Propaganda for guidance. Gleyo, on the other hand, wrote to the Propaganda in defense of the institute and Moÿe's administration of it. He insisted that the Christian Virgins in fact lived in dwellings in which "they are as if in a convent," and notwithstanding the youth of the schoolmistresses, their discipline was maintained by teaching in pairs. Moÿe also wrote to the Propaganda, arguing that the Virgins, although young, were able and dedicated; they took simple, not solemn, vows, and they never taught before mixed assemblies as the bishop claimed they did.[46]

The institute after 1784

Two years later, on 29 April 1784, the Propaganda issued new instructions for the regulation of Christian Virgins.[47] These instructions reaffirmed the 1744 rules established by Martiliat and added six new rules. The Propaganda advised abolition of the institute if it proved impossible to enforce these rules, indicating perhaps how marginal the institute was to the concerns of the church leadership. Nevertheless, the instructions also gave the Christian Virgins canonical recognition.

The regulations of 1784 prohibited the Christian Virgins from preaching or reading before assemblies including men, quoting the admonition in 1 Corinthians 14:34 that "women must be silent in the churches." The Propaganda ruled that women not be permitted to take a vow of chastity before the age of 25 and that such vows be temporary, renewable every three years. Ideally, those chosen for the work of teaching girls should be "advanced in years," if possible over 30, coincidentally the age at which women were thought in China to have lost their sexual attractiveness.[48] No woman was to be admitted to the institute unless she could be supported by her family. Finally, pupils were to be taught with circumspection in order to avoid attracting the attention of "the gentiles."

The regulations issued by the Propaganda reflected the concern the church has always had for maintaining control over the vocation of chastity, fearing that without regulation it could easily fall into heresy or fanaticism. The catechism written by Jean-Didier de Saint Martin declared, for example, that the state of virginity is more perfect and grander than the state of marriage because it allows one to resemble angels and have a more intimate union with God. Yet it must be inspired by God and be "in accordance with the decisions of the Church."[49]

Ironically, these regulations were issued just as an outbreak of persecution brought the church in Sichuan into turmoil. Bishop Pottier escaped capture, but four other French missionaries and several Chinese priests and lay leaders were arrested.[50] Gleyo died in prison. Moÿe, disillusioned by his conflict with his superiors, had in 1782 returned to France, where he learned of the decision of the Propaganda.

A twenty-year period of peace returned to the Catholics of Sichuan after the persecution. Saint Martin, who had succeeded Pottier as vicar apostolic in 1793, had been an early critic of the Institute of Christian Virgins. At the time of his death in 1801, however, he asked his coadjutor and successor, Gabriel-Taurin Dufresse, to publish a retraction of his earlier views.[51]

Saint Martin nevertheless sought to circumscribe further the activities of the Christian Virgins by adding his own regulations to the order after his consecration as vicar apostolic. He reaffirmed the Propaganda's prohibition of vows before the age of 25 and the requirement that Christian Virgins be supported by their parents. Schoolmistresses were to be at least 25. Missionaries were not actively to recruit Christian Virgins in their districts, and the number of schools in each district was to be limited. Saint Martin ordered that missionaries avoid meeting the women unless accompanied by two aged women or other missionaries in order to avoid scandal. He also ordered that no Christian Virgin or other woman serve a priest at a table, enter his room, or offer him tea or tobacco. Saint Martin also ruled that it was not necessary for Christian Virgins to learn how to write.[52] Reading, presumably, was enough.

At the beginning of Saint Martin's vicariate in 1793, the mission in Sichuan had 32 schools: 11 for boys and 21 for girls. Six years later 10 more boys' schools had been established, as well as 5 more for girls. Chongqing had 2 Catholic schools, one for boys in which religious books and Chinese classics were taught by male teachers, and one for girls in which only religious books were taught. Christian merchants supported the education of daughters of poor families. The schools taught by Christian Virgins clearly gave girls an opportunity unusual in Chinese society, where girls' access to education was rare outside of the upper class.[53]

In 1803 Dufresse reported that schools were flourishing. There were now more schools for boys than for girls, 35 and 29 respectively. This was an increase of 13 boys' schools and 3 girls' schools over the previous year alone. Clearly, the church was attempting to put more resources than before into the education of boys. The Catholic boys' schools were so popular, Dufresse reported, that even non-Christian parents sought admission for their sons. The girls' schools, however, did not attract non-Christian pupils.[54] Non-Christian parents seem to have been unenthusiastic about educating their daughters; in any case the girls' curriculum was more religious than the boys'.

Renewed persecution broke out in 1805, eventually resulting in the martyrdom of Dufresse and several Chinese Catholics in the 1810s. Nevertheless, the Catholic church in Sichuan survived and grew. In the 1840s the French traveler Abbé Huc noted that Sichuan was the province in which Christianity was most flourishing, and estimated that there were 100,000 Christians there.[55]

The Institute of Christian Virgins flourished into the twentieth century. By 1892 there were 1,060 Christian Virgins in Sichuan, and 434 in other areas under the missionary jurisdiction of the Société des Missions Étrangères in Yunnan, Guizhou, Guangdong, Tibet, and northeast China. There were 2,945 pupils studying in 231 schools directed by Christian Virgins in Sichuan, as well as six orphanages under their direction in the province.[56] There were 2,450 members of the Institute of Christian Virgins in 1925.[57] The institute began to decline in the twentieth century because of the introduction of more regular religious communities of women. As one historian notes, however, these congregations failed to fill the role held by the Christian Virgins because their constitutions prevented their members from living in villages outside of convents, effectively limiting the role they could play in society.[58] Nevertheless, the institute, consisting of a dwindling number of elderly women, still existed on the eve of the arrival of the People's Liberation Army in Sichuan in 1950.

Conclusion

The Institute of Christian Virgins originated as a Chinese initiative. The first Christian Virgins were Chinese women who chose not to marry but to dedicate themselves to a religious life. Although they first apparently limited themselves to a contemplative life, they eagerly accepted a mission of evangelism and social service in the 1770s.

The importance of the Christian Virgins in promoting the Catholic faith parallels the role of women teachers in the White Lotus sect.[59] In both religions women were less vulnerable to persecution than men, whom the state punished more severely for heterodoxy. Moreover, both the Catholic church and the White Lotus offered women an outlet for their religious fervor not available within Chinese orthodoxy. In addition, a religious vocation was probably the only respectable alternative to marriage for Chinese women, both Catholic and Buddhist. This is not to suggest, of course, that the Christian Virgins were not primarily motivated by piety and a call to service.

The institute certainly conflicted with certain Chinese practices and mores. It demanded celibacy in a society in which marriage was a moral duty, but required women to wait past the usual marriage age to take their vows of chastity. It engaged in teaching girls in a society in which girls' education was not valued.

In 1744 the church brought the Christian Virgins under its authority through Martiliat's rules. These rules gave the order canonical recognition while at the same time ending the Christian Virgins' autonomy and bringing them directly under the control of European missionaries. Thirty years later many women responded enthusiastically to Jean-Martin Moÿe's vision of an expanded role for them. The Christian Virgins began a work of evangelism and social service. The regulations instituted by the Propaganda in 1784 again circumscribed their role while recognizing their vocation. After 1784 the church channeled the women's efforts into teaching children rather than seeking converts among adult non-Christians. At the same time the church put ever greater resources into establishing schools for boys, which were not run by Christian Virgins. It appears that the church regarded the work of these women as marginal. Nevertheless, the Christian Virgins remained central to the growth and maintenance of the Catholic community in Sichuan through the education of girls.

Notes

Research for this chapter was supported by travel grants from the National Endowment for the Humanities and St. Olaf College. I am deeply grateful for the hospitality and assistance I received at the Société des Missions Étrangères de Paris, especially from Fr. Jean-Paul Lenfant, archivist; Annie Salavert-Sablayrolles, librarian; and Mgr. René Boisguerin. Jean-Paul Lenfant, Ann Waltner, and Jean-Paul Wiest commented on earlier drafts of this chapter, as did Gao Wangzhi, Charles Litzinger, and other members of the History of Christianity in China Project.

Sources from the Archives des Missions Étrangères, of the Société des Missions Étrangères de Paris, are indicated by the abbreviation AME, followed by volume number and page number.

1 Gourdon, *Catalogus cleri*, pp. 9–21.
2 Dufresse to MEP, 11 Oct. 1804, *Nouvelles lettres édifiantes*, 4: 94.
3 Entenmann, "Chinese Catholic Clergy and Catechists."
4 Launay, *Histoire de la Mission*, 1: 214. Launay indicates that the late-Ming Jesuit missionaries in Sichuan, Luigi Buglio and Gabriel de Magalhães, wrote of women who had "consecrated themselves to God." Launay does not cite a source,

however, and I have not found any such references in the writings of these missionaries.

5 Basset to Artus de Lionne, 17 July 1705, AME 407: 559.

6 Basset to Artus de Lionne, 17 Sept. 1704, AME 407: 485–89; Martiliat, Journal, May 1738, AME 434: 569.

7 Martiliat, Journal, Mar. 1733, AME 434: 489.

8 Martiliat to MEP, 13 July 1745, AME 434: 347–48.

9 Van Gulik, p. 50. Van Gulik's observation applies to the pre-Han period, before Buddhism with its vocation of celibacy was introduced to China, but such attitudes have nonetheless persisted.

10 A field study conducted in rural China in 1929–31 indicated that fewer than one woman in a thousand never married. George W. Barclay *et al.*, p. 610. Martiliat observed that marriage was nearly universal in China. Journal, Aug. 1734, AME 434: 519. Yet polygamy meant, of course, that some men had multiple wives and others none.

11 Famin, governor of Sichuan, memorial of Yongzheng 4/6/4 (3 July 1726), *Gongzhongdang Yongzheng chao zouzhe*, 6: 107–9.

12 Ly, 7 Sept. 1748, pp. 84–85. Ly's diary, written in Latin and sent by courier to Macao and thence to the Société des Missions Étrangères, is held in the Société's archives (AME 500).

13 Ly, "Relatio vexationum christianorum Mao-ping civitatis Fou-tcheou," *Journal d'André Ly*, pp. 306–7.

14 Ly, 9 Dec. 1755, p. 358.

15 Stockard, esp. chaps. 4 and 7.

16 Ly, "Relatio persequutionis christianorum Sin-Tou-Hien," *Journal d'André Ly*, p. 12.

17 Martiliat, Journal, Apr. 1733, AME 434: 492.

18 Ly, "Monita moralia ad presbyteros provinciae Sse-tchuen," 30 Nov. 1753; Journal, 15 Aug. 1757, *Journal d'André Ly*, pp. 258, 421.

19 Gleyo's account of his captivity, reprinted in Launay, *Histoire de la Mission*, 1: 406; see also "Extrait de la relation de la persécution qu'a essuié M. Gleyo, missionnaire apostolique de Séminaire des Missions Étrangères, dans la province de Su-tchuen en Chine 30 Mai 1769–27 Juin 1777," *Nouvelles lettres édifiantes*, 3: 44–88.

20 Ly, "Relatio persequutionis christianitatis Long-men-than et Ching-tsong-ping, oppidi Kiang-tsin suffraganei urbis Tchung-khing," *Journal d'André Ly*, p. 354. This persecution is examined in my other chapter in this volume, "Catholics and Society in Eighteenth-Century Sichuan."

21 For a discussion of widows in this period see Waltner, and Elvin.

22 Martiliat, Journal, Mar. 1733, AME 434: 489. After 1723, in fact, widows were eligible for honors if they had been widowed for as few as fifteen years. Elvin, p. 124.

23 Ly, "Infamia a Josephus Tchao sibi comparata," *Journal d'André Ly*, p. 9.

24 One of the Chinese priests in Sichuan, Antonius Dang Huairen, had served in Fujian in the 1720s, where his duties included supervising a group of "virgins dedicated to Christ." Martiliat to MEP, 13 July 1745, AME 434: 341.

25 Martiliat, Journal, Nov. 1744, AME 434: 733.

26 The Chinese text is *Tongzhen xiugui*; the Latin version is reprinted in Launay, *Histoire de la Mission*, 2: appendixes, 13–20. Later regulations for Christian Virgins are included in *Summa Decretorum*, pars prima, cap. 3, art. 5: De Virginibus.

27 *Yili*, 20.15b.

28 Gabriel Taurin Dufresse to his mother, 15 Aug. 1780, AME 1250: 116.

29 François Pottier, "Responsa ad questiones S. Congregationis de Propaganda Fide circa missionem Seu-tchuen," n.d., AME 436: 903. Internal evidence indicates that this report was written in 1765.
30 Launay, *Histoire générale*, 3: 141–46.
31 Martiliat, Journal, Jan.–Mar. 1745, AME 434: 740.
32 Martiliat to MEP, 13 July 1745, AME 434: 348.
33 Moÿe is the subject of several biographies. Father Jean Guennou kindly provided me with a photocopy of parts of his book. See also works by Marchal, Foucauld, Plus, Mary Generosa Callahan, and Tavard.
34 Marchal, p. 235.
35 Pottier to Steiner, 18 Oct. 1782, AME 438: 237–40.
36 Dufresse to Georges Alary, 4 Oct. 1782, AME 1250: 148; Dufresse to Alary, 30 Aug. 1789, AME 1250: 475. The aunts of Benedictus Sun are referred to as Lieu (Liu) Da guniang and Sun Da guniang. Da guniang (Great maiden) was evidently a title of respect for Christian Virgins.
37 Marchal, p. 230.
38 Moÿe, "Narratio rerum ad missionem in parte orientalis Su-tchuen et Koueitcheou attinentium pro anno 1778 finiente et sequenti," Archives of the Sacred Congregation for the Propagation of the Faith, East Indies and China, Scritture riferite nei Congressi, 1780, vol. 320, cited in Guennou, p. 221.
39 Moÿe to Propaganda, 27 July 1779 and 7 Apr. 1780, as cited in Mary Generosa Callahan, p. 142, and Marchal, pp. 359–61; Moÿe, "Narratio," cited in Guennou, p. 215.
40 Moÿe to Dufresse, 19 Aug. 1780, reprinted in Marchal, p. 441.
41 Ibid., p. 440.
42 Dufresse to Alary, 24 Sept. 1782, AME 1250: 148.
43 Pottier's report of Sept. 1782, quoted in Marchal, p. 462.
44 Pottier to Steiner, 18 Oct. 1782, AME 438: 237–40, esp. 238–39. See also Guiot, pp. 335–36, for excerpts from a letter from Pottier to Jean-Joseph Descouvrièrs, procurer of the Société des Missions Étrangères in Macao, 16 Oct. 1782.
45 Martiliat had noted a half-century earlier that marriages were usually contracted when the woman was 17 to 20 years old. Martiliat, Journal, Jan. 1734, AME 434: 519. On one occasion he celebrated a wedding for a woman of 23, "an old age for these parts." Her father had turned down earlier marriage offers from non-Christians, waiting for a suitable Christian match. Martiliat, Journal, June 1743, AME 434: 720.
46 Marchal, p. 468. The original letters, which I have not seen, are located in the archives of the Propaganda.
47 Instruction of the Sacred Congregation for the Propagation of the Faith to the Vicar Apostolic of Sichuan, 29 Apr. 1784, *Collectanea*, 1: 351 (document 59).
48 Elvin, p. 124.
49 Saint Martin, *Shengjiao yaoli*, p. 50a–b. There are many editions of this work, which was used well into the twentieth century. See also the French translation: *Doctrine de la Sainte Religion*, pp. 109–10. I am grateful to Annie Salavert-Sablayrolles of the Bibliothèque Asiatique des Missions Étrangères for bringing this work to my attention.
50 On this persecution see Willeke.
51 Dufresse to MEP, 11 Oct. 1803, *Nouvelles lettres édifiantes*, 4: 64.
52 Saint Martin, pastoral letter, 1 Sept. 1793, summarized in *Summa Decretorum*, pp. 47–49.
53 Dufresse to Denis Chaumont, 26 Sept. 1798, *Nouvelles lettres édifiantes*, 3: 323. See Rawski's discussion of female literacy, pp. 6–8.

54 Dufresse to MEP, 28 Oct. 1803, AME 1250: 988.
55 Huc, 1: 301.
56 Launay, *Histoire générale*, 3: 557, 576, 588.
57 Foucauld, p. 49.
58 Wiest, *Maryknoll*, p. 87.
59 See Naquin's work on the White Lotus tradition, particularly her *Millenarian Rebellion*, pp. 47–48, and "Connections Between Rebellions"; Overmyer, "Alternatives"; and Rosner, pp. 239–46.

30

Excerpt from 'CONVERSATIONS IN TARANGAMBADI

Caring for the self in early eighteenth century South India'[1]

Eugene F. Irschick

Source: *Comparative Studies of South Asia, Africa and the Middle East*, 23(1&2) (2003), 254–70.

In their commentary about the Tswana, John and Jean Comaroff have questioned the usefulness of conversion as an analytical category. In their work, they note that Protestant conversion activities were "decided by a serendipitous and superficial overlap of two very different orders of meaning and value." They also believe that "Given the mounting evidence of the 'shallow-rootedness' of the new faith, the meaning of conversion itself became debatable."[2] In this article I want to reintroduce the notion of conversion as a much more wide-ranging set of activities that questions the one-way orientation usually associated with conversion. In this narrative I want to respond to what Dipesh Chakrabarty has called the "more *affective* narratives of human belonging."[3] In the account that follows I wish to show that conversion is a process of examining one's life and physical body and changing it for both the missionary and for the target of conversion. The goal of this religious conversion, that is to say the conversion that the Christian missionaries wanted to bring about, was ultimately transformed not into converting the "heathen," but was a mechanism where the missionary was himself converted to a local way of thinking. The main project in the article is the way in which this conversion made the thinking of the locals and the missionary into a homogenous entity, where the missionary discovered in the local terms and thinking about health a fulfillment of his own religious conversion goals.

The major argument of the article is that a part of the chemistry of this conversion process involved the mutual invocation by the missionary and the local individuals of certain ways of thinking that were implicit in the local Tamil world. These ways of thinking or knowledges were available to be used, and could be relatively easily invoked, and therefore later became the central clement in the way by which this conversion of both the missionary and the locals expressed itself.

The health project that was implicit in this mutual conversion process ultimately was enhanced by many other forces and agents. It is of some interest that the Tamil cultural area where the missionary arrived in the early eighteenth century, by the twentieth century becomes one of the most modern in India and achieves zero population in the 1990's.

The long conversation between the missionary and the focus of his interest takes place on the Tamil coast in the southeastern part of the Indian sub-continent in the early years of the eighteenth century in a seaport called Tranquebar or Tarangambadi controlled by the Danish East India Company. [. . .]

Arriving in the middle of things

[. . .] Tarangambadi town consisted of a Danish port and fifteen villages in the late seventeenth century, only about 250 of the 6,000 people who lived there being Europeans. Most of the European soldiers were not Danes but, in fact, German.[9] Arriving on the coast just as the dominance of the Portuguese was beginning to wane, Wöllum Leyel, the Danish Commander from 1643 to 1648 also welcomed the Portuguese who were trying to get away from the Dutch. When the Portuguese were turned away by the Dutch and the English at Negapatam, St. Thome, Manar, and Sri Lanka they found refuge at Tarangambadi. It was natural therefore that the Portuguese language remained the local lingua franca from the middle of the seventeenth century well into the eighteenth century. Leyel, in addition, permitted the Portuguese to build a Catholic church in Tarangambadi "because we are anyway obliged to tolerate idols."[10]

In Tarangambadi Muslims were locally referred to as Moors. They were mostly Dakhni-speakers who originated from North India, Arabia, and the northeastern coast of Africa. Bartholomäus Ziegenbalg and Heinrich Pleutschau, the first two German Protestant missionaries, reported that these *maraikkaayars* and others were merchants "whose trade was greater than the people they called Heathens [i.e. the local Tamils and Telugus]." Ziegenbalg, the first Protestant missionary to India, at first wanted to believe that these Muslims were great enemies of the Christian missionary project.[11] Later evidence shows that both the local Muslims and he had many of the same religious and bodily projects in mind.

When Ziegenbalg and Pleutschau arrived in Tarangambadi in 1706, they also found themselves in a politically vulnerable position. Shahji, the Maratha raja or king of Tanjavur, was in the process of building a substantial economy based on rice. Contemporary evidence placed the rice production of Tanjavur at about 400,000 tons that came from 5,735 villages. According to some historians, this production can be considered a "not insignificant part of the subcontinent's total grain production."[12] Shahji harassed the Catholic Christians in his kingdom (just to the west of Tarangambadi) because he despised the methods employed by the Portuguese Catholic missionaries. Seven years previously, in 1699, Shahji had surrounded Tarangambadi with 14,000 cavalry and infantry.

In the event, arms from the British at Fort St. George helped the Danes to intimidate Shahji and his army.[13] This did not prevent Shahji from surrounding Tranquebar or Tarangambadi for six months in that year. Shahji also stopped the Danish slave trade that caused great economic loss to the Danish company.

Just two years prior to the arrival of these Protestant missionaries in Tarangambadi at the French port of Pondichéri, just to the north on the Tamil coast, Jesuits had tried to take over political control of the city. Jesuits had already been responsible for the palace revolution in Siam. Jesuits also wanted to establish a theocratic state in Pondichéri like that in Paraguay based on "authority derived from the position the order held in the favor of Louis XIV."[14] In Pondichéri, the Jesuits were responsible for antagonizing a temple crowd during a festival. "Forty thousand Hindus who attempted to leave the city were turned back by French sentries at the gates, which the French factor François Martin had ordered to be locked, and a revolt broke out which lasted for twelve days."[15]

Therefore, when Ziegenbalg and Pleutschau began to preach in Tarangambadi, this aroused the anxiety of the Danish commandant, Hassius. Hassius felt that Shahji, the raja of Tanjavur, would again interfere in Tarangambadi if the missionaries were to start a rebellion. In June 1707 Pleutschau preached a sermon in which he said, "You who are ruling, test yourselves, whether you do faithfully what you are commended to do, whether you prefer promoting the work of the Lord to hindering it, and whether you bother more about God's glory than your own." Hassius, the Governor, replied to Pleutschau, "Who has given you people permission to attack me from the pulpit and speak as if you are hindered in your ministry? In this way you could easily cause a rebellion."[16] Between November 19, 1707 and March 26, 1708 Hassius imprisoned Ziegenbalg to temper his enthusiasms. As a result, both Ziegenbalg and Pleutschau became more and more aware of their vulnerability in a site where the Maratha Raja of Tanjavur would not tolerate conversion and where Hassius would not consent to preaching that went against his political authority.

It is also of interest to understand what kind of local social system Ziegenbalg was surrounded by. One seventeenth century Tamil text celebrates both the bringing country. It also praises the practice of agriculture among the a group of agricultural *jatis* called *paLLis* who abused the higher *jatis* (sub-castes) while they say that the paddy that the *paLLis* produce is certainly good enough for the higher *jatis* to eat. Therefore, the story projected by the *MukkuuTar PaLLu* text is a very contentious one.[17] What is of equal importance for us is the formulation of organic dependence and cooperation, which this text and the discourse that produced it articulate:

> The areca nut tree, which crowds in, carries the young coconut of the coconut tree, which grows very high. The areca nut tree gives its nuts to the mango tree that has joined it. The mango gives its fruit to the jack fruit, which allows its own fruit to hang down. The jack fruit makes the banana tree bow down and causes the bunches (of bananas) to dip down. The branches of the pomegranate bear the banana tree. . . . / A lotus stretches up its head and touches a shoot of green ginger at the edge of the tank [lake]. The ginger that is steady touches the leaf of the turmeric gently and strokes it. That turmeric becomes affectionate with the ripening heads of paddy that are moving back and forth. That ripening grain gives its hand to the ripening sugar cane (vv., 25, 26)

According to this textual formulation, coherence and mutual dependence are critical for the continuance of Tamil society.

Ziegenbalg himself also wrote an account of contemporary Tamil society. In his assessment of this society, he emphasized not the differences between the brahmans and those later called non-brahmans, nor the difference between the so-called non-brahmans and those later called Dalits or "untouchables," but rather sought to present the whole society from "top to bottom" as a Shudra society.[18] Though he speaks about the "untouchability line" in his account, he gives the names of all the jatis or sub-castes in a consolidated list, with the "Shudra Brahmans" at the top all the way through groups who ordinarily live in the forest. Gita Dharampal-Frick contends that Ziegenbalg's presentation of Tamil society does not assert the existence of a rigorously structured system, but rather of a society that is growing organically around occupational differentiation, a formulation that mediates groups who were mutually dependent upon one another.[19] Ziegenbalg shows, for instance, that many groups, among them the "agriculturalist" *vellalas*, could cultivate the land if they sought to. Furthermore, he writes that persons from a variety of different *jatis* could, through hard work and intelligence, become persons of rank in positions such as kings, counselors, poets, schoolmasters, governors, or other high ministers. This was a society, according to Ziegenbalg, that was not at all rigid but allowed the individual considerable room for personal ambition. In many ways his picture is one that reflects the kind of formulation found in Cynthia Talbot's work on early fourteenth century Andhra where titles indicated individuals who had been successful in their ambitions.[20]

From our perspective, what is even more important is that Ziegenbalg's orientation does not particularly emphasize any specific group that represents either juridical power or authority. Rather, he wants to depict the society as an organic structure whose constituent elements are dependent upon each other. In fact, there is a sense where the formulation of the MukkuuTar PaLLu is very similar to what Ziegenbalg himself describes. Dharampal-Frick says that Ziegenbalg also brought to his empathetic study of Tamil society his own rural experiences of hierarchy in Lausitz where he was familiar with a similar, though not quite so variegated situation in the late seventeenth century. She writes that his analysis did not look on the Tamil social system as one in which the individual was paralyzed by a coercive ordering (Zwang-sordnung) but rather as a framework for trade and life that oriented and endowed individual life goals with considerable space for fulfillment. She considers that change is accordingly central to this Tamil system of group organization in the early eighteenth century.[21] It was into this competitive, relatively open and mobile social and political system that Ziegenbalg and his colleague Pleutschau came in 1706.

The nature of the project

Ziegenbalg wrote in 1709 that, "The Inhabitants [of Tarangambadi] are partly white *Europeans*, partly white tawny *Portugueze*, and partly yellow *Moors*; but for the most part, black-brown *Malabarians*. [Tamils]" Ziegenbalg, speaking of European ignorance of local conditions, noted that, "Very few white Europeans would be able to tell you the names of such towns and villages, which is why they often have seven other names which they have come up with arbitrarily." "Few of the white *Europeans* know the Names of these sundry towns and Villages [that Ziegenbalg has just mentioned, and is proud about knowing], which is the reason they frequently give them quite other names, according as their Fancy leads them."[22] Ziegenbalg mentions this to suggest that he is a different kind of person. He knows the names of the towns that he goes to and feels that he does not recall the name of a town "just out of Fancy." The point is that in his descriptions of much that he sees, he is defining himself by what he is *not.*

In the same context, Ziegenbalg penned an account of the various kinds of weather in Tarangambadi. "As for my self [in comparison to the other pale Europeans], the greater the Heat is, the better I enjoy my Health; it agreeing so well with my constitution, that I seldom as yet felt any inconveniency by it: Nay I should find it rather somewhat strange, if I should happen to return to *Europe* again in a cold, and chilly Winter."[23] The young Ziegenbalg (he was 24 years old in 1707) wants to show that though he was sick most of the time while he was in Europe, on the Tanjavur coast he was healthier than the other Europeans there.

When Ziegenbalg and his colleague Heinrich Pleutschau got to Tarangambadi they therefore found that they had problems articulating what they were. Over and over again they had to define themselves by exclusion. Though they had come with the presumption that their religion was morally superior to that of the local society, they were everywhere reminded that local people looked on them as hopelessly ignorant and unclean. For instance, in 1706, a few months after their arrival on the Tanjavur coast, Ziegenbalg wrote, "Truly, the *Malabarians* being a witty and sagacious people, will needs be managed with a great deal of Wisdom and Circumspection. Our School-Master argueth daily with us, and requireth good Reasons and Arguments for every thing. We hope to bring him over to the Christian Knowledge; but he is confident as yet, that one time or another, we shall all turn *Malabarians* and in this hope, he takes all the Pains Imaginable, to render things as plain and easie to us as possibly he can."[24] In other words, the old school master always hoped that the two missionaries would totally abandon Christianity and migrate to another, more Tamil, point of view.

Some local individuals were much more direct in their criticism of the missionaries. In March 1714, one local person who appears to have been a local Tamil merchant stood up and said that the local residents thought of themselves as a very happy, understanding people. Their society was well regulated. They didn't require anything that the body and soul needed. Therefore, they wondered why Europeans criticized their religion. Do we look like monsters? Don't we have as much understanding as you do? The things manufactured here are greatly in demand by Europeans. What would move us to change our religion?[25]

Naturally, there was a grand pre-history to these remarks that needs a fuller articulation. Even before they had converted anybody, the missionaries had to contend with the behavior of the resident Europeans in the port-city of Tarangambadi. For instance, one day when Ziegenbalg went outside the boundaries of Tarangambadi to the north along the coast to a neighboring town named Anandamangalam, he started talking to a group of people who had surrounded him. This was in 1709 before his colleague Pleutschau had left and before his later colleague Ernest Greundler had arrived. On that occasion he spoke to the group about the necessity to settle one's spiritual accounts with God daily, to eliminate any problem at the last judgement. One member of the group then asked him "Do all the Blanks [Whites, Blanken] understand what you say? Do they all speak as you do? What is the Reason, that coming amongst us they are bent on nothing but on doing of Mischief;

that having carouzed [caroused] it a while amongst us, and indulged themselves in excessive Drinking, they turn us out of our own Houses in their mad Pranks?" "Why can't you tell them the same Things you tell us?"[26] "This Heathen nation is naturally inclined to Candour and Honesty towards those that are of the same Religion with them," wrote Ziegenbalg in 1709," but then they shew but little Regard to our *European* Christians, among whom they have for these *Hundred* and *Fifty* Years past, observed innumerable bad and disorderly Doings."[27] Once, in 1707, when Ziegenbalg asked a group of listeners what they thought of the behavior of the European Christians, they would not answer until Ziegenbalg assured them that they would not be harmed for what they said. Then they said that, "they considered Christians to be a most stupid and ignorant people who never thought of God or of eternity." When Ziegenbalg asked them how they could say that when the Christians had a church there in Tarangambadi where singing and preaching went on three times a week, where all the Europeans were present. His listeners replied that they certainly heard and saw "us." But they "believed that the priests taught nothing in church but how to eat and drink, to game and ill-treat the Blacks." Local individuals "did not understand the Danish language in which the service was conducted but seeing the actions of the congregation immediately after it, never doubted but these were the lessons they had learned."[28] Again, some of Ziegenbalg's listeners asked him why he could not say the same thing to the European Christians as he had said to the local people. Ziegenbalg replied, "They have the Word of God in their Hands: They hear us preach constantly on *Faith* and *Repentance*; but they proving disobedient to what they hear, make ineffectual the Word that is preached to them. For this Reason we are now come to you; if perhaps the Word may have a better Effect upon you than it hath upon them."[29] Therefore, at the very beginning of his Tarangambadi experience Ziegenbalg wrote, "mistakes in our life as Christians are greater than what falseness we want to show them in theirs." He also concluded that for anybody who sought to move among the local people it was critical that they live a "clean life."[30]

Behavior among local Christians

In fact, it was commonly believed that the Europeans themselves, and particularly Christianity, had introduced dishonesty, drinking, and immorality into a pristine, untouched native world.[31] Even before he got to India, Ziegenbalg "discovered" the local people he called the "Hottentots" as a foil to local Christian society at the Cape of Good Hope. He wrote that the local Africans, "make us Christians ashamed in many Particulars. They are very kind to one another, and so communicative in their Love, that if one has something that is good, he shareth it among all the rest. They are content with very little, If you will give them a *Ducat* they will hardly take it, requiring only a *Groat*, by reason they don't use to spend more in a Day; and they are Unconcerned for the Morrow. They are very ready to serve one; If one giveth 'em a Groat, they will run as many Miles for it as you please. They are very faithful in things committed to their Care, and never pilfer the least Farthing from the Christians, tho' they should see great Store of Money about them. They are not seized with the Plague of *Ambition, Covetousness*, and of *anxious Cares* for the Belly. Like our Christians in *Europe*."[32] As soon as Ziegenbalg and Pleutschau arrived in Tarangambadi they discovered a variegated society that was characterized by openness and the possibility for personal fulfillment. But Tarangambadi was also a colonial port city partly based on the slave trade.

It is of interest that Ziegenbalg's and Pleutschau's earliest converts to Christianity were slaves that worked there. Moreover, much of the earliest concern of the missionaries was with what happened to the slaves once they had been converted to Lutheran Pietist Christianity. It goes without saying that much of the interaction with local society over conversion was with individuals in the lower reaches of that society. What made the question of behavior even more complicated for the missionaries was that they were part of this colonial society where meat was eaten and alcohol was consumed. Therefore, to establish moral superiority for themselves in this environment was extraordinarily difficult. More than anything else, the missionaries had to demonstrate that not only their form of religion, but the behavior that their religion engendered was superior to local religious and social manners.

Seen from this perspective, it was natural that missionary commentary about the "bad behavior" of local Christians litters the pages of the Hallesche *Berichte* or Halle missionary *Reports* and their personal correspondence. In addition, an important goal of both the "Malabarische Korrespondenz [Tamil Correspondence]" and the various "Conferences" that Ziegenbalg and Ernest Greundler set in motion was to learn exactly what were the feelings of local people toward local Christian demeanor. It is not, therefore, shocking to read that these inquiries and interchanges generated a vast array of comments from local people about what they felt was inappropriate in this conduct. Ziegenbalg noted that because these Christians lived in the charmed environment of a Danish colonial port they could not be criticized so readily. However, were the Christians to be in the adjoining kingdom of Tanjavur, they would be very severely criticized and mistreated.[33] That Ziegenbalg had to confine his conversion goals to people within the villages and urban region of Tarangambadi was a given from the start of his Tanjavur experience. Despite his great desire to convert people from outside Tarangambadi in the Tanjavur kingdom, he apparently attempted this only once. Ziegenbalg reported that soon after he got to Tarangambadi, he made a trip beyond the border of the Tarangambadi territory. At the edge of the Tanjavur kingdom he changed his black clothes and put on local white garments with a turban on his head. He also wore a white *ankavastiram* with a red stripe over his shoulder. In the course of his travel some officials of the Tanjavur raja recognized him, and told him that it was too dangerous for him to travel beyond the Tarangambadi borders. As a result he came back late that night, but concluded that it was not possible to travel in the Tanjavur kingdom without the permission of the raja.[34] It was clear both from this episode and others that Ziegenbalg wanted to be free of the constraints of the colonial environment that Tarangambadi presented. He also admitted that he found working with local Christians far easier than with resident Europeans. Moreover, he felt that the Christians in Europe could learn from the behavior of ordinary people on the Tanjavur coast.[35]

Naturally, the local people found both resident European and local Christian behavior intolerable. Christians (Europeans and locals) ate beef, used the left hand to eat after they had defecated, and used alcoholic drink.[36] One commentator, Alleppa, possibly the author of many of the responses to the missionary inquiry that came to make up the "Malabarische Korrespondez," wrote that Christians, "perform very few good works, give very few alms, have no penitences, willingly accept presents, drink strong drinks, illtreat animals and use them for food, care very little about bodily cleanliness, look down upon all others as inferiors and are very avaricious, proud and passionate. Indeed, our Brahmans say that the white people are descended from the giants, that they do not know the difference between good and evil but sin continuously."[37]

As a matter of fact, the kind of discipline that Ziegenbalg was seeking to articulate to his Tamil listeners was not akin to the "penances" in a society that sought to torture the body. On one occasion when Ziegenbalg was speaking about the need for people to become penitent, a brahman said that among "You Christians" no one had ever seen anybody who was penitent. He then gave lots of examples of local "penitents" who engaged in a variety of self-torturing behaviors. Ziegenbalg said this only showed that these atonements were not the will of god but were the will of man. He said that until they changed their behavior and heart none of the penances would mean anything. He also said that Christians did not undertake any unusual penance or ways of life.[38] The point here is that Ziegenbalg's idea of penance had more to do with a decision to change one's will and thinking rather than torment one's own body. A part of his thinking also implied the operation of capillary knowledges that did not honor the sovereign but expected each person to work for the development of a society on a microphysical basis.

Other movements occurred at the microphysical level to incite people to learn how to take care of their bodies to prepare them for a long and productive life. It was, therefore, during this same period that another equally important religious discipline that honored a group of saints called siddhars and that was popular among many men, acquired a following. The siddha system was a (right hand) tantric set of beliefs that was articulated by a series of individual saints many of whom wrote poems in the Tamil of ordinary people. Unlike the religiopolitical system described by David Shulman or by Susan Bayly, the siddha system oriented itself toward the microphysical needs of individuals. Interactions between locals and missionaries were part of a general movement to bring these knowledges into discourse. Siddha belief and practice was not based on scripture and was very hostile to the kinds of brahmanic religion articulated by texts called the Puranas, siddha practitioners believed that to attain *moksha* or *mukti* (Tamil for "salvation" or "release") it was necessary to have a healthy and strong body. According to Kamil Zvelebil, siddhas sought to suppress *bhakti* and were typified by anti-ritualism and anti-ceremonialism. There was also a stress on ethical principles and a quest for knowledge. It was quintessentially a socially radical movement. A critical part of siddha thinking was the need to pay great attention to one's body in order to make it strong and resistant to disease. Medicine and alchemy were accordingly critical parts of siddha preoccupation, siddhas emphasized moral behavior and right conduct. According to them the worst sins were anger, lust, and egoism.[39] Among the ranks of siddha practitioners were two Muslim saints. K. Kailasapathy considers that the siddha system and the Sufism that these Muslim saints represented "were responding to numerous varieties of local cultures in Tamil Nadu and taking up similar stances."[40] Therefore, siddhars were more concerned with the microphysical individual body and individual subjectivity than with temple religion and kingly juridical power. They were interested in both the care of the self and in ways to develop a civil society that argued the importance of having a strong and healthy body as technologies of the self not from the top-down but from below.

We know, for instance, that many individuals contested siddha systems of discipline and health in a large variety of contexts ever since the twelfth century. Moreover, even though siddhars attacked *bhakti* devotees, Padma Kaimal shows that it is possible to see a strong continuity between the divine and human body in *bhakti* portraiture as well. In her thinking, "divine images and human portraits may represent linked points along a continuum rather than a starkly contrasting opposition."[41] Kaimal concludes that in the various areas on which she worked

> the concept of the Self was integrally linked to the physical body, which in turn integrated all aspects of the devotee: emotions, spirituality, thought, ecstasy, and the peculiar marks of individuality. As the Self was fully integrated, so were the devotee and the lord perceived as joined by continuities. Through its physical idiosyncrasies and through communicative gesture, the body served as a bond rather than an obstacle to union with the perfect divine body.[42]

These struggles over the function of the body helped to create silences at the same time as they widened the currency of those knowledges themselves.

For Foucault, this "technological" enterprise involves several discrete activities. "Each person has the duty to know who [s]he is, that is, to try to know what is happening inside him [or her], to acknowledge faults, to recognize temptations, to locate desires; and everyone is obliged to disclose these things either to God or to others in the community and, hence, to bear public witness against oneself."[43]

At the same time, local siddhar thinking and practice was already oriented to the operation of these kinds of decentered capillary knowledges. Still, the care of the self implicit in the siddhar system had to be significantly altered in order to function effectively for a moral subject. But at the same time, siddhar emphasis on care of the body and not *torture* of the body to please Civam gave it more of a kinship to modern ideas of care of the self as a personal discipline that was bound to lead to a productive and long life

The Tamil land and Tamil culture as a local site

As soon as Ziegenbalg started studying Tamil and Tamil culture he was immediately struck by a large number of similarities between what he was studying and the kind of religious, social, and political phenomena to which he was accustomed in Europe. In many ways he was learning to localize his approach. By localize I mean a process by which he made Christianity appropriate to local Tamil usage. Likewise, as soon as he could articulate his localizing ideas in Tamil, he found that people to whom he spoke were seeking to relate what he said to their own cultural repertoires. Local responses suggested quite clearly that his verbalizing quickly evoked ideas and notions that seemed to have deep and formidable resonances in local culture. It seems clear that what Ziegenbalg was evoking were a large series of subjugated knowledges that bubbled up everywhere because they were now being used for new purposes to create a society from below. By thinking and studying in this way he was formulating a way that was also later adopted by the Hindu reformer Raja Ram Mohan Roy when he went to England.[44]

What Ziegenbalg said invoked this process of participation in knowledge production that had a history of struggle within Tamil society. Tamil society had for many hundreds of years been the site where conflicts arose about Jainism, Saivism, and many other religious systems. This conforms to Foucault's observation that these subjugated knowledges have "historical contents that have been buried and disguised." They are "a whole set of knowledges that have been disqualified [in the past] as inadequate to their task or insufficiently elaborated: naive knowledges, located low down on the hierarchy, beneath the required level of cognition or scientificity."[45] Foucault's formulations point to a long historical process where knowledges compete to find a place in scientific or erudite knowledge in society. Norbert Elias also argues that these subjugated knowledges only find their place in the society when they seem to reflect common everyday requirements.[46] Ziegenbalg's strategies in seeking to get the local people to change their lives required that he use words and phrases out of Tamil literature with which his hearers were more familiar than even he was. Since he wanted to see things from the inside, and his audiences understood this, his adoption of these Tamil words and phrases provoked a mutiny of subjugated knowledges that overtook and turned back on Ziegenbalg's own intentions.

Faced as he was by a European population (including some of the missionaries[47]) who broke all the local rules of cleanliness and proper decorum, Ziegenbalg spent more and more time learning Tamil, the language of most local people. In the same way as the "Hottentot" language that Ziegenbalg felt was "very uncouth, and a sort of Gibberish, which no Body can learn,"[48] most "Christians in Europe consider that the Tamil heathen are a very barbaric people who know nothing either in the matter of learning or moral usage. This is a result of the fact that Tamil is unknown." Ziegenbalg also admits to the fact that when he first got to Tarangambadi he could not imagine that Tamil was a completely regular language. As a result, he had many false conceptions about what the Tamils did, believing that they had "no civil or moral law." But as soon as he had been learning Tamil for even a short time and could speak with each and every one of them he was "gradually freed from this presumption." By this mechanism he felt that he could entertain better notions about Tamil and Tamil culture. As a result he came to the conclusion that Tamil books could be read and that among the Tamils precise philosophical disciplines were set forth somewhat like what would be sought after by the learned in Europe.[49] "Though they are in great error and thick darkness," he wrote,

> both with regard to their lives and teaching, yet I must declare that my conversations with them have often led me to deeper consideration of many subjects, and that both in theology and in philosophy I have learned much of which neither I nor other students had thought before. I remember that many learned people in Europe have written on the manner in which the heathen ought to be converted, but there was no difficulty in this, as there was no one but themselves to contradict them. If these men were to come here, they would find that for one reason, which they brought forward, the heathen would have ten to oppose them. It requires great wisdom to converse with such people, and to bring them to a conviction that their heathenism is false and our Christianity true. Neither Logic, nor Metaphysics, but God alone can give this wisdom.[50]

It is therefore clear that the more he studied Tamil and Tamil behavior the more the vaunted Western moral and intellectual superiority tended to collapse.

By the end of 1708 he and his Tamil teachers had read a total of 119 Tamil texts, all on palm leaf manuscripts, all the words joined together without any spaces between them and all without any punctuation. These Tamil teachers were either "the old teacher," who was always trying to make Ziegenbalg into a Malabarian[51] or the Company dubash known either as Allepa[n] or as Arumugam. In many ways, despite the fact that Ziegenbalg mentions Allepan very infrequently in his correspondence,[52] Allepan's function for both Ziegenbalg, and later Ernest Greundler, seems to have been similar in many ways to the role that Shankarayya played with Francis Whyte Ellis in the discovery of Tamil and Dravidian.[53] Allepan not only helped to teach Ziegenbalg and Greundler Tamil but also was the author of many of the letters written to the missionaries in the "Malabarische Korrespondenz." This teaching and authorship of "native letters" helped to communicate knowledges about local society. Allepan was historically placed to perform a series of critical historical functions at the given moment when Ziegenbalg and Greundler were in Tarangambadi. Both for the "old teacher" and Allepan the historical forces around them made them into individuals who articulated these enabling and coercive knowledges.

Conversion as care of the self – I

One definition that Ziegenbalg gave for the moral subject was the person who was transformed from within, whose goal was to seek salvation. He gave this definition to a series of individuals who were doing penance. He said, "If you have any hopes for salvation you must let yourself be placed by God in a position in which you will have the strength to avoid evil and do good."[54] As part of the same discussion with some individuals who were doing penance, he said, "you need to avoid sins and be able to do good. In this way a complete transformation will take place within you and you will become an entirely different person in heart, mind, disposition [Gemath], understanding, will and all the powers of the soul, so that everyone will be able to see, from your external behavior, that a spiritual change has taken place within you."[55]

Some of the people who were with him in this discussion replied,

> That is all very well, that you are concerned about us, and we can tell that you want to convert us to your Christian religion, but we have heard since we were little that no religion is worse than the Christian. It is true that we have never heard or read anything substantial in our language about your religion, but we can tell by the way Christians live that their religion is not good. And if only those make it to heaven (are those) who stick to the straight and narrow path that you have described, then not very many of you Christians will attain salvation. Every day we see things with our own eyes that are disgusting to us; surely God will be even more disgusted by such things. But please do not lose your temper when we tell you what we think.[56]

In fact, Ziegenbalg was well known for not losing his temper.

Ziegenbalg said that his hearers were making their decision on the basis of seeing how these Christians lived, not on the basis of Christian laws. These were Christians in name only and not in deed. Ziegenbalg asked the local people to look at their own lives and see whether he was a good example on the basis of the "word of God." These local listeners told Ziegenbalg that they had been informed that it was, in fact, only possible to attain salvation by refusing to adopt any belief at all, not to go to the temple nor perform any external ceremonies, but instead remain above all religions and to "honor the being of all beings." Ziegenbalg agreed that both TiruvaLLuvar and Shiva Paakkiyam [Civavaakkiyar] had written well about "the foolishness of your idolatry, your dirty rituals in the temples, a contempt for all things, striving for a virtuous way of life, and the internal and external composition of white people."

What was even stronger than a revulsion against white behavior was the feeling that the present was a time of great moral uncertainty. In many of these "Conferences," for instance, Ziegenbalg reported that his listeners often claimed that the world was turned upside down. In December of 1707 Ziegenbalg related a discussion with some people who said that "everything is confused," and they didn't know what to do. Ziegenbalg urged them to free themselves from this bewilderment. He felt that they should not use the "sorry state of the world" as a way not to do something about its whims.[57] For him, the project to become a good moral subject was more urgent. Again, in early 1708, Ziegenbalg recounted an incident where he was visited by a number of Muslims from the neighboring Tamil port-town of Negapatam. One of these Muslims was a "holy man" or "priest." It is clear in this and many other contexts that Ziegenbalg looked upon his work as a mutual activity that involved everyone in his particular universe. What is even more striking is that people heard about or found out about it and went to see him with a similar intent. One Muslim holy man recounted that there was impiousness among not only Christians, but also among Muslims and what we would later call "Hindus." Ziegenbalg replied that since both he and the Muslim were "priests" shouldn't they somehow try to see how they could restore the situation? Yes, replied the Muslim, but how can we do this in such disadvantageous circumstances? Ziegenbalg said that the first priority was to bring order into one's own life. We have to commit our bodies and souls to God, he said. If we begin by improving ourselves God will show us a way out of the corruption of the present. Next, the Muslim "priest" looked at Ziegenbalg and said that he had not wished to believe what he had heard about Ziegenbalg until that moment. However, now that he saw and heard him he was astounded to hear a Christian speak in this manner.[58] Again, at the end of July 1708, while Ziegenbalg was visiting a rest house or *chattiram* for travelers on his way back from a trip to a Dutch seaport called Negapatam, he had several more discussions with people about what they considered to be the sad state of the times. When he was there an old man stood up and said that it was the *Kaliyuugam*, the fourth stage of the world, when everything was confused and full of imperfections. According to Ziegenbalg, the old man said that there were so many different opinions about the nature of God and the names of God, a person did not know what to choose. When this period had passed, things would be again put right, all the people of the world would agree about these things.[59] In 1714 Ziegenbalg said that he was amazed to see that among Muslims there was a prophesy that there would be a great alteration in religious affairs and that they would be visited by men to undertake this change. The old "Hindu" schoolmaster said that the "Hindus" also had prophecies to the same purpose as the Muslims, "who have made great alteration in these Countries of late Years, In matters of Religion."[60] Wherever Ziegenbalg turned among the local population he was confronted by the feeling that the whole world was in turmoil.

In this "time of troubles," Ziegenbalg was particularly preoccupied in trying to discover the "fundamentals" of Tamil culture. One of the ways he undertook this project was by looking at Tamil aphoristic literature, akin to the work of C. P. Brown and M. W. Carr for Telugu. Brown's interest in Veemana was also in the "rejection of brahmanical privilege and hierarchy, ritual, and emphasis instead on cultivating the moral person in the body—even to the point that there's a strong alchemical component."[61] One aspect of Ziegenbalg's efforts found fruit in the translation of three works of Tamil "wise sayings" or "Tamil-Spruchweisheit."[62] These three were included in a work called "Malabarishe Sittenlehre, Kondci Wenden: oder, Malabarishe Moralia, Ulaga Nidi: oder, Weltliche Gerechtigkeit."[63] Kamil Zvelebil contends that this was probably the earliest translation from Tamil into a non-Indian language. Ziegenbalg's principal interest lay in understanding the relation between texts and behavior in Tamil society. In his account of "Ulaka Niiti" or civil law, Ziegenbalg wrote that he had translated it into German

> just to find out what kind of morality exists amongst such heathens. It is the first book the school children study, yet all those rules are never properly explained to them. Whenever I visit a school and ask some youngsters what certain things mean they are always unable to give me a satisfactory answer. The same happens in the case of other books dealing with ethics, they are learnt by heart but without proper understanding; just as we Christians often learn the Catechism by heart without understanding it.[64]

Ziegenbalg used his interest in this kind of literature to try to understand the weakness of his conversion appeal to Tamils. He noted, for instance, that another "morality book" "Muuturai" by Auvaiyaar,

> shows that even after the wretched fall of man those heathens had the Law written in their hearts. This fact manifests itself again and again in their literature, and I can truly say that I have found a much higher level of morality in their books and in their speech than was common among the Greek and Roman heathens. Therefore, if one leads a pious and virtuous life amongst them, they are in full agreement with us Christians and they love those who have devoted themselves to virtue; but if one tells them about Christ, the importance of baptism, and other things necessary for the attainment of bliss, they will not argue but at the same time they will refuse to accept one's word, saying that a man who leads a good life will reach a good place after his death, one who leads an evil life will find himself in an evil place of residence whether he was a heathen, a *Turk*, a Jew, or a Christian.[65]

Ziegenbalg was also the author of the first connected account of Tamil literature.[66] In addition, he wrote two works on what we would today call "Hinduism." One of them, *Geneologie der Malabarischen Goetter*, did not get a good reception back in Halle by August Hermann Francke, who felt that Ziegenbalg should have been spending his time converting the "heathen" instead of writing about their religion. It was worked over by many hands and was first published in Berlin in a mutilated version in 1791 and later fully in 1861.[67] Ziegenbalg also wrote another work called *Malabarisches Heidenthum* that he composed to correct some of the things he had written in the *Geneologie*. *Malabarisches Heidenthum*, unlike the *Geneologie*, was hardly touched by his successors in Germany, but also was not published until 1926.[68]

Two authors who seemed to be "fundamental" to Tamil culture and who at the same time argued the need for a moral life were TiruvaLLuvar and Civavaakiyar. In commenting on the work of Civavaakiyar, a fourteenth century Tamil siddhar poet, Ziegenbalg wrote that, "he did not believe in any religion but only in leading a virtuous life." At present the author [Shiva Paakiyam or Civavaakiyar], wrote Ziegenbalg, "had many devotees in the Tamil country." These followers only read the author's books and "pay no attention to the ceremonies performed in the temples in honour of the gods." Ziegenbalg said that

> I had many discussions with them; usually they agree with my idea of virtue [Ziegenbalg's notion of moral behavior] but just as they do not want to take note of their own gods and the different aspects of their own faith, in the same way they are also not interested to hear about Christ and the attitude of the Christian religion. I have met such people amongst the Moors . . . too. They lead a very restricted life and talk only about virtues.[69]

Ziegenbalg's testimony as to the popularity of Civava akiyar's work and thinking among all religious groups is enhanced by his statement that, "Parts of the Schiva paikkiyam [Civavaakiyar] are frequently found amongst the Malabaris [Tamils] and, since the disciples of the author know that their teacher's name is well respected by all Malabaris, they often compose such ethical works and bring them out under his name; this happens in Europe too."[70] Civavaakklyar's popularity at Ziegenbalg's time was a product of the operation of knowledges that were being taken up again in order to perform new historical tasks. One of these projects was to enhance an individual's subjectivity.

Ziegenbalg's experience shows that Civavaaklyar's ideas and words were part of a long historical struggle in which many contemporary devotees composed verses in his style and attributed them to Civavaakiyar. This also suggests that Civavaakiyar's ideas and words seem to have found a resonance in contemporary society as what Foucault calls an "insurrection of subjugated knowledges."[71]

Conversion as care of the self – II

The missionaries and their respondents spoke a great deal about the relation between political-juridical power or kinds of knowledge that we can call the technology of power and domination, and their other interest, which was in learning how to govern the self—conversion—or the technology of the self. This technology of "domination," says Foucault, "determines the conduct of individuals and submit[s] them to certain ends or domination, and objectivizing of the subject."[72] According to Foucault, the technology of the self, "permits individuals to effect by their own means, or with the help of others, a certain number of operations on their own bodies and souls, thoughts, conduct, and way of being, so as to transform themselves, in order to attain a certain state of happiness, purity, wisdom, perfection or immortality."[73] In effect, in Tarangambadi Ziegenbalg and those he worked with—Allepan, the old school teacher, women, the people in the crowds, brahmans, Muslims, and children—were preoccupied with the elements that made up the striving to be a moral subject, with the interface between the technology of the self and the technology of domination, with subjectivity.

These technologies of the self were a critical part of becoming a moral subject.[74] Ziegenbalg said that true conversion consisted in a changing of the will, so that one was not so willful and listened better without getting angry. This was so that one became more devoted to the deity. In one way he was speaking about the general project of the pietistic relationship of *Leib* and *Seele*—body and soul—so that one could learn how to live an orderly life as a moral subject. According to Ziegenbalg, this "conversion process," whereby one changed oneself, could not be undertaken by oneself alone. One needed the help of the deity. Ziegenbalg was reacting to several of his hearers who believed that they could enter upon the project of becoming a moral subject without becoming a Christian. There are several places in his book *Malabarisches Heidenthum* [Tamil Heathenism] of 1711 where he feels that the local "natural" religious behavior puts Christian comportment to shame. In 1709 he wrote that, "many Christians . . . could learn from them [local people]."[75] In Ziegenbalg's view, this "natural" moral behavior is based in large part on the ideas of the Tamil yogis or Tamil siddhars.

Once Ziegenbalg had discovered Civavaakiyar it was thereafter clear that the Tamil siddhars were engaged in a holistic project that had a number of similarities to the pietistic one that Ziegenbalg and the other missionaries "brought with them." One physician who articulated holistic ideas about the unity of *Leib* (body) and *Seele* (soul) was Christian Friedrich Richter (d. 1711). Richter's most important work was called *Kurtzer und deutlicher Unterricht von dem Leibe und Nateurlichen Leben des Menschen* [A Short and Clear Lesson about the Body and the "Natural" Life of Man] that appeared in Halle in 1705.[76] Richter provided Pietists from Halle with conception of "nateurlichen Leben." Correspondingly, it had an important technical significance for the missionaries as well. Richter wrote that just as when two things unite they produce a new thing, likewise when the body (*Leib*) and soul (*Seele*) unite they produce a new entity called the *nateurliches Leben*, which, because it has different characteristics, is called one's nature.[77] It was in part this technical meaning of the "nateurliches Leben" that informed Ziegenbalg's analysis of Tamil society and religion. Ziegenbalg and the other Pietists thought that their holistic insight into the relation of *Leib* and *Seele* was their exclusive preserve. It was also informed by the notion of "natural religion" that people like the Tamils were thought to have as a matter of definition. They would have innate knowledge of morality and a monotheistic god innately.[78] Therefore, the more Ziegenbalg read Civavaakyar and other Tamil works like Auvaiyaar's *Muuturai* the more he believed that Tamil "nateurlich" behavior, the joining of the body and the soul, was a function, at least in part, of this on-going Tamil micro-physical project.[79] Arguing that the siddhars appeal to their listeners not to undertake disciplines, ceremonies, and bathe themselves in water as a way to rid themselves from sin, he says instead that they emphasize the need to be silent. They stress steadfastness, holiness, and vigilance. They want people to be composed and calm.[80]

Ziegenbalg goes on to connect this orientation of the siddhars to a general tendency in the population to act in charitable ways in giving alms. He says that people seek not only to remove their sins but also act so as to reach salvation with certainty. Therefore, he said, one finds houses in every street and in all towns and cities where travelers rest and where strangers can live. People also provide water there for people to drink, an act that in India is considered an act of charity. He also notes that the few ordinary people one sees begging are those who are lame or blind or poor.[81]

For the siddhars and for Civavaakiyar in particular the physical body was not the site of decay but was something to protect and enhance. Kamil Zvelebil has written that, "The body is no longer a source of pain and temptation, but the most reliable and effective instrument of man is his quest to conquer death and bondage [for the siddhars]. Since liberation can be gained even in this life, the body must be preserved as long as possible, and in perfect condition."[82] Zvelebil also cites the *Tirumantiram*, by another siddhar named Tirumuular, (late sixth to early seventh century). Tirumuular writes, "Mistakenly I had believed the body to be imperfect / But within it I realized Ultimately Reality." "Those who let the body decay, destroy the spirit; / they will not attain the true, powerful knowledge, / I have learned the art of how to foster the body;/ I fostered the body, and I fostered the soul" (v. 725).[83] Civavaakiyar also believed in the great importance of a person's physical body. He wrote, "This simple body is the place where the Lord lives" (v. 272). Accordingly, therefore, the aim of *yoga saatanaa* is *kaayasitti* or the perfection of the body. Every siddhar was a "spiritual alchemist" par excellence and the goal of *yoga saatanaa* is *kaayasitti*, which means the cultivation of the body or "transformation of the body into immortal essence."[84]

Moreover, worshipping through the traditional religious texts had no value whatsoever for siddhars. More important was to have Sivam or Civam (not Civan) within you. He wrote, "When the time of death approaches, will the Vedas help? / It's enough to know god even for a second, and keep Civam inside you. / Then what kind of sickness can affect the body?" (v. 13). It is K. Kailasapathy's contention that the siddhas did not worship the personal god Sivan, but the abstract quality Sivam, which means "goodness" or "auspiciousness" and the highest state of god.[85] At one point, Civavaakiyar wrote that, "The quality of Civam is the Lord and me together" (v. 291).

What a siddhar sought was to bring Civam inside one, a little like lightning. In the same way as when "lightning develops, spreads and recedes, just like Civam who stays inside me, and comes back to me" (v. 124). What was indeed central to siddhar thinking was the necessity not to bathe in "sacred" tanks and visit "sacred" temples, but to have Civam within you. This is how Civavaakiyar said it: "You brahmans make the recitation of the Shaastirams sound like the law/ when the time of death approaches, will the Vedas help? / It's enough to know Civam even for a second, and keep it inside you/ Then what kind of sickness can affect the body? /Then you will get power, knowledge and moksha [mukti]" (v. 13). In another verse he wrote, "Oh dumb people who wander and run around the town, the land and the forest, suffering/ The highest of the highest is spread everywhere in the earth and the sky/ Know that the highest, is directly within you, remain with that feeling!" (v. 28). "Oh poor people who seek to bathe yourself in the sacred waters/Where is the place where the sacred waters are, . . . /After it is clear to you that the sacred waters are within you/ Then the sacred five syllables are the sacred waters itself, there is nothing more"(v. 64).[86] Moreover,

"Civam is indeed inside and you and you yourself can know and feel him" (v. 306).

Therefore, the goal is not frenetic religious activity outside yourself but rather inner stillness. Civavaakiyar wrote, "After Sivam enters my heart and makes it a temple/ I don't open my mouth before the people of the world (I am still)" (v. 32). Aside from learning how to remain serene siddhars believed that moral behavior and right conduct were very important. By far the worst sins are anger, lust, and egoism. According to Zvelebil, there is only one way to attain salvation and that is through adequate knowledge. In siddhar thinking knowledge consists in knowing the self. This is attained through practice and direct experiment, which can only be undertaken with the help of a guru.[87] However, the siddhar system was not really meant for women. In fact, siddhas were of the opinion that women were to be considered the most determined enemies of reform.[88]

Though women were offered various ways they could discipline their bodies in the Tamil religious system (such as remaining chaste as a way to protect their husbands in the reproductive world) women did not have access to *mukti* or salvation. For a very few women the discipline of being a *devadasi* or dancing girl associated with a temple allowed them to undertake a course of training to become dancers. According to the autobiographical *prabandamu Raadhika, Saantvanamu*, the author Muddu PaLani, writes in Tanjavur in the 1760s that a *devadasi*, besides learning the *Bhaarata NaTTiyam Shaastra*, would learn how to sing Telugu *deeshiya raagas*, how to play various stringed instruments, how to show the various moods in dancing, how to read poems, and how to compose them.[89] Muddu PaLani reports that not only was she a devotee of Rama but made donations liberally to pandits and scholars. Literary works were also dedicated to her. Her artistic associates praised her.[90] In the words of an early eighteenth century translator, Ziegenbalg wrote, "Many of these girls [*devadasis*] are of good Parts, and quick of Apprehension."[91]

But Ziegenbalg was greatly disturbed by the fact that *devadasis* were also seen as prostitutes. On one occasion, Ziegenbalg publicly denounced the life of the *devadasi* as one of great immorality even though he admitted that they were persons of great competence and learning.[92] It is clear, however, that Ziegenbalg was nevertheless anxious to encourage the women he met and the girls he was educating to a greater subjectivity. Ziegenbalg wanted to create a structure that incited women to speak. One of those mechanisms was his charity schools. Another was the chance to ask him questions when he spoke and to comment on what he said. In his commentary on the Tamil books, which he read to understand "the fundamentals of Tamil culture," Ziegenbalg mentions the *Bhaarata NaTTiyam Shaastra*, which was learned by the *devadasis*.[93] Among Tamil women, he wrote, the *devadasis* "alone know how to read and write the Malabari language, for usually one does not find women competent in this art except perhaps royal or noble personages."

Still, in the same breath he continues, "I have started a Malabari [Tamil] [charity]school in my house which has more girls than boys, and I am quite confident the girls will be able to hold their own in front of the boys."[94]

It is striking that Ziegenbalg was confronted over and over again by questions from women in the audience. Many of the interactions suggest that they considered him to be a siddhar adept. One day (27 July 1708) when Ziegenbalg was on his way back to Tarangambadi from Negapatam, he stopped at a *chattiram*, a rest house for travelers. On that occasion, one woman said to him that even in his last birth Ziegenbalg was a person of great understanding. Ziegenbalg said that he was born only once and that to think of repeated births was a way to delay changing your life by repenting. Another woman said that Ziegenbalg would never die and that he would live forever. Ziegenbalg said that this was wrong and that the only way a person could live forever was by becoming a part of the mystical body of Christ.[95] Likewise, according to siddhar thinking, an adept could remember his previous life.[96] Moreover, siddhars used a system of breath control to attain immortality.[97] Siddhars also spent effort on their bodies to make them mature.[98] Ziegenbalg's personal qualities also came under discussion in a number of different contexts, not all of them favorable to him. Some of the people who listened to Ziegenbalg found him and what he was trying to say rather overbearing. On one occasion, he told them that God was not responsible for sin and corruption but that each person was chargeable for changing this. Secondly, though it was true that some persons in Tamil society led estimable lives and were holy, it was up to them and not to those other people to change themselves. One hearer on this occasion said. "We accept such teaching with gratitude and are eager to hear more, but you should let us speak more, and insure us that you will not get angry if we object to something you say."

Ziegenbalg then said, "I said: you can tell me at any time what you object to and I promise not to get angry but instead to let it serve as a reminder. For just as I would like you to retain the things I tell you which your conscience convinces you are true, so I see myself bound in the same way to listen patiently to your objections to my teachings."[99]

In March 1714 a merchant told Ziegenbalg that the country did not need the values and practices of the West. At the end of the session the same merchant said, "I heartily beg Pardon for my contradicting you so violently: For I did it to no other end, but to see if I could once put you into a Fit of Anger; for many told me, that you were never seen to be in a Passion in any Publick Dispute." Ziegenbalg said that doctors never quarrel with their patients because their job is to cure the sicknesses of the body "with Gentleness and Sweetness of Behaviour; and 'tis mine to cure the Diseases of the Soul with all Long-suffering and patience."[100]

Ziegenbalg's interactions with local people indicate that he was both criticized and appreciated in a variety of contexts. It was a process in which what he was doing, his gestures, and what he said were continually being fitted into a series of subjugated knowledges that were newly becoming available and locally being used for new projects. What is important is that Ziegenbalg's participation and orientation in these local projects was coincidentally entirely appropriate to the kind of Tamil social system that he himself had formulated; one in which personal decision and choice was critical to the care of the soul, to the growth of subjectivity.

Foucault says that, "The individual is not to be conceived as a sort of elementary nucleus, a primitive atom, a multiple and inert material on which power comes to fasten or against which it happens to strike, and in so doing subdues or crushes individuals. In fact, it is already one of the prime effects of power that certain bodies, certain gestures, certain discourses, certain desires, come to be identified and constituted as individuals."[101]

What is clear is that Ziegenbalg came to be constituted as such an individual in early eighteenth century south India. His function was to take a historic role in Tarangambadi with specific gestures, behaviors, and discourses. This role was to get the local Tamils to look at themselves, to take care of themselves. This was the hermeneutic project. At the same time, his function was to be the focus of local questions about Western moral superiority. On one occasion Ziegenbalg was quoting a variety of Tamil religious works verbatim to convince his listeners that present Tamil society was religiously corrupt and degenerate. A listener to Ziegenbalg's discussion, a man, said that what he saw of Ziegenbalg's behavior showed clearly that his words were good but his actions, like those of the Tamils themselves, were bad. The point is that Ziegenbalg's adoption of Tamil words, phrases, and authors to convert them convinced local Tamils that they could see themselves and their projects in the gestures, actions, and discourse of Ziegenbalg. But his gestures and behavior also enabled the local Tamils to tell Ziegenbalg about himself. Ziegenbalg and the local people were often mirrors of what they were trying to evoke in each other. But by being a European who adopted Tamil gestures, words, and books he exemplified for local people what Europeans could be like.[102] At the same time, the kinds of interaction that this episode represents occurred in hundreds of other contexts and individuals as well.

Further incitements to discourse, decentering the project

In 1719 Ziegenbalg died. In 1720 his colleague Ernest Greundler also died. In the years that followed the missionaries and local people largely withdrew from each other. One historian of the Tarangambadi Mission recounts that, "If the Tranquebar Mission has been changed in our time into a mere school-institution, one cannot say but that the first Missionaries contributed to it, as they raised school-teaching to an undue eminence, and the free publication and preaching of the word seem to have fallen more and more into the shade."[103] In 1733, for instance some missionaries mentioned that their main dealings were with farmers (otherwise known as Paraiyar or Dalit) and towns people. With these people it was impossible, said the missionaries, to have a discourse (the word which they used in the *Hallesche Berichte*) with them on godly matters. And it was only when these people realized that the missionaries sought to be forthright with them (*dass mann treu mit ihnen mey-net*) that they make an attempt to have a discussion or ask a question.[104] In this connection they called the brahmans ""babblers and debaters" (*Schwaetzer und Disputirer*). Generally, they said, they found the exercise of having discussions in the open not useful since they found people who did not want what the missionaries offered. As a result the missionaries passed their homes by so that they did not "cast pearls before swine and have them trodden underfoot."[105] We cannot in any way say that dialogic productions came to an end. Rather there is much more evidence, in fact, that these discursive structures became more widely dispersed.

We know, for instance, that many individuals, but particularly the *paiTaarams* (priests who were not brahmans) deliberately sought out and purchased the palm leaf manuscripts of Civavaakiyar and systematically destroyed them. One German author in 1919 reported that "the works of the Siddhars [are] systematically distorted and destroyed by Saivite zealots, particularly the pandarams," because these writings spoke out so stridently against the religion that the *pandarams* believed in.[106] Another report from the middle of the nineteenth century, W. Taylor's *A Catalogue Raisonné of Oriental Manuscripts*, states that "the ascetics (Pandarams) of the Saiva class seek after copies of this power [i.e. Civavaakiyar's PaaTal] with avidity and uniformly destroy every copy they find, It is in consequence rather scarce and chiefly preserved by native Christians."[107] It is therefore clear that far from this "repression" eliminating knowledges, its effect was both to administer silences but also greatly to broaden and enhance knowledges about the discussion of Civavaakiyar's writing and that of the other siddhars both in the nineteenth and the twentieth centuries. Silences, after all, are not the limit of discourse but rather "an element that functions alongside the things said, with them and in relation to them within over-all strategies."[108] It is as a result of the conflicts that preceded and followed Ziegenbalg in Tarangambadi that these subjugated knowledges about the moral function of the microphysical body were brought into discourse, not only from siddhar sources but from a large variety of other sources as well. These incitements represented the intensification of the operation of local, capillary knowledges in thousands of different contexts.

In the nineteenth century, another siddhar named Ramalingaswami (d. 1874) became even more popular for many of the same ideas that Civavaakiyar was famous for. Like the siddhar Civavaakiyar, Ramalingaswami also scorned traditional religious "brahmanical" texts. He contended that these texts articulated a hierarchical social system where individuals were assigned positions, which he considered to be unjust. In much the same way as Civavaakiyar had also argued, Ramalingaswami presented a utopian notion of egalitarian society where Civan or Sivan "dances so that caste, religion, principles and other doctrinal differences may all disappear." Ramalingaswami was also famous for his interest in the need to take care of the body and the need to be compassionate to poor people who often suffered badly from starvation. In sum, like Civavaakiyar, Ramalingaswami presented ideas from below to encourage people to take care of their bodies and be compassionate to the weak.[109] In a sense he was both encouraging the development of a society but was also providing a model to the state from below, so that it could adopt projects that the society itself had begun to adopt and formulate for itself. Here again, Ramalingaswami's suggestions and formulations were articulations of many subjugated knowledges that became popular because, as Elias says, they served the urgent needs of the time.

Likewise, in the nineteenth century, after the absorption of Tanjavur into the Madras Presidency in 1799 and that of the remaining part of the Carnatic in 1801, the East India Company colonial slate took over juridical control of the area. As soon as the Company took possession of the Tanjavur area, it sought to develop techniques to "rectify" the problems that had arisen during the last days of the Tanjavur raja's rule and create a state that sought the welfare of the population. One British official, Collector Charles Harris, sought to typify the interaction between the state and society at this critical epistemic moment. He wrote, "The works of the inhabitants (for which they receive the [money] advances recommended in my letter. . . . The raising of the banks of the paddy fields, the digging of their small channels, the manuring of their fields . . . and their ploughing and sowing have had as much attention [as I could give them], and I have no doubt in a fortnight more *the united labours of the circar [the state] and people will have a most agreeable effect on the face of the country.* [My emphasis]"[110] Both the state and the society would thereby seek to protect property and produce both in Tanjavur and elsewhere.

Antonio Gramsci has pointed to this kind of society that is filled with individuals who are constantly engaged in creating a state after the model of the society. Gramsci himself wrote that, "If everyone is a legislator in the broadest sense of the concept, he continues to be a legislator even if he [or she] accepts directives from others—if, as he [or she] carries them out, he [or she] makes certain that others are carrying them out too; if, having understood their spirit, he [or she] propagates them as though making them into rules specifically applicable to limited and definite zones of living."[111]

Likewise, K. R. Subramaniam, the historian of the Maratha Tanjavur kingdom, thinking very much in the Gramscian mode before Gramsci himself formulated these things, noted: "The people [of twentieth century Tanjore District] are taught, albeit slowly, that the Government is theirs to make or mar, and they can no longer say 'what care we if Rama rules or Ravana rules?' " Subramaniam felt that the relationship between the society and the state had radically changed after the Maratha kingdom was incorporated into the Madras Presidency: "It is no longer its task to build temples and choultries, or present shawls to pandits and musicians. It has no Gods and does not belong to any caste." He also argued that

> There was a liberal spirit of toleration. Arbitration was cheap, quick and useful in its results. The local commonwealths went on undisturbed by central changes, and the evils of centralisation and overgrown officialdom were absent. Peace, the bulk of the people always enjoyed as only the capital was affected by the invasions. Justice, as it was administered, the people were eminently satisfied with. They were not *ruled* as they are to-day, and they felt the presence of the central Government only through its usual taxes and occasional benefactions. There was no army of clerks and civil officials who constitute to-day the second line of defense.[112]

What Subramaniam is speaking about is of course the growth of local capillary knowledges that bound both the state and the society together. I am suggesting that local microphysical subjugated knowledges about health and discipline were the basis of a development of society in both Tanjavur and Tamil Nadu generally, that gradually transformed the state from below. The sovereignty of the Maratha raja-state was never as strong or as monolithic as we have thought. At the same time, as capillary knowledges worked their way through the population, contrary to those who think otherwise, in Tanjavur and all over what became Tamil Nadu they began more and more to inform the relation of the state and the society. Therefore the creation of Gramsci's "hegemony" to produce consent and dominance was a result not of the juridical power of the state but the active technologies of the Tamil self operating as individual legislators. In the long term, these Tamil technologies of the self paved the way to enable Tamil Nad to reach zero population growth in the 1990s. For Tamils, development was freedom.

Notes

1 Different parts of this article were offered in a number of different contexts. In addition, many students, teachers, and colleagues aided me in helping me to complete this article by reading different versions of it or providing me with ideas, texts, instruction, and encouragement.

2 Jean Comaroff and John Comaroff, *Of Revelation and Revolution: Christianity, Colonialism, and Consciousness in South Africa* (Chicago: University of Chicago Press, 1991), I: 212–213.

3 Dipesh Chakrabarty, *Provincializing Europe: Postcolonial Thought and Historical Difference*," (Princeton: Princeton University Press, 2000?), 71.

[. . .]

9 Ulla Sandgren, *The Tamil New Testament and Bartholomaus Ziegenbalg*, (Uppsala: Swedish Institute of Missionary Research, 1991), 85.
10 Gerrald Duverdier, "Portugais ou Indo-Portugais, le choix des missionares de Tranquebar," (Fundacao Calouste Gubenkian, Lisboa-Paris, 1986), 115.
11 *An Account of the Religion and Learning and Government, Oeconomy etc. of the Malabarians: Sent by the Danish Missionaries to their Correspondents in Europe* (London: Joseph Downing 1717), 32.
12 Bayly and Bayly, "Eighteenth Century State-Forms," 80.
13 East India Company (English), Records of Fort St. George, *Diary and Consultation Book of Fort St. George, 1699* (Madras: Government Press, 1922), 18.
14 Elizabeth Lee Saxe, "Fortune's Tangled Web: Trading Networks of English Entrepreneurs in Eastern India, 1657–1717," Ph.D. dissertation, Yale University, 1979, p. 281.
15 Saxe, "Fortune's tangled Web," 281.
16 Quoted in Sandgren, *Tamil New Testament*, 92.
17 *MukkuTar PaLLu* (Cennai: Es. Rajam, 1959), v. 15.
18 W. Caland, ed. "Ziegenbalg's Malabarisches Heidenthum," *Verhandelingen der Koninklijke Akademie van Wetenschappen, Te Amsterdam Afdeeling Letterkunde*, Niewe reeks, Deel XXV, No. 3 (1926): 195–199.
19 Gita Dharampal-Frick, "Malabarisches Heidenthum: Bartholomäus Ziegenbalg ueber Religion und Gesellschaft der Tamilen," in *Missionsberichte aus Indien im 18 Jahrhundert*, ed. Michael Bergunder, (Halle: Verlag der Franckeschen Stiftungen zu Halle, 1999), 146.
20 Cynthia Talbot, *Precolonial India in Practice: Society, Region, and Identity in Medieval Andhra* (New York: Oxford University Press, 2001), 48–86.
21 Dharampal-Frick, "Malabarisches Heidenthum," 152.
22 *An Account of the Religion*, 2–4. Emphasis in original.
23 *An Account of the Religion*, 12.
24 B. Ziegenbalg letter 16 Sept. 1706, in B. Ziegenbalg, *Propagation of the Gospel in the East: Being an Account of the Success of Two Danish Missionaries Lately Sent to the East Indies for Conversion of the Heathens in Malabar*, Part I, 3rd Edition (London: Joseph Downing, 1718), 30–1.
25 *Hallesche Berichte* 9: 737–8, (10th Conf, 2nd ser., 14 Mar. 1714) Hereafter *HB.*
26 *An Account of the Religion*, 39–40.
27 *An Account of the Religion*, 57–8.
28 J. Ferd Fenger, *History of the Tranquebar Mission, Worked Out from the Original Papers*, (Madras: M.E. Press, 1906), 58.
29 *An Account of the Religion*, 39–40.
30 *HB* 1: 16, 22 Aug 1708.
31 See the remarks of Nicholas Dal in 1725 to the effect that in the West Indies Christians had learned hypocrisy, lying, treachery, indulgence, and various other vices which before their conversion were unknown. N Dal to Mission Collegium and A.H. Francke, 27 Sept. 1725, AFSt. /M IB2: 49, Frankesche Stiftung Archives, Halle, Germany.
32 B. Ziegenbalg and H. Pluetschau, *Propagation of the Gospel in the East Pt I*, Letter 30 April 1706, p. 12.
33 "The Heathens in these parts, being under the jurisdiction of His Majesty the King of Denmark, they dare not vent their Fury on those that espouse the Christian Religion: for the same Reason, they dissemble so far, as to speak well of them in our Presence. *An Account of the Religion*, 54.
34 *HB* 4:169 (11th of September 1709). It was not until the late 1720s that missionaries were allowed to travel in the Tanjavur kingdom. The famous missionary C. F. Swartz did not move to Tiruchirapalli and Tanjavur until 1762.

35 *HB* 3:133–4. (27th of August 1709).
36 *An Account of the Religion*, 6–8 and *HB* 7: 340–1.
37 Fenger, *History*, 46.
38 *HB*, 8: 558, (9[h] Conf. 5 March, 1708).
39 Kamil Zvelebil, *The Poets of the Powers* (London: Rider and Co., 1973), 29–30, 34, 64.
40 K. Kailasapathy, "The Writing of the Tamil Siddhas," in *The Saints: Studies in a Devotional Tradition of India*, eds. Karine Schomer and W. H. McLeod (New Delhi: Motilal Banarsidas, 1983), 407.
41 Padma Kaimal, "Passionate Bodies: Constructions of the Self in South Indian Portraits," *Archives of Asian Art*, XLVII (1995): 9.
42 Kaimal, "Passionate," 10.
43 Michel Foucault, "Technologies of the Self," in Michel Foucault, *Ethics: Subjectivity and Truth*, ed. Paul Rabinow, trans by Robert Hurley and others, vol. I of *The Essential Works of Michael Foucault, 1954–1984* (New York: The New Press, 1994), 242–3. Hereafter this will be cited as Foucault, "Technologies."
44 Lynn Zastoupil, "Defining Christianity, Making Britons: Rammohun Roy and the Unitarians," *Victorian Studies*, 44, no. 2 (Winter 2002): 222.
45 Michel Foucault, "Two Lectures," *Power/Knowledge*, ed. Colin Gordon (New York: 1980), 81–3.
46 "It may be," Elias writes, "that particular individuals formed them [subjugated knowledges] from the existing linguistic material of their group, or at least gave them new meaning [in the past]. But they took root. They established themselves. Others picked them up in their new meaning and form, developing and polishing them in speech or writing. Norbert Elias, *The History of Manners*, trans. Edmund Jephcott (New York: Pantheon Press, 1978), 7.
47 See the cases of Johann George Boeving and Martin Bosse. "Apologia" of B. Ziegenbalg and E. Greundler, 9 Sept. 1713, AFSt/M, II C5 and Martin Bosse to Sebastian Bosse, 18 Sept 1725, AFSt/M 1 B 2:39, Franckesche Stiftung Archives, Halle, Germany.
48 B. Ziegenbalg and H. Pleutschau, *Propagation of the Gospel in the East.* Pt. I, Letter of 30 April 1706, p. 12.
49 In one of his early letters back to Halle, Ziegenbalg, after describing his daily routine, noted that though the heathen or Hindus and the Muslims or Moors go along in their error and darkness, he had to admit that he often needed to reflect for a long time after their discourses. *HB*, I: 1, 15, 22 August 1708.
50 Fenger, *History*, 57.
51 Ziegenbalg, *Propagation of the Gospel in the East*, Part I, Letter 16 Sept. 1706 (London: Joseph Downing, 1718), 30–1.
52 Kurt Liebau, ed, *Die Malabarische Korrespondenz: Tamilische Briefe an Deutsche Missionare, Eine Auswahl*, (Sigmaringen: Thorbecke, 1998), 21.
53 Eugene F. Irschick, *Dialogue and History*, 101–2, Thomas Trautmann, "Hullabaloo about Telugu," *South Asia Research*, 19, no. 1 (1999): 61–2.
54 *HB*, 8: 542. (8th Conf. 31 January 1708).
55 *HB*, 8: 543. (8th Conf. 31 January 1708). I owe this passage to John Abromeit who found it and translated it.
56 *HB*, 8: 544. (8th Conf. 31 January 1708).
57 *HB* 8: 528 (5th Conf. 17 Dec. 1707).
58 *HB*, 8: 535–6. (7th Conf. 23 Jan. 1708).
59 *HB* 8: 597–8 (16th Conf. 28 July 1708).
60 *HB* 9: 673 (2nd Conf, 2nd ser., 16 Jan 1714).
61 Phillip Wagoner, personal communication, 7 September 2001. See also C. P. Brown, *Verses of Vemana* (New Delhi: Asian Education Services, 1991), first

published in 1829; and M. W. Carr, *A Collection of Telugu Proverbs* (New Delhi; Asian Educational Services, 1989).

62 H. W. Genischen, "Bartholomäus Ziegenbalgs Rezeption der Tamil-Spruchweisheit," *Neue Zeitschrift fuer Missionswissenschaft*, v.2, pt. 2 (1989), 81–92.

63 W. Caland, "B. Ziegenbalg's Kleinere Schriften," *Verhandelingen der Koninklijke Akademie van Wetenschappen, Te Amsterdam Afdeeling Letterkunde*, Niewe reeks, Deel XXIX, No. 2 (1926), 1–68.

64 Gaur, "Verzeichnis," 84–5.

65 Gaur, "Verzeichnis," 84–5.

66 Kamil V. Zvelebil, *Lexikon of Tamil Literature* (Leiden: E.J. Brill, 1995), 783.

67 Bartholomäus Ziegenbalg, *Geneologie der Malabarischen Goetter, aus eigenen Schriften und Briefen der Heiden zusammengetragen und verfasst . . .* (Madras: Society for Christian Knowledge, 1867). See also the interview of Prof. Daniel Jeyeraj by Theodore Bhaskaran, *Frontline* 25 (May 2001): 81.

68 Ziegenbalg, "Malabarisches Heidenthum," 1–291.

69 Albertine Gaur, "Bartholomäus Ziegenbalg's Verzeichnis der Malabarischen Buecher," *Journal of the Royal Asiatic Society of Great Britain and Ireland*, Parts 3 and 4, (1967): 77–8.

70 Gaur, "Verzeichnis," 78.

71 Foucault, "Two Lectures," 81.

72 Foucault, "Technologies of the Self," 225.

73 Foucault, "Technologics of the Self," 225.

74 Michel Foucault, *The Use of Pleasure* (New York: Vintage Books, 1990); Michel Foucault, "Governmentality," in G. Burchell, Gordon and Miller, *The Foucault Effect: Studies in Governmentality*, (Chicago: University of Chicago Press, 1991), 87–104, and Nikolas Rose, *Powers of Freedom: Reframing Political Thought* (Cambridge: Cambridge University Press, 1999).

75 *HB* 3:133–4 (27th of August 1709).

76 Eckhard Altman, *Christian Friedrich Richter (1676–1711): Artzt, Apotheker, und Liederdichter des Halleschen Pietismus*, (Witten: Luther-Verlag, 1972), 66–83. Later, this work comes to be called *Erkenntniss des Menschen.*

77 Richter, *Erkenntniss*, 80–81.

78 See Wilhelm Halbfass, *India and Europe: An Essay in Understanding* (Albany: State University of New York Press, 1988), 47–9.

79 Ziegenbalg, "Heidenthum," 75, 77–9.

80 Ziegenbalg, "Heidenthum" 77.

81 Ziegenbalg, "Heidenthum" 77–8.

82 Zvelebil, *Poets*, 31.

83 Quoted in Zvelebil, *Poets*, 76.

84 T. N. Ganapathy, *The Philosophy of the Tamil Siddhas* (New Delhi: Indian Council of Philosophical Research, 1993), 7, 9.

85 K. Kailasapathy, "The Writing," 313.

86 The syllables are (in the appropriate transcription), "ci, va, ya, na, ma" which, taken together, produce the very sacred mantra civaayanama, "obeisance to Shiva." Zvelebil, *Poets*, 141, fn. 104.

87 Zvelebil, *Poets*, 64–7.

88 Ganapathy, *Tamil Siddhas*, 197.

89 Muddu PaLani, *Raadhika, Saantvanamu*, ed. Bengaluuru Naagaratnamu (Madras: Vavilla Ramaswami Sastrulu and Sons, 1950), I: 59.

90 Raadhika, *Saantvanamu*, I:32.

91 *An Account of the Religion*, 29.

92 *HB* 8:548–9.

93 See the account of Muddu PaLani, *Raadhika Saantvanamu*, I:59.
94 Albertine Gaur, "Bartholomeus Ziegenbalg's Verzeichnis der Malabarischen Buecher," *Journal of the Royal Asiatic Society of Great Britain and Ireland*, Parts 3–4, (1967): 81.
95 *HB* 8: 603, (16th Conf.) 28 July 1708.
96 Kamil Zvelebil, *The Poets*, 61.
97 Zvelebil, *Poets*, 34.
98 *Cittar PaaTallkaL*, (Citambaram: Maaikavacakar Patippakam, 1987); Civavaakiyar, vs. 19, 153.
99 HB 8: 525–6, (4th Conferernce).
100 HB 9: 743, (10th Conf., 2nd ser., 14 Mar. 1714).
101 Michel Foucault, "Two Lectures," 98.
102 HB 9: 728, (8nd Conf., 2nd ser., 5 Mar. 1714).
103 Fenger, *History*, 60.
104 HB, Cont. 37, 4 Aug. 1733, IV, 62–3.
105 HB, Cont. 37, 4 Aug. 1733, IV, 62–3.
106 Heinrich Nau, *Prolegomena Zu Pattanattu Pillaiyars Padal* (Halle, 1919), quoted in Zvelebil, *Poets*, 20, fn. 14.
107 Three volumes, Madras, 1857–62, quoted in Zvelebil, *Poets*, 20.
108 Michel Foucault, *The History of Sexuality, Volume 1: An Introduction*, trans Robert Hurley, (New York: Vantage Books, 1980), 27.
109 Eugene F. Irschick, *Tamil Revivalism in the 1930s* (Madras: Cre-A, 1986), 86–8.
110 Coll. Charles Harris to BOR, 29 June, 1801, BORP, 1801, P/286/63, India Office Library, London.
111 Antonio Gramsci, "State and Civil Society," in *Selections from the Prison Notebooks of Antonio Gramsci*, trans. and edited by Quentin Hoare and Geoffrey Nowell Smith (New York: International Publishers, 1971), 266.
112 K. R. Subramanian, *The Maratha Rajas of Tanjore* (New Delhi: Asian Educational Services, 1988), p. 95.

31

CONVERSION, IDENTITY, AND THE INDIAN MISSIONARY

Keely McCarthy

Source: *Early American Literature*, 36(3) (2001), 353–69.

Narratives recounting the efforts to convert Indians were ubiquitous in the eighteenth century.[1] Missionary tracts, as Hilary Wyss terms such texts, were published by missionary societies, such as the Society for the Propagation of the Gospel, by churches, and by missionaries themselves, and they appeared as journals, letters, memos, and essays. They often recounted the difficulties involved in missions, speculated about missionary method, and looked hopefully toward the conversion of the "heathen." Indians, the objects of these proselytizing efforts, were not silent while missionaries attempted to convert them or while the debate over the social and legal status of Christian and non-Christian Indians raged in British America. Numerous Indians spoke out against conversion, and Indian resistance was the major barrier to Protestant missionary work.[2] But some Indians responded by embracing rather than rejecting Christianity, and a number even became missionaries, some officially ordained, others practicing as lay preachers.[3] As Harold W. Van Lonkhuyzen has observed, scholarship on Indian conversion still largely assumes that such conversions were forced (397). The figure of the Indian missionary, however, helps us to look at conversion from the perspective of the convert and to see conversion as more than a tool of assimilation. It forces us to grapple with the category of belief, as Gauri Viswanathan calls for in *Outside the Fold.* While the scant written records from Indian converts offer no definitive statement of belief, by looking at the figure of the Indian missionary, we can approach a better understanding of the role converts played in altering the religion they adopted, and we can better understand the competing desires within colonialism that would lead an Indian to choose the religion of the colonizer in the first place. The life and writings of the Reverend Samson Occom (1723–1792), New England missionary and teacher, Mohegan leader, and author, provide such an opportunity.

Occom's white contemporaries were proud of his accomplishments as a Christian preacher but were uneasy with his Indianness. The terms they used to describe Occom—"Pious Mohegan," "Indian preacher," "Red Christian," and "Praying Indian"—reveal the tensions between his two identities. On one hand, eighteenth-century British Americans found it unusual for an Indian to be pious, so the sometimes-mocking titles separate Occom from his Indian brethren. On the other hand, the names separate Occom from his *Christian* brethren—he could convert to Christianity, but in the eyes of whites he would always remain Indian. In either case, the titles reveal the prejudice Indians faced even when they tried to work within colonial systems. Moreover, they reflect the uncertainty whites felt over Indian conversion. In the seventeenth century, missionaries were generally optimistic about Indian conversion and assimilation. While there were abundant theories about the nature and cause of differences between Indians and Europeans, missionaries felt that "savagery was . . . a temporary condition," one that could be easily "overcome" with education and conversion to Christianity (Cheyfitz 114). Countless failed missions, Indian/colonist wars, and political propaganda that demonized Indians in order to promote land grabs and support military action against Indians led British Americans of the next century to see assimilation as a failure and even an impossibility. To many British Americans of the eighteenth century, differences between Indians and Europeans seemed insurmountable. This perceived gap in the fundamental nature of Indians and Europeans conflicted with missionary teachings about the universality of God's message, as well as with a Protestant missionary tradition that held that religious conversion was complete only if it was accompanied by cultural transformation (assimilation); in other words, if assimilation was impossible, so was true conversion. Eventually, even a converted Indian like the "Pious Mohegan" was seen as unable to be fully within Christianity. Occom's works, particularly "A Short Narrative of My Life," expose this trend toward racialization, countering it by privileging the dual identities of the Christian Indian. Occom demonstrates that there need be no contradiction between his Christian and Indian identities. In so doing, he rejects dominant British-American notions that there were necessary links between race and culture and between culture and religion.

Even as assimilation was called into question in the eighteenth century, missionary leaders such as Eleazer Wheelock, Occom's teacher and mentor and founder of the Indian Charity School (now Dartmouth College), held it out as a long-term goal, hoping that assimilation to western culture would aid Indian conversion to Christianity. And yet, faced with little success in converting or assimilating Indians, Wheelock and others sought different tactics. As he describes in his "A plain and faithful Narrative of the Original Design, Rise, Progress and present State of the Indian Charity-School"

(1763), Wheelock hoped that an Indian preacher like Occom could use Indian language and culture to slowly but successfully bring Indians to the Christian religion.[4] This would lead, Wheelock envisioned, to white missionaries becoming accepted among Indians. Once white missionaries, or "elder Brethren," as Wheelock referred to them, gained ground, they could work to assimilate the Indians.

Although Occom clearly disapproved of Indian missionaries being used as trailblazers for white missionaries, during his life there was some debate about his stance on assimilation. Perhaps afraid that Occom had gained too much respect in both the white and Indian communities, one critic charged that Occom demanded that his students assimilate and that he refused to speak in his Indian tongue or wear Indian garb.[5] And so he was criticized for being either too Indian or not Indian enough. The contradictions at the heart of the attempt to have Occom and others like him be simultaneously Indian and non-Indian can perhaps be explained as the "desire for a reformed, recognizable Other, *as a subject of difference which is almost the same, but not quite*," that Homi Bhabha describes (86). In his autobiographical sketch, Occom calls this exoticization what it is, racism: he is told that he is valued for his Indianness, but this means that his Indian identity is never forgotten by the outside world—he is a "poor Indian," a "despised creature," and the treatment he receives generally reflects this.

How do we make sense of Occom today? For centuries Westerners have sought to determine the definition of authentic "Indianness" for themselves, often finding it incompatible with western culture, including Christianity. In the twentieth century, the charge against Christian Indians was that they had abandoned their "roots," passively adopting the oppressor's religion. For this reason it might be tempting to find an ominous pun in one of the many spellings of Samson Occom's last name: Ockham, meaning "on the other side" in Mohegan (Deloss Love 21). Attempting to avoid such a reductive account, much postcolonial theory today agrees with Bhabha that narratives of converted or assimilated non-Europeans should be read as "anticolonial mimicry," as "moment[s] of civil disobedience within the discipline of civility" (121). Bhabha sees figures such as Christian Indians, who adopt some or all of European culture, as doing so in order to undermine that culture, mimicking in order to resist. Yet such theories do two things: first, they undermine the agency of the convert who has actively chosen to convert for the sake of belief; and, second, by framing the ultimate goal as critique, they fail to see the many, often subtle, ways converts alter the adopted religion and the cultures that hold it. Even James Axtell's nuanced account figures Indian conversions as mere political maneuverings, often as understandable attempts to avoid extinction, but not as statements of belief. Yet Occom, for example, does not approach conversion as *either* political critique *or* a sincere statement of religious sentiment; he resists the racism of British-American culture but does not critique Christianity itself. Instead of resisting

Christianity, Occom makes it his own, offering his alternative vision for the Indian in the eighteenth-century transatlantic world. He may have dressed like a Briton and mastered Latin, but he also wrote about Indian medical practices,[6] referred to Indian traditions, and used Indian languages in his work. His loyalties were to both sides as well: he supported Indians over colonial governments, and he preached the gospel until his death. For Occom there was no contradiction in these two positions.

In his old age Occom recounts a dream that reveals his vision of how Christian and Indian identities were compatible. Dreaming of the Reverend George Whitefield, then his late mentor and friend, Occom imagines him in the manner of an Indian spirit who encourages Occom to continue his often lonely and disheartening missionary work:

> Last Night I had a remarkable dream about Mr. Whitefield, I thought he was preaching as he use to, when he was alive, I thought he was at a certain place where there was a great Number of Indians and Some White People,—and I had been Preaching, and he came to me, and took hold of my wright Hand and put his face to my face, and rub'd his face to mine and Said, I'm glad, that you preach the Excellency of Jesus Christ yet, and Said, go on and the Lord be with thee, we Shall now Soon [be] done, and then he Stretched himself upon the ground flat on his face and reach'd his hands forward, and made a mark with his Hand, and Said I will out doe and over reach all Sinners, and I thought he Laugh'd
>
> Some were pleased, and Some were frightened, and after that he got up, Said to me I am going to Mr. Potters to preach, and Said will you go, and I Said Yes Sir and as we were about to Set out I awoke, and behold it was a Dream—and this Dream has put me much upon thinking of the End of my Journey.
>
> (Reverend Samson Occom, from a 1786 diary entry)[7]

Drawing upon the Indian belief that the spirits of elders visit the living to help them prepare for their end, Occom interpreted the dream as a premonition of his death (Peyer 97). The two men had been in each other's thoughts for a long time. In 1760, before he had even met Occom, Whitefield envisioned him: "Had I a converted Indian scholar that could preach and pray in English something might be done to purpose" (qtd. in Deloss Love 130).[8] In their visions, Occom and Whitefield reverse positions, as each turns the other into the self: Occom makes Whitefield into an *Indian* elder, and Whitefield imagines someone like Occom in Whitefield's own role of itinerant preacher. As Occom describes it, they see reflections of themselves in each other, as they stand face-to-face. They identify with each other through the common occupation of preaching, but Occom draws on more than

Christianity as a basis of sameness. He also uses Indian beliefs and conventions to imagine fluidity between Indian and western cultures: He can be a Christian preacher, and Whitefield can be an Indian elder. In Occom's dream, Whitefield authorizes Occom's work, reassuring him and showing respect for him, and Occom shows his approval of and respect for Whitefield by making him Indian. This vision characterizes Occom's career, throughout which he drew on Christianity and Indian culture, showing that they were not mutually exclusive.

But while the two men can identify with each other, their visions reveal a gap in the way each imagined the role for the Indian missionary. Occom, on one hand, was cognizant of his difference, remarking that it could be a barrier when dealing with the white community and an asset in his work with Indian congregants and students. At the same time, the dreams represent his philosophy that Indians and whites are essentially the same: their souls do not differ. The *limits* to that identification, in the eyes of whites, are hinted at in Whitefield's wish: what whites would find valuable about such a figure, as Whitefield knew, would be his difference, the novel juxtaposition, the seeming contradiction, of an *Indian* preacher. That the Indian preacher was to remain a novelty is reflected in the fact that Whitefield does not himself identify with Occom; he does not imagine himself as an Indian.

Occom's professional diary, especially the self-contained selection from it written September 17, 1768, and entitled "A Short Narrative of My Life," reveals his attempt to employ western conventions to defend Indians and, conversely, his use of Indian traditions to preach Christianity.[9] He makes these arguments by putting his missionary career in the context of his life as an Indian. The narrative has typically been read as an attempt to narrate a life, not just a career. Held up against traditional American autobiographies, such as Benjamin Franklin's, the work has been criticized for both its brevity and its content. Critics remark that Occom's entire life is not represented, and many call attention to odd absences, such as an account of Occom's ordination or conversion. The work thus does not conform to the typical American spiritual autobiography, which, as Patricia Caldwell notes, usually abounds in details of the conversion experience. It is not that Occom was unconcerned with the spiritual life or was more concerned with material existence; instead, Occom shows that these realities were in conflict for the Indian of his time.

Arnold Krupat argues that Occom's work is shaped by deeper structures, that the work's brevity and lack of detail about spiritual feeling are in line with tales Indians told about their lives, personal histories that were informed by a notion of the self that were markedly unwestern. Krupat explains that the western autobiography is informed by an individualistic notion of the self, which was not a part of Indian cultures:

> [T]he western notion of representing the whole of any one person's life—from childhood through adolescence to adulthood and old age—was, in the most literal way, foreign to the cultures of the present-day United States. The high regard in which the modern West holds egocentric, autonomous individualism—the "auto" part of "autobiography"—found almost no parallel whatever in the communally oriented cultures of Native America. (3)

While this is a provocative point about culture and about autobiography, the focus of Occom's narrative is entirely on self—just not an internal self. Community is mentioned but only to support Occom's claims about his authority and experience as a missionary.

But, finally, whether a western notion of the self informs Occom's autobiography is moot because Occom's "Short Narrative" is not an autobiography but a missionary text, an account of Occom's life in the context of his later career. Read as a missionary text—one of the many professional accounts of missionary work and methods—rather than as a secular or spiritual autobiography or a confession, Occom's emphasis on professional details and his omissions of spiritual ones make generic sense. Occom's work is neither of an Indian genre, as Krupat would have it, nor a canonical western one like the autobiography. Instead, it is informed by both Indian and European traditions. Reading Occom's narrative in the context of missionary texts helps us to see it as a product of the "contact zone," to use Mary Louise Pratt's term, as a work neither Indian nor western but straddling the two worlds.

Occom's narrative argues for recognition of his missionary work and points up the biases that keep him from gaining that recognition. Throughout the text Occom critiques the policies of missionary societies and the practices of white missionaries. A central claim is that white missionaries do not carry authority among Indian communities. He argues this with examples from his childhood and adult experience. Having stated that none of the children who studied alongside him at the Mohegan school learned anything, Occom recalls, "when I was about 10 Years of age there was a man who went among the Indian Wigwams, and wherever he Could find the Indian Children, would make them read; but the Children Used to take Care to keep out of his way" (12–13). As Occom describes it, the missionary does not have the authority in the community to order children to attend school or to encourage parents to compel their children to attend. Nor does the missionary possess an understanding of what might entice the children to attend school of their own accord.

Occom contrasts this scene with his own experience as a missionary at Montauk. He was not assigned this post by Wheelock or the Boston Commissioners; instead, having no employment at the time, he went to Montauk because a number of other Mohegans were going, and he stayed on as missionary and schoolteacher because "the Indians there were very desirous to have me keep a School amongst them" (14). His authority for taking this post, therefore, came directly from the Montauk Indians. In fact, the Indians at Montauk already had a minister assigned to them, a Mr. Horton, who spent some time at Montauk and more than half of his time at Sheenecock, which was about 30 miles from Montauk.[10] Like the British missionaries of Occom's childhood (who preached only "Once a Fortnight, in ye Summer Season"), Horton divided his ministry between two regions, having to perform the ministerial roles for both communities with no assistance until Occom arrived. Here Occom not only points out that white missionaries lack authority among Indians, he also calls attention to the missionary society's neglect of these communities, including the lack of funds to pay more missionaries.

Occom takes on the educational philosophy of white missionaries as well. Part of the recognition he deserves, Occom argues, comes from his unique approach to his work. Instead of thinking of Christianity and western culture as replacing Indian culture, Occom argues that Indian culture should be kept alive and even used to teach Christianity and the English language to Indians. And he directly criticizes the methods of white missionaries. Although a school was set up for the Mohegans during his childhood, Occom reports that "there never was one that ever Learnt to read any thing" (12). Occom learned some of the English alphabet only because the missionary would "Catch" the young Samson and "make [him] Say over [his] Letters."[11] Occom contrasts this image of the missionary grabbing little Indian children and forcing them to recite the English alphabet with his own work at Montauk, which he describes at length. With innovations of his own, such as flash cards and letter recognition games, Occom was successful (by his own account) in teaching his students what we would call phonics and from there teaching them to read and spell:

> I found Difficulty with Some Children, who were Some what Dull, most of these can soon learn to Say over their Letters, they Distinguish the Sounds by the Ear, but their Eyes can't Distinguish the Letters, and the way I took to cure them was by making an Alphabet on Small bits of paper, and glued them on Small Chips of Cedar after this manner A B & C. I put these Letters in order on a Bench then point to one Letter and bid a Child to take notice of it, and then I order the Child to fetch me the Letter from the Bench; if he Brings the Letter, it is well, if not he must go again and again till he brings ye right Letter. When they can bring any Letters this way, then I just Jumble them together, and bid them to set them in Alphabetical order, and it is a Pleasure to them; and they soon Learn their Letters this way. (15–16)

He also describes how several times a week he would use part of the school day for religious studies, which he often conducted "in [his] own tongue," thereby making it accessible to his students and reinforcing a bilingual education.

While bilingual teaching had been tried before (by John Eliot, for example), it was an unusual approach in the mid-eighteenth century (Szasz 178; Kellaway 149–57). Because they saw language as an expression of culture, more often missionaries of Occom's time agreed with John Sargeant, Sr., missionary to the Housantonic Valley Indians from 1734 to 1749, who emphasized the importance of Indians supplanting their native tongue with English: "I propose . . . to introduce the *English Language* among [the Indian children] instead of their own imperfect and barbarous Dialect" (qtd. in Peyer 60). For Sargeant, assimilation to British culture and conversion to Christianity were identical processes, together comprising the transformation from a savage to a civilized state. Although Occom never responded overtly to the policies of Sargeant or those who agreed with him, his narrative makes clear that his approach differs greatly from those of Sargeant and others like him.[12] Occom does not theorize his preference for a bilingual education, but he uses this technique throughout his career, and he finds value in teaching in both languages and even in teaching Indian children other Indian languages. This passage also conveys Occom's dedication, as he recalls how much time and thought he gives to evaluating how and how much his students learn. His remark that learning "gives Pleasure" to his Indian "Scholars" reveals the value Occom puts on learning and the attention he pays to his students. Finally, Occom claims authority over the privileged space of the school—the place that whites saw as the optimal site for *assimilation* to take place. Instead of using the school to bury Indian identities, Occom employs Indian language and tradition in his teaching, demonstrating to his pupils that they need not erase their past.

Recounting more than just educational advances among the Montauk, Occom reports, "Some Time after Mr. Horton left these Indians, there was a remarkable revival of religion among these Indians and many were hopefully converted to the Saving knowledge of God in Jesus" (16). While he does not explicitly state that he is responsible for this revival, the placement of the comment—immediately following an account of his work and how he laid the seeds for the conversion of the Montauk people—leaves the impression that Occom's endeavors have brought it on. The word "revival" not only aligns Occom with the Great Awakening and preachers such as Whitefield, but also suggests that the Indians had a prior religious dedication that had been neglected (though it is not clear whether that was a Christian or Indian religion). Mentioning Horton's departure in the same sentence suggests that he was an impediment to this resurgence of religious feeling. When taken with the statements that follow this one, it is clear that Occom is highly critical of Horton's inability to teach and convert.

Occom's comparisons tacitly serve to make a case for supporting more Indian missionaries. He implies that as an Indian he carries more authority than the white missionaries, that having the ability and desire to conduct school and services in English and the Indians' own language, he better understands how to teach Indian children, and that he has enjoyed more success in converting the Indians. These observations are similar to ones made by Eliot and later Wheelock and other white clergy, who supported the use of Indian missionaries. But whereas they often saw Indian missionaries as lesser substitutes for white missionaries, standing in until whites could gain authority and learn Indian languages, Occom saw more concrete advantages to Indian missionaries. He implies that his Indian identity makes him care more about his students, thus gaining the trust and respect of the Indians he is teaching, and that it gives him a unique perspective on his job, one that not only allows him to sympathize with Indian congregants but also helps him to formulate innovative teaching techniques. Moreover, Occom finds bilingual services and lessons valuable not because doing so is convenient or because he has lost hope that Indians can learn English but because he finds that it encourages dialogue, something that Wheelock, Eliot, and other white missionaries do not consider (or perhaps care about). Speaking in their own language, Indians could freely discuss Christian ideas and their responses to them and could even share this dialogue with other tribes.

In this way, Occom capitalizes on his Indian identity. Dana Nelson suggests one way to read that self-representation, seeing Occom as self-consciously representing himself as the commodity that he has been made into and then using that status to "sell" himself:

> [H]is representation of himself, as well as his physical presence in England for fund-raising, was to be commodified and used as a resource to benefit not him but the process that produced him. In his text Occom, as an Indian convert, is made generic and thereby fully exchangeable for others just like him. (54)

As Nelson demonstrates, Occom makes the implicit argument that his Indian identity makes him a valuable resource. But his self-promotion is more specific than Nelson shows. Nelson ignores Occom's critiques of white missionaries and his argument that Indian missionaries are *more* valuable than their white counterparts. Nelson's reading is symptomatic of a blind spot in much postcolonial criticism: the assertion that Occom's interests are essentially in conflict with "the process that produced him" does not leave space for Occom's agency for critique; it does not allow Occom to be within missionary culture and also a critic of it.

Occom's scheme of value is inverted by the Boston commissioners, who consistently make distinctions between Indians and Christians: they see Occom as Indian first and Christian second. Occom argues that the commissioners treated him as inferior to white missionaries. Having shown that he is a worthy missionary, in many ways superior to white missionaries, Occom expresses frustration at being practically forced to make this accusation:

> Now you See what difference they made between me and other missionaries; they gave me 180 Pounds for 12 years Service, which they gave for one years Services in another Mission.—In my Service (I speak like a fool, but I am Constrained) I was my own Interpreter, I was both a School master and Minister to the Indians, yea I was their Ear, Eye & Hand, as Well as Mouth. I leave it with the World, as wicked as it is, to Judge, whether I ought not to have had half as much, they gave a young man Just mentioned which would have been but 50*l*. a year; and if they ought to have given me that, I am not under obligations to them, I owe them nothing at all; what can be the Reason that they used me after this manner? (17–18)

Occom's parenthetical "I speak like a fool" has been puzzled over by practically every scholar who has written on the narrative. Nelson sees the remark as evidence of the "structural hegemony of colonialism that undercuts Occom's attempt to argue his own worth. . . . Just as he asserts a fuller worth *because* of his ability to speak his native tongue, he finds himself compelled to apologize for his lack of eloquence in English" (58). But instead of being undercut by colonialism, as Nelson suggests, Occom uses western, biblical allusions to defend himself and accuse colonialism. Rather than apologizing for his inadequate English, Occom is quoting the apostle Paul's second letter to the Corinthians, in which he defends himself against "false apostles," who have come to Corinth to displace Paul and his Gospel: "Are they Hebrews? so *am* I. Are they Israelites? so *am* I. Are they the seed of Abraham? so *am* I. Are they ministers of Christ? (I speak as a fool) I am more: in labours more abundant, in stripes above measure, in prisons more frequent, in deaths oft" (2.11:22–23).[13]

With his parenthetical remark "I speak as a fool," Paul acknowledges that it is foolish, inappropriate, for him, an apostle of Christ, to boast of his accomplishments; instead, he should "boast" of Christ. Yet, as Paul indicates, he is forced to defend himself in this way because the Corinthians are so blind as to believe the "false apostles" and therefore already think Paul a "fool." Paul asks the Corinthians to be patient in allowing him to defend himself (an act that he considers "foolish") and not to think him the fool: "Let no man think me a fool; if otherwise, yet as a fool receive me, that I may boast myself a little" (11:16). Occom uses the allusion to imply that he should not have to defend himself either, that to do so is to "speak like a fool." Yet he is forced to boast of himself in this way: "I am Constrained," he explains. The allusion to Paul's letter also intimates that Occom sees the white missionaries as "false," like the "false apostles" whom Paul is forced to defend *himself* against. Finally, the reference invokes Paul's complaint that he has preached to the Corinthians for free even when the "false apostles" took their money. Occom, too, has preached for free in some cases and practically for free in others, while white missionaries were paid at least enough to live.

But Occom's situation is also very different from Paul's, as Occom makes clear in the last paragraph. Paul's audience is simply foolish; Occom's audience is foolish in a particular way: they are prejudiced.

> So I am ready to Say, they have used me thus, because I Can't Influence the Indians so well as other missionaries; but I can assure them I have endeavoured to teach them as well as I know how;—but I *must Say*, "I believe it is because I am a poor Indian". I Can't help that God has made me So; I did not make my self so. (18)

The line "'I believe it is because'" is in quotation marks, perhaps for emphasis, perhaps to help link the line to Occom's earlier reference to the words of an Indian boy, who is beaten by his master:

> He Said, he did not know, but he Supposed it [the beating] was because he could not drive any better; but says he, I Drive as well as I know how; and at other Times he Beats me, because he is of a mind to beat me; but says he believes he Beats me for the most of the Time "because I am an Indian." (18)

By quoting the Indian boy, Occom emphasizes his own status as an outsider and a member of an oppressed population. The phrase in quotation marks also serves to emphasize that these words are now aimed at the missionary board, which is compared to a capricious and cruel master. What Occom finally "*must say*" is that he has been discriminated against, that the Christian world he has adopted is "wicked."

The world is not only wicked, but, paradoxically, the Christian world is often "savage," as Occom states explicitly in a 1761 journal entry:

> I have thought there was no Heathen but the wild Indians, but I think now there is some English Heathen. . . . Yea, I believe they are worse than ye Savage Heathens of the wilderness,—I have thought that I had rather go with the Meanest and most Dispis'd creature on Earth to Heaven, than to Go with the greatest Monarch Down to Hell, after a Short Enjoyment of Sinful Pleasures with them in this World—I am glad there is one defect in the Indian Language, and I believe in all their Languages they Can't Curse or sware or take god's Name in Vain in their own Tongue.
>
> (qtd. in Blodgett 57)

The allusion also invokes the context of Paul's letters as he writes to the heathen Corinthians, admonishing them for their loose morals. Reversing the civil/savage dichotomy, Occom calls attention to the irony in the heathen-like behavior of British Americans.[14] Implying that British Americans have much to learn from the Indians, Occom not only scolds British Americans for their hypocrisy, he characterizes the Indians as more civilized, more moral. The Indians' world is so far from the "English heathen[s']" blasphemous culture that they do not even have words for swearing.[15] In this diary passage and in his narrative, therefore, Occom ironically positions himself and other Indians as more legitimate Christians than British Americans.

His position as "despised" by British-American culture is not of his own making, as Occom makes clear by adding, "I did not make myself so." One meaning is that God made him, and neither he nor those he accuses should question God's work by treating him as a lesser human being. The line also indicates that Occom did not make himself an object of prejudice, that this comes from the outside world. He has done nothing to invite it. "I did not make myself so" is not a confession bemoaning his state. He shows that his Indianness is a problem only because whites make it so. In fact, for the rest of the narrative he has shown that being an Indian has helped him in his work. At the same time that he did not make himself "despised" or a "poor Indian," he *made* himself in a crucial sense, and this is a central claim of the narrative.[16] He has proven that he is an innovative teacher, a respected clergyman, a scholar, a father, and an industrious community leader, all in the face of material hardship and cultural prejudice from the white community.

The modesty in "I did not make myself so," like the modesty in "I speak like a fool," makes Occom's critique subtle. Yet the message is clear: Christian institutions have not done right by this new member of the faith; moreover, they have failed to realize the extraordinary value of Occom as a teacher and leader. Occom launches this critique not to undermine the missionary project or colonial governments but to argue for the inclusion of Indians in these institutions as well as to give British Americans a sense of what could come out of such inclusion—what they could learn from an Indian and what Christianity might look like if taught by a Mohegan.

Notes

I would like to thank Steve Newman, Vincent Carretta, George Williams, Robert Levine, Sue Lanser, and Ralph Bauer for comments on earlier drafts of this article. Versions of this essay were presented at the 2000 American Society for Eighteenth-Century Studies conference and the 2001 Society for Early Americanists conference. I would like to thank the SEA panelists, audience, and respondent, Hilary Wyss, for their valuable insights.

1 "Native," "Indian," and "Christian" are ambiguous and highly contested terms. The debate over naming continues in Native-American studies, literary studies,

anthropology and other fields as well as in local communities. I like Gerald Vizenor's term "postindian" to acknowledge the struggle of "natives" (Vizenor's word) against the various myths associated with the word "Indian." I choose to use the word "Indian," however, in part because my subject is these myths; therefore, I invoke them in order to explore them. But the word conjures more than myths. As Menno Boldt articulates in his study on Indians and self-government, "Indian" "has a constitutional, legal reality, and . . . it has also acquired a sociopolitical reality" (xiii). "Indian" was the term consistently used by both Indian and European authors of the eighteenth century, and in this way the word allows me to refer directly to both the myths and the realities associated with the use of the word in the eighteenth century. The term is useful because it refers to a historical position, a legal state, and a cultural heritage.

2 At least one Indian refutation of Christianity was published: "A Speech delivered by an Indian Chief, in America. In reply to a sermon preached by a Swedish Missionary, in order to convert the Indians to the Christian Religion" (London, 1739). According to the text, the speech was recorded in Latin by the Swedish missionary who turned the text over to the University of Upsala, asking the professors there "to furnish him with Arguments to confute the strong Reasoning of the Indian." In his essay, "Remarks Concerning the Savages of North America" (1784), Benjamin Franklin recounts a story similar to the one found in "The Speech delivered by an Indian Chief."

3 John Sassamon (Namasket preacher and translator near Mount Hope), John Hiacoomes (preacher at Martha's Vineyard), William Simonds (preacher and teacher at Dartmouth), Joseph Wanno (preacher at Manomet Ponds Plymouth), Oliver Peabody (preacher at Natick), David Fowler, and Joseph Johnson were a few of the many Indian preachers.

4 In the seventeenth century, John Eliot proposed that Indians become preachers to other Indians. While none were ordained, many of Eliot's students worked as preachers and translators.

5 In a letter to Wheelock, Samuel Hopkins quotes missionary "Mr. Hawley," who launches this critique. The letter is dated January 27, 1763.

6 *Ten Indian Remedies: From Manuscript Notes on Herbs and Roots, by Rev. Samson Occom as Compiled in the Year 1754*. Ed. Edward C. Lathem. 1964.

7 From Occom's journal, January 23–April 27, 1786, Wheelock Papers.

8 Whitefield was correct about the interest a figure such as Samson Occom would excite: when Occom traveled to England, upon Whitefield's enthusiastic request, he preached over 400 sermons and addresses in the course of two years (February 1766 to April or May of 1768). He won friends and followers, raised over 12,000*l*. for Eleazer Wheelock's Indian Charity School, and was recruited by the Anglican Church to join their clergy (he declined). There was opposition to Occom's trip from some colonial officials. It was feared that he would meddle in a controversy over land (called the Mason controversy), so reports were spread to discredit him. These included allegations that he was actually a Mohawk (considered more savage than the Mohegans, most of whom were Christian) and that he was illiterate. Occom wrote his autobiography in part to defend himself against these rumors.

9 Occom's "A Short Narrative" may have been intended for a public audience since in it he addresses the Boston Commissioners (a missionary organization), but whether or not Occom meant it for publication, the narrative was not published until the twentieth century. In 1982 it appeared in *The Elders Wrote: An Anthology of Early Prose by North American Indians, 1768–1931*, edited by Bernd Peyer. This is the text that I use.

10 This is most likely Azariah Horton (1715–1777), who was ordained by the New York Presbytery and was supported by the Society in Scotland for the Propagation of Christian Knowledge.

11 Although Occom does not name him, this missionary was John Barber (Szasz 192).

12 Occom did have a conflict with Sargeant's son when, in the late 1780s, John Sargeant Jr. arrived as missionary to New Stockbridge (he had been missionary to the Stockbridge Indians in Massachusetts since 1771), where Occom was already working. The power struggle between the two men divided the community into two camps and greatly upset Occom, especially when Sargeant received a handsome sum from the breakup of the New England Company and was made the "official" pastor to this community, which Occom had served for two years without any compensation (Peyer 87).

13 I am grateful to Vincent Carretta for bringing this allusion to my attention.

14 Occom, whose career spanned the American Revolution, consistently uses the word "English" to describe Britons and British Americans. I use "British Americans" to describe those Britons living in America during the second half of the eighteenth century (before and after the war).

15 As Stephen Greenblatt has shown, this is a colonial commonplace: Swift uses it in *Gulliver's Travels* to describe the Houyhnhnms' innocence; Aphra Behn uses it in *Oroonoko* to describe the innocence of the natives of Surinam; Montaigne uses it to describe the innocence of the "New World" natives in "Of Cannibals."

16 Michael Elliott makes a similar point about Occom's "making" and remaking" of himself (249).

Works cited

Axtell, James. *The Invasion Within: The Contest of Cultures in Colonial North America*. New York: Oxford Univ. Press, 1985.

Bhabha, Homi. *The Location of Culture*. London: Routledge, 1994.

Boldt, Menno. *Surviving as Indians: The Challenge of Self-Government*. Toronto: Univ. of Toronto Press, 1993.

Caldwell, Patricia. *Puritan Conversion Narrative: The Beginnings of American Expression*. Cambridge: Cambridge Univ. Press, 1983.

Cheyfitz, Eric. *The Poetics of Imperialism: Translation and Colonization from The Tempest to Tarzan*. New York: Oxford Univ. Press, 1991.

De Loss Love, William. *Samson Occom and the Christian Indians of New England*. Boston: Pilgrim Press, 1899.

Kellaway, William. *The New England Company, 1649–1776*. New York: Barnes and Noble, 1962.

Krupat, Arnold. *Native American Autobiography: An Anthology*. Madison: Univ. of Wisconsin Press, 1994.

Lonkhuyzen, Harold W. Van. "A Reappraisal of the Praying Indians: Acculturation, Conversion, and Identity at Natick, Massachusetts, 1646–1730." *New England Quarterly* 63 (1990): 396–428.

Nelson, Dana. "'(I Speak Like a Fool but I am Constrained)': Samson Occom's Short Narrative and Economies of the Racial Self." *Early Native American Writing: New Critical Essays*. Ed. Helen Jaskoski. Cambridge: Cambridge Univ. Press, 1996.

Occom, Samson. "A Short Narrative of My Life." *The Elders Wrote: An Anthology of Early Prose by North American Indians, 1768–1931*. Ed. Bernd Peyer. Berlin: Reiner, 1982.

Peyer, Bernd. *The Tutor'd Mind: Indian Missionary-Writers in Antebellum America*. Amherst: Univ. of Massachusetts Press, 1997.

Szasz, Margaret Connell. *Indian Education in the American Colonies*. Albuquerque: Univ. of New Mexico Press, 1988.

Viswanathan, Gauri. *Outside the Fold: Conversion, Modernity, and Belief*. Princeton: Princeton Univ. Press, 1998.

Wheelock, Eleazer. *A plain and faithful Narrative of the Original Design, Rise, Progress and present State of the Indian Charity-School at Lebanon, in Connecticut*. Boston: Richard and Samuel Draper, 1763.

Wyss, Hilary. "'Things That Do Accompany Salvation': Colonialism, Conversion, and Cultural Exchange in Experience Mayhew's *Indian Converts*." *Early American Literature* 22 (1998): 39–61.

WORLD CHRISTIANITY

WORLD CHRISTIANITY

Critical Concepts in Religious Studies

Edited by
Elizabeth Koepping

Volume II

Routledge
Taylor & Francis Group
LONDON AND NEW YORK

First published 2011
by Routledge
2 Park Square, Milton Park, Abingdon, OX14 4RN

Simultaneously published in the USA and Canada
by Routledge
270 Madison Avenue, New York, NY 10016

Routledge is an imprint of the Taylor & Francis Group, an informa business

Typeset in Times NR MT by Graphicraft Limited, Hong Kong
Printed and bound in Great Britain by MPG Books Group, UK

British Library Cataloguing in Publication Data
A catalogue record for this book is available from the British Library

Library of Congress Cataloging-in-Publication Data
World Christianity : critical concepts in religious studies / edited by Elizabeth Koepping.
p. cm.
Includes bibliographical references and index.
ISBN 978-0-415-46827-5 (set) – ISBN 978-0-415-47291-3 (1) –
ISBN 978-0-415-47290-6 (2) – ISBN 978-0-415-47289-0 (3) –
ISBN 978-0-415-47288-3 (4) 1. Christianity.
I. Koepping, Elizabeth.
BR121.3.W67 2010
270.09–dc22
2010006472

ISBN 978-0-415-46827-5 (Set)
ISBN 978-0-415-47290-6 (Volume II)

Publisher's Note

References within each chapter are as they appear in the original complete work

CONTENTS

VOLUME II

Acknowledgements ix

Introduction to Volume II **1**

PART 8
Nation, state and person in nineteenth-century World Christianity **11**

32 The Parsis of Bombay and Christian conversion, 1839–1845 **13**
JESSE S. PALSETIA

33 Cultivation, Christianity and colonialism: towards a new African genesis **28**
JOHN L. COMAROFF AND JEAN COMAROFF

34 Catholics in protest: lower-caste Christianity in early colonial Madras **51**
APARNA BALACHANDRAN

35 Excerpt from 'Christianity without civilization: Anglican sources for an alternative nineteenth-century mission methodology' **65**
SARA H. SOHMER

PART 9
Gender, education and conversion **79**

36 Missionary maternalism: gendered images of the Holy Spirit Sisters (SSpS) in colonial New Guinea **81**
NANCY LUTKEHAUS

37 **Young converts: Christian missions, gender and youth in Onitsha, Nigeria 1880–1929** 95
MISTY L. BASTIAN

38 **Excerpt from 'Devils, familiars and Spaniards: spheres of power and the supernatural in the world of Seberina Candelaria and her village in early 19th century Philippines'** 117
GREG BANKOFF

PART 10
Religion, ethnicity and the nation 135

39 **Conversion by affiliation: the history of the Karo Batak Protestant Church** 137
RITA SMITH KIPP

40 **The making of an ethnic collectivity: Irish Catholic immigrants in nineteenth-century Christchurch** 160
LYNDON A. FRASER

41 **The limits of religious ascription: baptized Tatars and the revision of 'apostasy,' 1840s–1905** 179
PAUL W. WERTH

42 **Religion and modernization in 19th century Greece** 201
NIKOS KOKOSALAKIS

PART 11
Local agents of mission 223

43 **Indians and the breakdown of the Spanish mission system in California** 225
GEORGE HARWOOD PHILLIPS

44 **Hidden but real: the vital contribution of Biblewomen to the rapid growth of Korean Protestantism, 1892–1945** 237
CHRISTINE SUNGJIN CHANG

45 **Kimbanguism and the question of syncretism in Zaïre** 253
WYATT MACGAFFEY

PART 12
Roman Catholic fields of engagement with Pentecostals 271

46 Excerpt from 'In the absence of priests: young women as apostles to the poor, Chile 1922–1932' 273
GERTRUDE M. YEAGER

47 Reinterpreting Chilean Pentecostalism 285
JUAN SEPULVEDA

48 Glossolalia and possession among Pentecostal groups of the Mezzogiorno 307
MARIA PIA DI BELLA

PART 13
Negotiating religious and political competition 321

49 The Lord of Heaven versus Jesus Christ: Christian sectarian violence in late-nineteenth-century South China 323
JOSEPH TSE-HEI LEE

50 Revolutionary anticlericalism and hegemonic processes in an Andalusian town, August 1936 340
RICHARD MADDOX

51 Orthodox mission in tropical Africa 368
STEPHEN HAYES

52 The spirit and the scapular: Pentecostal and Catholic interactions in Northern Nyanga District, Zimbabwe in the 1950s and early 1960s 383
DAVID J. MAXWELL

ACKNOWLEDGEMENTS

The publishers would like to thank the following for permission to reprint their material:

Oxford University Press for permission to reprint Jesse S. Palsetia, 'The Parsis of Bombay and Christian Conversion, 1839–45', revised by author 2009, originally published in *Journal of the American Academy of Religion*, 2006, 74, 3, 615–645.

Ohio University Press for permission to reprint John L. Comaroff and Jean Comaroff, 'Cultivation, Christianity and Colonialism: Towards a New African Genesis', in J. De Gruchy (ed.), *The London Missionary Society in Southern Africa* (Ohio University Press, 2000), pp. 55–72.

Sage Publications, India for permission to reprint Aparna Balachandran, 'Catholics in Protest: Lower-Caste Christianity in Early Colonial Madras', *Studies in History*, 2000, 16, 2, N.S., 241–253. Copyright Jawaharlal Nehru University, New Delhi.

Wiley-Blackwell for permission to reprint Sara H. Sohmer, excerpt from 'Christianity without Civilization: Anglican Sources for an Alternative Nineteenth-Century Mission Methodology', *Journal of Religious History*, 1994, 18, 2, 174–178, 180–181, 185–188, 195–197.

Nancy Lutkehaus for permission to reprint Nancy Lutkehaus, 'Missionary Maternalism: Gendered Images of the Holy Spirit Sisters (SSpS) in Colonial New Guinea', revised by author 2009, originally published in Mary Huber Taylor and Nancy Lutkehaus (eds), *Gendered Missions: Women and Men in Missionary Discourse and Practice* (University of Michigan Press, 1999), pp. 207–235.

Anthropological Quarterly for permission to reprint Misty L. Bastian, 'Young Converts: Christian Missions, Gender and Youth in Onitsha, Nigeria 1880–1929', *Anthropological Quarterly*, 2000, 73, 3, 145–158.

Journal of Social History for permission to reprint Greg Bankoff, excerpt from 'Devils, Familiars and Spaniards: Spheres of Power and the Supernatural in the World of Seberina Candelaria and Her Village in Early 19th Century Philippines', *Journal of Social History*, 1999, 33, 1, 37–55.

The American Anthropological Association for permission to reprint Rita Smith Kipp, 'Conversion by Affiliation: The History of the Karo Batak Protestant Church', *American Ethnologist*, 1995, 22, 4, 868–882.

Wiley-Blackwell for permission to reprint Lyndon A. Fraser, 'The Making of an Ethnic Collectivity: Irish Catholic Immigrants in Nineteenth-Century Christchurch', *The Journal of Religious History*, 1996, 20, 2, 210–227.

Wiley-Blackwell for permission to reprint Paul W. Werth, 'The Limits of Religious Ascription: Baptized Tatars and the Revision of "Apostasy," 1840s–1905', *Russian Review*, 2000, 59, 4, 493–511.

Sage Publications for permission to reprint Nikos Kokosalakis, 'Religion and Modernization in 19th Century Greece', *Social Compass*, 1987, 34, 2–3, 223–241.

Duke University Press for permission to reprint George Harwood Phillips, 'Indians and the Breakdown of the Spanish Mission System in California', *Ethnohistory*, 1974, 21, 4, 291–302. Copyright, 1974, the American Society for Ethnohistory. All rights reserved. Published by Duke University Press.

Taylor & Francis Ltd for permission to reprint Christine Sungjin Chang, 'Hidden but Real: The Vital Contribution of Biblewomen to the Rapid Growth of Korean Protestantism, 1892–1945', *Women's Historical Review*, 2008, 17, 4, 575–595. www.informaworld.com

Boydell & Brewer Ltd for permission to reprint Wyatt MacGaffey, 'Kimbanguism and the Question of Syncretism in Zaïre', in W. E. A. van Beek, Th. E. Blakely and D. L. Thomson (eds), *Religion in Africa: Experience and Expression* (Heinemann, 1994), 241–256.

The Americas for permission to reprint Gertrude M. Yeager, excerpt from 'In the Absence of Priests: Young Women as Apostles to the Poor, Chile 1922–1932', originally published in *The Americas*, 2007, 64, 2, 207–242.

Sage Publications for permission to reprint Juan Sepulveda, 'Reinterpreting Chilean Pentecostalism', *Social Compass*, 1996, 43, 3, 299–318.

Annales, ESC for permission to reprint Maria Pia di Bella, 'Glossolalia and Possession Among Pentecostal Groups of the Mezzogiorno', *Annales, ESC*, 1988, 4, 897–907. Translated by Olga Koepping.

Duke University Press for permission to reprint Joseph Tse-Hei Lee, 'The Lord of Heaven versus Jesus Christ: Christian Sectarian Violence in

Late-Nineteenth-Century South China', *positions*, 2000, 8, 1, 77–99. Copyright, 2000, Duke University Press. All Rights Reserved. Published by Duke University Press.

The American Anthropological Society for permission to reprint Richard Maddox, 'Revolutionary Anticlericalism and Hegemonic Processes in an Andalusian Town, August 1936', *American Ethnologist*, 1995, 22, 1, 125–143.

Missionalia for permission to reprint Stephen Hayes, 'Orthodox Mission in Tropical Africa', *Missionalia*, 1996, 24, 383–398.

Taylor & Francis Ltd for permission to reprint David J. Maxwell, 'The Spirit and the Scapular: Pentecostal and Catholic Interactions in Northern Nyanga District, Zimbabwe in the 1950s and Early 1960s', *Journal of Southern African Studies*, 1997, 23, 2, 283–300. www.informaworld.com

Disclaimer

INTRODUCTION TO VOLUME II

Colonies and councils: the consolidation of World Christianity

The readings in this second volume move from the increasing spread of mission Protestantism in the late eighteenth century to the 1947 establishing of the Protestant and Orthodox World Council of Churches and the 1959 calling of Vatican II in the Roman Catholic Church. The period saw two new recruits: the Euro-centred and therefore Christian world map added Australia and Oceania in the late eighteenth century; and the Pentecostal movement, gestating in Wales, Scotland and North America in the mid-nineteenth century, became a world movement reaching out from Korea, California, Chile and Wales from 1906. The threads set in Volume I, such as power, agency, training, representation, contextualization, ethnicity and gender, are as relevant in this as in the other volumes, along with as comprehensive a coverage as feasible.

The texts here benefit from and deal with two important issues which are indispensable for the study of World Christianity. The first is the greater breadth of sources in the wake of increased literacy and the increased availability of paper, writing implements and, throughout the twentieth century, the existence of, if not always access to, typewriters. While the elite in most regions were certainly privileged, if not downright powerful, and had long exerted a control over the written word, the spread of formal book-based education did enable bright (and fortunate) poorer youngsters to write, and write down lines for posterity, lines of dissent, criticism, approbation and rejection. While a considerable portion of those who joined the ranks of the literate also joined the winners, eliding their past, there is nevertheless a somewhat greater chance of unearthing the stories of the losers, stories from people who negotiated their way through changing socio-religious opportunities or restrictions by converting once, twice or thrice, by resisting, negotiating, acquiescing, by ignoring the various options, maintaining the ascribed tradition while achieving another, or appropriating and re-jigging proffered religions considered relevant to specific areas of their life.

The second issue is another great wave of colonization, primarily in Africa but also Asia, and two periods of formal decolonization which commonly, though by no means always, left the former masters with strong political, economic and religious influence, if not outright control. France gave up Haiti in 1808, while the other Latin American countries, colonized for over three hundred years, broke from Spain between 1810 (Colombia) and 1822 (Ecuador), with Brazil becoming free of Portugal in 1822. Given the pattern of Iberian governance, that had meant three hundred years of Roman Catholicism as the only officially accepted religion in each country. The taking of much of Africa, formally organized by European powers in the 1882 Treaty of Berlin, saw an increased Roman Catholic, Protestant and eventually Orthodox Christian presence in that continent, just as did (though more cautiously given the many major religions there) the extension of British, Dutch and French territories in Asia. The end of this volume is also the beginning of the end of most formal colonization. The Philippines, Taiwan, India, Sri Lanka, Pakistan, Burma, Indonesia and Korea were free at or soon after the end of the Second World War, Malaya and Ghana in 1956, leading to the swift (with some notable exceptions) dismantling of most remaining colonies within twenty years.

The demise of direct colonialism, however, did not see the ending of a Christian presence, perhaps expectable, had the assumption that people only converted to please or directly benefit from their colonial master held water. On the contrary, the faith expanded. But the modern period will be the subject of Volume III.

Part 8: Nation, church and the person in nineteenth-century World Christianity

The relationship between the person, their religion in the broad sense and the political unit to which they are affiliated is an important delineator of their identity, their rights and even their life-chances. Volume I showed that the European statehood pattern also privileged Christianity in certain colonial possessions in the sixteenth century and beyond. Yet privileging one version of the ordering of relations between individuals to the visible and less visible worlds has long been common. Rome before and after Constantine, Buddhist Japan after the final outlawing of Christianity in 1634, a Borneo village in 1896 against neighbours, modern Saudi Arabia: all followed '*Cuis regio, eius religio*'.

Stable ties between the person, the political unit and religion tended to be seen in social science as being so firm that it was change which demanded explanation; while that field now grasps that the 'unchanging nature' of a group is an ideological statement, not all scholarship does. Nevertheless, when a cluster of villages ceases to be the widest working unit as central government expands or a totally new power appropriates the region, the impact on all aspects of local lives has the potential to be profound. Foods, clothing, language use, to pick just three areas, may alter segmentally, as has *always* been the case; new ways of enculturating children may evolve, conflict with local mores commonly being managed; and the rank-ordering of particular families, lineages, ethnic groups is shaken. Or not, if the traditional elite successfully suborns the incomers by repelling or 'helping' them.

How mission workers of whatever origin and hue negotiate such issues is the subject of these three papers. They commonly (but not always) hoped people would sooner or later decide to become Christian and stay Christian once converted. To that end, they might discern and link up with power-holders, inadvertently or otherwise strengthening the latter's position; link up with amenable ethnic groups who, privileged by earlier literacy, could more readily climb the power ladder; or, often with difficulty, they could sidle up to a colonial government (though not all colonial servants or settlers were interested in either church doctrine and its rules), exchanging their own energy in social welfare and education for access, which saved the government money. Whatever the context and mode, power, agency, misunderstanding, hegemonic collusion, as well as exploitation of and by churches, are part of the mix.

Palsetia (Chapter 32) is concerned with the battle between a schoolmaster and the family of a Parsi youth who converted to Christianity. The boy chose: the family felt he could not or should not make such a decision. With some misgivings, the British-organized court decided for the boy on the innovative basis of his rights as an individual – which led to the withdrawal of some other children from mission schools lest their sons too be beguiled, misled or unfilial. As with nineteenth-century Hindu response to mission, Parsis quickly codified their tradition the better to defend it. The Comaroffs (Chapter 33) put forward another aspect of mission: carefully organized as an all-round enterprise for the body and the soul, Christian witness could civilize as it converted. To this end, herders were to become farmers, idle men supportive husbands of their hitherto overworked wives – and the marital power base altered. Tswana problems came as much from the missionaries as agents of economic change than of conversion. Balachandran discusses tensions between and agency exercised by groups of Paraiyar (outcaste) South Indian Catholics in Chennai (Chapter 34). That church, as often still today, was less bothered by the conflict between maintaining caste rules and Christian doctrine than the Protestants. She discusses the absence of religious exclusivism among Paraiyars, the objection of the church to their continued mixing with 'pagans', in which they were not supported by colonial government, and the very 'flexible' affiliation of followers to what outsiders might see as an exclusive club.

These first texts suggest tension over the new faith both between incomes and locals and among locals; the last paper, on Melanesia (Chapter 35), rather evokes Colenso's pragmatic and rational approach from Volume I. As Sohmer makes clear, Bishop Codrington used local languages to train local clergy to work in villages, maintaining the framework of local custom; his Melanesian Brotherhood remains a powerful and respected group of men, ordained and lay, working in the area.

Part 9: Gender, education and conversion

Church members worldwide are predominantly female: more women than men are actively linked to a church, identify as Christian even if inactive, and are prominent in conversion narratives. Being Christian may thus seem as gender-linked as wearing ear-rings. Until the 1858 ordination of a Congregational woman to the ministry, church services and structures were run by men: they still largely are. Yet there is a persistent 'red thread' of women's ministry from Phoebe and Junia, Theodor/a the Bishop through the deaconesses of Orthodoxy and the powerful Abbesses of the pre-medieval age such as Hilda, in charge of male and female religious, to the more recent nuns, deaconesses, single and married female missionaries of various denominations who worked in home and overseas mission. Their story was elided on a mosaic; subsumed under their husband's name if they married a fellow missionary, as occurred in most missions to Africa but interestingly not in the China Inland Mission; or constricted by increased cloistering after the Council of Trent. That story also includes women maintaining, or being assumed to maintain, alternative systems of knowledge alongside or beneath church ties.

Christianity, like other faiths with written sacred texts, developed a tradition of literacy. Ritual specialists sufficiently literate to read the liturgy and pass on the Word to the elite or the bright joining the class to obtain that or another job would have sufficed. Yet printing, the Renaissance and the Reformation, led to the more general use of Primers, short outlines of doctrine with a catechism,[1] in Europe and elsewhere, which became part of secular education. Increased demands for general as well as theological learning, and for every Protestant to read the Bible, expanded the provision of schools for boys and then for girls. To the extent that it was timely, feasible and locally acceptable (only basic schooling for girls was normal in EuroAmerica until at least the mid-twentieth century), that same pattern of education broadly obtained across the missionised world.

The teaching work of Lutkehaus's nuns in the New Guinea Mission from the 1880s was much desired by the then German colonial government, their way of being 'strong female people' the counterpart to the blunt masculinity involved in running the country: mission nuns, as some other female missionaries, were independent adults with opportunities (Chapter 36). Their charges too both followed and evaded their bidding. Changing continents, Bastian (Chapter 37) describes the gender-specific teaching organized by Church Missionary Society (CMS) missionaries of African descent for young converts in Nigeria from the late nineteenth century onwards. Men were to evangelize and run churches; women (as in the Britain of the usually unmarried missionaries) were to run the home; yet both were to separate themselves from 'pagan' Igbo society. Children were educated, including lessons in doctrine, though girls' lessons trained them more as domestic goddesses and eventual mothers than equal partners which, given the loneliness many Christian Igbo wives would live under, was scant preparation. That the outcome of this training and education would be an Igbo Christian elite was not intended by the mission – yet no convert (however they perceive that process) will be sure of the outcome if they are among the first to explore alternative gods.

Maintaining alternative knowledge rejected by the church or, at times, the state (exclusivism being as much ideological hope than fact) may also be a strongly female pattern, especially in areas relating to hearth and field. Such has been assumed and indeed, as Bankoff's paper (Chapter 38) indicates, feared and acted on. Seberina, who drew strength from her local shamanic power, was tried for heresy by the early nineteenth-century Filipino church, a Spanish institution of governance. Female power may be a chimera and female subversion a somewhat ineffectual means of charge; but 'witches' live on as fact or excuse for female suppression, whether by exclusion or 'special care'.

Part 10: Religion, ethnicity and the nation

Specific ways of 'being religious' can be part of or fundamental to the way one collection of people see themselves as similar to or different from others in terms of language and language use, expectations of proper behaviour in life and death and, albeit affected by class and gender, a shared memory. There may be an overlap, as in South Korea in the 1970s, between nation and ethnicity, just as nation and religion may seem one, Zambia and Tonga being Christian nations, Lutheranism and Roman Catholicism being, or assumed to be, the default faith in Denmark or modern Spain, respectively. Ethnicity and religion may interact to define one group as being different from (and usually better than) another. One outcome, however, is that religion may 'stand for' national problems and animosities in politics or economics, not because religion is inherently divisive, but because it can be readily harnessed to speak to and strengthen boundaries and privileges.[2] Violence expressed in faith words may also be safe shorthand for memories of oppression in other areas of life. Misapprehension about the place of violence in religion is thus rather common.

The Karo Batak became Protestant in the late nineteenth century, during the Dutch occupation of Indonesia, conversion being related to 'political pressure, ethnic pride or the quest for education', as Kipp puts it (Chapter 39). It was surely a matter of self-identity and then, as now, that means collective identity, Karo being almost by definition devout Lutherans, in clear contrast to the neighbouring Muslim Minangkabau or the Toba Batak. Kipp shows the dialectic between individual agency and the structure in which that agency is anchored, and the way in which being Batak contributes to resisting a largely Muslim state, just as being a Christian Hmong or Akha in Thailand, an Iban or Kadazan in Malaysia, a Karen or Chin in Myanmar, affirms minority ethnicity.

The maintenance of ethnic and religious difference was equally evident among Fraser's Catholic Irish in nineteenth-century New Zealand, the parish again offering each new immigrant when and as they wished a secure world parallel to that of the powerful Protestants (Chapter 40). As with other Christianities, we do not actually know whether or in what way these Irish Catholics in New Zealand were orthodox and devout, or exactly why each person identified as 'Irish and Catholic'. One outcome, though, common in diasporas, was a certain isolationism born both of experience and of holding on to an imagined past.

Werth's paper (Chapter 41) takes us to the Orthodoxy of the Tsarist state, when to be Russian was to be Orthodox in similar fashion to implicit and explicit expectations within the Spanish and Portuguese Empires. Muslims absorbed by conquest in Russia's imperial expansion thus had a problem. Tatars had been ascribed to Orthodoxy by the Russian state in the sixteenth and seventeenth centuries. Amid social, political and economic changes in the nineteenth century, thousands petitioned the state to be regarded as Muslim again. The state allowed such freedom to people 'ethnically' of a different religion – but not to individuals, until legal changes in 1905 allowed a return to the 'ethnically appropriate religion'. Orthodoxy in Greece is also, as Kokosalakis (Chapter 42) points out, the bearer of Greek ethnic identity, helped considerably by centuries of Muslim Ottoman occupation, during which church involvement was the safest way of resisting:[3] it is still the state religion. Doctrine and belief were less crucial markers than ascription, which could, as with any such close linkage, become part of the power and control system. Greek, Serbian and other Orthodox churches, just as Catholicism in Fascist Italy,[4] have run into problems for being too closely involved with the losing side.

Part 11: Local agents of mission

Recognizing that subordinated people may express themselves through intellectual scepticism, both their rejection as well as assent demands accepting that they reflect intellectually. This may seem too obvious to need stating. However, the writing of EuroAmericans in the past about 'others', whether a home minority (Roma, Australian Aborigines or Cree, for example) or a despised underclass,[5] and current common assumptions in 'cross-cultural contact' and the so-called South–South mission field suggest otherwise. While Social Darwinian ideology may be unfashionable, it, or the scarcely less crude attitudes it spawned, regularly informs assessment both within and between social groups. Where such beliefs obtain, it is all too easy to assume others are passive through incapacity or unconcern. This may inadvertently sideline efforts for social justice by colonial governments or (in modern times) international companies. Anger, resentment, dependency and opposition may thus be ignored or unappreciated.

The three papers here all relate in various ways to the recipients of mission and their own agency, their own contribution to their conversion, their church attitude and the continuation of any relationship there may be. Relating to the nineteenth century, the issues raised in the first paper continue to be relevant. Indian reserves in America were and until recently are paralleled by the 'total institutions' of homelands or government-run 'missions' in South Africa or Australia. Assumptions about the nature of women in late nineteenth-century Korean society continue to subordinate Christian women in that 25 per cent Christian country, their history and agency smoothly sidelined by the mainly male writers of Korean church history. The agency of Belgian Congolese during that appalling colonial era, which saw independent churches erupt from the misery (to the anger of the government) has been translated over the years into one of the largest and theologically most sophisticated African-originated churches in that continent and beyond, with a place at the World Council of Churches in Geneva.

As Phillips says (Chapter 43), the collapse of the Indian missions in California was attributed to greedy or incompetent Mexican officials, the contribution of Indians to the demise being ignored for, as they were 'stupid and improvident', agency was not attributed to them. Some were allowed to leave, provided they were judged 'mature' enough – another sign of the total institution. Far from leaving only after the mission had been secularized, the increase in Indian departures meant that not only the furious but also the apparently quiescent voted with their feet and left.

For Chang (Chapter 44), the apparent passivity of Korean women was as much imagined by both American and Korean writers on mission as a reflection of reality, ignoring both developments in mid-nineteenth-century Korea and the traditional, though rather hidden, female networks. How otherwise could the early Biblewomen have gone on long journeys alone had they not been used to positions of strength? She rejects suggestions that it was foreign female missionaries alone who emancipated them. Yet, however much work they did, however many bibles they sold or people they converted, their role was sidelined post hoc to that of, to use a EuroAmerican parallel, the butterers of bread and makers of tea at church functions.

McGaffey (Chapter 45) writes on the issue of syncretism among Kimbangu and linked churches in Congo (Zaïre at the time of his writing), which may seem rather a different issue from agency exercised by those in two religious worlds. It is not. Through the exercise of agency and intellectual negotiation in the area of what could be called 'overlap' between the French and the Kigongo systems, were that not to essentialize and fossilize them, individuals create a mode of relating to options which secures their social place. Without their own agency, this is not possible. Syncretism, so often in Christian contexts seen as negative, is rather the sign *par excellence* of personal agency. While that may be enough for missiologists to reject it, social science is woven from a different thread.

Part 12: Roman Catholic fields of engagement with Pentecostals

Inter-continental comparison can illuminate much about World Christianity, somewhat hampered by the tendency of theologians, missiologists and even social scientists to take the region or religion they know as the yardstick for assessing the probity and orthodoxy of the faith in all other places. The three papers in this section all relate to Pentecostal–Catholic juggling for place in Chile and Italy over the twentieth century. Both countries were independent of the Roman Church, but both, at the start of the century, were somewhat under Curial control; by the century's end, that position had altered radically. Chile in the period was a rank-ordered ethnically divided society, with firmly ruled haciendas worked on by peasants of various backgrounds, and increasingly insecure trading, small factories or craft work for the employed remainder. The elite were Spanish, with little or no Indian blood, the mestizos were of mixed origin, and Indians, such as Mapuche or Aruaca, lived in isolated rural settlements or missions when not moving to the fringes of the growing towns and cities. Pentecostal missions and churches began in Chile (98 per cent Catholic in 1906) before or at the same time as Azuza Street in 1907,[6] returning emigrants bringing it to Italy from America. Catholic apart from some Waldensian Protestants in the north and, according to Levi,[7] semi-pagans in the far south, interest was strongest among the rural and urban poor of class-conscious Italy.

The tensions in Chile Sepulveda (Chapter 47) writes of were long evident in the Catholic Chile of Yeager's text (Chapter 46): too few priests to celebrate the Eucharist regularly, let alone teach the faith in vast dioceses with poor internal communication. There was too a residue of anti-Catholic feeling against the conservative and elite Spanish nature of that church. The 80 per cent 'illegitimacy' rate of children born to the poor prevented those still 'living in sin' from taking the Eucharist. Auricular communion got round this to an extent – but getting round a problem was no solution. Church leaders, priests and religious usually regarded Popular Catholicism as an inadequate expression of faith which came close to syncretism. Methodism, from which Chilean Pentecostalism grew, had, like the Roman Catholic Church, become involved in school and liberal arts education, and appealed to the middle classes in a rather Anglican fashion, the latter serving either expatriates or Arauca Indians. Pentecostal developments did not go unnoticed by Chilean Catholics, as Yeager makes clear. Detailing Roman Catholic efforts to deal with their shortage of clergy and the recognition, by some at least, of the 'threat' from Pentecostalism, she also shows the position of women as almost substitute clergy recognized by the church: they taught, gave homilies, took services and efficiently organized the pastoral and social work of the church. Their work was for the church and its people – but the lively interest of Protestants and Pentecostals who went out all over the rural backwaters certainly propelled Catholic Action's 'movement for change' forward and, in the short term, supported women's work.

Di Bella's mid-century Italy also had residual or nascent anti-clericalism given both the nineteenth-century struggles for unity, opposed by the Papacy, and the 1929 Concordat between Mussolini and the Vatican, opposed by anti-Fascist Italians (Chapter 48). The Pentecostal message thus fell on fertile ground. Di Bella, an anthropologist rather than a historian, outlines the development of the new tradition in southern Italy, acceptance of which was affected to an extent by potential converts' appraisal of a missionary's financial success in the USA, and the process by which that initial and usually emotional move was routinized into a properly established church anchored in the community. Finally, she sets out both context and usefully detailed texts of *glossolalia*, enabling readers to see how 'Italians in rural areas use it to manage the problems of domination and hierarchy with which they concern themselves'.

Part 13: Negotiating religious and political competition

Reflecting the context in which they exist, it is to be expected that religions continually absorb not only the cultural and intellectual hue of each locality, but also the tensions, the quarrels and the divisions, be that between males and females, opposed families or ethnicities, classes, castes and combatants in civil or national wars. Where this is not the case, that religious tradition may alight but briefly in the locality. As we have seen thus far, Christianity, just like any other religion expanding from its heartland, had to fit in with but ideally not be totally absorbed by each resting place. It dealt with this issue in various ways, helped in the first fifteen hundred years by poor communications, little chance of doctrinal control at a distance and that vital ingredient, plenty of time.

The first two readings in this final part of Volume II look nationally and locally at everyday village politics which used newly available religious labels to continue old fights. They consider the effect of, on the one hand, a historically embedded commitment to a long-powerful and strongly government-supporting church and, on the other, inevitable loathing for that church by those opposing the government.

The Catholic–Baptist dispute in a late nineteenth-century Chinese-lineage village was linked both to national-level Christian political disputes between Baptists and Roman Catholics, as well as mutual theological suspicion, and to the long-set local animosity which made use of the two missions to raise the ramparts between them even higher, as Lee sets out in his article (Chapter 49). It is a useful approach, for it indicates how religion, and colonial Christianity at that, was used by people for ends which had little to do with belief in the Trinity. This is not to say they were not Christian – far from it – but that their being Christian, or deciding which version of

Christian, involved rational decisions which had much to do with local life and politics.

Anti-clericalism, in the sense of blaming the church for the failings of the government, so closely were the two seen, has already been picked up in discussion of the Philippines and Chile. While neither 1930s Catalonia nor Andalusia were exactly colonies of Madrid, Maddox (Chapter 50) sets out the relation between the Roman Catholic Church as supporter of the unelected Franco wielding his illegal and frequently abusive state power during the Spanish Civil War, and the Andalucian and Catalonian opponents, who, as a logical consequence, were strongly anti-clerical. Similar nineteenth- and twentieth-century patterns fuelled the growth of Protestantism in Latin America.

The final two papers relate to colonialism in Africa. A survey on Orthodoxy in that continent (Chapter 51) sees it very clearly as a rejection of West European-originating churches on the grounds that no Orthodox churches were linked to colonialism in Africa, that of Russians in nineteenth-century Central Asia being irrelevant to twentieth-century colonized Africans. This was one choice in which, exercising agency and acting independently of the mainline churches yet remaining within the world fold, Orthodox Africans outside Egypt were able to sidestep European clerical power. Certain individuals such as the Nigerian Bishop Crowther apart, Europeans had held on to the higher church offices almost to the end.

Maxwell's article (Chapter 52) takes us right to the end of the period covered by this volume, to Vatican II and decolonization in Africa, though not, sadly for that still ravaged country, peace for Zimbabwe. Then known under its earlier name of Southern Rhodesia, the Christian range includes 'Romans' and 'Ulstermen', and Pentecostals too. The outcome was influenced not only by the various versions of the faith which came in, and not only by each church's negotiation of the political context, but once again by the way the various Christian labels negotiated (or fought out) the differences and aspirations against each other.

Notes

1 See 'Laity Formation: The Role of Early English Printed Primers', *Journal of Religious History*, 18/2, 1994.
2 C. Muzzafar, *Universalism of Islam*, Penang: Aliran, 1984, p. 123.
3 A similar pattern existed in East Germany and Poland before 1989.
4 G. Parsons, 'National Saint in a Fascist State: Catherine of Siena 1922–43', *Journal of Religious History*, 1/32, 2008.
5 S. Thorne, 'The Conversion of Englishmen and Conversion of the World Inseparable', in Frederick Cooper and Ann Laura Stoler (eds) *Tensions of Empire*, Berkeley: University of California Press, 1997.
6 Chile counts among Wales, Korea, South Africa, Armenia and the USA as the start of the twentieth-century Pentecostal movement.
7 P. Levi, *Christ Stopped at Eboli* [1945], London: Penguin, 2000.

Part 8

NATION, STATE AND PERSON IN NINETEENTH-CENTURY WORLD CHRISTIANITY

32

THE PARSIS OF BOMBAY AND CHRISTIAN CONVERSION, 1839–1845

Jesse S. Palsetia

Source: originally published in *Journal of the American A cademy of Religion*, 74(3) (2006), 615–45; revised by author, 2009.

The 1830s marked a period of intense Christian proselytism and activity in Bombay in western India. From 1813, the British East India Company removed restraints upon Christian missions to operate within its jurisdiction in India, and a new age of Christian missionary activity and mission schools commenced. Between 1839 and 1845, the subject of Christian conversions reached a crescendo in Bombay, as the Parsi community challenged in the law courts Christian missionary conversion of Parsi children, demanded their return to the Parsi community, and sought the prosecution of missionaries for unlawful conversion.

This article examines the conversion case of Dhanjibhai Nauroji of 1839, and highlights the response of the Parsi community of Bombay to Christian proselytism and other aspects of the colonial environment. The case was a precedent in an Indian community legally challenging missionary conversion of Indian children, and it evinces the complexity of Western–Indian cultural encounters under colonialism. The conversion case highlights the cultural, intellectual and religious impact of the colonial environment on an Indian community, particularly in the urban setting, where social and culture contact was unavoidable and ongoing. Christian missionary activity formed one aspect of the complex economic, political, and cultural and religious ideological framework that constitutes colonialism. Indians sought to adapt to, adjust to, and challenge imperial culture, semiotics, and ideology. Furthermore, Indians both utilized existing mechanisms of traditional society and creatively appropriated imperial apparatuses in response to Christian conversion. The results were the emergence of cultural–intellectual struggles, accommodations, acquiescence to overpowering imperial ideologies, as well as reassessments of Indian tradition, culture, and ideology (Dirks 1992; Bayly 1998; Panikkar 2002).

The missionary impact

The opening of India had long been a goal of Christian missions desirous to spread Christianity to Indians. The spiritual and religious impact of Christian missions on Indian society was significant and consequential (Frykenberg 2003: 6–17). Christian missions also emerged as an effective vehicle for the spread of Western, and ultimately imperial, ideologies. For missionaries no less than for Liberals and Utilitarians, India was a crucible of experiment. Christian missionary efforts contributed to shaping the colonial milieu and exposed Indians to new ideological, social, and judicial pressures not experienced previously. During the eighteenth century, eastern and southern India had been the early centres of Christian missionary activity on the part of both Protestant and Roman Catholic missionaries and evangelists (Potts 1967; Ingham 1973). At places like Fort William and Serampore missions, the semiotics and hermeneutics of Christian apologetics in India developed (Young 1981: 13). In the nineteenth century, Bombay emerged as a centre of missionary activity and a place to apply methods to promote proselytism well honed elsewhere (Mitchell 1852; Hall 1836), education being one of the crucial early urban modes.

In 1829 John Wilson, a Scottish missionary, and his wife Margaret had begun their work in India and in 1832 they started a mission school in Bombay, renamed the General Assembly's Institution in 1835. The initial student population was forty-five Hindu and three Parsi boys, and the eve of the Parsi conversion case saw 230 pupils (*OCS*, August 1834: 203; November 1837: 523; June 1839: 210; David 1975: 26–7). The missionary emphasis on education in some measure was part of an internal debate among Christian evangelicals on the best means to promote conversion in India; at the same time, its impact was foremost felt by Indians (see WMMS 1890; Greenfield 1888).

The rise of mission schools and the culture contact they afforded also offered the prospects and forum for inter-religious debate between Christianity and Indian religions for some missionaries. Many missionaries made diligent efforts to learn Indian languages and investigate Indian religions. The scholarship of famous missionaries like William Carey, Alexander Duff, and John Wilson formed part of the larger Orientalist project to understand India, whether through governing or converting (Panikkar 2002). Missionary researches into Indian languages, religions, and traditions aimed to contrast Christian and Indian morality, and their critique of Indian religion through treatises and polemical argument formed one of the numerous techniques missionaries devised to interest, entertain, excite, and provoke Indians into contact with them (Ingham 1973: 55–83; Conlon 1999: 160). Bombay had long lagged behind other areas of India in inter-faith discussions; their inauguration in the 1830s drew considerable public notice and was reported in the Indian press (*Bombay Times*, 22 May 1830). However, Bombay emerged a centre of bitter confrontation rather than amicable dialogue as a radicalized Christian apologetic met a defensive Indian response (Young 1981: 21).

John Wilson's knowledge of Sanskrit religious literature, Persian, Marathi, Gujarati and Hindi had prepared him for inter-faith debate. He regarded the education of and debate with Indians on religion as part of a comprehensive strategy to prove both the value of education to conversion to Christian metropolitan critics and the truth of the Christian message to Indians. Wilson noted: "The more a knowledge of Hindooism . . . is possessed . . . the more forcibly will [the teacher] be enabled . . . to set for the authority and excellence of the doctrines of Christianity" (Smith 1879: 184). His denunciations of Indian religion deliberately aimed to challenge and best Indians in debate over religion, as he hoped "to rouse some apologist of the other side" (Smith 1879: 128). Towards this aim in 1830 Wilson started the *Oriental Christian Spectator* (*OCS*), a periodical containing commentaries on Indian religions from the missionary perspective, published until 1862 (*OCS*, June 1830: 186–95). Between 1831 and 1839, Wilson published works on the religions of Hindus, Parsis, and Muslims, including *First and Second Exposure of the Hindu Religion* and the *Parsi Religion* (Smith 1879: 110–12). Missionary influence, consequently, was significant in educating Indians, setting public discourse, and shaping the Bombay public sphere.

The Parsi response

Urban Indian interactions with the missionaries reflected a paradox, as urban Indians, while opposing Christian proselytism, eagerly sought to educate their children in institutions providing a Western-standard education for Western knowledge, training, skills, and status under colonialism. Furthermore, Indians sought institutions providing English-language education irrespective of the motives of those running them, including those of missionaries. This was particularly the case among Parsis. As Karaka writes of the Parsis and education, "No Parsee, whose means can afford it, will neglect giving [Western education] to his children" (Karaka 1858: 190).

Indian intellectual engagement of the missionaries in the urban setting also exposed the strengths and weaknesses of the Indian response. As Young notes, in Bengal and south India, Indians were familiar with the tradition of religious apologetics for over a century and had produced popular anti-Christian tracts indicating their ability and willingness to engage the Christian missionaries (Young 1981: 15, 19–22). Prior to the mid-nineteenth century in Bombay, Christian evangelists were clearly ahead of the game, being well educated and sophisticated in inter-faith debate, Hindus, Muslims, and Parsis quickly emerging as vociferous opponents of Christian propaganda. Between 21 and 24 May 1830, the Hindu convert to Christianity Ram Chandra debated the merits of Christianity over Hindu religion with the Hindu Laxman Shastri amongst some one hundred Brahmins and other Indians. Thereafter, other Hindu scholars debated with Wilson, including the scholar Mora Bhat Dandekar, usually presenting defenses of Hindu religion or argument by comparative analogy (Smith 1879: 62–8, 101; Young 1981: 25–31).

The Parsis of Bombay closely followed Wilson's debate with the Hindu community. Wilson had studied the religion of the Parsis, and between 1831 and 1839 had published writings and delivered lectures critiquing Zoroastrian doctrine and the character of the prophet Zarathustra (*OCS*, July 1831: 235; Wilson 1833, 1847; *OCS*, July 1842: 333–9). The Parsi editor of the Gujarati-language newspaper *Bombay Samachar* first engaged Wilson in inter-faith debate, criticizing Wilson for attempting to promote Christianity by attacking the religions of Indians (*OCS*, September 1831: 332–5). Other Parsis championed their religion with more passion than knowledge. In a letter to the newspaper the *Hulkaru and Vartman*, the Parsi editor Nowroji Dorabji Chandaru boasted that the conversion of a Parsi could not be dreamt of. His letter, however, contained many basic errors in his knowledge of Zoroastrians, and was ridiculed by Wilson (*OCS*, October 1831: 381–4). Parsi religious scholarship was unprepared to counter the Christian polemic, being limited among both clergy and laity to devotional observance, ritual and dispute resolution: in the course of the nineteenth century, knowledge grew as debate overcame ethnic and religious exclusivity.

Wilson had a tremendous impact on the Indian community of Bombay. The frenetic and defensive initial response of Indians to Christian polemics indicated the inroads Christian ideology made among Indians. What is significant about the Parsi response in Bombay is that traditional societal mechanisms emerged in response to the missionaries. By attacking the religion of Indians in the interests of promoting conversion, Wilson aimed to pierce Indians' self-confident beliefs and taboos, their "golden understandings" (Lederle 1976: 41). However, neither he nor other missionaries fully gauged the Indian reaction. Notwithstanding the continuing conversion of Indians, including at times high-profile conversions, missionaries in India raised barriers between themselves and Indian communities (Potts 1967: 207–44). Wilson's attitude of cultural and religious superiority elicited a like response among Parsis, challenging Christian proselytism through both traditional mechanisms and new ways adopted from the colonial environment. Parsi social control aimed to counter the missionary impact. How well Parsis and other Indians succeeded would affect both accommodation or resistance to Christianity and the process of internal change.

Parsi conversion case of 1839

On 1 May 1839, Wilson baptized a sixteen-year-old-male named Dhanjibhai Nauroji a Christian. A day later, a second boy of eighteen, Hormusji Pestonji, was baptized, in a further confronting of Parsi religious identity with the colonial environment, putting into question the Parsis' knowledge of their religion and ability to meet the religious criticism from the missionaries, and their ability to protect and regulate their community under British justice. It temporarily perturbed British–Parsi ties.

In 1832, Dhanjibhai Nauroji was brought to Bombay from provincial Gujarat by his uncle Heerjeebhoy Dadabhoy, who had looked after Dhanjibhai Nauroji and his mother and four sisters following the death of Dhanjibhai's father in 1827. In 1835, he was placed in Wilson's school, and on 19 April 1839 began living with Wilson at his residence (*OCS*, June 1839: 210). Hearing of the conversion, Dadabhoy sought to retrieve Dhanjibhai and when prevented from doing so by the missionaries took legal action. He applied for a writ of habeas corpus and the prosecution of Wilson before the Supreme Court of Bombay. In seeking the writ, he accused Wilson of breaching the terms and understanding under which Dhanjibhai had been placed in his care, and using "undue, improper, and fraudulent means to convert and seduce the said Dhunjeebhoy Nowrojee from the religious faith of his ancestors and family" (*OCS*, June 1839: 212). A writ of habeas corpus was granted on 3 May, ordering Wilson to produce Dhanjibhai before the Court on 6 May. At that time, Justice John Wither Awdry invited affidavits to be filed by both sides in the dispute by 11 May, with a final hearing and judgment to follow on 16 May. Until the final hearing, Dhanjibhai was permitted to stay where he pleased, and chose to stay with Wilson.

In his narrative of the events surrounding his conversion, written many decades following the event, Dhanjibhai Nauroji described the atmosphere on the appointed day: "The newspapers gave warning that Dhanji was today about to leave the religion of his fathers, and enter that of strangers. They violently denounced the baptism, and the Parsis moved heaven and earth to prevent it" (Nauroji 1909: 47). The reaction of the Parsi community to the baptism of one or two members of the community reflected the threat Indian communities felt from the Christian missionaries. As Panikkar notes, concern among Indians was most strongly expressed whenever religious beliefs and practices were perceived to be violated by the administrative measures undertaken by the colonial state or by the evangelizing efforts of Christian missionaries (Panikkar 2002: 82). The court case exposed the dichotomy of Indian and Western cultural outlooks as regards religion, the individual, and the community. The Parsis placed the collective's interest over that of the individual in matters of religion and community identity. Traditional society apprehended the concept of the individual as part of a complex family, social, and community network that was interdependent and from which identity derived. In this schema challenge to or weakening of one element imperiled the whole (Fruzzetti *et al.* 1982). Traditional society saw Christian conversion not as a matter of personal conscience and choice, as understood in Western culture, but rather as a challenge to the right to regulate and safeguard the community and caste. The dichotomy of cultural outlooks was expressed by P. C. Mazoomdar, noting that in seeking converts the missionary revolutionized, denationalized, and alienated Indians from their kith and kin (Mazoomdar 1883: 42–3). As a minority community, the Parsis remained particularly concerned to safeguard their religious identity within the larger Indian and colonial social environments. In appealing for the writ of habeas corpus and the prosecution of Wilson, the Parsis became the first Indian community in western India to challenge legally Christian missionary activity.

The Parsis employed both traditional and non-traditional mechanisms in defense of their cultural outlook and in response to the missionaries. The Parsi Panchayat effectively took the lead in the court case. The Panchayat was the internal government of the Parsis in Bombay. It was composed of the prominent Parsis of Bombay, both lay and clerical. The Parsi Panchayat adjudicated disputes among Parsis, issued regulations on Parsi social and religious matters, and was effectively the regulator of what it meant to be a Parsi. It also meted out punishment to Parsis, which could include barring a Parsi from the use of the social and religious facilities of the Parsi community (Davar 1949: 20–48; Palsetia 2001: 65–104). The Panchayat had pressured Heerjeebhoy Dadabhoy to go to court (*OCS*, June 1839: 222, 229). Dhanjibhai's conversion had compromised his uncle's situation among the Parsis, as by Parsi norms he had not supervised his nephew sufficiently to prevent him converting. Heerjeebhoy Dadabhoy had much to fear in having "permitted" the baptism of his nephew to take place. Parsi social codes of the nineteenth century called on all Parsis to maintain community norms, and sanctions fell as much on the relatives as on a Parsi malefactor. Displays of corporal punishment against those who breached community standards were not uncommon, and reflected the extent of Parsi social control (Davar 1949: 20–48; Jeejeebhoy 1953: 295–323; Palsetia 2001: 65–104).

Traditional society's harshest response often fell on the convert. The difficult situation of the Indian convert to Christianity has been well documented; and most often resulted in social ostracism from other Indians (Potts 1967: 207–244; Carson 1991: 125–55). The impulse to harm or forcefully to reconvert also formed part of traditional society's response. The *Bombay Gazette* of 10 May 1839 noted rumors during the conversion episode that the Parsis intended to seize Dhanjibhai and reconvert him. Dhanjibhai Nauroji described the scene at the courthouse on 16 May:

> When our carriage reached the Court House numbers of Parsis sprang forward and surrounded us; some seized the wheels of the carriage; some laid hold of the horses; and one violently wrenched open the

> carriage window, and began to try and drag me out . . . When we reached the verandah of the Court, the crowd was so thick that we could not get to the staircase. Two constables, one on either side, took me by the hand. The others pushed the people back with their fists. It was with the utmost difficulty that we succeeded in reaching the room where the trial was to be held.
>
> (Nauroji 1909: 51–2)

Even following the court case, Dhanjibhai describes plans by Parsis:

> One of these devices was to set fire to Dr Wilson's bungalow, and destroy us all. Another was to poison the food that came to us from the bazaar and so kill us. Yet another was to surround the bungalow night and day, in the hope of getting hold of us as we came out, so that they might carry us off to murder us. Such plans as these they, attempted to carry out, but all their plots failed and their hopes were frustrated.
>
> (Nauroji 1909: 57)

According to Dhanjibhai, life continued to be difficult for him and other Parsis for some time following their conversions (Nauroji 1909: 61–3).

The Parsi response to threaten the convert reflected the strength and weakness of their position. Ostracism, maltreatment, or forceful reconversion of a convert was intended to be a deterrent to community members. Invariably, some Parsi converts to Christianity went into the ministry, reflecting the select company that accepted them among their ranks (Nauroji 1909: 63). The weakness of traditional society's stance was also evident in the conversion case. Traditional society's unwillingness to appeal to the convert to return to the caste community in any heartfelt way foreclosed opportunities for reconciliation. Dhanjibhai notes Parsi attempts to influence him back to the community that ranged from promises of bribes and goodwill if he returned to threats of harm if he did not; all of which convinced him of the insincerity of their stance: "If I would come back to them, the Parsi leaders were willing to receive me, and would not let me be harmed in any way . . . but would on the contrary make me prosperous to the best of their power" (Nauroji 1909: 55–7). Traditional society, it appears, placed less value on the welcome return of a convert to the community than the deterrent value of harsh measures for future defections from the caste community. Most importantly, traditional society's unwillingness to appreciate the impact of Christianity on Indians proved a weakness. Dhanjibhai's willing baptism exploded both the Parsi conviction that conversions could not be dreamt of and the idea that culture-contact could be one sided. Dhanjibhai's embracing of Christianity indicated that society's pull on its members was not inviolable, that Indian converts made rational choices, and that Christianity could also engender a sense of community and social belonging among Indians (Frykenberg 2003: 9).

The predicament of the convert was at the heart of the conversion controversy yet had become secondary to the clash of cultural positions. Both Western and Indian cultural outlooks coincided in seeing the convert as "victim" whether of a benighted Indian religion whose sole purpose was to control its members or of a predatory Christianity that sought to chalk up converts. In reality, the convert could be victim and instrumentality of both cultural outlooks. For Wilson, the conversion of an Indian from a proud and influential community like the Parsis satisfied pious ambitions, inter-denominational competition, and was a visible return on the investment of the Scottish church in India: "The probable usefulness of [my] work in leading [Indians] to inquiry and in assisting future missionaries . . . ha[s] led me to come to the determination on the subject" (Smith 1879: 127). Equally, Dhanjibhai's conduct had greatly upset the Parsis, as he had renounced the religion of his birth and committed sacrilege in deprecating its symbols (*OCS*, June 1839: 216, 220, 249). The return of Dhanjibhai to the Parsis would have satisfied Parsi religious, social, and political concerns to be seen as a small but proud religious community capable of regulating and addressing the concerns of its members. By contrast, the feelings of the convert seem removed from the tumult around him. Unlike the motives of those around him, Dhanjibhai notes just one motive: "I had not left the Parsi religion for any transitory worldly advantage, but for quite a different purpose—to obtain the everlasting life which Christ bestows" (Nauroji 1909: 56).

The Parsis' response to the conversion was also novel among Indians, as they employed the apparatuses of the colonial milieu to combat the missionaries. The court case was a measure of how comfortable the Westernizing Parsis felt with British institutions in India. In initiating the court case, the Parsis were hopeful of a favorable response from the colonial environment, with which they had long held an advantageous collaborative relationship (White 1987). British power in Bombay had benefited the Parsis. In 1787, the British recognized the Parsi Panchayat as the internal government of the Parsis in Bombay. The Bombay government consistently supported the authority of the Parsi Panchayat in disputes between it and community members (Blue Pamphlets of 1843: 14–15, 57). Furthermore, the Parsis' loyalty and socio-political ties to the British had gained the Parsis privileges and concessions over the years. The *Hulkuru and Vartman* of 21 November 1832 commented that: "We state as our conviction that in all of India there is not a caste as clever as that of the Parsees; and so likely to be of service to the Government in times of difficulty or war" (GD 1832 17/262: 142). Prominent Parsi figures enjoyed close personal friendships with British businessmen and officials (Karaka 1884, 2: 113; Wacha 1920: 685, 763). The court case, consequently, was meant to confirm and exploit the "special relationship" the Parsis believed existed between the community and the colonial administration.

The Parsis' arguments in court presumed on Parsi–British ties. Dhanjibhai Nauroji notes the presence of the leaders of the Parsi Panchayat at the courthouse on 16 May: "At 11 o'clock the Judge took his seat, and then the twelve heads of the Parsi Panchayat, wild with excitement, made their appearance also. The Judge gave these gentlemen seats of honor with himself (Nauroji 1909: 52). Through affidavit testimony, the Parsis held their right to safeguard their community from the missionaries to be inviolable. They had placed their children in mission schools with a clear belief that their religion would not be interfered with. The Parsis maintained that unless Dhanjibhai was returned to his uncle "a great and unexpected inroad has been made upon their privileges as hitherto believed to be secured and guaranteed to them by the British laws" (*OCS*, June 1839: 233–5). With their appeal, a legal case became a case of political import. At the same time, underlying the Parsis' representations in court were assumptions based in traditional society. The Parsis asked the Supreme Court to recognize the precedence of their tradition. The Parsis' response to conversions was representative of the social, cultural, and religious norms that informed Indian society. Parsi tradition rested on internal rationalizations that gave tradition its shape and meaning: the need to safeguard the collectivity. It was based on normative understandings and conventions of conduct unique to the Parsis of India. It could appear seemingly irrational and superstitious to the uninitiated or, like Dhanjibhai, those who chose not to adhere to its norms. The prosecution reiterated Parsi sentiments: "What the Parsis deposed to as to their own customs, must be taken as matter of fact, and could not be displaced by the learning of any European gentleman . . . It was not in the minds of a people, who clung to their religious usages with such tenacity, to suppose the possibility of a conversion" (*OCS*, June 1839: 261). The prosecution's remarks encapsulated the Parsis' cultural outlook, and the understanding the Indian community sought to form an accommodation with British colonialism.

The limitations of the Parsis' stance, however, were exposed in the conversion case. In appealing to British justice the Parsis became subject to a new set of normative standards; ones which were inherently indifferent to Parsi political influence. The case raised the ambiguity of Parsi law under British jurisdiction and pitted the customs of an Indian community against the evolving traditions of English law and religious freedom in India. Dhanjibhai Nauroji's claim to be of age to determine his own fate put the weight of English common law against Parsi tradition. As the first conversion case to come before a court in western India, the Supreme Court examined all the relevant issues the Nauroji case purported to raise. These issues included: the welfare of the child and whether illegal restraint was employed on him by the missionaries; the character of the guardian seeking the writ of habeas corpus; the age of the child and his maturity in determining his fate; and the interests of parties other than the guardian in the case (Perry 1853: 107). The onus, however, fell on the Parsis to show that their traditions did not conflict with the welfare of Dhanjibhai. The Parsis had given scant consideration to the rights of the individual, as their foundational assumption was the interests of the community. This proposition proved inconsistent with the evolution of imperial and legal ideologies in British India. Furthermore, the Parsis were compelled to substantiate the very content of Parsi law. Their inability precisely to define Parsi law before a British court presented a difficulty. The laws of the Parsis were unlike those of other communities in India. No extant law code or body of substantive Parsi law existed. Parsi law was a combination of religious custom, Panchayat rulings, Parsi adaptations of local Indian usage and customs, and from the nineteenth century the application of English law (JD 1863 20/143: 215–29; Palsetia 2001: 197–200).

The Parsis' difficulties were characteristic of Indian adjustment to the rise of imperial power and ideology in India (Choksey 1971: 424). To state the case another way, the Parsis' difficulties represent colonialism's inability to fully understand Indian norms, resulting in the precedence of British norms over Indian ones. Thus, it was easy and convenient for defense counsel in the conversion case to question the basis for the court to consider the Parsis' claims:

> But it is pretended that there is some peculiarity in the Parsi law, which is to control the decision in this case . . . My Lord, *What is Parsi law?* Since I have been in Bombay, I have never been able to discover it; and I have never met with any man who had . . . At one time, as it suits their purpose, they adopt a custom analogous to Hindu law, at another time they adopt a custom analogous to English law. I think I may insist that the Parsis have no law, by which any decision can be formed regarding this case.
>
> (*OCS*, June 1839: 255–6)

The defense claimed the Parsis' sole goal in seeking the writ of habeas corpus was to reconvert Dhanjibhai, which was a proposition untenable in British justice (OCS, June 1839:259–60).

British justice ruled against the Parsis. Justice J. W. Awdry felt that he could not grant the writ of habeas corpus. Awdry was not satisfied that granting the writ and returning Dhanjibhai to the custody of his uncle contrary to his wishes was in the best interests of the boy. Heerjeebhoy Dadabhoy's motives were deemed suspect and lacking in parental feeling. John Wilson was cleared of any charges, as Awdry found Dhanjibhai had not been kept against his will. The Supreme Court deemed Dhanjibhai not of legal age to be free from paternal control but as sufficiently mature to decide his own company. Dhanjibhai immediately chose to go with Wilson (*OCS*, June 1839: 255–6). The Parsi decision was the first of many conversion controversies that came before the Indian law courts. By mid-nineteenth century, however, the rights of converts of majority or near-majority age where they could reasonably make independent decisions not to be returned to parental control were established in India (Perry 1853). Dhanjibhai was deemed of sufficient age and discretion to "own" himself.

The judgment in the conversion case had a tremendous effect on the entire Indian community of Bombay. The Parsis felt the greatest unease, as they believed their right to safeguard their community was in question. At the same time, the unintended consequence of the conversion case was to stimulate Parsi solidarity, and a process of reassessment within the Parsi community commenced as to the best means to safeguard its interests. A three-pronged response emerged that included: political agitation, intercommunity cooperation, and educational reform. Parsis joined by Hindus and Muslims drafted a petition styled the "Anti-Conversion Memorial," containing 2,115 signatures. It called on the Bombay government to move the Legislative Council of India and subsequently Westminster to ban missionary activities in India, to set twenty-one as the legal age of majority for children to decide their religious rights, and to disadvantage converts in terms of their rights of inheritance and parental authority. Ironically, the Government of Bombay rejected the petition, citing British policy not to interfere in Indian community matters (*OCS*, June 1839: 275; Wilson 1847:150–3).

More significantly, the second consequence of the conversion case was to activate intercommunity cooperation in Bombay. The expression of this cooperation was the withdrawal of Indian children from mission schools. The Parsis took the lead in removing all pupils from the General Assembly's Institution and other mission schools (*OCS*, June 1839: 280–1). The Marathi and Gujarati Hindu communities, impressed by the Parsi resolve, followed suit and removed their children from the schools (*Bombay Courier*, 24 May 1839). The Indian actions captured the attention of the public, especially the missionaries, as the Christian-run newspaper *Friend of India* of 30 May 1839 noted the strange religious confederation of "Parsees, Hindoos, and Mahommedans uniting for mutual defense against the proselytism of Christians" (*OCS*, June 1839: 287). The boycott had a tangible effect, as Dhanjibhai Nauroji noted the drop in the numbers of Indian pupils in the General Assembly's Institution from 500 to between 60 and 70 (Nauroji 1909: 59; *OCS*, February 1840: 57).

The withdrawal of Indian children from mission schools, at the same time, did not diminish the Indian regard for Western-standard education. In the immediate aftermath of the verdict, Indians placed their children in government-run schools that did not impart Christian education. Most importantly, the conversion judgment spurred Indian efforts to create an independent educational system. In 1849 the Sir Jamsetjee Jejeebhoy Parsi Benevolent Institution opened, which was the first indigenous educational institution in western India modeled on Western lines (Mody 1959: 133). The boycott of mission schools was reminiscent of traditional methods employed by Indians, particularly the commercial classes, in striking or closing down daily activities to protest grievances. In the context of the opposition to the missionaries, traditional Indian responses gained a novel significance. A sense of unity was forged among Indians disturbed over Christian conversions and the general intrusion of imperial ideologies in Indian society. In some measure, the intercommunity cooperation of mid-century, the rise of religious identity, and even nascent nationalism had their roots in the politics of the Parsi conversion case.

The controversy over the Parsi conversion case had not lessened the progress of Christian proselytism in Bombay. Indeed, the case in the Supreme Court of Bombay had legally redounded in the missionaries' favor. The conversion case, at the same time, was a precedent in Indians legally challenging Christian proselytism in Bombay, and the Parsi example was the model for other communities' resistance to conversions by way of the law courts. The tension between indigenous culture and imperial ideology continued to define cases of religious conversion. In the Parsi conversion case, Western normative standards and law trumped Indian caste and community norms. In future cases, British justice benefited Indians, particularly where parental rights over minor children were involved. At the same time, British legal standards determined the outcome (Perry 1853; *OCS*, December 1843: 597–624).

Conclusion: accommodation and resistance

One of the most important effects of Western culture on indigenous tradition was to promote internal debate over the modernization of tradition. The missionary influence intensified this process. Whereas missionaries could unite Indians in defense of tradition, they also added to sharpening religious debate and the gulf between Indian conservatives and modernizers (Oddie 2003: 178–81). In Bombay, debate cut across caste and socio-economic status and increasingly turned to interpreting custom amidst the pressures of the colonial milieu.

The Parsis of Bombay felt the attractions and challenges of the colonial environment in the first half of the nineteenth century. The Parsis accommodated or reconciled aspects of their normative standards to Western ideologies, particularly as related to the modernization of cultural outlooks. At the same time, they assumed a posture of resistance to Western religious, cultural, and legal norms at variance with their fundamental beliefs and traditions. Finally, the process and degree of Indian accommodation or resistance to Western ideologies would determine the nature of internal transformations of indigenous traditions. The Parsis are a paradoxical example of the preservation of identity amidst general assimilation. Their community identity and solidarity increased under colonialism, just as they were socialized to British political and cultural values, including using British models to safeguard core aspects of Parsi identity. For example, as English law confronted the ambiguities of Parsi law, the Parsis were compelled to standardize, codify, and modernize their personal laws. The result was the Parsi Laws of 1865 on intestate succession, inheritance, marriage, and divorce, which combined aspects of Parsi custom and current English law (Palsetia 2001: 197–226).

By the twentieth century, this process of Parsi accommodation to Western and modernizing ideologies made the Parsis the most Westernized, if not secularized, community in India.

At the same time, Parsi accommodation to Western ideologies did not entail acceptance of Christianity or religious modernization. The counterpart to the Parsis' social assimilation was the retention of an orthodox religious tradition. If the colonial milieu accelerated social change among the Parsis, it also intensified resistance both to external and internal religious changes. The Parsis continued to oppose Christian conversion (*Rast Goftar*, 9 October 1864). Significantly, resistance to Christianity in the above case spurred modernization. Parsis attended educational academies, started their own indigenous educational system, and made education a marker of identity. Parsi religious education was also improved, which included the better training of priests in new seminaries or *madressas*, and the religious education of youths. Educated Parsi reformers emerged at mid-century who would fundamentally reorient Parsi perceptions of their religion and heritage while leaving unaffected Parsi religious practices. By the twentieth century pluralism of religious outlook emerged, as Parsis adhered to liberal and orthodox religious viewpoints and began to debate vigorously community issues, including whether an endogamous community should permit conversion. Religious pluralism, however, did not translate to innovation in ritual or observance. The legal judgment in the conversion case had forestalled any internal religious debate on the proper rituals necessary to readmit converts to the religion (see Mody 1959: 126–57). Furthermore, the Parsis' endogamous nature rendered any debate on conversion unnecessary until the beginning of the twentieth century, when a famous convert case concerning the admission of a non-Parsi to the community reopened the issue, and resulted in the most divisive of community debates (Dhalla 1999: 122–35; Palsetia 2001: 226–76). Parsis maintain remains a progressive social identity grafted onto an orthodox religious identity.

The Parsi conversion case was one significant example of a process of self-inquiry and introspection taking place among many Indians in the nineteenth century. Indians' use of traditional and colonial norms in defense of their interests was indicative of their vigorous and creative engagement with Western ideologies. Ultimately, in the Parsi case the legal loss increased efforts to protect religious identity while continuing the process of cultural assimilation and social modernization already underway, illustrating the attractions and challenges the colonial environment posed in the nineteenth century.

References

Ballhatchet, Kenneth (1957) *Social Policy and Social Change in Western India, 1900–30*, Oxford: Oxford University Press.

Bayly, C. A. (1988) *Indian Society and the Making of the British Empire*, Cambridge: Cambridge University Press.

Blue Pamphlets of 1843 (1843) Bombay: Department of Archives, Government of Maharashtra.

Carson, Penelope (1991) "Missionaries, Bureaucrats and the People of India, 1793–1833," in Nancy G. Cassels (ed.) *Orientalism, Evangelicalism and the Military Cantonment in Early Nineteenth-Century India: A Historiographical Overview*, pp. 125–55, Lewiston, NY: Edwin Mellen Press.

Choksey, R. D. (1971) *Mountstuart Elphinstone the Indian Years, 1796–1827*, Bombay: Popular Prakashan.

Conlon, Frank F. (1999) "Visnubawa Brahmachari: a Champion of Hinduism in Nineteenth Century Maharashtra," in A. R. Kulkarni and N. K. Wagle (eds.) *Region, Nationality and Religion*, pp. 130–56, Mumbai: Popular Prakashan.

Davar, Sohrab P. (1949) *History of the Parsi Punchayet*, Bombay: New Book Company Limited.

David, M. D. (1975) *John Wilson and His Institution*, Bombay: John Wilson Education Society.

Dhalla, Homi B. (1999) "Contra Conversion: The Case of the Zoroastrians of India," in Christopher Lamb and M. D. Bryant (eds.) *Religious Conversion: Contemporary Practices and Controversies*, pp. 115–35, New York: Cassell.

Dirks, Nicholas B. (1992) "Introduction," in N. B. Dirks (ed.) *Colonialism and Culture*, pp. 1–25, Ann Arbor: University of Michigan Press.

Fruzzetti, Lina, Akos Östör, and Steve Barnett (1982) "The Cultural Construction of the Person in Bengal and Tamilnadu," in Akos Östör, L. Fruzzetti, and S. Barnett (eds.) *Concepts of Person: Kinship, Caste and Marriage in India*, pp. 8–30, Cambridge, MA: Harvard University Press.

Frykenberg, Robert Eric (2003) "Introduction," in Robert Eric Frykenberg (ed.) *Christians and Missionaries in India: Cross-Cultural Communication since 1500*, pp. 1–32, Cambridge and New York: Eerdmans Publishing Co. and RoutledgeCurzon.

General Department [GD] (1858) vol. 81/550, Bombay: Department of Archives, Government of Maharashtra.

General Department [GD] (1832) Vol. 17/262, Bombay: Department of Archives, Government of Maharashtra.

Greenfield, M. Rose (1888) *Education Versus Evangelization*, Amritsar.

Gupchup, Vijaya V. (1993) *Bombay: Social Change, 1813–1857*, Bombay: Popular Book Depot.

Hall, Gordon (1836) *Anecdotes of the Bombay Mission for the Conversion of the Hindoos*, London: Frederick J. Williamson.

Ingham, Kenneth (1973) *Reformers in India, 1793–1833*, New York: Octagon Books.

Irani, Pheroze K. (1963) "The Personal Law of the Parsis of India," in J. N. D. Anderson (ed.) *Family Law in Asia and Africa, Studies in Modern Asia and Africa, no. 6*, pp. 273–300, London: Allen and Unwin.

Jeejeebhoy, J. R. B. (1953) "Communal Discipline among the Bombay Parsees in Olden Times," in *M.P. Kharegat Memorial Volume*, vol. 1, pp. 295–323, Bombay: K.R. Kama Oriental Institute.

Judicial Department [JD] (1863) vol. 20/143. Bombay: Department of Archives, Government of Maharashtra.

Karaka, Dosabhoy Framjee (1858) *The Parsees: Their Manners, Customs, and Religion*, London: Smith, Elder and Co.

—— (1884) *History of the Parsis*, 2 vols. London: Macmillan and Co.
Lederle, Matthew (1976) *Philosophical Trends in Modern Maharashtra*, Bombay: Popular Prakashan.
Masani, R. P. (1960) *Dadabhai Naoroji*, New Delhi.
Mazoomdar, P. C. (1883) *The Oriental Christ*, Boston: George H. Ellis.
Mitchell, James Murray (1852) *In Western India: Recollections of My Early Missionary Life*, Edinburgh: D. Douglas.
Mody, Jehangir R. P. (1959) *Jamsetjee Jejeebhoy: The First Indian Knight and Baronet*. Bombay, Maharashtra: Evergreen.
Naik, J. V. (1995) "The Seed Period of Bombay's Intellectual Life, 1822–1857," in Sujata Patel and Alice Thorner (eds.) *Bombay: Mosaic of Modern Culture*, pp. 61–75, New Delhi: Oxford University Press.
Nauroji, Dhanjibhai (1909) *From Zoroaster to Christ: An Autobiographical Sketch of the Rev. Dhanjibhai Nauroji the First Modern Convert to Christianity from the Zoroastrian Religion*, Edinburgh: Oliphant, Anderson and Ferrier.
Oddie, Geoffrey A. (2003) "Constructing 'Hinduism': The Impact of the Protestant Missionary Movement on Hindu Self-Understanding," in Robert Eric Frykenberg (ed.) *Christians and Missionaries in India: Cross-Cultural Communication since 1500*, pp. 155–82, Cambridge and New York: Eerdmans Publishing Co. and RoutledgeCurzon.
Palsetia, Jesse S. (2001) *The Parsis of India: Preservation of Identity in Bombay City*, Leiden: E.J. Brill.
—— (2003) "'Honourable Machinations': The Jamsetjee Jejeebhoy Baronetcy and the Indian Response to the Honours System in India," *South Asia Research*, 23/1 (May): 55–75.
Panikkar, K. N. (2002) *Culture, Ideology, Hegemony: Intellectuals and Social Consciousness in Colonial India*, London: Anthem Press.
Perry, Erskine (1853) *Cases Illustrative of Oriental Life: Decided at H.M. Court at Bombay—The Application of English Law to India*, New Delhi: Asian Education Services (reprint 1988).
Potts, E. Daniel (1967) *British Baptist Missionaries in India, 1793–1837: The History of Serampore and Its Missions*, London: Cambridge University Press.
Rana, Framjee A. (1934) *Parsi Law: Embodying the Law of Marriage and Divorce and Inheritance and Succession Applicable to the Parsis in British India*, Bombay: A.B. Dubash.
Smith, George (1879) *The Life of John Wilson*, London: John Murray.
Wacha, D. E. (1920) *Shells from the Sands of Bombay: My Recollections and Reminiscences, 1860–75*, Bombay, Maharashtra: K.T. Anklesaria.
Wesleyan Methodist Missionary Society [WMMS] (1890) *The Missionary Controversy: Discussion, Evidence and Report*, London.
White, David L. (1987) "Parsi in the Commercial World of Western India, 1700–1750," *Indian Economic and Social History Review*, 24/2: 183–203.
Wilson, John (1833) *A Lecture on the Vendidad Sade of the Parsis Delivered at Bombay on the 19th and 26th of June, 1833*, Bombay.
—— (1847) *The Doctrine of Jehovah*, Edinburgh: William Whyte and Co.
Young, Richard Fox (1981) *Resistant Hinduism: Sanskrit Sources on Anti-Christian Apologetics in Early Nineteenth Century India*, Vienna: Institut für Indologie der Universität Wien.

33

CULTIVATION, CHRISTIANITY AND COLONIALISM

Towards a new African genesis

John L. Comaroff and Jean Comaroff

Source: J. De Gruchy (ed.), *The London Missionary Society in Southern Africa*, Cape Town: David Philip, 2000, pp. 55–72.

> Civilization . . . must originate and depend on the culture of the ground.[1]

Two things stand out clearly in the archives of the early LMS mission to the Southern Tswana, two motifs in the encounter between Europeans and Africans along this colonial frontier. The first was the evangelists' realisation that, if they were to 'civilise' and convert 'the Bechuana', they would have to begin on the terrain of everyday life.[2] In so far as it became evident that this 'native' world was not to be remade simply by smashing its idols and icons, or by means of theological argument, the civilising mission could not depend on didactic means to achieve its ends; Moffat, Livingstone and their brethren might have preached and prayed but, in the pragmatic matter of re-forming Southern Tswana, they vested most of their hope in a prosaic theatre of Protestant industry which set forth the mundane signs and practices of European modernity.[3] This show-and-tell was based on the faith that the Africans would be unable to resist the temporal benefits of civilisation;[4] being childlike and impressionable, they would learn readily by imitations.[5]

The second recurring motif in the encounter was the stress of the first generation of LMS emissaries on things material. For evangelists and abolitionists everywhere, as has often been remarked, commerce was the very antithesis of, and an antidote to, both slavery and primitive communism. In this regard, the missionaries took for granted that consumption and production were all of a piece;[6] that, tied together by the market, they were indissolubly bound up in the workings of advanced capitalist economy and society. If

Tswana were to gain entry into the modern Christian commonwealth, therefore, both – production and consumption – would have to be recast, each in relation to the other and both from the ground up. Hence Moffat's insistence that civilisation originated in 'the culture of the ground',[7] that civility had its genesis in the soil. Hence, also, Campbell's

> Till the present system shall undergo a complete revolution, [the Tswana] can never abound in grain, nor can it become an article of trade. The land that may be fairly claimed by each nation is capable of supporting more than twenty times the population, if the ground were to be cultivated . . .[8]

The 'complete revolution' was meant to be at once conceptual and concrete: a matter of culture and agriculture, of moral and material economics. In this essay, then, we look at the campaign of the colonial evangelists to revolutionise patterns of production among Southern Tswana, a campaign that shaped a new field of social and cultural distinction, a field of classes-in-formation. We trace out both the short-term impact of the mission outreach and the historical processes of the long run – sometimes surprising, often ambiguous, inevitably complex – which it unleashed.

The civilising mission and the culture of the ground

> There, on their pious toils their Master, smil'd
> And prosper'd them, unknown or scorn'd of men,
> Till in the satyr's, haunt and dragon's den
> A garden bloom'd, and savage hordes grew mild.[9]

The centrality of agriculture to colonial evangelism owed much to the close ties, sociological and imaginative alike, that bound the LMS missionaries to the displaced peasantry at home. In their theology, too, cultivation and salvation were explicitly associated[10] – *vide* Mark 4:3–32 – so that agrarian labours-and-scenes saturated spiritual discourses and vice versa. Thus, for example, Robert Moffat, professional gardener and farmer's son, told his readers how he and his brethren 'put their hand to the plough', preparing the arid African earth for a 'rich harvest of immortal souls'.[11]

But cultivation was not linked only to salvation. In the culture whence the missionaries came, it was connected to colonialism[12] and civilisation as well. Hear, again, Moffat: 'Let missionaries and schoolmasters, the plough and the spade, go together, and agriculture will flourish, the avenues of legitimate commerce will be opened . . . whilst civilisation will advance as the natural effect, and Christianity operate as the proximate cause of the happy change.'[13] Nor was this a fleeting vision. If anything, it grew more elaborate over time. At his ordination in Edinburgh in 1858, John Mackenzie, an LMS evangelist of the next generation, said: 'As to civilisation and the temporal interests of the people, I conceive that I am furthering both when I preach the Gospel . . . In order to complete the work of elevating the people, we must teach them the arts of civilized life . . . We must teach them to till their own land, sow and reap their own crops, build their own barns . . .'[14]

Given the African concern with cattle, it may seem odd that the early LMS missionaries seldom included pastoralism in their plans; indeed, they were notably silent on the salience of livestock in the Kingdom of Christ. This did not arise from an ignorance of the value of animals to Southern Tswana. Quite the contrary. The stress on the civilising role of cultivation, rather, flowed from an axiom as old as English colonialism itself: that sedentary agriculture was both a cause and an effect of civility and advancement.[15] 'The way to increase the productivity of both land and people in Africa', the Rev. W. C. Willoughby was to say in the 1920s, 'is to cultivate each by means of the other.'[16] Cattle and culture, ranching and refinement, on the other hand, seemed almost inimical. As long as it had no fixed abode, or did not accompany settled tillage, pastoralism excited visions of shiftless, shifty people wandering about sans property, propriety or a proper place in the body politic.

At the turn of the seventeenth century, Edmund Spenser had blamed the barbarity and belligerence of the 'wild Irish' on their semi-nomadic, pastoral pursuits.[17] In order to allay the threat they posed to England, and to bring them within the compass of its civilisation, they had to be made to live settled agrarian lives. The Bible might have spoken of a chosen people who herded at least as much as they tilled – a point not lost on Tswana – but, to the modernist imagination, evolution depended on cultivation. Like their contemporaries in England, the evangelists absorbed the axiom that agriculture made men peaceful, law-abiding and amenable to education. At once civil and servile. To wit, Livingstone blamed the lawlessness of 'the Boers' on the fact that they 'were more a pastoral than an agricultural race'.[18] Not for naught had Spenser warned an imperially minded England that all who live 'by [the] kepinge of cattel . . . are both very barbarous and uncivill, and greatly given to warr'.[19] From a purely evangelical perspective, too, mobile populations posed problems: Philip is reputed to have told his colleagues that, as long as people had 'no settled homes . . . it was easy for them to desert the means of instruction'.[20]

If the rude savage was to be refined, then, it would be tillage that would do it. As he sowed, nurtured and harvested his crop – all with enlightened techniques and tools – the Tswana yeoman would make himself anew. This agrarian revolution, as was often said, was intended to enable African converts to yield enough of a surplus to tie them through trade to Christian Europe.[21] The dark continent would become a 'fruitful field', a rich rural periphery of the metropolitan centres of civilisation abroad.[22] No more would it call forth the 'agonizing tears of bereaved mothers', the 'orphan's cry, the widow's wail'.[23] Not, that is, if their menfolk were restored to them as true husbandmen. Even in its most materialist moments, *circa* 1820–50, the civilising mission continued to ring, not merely of biblical pastorale, but also of romantic naturalism and abolitionist moralism. It also invoked many of the old tropes: Africa, savage and infantilised, devastated by bondage, its women dispossessed and its men laid low – all awaiting the white saviour to regenerate them so that they might once more harvest their own crops and 'sit under their own vine and fig-tree'.[24]

No matter that Tswana had never suffered slavery. In Nonconformist narratives of South Africa, *difaqane* served much the same imaginative function as did the slave trade further north. This period of upheaval in the 1820s, usually ascribed to the rise of the Zulu state and the subsequent predations of displaced warrior peoples,[25] had ostensibly robbed 'the native population' of its moral manhood and its capacity for self-determination – and had left it 'unprotected . . . without missionaries'.[26] Some of the peoples of the interior were badly disrupted by the turmoil of the times, yet most Southern Tswana had managed to grow some crops in temporary places of refuge, to recoup their herds, and to keep intact their political communities. But such subtleties went largely unspecified in the stark stories penned by the Christians. These told of soil strewn with blood and bones by 'warlike, wild tribes', of a wake of women and children left to wander about, barely surviving on wild fruit, locusts, and 'garbage'; even, added the horrified evangelists, on human flesh.[27] Here too we detect traces of the vision of Africa-the-Fallen, of its children as foundlings.

Such accounts did more than merely confirm the pained portraits of darkness and degeneracy circulated by philanthropists. They also justified the resolve of the clerics to 'train [the Bechuana] up in the habits of civilized life';[28] in particular, to teach them how to farm productively in the fields of God.[29] Hence the essential gesture in the imagery of colonial evangelism, one to which we keep returning:[30] the missionary, a black male convert at his back, tending an 'abandoned mother' in the bush. In most versions she is being handed the 'bread of life', long a European symbol of cultivated food – and, not coincidentally, the stuff of the sacrament and icon of the gospel.[31]

African agriculture: seeing, seeding, sowing, reaping

Superstition, socialism and agrarian aesthetics

The civilising mission might have portrayed Africa as uncultivated, even empty. But the early evangelists nonetheless expatiated on Tswana economy, taking care to underscore how much had to be erased or remade. Much of their commentary was a discourse of absence: it focused on the lack of ways and means taken for granted in European culture. Most notable were references to the want of money, itself assumed to be indispensable to an advanced economy; of markets or anything beyond rude barter;[32] of civilised crops, especially refined species of maize, corn or vegetables;[33] of irrigation[34] and all but the simplest implements and technologies;[35] of privately owned land;[36] and of any capacity for invention or self-improvement by the exercise of reason.

Still more striking than this discourse of absence, however, was the discourse of irrationalities that permeated mission texts and conversations: Tswana economy was portrayed as a repertoire of illogical, impractical, improvident means and ends. A noteworthy feature of this discourse was its obsession with the aesthetics of agrarian production and material life. Some evangelists were quite open in their disapproval of the 'disorderly' way in which Tswana put nature to use 'without regard to scenery or economy',[37] destroying the 'park-like appearance of the landscape'.[38] Many of them harped on the preference, in cultivation and construction, for the 'sinuous' and 'arc-shaped' over neat rectangular forms. Philip once likened Dithakong and its environs to an 'ant-hill',[39] but Mackenzie was most direct: '[Tswana] gardens and arable land', he lamented, 'are laid out in a manner which offends the eye of a European.'[40] Even as late as 1899, Willoughby claimed that Africans could not plough a linear furrow.[41] At issue here was not merely taste violated. Beauty, after all, was truth. And truth – in the form of rational, universal knowledge – opened the path from savagery to civility.

Again, the idea that civilisation expressed itself in squares and straight lines ran to the core of contemporary British culture. In *The Return of the Native*, for instance, Thomas Hardy contrasted the wildness of Egdon Heath, *circa* 1840–50 ('an uncouth . . . obsolete thing') to the 'modern' countryside 'of square fields, plashed hedges, and meadows watered on a plan so rectangular that on a fine day they look like silver gridirons'.[42] No wonder that Philip, in praising the progress of the Kuruman mission (*circa* 1825), chose to stress the 'taste' with which its rigidly rectilinear garden had been laid out. There was, he stated, 'something very . . . pleasing' in this place of 'rising beauty'.[43] By contrast, Tswana terrain was much less attractive, much less productive, much more like farmstead Ireland, *circa* 1815, which Halévy was to dismiss, stereotypically, as 'a disgusting sight . . . [there being] no vestige of a garden'.[44] But the putative irrationalities of Tswana economy were described in terms that went far beyond the aesthetic. Among the things most commonly remarked by the missionaries were (i) the prevailing politics of production; (ii) the unenlightened 'selfishness' of Africans; (iii) the savage 'superstition' and 'enchantments' said to saturate their material lives; and (iv) their 'unnaturally' gendered division of labor.

The Nonconformists regarded it as utterly beyond reason that chiefs should orchestrate the rhythms of agrarian production; that the annual cycle should be punctuated by collective rites; that cultivation should be seen to depend on a ruler providing spring rains to inseminate the land; that women should not be permitted to plant before the sovereign 'gave out the seed-time'; that each activity, from sowing to harvest, should begin with tributary toil on royal fields.[45] The evangelists might have asserted, throughout the century, that 'traditional' authority was on the wane, but they continued to complain about it. As late as 1900, Brown was to write, from Taung, that the local chief was still the channel 'through which the rain flows to the people. He still exercises the right of saying when the ploughing shall begin . . . Corn in some gardens may be fully ripe, and even wasting from ripeness; but the owners of these gardens dare not reap till the chief has given permission . . .'[46]

Another obstacle, equally irrational in the eyes of the Europeans, was summed up by Willoughby: 'The African', he declared, 'lives a simple socialistic life, subordinating his individuality to the necessities of the tribe.'[47] Hence his antipathy to 'healthy individualistic competition', to the maximisation of time and effort, and to self-possessed industry.[48] Tswana might have been crafty and duplicitous,[49] suspicious and jealous of each other.[50] And they might have been 'keenly alive to their own interests';[51] 'under the influence', Hodgson put it, 'of [the] selfish principled'.[52] But this was quite different from the kind of rational individualism that persuaded people to 'submit to the labour of cultivating the ground'.[53]

The allusion to rationality here picks up another theme in the discourse. Many of the evangelists spoke of the need to rouse the Tswana capacity for 'reason', thereby to counter 'savage superstition'. The latter, held Philip, flowed 'from confused ideas of invisible agency'.[54] These led the Africans to believe that successful cultivation depended on the observance of taboos; that female pollution could cause the clouds or the crops to abort; that the fertility of fields might be increased by the ministrations of medicine men.[55] Much to the annoyance of the missionaries, moreover, such beliefs had been placed as impediments in their way: 'Till lately, the missionaries have not been allowed to use manure for their gardens. It was formerly universally believed that if the manure were removed from the cattle-kraals, the cattle would die . . .'[56] From the standpoint of the LMS, the enchantments of savagery had yet another insidious side to them: they encouraged an irrational conservatism in the face of challenge and change, making Tswana reluctant to accept the most obvious proof of the superiority of civilised practices. Added Philip: 'it was against their practice to deviate from the customs of their ancestors. When urged to plant corn, &c., they used to reply that their fathers were wiser than themselves, and yet were content to do as they did: they also regarded every innovation as an insult to the memory of their ancestors.'[57]

But it was the division of labour – in particular, gendered relations of production – for which most opprobrium was reserved. Lichtenstein might have likened Tswana agriculture to that of the 'Mosaic forefathers'.[58] But the evangelists found the comparison altogether less happy. To them, African economy was 'topsy-turvy'.[59] The men, whose herds were tended by youths and serfs, looked to be lazy 'lords of creation':[60] their political and ritual activities were mostly invisible to the European eye, their leather work did not appear to be work at all, and their exertions as smiths went largely unremarked. Women, on the other hand, seemed to have been forced into what was properly male labour, building and thatching, digging and 'scratching' on the face of the earth like 'beasts of burden'.[61] Missionary accounts of women's toil were always tinged with disgust, and were often highly emotive. Mary Moffat observed that

> The women cultivate all the land, build the houses [and so on] . . . while the men . . . never condescend to lend a helping hand to them. Picture to yourself tender and gentle women . . . bending their delicate forms, tearing the rugged earth . . . dragging immense loads of wood over the burning plains, wherewith to erect their houses, thus bearing the double weight of the curse on both sexes.[62]

What is more, rather than till lands tied to the family home, they were sent to far-off fields for weeks on end, where they remained beyond the reach of the mission. Occasionally, too, existing relations of production sparked conflicts between the sexes that discomforted the Nonconformists and gave the lie to patronising talk of 'tender and gentle women'. Speaking of Batlharo, Wookey wrote, in 1873:

> the gardens belong to [females]. The cattle, sheep and goats belong to the men. Well, amongst the Badaro it seems some of the cattle had been troublesome in wandering into the gardens and destroying the women's corn. Accordingly, they determined to kill everything found in their lands. In doing this they were following a law to that effect made by a Batlaro chief; and for which also some women were cut off the church by Mr. Moffat. Numbers of cattle were hacked and killed in a most horrible manner, the women of the church taking a prominent part in the work.[63]

It is obvious why such incidents should have distressed the evangelists: hacking beasts to death, like toil far from home, was not their idea of a proper feminine activity. No wonder that the emissaries of LMS, like their Wesleyan counterparts, were so intent on confining Tswana women to house and hearth; on domesticating them, that is, within a world divided – socially and sexually – into public and private domains, sites of production and reproduction.

The missionaries were under no illusions that this would be easy. One had already learned as much at the turn of the nineteenth century, when he tried to set up a station along the Kuruman River. His request met with resistance from the local chief who, having heard news of Khoi converts to the south, feared the civilising lessons of the LMS.[64] Why? Because, the ruler insisted, they led to indigence. Twenty years on, Broadbent reported that Tswana listened to much of what he had to say but not to his advocacy of European agriculture: its division of labour 'opposed their ideas and habits'.[65]

He might have added that, to the Africans, European practices appeared as 'topsy-turvy' as did theirs to the evangelists.

The missionaries did not always see quite how unreasonable was their own discourse of irrationalities; quite how full it was of counter-examples which gave a very different impression of Tswana economy. For instance, Campbell recalled that, while travelling across Rolong country in 1820, he came upon 'several hundred acres of Caffre corn; many of the stalks were eight and nine feet high, and had a fine appearance'.[66] Earlier, he and his companions had passed 'extensive corn-fields on both sides of the road'. Giving voice to the observation of one group of Africans by another, the evangelist said that the Khoi in his party, themselves familiar with agriculture in the Cape Colony, 'were amazed at the extent of the land under cultivation, having never seen so much before in one place'. Moffat also offered counter-evidence, albeit of a different sort. The Kuruman station, he noted, was situated on 'light sandy soil, where no kind of vegetables would grow without constant irrigation'. By contrast, he added, 'native grain . . . supports amazing drought'.[67] In this light, claims for the superiority and rationality of European techniques must have puzzled Southern Tswana. All the more so since whites from the Colony kept entering their territory to purchase their surplus cattle and, later, crops. But their discourse of irrationalities is largely irrecoverable, save, as we have said before, from traces scattered inchoately between the lines of colonial texts – and from a variety of practical reactions, some of which we shall come upon as our account unfolds.

Metamorphosis and disenchantment

Livingstone once wrote of a young chief who, eager for the benefits of civilisation, wanted him 'forthwith to commence the work of metamorphosis by means of enchantments'.[68] In fact, the first generation of evangelists did resort to a technology of enchantment – involving, among other things, their almost magical gardens – to impress the power of their presence on the Africans. But when it came to reconstructing Tswana life over the longer run, the LMS missionaries were to speak repeatedly of disenchantment. They would advocate the 'rational' expenditure of effort, introduce such 'scientific' instruments as the plough, and try to replace the 'superstitious' practices of the vernacular ritual calendar with the secular logic of commodity cultivation.[69]

Given the recent misfortunes of British agriculture, the LMS might have given careful thought to its export to Africa. According to Lord Ernle, 1815–37 was 'one of the blackest periods' in the history of English farming.[70] Some have questioned Ernle's now dated account,[71] but it is clear that the state of the rural economy was highly (if variably) precarious, the condition of small farmers being the most disastrous of all.[72] And this notwithstanding the profitable years of the Napoleonic Wars, the zeal of the king and aristocracy for agriculture,[73] the modernist rhetoric of enclosure, growing mechanisation, and the rise of High Farming.[74] Goldsmith had been prescient – unwittingly, no doubt – when, in 1770, he had rhymed: 'But a bold peasantry, their country's pride/When once destroy'd, can never be supplied.'[75] Perhaps it was this sense of loss, this nostalgia for the British yeomanry on the part of the missionaries,[76] that fuelled the horticultural dreams and schemes for Bechuanaland. Like some clergymen at home,[77] they had great faith in the capacity of a garden allotment and hard work to raise up the rude.

The agrarian revolution began modestly, centring itself on the mission garden, that master symbol of civilisation and Britishness.[78] For a while this square of red earth stood between the evangelists and hunger.[79] More than merely a source of food, it was also an exemplary appropriation of space[80] and an icon of colonial evangelism. Represented as a triumph over rank nature, it usually began as a vegetable patch, grew to include an orchard, and was expanded by the addition of fields of wheat and other crops; in short, not exactly a garden at all in contemporary English terms, but paradise to those who saw, in the creation of the first mission stations, a new African Genesis.[81]

In the ideal scenario, this Act of Creation was played out, from the first, on land bought from Africans. The gesture of purchase was itself meant to have two effects: (i) to establish missionary agriculture on a bedrock of civilised practices, thereby (ii) to make it a palpable example to the Tswana of those very practices. In an optimistically spirited letter, dated 21 November 1823, Mary Moffat wrote: 'each individual is to purchase his own ground, the missionaries having set the example.'[82] While some chiefs agreed to 'sell' plots, the evidence suggests that they made little sense of this kind of transaction. 'The particulars of . . . sale', Livingstone confessed, 'sounded strangely in the ears of the tribe[s].'[83] As Archbell implies, the major effect of such 'particulars' seems to have been reflexive:[84] they persuaded the Europeans, who sometimes feared for the security of their venture, that the mission was firmly implanted on soil it actually owned.

Aside from being vital to the self-sufficiency of mission stations and households, the cultivation of the garden enacted the first scenes in the narrative of reconstruction. On this ground, the evangelists performed the principles of material individualism: the creation of value by means of self-possessed labour and scientific technique, the conversion of nature into private property, and the accumulation of surplus through virtuous toil. Robert Moffat's son John makes it clear that his father spent a good part of his daily round as a 'farmer'.[85] The point, he implied, was to provide a visible model for Tswana to mimic. No wonder that Edwin Smith was to describe Moffat sen. as 'one of God's gardeners'.[86] Or that George Thompson, a Cape merchant who spent time at Kuruman in 1823, should have admired 'the example [the LMS had] set before the natives of industry in cultivating the ground'.[87]

Perhaps the most vivid insight into this didactic spirit is provided by Samuel Broadbent, a Wesleyan whose agrarian pursuits paralleled closely those of the LMS missionaries:

> I and my colleagues had each enclosed a plot of ground, which we had of course, in English fashion, broken up and cleared of the roots of weeds, and then sown with Kaffir corn, which we had obtained from the natives, and with sweet cane and various kinds of beans, also melons and pumpkins . . . What became the subject of wonder and remark was the notorious fact that these and other vegetables grew much more luxuriantly, and were more productive, in our grounds than theirs. One day a number of respectable natives came to ask the reason of this difference . . .
>
> My first answer was, 'Your idleness.' 'How so?' they inquired. I said, 'You have seen that we have dug the soil ourselves; you leave it to your women. We dig deep into the soil; they only scratch the surface . . . Our seed, therefore, is protected from the sun and nourished by the moisture in the ground; but yours is parched with the heat of the sun, and, therefore, not so productive as ours.' I added, 'Work yourselves, as you see we do, and dig the ground properly, and your seed will flourish as well as ours.[88]

Here, in sum, were the four crucial lessons of the sacred garden. The first presented itself as purely technical: that successful cultivation required digging 'deep into the soil'. This was only possible with the plough – not with the hoe, which the Europeans saw as exotic and primitive.[89] As we have said, the fabrication of 'refined' implements, in public at times, was an essential piece of the evangelical drama everywhere in Bechuanaland.[90] These objects became iconic of Christian cultivation at large, at once instruments and symbols.[91] Thus S. M. Molema, Tswana historian and a devout Methodist, was to write that 'no single machine . . . [did] so much for the civilisation of the Bantu than the plough'.[92] Like the irrigation ditch and the well, agrarian appliances were as vital to the realisation of the Nonconformist worldview as they were to the material basis of the mission.

The second lesson lay in enclosure after the 'English fashion'. As Broadbent intimates, everything began with the founding of a fenced plot, itself the core of the imagined African farmstead of the future.[93] Within its rectangular confines lay the promise of great productivity, which is why Moffat was so delighted, in the late 1820s, to report that Kuruman – where 500 acres were brought under irrigation and neat smallholdings began to appear – had become an exemplary 'Goshen to the surrounding country'.[94]

The third lesson involved the contrast between idleness and labour. The evangelists sought by their own efforts to show that self-possessed toil was the key to a decent life. Profitable agriculture, connoting the cultivation of 'civilised' crops for both home consumption and the market, depended upon it. The essence of this lesson was to be found in the Letter of Paul to the Thessalonians 3:9–10, often invoked in mission preaching: '[We] give you in our conduct an example to imitate . . . If any one will not work, let him not eat.' And in Timothy 2:2–6: 'It is the hard-working farmer who ought to have the first share of the crops.' This celebration of labour, as we shall see, was integral to the practical theology, and to the theology of practice, at the core of colonial evangelism: 'Work, the gospel of work, the sanctity of work, *laborare est orare*', to work is to pray, as Aldous Huxley would put it at a later date and in a quite different connection.[95]

But, and here was the fourth lesson, not all toil was the same. The world of work envisaged by the missionaries entailed an entirely new division of labour. The relative value of male and female exertions could not have been more clearly stated. 'Luxuriant' productivity, proclaimed Broadbent, demanded mastery over field and furrow, not scratchings on the soil. Like all the evangelists, he believed it 'of great importance . . . to lead the minds of the Bechuana men to agricultural pursuits'.[96] The corollary: that, while their husbands became breadwinners, housewives ought to be confined to such 'homely' tasks as cleaning, childcare, cooking and sewing. This invoked the same ideal of gentility that had enclosed bourgeois European women in the domestic domain. And, in so doing, it revealed a contradiction in the objectives of the civilising mission. On one hand, the clergymen dreamed of a free and prosperous African peasantry. On the other, their values, firmly rooted in the age of revolution in Britain, presupposed the social order of industrial capitalism centred on the urban, middle-class household. Few Tswana women were to be embourgeoised, of course. Quite the contrary. Many had eventually to earn their livelihood as domestic workers in European settler homes, their servitude offering a bitterly ironic commentary on the evangelical model for the African family. Others were compelled to seek employment in the colonial economy, or were forced back into the arid fields of subsistence agriculture. But this was still a long way off.

Re-actions of the short run: from mockery to mimesis

What were the first reactions of Southern Tswana to the evangelical onslaught on their material practices? It is clear that they did not immediately take the lesson which the LMS and the Wesleyans alike tried to convey; namely, that the abundant yields of 'modern' agriculture were the product of a particular regime of hard labour and enlightened technique. One early response, it seems, was to conclude that the bounty of the mission garden flowed from the innate potency of the whites themselves. Thus, for example, Seleka-Rolong men vied to have their wives sow fields beside those of the Methodists[97] because, we are told, they believed that the fertility of these fields would overflow into their own, that sheer proximity to the Europeans might afford access to their agrarian powers. Given time to observe British horticulture, however, and the tenacity of the Nonconformists in essaying their methods, Southern Tswana soon began to differentiate the alien means of production from the personal capacities of their owners.

A second reaction to the agrarian challenge of the mission issued mainly from Tswana women. As some of the implications of European practices became discernible, they began to resist them by interrupting irrigation routines, damaging dams and stealing the fruits of the garden.[98] Patently, if men took to the fields, it followed that their wives would lose control over agriculture and its harvest, the very things upon which rested the well-being of their houses. The evangelists might have regarded the lot of African females as unduly arduous, their productive labours as 'unnatural'. But there is no reason to expect that these women would have seen matters in the same light. From their perspective, the horticultural innovations of the LMS gave plenty cause for fear. With some justification, as it would turn out.

Pragmatic though this response might have been, it was also shaped by a cultural vision, by a sense of the proper connections among production, gender and human capacity.[99] For a start, intensive agriculture involved hitching the ox to the plough, bridging the gendered gulf between cows and cultivation – marked by a taboo against women handling beasts – that ran to the very core of the Southern Tswana world, *circa* 1820. Yet Tswana were remarkably open to innovation and the exchange of cultural knowledge, and so it is not surprising that the evangelists' methods should have elicited their attention. Or that some people would have begun to experiment with them. In August 1821, Moffat recorded 'Queen' Mahutu's efforts to expropriate a valley that he and his brethren had sown with corn.[100] True, he would have preferred her husband, Chief Mothibi of the Tlhaping, to take over the operation; and he was quick to complain that she misused the land, watering it in the heat of midsummer when moisture was scarce. Also, as we observed a moment ago, her actions might have had more to do with the effort of women to sustain control over cultivation than with a desire to become a progressive farmer, European-style. Still, for the LMS this was one of the first signs of success.

More were to come. Philip, who always took care to describe 'the progress which rational ideas had made', tells how Tlhaping cynicism gave way to comprehension. When, in the early days at Kuruman, his brethren began to cut their irrigation channel, the Africans were unimpressed:

> Until they saw the water running into the ditch, they deemed it impossible, and treated the attempt with ridicule. But, when they saw it completed, their surprise was as great as their former scepticism . . . The Bechuanas are, however, now convinced of their error; and some of them are leading out the water to make gardens and corn-fields on an inclined plane . . .

On his next visit, in the mid-1820s, Philip 'had the satisfaction to see [the chief], with his people, and other Bechuanas, applying to the missionaries for seed-corn to sow on the lands then under irrigation. In reference, also, to a promise of the missionaries to plough some land, and train a span of bullocks for him, he manifested considerable pleasure.'[101] This, for the LMS, was a breakthrough: men, including a chief, were evincing interest in animal-driven plough cultivation. Soon after, the Seleka-Rolong leader, Sefunelo, approached the Wesleyans working among his people for seeds, 'which he promised to sow'.[102]

Once the sparks of an agrarian revolution had been kindled, thought the evangelists, there was nothing to stop its catching fire. Or so it seemed in the late 1820s and 1830s. Thus, in 1828, Mary Moffat commented that 'nearly all our poor people have reaped good crops of wheat . . . and some maize . . . They also grow much tobacco, which they exchange for cattle, karosses, &c.' 'I am astonished', she added, 'to see what the willing earth yields in so short a time.'[103] Her sanguine husband, in a letter written on the same day, predicted that 'Next year the crop will be much extended, [and] the station will rise to some importance in a temporal as well as a spiritual point of view';[104] note, again here, the insistence on the simultaneity of the secular and the sacred. Equally auspicious reports came from the Wesleyans a few years on. In 1842, at Platberg, Cameron observed that 'numerous gardens . . . have lately been walled in', and brought under cultivation; at Lishuani, 'sixty large gardens [had] been enclosed, and upward of two thousand trees planted.'[105]

The economic revolution was further off than the Europeans suspected, however, and it was not to take the course they anticipated. Sites of agrarian 'progress' were very restricted at the time, being confined to the immediate surrounds of the mission stations – and to those Southern Tswana who fell within their sphere of influence. Also, as Shillington has noted, not all Bechuanaland was ecologically amenable to agricultural intensification.[106] Especially towards the arid west, people had little option but to rely throughout the century on their herds (and, to a decreasing extent, on hunting). And the region had yet to feel the full impact of settler expansion, of unsettled subcontinental conditions and of a mineral revolution.

Cultivation and class: transformations of the long run

There was a sustained ambiguity in mid-nineteenth century accounts of Southern Tswana reactions to mission agriculture: the evangelists spoke of a tendency to cling to custom and resist enlightened self-improvement, but they also suggested that the techniques of modern farming were making rapid inroads, that an agrarian revolution was imminent. This counterpoint was not born of witting misrepresentation. Some features of the Tswana world did not give way easily: the gendered division of labour, the separation of herding from cultivation, the polluting effect of women on animals, and the difficulties this raised for hitching the beast to the plough. Also, some people were less disposed or able to experiment with European technologies: only those with sufficient livestock could use ploughs, or profit from taking surpluses and trade goods to distant markets. In short, the immediate impact of colonial evangelism on Tswana agriculture was highly variable, and it was the extremes of this variability that are reflected in the ambiguities of mission texts. This, in turn, raises the obvious question: was there any pattern at all in the way in which European means of production took root and worked their social effects? The answer, we suggest, is to be found in complex processes of class formation and cultural distinction. Before we explore these processes, however, let us lay out a brief *histoire événementielle* of agrarian change during the middle and late nineteenth century. It will serve to demonstrate the variabilities of which we speak, and prepare the ground for an analysis of social and material reconstruction.

Passing seasons, eventful years

As we have said, the evangelists saw the reconstruction of Tswana material life to depend on the entry of men into plough cultivation: from this was supposed to follow the privatisation of the soil, the emergence of the nuclear family 'farmstead', the ascendance of cropping over pastoralism; in sum, the rise of a 'true farming class'.[107] Despite early mission reports of the adoption of European techniques, however, this transformation did not occur at once. It was only after *difaqane* had disrupted production, and the viability of hunting and foraging had begun to decline, that males began to take to the fields in earnest.[108]

Eventually the plough would displace the hoe everywhere, save *in extremis.* According to Mackenzie, this was owed entirely to the LMS evangelists at Kuruman: 'Under the supervision of the missionaries, the natives learned a higher agriculture, and exchanged the hoe of their own ruder garden work for the plough and the spade. What had been done at Kuruman was imitated by the natives elsewhere.'[109] In fact, it was not so much imitation as culturally tooled pragmatism that commended the plough to Southern Tswana. Its capacity to enlarge the scale and yield of farming in this dryland, unreliable ecology was soon noted.[110] Among Tlhaping, for example, the harvests of those who went in for intensive agriculture grew markedly in the late 1830s; before that, there had been only three ploughs in the Kuruman valley. After 1838, when a trader settled on the station to cater to the demand for British goods, there was a steady increase in the ownership of implements and wagons,[111] most of them bought from the proceeds of grain sales.[112]

As productivity rose, some Tswana communities became regular exporters of European cereals. In 1844 the Rev. J. Ayliff wrote that Dutch farmers near the Orange River were 'passing out of the colony with wagons . . . to purchase wheat of the Bechuanas'.[113] Local produce was also finding its way to more distant markets. We cannot know, of course, what precise proportion of Southern Tswana men actually moved into plough cultivation at this time. Many did not, or could not, and among those who did the size and success of farming enterprises was uneven. As far as can be told, many women continued, in the 1850s, to sow and reap as they had long done. According to Mackenzie, 'two styles of agriculture' prevailed in the region: the 'old' and the 'higher'.[114] Even as late as 1865, he said, few ploughs were to be found in many parts of the country. Most gardens were 'being cultivated in the old way by women with the hoe'.

When men did invest in intensive cultivation, they soon seized control over the crop. Women, however, were not banished to the domestic domain. Prosperous farmers might have had male servants and clients take over activities involving animals, but they left the rest of the burden to females. Even those who planted limited acreages, sometimes with borrowed beasts, relied on their wives, daughters and unmarried sisters for crucial tasks – and then sold the harvest on their own account. In short, to the degree that males entered the arable sector, the gendered politics of production were radically altered. What is more, distinctions of wealth and status greatly widened. Because it was only stock owners who could plough extensively, and because the plough yielded the largest returns, the rich became steadily richer. If they did not immediately become poorer, others benefited little from agrarian innovations.

If the uneven impact of European agriculture was already discernible in the 1840s, subsequent reports disclose its ever more equivocal effect. On one hand they spoke of the 'improvement' of farming in many areas. Mackenzie, for example, observed that, at Taung as at Kuruman, irrigated crops were being grown and sold with success.[115] 'Bechuana', he complained, could still not make a straight fence or furrow, but they had taken great strides in adopting modern means.[116] This had subverted the hold of custom: old forms of 'vassalage' were now disappearing, abetted by the breakdown of royal trade monopolies, and the authority of retrogressive rulers was on the wane.[117] But Mackenzie also recorded unhappier corollaries of reform[118] – among them, that the widespread use of guns, purchased from the proceeds of cropping, had so depleted the game population that hunting yielded almost nothing to those who still needed it; that, when drought and disease threatened the livestock economy, on which tillage increasingly relied, many people were forced to survive by 'picking' at the ground; that, with more pasturage being brought under cultivation, powerful families were gaining control of a disproportionate amount of land. Mackenzie might also have noted the first signs of the erosion caused by ploughs to earth whose shallow fertility was not everywhere well suited to them.[119] The material bases of both poverty and inequality were being reconstructed under the impact of European commodity agriculture.

By the 1870s, the decade that saw the onset of the mineral revolution and the growth of the diamond fields around Kimberley, the local agrarian economy had become even more polarised. Some Tswana were well placed to supply the Kimberley market with fruits, vegetables and cereals, and wagon owners also profited from selling wood to the diggings.[120] Of those who expanded their ventures during these years, most were royals who had adopted the techniques of cultivation and accumulation taught by the evangelists.[121] Others were commoners who, on becoming monogamous[122] and entering the church, had been given irrigable mission land. They procured the necessary tools, used 'modern' methods and reinvested their income in their farming enterprises. But the ideal of advancement through commodity production was realised by relatively few. Travelling in the back reaches of Tlhaping territory in 1873, Holub discovered that a 'good, useful plough' was a 'rarity', and that only a handful of families raised cereals or had 'any transactions at the Kimberley market'.[123]

Those who could not buy ploughs or irrigate their fields were steadily reduced to dependency. Many lost all access to productive land, which was taken over by their wealthier compatriots.[124] The latter set about indebting their less fortunate kin and neighbours;[125] so much so that, among Tlhaping, 'roughly two thirds of the formerly free, town dwelling population . . . succumbed to a clientship status' in the years after the discovery of diamonds.[126] Those in the middle made a sustained effort to continue farming on their own account, supplementing their incomes if necessary by hiring themselves out.[127] But drought and the destruction of natural resources were driving more and more people into the labour market by the late 1870s. While Southern Tswana were attracted to urban centres for many reasons, the flow was accelerated by the annexation of Griqualand West to the Cape Colony, which led settlers, speculators and administrators to disempower chiefs and dispossess their followers of land and stock.[128] Not all the LMS missionaries were upset that Tswana were being drawn into wage employment. A few even took pride in the fact that they had been so well prepared to enter the workforce, especially as skilled farmhands.[129]

Some chiefdoms were less fractured and straitened by agrarian transformations. For example, the Hurutshe at Dinokana, who retained only a small territory after Boers had expropriated their land, raised some 800 (200 lb) sacks of wheat in 1875. Having benefited from the extraordinary system of irrigation canals dug many years before by David Livingstone, they grew more maize, sorghum, melons and tobacco each year, and sold all surpluses 'in the markets of the Transvaal and the diamondfields';[130] their success, moreover, seems to have been spread evenly across the population. But this was an exception rather than the general pattern. More typical was the case of the Tshidi-Rolong, among whom it was the industrious Christian community at Mafikeng, established in 1857, that made most use of the methods of intensive cultivation. By contrast to the rest of the chiefdom, its citizenry prospered, largely from the introduction of European cereals and from marketing semi-irrigated maize to the Transvaal.[131] By 1877, this town, with its 'farmsteads' and 'enclosures', supported considerable plough agriculture, and the spacious, colonial-style houses of its richer residents signalled a level of wealth very different from that of the general populace.[132]

This process of polarisation was accelerated by external events. In the late 1870s, the Tshidi chief, Montshiwa, ousted the neighbouring Ratlou from lands that blocked his way to the diamond fields, declaring that he now grew 'corn for the markets to get money'.[133] The Ratlou, joined by Boer freebooters with designs on Tswana terrain, responded by driving Montshiwa out of Sehuba, then his capital. Retreating to Mafikeng,[134] he and his followers had their herds and crops looted, to the extent that the Tshidi came close to mass starvation.[135] In time the town recovered, but it never regained its past affluence – that much was assured by further territorial wrangling and settler violence, followed by British annexation (1885) and the imposition of taxes; by a series of ecological reverses; and by the shift of the industrial centre to the Transvaal goldfields. While the local economy did not collapse, most families had become dependent on the labour market by the early years of the new century. Only the wealthiest survived the crises with fortunes intact.

Elsewhere, too, the 1880s and 1890s were times of transition in Tswana communities. Surveying Southern Bechuanaland from the Kuruman station, the Rev. A. J. Wookey confirmed that there was little hoe cultivation any more, and that some of those who farmed commercially were doing very well. All this, he added, had positive implications: chiefs no longer enjoyed 'despotic' power; 'bushmen' serfs had largely disappeared; and women, servants and other bondsmen, like the poor and aged, '[held] a far higher position' than before.[136] Crisp agreed that the burden of a Tswana wife had been eased. But, he added, 'she has also lost her perquisite. The husband now apportions to her so much as is required for food; the rest is his to sell.'[137] Freed from the communal obligations and arrangements that surrounded female cultivation in the past, most husbands marketed as much as they could. Men of lesser means often sold small amounts to meet immediate needs and to invest in cattle and other capital goods, only to find themselves short of food and funds later. Hunger became so rife in many places that some rulers decided to regulate vending, as they were to do in the Bechuanaland Protectorate.[138]

Wookey, who did not mention the rampant marketing of crops, discussed other developments that obviously worried him. Due to the sale of wood the country had been denuded, worsening soil erosion. And, as noted earlier, wild beasts had disappeared. But, most of all:

> Work amongst the men has become more general; in fact, with many, it is the only means of subsistence . . . The land question has become the pressing one of the day here, and some of the chiefs, in order to get out of their difficulties, have been giving away land to Europeans to such an extent that it is a serious question whether there will be any land left for the natives to live upon . . . The country itself is capable of producing far more than it does at

> present. There are many fountains lying unused; and all are capable of doing very much more than they are at present . . .[139]

Two forms of pressure were working away at the infrastructure of local economies: the seizure of territory by settlers and the concentration of fertile land in the hands of ever fewer families. For most Southern Tswana, the conditions of production were not promising, and increasing numbers ended up labouring for wealthier neighbours, for whites, or as self-employed artisans.[140] A handful took refuge around the LMS missions, which rented plots to 'tenants',[141] and others managed to scratch out a subsistence. But many were dispossessed of the means of an independent livelihood. Matters took a general turn for the worse in 1896 with the rinderpest pandemic that decimated herds across much of southern Africa. In its wake followed famine and illness, not helped by the fact that, in the hope of containing infection, the government prevented 'the natives of Bechuanaland' from selling poultry and firewood at the diamond fields and from shooting game.[142] Both pastoral pursuits and cultivation would recuperate in time, but not fast and never fully.

The dawn of the new century, then, saw most Southern Tswana well on the road to poverty and dependency. Their reverses had not occurred *in vacuo*, of course, but were part of a broader process in which black South Africans were drawn into the dominion of colonial South Africa; converted, in large part, into what Parson has called a 'peasantariat'.[143] The story is familiar: how colonial capitalists and Christians, settlers and statesmen, despite differences among themselves, found common cause in inducing large numbers of Africans into wage labour; how tax Britannica, the seizure of property, the manipulation of agricultural prices and other blunt fiscal instruments combined to make them reliant on supplementary cash incomes; how all but the wealthy had to subsist on an uneasy mix of female peasant production and the income of low paid male jobs, both being necessary, but not sufficient, to nurture a family; how a regulated labour force was reproduced by women 'at home', the countryside being made to bear the cost of sustaining a rising proletariat; how, in all this, the political economy of black and white, rich and poor, agrarian and industrial South Africa was integrated into a single, tightly knit structure.

Notes

This essay is an abridged and amended version of Chapter 3 of Comaroff and Comaroff, *Of Revelation and Revolution*, II. We are grateful to Hylton White for undertaking the task of editing the chapter down to less than half its original size; it is from his draft that the present version has been produced.

1 This epigraph comes from Schapera (ed.), *Apprenticeship*, p.188.

2 See D. Chamberlin (ed.), *Some Letters from Livingstone 1840–1872* (London, 1940), p.115, on the 'daily labours' of an LMS evangelist in southern Africa c.1848.

3 For comparison of the daily labours of LMS evangelists with the everyday routines of nearby Wesleyan missionaries during the same period, see W. C. Holden (ed.), *Reminiscences of the Early Life and Missionary Labours of the Reverend John Edwards* (Grahamstown, 1886), p.93.
4 Schapera (ed.), *Apprenticeship*, p.116.
5 W. C. Willoughby, *Race Problems in the New Africa: A Study of the Relation of Bantu and Britons in those parts of Bantu Africa which are under British Control* (Oxford, 1923), p.255.
6 See Philip, *Researches*, I, pp.204f.
7 Schapera (ed.), *Apprenticeship*, p.188.
8 J. Campbell, *Travels in South Africa: Being a Narrative of a Second Journey*, II (New York and London, 1822), p.60.
9 T. Pringle, in London Missionary Society, *Missionary Sketches*, [October 1828] no. 43: South African Library, Cape Town; South African Bound Pamphlets, no. 54.
10 Comaroff and Comaroff, *Of Revelation and Revolution*, I, p.80.
11 Moffat, *Missionary Labours*, pp.500, 588.
12 R. Delavignette, *Christianity and Colonialism* (London, 1964), p.8.
13 Moffat, *Missionary Labours*, pp.616–17.
14 Dachs (ed.), *John Mackenzie*, p.72.
15 I. Schapera (ed.), *David Livingstone: South African Papers, 1849–1853* (Cape Town, 1974), p.76.
16 Willoughby, *Race Problems*, p.181.
17 J. Muldoon, 'The Indian as Irishman', *Essex Institute Historical Collections*, 3(267–89), 1975:275. Ironically, by 1815, says Halévy, Irish pastoralists were wealthier than those who tenanted 'tillage farms'. But the graziers were despised, both by their compatriots and by Halévy, for their uncouth ways: among other things, they allowed animals to run free in the kitchens of their 'absurdly luxurious' homes. See E. Halévy, *England in 1815* (New York, 1961), p.208.
18 Schapera (ed.), *Livingstone: South African Papers*, pp.75–6.
19 E. Spenser, 'A Veue of the Present State of Ireland' (1596), in A. B. Grosart, *The Complete Works in Verse and Prose of Edmund Spenser*, IX (London, 1882–4), p.235.
20 Macmillan, *Bantu, Boer and Briton*, p.76.
21 Dachs, *John Mackenzie*, p.72; Bundy, *Rise and Fall*, p.39.
22 S. Broadbent, *A Narrative of the First Introduction of Christianity amongst the Barolong Tribe of Bechuanas, South Africa* (London, 1865), p.204.
23 Moffat, *Missionary Labours*, p.613.
24 Ibid.; Comaroff and Comaroff, *Of Revelation and Revolution*, I, Ch. 3.
25 Ibid., pp.42ff.
26 Philip, *Researches*, II, p.146; Holden, *Reminiscences*, pp.83ff.; Moffat, *Missionary Labours*, p.435.
27 Broadbent, *Narrative*, p.71.
28 Ibid., p.98.
29 Moffat, *Missionary Labours*, p.613.
30 Comaroff and Comaroff, *Of Revelation and Revolution*, I, Plates 4a and 4b.
31 For a comment on the connection between consumer goods and ideological signs, with special reference to bread as a religious symbol in Christian sacrament, see V. N. Volosinov, *Marxism and the Philosophy of Language* (New York, 1973), p.10.
32 Campbell, *Travels in South Africa*, I, pp.139ff.
33 Ibid., p.178; Schapera, *Apprenticeship*, pp.187–8.

34 Moffat, *Missionary Labours*, p.285.
35 Livingstone, *Missionary Travels*, pp.215ff.; W. Crisp, *The Bechuana of South Africa* (London, 1896), p.16.
36 Campbell, *Travels in South Africa*, II, p.150; Holden, *Reminiscences*, p.87.
37 Moffat, *Missionary Labours*, p.330.
38 Broadbent, *Narrative*, p.63.
39 Philip, *Researches*, II, p.121.
40 J. Mackenzie, *Ten Years North of the Orange River: A Story of Everyday Life and Work among the South African Tribes* (Edinburgh, 1871), p.92.
41 Rev. Willoughby, no date, p.28.
42 T. Hardy, *The Return of the Native* (London, 1963), p.181.
43 Philip, *Researches*, II, pp.114–15.
44 Halévy, *England in 1815*, p.210.
45 Comaroff and Comaroff, *Of Revelation and Revolution*, I, pp.146ff.
46 J. Brown, Taung, 1900, 'Report for 1900: Ten Years Review'. CWM, LMS South Africa Reports, 3–1.
47 Rev. Willoughby, no date, [b].
48 J. Mackenzie in A. J. Dachs, 'Missionary Imperialism: The Case of the Bechuanaland', *Journal of African History*, 13, 1972:652.
49 Moffat, *Missionary Labours*, p.254.
50 Mackenzie, *Ten Years North*, p.402.
51 Livingstone, *Missionary Travels*, p.21.
52 R. L. Cope, *The Journals of the Reverend T.L. Hodgson: Missionary to the Seleka-Rolong and the Griquas, 1821–1831* (Johannesburg, 1977), p.157.
53 Philip, *Researches*, II, p.356.
54 Ibid., p.116.
55 Mackenzie, *Ten Years North*, pp.385ff.
56 Philip, *Researches*, II, p.116.
57 Ibid., p.118.
58 O. H. Spohr (ed.), *Foundation of the Cape (1811) and About the Bechuanas (1807)* (Cape Town, 1973), p.77.
59 Crisp, *The Bechuana*, p.16.
60 Moffat, *Missionary Labours*, p.505.
61 M. Kinsman, '"Beasts of Burden": The Subordination of Southern Tswana Women, ca. 1800–1840', *Journal of Southern African Studies*, 10, 1983:46. The use of 'scratching' to describe African hoe agriculture – with all its faunal resonance – was not uncommon in contemporary European writings, hence the title of M. L. Pratt's essay, 'Scratches on the Face of the Country', *Critical Inquiry*, 12, 1985:119–43. As far as we are aware, it appears, for the first time, in connection with the South African interior, in Somerville's diary entry for 1 Dec. 1801 in E. Bradlow and F. Bradlow (eds.), *William Somerville's Narrative of his Journey to the Eastern Cape Frontier and to Lattakoe 1799–1802* (Cape Town, 1979), p.139.
62 Philip, 1828, *Researches*, II, p.139.
63 A. J. Wookey, Kuruman, 24 Sept. 1873. CWM, LMS South Africa Reports, 3–1.
64 Bradlow and Bradlow, *William Somerville's Narrative*, p. 143.
65 Broadbent, *Narrative*, p.105.
66 Campbell, *Travels in South Africa*, I, p.177.
67 Moffat, *Missionary Labours*, p.285.
68 Chamberlin, *Letters from Livingstone*, p.203.
69 For a statement of the LMS vision of agrarian transformation in Africa written with a century of hindsight, see Willoughby, *Race Problems*, p.181. Although part of an essay on 'native education', this passage captures the

missionary perspective on material improvement among 'a race whose feet are on the lower rungs of progress'.

70 R. E. Prothero (Lord Ernle), *English Farming Past and Present* (London, 1912), p.312.

71 E. L. Jones, *The Development of English Agriculture, 1815–1873* (London, 1968), pp.10ff.

72 See, for example, Halévy, *England in 1815*, pp.220ff.

73 Ibid., p.224.

74 See J. Caird, *High Farming, under Liberal Covenants, the Best Substitute for Protection*, 4th edn (Edinburgh and London, 1849).

75 O. Goldsmith, *The Deserted Village*, 1st edn (NewYork: D. Appleton, 1857), p.13.

76 Comaroff and Comaroff, *Of Revelation and Revolution*, I, p.75.

77 G. S. R. Kitson Clark, *Churchmen and the Condition of England 1832–1885: A Study in the Development of Social Ideas and Practice from the Old Regime to the Modern State* (London, 1973), pp.168ff.

78 Much has been written on the symbolic centrality of the domesticated landscape in nineteenth-century European self-imaginings; although, as Darian-Smith reminds us, 'the garden is a complex concept with a constantly changing meaning', one that defies 'stable figural representation': E. Darian-Smith, 'Legal Imagery in the "Garden of England,"' *Indiana Journal of Global Legal Studies*, 2, 1995:397; see also 'Introduction', in W. J. T. Mitchell (ed.), *Landscape and Power* (Chicago, 1994). Our concerns here, however, are less with its conceptual archaeology 'at home' than with its transposition to Africa.

79 A. J. Wookey, *Chronicle of the LMS*, p.303.

80 M. Alloula, *The Colonial Harem*, trans. M. Godzich and W. Godzich (Minneapolis, 1986), p.21.

81 For an account of the development of the LMS mission garden at Kuruman, see Schapera (ed.), *Apprenticeship.* Broadbent, *Narrative*, pp.104ff., gives a parallel description of the first Wesleyan station among Tswana.

82 Schapera (ed.), *Apprenticeship*, p.111.

83 Livingstone, *Missionary Travels*, p.21.

84 J. Archbell, Platberg, 2 Sept. 1833. WMMS, South Africa Correspondence (Albany), 303.

85 R. U. Moffat, *John Smith Moffat C.M.G., Missionary: A Memoir* (London, 1921), p.14.

86 Smith, *Moffat.*

87 V. S. Forbes (ed.), *Travels and Adventures in Southern Africa*, I (Cape Town, 1967), pp.96–7.

88 Broadbent, *Narrative*, pp.104–5.

89 Livingstone, *Missionary Travels*, pp.215ff; Crisp, *The Bechuana*, p.16.

90 See, e.g., J. Archbell, Cradock, 23 May 1831. WMMS, South Africa Correspondence (Albany), 303.

91 Volosinov, *Marxism*, p.10.

92 S. M. Molema, *The Bantu, Past and Present* (Edinburgh, 1920), p.119.

93 Broadbent, *Narrative*, pp.104–5.

94 Northcott, *Moffat*, p.148.

95 A. Huxley, *Point Counter Point* (London: Flamingo, 1994), p.217.

96 Schapera (ed.), *Apprenticeship*, p.113.

97 T. Hodgson, Matlwassie, 12 Jan. 1824. WMMS, South Africa Correspondence, 300.

98 See, e.g., Schapera (ed.), *Apprenticeship*, pp.52, 71ff.

99 Comaroff and Comaroff, *Of Revelation and Revolution*, I, pp.144ff.
100 Schapera (ed.), *Apprenticeship*, p.23.
101 Philip, *Researches*, II, pp.118, 113–14.
102 Cope, *Reverend Hodgson*, p.206.
103 Schapera (ed.), *Apprenticeship*, p.292.
104 Ibid., p.290.
105 J. Cameron, Platberg, 26 Sept. 1842. WMMS, South Africa Correspondence (Bechuana), 315–121.
106 K. Shillington, *The Colonisation of the Southern Tswana, 1870–1900* (Johannesburg, 1985), p.18.
107 Dachs, *John Mackenzie*, p.110.
108 A. Wyatt Tilby, 'Some Missionary Pioneers in South Africa', in A. R. Colquhoun, *United Empire: The Royal Colonial Institute Journal* (London, 1967), pp.190–5; Shillington, *Colonisation*, p.17; Broadbent, *Narrative*, p.105.
109 Mackenzie, *Austral Africa*, II, p.341.
110 I. Schapera and J. L. Comaroff, *The Tswana*, rev. edn (London, 1976); Shillington, *Colonisation*, p.92.
111 Northcott, *Moffat*, p.148.
112 Moffat, *Missionary Labours*, p.605.
113 Broadbent, *Narrative*, p.106.
114 Mackenzie, *Austral Africa*, II, p.168.
115 Ibid.
116 Mackenzie, *Ten Years North*, p.70.
117 Ibid., pp.90, 131.
118 Ibid., pp.70ff.
119 N. Parsons, 'The Economic History of Khama's Country in Botswana, 1844–1930', in R. Palmer and N. Parsons (eds.), *The Roots of Rural Poverty in Central and Southern Africa* (London, 1977), p.128.
120 Shillington, *Colonisation*, pp.66ff.
121 See A. J. Wookey, Kuruman, 23 May 1884. CWM, LMS Incoming Letters (South Africa), 42–3–C.
122 Mackenzie, in *Ten Years North*, among others, notes that mission land was only given to monogamous men, p.70.
123 E. Holub, *Seven Years in South Africa: Travels, Researches and Hunting Adventures, Between the Diamond-Fields and the Zambesi*, I (Boston, 1881), pp.125, 120.
124 See J. Mackenzie, Kuruman, 17 Feb. 1882. CWM, LMS South Africa Reports, 2–1.
125 Comaroff and Comaroff, *Of Revelation and Revolution*, I, pp.140ff.
126 Kinsman, '"Beasts of Burden,"' p.39.
127 Shillington, *Colonisation*, pp.63ff.
128 Ibid., pp.99ff.
129 Mackenzie, *Austral Africa*, II, p.341.
130 Holub, *Seven Years*, II, p.22.
131 Ibid.,I, pp.278–82; II, p.22.
132 Ibid., II, p.13.
133 Shillington, *Colonisation*, p.129.
134 Z. K. Matthews, 'A Short History of theTshidi Barolong', *Fort Hare Papers*, 1, 1945:20.
135 A. Anderson, *Twenty-five Years in a Waggon: Sport and Travel in South Africa* (London, 1888), p.117.
136 Wookey, *Chronicle of the LMS*, pp.303f, 306.

137 Crisp, *The Bechuana*, p.17; See also J. Brown, Taung, 1900, 'Report for 1900: Ten Years Review'. CWM, LMS South Africa Reports, 3–1.
138 I. Schapera, 'Economic Conditions in a Bechuanaland Native Reserve', *South African Journal of Science*, 30, 1933:647.
139 Wookey, *Chronicle of the LMS*, pp.304–5.
140 See, e.g., A. J. Gould, Kuruman, 16 Feb. 1891. CWM, LMS Incoming Letters (South Africa), 48–1–B.
141 J. Brown, Kuruman, 28 May 1898. CWM, LMS Incoming Letters (South Africa), 55–1–C.
142 An anonymous letter to the *Diamond Fields Advertiser*, 23 Feb. 1897, objected to the government regulations. See also J. Brown, Kuruman, 5 Jan. 1899, 'Report for 1898, Kuruman'. CWM, LMS South Africa Reports, 3–1.
143 J. Parson, *Botswana: Liberal Democracy and the Labor Reserve in Southern Africa* (Boulder, 1984).

34

CATHOLICS IN PROTEST

Lower-caste Christianity in early colonial Madras

Aparna Balachandran

Source: *Studies in History*, (N.S.) 16 (2) (2000), 241–53.

Studies of lower-caste conversions in south India have largely concentrated on mass movements in the nineteenth and twentieth centuries initiated by Protestant evangelical missionaries.[1] The tendency has been to view this phenomenon purely as the rejection of an oppressive caste system and the acceptance of a more egalitarian Christian ideology. A shortcoming of this perspective is to see the adoption of Christianity purely in terms of missionary ideas and activities, to homogenize lower-caste 'converts' and to grant them very little agency, both in the process of conversion and in their effort to define their meaning of Christianity. This precludes the possibility of a deeper understanding of religiosity and religious self-perception as not 'given' but produced through social and cultural processes.

I will attempt to address some of these problems in my essay in which I have analyzed two Catholic church disputes involving 'outcaste' Paraiyar congregations in early nineteenth century Madras to throw some light on how religious self-expression as a community was inherently informed by, and embedded in, the dynamics of everyday life in a growing colonial city. Lower-caste voices were very much a part of the urban public sphere in the Madras of this period. Petitions, memorials, court cases and cultural performances reveal that the Paraiyars negotiated, dealt with and contested the often conflicting definitions of 'community' that were imposed on them by the state and the church.

I will also be concerned with Catholicism, whose largely acculturative ideology in south India was a far cry from the fiery anti-caste sentiments of most Protestant missions from the 1850s onwards. I seek to historicize the ideology of the Catholic Church in south India, analyze its functioning and explore the relationship of Christian Paraiyars with Catholic ecclesiastical authorities, with 'Heathen' Paraiyars, and with the state.[2]

We will see that Catholicism fostered the mixing and borrowing of religious traditions and beliefs; at the same time the attitude of the colonial state and the politics of representation, which privileged 'traditional' categories like caste, meant that the notion of a Christian community as imagined by missionaries and ecclesiastical authorities was invariably questioned. Did this mean that pre-colonial and early colonial India was characterized by the interpenetration and overlapping of communal identities? I shall argue that this was not necessarily true. Harjot Oberoi, for instance, comments on the inherent ambiguity about the issue of religious affiliation at that time.[3] In fact, the early nineteenth century saw the Paraiyars of Madras collectively identify themselves as Christians in a variety of contexts; it was only that their version of Christian truth was at variance with that of mission and church authorities. Invariably, projects that are looking for a history of communalism see in 'fuzzy' religious traditions a lack of a defined religious identity among believers. I will suggest that syncretic religious traditions in the case of the Christian Paraiyars of Madras did not necessarily reflect an indeterminate religious affiliation.

Two Church disputes in early nineteenth century Madras

In the year 1812, the Judge of the Supreme Court of Judicature at Fort St George received a 'humble' petition from 'all the Christian Pariahs residing at St Thomas Mount' complaining against the conduct of the Bishop of Mylapore and the Priest of the Portuguese Mount Church. The petition declared that these two men had, contrary to the 'rules and regulations' of the Catholic Church appointed a most unworthy character, a man named Rayahmundoo as the head of the Christian Paraiyars. The petitioners also claimed that the Bishop's orders to punish them by excommunication for refusing to comply with his decision was extreme and unjust. Since their appeals to him had fallen on deaf ears, they now turned to the British Government, 'their sole Guardian Angel and Protector in the Coast of Coromandel'.[4]

The Tamil notice of excommunication, which had been put up in the Mount Church by the Priest, certainly appeared unequivocal in its tone. 'We,' stated the notice, 'have turned them [the 'rebel' Paraiyars] out of the Church without granting them anything that pretends to it'. Further, for good measure, the Christians from the town and Camp had been asked to keep away from the 'rebels'—'neither receive them for any business whatever nor keep their conversation'.[5]

The reply from the government was swift—it made it clear that the office of headman was a civil one and consequently not one which the church had any authority to fill. It considered that 'the Native Christians' were not guilty 'of any crime against morality or religion' and it therefore recommended that the order of excommunication be repealed.[6]

A month or so later, an agitated Bishop of Mylapore was to send a series of extraordinary documents to the government, which were to throw some startling new light on the affair. It appeared that the 'Christian Pariahs' of San Thome were in fact trying to appoint a 'Heathen' Paraiyar, a man named Cauden Cooty, as their caste head. Cauden Cooty himself had sent a petition to the Bishop putting forward his claim to headmanship. This petition was jointly signed by 'Heathen', Catholic and Protestant Paraiyars.[7] Cooty was supported by a man named Philip who claimed to be the present head of the Paraiyars and who expressed his desire to work with the former.[8] Outraged, the Bishop pointed out that investigations by the Vicar had proven that Rayahmundoo had held the post of headman for twenty-five years, in which period he had been found to be both 'diligent and attentive'. It was clear to him that the actions of Philip, Cauden Cooty and their supporters obviously had motives other than the welfare of their fellow Christians. The shocked Bishop declared that while he had no wish to interfere with the 'cast affairs' of the Paraiyars, he could not possibly condone a 'Heathen' being allowed to manage church affairs and administer the sacraments. To appoint a Gentile as the head of Christians was 'entirely against religion and offensive to God'. Would 'Heathen' law allow for a Christian head?[9]

Paraiyar congregations in other parts of Madras were to similarly bother church officials by their un-Christian relationship with 'Heathens'. A second incident was to take place two years later when the Governor of Madras was to receive yet another petition, this time from 'all the Christian Pariars of the Great Parcherry of Madras' who belonged to one of the city's Capuchin churches. The petitioners claimed that nine men of their caste had, with the support of the Superior of the Capuchin Church, 'wrongfully' appropriated the position of caste headmen. Now the nine had taken over the key ceremonial positions in the church's chief festival, the 'Assumption of the Blessed Mary', and had been the ones to receive the 'betel and nut' which was the prerogative of headmen. Further, the petitioners also complained that the Superior of Madras had deliberately, 'maliciously, on purpose' induced the Superintendent of Police to punish all those protesting against the proceedings with impunity to prevent any kind of untoward incident. The petitioners, who strongly opposed this move, were made to pay a fine of 20 pagodas in lieu of corporal punishment. The fact that the Superintendent of Police was present with his retinue of peons meant that everybody other than the petitioners meekly obeyed the nine 'usurpers' for fear of being thrown into prison as 'riotous vagabonds'.[10]

The Christian Paraiyars therefore made a series of appeals to the government. The very first one wanted the Superintendent of Police to cease interference in the internal affairs of the caste. After all, they argued, there were already persons of authority, instituted by the Archbishop of Goa and sanctioned by the government to regulate church affairs. They demanded that the government ensure that the festival be conducted according to custom and under the supervision of the Bishop of Mylapore.

The Superior of Madras was to send the government a detailed reply to this complaint. 'All the Christian Pariars', he claimed, 'were men of low character, one being a drunkard and none with the power to interfere with ecclesiastical affairs'. In fact, since their conduct was so reprehensible that 'no spiritual punishment would suffice' the men had to be handed over to secular police authorities. Further, the allusions to the superior authority of the Archbishop of Goa were unwarranted since the church was in fact answerable to quite another jurisdiction, that of the 'Propaganda de la Fide'. The Superior firmly declared that he had no knowledge that the nine men referred to as 'usurpers' in the petition were anything other than what they said they were; if indeed they were impostors, the Superior would have no hesitation at all in having them punished strictly. His motives in the whole affair were completely transparent; his only intention had been to prevent the interruption of church festivals and to stop the hurling of insults at heads of caste, an extremely serious offence. As far he could see, the only aim that the petitioners had in asking the Superintendent of Police not to interfere in the church's internal affairs was to allow the former to violently disrupt the proceedings of the church.[11]

When commenting on the dispute, members of the Capuchin Brotherhood who generally oversaw the celebration of Catholic festivals in Madras made some extremely revealing observations on Paraiyar headmen in general. These men, according to the Brotherhood, were not to be trusted; in this particular church they had, over a period of twenty years allowed thefts to go unchecked, and instead used a great deal of church funds for bribery of various kinds. Thus, they purchased 'cakes and fruits' for 'Portuguese and European Gentlemen' and even more shockingly, 'saltfish and snuff' for Chinniah Moodeliar, an influential 'Heathen' head. Most importantly, they collaborated with Chinniah Moodeliar and the other 'Heathens' of the area to build a wall across the Christian charity bazaar from which taxes for the church were raised. This increased the size of the adjoining Hindu bazaar and seriously affected the amount of funds that could be raised for the Church.[12] Thus, for the Brotherhood, the question of the legitimacy of the various claimants to headmanship was unimportant. All Paraiyars were ultimately untrue to the Catholic faith and church—why else would they unite with 'Heathens' in activities that were detrimental to the church's well being?

Christian Paraiyars in a 'heathen' world

Let us first locate the two churches we are considering, both historically and geographically. British San Thome, adjacent to the 'native' town of Mylapore, originally belonged to the Portuguese. The fame of San Thome rested on its association with the apostle, St Thomas, who is supposed to have reached martyrdom there. The Portuguese, whose king had been granted the rights of 'Padroado' or patronage and control over dioceses in the East, set up a monastic establishment at San Thome in 1522; by 1579 it had been fortified and had several churches which were under the authority of the Bishop of San Thome or Mylapore and the Archbishop of Goa. An observer in 1662 was to comment that the churches in San Thome included two that were dedicated to St John and the Virgin Mary where the 'Mahometans and Pagans' were instructed. It is quite possible that the Mount Church referred to in the 1812 dispute was one of these and that there were Catholic Paraiyars in Madras as early as the sixteenth century.[13] Portuguese missionary energies flagged in the seventeenth century and the Vatican supplemented it by creating, in 1622, a new institution called the 'Propaganda Fide'. The Capuchin Churches of Madras, which were mostly manned by French friars at this time, came under its jurisdiction.[14]

Why would Christian Paraiyars desire a 'Heathen' headman? Why would Christian Paraiyar headmen conspire with 'Heathen' notables to the detriment of their church? A probable answer is that the boundaries between 'Hindu' and 'Christian' traditions and beliefs were amorphous enough in the early nineteenth century to see the formal religious affiliation of the heads of caste as immaterial. The St Thomas Mount itself was venerated by people of all classes and religions. Legend had it that when St Thomas struck a rock on the Mount with his cane, he produced a gushing stream of water which, when drunk with faith, had the power to cure diseases. People of all faiths would regularly come to avail of this miraculous cure. A 'curious mixed worship' mentioned as far back as Marco Polo's time had also been a phenomenon at St Thomas Mount. In 1771, the Mount Priest complained of Paraiyars forcing an 'elephant (Ganesh?) flag' into the Christian churches there. The flag was declared 'abominable to all Christians' and the 'mark of paganism'. The Paraiyars of the area had to take an oath before the Governor, Lord Pigot, that they would never repeat their actions.[15]

Other than San Thome's extraordinary history as a syncretic shrine, the similarities and continuities between indigenous and Christian, particularly Catholic, traditions in south India was quite remarkable. As in the case with medieval Europe, Catholicism tended to appropriate 'pagan' festivals and ceremonies. In fact, a recent history of Catholicism in south India has pointed out that this feature often made Company officials speak of Catholicism and Hinduism in terms that saw them as synonymous, citing one extraordinary example where the money to pay Catholic priests in Poona came not from the Ecclesiastical Department but from the 'Trust for Charitable Grants to Temples'.[16] At one level, Catholic acculturation was to result in the curious incorporation of 'native', essentially higher-caste, style in the public functioning of the missionaries. The most notorious example of this was, of course, the Jesuit missionary, Robert de Nobili in the seventeenth century who lived the life of a *sanyasi*, wearing a sacred thread, refraining from eating meat and following the principles of ritual purity.[17]

At another level, Catholic festivals and ceremonies were startlingly similar to those of Hinduism.[18] Early nineteenth century Madras was witness to a series of conflicts between different urban groups over the appropriation of symbols as well as questions of ritual precedence. Important amongst these were the great temple disputes of the time as well as the recurring street violence linked to Right and Left Hand caste disputes. Lower-caste feasts like the Capuchin Church's 'Assumption of the Blessed Virgin' were occasions with similar symbolic value. Public displays of pomp and ceremony became sites where questions of honour were negotiated; the issues of who would receive the 'betel nut and leaf' which were symbolic gifts in 'Hindu' ceremonies, and who would assume positions of importance during these occasions became all important. In particular, the position of the Hindu head at the apex of a hierarchical caste group was echoed in the importance given to the headman in the Catholic Church. As we have seen, it appears that for the Paraiyars he was central to the administering of the sacraments, a function that represented the essence of the Christian faith. He played a key ceremonial and ritual role in all the Church's festivals and represented the dignity and honour of the congregation. It is not surprising, therefore, that both the disputes we have been discussing were concerned with the legitimacy and behaviour of the heads of the Paraiyars.

The modus operandi and ideology of Catholicism in south India certainly encouraged the borrowing and appropriation of 'Heathen' traditions by the Paraiyars of Madras. However, it has to be kept in mind that the theory of *accomodatio* privileged Brahmanism as the general social model of Indian civilization. Nobili's, for instance, was a top-down view of Tamil culture and religion where low-caste practices were merely aberrations of the Brahmanical ideal. Thus, while the Paraiyars of Madras could emulate and borrow from the great Tamil temple festivals, bringing a lower-caste flag into a church was, as we have seen, frowned upon. Further, there was a clear distinction in the minds of Catholic ecclesiastical authorities between the appropriation of the ceremonial style of the 'Heathens' and allowing the latter to be centrally involved in church affairs. The shock which the Bishop of Mylapore expressed in 1812 over the prospect of having a 'Heathen' caste head exemplifies this sentiment. Catholicism, however tolerant of 'pagan' traditions, could never allow a 'Heathen' to be the leader of men who had converted to the Christian faith.

The urban space and the lower castes

By 1800, Madras had been transformed from a fishing village to a modern metropolis that was the seat of government in south India as well as being a major centre of trade and industry. The lure of urban employment as construction workers, scavengers, peons and domestic servants to the city's European population attracted large numbers of Paraiyars from the neighbouring countryside to Madras. By the middle of the eighteenth century, Paraiyars constituted 10 per cent of the city's population,[19] and by 1830, at least forty identifiable untouchable settlements existed within Madras.[20]

Since much of the employment that the Paraiyars found in Madras was considered impure and defiling by the rest of the city's population, the sense that the community was 'untouchable', and their identification in terms of more rigid and essentializing caste norms than in the 'traditional' agrarian context, must have been heightened.[21] In addition, the policies of the colonial state meant that categories like caste became an inherent part of the politics of representation as well as the most convenient way to deal with the 'natives'. The practice that was to gain momentum in the late nineteenth century—the attempt to create a rationalized political whole by defining communities on the basis of caste and kinship at the expense of the local and the familial—had already begun at this time. At the same time, upholding the principle of caste was a logical part of a nervous Madras Government's policy not to disturb 'local custom'.

As a result, the nineteenth century saw purely secular concerns investing positions like the heads of caste with a new significance that went well beyond the interests of a particular religious group. Paraiyar caste heads in Madras became employment brokers who were paid to provide servants to Europeans. Urban employment, even if 'defiling' was very often an escape for the Paraiyars, traditionally agricultural labourers, from a very hard existence on land. By 1790, the Board of Police had decreed that:

> the Masters of Palanqueen Bearers and other Tribes or Casts [*sic*] of Pariah Servants shall pay one Fanam monthly for each Servant to the Heads of the respective Casts . . . and out of the above Allowance the Heads of Cast shall each employ a Conicopilla, who shall keep a register of all such Persons employed. . . . Any person requiring a Pariah servant of whatever denomination shall apply to the Head of Cast, who shall provide the servant required.[22]

Thus, the tussles over the nomination of caste heads in the colonial urban space became those over the economic and social privilege that urban employment offered. For a people who stood on the lowest rung of Tamil society, these must have been extremely significant considerations. There is clear indication that every avenue that the city offered for social mobility was being explored; it is surely possible to see the Christian Paraiyars' purchase of 'cakes and fruits' for 'Portuguese and European Gentlemen' as attempts to forge links with the city's new elite who were both less conscious of caste differences and were the ones to provide employment, the key to upward mobility.

The opening up of new kinds of public spaces, the courts, petitions and memorials, made for a greater collective articulation of lower-caste demands and grievances. The series of Paracheri petitions that began to appear from the late eighteenth century onwards are particularly rich sources for the examination of the sensibilities of urban Paraiyars. As the 'native' or 'Black Town' began to grow at a rapid rate, civic authorities often began to encroach on Paracheris—the residential areas of the Paraiyars—in order to facilitate development. As a result, many of the Paraiyars began to petition the government to intervene in their favour. Written in the name of the headmen of the caste, these petitions used the rhetoric of the history of their loyalty and even of their sacrifices for their European employers as a negotiating instrument in their demands for government protection.

The Paracheri petitions are especially interesting because while they represented the public articulation of the collective attributes and demands of the Madras Paraiyars, they also reflected the deep-rooted experience of being a Paraiyar in Tamil society. In a 1780 petition for instance, the fact of being an outcaste was cited as a reason for state protection: '. . . Your Petitioners are of the meanest Cast, and in case of troubles . . . if your Petitioners should be dispossessed of their Houses and the said Ground . . . no other cast will entertain them in their Houses within the bound edge. . . .'[23]

The Paracheri petitions also reveal the traditional importance of land in the consciousness of an essentially landless people. The reverence with which Paracheris were treated and the notion that within its bounds the Paraiyar was all powerful was reflected in the fact that even Brahmans were not allowed to enter them. If they did so, dung was thrown on their heads and they were driven out.[24] The assertion of territorial sovereignty and the exclusivity of the Paracheris gave all Paraiyars, regardless of religion, a physical space in which the highest in society were denied access, just as the Paraiyars themselves were disallowed from Hindu 'sacred' spaces.

Moreover, the interaction between 'Heathen' and Christian Paraiyars was considerable at this time. The project of large-scale Christianization of the Paracheris was to begin only a few decades later when large-scale Protestant propaganda was to take the lower castes by storm. Print culture in the form of handbills, tracts, pamphlets and cheap Bibles, as well as public preaching and reading during fairs and festivals, in market places and streets, and the setting up of schools and other Christian associations resulted in 'corporate' or mass conversions. This wave of conversion was encouraged by the strength of Protestantism's anti-caste ideology. Protestant missionaries were also to conduct anti-Catholic campaigns particularly because they saw the latter's toleration of caste and 'Heathen' practices as abominable. In our period, however, the formal lines of distinction between different kinds of Christianity appear to have been neither understood nor maintained: it is significant that the petition sent to the Governor in 1812 was signed not just by Catholic but Protestant Paraiyars as well.

Life in a Madras Paracheri, therefore, encouraged the spillover of everyday life into the realm of religion. Caste headmen did not merely administer sacraments, they stood for the opportunities for social mobility that the city had to offer and presided over residential spaces. It is in this context that we can grasp the significance of Cauden Cooty's petition to the infuriated Bishop of San Thome who could not understand why a man seeking a religious post should talk so much of inessentials and 'impertins'—'family affairs, jewels and the processions of weddings in Tamil streets'.[25]

Religious debate and the Company

Upholding the principle of caste was not just a way of ordering 'native' society; it was a logical part of a tentative Madras Government's policy in the early nineteenth century not to disturb customary practice. Missionary journals of the time commented bitterly on the fact that the Company went out of its way to provide both physical and material assistance to 'native' ceremonies and customs. Rev. Rogers, touring Madras in the late 1830s was aghast to find that it was the Company which paid for the oil which lit the lamps in the temples of the city;[26] equally astonished was a missionary who found that the 'native merchants' of Madras intended to persuade the government to direct the Collectors of various districts to assist the procession of Hindu holy men through their areas.[27] The Paraiyars must have known that their appeals to the Government to prevent interference in Paraiyar 'cast' affairs was a plea that would carry considerable weight. In both disputes, the notion that caste was not concomitant with religion but was an important constituent element of local custom meant that the policing of the jurisdiction of church authorities was a point that was constantly reiterated by the Paraiyars.

The nature of state support that different varieties of Catholicism received was an important factor in determining attitudes of the congregation towards the church authorities. Capuchin Churches had tended to excite a good deal of contempt amongst the British from very early times. In 1660, factors in Madras were to complain that the 'Capuchin friars used idolatrous rites and ceremonies all of which were inimical to the true Christian spirit'.[28] In the early nineteenth century, altercations with the French in south India as well as a fear of the radical influence of the Jesuits in the aftermath of the Revolution made the British extremely suspicious of the French friars in the Capuchin Churches around Madras. In 1790, the Capuchin Fathers of Madras had been accused by the Madras laity of maladministration of Church funds. The British quickly turned the situation to their own political account to put to rest their fear of sedition spread by Capuchin missions under the Propaganda de Fide. The government therefore, issued a notice that all Roman Catholic Churches had to obtain a licence from the Bishop of San Thome, the head of the Protuguese Church in South India. Further, the financial management of the church was taken away from the Capuchin Fathers and placed in the hands of influential Madras merchants.[29] It is extremely probable that the knowledge that their church authorities would not receive the wholehearted support of the government encouraged the Christian Paraiyars of Madras to revolt against them. Significantly, the 1816 dispute saw Capuchin Paraiyars invoke the authority of the Portuguese Bishop and not the Propaganda Fide in their appeals to the government. The structure of the Paraiyar case was therefore determined by the questions of state patronage and support.

Paraiyar Christians or Christian Paraiyars?

Neither the assimilative 'indigenized' Christianity of the Catholic Paraiyars of Madras nor the fact that 'caste' was increasingly the basic unit as far as social mobility was concerned, resulted in ambiguity or confusion as far as the self-perception of Christians was concerned. As much as Catholicism in south India was indigenized, it also produced some dramatic changes. For a people who stood on the feared and despised margins of Hindu society, the basic premise of a church dedicated to the religious welfare of its lower-caste congregation must have been a novel one. It was only as Christians that Paraiyars could hold central positions in their 'Hindu'-style festivals and feasts; as we have seen, as 'Heathens' the functions of the Paraiyars in the great temples of the Tamil country were the most menial and defiling. The Church and Catholicism empowered the lower castes and provided the structure within which the appropriation of tradition could take place. It is important not to underestimate thc impact of an ideology which theoretically granted salvation to all, on the consciousness of the lowliest in Tamil society. In fact when the occasion arose, the lower castes of Madras were willing to declare explicitly that they were not 'Hindus'. As early as 1707, during the course of a Right and Left hand caste dispute, the Company ordered various groups to declare their allegiance to either side. The low-caste boatmen of Madras were to declare that they had joined the disturbance because of:

> The instigation and ill advice of some designing people . . . whereas we are Christians, we belong to neither; and now that the Governour [*sic*] and Council promising that we shall have their protection and all priviledges as Christians, we solemnly promise that we will never hereafter adhere to any Casts of the Gentues.[30]

The language of the representations made by the Paraiyars is indicative of their appropriation of the moral language of mission Christianity. All their actions were seen as driven by the dictates of Catholicism and the Catholic Church; these included protests against church officials who obviously did not grasp the true nature of Christianity. In the San Thome dispute, the

Christian emphasis on personal morality was used as an argument against the nomination of Rayahmundoo to the post of caste headman. The fact that Rayahmundoo was an efficient head of caste was immaterial; the argument against him was that he was a 'person of bad conduct', that he had a son who had ill treated his own wife and kept a mistress. This attitude was in striking opposition to the Bishop's, whose only objection to Rayahmundoo was that he was not a Christian. For the Paraiyars the formal religious affiliation of the men who wished to be head of caste was unimportant; it was only essential that they be Christian in spirit. Interestingly, the Paraiyar insistence on a morally circumspect life is in striking contrast to what was usually seen as natural to their character—licentiousness. Thurston, for instance, quotes a well-known Tamil proverb which states that 'the palmyra tree has no shadow, the Paraiyan as no regard for seemliness'.[31]

We have seen how the Paraiyars of Madras collectively used the petition to articulate their demands; Christian Paraiyars were to also use the system to ask for their specifically Christian needs. This included a spate of petitions in the early nineteenth century asking for land to be granted to Christian Paraiyars for building chapels and for burial grounds. When they felt the situation demanded it, public expression of their Christian identity was not uncommon amongst the Paraiyars. Historians interested in the construction of communal identities have inevitably stressed the syncretic nature of Indian religions; strong religious identities have tended to be seen as necessarily demanding unbridled loyalty from their adherents and indicative of an antagonism towards other faiths. The Paraiyars of Madras were capable of combining 'Heathen'-style beliefs and traditions with the conviction that they were, above all, good Christians and true to the Christian creed. The prioritization of agency requires a focus on the nature of appropriation of religious traditions rather than their assimilative process. Seen in this light, what appear to be sudden expressions of communal separateness to us—the demand for more chapels or burial land, for instance—would, for the Paraiyars, possibly be no different in spirit from asking for a 'Heathen' caste head.

I will conclude by asking a few questions and offering some tentative answers. Can the kind of religious consciousness that we have been discussing be attributed to the fact that these incidents involved 'Heathens'—men and women that we would today call Hindus? More than any other religious group, Hindus have been called an 'imagined religious community'. The 'Hindu' identity, prior to the nineteenth century, is seen as essentially segmentary—its beliefs and traditions identified by language, caste, occupation, locality and sect. Was this ambiguous 'Hindu' identity responsible for the Christian Paraiyars of Madras being untroubled by the implications of their relationship with 'Heathens'?

There are indications that the Paraiyars' relationship with Islam was much more problematic. In early 1812, the same year as the San Thome dispute, a group of Paraiyars protested that the chapel land which they had occupied for a period of forty years was being claimed by the Muslim Nawab of Wallajahpet (Arcot) as his own. The Nawab's men, the Paraiyars claimed, had dug up the bodies of children buried in the disputed land with such violence that in one case, the 'guts of the child' came out. As Christians, the Paraiyars moaned, they deserved better than to suffer the 'tyranny of the moors'.[32] In another incident in 1832, groups of Christian Paraiyars were brought to trial for allegedly throwing pig's blood into a mosque at Nellore. On inquiry, it appeared that the incident was triggered by Christian attacks on mosques all over Madras Presidency at this time.[33] I will suggest that as in the case of Christanity, the strength and nature of Islamic identity varied according to context and social group. It is more plausible to see the above incidents as situations which the Paraiyars saw as requiring their active participation as Christians, and not as essentially anti-Muslim in nature. A great deal more probing is required into the relationship of the Paraiyars of Madras with popular Islam in the Paracheris of Madras.

By the middle of the nineteenth century, Protestantism had begun to sweep the Tamil country. With its fierce anti-caste ideology and astonishingly efficient propoganda machinery, it attracted vast numbers of Paraiyars to its fold. In the Paracheris of Madras the categories of caste and religion dissolved into one. As the service sector became saturated in Madras and as the government became increasingly concerned with the threat to peace that constant migration of the lower castes to the city posed, Protestant Christianity with its vast network of missionary-run schools and welfare associations became the key to social mobility. Communal boundaries hardened as tensions mounted, particularly in districts like Tirunelvelli where there were violent upper-caste Hindu protests at lower-caste corporate conversion. However, it becomes important to recognize that as powerful as the ideology of egalitarianism was, particularly in a context where the indignities and inequities imposed by the caste system were particularly severe, there was once again no straightforward acceptance of Protestant doctrine. Historians have been peculiarly unbothered by the palpable confusion of missionaries as they dealt with 'backslidings', frequent denominational changes and the retention of 'Heathen' practices. These questions require far greater probing. It is possible that a deeper understanding of the earlier century could provide valuable insights into this kind of research.

Notes

1 See for example, Robert Frykenberg, 'The impact of conversion and social reform upon society in south India during the late Company period', in C. H. Philips and M. D. Wainwright, eds, *Indian Society and the Beginnings of Modernization c. 1830–1850*, London, 1976.

2 When early Europeans, especially eighteenth century missionaries, used the term 'Heathen' or pagan they meant what we would today call 'Hindu'. It is important

to note however that at this time no exculsive orthodoxy defined what was 'Hindu' from what was not. For a discussion on the terms 'Heathen' and 'Hindu', see Frykenberg, 'The impact of conversion', pp. 190–91.

3 Harjot Oberoi, *The Construction of Religious Boundaries: Culture, Identity and Diversity in the Sikh Tradition*, Delhi, 1994, pp. 1–35.

4 'The Humble Petition of all the Christian Parriars residing at Saint Thomas Mount' Pub. Cons., Vol. 400A, 27 October 1812, Tamil Nadu State Archives (hereafter TNSA).

5 'Copy of a Malabar Public Notice Published in the Church of the Mount Church', Pub. Cons., Vol. 400 A, 27 October 1812, TNSA.

6 'Letter from the Government to the Acting Bishop of San Thome', Pub. Cons., Vol. 400 A, 27 October 1812, TNSA.

7 'From the Episcopal Governor regarding the "the Humble Petition of Cauden Cooty, head and the rest of the Christian and Heathen Pariahs of St Thomas Mount"', Pub. Cons., Vol. 400 B, 17 November 1812, TNSA.

8 'The humble Petition of Philip, Head of the Christian Pariars at St. Thomas Mount to the Episcopal Governor', Pub. Cons., Vol. 400 B, 17 November 1812, TNSA.

9 'From the Jose de Graca . . . Ecclesiastic Governor and Episcopal Administrator of the Bishopric of Mallapoor', Pub. Cons., Vol. 400 B, 17 November 1812, TNSA.

10 'The Humble Representation of all the Christian Pariars of the Great Parcherry of Madras', Pub. Cons., Vol. 422 B, 23 September and 4 August 1814, TNSA.

11 'Observations on the Petition presented by the Pariahs of the Paracherry of Madras to His Excellency the Governor in Council bearing date 6 August 1814', Jud. Cons., Vol. 423, 1814, TNSA.

12 'The humble representation of the Brotherhoods', Pub. Cons., Vol. 422 B, 23 September and 4 August 1814, TNSA.

13 See H. D. Love, *Vestiges of Old Madras*, Vol.1, London, 1929, pp. 286–339.

14 For details about the establishment of various Catholic missions in India, see Kenneth Balhatchet, *Caste, Class and Catholicism in India*, London, 1998.

15 In fact, the Paraiyars made yet another attempt to force their 'pagan' practices into the Mount Church—as soon as Pigot had sailed for Europe. See Love, *Vestiges*, Vol. 3 p. 41.

16 See Balhatchet, *Caste, Class and Catholicism*, p. 20.

17 For a discussion of Nobili's theory and practice of '*accomodatio*', see Ines G. Županov, *Disputed Mission: Jesuit Experiments and Brahmanical Knowledge in 17th Century India*, Delhi, 1999.

18 I am using the word 'Hindu' here because the traditions that we are discussing appear to refer to those which we would today call Hindu. It has to be kept in mind however that 'Hinduism' was not a part of the ethnographic reality of the country. It was not until the colonial period that the term acquired wide currency to refer collectively to the wide variety of religious communities, often with distinct, even opposing, religious practices. For an analysis of the 'construction' of the 'Hindu' identity see Robert Frykenberg, 'The emergence of modern Hinduism as a concept and as an institution with special reference to south India', in Gunther D. Sontheimer and Herman Kulke, eds, *Hinduism Reconsidered*, Delhi, 1989; Romila Thapar, 'Imagined religious communities'? Ancient history and the modern search for a Hindu identity, *Modern Asian Studies* (henceforth *MAS*) Vol. 23: 2, 1989, pp. 209–31; also useful is Oberoi, *The Construction of Religious Boundaries.*

19 *The Manual of Administration of the Madras Presidency*, Madras, 1885, pp. 68–69.

20 Susan Neild Basu, 'Colonial urbanism: The development of Madras city in the eighteenth and nineteenth centuries', *MAS*, Vol. 13: 2, 1979, p. 227.

21 For a discussion of untouchability in colonial urban spaces, see Susan Bayly, *Caste, Society and Politics in India from the Eighteenth Century to the Modern Age*, Cambridge, 1999, pp. 225–29.
22 'Proceedings of the Board of Police", in Love, *Vestiges*, Vol. 3, pp. 14–15.
23 Love, *Vestiges*, Vol. 3, p. 165.
24 Edgar Thurston, *Castes and Tribes*, Vol. 7, Madras, 1909, p. 88. Interestingly Thurston mentions that some Brahmans considered Paracheris as auspicious sites for their *agraharams*, their residential complexes. It appears therefore that village society had accepted the Paraiyar claims to Paracheri sacrality.
25 'From the Episcopal Governor regarding "the Humble Petition of Cauden Cooty, head and the rest of the Christian and Heathen Pariahs of St Thomas Mount"', Pub. Cons., Vol. 400 B, 17 November 1812, TNSA.
26 'Idolatory supported by the Indian Government', Extract from the journals of the Rev. F. Rogers, *Church Missionary Record*, Madras, 1840. pp. 197–98.
27 'Madras Superstition favoured by the Indian Government', Extract from the journals of the Rev. J.H. Elouis, *Church Missionary Record*, pp. 196–97.
28 Love, *Vestiges*, Vol. 1.
29 *Church Missionary Record*, Vol. 3, pp. 391–92.
30 Love, *Vestiges*, Vol. I.
31 Thurston, *Castes and Tribes*, Vol. 7, p. 117.
32 See letter from the Secretary to the Board of Revenue to the Governor, Rev. Cons., Vol. 193, 18 December 1812; also 'The Humble address of the Christian inhabitants of Wallajahpettah Near Triplicane' Vols 609 and 610, 5 May and 17 June 1813, TNSA.
33 See letter from the Collector of Nellore, Jud. Cons. Vol. 249, 24 August 1832, TNSA.

35

Excerpt from 'CHRISTIANITY WITHOUT CIVILIZATION

Anglican sources for an alternative nineteenth-century mission methodology'

Sara H. Sohmer

Source: *Journal of Religious History*, 18(2) (1994), 174–8, 180–1, 185–8, 195–7.

Scholarship on the missionary movement in the nineteenth century has, since the 1960s, demonstrated a commendable awareness of the manner in which the internalized cultural assumptions of Western missionaries influenced their interaction with the indigenous peoples they served.[1] The most cursory examination of the growing body of material that examines aspects of these assumptions reveals the hegemony of the 'Christianize and civilize' formula in the theory and practice of nineteenth-century mission. The message to be delivered to the deprived and the unenlightened of the world contained in more or less equal parts the word of God and the economic, social and political value systems of the West.

The nineteenth-century missionary movement might therefore be the very last place one would expect to look in the historical record for the appearance of the matrix of values that have come to be associated with the term multiculturalism. But in the complex area of cross-cultural interaction, we need to remember that the key element in this matrix—the ability to recognize worth and value in cultures other than one's own—is not the exclusive insight of the late twentieth century. Nor were ethnocentrism, cultural insensitivity and destructiveness the *only* responses European culture could muster in its encounter with the strange and the different. The presence of Europeans capable of assigning value to very different cultures is in fact persistent enough in the historical record of encounter to merit far more attention than it has received.[2] If our understanding of encounter is to have the proper shades and nuances, we need to recognize this recurring phenomenon and work out in detail the factors that enabled specific Europeans in specific circumstances to not only conceptualize 'otherness' as legitimate and valuable but to discover in their own cultural tradition intellectual validation and support for this response. In the case of Victorian England, despite the pervasiveness of the 'Christianize and civilize' formula, some missionaries proved quite capable of assigning value to indigenous cultures and of accommodating the Christian message to their needs. Their story has an important, if largely unrecognized, place in historians' efforts to come to a more complete understanding of cultural encounter in the nineteenth century.

This pattern of recognition and accomodation is evident in the work of individual missionaries in the field and even, from time to time, among the policy-makers of the missionary societies.[3] But both historians and Victorian observers of the British missionary effort have pointed to its particular prevalence and constancy among the three missions with ties to the High Church tradition of the Church of England: the Universities' Mission to Central Africa [UMCA] (founded 1858), the Anglican Mission to Papua (founded 1894) and the Melanesian Mission (founded 1849).[4] While none of these missions could claim to be overwhelmingly successful in terms of numbers converted,[5] they sustained an active, organized presence in Africa and the Pacific until the post-colonial era and provided the foundation for independent churches of continuing vitality in these regions. It hardly seems correct to dismiss their methods as atypical, short-lived oddities. This paper will examine the rather unexpected ways the leadership of one of these Victorian missions, the Melanesian Mission, mined both traditional Anglican theology and the Oxford Movement for the intellectual and spiritual resources needed both to sustain the missionary effort and explicate the very different world in which the mission functioned. What they took from Anglicanism obviously included the responsibility to christianize, but the concomitant obligation to civilize was largely absent.

The Melanesian Mission of the Church of England served the Solomon Islands, portions of the New Hebrides and other smaller island groups in the south-west Pacific from the initial exploratory voyages in 1848 of its founder, George Augustus Selwyn, the first Anglican bishop of New Zealand, until the inauguration of the Church of Melanesia as an autonomous province of the Anglican communion in 1975. Selwyn, a man possessed of almost frightening high levels of energy and an expansive vision of the role of the church, saw mission in the Pacific as a heaven-sent opportunity for the revitalization of Anglicanism. Freed from the fetters of its establishment status in England, the church could, in the larger context of the colonial sphere, realize its potential to become a spiritual force in the world. Despite the press of his duties as bishop of New Zealand, he wrote to William Ewart Gladstone, his friend from schooldays at Eton, of his intention 'to organize if possible some definite system for the evangelization of western Polynesia [Melanesia] including all the "News"—New Caledonia, New Hebrides, New Britain, New Ireland, New Hanover, and New Guinea—where, if it please God, I hope in ten years to shake hands with the Bishop of Borneo'.[6] Faced with the practical difficulty of covering such a vast field with very limited numbers of European missionaries, Selwyn determined from the outset to create a Melanesian ministry that could christianize from within the island community. To that end, he devised a rotation system whereby promising young Melanesians were brought by mission ship to spend part of the year training at the mission's boarding school and then returned to their home islands to teach. The hope was that after a number of years these scholars would evolve into a Melanesian clergy guiding the development of a Melanesian Christianity. Although the initial plan was Selwyn's, the fundamentals of the mission's philosophy and methodology were the work of John Coleridge Patteson (1827–71) whom Selwyn recruited for the mission in 1854 and who became the first missionary bishop of Melanesia in 1861. A thoughtful, scholarly man with a gift for languages, Patteson provided an intellectual depth and polish to the mission's methods that set it apart both in its own eyes and in those of many observers not otherwise particularly well-disposed to the missionary movement.

By most nineteenth-century standards, the mission was less than spectacularly successful at the business of garnering souls. After a forty-year monopoly on mission in Melanesia it could count among its followers less than 5 per cent of the total population.[7] When the British Solomon Islands Protectorate was established in 1893, its administrators indeed felt obliged to expedite the process of 'civilizing' the region by inviting the participation of missionaries of other denominations. But those who knew the mission's work were usually more impressed with the quality of its approach to indigenous peoples than its statistical failings. Sir Everard im Thurn, governor of Fiji from 1904 to 1911, for example, praised the Mission for its skilful blend of missionary zeal and proper anthropological methods.[8] The pioneer anthropologist William Halse Rivers saw in the mission's culturally sensitive evangelization a possible cure for the psychological malaise afflicting Melanesian society in the early twentieth century.[9] More recently, David Hilliard, the principal modern scholar of the mission, has noted Patteson's efforts to tie the methods he developed out of pragmatic necessity to theological principles. Patteson's mature mission philosophy thus took into account the distinction between the most fundamental doctrines of Christianity and those cultural additions that had to be modified if the faith was to have universal applicability.[10] Darrell Whiteman, in his recent study of the Melanesian Christians influenced by the mission's efforts, gives the Mission high marks for cross-cultural sensitivity and its conscious policy of indigenization, particularly in comparison with the other missionary enterprises in the area. He attributes this sensitivity, moreover, to the goals and ideals delineated by the mission's Victorian founders and sees later lapses into paternalism and hierarchical control as an unfortunate deviation from their priorities.[11]

Among members of the mission itself, the policies developed by Selwyn, Patteson and Patteson's closest associate in the field, the Rev. Robert H. Codrington (1830–1922), became virtual holy writ. The use of a Melanesian language as the teaching and liturgical language of the mission's schools, the rotation of Melanesian students between the mission school and their home islands, the emphasis placed on the development of a Melanesian clergy, and respect for local tradition and custom remained fundamental to the mission's approach long after the isolation of the early years had disappeared.[12] Hence, Arthur Innes Hopkins, who joined the Mission in 1902, clearly reflected the position of his boyhood hero, Bishop Patteson, when he wrote:

> The differences that look so tremendous are really superficial and due to their [Melanesians] so different environment, mental and spiritual and physical. To treat them as fellow human beings, not a separate caste, is the great secret of real approach . . . The sophism civilize first and Christianize afterwards is a shallow, unintelligent attitude.[13]

Such comments suggest a need to reassess the perception that Victorian missionaries uniformly reflected the paternalism, aggressiveness and assumptions of superiority characteristic of Western attitudes toward the non-European world. But where in the Victorian world did this alternative perspective originate and what sustained it through years of effort and considerable frustration? Those who have acknowledged the unique qualities of the Victorian High Church Anglican missions have credited the relatively high level of education found among their members as the source of their more sensitive approach to indigenous peoples. Certainly, the percentage of missionaries holding university degrees was relatively greater in the Melanesian Mission and the UMCA (although not in the Anglican Mission to Papua) than in evangelical missions,[14] and their leadership saw the university-educated individual as the ideal missionary. Although Bishop Patteson in practice often worked with young laymen from less than elevated social backgrounds, his ideal recruit continued to be a paragon of education, resourcefulness, common sense, athletic prowess and piety who could only have come from his own public school–university background (Eton, 1845; Balliol College, Oxford, 1849): 'A very few men,' he wrote, 'well-educated, who will really try to understand what heathenism is and will seek . . . to work honestly without prejudice and without an indiscriminating admiration for all their own national tastes and modes of thought. We need only a few.'[15]

This is a far cry from the assumption of the great evangelical mission societies at the beginning of the nineteenth century that 'humble men full of zeal' could fill the missionary role.[16] The first London Missionary Society expeditions to the South Seas relied heavily on pious artisans with very limited education and no specific training for their task. Even after the need for further education had been conceded, the curriculum the societies deemed appropriate for aspiring missionaries could hardly foster an understanding of 'what heathenism is'. The goal of missionary training at such institutions as the training college of the evangelical Anglican Church Missionary Society at Islington was not so much to provide future workers in the field with expertise for ministering to the heathen as to enable men of lower social status to hold their own with their fellow clergy at home.[17] [. . .]

[. . .] Patteson indeed went to considerable pains not to be credulous. Despite their physical removal to the south-western Pacific, both Patteson and Codrington kept apprised of intellectual issues to a degree that astonishes when one considers the demands of their missionary duties. Patteson never returned to England in the years between his departure for the mission field in 1855 and his murder by the islanders of Nukupu in 1871, but his reading in Melanesia included a wide range of current and often controversial works that challenged traditional views of biblical authority, history and the natural world. He knew Sir Henry Maine's *Ancient Law* (1861), with its emphasis on the connection between the very earliest legal concepts and modern perceptions, and Sir John Seeley's controversial interpretation of the life of Christ, *Ecce Homo* (1865). *Essays and Reviews* (1860), an attempt at a more open interpretation of Christian truth that brought down heresy charges on its authors, found its way to Melanesia, as did the writings of such innovative biblical scholars as Joseph Lightfoot and Brooke Westcott.[21]

Patteson's and Codrington's work among the peoples of Melanesia further fuelled their involvement with the intellectual world of nineteenth-century England. New developments in philology, ethnology and comparative mythology had, for the missionary in the field, an immediacy and a relevance that went beyond mere scholarly interest. Patteson wrote to his sister early in his missionary career: 'You will wonder at my asking for more books but the fact is that certain works appear from time to time that one's own particular occupation make especially interesting, and moreover, certain fresh wants are created by the very work one is pursuing'.[22] Both he and Codrington corresponded with the well-known philologist Friedrich Max Mueller. Codrington, who was headmaster of the boarding school on Norfolk Island and provided direction for the mission from Patteson's death in 1871 to his retirement from the mission field in 1887, served as an informant to the anthropologist Edward B. Tylor and was himself the author of definitive works on the languages and culture of Melanesia.[23]

But in striving to come to terms with either nineteenth-century intellectual challenges or exotic environments these educated men of faith acquired far more than new information. They also formed very distinctive habits of mind—habits that included careful examination of sources, a willingness to utilize different types of evidence, an enlarged sense of historical time and a strong preference for the comparative. While we recognize that these habits of mind played an important role in questioning traditional religious values, we tend to forget that, once formed, they could also be used to defend and revitalize an Anglicanism that, in the view of many committed men and women, still had a critical, stabilizing role to play in a world that was changing at a dizzying pace. Defined by both their faith and the new critical perspectives they had acquired, such individuals found in Anglicanism an important (perhaps the most important) intellectual and emotional resource for the mission enterprise itself *and* a mission methodology that sought to incorporate rather than destroy indigenous culture.

Before examining in detail the relationship between particular aspects of Anglican belief and the approach to mission they developed for Melanesia, it might be advisable to examine the basic affinity the mission's founders perceived between mission and Anglican tradition. What, in other words, in that tradition might initially appeal to intelligent, educated men considering the missionary life? In providing an answer, it is necessary to consider the subtle differences between the motivation of these missionaries and their more familiar Evangelical counterparts. 'The key to the understanding of most missionary activity,' as Neil Gunson succinctly puts it, 'is revivalism.'[24] In the Calvinist context, eighteenth-century religious revivalism produced not only the conviction of salvation but an eagerness to provide tangible proof of redemption from guilt and sin—a phenomenon that dovetailed nicely with the older Calvinist tenet of the evangelization of the world as a precondition of the coming of the millennium. For those who identified with the Methodist component of revivalism, the conversion experience elicited an intense 'love to God' which, by extension, meant a new concern for the souls of His creatures. In either case, revivalism and the conversion experience provided a meaningful theological/spiritual framework for 'the great century of advance' in mission.[25] [. . .]

[. . .] The relationship between Melanesians and missionaries, as Patteson saw it, was less that of the elect pointing out the error of their evil ways to wretched sinners than that of reasonable, spiritual men helping God's creatures realize themselves more fully. This could be accomplished through the slow and undramatic exercise of sound learning, reason, patience and the ministrations of the Church. The imposition of forms which might signify 'progress' to outsiders (for example, Sabbath observance, the wearing of clothes, the abolition of dancing and other local practices) had, in fact, little relevance for indigenous peoples themselves.

All of this seemed so basic to Patteson even at the outset of his work in Melanesia that ordinary mission methods completely appalled him:

> the almost inconceivable ignorance or neglect of these basic truths underlies I am satisfied the systematic teaching of some missionary

> societies. It seems as if common sense and ordinary observation were to be regarded as 'unspiritual leaning on the arm of flesh': as if the knowledge of the human heart and the application could never be practically taught and learned.[39]

The old Puritan failure to recognize variety and potential, to underplay reason and practical knowledge of man, and to confuse form and substance were, for Patteson, the main sources of mission failure everywhere. The Anglican tradition as embodied in Hooker's writings, by contrast, provided a world view in which natural law and reason as well as Scripture and revelation served as sources of truth, and all men aspired to the perfection of God. The possibility could at least be entertained that an indigenous culture could create something worthwhile even without the benefits of Christianity. The role of Christianity was to complete and enhance; it did not always need to replace or destroy.

The eighteenth-century divine Bishop Joseph Butler actually addressed the issue of mission directly. His sermon for the anniversary meeting of the Society for the Propagation of the Gospel in 1738 stressed the need for patience and steadfastness in the absence of the spectacular successes critics of mission appeared to demand. The bare establishment of the faith was in itself important. 'Progress' in mission ultimately depended on Providence far more than the schemes of men.[40] Patteson, who shunned publicity for the mission out of fear of the public demand for results, must have found this comforting. But his affinity for Butler was based on more than Butler's rather marginal concern with mission *per se.* [. . .]

Although Patteson would hardly have had any quarrel with Butler's *a priori* assumption of the existence of deity, he was too close to the intellectual life of his own day to base his admiration of Butler on a wholesale acceptance of an orthodox theological position. However dated Butler's theology might have been, in his approach to changing conditions and new challenges and in his ethical theory there remained much to appeal to the Victorian Christian. Butler provided the best Anglican example of what Hans Frei has called 'mediating theologians'. These—and Frei includes in this group such diverse figures as John Locke, Ernst Schleiermacher and Rudolf Bultman—espoused the view that for religion to be meaningful it has to be understood through general experience. While the unique truth of Christianity depends on divine revelation, this 'miracle' has to be appropriate to the human condition and address human concerns. The role of the mediating theologian (or for that matter, the missionary) is therefore not so much to 'prove' the Gospel as to point out its meaningfulness and to mediate between the direct experience all people recognize and the specifics of Christian thought.[45]

In Butler, the method of mediation centred on analogy or the process of applying the understanding of the familiar to an unfamiliar concept/object which has, nonetheless, some points of similarity. Again, the possibilities for the application of this hallowed Anglican intellectual position to mission methodology are quite apparent. Christian understanding must be built on the familiar, on existing belief. The Gospel must be presented in such a way that its relevance is apparent to general human conditions. Codrington wrote:

> What I try myself to do is to make them (Melanesians) see a reason for believing in one God . . . also to make them see that they themselves, without any teaching from us, know and recognize the distinctions of right and wrong and feel the need of some higher association than their own.[46]

[. . .] For the leaders of the Melanesian Mission the assumption of the innate ability of all people to make moral distinctions was fundamental. It is important, moreover, to realize that this view was not acquired after a long exposure to indigenous peoples but formed part of their intellectual assumptions when they arrived in the field. In 1856, shortly after his arrival in New Zealand, Patteson was already firmly of the opinion that 'the capacity for the Christian life is there; though overlaid it may be with monstrous forms of superstition or cruelty or ignorance, the conscience can still respond to the voice of the Gospel of Truth'.[48]

That being the case, the concept of 'savage' had little meaning. Neither the moral failings nor the moral successes of Pacific islanders differed in any essential way from those of Europeans. After three years in the mission field Patteson wrote:

> It is strange to be living so peacefully among nations accounted savage and fighting each other while you highly educated and civilized individuals act your barbarism on a more exalted scale and with a far greater refinement. It is very savage indeed to spear 3 or 4 men, but exceedingly valiant to leave about 3,000 dead on a field slain by the Enfield rifle . . . What scene in Melanesia ever exceeded the horrors of the sack of a town by British troops?[49]

This fundamental perception of moral consciousness may also have influenced the mission's approach to teaching and, ultimately, to the decision to rely on an indigenous clergy. For if islanders failed to recognize Christian truth the fault did not rest with them. They had the capacity to make moral judgements, and if they did not do so the mission personnel could explain away their failings in terms of either harsh living conditions or inappropriate presentation of truth. The missionary Richard B. Comins, for example, reporting of bigamy and infanticide in the Solomon Islands in 1886, urged his readers to consider the marginal economy and the depressed status of women in creating these evils rather than assume depravity and perversity in

Melanesians.[50] Far more often failure was tied to inappropriate presentation of Christian truth.

Melanesians, Patteson believed, demonstrated that they could think perfectly well if principles were put in terms they understood. And despite the mission's use of Mota and other Melanesian languages, its sensitivity to existing belief, and the patient, long-range nature of its goals, he was never certain a European missionary could bridge the gap in communication. An indigenous clergy was another matter. George Sarawia, the first ordained Melanesian clergyman, had, in Patteson's view, a decided advantage, based not just on language ability, but on his mastery of such cultural subtleties as the language of gesture and expression.[51] Later members of the mission continued to support this position. Alfred Penny, a Cambridge graduate who served in Melanesia from 1875 to 1886 attributed any success for Christianity in the islands solely to the use of islander teachers and clergy.[52] Comins, who served the mission from 1877 to 1912, maintained that training 'an army of native teachers' had to remain the mission's first priority—a concept that did not, he noted, seem to commend itself to other missionary groups.[53] [. . .]

[. . .] While the Evangelical mission model everywhere stressed the Christian home and family, the High Church missions saw themselves in terms of the religious community. Visitors to the mission stations of the UMCA reported the atmosphere of a college devoted to plain living and high thinking as opposed to the Evangelical Protestant stations where family life necessitated a far greater reliance on Western life-styles.[88] In the UMCA and the Anglican Mission to Papua, both heavily influenced by Anglo-Catholicism, the model extended to celibacy for the term of mission service and either no salary at all or a very limited stipend.[89]

The Melanesian Mission never went quite so far. Although Patteson and Codrington never married and lived exclusively on their private incomes, other members of the mission did marry while in service, and their wives were welcome at Norfolk Island. Mission members also received stipends, albeit rather Spartan ones. Yet the early Church model clearly had an influence, particularly in the organization and operation of the Norfolk Island school, St Barnabas'. In describing St Barnabas' to his aunt in 1867, Codrington likened it to the ancient monasteries of England and Germany in its view of work and education.[90] The daily routine indeed had a monastic orderliness, with daily services and classes interspersed with work on the mission farm and meals of plentiful but decidedly plain food. Melanesian scholars and the European staff shared the work, and the entire mission sat down together for meals.[91] When discipline was required, Patteson found the example of the early Church most efficacious. A council of Melanesian communicants sat in judgments on the transgressor and determined appropriate punishments. Usually this involved banishment from services for a stated period. If the culprit was a Melanesian teacher, he might also be barred from teaching and sitting at the 'high table' of the dining hall with the rest of the mission staff. While Patteson admitted that this sort of Church discipline for social behaviour might not be appropriate everywhere, he found that the methods employed by the early Church worked marvellously well in Melanesia.[92]

Patteson's view of indigenous clergy and his belief in the need for specialized knowledge of human culture also benefited from the early Church model. He referred to the example of the early Alexandrine teachers who analysed existing belief systems in order to discover the appropriate means of introducing Christianity, a practice he found sadly lacking in most missions of his own day. 'It is not always easy to be patient and to remember the position which the heathen man occupies and point of view from which he must regard everything brought before him,' he maintained.[93] Yet the earliest Christian missionaries and teachers had taken care to come to just such an understanding and thus provided a most instructive example.

Ironically, having utilized the early Church model to support the concept of sophisticated cultural understanding, Patteson also found there arguments for the effectiveness of an indigenous clergy with limited formal training. The entire matter of the training and education of the indigenous clergy was problematic. Patteson shared the Oxford Movement's view of the importance of the clergy, both for their role in the administration of the sacraments and as the chief educators and spiritual leaders of their flocks. Thorough training in theology, Church history, and the languages necessary for Biblical studies assumed critical importance. In his own preparation for ordination and in that which he and Codrington provided for the European ordinands of the mission, he insisted on rigorous standards. Both he and Codrington felt satisfied that their ordinands acquitted themselves as well or better on ordination exams as their English-trained counterparts.[94] But should this standard be applied to the Melanesian clergy?[95] Despite his confidence in their ability and intelligence, Patteson thought not. Their job did not entail teaching theology to educated Christians. They had, rather, to convey the elements of Christian truth to people completely ignorant of the entire phenomenon. 'If they can state clearly and forcibly the very primary leading fundamental truths of the Gospel and live as simple-minded humble Christians, that is enough indeed,' Patteson concluded.[96] And again, he found his point of reference for this conclusion in the Church's earliest missionaries. Many of these men, Patteson noted, had scarcely been literate and had yet accomplished much of value.[97]

Given the size of the Melanesian mission field, this view of the indigenous clergy had obvious pragmatic appeal, but Patteson saw in it something more compelling. A Melanesian clergy was the only possible way of ensuring the proper communication of Christian truth and, consequently, the proper establishment of a Melanesian Church. 'We cannot be to them what a well-instructed fellow-countryman may be. He is near to them. They understand him. He brings the teaching to them in a practical and intelligible form.'[98]

As long as the Christian message came only from Europeans, it ran the risk of being perceived as the foreigner's religion and not as God's universal gift. Thus, in 1868 when George Sarawia took his ordination vows in Mota alongside Charles Bice who took his in English, Patteson expressed his overwhelming feelings of hope and thankfulness at the realization of a Melanesian clergy.[99] That he could do so was in no small degree a measure of his understanding of his own Anglican tradition—a tradition that, thanks to both the orthodox Anglican divines of past centuries and the Tractarian interpreters of the nineteenth century, provided this Victorian missionary with a critical framework for the development of his own religious life, the methodology of the Melanesian Mission, and the vision of a truly Melanesian Christianity.

Notes

1 E.g., *Mission, Church and Sect in Oceania*, James Boutilier, Daniel Hughes and Sharon Tiffany (eds), 1978; Neil Gunson, *Messengers of Grace: Evangelical Missionaries in the South Seas, 1797–1860*, Melbourne 1978; Mary T. Huber, *The Bishops' Progress: A Historical Ethnography of Catholic Missionary Experience on the Sepik Frontier*, 1988; Diane Langmore, *Missionary Lives: Papua, 1874–1914*, Honolulu 1988; Patricia Grimshaw, *Paths of Duty: American Missionary Wives in Nineteenth-Century Hawaii*, 1989; Mary Zwiep, *Pilgrim Path: The First Company of Women Missionaries to Hawaii*, 1990; David Hilliard, *God's Gentlemen: A History of the Melanesian Mission, 1846–1942*, St Lucia, Queensland 1978; Robert Strayer, *The Making of Mission Communities in East Africa: Anglicans and Africans in Colonial Kenya, 1875–1935*, Albany, New York 1978; Darrell Whiteman, *Melanesians and Missionaries: An Ethnohistorical Study of Social and Religious Change in the Southwest Pacific*, Pasadena, California 1983; Jean and John Comaroff, *Of Revelation and Revolution: Christianity, Colonialism and Consciousness in South Africa*, 1991.

2 As Garry Wills put it in his recent review of current scholarship on Christopher Columbus: 'we should have had a major biography of las Casas [Bartolome de las Casas, 1474–1566, Dominican defender of New World Indians and critic of the consequences of the Spanish Conquest] rather than the two-hundredth book on Columbus'. Garry Wills, 'Man of the Year', *New York Review of Books*, 21 November 1991.

3 For examinations of this question in the more evangelical Church Missionary Society, see, e.g., Strayer, *The Making of Mission Communities in East Africa*, and C. Peter Williams, *The Ideal of the Self-governing Church: A Study in Victorian Missionary Strategy*, Leiden 1990.

4 See Langmore, *Missionary Lives*, Honolulu 1989; David Neave, Aspects of the History of the Universities' Mission to Central Africa, 1885–1900, MA thesis, University of York 1974; David Wetherell, *Reluctant Mission: The Anglican Church in Papua New Guinea*, St Lucia, Queensland 1978.

5 The Melanesian Mission, founded in 1849, set the number of its adherents at about 14,000 or less than 5 per cent of the population it served in 1895. David Hilliard, 'Bishop G. A. Selwyn and the Melanesian Mission', *New Zealand Journal of History*, Vol. IV, October 1970.

6 G. A. Selwyn to W. E. Gladstone, July 1853, Gladstone-Selwyn correspondence, Gladstone Papers, The British Library, London. Series 44–299 ff.

7 David Hilliard, 'Colonialism and Christianity: The Melanesian Mission in the Solomon Islands', *Journal of Pacific History*, Vol. 9, 1974, p. 101.
8 Everard im Thurn in *Essays on the Depopulation of Melanesia*, W. H. R. Rivers (ed.), Cambridge 1922, p. vi.
9 Rivers, in *Essays on the Depopulation of Melanesia*, pp. 94–110.
10 Hilliard, *God's Gentlemen*, p. 56.
11 Whiteman, *Missionaries and Melanesians*, p. 425.
12 Melanesian scholars initially attended St John's at Kohimarama, New Zealand.
13 Arthur Innes Hopkins, Autobiography, unpublished manuscript, Australian National University microfilm, The Melanesian Mission, 1900–1925, pp. 15–16.
14 Roughly half of those who joined the Melanesian Mission between 1850 and 1900 held university degrees, as did a third of the UMCA missionaries of the same period. Hilliard, *God's Gentlemen*, p. 125.
15 J. C. Patteson to his cousin, Derwent Coleridge, 8 August, 1863, in Charlotte Yonge, *Life of John Coleridge Patteson, Missionary Bishop of Melanesia*, 2 vols, London 1874, Vol. 2, p. 67.
16 Sarah Potter, 'The Making of Missionaries in the Nineteenth Century: Conversion and Convention', *A Sociological Yearbook of Religion in Britain*, Vol. 8, 1975, p. 113.
17 C. P. Williams, '"Not Quite Gentlemen": an Examination of "Middling Class" Protestant Missionaries from Britain, c. 1850–1900', *Journal of Ecclesiastical History*', Vol. 31, 1980, p. 104.
[. . .]
21 Yonge, Vol. 2, p. 250.
22 J. C. Patteson to his sister, 2 August 1857, Patteson Papers, United Society for Propagation of the Gospel [SPG] Collection, Rhodes House Library, Oxford (microfilm, Hamilton Library, University of Hawaii at Manoa).
23 See *The Melanesians: Studies in their Anthropology and Folk-lore*, London 1891, reprint edn New York 1972; and *The Melanesian Languages*, Oxford 1885.
24 Gunson, *Messengers of Grace*, p. 47.
25 Sidney H. Rooy, *The Theology of Missions in the Puritan Tradition*, Grand Rapids, Michigan 1965, p. 321.
[. . .]
39 J. C. Patteson to his sisters, 23 September 1869, Patteson Papers, SPG Collection.
40 *The Sermons and Remains of the Right Rev. Joseph Butler*, E. Steere (ed.), London 1862.
[. . .]
45 Hans W. Frei, *The Eclipse of Biblical Narrative: A Study in 18th and 19th Century Hermeneutics*, New Haven, Conn. 1974, pp. 128–9.
46 Robert Codrington, in *The Island Voyage*, annual report series for the Melanesian Mission, 1874–1890, Ludlow 1875, p. 27.
[. . .]
48 Yonge, *Life of Patteson*, Vol. 1, p. 298.
49 J. C. Patteson to his sister, 27 August 1859, Patteson Papers, SPG Collection.
50 Richard B. Comins in *The Island Voyage*, 1886, p. 38.
51 J. C. Patteson to his sisters, 2 May 1867, Patteson Papers, SPG Collection.
52 Alfred Penny, *Ten Years in Melanesia*, London 1887, p. 210.
53 R. B. Comins in *The Island Voyage*, 1878, p. 28.
[. . .]
88 Neuve, Aspects of the History of the Universities' Mission to Central Africa, pp. 189–202.

89 Neave, Aspects of the UMCA, pp. 108–110, and Langmore, *Missionary Lives*, p. 89.
90 Codrington Papers, series 4, Rhodes House, Oxford.
91 E. S. Armstrong, *The History of the Melanesian Mission*, London 1900, p. 109.
92 J. C. Patteson to Sir George Pohlman, 25 January 1869, Yonge, *Life of Patteson*, Vol. 2, p. 352.
93 J. C. Patteson to Charlotte Yonge, July 1865, Yonge, Vol. 2, p. 152.
94 Codrington Papers, series 29.
95 It is interesting to note that Patteson and Selwyn reached very different conclusions on this issue. Despite his regard for the Maoris, Selwyn failed to develop a Maori clergy largely out of a high church concern to guard the standards of the priesthood, standards that he felt had to be consistently and universally applied. C. P. Williams, *The Ideal of the Self-Governing Church*, p. 21.
96 J. C. Patteson, Yonge, *Life of Patteson*, Vol. 2, p. 494.
97 J. C. Patteson to his sisters, August 1868, Patteson Papers, SPG Collection.
98 J. C. Patteson to Charlotte Yonge, 25 December 1867, Yonge, Vol. 2, p. 292.
99 J. C. Patteson, diary entry, June 1868, Yonge, Vol. 2, p. 324.

Part 9

GENDER, EDUCATION AND CONVERSION

36

MISSIONARY MATERNALISM

Gendered images of the Holy Spirit Sisters (SSpS) in colonial New Guinea

Nancy Lutkehaus

Source: originally published in Mary Huber Taylor and Nancy Lutkehaus (eds), *Gendered Missions: Women and Men in Missionary Discourse and Practice*, Ann Arbor, MI: University of Michigan Press, 1999, pp. 207–35; revised by author, 2009.

This essay describes the gendered dimensions of the work of the Holy Spirit Sisters (also known as the Sisters Servants of the Holy Spirit, or SSpS), a German Catholic order of missionary nuns who arrived in colonial New Guinea in 1899. The term "maternal" has multiple meanings. It refers to the role of missions in New Guinea within a colonial division of labor; to the formal goals and stated ideology of the Holy Spirit Sisters; and to the Sisters' actual behavior. The different meanings of missionary maternalism are discussed in relationship to social, political, and economic conditions in Europe and colonial New Guinea. While maternal activities and maternalism remain important aspects of the Holy Spirit Sisters' present-day identity, post-colonial changes worldwide have led to the Holy Spirit Sisters' constitution of themselves as a multicultural institution and to concomitant shifts in their relationships with Papua New Guinea women.

Missions as 'maternal' colonial institutions

Scholars interested in colonial studies and the role of missionaries in the colonial enterprise have increasingly challenged the prevailing sentiment among many Western scholars that missionaries simply reproduced the hegemonic values and roles of the colonizer.[1] We are beginning to acknowledge that the mission of missionaries has sometimes put them at cross-purposes with colonial officials, plantation owners, traders, and, in some instance, other missionary organizations.

"A . . . common source of suspicion of missionaries," the historian Lacey notes, "stemmed from their educational work. To Europeans who recruited or employed labour, mission educated people were shrewd and untrustworthy" (1972: 776). This attitude was not always the case, however; initially missionaries were welcomed to the colony *precisely* because of their willingness and ability to teach. In many missions teaching women and children, in particular, was seen as the responsibility of women, whether missionaries themselves, wives of missionaries, or lay religious personnel. For the Holy Spirit Sisters, who were affiliated with the Society of the Divine Word (SVD), the education of children and women was one of their primary tasks. While SVD priests and brothers proceeded to establish mission plantations and to build churches, the SSpS Sisters quickly organized schools.

It is useful to characterize the initial role of missions in the colonial enterprise in New Guinea as "maternal," as opposed to the "paternal" roles of the colonial state and the plantation system, the predominant economic base of colonial New Guinea. This designation may go against the grain of how many of us commonly think of missions in general, and Catholic missions in particular, i.e. as institutions that replicate the hegemonic values, beliefs, and practices of the patriarchal Western societies and churches of which they are a part. However, "maternal"—used here in the sense of a focus on care-giving and nurturance, on the upbringing and socialization of children, and on the development of "inner" qualities of morality and spirituality, all pursued in a compassionate manner—may be a revealing trope through which to analyze the missionary endeavor in general and the SVD and SSpS missions in particular.

This is in part because of the emphasis placed on the role of the missions in the education of indigenous men, women, and children by both the missionaries themselves and the colonial government in New Guinea. In contrast to the economic, military, and political activities pursued by planters and government agents, the spiritual and material educational tasks performed by the missionaries were deemed of necessary, but subordinate, value; much like the then current perception of the role of the mother in the socialization of children within the family, and the contribution of motherhood to the nation-state.[2] Colonizers (including missionaries) often referred to local people as "children" who needed to be socialized into the customs of Western society. In general, according to nineteenth-century middle-class European thought, women were better suited to socializing children than men.[3] Thus, by analogy, missionaries were like mothers preparing their children to become good citizens and laborers.

Germans in New Guinea: "internal" versus "external" education[4]

Several years before Germany's annexation of northeastern New Guinea in 1884, Friedrich Fabri, Director of the Rhenish Mission Society, suggested that successful colonization depended upon missionaries since they alone were capable of "regenerating the uncivilized, still barbaric peoples" through their ability to influence natives "mentality, intelligence and moral and religious conceptions" (Fabri, quoted in Firth 1983: 136). While planters, traders, and officials would undertake the external education of the colonized people, the missionaries would work internally to insure a ready acceptance of European values (Firth 1983). Fabri suggested a complementarity between missionaries and secular actors in the colonial division of labor, a marriage of mutual convenience between representatives of the church and the colonial state. The separation Fabri identified between "external" and "internal" education can also be thought of in gendered terms: the "external" or public work—that of the planters, traders, and government officials—being more "masculine," and the "internal" work, whether performed by male or female missionaries, because it related to spirituality and the inner dispositions of the villagers, more "feminine."

An additional value of the missionaries to the German colonial administration was that they achieved their conversions and socialization peacefully, in contrast to the violent disciplinary force often exhibited by the colonial state (Firth 1983: 136). This is another way in which missions can be considered "maternal," for, according to gender stereotypes of the time, men—and by extension such male institutions as the colonial state—were viewed as more inherently aggressive and violent in nature than women. This metaphoric extension of gender reflects notions about the differences between the sexes (*Geschlechtscharakter* or 'the character of the sexes') current in nineteenth-century Germany (Hausen 1981: 56).

If it was the missions' primary task to civilize the inner dispositions of the unruly savage, to socialize the barbarian into the customs and beliefs of Western culture, they could be considered to be more "maternal" in character than other "externally" focused colonial institutions.

This gendered characterization of colonial institutions and the colonial division of labor also reflects past and present Western images of the Christian church and religion. Within Catholicism itself, for example, the Jesuit scholar Walter J. Ong has written that "[t]he Church is sexually defined. To the psyche, the Church is always feminine, the Holy Mother Church. Psychoanalytically as well as theologically there is no way to have a 'Father Church' . . ." (1981: 178).[5] He goes on to suggest that in patriarchal societies "even an all-male clergy is likely to be regarded by other males as somewhat feminine because of the close alliance with the feminine church" (ibid.).

Blurred categories: missionaries and plantations

In reality, of course, the boundary between missionaries and other colonial actors was more blurred than either the internal/external or maternal/paternal dichotomy implies. Precisely because of this blurring tensions arose between the missions and other colonial institutions. There was no doubt in the minds of the German colonial government that evangelization was a means to a practical end, the preparation of natives as a willing and docile labor force, and that the missionaries were to teach the villagers practical as well as spiritual skills.

The Society of the Divine Word missionaries themselves made a distinction between "spiritual" and "practical" work (Huber 1988). Ironically, despite the mission's own emphasis on spiritual work, the ability of the missionaries to accomplish their spiritual work in New Guinea meant that initially they spent much of their time on material matters—in terms of both the physical establishment of the mission in New Guinea and of the education of laborers (Firth 1983: 153). According to the colonial government, the more "masculine" a mission was in its activities, it seems, the better—as long as the missionaries performed their tasks in a "maternal" (i.e. non-violent) manner.

This benign attitude towards the missionaries changed after World War I when Australia took over control of the Territory of New Guinea from the Germans. Then not only were Australian settlers in New Guinea suspicious of the missionaries' educational work, but "[t]here was also the suspicion that with such a large number of German personnel in some missions the local people might be under the influence of seditious ideas" (Lacey 1972: 780).[6]

Why, despite the public's suspicions—and possible resentment of mission plantation holdings—were German missionaries allowed to stay? It appears that the primary reason was because of the usefulness of their nursing and teaching activities—many of which were in the hands of women (Lacey 1972: 779).[7]

Maternalism extended: the Holy Spirit Sisters and social motherhood

A second meaning of "maternalism" refers specifically to the work of the Holy Spirit Sisters and their gendered missionary roles as nurses, teachers, pastoralists, and domestic helpmates to the priests and brothers on mission stations worldwide. As has often been noted, during the nineteenth and early twentieth centuries middle-class European and North American women were commonly seen as having a special role to play in missionary endeavors that was justified on the basis of the "natural" tendencies of their sex. These tendencies included maternal nurturance and women's exalted role in Christian societies as the bearers of moral uplift, in contrast both to men and to the role of women in "heathen" societies (Grimshaw 1989).

This attitude towards women was also prevalent in Germany (Allen 1991; Frevert 1989). The SSpS order was founded in 1889, a period in German history when feminists and other groups of women were articulating a new notion concerning the value of motherhood: an extension of woman's biological nature into the realm of public good known as *Mütterlichkeit*, or "social motherhood."

According to nineteenth-century sexual stereotypes prevalent in Germany, physiological distinctions between the sexes were used to describe the mental characteristics distinctive of men and women. These stereotypes mixed biology, social destiny, and inner nature and were intended to form a typology of the characteristics of men and women. Reduced to the essential contrast, men's nature destined them to be concerned with social production, while women were destined for the private world of reproduction (Hausen 1981: 55). These stereotypes or 'characters of the sexes" (*Geschlechtscharakter*) formed the basis for a debate at the turn of the century about the relationship of motherhood, child-rearing, and family life to the welfare of the state (Allen 1991).[8]

While many contemporary feminists have argued that a woman's biological role as childbearer has been used to limit women's social and economic possibilities, in the context of nineteenth-century Germany motherhood provided a model of empowerment and ethical autonomy (Allen 1991: 2; Frevert 1989). During this period in Germany, the mother–child bond became the basis of a concept of social morality that linked the individual woman to the larger community, as feminists, citing the importance of child-rearing and maternal duty, argued that these functions should be incorporated into public policy, creating a role of 'public motherhood' (the creation of kindergartens—or 'children's gardens'/play areas—was one result of this movement) based on the notion of 'extended motherliness' (*Mütterlichkeit*) (Allen 1991: 2; Frevert 1989: 126). Moreover, they continued, because women were best suited for the maternal role, logically they should also be responsible for fulfilling the role of "public motherhood."

The idea of motherhood as a source of ethical authority, although derived from a biological model, was not merely a product of biology; it was adopted by many women who were not biological mothers, "sometimes in order to avoid biological motherhood" (Allen 1991: 12). The characteristics of maternalism (nurturance, emotional empathy, compassion) and other female characteristics, bourgeois German women argued, were important antidotes to the "masculine" characteristics of modern technology and industry. Society as a whole was thus seen as needing "feminine cultural influence" in order to mitigate various deleterious effects of the modern world, such as housing shortages, the break-up of the family, alcoholism, and prostitution (Frevert 1989: 126–7).

Although Catholic women were under-represented in the German feminist movement (Allen 1991), it is not unreasonable to see both Catholic convents and women's mission orders as the spiritually inflected institutionalization of the practice of "social motherhood" promoted by secular women's organizations in nineteenth-century Germany.[9]

Missionary maternalism

Fr. Arnold Janssen, the founder of the Society of the Divine Word mission, recognized early on the special need for women in his mission endeavor. According to the story that the Holy Spirit Sisters recount of the origin of their order,[10] two women from Germany—Hendrina Stenmanns and Helena Stollenwerk—who had come to work for Father Janssen as kitchen staff for the SVD mission in Steyl, Netherlands,[11] were catalysts in getting Janssen to found a women's missionary order. Wanting to play a more important and immediate role in the missionary project than that of menial assistants to the priests and brothers, they begged Janssen to allow them to perform missionary work too. Janssen conceded to their request and by 1889 he had established two separate female orders at Steyl, the Contemplative Nuns and the missionary order the Sisters Servants of the Holy Spirit.

The origin story of the SSpS nuns is evidence of the historically subordinate relationship of Catholic women to men. As women did not have the authority to create a mission order themselves, they were dependent upon Janssen to establish an order for them. The story is also a charter for the principle of separate, but complementary, spheres and a gendered division of labor in the mission culture of the SVD and SSpS orders. Finally, the story also contains within it a seed of female autonomy, for ultimately Janssen decided to create an affiliated, yet structurally independent, female organization.

The mission calling

At the end of the nineteenth and the beginning of the twentieth centuries, it was unusual for a woman not to marry, and more unusual yet for her to become a nun, let alone a missionary sister. What might have motivated a young Catholic woman around the turn-of-the century in Germany to become a Holy Spirit Sister and how might she have expressed and acted upon her desire? As the following excerpts from an interview with Sister Maria suggest, a spiritual calling—in her case made manifest by a family crisis—lies at the heart of her decision:[12]

> The eldest daughter in a rural family of four children, Maria's decision to join the Holy Spirit Sisters at Steyl was precipitated by what she felt to be the impending death of her mother. She had been thinking about dedicating her life to Jesus, she said, ever since she had been confirmed at age eleven. When she was eighteen, her mother nearly died of cancer. While her mother lay in the hospital, Maria prayed to the Lord and asked him that her mother live at least another year. If her mother lived, she said, she would enter the convent. When her mother recovered, Maria took her recovery as

> a sign that the Lord had answered her prayers and that she was to become a nun.
>
> Around the time of her mother's illness, Maria happened to read a copy of the *Steyler Missionsbote* that her grandmother received from the SVD mission. The description of the missionaries' work in far off China, Africa, and New Guinea caught her imagination. Although she could have gone to one of the five convents in the area near her home, a rural farm community in Westphalia, Maria decided to go to Steyl instead because it was a missionary sending order.
>
> What had clinched the matter for her was that the SSpS sisters would accept her even though she was only nineteen. She was impatient and did not want to wait until she was twenty, the age required by some of the other convents.

Maria's narrative tells us that even prior to the crisis of her mother's illness she had been contemplating the idea of "dedicating her life to Jesus." As the Holy Spirit Sisters sometimes express their commitment to their vows of chastity, poverty, and obedience in terms of their dedication, or marriage, to Jesus, Maria is indicating that since her confirmation she had been interested in the possibility of becoming a nun. That spark of interest becomes transformed into a spiritual calling that permits, indeed requires, that she become a nun. In a time of personal crisis—the serious illness and potential death of her mother—Maria prayed to God for his help. She told herself that if He answered her prayers—if her mother did not die—out of gratitude she would dedicate her life to serving God by becoming a nun.

Looking beyond Maria's own words, we might also see in this story a young girl fearful that if her mother died duty would require her, as the eldest daughter in the family, to assume her mother's role as the female head of her father's household. Her mother's premature death would prevent her from leaving home and pursuing her desire to become a nun. But, if her mother lived, her family might well understand the nature of her gratitude and her spiritual motivation to leave home to join a convent. Fear of her mother's death, despite her recovery, might also explain Maria's eagerness to enter a convent as soon as possible. Indeed, her mother died two years later, after Maria had already become a novitiate, and her father allowed her to remain at Steyl.

Maria's story is typical of the accounts of other SSpS Sisters her age and younger who came to New Guinea prior to and immediately after World War II. In these narratives the Sisters decide to leave home either because of a strong spiritual calling or because of a desire to be trained as a teacher or nurse, or both. Several of the Sisters commented that becoming a nun was the only way in which they could receive training in medicine and nursing. At the time, the role of missionary offered women opportunities for work, travel, and independence that they would not have had had they remained at home. Reading accounts written by missionary sisters in the *Steyler Missionsbote* had fueled several sisters' imaginations and desire to travel to foreign lands rather than enter convents in Germany. Some of the Sisters also spoke of their fondness for their role as care-givers and mother to many children. They expressed this maternal role, however, in relationship to Jesus: "Like Jesus, the Sisters recognize the special needs of women," "Like Jesus, the Sisters were teachers," "Like Jesus, the Sisters help the sick."[13] Thus, they subscribe to a notion of maternalism based upon the model of Jesus as the caretaker of humanity in general.

Reality versus rhetoric: "maternalism" in action

As the followiing incidents show, the Sisters' behavior was more varied and nuanced than that delineated by either the rhetoric of social motherhood (*Mütterlichkeit*) or nineteenth-century notions of the "character of the sexes" (*Geschlechtscharakter*). Instead, aspects of nationalism, race, sex, and religion intertwined in the context of colonial New Guinea to allow for and necessitate different modes of maternal behavior than those prescribed by the ideologies of the time. These accounts were recorded in the chronicle the Sisters kept at the mission's outstation on Manam Island.[14] Following Jolly (1993), I use the term "maternalism" here not as a female-centered substitute for the male-centered concept of paternalism, nor simply as the gentle/violent contrast in character or demeanor suggested in the previous discussions, but rather to indicate a different construction of sociality based on the different way that race, class, and gender intersected for European women, and, in particular, for the Holy Spirit Sisters, who were embedded within the patriarchal structure of the Catholic Church and the German Society of the Divine Word.

Missionary maternalism in practice

By the eve of World War I there was an almost equal number of nuns in northern New Guinea as of priests and brothers combined. Of the 91 SVD missionaries and SSpS nuns in German New Guinea in 1913, 43 were sisters, 26 were priests and 22 were brothers (Sack and Clark 1980: 144). Throughout the course of their presence in Papua New Guinea, the SSpS Sisters' primary tasks have been teaching (reading, arithmetic, geography), nursing, domestic training, and religious education. Additional responsibilities included cooking, washing, and housekeeping for SVD priests and brothers living in separate quarters on the mission station. Depending upon the size of the station, like traditional wives the Sisters have often been expected to perform both sets of duties, assisted by local girls. On the smaller mission stations, with only three or four Sisters, it was not uncommon for a nursing or teaching sister to return to the convent at the end of the day and help prepare dinner for the priest(s), brothers, and other sisters. At the larger convents, there was a division of labor among the Sisters such that one or two were designated as "kitchen" or "domestic" sisters, whose main responsibilities were cooking or housekeeping chores. Local girls always lived in a separate dormitory in the convent compound or came daily from nearby villages to work. They either were paid wages or received their board and lodging plus some clothes in exchange for their labor.

Under the trying conditions of an unhealthy climate, lack of supplies, and dependence upon their own subsistence gardens for fresh food, the Sisters pursued their primary work as teachers and dispensers of medical aid. They were particularly concerned with maternal and infant care, traveling by boat or horseback to conduct open-air baby clinics. While they were focused on teaching children to read and write, they were also equally intent on teaching as a means of recruiting new members to the Catholic Church.

Maternalism imposed

At mission outstations such as Manam Island, where the following incident took place, the Sisters' attempts at eliminating local customs such as the practice of infanticide posed a quandary for them: local beliefs prohibited village women from raising a newborn baby when a mother died in childbirth or when an illegitimate child was born, yet the Sisters were not able to assume the role of surrogate mother themselves.[15]

As the following incident reveals, in order to impress upon villagers the need to stop infanticide the Sisters sometimes acted aggressively towards the birth mothers. The text was recorded in 1931, six years after the missionaries had settled on the island:

> In Oaia [Village], there was a young woman who had an illegitimate child. We tried to get her to keep the child and not kill it. We baptized it, but a short while later on, the child was dead. We do not know whether the child's mother had killed it or not. I went over to the village to get her. I went into the house after her, but she ran away. I threw bowls and pots after her, which all broke to pieces.
>
> During the night I went there again, accompanied by some girls. Again, the young woman saw me too soon and was able to escape. So I kicked down the little birth house [*boaruku*] and destroyed it. "Come now and sleep in your destroyed house, if you like!!" I called out after the woman.[16]

Here is a dramatic example of the manner in which the Sisters gradually began to change Manam attitudes towards childbirth and infanticide, not simply by preaching tolerance and respect for human life, but also by forceful demonstrations of their belief in the validity of their convictions. It also reveals that they could be far from docile women when intent upon enforcing what they saw as the Lord's word. Like the priests, who also found themselves sometimes forced to use violence to insure their authority, the Sister showed no hesitancy in using physical force to impress upon the wayward woman—and the other villagers—the strength of her moral convictions.

Protection of local women and girls

As the following incident reveals, in addition to education and employment the Sisters also offered village girls the option of temporary sanctuary at the convent, helping to protect them from arranged marriages with unsuitable partners second wives:

> On November 13 and 14 [1931], the *Kiap* was here.[17] They took away our little Maria from Kuluguma [village]. She was barely fifteen. The *Tanepoa* from Kuluguma has promised her to Paisi, a relative of his, who works as a Police Boy in Madang [the Provincial capital]. But Maria did not want to go. For this reason she came to us six months ago, hoping that we would help her. She went to mass and communion almost every day . . .
>
> Now the villagers have come and said that she has to come home . . . Maria's first words were: "I don't want to." She began to cry bitterly . . .
>
> I said that Paisi himself should come and that I wanted to speak with him . . . Then I said to Maria, "If you want, you may go and marry him for he has no other wife so far . . ." When we saw that she did not want to go, we let her be . . .
>
> At 5:30 in the morning the impertinent police boy came with a gun and an official piece of paper. This contained an accusation against us . . . and a summons for Mariay . . . We wanted to defend ourselves against unjust accusation and if possible help Maria in her predicament . . . Then [the kiap] asked the girl what kind of work she was doing. She said that she was working in the garden . . ." We, I know what kind of work she is doing at the Sisters'," he said, "and that's supposed to be education!" . . .
>
> . . . The length of the lawful conversation gave the people enough time to frighten Maria. Finally Maria was asked once more if she wanted Paisi, to which she answered, "Mi laik" ["I like" or "I want"] and she began to cry loudly. At that time she was ordered to go to Paisi's relatives in the village . . . Once again injustice was victorious. We could do no more but to pray for the girl.[18]

Stories like this one were probably common on Manam at that time, since young women had little say in their marriage arrangements. What is different about this particular case is the role the Holy Spirit Sisters played, or attempted to play, in altering the outcome. The Sisters' account reveals the constraints they faced in their struggle to support Maria in her desire not to marry Paisi. On the one hand, they were able to offer her a temporary haven away from home, as well as their backing of her choice not to marry, and thus the hope of success. These were probably not of insignificant value to young Manam women, as many of them sought out the Sisters' support. However, we also see the limits to the Sisters' effectiveness in confrontation with the European kiap. They could offer Maria support, but they could not overturn Manam male hegemony when coupled with the authority of the colonial state.

Conclusion

As the above incidents show, many factors constrained and shaped the nature and effectiveness of the Sisters' goals and behavior. Most important among these were the strength of indigenous customs and beliefs, the limitations posed by the physical constraints of a rugged tropical frontier environment, and the subordinate position of German missionaries within the colonial social structure of Australian New Guinea.

Many of the Holy Spirit Sisters' aims and actions, as well as the activities of missions in general, can be characterized as maternal; that is, showing concern for the care and nurturance of children, for the education of girls and women, and expressing a focus on the creation of good (Christian) families. Both the SVD and the SSpS missionaries felt that women were best suited to these tasks. Hence, early on Holy Spirit Sisters came to New Guinea to work in tandem with the SVD priests and brothers.

In New Guinea the Sisters experienced a greater personal freedom than they would have had they followed the traditional roles expected of them in Germany at the time. However, while conditions in New Guinea allowed SSpS Sisters unanticipated opportunities for personal independence (for example, several of the Sisters commented on the pleasure they took in going off on clinic patrols on horseback by themselves—usually accompanied by at least one local girl) and achievement, the gendered division of labor within the SVD and SSpS organizations still hove to the nineteenth-century model of men's and women's appropriate gendered roles. This gendered dichotomy also replicated the subordinate role of women within the hierarchy of the Catholic Church.

However, the education, as well as the opportunities for work and travel, that the Sisters provided local women and children did not simply reproduce hegemonic ideas and values; they were also the source of new ideas and concepts of the self, and of self-worth. Although Maria from Kuluguma village failed in her attempt to avoid an unwanted marriage, other Manam girls were able to successfully use the sanctuary and support of the Sisters.

Moreover, although the Sisters encouraged local women in the development of Christian families, they had themselves rejected marriage and actual motherhood. Thus, simply by the example of their own lives, the Sisters were an alternative model of womanhood for New Guinea women.

Thus, one of the consequences of the presence of the Holy Spirit Sisters in Papua New Guinea was to create a space for indigenous women to experience new female roles, celibate and otherwise. This knowledge and the opportunity to gain new skills opened new directions—both secular and spiritual—for women to pursue besides the traditional role of village wife and mother. Many New Guinea women have continued their education beyond primary school and become teachers or nurses. There is also a small number of young Papua New Guinea women who have chosen to become missionary nuns themselves, and the first indigenous Holy Spirit Sister was recently sent abroad. Almost one hundred years later a circle has been completed: a Papua New Guinean SSpS Sister is now on a mission of her own (Lutkehaus 2007).

Acknowledgments

The research for this article was conducted under grants from the Wenner-Gren Foundation for Anthropological Research (Grant No. 5569), a Zumberge Faculty Research Stipend from the University of Southern California (USC), and a Grant from the USC Gender Studies Program at USC. I would like to thank the Holy Spirit Sisters on Manam Island and Alexishafen in Papua New Guinea who generously gave of their time to talk with me, as well as the Sisters in Steyl, Netherlands, Wimbern, Germany, and Rome who allowed me access to their archives and their memories. This article is a shortened version of a similarly titled article published in Mary Huber and Nancy Lutkehaus (eds.) (1999) *Gendered Missions: Female and Male in Missionary Discourse and Practice*, Ann Arbor: University of Michigan Press, pp. 207–35.

Notes

1 See Comaroff and Comaroff 1991; Hunt 1990; Kipp 1990; Thorne 1997.
2 See, for example, Anna Davin's "Imperialism and Motherhood," 1997.
3 See, for example, Grimshaw 1989; Allen 1991.
4 This article focuses on the Holy Spirit Sisters prior to 1945 in the German Territory of New Guinea (1884–1914). Subsequent to World War I, this region became part of the Australian Territory of Papua and New Guinea.
5 Ong also says that "The overwhelming femininity of the Roman Catholic Church from the human side suggests that a male clergy is basically not a characteristic of the Church so much as a countervailing feature" (1981: 178). Ong's work is analyzed by Peter McDonough in an article that discusses gender roles and hierarchy in contemporary Catholicism (McDonough 1990).
6 During the 1930s, Germans comprised the largest number of expatriate missionaries in New Guinea outside of Australians (Lacey 1972: 779).

7 Vocational training in skills considered appropriate to men, such as carpentry, printing, ship-building and seamanship, etc., was taught, for the most part, by the brothers.
8 According to Frevert, "Even in the late 19th century women who subscribed to the bourgeois movement [in Germany] firmly believed that the female sex was without exception "destined for motherhood', and that this destiny determined women's physical and psychic constitution" (1989: 126).
9 See, for example, Prelinger's (1987) *Charity, Challenge and Change: Religious Dimensions of the Mid-Nineteenth Century Women's Movement in Germany.*
10 This story has been published in several languages and is available through the SSpS convents.
11 Due to Bismark's anti-Catholic policy (*Kulturkampf*) in Germany at the time, Fr. Arnold had been forced to locate his fledgling mission order across the border in Steyl, Netherlands. The mother house of the SSpS is now in Rome.
12 Born in Germany between 1907 and 1911, Sister Maria died in Papua New Guinea in 1993. I spoke with her there in 1992.
13 *The History of the Holy Spirit Sisters in Papua New Guinea* (n.d.), pp. 1–2.
14 The chronicles are official documents that the Sisters are required to keep as a record of important events in the life of the convent.
15 For more detailed information about Manam Island, see Lutkehaus 1995.
16 *Chronicle of the Sisters Servants of the Holy Spirit*, Herz Jesu Convent, Bieng Catholic Mission, Manam Island, Papua New Guinea: 1924–1974, unpublished ms., p. 28.
17 *Kiap* is the Melanesian Pidgin term for an Australian colonial officer.
18 *Herz Jesu Convent Chronicle*, Manam Island, pp. 30–4.

References

Allen, Ann Taylor (1991) *Feminism and Motherhood in Germany, 1800–1914*, New Brunswick: Rutgers University Press.

Comaroff, Jean and John L. Comaroff (1991) *Of Revelation and Revolution: Christianity, Colonialism and Consciousness in South Africa*, vol. 1, Chicago: University of Chicago Press.

Davin, Anna (1997) "Imperialism and Motherhood," in Frederick Cooper and Ann Laura Stoler (eds.) *Tensions of Empire: Colonial Cultures in a Bourgeois World*, pp. 87–151, Berkeley: University of California Press.

Firth, Stewart (1983) *New Guinea under the Germans*, Victoria: Melbourne University Press.

Frevert, Ute (1989) *Women in German History: From Bourgeois Emancipation to Sexual Liberation*, Oxford: Berg (Original German edition 1986).

Grimshaw, Patricia (1989) *Paths of Duty: American Missionary Wives in Nineteenth Century Hawaii*, Honolulu: University of Hawaii Press.

Hausen, Karir (1981) "Family and Role-Division: The Polarization of Sexual Stereotypes in the Nineteenth Century—an Aspect of the Dissociation of Work and Family Life," in Richard J. Evans and W. R. Lee (eds.) *The German Family*, pp. 51–83, Totowa, NJ: Barnes and Noble Books.

Huber, Mary Taylor (1988) *The Bishop's Progress: A Historical Ethnography of Catholic Missionary Experience on the Sepik Frontier*, Washington DC: Smithsonian Institution Press.

Hunt, Nancy Rose (1990) "Domesticity and Colonialism in Belgian Africa: Usumbura's Foyer Social, 1946–1960," *Signs* 15(3): 447–74.

Jolly, Margaret (1993) "Colonizing Women: The Maternal Body and Empire," in Sneja Gunew and Anna Yeatman (eds.) *Feminism and the Politics of Difference*, pp. 103–27. Boulder: Westview Press.

Kipp, Rita Smith (1990) *The Early Years of a Dutch Colonial Mission: The Karo Field*, Ann Arbor: University of Michigan Press.

Lacey, R. L. (1972) "Missions," in Peter Ryan (ed.) *Encyclopedia of Papua and New Guinea*, pp. 772–82, Melbourne: Melbourne University Press.

Lutkehaus, Nancy (1995) *Zaria's Fire: Engendered Moments in Manam Ethnography*, Durham, NC: Carolina Academic Press.

—— (2007) 'In the Way' in Melanesia: Modernity and the New Woman in Papua New Guinea as Catholic Missionary Sister," in John Barker (ed.) *Dilemmas and Exemplars: The Anthropology of Morality in Melanesia*, pp. 149–67, London: Ashgate Publishers.

McDonough, Peter (1990) "Metamorphoses of the Jesuits: Sexual Identity, Gender Roles, and Hierarchy in Catholicism," *Comparative Studies in Society and History* 32(2): 325–56.

Ong, Walter J. (1981) *Fighting for Life: Contest, Sexuality and Consciousness*, Ithaca, NY: Cornell University Press.

Prelinger, Catherine M. (1987) *Charity, Challenge, and Change: Religious Dimensions of the Mid-Nineteenth Century Woman's Movement in Germany*, New York: Greenwood Press.

Sack, Peter and Dymphna Clark (eds.) (1980) *German New Guinea: The Draft Annual Report for 1913–14*, Trans. Peter Sack and Dymphna Clark, Canberra: The Australian National University.

Sisters Servants of the Holy Spirit (SSpS) (n.d.) *The History of the Holy Spirit Sisters in Papua New Guinea*, printed pamphlet, Papua New Guinea.

Thorne, Susan (1997) "'The Conversion of Englishmen and the Conversion of the World Inseparable': Missionary Imperialism and the Language of Class in Early Industrial Britain," in Frederick Cooper and Ann Laura Stoler (eds.) *Tensions of Empire: Colonial Cultures in a Bourgeois World*, pp. 238–62, Berkeley: University of California Press.

37

YOUNG CONVERTS

Christian missions, gender and youth in Onitsha, Nigeria 1880–1929

Misty L. Bastian

Source: *Anthropological Quarterly*, 73(3) (2000), 145–58.

> When African children of both sexes roam about at will indoors & out-of-doors without clothing of any kind, until in some cases 18 years of age, & when Christian mothers allow the same unclothed condition to prevail among their own young ones, the innocence of infancy is lost at birth, & how is it possible for the young people to be either pure in thought or chaste in deed? When the older girls & women are unclothed to the waist, & when even among Christian mothers an upper covering is considered a "fad," rather than an act of decency, is it to be wondered at that the young men fall an easy prey to the enticements of the girls? The African Christian woman has yet to learn her responsibility in this direction, & we trust that the Missions to Women held during the year in this District & elsewhere—to be followed by a Conference of Women on Social & other subjects next year at Onitsha—may lead women to see their duty in this matter of Social Purity. (From Annual Letter, dated December 18, 1909, by Rev. J. C[raven]. R. Wilson)[1]

In the late nineteenth century and early decades of the twentieth Church Missionary Society (Anglican) missionaries, both of African and European descent, became interested in gaining converts among Igbo-speaking women in southeastern Nigeria. Schooling was an integral part of the conversion process. This education was perceived by the missionaries as a concomitant training to that of young, Igbo-speaking men. Igbo men were seen as the deepest foundations of the Anglican church in southeastern Nigeria. Europeans never really considered Nigeria a proper location for settler colonization but an experiment in indirect rule from its inception. So these young men were trained not only to be catechists and layreaders by their CMS missionaries but eventually to become missionaries and priests to a chain of indigenous congregations, stretching across the very populous Igbo-speaking region. During this same period girls were trained in the doctrines of the Christian faith, to become the "helpmeets" for their Christian male contemporaries and proper mothers of the next Christian (hopefully Anglican) generation. Women, therefore, mattered to CMS missionaries both as the domestic purveyors of an Anglican culture and as exemplars for women's christianization throughout the Nigerian southeast. While Anglican Igbo women, too, were to be missionaries of a sort, their mission was to be bounded by the walls of their European-style homes or, at most, kept to specific Christian localities over which their husbands held priestly sway.

I contend in this article that CMS missionization in Onitsha and other parts of the southeastern region of what is now known as Nigeria, was therefore based on developing quite separate and gendered body/mind disciplines for Igbo "youth" which were then meant to be extended into adulthood and on to the next generations. Indeed, I suggest ways these body/mind disciplines themselves, based on an amalgam of contemporary European as well as Igbo gender categories, helped to develop a new and separate category of personhood among Igbo-speakers. This was called, in some locations, *ndi kris*, the Christian people—a group that was generally youthful and otherwise marginal to ordinary Igbo social life in the period. The making of ndi kris was therefore also the making of "youth" as a cultural category in this part of West Africa, demonstrating how western gender regimes along with local ones were essential for that category's development and dissemination. I will therefore also discuss what the development of this socially separate, gendered, and youthful category of persons meant for Onitsha Igbo society at large, as well as use the material to problematize not only western notions of gender but, indeed, to discuss how "youth" itself is meaningfully constituted in the theoretical literature.

Constructing young converts: the CMS and gendered problems of conversion

Early CMS missionaries in southeastern Nigeria were mostly repatriated Igbo and Yoruba men from Sierra Leone, the children of people rescued from the transatlantic slave trade.[2] The social persona of these young men was itself therefore formed by a process of conversion to Christianity and mission education, mostly in Freetown during the mid-nineteenth century. Missionaries of African descent were recruited in an evangelical campaign in that city by Anglican Bishop Samuel Crowther (a repatriated Yoruba speaker) during the 1860s and 70s.[3] The new Niger Mission was an experiment for the CMS—the first time that the established English church had approved indigenous missionization. The mission's ultimate success or failure was carefully watched by CMS administrators in London. Because of its symbolic importance to the growing numbers of Christians in West Africa as well as its experimental status in the eyes of the Anglican Church, Crowther and his colleagues chose to begin the Niger Mission in the well-known river port of Onitsha. It was distant enough inland from the coastline of the Bights of Benin and Biafra to work outside the surveillance of most European colonialists but connected to coastal trading ports via the Niger so that supplies and correspondence could still be transported.

CMS missionaries first appeared in Onitsha, on the eastern banks of the Niger River, in the 1860s—partially in response to Bishop Crowther's shrewd economic and political assessment of the future importance of the town for European colonialism. When the first missionary (the Rev. Taylor, a repatriated Igbo) arrived, however, he found that Christian evangelism in the town would be difficult and fraught with dangers. *Ndi onicha* (Onitsha people) eagerly accepted European merchandise and were already involved with the representatives of European trading firms. They were, however, highly skeptical of the offer of a new religion, particularly once they discovered that African CMS missionaries were accorded little respect by western traders. This meant that important Onitsha elders kept their distance from the missionaries, although a few treated the Christian evangelists like obnoxious but amusing pets.[4] The first, tentative converts were thus drawn from the ranks of Onitsha's more marginal populations: domestic slaves (*ndi oru*) attached to European trading compounds, a very few *ndiani* (freeborn, literally "people of the earth/soil") women who were widowed or impoverished, as well as a small number of children who were sent by ndi onicha to find out what was happening with these strange, new Africans who dressed like and spoke the same language as the Europeans. By the late 1870s the missionaries realized that they had little hope of success among Onitsha elites. They busied themselves buying enslaved children, rescuing twins (who were supposed to be cast into the *ofia ojoo*, the "bad bush," as abominations), and taking in the equally abominated mothers of twins, as well as ministering to the youthful African workers associated with the European "factories" (warehouses) along the riverside. It was these, mainly young converts, with nowhere to go and little to lose in their connection to the missions, who would form the most permanent, early congregation.

Not only was the fledgling congregation made up of marginal people residing in and around the town, but it was a fragile group, highly susceptible to any shock. During the late 1870s, for example, the CMS mission in Onitsha—whose interest in twins (*umu ejima*), so-called sacred slaves (*ndi osu*) and other outcasts was now apparent and the cause of some disquiet in Onitsha's main "village" of Inland Town—was almost destroyed by a series of witchcraft accusations leveled against the congregation by two former domestic slaves.[5] Although, from archival evidence, there is a hint that these women may have been coerced to "confess" their witchcraft and implicate the mission, the very notion that Christians were really witches setting up shop by the Onitsha riverside ensured that it would be twenty more years before the Anglican church made serious inroads into converting the local population. Indeed, rumors persisted of witchly doings at the old CMS compound through the late 1980s when I did fieldwork in Onitsha, so it could be said that the mission never fully recovered its reputation, even a hundred years after the event.

The Niger Mission's greatest success in Onitsha came through its early decision to educate local boys (and, by the 1890s, some girls) in basic English literacy and western numeracy. Although male and female elders continued to shun the church throughout the latter half of the nineteenth century and forbade their dependents to spend time there on Sundays, the spectacle of a small number of young boys sitting over their slates doing arithmetic and learning to speak a smattering of English proved enticing. Ndi onicha quickly deduced the usefulness of a cadre of young men, owing their allegiance to the *Obi* (king of Onitsha) and his *imobi* (court), who could interpret and keep accounts in the recently introduced western style.[6] A small number of ndiani women, who had been involved in the mission since the witchcraft episode, against the better judgment of the kingly court, were now quietly encouraged to send their sons to the mission school to see what they could learn. One of these young men, Isaac Mba, became the CMS's star convert and pupil. He went on not only to become literate in English but to assist in the translation of the Bible into Igbo, as well as to teach in CMS schools before being exiled for the unforgivable mission crime of polygyny.[7] Although one of the first and most talented, Mba was soon followed by a flood of boys. It became fashionable by the late 1890s for Onitsha ndiani boys to spend as much of their days as possible in the CMS compound —even when school was not in session.

Boys who were taught at CMS schools also received training in the Christian religion—not as a secondary set of lessons but as the centerpiece of their education. This was an unexpected consequence of mission schooling, as far as Onitsha elders were concerned, and soon became an unwelcome one as the boys lectured their seniors on such topics as "idol worship" and polygynous relations. One response to male missionization was for wily elders to implicate their own children in polygynous unions and estrange them from the church, as in the case of Isaac Mba. Senior men's control over bridewealth and access to marriage partners proved to be a major stumbling block for maintaining Christian conversion among the missionaries' pupils by the 1890s.[8] As male students like Isaac Mba matured, they clearly needed to marry someone. The CMS's relative lack of interest in the cultivation of marriageable girls made the mission compounds a masculinist preserve and a place where female companionship was almost unknown. Mba was not the only young convert who strayed, however unwittingly, from CMS Christian teachings in his search for a lover or wife, and a veritable war ensued between the missionaries and Onitsha elders over the hearts and minds of younger men, using young women as pawns. (See Wilson quote, above.) After the desertion of Mba and a few other, favored young male converts, senior missionaries began to intervene in the possible marriages of their catechists, actively corresponding with one another over the question of which converts might productively take on the responsibilities of marriage and when they should wed.[9] With the need for their converts to marry within the church if the congregation was to be maintained and reproduced, missionaries were forced to reconsider the importance of women for their mission and to take a serious interest in girls' education for the first time during this decade.

Because of complicated internal CMS politics which there is no space to go into here, the 1890s also saw the phasing out of Africans and the introduction of British clerics and layworkers into the Niger Mission.[10] Since the population of British CMS missionaries at this period invariably included a few adventurous women as nurses and elementary school teachers, this also meant that some female missionaries soon found their way up the Niger to Onitsha.[11] These women missionaries, who appear from their correspondence and clearly ideological programs to have been (somewhat covert) Christian members of the first wave of feminism, at once made girls' training their special mission.[12] By the 1910s, a scant twenty years after British women's arrival on the southeastern Nigerian scene, almost no male missionary had anything to do with the education of Igbo girls. Indeed, girls' educational establishments were by then constructed outside the environs of Onitsha proper, away from "harmful influences" on the Waterside, where most male CMS missionaries lived and worked and where Igbo boys and young men were constantly in attendance.

Female separatism was not only encoded in women's missionized space in the 1900s but in the very mode of girls' education. Where the boys' school curriculum included such coursework as New and Old Testament classes, English poetry, arithmetic, geography, physiology, hygiene, and first aid, all taught in English after the elementary forms, using English textbooks,[13] girls were instead taught to read enough Igbo to understand their Bibles and hymn-books. Indeed, they were rarely introduced to the English language prior to the 1920s, unless marked out to become pupil teachers or special students at CMS "ladies'" academies in Lagos or Sierra Leone. Girls were also taught a plethora of domestic courses meant to hone their skills to become proper Christian homemakers and housewives. Pamela Row, one of the missionaries at the Girls' Training School at Umudioka (outside of Onitsha, but a location where many Onitsha girls were educated), described the typical girls' training regime in her Annual Letter of 1909:

> The girls do a great deal of practical work; what with washing, ironing, cooking, sweeping, fetching wood & water, their days are fully occupied. We try to do as much outside work as we can. . . .[14]

By the 1910s converted Christian girls and young women were sent to these establishments not only by their parents but by their prospective, Christian fiances, who were expected to pay all their fees (as part of the bridewealth special to ndi kris) as well as for their food and lodging. Young Christian men with an eye to advancement within the CMS and colonial administrative hierarchy were already becoming convinced at this early period of the need for Christian, relatively sophisticated wives who could offer domestic support to their husbands in a manner approved by the Europeans. Such wives were considered by men a token of youthful male success within the emerging colonial class structure and were, indeed, an integral part of the development of an elite, Christian class.[15]

It is also clear that the development of such a new class within Igboland did not go unnoticed outside Christian ranks. The potential pragmatic benefits of the missionized girls' coursework became so well understood outside CMS enclaves that a number of non-Christian parents, hoping for a larger bridewealth and connections to the increasingly well-to-do Christian families, eventually were willing to send their daughters to Umudioka and other similar locations. Igbo-speaking parents sent their daughters away knowing full well that this would mean the girls would be christianized and effectively cut off from *omenani* ("tradition," literally "respect for the earth"). From the point of view of the missionaries, the girls' training centers were therefore a huge success—particularly since it was discovered that local people would pay more willingly for this practical, domestic training than for the more expensive, technical, religious education that boys were offered. Many more boys, it appears, studied on scholarships paid for by Anglican congregations in the U.K. than did girls.[16] The girls' training centers became largely self-supporting; partially a function of the separatist ideologies of the women missionaries and partially a function of a reluctance, on the part of "home" congregations, to promote African girls' education of any kind.[17] This reluctance could be a sign that British outside the colonies were aware of the usefulness of mission education to transform the class situation of the colonized, or simply a sign of late Victorian ambivalence about women's education more generally. Whatever this lack of support for girls' education meant to those living in the metropole, however, it had serious ramifications for the development of categories of youth and gender within the CMS mission sphere.

Within the emerging Christian community in the Nigerian southeast during this period, a community which was predominantly youthful and alienated from both its elders and non-Christian peers, this separate and unequal training meant that boys and young men were necessarily considered by the missionaries to be the superior members (even if they brought in less money for the mission coffers). Boys and young men were given scholarships and more prestigious coursework, and they were being groomed as catechists for future mission work. Girls and young women were constantly told that their duties as converts lay in providing decent, Christian homes for their future husbands and children.[18] Later, in the 1920s, when the demand for girls' training grew too great for CMS missionaries to handle on their own, some would lament that they had trained young women too well in their domestic roles:

> At St. Monica's School [descendant of Umudioka Girls' Training School, above] the pressure is getting utterly beyond the physical powers of the Staff. The work now falling upon the ladies cannot be done in the time of mortal disposal. The School has been brought under Government Inspection practically on the orders of Salisbury Square [headquarters of the CMS in London], and the work has doubled in consequence. The impossibility of maintaining a responsible native staff aggravates the situation. The girls as soon as they become really effective leave on account of marriage. Three senior members of the native staff have gone during the last few months and only one responsible native teacher remains at the moment. Native girls cannot be found yet who are prepared to consider any other career but that of wife and mother, hence the school has to depend on European workers which is the opposite to the work in the charge of men. Boys can be got by the score but not girls.[19]

By this time, ndi kris in Onitsha subscribed to different and more distinct gender boundaries than those existing between their parents and grandparents. Girls and young women opted out of many community events where their female elders had important, public roles and had learned that their own power must be firmly based in domestic responsibilities under male heads of household.[20] Most Igbo societies were both patrilineal and exceedingly patriarchal before the advent of the Christian missions and colonialism more broadly, but women did have, through their interactions in the marketplaces of their marital towns and as daughters of particular patrilineages, many connections outside the marital household (Uchendu 1965; Amadiume 1987). Certainly some Igbo-speaking women could become priestesses, prophets, and *ndi dibia* (healers/diviners), as well as, in Onitsha, take on the important roles of "mothers of the town" or "market queen" (*omu*) and be members of female title societies. (See Helen Henderson 1969 for a full discussion of these roles.)

These connections enabled Igbo women in the immediate precolonial and early colonial periods to establish themselves as important personages in their own right as well as to know other women and men, across the generations as well as across space. Christian girls and young women were not encouraged to make these connections or to take on these social roles, even after they matured, because they could not participate in the "pagan" ritual practices that were an important part of each activity. Some Christian girls may have used this severing of ties to the older women's community (*umunwaanyi*) to their individual advantage, or as a marker of their resistance to "outmoded" ways. We see in the footnoted quote above, however, they were also more isolated within their households and consequently more bonded to the fortunes of their husbands than ever before.

The despised and misunderstood minority: Igbo Christian girls and young women in the early twentieth century

Female missionaries, perhaps acting out of their own experiences of domestic isolation as well as Christian feminist principles, tried to mitigate this isolation somewhat by establishing women's groups at school. One such group was the Scripture Union, for those women who could read their Bibles and by encouraging Christian women who had graduated from their training to meet periodically as "Old Girls" or members of Christian women's associations. In the early 1900s regular Women's Conferences were established by joint committees of female missionaries and prominent Old Girls. The first of these conferences was held in January, 1910, at Ozala, on the Waterside in Onitsha, where CMS women missionaries maintained a residence and offices in conjunction with the main, and mostly male-dominated, mission compound. Over seventy women, youthful and married to CMS-educated men, attended the conference, many coming from what were then formidable distances. Besides prayers and lengthy discussion of the future of mission education for women in the Igbo-speaking areas, the Old Girls were encouraged to discuss their personal situations. The writer of the official report of the conference (probably one of the women missionaries) noted that

> Some of the women spoke very well and most were eager to give messages from their town and to tell out their difficulties. Prayer was asked in almost every case and difficulties in connection with the heathen, the Government, and the Roman Catholics were spoken of besides those of a more private nature. One was impressed with the fact that although we are winning some, Christians in this country are the despised and misunderstood minority.[21]

As the Igbo attendees were clearly among the most activist and committed Christian converts, one may have some sense from the above of their everyday circumstances, once the converted women moved away from the secluded and supportive atmosphere of the girls' training centers. From the Aba Commission's *Notes of Evidence* in 1930 we know that missionized women sometimes banded together in their marital towns in groups that became known as *mikiri* ("meetings;" see also Green 1964 and Van Allen 1976). These mimicked, in many respects, other indigenous women's groups, particularly savings collectives and the dance groups (based on something like age-grades) whose *egwu* (songs/dances) would otherwise have content offensive to Christian sensibilities.

CMS missionized girls and women during the early 1900s needed these support groups, not only to maintain and enlarge upon what they had learned in their schools, but to give them some prestige in what could be hostile living environments. It appears that many girls throughout Igboland had risked the wrath of their parents, even at times nominally Christian parents, to apply for training at the mission schools during the early period of the intensification of girls' missionization—perhaps with an eye to making a Christian marriage of their own choice. We have, for instance, CMS missionary Frances Dennis's testimony on women who expressed an interest in the western Igbo missions during the first years of the century:

> Such was the state of the women when we went to Idumuje Ugboko in 1902 and they were quite content—the work among them was most discouraging from the first—while many young men came forward for Baptism and were baptized [,] only one old woman could be baptized with the exception of two young girls who were betrothed to Christian men and went away to the Girls' School at Iyienu & were married last year. There was apparently no hope for the women [,] fanning any desire in their hearts to be good only brought them into great trouble—the chiefs and the native courts were strongly opposed to any reform and in several cases when girls persisted in their refusal to marry heathen 'husbands' and wish to marry Christian men. The native courts were appealed to and judgment was given against the women.
>
> Meanwhile the young converts were breaking away from this bad custom seeking young girls to whom they could be married in Church.
>
> Clearly things could not go on as before & for many months in 1905 there was chaos in Idumuje Ugboko. Public opinion was all against the women who wanted to be good & there were no Christian parents to be willing for their girls to release themselves from old bonds made for them—I was several times awakened by the screams of girls being dragged away to neighbouring towns to men whom they hated. Many flung themselves upon our protection—one or two girls 'devoted' to the house persuaded their fathers to allow them to marry went to the Girls' School at Iyienu with others whose 'husbands' had been prevailed upon to receive the dowry back again.
>
> Towards the end of the year Bishop Tugwell made representations to the Govt Officials which led them to see that something must be done to make a law in favour of the women. It was to the effect that no young girl should be forced to marry a man to whom she had been betrothed as a child never having lived with him, and any young man wishing to marry her could do so by paying the dowry

> into the native court to be repaid to the former 'husband'. So the women have been saved—Praise God.[22]

Although the majority of Igbo-speaking girls during this period were unlikely to approach the missions, Dennis' account shows us that some were not only willing to take the risk of offending their parents and destroying their patrilineally arranged marital opportunities, they had determined upon it. For Dennis, of course, these were the "women who wanted to be good," but from the point of view of Idumuje Ugboko elders, they must have seemed young hellions, bent on destroying proper gender relations along with carefully constructed networks of alliance and affinity. The picture of girls dragged screaming into the night was constructed by Dennis to woo potential CMS donors for a girls' training institution in western Igbo. Nonetheless, there remains in the account something of the horror and embarrassment that must have been felt by every participant in these evening dramas. Nothing could have been farther from the expectations of western Igbo parents in relation to their female children's behavior; nothing could have been more agonizing for Igbo girls than to have their well-known rights of marriage refusal (Uchendu 1965: 52–53) publicly flaunted. For those Idumuje Ugboko residents who were not directly involved, the piteous sobbing, pleas, and loud arguments between missionaries and long-suffering parents must have been completely disruptive of the town peace—something that would have confirmed that the missions had brought abomination along with their books and new religious practices.

Even devoted missionaries like Miss Dennis seemed nonplused by the reaction of girls and their parents alike; the CMS's belated focus on girls had stirred up something unexpected and clearly powerful. Frances Dennis, trained by her own culture to be obedient to her elders, including senior administrators in the CMS itself, is obviously torn in her account between a belief that western Igbo parents had responsibility for and authority over their children and her equally strong sense of the importance of the Christian mission for the people's personal salvation. Partially because of this struggle within their consciousness, it appears, CMS missionaries did not all take up the cudgels fiercely for their "wayward" female charges but surrendered the majority of them back to their lineage mates for marriages that—from Dennis's use of punctuation ("'husbands'")—the Anglicans did not consider legitimate. The metaphors of marriage and women's submission were simply too engrained, and the lack of funding for girls' training too overwhelming, for missionaries fully to embrace the radical step of emancipating jural minors from the power of parents and other elders, even to spread the gospel.

This did not, as we can see from Wilson's quote at the beginning of this article, keep male Christian missionaries from holding local women and girls responsible for leading male youth astray in Igboland. Igbo-speaking boys were so valued as converts that their sexuality and marriage interests were to be catered to at all costs. Young Igbo women's bodies and sexuality, conversely, were perceived as snares that could entangle the missions in dangerous local politics as well as destabilize the "young converts" who were expected to lay the foundations of the Anglican church throughout Igboland. Although largely unspoken, the need to maintain the girls' training centers at some distance from the homes of the centers' inmates was not only a statement about checking girls' perilous sexuality and policing their improperly bounded bodies, but of maintaining some secrecy about the transformation in gender relations being effected by the missions. This transformation would find its clearest expression in new models of youthful female behavior.

Before discussing this transformation at any length, however, it should be made plain that the western category of "girl" was not one that would have seemed common sense to Igbo-speakers in the early 1900s. The model of girlhood, or female adolescence, that missionaries imported from Britain during this period was marked by specific body practices—notably putting up one's hair and lowering the hemlines of one's skirts—keyed to the onset of menstruation or certain calendrical celebrations (for example, "sweet sixteen" birthday parties).[23] Although menstruation was an important marker for Igbo female personhood as well, it was not construed as the beginning of "adolescence," if we consider this a period of relative freedom before marriage and adult responsibilities, or as marking a particularly poignant moment in a sentimental construction of "girlhood." Instead, menstruation among Igbo-speakers enabled the partial fulfillment of a marriage process that may have begun some years earlier. Menstruation could be marked by taking on the dress and hairstyles associated with full, married womanhood—that is, the wearing of cloth around the waist and discarding the elaborate, semipermanent constructions of hair and mica-flecked mud as well as some of the adornments that demarcated unmarried status.[24] In some Igbo-speaking areas, menstruation and/or the growth of breasts was the signal for the placement of young women in "fattening houses" (*nkpu*; see Basden 1966: 73–75), a ritual process of seclusion and beautification that might last several Igbo four-day weeks or even months at a time. Emergence from seclusion did not mark a beginning of a liminal period of adolescence but, once again, marriage and the bearing of children, quite often at a chronological age felt by the British to be too young for such a responsibility. Christianizing young women also meant turning people who qualified as candidates for full adulthood in Igbo into "girls" in order to preserve them for a short time from marriage and for a western domestic education.

The CMS missionaries therefore had to respond to their own ambivalences about both the centrality of marriage to Christian culture (most of the women missionaries were unmarried while in the Niger Mission) and the need to establish a proper, liminal period of "youth" or "girlhood" for christianized women to prepare them for their duties as wives and helpmeets to Christian husbands. Older women were welcome as converts, but the missionaries were constantly disappointed at how little influence such women seemed to hold over their "heathen" husbands, at least in terms of evangelism. It became apparent during the early period of missionization that converted older women were likely to be peripheral in their husbands' households, whether as mothers of twins, barren women, or women too sick to be fully productive as farmers or traders. Younger women and girls proved more important to the long-range plans of missionaries, just as they were crucial to the plans of fathers and lineage elders. By the early 1900s young women were thought by the missionaries to be more malleable and interested in new ideas and commodities—ripe for conversion as well as indoctrination into other Europeanized activities. Missionaries' focus on young women's conversion was also seen as an investment in the future of the church. The children of Christian women had already proved to be the foundation of the Anglican church in the forty years since its inception in Igboland, and CMS missionaries were eager to maintain a hold on the imaginations of children to come through their mothers' examples of faith.

Besides having souls that missionaries could save for Christ, however, these young women also provided much needed domestic services for the busy Europeans and a ready-made set of potential "role models" for other women in the community. They were, in return, educated to attract the young, christianized men who were gaining status and wealth throughout Igboland. Among the mission girls' virtues for the *arriviste* male Christians were their basic understanding of Christian tenets, their adherence to "modest dress" (frocks that covered those offending bodies from neck to ankles), and their expressed willingness to live in the domestic isolation of a Christian, monogamous household. Missionized women were also trained to assist their Christian catechist fiancés in low level evangelical work among the Igbo unconverted. Not least of their work was offering support for the men's Christian ideals within their households and, as noted above, by training Igbo Christian children in the tenets of their new faith and under a domestic regime modeled on that of contemporary Europe. Some of these children were their own, but young Christian wives were later encouraged by the missions to engage in a form of fosterage. They would take in a few of the children of other, aspiring families and train them about Christianity, sanitation, and the proper care of a "modern" household. These children would act as household help for their foster mother while gaining access to the Christian networks that could eventually mean school, employment with the colonial administration or, at least, an enhanced understanding of the new regime.[25]

This model of domestic support and dependency was completely unlike what was expected of the unconverted Igbo woman. Such a woman was more likely to live separately from her husband, with her children, inside a polygynous or extended family household and to attend to women's business, only engaging in a discussion of men's affairs under very special circumstances. Nonetheless, ordinary Igbo women of the period had allegiances that extended beyond their marital households, whether through continued participation in their natal patrilineages or through the relations developed in trade or among other "wives of the village." Missionized women were actively discouraged from spending too much time with Igbo-speaking women of their own lineages or households who refused to convert. They were also discouraged from becoming overly familiar with women or men who had converted to Catholicism or one of the indigenous Christian churches springing up around southeastern Nigeria in the early years of the twentieth century. (See quote above on the antagonism between the CMS and its Catholic counterpart, the Holy Ghost Fathers.) The ties created within *Anglican* mission schools or training centers were supposed to take the place of all culturally significant relations with other women. For instance, CMS women missionaries walked a fine line between being seen as taskmistresses and having a somewhat strained friendship with their pupils and Old Girls, while young women in the schools were encouraged to be both competitive and cooperative with one another through an extracurricular program that ultimately included, besides the domestic labor outlined above, team sports, drill, and, by the 1920s, European women's institutions like the Girl Guides and the YWCA.[26]

Missionized men who showed some interest in evangelism were, by the 1910s, often sent off to villages at some distance from mission centers like Onitsha in order to prepare the way for more professional missionaries or to demonstrate their own fitness for more evangelical responsibility. Their young, recently trained wives would either accompany them directly or be sent for after completing their course.[27] Wives' immediate duties included assisting their husbands in setting up Bible studies as well as developing a model, Christian home for the "heathens" to emulate. This they had to do out of materials that were available to a stranger couple on a stringent budget, without many village-level resources (such as ready access to farmland or seed crops) or the materials of the mission schoolrooms they themselves had only recently quitted. Since there are a number of dialectical variations in what we today call the Igbo language,[28] it is possible that most of these young women were isolated not only by their adherence to the new religion, their manner of dress, and their reluctance to take part in markets or "pagan" women's organizations, but by language as well. Even in Onitsha, where there was a good deal of missionary support for the Old Girls and where the Niger Mission had been based for half a century, young Christian women might find their lot overwhelming, as in this excerpt from a woman missionary's letter to her London-based superior:

> I also spent a few days in Onitsha Town in the house of one of our newly married girls. She was trying to do her best to help her husband in the work but I realized how difficult it was for her. There were a few Christian women all her seniors so it was difficult for her to suggest to them new meetings or means of help. She said to

> me if I speak to the heathen they say to me 'why do you tell us to follow God look at your own father how he has gone back from following God'—It was true her father is a backslider. These things showed me how hard it must be for these young girls to witness for Christ & not get discouraged. We try hard to prepare them & to strengthen their characters in every way possible. We ask also for your prayers that God will put His Spirit within them that they may be all He wants them to be.[29]

In some cases the husbands were sent back to their natal region, but these were probably not villages familiar to the young wives. The fact that the CMS training centers took in girls from all parts of the Niger Mission therefore meant that missionaries were, however inadvertently, maintaining Igbo requirements of exogamy for many of the new Christian marriages. The missionaries, also like Igbo patrilineal elders, expected their charges to make alliances of duty rather than the "love matches" of sentimental western fiction, and many of those who married out of mission schools and training centers knew each other very slightly. Some girls who were placed in CMS training, under the impression that they would eventually marry specific Christian men, found themselves married instead to strangers when their original partners backed out of the agreement or professed themselves dissatisfied with the girls' progress.[30] Young women who had thrown themselves wholeheartedly into the CMS enterprise of training might also find that their pasts, before Christian conversion, were held against them by their husbands (even in the tight Christian marriage market) as well as by their new neighbors. For example, girls who had been rescued twins or had been at an early age dedicated to village deities (so-called sacred slaves, *ndi osu*) found that their prospects were limited, even with the valued CMS training. Converted Onitsha Igbo men did not look with any favor upon girls from the interior Igbo areas, and the majority of converted girls during the early years of the twentieth century were former domestic slaves (ndi olu) or ndi osu who had been taken into missionary care at an early age. This led to a shortage of acceptable marriage partners in Christian Onitsha and gave the educated converts one more reason to leave the CMS and go in search of employment at the newly opening offices of the colonial administration.[31] Young men with connections to Onitsha aristocracy were particularly apt to move away from the CMS over questions of marriage, since their future prospects within the town's social system could be completely destroyed if they married female slaves, twins or young women dedicated to the Igbo deities (*osu*).

If such marriages were a problem among the urban sophisticates of Onitsha, they were perceived as utterly abominable in the towns and villages of rural Igboland. Women who associated with these "tainted" Christian wives, or who allowed their children to play with the children of such abominable marriages, would have been considered a danger to their own households and to the town at large. The girls were secluded by their religion and a hybrid material culture made up of valuable European commodities and familiar Igbo domestic objects used in new ways, their possibly truncated understanding of the local Igbo language, some of the girls' backgrounds in problematic Igbo institutions, as well as by their Europeanized models of monogamy and "nuclear family" domesticity. It should, therefore, come as no surprise that youthful Christian women became the "despised minority" throughout the Igbo-speaking region.[32] Doubly strangers in the villages where they were sent by the CMS and without the protections of masculinity or western education that characterized their husbands, these young women were peculiarly vulnerable in every social situation.[33] Although missionized women would eventually predominate in Igbo-speaking towns and villages during the years after 1929,[34] the first Old Girls and their daughters faced discrimination and what sounds like crushing loneliness. The fact that they continued in their lay work, usually without much support from the Niger Mission's "home" base in London and in the face of their severe social isolation, is a tribute to these young converts' personal perseverance, thorough indoctrination in and devotion to the "new ways" of Christianity.

Conclusions

One of the primary ways that "youth" is described in the theoretical literature in both sociology and, more lately, anthropology is in terms of lack. It may be a lack of the privileges of adulthood, a lack of adulthood's responsibilities, or, even among those theorists who have "youth's" interests squarely at heart, a lack of voice to describe their own social lives.[35] Perhaps this is true of youth cultures in the west at the end of the twentieth century, but it was clearly not the case of the emerging missionized Igbo youth culture described above. I would like to suggest, in this conclusion, that lack, or nullity, is a highly implausible base upon which to build any social group. What the CMS missionaries seemed to see, as they looked for and helped to create "youth" among the Igbo-speaking peoples of the Nigerian southeast, was plenitude rather than lack: Igbo young people, as the missionaries hopefully constructed discourse about them, were filled with potential—not all of it good, but potential nonetheless.

This had something to do the desire for a Christian futurity that missionaries imposed on the clever, strong, curious, and willful young Igbo who found their way into the CMS's schoolrooms and compounds. We may also wonder what part was played in the development of a mission focused so narrowly on youth by the fact that most of the British members of the Niger Mission were denied the society of their own children, whether because they never married, like the majority of the CMS women missionaries while in the field, or because they maintained families in the United Kingdom, like a number of the male missionaries.[36] As we have seen, missionaries had little choice in the matter: older, socially adept Igbo-speakers were largely unsusceptible to the Christian message in the early years of the Niger Mission, and there was a willingness to put at least some younger people forward as what we might call "test cases" when it was clear that mission education might lead to employment and advancement in the burgeoning colonial system. It is not clear that the CMS missionaries, male or female, fully thought through the implications for conversion and western-style education for their charges. However, from the surprise and displeasure of Europeans in later years as they confronted the fruits of mission labor in southeastern Nigeria, we may infer that the development of a new, elite class of the colonized was an unexpected result of CMS efforts.[37]

However little the development of an elite had been expected, though, other European categories of personhood were more purposefully implemented. The separate disciplines of the male-dominated schoolroom and the girls' training institutions, and, indeed, the focus on education that missionaries found to be most successful for gaining converts, were all geared—from their antecedents in European culture—to developing "youth" as a socially meaningful category, along with "Christian" and, perhaps, "modern" persons. In these new, Christian dominated spaces, young people did not only "learn to labor," in Willis's (1977) phrase, but they learned to see themselves as separate from their Igbo-speaking elders and to appreciate and desire ideas and commodities outside those elders' experience.

While this may have been liberating for some missionized young people, it was not—as I hope to have shown—an unmitigated blessing for all. Young Igbo women's experience of mission modernity, for instance, may have freed them from the surveillance and control of patrilineage mates, but it did not free them from surveillance and control more generally. Becoming a "Christian girl" in Igboland during the early years of this century was not tantamount to living the lifestyle of a pampered Edwardian, middle-class adolescent. If anything, their movements were more greatly curtailed, first in the isolated girls' institutions, where their every waking moment was scheduled and supervised by women missionaries and their local assistants. From these institutions, most women converts then moved directly into marital households, where the husband was meant to be the unquestioned head, and where they could have fewer outside contacts or allies than in a so-called traditional Igbo marriage.

Paradoxically seen as more weak by the missionaries, but objectively less protected by their new gender roles or "practical" education, a scarce but consistently undervalued commodity in the cultural economy of the CMS mission, Christian female youth in this period nonetheless somehow managed to flourish. And they underwrote the ongoing missionization of rural Igboland through their school fees, unpaid domestic labor, lay church work, and the bearing of children who would be raised in households where the Christian mores of the CMS missionaries were the norm rather than the exception.

This is what Mitchell (1988: 113), writing about the nineteenth-century British colonial perception of Egyptian women and their need for education, calls the discourse of "modern motherhood." Modern motherhood, in this sense, placed the onus for "civilizing" the colony on its women, forcing them into an engagement with the colonial and (in the present case) mission apparatus through school, but only in order to send them back into "the home" with a new set of domestic priorities. Perhaps we need to explore the notion of "modern motherhood" further, however, since its consequences were not always as negative as they might appear at first glance. The Igbo-speaking Christian schoolgirls of the early 1900s became the elite, Christian matrons of the 1930s and the mothers of women who, during the next three decades, took an active part in Nigeria's struggles for independence, women's suffrage, free universal primary education, and the Biafran civil war (Mba 1982). In this instance, at least, becoming a "civilized youth" meant anything *but* lack, and the construction of a new set of gender standards during missionization would make a dramatic impact on the history of a twentieth century African nation-state.

Acknowledgments

I would first like to acknowledge the invaluable assistance of my student researcher, Ms. Estelle Sohne, during the summer of 1997. Estelle not only brought the liveliness of her personality and the sharpness of her intellect to bear on the CMS materials we read together in Birmingham that year, but she offered the perspective of a young African woman who is living with the aftermath of her ancestors' Christian mission training.

Notes

1 G3 A3/O 1910, item 23. Unless otherwise denoted, all of the Church Missionary Society materials in this article come from the CMS Archives, University of Birmingham, UK.

2 See, among others, Curtin 1969: 244–246 for data about the numbers of repatriated slaves living in and around Freetown in the mid-nineteenth century.

3 For a refreshingly Igbocentric view of Crowther and his Niger Mission, see Kalu 1996; 81–89.

4 The Rev. John Buck's 1872 diary (C A3/O9) testifies to this fact of Onitsha mission life. At one point the Odu of Onitsha (one of the king's advisors) tried to force Buck to drink with him.

5 G3/A3/0 1890, written in Crowther's hand, dated July 1890, "Statement of Okuwan in an open air Meeting in the market place at Onitsha." Okuwan was the witch who Crowther personally heard confess during this event. For an analysis of this document and what it reveals about gender and social class in Onitsha during the 1890s, see Bastian 1999.

6 By 1901 the desire among ndi onicha for young men's education had grown so large that the missionaries requested permission from their home office to institute classes in both "infant" and secondary school. Fearing that these

extraordinarily well-educated young men would wish to take their knowledge out of the church and work for the colonial administration or trading organizations, Salisbury Square (CMS headquarters) denied the request and instructed its missionaries to instruct students up to secondary school level in "the vernacular" as much as possible.

7 Isaac Mba did not, in fact, marry polygynously on his own, but was married to a second wife by his father (against his will and outside his knowledge). His letter of explanation is one of the most heartfelt from any convert in the CMS archives.

8 This was hardly unique to the Onitsha Igbo case. The Comaroffs (1991: 140 *passim*) describe very similar elder resistance to mission interference in Tswana marriage patterns.

9 This was completely in keeping with CMS policy for its African and European missionaries alike, all of whom were required to receive permission from the home office in Salisbury Square before taking a wife or husband.

10 See Kalu 1996: 88 for some discussion of the internal politics of African and European CMS missionaries.

11 One such woman was Edith Warner, who would go on to found the first girl's training institution in the Nigerian southeast. See Basden 1927 for Miss Warner's mission biography.

12 This was, of course, the period of the "New Woman" in Britain and the United States. However, it seems unlikely that the women missionaries—unorthodox as they might appear to the population at large in their desire for travel and spiritual work among Africans—would have lightly taken on the appellation.

13 G3/A3/0 1909, item 72, "Precis of the Response of the Education Sub-Committee on the Oka Training Institution." Amadiume (1987: 134–136) also notes the exclusion of Igbo women from equal educational opportunities during this period.

14 G3 A3/O 1910, item 126.

15 This was, of course, a common enough occurrence in West Africa. See Mann 1985 for a discussion of marriage and class among elites in colonial Lagos and Moran 1990 for more on the concatenation of class and "civilization" for women in Liberia. Karen T. Hansen's edited volume on *African Encounters with Domesticity* (1992) contains a number of essays that are complementary to the points made in this article.

16 In 1909 fifty-one girls were enrolled in the Girls' School at Umudioka, all being maintained there by a four-shilling per month contribution from prospective husbands or their own families.

17 Women missionaries did attempt to solicit money from home congregations, as did their male counterparts, often making particular pleas on the behalf of local women. See, for example, G3 A3/O 1903, item 14; "A Journey to Idumuje Ugboko" by Miss M[ary]. Elms (Onitsha, Southern Nigeria, West Africa, December 7th 1902).

18 See, for example, G3/A3/0 1910, item 18; Pamela Row, Annual Letter on the Girls' School, Dec 4th, 1909:

> Lessons are not considered the most important thing here; most of the girls leave us to get married & what we want them to learn is to live a consistent Christian life in their own homes.

This emphasis was not peculiar to southeastern Nigeria; see Schmidt 1992: 131–40 and Coquery-Vidrovitch 1997: 144–146, for strikingly similar missionary sentiments in what were, during the same period, Southern Rhodesia and the Belgian Congo.

19 G3 A3/0 1926, item 46; letter from Rev. George T. Basden to H. D. Hooper, dated August 5, 1926.

20 Sylvia Leith-Ross (1936: 296) in the early 1930s recorded an interesting conversation with a male informant on this topic:

> He [Leith-Ross's informant] merely explained that the boy who goes to a Mission school takes it for granted that becoming a Christian is a corollary to becoming a scholar and will automatically and unreasoningly go through the requisite forms without thought or question. Pursuing the subject, he stated that some girls, other than schoolgirls who would pursue the same course as their brothers, would also become Christians for the unexpected reason that it was "less trouble." Questioned more closely, he reminded me of the innumerable family and social obligations a pagan girl is under. She must take part in the girls' dances, which, with all the rehearsals, represent a good deal of physical exertion; she must pay the proper visits, at the proper times, help cook at festivities, condole with the bereaved. The Christian girl says: "I am a Christian. I have nothing to do with this," and sits quietly at home. It is true she has to go to church on Sunday but there again "she can sit down, then she comes home and her duties are finished."

21 From G3 A3/0 1910, item 39; "Report of the First Women's United Conference, Onitsha. Jan. 18–20, 1910." The style of the Report is well-represented by the following passage:

> We met on Wednesday expecting great things, and were not disappointed. Miss Dennis' address on women's position and influence reached the highest point in the Conference and one could see the eager longing in the faces of the women to reach up to something more nearly approaching the ideal women.

22 G3 A3/0 1906, item 103; Frances Dennis, "Young Women's Institution for the Asaba Hinterland"

23 See Brumberg 1997, particularly pp. xvii–xx and 1–56, for a detailed discussion of transformations in notions of adolescence, puberty and the social construction of western girls' bodies during the late nineteenth and early twentieth centuries.

24 Unmarried Igbo women during this period were not supposed to wear cloth, particularly around their waists or wrapped around their hair.

25 For a fascinating portrait of such fosterage, see 'Wole Soyinka's (1989) description of his mother's duties in a 1940s CMS parsonage in southwestern Nigeria.

26 See G3 A3/O 1925, item 24, "St. Monica's School Report, 1924," by P[amela]. R. Row.

27 This new form of Igbo domesticity was noted approvingly by CMS officials in the early 1900s:

> In the young women of the Country lies the hope of the Church; they are all unconsciously the life of the Church or its bane. But here in this Ibo Country the young women appear to be full of promise. Those who have gone forth from the School of which Miss Warner is the head, and have become wives of Agents are doing valuable work. There is not the tendency to trade on their part which one notices in some districts, and they appear to regard the work of their husbands as their work to which

> they devote themselves whole-heartedly (G3/A3/0 1907, item 91, letter from Bishop Tugwell to CMS administrator Baylis, dated September 24th, 1907).

28 Echeruo (1998: xv) suggests that there are only two major dialect zones of Igbo, Onicha (Onitsha) and Owerre (Owerri), but within these zones today important dialectical variations exist from town to town, sometimes even from city quarter to city.

29 G3 A3/0 1910, item 125; "Miss Martin's Annual Letter, Girl's Training School, Umudioka, Nov. 1910."

30 G3 A3/O 1905, from "E[ducation] C[ommittee] Minutes," Onitsha, Feb. 1905:

> A letter from Jacob Mmegafu was read objecting to the suggestion that he should pay part of the cost of the education of a fiancee whom he now felt no desire to marry. The E. C. decided that Jacob must pay 2/6 monthly for one year.

31 See G3/A3/0 1909, item 31; letter from Smith to Secretary Baylis, dated Onitsha, March 22, 1909.

32 See Ugwu-Oju's (1995) account of her mother's life for a better understanding of the problems faced by a young Christian (in this case, Catholic) but also osu Igbo girl of the early twentieth century.

33 If there is any doubt that Christians felt oppressed by their neighbors, one might do well to read the testimony of Nnochiri Oriaku, a man from Uzuakoli:

> Among the boys of my age, I was the first to have a woman to wife. It was rather premature that I should have a wife at that age, but custom overlooked my tender age and made me inherit, of all things, the wife of my dead elder brother. When the persecution of the Christians was in vogue, I ran with my inherited wife to Ogboko Ozuitem in 1913. Then at Ogboko Ozuitem lived one huge and influential man, Mazi Onwukwe Anyaogu by name, who was a pious and devoted Christian. He made his house a place of refuge for persecuted Christians (Isichei 1978: 298–299).

34 Amadiume 1987: 119–133 gives an account of Igbo Christians' rise to prominence in Nnobi, a town not too distant from Onitsha. She, very rightly, sees that this rise came at the expense of women's social position in Nnobi and elsewhere in the Nigerian southeast and makes a very interesting argument for how a Christian insistence on masculine deities undermined Igbo women's political and religious power.

35 See, for an example of well-meaning theoretical discourse, James 1995: 46, who talks about the need to see

> the cultures of childhood and youth, not as subcultures seemingly fixed in their opposition to the adult world or in jeering mockery of it, but instead as Geertzian contexts within which the generational experience of being denied access to and participation in central social institutions can be thickly described.

36 Edith Warner died unmarried, after over thirty years of missionary work among Igbo-speakers.

37 Sylvia Leith-Ross published a diary she kept in Onitsha during 1937, discussing her experiences with ndi onicha (Onitsha people), particularly with the emerging Onitsha elite. Her description of Ibeze, her landlord, is fairly representative of the disdainful bemusement felt by British colonialists towards the products of mission education:

> As in many others, I've seen in Ibeze a hunger and thirst after a righteousness which has no specifically religious connotation, but is a strange mingling of snobbery and sincerity; an intense desire for "civilization," the mirage always on the horizon of those who have come into even the slightest contact with the white man, Leith-Ross 1943.

References cited

Aba Commission of Inquiry. 1930. Notes of evidence taken by the Commission of Inquiry appointed to inquire into the disturbances in the Calabar and Owerri Provinces, December, 1929. London: Government Printing Office.

Amadiume, Ifi. 1987. *Male daughters, female husbands: Gender and sex in an African society.* London: Zed Books.

Basden, George T. 1927. *Edith Warner of the Niger: The story of thirty-three years of zealous & courageous work amongst Ibo girls & women.* London: Seeley, Service and Co.

——. 1966[1921]. *Among the Ibos of Nigeria.* London: Cass.

Bastian, Misty L. 1999. "The daughter she will eat agousie in the world of the spirits": Confessions of a witch in missionized Onitsha, 1890. Paper presented to the XVth Satterthwaite Colloquium on African Religion and Ritual, April, Satterthwaite, UK.

Blunt, Alison. 1994. *Travel, gender, and imperialism: Mary Kingsley and West Africa.* New York: Guilford Press.

Brumberg, Joan Jacobs. 1997. *The body project: An intimate history of American girls.* New York: Random House.

Callaway, Helen. 1987. *Gender, culture and empire: European women in colonial Nigeria.* Urbana: University of Illinois Press.

Comaroff, Jean and John Comaroff. 1991. *Of revelation and revolution. Vol. I: Christianity, colonialism, and consciousness in South Africa.* Chicago IL: University of Chicago Press.

Coquery-Vidrovitch, Catherine. 1997. *African women: A modern history.* Boulder CO: Westview Press.

Curtin, Philip. 1969. *The Atlantic slave trade: A census.* Madison WI: University of Wisconsin Press.

Echeruo, Michael J. C. 1998. *Igbo-English dictionary.* New Haven CT: Yale University.

Green, M. M. 1964. *Ibo village affairs.* New York: Praeger.

Hansen, Karen T., ed. 1992. *African encounters with domesticity.* New Brunswick NJ: Rutgers University Press.

Henderson, Helen Kreider. 1969. Ritual roles of women in Onitsha Ibo society. Ph.D. Dissertation, University of California, Berkeley.

Isichei, Elizabeth, ed. 1978. *Igbo worlds: An anthology of oral histories and historical descriptions.* Philadelphia PA: Institute for the Study of Human Issues.

James, Allison. 1995. Talking of children and youth: Language, socialization and culture. In *Youth cultures: A cross-cultural perspective*, ed. V. Amit-Talai and H. Wulff. New York: Routledge.
Kalu, Ogbu U. 1996. *The embattled gods: Christianization of Igboland 1841–1991.* Lagos: Minaj Publishers.
Leith-Ross, Sylvia. 1936. *African women: A study of the Ibo of Nigeria.* London: Farber.
——. 1943. *African conversation piece.* London: Hutchinson.
Mann, Kristin. 1985. *Marrying well: Marriage, status and social change among the educated elite in colonial Lagos.* Cambridge: Cambridge University Press.
Mba, Nina Emma. 1982. *Nigerian women mobilized: Women's political activity in southern Nigeria, 1900–1965.* Berkeley: University of California.
Mitchell, Timothy. 1988. *Colonising Egypt.* Berkeley: University of California Press.
Moran, Mary H. 1990. *Civilized women: Gender and prestige in southeastern Liberia.* Ithaca NY: Cornell University Press.
Schmidt, Elizabeth. 1992. *Peasants, traders and wives: Shona women in the history of Zimbabwe, 1870–1939.* Portsmouth NH: Heinemann.
Soyinka, 'Wole. 1989. *Aké: Years of childhood.* New York: Harper Collins.
Uchendu, Victor C. 1965. *The Igbo of southeast Nigeria.* New York: Holt, Rinehart and Winston.
Ugwu-Oju, Dympna. 1995. *What will my mother say?: A tribal girl comes of age in America.* Chicago IL: Bonus Books.
Van Allen, Judith. 1976. "Aba riots" or Igbo "women's war"? Ideology, stratification, and the invisibility of Women. In *Women in Africa: Studies in social and economic change*, ed. N.J. Hafkin and E. G. Bay. Palo Alto CA: Stanford University Press.
Willis, Paul. 1977. *Learning to labour.* Farnborough: Saxon House.
Wulff, Helena. 1995. Introducing youth culture in its own right: The state of the art and new possibilities. In *Youth cultures: A cross-cultural perspective*, ed V. Amit-Talai and H. Wulff. New York: Routledge.

38

Excerpt from 'DEVILS, FAMILIARS AND SPANIARDS

Spheres of power and the supernatural in the world of Seberina Candelaria and her village in early 19th century Philippines'

Greg Bankoff

Source: *Journal of Social History*, 33(1) (1999), 37–55.

Historians are rarely permitted insight into the inner world of the imagination of those long dead. While the activities and deeds of a prominent few are well documented, the jumble of desires, fears and beliefs with which they perceived and attempted to make sense of the world around them is little understood. This is especially so in the case of the common people whose lives, let alone thoughts, are often the subject of historical speculation, especially in the non-western world where written records are few and their preservation haphazard.

The trial, then, of Seberina Candelaria is deserving of our attention in all these respects. She is a young woman aged twenty-two, otherwise historically unremarkable, illiterate, from a largely insignificant rural community, Obando, north of Malabon and west of Polo, in the province of Bulacan on the archipelago's principal island of Luzon, who, in 1808, is arraigned before an ecclesiastical court accused of associating with the Devil who appears to her in the form of a demonic familiar. The detailed transcripts of this case, that extend to nearly seventy closely hand-written pages, contain not only Seberina's compelling account of how she entered into compact with the Devil, but also the evidence of her neighbours and fellow villagers who sought to know the future or that which was hidden from them by currying favour with her familiar. As the case unfolds, the proceedings also provide insight into the beliefs and opinions of her examiners, revealing to what extent the Enlightenment had penetrated ecclesiastical views in the Philippines by the turn of the nineteenth century.

While the nature of the power structure within municipalities has been the object of considerable scholarship,[1] the question of dissent and opposition in the village has received far less attention apart from the figure of the *tulisan* or bandit as social avenger.[2] But James Scott and Michael Adas write about another type of resistance, those commonplace forms of protest that popular struggle takes when it does not seek to openly confront the forces that dominate. What the former calls *weapons of the weak*[3] and the latter *avoidance protest* include[4]: foot dragging, dissimulation, false compliance, pilfering, feigned ignorance, slander, arson, sabotage and the like. These models have subsequently been applied to more contemporary rural conditions in the Philippines.[5]

However, Scott carried this notion of a dissonant political culture one step further to embrace not only actions but also the alternative meanings given to public texts and those words of anger, revenge or self-assertion spoken by subordinates out of earshot of their *betters*.[6] These *hidden transcripts* most certainly masked acts of defiance but also functioned "as a barrier and a veil that the dominant find difficult or impossible to penetrate."[7] Here the scholar stands poised at the threshold of historical consciousness, how people perceived the world around them in the past, where sources that had been previously sparse now become virtually non-existent. The Philippines, in this respect, is actually more fortunate than many other societies in Southeast Asia, in that a considerable body of early lexicological and vernacular religious material has survived from which fascinating insights into the popular imagination have been inferred.[8] But sources such as the detailed transcripts of a trial for demonic possession remain rare and are deserving of close historical scrutiny.[9]

Witches and devils

Before examining the case of Seberina Candelaria to see what light it sheds on the supernatural beliefs of a rural Tagalog community in the early nineteenth century, the concept of witchcraft both in western and indigenous societies requires some explanation and historical elaboration. The witch has alternately either been regarded as primarily a delusional figure or been accepted as fact in Christianised Europe.[10] The existence of the Devil was not doubted before the scientific rationalism of the nineteenth century but his powers have been variously assessed at different times. Thus the thesis that demonic action was real but essentially psychological or spiritual in character, sometimes referred to as the Augustinian doctrine, prevailed throughout much of the Middle Ages. Weak minds, particularly, it was thought, those of women, were liable to be deceived by blandishments and vain imaginings.

Gradually this view was replaced by one in which theologians, beginning with Thomas Aquinas in the thirteenth century, no longer believed that the Devil's power was limited to simply the mental sphere but had a real existence in the form of magic performed by practitioners in the black arts who worshipped and entered into a covenant or pact with the Devil.

By the late fifteenth century, witches, far from being poor deluded individuals, were now considered dangerous criminals who used their powers of enchantment, spell and sorcery to bring about death, disease and misfortune to their neighbours. While there were marked variations among countries and even among regions, the systematic persecution of witches came to be regarded not only as a religious duty but as the civic responsibility of ecclesiastical authorities. The publication of *Malleus Maleficarum* (Hammer of Witches) in 1487 established witchcraft as primarily a social crime of malefice and provided the manual by which the great witch-hunts of the sixteenth and seventeenth centuries were conducted, reaching a climax between 1575–1650.[12] Prosecutions continued into the early eighteenth century until beliefs in the actual demonic powers of the witch were supplanted by the conviction, borne of the Enlightenment, that witchcraft was simply the popular derangement of ignorant people, only to be finally dismissed as pure fantasy in the twentieth century.[13] [. . .]

[. . .] An important aspect of the Spanish conquest and incorporation of the Philippines, largely overlooked by historians, is that these events took place at the height of the great witchcraft persecutions. While more witches were burnt at the stake in France and Germany, nonetheless there were notable witchcraft trials in Spain at the start of the sixteenth and seventeenth centuries, especially in the Basque provinces.[18] The prevalent theological opinion on witchcraft must have influenced the way in which the early missionary fathers viewed the religious practices they encountered in the islands after 1565. More especially, the disappointing experience of the Americas, where idolatrous practices thrived despite the early enthusiasm with which tens of thousands of indigenous peoples had flocked to seemingly embrace the Holy Faith, must have proved a salutary admonition to many. As apostasy was increasingly seen as the Devil's handiwork, local inhabitants were no longer regarded as ignorant simpletons but as members of a counter-Church with its own parodies of Christian rites: 'excrements' instead of sacraments, female as opposed to male ministers.[19] It is from a theological perspective formulated in the context of the great European witch-hunts and confirmed by their recent experience in the Americas that the missionary orders embarked on the conversion of the Philippines and approached the religious practices of the archipelago's inhabitants. What they found, of course, only seemed to confirm the worst of their fears, with many of the early missionaries regarding the Indios as being in the Devil's service.[20]

Early accounts of the islands suggest that the various peoples of Luzon and the Visayas were mainly Animist, venerating the spirits of nature and those of their ancestors while placating a host of malevolent ones.[21] There were reportedly no temples or gathering places set apart for worship though certain topographical features or groves were held to be the preserve of particular spirits.[22] Sacred effigies, however, were commonplace and revered in most homes being referred to variously as *anitos* or *divitas* and being variously associated with war, health, agriculture, fisheries and the like and to which sacrifice and offerings of perfume and food were made. More important ceremonies were performed by a numerous class of professional celebrants, mainly women, known as *catalonans* (Tagalog) or *babaylanes* (Visayan) in private homes or at feasts in specially prepared bowers erected for that purpose close to the host's house.[24] Though many priestesses evidently inherited their office, ties of kinship might also be adoptive and all served a noviciate before officiating at rituals, for which services they were paid, reference being made to their rich attire, jewels and wealth.[25] [. . .]

[. . .] Apart from divination and auguries usually performed on animal entrails,[32] the priestesses were also consulted as physicians.[33] Evidently, many had extensive knowledge of herbs whose properties were used medicinally to cure disease which, no doubt, contributed to their status.[34] But their station in indigenous society remains more difficult to gauge. Spanish missionary sources attempt to decry their influence: Fr Colin contending that "they were not honoured or esteemed" but considered "an idle lot who lived by the sweat of others."[35] Pedro Careen, on the other hand, while dismissing the priestesses as "a band of worthless women," goes on to deplore their "tyrannical hold" upon the village "by various means and plots compelling many to repair to them upon every occasion."[36] However, their function as intermediaries with the spirit world, often on behalf of the sick, combined with their medicinal skills, confirm the role of these women as shamans whose importance would be considerable especially within societies without highly developed superordinate forms of social control.

Certainly most of the missionary fathers thought these women dangerous influences and considered them responsible for the regular incidences of apostasy with which they had to contend. In the first place, the priestesses were held to derive their powers from the Devil with whom they were in communication.[37] They were blamed for the governmental and religious institutions of the country "founded on tradition, and on custom introduced by the Devil himself" through their offices.[38] All the inhabitants, therefore, were 'in the service of the devil,' "a people abandoned by the hand of God and governed by the devil in accordance with his laws."[39] Despite the initial willingness of many indigenous people to embrace Christianity, apostasy was rife and priests were urged to be on their guard against backsliders.[40] Many pre-Christian rites were maintained in secret[41] under a veil of silence and subterfuge to conceal such worship from the notice of local priests.[42] On some other occasions, however, their practice provided the nucleus about which more serious opposition to Spanish rule coalesced, as in the revolt on Bohol in 1622.[43]

Spanish authorities were uniformly hostile to the maintenance of pre-Christian practices. Parishioners were urged to abjure such rites and denounce all sorcerers, witches, magicians and apostates on pain of being 'punished most severely'.[44] In particular, children, receiving instruction in the local *convento*, were exhorted to report the activities of their parents and elders to the parish priest and then often used to desecrate sacred artefacts by throwing them into the privies and urinating and defecating over them.[45] In the most extreme cases, there is also evidence that some celebrants were burnt "in order that, by the light of that fire, the blindness in which the divata had kept them deluded might be removed."[46]

Despite the severity of Spanish responses on occasions and the increasing consolidation of the colonial regime during the seventeenth and eighteenth centuries, there is no indication that pre-Christian rites and practices ceased, though they certainly became more clandestine. Incidences of such worship uncovered among the Zambals in 1683 were said to involve 'the principal people of the village'.[47] Mid eighteenth century Augustinian and Dominican missions to the Visayan islands report the presence of 'wizards' able to change themselves into crocodiles or other animals to commit murder, and of sorcerers whose magic is able to cause or cure various sicknesses.[48] A fascinating account of the continuing widespread prevalence of these beliefs and practices is contained in a supplement to *El Renacimiento*, a Manila newspaper, written by José Nuñez in 1905.[49] The author recounts his own experiences with regard to witchcraft and the existence of witches which he calls *mangkukulams*. Remaining entirely sceptical himself ("I have not come to believe in, or to be convinced of, the existence of witches in Filipinas"), he nonetheless concludes that "such beliefs continue to exist in the popular mind."[50]

Nor have these kinds of beliefs apparently disappeared as a result of the dramatic political, social and economic upheavals of the twentieth century. The anthropologist, Richard Lieban, recorded 111 cases of sorcery and malign magic in Cebu, the Philippines' second largest city, and on the neighbouring island of Negros during the 1960s.[51] Moreover, there appears to be a remarkable continuity in the types and forms of practices described by these authors spanning the centuries from the initial accounts of the early Spanish missionary fathers to Lieban's study four hundred years later. In other words, far from being supplanted by the introduction and near universal adoption of Christianity in the northern and central islands of the archipelago, the evidence suggests that such beliefs remained commonplace in many parts of the Philippines, especially in rural areas. It is in this context, then, that the circumstances surrounding the trial of Seberina Candelaria need to be considered.

The supernatural world of Seberina Candelaria

Charges accusing Seberina of consorting with a *duende* or demon familiar were laid before the *vicario foráneo*, the bishop's representative at the district level and the lowest level of the judicial structure in ecclesiastical matters, in the *casa parroquicd* of Obando on 4 June 1808.[52] It was averred that her familiar was able to determine the identity of thieves, the whereabouts of lost items and other marvels during nightly gatherings held in the town and throughout the district. Many people had been attracted to these assemblies, bringing with them money and candles as offerings in the hope of securing an auspicious response to their questions. As a result of these allegations, the judge ordered the arrest and confinement, incommunicado, of Seberina, her husband, Sebastian, and their various accomplices while an investigation of these events was made.[53]

The evidence collected during the course of the inquiry includes the frank and detailed statement of the defendant herself, and this provides one of those rare opportunities enabling the reader to enter into the consciousness of someone alive two centuries ago and to experience the world, if for however briefly, as she did. Seberina describes how she was followed one day as she was returning home from Polo, the nearest town, after prayers. As her pursuer drew close by, she perceived it "to be a man or such she took it to be" and she addressed him, asking him why he was following her in this manner when she was a married woman. He responded by making crude aspersions casting doubt on her marital status, and then the two proceeded on their way as before. Nothing else untoward took place until Seberina approached the house of her mother-in-law when a nearby tree suddenly began to shake so violently that she thought it would fall on top of her. Other strange things then began to happen: sand was continually flung about the house and objects mysteriously moved but there was no more sign of the man. Some days later, however, a small figure, no bigger than half a vara (1 vara = 0.836 metres), appeared to her while she was working in the family field (*sementera*).[54] He offered her a golden rosary and a purse of money and grew angry when she refused them, pinching her, throwing sand into her eyes and calling her mad. After this, he appeared most days at sunset, telling her that he was a demon familiar and that his name was Isac.[55]

When Seberina returned to Obando, the familiar followed. From this time on, Isac conversed with her frequently, answering any question she put to him. Soon the news spread and people started coming to the house to consult him, offering money in return for information about the whereabouts of lost or stolen items. Few, however, claimed to have seen the familiar, and those that did reported only a shape dimly perceived in a dark corner. Certainly, there are no other descriptions of his appearance. But everyone heard him: witnesses' testimonies describe a great variety of voices—thick and muffled, thin and clear, small 'as if faked by someone'. Often these voices appeared to originate outside the room, from beneath the floor or above the ceiling. Sometimes Isac sang, entertaining his audience with verses from popular or amorous ballads though it was not always possible 'to understand what he said in his song'. At other times, he would abuse them, mouthing 'kitchen remarks', making obscene allusions to his and their genitalia, and commenting on the activities of spouses in the absence of their partners. Usually he danced: both the executed steps of formal dances but also wild cavorts and capers to the sound of castanets and drum. Again these activities were mainly heard rather than seen, taking place in a darkened alcove or nook where visibility was poor. However, several witnesses insist that it was impossible for Seberina to have played a role in the production of these sounds and that she could always be seen at some distance from where the noise emanated. All these gatherings took place after dark.[56] [. . .]

[. . .] While Seberina's visits conferred a certain local notoriety on her, they may also have become something of a necessity. Her husband, Sebastian, arrested along with her but against whom charges were subsequently dropped, had begun to beat her. He wanted an end to these nightly entertainments in what was his mother's house. Perhaps, too, there was a degree of maternal rivalry or pressure. Seberina tried to put a stop to these visitations "but she did not know how to and he [the familiar] always came anyhow."[58] Events now begin to elude her control. People in the village and the surrounding district become alarmed. The evidence of Fulgencio de San Juan, a local chorister, clearly strikes the note of unease that many felt despite due reservations that should be given to the nature of his occupation and the context of the venue in which he spoke. A witness to one of these nightly events, he says how: "seeing the futility of these happenings, some false, others true, and that in all cases that it might be wrong to be present at such gatherings . . . he left."[59] Others, however, were not content with merely withdrawing: the *fiscal*, Don Luis Navarro, known as Maestro Luis, denounces her to the parish priest and she is arrested.[60]

But the matter does not end with Seberina's confinement to the stocks in the local *casa real* or town hall. Isac pursues her even there, exchanging filthy innuendoes with the guards over possible marriage partners for Alin Vela, the village's *bieja loca* ('mad old woman') and other such inanities. On the next night, she confronts him, demanding an explanation for her present sufferings, including, it seems, a whipping. Finally, she tells him to leave her alone and begins to recite the Creed. Pandemonium then breaks out. There is a deafening noise, so loud that the guard outside thought that 'the house was falling down', as Isac hurls a large piece of wood at her (described by the jailer as 'too heavy for Seberina to have handled'), missing but hitting the door. She cries out for help as he begins to lift the stocks but the guard arrives at this moment with a light to find her "trembling all over her body and so cold that he thought she was at her last breath."[61] And from that moment on she never sees nor hears from Isac again.

The supernatural world of the village

The testimony of Seberina Candelaria provides valuable insight into the world view of the rural population of the Philippines at the start of a century of change and transition that was to prove so influential in shaping that society. It also raises serious questions about the degree to which Christianity had displaced earlier beliefs after more than 200 years of friar evangelisation and mission in the archipelago, suggesting the continuance of another level of reality that was only lightly, if at all, touched by the ministrations of the Church. But the priest was himself an important part of the village world, and the deliberations of Seberina's inquisitors disclose much about their attitudes and perspectives and, in the process, indicate the increasing gulf that separated them from their parishioners.

An essential first step in this inquiry is to consider the extent to which Seberina Candelaria's views represent those of the majority rural population at the time: to determine that she was not simply a delusional psychotic but that her lore formed part of a wider belief system shared by many if not most of her neighbours. More significant than simply the number of people who evidently attended the nightly gatherings is the social status of those who came to ask questions of the familiar. The identity of those called to give testimony at Seberina's trial reveals that many belonged to the principalia or local village elite, precisely the people one might expect to have been most exposed to Christianity and Hispanic culture over the last two centuries.

One of the principal venues for Seberina and Isac was the home of Don Fernando Caguia, the *gobernadorcillo* or municipal administrator and magistrate of Obando. In particular, his wife was very solicitous of her husband's health and good fortune. Among the distinguished visitors to the house was Don Josef Thoribio of Polo, better known as Captain Biyo, who came on four consecutive nights to inquire after the whereabouts of his dead son's horse. Biyo recounts how he came to Obando to light a candle to Santa Clara in the church there but, after hearing the news and seeing the 'great concourse of people' at Don Fernando's, had decided to ask the familiar on his own behalf. After paying two *reales* to Seberina, he was told the animal could be found in Bigaa but, unable to locate the beast there he returned a second and then a third time to be told it had moved to Tinaferos and then Santol. Angrily, Biyo returned on yet a fourth night offering to pay two *pesos* if the familiar would tell him for certain where the horse was or have it brought back to him.[62] [. . .]

The participation of the principalia in the maintenance of such practices remains intriguing. Earlier evidence suggests a fairly close relationship between celebrants at pre-Hispanic religious ceremonies and local elites. An account written in 1683 specifically identifies native priests or babaylanes as drawn from the 'principal people of the village'.[65] Certainly the cleric involved in Seberina's case expresses deep concern about the extent of the elite's role, even accusing the gobernadorcillo and principales of Obando as her 'accomplices'. The vicario foráneo blames the prevalence of these types of cases on the fact that municipal officers were Indios and, the more one reprimanded or exhorted them to take firmer action, "the more they are the first to hide such things."[66] Possession by a demonic familiar, then, was evidently not regarded by this churchman as unique or particularly exceptional.

Instances of similar and related practices are also revealed in the vicario foráneo's report to the archbishop in Manila. While a missionary in the uplands, he had come upon another case whereby an eight year old girl had been possessed by a demonic familiar who appeared to her in the shape of a 'black (*Negrito*) child'. He describes how this spirit managed to win the confidence and trust of the child, becoming its friend and playmate "but without losing any occasion on which to instruct her in the most obscene entertainments." It took the priest over two years to convince the girl about the nature and true identity of her companion and to teach her to conduct herself "with all the judgement of a good christian adult." The priest then consoles himself with the reflection that her death, at the age of ten, was an occasion of much edification to the entire mission.[67]

In still another part of his letter to the prelate, the priest relates what he knows about other forms of divination commonly practised within his parish. In particular, he recounts how people who have lost things or had them stolen will frequently consult a diviner who places a light in the middle of a reed tray or sieve (*bilao*) about which are placed playing cards and other objects. The whereabouts of missing items are inferred from the inclination of the flame towards the objects on the bilao.[68] Similar practices were witnessed by Antonio Mozo and Tomás Ortiz during the eighteenth century but, in these instances, the divinations were performed by shaking the sieve.[69] Far from being a world in which such ideas were considered to be arcane relics of customary tradition, the vicario foráneo's report suggests that many indigenous people held a more diverse world view than might be supposed from their outward adherence to Christianity.

This impression receives further reinforcement by a comparison of the activities surrounding Seberina's possession as related in the transcripts of her trial with the accounts of ritual practices performed by babaylanes as described by the early missionary fathers. The importance of music is particularly evident to both but so is the apparent strange symmetry of harmonics between the instruments despite the separation of centuries: the often uncoordinated beat of castanets and drum to which Isac performed[70] and the irregular cadence of bell, gong and kettle-drum to which the priestesses danced.[71] Song, too, appears to play a central role in both descriptions. Several witnesses make mention of the familiar singing a broad range of verses from canticles to amorous tunes,[72] and song was also a noted part of the ceremonies at which babaylanes were celebrants.[73] Again many of those who testified at the trial of Seberina remarked on the unusual characteristics of the familiar's voice just as an earlier report describes such voices as emanating from 'a hollow reed'.[74] Given these similarities and those of venue (private homes), activity (divination) and participation (including local dignitaries), there would appear to be some doubt as to how Seberina was regarded by her local community: as a woman possessed by a demonic familiar within a Christian cosmology of God and the Devil, as an officiating celebrant within a tradition of customary beliefs with its origins in the pre-Hispanic period, or as something of both. Even the outward manifestations of Christianity may need examination as being more in the minds of Seberina's sacerdotal interlocutors than in her own or those of her fellow villagers.

However, such an interpretation gives insufficient recognition to the impact of centuries of Christian evangelisation in the Philippines and to the way in which elements of power external to those societies were often selectively incorporated within local communities to create new cosmologies that were neither wholly foreign nor wholly customary. Dieter Battels argues that the Ambonese responded to Europeans by absorbing elements of the newcomers' beliefs thought to confer access to sources of power previously unknown, eventually syncretising them into a system in which traditional elements were preserved. Rather than invalidating customary beliefs, such new knowledge served only to enrich the Ambonese conceptualisation of the universe, so that elements of both systems were retained without any apparent contradiction.[75]

Certainly, there are aspects of both customary and Christian beliefs in Seberina's case. In response to repeated questions about Isac's identity, she eventually calls him a 'tianac', a mischievous and diminutive sprite or dwarf common to the folklore of Tagalog, Bikol and Visayan traditions and described by both Mozo and Ortiz in the eighteenth century.[76] Indeed, there are a number of striking similarities between Seberina's experience with Isac and the explanation of such phenomena given by Tomás Ortiz. However, despite her evident association of the familiar with a figure from indigenous cosmology, she can only succeed in liberating herself from his influence through recourse to the Christian profession of faith, by reciting the Creed.

These two belief systems, the native and the foreign, become even further blurred in the form of Isac himself. While the figure of a tianak is variously depicted as dark with horns, fangs, long pointed ears and angular features,[78] Seberina's familiar is imbued with all the characteristics of her colonial 'masters'. She describes him as dressed like a Spaniard, wearing a beret and bearing a *palo* or staff of office.[79] Nor does Isac simply perform just any old dance but specifically *la marcha*, the *bolero* and *fandangos*, all eminently Spanish steps and all to the accompaniment of castanets.[80] It would seem that devils, familiars and Spaniards had become one—at least in the cosmology of Seberina Candelaria and her village. A somewhat similar transcultural association has been noted among medieval Christian communities in Europe to whom the Devil was often manifested as a Moor.[81]

But more is going on here than simply the 'colonisation of the indigenous spirit world' as Hispanic and Christian forms take on shape and substance within local belief systems. The very symbols of Spanish power, both its secular might and spiritual prowess, have been appropriated and incorporated into native concepts of power. At their initial meeting on the road from Polo, Seberina is offered a rosary, a visible manifestation of the power of the Catholic Church, by Isac whom she perceives to be a tianak, an indigenous malevolent sprite but who wears European clothes and bears the staff of colonial office. The fact that Seberina may be representative of a long tradition of female intermediaries with the spirit world known all over the archipelago from pre-Christian times should not obscure an appreciation of her ability to tap these new sources of power, ones, moreover, that were external to her community and whose acquisition conferred on her a higher status than she had enjoyed previously. While priestly office was mainly limited to elite groups within society, such restrictions may have had no weight when it came to tapping previously unknown sources of power. Thus, as Bartels notes on Ambon, "new powers can be attained by anyone, regardless of previous position in society and this can have a great effect on the social structure."[82] It may be no coincidence that the person who eventually denounced Seberina to the authorities was a member of the principalia, Maestro Luis, who might have felt that his own and his peer's influence in the community was increasingly being eroded by the sway of this woman.[83]

The possibility of competition between Seberina and a local authority structure dominated by men raises another aspect of her appropriation and incorporation of new sources of power. The *conquistadores* brought with them a very different concept of gender construction that emphasised Catholic mother-centred definitions of womanhood and affected relations between the sexes, restricting women's activities largely to the private sphere. The public sphere was defined as masculine. In other words, the Spanish colonisation of the Philippines involved not only the physical subjugation of the indigenous peoples to Europeans but also the cultural subjugation of women to men.[84] Few women wielded any form of public power within colonial society and what little they did exercise was mainly dependent on their intimate access to men in positions of authority, such as the mistress of a parish priest.[85]

Not only is Seberina able to tap into Hispanic and Christian forms of secular and spiritual power but she uses this new source to give her greater influence outside a male dominated authority structure. As Seberina becomes a centre or focal point of an alternative means of accessing power within her village, she, intentionally or otherwise, invests herself with the symbols and trappings of recognised authority. At any event, her activities are increasingly seen as a threat to the male monopolisation of power wielded by the gobernadorcillo and ultimately the parish priest. Not that the secular and spiritual were clearly differentiated within her mind: Isac both bears a staff of office and offers her a rosary. In a short period of several months, Seberina comes to exercise a form of influence that a young woman of twenty-two could not hope usually to have in her community. Ultimately, however, she transgresses too many boundaries and is brought low. Beaten and admonished by her husband, denounced by Maestro Luis and imprisoned, assaulted and then abandoned by Isac, Seberina is found by the guard cold and quivering on the floor of her prison cell, a forlorn and rather pathetic figure.

Where in all these happenings surrounding the case of Seberina Candelaria at Obando is the Spanish priest? Despite the fact that he has long been considered the most knowledgeable of royal officials, versed in the language and customs of the indigenous peoples through long residence in one locality, he seems a very remote and distant figure: unaware, unless so informed, of the activities of his parishioners; understanding little of the belief systems by which members of his flock made sense and operated in the world about them. While the outward forms of Hispanic power and Christianity may have been integrated into an indigenous cosmology, the priest remained an outsider: a potent symbol, certainly, in much the same way as a sacred grove, an ancestral shrine or a hallowed landmark but external to the daily round of the village.

The distance between priest and his congregation only widened in the eighteenth century as the effect of the Enlightenment increasingly influenced European perceptions of supernatural phenomena and witchcraft came to be viewed as more delusional, the product of the mind rather than of magic and the black arts.[86] While the early missionary fathers had decried the foul works of the Devil in the archipelago, Seberina's examiners take a somewhat more 'scientific' view of the affair, one indicative of the extent to which the ideas of the Enlightenment had already penetrated the rural Philippines by 1808. To Fr Casimiro Tembleque, parish priest of Obando, Seberina's familiar is nothing more than "the delusions of a 'weak mind' (*fantasia debil*) so common to her sex" and he initially counsels her simply to "arm herself with the shield of faith," blesses and admonishes her to hear mass frequently, take communion and recite the rosary. Later, however, when he discovers that the case is well known throughout the locality, he realises firmer action is called for. Even so, he refers to the situation as a "strange case . . . difficult to believe in without such evident proofs" but feels that it "should be dealt with by the full rigour of the law, since not only does it deal with a loss of faith . . . but its consequences are very prejudicial to public morals and good order."[87] In other words, Seberina should be proceeded against not only because of anxiety about her or her fellow villagers' immortal souls but because her actions disturb public order within the community!

As a more rationalist approach permeated Catholic theology during the nineteenth century, concern over uncovering the demonic practices associated with witches is replaced by a conceptualisation of the Devil as the arch-beguiler, the spinner of deceits and the master of duplicity against whom the unwary need to be constantly on their guard. As mental delusion supplants witchcraft, the gap between the Spanish priest and his indigenous parishioners, between a system of beliefs imbued with the new ideas of the Enlightenment and a native cosmology that has selectively appropriated and incorporated Hispanic and Christian symbols, would only appear to have widened.

Conclusion

The case of Seberina Candelaria and others like her make the historian more aware of the complexities of writing colonial histories that are unable to penetrate the surface layer of historical representation and fail to reach beyond the level of action to the realm of consciousness. Here, of course, the ground becomes very slippery. James Scott identifies one path through this morass by focusing on what he calls the hidden transcripts or the alternative meanings given to public texts that can cloak a dissonant political culture behind a veil of seeming compliance. According to this mode of analysis, the events that take place in Obando can certainly be interpreted as representative of a latent hostility against a colonial order sustained behind the facade of Christianity: devils, familiars and Spaniards are, after all, one in Seberina's consciousness. And the widespread attendance at the nightly gatherings, the conspiracy of silence that surrounds these activities for months, and the evident isolation and relative impotence of the priest only cast serious doubts over the penetration and effectiveness of Spanish rule in the Philippines after more than two hundred years of colonisation and evangelisation.

But there would also appear to be so much more going on here than simply popular defiance at a colonial system: Scott's hidden transcripts seem a useful but somewhat crude analytical device if confined purely to examining the relations between ethnic, racial or class groups in Obando. Seberina's case is not only about domination and the forms of resistance between indigenous peoples and the Spanish but is also about gender relations in her community. Possession by a demonic familiar grants her the opportunity to manipulate an alternative source of influence outside the male dominated authority structure that was not usually available to women of her age and position in that society. Ultimately it will also create a backlash that overwhelms and then crushes her.

However, in the final analysis, the case of Seberina Candelaria is about how power is abstracted in a rural community during the late eighteenth and early nineteenth century Philippines. And here, perhaps, is its most valuable historical insight. Far from overturning the previous belief systems, it suggests that the forms and symbols of Christianity had themselves been appropriated and incorporated within a pre-Hispanic mythology and tradition of mainly female priestesses. The result was neither wholly indigenous nor wholly exotic but the formation of a hybrid cosmology. Moreover, this cosmology was, in some ways, even further removed from the ideas of the Enlightenment than the Christianity of the early missionary fathers, who had at least shared with their converts more of a belief in the supernatural means of manipulating reality.

Nor is it possible to gauge just how commonplace such hybrid cosmologies were given the relative paucity of the historical record for the period. Jerry Bentley argues that the simple effort to communicate any beliefs and values across cultural boundaries "almost inevitably entailed a certain amount of syncretism, since the explanation of foreign concepts required some degree of comparison and assimilatation to familiar ideas."[88] If such is the case, then the encounter between Christianity and indigenous belief systems did not involve the wholesale acceptance of an alien religious system by the native populations of the archiplegao, but rather its selective adoption and adaption in which the former's original elements were fractured, restated in new terms, endowed with different meanings, and assembled in a new way that made sense and gave significance to the latter's cultural point of view.[89] Colonial society, then, may have been full of 'Seberinas' whose existence, however, remained hidden to all but the most discerning among Spanish religious and secular authorities.

Whether Seberina Candelaria herself was a bored young woman seeking local notoriety and importance within her community, a psychotic who heard voices, or a latter-day priestess in the time-honoured tradition of the babaylanes is a matter of personal and, perhaps, cultural interpretation. However, not only does her case permit the historian a rare glimpse into the inner world of a young woman and the imagination of her fellow villagers alive nearly two hundred years ago, but it also raises serious doubts about the extent of Spanish control over the rural Philippines.

Notes

1 Greg Bankoff, "Big Fish in Small Ponds: the Exercise of Power in a Nineteenth Century Philippine Municipality," *Modern Asian Studies* 4, 26 (1992): 679–700.

2 Greg Bankoff, "Bandits, Banditry and Landscapes of Crime in 19th Century Philippines," *Journal of Southeast Asian Studies* 29, 2 (1998); Isagani Medina, *Cavite Before The Revolution (1571–1896)* (Quezon City, 1994) pp. 59–105; and David Sturtevant, *Popular Uprisings in the Philippines 1840–1940* (Ithaca and London, 1976) pp. 115–138.

3 James Scott, *Weapons of the Weak. Everyday Forms of Peasant Resistance* (New Haven, 1985) p. 29.

4 Michael Adas, "From Footdragging to Flight: The Evasive History of Peasant Avoidance Protest in South and South-East Asia," *The Journal of Peasant Studies* 13, 2 (1986): 64–86.

5 Brian Fegan, "'Tenants' Non-Violent Resistance to Landowner Claims in a Central Luzon Village," *The Journal of Peasant Studies* 13, 2 (1986): 87–106 and Benedict Kerkvliet, "Everyday Resistance to Injustice in a Philippine Village," *The Journal of Peasant Studies* 13, 2 (1986): 107–123.

6 James Scott, *Domination and the Arts of Resistance. Hidden Transcripts* (New Haven and London, 1990).

7 James Scott, *Domination and the Arts of Resistance* p. 32.

8 Vincente Rafael, *Contracting Colonialism. Translation and Christian Conversion in Tagalog Society Under Early Spanish Rule* (Ithaca and London, 1988) and Reynaldo Ileto, *Pasyon And Revolution: Popular Movements In The Philippines, 1840–1910* (Quezon City, 1979).

9 These trial transcripts comprise the initial statements made in secret by Seberina Candelaria and her fellow villagers before the ecclesiastical tribunal held in Obando, that tribunal's writs and orders, a summary of the case referring the matter to a higher court, an accompanying letter from the parish priest, and the evidence of the spiritual interrogators in the convent where Seberina is ultimately confined. However, it is impossible to determine whether these initial statements were actually the product of interrogation or simple declarations.

10 A more graduated picture of witchcraft is presented by Stuart Clark who views changes in such beliefs in terms of their relationship to the wider intellectual life of Europe. Stuart Clark, *Thinking With Demons. The Idea of Witchcraft in Early Modern Europe* (Oxford, 1997).

12 This work was compiled by two German inquisitors, Jacob Sprenger and Heinrich Institoris, subsequent to the papal bull of Innocent VIII, *Summis desiderantes effectibus*, authorising the persecution of witches in certain dioceses in 1484.

13 Norman Cohen, *Europe's Inner Demons. The Demonization of Christians in Medieval Christendom* (Pimlico, 1993); Julio Baroja, "Witchcraft and Catholic Theology" in Bengt Ankarloo and Gustav Henningsen (eds.) *Early Modern European Witchcraft. Centres and Peripheries* (Oxford, 1990) pp. 19–43; and G. R. Quaiffe, *Godly Zeal and Furious Rage. The Witch in Early Modern Europe* (London and Sydney, 1987).

18 Gustav Henningsen, *The Witches' Advocate. Basque Witchcraft and the Spanish Inquisition (1609–1614)* (Reno, 1980) pp. 22–23.

19 Fernando Cervantes, *The Devil in the New World. The Impact of Diabolism in New Spain* (New Haven and London, 1994) p. 25.

20 Diego Aduarte, "Historia de la Provincia del Sancto Rosario de la Orden de Predicadores, Manila, 1640" in Emma Blair and Alexander Robertson (eds.), *The Philippine Islands, 1493–1898* (Mandaluyong, 1973) volume 31, p. 73.

21 Pedro Careen, "Relación de las Islas Filipinas, Roma, 1604" in Blair and Robertson, *The Philippine Islands* volume 12, pp. 264–265.

22 Diego de Bobadilla, "Relation of the Pilipinas Islands by a Religious Who Lived There For Eighteen Years, 1640" in Blair and Robertson, *The Philippine Islands* volume 29, p. 285; and Pedro Careen, "Relación" pp. 206, 268, 272–273.

24 Other contemporary commentators note that officiates were frequently also male or *asog*, effeminate men possibly transvestites. Luis de Jesus, "Historia General de los Religiosos Descalzos del order . . . S. Augustin, Madrid, 1681" in Blair and Robertson, *The Philippine Islands* volume 21, p. 203 and Alcina as quoted in Evelyn Cullamar, *Babaylanism in Negros: 1896–1907* (Quezon City, 1986) p. 18.

25 Pedro Careen, "Relación" p. 270.

32 Pedro Colin, "Labor Evangélica, Madrid, 1663" in Blair and Robertson, *The Philippine Islands* volume 4, p. 76.

33 Luis de Jesus, "Historia General" p. 207 and Pedro Careen, "Relación" p. 269.

34 Antonio de Morga, "Sucesos de las Islas Filipinas, Mexico 1609" in Blair and Robertson, *The Philippine Islands* volume 16, p. 131 and Miguel de Loarca, "Relación de las Yslas Filipinas, Arrevalo, 1582" in Blair and Robertson, *The Philippine Islands*, volume 5, p. 163.

35 Pedro Colin, "Labor Evangélica" p. 77.

36 Pedro Careen, "Relación" p. 271.

37 Juan Mendoza, "History of the Great Kingdom of China, Madrid, 1586" in Blair and Robertson, *The Philippine Islands* volume 6, p. 147 and "Resume 1521–1569" p. 139.

38 Pedro Careen, "Relaci6n" p. 263.
39 Diego Aduarte, "Historia de la Provincia del Sancto Rosario" volume 30, p. 296 and volume 31, p. 73.
40 Diego Serrano, "Edict of Fray Diego Garcia Serrano. Archbishop of the Philippines, 1622" in Blair and Robertson, *The Philippine Islands* volume 21, p. 60.
41 Pedro Careen, "Relación" p. 271.
42 Tomás Ortiz, "Práctica del Ministerio, 1713–42" in Blair and Robertson, *The Philippine Islands* volume 43, p. 106.
43 Murillo Velarde, "Historia de Philipinas, 1674–83" in Blair and Robertson, *The Philippine Islands* volume 38, p. 88.
44 Diego Serrano, "Edict" p. 61.
45 "Historia del Santissimo Rosario, Manila, 1742." in Blair and Robertson, *The Philippine Islands* volume 43, pp. 52–53.
46 Murillo Velarde "Historia de Philipinas" p. 93.
47 "Santissimo Rosario" p. 52.
48 Antonio Mozo, "Later Augustinian and Dominican Missions, Madrid, 1763" in Blair and Robertson, *The Philippine Islands* volume 48, pp. 113–114.
49 The article was included in the document series compiled by Emma Blair and Alexander Robertson with the following notation from the authors: "It is deserving of a place in this series, as showing what is actually believed at the present time among some of the ignorant Filipinos." Blair and Robertson, *The Philippine Islands* volume 43, p. 312.
50 José Nuñez, "Present Beliefs and Superstitions in Luzon, 1905" in Blair and Robertson, *The Philippine Islands* volume 43, pp. 310–319. Another Manila newspaper, *La Democracia*, carried an item on 29 August 1903 reporting the hanging of men accused of killing a witch.
51 Richard Lieban, *Cebuano Sorcery. Malign Magic in the Philippines* (Berkelgy and Los Angeles, 1967).
52 The vicario foráneo was invested with both executive and judicial powers, though his authority in criminal matters was limited to a preliminary investigation of the case and the preparation of a *sumario* or initial report for referral to the diocesan court of the bishop or archbishop that acted as the court of first instance in all matters that fell within ecclesiastical jurisdiction. Greg Bankoff, *In Verbo Sacerdotis: the Judicial Power of the Catholic Church in the Nineteenth Century Philippines* (Darwin, 1992) pp. 8–9.
53 "Causa Contra Seberina Candelaria N[atural] de Obando por Sociedad con un Diablo Familiar," Archive of the Archdiocese of Manila, Asuntos Criminales, Box 1808–1819, file 1808–1811A, pp. 1–4.
54 The sementera would often be at a considerable distance from the family house and those working in it might spend several nights there, especially at certain times of the agricultural cycle such as before the harvest.
55 "Causa Contra Seberina Candelaria" pp. 17–18.
56 "Causa Contra Seberina Candelaria" pp. 4–16. There is some difficulty in establishing the extent of Seberina's healing powers as the Spanish text repeatedly uses the verb *hilotearse* and the noun *hiloteo* for which no satisfactory translation has yet become available. The context, however, in which the words occur strongly suggest that the meaning has to do with restoring health. "Causa Contra Seberina Candelaria" p. 18.
58 "Causa Contra Seberina Candelaria" p. 18.
59 "Causa Contra Seberina Candelaria" p. 9.
60 The fiscal or *fiscalillo* was an ecclesiastical official introduced into the Philippines from Mexico during the late sixteenth or early seventeenth century whose duties

combined those of a sacristan and religious secretary. Unofficially, however, they acted as the moral guardians of their villages, admonishing irregular behaviour in the community, confirming that parishioners had valid reasons for not attending mass and checking that people observed Christian tenets in their daily lives. They were also the priest's henchmen and chief advisers on all matters local, inflicting corporal punishment or other penances on those deemed to merit such correction and providing what information might be required on the character and reputations of parishioners. Traditionally the office was held by the *principalia* or prominent members of the community. Greg Bankoff, "Big Fish" pp. 693–695 and Greg Bankoff, *In Verbo Sacerdotis* pp. 23–24.

61 "Causa Contra Seberina Candelaria" pp. 13–14, 18–19.
62 "Causa Contra Seberina Candelaria" p. 15.
65 "Santissimo Rosario" p. 52.
66 "Causa Contra Seberina Candelaria" pp. 24–26.
67 "Causa Contra Seberina Candelaria" p. 25.
68 "Causa Contra Seberina Candelaria" p. 26.
69 Antonio Mozo, "Later Augustinian and Dominican Missions" p. 115 and Tomás Ortiz, "Práctica del Ministerio" p. 109.
70 "Causa Contra Seberina Candelaria" p. 10.
71 Luis de Jesus, "Historia General" p. 203.
72 "Causa Contra Seberina Candelaria" p. 13.
73 Luis de Jesus, "Historia General" p. 203 and Juan de Plasencia, "Customs of the Tagalogs" p. 190.
74 "Resume 1521–1569" p. 139.
75 Dieter Bartels, "Politicians and Magicians: Power, Adaptive Strategies, and Syncretism in the Central Moluccas" in Gloria Davis (ed.), *What is Modern Indonesian Culture?* (Madison, 1976), p. 283.
76 Antonio Mozo, "Later Augustinian and Dominican Missions" p. 115 and Tomás Ortiz, "Práctica del Ministerio" p. 107. The tianak or patianak (also referred to as dwende) in Tagalog is synonymous with the Bikol *patyának*, the fusion of an untimely discharged human foetus and a tiny black bird whose mournful wailing resembles that of an infant, and the Cebuano *mantiyának*, a supernatural being of a brownish hue who preys on new-born infants.
78 John Wolf, *A Dictionary of Cebuano Visayan* (Manila, 1972) p. 670 and Merito Espinas, "A Critical Study of the Ibalong, The Bikol Folk Epic Fragment," Unitas 41, 2 (1968) p. 183.
79 "Causa Contra Seberina Candelaria" p. 17.
80 "Causa Contra Seberina Candelaria" p. 17.
81 Norman Cohen, *Europe's Inner Demons* pp. 25–26.
82 Dieter Bartels, "Politicians and Magicians" pp. 284–285.
83 "Causa Contra Seberina Candelaria" p. 12.
84 Greg Bankoff, "Households of Ill-Repute: Rape, Prostitution and Marriage in the Nineteenth Century Philippines," *Pilipinas* 17, Fall (1991): 35–49.
85 Greg Bankoff, "Big Fish" pp. 695–697.
86 Robin Briggs, *Witches & Neighbours. The Social and Cultural Context of European Witchcraft* (1996) pp. 378–380.
87 "Causa Contra Seberina Candelaria" p. 24.
88 Jerry Bentley, *Old World Encounters. Cross-Cultural Contacts in Pre-Modern Times* (New York 1993) pp. 15–16.
89 Jerry Bentley, *Old World Encounters* p. 16.

Part 10

RELIGION, ETHNICITY AND THE NATION

39

CONVERSION BY AFFILIATION

The history of the Karo Batak Protestant Church

Rita Smith Kipp

Source: *American Ethnologist*, 22(4) (1995), 868–82.

Theories of conversion have often stressed either psychological or sociological factors, but viewing conversion as the public declaration of a new identity and incorporating the element of time afford a way to synthesize these approaches. Although conversions to Christianity in the Karo Protestant Church, legacy of a Dutch Reformed mission, were often prompted by political or pragmatic considerations and reinforced an ethnic identity in contrast to a Muslim majority, religious life for many Karo has been transformed over the long run.

The Karo, the northernmost of the Batak groups in highland Sumatra (Indonesia), are today a religiously plural society, although the majority identify as Christians. Karo Christianity, like Christianity elsewhere, is fragmented into many denominations, including Catholics and the rapidly growing Pentecostal groups. By far the largest denomination, however, is the Karo Batak Protestant Church (GBKP), an explicitly ethnic church. The GBKP is the denomination with which I have had the most contact during my years of research on the Karo. I have always lived in the homes of families who were GBKP members, with the exception of one Muslim family. As a result, I have attended countless GBKP Sunday services as well as midweek devotionals held in private homes, women's group meetings, choir rehearsals, and special events such as ordinations and commemorative celebrations. These experiences have convinced me that Christianity is far more than skin deep for many Karo, and far more than a Sunday observance. Some Karo Christians are avid students of the Bible, and many find guidance and comfort in it and in their church community.

Here I seek to understand how the faith of many GBKP Christians can be reconciled with a historical account in which conversions appear to be motivated by political pressures, ethnic pride, or the quest for education.[1] Although inspired more often by short-term expediencies than by religious understanding and conviction, these conversions entailed the consequence that today the majority of Karo are Christian, many of them devoutly so. How can we account for the Karo's *religious* transformation, given that both conversion narratives and the sociohistorical context suggest that converts joined the GBKP for practical and political reasons?

Personal stories from the colonial era suggest that people were usually first drawn into the Christian orbit through their self-interest, especially by their desire for literacy. Some continued their education, becoming employees of the mission as teachers, nurses, or evangelists. In 1983, pursuing research on the early history of the Karo mission, I conducted interviews with over 20 elderly people who had had connections of some sort with it. I spoke with former students of the missionaries and with people who had worked in missionary households. Some had been school teachers or evangelists; others were the children of such teachers and evangelists. I usually began by asking about the person's life history, tape recording and later transcribing the interview. With the exceptions of one woman who described her father's struggle with "Setan" before becoming a Christian and some who spoke of converting despite objections from their families, there were no noteworthy conversion stories. Speakers often told about attending a mission primary school, then continuing their education or becoming workers in a missionary household, and finally becoming teachers or evangelists, as if the whole thing had been an unpremeditated process of taking one step after another.

The following is an example in the form of notes from my interview of a man whom I will call Samuel, born around 1900 in Pancur Batu, a town not far from the city of Medan. Samuel was employed by the mission only for a brief period, spending most of his teaching career in government schools, but he was an active church participant and sometimes preached when a congregation asked him. He describes both his own and his father's conversion in a matter-of-fact style that is typical of these narratives:

> There was no school in Pancur Batu, but a teacher who worked for the mission came to offer night classes. Samuel tagged along with his father who attended these. (Samuel did not remember the name of this teacher, but presumed that he would have had only three years of formal education, like all the teachers of that early era.) Imitating his father, Samuel learned to read and write a little.

> Once Samuel's father could read and write, the teacher asked him to become a Christian. "If I become a Christian, what will it mean?" his father asked. The teacher said he would first study at Sibolangit [a mission post with a full primary school of several grades], then he could move to Tambunen village and become a teacher himself. When his father talked it over with other villagers, not one wanted him to do it. [Why? I pressed.] That was just the general feeling. People knew some Batak script, but did not think it was necessary to learn the Dutch script. But Samuel's father's agnatic kin agreed, so his father went to study at Sibolangit. Eventually his father took the family to Tambunen, where he taught school, and they lived in a traditional house with three other families. Samuel studied in his father's classroom for three years until his father was transferred to another village. About nine years old at the time, Samuel stayed on in Tambunen with friends so as to be closer to Sibolangit where he could continue his own education. It was five kilometers away, so he had to leave his house at six o'clock in the morning and run to get there in time for school. After two years of that, the wife of missionary Neumann invited him to stay with them in Sibolangit and work for his keep.
>
> After he finished the fifth grade, Mrs. Neumann asked if he would like to continue at Raya, where a teacher's training school had been started. "Ask your parents," she said. His father said, "Do as you wish," so he went to Raya, applied, and was accepted. Students lived five to a room in a simple "dormitory" with woven bamboo walls and an *atap* [palm leaf] roof. Samuel arrived at Raya in 1916, the year he became a Christian. "Only if you were a Christian could you become a student there." He studied for four years, graduating from the program in 1919, and he took his first teaching job at Sibolangit in 1920. He had taught for only two or three months when the mission closed all its schools and he was out of a job. He took up farming then, becoming "like the people of the village," but some years later the district government opened primary schools so he began to work as a teacher again. [Narangi Peranginangin, personal communication, July 24, 1983]

Narratives such as this contrast with others I recorded in 1986 while attempting to grasp the dimensions of Christianity outside the GBKP in Karoland. I interviewed three Karo preachers in the Gereja Sidang Rohulkudus Indonesia (GSRI), a Pentecostal sect started by a Karo man and now claiming some 14,000 members in the North Sumatra region. These Pentecostal evangelists spontaneously recounted numerous conversion stories in great detail. Each story traced a similar pattern describing either a string of serious, intractable illnesses, depraved living, depression and angst, or some combination of these problems, followed by an encounter with the Holy Ghost and its "baptism by fire" that had healed and totally reoriented the individual's life. Whether speaking with GBKP old-timers who had become Christian in the missionary era or with young GBKP Christians, I had never encountered stories such as these before, but I had never noticed the *absence* of GBKP conversion stories until struck by this contrast of the two Christian traditions.

The contrast between GBKP and Pentecostal conversion stories derives in the first instance from theological contrasts between different Christian traditions. Clergy or missionaries who convey different Christian traditions bring about religious change in correspondingly different ways. In general, the more orthodox or fundamentalist the theology, the more the evangelical focus aims at an individual, emotional conversion, while liberal Protestant missions are more comfortable with a long-term approach aimed at church formation (e.g., Rubingh 1969; Verkuyl 1978). Furthermore, a single church or mission organization may exhibit different evangelical strategies through its history (Huber 1988). Like many other Pentecostal groups in Indonesia, the GSRI traces its source to Bethel Temple in Seattle, whereas the GBKP developed from a mission run by the Dutch Missionary Society (Nederlands Zendelinggenootschap, or NZG). The pragmatic cast of GBKP conversion narratives is a legacy of this liberal Protestant mission.

NZG missionaries did not try to incite conversion as a dramatic, emotional transformation of the person.[2] Rather, they sought a formal commitment of aspirant Christians, symbolized in the sacrament of baptism, a rite that did not occur without a sufficient period of study. Children born to Christians, however, were routinely baptized as infants. In its first century, beginning in 1797, the NZG emphasized evangelical individualism, a strategy stemming from an ambivalence toward the church, a site of doctrinal disputation and bureaucratic ossification (Van Randwijck 1981). In a speech at a missionary conference in 1901, however, NZG Director J. H. Gunning departed from this tradition, quoting a German mission theorist (Gundemann) to the effect that the goal of evangelization cannot be to change the individual first, and that "[m]issions cannot do otherwise than establish folk churches" (Gunning 1901:305). He went on to advocate the dual approach of moving individuals toward conversion and establishing Christian *gemeente.* The term *gemeente* denotes both secular community and religious congregation, but here connotes especially Christendom as community. New economic links between missions and the colonial government in the early 20th century were enabling missionaries to involve themselves more widely than before in medical care, education, irrigation, and other development projects. These social services, only indirectly evangelical, were rationalized as part of gemeente-forming, by its nature a long-term goal.

Conceptualizing conversion

Two authors of a review article on the sociology of conversion conclude that radical personal change "remains at the core of all conceptions of conversion, whether theological or social scientific" (Snow and Machalek 1984:169). The emphasis on conversion as an intensely personal religious *experience* goes back to James (1902); and scholars have often explained such experiences with reference to stress, deprivation, or other negative predisposing factors (cf. Cucchiari 1988; Dawson 1990; Richardson 1985). Like Nock (1933), some contemporary scholars of conversion in religion and sociology presume that without a deeply personal reorientation, conversion has not occurred (e.g., Heirich 1977).

Anthropologists and historians, however, usually speak of conversion as a social or political phenomenon. It may, indeed, be the action of a collectivity such as a kin group or a village. Some writers link conversion explicitly to political and material advantages or to a quest for intangibles such as dignity. Spiritual aspirations, values, and even the beliefs of converts may appear to change little if at all. The politics of colonial domination, of status conflicts, ethnicity, gender, caste, or class are used to explain why certain groups or whole areas find a new religion attractive (e.g., Colson 1970; Comaroff 1985:150).

Considering the ambiguity of "conversion," the Comaroffs have suggested that we scrap the term altogether (1991:248–251). More commonly, however, anthropologists prefer to narrow or specify "conversion" to indicate merely the public, formal change of affiliation, leaving motivation, beliefs, and other inner experience explicitly moot (e.g., Aragon 1992:372; Firth 1970:321):

> The most necessary feature of religious conversion, it turns out, is not a deeply systematic reorganization of personal meanings but an adjustment in self-identification through the at least nominal acceptance of religious actions or beliefs deemed more fitting, useful, or true. In other words, at the very least—an analytic minimum—conversion implies the acceptance of a new locus of self-definition, a new, though not necessarily exclusive, reference point for one's identity. [Hefner 1993a:17]

Robert Hefner, introducing an important collection called *Conversion to Christianity*, draws from reference group theory to conceptualize conversion as a commitment to a new identity, but it is clear from his own ethnographic materials on Christians in East Java (Hefner 1993b) and from that of other contributors to the same collection that a convert's new identity may at first be lightly worn and only dimly understood. Reference group theory implies that people accept identities via a positive process of claiming for themselves similarities to a group or category of persons. Hefner's own ethnography suggests that the East Javanese conversions were fueled even more insistently by a wish to affirm or enhance *differences*, in this case differences between Muslims and non-Muslims, lowlanders and highlanders. In fact, the new religious identity one claims may be far less sharply understood than a negative image from which one hopes to distance oneself. What being a Christian or a Muslim means is then rethought and renegotiated over the years, partly from a drive to make lives fit more consistently the categories that frame them and partly because the political economies of religious identities keep shifting (e.g., Bowen 1993):

> The cultural knowledge embodied in a complex religion is always larger than any individual's understanding. . . . Over the long run, then, conversion (or, similarly, a child's learning of the faith) may have conceptual implications of which the individual is unaware. In other words, the allegiance professed early in conversion may be preliminary to a more radical and unanticipated resocialization. [Hefner 1993b:120]

Hefner insists on the interpenetration of psychological models of conversion with sociopolitical ones (1993a:23). Starting from either a psychological or sociological vantage point, scholars have sometimes succeeded in synthesizing those two angles of vision. For example, some scholars have asked whether experiencing certain events and situations or occupying certain social positions might not make individuals more responsive to the rhetoric of conversion or more amenable to the "psychological magic" of rituals that disrupt ordinary reality and reorient persons toward new realities (Whitehead 1987). Others have noted that religious experiences, like any others, are socially constructed (Snow and Machalek 1984:176). As is obvious from the difference between GBKP and Karo Pentecostals' conversion stories, whether individuals experience a dramatic reorientation or not and the ways conversion is cast, comprehended, and later recounted have much to do with the tradition of the group they are joining (see also Harding 1987; Schneider and Lindenbaum 1987).

Historians and anthropologists most often succeed in showing the interpenetration of psychological and sociological factors in conversion when they depict conversion as a product of time (e.g., Beidelman 1982; Berkhofer 1965; Boutilier *et al.* 1978; Bromley and Shupe 1979; Firth 1970; Sahay 1968; Shinn 1987; Taylor 1987). That is, rather than starting from an electrifying personal experience as the beginning of religious change, they describe affiliating with a new religion as one part of a process that may have begun with a changed socioeconomic environment and may end in the eventual transformation of personal, religious experience for some or all members of a community. Only a few persons may decide to adopt a new religious identity at first, and for reasons that have little to do with faith. The children of those pioneers who remain true to their commitment, however, grow up in a new religious environment. Over generations the process of accommodating the new religion to local culture and local conditions may entail changes in the religious system itself, what we usually call syncretism or indigenization (e.g., Barker 1993); alternatively, people strive for greater consistency or orthodoxy through periods of rationalization, revival, and reform (e.g., Bowen 1993). Through a long dialectic of blending indigenization and purifying reformation, the forms and qualities of religious experience in a community may change utterly.

The synthetic vision of religious change I suggest here draws insights from practice theory. Practice theory of the past decade has tried to create a synthesis between what sociologists term macro- and microtheories (e.g., Knorr-Cetina and Cicourel 1981). Both structural accounts that lose sight of individuals' agency and ethnomethodological accounts of individual agency abstracted from larger structures have been exposed as one-sided. Practice approaches strive to see how individuals' agency either reproduces or changes the larger systems in which those individuals act. Giddens (1984) has tried to spell out how action and intentionality reproduce systems, a process he calls structuration; Sahlins (1985) shows how action, carried out in terms of prior structures and categories of some kind, always risks the transformation of those structures and categories. In these approaches actors are portrayed as pursuing goal-directed transactions with other actors and with their environments, yet these transactions often produce results or consequences not encompassed in the actors' goals (Ortner 1984).

Tracing the spiraling loop of agency and structure entails a historical perspective. The history of GBKP conversions shows how new structures (here an indigenous church) emerge as a consequence of individual agency (expedient conversions) and how the new structures then shape new forms of experience (in this case, religious life). The bifurcation of psychological and sociological approaches to conversion reflects different emphases on the two poles of structure and agency. While it may be appropriate at times to analyze either the individual agency of converts or the structural setting that contextualizes that agency, it is also useful to conceptualize conversion as a "dialectical process" (Ranger 1987) encompassing both elements.

Acknowledging the fundamental religiosity of the faith of many GBKP Christians today, I present historical data showing that the road to religious change has converged with other kinds of roads, the mapping of which takes us well outside the realm of religion. Identity politics in colonial and post-colonial Indonesia are especially central to this story. Actions for the short term (affiliating with a new religion) went beyond the designs of the actors as GBKP Christians in concert and, in the long run, created a church that imbued contemporary religious life with a particular form and color.

The growth of Christianity among the Karo: "the seed that grew"[3]

The story of GBKP growth suggests a complex power dynamic that encompassed both ethnic politics and the politics of state domination; at first the domination was that of a colonial state (which the Karo steadily resisted) and later became that of a developing, militaristic one. Ironically, the Indonesian nation-state, the largest Muslim country in the world, has had more success at stimulating the Karo's conversion to Christianity than the Dutch colonialists had. In any case, incentives for conversion in all periods appear to derive more frequently from the quest for literacy, calculations of material advantage, or political protection than from deep religious conviction.

While the majority of the Karo are Christian, it is impossible to know the exact percentage because the government does not collect census data on ethnicity. In the district that is the Karo's highland home (Kabupaten Karo), Christians in all denominations comprised about 67 percent of the population in the 1980 census (Kabupaten Daerah Tingkat II Karo 1981). Most people who live in Karoland are ethnically Karo, but Indonesians of many other ethnic groups live there as well, especially in the two largest towns. Many of these immigrants make up the 18 percent identifying themselves as Muslim in 1980. Animists were about 12 percent in 1980, and these were probably all Karo.[4] The population of the district was approaching 300,000 at that time, but fully as many Karo live outside Kabupaten Karo as in it. Karo also live in rural areas in districts adjacent to Kabupaten Karo, and since the 1950s have migrated in ever larger numbers to Medan, Jakarta, and other urban areas throughout the country. Karo who live in urban areas, furthermore, are overwhelmingly Christian or Muslim.

Numbers, of course, do not measure faith or commitment. Because identifying with one of five officially approved world religions is all but imperative in contemporary Indonesia, many Karo Muslims and Christians are merely nominal adherents, as is suggested by their lack of participation in organized religious life. Some of these Muslims and Christians participate in animist rituals instead, but many are simply not observant of any religion. As everywhere, Karo Christians run the gamut from lapsed or indifferent to deeply devout. Many of the GBKP church buildings—as well as those of other Christian denominations—are totally full for Sunday services throughout Karoland. In the towns and cities GBKP congregations often provide two Sunday morning services to accommodate the large number of worshipers. For the faithful, Christianity shapes the routines of daily life, and the interpretation of events and relationships, history and the future.

The first converts to Christianity, five men and one woman who were members of the same family, were baptized in 1894 under the auspices of a mission post run by the NZG that had been established there four years earlier (Kipp 1990:134–135). There are no surviving records of what these six believed or felt, but we do have some glimmer of how their neighbors perceived their conversion. Other Karo wondered what the converts' salaries were going to be now that they were "coolies" of the missionary. The converts' new affiliation as Christians suddenly called into question their responsibilities toward their village headman and toward the Muslim sultan who claimed them as subjects. People wondered when the Dutch would conscript them to fight in the war against Aceh. The first baptisms were widely interpreted as a quite literal brainwashing that made the converts lackeys of the Dutch (Kipp 1990). Unfortunately we do not know whether the converts understood their conversion as a spiritual transformation or at least a spiritual commitment (which is how the missionaries understood it) or whether they were motivated (as their neighbors assumed they were) by the hope for political and economic advantages.

As it turned out there were not many political and economic advantages to becoming a Christian, and relatively few Karo did so during the colonial period. Karo Christians, however, do not explain the slow growth in their numbers during the colonial era in these terms. They say instead that the Karo resisted becoming Christian because they thought of Christianity as a Dutch trait. The Karo resented colonial taxation, which was relatively steep in their case (Reid 1979:57), and they were extremely wary of the land-hungry European plantations that skirted the Karo highlands on the East. These plantations were the mission's primary patrons in its early years. "In the turbulent 1940s," Reid says of the Karo, "they would become the most whole-hearted supporters of revolution against the Dutch" (1979:57). Missionary letters or reports often described the Karo as cynical and distrustful, attitudes that the missionaries felt stood in the way of their receptivity to the Gospel. Colonial-era Karo, resisting identification with their colonial overlords, and fearing especially to be drafted as soldiers for the Dutch, also resisted affiliating as Christians.

During the first decade of the mission, 1890–99, work was confined to the foothills between Medan and the Karo Plateau, and only 25 persons were baptized. In the next decade, some 500 baptisms occurred in a period that coincided with the mission's move to the more densely settled Karo highlands once these were annexed and pacified (Neumann 1941). The following decade, 1910–20, was one of losing ground, however, for baptisms did not stay ahead of the deaths and other attrition at some posts (e.g., Neumann 1915). Nor did the picture improve much during the 1920s, which began with the drastic step of closing all the mission's primary schools because attendance was so low. Frustration and fault finding often set the missionaries to quarreling with each other but still the mission hung on, continuing to train evangelists, nurses, and, eventually, schoolteachers once again. In the 1930s the number of baptisms began to increase slightly. The peak year in the precolonial period came in 1940, when almost 500 people were baptized in one year. At the end of that year, however, the total number of Christians under the mission's wing, after nearly fifty years of missionary work, was only 5,347, still a small minority of the Karo people (Cooley 1976).[5]

The NZG was slow to see the inevitability and necessity of replacing the mission installations with independent folk churches. This may have had something to do with their suspicion of churches as organizations. In the Karo case, at least, the NZG was unusually late in training an indigenous clergy. While the missionaries began to talk about church formation in the 1920s, they got down to hammering out the ecclesiastical and liturgical outlines of an indigenous church only when war threatened to remove them from the local scene altogether. Their internment by the Japanese left the fledgling church with only two ordained ministers and with teachers, evangelists, and a laity that had never been taught to lead and manage a modern bureaucratic organization.

In the revolutionary era of the 1940s, including the Japanese occupation and the struggle for Indonesian independence, all the old questions about Christian affiliation and political loyalty came rushing back. Were the Christians Dutch loyalists, as many Karo had suspected all along, or would they stand with the revolution? Christians did not repudiate their religion in this period, but some told me they did destroy pictures of themselves in the company of missionaries or other evidence that would suggest they had been too friendly with the colonialists. In this decade of war and revolution the church grew not at all. Given the conditions of the times and its lack of resources and leadership, however, its mere survival was remarkable (Cooley 1976; GBKP Panitia Jubileum 1990).

The removal of the missionaries and the colonial order of which they had been a part changed the identity politics of becoming a Christian. The Dutch presence and power had greatly mitigated the impact of older sources of power—Muslim chiefdoms and sultanates—with which Karo had interacted and that they had resisted throughout their history. The Acehnese to the northwest had attempted to incorporate and convert the highland Karo in the 17th century. Along the east coast, the Malay sultans viewed many lowland Karo as their subjects, but these lowlanders did not necessarily concede to subjugation (Pelzer 1978). The Dutch controlled the Sumatran Malays via a form of indirect rule utilizing the sultans, but after 1888 they administered the Batak directly through Dutch civil servants *(controleurs).* The colonial authorities also allowed missionaries entry into Batak regions but not Malay areas, where their presence might have incited Muslim resistance. Through missionaries and civil servants Karo thus had a direct link to Dutch power but they also chafed under a more direct surveillance. They played one would-be master against the other, using the Dutch to wrest concessions from the sultans and the threat of converting to Islam to worry the Dutch. But Indonesian independence took the Dutch out of the picture. Defending Karo interests and Karo identities against a Muslim majority then came all the more clearly into focus.

Christian missions in mainland Southeast Asia and in Indonesia have enjoyed their greatest successes in areas not previously claimed by the majority religion (Keyes 1977:21, 102). Miao conversion traces to a desire for literacy and a wish to maintain a conceptual distance between themselves and the majority; for the Hmong becoming Christian was "a way of remaining Hmong *without* being absorbed by the Thai state" (Tapp 1989:89). Kammerer's (1990) assessment of the recent turn of the Akha to Christianity is similar; she finds little "change of heart" in these Akha Christians. In these cases people seem to take up a new religion partly to preserve an ethnic identity.

The politics of ethnicity certainly influenced the Karo turn to Christianity as well. Before Christianity was an option, conversion to Islam had signaled a Karo's political and ethnic transformation. Karo had been linked historically to the Malay sultanates through trade, mercenary roles, sharecropping, and occasionally marital alliance, and many Karo lived in the lowlands near the centers of these sultanates. In precolonial times and well into the colonial era lowland Karo who converted to Islam changed ethnic identity and political loyalty, becoming Malay (Jawi). New Muslims dropped their Karo clan names and became subjects of the sultans. Despite its frequent violation the boundary between Karo and Malay remained no less sharp, outlined by the diacritical marker of religion (Kipp 1993). Probably because conversion to Islam had formerly registered a lowlander as a subject of a sultan or raja and also implied a change of ethnic identity, conversion to Christianity was at first confused with loyalty or service to the Dutch. Although the missionaries tried verbally to dissociate Christianity from its political entanglements, their own actions often implicated the new religion with colonial interests (Kipp 1990). Colonial-era Karo thus resisted Christianity as a Dutch trait or as a sign of loyalty to the Dutch.

After independence, and once local Christianity came under local Karo control, many Karo began to find church membership more attractive. Cooley (1976:68) presents a graph of church growth that shows a marked takeoff during the 1950s. Karo migration to the cities was barely beginning in this era, but those who left the highlands for city life were especially likely to convert. The village kinship network and agricultural cycle, ancestors' graves and localized nature spirits—elements that had been bound up with observance of the traditional religion—could not be easily transported to the new urban setting (Kipp 1987; Steedly 1993). From the beginning the missionaries had encouraged the use of the Karo language and dress as ethnic insulators against Malay/Muslim influence. In the postindependence cities of Indonesia, the Karo Batak Protestant Church became a center of community life as *Karo.* Church events were one of the few public contexts in which Karo speakers could enjoy hearing and speaking their language. The church's activities for children and adolescents, its choir groups and prayer groups, and its holidays and other commemorations became a magnet for urban Karo. In the ethnically heterogeneous urban context, and especially in Javanese cities where Karo are quickly labeled as Batak (a word with many negative associations), GBKP membership gave migrants access to the supportive companionship of other Karo (Kipp 1993).

Ethnic politics are only one dimension of the politics of religion in Indonesia. Also significant are the politics of nationalism and the government's fear of class consciousness. Cooley's graph soars skyward during the decade of the 1960s, and precisely after 1965. For the GBKP this was an era of "mass conversions," as it was in several other areas throughout Indonesia—especially where, as in Karoland, Communism had been strong before 1965 (Grothaus 1970; Pedersen 1970). The abortive coup of the Communists in Jakarta on September 30, 1965, gave way throughout Indonesia to the violent crushing of the Partai Komunis Indonesia (PKI) by execution and incarceration. In this atmosphere people rushed to identify with one of the recognized religions as a badge of innocence. But the mass conversions of the post-1965 era were not an entirely spontaneous, grassroots response. The governor's office of North Sumatra, the military, and the Council of Churches (of which the GBKP was a member) cooperated to fund flashy evangelization tours, complete with brass bands and choirs, that held rallies in the villages of Karoland to recruit converts (Pedersen 1970:190). The government decided that "the making of believers was the unmaking of Communists" (Thomson 1968:8), and, looking toward the future, that building religious faith would temper the impulses toward a class-based revolution. Having counted only 33,240 in 1966, the GBKP claimed 100,000 members by 1970 (Grothaus 1970).

During the postcoup period, Muslims in Karoland also experienced substantial growth, although not on the same order of magnitude as the Christians. The governor of North Sumatra and the *bupati* (district head) of Karoland, both of whom were Karo, were removed from office shortly after the events in 1965 because of their suspected complicity with the Communists. The man appointed as the new bupati in Karoland was a Muslim and was not a Karo. He publicly announced the dissolution of the PKI and all related groups. As elsewhere in the country, the retribution and rounding up of Communists in Karoland were carried out largely by Muslim youth groups.[6] Muslims in Karoland numbered just over 24,000 in 1966, although many of these were non-Karo immigrants living in the major towns. By the end of 1970 the number of Muslims in Karoland had grown to 31,775, suggesting that they, too, experienced some gains from the postcoup terrors that drove people to declare a religion (Martadi n.d.). But the ethnic dynamic in this locale, namely the Karo animists' search for protection against groups that were mainly Muslim and in some measure non-Karo, meant that the animists were more likely to turn for succor to a Christian affiliation than to a Muslim one and to identify themselves in contrast to their persecutors.

Since 1965 the government has encouraged animistic peoples to adopt an *agama* (organized religion) in order to demonstrate that they are modern, trustworthy citizens (i.e., not Communist sympathizers). Identity cards specify religious affiliation, and it is impossible to work in the civil service and difficult to get permits and licenses without being Muslim, Christian, or a member of one of the other officially recognized religions (Kipp and Rodgers 1987). The politics of religion in Indonesia create the incentives for abandoning traditional religions; the politics of ethnicity may then predispose people like the Karo to choose a minority religion rather than joining the Muslim majority. At times these conversions seem to result from a matter-of-fact assessment of the impossibility of maintaining the traditional religion given the political and technical requirements of the modern world (e.g., Hoskins 1987:142; Volkman 1985:132).

GBKP Christians, being far from blind to these political considerations, interpret events and history within the intellectual tradition of Reformed Christianity, in which structural constraints such as this appear to be part of God's design (e.g., Kipp 1990:37–38). The account cited below is from a tape-recorded interview with a retired GBKP clergyman. We were discussing the history of the church, comparing especially the colonial with the post-colonial rate of growth. When I asked what he thought was most important in this history, he responded:

> In this portrayal of the Gospel? I would say it is the mercy of God toward the Karo people. The Karo were closed in, insulated, separated from other people, because we were in between powerful political realms—Aceh, Sisingamangaraja [Toba Batak], and Malay. We were squeezed in the middle and could not move. Because of the power of God, of the Gospel, we can be loose, we can be free. He has given us faith and belief since the Gospel has come. If we are to make the history of the church, that is the first thing I would note: that through the mercy of God—full of mystery, dynamic, and full of challenges—through this we entered into New Life. [Ngantan Munte, personal communication, July 29, 1983]

For this man, the ethnic dynamic by which the Karo became Christian, far from undermining the religious significance of all those particular choices, was evidence that God had been working in history to prepare this people's receptivity. In his view it is less remarkable that the Karo chose the Christian God than that the Karo, first, were chosen.[7]

Migration out of Karoland into the cities, especially outside Sumatra, has increased significantly since 1970 (Bangun 1986). The GBKP continues to grow faster in urban areas than in the Karo highlands, and the leadership of the church makes a concerted effort to found new congregations in cities or suburban areas when Karo first begin to move there (Pandita A. Ginting-Suka, personal communication, June 20, 1983).[8] While there is no terror motivating conversion, as there was in 1966 and 1967, the political and social pressures to claim a religious affiliation are still strong, especially for Karo who attend universities or work in urban settings. Thus, the GBKP has continued to expand in the last two decades despite the fact that it has also begun to lose members to Pentecostal and other Protestant denominations.[9] At a groundbreaking in 1990 for a church and office complex in Jakarta, the current head of the church said that the membership of the GBKP was now 250,000.[10]

The missionaries left behind only a minority who were Christian. The members of this minority, however, were nearly all literate, poised to take advantage of the opportunities of the postrevolutionary era in which upward mobility has been linked to urban migration. The elite, the highly educated, and the middle class of Karo society are thus for the most part Christian. Under missionary direction, Karo teachers and evangelists began the process of rethinking Karo traditions in order to separate out what conflicted with religion (Kipp 1974). The carving up of life into secular customs and sacred obligations happened elsewhere in Indonesia under missionary direction (e.g., Volkman 1985) as much to preserve people's linguistic and cultural distinctiveness from the Muslim majority as to exorcise pagan practices. Animists do not agree that the world can be apportioned so neatly into spheres of agama (religion) and *adat* (custom), but they no longer operate from a social and economic position that gives weight to their viewpoint (Steedly 1993). Gradually interpreting and internalizing the new religion for themselves, Christian Karo have also arrived at a more self-conscious view of the traditions they select to define themselves as Karo (Kipp 1993). A self-conscious ethnic identity is one result of this rethinking, along with a deeper understanding of what it means to be a Christian.

If faith seems irrelevant to most GBKP conversion narratives, it does lie in and between the lines of the life histories of Karo Christians in the colonial period. Christians' minority status and their association with the Dutch marked them as objects of suspicion and made their lives difficult. Evangelists traveled by foot before the revolution and were often at the mercy of strangers for food and shelter. The wages of school teachers and evangelists were not sufficient to support their families, who had to farm to make ends meet, but neighbors envied their salaries, however meager, and the fact that these men seemed to "eat" (i.e., make a living) without doing much that resembled work as the Karo knew it. Wives and children of the evangelists and teachers recall the frequent transfers of mission employees as a special hardship. Balancing the social strains of Christians in their kin groups and local communities was the emergence of a new kind of community, the

Christian gemeente. Evangelists' conferences and other special gatherings, weekly worship, a yearly calendar of religious holidays, and the policy of requiring Christians to marry only Christians all contributed to an emerging sense of community within Karo society.

Young Karo growing up in Karoland today where being a Christian is taken for granted now face challenges rather different from those their Christian parents and grandparents faced. All young people have some formal education and have often seen something of the world outside Karoland, a world they also know through newspapers, radio, and television. Their sense of the world is macrocosmic in comparison to the microcosm of village life two generations ago (Horton 1971, 1975). Figuring out what life *means* is the challenge young Indonesians of any faith now face in a newly self-conscious manner. The universalist faiths claim to provide answers.

Here, for example, are some notes I took in 1986 after two casual conversations with a young divorced woman, D., whose coffee shop I frequented. An active member of one of this town's GBKP congregations, she had named her coffee shop Mother's Prayer, and she kept close company with a female evangelist. D. was a third-generation Christian, the granddaughter of a man who had been converted by the missionary J. H. Neumann. She supported a very elderly disabled aunt who also worked in the shop, and who was often party to our conversations.

> *14 October 1986, Kabanjahe* D. said she had recently asked her aunt [who was present] about the meaning of life. We get up in the morning to work all day to eat, then go to bed and start over the next day. In the end, we die. She said her aunt did not have an answer. They began to hash it over again right there. The aunt reasoned that we work to educate our children, to eat, and so on. She seemed unable to understand the depth of her niece's concern with the futility of it all. I asked D. what she thought the meaning of life might be, and she answered, "I don't know yet," but then went on to say that she guessed God knew, and he had created us for his glory. Her mood in all of this was gay, however, not pessimistic as I have seen her sometimes. She seemed to be pulling me into this ongoing conversation partly to tease the older woman, who could not fathom what we two younger women could see—that the meaning of life is not given.
>
> *16 October 1986* Today D. raised the same issues, but in a more somber tone. [The aunt was not there.] She had suffered much and had often wished to go away where no one knew her. Ever since she was small, she had fantasized about going away to a foreign country. She had been Christian all her life because her parents and grandparents had been. She prayed before meals and before going to sleep at night, but these were just automatic. As a child, you don't

> understand why you do these things, she said. Recently she had spoken with a minister from Manado who was visiting the GBKP. He understood her doubts and had taken her questioning of life seriously. He was able to explain things to her in a way that had been comforting. He was the one who explained that all creation was for the glory of God.
>
> The Christian environment in which D. participated did not make her immune to existential dilemmas, but at this point it still remained the environment in which she sought answers to life's deepest questions.

Conclusion

Practice theory encourages us to link microprocesses of consciousness and agency with macropatterns of society and culture by attending to change and stasis over the long term (Bourdieu 1977). This has turned anthropologists increasingly toward research on local histories (e.g., Comaroff and Comaroff 1991; Hefner 1990; Ortner 1989; Sullivan 1989). I have examined GBKP history in order to link expedient affiliations with the church's eventual success and, at the experiential level, with the transformation of religious life. GBKP statistics on membership, attendance, and the church's great physical and material resources—and, at the microlevel, the sincere prayer of someone seeking God's wisdom in a difficult moment—bespeak how the faith of many Karo has changed since that day in 1894 when six people (for reasons that remained obscure even to their closest neighbors) publicly declared themselves to have taken on a new religion.

Practice theory urges that agency and structure are best understood in relation to each other, suggesting a corrective to the bifurcated approach to conversion in the literature. Approaches that focus too exclusively on the individual's religious experience miss the potential social and personal impact of any decision to change religious allegiance, even if the change is merely nominal. Similarly, accounts that reduce conversion to affiliation and its short-term benefits, or those that depict only the social predispositions and consequences of this act, undervalue the religious implications of what has happened or, more precisely, what may happen. Many colonial-era Karo Christians were baptized as young men and women seeking access to mission schools but came to interpret their lives through a new faith. As actors try to reconcile the new label of Christian with their changing experiences and knowledge, interpreting their lives in terms of a growing understanding of what is written as word, formerly nominal Christians may become Christians of conviction.[11] Their children, in contrast, grow into a faith, grow away from it, or reformulate it for themselves in response to their own search for comfort and meaning.

This historical exercise has sought the connections between religious experience and structural forms. First, structures such as different church traditions influence the conversion experience. In turn, particular kinds of faith and religious experiences grow from participating in these churches. The missionaries of the Dutch Missionary Society looked at conversion as a public commitment rather than as a suddenly transforming emotional experience, a tradition that GBKP members perpetuate in their own conversion narratives. Affiliating with the mission, small numbers of colonial-era Karo became literate, learning new conceptions of time, history, and value along with Bible stories and hymns. Because being a Christian at that time connoted, if not a Dutch identity, at least a loyalty to the Dutch, most Karo wanted nothing to do with it. When the Dutch were eventually forced out of the picture, however, the press of the surrounding Muslim majority gave the Karo's old resistance to Islam a new urgency. While some Karo did choose Islam, far more opted for Christianity in the era of independence, a choice that marked and preserved ethnic identity in a way that becoming Muslim in this context could not have done. The GBKP is the only explicitly ethnic Karo church. Prominent since 1965 are the blatantly political and pragmatic motives for affiliating as a Christian in a polity that still ranks Communism as "public enemy number one" (Abdullah 1981).

Attracted to the literacy provided in mission schools in the colonial era, trying quite literally to save their lives in the bloodbath after 1965, or seeking a job and a friendly community in the rush to the cities since 1970, the majority of Karo have chosen to become or remain Christian. Ethnic consciousness, political dangers, state encouragement, and the quest for education explain why many Karo became Christian but not necessarily what being a Christian means to them. For some it means that they have come to see history and their own existential dilemmas through a lens of faith. What appears to the anthropologist as the structures predisposing agency (ethnic rivalries and political purges) appears to them as the mercy of God molding human action.

Acknowledgments

I conducted field research from 1972 through 1974 over an 18-month period. I carried out additional research for durations of several months or weeks in 1983, 1986, 1989, and 1990. I wish to thank the Fulbright Foundation and Kenyon College for financial support on those trips. The historical research was conducted in the Netherlands during 1980–81 under an NEH fellowship. A version of this article was presented at the annual meeting of the American Anthropological Association in 1991. Robert Hefner, the discussant in our session, provided detailed commentary that was very helpful. I also appreciate suggestions from Richard Kipp, Don Rogan, and Howard Sacks.

Notes

1 Although the term *faith* carries meanings peculiar to Christianity, I use the term analytically to mean that melding of ethos and worldview that characterizes religion in general (Geertz 1966; 1968:2).
2 See Weber's contrast of Luther and Calvin on the matter of feelings and emotions (1958:102, 113–114).
3 The history of the GBKP has appeared as one of a series of church histories commissioned by the Indonesian Council of Churches and edited by Frank Cooley called *Benih yang Tumbuh (The Seed that Grew)*. My article cannot deal with that history in any detail, nor can I offer a full account of the contemporary church, its organization, leadership, and the scope of its operations. Readers interested in these topics might consult Pedersen 1970 and Rae 1994.
4 Official statistics are deceptive here too. Some Karo who practice the traditional religion are now officially listed as Hindu. Like the Balinese, they have undergone a process of "internal conversion," rationalizing and transforming their religion as Hinduism (Geertz 1973; Steedly 1993).
5 Total Karo population at the time was around 180,000 in 1936 by one missionary's estimate, making the 5,000 members of the church around 3 percent of the total (Van Muylwijk 1939).
6 In Karoland, two Muslim youth groups, Kesatuan Aksi Pemuda Pelajar Indonesia (KAPPI) and Kesatuan Aksi Mahasiswa Indonesia (KAMI), were particularly involved in these retributive actions.
7 The Biblical idea of a "chosen" people finds diverse expressions in the Christian world. See, for example, Schama 1988:45 on the Dutch.
8 Pandita A. Ginting-Suka was chairman of the GBKP from 1964 to 1989.
9 Pentecostal styles of Christianity have been attracting small numbers of Indonesians since the 1930s, and are today perhaps the fastest growing sector of Indonesian Christianity.
10 This figure includes GBKP in cities everywhere as well as in Karoland and may be a little high, but not markedly so. No one knows for certain how many total Karo there are, since census data do not include ethnicity. Estimates run between 800,000 and a million. If so, this figure on GBKP membership is not terribly inflated.
11 Fischer (1973) notes the importance of literacy in this gradual process of religious change.

References cited

Abdullah, Taufik
1981 The Sociocultural Scene in Indonesia. *In* Trends in Indonesia, II. Leo Suryadinata and Sharon Siddique, eds. Pp. 65–76. Singapore: Singapore University Press.

Aragon, Lorraine V.
1992 Revised Rituals in Central Sulawesi: The Maintenance of Traditional Cosmological Concepts in the Face of Allegiance to World Religion. Anthropological Forum 6:371–384.

Bangun, Tridah
1986 Perseketuan Orang Batak Karo di Daerah Perantauan. (The Communion of Karo Batak People in Areas of Migration.) *In* Seminar Kebudayaan Karo

dan Kehidupan Masa Kini. (Seminar on Karo Culture and Contemporary Life.) Sarjani Tarigan, ed. Pp. 192–210. Medan, Indonesia: Panitia Penyelenggara Seminar Kebudayaan Karo dan Kehidupan Masa Kini.

Barker, John
1993 "We are Ekelesia": Conversion in Uiaku, Papua New Guinea. *In* Conversion to Christianity. Robert W. Hefner, ed. Pp. 199–230. Berkeley: University of California Press.

Beidelman, Thomas O.
1982 Colonial Evangelism. Bloomington: Indiana University Press.

Berkhofer, Robert F.
1965 Salvation and the Savage. New York: Atheneum.

Bourdieu, Pierre
1977 Outline of a Theory of Practice. New York: Cambridge University Press.

Boutilier, James A., Daniel T. Hughes, and Sharon W. Tiffany
1978 Mission, Church, and Sect in Oceania. Lanham, MD: University Press of America.

Bowen, John
1993 Muslims through Discourse. Princeton: Princeton University Press.

Bromley, David, and Anson Shupe
1979 Just a Few Years Seem Like a Lifetime: A Role Theory Approach to Participation in Religious Movements. *In* Research in Social Movements: Conflict and Change. Lewis Kriesberg, ed. Pp. 159–185. Greenwich, CT: JAI Press.

Colson, Elizabeth
1970 Converts and Tradition: The Impact of Christianity on Valley Tonga Religion. Southwest Journal of Anthropology 26:143–156.

Comaroff, Jean
1985 Body of Power, Spirit of Resistance. Chicago: University of Chicago Press.

Comaroff, Jean, and John Comaroff
1991 Of Revelation and Revolution: Christianity, Colonialism, and Consciousness in South Africa. Chicago: University of Chicago Press.

Cooley, Frank L., ed.
1976 Benih Yang Tumbuh IV. (The Seed That Grew, IV.) Suatu Survey Mengenai Gereja Batak Karo Protestan. (A Survey concerning the Karo Batak Protestant Church.) Jakarta: Dewan Gereja-gereja di Indonesia.

Cucchiari, Salvatore
1988 "Adapted for Heaven": Conversion and Culture in Western Sicily. American Ethnologist 15:417–441.

Dawson, Lorne
1990 Self-Affirmation, Freedom, and Rationality: Theoretically Elaborating "Active" Conversions. Journal for the Scientific Study of Religion 29:141–163.

Firth, Raymond
1970 Rank and Religion in Tikopia: A Study in Polynesian Pragmatism and Conversion to Christianity. London: Allen and Unwin.

Fischer, Humphry
1973 Conversion Reconsidered: Some Historical Aspects of Religious Conversion in Black Africa. Africa 43:27–40.

GBKP Panitia Jubileum 100 Tahun (GBKP Committee for the Centennial Celebration)
1990 Selamat Jubileum 100th GBKP. (Happy Centennial Celebration of the GBKP.) Medan, Indonesia: Moderamen GBKP.

Geertz, Clifford
1966 Religion as a Cultural System. *In* Anthropological Approaches to the Study of Religion. Michael Banton, ed. Pp. 1–46. London: Tavistock.
1968 Islam Observed. Chicago: University of Chicago Press.
1973 "Internal Conversion" in Contemporary Bali. *In* The Interpretation of Cultures, by Clifford Geertz. Pp. 170–189. New York: Basic Books.

Giddens, Anthony
1984 The Constitution of Society. Cambridge: Polity Press.

Grothaus, Werner
1970 80 Jahre Karobatakkirche. (Eighty Years of the Karo Batak Church.) In die Welt für die Welt. 6(8–9): 1–11.

Gunning, Jan Willem
1901 Evangelisatie of Christianisatie? Referaat mede naar aanleiding van reis indrukken in Indië, gehouden op de Nederlandsche Zending-Conferentie te s'-Gravenhage op 18 Oktober 1901. (Evangelization or Christianization? A Lecture Presented with Reference to Travel Impressions of India, Held at the Dutch Mission Conference at s'-Gravenhage on October 18, 1901.) Mededeelingen NZG 45:297–344.

Harding, Susan
1987 Convicted by the Holy Spirit: The Rhetoric of Fundamental Baptist Conversion. American Ethnologist 14:167–181.

Hefner, Robert W.
1990 The Political Economy of Mountain Java: An Interpretive History. Berkeley: University of California Press.
1993a Introduction: World Building and the Rationality of Conversion. *In* Conversion to Christianity. Robert W. Hefner, ed. Pp. 3–44. Berkeley: University of California Press.
1993b Of Faith and Commitment: Christian Conversion in Muslim Java. *In* Conversion to Christianity. Robert W. Hefner, ed. Pp. 99–125. Berkeley: University of California Press.

Heirich, Max
1977 Change of the Heart: A Test of Some Widely Held Theories about Religious Conversion. American Journal of Sociology 83:653–680.

Horton, Robin
1971 African Conversion. Africa 41 (2):85–108.
1975 On the Rationality of Conversion. Africa 45:219–235, 373–399.

Hoskins, Janet
1987 Entering the Bitter House: Spirit Worship and Conversion in West Sumba. *In* Indonesian Religions in Transition. Rita Smith Kipp and Susan Rodgers, eds. Pp. 136–160. Tucson: University of Arizona Press.

Huber, Mary Taylor
1988 The Bishops' Progress: A Historical Ethnography of Catholic Missionary Experience on the Sepik Frontier. Washington, DC: Smithsonian Press.

James, Williams
1902 The Varieties of Religious Experience. New York: Longmans.

Kabupaten Daerah Tingkat II Karo
1981 Monographi. (Monograph.) Paviliun Pemerintah Daerah Tingkat II Karo di Pekan Raya, Sumatera Utara.
Kammerer, Cornelia Ann
1990 Customs and Christian Conversion among Akha Highlanders of Burma and Thailand. American Ethnologist 17:277–289.
Keyes, Charles F.
1977 The Golden Peninsula. New York: Macmillan.
Kipp, Rita Smith
1974 Karo Batak Religion and Social Structure. Sumatra Research Bulletin III (2):4–11.
1987 Karo Batak Rice Rituals Then and Now. *In* Cultures and Societies of North Sumatra. Rainer Carle, ed. Pp. 253–273. Berlin: Dietrich Reimer Verlag.
1990 The Early Years of a Dutch Colonial Mission: The Karo Field. Ann Arbor: University of Michigan Press.
1993 Dissociated Identities: Ethnicity, Religion, and Class in an Indonesian Society. Ann Arbor: University of Michigan Press.
Kipp, Rita Smith, and Susan Rodgers, eds.
1987 Indonesian Religions in Transition. Tucson: University of Arizona Press.
Knorr-Cetina, Karin, and Aaron Victor Cicourel
1981 Advances in Theory and Methodology: Toward an Integration of Micro and Macro Sociologies. Boston: Routledge and Kegan Paul.
Martadi, E.
n.d. Sejarah Masuk dan Perkembangan Agama Islam di Tanah Karo Simalem. (The History of the Entrance and Development of the Muslim Religion in Karoland.) Unpublished manuscript.
Neumann, Johann Heinrich
1915 Het 25-jarig Bestaan der Deli-Zending. (The 25-Year Existence of the Deli Mission.) Mededeelingen NZG 59:107–110.
1941 De Zending Onder de Karo-Batak. (The Mission among the Karo Batak.) Zendingsblad voor Nederlands-Indië. 2de Jaargang:162–169.
Nock, Arthur
1933 Conversion: The Old and the New in Religion from Alexander the Great to Augustine of Hippo. New York: Oxford University Press.
Ortner, Sherry
1984 Theory in Anthropology since the Sixties. Comparative Studies in Society and History 26:126–144.
1989 High Religion: A Cultural and Political History of Sherpa Buddhism. Princeton: Princeton University Press.
Pedersen, Paul
1970 Batak Blood and Protestant Soul: The Development of National Batak Churches in North Sumatra. Grand Rapids, MI: Eerdmans.
Pelzer, Karl
1978 Planter and Peasant: Colonial Policy and the Agrarian Struggle in East Sumatra, 1863–1947. The Hague: Nijhoff.
Rae, Simon
1994 Breath Becomes the Wind: Old and New in Karo Religion. Dunedin, New Zealand: University of Otago Press.

Ranger, Terence
1987 An Africanist Comment. American Ethnologist 14:182–185.
Reid, Anthony
1979 The Blood of the People. Kuala Lumpur: Oxford University Press.
Richardson, James T.
1985 The Active vs. Passive Convert: Paradigm Conflict in Conversion Recruitment Research. Journal for the Scientific Study of Religion 24:163–79.
Rubingh, Eugene
1969 Sons of Tiv. Grand Rapids, MI: Baker Book House.
Sahay, Keshari N.
1968 Impact of Christianity on the Uraon of the Chainpur Belt in Chotanagpur: An Analysis of Its Cultural Processes. American Anthropologist 70:923–942.
Sahlins, Marshall
1985 Islands of History. Chicago: University of Chicago Press.
Schama, Simon
1988 The Embarrassment of Riches. Berkeley: University of California Press.
Schneider, Jane, and Shirley Lindenbaum
1987 Frontiers of Christian Evangelism: Essays in Honor of Joyce Riegelhaupt. American Ethnologist 14:1–8.
Shinn, Larry D.
1987 The Dark Lord. Philadelphia: Westminster Press.
Snow, David A., and Richard Machalek
1984 The Sociology of Conversion. Annual Review of Sociology 10:167–190.
Steedly, Mary Margaret
1993 Hanging without a Rope: The Politics of Representation in Colonial and Post-Colonial Karoland. Princeton: Princeton University Press.
Sullivan, Paul
1989 Unfinished Conversations: Mayas and Foreigners between Two Wars. Berkeley: University of California.
Tapp, Nicholas
1989 The Impact of Missionary Christianity upon Marginalized Ethnic Minorities. Journal of Southeast Asian Studies 20:70–95.
Taylor, William B.
1987 The Virgin of Guadalupe in New Spain: An Inquiry into the Social History of Marian Devotion. American Ethnologist 14:9–33.
Thomson, Alan
1968 The Churches of Java in the Aftermath of the 30th September Movement. Journal of South East Asian Theology 9:7–20.
Van Muylwijk, Jacobus
1939 De Karo-Batak-Zending. (Karo-Batak Missions.) Nederlands Zendelinggenootschap archives. (Deli Zending.) Typescript.
Van Randwijck, Steven Cornelis Graaf
1981 Handelen en denken in dienst der Zending. (Acts and Thoughts in the Service of Mission.) s'-Gravenhage: Uitgeverÿ Boekencentrum.
Verkuyl, Johannes
1978 Contemporary Missiology. Grand Rapids, MI: Eerdmans.

Volkman, Toby Alice
1985 Feasts of Honor. Urbana: University of Illinois Press.
Weber, Max
1958 The Protestant Ethic and the Spirit of Capitalism. New York: Charles Scribner's Sons.
Whitehead, Harriet
1987 Renunciation and Reformation: A Study of Conversion in an American Sect. Ithaca, NY: Cornell University Press.

40

THE MAKING OF AN ETHNIC COLLECTIVITY

Irish Catholic immigrants in nineteenth-century Christchurch

Lyndon A. Fraser

Source: *Journal of Religious History*, 20(2) (1996), 210–27.

On a spring day in September 1886, Patrick Henley, president of the New Headford branch of the Australasian Hibernian Society, offered a purse of sovereigns to a man of 'sterling and undying patriotism' whom he described as 'our dear *Soggart Aroon*'. The recipient of the gift was Thomas Walsh, a young secular priest born in Mooncoin in the diocese of Ossory, educated at the University school, Waterford, and the Missionary College of All Hallows, Dublin, prior to his ordination for the New Zealand diocese of Wellington in 1883.[1] Appreciative of the generosity and deference displayed toward him, Walsh phrased an eloquent reply in language that struck a deep chord with the Irish audience gathered to witness this symbolic exchange: 'What an apt and striking appellation your society bears! Catholic would not be sufficient — Hibernian is enough. Both united embrace everything of which a Catholic Irishman should be jealously proud . . . Hibernian is your name, Catholic is your sirname [sic].'[2]

The explicit synonymy of the terms 'Irish' and 'Catholic' in Walsh's rhetoric has much wider significance for emigrants who made their way to Christchurch in the nineteenth century than this stylised encounter suggests. During the 1870s and 1880s the language of ethnicity penetrated immigrant perceptions to an unprecedented degree, constituting something of a 'grand controlling metaphor' that located whole bodies of social practices on an intelligible experiential map.[3] In the city and its environs, the parish church became the central institution in local Irish Catholic life, and around it a wide variety of formal associations were erected to nourish the cultural, spiritual and social needs of its members. For the majority of newcomers, religion emerged as the primary origin and expression of Irish identity, a source of comfort and continuity that held forth a promise of spiritual and political redemption in the future. This lay interpretation of Irishness was reinforced with varying degrees of intensity by clerical leaders, who viewed the metaphor of Irish nationality within a predominantly religious frame of reference and extolled the virtues of a holy and cruelly oppressed 'Isle of Erin'. By the late nineteenth century, the creative synthesis of formal religion and Irishness had enveloped Irish Catholics in a comprehensive network of personal relationships, parish organizations and ethnic institutions which provided some unanimity of communal purpose and obscured potential class conflict. Notwithstanding the diversity of outlooks and interests within the group, religious identification offered a useful resolution of ethnic tensions and traditions, while ensuring the continuing vitality of a separate spiritual, educational and social life alongside the dominant local system.[4]

The transition 'from immigrants to ethnics' requires critical dialogue with the process of group ethnicization. In carrying out this difficult analytic task, I want to avoid the essentialist emphases found in the work of some Irish-American historians.[5] My quarrel with these scholars is that they rest their quasi-mythic sagas on the mistaken assumption Irish emigrants arrived in the New World with a well-developed national spirit and a patterned system of communal affiliation that was either predestined or static over time. We cannot take cultural continuity for granted in this way, nor should we attribute innate organizational powers to an underlying subculture. Ethnic identity, after all, is a culturally constructed set of usages adopted by people in their day-to-day relationships with one another and the society around them.[6] We would do well to remember that it is a contested choice, defined by people as they live their own history, and not, in the final analysis, a primordial 'given' of social existence.

In what ways were aspects of an inherited Old World culture 'handled' by the Catholic Irish immigrants in Christchurch? How do we account for the process of ethnic consciousness-making in a colonial context? In this article, I want to suggest that the formation of heightened ethnic awareness among the group was a complex phenomenon shaped by the constant interaction of Old World cultural resources and expressive symbols with colonial social settings. After moving from one place to another, migrants needed to reestablish networks of personal affiliation, a project that entailed a choice between the people that they left and those that they met. There was nothing inevitable about this process. Pre-migration classifications belonged to various points of origin and newcomers did not simply transport a collective identity across the oceans in their cultural baggage.[7] Rather, their self-definition, at first, reflected a range of regional and village loyalties, or kinship ties. Which of these attachments they chose to pursue, and what meaning they gave to other affiliations, depended upon a number of critical factors, including patterns of migration, local opportunity structures, and external discrimination.

Nineteenth-century Irish migration to Christchurch differed markedly from movements to North American and Australian destinations in its timing and composition. The city itself was not established, let alone settled, prior to 1851 and though small numbers of Irish migrants drifted into the provincial capital during the first decade, significant groups did not arrive until much later. The cost of passage to the colony, which ranged as high as £18 to £24 in the mid-1850s, was beyond the scant resources of most Irish emigrants, even when subsidized by the provincial government, and it compared poorly with existing fares to North America. Moreover, provincial leaders and administrators displayed considerable ambivalence toward immigration from Ireland, fearing that an influx of Catholic Irish would introduce a plethora of social problems including higher rates of drunkenness, violence and sectarian animosities. Successive emigration agents appointed to act for the province of Canterbury in London did little to formally attract, select or arrange for the transport of immigrants from Ireland and concentrated their limited recruitment efforts on districts located in north-east Ulster.[8]

Nonetheless, the supply of labour in the province seldom equalled the demand, particularly during boom periods such as 1857–64. As a result, rigorous selection criteria underpinning provincial immigration programs were periodically relaxed to attract sufficient numbers of agricultural labourers, shepherds and domestic servants. In addition, intending immigrants were encouraged to sail to Canterbury by various financial subsidies designed to alleviate the hardship and cost of the journey. These inducements held obvious appeal for impoverished Irish men and women who were better able to raise the few pounds towards their fares. Once in the city, they could then take advantage of a nomination system to secure passages for relatives or friends. These changes not only made Canterbury more competitive with North American destinations and other Australasian colonies, but opened the gates to significant numbers of Irish immigrants.

Few Irish-born Catholics ventured to the province before 1859. Census figures from 1854 indicate that only 2.8 per cent of Canterbury's inhabitants subscribed to the Catholic faith, and of these nearly half were French-born settlers and their children residing in the district of Akaroa. By contrast, English colonists comprised 84.5 per cent of all inhabitants, a figure almost matched by the proportion of Anglicans (82.8). Still less than 3 per cent of the province's population at the end of the preceding decade, the bulk of Irish Catholic movement to the region took place during the period 1860–80, with particularly large infusions between the years 1862–5 and, more especially, 1871–9 (Table 1). The Census of 1861 reveals that the group constituted around 5 per cent of the provincial population, a figure that had increased to 10.3 per cent by 1878. Thereafter the proportion of Catholic Irish and their offspring remained relatively steady, increasing only marginally by the turn of the century (11 per cent).[9]

Table 1 Provincial proportions of Irish Catholic immigrants by date of arrival in the colony, 1855–1918.

	1855–61	*1862–5*	*1866–71*	*1872–9*	*Post-1880*
Ulster	14.7	24.8	26.9	33.1	21.7
Leinster	34.5	14.0	16.0	13.9	20.5
Connaught	10.3	22.1	17.9	7.8	22.4
Munster	40.4	39.2	39.1	45.2	35.4

Table 1 is based on a prosopographical study of all Irish Catholic immigrants whose deaths were registered at Christchurch between the years 1876 and 1918. This sample comprised a total of 1,434 individuals, of whom 700 were male and 734 female. Systematic record linkages were undertaken between death certificates, probate files, passenger lists and church registers, while additional qualitative information was gathered from genealogies, newspapers and archival repositories.

Birthplace data was unavailable for 232 persons, or 16.2 per cent of the total sample ($N = 1{,}434$), while details about date of arrival were not established in 150 cases (10.5 per cent). *Sources*: Christchurch Registry of Births, Deaths and Marriages; Probate Files, CH 171, National Archives, Christchurch; Passenger Lists, Im-CH 4 and Im-15, National Archives, Wellington; Transcript of the Baptismal and Marriage Registers of The Cathedral of The Blessed Sacrament, Lyttelton and Shand's Track, Canterbury Public Library.

In terms of its Irish regional origins, over two-fifths of Christchurch's Catholics were associated with districts in Munster (see Table 1). Emigrants from County Tipperary were numerically greater than elsewhere, but Cork, Limerick and Kerry all ranked in the first five sending counties. Although the proportion of persons from Connaught was relatively light (14.4 per cent), County Galway was only marginally second to Tipperary as a source of emigrants and maintained close ties with Christchurch throughout the nineteenth century. Leinster, like its western counterpart, contributed a small share of total numbers (17.3 per cent), but Dublin proved an exception to the wider picture and forged enduring links with the city by the early 1860s. In Ulster, on the other hand, Counties Antrim and Tyrone were well represented among the immigrants, but movement from the north does not become apparent until after 1862. From this point onward, the composition of Christchurch's Irish population acquired an increasing infusion from the north, while retaining a south-western orientation forged during the period 1859–65.

Initially, at least, these newcomers displayed few signs of intensified ethnic awareness. The migrant stream comprised quite distinct elements, each of which had different backgrounds, loyalties and attachments according to their regional origins, time of exodus and position in the life cycle. Diverse and disorganized, they brought with them a wide variety of perspectives, motivations and opinions. Moreover, the majority of immigrants were absorbed in building lives of their own within rather narrow boundaries, and lacked either the numbers or socioeconomic resources to provide a strong basis for Irish ethnicity. Scattered widely, internally factionalized and without effective clerical or lay leadership, they confronted obstacles which militated against the maturation of group consciousness or shared interests that could be used to effect group mobilization.

Despite initial fragmentation, the presence of informal and formal structures within the nascent ethnic community had the potential to keep immigrant social relations inside its boundaries. In particular, the existence and centrality of family-oriented migration chains in the movement of Irish to the city provided circumstances well suited to the development of ethnic institutions.[10] These private, interpersonal bases of group action were extended as newcomers endeavoured to reconstruct the foundations of inherited culture in the context of daily social life through the perpetuation of friendship ties, marriage, residential bonding, household formation and so on. Informal group activities of this kind broadened the attachments of members of subgroups beyond the realm of their immediate kin and constituted an important prerequisite for the subsequent rise of ethnic association patterns and institutions. The establishment of churches, sectarian schools, confraternities and mutual-aid organizations not only widened the structural separation of Irish Catholics in a formalistic sense, but also furnished public bases for a flourishing ethnic social substructure. This expansion, in turn, fed on both formal and informal streams of activity, each of which reinforced the other by increasing the cohesiveness and solidity of already existing associative networks.[11]

During the early years of Catholic settlement, informal patterns of social bonding came to be expressed spatially in rural neighbourhoods on the periphery of the city, where localized, Old World loyalties were maintained in small, clustered settlements. At Broadfields, for example, a tightly woven group of colonists settled in an area which extended along Shand's Track as far as present-day Lincoln. The first Catholic arrivals in the district had made the voyage out on three ships, the *Clontarf*, the *William Miles* and the *Chrysolite*, and most had strong associations with Nenagh, County Tipperary. These bonds were strengthened subsequently as newcomers brought out by family and friends joined the pioneering cohort, a process that spanned a period of fifteen years. Similar settlement patterns emerged in other areas, with particularly strong contingents of Catholic Irish clustering around Halswell, Leeston, and Bingsland.[12]

Neighbourhood communities like these drew immigrants together in tangled webs of kinship relations and mutual support, enabling fragments of older social networks to be re-established in the colony. In many cases settlers had known one another quite intimately prior to the moment of migration, while some had forged connections with receiving networks through information acquired at home or in Australia. Once in the community, all had their social relations sharply prescribed by membership of the group. Clustered settlements of this type fostered a high degree of cultural continuity and may even have imparted a profound sense of detachment from the host society. Yet residential bonding represented more than a defensive strategy.

Engaged in small-scale dairying or subsistence agriculture on holdings that were seldom greater than twenty acres, most of these newcomers eked out a very precarious existence even with the assistance of relatives and friends. A reliance on familial ties, together with the nascent fusion of ethnicity and kinship, was a purposeful activity that allowed the immigrants to bring a constraining environment into closer conformity with their purposes.

Not all Irish Catholics, of course, lived in rural kinship communities of this type. For many, the casual, intermittent nature of wage labour in Canterbury encouraged an itinerant way of life, and people moved from location to location, and job to job as circumstances or seasons demanded. The need for constant geographical mobility was especially pressing for unlanded male workers, whose services were eagerly sought after from spring to autumn on the larger farms, estates and runs, but no longer required during the bleak winter months.[13] With few marketable skills or capital upon their arrival, Irishmen secured only a tenuous foothold in the province's secondary labour market, working as labourers, harvesters, ploughmen and general farm hands.[14] This type of work demanded a great deal in terms of strength and tenacity, but little in the way of skill or experience. The instability and irregularity of these low-paying jobs restricted the range of opportunities available to male immigrants and encouraged the adoption of various strategies to supplement meagre incomes, including a willingness to move about regularly in search of work.

Persistent insecurity also obliged a greater reliance on the paid and unpaid activities of women, whose contributions to the domestic economy formed part of a larger pattern of familial and kin mutual support with its origins in Ireland. Irish housewives not only took responsibility for household chores, but cared for the family dairy cow and took in boarders. Their labours, meanwhile, were further supplemented by their daughters who went into domestic service from an early age, considerably boosting household incomes with their wages. The survival of a strong female role within the Irish Catholic family considerably extended the range of strategies available for coping with economic uncertainty in a new environment and was a crucial factor in facilitating group social mobility.[15]

A perpetual shortage of domestic servants in the province meant that there was much less variation in demand for the services of Irish women over the course of the year and from year to year, a pattern that held even in times of economic recession.[16] Single Irish women on assisted passages, like those of other nationalities, were quickly engaged by affluent Canterbury families, sometimes less than twenty-four hours after their arrival at the Immigration Barracks.[17] Moreover, the level of remuneration which they could expect to receive for personal service remained steady throughout the 1860s and 1870s. Girls aged from twelve to fifteen years of age, for example, earned between £12 and £15 per annum, while their counterparts aged sixteen to eighteen obtained up to £25.[18] In general, wages during the period ranged from £15 to £40 per annum depending on the age, experience and quality of an individual worker.[19]

Domestic service in the homes of the well-to-do may have placed Irish Catholic women under the close scrutiny of their employers, but their position was relatively secure compared to the chronic fluctuations of the male labour market. In consequence, these women were able to accumulate savings with which they brought over relatives from Ireland, supported devotions in the Catholic church, and provided a nest-egg for marriage. Furthermore, live-in help furnished important fringe benefits such as full board and lodging, or gifts of discarded clothing and furniture which were no longer of use to their employers. Although ties of affection may well have developed between some householders and their servants, Irish Catholic women seldom stayed in a situation for long. Many single women married within the first two years of residence in the colony, while most eagerly exploited the insistent market demand for female workers inside domestic and personal service by changing engagements frequently in response to working conditions and familial obligations.[20]

Transience was a pervasive facet of immigrant life for both sexes but it did not lead to atomization or a breakdown of familial cooperation. Irish migrants were well accustomed to patterns of temporary itinerancy and responded to situational exigencies with resilience and tactical virtuosity. Although recurrent economic uncertainty may have sharpened feelings of ambivalence toward colonial life, it also promoted a dependence on collectivist strategies. In particular, migrants made extensive use of informal ethnic and kinship networks which provided advice and information about work and accommodation, and material assistance in times of need. During the summer, for example, Catholic Irish families and individuals maintained close contacts with kinfolk as they moved together around the countryside in search of employment, while newly arrived settlers were often met by relatives with whom they went to live as boarders.

Indicative of this larger pattern of mutual support was the high esteem with which localized kin ties were held among the group. This preference is clearly reflected in the baptismal registers of the Church of the Blessed Sacrament at Barbadoes Street, founded in 1864.[21] The grant of godparentage implied a great deal of trust on behalf of parents toward certain named individuals who agreed to provide for the child in the event of anything happening to the parents. It is significant that immigrants invariably chose Irish Catholic friends to act as sponsors where immediate relatives were unavailable, thereby placing these Active kinship ties on the same level as familial collectivism.[22] Such types of interaction created sets of enduring social relations shaped by very specific values and beliefs, which in turn strengthened an emergent ethnic subculture.

The effectiveness of the interpersonal connections which bound immigrants together in tangled webs of mutuality were further extended by high rates

Table 2 Irish Catholic marriage patterns, Christchurch, 1860–89.

Sex	*1860–9*		*1870–9*		*1880–9*	
	N	*%*	*N*	*%*	*N*	*%*
Female						
Endogamous	44	69.8	57	73.0	28	71.8
Exogamous	19	30.2	21	27.0	11	28.2
Male						
Endogamous	38	95.0	50	98.0	24	96.0
Exogamous	2	5.0	1	2.0	1	4.0

Sources: Transcript of the Marriage Register of the Church of the Blessed Sacrament, Canterbury Public Library; Christchurch Registry of Births, Deaths and Marriages; Passenger Lists, Im-CH 4 and Im-15, National Archives, Wellington.

of in-group endogamy. The selection of a marriage partner not only entailed the formation of certain loyalties and moral obligations, but also represented a vital means for the development of primary relations or alliances between groups and individuals. In their matrimonial behaviour, Catholic Irish immigrants constructed and maintained a clear social distinction between those who belonged to an inner circle and those who did not. Not surprisingly, Catholic clergy actively encouraged and perpetuated this pattern within their administrative boundaries, using both the pulpit and the weight of their spiritual authority to inhibit exogamous unions with members of other groupings.[23]

While it is difficult to calculate the precise degree of endogamy among Irish Catholics, data adduced from vital events sources and church registers indicates a strong preference for endogamous unions (Table 2). In a sample of 296 marriages from the period 1860–89, nearly all single male immigrants selected partners from within the group (96.6 per cent), an extraordinary level of endogamy considering that Catholic men outnumbered women in the province until the mid-1880s.[24] By contrast, a larger proportion of women chose partners outside their ethnic marriage field (28.3 per cent), though about one-quarter of these still married Roman Catholic men. As many as one-half of the remainder sought and obtained dispensations for mixed marriages before a Catholic priest. In these cases, the non-Catholic partner promised to respect the faith of the Catholic and agreed to bring up the children as Catholics. Overall, the marriage behaviour of immigrant women was still highly endogamous throughout the period under consideration, even though a significant minority were prepared to cross ethnic boundaries and select mates from outside the emerging group.

The analysis of Catholic Irish marriage behaviour indicates the existence and maintenance of a remarkably strong sense of social identification based on ethnicity. By selecting companions from within their own group, immigrants not only sharpened the distinctiveness of the emerging ethnic community, but also cemented alliances between diverse social networks which were consequently redefined and reshaped. Ethnic endogamy greatly deepened informal social interaction among Irish Catholics and facilitated the development of group endo-culture. As a result, older existing kinship and associative fragments were superseded by more solidified, expansive social networks encompassing major segments of the new community.

How, then, can we account for these expressions of ethnicity in the patterning of Irish group relations? A plausible explanation for this process is that it constituted a defensive reaction against anti-Irish prejudice. As I noted earlier, there was considerable ambivalence toward the Irish in Canterbury and they were generally regarded as undesirable immigrants, especially during the 1860s. The settlement's founders, the Canterbury Association, had sought to establish a balanced, agricultural settlement restricted to members of the Church of England which they hoped would replicate the social and economic hierarchy of the English rural community.[25] Such a scheme had little use for the sons and daughters of west Munster tenant farmers or Connemara labourers. Nonetheless, the aspirations of leaders of the Association were not realised and religious exclusiveness was an ideal soon abandoned by provincial administrators who needed to satisfy a persistent demand for agricultural labourers, shepherds and domestic servants.[26] While immigrant recruitment was never intended to extend 'beyond the pale', the attraction of subsidized passages, reasonable wages and cheap land lured a steady stream of Irish Catholics to the colony throughout the 1860s and 1870s.

To what extent, however, did Catholic Irish immigrants face unfair discrimination in the cradle of Protestantism? Many non-Catholic settlers brought with them a vast reservoir of distorted, negative stereotypes about Irish Catholics, and looked upon their fellow colonists with a mixture of curiosity and suspicion.[27] In general, Victorian Protestants deeply distrusted Roman Catholic clerics and institutions, particularly the convent and the confessional, and could neither accept nor understand the ideal of priestly asceticism. As Philip Ingram has convincingly argued, the idea of a celibate priesthood seemed to contravene the authority of marriage and the family for those exposed to tales of clerical promiscuity in popular essays and novels such as *Maria Monk*.[28] Anxieties about priestly intent permeated all social classes in Victorian Britain and provided fertile ground for the growth of anti-Catholicism. Moreover, the rituals of the church and its religious pageantry offended fragile Protestant sensibilities, and fostered a widespread view that these aspects of Catholicism blunted the moral feelings of its adherents and blighted them with the stain of idolatry.

There is no evidence to suggest local immigrants faced prohibitions of the type encountered by Irish-Americans along the eastern seaboard of the United States, where the 'NINA' ('No Irish Need Apply') syndrome was firmly entrenched. But it is clear that a certain amount of anti-Irish and anti-Catholic prejudice and bigotry existed in Christchurch throughout the nineteenth century. The provincial government, for example, attempted to stem the flow of assisted migrants from southern Ireland during the 1860s, while attentive audiences gathered to hear 'reformed priests' like the apostate Catholic, Pastor Charles Chiniquy, who visited the region in 1880.[29] Provincial leaders castigated the Irish as a particularly troublesome, disorderly people, prone to excessive drunkenness and rowdyism.[30] Moreover, employers of domestic help complained bitterly about the inability of single Irishwomen to carry out the duties associated with their position. *The Press*, for example, noted in 1867, that a householder

> is compelled either to do without a servant at all, or to pay for idle, ignorant, unskilled . . . [h]ousemaids who have never handled a broom, cooks who scarcely know the difference between roast meat and boiled, and whose highest practical achievements in the art have been limited to preparing potatoes . . . for the Sunday dinner in the wilds of Connemara.[31]

A similar view of defective, witless Irish female domestic is evident in English writer Sarah Amelia Courage's depiction of her 'stolid and faithful' maid.[32] 'Mary' was a 'respectable farmer's daughter, too proud, she said, (or too incompetent) to go to service at home'. Courage considered her to be 'clean' but lacking method in her work: '[s]he was very willing and warmhearted, like all the Irish, and those good qualities covered a multitude of sins'.[33] Equally revealing is the narration of Mary's 'many blunders' at Cashel Street. 'On one occasion,' Courage wrote,

> not feeling very well, I went to my room to lie down, and told Mary if anyone called that afternoon to say I was not at home. Two ladies called together, and Mary said I was not at home. They asked if she knew how long I should be away. Mary said no, but she would go and ask me; and, suiting the action to the word, she left them standing on the doorstep and, knocking at my bedroom door, asked me when I should be in. I was vexed, but I had them shown in and explained matters.[34]

This passage is worthy of closer examination. On one level, the incident is amusing and trivial. But on another it depends upon prior categorization of stereotypical Irish behaviour which is then empirically verified and given 'objective' existence by Courage's observations. Many local Protestants would have readily identified with this satirical portrait. Some might also have found a great deal of explanation for Mary's deficiencies in her refusal to venture 'up country [because] her people . . . didn't like her to go so far from the Roman Catholic church'.[35]

These negative images of Irish Catholics suggest that sectarianism formed an important subterranean influence in daily relations between immigrants and the dominant local culture. For the latter, a visible Irish presence served as a constant reminder of what colonial society must not become. This opinion gained credence on those occasions where newcomers engaged in sporadic outbursts of antisocial behaviour. The eruption of Old World hostilities in Christchurch's Boxing Day riot of 1879, when about thirty Irish males armed with pick handles attacked an Orange procession, greatly heightened anti-Catholic sentiment in the colony.[36] The increasing number of Irish arrivals, the problematic nature of Irish male drinking, and the initial concentration of migrants in unskilled occupations were also factors which contributed to Protestant fear and antagonism. At the same time, predominant representations of Catholic Irish as a wayward people — as something distinctly 'other' — delineated the outer edges of local social life.[37] By interpreting the group as a social threat, Protestants exacerbated the cultural distance separating these newcomers from the wider community and thereby increased the likelihood of sectarian conflict.

What was the effect of these negative attitudes on the immigrants themselves? The reaction of Protestant settlers to the religion, cultural background and social values of their neighbours catalysed a significant degree of ethnic group defensiveness. Whether real or imagined, anti-Catholic and anti-Irish prejudice played a major role in the process of ethnicization. It led more assertive Catholic agitation over religious issues such as denominational schooling or the defence of Catholic doctrines. And it sustained a mood of suspicion which was expressed in a reflexive turning away from the surrounding non-Catholic society.

This siege mentality was intensified in the 1870s and 1880s by the demeanour of newly arrived Irish secular clerics such as Bishop Patrick Moran of Dunedin. The polemical style that these men introduced to New Zealand was deeply influenced by Old World historical analogies, traditions and emphases. A backdrop of centuries of economic and political domination by English Protestants, of failed uprisings, grinding poverty and religious suppression, had bestowed an image of historical misfortune that was deeply etched into the collective memory of the island's Catholic masses. When linked with a passionate commitment to Roman Catholicism, this legacy was not an affliction but a strategic tool capable of being transformed to serve new purposes where the need arose. Moran, especially, skilfully manipulated powerful myths and symbols associated with Ireland's subjugation and reinterpreted perceived threats to the group as a continuation of the historic wrongs suffered at the hands of the hated English. This was particularly evident in relation to education. In his Lenten Pastoral of 1873, for example, the bishop castigated the provincial education ordinances of Otago and Canterbury as 'so many penal laws, and virtually a repeal pro tanto of the Emancipation Act. We cannot regard them in any other light than as a re-enactment of some of the provisions of the odious, impolitic, and cruel penal code.'[38]

The battle of faith and morality was to be fought in the classroom.[39] At stake, Moran believed, was not simply the principle of distributive justice, which required that those who were taxed for purposes should have their taxes spent on the schooling of their children. More importantly, education entailed an initiation into a holistic view of life that was, in turn, part of a wider preparation for death and therefore a proper function of the church. In developing these aspects of his religious ideology, Moran drew especially upon the *Syllabus of Errors*, published by Pope Pius IX in 1864, which specifically condemned the proposition that the entire administration of public schools belonged to the civil authority.[40] In the course of mobilizing Irish colonial Catholicity, however, he relied so heavily on a brooding sense of oppression and impending crisis that other, more subtle emphases were almost completely obscured. The tone of the Catholic weekly, *The New Zealand Tablet*, founded by Moran in 1873 to defend the faith and argue a case for government support of parochial schools, extended the influence of this brand of militant Irish Catholicism and provided an important forum for debate over the direction of the Catholic Church in New Zealand.[41]

That an overwhelmingly Irish-born laity in the city were receptive to this brand of strident Catholic triumphalism, as well as its evocations of Irish spiritual superiority, attests to the reactive dimension of their ethnicity. Yet the temptation to explain group ethnicization solely in terms of prejudice and discrimination would be misconceived. In light of the social circumstances of Irish daily life in Christchurch, the emergence of a workable Irish Catholic identity was as much a positive accomplishment as a retreat from hostility and contempt. This does not mean that it was entirely self-created, because this process owed a great deal to the perception and ascription of outsiders who simply lumped the newcomers together as 'Catholic Irish'. Rather, I am suggesting that examination of the group's inner experience and development leads to a richer understanding of how this self-definition converged with the views of others. Inter-ethnic conflict was certainly crucial in heightening a sense of shared ethnicity. But so too were patterns of chain migration, the limits imposed by the local economy, and the controversies which raged within the nascent Catholic community itself. Internal friction, in particular, helped to sketch the basic parameters of group life and stimulated ethnic self-understanding by effectively deepening the involvement of immigrants in Irish ethnicity.

A long struggle by Christchurch laity for Irish priests and bitter divisions between religious and secular clergy over the control of church affairs played an important role in fostering and reinforcing group identities. Essentially, these disputes arose from a fundamental cleavage within Catholic circles over the shape that Roman Catholicism should assume in the colony. On one hand, Irish secular priests and lay leaders sought to assimilate colonial Catholicity into an Irish spiritual empire and envisioned a religion that primarily expressed Irish interests and Irish attitudes. Theirs was an undeniably narrow and parochial faith, but it resonated with an extraordinary degree of richness and its religious style and leadership held a great deal of popular appeal. Advocates of this position creatively fused Tridentine Catholicism with Irish nationalism and vigorously emphasized the ethnic needs of local communicants. To achieve their goals they sought to erect the structure of a strong, fully active Catholic community centred around an Irish bishop, a network of parishes with permanent churches and a school system run by Irish teaching orders.

The Society of Mary, which had held responsibility for the spiritual needs of the region since 1849, considered a strident Irishness incidental to setting up a missionary Church in a new environment. The Marists did not differ in theological or doctrinal understanding from their clerical opponents, but they stood resolutely within the mainstream of international Catholicism and generally embraced a broader, more ecumenical approach to the Canterbury mission. Furthermore, they viewed themselves as itinerant missionaries whose task was to prepare the ground for the establishment of a diocese. After this goal was accomplished the Marists intended to withdraw from parochial work and undertake pastoral responsibilities more in keeping with their spiritual vows. In theory, this approach should have been complementary to that of their secular co-workers. In practice, however, the transition from mission to diocese was not accomplished without considerable acrimony. By the late 1870s, the Society of Mary elected to retain control over the direction of Christchurch, rather than surrender it to a rival tradition of ultra-Irish bishops and domineering Irish clerics.

The roots of controversy over episcopal control of the province's flourishing entrepôt were deep-seated and represented part of a wider ongoing, adamantine struggle between rival Catholic traditions. In Australia, a succession of ultra-Irish bishops had been appointed through the influence of Paul Cullen, Cardinal Archbishop of Dublin, and all were openly contemptuous of religious orders earlier in the field. Fired by grandiose visions of an Irish spiritual empire, these newcomers triumphantly seized control of the Australian Catholic Church from the English Benedictine pioneers and defined the religious scene in terms of Irish experience.[42] The resolution of this conflict in favour of secular priests and Irish episcopal authoritarianism had clear implications for New Zealand. Indeed, the appointment of the Irish bishops Patrick Moran and Thomas Croke to the sees of Dunedin and Auckland in 1869 and 1870 seemed to indicate that Rome intended to establish a distinctly Cullenite hierarchy in the colony. Unlike their Benedictine counterparts across the Tasman, however, the Society of Mary was not so easily superseded.

A central issue in the evolving dispute was the fact that the region's spiritual affairs were administered from Wellington. In 1849 *Congregatio de*

Propaganda Fide had sought to end a protracted dispute between Bishop Pompallier and the Marist General, Father John Claude Colin, by dividing authority in the colony at the thirty-ninth degree of latitude.[43] The Marists were removed to the newly created diocese of Wellington, encompassing one-half of the North Island and the whole of the South Island, while Pompallier was established as resident bishop in the northern diocese of Auckland with responsibility for the Maori mission. This instruction effectively left a French bishop, Philip Viard, in charge of a large southern pastorate that was rapidly being peopled by Irish migrants and for which he had insufficient resources at his disposal. Between the years 1850 and 1859 there were no resident priests stationed in Canterbury, and though visits were taken to the region by French clerics these were infrequent. It was not until mid-1860 that Viard obtained the first resident priests for Christchurch, following repeated petitions to Rome and the arrival of additional Marists for the first time in sixteen years.[44] Fathers Séon and Chataigner took charge of Christchurch and began a long period of pastoral labours by genteel French clergy, whose spiritual control of the region remained unbroken until 1877.[45]

These pioneer churchmen received cooperation from local congregations, but they were unable to achieve the degree of sympathy and close identification that the laity reserved for priests of their own nationality.[46] In short, the encounter between French apostolic labourers and their Irish flock forced the latter to confront the idea of their ethnic identity. By the 1870s underlying tensions within local Catholic circles were such that lay critics felt compelled to agitate for an Irish bishop and the provision of a sufficient number of Irish priests. Why, they asked, was Christchurch the only one of four main centres without a bishop at a time when the province had emerged as the colony's prime arable region, with a flourishing commercial centre?

Lay dissatisfaction with distant Marist suzerainty and its 'foreign clerics' was understandable. Whether or not they had sailed directly to the colony, most of the immigrants had left Irish communities at a time when they had become increasingly defined in terms of religious belief and emotion.[47] The state of spiritual affairs in Canterbury, in comparison, must have been a considerable disappointment, even for those who had experienced colonial life at other points of destination. Priests were encountered infrequently and the institutional structure of local Catholicism was much less effective and enclosing than that of Irish communities. No doubt there were some newcomers who appreciated this lack of clerical interference. Under the circumstances, it was relatively easy to drift away from the church, confident in the belief that familiar spiritual services were always available should the need arise. Among some sections of the laity religious practice became more instrumental in character and emphasized concrete ends rather than ceremonial observances. Quiet devotional aspects of faith were retained and Catholics remained firmly attached to the rites of baptism, marriage and extreme unction. But many placed considerably less importance on regular attendance at Mass, confession and communion except during Missions, when churchgoing tended to increase dramatically. Others were simply unable to approach the sacraments on a regular basis because of the nature of their work or the location of their residence.[48]

Despite these problems it would be wrong to characterize the laity as indifferent to their spiritual duties. Neither docile nor subservient, ordinary immigrants were capable of extraordinary creativity and personal initiative. They responded in various ways to the situation that confronted them and played a major role in shaping the Catholic churches, private devotions and institutions that developed in the province. Local historians have too easily obscured the fact during the 1860s, in particular, a predominantly Irish laity working in seasonal, unskilled occupations provided the resources necessary to construct a rudimentary Catholic institutional presence in the colony.[49] At the same time, members of local congregations generously donated what little spare time, money and labour they had to assist their priest practitioners in meeting spiritual objectives and providing essential services. When the efforts of local clergy fell short of immigrant expectations the laity articulated deep-seated local grievances against the Society of Mary and its administration of the region.[50] By engaging in the debate over the future direction of colonial Catholicism and enthusiastically fashioning an ethnic stance toward the group's internal difficulties, parishioners belied the notion that they mindlessly accepted the counsel of their priests. As emigrants they had left Ireland for something it could not give, but as colonials they recognized in the strong affirmation of Catholic Irishness an invaluable mechanism with which to shape outcomes and interpret the group's problems and obligations.

The appointment of an English-born Marist bishop, John Joseph Grimes, to Christchurch and Archbishop Francis Redwood's subsequent demotion of a popular Irish secular priest, Father James O'Donnell, for organizing a secular petition to Rome merely intensified Irish antipathy to the Marist order in Canterbury.[51] Yet these ongoing controversies did not diminish the position of the parish church as the central social and spiritual focus of Irish Catholic life in the region. On the contrary, internal conflict greatly strengthened immigrant solidarity around a reified Irish Catholic identity and successfully overrode possible class antagonisms. The struggle between clergy and parishioners formed an integral part of parish life, just as it had in Ireland, and demonstrated the limits of clerical authority. Moreover, persistent criticism of the Society of Mary forced the order to adopt a position that one historian has described as 'more Irish than the Irish themselves'.[52] The introduction of Irish-born Marists and teaching orders was an important step in this direction. Most importantly, however, Marist clergy were increasingly inclined to appeal to the ethnic sensibilities of laity in order to sustain some influence over their activities.[53] This, in turn, further deepened involvement in Irish ethnicity by encouraging greater intimacy with the Catholic church, as well as a greater degree of social isolation and structural separation.

'Ethnicization' did not unfold evenly among Catholic Irish immigrants, nor indeed was it a sudden eventuation. Instead, the process involved a gradual self-realization of a shared ethnic heritage that was sharpened in the course of daily interaction with the host system. This growing perception of peoplehood was not without some undesirable features. It was, above all, introspective and frequently fostered attitudes of mistrust and antagonism toward 'outsiders', even where they professed the same faith. The prevalence of dichotomous us-against-them thinking was only intensified in public life, where sectarian animosities drove Irish Catholics together into defensive organizations. Immigrant leaders, meanwhile, depicted their rank-and-file clientele as an embattled minority and manipulated nationalist symbols in the practical defence of Catholic interests against real and imagined adversaries. Efforts to unite the immigrant community in this way, however, had the unintended consequence of moulding a mental ghetto which reinforced Orange kinds of Protestantism and erected barriers that proved difficult to dismantle.

Nonetheless, there was a more positive side to the flowering of ethnicity. When they arrived in Canterbury newcomers had little to offer other than their labour, but they brought with them an essential resource for group formation in the shape of their religion. Roman Catholicism was primarily a system of beliefs buttressed by an appeal to supernatural realities which supplied its adherents with a coherent world-view and morality. But it also provided the foundations of a stable institutional structure capable of supporting popular mobilization and thus represented a powerful means to effect a creative response to the situational exigencies of the present. Its efficacy was overlayered by Old World folk memories of exploitation, suffering and persecution under English colonial administration, an image of historical misfortune that belied a long-established tradition of defensive unity in face of external threat. This shared ethno-religious heritage, along with the similarity of immigrant lifestyles, a fundamental concern with familial security and the high degree of interpersonal association engendered by work relations and strong kinship ties, facilitated the development of group awareness in Christchurch. These informal ties proved a vital prerequisite for a more militant brand of ethnic consciousness that arose during the 1870s and 1880s in the context of sectarian tensions and an internal dispute over the direction of Roman Catholicism in the colony. As a consequence, the immigrants gradually discarded narrow regional affiliations and began to perceive themselves in terms of a broad ethno-religious grouping that was intelligible, if more than a little worrying, to outsiders. And, from this perspective, the crystallization of ethnic awareness among Irish Catholics in the city was an example of 'emergent ethnicity' — in the process of *becoming*.[54]

Notes

1 Kevin Condon, *The Missionary College of All Hallows, 1842–1891*, Dublin 1986, p. 347.
2 *New Zealand Tablet*, 1 October 1886.
3 For a brilliant discussion of 'metaphor' in historical ethnography, see Rhys Isaac, 'A Discourse on the Method', in *The Transformation of Virginia, 1740–1790*, Chapel Hill NC 1982, esp. pp. 323–5, 347, 349–51.
4 See Lyndon A. Fraser, Community, Continuity and Change: Irish Catholic Immigrants in Nineteenth-Century Christchurch, PhD thesis, University of Canterbury, 1994.
5 See, e.g., Oscar Handlin, *Boston's Immigrants 1790–1865: A Study in Acculturation*, Cambridge MA. 1959; William V. Shannon, *The American Irish*, New York 1964; Lawrence J. McCaffrey, 'The Irish-American Dimension', in Lawrence J. McCaffrey, Ellen Skerret, Michael J. Funchion and Charles Fanning, *The Irish in Chicago*, Urbana 1987.
6 Gordon Darroch, 'Half Empty or Half Full? Images and Interpretations in the Historical Analysis of the Catholic Irish in Nineteenth-Century Canada', *Canadian Ethnic Studies*, Vol. 25, 1993; Kerby M. Miller, 'Class, Culture, and Immigrant Group Identity in the United States: The Case of Irish-American Ethnicity', in *Immigration Reconsidered: History, Sociology, and Politics*, Virginia Yans-McLaughlin (ed.), New York 1990, p. 98.
7 I am indebted here to Charles Tilley, 'Transplanted Networks', in *Immigration Reconsidered*, Yans-McLaughlin (ed), pp. 85 and *passim.*
8 See Fraser, Community, Continuity and Change, ch. 1.
9 *Canterbury Gazette*, 1 July 1854, 4 June 1862; *Statistics of New Zealand*, 1859, pp. iv–v; *Census of New Zealand*, 1878, Table vi, p. 257, and 1901, Table vi, p. 88.
10 See Fraser, ch. 1.
11 The distinction between formal and informal social organization in relation to ethnic communities is discussed by Raymond Breton, 'Institutional Completeness of Ethnic Communities and the Personal Relations of Immigrants'. *American Journal of Sociology*, Vol. 70, No. 2, September 1964, pp. 193–205.
12 Im-CH 4/29, 4/31 and 4/35, National Archives, Wellington (hereafter NA-W); Land Registry Office, Christchurch.
13 R. H. Silcock, Immigration into Canterbury under the Provincial Government, MA thesis, University of Canterbury, 1964, pp. 70–1.
14 See Immigration Officer's Reports, ICPS 1491/1861, 760/1865, 1501/1867, 59/1869 and 170/1871, National Archives, Christchurch (hereafter NA-CH); Marshman to Provincial Secretary, 25 July 1861, ICPS 1739/1861, NA-CH; Provincial Secretary to Duncan, 29 August 1873, ICPS 1447/1873, NA-CH.
15 See Fraser, ch. 5.
16 Charlotte Macdonald, Single Women as Immigrant Settlers in New Zealand, 1853–1871, PhD thesis. University of Auckland, 1986, pp. 43–4.
17 Immigration Officer's Reports, ICPS 1950/1864, 1117/1866, 946/1868, 59/1869 and 460/1871, NA-CH.
18 Immigration Officer's Reports, ICPS 1117/1866, NA-CH.
19 Immigration Officer's Reports, ICPS 1491/1861, 112/1866, 323/1867, 1095/1867, and 946/1868, NA-CH. See also Immigration Officer's Report, 31 March 1876, Im-CH 5/4, NA-W.
20 Macdonald, Single Women, pp. 206–45.
21 Transcripts of the Baptismal Registers, Church of the Blessed Sacrament, Canterbury Public Library.

22 This practice is comparable to that described by Maureen Molloy in a study of the Highland Scots community in nineteenth-century Waipu, 'Friends, Neighbours, and Relations: The Practice of Kinship in Waipu, New Zealand, 1857–1917', *Journal of Family History*, Vol. 14, No. 4, 1989.

23 Circular of the Right Rev. Dr Redwood, Bishop of Wellington, to his Clergy, 6 June 1876, Marist Archives Wellington (hereafter MAW); Redwood to Chareyre, 23 January 1877, Wellington Archdiocesan Archives (hereafter WAA); *New Zealand Tablet*, 12 April 1878; Redwood to Ginaty, 11 January 1878, MAW.

24 In 1867 there were only 519 Catholic females for every 1,000 males in Canterbury, a ratio that had increased to 785 per 1,000 in 1878, and 962 per 1,000 by 1886. *Census of New Zealand*, 1867, 1878 and 1886.

25 L. C. Webb, 'The Canterbury Association and its Settlement', in A *History of Canterbury, Volume 1: To 1854*, James Hight and C. R. Straubel (eds), Christchurch 1957, pp. 135–233.

26 Silcock, Immigration into Canterbury, pp. 5–10, 23.

27 Some evidence for this assertion can be found in shipboard diaries. English-born Fanny Horrell, for example, sailing to Lyttelton aboard the *Piako* in 1878, described her co-travellers in this way: 'My mess mates are all English girls and respectable, but there are some queer looking characters here. I don't think I should be very comfortable if I had to mess with some of them. There are a great many Irish Roman Catholics. They do make a fuss over their prayers, saying "Mother Mary of God pray for us".' See The Journal of Fanny Horrell, 129/64, Canterbury Museum Archives; Im-CH 4/172, NA-W.

28 Philip Ingram, 'Protestant Patriarchy and the Catholic Priesthood in Nineteenth-Century England', *Journal of Social History*, Vol. 24, No. 4, Summer 1991.

29 Michael O'Meeghan, *Held Firm By Faith: A History of the Catholic Diocese of Christchurch, 1840–1897*, Christchurch 1988, pp. 135–9.

30 R. L. N. Greenaway, Henry Selfe Selfe and the Origins and Early Development of Canterbury, MA thesis. University of Canterbury, 1972, pp. 200–1; Henry Selfe Selfe to Provincial Secretary, 24 April 1861, ICPS 1378/1861, NA-CH; Provincial Secretary to Marshman, July 9 1862, CP 605/2, NA-CH; John Marshman to Provincial Secretary, 24 January 1863, ICPS 647/1863, NA-CH.

31 *Press*, 12 April 1867, p. 2.

32 Sarah Amelia Courage, *Lights and Shadows of Colonial Life: Twenty-Six Years in Canterbury New Zealand*, Christchurch 1976, p. 31.

33 Courage, *Lights and Shadows*, p. 26.

34 Courage, p. 26.

35 Courage, p. 34.

36 See Sean G. Brosnahan, "The "Battle of the Borough" and the "Saige O Timaru" ', *New Zealand Journal of History*, Vol. 28, No. 1, April 1994.

37 I am indebted here to Kai Erikson, *Wayward Puritans: A Study in the Sociology of Deviance*, New York 1966.

38 Patrick Moran, Lenten Pastoral, 1873, Dunedin Diocesan Archives (hereafter DDA).

39 Moran, Lenten Pastoral, 1872, DDA.

40 Hugh M. Laracy, The Life and Context of Bishop Patrick Moran, MA thesis, Victoria University of Wellington, p. 107.

41 *New Zealand Tablet*, 3 May 1873.

42 See Patrick O'Farrell, *The Catholic Church and Community: An Australian History*, Kensington 1985, esp. chs 2 and 4. See also O'Farrell, *Vanished Kingdoms: Irish in Australia and New Zealand: A Personal Excursion*, Kensington 1990, ch. 4.

43 O'Meeghan, *Held Firm by Faith*, p. 53. Father Colin wanted better spiritual and material care of his men than the bishop was providing, and refused to send more Marist priests until the situation was resolved.

44 Lillian G. Keys, *Philip Viard, Bishop of Wellington*, Christchurch 1968, pp. 124–30. Father Petitjean said the first Mass at Christchurch on Pentecost Sunday, 31 May 1857.

45 Séon to Provincial Secretary, 28 June 1860, ICPS 420/1860, NA-CH.

46 Neil Patrick Vaney, The Dual Tradition: Irish Catholics and French Priests in New Zealand — the West Coast Experience, 1865–1910, MA thesis. University of Canterbury, 1976, p. 117.

47 On the so-called 'devotional revolution' see Emmet Larkin, "The Devotional Revolution in Ireland 1850–1875', *American Historical Review*, Vol. 72, No. 3, June 1972; David W. Miller, 'Irish Catholicism and the Great Famine', *Journal of Social History*, Vol. 9, No. 1, Fall 1975; S. J. Connolly, *Religion and Society in Nineteenth-Century Ireland*, Dublin 1985, pp. 7–14, 47–60.

48 See, e.g., Diocesan Return for the Parish of Darfield, 13 August 1892, Christchurch Diocesan Archives (hereafter CDA).

49 See Barry Samuel Allom, Bishop Grimes: His Context and Contribution to the Catholic Church in Canterbury, MA thesis. University of Canterbury, 1968; Brendan P. Daly, The Founding of the Roman Catholic Diocese of Christchurch, 1840–1887, PG Dip. Theology, Christian Thought and History (2), CDA.

50 See Fraser, Community, Continuity and Change, ch. 2.

51 James Joseph O'Donnell, born in Glenroe, County Limerick, in 1855, was educated at Mt Melleray and All Hallows and ordained by the bishop of Cork on June 24 1880. He was demoted from the parish of Ahaura and sent to Christchurch by Archbishop Redwood for his part in organizing the petition. Le Menant to Sauzeau, 3 November and 17 November 1887, CDA; Le Menant to Redwood, 22 December 1887, CDA; Redwood to Grimes 21 July and 27 October 1887, MAW.

52 Rory Sweetman, The Catholic Church in Nineteenth-Century New Zealand, unpublished paper delivered at the Canada–New Zealand Comparative Seminar, University of Edinburgh, 10 May 1985, p. 13.

53 See, e.g., the address to Bishop Grimes prepared by the French priest, Le Menant des Chesnais: 'We are truly jubilant today to have you in our midst . . . The devotedness of the Irish race to their pastors is proverbial all over the world, and the numerous assembly which now fills the walls of this Cathedral is a manifest proof that, in these Canterbury Plains, the spirit of the great Patriarch of Ireland is still alive, and as strong as in the beautiful but most cruelly oppressed Isle of Erin." Le Menant, *Address*, 31 January 1888, CDA.

54 William L. Yancey, Eugene P. Eriksen and Richard N. Juliani, 'Emergent Ethnicity: A Review and Reformulation', *American Sociological Review*, Vol. 41, No. 3, June 1976.

41

THE LIMITS OF RELIGIOUS ASCRIPTION

Baptized Tatars and the revision of "apostasy," 1840s–1905*

Paul W. Werth

Source: *Russian Review*, 59(4) (2000), 493–511.

Signifying the repudiation of Orthodox Christianity in favor of another faith, the concept of "apostasy" (*otpadenie* or *otstupnichestvo*) constituted a powerful rhetorical, legal, and administrative tool for the Orthodox church and the imperial Russian state in policing the edges of the empire's Orthodox community and consolidating an otherwise weakly integrated Russian polity. Yet despite its firm foundation in church and civil law, the precise contours of "apostasy" became increasingly unstable as the nineteenth century progressed. By tracing the transformation of this concept through the experience of one particular group of religious defectors—baptized Tatars—this essay elucidates a process whereby the religious self-definitions of imperial subjects came gradually to supplement and condition a more traditional emphasis on law and bureaucratic ascription in the matter of establishing confessional affiliation. Faced with baptized Tatars' tenacious striving for official status as Muslims, imperial authorities increasingly felt compelled to recognize a social reality that defied official prescription and to acknowledge that religious conviction represented a component of confessional identity. Yet many officials simultaneously retained older perspectives that privileged Orthodoxy and construed religious status as a matter of communal affiliation rather than individual belief. I conclude that the tensions and contradictions characteristic of this incomplete transition remained inscribed in new laws promulgated in 1905, which ostensibly introduced a more liberal approach to the issue of religious tolerance. Particularly as concerned non-Christian faiths, the assertions of imperial subjects remained only one of several considerations in evolving official conceptions of religious affiliation.

Beyond investigating the concept of apostasy specifically, this essay addresses broader tensions in Russia between ascriptive identity as imposed by state authority and self-definitions reflecting subjective beliefs, outlooks, and aspirations.[1] To the extent that religious labels in Russia reflected a combination of communal affiliation, legal identity, and belief, examination of "apostasy" offers valuable insights concerning the interplay of formal ascription and personal assertions in the formation of social identity. Moreover, in its attempt to highlight complexities in the emergence of privatized notions of belief and conviction, this essay reveals ambiguities broadly characteristic of the attempt to establish a modern liberal order in Russia, whereby abstract civic values of the Enlightenment were fundamentally tempered by indigenous Russian cultural strains and practices.[2] As we shall see, imperial officials for the most part remained unable to accept the proposition that individual autonomy should form the basis for social life.

Apostasy in law and administrative practice

Following Muscovy's conquest of the Kazan Khanate in 1552 and again in the mid-eighteenth century, representatives of the Russian state and church formally baptized significant numbers of Tatars in the Volga-Kama region into Orthodoxy. Settled primarily in Kazan, Simbirsk, Viatka, and Ufa provinces, baptized Tatars numbered close to seventy-five thousand by the mid-1860s.[3] Yet to the extent that these "converts" had accepted baptism either under coercion or in order to receive material benefits offered by the state, many of them continued to spurn Orthodoxy in the nineteenth century, either by simply ignoring their "Christian obligations" or by openly repudiating their Orthodox status altogether in petitions to ministers and the emperor requesting formal recognition as Muslims.[4] Such requests culminated in the late 1860s, when over ten thousand baptized Tatars, motivated by rumors about a tsarist law permitting them to return to Islam, filed petitions, adopted "Tatar" clothing and names, and (in the case of men) shaved their heads and donned *tiubeteiki* (skull-caps). Though apostasy by no means affected all baptized-Tatar communities, its impact was sufficiently broad to produce fears among Orthodox officials about the Islamization of virtually all the non-Russians of the Volga-Kama region.[5]

Though its causes were complex, apostasy can be ascribed to a combination of the superficial nature of the original conversions, persistent cultural similarities between baptized and Muslim Tatars, the relative absence of religious texts and liturgy in native languages, the preaching of itinerant Sufis in the region, and emerging patterns of migrant labor that brought baptized Tatars into increasing contact with Muslim communities.[6] Moreover, as a result of the decentralization of state-peasant administration in 1866, whereby self-government of local peasant communities largely replaced the oversight of the Ministry of State Properties, their minority position within predominantly Muslim volosts divested many baptized Tatars of both the desire and the ability to maintain their particularity vis-à-vis their Muslim counterparts.[7] In these conditions apostasy became a fairly simple matter: one went to the volost board, inscribed oneself "with Tatar name," and rejected Christianity. Apostates informed remaining baptized Tatars that they "can be completely Tatars without fear," thereby investing the movement towards Islam with greater momentum.[8]

Yet if the adoption of an Islamic identity was both desirable and increasingly possible in practice, the state continued to privilege ascriptive religious identity over subjective religious assertions and therefore construed these baptized Tatars as "apostates" from Orthodoxy in violation of existing legal codes. Imperial law required converts to give a solemn promise upon baptism "to remain always invariably obedient to [the Orthodox Church]" and obligated all Orthodox Christians to baptize and raise their children in Orthodoxy (even if only one parent was Orthodox).[9] "Apostasy" from Orthodoxy, even in favor of another Christian faith, was strictly forbidden, and thus Orthodox status became both hereditary and unalterable. Furthermore, while extending certain religious protections to Muslims and other non-Orthodox subjects, Russian law simultaneously limited religious freedom in order to safeguard the "supreme and ruling" status of Orthodoxy, for example by prohibiting non-Orthodox proselytism in the empire.[10]

Notably, the law assumed that it was not the individual who believed, but rather the community as a whole: "All peoples (*narody*) that inhabit Russia praise God Almighty in various languages in accordance with the law and confession of their forefathers."[11] According to the legal scholar M. A. Reisner, Russian law on religious toleration was deeply rooted in the incorporation of various peoples into Muscovy, which required the recognition, on some level, of their cultural specificity. "This was toleration not of faith, but of these or those tribes or peoples with all their customs and habits and, among other things, their faith." Russian law, he thus concluded, construed religion "primarily as a foundation for nationality, as the spiritual nerve of various tribes and peoples, and not as one or another kind of relationship of a person to God."[12] Thus while the state reserved the right to promote conversion to Orthodoxy, it viewed specific non-Orthodox faiths as being essentially inherent to particular communities that we today would be inclined to identify in ethnic or national terms.[13] In short, the law offered basic religious toleration (*veroterpimost'*) to recognized religious groups, but not freedom of conscience (*svoboda sovesti*) to the individual.[14]

The perspective on religion as an organic communal attribute helps account for tensions in official views of conversion to Orthodoxy. On the one hand, there were significant assimilationist assumptions regarding such conversion, as well as an array of privileges established by the state precisely in order to encourage *inovertsy* (non-Christians) to adopt the Orthodox faith. At the same time, latent doubts about the transformative power of conversion persisted, so that the *origins* of a convert, especially if he was one of a group of neophytes, remained an important part of his ascriptive identity and underscored his liminal status with respect to Orthodoxy. Thus the term *novokreshchenye* (newly converted) served as a basic category to describe converts and even their descendants for decades after their actual baptism.[15] And by the second half of the nineteenth century, the expression *kreshchenye inorodtsy* (baptized aliens), by referencing simultaneously inclusion and exclusion, offered another way of highlighting the ambiguity of converts' liminal state.[16] Thus much like Hindu converts to Christianity in colonial India, *kreshchenye inorodtsy* in Russia remained relationally placed vis-à-vis the community they had ostensibly left behind.[17] The irony is that while this language betrays fundamental doubts about the depth of converts' allegiance to Orthodoxy, for legal and administrative purposes converts continued to be regarded unambiguously as Orthodox Christians.

According to the criminal code, each case of apostasy involved two potentially adjudicable acts. In the first place, by article 185 of the criminal code, apostates from any Christian confession to a non-Christian faith were to be turned over to religious authorities "for admonitions and persuasion," and could be deprived of their rights and property, and even lose their children to temporary guardianship, until they returned to Christianity and promised to remain there without deviation.[18] The code meanwhile ascribed a higher degree of criminality to those attempting to lure Christians into non-Christian religions "through instigation, seduction, and other means," depriving them of all rights and sentencing them to hard labor in exile for a period of eight to ten years (article 184).[19] Through the concept of "seduction" (*sovrashchenie*), the law drew a clear distinction between instigators, who were supposedly conscious of their guilt, and the "seduced," who presumably lacked criminal intent and required only admonition.[20] Accordingly, "seducers" were actually punished, while the "seduced" simply endured certain disabilities until they finally submitted.

In practice, there were substantial impediments to the enforcement of these laws. It was often difficult to prosecute cases of apostasy and "seduction" successfully because of the high standards of evidence required by the law. Tatars' "resourcefulness and cunning," allegedly involving bribery, witness-tampering, and intimidation, represented a fundamental obstacle to effective prosecution and necessitated the abandonment of many cases.[21] In general, as one district police chief explained, baptized Tatars "like the judicial ceremony [because] one will always find a possibility there of emerging from the water dry, of dragging the case out for a long time, and during this time of being in freedom and having the possibility to agitate."[22] The result was that even figures whom the administration regarded as obvious "instigators" were freed from judicial proceedings due to lack of sufficient evidence.[23]

Moreover, some officials harbored reservations about the appropriateness of articles 184 and 185 in the cases they encountered. While acknowledging that seduction of baptized Tatars by Muslims constituted a violation of the law, some officials rejected the notion that the mass of apostates could actually be divided into "instigators" and "seduced," since they were all officially Orthodox. Thus the head of the Judicial Chamber in Kazan province contended that article 184 was "very harsh and even unfair," since the ostensible "seducers" constituted merely an expression of the general mood among baptized Tatars.[24] Others, like Minister of Internal Affairs P. A. Valuev, were skeptical that one could ascribe criminal motivations to the mass of baptized Tatars under prosecution. If the apostasy had involved Russians who had long been Orthodox, he argued, "then obviously, in such a case, the seducers and seduced alike would be subject to the full harshness of the law, without leniency." But the reports indicated that the prevailing circumstances—baptized Tatars' kinship with Muslim Tatars, their inability to understand Russian, and the weak influence of the Orthodox clergy—"did not allow the population the possibility of establishing themselves in Orthodoxy."[25] The Kazan Chamber of State Domains likewise contended that "religious education and inculcation of Christian ideas among the baptized Tatars were always neglected, and one cannot blame Tatars themselves for this."[26] In short, implicitly expressing apprehensions about the predominance of legal-ascriptive categories over self-definition, some officials doubted that what they were observing could actually be considered apostasy in the sense that the law code intended, precisely because most baptized Tatars had never been Christians in anything but the most formal sense.

Finally, especially after 1866, the large number of apostates greatly complicated the task of handling cases successfully. One official openly doubted that it was possible to submit almost eight thousand people to religious exhortation and to deprive them of their rights until they embraced Orthodoxy.[27] The governor of Simbirsk province likewise held that this law was not appropriate "to masses of peasant population" and thus "cannot make any impression on them whatsoever."[28] Evidence suggests that the verdicts that did result from court cases were only partially carried out, if at all.[29] In some cases, it was simply dangerous to attempt to admonish apostates as provided in the law, as they increasingly challenged and threatened Orthodox clergy.[30] Over the course of the 1870s, clergy in many cases abandoned attempts to persuade apostates to return to Orthodoxy, leaving them without any real punishment in many cases. Existing law was thus ill-suited for handling apostasy to Islam on such a grand scale.[31]

Partly as a result of these difficulties, state authorities supplemented legal provisions with a range of administrative measures. Already in the 1830s and 1840s, many Tatar apostates had been resettled to Russian villages in order to eliminate the influence on them of local Muslims and to bring them into greater cultural contact with Russian communities. Though construed as a beneficial measure rather than a form of punishment, this policy of course inflicted tremendous economic and emotional hardships, and apostates naturally resisted resettlement by absconding or returning to their old villages surreptitiously.[32] Similarly, in 1866 many officials felt that the judicial measures listed above should be replaced or supplemented by administrative methods for counteracting apostasy—in particular the immediate exile without trial of alleged "instigators" to Siberia.[33] While court cases were lengthy and required formal evidence, "administrative-repressive measures" allowed authorities to identify and exile perceived troublemakers by less stringent criteria (and thus more quickly). The ostensible goal of these measures, as the Ministry of Internal Affairs (MVD) asserted, "is not so much the application of harsh punitive measures to the defendants, as it is *the suppression of the arising movement through the removal* of the principal instigators from their place of residence, for the elimination of their harmful influence on the mass of baptized Tatars."[34] In short, the government was not limited to the measures in the criminal code, especially if it could justify its actions in prophylactic, as opposed to punitive, terms.

In fact, before the 1860s, even the judicial handling of cases of apostasy had involved a distinctly administrative dimension, thus confirming the proposition that the distinction in Russia between law and administration remained vague.[35] Beginning already in 1823, cases of apostasy enjoyed a special status exempting them from the usual judicial route: instead of executing the verdicts of the courts, local governors were required to submit those verdicts to the MVD in St. Petersburg for further review.[36] Many decisions and guidelines on these issues were subsequently worked out in an extralegal fashion by the Secret Committee on schismatics, whose purpose was to create a consistent and unified policy with respect to sectarians, schismatics, and apostates.[37] In 1836, cases of Tatar apostasy came under the jurisdiction of the Secret Committee (as did all cases of "seduction" from Orthodoxy in 1839), and the committee made a number of significant decisions on Tatar apostates.[38] Thus while authorities responded to the specifics of Tatar apostasy, they situated the issue of apostasy within the larger context of religious dissent in Russia, and as a result the policies and practices adopted with respect to apostasy were subject, to some degree at least, to the logic dictating policy on schism.

The reform period in the 1860s altered the approach to apostasy considerably. In the first place, Alexander II, objecting to the treatment of schismatics (and by extension apostates) as "a kind of particular *soslovie*" exempt from the general laws and policies of the empire, proposed limitations on the Secret Committee's activities. A less surreptitious order for dealing with apostasy was duly established, whereby cases superseding the competence of the MVD were submitted to the Committee of Ministers.[39] Regarding Tatar apostates specifically, more profound changes occurred around 1870, when the new judicial statute of 1864 went into effect in Kazan and neighboring provinces, considerably restricting the scope of administrative interventions. In 1869, with an eye toward the new order that the statute would introduce, the MVD and the Ministry of Justice agreed that those apostates and "seducers" who had been sentenced to hard labor in the aftermath of 1866 should simply be exiled to Siberia immediately, while the objects of lesser verdicts (for example, admonition) should be released altogether in light of the time they had already spent in prison waiting for their cases to be heard.[40] Thus by 1870 the courts had largely completed the sentencing of the apostates of 1866, and the government had officially discouraged local clergy from seeking the aid of police officials, "whose interference in matters of freedom of conscience is hardly useful," enjoining them to rely instead on the moral power of persuasion.[41] In 1876 even the Kazan Ecclesiastical Consistory asked to be relieved of the duty of keeping track of those Tatars who had apostatized in the years 1811–63.[42] The laws cited earlier were still in effect, but it does not appear that anyone, aside from some missionaries, was interested in applying them.

The result of this retreat was a resurgence of apostasy in the early 1870s, as baptized Tatars became convinced that local authorities had no real basis for preventing their return to Islam. As one religious superintendent reported from Kazan diocese in late 1869, apostates claimed "that many Tatars . . . though they were judged and sat in jail for apostasy from the Christian faith, have now been released and live freely as Muslims."[43] The Archbishop of Kazan concluded that "the main reason for the new repetitions of apostasy is the failure to punish the earlier apostates," who were now free to disseminate the notion "that the authorities who judged them have allowed them to stay in Mohammedanism."[44] With authority decentralized and the government reluctant to pursue court cases, the possibilities for counteracting apostasy were extremely limited, and local missionaries were for the most part left to their own devices to deal with the problem.[45]

While focusing their attention on the establishment of schools and translation of religious texts into native languages,[46] these missionaries nonetheless sought to draw the government's attention to the local distribution of power, by which Muslims allegedly exploited their control of local communal assemblies to block the establishment of churches and government schools and to put pressure on baptized Tatars to join the apostasy.[47] Stridently contending that on the local level Islam enjoyed unfair advantages over Orthodoxy, missionaries accordingly called for stricter guidelines in the constitution of the peasant administration and greater control over the construction of mosques.[48] However, central authorities in the MVD rejected such calls as impracticable infringements of Muslims' legally established electoral rights that were likely to invoke disturbances and to incite "fanaticism."[49] Thus while central authorities agreed that apostates could be prohibited from holding local posts, they produced only a vague call for "supervision," so that such posts, "to the extent possible," be filled by Russian villagers and not by "Muslim fanatics."[50] When the Committee of Ministers took up the issue of apostasy in 1884, it explicitly rejected calls for more direct government intervention and decided merely to sustain support for the network of religious schools that local missionaries had established in a semi-official capacity.[51] In short, faced with the various exigencies of post-Emancipation society and politics, and increasingly convinced of the futility and unsuitability of using administrative measures in matters of faith, the government declined to stir up trouble with the empire's Muslim population for the sake of a few thousand baptized Tatars.

The result of these developments was a stalemate of sorts. Though the state had little means with which to compel the apostates' submission, it could still withhold the one thing that the apostates truly wanted: formal recognition as Muslims. As a result, the apostates occupied a strange and nebulous legal space somewhere between Christianity and Islam. They could not hold any local office, since they were unwilling to take the Christian oath that their religious status required. Children of apostates were not allowed to marry Muslims. Mullahs were not permitted to perform marriages and keep registers (*metricheskie knigi*) for apostates, since this would constitute their recognition as Muslims. Petitioners spoke increasingly of the fact that they could not conclude a legal marriage and that their children were therefore illegitimate. They were excluded from inheritance and could not prove their age and social status, which was especially problematic with respect to the military draft.[52]

This strange state of affairs was equally confusing for Russian authorities. The Kazan governor explained that on account of the "confusion of the record-keeping [on apostates] . . . the collection of information on cases about them is extremely difficult and gives rise to extended correspondence."[53] Local authorities were confused about whether they should make special lists for apostates and which names they should enter into the list: many apostates had no Russian names (since they had never been baptized), while the use of Tatar names would create the impression that they had been recognized as Muslims. Moreover, any attempt to collect information about apostates aroused their hope that their aspirations were finally about to be fulfilled.[54] Thus authorities had to perform a tortuous balancing act of creating some kind of administrative order for apostates that would nonetheless not produce the impression that they were now formally Muslims. This awkward situation provided substantial incentives for a modification of the category of apostate.

Self-ascription and the revision of apostasy

By the 1880s the supplicants in petitions were increasingly children and grandchildren of previous apostates, raised as Muslims without baptism.[55] In their petitions they accordingly emphasized that they themselves were not apostates and should not be treated as such. They recounted that "these so-called apostates are nothing other than the children and in general the descendants of Muslim Tatars, and despite all the strenuous efforts of the Christian clergy [they] have remained adamant and in the majority of cases converted again to Islam, after which their children were not baptized by Christian ritual."[56] Noting that several generations had passed since the apostasy, another group wrote: "Judging by this, what are we guilty of? If indeed our ancestors apostatized from the Orthodox faith to the Mohammedan, we were not yet even on the face of the earth, and no one taught us the Orthodox faith."[57] In short, a generational shift had occurred, whereby most of those still considered apostates in a legal sense had virtually no connection whatsoever with the church and religion from which they were renegades in a strictly legal sense. In most cases, however, the government rejected or simply ignored their petitions, remarking that they did not merit satisfaction. As a result, many of these Tatars filed multiple petitions to various government agencies, virtually always to no avail.

Yet the persistent claims of these second- and third-generation apostates were not entirely without effect. Despite the assumptions about religious identity described earlier, imperial authorities slowly began to accord self-ascription a more significant place in the matter of determining religious status. Thus as Peter Waldron and Laura Engelstein have noted regarding sectarianism, by the 1870s or so state authorities increasingly left the issue of religious belief beyond the scrutiny of the courts, even while continuing to criminalize open manifestations of false dogma (such as processions and public preaching).[58] In particular, a new regulation on Old Believers in 1883 attempted to establish basic conditions necessary for their religion to function, thus acknowledging a realm of private belief beyond the state's purview. Similarly, in 1881, despite its general reluctance to allow the conversion of "pagans" to Islam, the state did permit such conversion to a number of "pagans" and considered more general legislation on this question.[59] Though commitments to the privileged status of Orthodoxy prevented more than tentative steps along this trajectory, nonetheless these provisions reflected at least an implicit recognition that subjective assertions of religious belief were an undeniable part of religious identity. The aspirations of baptized Tatars to return to Islam could hardly fail to converge with this developing discourse. Indeed, already in the immediate aftermath of the 1866 apostasy, the governor of Simbirsk province asked, "Would it not be better to let the poor Tatars believe as they think proper, and would not tolerance instead of persecution diminish the fanaticism and perhaps the spread of the prohibited [sic] religion itself?"[60]

Others, meanwhile, began to contemplate the possibility of granting apostates Muslim status out of concern for administrative efficiency. In 1882 the governor of Kazan province, less out of a principled sense of religious tolerance than a desire "to be rid of" (*izbavit'sia ot*) apostasy as a chronically recurring problem, held out the idea of recognizing those who had apostatized before a certain date as Muslims ("although not openly"), which would allow the police to restrain more effectively the remaining baptized Tatars from visiting mosques and sending their children to Islamic schools.[61] In 1895 a special Editorial Committee for a new criminal code, contending that the law's deprivation of rights of apostates created too much confusion to be included in the newest edition of the code, called for the exclusion of article 185 (punishment for apostasy) from the new code, leaving the matter entirely to religious authorities.[62] Also in 1895 the Samara governor was even prepared to recognize one set of petitioners as Muslims, since they were not listed in parish registers and did not have even grandparents who had officially been considered Christian.[63] These arguments centered above all on the practical hardships engendered by the government's intransigent stance on the issue of apostasy, but they also implicitly recognized that there was a compelling social reality that resisted efforts to subordinate it to official dictates.

Most ecclesiastical figures continued to maintain that even the grandchildren of apostates should not be separated from the church, adding that the recognition of some as Muslims would produce a massive exodus of non-Russians from Orthodoxy. As Over-Procurator K. P. Pobedonostsev wrote in 1898 on the basis of reports from local bishops, "granting to all apostates the right to confess Mohammedanism will constitute a victory for the bitterest opponents of Christianity—Muslims—will strengthen their fanaticism and propaganda, and will serve as a seduction for all those who are weak and unsteady in the faith, and in any case threatens great harm for the Holy Church."[64] Though forced to admit that one set of petitioners were "Mohammedans in the full sense of the word," the Kazan archbishop similarly argued in 1895 that granting Muslim status would constitute "a great loss for the Orthodox Church."[65] Likewise, prominent missionaries such as E. A. Malov and N. I. Il'minskii remained adamantly opposed to sanctioning apostates' return to Islam. Even as he acknowledged that many baptized Tatars were Christians "in name only," Malov nevertheless argued in 1865 that formal Christian status constituted a fundamental starting point for Christianization: "While baptized Tatars remain Christians, even if only in name, and at peace, if only ostensibly, with the church, there is still hope of bringing them to their senses and affirming them in Christianity, while after their official apostasy into Mohammedanism, their conversion to Christianity will be as difficult as that of present Mohammedans."[66]

Yet even among clerics there were doubts about the appropriateness of continued intransigence. Already in 1858, Bishop of Cheboksary Nikodim expressed his conviction that it was "an unjust affair to attempt ever more forcefully to prove to a Tatar that he is a Christian, when he himself says that he is not a Christian and when he begs the Sovereign not to be considered a Christian (*ne byt' i ne nazyvat'sia khristianinom*)." It would be better, Nikodim contended, "to terminate all persecution of these Tatars for their apostasy to Mohammedanism, not to foist Christianity onto them forcefully, but to wait and see whether the Lord Himself doesn't provide some kind of opportunity, and then to make use of that."[67] In 1895 the bishop of Samara acknowledged with respect to two families that, because they had Muslim names and were not entered into Orthodox parish registers, their apostasy could be considered "completed" (*sovershivshimsid*) and their children should be released from Christianity.[68] Most remarkably, having received such opinions from local bishops, even Pobedonostsev was prepared to have the petitioners' requests satisfied, thereby signaling his willingness to compromise in certain particular cases, even as he remained resolutely opposed to more general reform of the apostasy issue.[69]

As a result of this growing willingness to compromise, petitioners from three villages actually received satisfaction in 1894–95, due to the extremely tenuous nature of their connections to the Orthodox Church.[70] By contrast, while a commission established in Kazan by 1896 investigated the "religious condition" of baptized Tatars and contemplated ways of bringing them more deeply into the Orthodox fold, other petitions were rejected until 1905 with the simple justification that "the petitioners are among the descendants of baptized Tatars who have apostatized from Orthodoxy."[71] While the work of the commission in Kazan slowly proceeded, all incoming petitions were shelved, and thus nothing substantial in their situation changed until the Committee of Ministers took up the question of religious tolerance early in 1905. Thus the door for return to Islam was opened a crack in 1895 but then closed again until 1905.

Though 1905 undeniably marks a major watershed in the religious history of Russia, the new law of religious toleration promulgated on 17 April was not entirely the product of the revolutionary events of that year. To be sure, by spring the autocracy was under assault by societal forces, which made the government eager to resolve the issue of religious tolerance. Muslims took advantage of the augmented possibilities for political expression to organize and to submit petitions to the government requesting greater religious toleration, reform of the administration of Muslims, and permission for Tatar apostates from Orthodoxy "to confess Islam openly and freely with the right of their registration within the Muslim community."[72] But while the promulgation of the April laws owed something to this revolutionary context, the evolving policy on apostasy described above suggests that the laws completed and codified a shift that the government had been in the process of making for some time. Indeed, commitments to greater religious tolerance had already been expressed in earlier imperial decrees, which promised "to strengthen the steadfast observance . . . of the guarantees of religious toleration contained in the Fundamental laws of the Russian Empire" (February 1903); to review statutes on the rights of sectarians, non-Orthodox and non-Christians; and more immediately "to take now in the administrative order appropriate measures for the elimination of all constraints on religious life not directly established by law" (December 1904).[73]

In response to the *ukaz* of 1904, the issue of apostasy was taken up in the spring of 1905 by the Department of Religious Affairs of Foreign Faiths, the subdivision of the MVD responsible for administering the religious matters of the empire's non-Orthodox populations. The department's acting director, M. E. Iachevskii, identified three principal groups of "recalcitrants" (*uporstvuiushchiia*) and "apostates from Orthodoxy" whose situation demanded the most immediate attention: baptized-Tatar apostates; former Uniates who had been forcibly incorporated into Orthodoxy after the elimination of the Uniate church in 1839 and 1875; and Estonian and Latvian peasants who had converted to Orthodoxy in the 1840s for predominantly economic reasons.[74] Underscoring the role of material concerns over religious conviction in the "conversion" of these groups, Iachevskii concluded that "the phenomena of apostasy from the ruling church that has arisen in the nineteenth century have been directly dependent on those abnormal circumstances in which the acceptance of Orthodoxy by *inovertsy* in Russia occurs." Iachevskii accused the government of ignoring the "unconscious or forced conversion" and of naively believing that a combination of missionary activity, schooling, and time would triumph over apostates' dark religious prejudices. Concluding his discussion of Tatar apostates, Iachevskii argued that the many petitions and the "complete alienation of the petitioners from association with the Orthodox church and everything Russian must be recognized as clear proof of the hopelessness of all attempts to return those people to the bosom of the Orthodox church." The obvious solution was to grant these unfortunate "recalcitrants" and apostates the right to choose their faith freely, thus hindering "the further advancement of this chronic ailment."[75]

The Tatar apostates' cause was aided by a generally positive evaluation of Muslims in the Committee of Ministers in its further deliberations leading to the April laws. Indeed, in 1905 the committee concluded, contrary to the arguments of many missionaries and some officials about Muslims' "fanaticism" and hostility to Russian civilization, that the empire's Muslims had always fulfilled their duty to the state, had not presented any political challenges, and had never proselytized among Russians. "Moreover, despite some remaining differences in external and internal way of life, this population has become intimate with Russia (*srodnilos's Rossieiu*) and has become completely friendly with her. These historically constituted relations should be valued, and one should avoid ruining them."[76] Particularly disturbing for the committee was the fact, underscored by petitioners themselves, that their strange position left them without any access to clergy and houses of prayer. Unable to attend mosques legally or to receive religious rites from Islamic clergy, and thoroughly alienated from Orthodox religious institutions, apostates had no possibility to develop their religious lives or to sanctify (or even legalize) their marriages and the births of their children. As the committee itself recognized, "these stubborn ones and apostates remain entirely without religion."[77] The committee could hardly fail to recognize "the moral sufferings experienced by people who remain without any spiritual consolation in the difficult moments of life," and indeed it acknowledged that particular attention should be directed toward baptized Tatars, since "those unfortunate people lead a very miserable life, located between two confessions."[78] Apostates' lack of access to religion, particularly in a time of revolutionary turmoil, was intolerable and dangerous also for simply political reasons: "There can scarcely be a less desirable element in a state than subjects without religion, that principal foundation of morality; such people can all the more easily become fertile soil for the birth of sedition and lawlessness of every kind."[79]

For our purposes, the most important aspect of the new law in 1905 was the legal permission it granted apostates to return to their original religions.[80] But while this law fully legalized conversion from Orthodoxy to other Christian religions, it continued to impose certain restrictions on the transfer to non-Christian religions, thus upholding a fundamental distinction between Christian and non-Christian faiths.[81] Declaring its commitment to the "supreme and ruling" status of the Orthodox Church, the Committee of Ministers insisted that "direct permission" for Orthodox Christians to accept non-Christian faiths "would not conform with the deep recognition of the truth (*istinnost'*) of the principles at the base of the faith of Christ." Even while acknowledging that a convert to a non-Christian faith should not endure any "repressive" measures, the committee insisted that unfavorable civil disabilities should remain in place, "as a result of the nonrecognition by the state that such a transfer has occurred." Thus even in the heady atmosphere of 1905, the state refused to recognize the conversion of Orthodox Christians to non-Christian faiths. Yet the Committee nonetheless felt compelled to make an explicit *exception* (*iz"iatie*) for baptized-Tatar apostates and a few other "comparatively insignificant groups of apostates" (Abkhazians, trans-Baikal Buryats, "and so on") who "in reality" confessed non-Christian faiths.[82] The new law accordingly granted the right of exclusion from Orthodoxy explicitly to "those people who are ascribed as Orthodox, but who in reality confess that non-Christian faith to which they themselves or their ancestors belonged before their adherence to Orthodoxy."[83]

This rather convoluted formulation thus allowed baptized non-Russians to return *only* to their historic religion, thereby upholding the idea of national religions referred to above.[84] More subtle was the requirement that the affected party "in reality confess" the faith to which he wished to be ascribed. While the law itself left this phrase largely undefined, a subsequent MVD circular of August 1905 attempted to clarify what it should mean in practice. In each case the local governor was to ascertain whether the given person or his ancestors "truly belonged to that non-Christian religion, which the petitioner claims to profess and to which he wishes to be ascribed." Should it prove difficult to establish this circumstance definitively, "administrative authorities limit themselves to ascertaining whether the petitioner truly deviated from fulfilling the rituals of the Orthodox Church prior to the appearance of the *ukaz* of 17 April 1905."[85] In other words, if apostasy was demonstrably manifest *prior* to 1905, the apostate could expect satisfaction. In contrast, the law of 1905 refused to condone apostasy that occurred *after*, or *as a result of* the new law. At least with respect to non-Christian religions, then, the idea was to open the floodgates momentarily, to release all the accumulated apostates, but by no means to encourage further hemorrhage by leaving matters open for others. To the extent possible, the state wanted a controlled transfer of incorrectly ascribed religious populations, and not religious anarchy. Thus while making an important concession to the power of religious conviction, the state stopped decidedly short of allowing belief actually to serve as the primary foundation for religious identity, at least as regards non-Christian faiths.

Despite these qualifications on the law, it does not appear that Tatar petitioners encountered difficulty receiving Muslim status. Muslims in Kazan paid for the large-scale distribution of copies of relevant sections of the 1905 law and printed petitions in which apostates needed only to fill in their names and villages.[86] From 1905 to the beginning of 1909, close to fifty thousand apostates finally received official recognition as Muslims and were ascribed to local Muslim parishes.[87] Although some sources speak of an immense apostate movement in the aftermath of 1905, S. Bagin was probably closer to the mark when he estimated that this period saw only about three thousand "new apostates," the rest being those who had severed their ties with Orthodoxy long before.[88] Notably, the majority of formally Christian Tatars (over one hundred thousand) did not apostatize formally, and at least a portion of them developed substantially stronger attachments to Christianity and began to articulate a more conscious, politicized sense of *Kräshen* (baptized-Tatar) particularity that lasted into the Soviet period.[89]

It may be tempting to see in the state's final capitulation to baptized-Tatar apostates a triumph of the principles of religious freedom and individual autonomy. Yet the account here suggests that other, less exalted concerns were perhaps more important in bringing about this revision of apostasy. To be sure, there was by 1905 a certain willingness to afford belief a more prominent place beside formal ascription in the determination of religious affiliation, and the October Manifesto (17 October 1905) notably used the phrase "freedom of conscience" rather than merely "religious tolerance."[90] Even those who tenaciously opposed apostates' recognition as Muslims tended to agree that religious belief—that is, conscious acceptance of Christian "truths" independent of coercion—should replace mechanical and unreflective execution of "Christian obligations" under the threat of punishment.[91] But similar to the way in which the abolition of the knout in 1845 was motivated less by an espousal of Enlightenment ideals than by officials' recognition of their inability to control public reactions to the spectacle of knouting, the revision of apostasy in 1905 grew as much (or more) out of a desire to simplify administration and to "be rid of" the problem of apostasy as it did out of a principled commitment to allow the articulated beliefs of imperial subjects to determine formal religious status.[92] And if 1905 represented an admission on the part of the state that its determination to regulate subjects' religious affiliations was unequal to the tenacious aspiration of apostates to rejoin the Islamic community, the new order also represented an opportunity for church and state to reinitiate the process of Christianization with an ostensibly untainted pool of baptized Tatars. In this sense, one could certainly argue that the church was liberated from the apostates as much as vice versa. When one considers that few of the promises for substantial legislative change made in the manifestos of 1905 actually came to fruition,[93] one is hard-pressed to conclude that the "conversion" of government officials to a liberal conception of religious freedom was anything more than partial. Rather, the revision of apostasy represented a compromise that imperial officials made, in some cases willingly but for the most part reluctantly, with the culturally distinct and often tenacious Tatar subjects they deigned to rule.

Notes

* An earlier version of this essay was presented at the Twenty-ninth AAASS Convention in Seattle (November, 1997). Support for the research was provided by the International Research and Exchanges Board, with funds provided by the National Endowment for the Humanities, the U.S. Information Agency, and the U.S. Department of State, which administers the Russian, Eurasian, and East European Research Program (Title VIII); the American Council of Teachers of Russian; the Social Science Research Council; and the Kennan Institute for Advanced Russian Studies. For critical readings of earlier drafts of this essay I wish to thank Boris Anan'ich, Phillip Skaggs, David Tanenhaus, Nicholas Breyfogle, Abby Schrader, Golfo Alexopoulos, Laura Engelstein, William Rosenberg, two anonymous readers for *Russian Review*, and above all Jenifer Stenfors, who to my great sorrow died of cancer before this article could be published.

1 Among the most important general works addressing this issue are Gregory Freeze, "The *Soslovie* (Estate) Paradigm in Russian Social History," *American Historical Review* 91 (February 1986): 11–36; and Elise Kimerling Wirtschafter, *Social Identity in Imperial Russia* (DeKalb, 1997). Consider also the contradiction in the Soviet period between ascription and Marxist class, as analyzed by Sheila Fitzpatrick, "Ascribing Class: The Construction of Social Identity in Soviet Russia," *Journal of Modern History* 65 (December 1993): 745–70.

2 The complexities connected with liberalism in Russia have been examined in some detail through the prism of sexuality by Laura Engelstein in *The Keys to Happiness: Sex and the Search for Modernity in Fin-de-Siècle Russia* (Ithaca, 1992); and through the person of Miliukov by Melissa Kirschke Stockdale in *Paul Miliukov and the Quest for a Liberal Russia, 1880–1918* (Ithaca, 1996).

3 E. A. Malov, "Statisticheskiia svedeniia o kreshchenykh tatarakh Kazanskoi i nekotorykh drugikh eparkhii, v volzhskom basseine," *Uchenye zapiski Kazanskago universiteta*, vyp. 3–4 (1866): 311–20, 321–87; and D. M. Iskhakov, *Istoricheskaia demografiia tatarskogo naroda, XVIII–nachalo XX vv.* (Kazan, 1993), 93–98.

4 In the eighteenth century and into the nineteenth, the state offered direct material goods to new converts, and baptism was accompanied by a three-year exemption from all taxes and a lifetime exemption from military service. On the conversions see Apollon Mozharovskii, *Izlozhenie khoda missionerskago dela po prosveshcheniiu kazanskikh inorodtsev s 1552 po 1867 goda*, Chteniia v Imperatorskom obshchestve istorii i drevnostei rossiskikh pri Moskovskom universitete, vols. 112–13 (Moscow, 1880); Chantal Lemercier-Quelquejay, "Les missions orthodoxes en pays musulmans de Moyenne- et Basse-Volga, 1552–1865," *Cahiers du Monde russe et soviétique* 8 (Juillet–septembre 1967): 369–403; Michael Khodarkovsky "'Not by Word Alone': Missionary Policies and Religious Conversion in Early Modern Russia," *Comparative Studies in Society and History* 38 (April 1996): 267–97; I. K. Zagidullin, "Khristianizatsiia tatar Srednego Povolzh'ia vo vtoroi polovine XVI–XVII vv.," *Uchenye zapiski Tatarskogo gosudarstvennogo gumanitarnnogo instituta* 1 (1998): 111–65; and idem (Ildus Zahidullin), "La conversion à l'orthodoxie des tatars de la région Volga-Oural, aux XVIIe–XVIIIe siècles, et ses causes économiques et sociales," in *L'Islam de Russie: Conscience communautaire et autonomie politique chezles Tatars de la Volga et de L'Oural depuis le XVIIIe siècle*, ed. Stéphane A. Dudoignon, Dämir Is'haqov and Räfyq Möhämmätshin (Paris, 1997), 27–64.

5 There is a tendency in the sources—and therefore in the historiography—to focus overwhelmingly on baptized-Tatar communities that either apostatized or exhibited inclinations in that direction, and thus to ignore numerous communities with stronger attachments to Christianity or to pre-Islamic practices. For more on this issue see Paul W. Werth, "From 'Pagan' Muslims to 'Baptized' Communists: Religious Conversion and Ethnic Particularity in Russia's Eastern Provinces," forthcoming in *Comparative Studies in Society and History.*

6 It is not my goal here to address in detail either the specific sources or the dynamics of the apostasy, but see Jean Saussay, "L'apostasie des Tatars Christianisés en 1866," *Cahiers du Monde russe et soviétique* 9 (Janvier-mais 1968): 20–40; Agnès Kefeli-Clay, "L'Islam populaire chez les Tatars Chrétiens Orthodoxes au XIXe siècle," *Cahiers du Monde russe* 37 (Octobre–décembre 1996): 409–28; idem, "Constructing an Islamic Identity: The Case of Elyshevo Village in the Nineteenth Century," in *Russia's Orient: Imperial Borderlands and Peoples, 1700–1914*, ed. Daniel Brower and Edward Lazzerini (Bloomington, 1997), 271–91; Kefeli-Clay, "Une note sur le rôle des femmes tatares converties au christianisme dans la réislamisation de la Moyenne-Volga, au milieu du XIXe siècle," in *L'Islam de Russie*, 65–72; and Paul W. Werth, *At the Margins of Orthodoxy: Mission, Governance, and Confessional Politics in Russia's Volga-Kama Region, 1825–1917* (forthcoming, Cornell University Press).

7 On the reform of state peasants see N. A. Khalikov, *Zemledelie tatar srednego Povolzh'ia i Priural'ia XIX–nachala XX v.* (Moscow, 1981), 14–22; and N. M. Druzhinin, *Russkaia derevnia na perelome, 1861–1880 gg.* (Moscow, 1978), 103–13. On growth of Muslim influence after the reform see Rossiiskii gosudarstvennyi istoricheskii arkhiv (RGIA), f. 821, op. 8, d. 743, l. 182ob., and d. 759, ll. 70–75; and "O kreshchenykh tatarakh," *Sovremennyi listok* 39 (14 May 1866).

8 "Prichiny otpadeniia kreshchenykh tatar ot khristianstva," *Missioner* 10 (1874): 105, RGIA, f. 797, op. 41, otdel 2, stol 3, d. 178, l. 4. See also V. Timofeev, "Poezdka v prikhody kreshchenykh tatar po povodu poslednikh otpadenii v magometanstvo," *Pravoslavnoe obozrenie* (1872): 478.

9 *Polnoe sobranie zakonov Rossiiskoi Imperii* II (*PSZ*II), vol. 16, no. 14409 (1842), article 25. Each Orthodox husband/father was required to ensure that his wife

and children did not accept another faith. See *Svod zakonov Rossiiskoi Imperii* (1832), vol. 14, art. 41; and Ardalion Popov, *Sud i nakazaniia za prestupleniia protiv very i nravstvennosti po russkomu pravu* (Kazan, 1904), 317.

10 *Svod zakonov* (1832), vol. 1, chap. 1, arts. 44–45; ibid., vol. 14, arts. 40–41, 73. In 1851 representatives of non-Orthodox Christian religions received the possibility of proselytizing among pagans with the emperor's permission (*PSZ*II, vol. 26, no. 24820 [1851]), a privilege that was eventually extended to proselytism among Muslims as well (Popov, *Sud i nakazaniia*, 314). For a broad treatment of legislation regarding Muslims specifically see Aidar Nogmanov, "L'évolution de la législation sur les musulmans de Russie, de la conquête de Qazan à la guerre Crimée (1552–1853)," in *L'Islam de Russie*, 115–30.

11 *Svod zakonov* (1832), vol. 1, art. 45.

12 M. A. Reisner, *Gosudarstvo i veruiushchaia lichnost': Sbornik statei* (St. Petersburg, 1905), 406–7, 196. See also Nicholas B. Breyfogle, "Heretics and Colonizers: Religious Dissent and Russian Colonization of Transcaucasia, 1830–1880" (Ph.D. diss., University of Pennsylvania, 1998), 31–35. Or, as Pavel Miliukov wrote, "Neither the state nor the church had foreseen that it was possible to choose a religion according to one's personal conviction. Faith was regarded as something innate, inseparable from nationality, a second nature, so to speak" (cited in John W. Slocum, "The Boundaries of National Identity: Religion, Language, and Nationality Politics in Late Imperial Russia" [Ph.D. diss., University of Chicago, 1993], 70).

13 Note that the institution charged with administering non-Orthodox faiths in the nineteenth century—the Department of Religious Affairs of Foreign Faiths—construed them explicitly as "foreign" (*inostrannye*).

14 For more on this distinction between toleration and freedom of conscience, see Reisner, *Gosudarstvo*, 390–423; and Peter Waldron, "Religious Toleration in Late Imperial Russia," in *Civil Rights in Imperial Russia*, ed. Olga Crisp and Linda Edmondson (Oxford, 1989), 103–19. For a complete compilation of active law on religion see Ia. A. Kantorovich, *Zakony o vere i veroterpimosti* (St. Petersburg, 1899).

15 Indeed, the term *novokreshchenye* operated even as a social category for converts that replaced the designation "peasant," which itself had significant religious connotations (*krest'ianin* = "Christian"). See Werth, *Subjects for Empire*, 189–90.

16 On the inability of conversion to overcome *inorodtsy* status, and for an insightful consideration of the problem of *inorodtsy* generally, see John W. Slocum, "Who, and When, Were the *Inorodtsy*? The Evolution of the Category of 'Aliens' in Imperial Russia," *Russian Review* 57 (April 1998): 173–90.

17 Gauri Viswanathan, *Outside the Fold: Conversion, Modernity, and Belief* (Princeton, 1998), 115. Viswanathan shows how Hindu converts to Christianity were treated as Hindus by the colonial courts and administration in certain contexts, because it was assumed that their conversion did not obviate indigenous customs, usages, and manners.

18 *Ulozhenie o nakazaniiakh ugolovnykh i ispravitel'nykh* (St. Petersburg, 1866), art. 185. The law did not clearly indicate what should occur if admonition failed to achieve its goal. See Popov, *Sud i nakazaniia*, 349.

19 *Ulozhenie o nakazaniiakh*, art. 184. The term of hard labor was increased to twelve to fifteen years if the guilty party had resorted to force or coercion in promoting apostasy.

20 According to V. N. Shiriaev this notion of "seduction" was a unique feature of Russian criminal law. See his *Religioznyia prestupleniia: Istoriko-dogmaticheskii ocherk* (Iaroslavl', 1909), 377.

21 RGIA, f. 821, op. 8, d. 763, ll. 29–31; Natsional'nyi arkhiv Respubliki Tatarstan (NART), f. 1, op. 3, d. 229, ll. 53–54ob.
22 NART, f. 1, op. 3, d. 228, ll. 139ob.–140.
23 Most dramatically, a certain Galim Samigulov, whom local authorities identified as being at the vortex of instigation during the 1866 apostasy, was acquitted on the charges brought against him (RGIA, f. 821, op. 8, d. 780, 1. 10ob.). He was, however, subsequently subjected to administrative exile.
24 Ibid., d. 763, l. 42ob.
25 Ibid., ll. 119–19ob.
26 Ibid., d. 759, ll. 70–75.
27 Ibid., d. 763, ll. 54ob.–55.
28 Ibid., d. 780, ll. 6ob., 10. See also ibid., d. 763, ll. 120–21.
29 Ibid., d. 774, ll. 39–40ob. This refers above all to verdicts under article 185. Over twenty people were actually exiled to Siberia.
30 RGIA, d. 796, op. 172, d. 2667, l. 140, op. 167, d. 2271, l. 35ob., and f. 821, op. 8, d. 794, l. 145ob.; "Izvlechenie iz otcheta Vysokopreosviashchennago Antoniia, Arkhiepiskopa Kazanskago i Sviiazhskago, o sostoianii Kazanskoi eparkhii za 1872 g.," *Izvestiiapo Kazanskoi eparkhii* 16 (1873): 512.
31 Ia. B. [E. A. Malov], "Russko-gosudarstvennyi vzgliad na otpadanie inorodtsev-khristian v mukhammedanstvo," *Tserkovnyi vestnik* 23 (1876): 10. In at least one instance this dearth of legal provisions impelled an observer to argue for the application of laws originally intended for the most "fanatical" schismatics and heretics to Tatar apostates. See E. N. Voronets, "K voprosu o svobode very i o sovremennykh, vnutri Rossii otpadeniiakh ot khristianstva v magometanstvo," *Pravoslavnyi sobesednik* 1 (1877): 226–58.
32 An enormous number of archival files address this issue, such as NART, f. 1, op. 2, dd. 943 and 1225, and f. 4, op. 72, d. 12; and RGIA, f. 797, op. 15, d. 35644. See also E. A. Malov, "Prikhody starokreshchenykh i novokreshchenykh tatar v Kazanskoi eparkhii," *Pravoslavnoe obozrenie* 17 (1865): 449–94; and ibid. 18 (1865): 283–308, 477–513. Almost all such resettlements occurred within Kazan province, from one district to another.
33 On the debates concerning the merits of administrative and judicial means of action see Werth, *At the Margins*, 160–65.
34 RG1A, f. 821, op. 8, d. 763, l. 161ob.
35 For a general discussion on the tensions between administrative measures and judicial procedure in Russia see Engelstein, *Keys to Happiness*, esp. 19–28.
36 *PSZ*II, vol. 9, no. 7440 (1834); *Sobranie postanovlenii po chasti raskola* (*Sobranie*), vol. 2 (St. Petersburg, 1858), 179–80; *Obzor meropriiatii Ministerstva vnutrennykh del po raskolu s 1802 po 1881 god* (St. Petersburg, 1903), 77. Beginning in 1838 these verdicts were also to be approved by the emperor himself (*PSZ*II, vol. 13, no. 10872 [1838]).
37 On the creation of this committee toward the end of Alexander I's reign see Breyfogle, "Heretics and Colonizers," 57–58. A directive in 1838 called for the creation of such committees, consisting of the local bishop, governor, and representatives of the Ministry of State Properties, in each provincial capital. Committees were accordingly created in the 1840s in various provinces (*Sobranie* 2:89, 128–29, 314–16). See also *Izvlecheniia iz rasporiazhenii po delam o raskol'nikakh pri Imperatorakh Nikolae I i Aleksandre II* (Leipzig, 1882), 5–7.
38 RGIA, f. 797, op. 15, d. 35644, ll. 48–54. On the transfer of Tatar apostasy to the committee see *Sobranie* 2:682; and RGIA, f. 821, op. 11, d. 11, l. 113.
39 *Sobranie* 2:678–84.

40 RGIA, f. 821, op. 8, d. 763, l. 161ob., and d. 771, ll. 3–4. In one district (Tetiushi), investigations continued through the 1870s but were abandoned in 1879 due to a dearth of evidence (ibid., d. 794, ll. 6, 12–14).

41 Ibid., d. 743, l. 76, and f. 797, op. 39, otdel 2, stol 3, d. 93.

42 Though the Synod never officially approved the Consistory's request, it appears as though this policy was more or less adopted (RGIA, f. 796, op. 163, d. 1231, op. 172, d. 2667, and f. 821, op. 8, d. 788). In any event, by the end of 1876 the Consistory had instructed local clergy to keep track only of the numbers of children born of apostates, instead of more complete church records. See "Kak pisat'v dukhovnykh vedomostiakh detei otpavshikh," *Izvestiia po Kazanskoi eparkhii* 24 (1876): 727–28.

43 RGIA, f. 821, op. 8, d. 763, ll. 238–39.

44 Ibid., l. 268.

45 On the apostasies see NART, f. 4, op. 98, d. 34; RGIA, f. 797, op. 41, otdel 2, stol 3, d. 178, and f. 821, op. 8, d. 763, ll. 261–300, and d. 767; and Timofeev, "Poezdka."

46 These missionary efforts centered above all on the semiofficial Brotherhood of St. Gurii, which was established in 1867 and included many of the region's most prominent religious figures and educational specialists. See M. A. Mashanov, *Obzor deiatel'nosti "Bratstva Sv. Guriia" za 25 let* (Kazan, 1892); Isabelle Teitz Kreindler, "Educational Policies Toward the Eastern Nationalities in Tsarist Russia: A Study of Il'minskii's System" (Ph.D. diss., Columbia University, 1969); and Robert Paul Geraci, "Window on the East: Ethnography, Orthodoxy, and Russian Nationality in Kazan, 1870–1914" (Ph.D. diss., University of California, Berkeley, 1995).

47 See, for example, the account by Gr. L'vov, "Religioznoe sostoianie otpadshikh tatar v der. Iangil'dinoi, Cheboksarskago uezda," *Izvestiia po Kazanskoi eparkhii* 21 (1896): 406–11.

48 Russian law required that each Muslim parish consist of at least two hundred male revision souls, and also that each new mosque be determined "necessary" and not constitute a source of "seduction" for nearby Christians (*Svod zakonov* [1857], vol. 12, arts. 260–61). Missionaries claimed that these laws were being violated, and that some mosques had been constructed to serve far fewer than the established two hundred souls. See in particular E. A. Malov, "O tatarskikh mechetiakh." *Pravoslavnyi sobesednik* 3 (1867): 285–320; and ibid. 1 (1868): 3–45. See also idem, "Ocherk religioznago sostoianiia kreshchenykh tatar, podvergshikhsia vlianiiu magometanstva: Missionerskii dnevnik," *Pravoslavnyi sobesednik* 3 (1871): 250, 398; "Zapiska N. I. Il'minskago po voprosu ob otpadeniiakh kreshchenykh tatar Kazanskoi gubernii v 1881 g.," *Pravoslavnyi sobesednik* 2 (1895): 274; and RGIA, f. 821, op. 8, d. 743, l. 96–98.

49 RGIA, f. 821, op. 8, d. 743, ll. 119–28. By contrast, pagans had been prevented from serving as volost and village heads in mixed areas already in 1835, and there were various restrictions on schismatics as well. On pagans see *PSZ*II, vol. 10, no. 8021 (1835). On schismatics see *Obzor meropriiatii*, 68–69.

50 "Perechen' ogranichitel'nykh postanovlenii po dukhovnym delam inoslavnykh i inovernykh ispovedanii," RGIA, Pechatnye zapiski, folder 2349, p. 20.

51 RGIA, f. 821, op. 8, d. 743, ll. 180–89ob.

52 Ibid., d. 788. At draft selection, apostates' ages were determined by appearance.

53 Ibid., d. 790, l. 84. Religious figures registered similar complaints (ibid., f. 796, op. 172, d. 2667, l. 125).

54 RGIA, f. 821, op. 8, d. 788, l. 115ob.

55 RGIA, f. 796, op. 172, d. 2667, ll. 20–23, 129–32. These children of apostates were responding to the Kazan Consistory's decision to end correspondence

about them (1876), which they construed as the long-awaited permission to confess Islam.

56 RGIA, f. 821, op. 8, d. 774, ll. 56–56ob.

57 RGIA, f. 796, op. 172, d. 2667, l. 2ob.

58 Waldron, "Religious Toleration," 110; idem, "Religious Reform after 1905: Old Believers and the Orthodox Church," *Oxford Slavonic Papers*, New Series 20 (1987): 114; Laura Engelstein, "From Heresy to Harm: Self-Castrators in the Civic Discourse of Late Tsarist Russia," in *Empire and Society: New Approaches to Russian History*, ed. Teruyuki Hara and Kimitaka Matsuzato (Sapporo, 1997), 16. In certain respects this distinction in fact signaled a return to the policy of Alexander I in the first part of his reign (See Breyfogle, "Heretics and Colonizers," 35–48).

59 On the 1883 regulation see Waldron, "Religious Reform," 114–15, who notes that the state's concessions to Old Belief were motivated principally by the reluctance to antagonize a group that it now recognized as a highly conservative force, deeply attached to Russia. See also K. K. Arsen'ev, *Svoboda sovesti i veroterpimost'* (St. Petersburg, 1905), 61–85. On "pagan" conversion to Islam, which had never actually been prohibited by law, see Paul W. Werth, 'Tsarist Categories, Orthodox Intervention, and Islamic Conversion in a Pagan Udmurt Village, 1870s–1890s," in *Muslim Culture in Russia and Central Asia from the 18th to the Early 20th Centuries*, vol. 2, *Inter-Regional and Inter-Ethnic Relations*, ed. Anke von Kügelgen, Michael Kemper, and Allen J., Frank (Berlin, 1998), 385–415.

60 RGIA, f. 821, op. 8, d. 759, l. 242.

61 See "Zapiska," 262.

62 RGIA, f. 796, op. 172, d. 2667, ll. 130–31. The committee's conclusion was based partly on the idea that it was inappropriate for criminal courts to sentence people to "church repentance," that is, to "admonitions and reasoning," since such "crimes" were to be handled exclusively by ecclesiastical courts.

63 RGIA, f. 821, op. 8, d. 790, l. 164ob.

64 Ibid., d. 788, ll. 113ob.–14. Pobedonostsev was citing almost verbatim from a report by the Archbishop of Kazan (RGIA, f. 796, op. 172, d. 2667, l. 134ob.).

65 RGIA, f. 821, op. 8, d. 790, l. 57ob.

66 Malov, "Prikhody," 451. N. I. Il'minskii similarly wrote in 1883 that since measures for Christian education were still weakly developed, apostates "must be restrained and held [within the church] at all costs" (cited in Kreindler, "Educational Policies," 103).

67 Cited in Malov, "Prikhody," 509.

68 RGIA, f. 821, op. 8, d. 790, ll. 33ob.–34. The Department of Religious Affairs of Foreign Confessions nonetheless rejected the petition.

69 Ibid., ll. 59, 94, 168.

70 RGIA, f. 821, op. 8, d. 788, l. 113ob., and d. 790, ll. 37–59, 85–94, 163–68. The villages were Novaia Kadeeva (Chistopol' district), Risovaia Poliana (Spassk district), and Novaia Mansurkina (Buguruslan district). Some other petitions also found satisfaction in 1896 and 1898, but only in the complete absence of evidence of connections to the Orthodox Church. In the three cases above, by contrast, the petitioners were identified explicitly as descendants of apostates and were thus not legally entitled to satisfaction. I cannot say with complete certainty, however, that these were the only petitioners to receive satisfaction at this time.

71 RGIA, f. 821, op. 8, dd. 794–95. Eighty-three new petitions were filed again in 1895–98 alone, following the successful petitions in 1895. Details on the formation of this commission are in RGIA, f. 796, op. 172, d. 2667, ll. 125–243.

72 "Dokladnaia zapiska upolnomochennykh Kazanskago musul'manskago obshchestva, Predsedateliu Komiteta Ministrov," RGIA, Pechatnye zapiski, folder 2349,

p. 7. For more details on the political activities of Muslims during and after 1905 see S. M. Iskhakov, "Revoliutsiia 1905–1907 gg. i rossiiskie musul'mane," in *1905 god: Nachalo revoliutsionnykh potriasenii v Rossii XX veka* (Moscow, 1996), 192–210; Azade-Ayse Rorlich, *The Volga Tatars: A Profile in National Resilience* (Stanford, 1986), 104–22; and Diliara Usmanova, *Musul'manskaia fraktsiia i problemy "svobody sovesti" v Gosudarstvennoi Dume Rossii (1906–1917)* (Kazan, 1999).

73 *PSZ*III, vol. 23, no. 22581 (26 February 1903); ibid, vol. 24, no. 25495 (12 December 1904).

74 On the elimination of the Uniate church see M. Koialovich, *Istoriia vozsoedineniia zapadnorusskikh uniatov starykh vremen* (St. Petersburg, 1873); and Theodore R. Weeks, "The 'End' of the Uniate Church in Russia: The *Vozsoedinenie* of 1875," *Jahrbücher für Geschichte Osteuropas* 44:1 (1996): 28–39.

75 "Zapiska ob otpavshkikh iz pravoslaviia v inoverie," RGIA, Pechatnye zapiski, folder 2349 (citations from pp. 8, 11, 12, 72, 9).

76 "Osobyi zhumal Komiteta Ministrov 22 fevralia i 1 marta 1905 o poriadke vypolneniia punkta 6 Imennago Vysochaishago ukaza 12 dekiabria 1904 po voprosam, kasaiushchimsia inoslavnykh i inovernykh ispovedanii," RGIA, Pechatnye zapisiki, folder 2349, p. 22. This is not to say that state officials had no apprehensions about Islam. But a more thoroughgoing Islamophobia on the part of the secular government appears to have been a development principally of the post-1905 period, when a combination of Muslim deputies' oppositional stance in the Duma, a more dynamic Islamic reform movement, and the Young Turk Revolution in the Ottoman Empire inclined government officials to view Muslims, especially in the Volga region, in more dangerous political terms. The most thorough treatment of this process is Elena Vorob'eva, "Musul'manskii vopros v imperskoi politike Rossiiskogo samoderzhaviia: vtoraia polovina XIX veka–1917 g." (Cand. diss., European University, St. Petersburg, 1999); idem, "Musul'manskii vopros v Rossii: Istoriia problemy," paper delivered at the conference "Imperiia i region: Rossiiskii variant" (Omsk, luly 1999). See also Robert Geraci, "Russian Orientalism at an Impasse: Tsarist Education Policy and the 1910 Conference on Islam," in *Russia's Orient*, 138–61; and Serge Zenkovsky, *Pan-Turkism and Islam in Russia, 1905–1920* (Cambridge, MA, 1960).

77 The deliberations of the Committee of Ministers on these questions in the winter of 1905 are reproduced in N. P. Solov'ev, *Polnyi krug dukhovnykh zakonov* (Moscow, 1907) (citation is from p. 12). The committee here was referring to former Uniates and Latvian converts as well as to Tatar apostates.

78 "Postupivshee k Ministru Zemledeliia i Gosudarstvennykh Imushchestv zaiavlenie magometan," RGIA, Pechatnye zapiski, folder 2349, p. 4.

79 Solov' ev, *Polnyi krug*, 13.

80 Because the Russian government had done away entirely with the Uniate church, former Uniates only had the option to become Catholics. See Theodore R. Weeks, *Nation and State in Late Imperial Russia: Nationalism and Russification on the Western Frontier, 1863–1914* (DeKalb, 1996), 175–76.

81 *PSZ*III, no. 26126 (17 April 1905), art. 1; Waldron, "Religious Toleration," 111–12; idem, "Religious Reform," 116–19. To the extent that 1905 witnessed the elaboration of a firmer distinction between Christian and non-Christian faiths, sectarians were at least on the "correct" side of this divide, and thus received something close to the status of a recognized non-Orthodox Christian faith (*inoslavnoe ispovedanie*) (Reisner, *Gosudarstvo*, 420).

82 Solov'ev, *Polnyi krug*, 11–14.

83 *PSZ*III, no. 26126 (17 April 1905), art. 3. Notably, this provision was included explicitly "as a supplement" to the two previous articles of the new law, which concerned non-Orthodox Christians.

84 Even so, baptized Maris in Viatica province seeking to return officially to paganism almost all had their petitions rejected (Gosudarstvennyi arkhiv Kirovskoi oblasti [GAKO], f. 582, op. 149, d. 136, and f. 582, op. 150, dd. 60, 73, 118).
85 The circular (no. 4628) is in RGIA, f. 821, op. 8, d. 795, ll. 102–3.
86 S. Bagin, *Opropagande Islama putem pechati* (Kazan, 1909), 9. The numerous copies of these petitions are in several files in NART, f. 2, op. 2, dd. 12720–24, 12732–33, and 12736.
87 "Svedeniia o chisle lits, otpavshikh za vremia s 17 aprelia 1905 g. po 1 ianvaria 1909 ot gospodstvuiushei very," RGIA, Pechatnye zapiski, folder 2349.
88 S. Bagin, "Ob otpadenii v magometanstvo kreshchenykh inorodtsev i o prichinakh etogo pechal'nago iavleniia," *Pravoslavnyi sobesednik* 1 (1910): 125–27. Even some of the villages that Bagin lists as having "new apostates" had in fact earlier been the scenes of apostasy.
89 I explore the development of this *Kräshen* ethnoreligious identity in "From 'Pagan' Muslims to 'Baptized' Communists."
90 Waldron, "Religious Toleration," 112; idem, "Religious Reform," 117–18.
91 Werth, "Subjects," 208–10.
92 Abby M. Schrader, "Containing the Spectacle of Punishment: The Russian Autocracy and the Abolition of the Knout, 1817–1845," *Slavic Review* 56 (Winter 1997): 613–44.
93 Usmanova, *Musul'manskaia fraktsiia*, 81–127; Waldron, "Religious Reform," 122–39.

42

RELIGION AND MODERNIZATION IN 19TH CENTURY GREECE

Nikos Kokosalakis

Source: *Social Compass*, 34(2–3) (1987), 223–41.

1. Introduction

The purpose of this paper is to explore the background of the relation of religion and modernity in Greece from a historical and cultural perspective. As in most parts of the world so in Greece modernity has had a serious impact both on the church as an institution and on religious culture at large. Secularization[1] as defined by Wilson (1982: 149) has been a dominant process in Greek society and culture since independence and even before. Compared with other European countries, however, Greece is less secularized and the decline of religion as well as the advancement of modernity present certains idiosyncratic patterns. This, of course, is not surprising since neither the Reformation nor the Enlightenment, which are generally regarded as the springboards of modernity, affected Greece directly as indigenous cultural movements. But there are many other historical, cultural and social-structural reasons which account for the cultural specificity of modern Greece.

Up to now, in most western societies at any rate, the process of industrialization and social differentiation and the advancement of science and technology has gone hand in hand with the separation of church and state and the decline of the influence of religion in political life at large. On the cultural plane too the whole process has been parallel to the evolution and growth of individualism on the one hand and cultural pluralism on the other. In other words, modernization, industrialization, secularization, individualism, cultural pluralism and the separation of religion and politics have been progressive, parallel and inextricably linked developments in western societies. There have been, of course, variations within these developments which Chadwick (1975) and Martin (1978) have clearly described. But, as their analysis shows, the mainstream culture and social structure in the west as a whole has been moving along the same path of social change. Namely the path of modernity.

Now, it is my argument in this paper that for various special, historical and cultural reasons this has not been the case in Greece. Let me state some of these reasons here before I go on to elucidate them in the general discussion. Greece, unlike most western societies presents a cultural idiosyncrasy and homogeneity which are the result of the close, some would say inseparable, connection between Hellenism and Greek Orthodoxy over two millennia. As a consequence, Orthodoxy in Greece, like Judaism in Israel and Roman Catholicism in Poland, has been both an essential part of the mainstream culture and a central bearer of ethnic identity. Indeed, before the Greek Revolution in the 1820s Greek identity was largely defined in terms of the Orthodox religion. Moreover, Greek identity was also defined in opposition to Western Christianity whether Catholic or Protestant, on the one hand, and to Islam on the other. It is important for our discussion to draw attention to the fact that the Greek Orthodox East and the Latin West were locked in theological and political conflict throughout the middle ages and even before. But suspicion and even hostility towards western ideas, whether religious or secular, increased during the Ottoman occupation when the Church was the sole institution managing the social, cultural and political affairs of the enslaved Orthodox Christians. Yet, Greek culture, because of its classical Hellenic roots, is essentially compatible with and even a precursor of the rationalism of modern western culture. Similarly there is nothing anti-rational or anti-scientific in the essence of Orthodox Theology and the Orthodox ethos itself. However, it is important to emphasize that Orthodox religious culture is essentially different from both Protestantism and Roman Catholicism.

On the political plane, because of its cultural and historical role, Greek Orthodoxy has been, implicity or explicity, one of the central ideological pillars of the modern Greek nation state. This is most obvious in the area of Church, state relations, which are unique in Europe and perhaps in the world. The Orthodox Church, which nominally represents about 97% of the population in the country, is not just the established church but has been since 1833 virtually a department of the state. As a consequence of the constitutional position of Orthodoxy as the official religion of the country the Orthodox Church has lost its essential institutional autonomy to the state. The hierarchy, however, seems prepared to pay this price as long as it enjoys constitutional and legal protection to maintain its religious hegemony over Greek society. This explains the hostile attitude of the clergy especially towards the various sects and Jehovahs' Witnesses in particular.

Other crucial factors unique to the political history of modern Greece have contributed to maintain the close nexus of Orthodox religion and Greek society. The political fortunes of modern Greece have, to a significant degree, been determined by foreign intervention and by international political forces and interests. As a result religion and the Church have always been closely involved with the power-political struggles of the country whether internal or external. Religion in Greece has been an important and potent medium of social and ideological control and has been used as such by the state. It is because of this that popular religiosity and even magical and superstitious practices can and do easily acquire political significance.

All these and other factors I shall thus try to explore in the discussion that follows. Combined, these factors may account for the specificity of religious culture in Greece and the ambiguous role of that culture in the process of the modernization of the country over the last 150 years. In her search for an identity in the modern world Greece experienced and continues to experience severe tensions which arise from her long and rich cultural history and from her struggle to emerge as a modern independent nation. In these tensions and struggles religion has featured very prominently as a cultural historical force. As such it has played a full role in the symbolization and mediation of power and has been in turn severly politicized while at the same time trying to transcend the formal rationalist procedures of modernity. According to the general criteria of modernity Greece is now a modern society. Yet, Greece is not and does not seem to want to become a western society, but is ambiguously placed between east and west. Greek Orthodox Christianity expresses that ambiguity par excellence.

Perhaps, it is worth pointing out at this juncture that this cultural specificity cannot be accounted for either by Marxist or by functionalist sociological theories. Marxist theories, ultimately attempt to reduce all cultural specificities to economic structures and transformations of classes. Functionalists on the other hand wish to account for all cultural configurations in terms of social differentiation and the social evolutionary pattern of the west which, according to Parsons (1966), all modern societies will undergo eventually. Neither of these theoretical schemes can explain the cultural specificity of Greece. The tensions which religious culture and Greek ethnic identity have been experiencing over the last hundred and fifty years can be better understood, I suggest, in historical terms and in the context of the dialectic between culture and society in the era of nationalism and the modern nation state.

2. The cultural specificity of Greek Orthodoxy

One of the crucial historical reasons which may account for the cultural idiosyncracy of modern Greece amongst the rest of European societies is the fact that the Reformation had no cultural or political impact on occupied Byzantium. The famous patriarch Kyrillos Loukaris (1572–1638) had many contacts with various Protestant churches but his whole aim was to defend Orthodoxy from Roman Catholic infiltration and also to promote Greek education. The polarities between Roman Catholicism and Protestantism and the concommitant cultural and political conflicts, which were at the heart of the Reformation in most European territories, were on the whole absent from the Greek Orthodox World.

For historical reasons to be discussed later, the fusion of popular and official religion and their relation to politics was strengthened, which is exactly the opposite of what happened in the West after the Reformation. The immediate purpose and function of the Reformation was to eradicate the mediate religious symbolism and practice at both the popular and official ecclesiastical level. Keith Thomas (1971) has shown how the Reformation affected mystification and magic in English society during the 16th and 17th centuries. The process of eradication of traditional religious symbolism and magico-religious practices, as D. Starkey (1977) has argued, was not just assisted but initiated by Henry the VIII who introduced his own politico-religious symbolism. As Geertz (1977) has shown, the same was the case later with Elizabeth the I. The Tudors imposed their own religico-political rituals not just because they saw in popular religion obscurantism and superstition but because that religion was the vehicle of Papal political power. The Reformation, of course, introduced the rationalist principle into the realm of religious faith and practice. Even in Catholic territories this rationalist principle pertained to religious culture because of political and economic processes. As Weber so well documented, rationalization in the realm of religious culture has been at the same time the central principle of economic development and political culture in the west.

That specific Protestant, western rationalism, however, was foreign to Eastern Orthodoxy. The crucial point is that there was no Reformation in the Orthodox Church. To the extent that western rationalism was introduced into the Orthodox faith and practice it came, as we shall see, later at the end of 18th century but only marginally. The church on the whole was against western rationalism. Yet the point I shall be trying to make in this essay is that it was not the church's attitude or the cultural nature of Orthodoxy by themselves which affected the process of modernization in Greece. It was rather the specific combination of the Orthodox cultural tradition with the political ethnic and national aspirations of the newly-born state which determined the evolution of cultural patterns in Greek society. The state, especially in the beginning, attempted to function on imported western-style institutions but it was in its own interest to maintain the traditional fusions between official and popular religion. Religion functioned as a factor of social control which cut across conflicting interests and substantive socio-economic cleavages. But more importantly religion was the central ideological factor underpinning the national aspirations of all sectors of Greek society. After all the gradual liberation of modern Greece from Ottoman rule took almost a hunderd years. Thus in a peasant agricultural society, which was largely governed by foreign interest and a foreign imported King, the passionate ideas of the famous scholar A. Korais that Greece should be based on Greek classical values and the political ideas of the Enlightenment had little appeal for the political elite of the country and little chance of realization. Instead, the Church became subordinated to the State and Byzantine culture continued to play an important role in Greek politics.

Apart from these historical reasons, which will be discussed later, the cultural specificity of Greek Orthodoxy is implicit in the character of Orthodox religiosity itself and in the process of interaction between the institution and the public. One of the remarkable features of the Orthodox Church throughout its long history has been its capacity to absorb into its own structures popular religious culture and even the magic and superstition of peasant communities. In a subtle and flexible way Canonical procedures themselves have always depended on popular faith. Even when established doctrine and Canon law conflicted with certain aspects of such faith and practice the principle of *economy* (Oikonomia) (Fouyias 1983: 207–310) has always been used. This is an ancient practice in the Eastern Orthodox Church which in fact meant that the institution had to compromise in order to accommodate transgressions against established doctrine and practice on certain occasions. The Apostolic Canon 46, for example, states that if a bishop or priest accepts the baptisms of heretics he should be unfrocked. But later in the 4th Century the Second Oecumenical Council and subsequent Councils accepted the baptism of heretics as valid on the principle of *Oikonomia.* This flexible principle has been very important for the incorporation of popular faith and practice into the institution and the avoidance of rigid legalism by the church. Greek Orthodoxy in this respect differs significantly from Roman Catholicism where doctrine and Canon Law has always functioned in a certain strict legalistic manner. Even the "diffused religion" of contemporary Italy which Cipriani (1983: 80) so well describes "draws its origins solely (or almost) from ecclesiastical doctrine".

In Greek orthodox religiosity by contrast there is a tenuous relationship between the individual and the Church as an institution. The reciprocal relationship between the individual and the institution takes place in the context of a framework of rules and principles but it is up to the individual to follow them. Ethical transgressions especially are the responsibility of the individual and it is only in exceptional cases that a person will be denied participation in the sacramental life because of them. Participation in worship itself is not obligatory and Church attendance as such is not considered as an index of religious committment. J. Campbell (1976: 321) has astutely observed how the highly religious *Sarakatsani* shepherds of a Greek mountain community paid lipservice to organized worship and had little or no knowlegde of formal ecclesiastical doctrine. The latter is generally true for the large majority of the Greek population.

The Church in general is not primarily concerned to impose rules of religious conduct and belief but to accommodate and guide the perceptions and the religious and psychological needs of the people in the context of the human condition. The informal unity of the Orthodox Church largely depends on its tolerant attitude to grass roots faith and practice. Orthodox theology itself and the Orthodox traditions generally have greatly contributed to this unity by allowing quite a lot of religio-ethical space and hence freedom and responsibility to the individual and collective religious consciousness. The notion of holiness itself is popularly emergent rather than institutionally derived. Note, for example, the process by which Saints are declared. The Synod of the Oecumenical Patriarchate may recognise and declare a saint as such only after a particular community and the wider society has, for a long time, sometimes for more than a hunderd years, revered a particular person as holy. A relatively recent case in Greece is that of St. Nectarios, a Bishop on the island of Aighina who died in 1920. His reputation as a holy man was widespread while still alive. However, gradually after his death his veneration as a saint grew nationally and increasingly the attribute of thaumatourgos (miracle-working) has been attributed to him. After his indubitable recognition as a saint by the public at large the synod of the Oecumenical Patriarchate declared him such in 1961. Now he is one of the most, if not the most highly venerated saints in the country.

These specific cultural features of Orthodoxy, which I have just outlined, indicate that it can be accommodated and even manipulated within specific ethnic and political orientations but as a cultural idiom per se it is neither anti-modern nor is it incompatible with modernity. One indication of this is that no conflicts between religion and science arose in the Orthodox Church as they did in the west. Also, other conflicts which have to do with specific ethical issues such as contraception, abortion, homosexuality etc., are usually fought or resolved primarily at the level of individual consciousness, with the church structures and teaching acting as a guide. It would be wrong therefore to consider Orthodoxy and modernity as opposed cultural principles. Besides the cultural character of religion can hardly be analyzed outside the general socio-cultural, economic, historical and political context in which it belongs.

3. The ethnic character of Greek Orthodoxy

A marriage between the Greek classical and Hellenistic culture on the one hand and Christianity on the other is believed to have taken place in Greek society during the first two centuries. Some scholars locate that union in the New Testament itself, most of which was written in Greek[2], and in St. Paul's Hellenistic education in particular. They point to the historical fact that the churches of Asia Minor and of today's mainland Greece were established by St. Paul and other Apostles. This union between Christianity and Hellenism was strengthened, indeed, consolidated in 330 when the Emperor Constantine transferred the capital of the Empire from Rome to

Constantinople. Christianity then became not only *religio licita* but also the offical religion of the state. In a theological, philosophical and cultural context the connections between Hellenism and Christianity were formally worked out, particularly by the Cappadocian fathers[3] during the fourth century. The significance of these connections has been discussed ever since by theologians, historians and even social scientists. Parsons (1979), for example, sees this union of Christianity with the Greek intellectual spirit during the fourth century as basic to the evolution of religious and economic symbolism in modern society at large.

For the evolution of the Byzantine and modern Greek culture, of course, the importance of these connections is recognized by all Greeks, although there are varying, and sometimes diametrically opposed interpretations of their value for modern Greek identity and society. Many Greeks, especially clergymen and some academics and politicians have cause to believe and argue that the marriage beetween Hellenism and Greek Orthodoxy is indisoluble and that it constitutes the very basis of both Greek ethnic identity and the unity of the Greek nation. Others, some intellectuals in particular and politicians of the left, maintain that it is only a historical relic but it has been used as a tool of political convenience and has served as an obstacle to the modernization of Greek society. But be that as it may, the fact remains that religion has had and continues to have real consequences for Greek society, especially at the juncture of culture and politics. It is certainly true that Greek Orthodoxy has been one of the main cultural factors at play in the tensions experienced over the shaping of the ethnic identity of modern Greeks.

Historical events within the unfolding of Greek history have sometimes strengthened the Hellenic and sometimes the Christian dimension of Greek culture but have never separated them completely. Rather external forces have contributed to strengthen and consolidate the fusion between the religious and the ethnic factor. Because of the conflicts between the Eastern and Western church, which was also a conflict about political power, after the schism in 1054 the Greeks of Byzantium started calling themselves Hellenes. Thus the 11th century in Byzantium not only represents an emphasis on Hellenic identity as a defense mechanism of a weak and vulnerable empire threatened on all its frontiers, but also a historical landmark for the consolidation of the cultural and political distance and mistrust between the Greek Orthodox East and the Latin Catholic West. The mistrust gradually became a cultural gulf due to subsequent historical events like: the Crusades; the imperialist tendencies of the church of Rome and the supremacy of the papal authority (Stefanides 1959: 370–396); the Venetian occupation of much of today's Greece; the Uniate efforts to proselytize Orthodox members during the Ottoman occupation etc. Since the establishment of the Greek state in the 1820s the cultural distance and mistrust of the West has continued to the present day because of the constant intervention in Greek affairs by one or another western power.

These historical events had a hardening impact at both the official theological and the popular cultural level and contributed to sharpening the boundaries of ethnic identity. Historically then the fusion of religion and ethnicity was strengthened and consolidated in order to serve as a shield against external threatening forces but also in order to carry forward the survival of the nation (to genos). Svoronos (1975: 22), one of the sounder contemporary Greek historians, remarks that the idea of Orthodoxy, which was always the dominant Byzantine ideology, became, after the Ottoman conquest, inseparably linked to the idea of the nation (to genos). During the four centuries of the Ottoman rule the church was the institutional vehicle which carried the ethno-religious identity of the Greeks and became a cultural symbol and a bridge between Byzantium and modern Greece.

But the civil role of the Church was not less important and must be understood in a historical context. It is well known, (Watt, 1968: 49) that it was Islamic policy, going back to the time of the Prophet Muhammad, to allow the indigenous conquered populations practice of their religion and the ownership and cultivation of their lands in return for fiscal obligations and allegiance to the Islamic political authority as prescribed by Islamic law. The civil authority of the Orthodox church was derived mainly from the fact that it formed a mediating organization between the Sultans and the Orthodox subjects. The Sultans recognized the Oecumenical Patriarch as the chief *(millet-bashi)* of the Orthodox *millet*[4] who were free to practice their religion but in return the patriarch guaranteed their obedience to the Sultan and the collection of taxes (Clogg 1979: 18–19). These privileges and obligations of the Patriarch were legally established and promulgated by special documents called *Berat* and *Firman* (Papadopoulos 1968: 201–229). So the Patriarch, the bishops and the lower clergy, apart from their spiritual authority, also exercised a civil authority not only for the Greeks but for all the other Orthodox ethnic groups. Apart from this civil function the church was also exercising full juridicial authority concerning matters of marriage, divorce, dowry, property, inheritance and so on. The church also carried responsibility for education, the transmission of the Greek language, and also welfare.

Economically too the church became strong during the Ottoman rule. Because church property was not confiscated, and also for devotional reasons, many people transmitted their lands to the church and the monasteries. Such land, some of which is still owned by the church, became subsequently a bone of contention between church and state and continues to be so to the present day. Most church lands, however, were gradually passed on to the state and to the landless peasantry since independence.

So the combination of religious, ethnic and civil functions in the hands of the church and the daily interaction of the clergy with the people at all social levels generated an ethos of reverence towards ecclesiastical office which became deeply rooted in the masses of enslaved Christians. The prestige of the church was also enhanced by the fact that up to the 18th century she was, according to Svoronos (1975: 57), liberal, humanistic and often revolutionary. On the other hand, the concentration of civil, religious and political functions in the hands of the higher clergy, and their ambition for promotion to higher office meant that the more unscrupulous of them got involved in corrupt dealings with the High Porte. They became part of the ruling elite and were on the whole highly conservative and inimical to new western ideas. To many educated Greeks of that time, especially those who were influenced by the Enlightenment, this was distasteful and turned them against the church hierarchy and even against the Byzantine tradition itself. R. Clogg (1976: 257–276), in fact argues that there was widespread anti-clericalism in pre-independence Greece. He also produces some evidence to show that anti-clericalism was not confined to the intelligentsia but also characteristic, to a considerable extent, of the mass of the Greek people. His evidence for this, however, is insufficient. In any case, one must distinguish the possible attitudes of the peasantry and the small urban sector towards some members of the higher clergy from their undoubted and deep respect for the Orthodox Church. Be that as it may, it is true as Dimaras (1969) shows that the ideas of the Enlightenment had wide appeal amongst Greek intellectuals in the second half of the 18th century. The anti-clericalism of such intellectuals, however, must be distinguished from the anti-clericalism of western intellectuals especially in France at that time. Such intellectuals were not irreligious. Neither were they against the ethnic character of the Orthodox church but were fighting the cultural obscurantism of the higher clergy and their attachment to the status quo.

The fundamental preoccupation of the Greek church and of Greek thought throughout the period of occupation, as Svoronos points out (1975: 22) was the protection of orthodoxy from the threat of Islam as well as from western propaganda. The defense mechanisms of ethnic identity and the national idea strengthened even further the already strong fusion between popular culture, official religion and the political fortunes of modern Greece. From the 15th to the 19th centuries the Church was the sole cultural and political agent of the nation. The church was also actively involved in the ethnic resistance, during the 16th and 17th centuries in particular, at the cost of high sacrifice and martyrdom of high and low clergy. Despite the corrupt dealings of many high clergymen with the Ottoman authorities, the prestige of the church was enhanced in the popular mind because of her central role in the war of independence. More than 6000 priests and a large number of bishops were killed during the revolution and the Patriarch Gregorios V was martyred in 1821 (Frazee 1969: 101, Woodhouse 1952). Although the role of the church during the Greek uprising has been at times exaggerated the fact remains that the church's contribution was outstanding. This was not because the church was or is a revolutionary church but because she was and continues to be a church tied to the ethnic identity of the Greeks.

It is precisely because of its ethnic character and its subsequent close attachment and subordination to the Greek state that her role, in the process of modernization of Greece during the last 150 years, has been ambiguous. The church as an institution has been used by conservative, reformist fascist and socialist regimes alike in order to promote the nationalist Greek ideal as each of these regimes interpreted it. Let me mention two or three of the latest examples. The dictatorial regime of the colonels, who usurped power in 1967, used the church in order to promote their version of "Greek-Christian civilization". Karamanlis, the conservative but democratic politician, was known to be in favour of the separation of the church from the state during the late 1970s. However in his message in the fourth clergy-laity conference of the Greek Orthodox Archdiocese of Australia held at Sydney 25–28th January 1981 he stated "The nation (to ethnos) and Orthodoxy . . . have become in the Greek consciousness virtually synonymous concepts which together constitute one Helleno-Christian civilization"[5]. He sent the same message a year later as President of Greece to the twenty-sixth clergy-laity conference of the Orthodox church in America in 1982. "Orthodoxy by enriching the shining cultural tradition of classical antiquity constituted with it the strong spiritual and ethical foundation of Hellenism; the substance which holds it together; its giver of light; and also its strength . . . For this reason the concepts of Hellenism and Orthodoxy have been interwoven inseparably in the consciousness of the nation". The socialist party PA.SO.K. in its electoral manifesto before the 1981 election proposed the "administrative separation[6] of church and state" but at the same time it stated that "the bonds of the church with the nation (to ethnos) must be preseved". However while in power PA.SO.K. did not introduce any change in the status quo and has more harmonious and even tighter relations with the church than previous right wing governments. Indeed Prime Minister Papandreou went so far as to declare the Virgin Mary patron of the armed forces in August 1982.[7]

The ethnic character of Greek Orthodoxy is also clearly reflected in various aspects of social and cultural life and in civil and religious rituals. The Greek constitution itself states that the official religion of the country is the Eastern Orthodox. All Greek constitutions (except that of 1927) — and there have been many revisions of the constitution — open with the invocation: "in the name of the Holy Homoousios and Undivided Trinity". Significantly on the draft for the constitution of 1975 the invocation of the Holy Trinity was ommitted and replaced by the statement "form of the policy and individual and civil rights". A church history Professor of Athens University (Feidas 1976) has seen in this plan: a serious attempt to secularize the constitution; a decisive step towards the separation of church and state; and an emphasis on the rights of the individual at the expense of the cultural unity of Greece. However the reactions from ecclesistical and other circles against these constitutional changes were so strong that none of them was implemented. The ethnic character of Greek Orthodoxy then, and its specific relation to the Greek state may account in large measure for the ambiguous relationship of religion and modernity in Greece which we shall explore a little further below.

4. The church and the ideas of the Enlightenment

The civil and administrative authority, as well as the ecclesiastical jurisdiction of the Oecumenical Patriarchate, ceased to apply in Greece soon after her independence. As mentioned earlier, already before independence the ideas of the Enlightenment were widespread amongst Greek intellectuals (some of them clergy), who questioned the cultural hegemony of the Patriarchate. For many of them in fact Byzantium had meant a period of obscurantism, superstition, barbarity and corruption the very antithesis of the values of the Enlightenment.

A secular, Hellenic, rationalist and nationalist spirit had been cultivated and promoted by some eminent Greeks for some time, especially in the diaspora. Adamandios Korias, the son of a merchant from Smyrna who settled in Paris, is generally acknowledged as the most important protagonist of that spirit (Dimaras 1953). He visualized the rebirth of Greece and her identity in the modern world not on the basis of Byzantine religious culture but in the context of a secular political society guided by the old Hellenic spirit and rational, humanistic and philosophical values. He did not, however, advocate a return to antiquity either in language or in literature but a rational application of the spirit of classical Greece in a modern social and political context. Yet he was not a secularist but tried to steer a course between what he termed the Scylla of superstition and the Charybdis of atheism (Clogg 1979: 40). He was above all a liberal and a reformist and thus a strong advocate of modernity.

Secular tendencies amongst intellectual circles were strong if we judge from the large number of publications of a secular character which appeared in Greek during the first two decades of 19th century.[8] There were also many translations of the French Encyclopaedists, and of other western philosophers and scientists. Some sections of the small Greek middle class turned to the Greek classics and even baptised their children by giving them not the names of Orthodox saints as was generally the practice but names of ancient Greek deities, philosophers, writers and politicians. These tendencies, which emphasised the secular and rational strand of Greek culture, were congruent with the secular spirit of the time and the subsequent secularization and modernization of European societies. They were also congruent with the ideas of the European philhellines, such as Lord Byron for instancce, and the general revival of neoclassisism which was then sweeping Europe in the realm of intellectual ideas and in architecture. As Jenkyns (1980) has convincingly argued Victorian culture was saturated with the spirit of ancient Greece.

Yet, the point which must be made most emphatically is that both the Enlightenment and the revival of classical ideas were not endogenous to the Greek society of that time. Although the classical Greek civilization has always been latent in Greek culture, the modernizing ideas of the Enlightenment were imported into Greece and touched the general Greek population only marginally, if at all.

The church on the whole took a negative and in some cases reactionary stance towards these ideas and also towards the revival of classicism. Clogg (1975: 267) quotes from an encyclical issued by the Synod of the Oecumenical Patriarchate in 1819 which shows this. Young men, according to the encyclical, would derive little benefit from "algebra and cubes and cube roots, and triangles and triangulated tetragons, and logarithms and symbolic logic, and eliptical projections, and atoms and vacuums, and whirlpools, and power and attraction and gravity . . . and myriad of such kind and other monstrous things . . . if, as a consequence, in speech they are barbarians, if they are ungrammatical in their writings, ignorant in the things of religion, degenerate and frenzied in morals, injurious to the state, obscure patriots and unworthy of their ancestral calling . . . ?" The church then was not sympathetic to the ideas of the Enlightenment and in some cases was conservative to the point of obscurantism and reaction. This is shown by the clash of the synod of the patriarchate with modernists such as Methodios Anthrakitis, whom she condemned twice, Eugenios Voulgaris and Adamantios Korais amongst others, who were not atheists.

Yet, the stance of the church must be placed in the general context of the conflicting ideological and cultural trends which have been characteristic of modern Greek history to the present day. The cultural and theological position of the church was then, and to a certain extent still remains, that Orthodoxy constitutes the basis of Greek ethnic identity as well as the true and unchanged continuation of the apostolic Christian faith. The ideas of the Enlightenment, especially in their atheistic form, were clearly incompatible with this position. Moreover, because of the historical relations between Eastern and Western church, western ideas in general were viewed with suspicion by the Orthodox hierarchy. Orthodoxy as such, however, as we have seen is not incompatible with the scientific ethos of modernity and classical antiquity and, according to the Greek fathers, was viewed as complementary to the Christian faith.

But there were other more substantive sociological reasons which explain why the progressive ideas of the Enlightenment were not accommodated in Greek society and culture at the time. Economically, politically and culturally Greek society, before and after the Revolution (1821), was unable to adopt rational, modernizing ideas and programmes. Such ideas were clearly romantic and utopian in the face of Greek social reality as philhellines such as Byron and others discovered. The mass of Greek people were illiterate and landless peasants who were steeped in the Byzantine tradition and the superstitions of a rural society.

Over 60% of the population was rural and 80% of the rural families had no property at all. The rest owned small holdings of between 1/2 and 1 acre in the mountainous areas and the richer ones between 5 and 20 acres in the fertile planes (Svoronos 1975: 79). Both in the time of Kapodistria (1827–1831) and King Otto (1833–1862), land distribution and reform remained the crucial problem. Up to 1856 out of 721,000 acres of national lands only 28,000 acres were distributed to the peasantry and even those went to the stronger ones (Svoronos, ibid).

The lower clergy too were propertyless and without education. Frazee (1969: 101) reports that according to estimates only one percent of the priests knew how to write their names. The general population was equally uneducated although there was a small middle class who were aspiring to give their offspring a good education and there was a substantive intellectual sector who lived in the diaspora. Besides, socio-cultural developments in Greece throughout the 19th century were crucially influenced by a multiplicity of conflicting interests and ideological currents both internal and foreign. Certainly what determined modernization and social change in Greece were not the ideas and ideals of the Enlightenment and classical Greek civilization but harsh and conflicting political, ideological and economic realities and interests. After the assasination of Kapodistria, the first governor, Greece was governed by an imported monarchy[9], an imported administration and even an imported army. The "Protecting Powers" exercised such an influence on the newly born Greek state that the first political parties were appropriately named the "English party", the "French party", and the "Russian party". Supporters of these parties represented nascent class structural features of Greek society but above all the parties represented corresponding foreign influences and interests.

5. The church and the Bavarian administration

After the Revolution the ethnic character of the church was enhanced. It became in fact a national church closely tied to the state. In the history of the transformation of religion and politics and church and state relations in the 19th century the Greek case is, perhaps, unique. Psomas (1978: 57) aptly remarks that "The usually thorny problem of determining the relations between the state and the church was settled by Maurer almost uneventfully, despite his rendering the church completely subservient to the state". Soon after the arrival of the young Bavarian King Otto the regent Maurer appointed a seven member commission[10] to prepare a report aiming towards a constitutional charter for the church of Greece. His main objectives were: to declare the church independent of the Oecumenical Patriarchate and to subject her to the monarchy according to the Bavarian prototype where the King was also the "supreme Bishop" (Frazee: 106). He also proclaimed that the church should be modernized and the educational standards of the clergy should be improved. The first constitution of the church (July 1833)[11] which was based on the report (ecthesis) of the commission adumbrated these objectives.

The church was declared autocephalous, that is independent from, but in communion with, the Patriarchate of Constantinople. This declaration, however, was without the consent of the Patriarchate. A number of Greek theologians and church historians have argued that the declaration was against the Canon law of the Orthodox church and against established ecclesiastical practice (Konidaris 1971: 35). Other Orthodox churches had declared themselves autocephalous in the past but always with the consent of the Patriarchate. This was for instance the case with the church of Russia. The Patriarchate, however, did not declare the church of Greece schismatic as it did later in 1871 with the church of Bulgaria. Again in both cases ethnic reasons account for these facts.

According to the constitution the autocephalous church of Greece recognized "no other head except Jesus Christ" but was to be administered by the Holy synod which was under the authority of the King. A layman was to serve in the five member Synod as the King's representative (Vassilikos Epitropos) who carried in fact significant power as no act of the Synod was valid without the approval and signature of the King's administration. The church thus became absolutely subordinated to the state, an act which has influenced crucially not just church and state relations to the present day but also the church's attitude to modernization and social reform.

Despite its declared intention to modernize the church and to improve the educational standards of the clergy the Bavarian administration adopted in fact antiquated and even reactionary policies towards the church. In church administration as in education and social organization as a whole the regency council adopted a highly centralized system according to French and Bavarian prototypes. Maurer's first policy of modernization and rationalization of church organization and resources involved a devastating attack on the monasteries and their properties. In the process of modernization parallel attacks on monastic institutions and their properties had taken place in various parts of Europe since the Reformation but in the Greek case they were totally inappropriate and culturally out of place. Out of 593 monasteries, of the small Greek dominion at the time, 412 were closed and their properties confiscated and passed to the Crown. There were over 2,000 monks then in Greece who, by Royal decree, had to be accommodated in 148 monasteries. The much smaller number of nuns had to be accommodated in three monasteries and there was a fourth temporary one for excess numbers (Government Gazette 15/1834 p.123).

Opposition to these measures was widespread. Many clergy and monks were exiled but the church was impotent to act because the synod was totally ruled by the throne. The synod in fact issued an encyclical to all the clergy and lay people in order to passify their feelings which were running high. The encyclical suggested that "the policies on the monasteries are acts of salvation loved by God, they intend your benefit and the enlightenment of your children, the amelioration of the clergy and the true shining of the church. Nothing was enacted against religion and nothing will ever be done to harm it. That is and will always be the will of our Christ-loving king, which he expressed as soon as he set foot in his new country". (Strangas, vol.I, 1969: 81).

Nothing, however was done to educate the illiterate lower ranks of the clergy nor were the proceeds from the confiscated properties[12] in any way used to modernize the church. Instead an influx of missionaries and biblical societies from the west were allowed to operate freely in the country. The work of the missionaries and the biblical societies were seen by the people, the clergy, and by the synod itself as an attempt to protestantize the country. In a written formal protest to the administration the synod pointed out that the literature distributed by the biblical societies, far from educating the people, were against the intercession of the saints, the icons and even the doctrines of the Orthodox church (Strangas, vol.I, 1969: 93). The administration, however, ignored the appeal by the Synod. In some parts of the country there were explicit and even violent protests. In the island of Syros for instance the inhabitants attacked and attempted to burn the school of Hildner demanding the deportation of foreign missionaries. It was only with the intervention of the army and a warship that the violent protests were contained (K. Oikonomos 1857: 344).

The regime had no understanding of the indigenous religious culture. As they attempted to adapt western legal and cultural norms to Greek society as a whole their original aims of westernization and modernization of the country were compromised and failed (Legg, 1969: 54). The influence of external forces throughout the period of Otto was in fact such that, according to Svoronos (1975: 79), one gets the impression that the Greeks were completely absent from the formal political procedures.

The antagonisms of the protecting powers amongst themselves over Greece, and the policies of the Bavarian administration contributed to produce a revival of the Orthodox ethos at both a formal theological and a popular level. The former was expressed in the formation of the Philorthodox society, in the writings of K. Olkonomos who was earlier a strong advocate of the Enlightenment and in the condemnation of the unorthodox teachings of Theophilos Kairis. The latter was expressed in the revival of old traditions and messianisms as portrayed in the editions of the oracles of Agathangelos and the deep popular religiosity of Makriyannis (P. Kitromilides 1984: 31). Makriyannis, himself, who initially was friendly with the King, who in fact, acted as godfather to one of his sons[13], was now in conflict with him over the injustices, discrimination and clientilistic politics of his administration. (Makriyannis 1966: 150, 154).

The Bavarian administration then with its complete subjugation of the church to the state and by its indifference to the proseyletizing activities of the bible societies contributed to the revival of the old hostility against western ideas and to sharpening the boundaries between Greek orthodox and western culture.

6. The fusion of national aspirations and religious culture

By 1840 it was obvious that Greece was unlikely to develop along the cultural patterns of modernization prevalent in western Europe. Industrialization was virtually absent and the whole structure of the econmy was clearly pre-capitalist. The whole political edifice too was functioning not on the basis of political parties with specific political objectives and policies but in the context of personalized clientilistic politics which expressed the web of powerful family relations and interests. Political parties, as mentioned earlier, did exist but on the whole they reflected the interests of the antagonisms of foreign powers and functioned outside any constitutional framework (Petropoulos 1968). Both Kapodistria and the King's administration intended to modernize the country along the European prototype but the regency especially proved entirely inept as they attempted to impose changes from above without changing the social infrastructure. Otto's administration was on the whole very conservative and oligarchic. It was only after severe pressure from the grass roots and the intervention of the army on September 3rd 1843 that he was forced to concede a constitution. As the King was Catholic and without an heir one of the significant provisions of the constitution was that the successor to the throne must be Orthodox. The second article of the constitution also promulgated that the church of Greece should be administered on the basis of the holy canons of the Orthodox church and according to the holy Orthodox traditions.

Apart from the fact then that the whole socio-economic and political structure of the country was not conducive to western style modernization the ideological and cultural currents also pointed to a totally different direction. The aspirations of Korais, therefore, that Greece should be established and flourish in the context of modern European cultural values seemed by the mid-nineteenth century unrealizable. Instead, a romantic Greek nationalism was born which was largely underpinned by the religious culture of Byzantium which constituted a bridge between ancient and modern Hellenism. In 1844 John Kolettis, a politician favoured by the King, articulated the doctrine of "the Great Idea" (Megali Idea). Broadly speaking the basis of this doctrine consisted in a romantic vision of re-establishing modern Greece within its pre-Ottoman occupation boundaries. The King became very a ardent supporter of this vision and so did most Greek people. As Clogg (1979: 76) states: "Almost all Greeks subscribed to this vision, the only argument being as to how it might best be implemented". The successes, the failures, the disappointments and the tragedies in attempting to implement the "Great

Idea" will not concern us here. I only wish to emphasize that the vision revived the historical connections between Orthodoxy and Hellenism and constituted a fusion which became the basic cultural orientation of modern Greece.

A number of historical and cultural factors contributed to this. The 19th century, it is well known, was the period when modern nations struggled to consolidate their cultural and historical roots. For a new state like Greece it was imperative that the historical continuity of her cultural identity, going back to classical and ancient Greece, should not be doubted. Yet, the cultural historian, Falmerayer put forward theories to question precisely that. The reaction inside and outside Greece was very strong. Spyridon Zampelios (1852: 464) coined the term "hellenochristianikos" (Greek-Christian), in order to point to the unbroken continuity between ancient Greece, Byzantium and modern Greece. A little later, in the 1860s, K. Paparrigopoulos produced a full and detailed history of Greece from antiquity to his time in order to make explicit and protect the continuity of Greek civilization. At the same period N. Politis turned to the study of Greek contemporary popular culture and Greek folklore where he discovered ancient Greek and Christian elements intertwined in abundance. By these efforts Byzantium and the Orthodox church were fully reinstated as essential strands of modern Greek identity and culture. For the mass of the Greek people, of course, Orthodox religiosity had always been an essential part of their cultural identity.

In 1850 the Oecumenical Patriarchate officially recognized and declared the church of Greece independent by issuing a document called "Synodikos Tomos" (Synodical Volume). It was, however, the Greek government which formally requested from the Patriarchate, "on behalf of the Greek people and the church", to recognize the church of Greece as autocephalous. The recognition was greeted with great enthusiasm by political and ecclesiastical circles. It clearly added ideological strength to the national aspirations and the ethnic ideology of the Greek state. It also normalised church and state relations internally and the relations of both with the Patriarchate. The only formal protest against the recognition came from the Archimandrite Theoklitos Pharmakides who was the secretary of the Synod and an influential figure in the church during the Bavarian administration. The role of Pharmakides throughout that period seemed very ambiguous. On the one hand he appears an ardent nationalist and on the other an obedient servant of the Bavarians. One of the reasons which may explain his strong reaction against the "Synodikos Tomos" may be that he was one of the main architects of the unilateral declaration of the independence of the Church of Greece from Constantinople in 1833. There were however deeper ideological and political reasons behind his stance.

The normalization of relations between the Greek state, the church and the Patriarchate of Constantinople had a substantive effect on the economic progress and the modernization of Greece. The Patriarchate continued to exercise civil anthority for the Greeks of the Ottoman empire throughout the 19th century. This section of Greeks was well know for its economic entrepreneurial activities. As Svoronos (1975: 91) points out: "Constantinople and not Athens was the economic capital of Greece throughout the 19th century". The section of Greeks who were still under Ottoman rule was much larger than that of independent Greece.[14] The economic cooperation between the two sections after 1850 had an immediate and significant effect on the economy of the country. The Greeks of the Ottoman empire, sensing the various nationalist movements in the Balkans and the emerging nationalism of the young Turks, transferred substantive capital to Greece (Svoronos ibid: 100). Thus the foundations of industrial and banking activity were strengthened, and commercial activity was increased, which was followed by the emergence of an urban middle class. In parallel the state launched projects of modernization in communications, transport, the ports, the railways and other public works like the opening of the canal of Corinth (1882–1893) etc.

But apart from the economic sphere, the cooperation between the Greeks of the kingdom and those of the diaspora also strengthened Greek cultural unity. The University of Athens, established in 1837, became after 1850 a cultural center for the whole of Hellenism and for the intellectuals from Constantinople in particular. For ethnic rather than religious reasons the Faculty of Theology occupied a prominent and privileged position by promoting the ethno-religious identity of Greece. The cultural homogeneity of the country was further enriched and strengthened after 1864 when the Ionian islands with their rich religious and cultural heritage were ceded to Greece from Britain.

Thus both in the economic and cultural sphere the ethno-religious fusion had a significant and visible impact. In the political sphere also a more progressive, democratic and liberal politics came into being. This led to the fall of the oligarchic regime of King Otto, who was forced to leave the country in 1862, and the adoption of a liberal democratic constitution in 1864 under King George the I. At the same time it must be emphasized that this ethno-religious fusion was destined to play a very complex and at times very destructive, negative and reactionary role in internal Greek politics from that time on. The analysis and evaluation of that role lies outside the scope of this paper. The purpose of the paper rather was to show how the specific configuration of religious culture and Greek nationalism in the 19th century set the political and ideological parameters of the development of modern Greece. The extent to which this purpose has been achieved is, of course, for the reader to assess.

Notes

1 The secularization process according to Wilson applies both to social institutions and to consciousness and he defines it as "that process by which religious institutions, actions, and consciousness, lose their social significance".

2 Only St. Mathew's Gospel was written first in Aramaic but was translated into Greek by the time it was incorporated into the Canon of the New Testament.

3 Such was the impact of St. Basil, St. John Chrysostan and St. Gregory on the amalgamation of Hellenism and Christianity that both the Greek Church and the State adopted them as patrons of Greek letters and education. During the present century their influence as patrons of education has been strengthened. In Greece and throughout the Greek diaspora all educational institutions and churches hold the 30th of January as a special educational and religious holiday. The memory of "the *Three Hierarchs*" is honoured and celebrated with ceremonies and speeches as the symbol of the unity of Hellenic and Christian values.

4 The Ottomans had organised their subjects according to religious groups called millets (Clogg 1979: 19).

5 Newspaper *Orthodox Typos* 9th February, 1981, p.4.

6 PA.SO.K. Manifesto, *Contract with the People* Athens 1981, p.45.

7 Prime minister Papandreou, accompanied by members of his Cabinet, visited the popular shrine of the Virgin Mary in Veroia Northern Greece, known as "Panaghia Soumela" on the feast of the Dormition 15th August 1982. In the midst of about 100,000 people he knelt in front of the icon of the Virgin and then delivered a short sermon extolling her popularity and the connection of popular values with the popular socialist ideals of the Government. At the same time he declared the Virgin patron of the armed forces (he is also Minister of Defense). After the service, at a banquet given in his honour by the armed forces, the prime minister said "It is not strange that the Mother of God is identified with our armed forces. This relationship derives from the history of our people and our race and we cannot forget it without having to pay a serious price . . . Today it is at the same time the day of the armed forces. Indeed, I believe, that it was a good choice this day — the 15th of August — to be designated as the feast of the armed forces".

8 According to Clogg (1979: 36) 1300 Greek books were published during that period and some editions ran to several thousands.

9 After the assassination of the first president of Greece, T. Capodistria, the protecting powers Britain, Russia, France and Bavaria convened in May 1832 and offered the monarchy to Prince Frederic Otto of Wittelsbach, the seventeen year old son of King Ludwig of Bavaria. He was accompanied by a three-man regency council consisting of Count Joseph Von Armansberg, Professor Georg Maurer and General Karl Heidock. For details see R. Clogg (1979: 70).

10 Maurer personally selected the members of this commission which consisted of three clerics and four laymen. The clerics were: the refugee bishops of Elaias Paissios, and Ardameriou Ignatios, and the Rev. Theoklitos Pharmakides. The laymen, all well known men of letters, were: P. Notaras, K. Schinas, Skarlatos Byzantios and Spyridon Trikoupis who was appointed chairman of the Committee.

11 This constitution carried the title "Declaration of the Independence of the Greek Church" and was published in the Government Gazette no. 23, p.189–174.

12 Even sacred objects, used in worship, such as chalices, icons, vestments, etc., were sold on the street bazaars at ridiculous prices. Such acts were seen as blasphemous by large sectors of the public whose religious sensitivities were seriously wounded. (Newspaper *Athena* no. 434, p.1765,1837.

13 This was not correct according to Orthodox practice and is not accpeted by the Orthodox church even today. The church, however, was impotent to resist this practice which was widespread by 1835 for political clientilistic purposes. On October 23rd 1836 the synod issued an encyclical against this practice. The editor of a religious magazine «Priest Monk» (Ieromonachos) Germanos, who spoke against

it was exiled to the island of Skiathos by the administration. (Newspaper *Athena* No. 390–93, p.1592–1604, 1836.

14 In 1840 Athens had about 26,000 inhabitants whereas Constantinople had about 120,000 Greeks. In 1861 the total population of the Greek state was 1,100,000 whereas the Greek population still under Ottoman rule and of the British ruled Ionian islands was three times that (Statistical Year Book of Greece 1970, p.18).

Bibliography

CAMPBELL J. (1976) *Honour Family and Patronage: A study of institutions and moral values in a Greek mountain community*, Oxford, Oxford U.P.

CHADWICK O. (1975) *The Secularization of the European Mind in the 19th Century*, Cambridge, Cambridge U.P.

CIPRIANI R. (1983) "Religious Influence on Politics in Italy", *Acts of 17th International Conference on the Sociology of Religion*, London.

CLOGO R. (1976) "Anti-Clericalism in Pre-Independence Greece C. 1750–1821", in D. Baker (ed.) *The Orthodox Churches and the West*, Oxford, Basil Blackwell.

CLOGG R. (1979) *A Short History of Modern Greece*, Cambridge, Cambridge University Press.

DIMARAS C. T. (1953) *A. Korais and His Era*, Athens Basic Library, (in Greek).

DIMARAS C. T. (1969) *La Grece au temps des lumières.* Geneva.

FEIDAS V/ (1975) *Church and State Relations in Greece*, Athens (in Greek).

FRAZEE A. (1969) *The Orthodox Church and Independent Greece 1821–1852.* Cambridge, Cambridge University Press.

FOUYIAS M. (Archbishop) (1983) *Theological and Historical Studies* Vol. III Athens. (in Greek).

GEERTZ C. (1980) *The Victorians and Ancient Greece* Oxford, Blackwell.

KITROMILIDES P. (1984) "Ideological Currents and Political Demands: Aspects from 19th Century Greece" in D. Tsaousis (ed.) *Aspects of Greek Society in 19th Century* Athens, Estia (in Greek).

KONIDARIS G. (1971) *Landmarks of Ecclesistical Polity in Greece from Kapodistrias to the Present* Athens (in Greek).

LEGG K. (1969) *Politics in Modern Greece* Stanford, Stanford University Press.

MAIRIYANNIS J. (1966) *The memoirs of Genral Macriyannis* Ed. and translated by H. A. Lidderdale, London, Oxford University Press.

MARTIN D. (1978) *A General Theory of Secularization* Oxford, Blackwel.

OIKONOMOS K. (1857) *Ta Sozemana Vol II* (Athens) in Greek.

PARSONS T. (1966) *Societies: Evolutionary and Comparative Perspectives* Englewood Cliffs, Prentice Hall. (1979) "Religious and Economic Symbolism in the Western World" in H. M. Johnson (ed.) *Religious Change and Continuity*, Washington, Jossey Bus Publishing Company.

PAPADOPOULOS T. (1968) "Orthodox Church and Civil Authority" *Contemporary History* XV.

PETROPOULOS J. (1968) *Politics and Statecraft in the Kingdom of Greece 1833–1843* Princeton, Princeton University Press.

PSOMAS (1978) *The Nation the State and the International System: The Case of Modern Greece*, Athens.

STARKEY D. (1977) "Parallel or Divergence: Monarchical Symbolism during the Reformation and After" *Acts of the 14th International Conference on Sociology of Religion* Strasbourg.

STEFANIDES V. (1959) *Ecclesiastical History* Athens, Astir. (in Greek).

SVORONOS N. (1975) *Review of Modern Greek History* Athens, Thermelio (in Greek).

THOMAS K. (1971) *Religion and the Decline of Magic*, London, Allen Lane.

VEREMIS T. (1983) "State and Nation in Greece 1821–1912" in D. Tsaousis (ed.) *Hellenismos Hellenicotita* Athens, Estia.

WATT M. (1968) *Islamic Political Thought*, Edinburgh, Edinburgh University Press.

WILSON B. (1982) *Religion in Sociological Perspective*, Oxford, Oxford University Press.

WOODHOUSE C. M. (1982) *The Greek War of Independence: Its Historical Setting* London.

ZAMPELIOS S. (1857) *Asmata Dimotika tis Hellados* Athenis (in Greek).

Part 11

LOCAL AGENTS OF MISSION

43

INDIANS AND THE BREAKDOWN OF THE SPANISH MISSION SYSTEM IN CALIFORNIA

George Harwood Phillips

Source: *Ethnohistory*, 21(4) (1974), 291–304.

Writing in 1769, a Franciscan missionary asserted that the California Indians were "without religion, or government, [having] nothing more than diverse superstitions and a type of democracy similar to that of ants." Similarly, in 1851 an Anglo-American visitor to California claimed that "the extreme indolence of their nature, the squalid condition in which they live, the pusillanimity of their sports, and the general imbecility of their intellects, render them rather objects of contempt than admiration" (Forbes 1964:16).

Because statements such as these abound in the primary documentation, it is not difficult to understand why historians (often the prisoners of their source materials) have considered the Indians of California to be backward and inferior. Thus in 1930 Fr. Zephrin Engelhardt, the author of a dozen or so books on the California missions, could write that "all accounts agree in representing the natives of California as among the most stupid, brutish, filthy, lazy and improvident of all the aborigines of America" (1930b:245). In the 1953 edition of his textbook, *California*, John Caughey wote:

> The Californians lacked the military cunning and ferocity that inspired respect for the Indians of the Plains and Eastern Woodlands. They were not such expert craftsmen in woodworking as their neighbors on the Northwest Coast, nor had they so interesting an art form or so highly developed a social system. They were obviously inferior to the Pueblo Indians in the Southwest, who had developed multistoried buildings, agriculture and irrigation, excellent textiles and pottery, and a complex social organization.
>
> (1953:19)

And as recently as 1966 Florian F. Guest stated that California Indian existence was "haphazard, irresponsible, brutish, benighted, and barbaric" (1966:206–207).

When Indians are viewed as either stupid and brutish or just culturally inferior, their historical importance is not appreciated. Even those historians genuinely sympathetic to the Indians seldom consider them to be anything more than passive observers of their own demise, doing little to alter the conditions imposed by succeeding waves of Whites and thereby playing an insignificant role in the historical process.

This picture of Indian passivity (and thereby historical unimportance) is no more clearly drawn than in the events known as the secularization of the California missions. During the late 1820's and 1830's, the Mexican government passed a number of laws that, while not intending to destroy the mission system, were designed to reduce the powers of the Spanish missionaries, to break up the mission estates, and to distribute lands and goods to the neophytes (as the Indian converts were called) and to deserving Mexicans. By the 1840's the mission system in California was in ruins.

Historians have attributed the collapse solely to the activities of land-hungry Mexican officials and aristocrats who cheated the neophytes out of their promised lands. They give no recognition to the possibility that the neophytes themselves might have played an active role in the process of breakdown. For example, according to Andrew F. Rolle, during secularization "the mission Indians stood apathetically by as deeply confused, helpless witnesses" (1963:158). Furthermore, most historians claim that secularization forced the neophytes to leave the missions. To Hubert Howe Bancroft, "the mission, broken up and despoiled, no longer afforded shelter to its children, save a few of more solid character. . . . The rest had been dispersed to seek refuge among the settlers or in the wilderness" (1888:241–242). Similarly, Robert Glass Cleland has stated that secularization "scattered the partly civilized neophytes like sheep without a shepherd" (1941:22–23).

This paper challenges these views. It will be shown that most of the neophytes were not forced to leave the missions during secularization but withdrew willingly and thereby played an important and active role in the breakdown of the missions system. To support this assertion, it will be necessary to discuss neophyte behavioral patterns and mission social structure by drawing upon both historical documentation and sociological theory. Following the concepts of the social anthropologist M. G. Smith and the sociologist Erving Goffman, the mission will be analyzed as a plural institution.

The plural society and the total institution

To M. G. Smith, population groups found within societies sometimes form distinct cultural sections. According to the distribution and function of its cultural sections, a society will exhibit either heterogeneous or plural features.

A heterogeneous society contains distinct cultural sections and manifests varying degrees of social, political, and economic differentiation. But the majority of the population forms a cultural section that shares a common belief in the society's traditions and institutions (Smith 1969a:56). Those sections represented by minorities usually present no serious threat to the social order. In the plural society, however, a cultural section representing only a minority of the population regulates the affairs of the inclusive unit. Perpetually occupied in preserving its economic, social, and political supremacy, the dominant cultural minority often maintains its position through serfdom, peonage, slavery, colonialism, or through a restricted political franchise (Smith 1969a:38). Thus, in a plural society the majority of the population are not citizens but subjects (Smith 1969a:33).

Since individual mobility and collective assimilation are minimized, it is virtually impossible to transfer from one cultural section to another (Smith 1969b:96; Smith 1969c:431–437). There is, of course, interaction between members of the distinct cultural sections and assimilation sometimes takes place. Some acculturated members of the dominated section even align themselves with their rulers as trusted but expendable aides and assistants. But most subjects are reduced to frustration and dissidence, since social identity is ascriptive and sectional in base (Smith 1969a:57–58).

If the plural society is to remain stable, sectional identities and boundaries should be preserved by maintaining religious, familial, educational, occupational, economic, and political inequalities. And the cohesion and superior organization to which the rulers owe their initial dominance should be continued through collective action that preserves their exclusiveness (Smith 1969a:54–55). Because of its sectional inequalities, however, the plural society is subjected to severe structural strains. Any change in intersectional relations produces changes in the inclusive unit (Smith 1965:14–15). And if the position of the dominant minority is weakened, control over the total unit becomes uncertain. As a result, the dominated majority will often blatantly challenge the authority of their rulers (Smith 1969a:58).

Similar to the plural society is the total institution as defined by Erving Goffman. Fundamentally, it is an organization in which the majority of members, the inmates, are controlled by a small supervisory staff. The responsibility of the staff is not the guidance or periodic inspection of the inmates, as in many employer-employee relations, but surveillance. Because of the sharp divisions within the institution, staff and inmates may stereotype one another. The staff may view the inmates as untrustworthy, bitter, and secretive, while the inmates may see the staff as condescending, high-handed, and mean (Goffman 1962:6–7).

Before incorporation into a total institution, the inmates had a conception of themselves that was a result of the social arrangements they found in their home environment. Upon entrance, however, this conception begins to change, and in some institutions the process is intensified when the inniates are forced into a series of abasements, degradation, humiliations, and profanations of self (Goffman 1962:14). Because most members of the staff have the right to inflict punishment, the inmates may live with chronic anxiety about breaking the rules (Goffman 1962:42). Thus, for many, the full meaning of being inside a total institution does not exist apart from the desire to get out (Goffman 1962:14).

It is evident that Smith and Goffman are discussing very similar types of social structures. However, while Smith is dealing at the most inclusive level of political and social organization, Goffman is concerned with the social structure of subordinate units. The Republic of South Africa and many present-day ex-colonial countries constitute plural societies (Smith 1969c:429). The total institution is represented by penitentiaries, slave plantations, mental hospitals, and monasteries to mention only a few (Goffman 1962:4–5). As will become apparent, the mission clearly fits the model of Goffman's total institution and possesses most of the characteristics of Smith's plural society. Because it lacked societal inclusiveness, Smith would probably identify the mission as a community. But since the concepts of both scholars are being utilized, perhaps the compromise term "plural institution" might best be applied to the Spanish mission.

The mission as a plural institution

The mission was the principal vehicle of the Spanish colonization of Alta California, not because it was thought to be the most suitable institution for the undertaking but because the Spanish lacked the men and motivation to engage in a large scale colonization effort. Actually, the acculturated Indians were to preserve California for the Spanish crown. By congregating them into the missions, by converting them to Christianity, and by teaching them the arts and sciences of Europe, missionaries would make the Indians become the region's main colonizing force. Once an area had been effectively transformed, the missionaries would move on to new frontiers.

Because the Spanish provincial government issued few land grants to private individuals, the missionaries could claim as much territory as they thought they could administer. The general area controlled by each mission was arranged between church and government officials; fixed boundaries were not deemed necessary. Since the missions were regarded as only temporary establishments, eventually to be turned into pueblos, titles were held by the Spanish crown (Beattie 1942:4). Only the mission itself, comprising the buildings, cemetery, orchards, and vineyards, belonged exclusively to the Catholic Church (Servín 1965:136). The missions were, however, semi-independent of the provincial government, for only in cases of serious crime did the state assert its authority (Guest 1966:208).

Many of the so-called Spaniards who arrived in Alta California, beginning in 1769, were of mixed ethnic and racial backgrounds. But as *gente de razón*, or people of reason, they considered themselves distinct from and superior to both the unconverted and Christian Indians. Their group identity was shaped not so much by their common interests as by their insignificant numbers, for they formed only a tiny minority at any one mission. In 1816, for example, the *gente de razón* at Mission San Buenaventura totalled only thirty souls (Engelhardt 1930a:42).

At most missions, however, the neophyte population averaged between 500 and 600 persons and sometimes ranged between 1000 and 2000 (Cook 1943:84–87; see also Cook 1940). Large numbers of Indians were needed to keep the missions operating. Neophytes planted, tended, and harvested wheat, barley, corn, peas, beans, and various other crops. Mission equipment was produced in the shops where the neophytes made bricks, tiles, pottery, shoes, saddles, hats, clothes, candles, and soap. Indians also tended the herds of cattle, sheep, and horses that grazed on the numerous ranchos possessed by each mission. Carpentry, tanning, shearing, spinning, and blacksmithing were other tasks undertaken by the neophytes (Engelhardt 1930b:261–262). They were, indeed, the economic backbone of the mission system.

Some neophytes, moreover, occupied positions of authority. In 1779 the governor of California issued a decree stating that the resident Indians at each mission should elect from their own ranks two *alcaldes*, or magistrates, and two *rigedores*, or councilmen (Engelhardt 1927:44). However, the "Spaniards" made sure that only the most acculturated and the most favored became mission officers. This point is emphasized by a neophyte, Pablo Tac, who noted that the padres "appointed alcaldes from the people themselves that knew how to speak Spanish more than the others and were better than the others in their customs" (1958:17).

Apparently the alcaldes took their work very seriously. A visitor to Mission San Luis Rey remarked that they "are very rigid in exacting the performances of the allotted tasks, applying the rod to those who fell short of the portion of labor assigned them" (Pattie 1930:347–348). Another visitor to the same mission reported that while the majority of the neophytes attended mass on their own, "it was not unusual to see numbers of them driven along by alcaldes, and under the whip's lash forced to the very doors of the sanctuary" (Robinson 1846:25–26). According to an early Anglo-American resident, the alcaldes where chosen from the most lazy, the padres being of the opinion that they took great pleasure in making the others work. "They carried a wand to denote their authority, and what was more terrible, an immense scourage of raw hide, about ten feet in length, plaited to the thickness of an ordinary man's waist! They did a great deal of chastisement, both by and without orders" (Reid 1968:85).

Those neophytes who disobeyed the alcaldes or the padres were subjected to varying degrees and different kinds of punishment. Writes one Franciscan:

> The punishments resorted to at Santa Barbara are the shackles, the lash, and the stocks, but only when we find that corrections and reproofs are unavailing. Seldom are the women punished with any of the above instruments but the stocks. . . . A man, a boy, or a woman, runs away or does not return from the excursion, so that other neophytes must be sent after them. When such a one is brought back to the mission, he is reproached for not having heard holy Mass on a day of obligation. He is made to see that he has of his own free will taken upon himself this and other Christian duties, and he is warned that he will be chastized if he repeats the transgression. He runs away again, and again he is brought back. This time he is chastized with the lash or with the stocks. If this is not sufficient, as is the case with some who disregard a warning, he is made to feel the shackles, which he must wear three days while at work. This same punishment is meted out to such as are caught in concubinage.
>
> (Engelhardt 1923:80–81)

The documentation clearly demonstrates that Indian discontent with mission life was prevalent from the very inception of the system and was often manifested in fugitivism. In 1779 a padre admitted that even those Indians who were on the sick list, thereby receiving the best care the mission could provide, ran away. "The majority of our neophytes have not yet acquired much love for our way of life; and they see and meet their pagan relatives in the forest, fat and robust and enjoying complete liberty" (Guest 1966:209). In 1819 a missionary lamented that "the spirit of insubordination, which is rampant in the world at large, has reached the Christian Indians. A considerable number have withdrawn from the mild rule of the friars" (Engelhardt 1930b:33–34). An Englishman who visited California in the mid-1820's mentioned that "after they became acquainted with the nature of the institution, and felt themselves under restraint, many absconded. Even now, notwithstanding the difficulty of escaping, desertions are of frequent occurrence" (Beechey 1831:360).

Because the Indians were continually withdrawing from the missions, sometimes to return on their own, other times to be brought back by force, the neophyte population was never static, and so valid information on desertion rates is most difficult to come by. But according to Sherburne Cook, of the over 81,000 Indians who had been baptized by 1831, nearly 3500, or one out of twenty-four, had successfully escaped. And from 1831 to 1834 some 2000 more neophytes "illegally" withdrew from the missions (Cook 1943:58–61). Ironically, however, the life of the mission system, or at least the lives of individual missions, may have been prolonged because of the high rate of desertion. The missions witnessed few serious uprisings, presumably because those who were the most discontented and thereby potentially the most dangerous had an alternative to violence.

It should be apparent that the Spanish mission in California possessed all the characteristics of the plural institution. The "Spaniards," represented by two priests, a few soldiers and laymen, comprised the institution's staff whose primary occupation, given the problem of fugitivism, was surveillance. As the dominant cultural section that formed only a tiny minority of a mission's population, the "Spaniards" saw themselves as superior in all ways to the Indians and often viewed them as untrustworthy and secretive.

In contrast, as the inmates of the mission, the neophytes formed a cultural section that constituted a population majority with distinct burdens and disabilities. Since social identity was ascriptive, there was no way in which the neophytes could change their sectional status. Even those who adopted much of Spanish culture and became alcaldes were prevented from transferring into the dominant cultural section. The cruelty they exhibited toward their fellow neophytes is probably a reflection of the frustrations they felt at being rejected by the very group they sought to emulate and please. Subjected to various kinds and degrees of punishment, many neophytes were degraded and humiliated and certainly must have regarded the "Spaniards" and their trusted Indian assistants as mean and high-handed. Large numbers probably lived with chronic anxiety about breaking the rules. And for many, full meaning of being inside the mission probably did not exist apart from the desire to get out.

The breakdown of the mission system

By the 1820's, fugitivism, disease, and a declining mission birth rate were drastically reducing the neophyte population. For example, Mission San Juan Capistrano claimed a total of 1361 neophytes in 1812, but by 1820 the number was down to 1064, and by 1830 it had dropped to 925 (Engelhardt 1922:175). Unless the padres had been able to tap new population centers, it seems likely that the mission system would have come to a gradual and unspectacular conclusion. As it was, political developments in Mexico hastened its demise in a most sudden and dramatic way.

When the Mexican war for independence broke out in 1810, the annual stipend of 400 pesos issued to each missionary by the Viceroy of New Spain was terminated, and the missions were subjected to taxation and forced requisitions by the provincial government. Thrown back on their own resources, many of the missions subsisted by selling hides and tallow to American and English sea merchants. The end of the war in 1821 failed to improve the situation, for the new Mexican government, facing grave financial problems, was unable to send more than token assistance (Hutchinson 1965:335–336).

The Mexican government, however, was not unconcerned as to the condition of the Indian. Infused with the egalitarian and humanitarian beliefs of the day, it sought to improve the lot of all the Indians within its vast territory. Government officials realized that only when released from their servile position in society would the Indians become useful citizens of Mexico (Hutchinson 1965:340). Consequently, the first Mexican governor of California issued a Proclamation of Emancipation on July 25, 1826, which stated that certain neophytes within the military districts of San Diego, Santa Barbara, and Monterey would be released from missionary supervision. To be set free, however, were only those whom the Franciscans thought capable of supporting themselves (Engelhardt 1922:81–82).

Neophyte response to the proclamation varied from mission to mission, but many Indians took immediate advantage of their new freedom. "In my former visit to this country," wrote an English sea captain in 1828,

> I remarked that the padres were much mortified at being desired to liberate from the missions all the Indians who bore good characters, and who were acquainted with the art of tilling the ground. In consequence of their remonstrances the government modified the order, and consented to make the experiment upon a few only at first, and desired that a certain number might be settled in the proposed manner. After a few months' trial much to his surprise, he found that these people who had been always accustomed to the care and discipline of schoolboys, finding themselves their own masters, indulged freely in all those excesses which it had been the endeavor of their tutors to repress, and that many having gambled away their clothes, implements, and even their lands, were compelled to beg or plunder in order to support life. They at length became so obnoxious to the peaceable inhabitants, that the padres were requested to take some of them back to the missions, while others who had been guilty of misdemeanor were loaded with shackles and put to work.
>
> (Beechey 1831:582–583)

Cutting through the paternalism and ethnocentrism of this statement, one realizes that the neophytes were not exhibiting the behavioral patterns of disobedient school boys but were manifesting the kind of psychological disorientation that often accompanies decolonization.

In August 1833, the Mexican government passed a law which secularized all the missions of Alta and Baja California. The governor of Alta California delayed implementing the law until a year later when he issued his own secularization decree. It stated that the missionaries were to relinquish all secular control over the neophytes and were to perform only religious duties until replaced by parish priests. The missions were to be converted into pueblos and their lands distributed among the neophytes. Each head of a family or adult male over twenty years of age was to receive thirty three acres of land. Half the missions' livestock, tools, and seeds were also to be distributed among the neophytes, but all surplus lands, cattle, and other property would become the responsibility of the missions' civil administrators who would be appointed by the governor. Furthermore, according to the decree, the government possessed the right to force the neophytes to work in the vineyards, orchards, and fields that remained undistributed. Indians could not sell or otherwise dispose of their newly acquired property. If an owner died without an heir, his lands would revert to the state (Hutchinson 1969:255–260).

At many of the missions, the majority of the neophytes exhibited no interest in acquiring mission lands or in having anything more to do with the system. For example, in 1834 the newly appointed civil administrator of Mission San Luis Rey complained of neophyte disobedience.

> These Indians will do absolutely no work nor obey my orders. In consequence, though the season for sowing the wheat is at hand, and the necessary plows have been prepared, I must suffer the pain of being obliged to suspend work for want of hands. The men have mistaken the voice of reason and even of the authority which orders the work, for they declare they are a free nation. In order to enjoy their obstinancy better, they have fled from their houses and abandoned their aged parents, who alone are now at this ex-Mission.
>
> I have sent various alcaldes to the sierra in order to see if, with sweetness and gentleness, we might succeed in having them return to their homes; but the result was the opposite of my desires. Nothing would suit them, nothing would change their ideas, neither the well-being which must result for their good behavior, nor the privations which they suffer in their wanderings. All with one voice would shout, 'We are free! We do not want to obey! We do not want to work!' (Engelhardt 1921:96–97).

In 1835 an English visitor to California predicted a quick end for the missions. The neophytes "have been compelled to live under a restraint they could not bear. . . . I believe a great deal both of force and fraud were used in congregating them together in the missions; and the moment that force shall be altogether withdrawn, I have no doubt that the majority of them will return to the woods" (Coulter 1925:67). Indeed, once force was withdrawn, the termination of the mission system came rapidly. Most of the neophytes either sought work on the great Mexican ranchos then being carved out of mission territory or wandered into the towns, such as Los Angeles, to work intermittently and to drink and gamble. Others trekked inland to join independent Indian societies. Between 1834 and 1843, it is estimated that the neophyte population declined from over 30,000 to under 5000 (Jones 1850:27).

Conclusion

Eurocentric in their attitudes and often prisoners of a biased documentation, historians generally view the Indian as having played only an insignificant role in California history and no role at all in the collapse of the Spanish mission system. Their commonly held position states that the mission system was brought to an end by the activities of land-hungry Mexican officials and aristocrats who forced the neophytes to leave the missions by cheating them out of their promised lands. This view, however, overlooks the documentation that discloses neophyte behavioral patterns and it fails to acknowledge the importance of mission social structure in determining neophyte activity.

It will be recalled that the plural institution is characterized by sectional divisions in which a dominant cultural minority, the staff, regulates the affairs of the entire unit. If the structure is to remain stable, sectional identities and boundaries should be preserved and the cohesion and superior organization of the rulers maintained. Changes in intersectional relations, however, produces changes in the entire unit, and once the position of the staff is weakened, control over the institution becomes uncertain. The dominated cultural majority, the inmates, will then often blatantly challenge the ruling section.

Exhibiting social and political inequalities in which "Spaniards" and Indians formed distinct cultural sections, the mission, from its inception, was subjected to perpetual structural strains. This is most clearly seen in the continuous process of withdrawal. But significant changes in intersectional relations did not occur until the secularization laws stripped the staff of each mission of its temporal powers and thus gave the inmates new alternatives of action.

Some of the neophytes attempted to salvage whatever they could from their years of labor and were often cheated out of their promised lands and driven from the missions. But contrary to established opinion, most were not forced to leave, but withdrew willingly. This was in keeping with much of their past activity, for the withdrawal taking place after secularization represents an intensification of a process that had been going on throughout the entire mission period. Prior to secularization, however, escape was usually a matter of individual initiative. Afterwards, the neophytes could blatantly challenge the authority of their now politically emasculated rulers by withdrawing *en masse* with little fear of capture and punishment.

Their action was a near unanimous rejection of an oppressive social system, the final and most dramatic manifestation of a long-standing and very profound discontent. Furthermore, it demonstrates that the neophytes played an important role in the breakdown of the Spanish mission system in California. Far from being passive observers of their own destruction, doing little if anything to alter their colonized status, the neophytes were active agents in the historical process and deserve to be recognized as such.

References

Bancroft, Hubert Howe

1888 *California Pastoral 1769–1848.* San Francisco: The History Company.

Beattie, George W.

1942 Mission Ranchos and Mexican Grants. *San Bernardino County Historical Society*, Vol. 2, pp. 2–4.

Beechey, F. W.

1831 *Narrative of a Voyage to the Pacific and Beering's Strait in the Years 1825–1828, Pt. I.* London: Henry Colburn and Richard Bentley.

Caughey, John

1953 *California.* Englewood Cliffs: Prentice-Hall, Inc.

Cleland, Robert Glass

1941 *The Cattle on a Thousand Hills: Southern California, 1850–1870.* San Marino: The Huntington Library.

Cook, Sherburne F.

1940 Population Trends among the California Mission Indians. *Ibero-Americana*, no. 17. Berkeley: University of California Press.

1943 The Conflict between the California Indian and White Civilization: I, The Indian Versus the Spanish Mission. *Ibero-Americana*, no. 21. Berkeley: University of California Press.

Coulter, Thomas

1925 Notes on Upper California. Reprinted from *The Journal of the Royal Geographical Society*, 1835. Chicago: Aldine Book Company.

Engelhardt, Zephyrin Fr.

1921 *San Luis Rey Mission.* San Francisco: The James H. Barry Company.

1922 *San Juan Capistrano Mission.* Los Angeles: The Standard Printing Company.

1923 *Santa Barbara Mission.* San Francisco: The James H. Barry Company.

1927 *San Gabriel Mission and the Beginnings of Los Angeles.* San Gabriel: Mission San Gabriel.

1930a *San Buenaventura: The Mission by the Sea.* Santa Barbara: Mission Santa Barbara.

1930b *The Missions and Missionaries of California, Vol. II, Upper California, Pt. I.* Santa Barbara: Mission Santa Barbara.

Forbes, Jack, ed.

1964 *The Indian in America's Past.* Englewood Cliffs: Prentice-Hall, Inc.

Goffman, Irving

1962 *Asylums: Essays on the Social Situation of Mental Patients and Other Inmates.* New York: Doubleday and Company, Inc.

Guest, Florian F.

1966 The Indian Policy Under Fermín Francisco de Lasuén, California's Second Father President. *California Historical Society Quarterly*, Vol. 45, no. 3, pp. 195–224.

Hutchinson, C. Alan

1965 The Mexican Government and the Mission Indians of Upper California, 1825–1835. *The Americas*, Vol. 21, no. 4, pp. 335–362.

1969 *Frontier Settlement in Mexican California: The Hijar-Padres Colony and Its Origins, 1769–1835.* New Haven and London: Yale University Press.

Jones, William Carey
1850 *Report on the Subject of Land Titles in California.* Sen. Ex. Doc. no. 18, 31st Cong., 1st Sess., Washington D.C.

Pattie, James C.
1930 *The Personal Narrative of James C. Pattie of Kentucky.* Edited by Timothy Flint. Chicago: The Lakeside Press.

Reid, Hugo
1968 *The Indians of Los Angeles County: Hugo Reid's Letters of 1852.* Edited by Robert Heizer. Los Angeles: Southwest Museum.

Robinson, Alfred
1846 *Life in California during a Residence of Several Years in that Territory.* New York: Wiley and Putnam.

Rolle, Andrew F.
1963 *California: A History.* New York: Thomas Y. Crowell Company, Inc.

Servín, Manuel P.
1965 The Secularization of the California Missions: A Reappraisal. *Southern California Quarterly*, Vol. 47, no. 2, pp. 133–149.

Smith, M. G.
1965 *The Plural Society in the British West Indies.* Berkeley and Los Angeles: Univeristy of California Press.
1969a Institutional and Political Conditions of Pluralism. In *Pluralism in Africa*, pp. 27–65. Edited by M. G. Smith and Leo Kuper. Berkeley and Los Angeles: University of California Press.
1969b Pluralism in Precolonial African Societies. In *Pluralism in Africa*, pp. 91–151. Edited by M. G. Smith and Leo Kuper. Berkeley and Los Angeles: University of California Press.
1969c Some Developments in the Analytic Framework of Pluralism. In *Pluralism in Africa*, pp. 415–458. Edited by M. G. Smith and Leo Kuper. Berkeley and Los Angeles: University of California Press.

Tac, Pablo
1958 *Indian Life and Customs at Mission San Luis Rey.* Edited and translated by Minna and Gordon Hewes. San Luis Rey: Mission San Luis Rey.

44

HIDDEN BUT REAL

The vital contribution of Biblewomen to the rapid growth of Korean Protestantism, 1892–1945

Christine Sungjin Chang

Source: *Women's Historical Review*, 17(4) (2008), 575–95.

Introduction

This article aims to describe and assess the contribution of Biblewomen[1] to the rapid growth of Protestant Christianity in Korea from the late nineteenth century (the late *Chosŏn* period) until the end of the Japanese occupation of Korea in 1945. It seeks to demonstrate that Biblewomen and Christian women leaders more broadly were active subjects or agents in the development of Korean Protestantism, rather than the passive objects of evangelism or performing purely subordinate functions. These women's stories should be viewed as a creative source for a new scholarship, providing a Korean historical perspective on female faith and activism at the grassroots. Such research can make a valid contribution to both the larger field of women's studies in Korea and contemporary global analysis of the role of women in mission

Those described as 'Biblewomen' by Western missionaries are known mainly as *chŏndo puin* by Korean people, their precursors being *puin kwonsŏ*: '*chŏndo*' means 'evangelistic' and '*puin*' 'married woman' or 'lady'. *Chŏndo puin* therefore denotes a woman who works in evangelism, *puin kwonsŏ* being simply 'a woman who sells Bibles'. The first reference to Korean Biblewomen in English appears in the Annual Reports of the British and Foreign Bible Society (BFBS) in 1892,[2] which give the number of *puin kwonsŏ* in their Korean mission between 1898 and 1913. Important achievements of Biblewomen in the areas of education, evangelism and medical mission are regularly presented in the documents of (mostly American) 'Women's Work for Women'. According to a recent survey, Biblewomen in Korea numbered 1,215 in total between 1895 and 1945, 717 with the

Methodist Church, 209 among Presbyterians, 138 in the Holiness Church and 151 women in other churches.[3]

This brief introduction first aims to provide a critical reconstruction of the cultural landscape from which the Biblewomen emerged. It could be argued – though there is no space to develop this further here – that Korean women had historically played a vital role in pre-Christian society as transformers or interpreters in the indigenisation of religions, both for Shamanism, in which many of the leaders (*moodangs*) were female, and the popular folk Buddhism of the *Chosŏn* era. Biblewomen were created not by mission initiative alone, indigenous forces of social transformation being enhanced by missionaries.

The body of the article falls into three main sections, roughly denoting three periods which to some degree overlap and shade into one another in their portrayal of the history of Korean Biblewomen. The first presents the contribution of *puin kwonsŏ* to the early Protestant mission, particularly emphasising their role in disseminating and indigenising biblical knowledge through the *Ŏnmun* form of the Korean language that was used by women and people of lower social status. The second part demonstrates that *chŏndo puin* in reality played a leadership role in the indigenous development of Korean churches despite sex discrimination, cultural prejudice and religious competition. The final, rather abbreviated section shows the social roles of *chŏndo puin* as Christian teachers, nurses, counsellors and doctors who were distinguished from ordinary Korean women of the period.

Biblewomen and American missionaries in early Korean Protestantism

American women's activism in mission from the nineteenth to the early and mid-twentieth century has attracted scholarly research into both their distinctive contribution and their relationships with male missionaries and mission societies.[4] Some have been concerned with possible links to the feminist movement in places like Korea. Dana Robert, for instance, argues that the work of American missionary women, although it seemed subordinate, was not submissive, and introduced equality and freedom to indigenous women – which only the Christian gospel gave them.[5] On the other hand, the Korean feminist Yi U-jŏng insists that American women contributed little to the emancipation of local women because they could not overcome the straitjacket of the Western male-dominated Christianity of the period.[6] These claims point to contrasting perceptions within missiology about the significance of the American female influence.

Why be concerned about this in considering Korean Biblewomen? The overriding numerical importance of missionaries from the United States compels our attention. According to a Korean-compiled list, women constituted over 80 per cent of the total number of US missionaries in Korea from 1884

Table 1 Missionaries in Korea 1884~1945: Nationality and Numbers.

Nationality	*Number of missionaries*	*% of total*
America	1,059	69.8
Britain	199	13.0
Canada	98	6.4
Australia	85	5.6
Other	88	5.2
Total	1,529	100.0

Source: Kim Sŭng-tae and Pak Hye-jin, *Naehan sŏnkyosa chŏllam* [A Sourcebook of Missionaries in Korea, 1884–1984], p. 4.

to 1945, that is, 825 out of 1,059, a number which also included missionaries' wives.[7] Table 1 shows the dominance of American missionaries.

In assessing the 'feminist issue', I shall focus on the period between 1886, when modern education for Korean women was introduced with the establishing of Ehwa Girls' School by missionary Mary F. Scranton, and 1910, when Korea was annexed and occupied by Japan, forcing missionaries to change their strategies. American mission women went through a painful process of enlightenment. This had some remarkable results such as female higher education and job opportunities, as well as elite leadership roles for Korean Christian women in their churches and society. Nevertheless, the Americans were circumscribed both by their limited ideas and the existing system. The purpose of Christian mission at the turn of the twentieth century, I would argue, was not 'equality' between men and women but 'evangelism' of the unconverted. Egalitarianism in mission was defined by 'metaphysical human equality' rather than gender equality.

However, the interests of Korean women were different from those of American missionary women. They were living through a period of transformation from feudalism to modernism. From 1800 onwards, Korean society was in chaos, so that by 1860, the reputation of the *Chosŏn* dynasty had been fatally damaged. Queen Myongsong recognised the past folly of sealing off Korea, and in 1873, she accepted the proposal to reform Korean society along Western lines, readily admitting Western culture, especially to improve women's capacities. For instance, she was willing personally to name mission schools for Korean girls and hospitals for Korean women, sometimes supporting them financially.[8] There was likewise an idea of emancipation for women in the *Tonghak* reform movement of the same period.[9] Its notions of 'equality of educational opportunity', implying that women could acquire knowledge on the same footing as men, made another crucial input into the early feminist movement in Korea, alongside female mission education.

Thus, in this cultural and religious encounter, Korean women were very focussed on their own emancipation and social status in a reformed Korea, while American missionary women aimed to Christianise Korea and extend the female professional arena. Yet American domestic ideology and the concept of 'true womanhood' hindered female advance in Korean society because women's role was defined in terms of being wives and mothers at home, even though not all American missionary women were wives. The new Korean female leadership emerged under the name of 'New Women' through the work of missions in education, medicine and evangelism. But this enhanced agency grew within set parameters with real tension at times between the female recipients and the providers of 'liberation'. In addition, Korean Christian women were on the bottom rung of the hierarchy of the Korean church, with American male missionaries at the top.

While BFBS annual reports enumerated *puin kwonsŏ* for over two decades after 1892, totals suddenly decline after 1920, which a Korean historian attributes to a rapid increase in church development in that era.[10] Eventually, female Scripture-sellers became generally known as *chŏndo puin* (women evangelists), as they came to be more widely involved in teaching new believers about their faith. The activities and importance of *chŏndo puin*, my second major focus, came to the fore particularly after the Korean Awakenings in the early 1900s, a trend continuing to the end of the Japanese occupation in 1945. I examine their significant role in Protestant church growth through prayer meetings, the self-management of church life, Sunday school development, women's societies and primary outreach. The evidence reveals that although the *chŏndo puin* were well trained and capable, they could not rise to higher levels of institutional leadership. As women, they were given only limited recognition by the missionary societies and churches, operating under a glass ceiling, as the career of Sadie Kim will show.

Thirdly, analysts have suggested that Protestant missions had a positive social impact on Korean society, especially for women. However, Christianity also led to the replication of feudal classes within the *chŏndo puin*, Korean women being separated by education and employment stereotypes similar to those found in the traditional *Chosŏn* class system. Nevertheless, whether we look at surviving the Japanese occupation, or working for church institutions, *chŏndo puin* as social leaders had an important impact on Korean society, based upon their Christian background, with both positive and negative results for Korean women. The strikingly gifted but controversial Hwalran [Helen] Kim is briefly taken as exemplar.[11]

Mere 'extra' or lead actress? The work of *puin kwonsŏ* as a basis for the evangelisation of Korea, 1892–1920

From the middle of the nineteenth century, Biblewomen were proving their importance in world mission. In mid-Victorian Britain, 'Bible Mission-Women' were called the new evangelists.[12] In the American mission to Asia, missionaries sometimes called the native female agents Biblewomen and Bible readers. By the 1890s, the British and Foreign Bible Society's employment of Biblewomen in South Asian missions seemed particularly well established, although, mid-decade, none were yet listed for Korea. Of the 429 BFBS Biblewomen noted in 1895, a substantial 310 worked in India and 76 in Ceylon, alongside 4 in Mauritius and the Seychelles. There were 32 based in the Middle East (Syria, Palestine and Egypt), while China had 5 and the Straits 2. This represented a continued increase, returns being received from 27 more women than in 1892–3. They were reading the Bible to 26,560 native women a week on average, '4,546 a week more than before', while 1,549 indigenous women whom they taught 'had attained, within the year, the power of being able to read the Scriptures for themselves'. In total, the Society's Biblewomen in these areas outside Korea had circulated 15,263 Bibles, Testaments or detached books of Scripture that year.[13]

By 1898, Korea was featuring in a modest way in the East Asian deployment of BFBS Biblewomen, opening a new chapter in the history of the Bible Society's foreign labours. Korea provided ten Biblewomen alongside the five then at work in Japan and 28 in China. These Korean church-workers were reading to 104 women per week, on average, and had sold 390 portions of Scripture.[14] By the end of the nineteenth century, *puin kwonsŏ* in the Korean mission field were beginning to be recognised as vital agents of Christian evangelisation, similar to those in India, China and elsewhere.

A further factor that raised the profile of Biblewomen was that Korean missions were fortunate enough to have a vernacular Bible which had been translated into Korean orthography by the important linguistic pioneer, Rev. John Ross (1842–1872), who was working in Manchuria as a Scottish missionary. After visiting the 'Corean Gate', the customs house in Manchuria on the route between Korea and China and a crucial place for missionaries to meet Koreans easily,[15] he recognised the need for a mission to Korea. His mission philosophy reflects just how vital a contribution Bible translation was. He insisted on native people being involved in mission work in their own country, for which they needed to be able to listen to readings from the Bible in their own language and later read the Bible for themselves. To this end, he employed Korean scholars and middle-class men to achieve his aim. Although he had not planned any women's participation in his work, he nevertheless triggered a very important development in female evangelisation. Before the authorised version of the Bible in 'standard Korean', issued by the 'Permanent Executive Bible Committee' in 1900, the Ross translation, written in the *Ŏnmun* orthography version of Korean,[16] had already spread to Korean women readers.[17] This Ross Bible, in the 'everyday Korean' of the vast majority of the population, proved crucial for Korean Biblewomen's enthusiastic activities that had already started in the 1890s. The popular translation could be said to have led directly to the creation of a mission agent, the *puin kwonsŏ* or Biblewoman, who would be responsible for its successful circulation.

Most *puin kwonsŏ* came from poor or lower class backgrounds. Many were also widows who had sometimes lost both children and husband. Notwithstanding such hardship, they served the Korean mission well in the face of social prejudice, religious conflict, physical difficulties, sexual discrimination and economic problems.[18] *Puin kwonsŏ* mainly worked at selling Bibles, portions of Scripture, Testaments and copies of doctrine. They were also more involved than their evangelist successors in teaching Korean orthography, reading Scripture to illiterate people and initiating Bible circulation. The number of Scripture portions sold by *puin kwonsŏ* from 1897 to 1904 virtually doubled every year other than 1899, rising from 258 to 5,253 in seven years. Some of their later activities shaded rather into the *chŏndo puin* type: Maria Shin served as *chŏndo puin* in the isolated border region between China and Korea from 1923, while Shin Kyung Kim became the female evangelist in the Kosan Yi Church on Chejoo Island in South Korea in the same year. Likewise, Miriam Yi was sent out as a woman evangelist by Hambook presbytery in North Korea in 1930.[19]

The North American Protestants trained their Biblewomen in a variety of short-term, *ad hoc* ventures as the twentieth century opened, in order to deepen their religious understanding and enable higher quality work. In 1900, for example, the first school for *puin kwonsŏ* was started by the Methodist Episcopal Mission (North), as Rev. W. B. Scranton told a Bible Society colleague:

> We have found that our Biblewomen, though, according to their present ability, doing good service, yet fall short of what we desire for them. We have therefore begun in a modest way a Biblewoman's School . . . At present we have an average attendance of ten or twelve and the interest in deeper study and instruction is good.[20]

Likewise, the American Presybterians held a 'Bible Women's Training Class' for two weeks in May in Sungjin province in 1907, while in 1910, there were women's Bible training classes in six different areas of Korea, mustering impressively high attendance. Presumably, these drew on new female church members more broadly too, not just Biblewomen, since participants numbered 500 in Taegu, 150 in Kimhae and Busan, 300 in Seoul, 500 in Jaeryŏng, 600 in Pyongyang and 650 in Sunchŏn.[21] Through such systematic training, *puin kwonsŏ* came to possess their own practical skills and occupy a definite position, even though, officially, they were regarded as lower than male converts and virtually powerless. Yet the BFBS continued to evaluate the work of *puin kwonsŏ* positively and employed more and more of them in cooperation with American and Canadian mission societies in Korea. As a BFBS commentator observed just before the First World War, '"What would we do without these women?" During last year we supported an average number of 33 women, who sold 8,884 volumes.'[22]

From around 1915, the initial primary arena of *puin kwonsŏ* slowly reduced. There are two possible reasons for this. The first is the growing importance of commission-based sales (generally by men running urban bookstores) across the decade after 1915, according to a recent survey of colporteurs.[23] In 1916, of the total Korean sales figure of 826,635 Bibles and Scripture portions, 20,081 came from commission-sellers. By 1925, on the other hand, commission-sellers accounted for a larger number – 25,816 – of the (lower) total of items sold, which came to 611,476. Secondly, as Korean churches, schools and hospitals developed institutionally as the twentieth century advanced, utilising better trained and educated female evangelists or *chŏndo puin*, the old-style *puin kwonsŏ* had to extend their role beyond simply selling Bibles to take on evangelisation in the field. For more idea of the real challenges and achievements of early *puin kwonsŏ*, it is worth examining the life story of a representative example in detail.

Tabitha Won, **puin kwonsŏ:** *a mission legend and the mother of peace*

In 1916, Mrs L. L. Young of the Canadian Presbyterian Mission paid warm tribute to the childless widow Tabitha Won, who deserved 'a full share of credit' for recent evangelistic developments. The year she turned sixty, 1910, Tabitha entered a new life as a Christian.[24] For her, everyone who lived in Korea without knowing Christ was a potential target, giving meaning to her life of evangelism. She learnt the Korean *Ŏnmun* script to read the Bible and communicate with non-believers, and at 63, became a *puin kwonsŏ* supported by BFBS. In her first month, she travelled 267 miles on foot, over hard mountainous roads in cold autumn winds, selling 40 Gospels, five New Testaments, one Old Testament, and sundry portions of the Bible, and preaching to 79 people.[25] She made monthly reports of the large numbers of Korean non-believers reading and hearing the Word until her death in 1925.[26]

As a group, *puin kwonsŏ* were vital to Korean mission, not as passive assistants to missionaries or male native pastors, but self-organising, independent, religiously creative mission agents whose presence and contribution were essential. It could be argued that their evangelistic journeys undertaken for Scripture circulation provided the basis of the establishment of Korea's Protestant churches. What also happened, in the wake of this initial foundational period, was that the importance of *puin kwonsŏ* in mission, the classic pioneering Biblewoman, was superseded by the rise of female church leaders who played a powerful role under the title of *chŏndo puin*, women evangelists, as Korean churches developed further, into the 1920s. It is to their work that we turn now.

Submissive assistants or essential leaders? The practical leadership and evangelism of *chŏndo puin* as part of Korean church growth

Chŏndo puin were church leaders who contributed to the development of Korean Protestantism in the period when the churches were interpreting Christianity according to their own lights via the 'Awakening' movements of 1903–1910. These spiritual revivals changed the pattern of missionisation from collective social reform to the religious fervour of individual salvation. The trend rapidly had an impact on Korean women. American missionary women were surprised by the religious eagerness of Korean women during the Awakening, seeing them as inferior to Korean men in terms of intelligence, but their superiors in respect of deep faith, religious experience and spirituality. The Americans themselves responded eagerly to the growing fervour – a number of female missionaries being involved in the Korean Great Awakening prayer meetings at Wonsan from 1903.[27] One such missionary woman enthused thus about the revival and its transformative impact on a Biblewoman colleague:

> We had gone with the Bible woman into the home several weeks previous to his [Dr. Hardie's] coming, telling the women of the proposed services and urging them to so arrange their work as to make church-going the business for a week. What a wonderful week that was! Though having attended many blessed revival services at home, we had never before seen such intense conviction of sin, such marked manifestation of the Spirit's presence and power . . . During the service she [the Korean Biblewoman] arose and made what must have been for her a most humiliating confession and since that time her development into a most aggressive Christian worker has been truly marvellous.[28]

Against this changing background of intensifying spirituality, Biblewomen were redefined as not merely *puin kwonsŏ* (female booksellers) but also *chŏndo puin* (women evangelists). Establishing churches, leading prayer meetings, teaching Bible classes, caring for believers or newcomers, and managing Sunday schools were the basic elements of developing church life. *Chŏndo puin* were deeply involved in this work and achieved great results. Furthermore, they began to organise collective female Christianity: women's meetings that assisted with administration, finance and church services.

The number of local women's church societies proliferated after the first decade of the twentieth century, while their wider organisational structure also became more complex and coherently unified. As a survey of women's societies (*Puin Jŏndohoe*) from 1908 to 1928 shows, the initial local associations were founded in key cities like Pyŏngyang (1908), Sunchŏn (1909),

Ŭiju (1910), Wonsan (1911), Kangkae (1912) and Chilsan (1914), with branch societies in other churches and regions in due course. The first united women's society with a substantial, national structure began with Pyŏngbuk YŏJŏndohoe Yŏnhaphoe in 1915, to be followed by eight others over the next decade or so, with two of them founded, for example, in 1926.[29]

This network of Korean Christian women's groups at the local, regional and national level, built up over a twenty-year period, also played a great role in supporting the evangelistic work of *chŏndo puin.* They even sent them to other countries: Kim Sun-ho was the first Korean female missionary in Shantung, China, sent by the Pyŏng Yang Women's Society of the General Assembly of the Presbyterian Church in Korea.[30] This expansion of the arena of the female evangelists was a sign that the women's societies themselves were becoming more systematically organised and powerful, just as *chŏndo puin* were gaining more official leadership status and stable help.

In the process, some training schools and Bible Institutes, like the one for women in Pyongyang in 1905, continued to enhance the more 'professional' education of the female evangelists as their careers developed beyond mere Bible-selling and simple exposition. Between 1904 and 1906, at the beginning of Korean Awakening, the Methodist Episcopal Church held some six 'Bible Institutes', teaching nearly 350 women each year, with between 26 and 33 Biblewomen involved, while nine Biblewomen attended a 'Training School' aimed exclusively at them. Strikingly, in 1906 a leading *chŏndo puin,* Sadie Kim, was one of the speakers at such an 'Institute' alongside the American Methodist women, as the programme records.[31]

Increasing Biblewomen's official training and certification enhanced their standing in practice as church leaders, not only among women but also with men and children. However, while their improved access to information and skills was respected by missionaries, male pastors and the wider Christian community, sex-discrimination did still exist. Male-centred churches had glass ceilings blocking women in the Korean institutional hierarchy. Low salary levels for *puin kwonsŏ* were one sign of the long-standing under- or devaluation of women's contribution from the late 1890s onwards. In 1910, the average salary of *puin kwonsŏ* was 7 won per month: seemingly, little changed for two decades, since it was 5–10 won in 1929. By 1935, the situation had improved, with the women's earnings at about 150 won (around $5 at that time).[32] The basic Biblewomen's pay was less than that of *chŏndo puin* in the 1920s, yet even that was meagre: an average 20 won for women evangelists, even after graduating from Bible institutes or schools higher than local Bible classes. How does this modest amount compare with the monthly salary of male pastors in the same period? In 1922, such men were earning between 70 or 80 won to 100 won. A press article highlighted the gender disparity (despite often similar training) in a period 'when people claim the equality of men and women', pointing out, 'This issue is not recent. Several years ago, we had complained that the salary was very deficient.'[33] This discouraging treatment in the church field led *chŏndo puin* to argue the issue repeatedly with local churches or denominations in the early 1930s.

A powerful example of the denigration these energetic women faced – and their riposte – comes in the public and vocal protest of *chŏndo puin* Chŏng Mariah, voiced in *Kidokshinbo* [The Christian Newspaper] in 1930. The unflattering or demeaning nickname the women had acquired particularly irked her:

> From my childhood onwards, I kept up my Christian belief until I became an *Yŏjundoin* [*chŏndo puin* or women evangelist] for twenty years. The nickname of *Yŏjundoin* is 'dusting cloth' . . . I go to some homes for prayer, work as a mortician at the funerals, help as a midwife so my women give birth easily to babies, teach home education, educate children, read Bibles, and teach Korean orthography in the country churches isolated thirty or forty *lis* away from cities. Furthermore, I visit wedding ceremonies, funerals and very depressed families. My work of various visitations seems like a dusting cloth. However I must tell you that there wouldn't have been any clean houses without a dusting cloth.[34]

The work of the *chŏndo puin* in sustaining the church and keeping things in good order might be dismissed as seemingly purely 'domestic' or mundane, just an extension of the longstanding female responsibility for cleaning, just a 'dusting cloth' of little worth. Yet, in the humble perception of ordinary people, *chŏndo puin* had worked diligently, their hearts enthusiastic for evangelism. Women like Chŏng Mariah found their own identity and, in a reasonable manner, asserted their value to the churches. Notwithstanding their essential but taxing contribution to church development in a time of growing crisis, the treatment they frequently had to endure was utterly deplorable, in terms of marked differences in salary and working conditions from those enjoyed by male Korean leaders. In order to understand the lives and activities of *chŏndo puin*, we need again to look at an individual example, Sadie Kim, who was very active and devout.

God's messenger and female leader, **chŏndo puin** *Sadie Kim*

Sadie Kim was born on 17 October 1865 in Pyŏngnam province, in the northern part of Korea. She was married twice, first to a Mr Jung at 16 years old and in 1888 to Kim Jung-kyŏm who was from the Yangban class in Pyŏngyang. The source of her Christian belief, as recounted in her life-story by Methodist missionary wife Mattie Noble, was her second husband's cousin, Oh Suk-hyŏng, who had been a serious gambler and was then converted to Christianity by an earlier Methodist missionary, W. J. Hall. Oh persuaded her to go to church for her family's sake, which she began to do.

However, her husband was not happy about this and sometimes reasoned with her not to believe in God.[35] Nevertheless, she prayed for him. At last in the autumn of 1895, he had a spiritual experience, after which Sadie and her husband enthusiastically participated in Pyŏngyang church from 1896.[36] She, as Won, learnt *Ŏnmun* and studied Bible stories and Christian doctrines, graduating from 'Pyong Yang Bible Institute' in 1908. In 1899, she was officially supported by the Women's Society of the Methodist Episcopal Church of the USA as a Biblewoman, *chŏndo puin.* During work trips, she tackled a wide range of tasks for the church: selling Bibles and books of doctrine, visiting wedding ceremonies, dealing with the dead in funeral homes, and helping with housekeeping in family homes where she was in charge. Furthermore, the main objects of her evangelism were particularly isolated classes of women in Korean society such as widows; *kisaeng* (dancing women or prostitutes for *Yangban* or middle class men); and *mudang* (female shamans).[37]

The scale of Sadie Kim's pastoral and evangelistic work is clear. According to MEC mission reports, she visited an average of 1,500 to 3,000 Korean homes and gained 30 new converts per year, worked in Pyŏngyang Sunday schools from 1911 to 1915, ran a Sunday meeting for married women in Pyŏngyang (1911), led 82 prayer meetings (1913) and organised missions herself.[38] She was a leading member of the ecumenical society of Methodist and Presbyterian women, *Daehan Yaeguk Puinhoe* [the Korean Patriotic Ladies' Association] from June 1919, opposing Japanese power. Consequently, she was tortured by the Japanese police for around two years.[39] After her release from jail, she resumed her highly significant evangelistic work. In 1924, the year before her retirement at sixty, she led 22 Bible classes, evangelised a female shaman and reportedly won some 800 new believers to the church.[40] She stands here for the many women who remain unacknowledged.

New elite or social reformers? *Chŏndo puin* as social leaders obedient to the authorities in the late *Chosŏn* period and under Japanese occupation

In respect of social activities and involvement, *chŏndo puin* went through difficult times, confronting Korean traditionalist views, the changing political situation and Japanese persecution, despite all of which they played a significant role in Korean society. At the beginning of the era of modern education and the movement for enlightenment, they stood between the conflicting understandings of missionaries and Korean leaders about modern Western-style education. The former wanted to use education as the most effective tool of Christian mission while the latter sought missionaries with Western medicine and modern technology only in order to develop a new and modern *Chosŏn* dynasty. In these ambiguous times, some wonderful professional women emerged from *chŏndo puin* origins, women like Hahr

Nan-sa (1875–1919), the first Korean university graduate,[41] and Korea's first female doctor, Kim Park (1876–1910).[42] Accordingly, *chŏndo puin* who were educated and working in mission schools had to embrace or negotiate two discourses with differing aims, and satisfy both sets of expectations.

Chŏndo puin and other Christian female leaders established their own schools to achieve their chosen aims, which, predictably, made them social pioneers in the period of Korean reform. However, their experience in the practical social and educational fields was not that different from what happened in conservative church contexts: sex-discrimination was again prominent. Female teachers earned lower salaries and achieved a lower status in schools. Nurses and doctors were also treated less well and had to endure being treated as objects, as in traditional Korean society. Working for themselves or caring for girls within their own sphere, they did eventually come to dominate their own particular areas of education and the professions.

During Korea's political difficulties of the 1910s, educated *chŏndo puin* had a chance to reach a level nearly equal to that of men. In the initial moments of Korean independence, the support and, indeed, leadership of Christian women was very helpful, giving them considerable social power and spiritual influence in educational settings.[43] When Shinto worship and nationalist veneration of the Japanese emperor and flag were being enforced by the Japanese government in the late 1930s, alongside control of Korean educational institutions, including mission schools and colleges, two kinds of *chŏndo puin* emerged: for and against the worship.[44] As Korean churches surrendered to the strong religious persecution after 1938, Christian leaders had to determine how they would act. While some followed seemingly irresistible official orders from above, other refused. There have been many historical evaluations of the varying paths taken, but whatever road they chose, Christians negotiated a challenging context. Certain *chŏndo puin* supported Japanese policies and, from the nationalistic point of view, betrayed a number of their fellow Koreans, earning lasting blame and opprobrium: Hwal-ran Kim was one.

A tragic **chŏndo puin,** *Kim Helen Hwal-ran (1899–1970)*

As the first Korean woman PhD graduate and the first Korean president of the prestigious Ehwa Women's College, Hwal-ran Kim was an enormously powerful and respected figure in Korean society. At the time of the 1919 First Independent Movement, she was a teacher at Ehwa, but was deeply involved with underground organisations working for Korean independence, as a result of which she had to elude the Japanese police for a year. By her account, her job was to transfer money from mission schools and churchwomen's societies to the main organisation for Korean independence.[45] In addition, as a notable Christian evangelist, she led her Ehwa students to northern areas of Korea such as Pyŏngyang and Shinweejoo in the 1920s, trips that combined Christian propagation with nationalistic fervour. All this meant Korean people could not help but respect her in this period, while to most Korean girls, she was the ultimate role model. In addition, she was passionately committed to Christian social organisations, helping to establish the YWCA with Ryu Kak-kyŏng and Kim Pil-rye in May 1922. She was also deeply involved in Keunwoohwae, the patriotic women's group, which linked up with female socialists to free Korea from Japan on 27 May 1927. After trouble with the socialists in 1928, however, she left the group in order to work in Christian organisations, becoming President of Ehwa.[46]

From 1937, the Japanese government forced her to take a pro-Japanese stand. This had an enormous impact because she was such a widely respected Christian social leader and had already achieved prominence in anti-Japanese groups. Using her was a real propaganda coup for Japanese colonial policy in Korea. She helped raise money for the Japanese war effort and used her oratorical gifts to encourage especially the young to enlist for the Pacific War. She used the Japanese form of her name, and united the Korean and Japanese YWCAs in 1938. By the end of the Japanese occupation, she was viewed as a traitor to the Korean nation and an anti-Christian apostate.[47]

Conclusion

Using the history of *chŏndo puin* as the paradigm, this research has presented a new trajectory for reading the history of Protestant Christianity in Korea. My larger study sought to analyse the question of why *chŏndo puin's* stories had been neglected or ignored in Korean church history until now and what implications this has had both for that history and the present. *Chŏndo puin* were considered 'lower status' people in society, and female, despite representing the majority of Korean Christians. Throughout history, elite groups have been in the minority but extolled as major actors, used to 'tell the story of all others'. True to this pattern, the existence of *chŏndo puin* has been effectively eliminated from existing historical accounts, which assume that ordinary Korean Christian female leaders were unimportant to ecclesiastical historical scholarship, and even to the life of the church itself.

By contrast, my focus here falls deliberately on a number of elite as well as marginalised and ordinary women who developed Korea's Protestant Christianity in the context of mission and churches. Any such analysis needs both to confront and overcome three familiar dichotomies which set contrasting perspectives up against one another: Western imperialistic versus Third World; male versus female; and the powerful versus the powerless. Blinkered viewpoints make for erroneous, unpersuasive history. Due and balanced attention needs to be paid to both sides of the female encounter between missionaries and indigenous societies, with church history approached in a more gender-sensitive and sociologically aware manner, to combat both existing male elite-centred histories, dualistic feminist accounts and imperialistic, sexist or class-based views. The historical perspectives of Korean women and the leadership of *chŏndo puin* still have a significant part to play in the analysis of female missiology and Korean church history.

Notes

1 The material presented here draws extensively on SungJin Chang (2005) *Korean Bible Women: their vital contribution to Korean Protestantism 1895–1945* (PhD, University of Edinburgh).

2 See entry on Korea in British and Foreign Bible Society (BFBS) (1892) *The Eighty-Eighth Annual Report of the British and Foreign Bible Society (BFBS AR)* (London: BFBS), p. 249.

3 Kim Seung-tae (1999) *Han'guk Kyohoe Chŏndo Puin Charyŏchip* [Documentary Lists of Biblewomen of the Korean Church] (Seoul: Research Institute of Korean Christian History [RIKCH]). All translations from Korean in this paper are the author's own.

4 See Dana Lee Robert (1996) *American Women in Mission: a social history of their thought and practice* (Macon, GA: Mercer University Press).

5 Dana L. Robert (2002) *Gospel Bearers, Gender Barriers: missionary women in the twentieth century* (New York: Orbis), pp. 11–13.

6 Yi U-jŏng (1985) *Han'guk kidokkyo yŏsŏng paeknyŏn ŭi paljagu* [100 Years in the Footsteps of Korean Christian Women] (Seoul: Minjungsa), pp. 31–33.

7 Kim Sŭng-tae and Pak Hye-jin (1994) *Naehan sŏnkyosa chŏllam* [A Sourcebook of Missionaries in Korea, 1884–1984] (Seoul: RIKCH).

8 Chung Chong-rang (1987) *Ehwa paengnyŏn sa* [One Hundred Years of the History of Ehwa] (Seoul: Ehwa Women's University Press [WUP]), p. 42.

9 Chŏng Yo-sŏb (1979) *Han'guk Yŏsŏng Undongsa* [The History of the Korean Women's Movement] (Seoul: Jungwoomsa), p. 20, argues that *Tonghak* opposed the male-dominated view of Korean women centred in upper-class Confucianism. Its twelve-point demand for reform included 'permitting widows to remarry'. The movement 'made Korean women awaken and consoled them'. Kim Yŏng-Duk (1971) *Han'guksa Tamgu* [The Study of Korean History] (Seoul: Eljimunhwasa), pp. 61 and 221–2, likewise assesses *Tonghak*'s respect for women as the starting point of women's liberation from feudalism in Korea.

10 Yi Man-yŏl, *Han'guk Kidokkyo wa Minsokweesik* [Korean Christianity and Nationalism] (Seoul, Jisiksanubsa, 2000), pp. 356–374, suggests three reasons: the rise of commission sellers; the increasingly stability of the Korean church; and the vigorous activities of *chŏndo puin.*

11 In addition, I have used other primary sources in Korean and English; and periodicals like *The Korean Mission Field (KMF), The Korean Review, The Korean Repository*, Minutes of the Annual Meeting of Korean Mission in the Methodist Episcopal Church (1898–1913), *Korean Christian Magazine, Korean Methodist Magazine* and *Victorious Lives of Early Christians in Korea* (Seoul: The Christian Literature Society), where there is some direct storytelling from early *chŏndo puin.*

12 See Anon. (1861) *A Few Words to Bible Mission-Women* (London: Wertheim, Macintosh, and Hunt), pp. 6–8: to introduce women and children to the Bible; to help and educate the poor; to evangelise.

13 Anon. (1895) Bible Women in the East, *The Ninety-First BFBS AR* (London: BFBS), p. 232.

14 Ibid., p. 217.

15 Young-Jin Min (1998) Ross yuk lukabokŭmse ŭi sŏjisahang kwa pŏnyŏk ŭi sŏngkyŏk [A Bibliography and List of Traits of the Translation of Luke, Ross Version Gospel], *Sŏngkyung Wonmun Yŏngu* [Research on the Original Text of the Bible], 2 (February), p. 135.

16 This orthography's official name is *Hunminjungŭm*, a 'right script for teaching people', invented by 1443. Initially an elite script, its use quickly descended the social scale, leading to its description as 'an indecent orthography which was a tool for writing spicy talk or stories'. In *Chosŏn* society from 1446 to 1910, Korean men almost exclusively used Chinese characters for reading and writing, *Ŏnmun* being employed by those few high-class women who were educated. Yi Hyŏn-hi (1982) *Han'guk Kŭndae Yŏsŏng Kaehwasa* [The History of Women's Enlightenment in the Modern Period of Korea] (Seoul: Ewoo Monhwasa), p. 12.

17 'My interest in the people deepened with the progress of the year and as, after many amusing and futile attempts, I was able to find a clue to their language, I resolved to have the Scriptures in part or wholly translated into that language. This resolution was all the more decisive on discovering that everybody in Corea knew their beautifully simple phonetic alphabet, that "even all the women and children could read it."' Rev. J. Ross (1883) Corean New Testament, *The Chinese Recorder and Missionary Journal*, XIV (November–December, Shanghai), p. 491.

18 Anon. (1902) Bible Women, *The Annual Report of the Foreign Mission Committee*, p. 143.

19 Sources as for Table 3.

20 Anon. (1901) Our Biblewomen in Korea – Mr. A. Kenmure's Report for 1900, *The Bible Society Reporter* (April), p. 88.

21 *The Annual Report of the Board of Foreign Mission of the Presbyterian Church in the United States of America*, 1910.

22 Korea – Biblewomen, *BFBS AR* (1913), pp. 361–362.

23 Yi Man-yŏl' Kwonsŏ edaehan Yŏngu [Research on Colporteurs], *Han'guk kidokkyo wa minsokweesik* [Korean Christianity and Nationalism], p. 118.

24 Ibid.

25 Biblewomen, *BFBS AR* (1913), p. 362.

26 Kim Seung-tae [Documentary Lists of Korean Bible Women], p. 255.

27 J. L. Gerdine (1934) More Pioneers of Korea, in Charles A. Sauer (Ed.), *Within the Gate* (Seoul: YMCA Press), pp. 48–49.

28 Miss M. R. Hillman (1906), A Wonderful Week, *Korea Mission Field (KMF)*, II(10, August), p. 183.

29 Joo Sun-ae (1979) *Changnokyo yŏsŏng sa* [The History of Presbyterian Women] (Seoul: Editorial Committee National Organization of Korean Presbyterian Women), pp. 135–136.

30 Helen K. Bernheisel (1932) Their First Missionary, *Women and Missionaries*, Vol. 8, p. 429.

31 Mattie Wilcox Noble (1906), Report of Evangelistic Work, Bible Institutes, and Three Day Schools, Pyeng Yang, *The 18th ARKWC (MEC)*, p. 61.

32 Louise B. Hayes, The Korean Bible Woman and her Work, *KMF* (July 1935), p. 151.

33 *Maeilshinbo* [The Daily Newspaper], 17 September 1922, p. 17.

34 Chŏng Mariah in Kyongsŏng [an old name for Seoul], Yŏjŏndoin ŭi Sŭngriggaji [Toward the last victory], in an article on Yŏjundohoe bulpyongkwa Heemang [The Complaint and Hope of *chŏndo puin*], *Kidokshinbo* [Christian Newspaper], 1 January 1930.

35 Mrs. W. A. Noble (Ed.) (1927) Mrs. Sadie Kim, in *Victorious Lives of Early Christians in Korea*, pp. 128–130.

36 Ibid., p. 133–134.
37 Mattie W. Noble (1907) The Report of Mrs. W. A. Noble, *The 19th ARKWC (MEC)*, p. 75.
38 Kim and Yang [Documentary Lists of Korean Bible Women], p. 166.
39 *Kidokshinbo*, 30 October 1919.
40 Kim and Yang [Documentary Lists of Korean Biblewomen], pp. 165–6, and sources for Table 4.
41 For more detail, see Nansa K. Hahr (1911) A Protest, *KMF*, 7 (12, December), pp. 352–353.
42 See Anon. (1908) Copy of the Sketch of Woman's Medical Missionary Work Placed in the Corner Stone of the New Hospital, Pyŏngyang, May 20, 1908, *KMF*, 7, pp. 109–110, and H. B. Montgomery (1910) *Western Women in Eastern Lands* (New York: Macmillan), pp. 120–121.
43 United prayer meetings, with around one hundred participants each, took place in Presbyterian and Methodist mission schools. Chung Chong-rang (1968) *Ehwa Palshipnyŏnsa* [Eighty Years' History of Ehwa] (Seoul: Ehwa Women's College), pp. 425–427.
44 There were several trials of Christians for defending their own faith. A good example is an ecumenical women's anti-Shinto movement at the time of Women's World Day of Prayer meeting in 1941. See Cho Sun-hae (1996) 1941 nyŏn Manguk Puin Kidohoe Sagun Yŏngu [Researching the Women's World Prayer Meeting Event], *Han'guk kidokkyowa yŏk sa* [Korean Christianity and History], 5 (September), pp. 117–130.
45 Kim Hwal-ran (1999) *Ki Bipsuk ŭi Jagŭn Sengmyŏng* [The Little Life in the Light] (Seoul: Ehwa WUP), p. 101.
46 Kang Jŏng-suk (1999) *Chinilpa 99in* [The 99 Pro-Japanese people], Vol. 2 (Seoul: Banminjokmoonjaeyeongooso), pp. 275–283.
47 In Kim Seng-tae's list of *chŏndo puin*, her name does not appear. For further detail, see also Kim Jung-uk (1977) *Kim Imonim Hwal-ran* [My Mother's Sister, Hwal-Ran Kim] (Seoul: Junwoosa) and Kim Uk-gil (1959) *Kim Hwal-Ran Paksa Somyo* [A Portrait of Dr Hwal-Ran Kim] (Seoul: Ehwa WUP). This complex and well-documented story merits fuller treatment than I can give it here.

45

KIMBANGUISM AND THE QUESTION OF SYNCRETISM IN ZAÏRE

Wyatt MacGaffey

Source: W. E. A. van Beek, Th. E. Blakely and D. L. Thomson (eds), *Religion in Africa: Experience and Expression*, London: James Currey; Portsmouth, NH: Heinemann, 1994, pp. 241–56.

Although the word "syncretic" is commonly applied to religious, little thought has been given to the origins and specific features of syncretism. The term is in fact ambiguous, since it is taken to indicate a particular kind of religion or religious situation, characterized by the combination of heterogeneous elements; yet on the other hand, all culture, and *a fortiori* all religion, continually draws upon foreign elements. Citing a study of syncretism by J. H. Kamstra, Michael Pye observes that "to be human is to be a syncretist" but that "most practitioners of the study of religion are strongly influenced by Christianity and tend to see syncretism as an illicit contamination, as a threat or a danger, as taboo, or as a sign of religious decadence". Ambiguity in scholarly usage thus conceals an implicitly adverse judgment: "syncretism" has become a pejorative term, applicable only to situations of which one disapproves (Pye 1971:83–93).

Such usage is conspicuous in the history of European comment on Kimbanguism, one of the world's best-known religious movements, initiated in Lower Zaïre (then Lower Congo) in 1921 by the Kongo prophet Simon Kimbangu. This region was the object of intensive Protestant and later Catholic mission work from the 1870s onward. In 1908 it was incorporated into the Belgian Congo. The movement of 1921 aroused widespread popular enthusiasm but was rapidly suppressed by the Belgians, who imprisoned Kimbangu and his followers (Andersson 1958; MacGaffey 1983). Repression continued until 1959, when the sons of Kimbangu were recognized by the government as the leaders of the Church of Jesus Christ on the Earth by the Prophet Simon Kimbangu (EJCSK). This organization, now reputedly the largest African-founded Protestant church, belongs to the World Council of

Churches and is one of the three publicly recognized churches of modern Zaïre, the others being the Catholic and the united Protestant Church of Christ in Zaïre (ECZ).

EJCSK, however, though the largest, is by no means the only church claiming the spiritual legacy of Kimbangu. Conspicuous among the many others is a group of similar movements centered in Manianga, in the northern part of the province: in the literature on Kimbanguism this tradition is called *ngounziste* in French ("Ngunzist" in English), from the Kikongo *ngunza* [prophet]. Its constituent churches have usually called themselves by some variant of the term Church of the Holy Spirit [Dibundu dia Mpeve a Nlongo, or DMN].

The history and internal variation of Protestant Christianity in Lower Zaïre therefore present us with three kinds of churches, which we may think of as three concentric circles: First, at the center, "orthodox" churches controlled until recently by the American Baptist, British Baptist, and Swedish Evangelical missions, now united with other "communities" in the ECZ. Second, the independent EJCSK, the major organized result of the Kimbanguist movement of 1921. Third, a number of lesser offshoots of Kimbanguism, of which (for the purposes of this chapter) the Ngunzist DMN group are the most important.

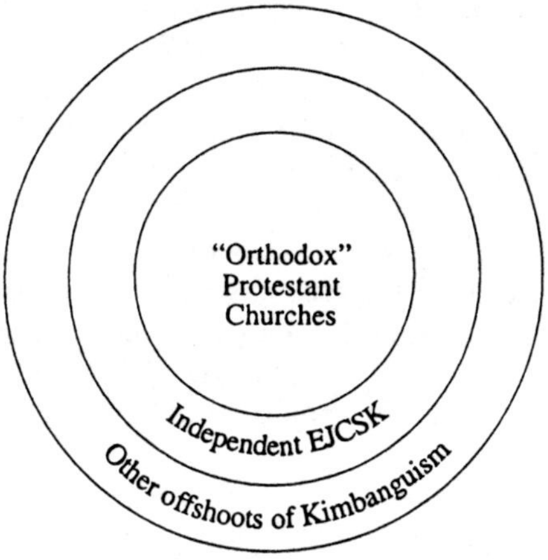

Figure 1 Protestant Christianity in Lower Zaïre [Bas-Zaïre].

Relations among churches in these three categories have always been political, both in the sense that they are schismatic and competitive and in the sense that they have been rivals for the favor of the government, colonial and postcolonial, upon which they all depend. Political discrimination (intended, that is, to defend the boundary of a particular corporate organization) is evidently a factor in the attitude of two of the principal commentators on Kimbanguism, Efraim Andersson and Marie Louise Martin, though their interests differ (Andersson 1968:77, 131–142, 158–161; Martin 1975). Andersson, though acknowledging and effectively documenting "the legacy of popular religion" among practicing members of the Swedish mission church in northern Kongo, still asserts that he can identify the "essential difference between paganism and Christianity". The difference is especially elusive when the mission church is compared with what Andersson calls "the sects", that is, the cluster of movements that eventually gave rise to EJCSK and the DMN churches. Within the Swedish mission church itself, especially in 1947 and 1955, individuals and movements emerged—bearing all the characteristic signs of ecstatic prophetism—who are nevertheless accepted, by Andersson at least, not only as Christian but as having brought special benefits to the rest of the church.

In 1921, some missionaries of the Baptist Missionary Society, to whose church Kimbangu originally belonged, had a good opinion of his work, although it is doubtful, given the strength of Belgian and Catholic sentiment at the time, that the mission as a whole, even if it wanted to, could have embraced the new movement (Desroche and Raymaekers 1946:117–162). In 1969, however, EJCSK was admitted to the World Council of Churches, as a result of reports rendered by Martin, among others, whose own religious background (Moravian) is similar to Andersson's evangelical Lutheranism. Martin's defense of EJCSK constantly distinguishes between it and "Ngunzism", which means in effect all the features of Kimbanguism in general of which she disapproves because they are "syncretic". Once again, the distinction is difficult to maintain and requires sustained special pleading: speaking of EJCSK, she says, "I myself was amazed to see how extensively ancient patterns of thought were transformed on the basis of the Gospel and vested with new content without succumbing to the danger of syncretism" (Martin 1975:x, 73).

It is easy to illustrate the difference between "ancient patterns" and the gospel, as both Martin and Andersson do, the latter with the benefit of extensive knowledge of the language and of the indigenous religion. Personal familiarity with Ngunzism would enable them to cite many examples of moral benefits and deeply thoughtful Christian piety there too, however. And of course scandalous misuse of the gospel can be documented in any European Christian mission or church by anyone disposed to do so.[1] A weekday evening service at EJCSK's holy city of Nkamba, birthplace of the prophet, or in some little congregation remote from the hoopla of the church's special festivals for foreigners can be an impressive and moving display of the austere dignities of the Protestant faith, but so can the equally disciplined early morning service of an Ngunzist church at its own holy city. It is equally impressive to listen to the advice given to a woman in distress by a DMN elder, into which is woven his knowledge of the Bible, of humanity, of oppression (the walls of his house bear the mark of Belgian bullets), and his belief in spiritual guidance and relief. In their unorthodox and often spectacular rites the DMN churches worship God with a vitality and exaltation that many a Protestant pastor of unimpeachable orthodoxy would envy, combining worship with concern for the social and psychological well-being of individuals.

It is not my intention, however, to extend the benefits of special pleading more generously than others have done. I wish to argue that the inadequacy of "syncretism" is derived from the inappropriate theory of meaning implicit in it.

In the article previously cited, Pye advances the view that the distinctive feature of syncretism is ambiguity of meaning (e.g., as exhibited in the situation studied, not in the usage of scholars). With reference to Shinto-Buddhist syncretism in particular, he says: "The elements under consideration became ambiguous. They were able to bear two distinct meanings: depending on the different points of view of the people involved with them" (Pye 1971:92). Such syncretism he thinks must necessarily be temporary. Since the traditions move all the time, meanings are continually refashioned. Pye's explanation for this dynamism is animistic ("the urge which many religions have to move out and to move on"), but he also postulates that within the individual consciousness "the ambiguous clash of meanings demands some resolution" (Pye 1971:92). He anticipates three possible resolutions of the ambiguity: assimilation, by which one meaning eliminates the other; fusion, in which a new religion emerges; and dissolution, a drifting apart of the two meanings. Such resolution, though effective for individuals, may not prevent other individuals from experiencing in turn the clash of meanings, so that "syncretistic situations may persist for a long time and even indefinitely, even though they are . . . intrinsically temporary" (Pye 1971:92–93).

The assumption that clashing meanings demand resolution, formally known as the theory of cognitive dissonance, remains unverified. In practice, people seem to tolerate high levels of cognitive cacophony. In retrospect, the theory (as applied to the study of religious change) can be seen as profoundly ethnocentric: our civilization has been so much influenced by the technology of literacy that we have come to think of the activity of the human mind itself as being like that of the scholar confronting the printed page (Greenwald and Ronis 1978:53–57). Jack Goody points out that widely disseminated books, archives, and records of every kind have made science itself possible, precisely because they intrude upon our discourse and force us to take note of discrepant statements (Goody 1977). Pye writes as though meaning were defined, for a believer, by something akin to a dictionary of his faith; the syncretist, finding the same "word" given different meanings in the "dictionaries" of Shintoism and Buddhism, feels compelled to seek some resolution.[2] In general, believers who are not scholars are uncertain of their beliefs and are inconsistent in their responses to questions about belief. The sense they have of "meaning" in their religion may develop at several levels of consciousness but certainly includes as an important element the sense of satisfactory communication with others in ritual. Ritual itself is a social event, takes place in a wider social context, and presupposes the values and meanings constitutive of community life in that place and time. It presupposes, for example, a certain routine to the week or the year; a certain allocation of resources; a division of social labor between men and women, adults and children; and common assemblages of visual and verbal symbols in which these distributions are signified.

The linguistic philosopher John R. Searle argues that "large tracts of apparently fact-stating language" depend for their meaning on the constitutive rules of the institutional context in which the utterances occur. The actors' sense of communicated meaning is at least partly a function of their ability to produce an intended effect, action consistent with pertinent institutional conventions. The parties to communication may not in fact share, "in their heads", exactly the same sense of what has been communicated (Searle 1969:50). As Edmund Leach says, "Just as two readers of a poem may agree about its quality and yet derive from it totally different meanings, so, in the context of ritual action, two individuals or groups of individuals may accept the validity of a set of ritual actions without agreeing at all as to what is expressed in those actions" (Leach 1954:86).

Syncretism and social pluralism

Although syncretism of some kind is a universal property of culture, religious situations that most often attract the label are particularly likely to occur in plural societies, that is, societies in which two or more institutional sets ("societies") exist within a single governmental framework. All colonial and postcolonial states are plural societies, although not all plural societies are colonial (Smith 1974).

The Belgian Congo, created in 1908, incorporated a large number of indigenous societies in a new political framework of European bureaucratic type. Kimbanguism arose in one of these, that of the Bakongo of the Atlantic coastal region. Kongo society was characterized by matrilineal descent, an economy of subsistence agriculture on which was superimposed a considerable volume of trade between the coast and the interior, and a cosmology in which the influence of the spirits of the dead upon the living was mediated by chiefs, priests, magicians, and witches. Institutions of this kind are not readily understood by Europeans, who expect anthropologists to interpret them (MacGaffey 1970a). The institutions of the colony itself, on the other hand, were relatively familiar; they included Roman-Dutch law, capitalist industry, bureaucratic government, and Catholic and Protestant Christianity. The dominion of this second or bureaucratic sector over the first or "customary" sector was governed by a policy known somewhat misleadingly as "indirect rule", whereby customary institutions were tolerated and even strengthened, provided that they conformed to what the Belgians described as universal moral norms. In fact, since the political and economic conditions of existence of customary institutions were entirely different from what they had been before, these institutions represented the social adaptation of the Bakongo to colonial rule in the twentieth century. What is important about them is not that they were "traditional", since they were no more so than those of the bureaucratic sector, but that they were maintained in their difference and subordination by the colonial regime, as a matter of policy.

Each of these sets of institutions presupposed a distinct cosmology and employed its own group of cultural codes. The bureaucratic sector was predicated upon a linear concept of time and, during the colonial period, on the reality of race. The cosmology of the customary sector presupposed a repetitive cyclical or spiral concept of time and included the belief that blacks, when they die, go to Europe or America, where they become white, and whence they may return to Africa as ancestors or ghosts, for good or evil purposes. The cultural codes included contrasting rules about such things as gestures, social precedence, and proper dress for men and women; the most important communicative resource was of course language, whether French or Kikongo, in each case closely tied semantically and practically to the respective institutional sets. In neither of these cosmologies are such concepts as the unilinear course of time, the reality of race, or Europe as the land of the dead, scientifically necessary or transcendently true. In each instance, the content of the cosmology can be related to the organization of the society, in conjunction with which it shapes the experience of the members, "formulating conceptions of a general order of existence and clothing these conceptions with such an aura of factuality" that the moods and motivations it establishes "seem uniquely realistic" (Geertz 1966; MacGaffey 1978a).

Between 1908 and national independence in 1960, Bakongo were progressively assimilated into the bureaucratic sector. They were converted to Christianity, educated in the European fashion, induced to work for wages, and subjected to taxation. They participated in state, church, and industry, however, on an entirely different footing from Europeans and remained subject, in their private lives, to Kongo institutions connected with matrilineal descent and the "customary" codes regulating marital, interpersonal, and local relationships. That is to say, the Bakongo under colonial rule belonged to two societies, not one, in which "meaning" with respect not only to matters of religion but to all matters of social purpose, identity, and ontology were expressed in different languages (Kikongo and French) and with different assemblages of symbolic practice.

It follows that whenever Kikongo speakers and French speakers interacted in contexts other than those in which only the most perfunctory or practical meanings were at issue, a high level of shared misunderstanding was institutionalized. A special colonial vocabulary, neither French nor Kikongo, was developed to mediate this noncommunication; in religion, some of its most useful words were *nlongo*, which meant "holy" to Europeans and something like "taboo" to Africans; *sumuka*, "to sin" or "to violate a taboo, to pollute"; *nkadi a mpemba*, "the Devil" or "a vengeful ghost"; and so on (Janzen and MacGaffey 1974). Since communication consists as much of interaction as language, a like ambiguity also characterized action, including ritual, but extending into all institutional contexts, not just religion (Doutreloux 1967:261).

The real semantic dissonance that inevitably arises in plural societies is part of a more general conflict of purposes arising on the political level. The separation of the sectors and the dominion of one over the other are maintained by continuous political activity. As Pye observes, the possible resolutions of the tension include assimilation (one meaning eliminates the other), fusion (a new religion emerges), and dissolution (drifting apart of the two systems). The fact that syncretic situations may persist indefinitely (even though, according to the concept of cognitive dissonance, they are "intrinsically temporary") is due, Pye explains, to the continual recurrence of syncretism in the minds of new individuals. According to the sociological perspective, however, ambiguity can be expected to persist in plural societies as long as the plural constitution itself persists, and its resolution depends on political rather than cognitive processes.

Syncretism and EJCSK

The social context of kimbanguism is the structural pluralism of a colonial state in which two separate institutional sets are maintained, one of them politically and economically subordinate to the other. The form of this relationship persisted after independence, although the class structure of the population changed: the African foremen and clerks of companies, missions, and government replaced Europeans as the managers of these organizations, and thus of the state. Meanwhile, almost all Zaïreans continue to live by two sets of rules, consciously and visibly segregated; in all public contexts, the truths of the bureaucratic institutional set dominate those of the customary set, which are only tolerated insofar as they can be represented, in French, as conforming to the categories of the bureaucratic world.

Religion among the Kikongo-speaking peoples in Zaïre can be represented diagrammatically as two overlapping circles, B and C, with a common area, X. The language of B is French; and its institutional structure, which gives meaning to both language and behavior, is "bureaucratic". The language of C is Kikongo, and its institutional structure is "customary". Items of belief and practice that fall in the common area, X, can be interpreted in either French or Kikongo and therefore have alternative meanings; items belonging to B or C but not falling in X are those that can readily be described only in French or in Kikongo, respectively. EJCSK, which began as a popular movement located in C, so to speak, has moved since 1959 increasingly into B (arrows in Figure 2). This movement was largely forced by political

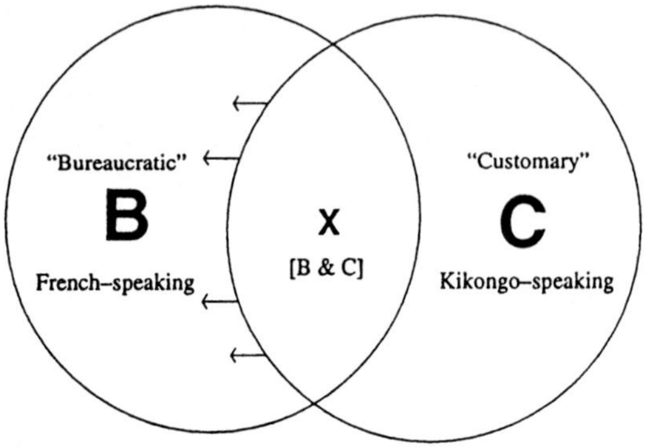

Figure 2 "Bureaucratic" vs. "customary" religion among Kikongo-speaking peoples in Zaïre.

considerations and has had its costs as well as its advantages. The leadership is conscious of the ambiguities involved, and its propaganda apparatus has been outstandingly successful in manipulating them before both Kikongo- and French-speaking audiences. These manipulations are socially and politically necessary and cannot be reduced to either theological ignorance or dishonesty.

Let us consider a concrete example. The rules of the church (EJCSK n.d.), in addition to the Ten Commandments, are

1 Respect the government (Romans 13:1–3).
2 Love everybody, even your enemy (Matthew 5:43–45).
3 No smoking, whether tobacco or hemp.
4 No alcohol.
5 No dancing or attendance at dances.
6 Do not bathe naked or sleep naked.
7 No quarreling.
8 No use of charms or magic.
9 Pay taxes.
10 Do not harbor resentment.
11 Everybody must admit his or her illdoing, before witnesses.
12 The only food taboos forbid eating monkey or pig.

All of these rules can be seen as making sense in either European (Francophone) or African (Kikongo) terms, but some fit much more easily into the one than the other, and the meaning of all of them changes according to the perspective. Rule 1, respect for government, is the least ambiguous and might seem to entail Rule 9, payment of taxes. In fact, taxation is a bureaucratic practice, to which the people have become accustomed in this century, but which they continue to resent, commonly (and with some justice) seeing it as a forced levy benefiting the governing class; they contrast it with personal, "voluntary" presentations, as to a chief or patron. Rules 3, 4, and 5 conform to Protestant (Baptist) morality but also make sense in indigenous terms; dances in particular are recognized, not as immoral in themselves, but as occasions for immorality. Rule 8, against magic, makes sense either in European terms ("no superstition") or in Kongo terms ("no self-seeking truck with the occult"). Rules 2, 7, 10, and 11 seem to be merely good moral advice but attract attention by their redundant multiplicity; in fact, in Kongo perspective, they are prescriptions against witchcraft, or against the attitudes from which witchcraft can unconsciously arise.

Rules 6 and 12 cannot easily be justified in French, and Kimbanguist attempts to do so are notably unsatisfactory. As to not bathing or sleeping naked, Kimbanguists say that persons of the opposite sex may pass by the bathing place or the house might catch fire, forcing the unprepared sleeper to expose himself or herself to the public. To the extent that these are real dangers, everybody confronts them, and there is no reason why common-sense precautions should be made into rules of the church. Members of other churches observe the same rules and more readily explain that in the reflecting surface of water one can see and be seen by the people of the other world, "the angels", some of whom are of the opposite sex; likewise, religious people expect to be visited by "angels" in their sleep. As a high-ranking minister of the Church of the Twelve Apostles said, describing a remarkable experience, "I had just lain down to sleep when the angel of the Lord appeared before me in a great shower of sparks; fortunately, I was wearing a good pair of underpants". In Kikongo, these "angels" are the dead [*bafwa*].

The taboo against pork is explained by Kimbanguists variously as based on Mosaic law, the story of the Gadarene swine, the filthy eating habits of pigs, or the risk of parasites and disease. The inadequacy of these explanations is obvious. Closest to the real reasoning is the story of the Gadarene swine, into which evil spirits fled from Jesus; domestic pigs are favorite repositories in which witches imprison the souls of their victims, and to eat domestic pork is to risk involuntary participation in witchcraft feasts.[3] Kimbanguists are allowed to eat wild pig. Likewise, as the head of the church, Joseph Diangienda, explained to me, "There are two kinds of monkey; one of them is forbidden, but the other we can eat". He did not elaborate, but Andersson explains that, of the two kinds, *makaku* (or *nsima*) monkeys live in bands, whereas *nsengi* monkeys go in pairs, as man and wife, and are believed to be human beings in disguise [*bituzi*] (Andersson 1958:176).

Kimbanguist theological accounting is not just a matter of keeping two sets of books. The church must participate in one or both of two institutional sets, each of which requires certain adaptations of organizational form and practice, and of interpersonal behavior, as well as language. For EJCSK to survive it had to develop a bureaucratic structure, a fiscal system, a school system, and various formal protestations of faith. More recently, the expectations of Protestant theology, upon which international and local support for the church is to some extent conditional, have pushed it to adopt a communion service, celebrated for the first time in April 1971. Such a move could be costly if it violated popular conceptions. As Andersson explains, the communion, even in its Baptist form (commemorative rather than sacramental), is inconsistent with popular notions of sin, grace, and salvation, even as they are found within the mission churches (Andersson 1968:148–153, 169–171). Popularly, the kingdom of God "on earth" is a matter of freedom from affliction. Affliction is caused by breaking cult rules [*sumuka*] or by witchcraft, although orthodox Protestant pastors struggle to convince their congregations that afflictions are in fact caused by "Satan", who has become a kind of aggregate, all-purpose witch. Communion, even within the mission churches, is often regarded as an ordeal to detect and punish witches, and like all such ordeals can be misused by the clergy, should they themselves happen to be witches. In 1966, certain Kongo pastors who were vigorous upholders of mission orthodoxy against all forms of prophetism regarded the communion as an item of European culture not necessary to true Christianity and thought that in an age of increasing independence from missionary control it should be abolished.

The EJCSK's introduction of communion had therefore to be carefully prepared, though we do not know what considerations occupied the thoughts of the leadership. In the domain of bureaucratic discourse, the church first uttered a theological explanation, written by the Secretary General. Less readily intelligible to the foreign observer was the performance, once only, of a special preparatory ritual, in which M. Diangienda himself or one of the priests [*sacrificateurs*] "sealed" each of the faithful on the forehead with the sign of the cross in Nkamba water (Martin 1975:161, 179–182). No explanation for the ritual or its origin was made available to outsiders, but the gesture, of Catholic origin, has long been used by Diangienda as a blessing and is popularly understood as having a beneficial effect on the recipient's *lusunzi* [his soul or life-chance], situated in his forehead [*ndunzi*]. The soul itself is often represented, in indigenous art, by a cruciform design.

Communion is supposed to be received three times a year: April 6th (the feast of the prophet's manifestation), October 12th (the date of his death), and Christmas. The omission of Easter, for which April 6th effectively substitutes, is interesting. The feast is celebrated only by the head of the church, Diangienda. In practice, Kimbanguists partake only if they are in Kinshasa (the capital), Nkamba (the New Jerusalem), or Kisangani (the third city of Zaïre); by 1980, communion had been celebrated only twice.

After 1960 the church lost much of its popular support by curtailing ecstatic and healing practices incompatible with its organizational needs; people began to say that it was nothing but another mission church. In 1972, in an effort to renew its spiritual vitality and discipline, EJCSK introduced a new observance—the retreat. Biblical precedents were cited for this new institution, which Kimbangu was also said to have foretold. Retreats took place deep in the forest, or at another place free of distractions. Kimbanguists were supposedly required to attend once in a lifetime, but members of other churches and faiths were welcome. A retreat lasted from Tuesday to Saturday and was marked by frequent prayers, a fast of three days' duration, Bible study, confession of sins, and other exercises expected to renew contact with the Holy Spirit as in the old days at Nkamba in 1921.

Every night, men and women slept separately at their camp in the forest, and watches were appointed of nine men and nine women (or 3, 5, or 7, but not an even number) to pray in turn throughout the night. Public confessions were heard throughout the morning, and then the participants, in odd-numbered groups, moved still deeper into the forest to pray and sing hymns. Everybody made the sacrifice of not eating, drinking, or washing for at least one day, some for two or three. Now and again someone would become possessed [*lauka*] and run shrieking to one of the pastors to confess something he or she had kept back; not to confess was to risk mental illness or even death. In the forest, people began to see visions [*mambu mamanene mangitukulu*]: "the crucified Christ, or you might see a huge eye which was perhaps the eye of God, we don't know". People spoke in strange tongues, such as English, which were intelligible to others though not to the speaker. The reports of visions were written down and transmitted to the central office of the church.

The institution of the retreat testified to the church's capacity for adaptive renewal but entailed its own risks. The closer the church reached towards the energy locked up in the real authenticities of indigenous culture, the sharper its rivalry with competing systems of spiritual guidance necessarily became. It is not surprising, therefore, that dealing with magicians and resorting to charms ("fetishes") were important and frequent themes of the confessions (MacGaffey 1976:40–43).

Syncretism and Ngunzism

Though prayers and dreams may remain private matters, the process of healing intrudes into the public domain in any society. Where life or social competence is at stake, therapy is subject to supervision in more than one public context; it is accordingly difficult for the practitioners, while it affords privileged opportunities to observe the structure of pluralism.

In Zaïre, as also in much of Africa from Nigeria to the Republic of South Africa, the rituals of prophetic churches commonly reveal two phases (see Kiernan 1976:356–366). The first phase consists of an ordinary Protestant service: hymns, prayers, Bible reading, and sermon. The second phase, marked by the appearance of the prophet himself, and by other changes of personnel, music, and spatial organization, is devoted to specifically prophetic activities and is highly ambiguous. The usual prophetic activities include oracular prediction and revelation [*mbikudulu*], ecstatic manifestations, prophylactic blessings, spiritual healing, "war" with hostile spirit forces, and, in Ngunzist (DMN) churches particularly, a form of spiritual testing and confirmation known by the French word *bascule* [weighing] (Janzen and MacGaffey 1974, no. 48). All of these practices are justified by reference to biblical texts, as are the practices of American Protestant churches. The participants think of themselves as Protestants or Catholics (the theological differences between the two mean little to most Zaïreans). When asked why their practices differ from those of mission-related churches, they argue that they have restored elements that the missions have improperly excluded. From their point of view, "true Christianity" is coterminous with the C sector of Figure 2, and all elements of B, or mission Christianity, that fall outside of X, the common area, are "syncretic" (improper) European additions.

Nevertheless, the contents of DMN rituals also closely parallel those of indigenous Kongo priests [*nganga*, singular]. One individual observed in Matadi in 1970 would enter in solemn procession with six or seven acolytes, most of them women dressed in white as nuns. He himself wore a white soutane and carried a staff resembling a crozier. The hymns sung by the congregation described the activities in progress:

> He is awake, has put on his robe,
> See the dawn!
> The lost sheep I seek,
> The white and the black,
> God's prophet is awake.

As the prophet invoked a blessing on water contained in a number of clear glass bottles, he and his acolytes trembled spectacularly and uttered ecstatic cries. Evidently imitating Catholic communion, the prophet poured a little water from a cup into the mouth of each acolyte, remarking that "all those who have received water to drink shall be saved" and afterwards rinsing his hands and drying them on a napkin that was folded and placed on top of the cup. He would then proceed to divination, saying, "Hark! The time for prophecy has come!" (Janzen and MacGaffey 1974, no. 22; MacGaffey 1983:159–177).

The glossolalia, trembling, and divination while in a state of possession can all be matched in the nineteenth-century rituals of *nganga manga*, *nganga ngombo*, *nganga ntadi*, and others intended to "sniff out" [*fyela*] witches. The Matadi prophet even referred to himself as *mfyedi* [diviner]. In the past, the ecstatic acolytes were called *mintombo*, from *tombula* [to raise up] spirits. The list of parallels also includes treatment by means of blessings, potions, and ablutions; divinatory inquiry proceeding through a series of alternatives (natural causes or witchcraft; if witchcraft, from the maternal or paternal side of the family?, etc.); the use of songs describing the proceedings; and the techniques of raising excitement by an increasing volume of music and the interpolation of increasingly specific revelations alternating with glossolalia. A Kongo anthropologist describes the work of *nganga ngombo* as follows:

> After a while one would see trembling and changes of behavior among those present, especially in the case of the one holding the pot of fetishes [medicines]. These signs manifest that at that moment the *nkisi* dwell in everybody who is trembling. And that is a good thing, because this is the means whereby the possessed (*habitées*) do whatever the possessing spirit tells them to do or say. If the *nkisi* tell them to go to the river in the middle of the night, they will run there. Being possessed, their voices change quality, and some of them speak Lingala or some other language instead of their own Kindibu dialect of KiKongo. Under the influence of the *nkisi* they reveal the names of witches and the history of witchcraft in the family in question, and also what should be done to effect healing and restore peace, prosperity, and fertility.
>
> (Buakasa 1968:153–169; cf. Cavazzi da Montecuccolo 1965:181–183)

In the basic healing technique of DMN churches, the healer circles the patient, flapping a towel and laying hands on the head or afflicted part, with invocations and much trembling. Some healers puff and blow, to add to the wind [*mpeve*] created by the flapping towel, or spread the towel over the sufferer. The towels used have been specially blessed for the purpose. Such towels and other cloths, including flags, have replaced animal skins and raffia cloths formerly used in the same way. In 1700 a Capuchin missionary described healing procedures he had observed:

> Then they take the skins of certain animals with which they touch the patient all over, and from time to time they shake him and strike him, saying that these skins will draw out the evil that has seized upon him. To signify this, the fetisher snaps and shakes the skins to shake out the evil adhering to them.
>
> (Cuvelier 1953:131)

In the nineteenth century, similar rituals were performed by *nganga mvutudi*, *ntombodi*, or *ntadi* to "return the soul" of a patient, the sign of success being that the priest was able to lay a raffia cloth on the patient's head [*tensikisa lubongo ku ntu mbevo*] (MacGaffey 1986:239). More examples of similar parallels could be given, and they form the basis for arguments that the modern prophet is merely a witchdoctor in Christian clothing. The prophets themselves, however, continually draw a sharp distinction between themselves and the *nganga n'kisi* [peddler of charms and magic] (Andersson 1958:3). Prophetic ritual practice, in contrast to that of the magician, stresses the use of plain water instead of herbal concoctions in palm wine. In this connection the whiteness of enamel vessels and the clear glass of the bottles used is important. Ritual clothing is plain white, with at most a few touches of red and an occasional embroidered sign. This whiteness is a powerful iconoclastic statement of purity, clarity, transparency, and sincerity, symbolizing the prophet's commitment to openness and publicity, as opposed to the particularism and murky secretiveness of self-serving magic. As one prophet said, "The Holy Spirit in a man is like water in a glass, hiding nothing".[4]

The resort to whiteness is no doubt partly an accommodation to censorship—holy water and white robes are acceptably Christian, whereas body paint and animal skins would declare their origin—but it is not simply protective coloration for covert "paganism"; a distinction is being made, within the implicit structure of indigenous religion, between beliefs and practices associated with the pursuit of personl advantage and those that assert the priority of public interests and values. Trance, glossolalia and the like are metaphorical expressions of the prophet's direct commission from God [Nzambi], in whose name and with whose power he purports to act. The charms of the magician, on the other hand, are bought and sold and stand for the pursuit of self-interest, which Kongo thought associates with witchcraft. This tension between public and private values is fundamental to the religion of most of Bantu-speaking Africa and can be discerned in Kongo history at least as far back as 1700 (MacGaffey 1970b:27–38, 1977:177–193).

Other Christian Churches

In effect, Bakongo assimilated the missionary condemnation of indigenous religion, described as "sorcery", "superstition", and the like, to their own standing distrust of all dealings with the occult not subject to public discipline. This misunderstanding persists to the present day and does not differentiate Kimbanguists or Ngunzists from other Kongo Christians, Catholic or Protestant. Collectively resolving in the name of Christianity to return to the right way, they enthusiastically adopted the moral prescriptions, rituals, and scriptures brought by the missionary, to the extent that they could read in them values they already respected. In the era of decolonization, the ambiguity of this conversion is much debated, notably by Catholic intellectuals in Zaïre. On the one hand, Zaïreans feel that they have always known God; as a government spokesman put it, "The missionaries expected to convert us to a faith, whereas they merely converted us to a kind of rite different from our own". On the other hand, as one of the leading intellectuals has written: "Catholic, universal, whatever you like, the problem remains: Catholicism is a religion marked by the West even in the understanding of the message. Carried, sustained as it is by European structures, it is hardly possible to love it without committing oneself in the history of the world" (Mudimbe 1973:35). From this dilemma arises the active contemporary movement towards an "African theology" (Inongo 1973:216; Mudimbe 1973:35; Tshibangu 1974).

According to Cardinal Malula, archbishop of Kinshasa, "Eight tenths of the life of our people is governed by the belief in witchcraft, divination, and dreams. This is a fact. After 80 years of 'evangelization', and despite all the condemnations of our 'civilizing masters', this sole fact should give us pause" (Malula 1977:5). Lufuluabo, a Franciscan priest, in the book to which the Cardinal prefaces these words, explains that the faithful, despite all the sermons they have heard, believe firmly in sorcery; to escape its effects, they turn not to their priest but to a diviner. The clergy are thus isolated from their flock in their moments of greatest spiritual need. "I know that we will make no true progress until we question the [European-derived] massive and summary condemnation of so-called superstitions, in which practically all African values are included" (Lufuluabo 1977:8).

Lufuluabo later got into trouble with the Catholic Church for practicing divination himself, and the problem continues to vex the best theological minds in the country. The respected scholar Vincent Mulago argues that for those who truly understand the essence of Christianity and African tradition there can be no contradiction between them (Mulago 1981:41). In the same issue of the same journal, Bimwenyi, Secretary-General of the Episcopal Conference of Zaïre, contradicts Mulago and gives sophisticated expression to Lufuluabo's point of view. He vigorously asserts that the Church as at present constituted is fundamentally alien to Africa, where Christian communities

> pray to God in a liturgy that is not their own, live according to a moral order which is not a transformation, by the grace of God and the breath of the Spirit, of their own former order. They are ruled by a canon law which is not a law born of the conversion to Christ of the socio-juridical realities immanent in the universe to which they belong. . . . If they reflect, they do so according to philosophical and theological systems generated by the meditation and reflection of other Christian communities that have evangelized them.
>
> (Bimwenyi 1981:49, English translation mine)

Protestant churches, on the other hand, traditionally emphasize individual inner redemption ("finding Christ"). In principle, the cultural embeddedness of the gospel is irrelevant to this view of salvation and pastoral practice. Insofar as the mission elements of the Protestant churches have identified a theological problem in the events of recent years, it seems to be that of "ecumenism"; having undergone enforced unification in the Church of Christ in Zaire, some of them are worried that they are being drawn into excessively close contact with others whose sense of salvation does suffer, in their view, from its cultural embeddedness.

Conclusion

The issue of syncretism in Zaïrean religion is thus more complex than at first appears. All of the several organizations calling themselves Christian show the results of centuries of cultural diffusion; but that is not what the issue is about. "Syncretism", with the implicit meanings of "deviance" and "covert paganism", has been used pejoratively by groups in a position to make the accusation effective against African-founded or "independent" churches. The members of those churches, contemplating the theology and practice of established Christianities, find them, too, to be syncretic in the same sense but lack the power to make their accusation stick. So far, then, we have the B and C of Figure 2, with the area of agreement, X, but this diagram represents only the conscious, reciprocal evaluations of the parties.

My thesis, grounded in the analysis of the social pluralism prevailing in Zaïre, is that the difference between Christianity as apprehended in bureaucratic and customary terms, respectively, goes far deeper than conscious evaluations, subjectively perceived differences, and cognitive dissonance. It is a matter of radically different cosmologies experienced not as theories of time, life, race, and the like but as the lived realities of contrasting institutional systems.

Secondly, I have argued that these incompatible cosmologies are entertained by the same people, no matter what their religious affiliation; they refer to the two contrasted social contexts in which all Zaïreans are to some extent engaged. The incompatibility of the two emerges most clearly in discussions by intellectuals of the intractable problem of witchcraft.

Only if belief and meaning were entirely independent of social practice and institutional context could Christianity ever be diffused without changing in form and content, and thus giving rise to new syncretisms. This is not evidence of human weakness, but the paradox of "the Word made Flesh". It may be a valid question in comparative ethics or Christian theology to discover whether the same truths are compatible with different forms, or the conditions in which members of different societies can share the same transcendent meanings, but inquiries of this kind must not be directed invidiously towards selected churches or religions. The orientations and commitments of the ordinary membership of all these churches, whether mission-related or not, are generally similar, no more and no less marked by syncretism than churches elsewhere.

Neither the debate about syncretism nor the practices to which the debaters variously refer are likely to be abolished by argument or preaching. The problem, I have argued, is political, as are the forces that created it and will put an end to it. The government of Zaïre has been struggling by legal and administrative means to abolish institutional pluralism, which it describes as a racist legacy of the colonial past. According to the letter of the law, all "traditional" forms of kinship and land tenure have been replaced by uniform national institutions; in practice, not the law but the uncertain progress of capitalism is slowly bringing about a society divided no longer by pluralism but by class (Axelson 1970:274–289).

A corresponding cultural homogenization of Kimbanguist doctrine and practice is taking place. The mimeographed *Essence de la Théologie Kimbanguiste*, circulated in 1980, aligns EJCSK with evangelical Protestantism in its theology of baptism and salvation, but explicitly dissociates itself from that tradition in accepting the doctrine of the Real Presence of Christ in the Eucharist (although, as we have seen, the Eucharist is not central to Kimbanguist worship). On the other hand, the new doctrine omitted most of the features, conspicuous in earlier versions, that could be traced to ancestral Kongo religion.

Notes

1 Early American Baptist (ABFMS) correspondence provides an example of what surely should be called syncretism: "Divine Providence has evidently placed the Anglo-Saxon (perhaps Teuton) race in the forefront of the battle to be pioneers of the Gospel" (Harvey to Duncan, 11 October 1893; cited by Kimpianga kia Mahaniah, 1975). Surely the battle was to spread the gospel, not to be pioneers.

2 In fact, according to recent studies, most Japanese are unaware of the theological incompatibility of Shintoism and Buddhism, treating "ancestors" and "buddhas" as two different names for the same thing (Newell 1976).

3 Western Kongo legend says of the *basi kintiemuna*, "the wide-awake people", that is, those who are awake at night, or witches, that "if they speak of eating pork they have a cannibal feast in mind". *Kintiemuna* literally means "firefly", a sign of witchcraft (Bittremieux 1936:19).

4 The same values are explicit in the religions of many other Bantu-speaking peoples. "What is good, for Ndembu, is the open, the public, the unconcealed, the sincere" (Victor Turner 1975:239; see also Fry 1976:27).

References

Andersson, Efraim (1958). *Messianic Popular Movements in the Lower Congo.* Studia Ethnographica Upsaliensia 14. Uppsala: Almqvist and Wiksells.

——. (1968). *Churches at the Grass-Roots.* London: Lutterworth.

Axelson, Sigbert (1970). *Culture Confrontation in the Lower Congo.* Falkoping, Sweden: Gummessons.

Bimwenyi, Kweshi O. (1981). Inculturation en Afrique et attitudes des agents de l'évangélisation. Aspects du Catholicisme au Zaïre. Special issue. *Cahiers des Religions Africaines* 14(27–28):49ff.

Buakasa, Gérard (1968). Notes sur le kindoki chez les Kongo. *Cahiers des Religions Africaines* [Kinshasa] 2(3): 153–169.

Cavazzi da Montecuccolo, G. A. (1965). *Descriçao histórica dos tres reinos do Congo, Matamba e Angola.* Vol. 2. G. Maria de Leguzzano, trans. and annotator. Lisbon: Junta de Investigações do Ultramar.

Doutreloux, Albert (1967). *L'ombre des fétiches.* Louvain, Belgium: Nauwelaerts.
Fry, Peter (1976). *Spirits of Protest: Spirit Mediums and the Articulation of Consensus amongst the Zezuru of Southern Rhodesia.* Cambridge: Cambridge University Press.
Geertz, Clifford (1966). Religion as a Cultural System. In *Anthropological Approaches to the Study of Religion*, 1–46. Michael Banton, ed. London: Tavistock.
Inongo, Sakombi (1973). L'authenticité à Dakar. *Cultures au Zaïre et en Afrique* [Kinshasa] 1:216.
Janzen, John M., and Wyatt MacGaffey (1974). *An Anthology of Kongo Religion.* Lawrence: University of Kansas Press.
Kimpianga kia Mahaniah (1975). The Background of Prophetic Moments in the Belgian Congo. Ph.D. dissertation. Department of History, Temple University.
Leach, Edmund R. (1969). *Dialectic in Practical Religion.* Cambridge: Cambridge University Press.
Lufuluabo Mizeka (1977). *L'anti-sorcier face à la science.* Mbujimayi, Zaïre: Editions Franciscaines.
Malula, Cardinal (1977). Preface. In *L'anti-sorcier face à la science.* Lufuluabo Mizeka. Mbujimayi, Zaïre: Editions Franciscaines.
Martin, Marie-Louise (1975). *Kimbangu: An African Prophet and His Church.* London: Heffer.
MacGaffey, Wyatt (1970a). *Custom and Government in the Lower Congo.* Los Angeles: University of California Press.
——. (1970b). The Religious Commissions of the BaKongo. *Man* n.s. 5(1):27–38.
——. (1976). Kimbanguism: An African Christianity. *Africa Report* 21(1):40–43.
——. (1977). Cultural Roots of Kongo Prophetism. *History of Religions* 17(2): 177–193.
——. (1978a). African History: Anthropology and the Rationality of Natives. *History in Africa* 5:101–120.
——. (1983). *Modern Kongo Prophets: Religion in a Plural Society.* Bloomington: Indiana University Press.
——. (1986). *Religion and Society in Central Africa: The BaKongo of Lower Zaïre.* Chicago: Chicago University Press.
Mudimbe, Valentin Y. (1973). *Entre les eaux: Dieu, un prêtre, la révolution.* Paris: Présence Africaine.
Mulago, Vincent (1981). Evangélisation et authenticité. Aspects du Catholicisme au Zaïre. Special issue. *Cahiers des Religions Africaines* 14(27–28):41.
Newell, William H., ed. (1976). *Ancestors.* Chicago: Aldine.
Pye, Michael (1971). Syncretism and Ambiguity. *Numen* 18(2):83–93.
Tshibangu, Tharcisse (1974). *Le propos d'une théologie africaine.* Kinshasa: Presses Universitaires du Zaïre.
Turner, Victor W. (1967 [1959]). *The Forest of Symbols.* Ithaca: Cornell University Press.
——. (1968). *The Drums of Affliction: A Study of Religious Processes among the Ndembu of Zambia.* Oxford: Clarendon.
——. (1969). *The Ritual Process: Structure and Anti-Structure.* London: Routledge & Kegan Paul.
——. (1975 [1962]). *Revelation and Divination in Ndembu Ritual.* Ithaca, New York: Cornell University Press.

Part 12

ROMAN CATHOLIC FIELDS OF ENGAGEMENT WITH PENTECOSTALS

46

Excerpt from 'IN THE ABSENCE OF PRIESTS

Young women as apostles to the poor, Chile 1922–1932'

Gertrude M. Yeager

Source: *The Americas*, 64(2) (2007), 207–42.

The Roman Catholic Church in Chile first acknowledged its inability to pastor its flock in the 1920s because of an acute shortage of priests.' Alberto Hurtado Cruchaga, SJ addressed the clerical crisis in a 1936 article, *La Crisis Sacerdotal en Chile.* When critics found his analysis "exaggerated," he conducted a survey of Chilean religious practices and published the findings in a controversial essay entitled *Es Chile un pais catolico?* which is said to have earned him the wrath of the hierarchy because it called attention to the woeful neglect of pastoral duties especially among the rural and working class populations.[1] This empirical data demonstrated that the Catholic Church in Chile had 451 parishes, some of which contained several towns and villages scattered over a thousand square kilometers with 10,000 parishioners to be ministered to by a single priest.[2] Hurtado's solution—a larger and better-educated clergy—was a long-term solution to an urgent problem that would never be achieved. In the gendered world of Chilean Catholicism, the task of pre-serving the faith fell to young laywomen.

In 1921 newly consecrated Bishop Rafael Edwards Salas returned to Chile from Rome with orders to organize Catholic Action. A decade before Catholic Action officially began in Chile, for its foundation date is given as 1931, Edwards launched the *Asociacion de la Juventud Catolica Feminina de Chile,* [hereafter AJCFCh] and helped to transform a generation of teenage girls into religious activists and apostles to the poor. The AJCFCh updated and genderized missionary strategies. It combined traditional ingredients from the female religious recipe book with contemporary organizational and propaganda techniques to reach its audience of mostly women and children. The priest shortage allowed AJCFCh members to organize and improvise community worship in ways that resembled prototypes of Christian Base Communities.

The AJCFCh required members to assume a public role that coupled social action with catechization. In the process young women acquired the tools and training to participate more fully in civil society because the AJCFCh functioned as a species of voluntary society that organized young women along both horizontal and vertical networks into a national force beginning at the grassroots level. In "Religion: A Movement and an Ideology" Antonio Gramsci, a dedicated Church watcher because of its central role in Italian politics, historicizes Church reliance on lay participation. He depicts the Catholic Church between 1890 and 1930 as an institution struggling for survival, plagued by internal divisions, yet able to renew itself by inventing survival strategies such as Catholic Action, a movement that first appeared in the 1840s and relied on lay participation. Gramsci posits that when the Catholic Church faces marginalization or a reduced social role, it develops new strategies and recruits new cadres. Because neither Social Catholic thought nor Catholic Action was compulsory for all Catholics, he considered both to be voluntary in nature.[3] To extend Gramsci's idea, if the perceived threat to the institutionalized Church is great enough, it will recruit laywomen as actors, a strategy well documented in recent historiography on Chilean women and religion.[4]

In Chile as elsewhere in Latin America, especially in the 1920s and 1930s, most of the people in the pew were women. According to Hurtado's 1939 survey of religious practices nine percent of Chilean women and 3.5 percent of Chilean men attended Mass regularly, while ninety percent of all Chileans remained outside the Churchy.[5] Although the two most famous contemporary Catholic figures, St. Teresa of the Andes and Father Hurtado, were contemporaries, born in 1900 *and* 1901 respectively, they are depicted as representing distinct spiritual eras. Teresa symbolizes the romantic suffering Christ of nineteenth century, while Hurtado represents the virile and human Christ of the post-1930 period.[6] Such a chronological gerrymandering of the Chilean religious landscape rests on a gender component that identifies the cloister and reparation spirituality with women and social justice with men.[7]

The canonized Father Alberto Hurtado SJ who in his roles as apostle to the poor, eloquent critic of the conservative hierarchy, mentor of *Accion Catolica,* founder of *Hogar de Cristo* and confessor to the *Falagne Nacional,* the precursor to the present Christian Democratic Party, best personifies a vigorous and manly Catholicism.[8] The 1992 canonization of Teresa of the Andes by John Paul II to commemorate the quinticentennial of the catechization of the Americas seemed to be a spiritual message out of tune with contemporary Latin American Catholicism, but it created a female counterpoint to Hurtado. Juana Fernandez, who took the religious name of Teresa of Jesus, and who died in a Carmelite cloister at the age of nineteen from typhus, closely resembled Catholic heroines from the past and had no ties to Liberation Theology.[9]

A periodization scheme based on Hurtado's links to the *Juventud Catolica Chilena* generation permits scholars to ignore *Accion Social Catolica.* In the first decades of the twentieth century this Church-sponsored movement supported progressive social legislation. Motivated by traditional sentiments of paternalism and Christian charity, it received the blessings of the hierarchy and became closely identified with the Conservative Party and traditional elites.[10] Social Catholicism also turned Chilean women into religious activists.[11]

Models and rituals of female spirituality

As girls reached adolescence and prepared for marriage they often attended special retreats to discern their true vocation. Close ties between elite women and religious sisters made the convent an attractive alternative to marriage." By the early 1900s girls from good families were expected to teach catechism classes to the unchurched. Such religious duties did not take vacations. Elite girls who summered at the shore or on a family hacienda made the children of fisherman and *campesinos* the focus of their zeal. Teresa Ossandon, long-time president of the AJCFCh, used her tennis fame to attract converts and taught catechism to the boys and other adult employees at the Lawn Tennis Club, but the summer mission was the principal apostolate that required female participation.

The annual mission, a Catholic version of a revival, coincided with the family's summer visit and brought a priest to the estate once a year. Religious scholars have used the terms Folk/ Pagan Catholicism to describe the religion most Chileans practiced in the early 1900s.[12] The absence of churches and clergy transformed the faith into something practiced and nurtured by women and it consisted of home-based worship and improvised liturgies. Most people did not attend the Mass regularly because it was unavailable and even if they did, the liturgy had little importance to them. With the Mass in Latin and literacy rates low, most Chileans in the 1910s had less than four years schooling, and the use of prayer books still a novelty, except for the upper classes, the people in the pew even if present at Mass, were usually engaged in highly individualized worships.[13] More Chileans identified with Catholicism through reciting the rosary than Mass attendance.

The women of the family took charge of all details of the rural mission. They cleaned the chapel, washed the altar linen and if there was a harmonium, a small organ-like instrument, they had it tuned. If numbers permitted, they formed a small choir and taught hymns. Then they toured the estate, often on horseback, taking an informal religious census for workers did not live in a village, but families were scattered throughout the estate; some were stockmen and herders, others farmers. The older girls of the family prepared children for First Communion by teaching them the catechism; often they used treats to reward learning and lured children to class with raffles. They sewed special clothes, such as veils and white frocks, purchased medals, rosaries, holy cards and other sacramentals and had the staff prepare a tasty breakfast with sweets and hot chocolate to be served after the Mass. The ministry extended to adults as well; the girls arranged for the baptisms of children born within the year and for marriages. The hardest task was getting the men to church; and it was harder yet to convince them to receive the sacraments. Often they refused to have their common law unions blessed or their children baptized, or grant permission to their wives to attend church.[14]

All this had to be accomplished before the arrival of a circuit-riding clergy who administered the sacraments and stayed in residence for about a week. The missionaries were usually foreign born; during the early 1900s they were principally Spanish and by the 1930s they were often Canadian or from the United States. A priest writing in 1938 said that Chileans recognized three sacraments: baptism, confirmation and procession.[15] Devotion to the saints and the Virgin took precedence over attending Mass and receiving the Eucharist. The religious rituals of the mission formed a matrix of a more general festival that included games, races, special foods, dancing and ended with a solemn procession in which *huasos* (cowboys), decked out in full riding regalia escorted the Eucharist to altars decorated with flowers and silver objects such as plates set up around the property. The rural mission allowed young women to function as and see themselves as apostles. These traditions and practices became the foundation upon which the AJCFCh constructed its missionary activities to the urban and rural poor.

The Association of Young Catholic Women of Chile

Of the institutions chartered by Edwards, the Association of Young Catholic Women of Chile was among the most successful. When in May 1922 AJCFCh held its first national congress in Santiago, Edwards explained to a receptive audience of several hundred young women that the function of AJCFCh was to organize an army of volunteers for action, propaganda and teaching the gospel. In her convention address Amalia Errazuriz likened the AJCFCh to a phalanx of young women who would march forward in a disciplined manner to pursue the highest goal. In study groups *(circulos de estudios)* sponsored by the association they would be formed into women of faith and action without losing the first title "woman of the home."[16]

The AJCFCh owed much of its success and energy to its first president, Teresa Ossandon whose life and career did not conform to traditional models of female piety, but reflected modern notions of Chilean womanhood.[17] In 1917 when she was fifteen Teresa won her first national tennis title in the youth division; between 1918 and 1927 she won the National Women's Tennis Championship four times. Tournament competition developed her self-confidence. Having lost matches as she pursued the national tennis championships, she accepted setbacks and did not lose her focus. Tennis made her a celebrity, and she used her name recognition to advance her cause.

Organized at the parish level the AJCFCh chapter served as the arms and legs of the local priest. It was also an umbrella organization that sponsored a myriad of activities for members. The longest list was under Parish Action: apostolic works, catechists, *patronatos,* and attendance at Forty Hours Devotions or Adoration of the Blessed Sacrament, staffing of missions and retreats. Organization at the parish level became more important after the separation of church and state in 1925.[18] Such a definition would send all but the most devout or most acutely bored fleeing. Girls were suspicious of being "roped into a religious scam."[19] Weekly it added new chapters and increased participation in the national conferences sponsored by the *Union Social de los Catolicos de Chile* and Marian conferences that addressed the role of Chilean woman in modern times. In October, 1926 3000 young women attended the fourth national congress.[20] Two years later the AJCFCh had 240 centers and 10,000 members.[21]

As catechists AJCFCh members taught the faith in working class neighborhoods, mining sites and rural villages. Missionary work allowed association members structured contact with the urban poor and rural people, and to learn first hand the social conditions in which the majority of Chileans lived. Its success rested on the continuous recruitment of young women, house-to-house canvassing and regular home visitations. In 1928 AJCFCh members taught catechism to 100,000 children and women and in Santiago over 3000 children received First Communion in huge services held in public parks. The AJCFCh took a practical approach to teaching the catechism by acknowledging that preparation did not require years of specialized study. It was more important for the classes to be interesting because children had a ten-minute attention span.[22] Of the 400 centers in operation that year only half functioned under the guidance of a priest.

The AJCFCh sought to establish chapters in towns and villages without a parish. In the absence of priests it fell to organizers to find a single girl who would lead them to a dozen more. A chapter depended on a group 12 to 15 dedicated workers. Membership requirements were minimal. Usually a girl needed to be Roman Catholic and possess some strength of character; the daughters of fisherman and inquilinos made great catechists. At times these minimum requirements could not be met because many girls were neither raised in Christian homes nor taught by nuns. Many had not received the sacraments. Yet in 1929 the AJCFCh had two successful centers in which no members had made their First Communion.[23] As Ossandon traveled the length of Chile many times organizing AJCFCh chapters, she recorded in her diary a realistic and bleak picture of Chile's religious landscape. In 1929 she wrote: "The rural towns present a spectacular failure for the faith. The indifference of Catholics, Protestantism, the failure to receive the sacraments, the atheism of many and lastly, the shortage of priests. . . . There are many towns, even large ones with no priest, completely abandoned."[24]

She shared these images with others through *Hacia el Ideal,* in speeches and other writings. In 1929 she began thinking systematically about evangelical work and the social conditions in which most Chileans lived.[25] Inspired by scripture, association members descended in pairs on *caserlos* and rural villages and knocked on doors. Because previous attempts to entice mothers to send their children to the local church for religious instruction had failed, the AJCFCh took catechism classes directly to the homes of the poor. She wrote that the greatest obstacle to missionary work was "our prejudice against the poor." She instructed AJCFCh members to imitate Christ and embrace the disadvantaged.[26] Social Catholic teachings of the early 1900s focused on the worker and addressed the dislocations associated with industrialization and urbanization, but offered little practical advice as how to precede in rural Chile, a vast area that contemporary churchmen as well as modern scholars have classified as pagan and or irreligious.[27] In truth, rural Chile also experienced modernization although at uneven rates. Mining areas attracted Socialist, Anarchist and Protestant organizers who, like their Catholic counterparts, viewed the religious practices of the people as barbarous, fanatic, vicious and pagan.[28] Rituals such as dancing for la *Virgen de la Tirana* and Judas Burnings on Good Friday embarrassed clergy who desired to replace such practices, which they viewed as religious artifacts from the colonial era with a modern Christocentric Catholicism.[29] The absence of priests in the countryside made rural Chile ripe for conversion to either Communism or Protestantism. In Laja Ossandon entered in her diary: "There is no religious spirit here . . . the town is very *mascimalista.* Recabarren spoke here, out-side the church and denounced religion. . . . The mining camp lacks a religious spirit and morality; it has been the site of labor unrest and agitation for four to five years. Luis Recabarren and other labor leaders have been busy planting anarchist ideas. The priest had said that both men and women protest and shout against all order, authority, religion. They stoned the church, wave red flags in their marches. The mining camp is paralyzed. There is no work, but the miners won't leave, there are only 3000 left of the original number of 10,000."[30] "We have seen how Protestants succeed in a town. Why? It is because of the individual effort that they make. They are concerned with a single individual person, until that person is completed convinced, and then who becomes an apostle who then goes and does the same thing. They are not interested in staging great assemblies, but they go door to door and suffer all types of insults."[31]

Contulmo was a town in the south populated mostly by German Protestants, located in the heart of the Cordillera de Nahuelbuta in Arauco, hours from Canete. There the chapter had nineteen members and a modest chapel where members recited the rosary and taught catechism on Sundays when there was no priest. The girls called the people to worship by ringing bells in the streets. On the rare occasion that Mass was offered, the girls informed the population throughout the countryside and on the Indian reservation. They prepared a list of baptisms and marriages for the priest and even portioned out medicine. Through much of rural Chile, Mass was limited to the period of the rural mission or at best a priest came once a month weather permitting.[32] In Antilue, another village without a parish, AJCFCh members rented a site and began to hold Sunday services. They then bought a few statutes and created a chapel that in time attracted the weekly visit of a priest. Later the association purchased a car to transport the Sisters of Charity that staffed the hospital to daily Mass.[33]

The religious writings of Chilean women

The religious writings of Chilean women demonstrate that they did not merely internalize or memorize the teachings of the "Fathers of the Church", but interpreted Catholicism through the filter of gender. The women-centeredness of the writings gives them contemporary resonance. Amalia Errazuriz de Subercausex, an eminent Catholic activist, president of the Liga de Damas Chilenas, author of seven books and numerous essays and mentor of AJCFCh, wrote *Nuestra Iglesia,* a history of the Catholic Church in which she described it as an organic society and "not a collection of powerful clergy."[34] She did not mourn the "the passing of the imperial church because it had little interest in the fate of man." Neither did she distinguish between the laity and the priesthood; both belonged to the same flock under the authority of the same shepherd.[35]

Errazuriz placed Mary, the mother of Jesus at the center of the creation of the Church on Pentecost Sunday. Mary consoled and strengthened the apostles who behaved like a group of desolate orphans after the Crucifixion, a flock without a pastor. The apostles in the company of Mary prayed and when the Holy Spirit descended upon them, the Catholic Church was born. Mary was Christ's most perfect apostle. Mary was the Church's queen and mother. Peter became its visible head of state and the other apostles, administrators, governors. Bishops, the disciples and women were the faithful members of this new society.[36]

In *Nuestra Iglesia,* Errazuriz acknowledged the role women played supporting and organizing the infant Church by offering their homes and fortunes. Praxedis and Prudence, whom Errazuriz identified as daughters of a Roman senator, aided Peter when he arrived in Rome. They also nurtured the poor and buried the dead. Women and children were martyred along with men in the early persecutions and served as missionaries.[37] Errazuriz lived in Rome when her husband, Ramon Subercausex served as Chilean ambassador to the Vatican. She visited the Basilica of St. Praxedis, which was then a destination for pilgrims because it contained the remains of many early martyrs. Today scholars believe it marks the site of an early home church. About 822 Pope Paschal I erected the mosaic chapel to honor his mother, "Bishop" Theodora. It contains a mosaic that depicts Mary, the Mother of

Jesus, Pudentiana, Praxedis and Theodora Episcopa, which ratifies "the ministry of early women leaders."[38]

As a married woman and mother, Errazuriz preferred to think of the Church as the House of God rather than the Kingdom of God because the phrase suggested to her an intimate space that nurtured close, loving relationships.[39] The AJCFCh took this concept and gave it a social dimension. Teresa Ossandon wrote in *Hacia el Ideal* that members use the challenges of home life to develop the necessary skills of an apostle. Contradictions formed the basis of family life, so good daughters, especially the oldest daughter who often acts a second mother and hears all the confidences, demonstrated their "love of God" by providing a link between parents and the other siblings. In these small acts they practice social justice and charity and soothe over domestic problems.[40] Using the powers of persuasion, a daughter convinced her father to invest 3000 pesos to improve the cottages of his tenants rather than enlarge the living room.[41]

Errazuriz embraced the social gospel message of the Catholic Church and likened Leo XIII's encyclical, *Rerum Novarum* to the Magna Carta for Christian workers. The Christian Utopia was short lived because man soon forgot his generosity and his disinterest in material goods. Its collapse resulted in the creation of social classes, discrimination based on wealth and eventual class conflict. The conditions in which urban workers lived distressed her. Low wages forced women to work outside the home and jeopardized the family. She rejected socialism as a solution to the social inequality caused by industrialization. Errazuriz challenged young women to dedicate themselves to alleviating human misery through acts of charity and service to society[42]

In its publications the AJCFCh co-opted the language of action and referred to its members as missionaries and apostles. *Hacia el Ideal* encouraged young women to dedicate themselves to the task of a catechist, for the primary duty of an AJCFCh member was to plant and nurture the seeds of faith. Priests baptized the children, but women cultivated their virtues. "We cannot be priests, but we can be better than men"[43] and serve the Church by preparing people to receive the sacraments. Articles even reminded readers that the "sanctity of Christ," not the "virtue of priests," formed the foundation of the Catholic Church.

Conclusions

Marciano Barrios Valdes considers the 1920s as the "transformational decade" for Chilean Catholicism, because it marked the Chilean Church's dependence on youth. To him the faith taught by Catholic Action sustained the Catholic Church in Chile until the 1960s.[44] An androcentric term such as Catholic Action not only renders female participation in catechization invisible, but obscures Catholic Church initiatives to modernize female roles in Chilean society. This essay has demonstrated that in the decade prior to the establishment of Catholic Action, young women made up the majority of catechists. Church officials encouraged them to step into new Church ministries and into the public sphere. In 1921 an article appeared in *Revista Catolica* that stated that the ideal ministry for young women was to teach the catechism to the urban and rural poor.[45] By 1929 just in Santiago AJCFCh members taught the catechism to over 100,000 children.

That same year the *Revista Catolica* reported the Chilean Church faced a pastoral crisis and offered suggestions to clergy to improve participation. To catechize women it recommended that the Church should use the AJCFCh because it is "best we have. Its members could take the catechism to rural villages and urban conventillos. Bishops could captain these legions."[46] The martial language attests to the seriousness of the challenge. In addition to being "Brides of Christ," the Church encouraged young women to enlist as "Soldiers of Christ" in this war about religious indifference.

Gramsci's observations about the Catholic response to institutional challenges hold true in the Chilean case. Bishops mobilized female laity as a solution to the priest shortage. By harnessing the energy of female youth, the Catholic Church sanctioned new roles for women that prepared them for fuller participation in civil society. The training AJCFCh members received—organizing and marching in mass rallies, publishing a journal, public speaking, forming nation-wide networks and house-to-house canvassing—would serve them well when suffrage came. The Church encouraged female youth to volunteer and participate in a wide range of social justice missions. It educated them formally in the issues of social gospel through *semanas sociales* and informally, and perhaps more potently by promoting home visitations and teaching in the popular barrios. By 1929 the AJCFCh was the largest and the best-organized female association in Chile.[47] When it was absorbed into Catholic Action in 1931, it had introduced a generation of young women to social action and defending the faith in the public arena. That same year, Chilean women voted for the first time in national elections.[48]

As it faced mass indifference to its message and increasing competition from socialism and Protestantism, the Chilean hierarchy explored new ways of being Church.[49] Training in forensic archeology is not required to discern the skeletal remains of an early prototype of the Christian Base Community. Teresa Ossandon wrote that it was not uncommon in Chile to meet people who have never seen a priest. As catechists AJCFCh members assumed responsibility for preserving the faith. During these lean years the content of the Catholic faith was greatly reduced. Even Father Hurtado, who criticized popular religious practices, wrote that a flicker of faith remained within the people. While Chileans neither attended Mass nor married in the Church, they baptized and confirmed their children and venerated the saints.[50] AJCFCh members went about their missionary work by tapping into popular religious traditions in the hopes of reinvigorating local piety.

Where churches did not exist, young women assumed the role of pastors. When the Eucharist was unavailable, they created and led worship services built around reciting the rosary, other familiar prayers and a reading from scripture. They used local traditions such as Nino Dios in Malloco, a centuries old miraculous image of a campesino child said to be from Cuzco, which the local population venerated. Teresa Ossandtin took exception to the low opinion many Church officials continued to voice about the spirituality of most Chileans. She wrote that Chileans were essentially good. They believed in God, practiced Christian charity and prayed to Mary she reminded *Revista Catolica* readership. Well ahead of her time, Ossandon was suggesting that Church officials recognize local religious mentalities as a cultural resource and use them to replenish faith.[51] In 1931 Chilean bishops commissioned the AJCFCh to assume direction of a new Church crusade to popularize Bible reading Catholics because of Protestant inroads,[52] and set a goal to establish an AJCFCh chapter on every fundo in Chile to target young campesinas.[53]

Bishops encouraged young women to enlist as "Soldiers of Christ," but the writings of Catholic activists suggest they found in gendered readings of Church history and Christian scripture a rationale to transform themselves into Apostles of Christ.[54] AJCFCh members identified the parish as their principal site of action because it functioned, "like a caring mother for a prodigal child."[55] Members saw themselves as true apostles of Christ and identified with the Samaritan woman with whom Jesus had a lively conversation at Jacob's well. Jesus recognized that the woman had a good heart and filled it with grace. The woman then returned to town and told the people to go and see the Man who knows many things and through her effort thousands converted. In a similar spirit, the AJCFCh member asked Jesus for the water of life to quench her thirst and prepare her to Christianize society.[56]

Notes

1 Fidel Araneda Bravo, *El clero en el acontecer politico chileno 1935–1960* (Santiago: Editorial Emision: 1988), Chapter 6 "Alarma en el clero conservador," pp. 35–43 and Alberto Hurtado Cruchaga, Si, *Es Chile un pals catolico?* (Santiago: Editorial los Andes, 1992).

2 Alberto Hurtado Cruchaga, SJ, *Humanismo Social* (Santiago: Editorial los Andes, 1994), pp. 66–67.

3 Antonio Gramsci, *Further Selections from the Prison Notebook,* Editor /translator, Derek Booth-man (Minneapolis: University of Minnesota Press, 1995), pp. 1–137.

4 Chilean scholarship dates women's participation in Church-affiliated lay institutions and civil society to the late 1830s: Maximiliano A. Salinas Campos, *El laicado catolico de la Sociedad Chilena de Agricultura y Beneficencia 1838–1849* (Santiago: Universidad Catolica de Chile, 1980), Erika Maza Valenzuela, "Catholicism, Anticlericalism and the Quest for Women's Suffrage in Chile," The Helen Kellogg Institute for International Studies, Working Paper Series, Working Paper 214, December, 1995, and Erika Maza Valenzuela, "Liberals, Radicals and Women's

Citizenship in Chile, 1872–1930," The Helen Kellogg Institute for International Studies, Working Paper Series, Working Paper #245, November, 1997. Erika Kim Verba's, *Catholic Feminism and the Social Question in Chile, 1910–1917: The Liga de Damas Chilenas* (Lewiston, NY: Mellen Press, 2003) documents that great numbers of elite Chilean women voluntarily joined and enthusiastically supported the *Liga de Damas Chilenas.*

5 Alberto Hurtado, *Es Chile un pals catolico?*, p. 64.

6 Marciano Barrios Valdes, *La espiritualidad chilena en tiempos de Santa Teresa* and his *La espiritualidad chilena en los tiempos del Padre Hurtado, 1931–1961.*

7 Paula M. Kane, "'She offered herself up': The Victim Soul and Victim Spirituality in Catholicism," *Church History* 71:1 (March, 2002), pp. 80–119.

8 Other priests associated with creating the progressive church include Fernando Vives SJ and Oscar Rucker.

9 Gramsci writes that the timing of canonizations reveals much about the papal agenda. The canonization of Teresa began to move forward during the presidency of Salvador Allende. Her beatification and canonization came about when the papacy was in the process of censoring Liberation Theology.

10 Maria Antonieta Huerta M., *Catolicismo Social en Chile.*

11 Erika Kim Verba's, *Catholic Feminism and the Social Question in Chile, 1910–1917: The Liga de Dumas Chilenas*, documents how great numbers of elite Chilean women voluntarily joined and enthusiastically supported the *Liga de Damas Chilenas.*

12 Cristian Parker, "Anticlericalismo y religion popular en la genesis del movimiento obrero en Chile 1900–1920," *Revista Mexicana de Sociologta* XLIX:3 (jul-sept 1987), pp. 185–204, and Maximiliano Salinas Campos, *Historia del Pueblo de Dios en Chile* (Santiago, Ediciones Rehue, 1987).

13 Ann Taves, *The Household of Faith, Roman Catholic Devotions in Mid-Nineteenth-Century America* (South Bend, IN: Notre Dame University Press, 1986). This observation is also true for Chile. For reference to literacy figures see Hurtado's *Humanismo social.*

14 References to female participation in rural missions are found in the diaries of Teresa de los Andes and Teresa Ossandon, in Ossandon's published works, in works about St. Teresa and throughout *Hacia el Ideal.*

15 Alberto Hurtado Cruchaga Si, *Humanismo social*, p. 49.

16 *Hacia el Ideal* I:1 August 1923.

17 Juan Carlos Ossandon Valdes, "Teresa Ossanddn Guzman," *Anuario de Historia de la Iglesfa en Chile*, 14 (1996), pp. 81–94; "Una famosa tenista," *La Segunda*, 18 January 1989, pp. 20–21. Unpublished sources include an obituary written by the Prioress of Holy Spirit Monastery and a biographical sketch written and circulated by her brother, Father Arturo Ossandon, shortly after her death; these as well as her diary, are presently housed in Holy Spirit Monastery located in Auco, Chile.

18 *Hacia el Idea*, III:24 March 1926.

19 Teresa Ossandon, *Par Nuestra Fe o relatos de una social* (Santiago: Imprenta La Ilustracion 1928), 3ra edici6n.

20 *Hacia el Ideal*, III:28 August/September 1926.

21 *Hacia el Ideal*, V:40 April 1928.

22 *Hacia el Ideal*, IV:24 June 1927. Also see Teresa Ossandbn's *Manual del Dirigente de la Asociacion Juventud Catolica Feminina de Chile* (Santiago: Imprenta Rapid, 1936), and *Por Nuestra Fe o relatos de una socia.*

23 *Hacia el Ideal*, VI:53–54 September/October *1929.*

24 Teresa Ossandon, Diario, *2* August, *1929.*

25 Teresa Ossandon, Diario, *2* August, *1929.*

26 *Hacia el Ideal*, VI:53–54, September–October, 1929
27 Cristian Parker Gumucio, *Anticlericalismo y religion popular en la genesis del movimiento obrero chileno en Chile*, 1900–1920 (Santiago: CERC, *1986*). This essay is more easily accessed through *Revista Mexicana de Sociologia*, XLIX, *3*, *pp.* 185–204. Maximiliano Salinas Campos, *Historia del pueblo de Dios en Chile*, and "Cristianismo popular en Chile, 1880–1920, un esquema sobre el factor religioso en las clases subalternas durante el capitalismo oligarquico," *Nueva Historia*, 3:12 (1984). Father Hurtado used the term "paganization of the masses" in *Humanismo social*, p. 61.
28 Cristian Parker Gumucio, *Anticlericalismo y religion popular en la genesis del movimiento obrero chileno en Chile.*
29 Cristian Parker Gumucio and Maxilimiano Salas Campos, "Cristianismo popular."
30 Teresa Ossandón, Diario, 29 July 1929.
31 Teresa Ossandón, Diario, 2 August 1929.
32 *Hacia el Ideal*, VI:53–54, September/October, 1929.
33 *Hacia el Ideal*, IX:65 March/April, 1931.
34 Amalia Errázuriz de Subercaseaux, *Nuestra Santa Iglesía*, introduction.
35 Ibid.
36 Ibid., pp. 112–114.
37 Amalia Errazuriz de Subercaseux, *Nuestra Santa Iglesia.*
38 "Rome pilgrims view evidence of women bishops, priests in the early Church," *Churchwatch*, May–June, 2006.
39 Amalia Errazuriz de Subercaseaux, *Nuestra Santa Iglesia.*
40 *Hacia el Ideal*, 6:49 April 1929. "En La Vida de la familia: La Contradiccion."
41 Ossandon, *Salvar or las vacaciones de Cecilia*, pp. 71–72.
42 Amalia Errazuriz de Subercaseaux, *Roma del Alma*, Rome: 1909, Vol. 9, pp. 112–115. "I see disinherited poor, the sick, men who are overwhelmed, with their souls hardened and brutalized . . . women exasperated from the need to help their spouses, who leave their children to earn a few cents in the streets. I see the rich egotistical man who has everything, looking down on the poor who lack everything and insulting the poor to their face with gross language. . . ."
43 *Hacia el Ideal*, IV: 35 July, 1927.
44 Barrios Valdes, *La espiritualidad en los tiempos del Padre Hurtado.*
45 *Revista Catolica*, 29:651 1 January, 1921, pp. *29–43.*
46 *Revista Catolica 29:651* 1 January, 1929; "Oratoria Sagrada," Conferencia Sacerdotal pp. *29–43. Hacia el Ideal*, IX: *65* March/April 1931.
47 *Hacia el Ideal*, September–October, *1929.*
48 "Mujeres de Chile," *Revista Catolica*, 31: 711 *3* October 1931, pp. *539–541.*
49 "La mision social del clero en la Enciclica 'Quadragismo Anno,'" *Revista Catolica*, 31:714, *21* November 1931, pp. *715–719.*
50 Alberto Hurtado, *Humanismo Social*, pp. 48–49.
51 "Sugerencias para una tema sobre misiones en los caserios y campos de Chile," T.O.G. *Revista Catolica* XLIV:967 August, September, October 1953, pp. 759–762.
52 "Al Pasar," *Revista Catolica* 31:701 9 May 1931.
53 "Programa de trabajos para este ano, organization de joven obrera y campesina," *Hacia el Ideal*, XI.
54 *Hacia el Ideal*, IV:35 July, 1927.
55 Teresa Ossandon, *Manual de la Dirigenta de AJCF*, p. 40.
56 "Reseiia del IX Congreso Nacional," *Hacia el Ideal*, X:85 September/October, 1933.

47

REINTERPRETING CHILEAN PENTECOSTALISM

Juan Sepulveda

Source: *Social Compass*, 43(3) (1996), 299–318.

It has been customary in sociological literature to consider Latin American Pentecostalism as a sort of mechanism of adaptation to socio-cultural changes.[1] As those changes — generally described as a process of transition from a fundamentally agrarian, religious, traditional and authoritarian (feudal) society, to a society which is basically urban, industrialized, secularized, modern and democratic — are thought to be the result of the increasing influence of the Anglo-Saxon world on Latin American affairs, Pentecostalism has also been seen as a movement controlled from the USA.[2] In a recent newspaper article on the Chilean experience, Richard Gott follows this line of interpretation quite plainly:

> These strange and interesting developments in the religious life of the Latin American continent do not of course take place in isolation. They are part of a much wider change in society whereby Latin America has finally recognized that its future lies in tandem with the US. It sees itself as part of the Protestant American hemisphere and no longer as some strange extension of Catholic Europe.[3]

In this article it is argued that the main interest of the Chilean experience lies precisely in the fact that it dispels this kind of sociological oversimplification. Chilean Pentecostalism is better understood when it is seen as a chapter in the religious history of the *bajo pueblo*.[4] Furthermore, the ways in which Pentecostals as individuals relate to society, and specifically to politics, has to be seen in the light of the wider socio-political behaviour of the bajo pueblo. Finally, the ways in which Pentecostal Churches, as institutions, relate to the state and current politics, have to be analysed in the context of the conflicts within the national "religious field".[5]

Pentecostalism in the religious history of the Chilean Bajo Pueblo

Protestant missionary efforts in Chile started soon after the struggle for independence from the Spanish crown weakened the religious monopoly of the Catholic Church.[6] But in 1907, 86 years after the first Protestant missionary had arrived in Chile,[7] a national census showed that Catholics made up 98.1 percent of the total population, Protestants one percent, people of unknown religion 0.8 percent, and non-believers 0.1 percent.[8] These figures suggest that up to this year, Protestantism had had but little impact in Chilean society. If one takes into consideration the following 85 years, an extraordinary change emerges: the national census of 1992 showed that Protestants (Evangelicos and Protestantes together) had reached 13.2 percent of the population aged 14 years or older.[9] The bulk of this change is accounted for in the growth of Pentecostalism among the urban and rural lower classes, that is, within the bajo pueblo.[10]

Commenting on the religious situation of the bajo pueblo by the end of the last century, the historian Gabriel Salazar writes:

> The tendency shown by the [Catholic] church to associate formally with the mercantile patricians (in spite of the latter's growing, schismatic secularism) and to define itself as an instrument of domination and social control left the bajo pueblo in a rather uncomfortable position relative to religious culture. For example, their poverty prevented many peons [itinerant, unskilled workers] from having a family in the conventional sense. Many, therefore, lived in permanent celibacy or in transitory, illicit unions. In so doing, they violated the law on a fundamental point: perpetual and monogamous matrimony. This violation continued for almost two centuries, so that more than 80 percent of the popular class consisted of natural or illegitimate children. Additionally, the poor could not pay the high fees for marriages and funerals. They could not tithe, give the first fruits, or pay the other ecclesiastical taxes for the maintenance of the church. The rigid moralistic and mercantilistic attitude of the church prevented the legalization of relations among the poor in conformity with the canons of the universal–national culture. Inevitably, the bajo pueblo, especially the men, ended up adopting a reticent, ironic, and detached attitude toward this culture. Women were frequently made the objects of denunciation, persecution, or even deportation, especially if they were accused of adultery, prostitution, or impiety. Marginal to the formal heart of Catholic culture, the popular sectors developed religious forms more congruent with their own type of sociability — never, however, risking a complete break with the church.[11]

Such religious forms are generally labelled "popular Catholicism", whose roots go back to medieval popular religion, in turn reshaped by contact with Indo-American cultures. It is our contention that after 1910, Pentecostalism offered to the bajo pueblo the first real chance to develop a "religious form more congruent with their own sociability" involving a "complete break" with both the Catholic Church and the (mostly foreign) Protestant Churches. What follows is an attempt to provide some historical support to such a contention.

Chilean Pentecostalism is the result of an independent development, contemporary to that of Azuza Street, Los Angeles, generally considered the cradle of modern Pentecostalism. It was the result of a movement of spiritual revival which started in the Methodist Episcopal Church of Valparaiso in 1902, and reached its peak in the years 1909 and 1910, involving the two main churches of Santiago as well. In the annual Methodist Episcopal conference held in February 1910, the doctrinal claims of the revivalists were condemned as being "anti-methodist, contrary to the Scriptures and irrational", and the three groups, along with their spiritual leader, the missionary pastor of Valparaiso, the Rev. Willis Hoover,[12] were virtually expelled from the Methodist communion. The three groups, therefore, founded the Iglesia Metodista Pentecostal (Pentecostal Methodist Church), the trunk of a tree that later produced innumerable independent branches.

It is clear that all through the events which broke the unity of the Methodist Church in Chile during the years 1909 and 1910, there were doctrinal issues at stake.[13] The claim that the baptism of the Holy Spirit was a necessary complement to justification and sanctification was highly influential on the direction the revival took after 1907.[14] There was also the question of whether the "signs and wonders" of the work of the Holy Spirit were things of the past, that is, restricted to the apostolic era,[15] or available, even necessary, to the Church in all ages. But, as Hoover himself kept saying, the division was not caused so much for doctrinal reasons as for conflicts over practices and church government.[16] Leaders of the Iglesia Metodista Pentecostal told Walter Hollenweger: "The difference between the Methodists and us does not lie in a different doctrine. It is just that they have merely the Methodist doctrines whilst we experience them."[17] In fact, Chilean Pentecostalism accepts the 25 articles of faith of the Methodist Episcopal Church with no alteration; practises infant baptism; continues with minor adaptations the Methodist system of church government and organization; and uses the old Methodist Manual for worship and special ceremonies. This closeness to Methodism differentiates Chilean Pentecostalism from that of the USA.

Some scholars have suggested that the conflict should be understood as a clash of "mentalities"[18] or a "cultural clash".[19] In line with that interpretation, I have suggested elsewhere that there were two main aspects of the conflict, namely:

1 Conflict between a religiosity centred in the "objectivity of dogma", in which faith consists of formal, conscious and rational acceptance of determined beliefs or doctrines, and a religiosity which gives primacy to the subjective experience of God, in which faith is a response to a kind of possession of one's being by the divine;
2 A conflict between a religion mediated by specialists of the cultured classes (an illustrious clergy) and a religion in which the poor, simple people have direct access to God and in which that relationship can be communicated in the language of feelings and the indigenous culture.[20]

To validate this analysis, however, it is necessary to show that both cultures were already present within the Methodist Church. Otherwise, it would be an anachronistic projection of a situation typical of late Pentecostalism back to the time of the Methodist revival. Furthermore, if we find some evidence that simple people bearing a popular culture were indeed members of the Methodist Church, then it should be explained how they made their way into an Anglo-Saxon religion embedded, as it seems to have been, in the rationalism of the late 19th century.

Hoover, the main source of descriptions of Pentecostal origins, despite some references to the social provenance of those converted when the revival was already in motion,[21] shows little interest in the social background of its protagonists. It has been pointed out, however, that the abundant correspondence of lay participants in the movement quoted by Hoover suggests that many of them had a level of formal education far beyond the reach of the bajo pueblo.[22] The work of J. B. A. Kessler,[23] despite being fairly criticized for mixing "theology and church history" and for being "full of moral and theological statements and judgements",[24] has proved to be very helpful in this matter. His thorough archival research, as well as his "special reference[s] to the problems of division, nationalism and native ministry"[25] provide many hints on the socio-cultural nature of the conflict.

A letter sent by Florence Smith, a Presbyterian missionary in charge of the school in Valparaiso, to Robert Speer, the secretary of the board in New York (22 January 1906) offers a good point of departure for the analysis:

> Undoubtedly the Chile mission (Presbyterian) is far and away ahead of the M.E. church in education, culture, sound judgment and wordly wisdom. Personally they are all charming gentlemen, but oh Mr. Speer we do lack warmth of spiritual life and love, or it is that we do not know how to express the warmth and the love we feel. Mr. Hoover, the M.E. missionary in charge of the work here, is a man of one idea. He is not too cultured to call the Chileans brothers. He is narrow, even bigoted, but I believe he can truly say: "This one thing I do" and "I count all but loss that I may win the Chileans to Christ." He is inordinately proud of the remarkable

> success of their work — to us offensively so! There is a great deal of froth and bombast and other defects it is easy to point out, but the fact remains, the poor have the Gospel preached to them.[26]

It is clear from the date that this letter was written during the early stages of the revival. So, the comments refer not to a "Pentecostal" but to the Chilean Methodist Church. Hoover is presented as a good example of what appears to be typical of early Methodist work in Chile. In this portrait, two "cultures" or "mentalities" emerge, one (educated, cultured, rich in sound judgement and wordly wisdom, but lacking a bodily language to express feelings) represented by the Presbyterian mission; and another (poorly cultivated, narrow, "bigoted", "frothy and bombastic", to express feelings) represented not by the Pentecostals, but by the Methodist Church itself, its missionaries (at least some of them) included. The final statement makes it clear that through the latter, "the poor have the Gospel preached to them".

Kessler mentions a number of facts which support the impression that Hoover was not an isolated case, but something like the best example within a general tendency. For instance, the Presbyterian mission had taken great pains to raise and prepare a "native ministry". However, eventually the best of their national workers felt compelled to leave the Presbyterian mission and passed to the Methodist Church. Such was the case of Juan Canut (1846–1896, born in Spain but converted in Chile),[27] whose fame and success as Methodist preacher and founder of churches was such that even today the nickname given by the common people to the Protestants is *canutos.* In September 1905 Robert Elphick, another national worker, decided to leave the Presbyterians to join the Methodist Church. Although Elphick himself understood his problems with the Presbyterian Church as "doctrinal", one of the missionaries pointed out the problem of "methods and manners":

> He [Elphick] is by temperament a Methodist and their methods and manners suit him better than ours. I am quite convinced that those methods and manners are quite adapted to many of the people; better perhaps than our own for the great majority of the Chilean people.[28]

Kessler also reflects on the fact that the work in Spanish of the Methodists met with considerably more opposition than that of the Presbyterians. This could be interpreted as an indication that the two Churches were trying to find their place in different sectors of Chilean society, the Presbyterian in the "cultured" middle class, the Methodist among the poor and "uncultured": "The uneducated people in Chile were fanatical whereas the cultured class were liberal and seemed to be much more open."[29] Despite his derogatory language, Kessler seems to point in the right direction. To be sure,

Protestant preaching was full of criticism of "popular Catholicism".[30] While this kind of criticism might of course have been hurtful to the bajo pueblo, thus their reaction, in liberal circles it might have rather produced sympathy. But despite the opposition the Methodists confronted, it seems that their "methods and manners" allowed them to win some hearing among the poor.

We have, then, sufficient evidence to say that, by the turn of the century, a clash between two "mentalities" or "cultures" was developing within Chilean Protestantism. At first, this conflict expressed itself in the different missionary strategies of Presbyterians and Methodists. That the early Methodist work showed "methods and manners" better suited to the Chilean people is explained by the fact that it started as the independent and self-supporting missionary project of William Taylor,[31] with no official backing from the Methodist mission board. The first generation of Methodist missionaries "tended to be drawn from the less cultured, revivalist fringe of the Methodist church in the United States",[32] therefore most of them felt more comfortable working with simple people than with the "cultured" middle class. The opinion of the leader of the Presbyterian Church, David Trumbull, that "the Taylor mission as a Gospel agency in Chile is not worth a rap. It has rather brought missions in discredit"[33] certainly reflects the failures of the early beginnings, but also reveals a sort of cultural contempt.

However, after the Methodist mission board had taken over the work,[34] and especially after Taylor's death, the new generation of missionaries arriving in Chile was educated with "the conviction that revivalism no longer adequately expressed Christianity in the modern world".[35] The Methodist Episcopal Church had attained an established position in North American society, and its emissaries were now preachers of progress and modernization. As this new generation reached high positions in the local hierarchy, the "official" self-understanding of the Methodist Church came closer to that of the Presbyterians, and the conflict of "mentalities" became sharper within the Methodist Church. Kessler's assertion that the "wise action" of the General Conference of 1884, which marked the beginning of the takeover of the Chilean work, helped to overcome the old disagreements between Taylor's mission and the North American Church, and in Chile "led to unity on a broadened basis"[36], can hardly be defended. On the contrary, the way in which the revival was handled by the Methodist hierarchy can be understood as a late outcome of the co-option of Taylor's self-supporting mission by the North American Church.[37] If some of the Taylor missionaries did not follow their "Chilean brethren", as Hoover did, this is understandable because of the hardships of going independent from the mission.

What has been said so far indeed reveals elements of a clash between an "official" (educated, rational, modern) culture and a "popular" (uncultivated, oral, traditional) culture. This conflict was already present in the missionary "home base", but it manifested itself more sharply in the "mission field".

So far, the dividing line appears to be more determined by differences of socio-cultural background than by nationality. Are there, moreover, any elements of a tension between a "foreign culture" and the "local culture"? In other words, could the conflict be understood as an expression of the search for an "indigenous church"?

Hoover himself was far from being an advocate of "church indigenization". When explaining the motives of his resignation to the Methodist Church, he declared with emphasis: "Nobody should think that there is something of nationalism in this action. May God forgive us for such a thought and free us from that wrong."[38] Although in matters of worship and spiritual life Hoover was always remarkably willing to put himself at the same level as or even under the guidance of his Chilean sisters and brothers, in matters of Church government he had far less confidence in them. Actually, as he was getting older, he tried hard to find a way of putting Chilean Pentecostalism under the authority of the North American movement, or at least, a North American Pentecostal leader as his successor.[39] He continued as Superintendent of the Iglesia Metodista Pentecostal until the struggle for power divided it between 1932 and 1934,[40] and in the same position in the Iglesia Evangélica Pentecostal (Evangelical Pentecostal Church), formed by those who supported him, until his death on 27 May 1936. To this day, the Iglesia Evangélica Pentecostal is reluctant to accept in its temples musical instruments other than the sober organ, another sign of Hoover's legacy in matters of indigenization.

However, Hoover's personal opinion does not mean that behind the Methodist division there was no move toward "indigenization". The "self-supporting mission" which created the background for the revival and the further development of Chilean Pentecostalism was in itself a sort of "experimental model" for an indigenous mission. In his *Pauline Methods of Missionary Work*,[41] published only two years after the beginning of his South American experience, Taylor argues that "the goal of Pauline mission is independent churches that are self-supporting, entrusted with their own governance, and committed to an evangelistic style that enables them to grow according to their own cultural patterns."[42] This small essay on missionary theory is remarkable not only for having being written 33 years before Allen's *Missionary Methods: St. Paul's or Ours?*,[43] but also because it was part of an ongoing missionary experiment designed in opposition to those who "claimed that the mission board structure was the modern approach to mission."[44]

We do not know whether all of Taylor's missionaries in Chile were familiar with his theories,[45] but the spirit of his approach was indeed present in those working in Spanish. This spirit seems to have permeated early to the Chilean workers of the Presbyterian Church as well. One could easily see the Methodist revival within the context of a wider search for reshaping the life of the Churches into the local "methods and manners".

The Presbyterian Church of Concepción, for instance, which was in the charge of a "national worker", Tulio Morán, was following a path quite different from that of the mission. Morán's temporary illness in 1907 gave the mission the opportunity to send a new missionary, James McLean, to put things in order. One of McLean's first reports reads:

> This congregation is nondescript in relation to any system of doctrine or policy. In government they are Congregationalist; as concerns baptism, ultra immersionists; in worship, fiery Methodists. Hostility to the rich and educated extends a warning finger, an exaggerated type of communism repels the sane enquirer, and the relinquishing of voters' rights makes Christ appear in a false light to a liberty-loving citizen who prizes his blood-bought franchise. Can we not do something for the rich and polished sinners for whom Christ died?[46]

As the cause of such a development was thought to be the "lack of supervision" by the mission, an experienced missionary, William Boomer, was moved to Concepción, and Tulio Morán became his associated minister. The situation ended in Morán's resignation and the division of the Church.[47] Morán and those who followed him later joined the Pentecostal movement. In a different development, H. L. Weiss, the founder of the Christian and Missionary Alliance in Chile, reported to Chile Evangélico (Concepción, 10 December, 1909), how the revival reached their own churches in Valdivia. In his letter, Weiss tells the readers how humiliating it was at first for them, the foreign pastors, to see local laywomen interceding for them. "Pastors are the first ones to resist the Holy Spirit and the last ones to humiliate themselves to the dust."[48] It seems that the fact that the "foreign pastors" of the Christian and Missionary Alliance bowed — as Hoover did in Valparaiso — to the "methods and manners" of the national members of their congregations, prevented the division. In this case, the revival was welcomed within the church structure.

Therefore, the understanding of the conflict as a "cultural clash" seems to have solid grounds, and the "cultural factor" will play a major role in the further development of Pentecostalism. Despite Hoover's rejection of "nationalism" as a legitimate motive for separation from the Methodist Episcopal Church, the division forced the new movement to rely on national resources, both human and material, for its future development. Except for Hoover, all the ministry and leadership of the new church had to come from the converted Chileans, most of them reared in the context of popular Catholicism. It was then inevitable that an unconscious process of cultural adaptation of the Protestant message and the ways of church life had taken place. William E. Carter was the first to notice that this adaptation had proceeded through a complex relation of rejection and continuity:

> . . . not only has Pentecostalism known how to meet a felt need; it has known how to fit its ritual into the culture, while yet maintaining its unquestionably unique identity. For example, its church buildings may be on deserted side streets. But it follows the traditional pattern of religion in the plaza, by constantly holding open air meetings there. It rejects the traditional saint's day processionals, but it preserves the basic idea that one should process in religion. One sees immense groups processing from the evening plaza rally to their Pentecostal temple, singing songs that are accompanied by guitars and that come straight out of the popular music of the masses. It instructs its members to refrain from the frequent evening visits with friends in the neighbourhood bar. But it offers, in its place, nightly, informal services with one's friends at the local temple. It retains extended, private prayer, but it dictates that it should be done in a clearly audible voice. It rejects miraculous healing through the saints, but it claims that divine healing may be easily had by direct prayer to God.[49]

Because Carter's observations show very well how this dynamic of rejection and continuity works, further examples are not necessary. However, some aspects of his interpretation need some discussion and clarification. In the first place, one gets the impression that there was a "unique Pentecostal identity" already defined or finished before it entered into contact with the local culture, and that this identity has been maintained without essential change throughout the process of adaptation. Such an idea is dispelled by the simple fact that Pentecostalism did not arrive in Chile as a ready-made missionary product. One should rather see what Chilean Pentecostalism is, that is to say, its identity, as one result of the complex relation of continuity and discontinuity between the Protestant tradition received from the missionaries, popular Catholicism, and the local culture as a whole.

In the second place, one gets the impression that, as a rule, Pentecostalism adopted *forms* but never *contents* from the local religious culture. This would mean that the doctrines received from the missionaries have always been maintained pure, but only dressed with local clothes. However, this theoretical, clear-cut distinction between content and form proves to be more difficult in practice. A case in point is the last of Carter's examples, that is, healing. The importance of healing could be seen as a sort of "point of contact" between primitive Christianity, revivalist Protestantism, popular Catholicism and Amerindian religiosity. In Chilean popular Catholicism, religious healing operates through the institutionalized practice of the *manda*: when people appeal to a local saint, virgin, or *animita* (small shrine located in the place where somebody suddenly died by accident or murder), for curing of diseases suffered by themselves or by relatives, they promise to perform different kinds of religious duties or sacrifices (lighting of candles, pilgrimage, etc.) if the saint/virgin/animita actually responds to their plea. When healing is experienced, failure to comply with the promise means the danger of becoming ill again. Although Pentecostalism denies that saints, virgins or animitas have real power to heal (only God heals), one can recognize the structure of the manda in many testimonies of Pentecostal conversions related to healing experiences: the faithful attendance at the church or the discharge of other Pentecostal duties (like evangelization), as well as the abandonment of mundane vices, is presented as the fulfilment of a promise made before God when pleading for healing from a serious disease. New episodes of illness are actually interpreted as caused by the failure to comply with the promise, or by the relapsing into old vices. Here, we have not only traditional religious forms, but also religious meanings surviving in Pentecostalism. Those meanings bear implications for the understanding of God and his grace which might look quite unorthodox from a classical Protestant point of view.

Finally, it might appear that the process of adaptation to the local culture has been quite smooth and homogeneous. However, another of Carter's examples shows that the process has been much more problematic, and that some adaptations have been contested for other groups within Chilean Pentecostalism: the adoption of instruments and styles of popular music. The portrait, already classical, of Chilean Pentecostalism through the image of a group of poor, cheaply but well dressed mestizos singing to the Lord accompanied by guitars, mandolins and tambourines,[50] overlooks the fact that the second biggest Pentecostal Church, the Evangélica Pentecostal, regards the use of those instruments as an undue concession to "the world".

Unlike others, this adaptation seems to have been the result of a conscious move toward "Chilenization". Manuel Umaña, the pastor of the 1st Church of Santiago, and later on the leader of the Iglesia Metodista Pentecostal, asked Genaro Ríos, a popular artist who had joined the church in 1930, to form a church band. Ríos, along with his two brothers, adapted existing hymns into the style of popular music, and introduced them with his instrumental accompaniments into the services in 1931.[51] At first, this innovation was not only rejected by those churches which a couple of years later followed W. Hoover to form the Iglesia Evangélica Pentecostal, but also by some of those who supported Umaña during the power struggle which led to the great division. In fact, the 1936 conference of the Iglesia Metodista Pentecostal (two years after the division) decided to expel the Ríos brothers from membership,[52] so they formed a separate Church, the Ejercito Evangélico de Chile (the Evangelical Army of Chile). However, as the innovation was readily accepted by laypeople and soon proved to have great appeal to those outside the Church, it gradually became a standard practice in the Iglesia Metodista Pentecostal and in many other younger Pentecostal Churches. The fact that the Iglesia Evangélica Pentecostal to this day rejects the use of popular instruments, does not mean that the old imported Protestant style had been maintained. While the instrumental Pentecostal music resembles the musical taste of the peasantry of Central Chile, which is very much a Mexican import, the singing in many Evangélica Pentecostal churches resembles the moanlike style of southern Chilean folklore, which often lacks instrumental accompaniment.

The foregoing discussion has shown that although the explicit motives of the Chilean Pentecostal revival were largely typical of all movements of religious reform or renewal (going back to the sources), underneath the surface there was a much more implicit process going on, that is, a sort of reappropriation of Christianity by the bajo pueblo. Through Pentecostalism, the bajo pueblo asserted their right to reshape the Christian experience and church life according to their own "methods and manners", or, as Gabriel Salazar (Note 4) put it, according to "their own type of sociability".

Chilean Pentecostalism and the world of politics

I have argued that Pentecostalism entered Chilean history as a part of the religious history of the bajo pueblo. Taking that into account, one should understand the relation of Pentecostals to politics in the light of the relation of the bajo pueblo as a whole to politics. My purpose in the second part of this article is to apply such a perspective to challenge or re-evaluate the most common sociological clichés regarding the "social ethic" of Chilean Pentecostalism: "opium of the people", "social strike", "social conformism", "religious justification of the status quo", "haven of the masses".

Before I begin, some words about the history of Chilean Pentecostalism are needed. Because after the great division of the years 1932–1934, an increasing number of offshoots grew from both Churches, the Metodista Pentecostal and the Evangélica Pentecostal, it is difficult to speak of the history of Chilean Pentecostism as a single movement. That history tends to be a plain chronicle of the successive divisions from one or other of the main branches, or simply a focus on a particular denomination. However, taking into consideration more general evidence such as the trends of growth, one could suggest or underline some stages in the development of Chilean Pentecostalism. As the figures for growth are taken from the national censuses,[53] one should bear in mind that they include Protestants as a whole.

1910–1930 (1932–1934)

During this period, the rate of Protestant growth was still low, mainly because the bulk of the congregation of the first Pentecostal Churches came out from Methodist and Presbyterian Churches. This was a period of organization as independent Churches, so most of the adaptations of the

Methodist inheritance, as well as the innovations in terms of methods and styles of Church government, ministry and self-support, were established. The year 1930 indicates the date of the last census which showed a low rate of growth. A more internal mark for the end of this first stage would be the date of the great division (1932–1934).

1930–1960 (1964)

During this period, the absolute number of Protestants approximately doubled each decade: the beginning of the so-called "Pentecostal explosion". One could also think that the process of adaptation analysed in the first part of this article took place mostly in this period. This possibility is supported by Kessler's suggestion that after the schism freed the Iglesia Metodista Pentecostal from Hoover's influence, "this denomination became more typically Chilean."[54] It is also during this period that foreign Pentecostal Churches started their missionary work in Chile.[55] Although these Churches are by now Chilean in leadership and finances, a clear difference remains between the two types of Pentecostalism, particularly regarding cultural adaptation, social insertion and theological articulation. An illustration of this difference is the fact that in Chile the members of the Pentecostal Churches of missionary origin would tend to identify themselves by the name of their denomination, instead of using the general label of "Pentecostal", which is reserved to the followers of Chilean Pentecostalism. Again, the year 1960 simply indicates the date of the census. An alternative date for the end of this stage would be 1964, when the Christian Democratic Party took power, marking the beginning of considerable changes in the life of the bajo pueblo.

1960–1970 (1973)

As during this decade Protestantism grew at a considerably lower rate, this period could well be considered as a time of stabilization and institutionalization. As this stage will be considered in more detail later, I shall content myself by saying that during the 1960s major changes in the life of the bajo pueblo occurred from which new challenges to Pentecostalism emerged. Signs of institutionalization included the beginning, with the exception of the Iglesia Evangélica Pentecostal, of Pentecostal involvement in ecumenical, or more exactly, interdenominational activities and in social programmes. The year 1970 was the date of the census as well as the last year of the Frei (Senior) government. However, a better date to indicate the end of this stage would be 1973, the year of the coup d'etat, because during the Unidad Popular government the trends of both the political life of Chilean society and Pentecostal life were very much in line with the previous years.

1973 onwards

A new wave of Pentecostal expansion started, with a rate of growth similar to that of 1930–1960. A chief characteristic of this period is the emergence of Pentecostalism into public life and politics. This trend is continuing.

If one sees the history of the Chilean political system in the 20th century as a progressive integration of new social sectors into the democratic life of the country, one soon realizes that up to the beginning of the 1960s those sectors we have described as the bajo pueblo had been generally excluded from any kind of political or even labour organization. The traditional Liberal and Conservative Parties were expressions of different factions within the upper classes. The Radical and much later the Christian Democratic (former Falange) Parties were mainly expressions of the middle class, which started to emerge toward the end of the last century. The increasingly popular Communist and Socialist Parties were expressions of the skilled proletariat of the still tiny industrial sector of the economy to which the labour unions were also restricted. For the heterogeneous, "marginal", unskilled sectors forming the urban and rural bajo pueblo, there was no opportunity of social participation other than the street or the Quinta de Recreo (the local bar). They watched the processes of "democratization" and "modernization" of Chilean society from the sidelines.

Lalive's image of "refuge of the masses" is perhaps an adequate account of Pentecostalism up to the beginning of the 1960s.[56] Indeed, it offered to those on the margins of society a protective community and also a new meaning for life. But the image is misleading if what is meant is that Pentecostalism prevented people from participating in social or labour organizations. For the bajo pueblo, this kind of organization simply did not exist. However, the situation began to change with unforeseen velocity in the early 1960s. Chile was transforming itself into a social laboratory for confrontation between reform advocates and those favouring revolution.[57] The Christian Democratic Party, representing the reform alternative, took power in 1964. It needed to build a strong base among the lower classes to counterbalance the hegemony of the left (Communist and Socialist) in the worker movement. So began an impressive work of social engineering by the state, aiming at integrating those on the margins, the bajo pueblo, with those in the mainstream of society. Empowered by the Agrarian Reform Law of 1965, the state moved strongly toward organizing labour in the agrarian sector.[58] With the legal creation of Juntas de Vecinos (neighbourhood organizations) and other types such as women's centres,[59] the state began the process of co-optation, aimed at taking over the grassroots movement which had begun developing on the margins by means of land invasions supported by the left. The issue to which these organizations devoted themselves was the provision of housing, a crucial aspect in the life of the "excluded".

In the last years of the Frei (senior) government the socio-political climate turned more conflictive and polarized. The lack of co-operation of the economic elite made it impossible for the government to carry out its social programmes, especially the provision of more housing. The frustration of expectations caused the *movimiento poblacional*, originally mobilized to support government policies, to move to the leftist opposition. In this context the electoral victory of Unidad Popular, which represented the revolutionary alternative in the dilemma of how to address change in Chile, took place. The three years of the government of Salvador Allende, head of Unidad Popular, were characterized as much by heightening of expectations of social change and of a greater social participation by the popular sectors, as by deepening of political cleavages and increase in belligerence in political conflict. Politics became all-absorbing and divisive for people.

There is no comprehensive study of how Pentecostals related to politics during those intense nine years of Chilean history. However, drawing from some scattered observations[60] and from formal and informal conversations with Pentecostal pastors and lay leaders, we can produce a provisional picture.

There are no grounds for thinking that Pentecostalism as a block acted against the current of social participation. It seems that a variety of factors, including the characteristics of a particular area, of the Pentecostal community in that area, of its leadership, etc. acted in favour of or against Pentecostal involvement in social organizations. For instance, in places where population groupings were small and the level of formal education lower, as in rural or semi-rural villages or small towns, the scarcity of human resources with some kind of organizational experience made it easier for members of Pentecostal Churches and even pastors to reach positions of leadership in the new social organizations. In turn, this made it easier for Church members to join those organizations. It was a different situation in the context of big urban popular neighbourhoods, often with a higher rate of social problems and delinquency. As a protective measure for the newly converted, Pentecostal Churches tended to hold services every night, and to fill the free time of their members with evangelistic activities, so that no spare time was available for other kinds of social commitment. In this context, cases of Pentecostal participation in social organizations tended to be more isolated, and to some extent involved conflicts of loyalty. In any case, only a minority of Pentecostal membership had an active participation in social organizations. But it is debatable whether this small proportion was significantly different from the level of participation of their non-Pentecostal neighbours.

Full membership in political parties, however, is generally regarded by Pentecostals as incompatible with Church life,[61] not only because both militancies are highly time-consuming, but also because political militancy could force them to compromise some key aspects of their life style. But this rejection of membership of political parties should not be understood as an absence of political views.

Analysing Pentecostals' political preferences is also difficult because of lack of information. Given the strong identification of the Christian Democratic Party with the social doctrine, and even with the pastoral policies of the Catholic Church, it is very unlikely that this party received substantial support from the Pentecostal electorate in the presidential election of 1964. Traditionally, most Protestants supported the Radical Party, seen as representative of the ideals of religious freedom and total separation between church and state. But because in the 1964 election the Radical candidate was supported by the right, it is probable that many Pentecostals gave their vote to Salvador Allende. As the Radical Party joined Unidad Popular for the 1970 election, it is likely that Salvador Allende received substantial support from the Pentecostal electorate. An indication of that may be a survey carried out in relation to the 1971 local (municipal) elections, in the Santiago congregations of the Iglesia Metodista Pentecostal: 77 percent gave their vote to Unidad Popular; 19 percent to the Christian Democratic Party; 4 percent to the National Party (Right).[62] One might conclude that Pentecostal political preferences did not differ significantly from those of their neighbours, except in that the "anti-Catholic motive" prevented many Pentecostals from supporting the Christian Democratic Party, making their support for the left stronger than that of their neighbours.

The lower rate of Protestant growth during the 1960s should also be understood as a by-product of the increasing level of social participation during those years. The climate of rising expectation for social change acted as powerful magnet for participation in social organizations, so that for the first time Pentecostalism suffered real competition. While some Churches reacted to this kind of pressure in a defensive way, that is, preventing their members from joining social organizations, others saw the pressure as a challenge to adapt themselves to the new times. A simple example of adaptation is the reduction of the number of services during the week, to produce spare time for other activities.

Some external factors also influenced the way in which Pentecostal Churches faced the challenge. The creation in 1958 (with strong support from the Church World Service, the National Council of Churches of the United States, and Lutheran World Relief) of Ayuda Cristiana Evangélica, a Protestant relief organization, helped to involve many Pentecostal communities in distribution of relief (food, clothes, etc.) to poor people, or to victims of the frequent floods and earthquakes.[63] From this experience some Pentecostal Churches started to consider "service" as a dimension of their mission. On the other side, some Conservative Protestant organizations made considerable efforts to influence Pentecostal Churches to oppose social change. Particularly during the government of Unidad Popular, the bulletin *La Voz de los Mártires* and copies of R. Wurmbrand's *Torturado por Cristo* were widely distributed free of charge to the leadership of the Churches. But this campaign aimed to involve Pentecostals in "anti-communist" politics rather than to call them to withdraw from politics.

This provisional balance in the way in which Pentecostals related to politics during the years 1964 to 1973 suggests that the social and political behaviour of Pentecostals as individuals did not differ significantly from that of the bajo pueblo as a whole, and that Pentecostal Churches as such showed the first signs of awakening to public life. Pentecostalism certainly did not operate as a major obstacle to social change. At any rate, one could say that Pentecostalism kept its identity as a religious community, appealing mainly to those who approached life's problems with a religious perspective.

Things changed drastically again with the 1973 coup d'etat and the subsequent 16 years of military rule. This aspect of Chilean history is well documented[64] and I shall take up only two important dimensions relating to the religious field. First, the government's making illegal and systematically repressing political parties and social organizations, together with social consequences of the difficult economic adjustment begun by the military, produced indirectly in the general populace a shift toward the Churches. Particularly in the popular sectors, the churches, in as much as they were the only places authorized for meetings, were filled with people seeking protection, spiritual support, meeting houses, and the like. Second, the historical and social weight of the Catholic Church turned itself into the principal bulwark in the defence of human rights, and, as a consequence, became the voice of denunciation of the violation of rights. This produced the first great crisis of relations between the Catholic Church and the state since the era of national independence.

It was this withdrawal of religious and moral support by the preponderant Church which drove the government to look for moral support in the second religious force in the country. So, the scenario was prepared for a rapid emergence of the Protestant world, Pentecostals contributing the bulk, into public life or politics: official and public meetings with the military authorities offering support and recognition; "Evangelical Te Deums" held in the "Evangelical Cathedral", meant to be thanksgiving for independence (18 September 1810), but openly presented by the government as thanksgiving for the Pronunciamiento Militar (11 September 1973) — all with the maximum of publicity. Those Protestant sectors (Pentecostals included) who felt misrepresented by this new political agenda were forced to emerge in the public space to make clear their own perspective, initially with little impact on the press.[65]

If this search for moral support found a ready partner within an important sector of Protestant leadership (not exclusively Pentecostal), this was not principally because of political affinity, but rather for reasons relating to the struggle for "religious power". Despite the fact that the political constitution of 1925 separated the church from the state, the Catholic Church retained a powerful position in Chilean society: its cultural power, as well as its influence in the political life of the country, made "religious equality" something of an illusion. Protestants continued to be regarded as "dissenters", and many people, especially the middle and upper classes, looked down on them. This religious discrimination, coupled with the reality of social exclusion, caused Pentecostals to grow up with the feeling of being 'second-class citizens". The main motive for any sort of organized Protestant intervention in public life has long been the struggle to overcome this religious discrimination, to obtain recognition from the state. While the position of the Catholic Church in society is contested by Protestants, at the same time it represents the only model of what it means to be recognized by the state. That this struggle for "religious power" was behind the support to the military regime is illustrated in the number of practices copied from the Catholic model: the building of a cathedral, the organization of a Te Deum (keeping the Latin designation), the importance given to the presence of the authorities and dignitaries in the temple. The military government, on its part, was ready to provide this sort of symbolic recognition plus other facilities for the day-to-day work of evangelical pastors. But it was not ready to risk a deeper break with the Catholic Church by promoting real changes regarding religious equality.

The continuation of all this practices after the re-establishment of the democratic system in Chile confirms that they were not designed to support a government of a particular ideology, but were a statement of the new place in society of Protestants or Pentecostals: "We are no longer second-class citizens."

Conclusion

As early as 1961 Eugene Nida[66] suggested that Latin American Pentecostalism should be seen as an expression of an "indigenous Christianity". On the one hand, this means that the religious character of Pentecostalism should be addressed more clearly. To reduce Pentecostalism to a mechanism of social adaptation may perhaps show something of what Pentecostalism does, but nothing of what Pentecostalism is.[67] On the other hand, this means that to "locate" Pentecostalism in the context of the struggle of the mestizo and indigenous underclasses, the bajo pueblo, to reassert their cultural identity and their "religious self-determination" could be far more illuminating than constantly re-hashing "conspiracy theories", or imagining Pentecostalism as a squadron in the battle between Anglo-Saxons and Latins, foxes and hedgehogs,[68] modernists and traditionals.

I hope that I have successfully demonstrated the importance of this approach for Chilean Pentecostalism. Its application to situations elsewhere in the world should be the subject of further debate.

Notes

1 The classics are Emile Willems, *Followers of the New Faith. Culture Change and the Rise of Protestantism in Brazil and Chile*, Nashville, TN, Vanderbilt University Press, 1967; and Christian Lalive d'Epinay, *Haven of the Masses. A Study of the Pentecostal Movement in Chile*, London, Lutterworth Press, 1969. More recent is David Martin, *Tongues of Fire. The Explosion of Protestantism in Latin America*, Oxford, Basil Blackwell, 1990.

2 That this sort of "conspiracy theory" is quite old is shown by J. Samuel Escobar, "Conflict of Interpretations of Popular Protestantism", in Guillermo Cook, ed., *New Face of the Church in Latin America*, pp. 112–134, especially pp. 117ff, New York, Orbis Books, 1994.

3 "The Latin Conversion", in *The Guardian Weekend*, 10 June 1995, pp. 14ff (here p. 27).

4 This expression, which could be translated as "lowly" or "humble" people, was at the turn of the century the common designation of the lower classes of Chilean society. Having the same descriptive connotation as "lower classes", the expression also connotes the sort of cultural and moral judgement that the mainstream of society had about the lower classes. The expression has been brought into historical research by Gabriel Salazar, "The History of Popular Culture in Chile: Different Paths", in Kenneth Aman and Cristián Parker, eds, *Popular Culture in Chile. Resistance and Survival*, pp. 13–39, Boulder, CO, Westview Press.

5 The concept of "religious field" makes reference to the totality of religious institutions acting in a pluri-religious society, and the conflicts and tensions between them, especially with regard to their ability (or inability) to establish relations of mutual legitimation with the state. Cf. Otto Maduro, *Religión y conflicto social*, Mérida, 1978.

6 Hans-Jürgen Prien, *La historia del cristianismo en América Latina*, Salamanca, Ediciones Sígueme, 1985, pp. 434–438; 585–597.

7 James Thomson, a Scottish Baptist minister, representative of the British and Foreign Bible Society and the Foreign School Society, came to Chile in 1821 in response to an invitation from Bernardo O'Higgins, the first "Supreme Director" (1818–1823) of the Chilean nation. See J. B. A. Kessler, *A Study of the Older Protestant Missions and Churches in Peru and Chile*, Goes, Oosterbaan & le Cointre N.V., 1967, pp. 19–23.

8 Figures quoted from Cristián Parker, "Christianity and Popular Movements in the Twentieth Century", in Aman and Parker, eds., op. cit. Note 4, pp. 41–65, here p. 43.

9 Cristián Parker, "Radiografía a la religión de los chilenos", *Mensaje* 428 (1994): 178–181.

10 Traditional Protestant Churches seem to have grown at a rate hardly higher than that of the Chilean population as a whole, and in some cases even lower: cf. Lalive, op.cit. Note 1, pp. 16ff.

11 Ibid., pp. 23f.

12 Hoover's written testimony is still the main source for the origin of Chilean Pentecostalism. Although finished in 1931, the book was first published after his death: *Historia del avivamiento pentecostal en Chile*, Valparaiso, Imp. Excelsior, 1948.

13 Kessler, op.cit. Note 7, pp. 124ff.

14 In 1907 Mrs Hoover received a pamphlet which contained this claim. The pamphlet, describing a revival which had taken place in the girls' home of Pandita Ramabai at Mukti, India, had been written and sent by Minnie Abrams,

Mrs Hoover's old classmate at the Chicago Training School. Hoover, op.cit. Note 12, p. 14.

15 The opinion generally accepted within the western theological tradition since St John Chrysostom (4th century), that the charismata were gifts temporarily given to the early Church because of its weakness, was maintained by Luther and Calvin (see José Comblin, *The Holy Spirit and Liberation*, New York, Orbis Books, 1987, pp. 35ff). Wesley seems to have separated himself from that tradition (Donald Dayton, *Raíces teológicas del pentecostalismo*, Buenos Aires, Nueva Creación & Eerdmams, 1991, pp. 25f). However, Robinson, the pastor of the 2nd Methodist Church of Santiago, wrote an editorial article in *El Cristiano* (18 October 1909) defending the "traditional" opinion, making the further statement that the work of the Spirit was "rational".

16 Ibid., pp. 70–71; 74; 81–82.

17 W. Hollenweger, "Methodist's Past in Pentecostal's Present", in *Methodist History* 20(4) (1982): 169–182, here p. 176.

18 Lalive, op.cit. Note 1, p. 10.

19 Hollenweger, op.cit. Note 17, passim.

20 "Reflections on the Pentecostal Contribution to the Mission of the Church in Latin America", *Journal of Pentecostal Theology* 1 (1992): 93–108, here p. 95.

21 He makes reference to the conversion of many humble people, some of them outlaws, but also to the attraction the movement had for some "gentlemen of dignity and serious young men" (Hoover, op.cit. Note 12, p. 43).

22 M. Canales, S. Palma and H. Villela, *En tierra extraña II*, Santiago, Amerinda-SEPADE, 1991, p. 24.

23 Op.cit. Note 7, passim.

24 F. H. Kamsteeg, "Prophetic Pentecostalism in Chile", PhD dissertation, Amsterdam, Vrije Universiteit, 1995, p. 56.

25 This is the subtitle of Kessler's book.

26 Kessler, op.cit. Note 7, p. 105 (emphasis mine). This letter is also commented on by W. Hollenweger, op.cit. Note 17, p. 170.

27 Ibid., pp. 49–50, 52–54, 101–102.

28 Garvin's letter to Speer dated 2 October 1905, quoted by Kessler, ibid., p. 63.

29 Ibid., p. 48. See also pp. 46 and 100.

30 One of the literary debates which made David Trumbull, the founder of the Presbyterian Church in Chile, popular in liberal circles, was related to a procession with the image of Saint Isodorus, the patron saint of the rain, held in Valparaiso during a prolonged drought. Ibid., p. 44.

31 Ibid., pp. 96–108; David Bundy, "The Legacy of William Taylor", *International Bulletin of Missionary Research* (October 1994): 172–176.

32 Kessler, op.cit. Note 7, p. 103.

33 Letter to Gillespie dated 17 January 1888, quoted by Kessler, ibid., p. 100. Kessler justifies Trumbull's criticism on the ground of what he considers Taylor's total lack of provision for those missionaries who could run into difficulties (pp. 99f.). He did not realize that this lack of provision was not the result of Taylor's improvisation, but rather the expression of his conscious missionary theories and policies (cf. Bundy, op.cit. Note 31, p. 174).

34 During the 1880s the Methodist Episcopal Church had initiated a strategy to bring Taylor and his missionaries working in South America, Asia and Africa back to the flock. In 1882 the General Missionary Committee asked them to "locate" in local churches, Taylor becoming a member of a local church in South India. The 1884 General Conference celebrated in Philadelphia, which Taylor attended as delegate of the South India Conference, elected him missionary bishop for

Africa. As part of the new arrangement, the Mission board agreed to continue the "self-supporting" policy on the west coast of South America. Under the new circumstances, the groups in Chile started to organize themselves into Methodist Churches as early as 1886, and by 1903, the year of Taylor's death, they were all working under the board's control. Kessler, op.cit. Note 7, p. 175; Bundy, op.cit. Note 31, p. 175.

35 Kessler, op.cit. Note 7, p. 111. It is worth noting that this new thinking represents a major change in North American Protestantism. According to W. Hudson, the characteristic core of North American Protestantism was, before the rise of liberalism, the reinterpretation of Christianity in terms of evangelicalism and revivalism: "Evangelicalism was a theological emphasis upon the necessity for a conversion experience as the beginning point of a Christian life, while revivalism was a technique developed to induce that experience" (*American Protestantism*, Chicago, University of Chicago Press, 1961, p. 78).

36 Ibid, p. 103.

37 It may be argued that without the financial support of the North American Church, Taylor's mission would hardly have survived. That is possibly true, but it is also true that the North American Church was not prepared to support the Chilean Church as self-governing.

38 Op.cit. Note 12, p. 74. Hoover's position against "church nationalism" could well be the result of his own experience. In September 1895, when Hoover returned to Iquique after his furlough in the USA, he found that A. Vidaurre, the Chilean worker in charge of the church during his absence, did not want to submit himself to the authority of a foreign missionary. So Vidaurre left the Methodist Church with most of the congregation. Hoover had to start again from nothing, in which he succeeded. Kessler, op.cit. Note 7, p. 109.

39 Ibid., pp. 281 and 300. Doctrinal differences (the question of infant baptism, the forms of baptism, in other words, the Methodist legacy) prevented Hoover from going further. To be sure, he would have found a bigger "stumbling block" in the opposition of the Chileans to that solution.

40 There was also an accusation of immorality against Hoover. However, Kessler shows clearly that although Hoover eventually "confessed his guilt", this accusation was subservient to the power struggle. Kessler, op.cit. Note 7, pp. 303–307.

41 Philadelphia: National Association for the Promotion of Holiness, 1879.

42 Bundy's synthesis, op.cit. Note 31, p. 174.

43 London: World Dominion Press, 1912.

44 Bundy, op.cit. Note 32, p. 174.

45 Except through Goodsil F. Arms, who wrote the book *History of the William Taylor Self-supporting Mission in South America*, New York: Methodist Book Concern, 1921. Arms was, before the division, a close friend and supporter of Hoover.

46 James McLean's letter to Speer dated 10 June 1907, quoted by Kessler, op.cit. Note 7, p. 66.

47 Kessler's comment on this incident is worth quoting:

The basic trouble was not, however, a lack of supervision, but a surplus of United States nationalism. As soon as the missionaries discovered that the church practice in Concepción was irregular, they reacted against what they felt was a failure to conform to the Gospel by asserting their Presbyterian law. The missionaries forgot that this law had arisen as a result of an attempt by European or Anglo-Saxon people to conform to the Gospel in their own environment. (Ibid., p. 67)

48 Letter republished in *Evangelio y Sociedad* 15 (1992): 32–33 (translation mine).

49 Quoted by Lalive, op.cit. Note 1, p. 63, from I. Vallier (Project Director), Anglican Opportunities in South America, New York, Bureau of Applied Social Research, Columbia University (mimeo), p. 24. Consistent with his interest in structural change, Lalive himself applies this paradigm of continuity and discontinuity (rejection) to the analysis of the relation between the Pentecostal community and what he sees as the basic institution of traditional society: the *hacienda* (the land estate). According to him, the structure of the Pentecostal community, with its face-to-face relationships, resembles the structure of the hacienda; while the pastor, and the kind of authority he enjoys, resemble the figure of the *patrón.* The element of discontinuity is that the Pentecostal community does not reproduce the class structure of the hacienda: in the Pentecostal community, both the congregation and the pastor belong to the same social class (op.cit., pp. 32–33, 82–84, 129–132)

50 See, for example, the full-page photograph in the cover story of *The Guardian Weekend*, 10 June 1995, p.15.

51 Kessler, op.cit. Note 7, p. 309.

52 Ibid., p. 309.

53 The percentages of Protestants in national censuses since 1907 are: 1907, 1%; 1920, 1.4%; 1930, 1.4%; 1940, 2.34%; 1952, 4.06%; 1960, 5.58%; 1970, 6.18%; 1992, 13.2%. The census of 1982 did not ask about religious affiliation. The census of 1992 asked only the population 14 years or older.

54 Op.cit. Note 7, p. 309.

55 Asambleas de Dios Autonóma, Sweden (1937); Asambleas de Dios, USA (1942); Iglesia Cuadrangular (Foursquare) (1945); Iglesia de Dios (1950); Iglesia de Cristo (1952); the latter three from the USA as well.

56 In fact, most of Lalive's fieldwork took place in 1965, when the situation for the bajo pueblo in terms of real opportunities for social participation was just starting to change.

57 See William V. D'Antonio and Frederick B. Pike, *Religion, Revolution, and Reform: New Forces for Change in Latin America*, New York, Praeger, 1964.

58 In contrast to 1964 (the year of Eduardo Frei Montalva's election as President) when from a total of 335,537 agricultural day workers only 1647 (0.49%) belonged to labour unions, in 1972, of a total force of 335,343, those unionized numbered 207,910 (62%). Manuel Castells, *Reforma agraria, lucha de closes y poder popular en el campo chileno*, Santiago, CIDU, mimeo, 1972.

59 Until the middle of the 1960s the popular movement was concentrated in the workers' movement. By 1972 it had expanded and it was estimated that there were about 800,000 members of neighbourhood and village movements within a vast network of territorial organizations up and down the country. This amounted to a greater number than all rural and urban workers' unions. Manuel Castells, "El movimiento de pobladores y lucha de clases en Chile", in *Revista Latinamericana de Estudios Urbanos Regionales* (EURE) 3(7) (1973): 9–35.

60 See for example Irma Palma, ed., *En tierra extraña: itinerario del pueblo pentecostal chileno*, Santiago, Amerinda, 1988, which contains interviews with 10 Chilean Pentecostal leaders.

61 Cf. Lalive, op.cit. Note 1, pp. 106ff.

62 Hans Tennekes, *El movimiento pentecostal en Chile*, Iquique, CIREN, 1985.

63 See the chapter "Ecumenism of Trial" in Lalive, op.cit. Note 1, pp. 161–190.

64 Two lengthy accounts are provided by Pamela Constable and Arturo Valenzuela, *A Nation of Enemies: Chile under Pinochet*, New York, Norton, 1991; and Mary Helen Spooner, *Soldiers in a Narrow Land: The Pinochet Regime in Chile*, Berkeley, University of California Press, 1994.

65 On the subject of Protestants during this period, see Humberto Lagos, *Crisis de la esperanza. Religión y autoritarismo en Chile*, Santiago, Presor/Lar, 1988.
66 "The Indigenous Churches in Latin America", *Practical Anthropology* 8 (1961): 97–105.
67 Cf. Francisco C. Rolim, "Pentecôtisme et société au Brésil", *Social Compass* 26(2/3) (1979): 345–372, here p. 346.
68 See Claudio Véliz, *The New World of the Gothic Fox: Culture and Economy in English and Spanish America*, Berkeley, University of California Press, 1994.

48

GLOSSOLALIA AND POSSESSION AMONG PENTECOSTAL GROUPS OF THE MEZZOGIORNO*

Maria Pia di Bella

Source: *Annales, ESC*, 4 (1988), 897–907; translated by Olga Koepping.

The gift of tongues, or 'glossolalia', is a religious phenomenon, mystical or paranormal, which leads to some people being able to express language which can be heard or even understood as a language that does not exist, and to use their own language so that their listeners will be at their command and as if under a spell.[1]

This phenomenon, which occurred many times in the religious centres of Ancient Greece and which we can rediscover in our time in several 'primitive' religions (May 1956: 75–96), for example shamanism, is also present in the Old Testament, in form of prophecies (I *Sam.* X, 5–13; XIX, 18–24). The New Testament gives it a large significance, first in the *Acts*:

> When the day of Pentecost arrived, they were all together in one place. And suddenly there came from heaven a sound like a mighty rushing wind, and it filled the entire house where they were sitting. And divided tongues as of fire appeared to them and rested on each one of them. And they were all filled with the Holy Spirit and began to speak in other tongues as the Spirit gave them utterance.
>
> (Acts II, 1–40)

In the first letter to the Corinthians (XII, 27–30; XIV, 2–6, 18–19, 39–40), the apostle Paul mentions it at length but in an ambivalent way.

Although he did not intend to forbid a phenomenon which was showing rapid growth across different Churches at the point of conversions, he did want the faithful to explain to their new recruits the message of this new religion in a comprehensible way, in their everyday speech. It was only in

177 that the Church put a stop to the phenomenon of speaking in tongues, by excommunicating Montan and his sect, all of whom believed in the concept of 'glossolalia' as tangible proof of the gift of the Holy Spirit. This ended its daily and widespread practice.

In the subsequent history of the Church, glossolalia appeared only in dissident groups, mendicant orders, French Jansenists, Camisards, followed by early Quaker groups, some of the first adherents of Methodism, the Shakers and the apostolic Catholic Church (Irvingites). It was in the United States, around 1900–6, that various elevations to sainthood gave rise to several Pentecostal groups and the phenomenon of glossolalia was rediscovered within their group. It is this rediscovery of the phenomenon which has contributed to its striking expansion in the world (between eight and ten million members in 1988).

Creation and development of Pentecostalist groups

At the end of the Second World War, small groups of Protestants appeared in southern Italy. Although the exact number of adherents of new faiths was negligible, the large number of these groups and their survival within a very conservative Catholic environment rapidly became a problem, starting a debate and venomous press campaigns between Italian Catholics and laypeople throughout the 1950s. Later on, this phenomenon would attract the attention of some researchers (Cassin 1956; Miegge 1959; Lanternari 1969; Castiglione 1972).

This study of the emergence of the new doctrine within a rural environment started at Accadia in Apulia, a centre for Oneness Pentecostalism, and later extended to other villages where this doctrine developed: Gesualdo, Villanova (Campania), San Fele (Basilicata), Randazzo, Marsala (Sicily).[2] Moreover a comparison has been drawn with certain Trinitarian Pentecostalist groups in the neighbouring Apulian towns of Anzano and Monteleone. The introduction of Pentecostalism and its development in a rural environment clearly followed the same pattern in these different locations. Three distinct phases could be discovered in the process, each marked by resistance to rural local values.

The first phase, that of conversions, consists of the arrival of a missionary in the village, his (or her) strong proselytizing aimed at his family. The first baptisms, often in groups, were usually associated with difficulties and persecution of the fledgling group by the villages, the local clergy and the authorities. It is clear that in all the studied communities the type of missionary is always the same: he is an Italian born in the village to which he is returning, having emigrated to the United States in his youth (or more rarely to Latin America). In his adopted country, his conversion to Pentecostalism will often have facilitated his integration (Wilson 1970). As a profound believer, he sees Pentecostalism as having given him 'salvation' through baptism and above all through the presence of the Holy Spirit in his body, which manifests itself in the 'gift' of glossolalia. As soon as he is aware of his difference, he sees it as his duty to return home to 'save' his family. They react to the new doctrine according to the opinion they have of the missionary: if he has the reputation of having 'succeeded' in the United States, the family will convert as a whole (Accadia, Anzano, Gesualdo, Marsala); if he has the reputation of having 'failed', they will reject his attempt (San Fele). He will also try to expand the circle of converts, but will not look very far, as, with the exception of some distant blood relations, his ambition is limited to the conversion of friends and clients. The personal reputation of the missionary and the social status of his family decide the size of the circle of converts: the more modest their origins, the smaller the group will be.

This first phase is characterized by its emotional intensity; added to the family reunion after years of distance is the discovery of a new doctrine which allows its followers to feel closer to Jesus, thanks to the 'gift' of glossolalia. Indeed, it gives its followers (some of whom are already deeply religious, others rediscovering faith through this new mode of expression) the certainty of being 'saints', 'elected' by Jesus, and thus the power of recouping their social exclusion for themselves and in the eyes of their fellows citizens. The ostracism which these small groups were forced to undergo until 1954 also contributed to the development of the emotional character of this first phase.

The second phase, of rupture or consolidation, appears to be decisive to the entrenchment of the new faith. It is characterized either by the entrusting of the group to a pastor, usually chosen by the missionary himself, who will replace him in his absence (Accadia, San Fele) or who will take on his authority (Anzano, Marsala), or by the final installation of the missionary (Gesualdo, Randazzo). The transfer of this authority from the missionary to the pastor, and particularly the choice of pastor, appears to be fundamental to the survival and flourishing of the group. If the missionary chooses to appoint a pastor outside his family of origin and its blood relations, he is thereby risking his future: the offended men of his family withdraw more or less from meetings and collective rituals in order to separate themselves from the 'outsider' pastor, and force their wives to do the same (Accadia). However, if the pastor is chosen from within the family of the missionary (Anzano, Marsala) the group unites, even in certain respects forming a community. The defection of some followers or, on the other hand, their solidarity means that at this stage they appear to freeze and, due to a lack of encouragement or because they have reached a limit, they give up the proselytizing which characterized the previous phase. However, by consecrating an old house as a temple (Accadia, San Fele, Gesualdo) or building a temple mainly financed by the missionary (Villanova, Randazzo), they give themselves a seat and make their position official.

The third phase, that of institutionalization, is demarcated by the construction of a second temple, intervillage regroupments (Accadia with Randazzo and Marsala; Gesualdo with Villanova and San Fele) and the affiliation with an Evangelical institutional church (Accadia is affiliated with the United Pentecostal Church of Europe and the British Isles, Gesualdo with the Chiesa Apostolica della Fede in Cristo Gesù, Anzano with the Assemblee di Dio). It is in fact at this stage that the followers, who need to visit each other and help each other, come to consolidate their groups.

This first initiative leads to a wish to join an Evangelical Church. They take the necessary steps, receive visits from official missionaries and progressively affiliate themselves to the Church of their choice. At the same time, the older members must face the problem presented by the second generation: converted at a young age or born after the creation of the group, the young members have difficulty finding an evangelized partner in their home environment when they reach marriageable age. They therefore have three choices: marrying outside the group and automatically being excluded from it, converting their partner and introducing him or her into the group, or deciding not to marry except 'in the religion'. In the latter case, if no candidate appears in their own village they will entrust their elders with the search for someone among other followers of the same Church, by distributing photographs of themselves.

Interpretation of the phenomenon of glossolalia in the southern region

The gift of tongues in the Italian south has the same significance as it does in *Acts*: it is the descent of the Spirit onto the believer, the only proof, for the autochtones, that the believer has been 'saved' being this tangible mark of his 'sainthood'. In the groups studied, the believers who received the 'gift' manifest it primarily during the periods of prayer. However, in Accadia more than elsewhere, the believers speak 'in tongues'. Under the spiritual leadership of a missionary woman, they pray on their knees for around forty minutes during the prayer period, while in the other places studied, where it is men who lead, they only stay kneeling for ten minutes at the most. This constraint imposed by the female missionary does not seem to weigh on the participants; on the contrary, it is a much loved moment in which the followers like to get out of themselves (Di Bella 1982).

On an individual level, the gift of glossolalia is experienced by the believer as a doubly significant act; at the moment when he or she feels that he is expressing a verbal message in what he imagines to be a language foreign to him, he thinks that the Holy Spirit has chosen him to deliver his message to the world, through him. At the same time, he imagines that he has been designated a 'saintly' person in the eyes of all present, worthy of receiving in his body 'His' message, and that He will therefore 'save' him in Eternity. Because of the personal contact established between the Holy Spirit and the believer, no person can be considered responsible for the conversion of the believer, the missionary and/or the pastor being just the catalysts, individuals who brought the 'word' and showed the 'way'; but nothing more. The conversion is in fact justified by conscious or unconscious vocation (often announced by a dream), or a recovery judged to be a miracle – it is thought to be a response to a personal call which the believer cannot refuse.

Indeed, for the members of the group in Accadia, only 'speaking in tongues' determines belonging to the group; if baptism serves to establish a division between the believer and the rest of the village (or the world), 'speaking in tongues' contributes to a differentiation within the group itself between the real and the false believer. This can lead to the creation of barriers between the believers themselves. In this way a marriage between a believer who has the 'gift' of glossolalia and a person who does not have it is seen negatively: although not forbidden, it will often be postponed in the expectation that the 'gift' will be bestowed on the partner. Those believers who do not make visible and repeated efforts to receive the 'gift' are almost excluded, while those who, despite their diligence, do not receive it elicit pity and sympathy. Although in Accadia this internal division does not appear to conform to a fixed pattern, in the other groups it seems to create a hierarchy: only the pastors and their close associates possess this 'gift' which the mass of believers is without. Because of this fact the position of pastors is very strong and their decision-making powers are almost uncontested (Anzano, Gesualdo, Villanova, San Fele).

Glossolalia, involuntary emission of a verbal message without apparent meaning in the everyday language of the speaker, is interpreted as one of the *signs* of the presence of the Holy Spirit in the body and the soul of the believer. The mark of this presence is precisely the 'non-sense' of the message, non-sense which shows the believer to be 'other' – chosen, saved, sainted, body-tabernacle chosen before others to receive the Holy Spirit. Glossolalia therefore establishes a difference between the 'saved' faithful, equal amongst themselves, and those who are not.

This is how a believer in Accadia describes his first baptism in Spirit:

> For two days there were long religious discussions between the Pentecostal missionary woman, the sergeant and the cadet of the Salvation Army; I was there and by listening I understood what was right and I said to myself, 'Lord, why do you not baptise me too?' Without saying anything to the others, when the moment came to pray to the Lord, I felt a fire heat from the tip of my toes throughout my body, and in this heat I felt a great joy to be able to glorify God. For about twenty minutes I stayed in the same position. When the prayer was over I had already forgotten about their discussion, but I started to think about what had happened. I didn't ask the missionary anything else, I felt such happiness and joy in myself that I didn't even have the will to leave and go home – it was about two hours later that I left.

> The following day I returned; the weather prevented me from going, it was an evening of bad weather, one couldn't even leave the house and there was also some prevention by the family: 'You, where are you going?', but I had a strong desire to go and pray because I had found something that was not part of this world. So I arrived at the missionary's house, where there were five or six people. When we were praying, after five or six minutes, I was overtaken – I had my eyes closed, certainly – I saw something like a light, mysterious and white, and the strong heat of the previous evening, but seven times stronger. I was within a light that I can't describe and then I realized that my tongue was speaking a language that I didn't even know. My body stayed immobile, as if dead, for about three hours, all the time I wanted to pray and I prayed and prayed, but I didn't understand the words, I didn't understand what I was saying. After that manifestation I was sure of having found the full doctrine, of being on the right path. I thanked God for what had happened. The missionary, when I asked her, gave me the chapter numbers of the Scriptures which corresponded to what had happened because she had also not understood the language I had been speaking. It was only then that I understood that it was the Spirit of God who had also taken over my body.

Other charismatic phenomena are usually associated with glossolalic episodes; the most frequent are the gift of interpretation, which is a capacity to translate into normal language the flow of glossolalic words or phrases uttered by others. There is also the gift of prophecy, of healing by the laying on of hands and finally the performance of miracles.

Glossolalic practice of the Pentecostal group of Accadia

The phrases which the members of the Pentecostal group of Accadia speak 'in tongues' and the trance-like movements which accompany them take place mainly during the four weekly ceremonies which the group organizes. Held on Wednesdays, Fridays, Saturdays and Sundays, they last a minimum of two hours. During three of these ceremonies, called *ammaestramento* (Wednesday) and *culto* (Friday and Sunday), there are two occasions when the faithful can express themselves physically and verbally, for approximately twenty minutes each time: these are the times reserved for prayer to the Holy Spirit. The fourth ceremony, which takes place on Saturdays, is called *preghiera allo Spirito Santo*, because it is entirely devoted to the Holy Spirit. Although the glossolalic trance only takes place in the course of the intercessions dedicated to praying to the Holy Spirit, it is nonetheless possible for worshippers who wish to express themselves outside these times, or who fail to stop their gesticulating or speech in time for the end of prayer, to disturb or reverse the order of the ceremony.

The prayers to the Holy Sprit are said by the faithful kneeling on the floor, against wicker chairs, with their back turned away from the wooden pulpit which serves as a platform within the small place of worship. For the rest of the service the worshippers stay seated, rising to affirm their faith or to sing the first or last hymn. When kneeling, the worshippers concentrate, their elbows on the chairs and faces hidden in their hands. After several minutes each of them chants prayers independently and loudly, forming a powerful and dissonant choir, in which one can discern some common phrases:

> Holy! Oh Hallelujah! Glory be to your name, for you are great and powerful, in the name of Jesus do not abandon me, fulfil your work through me; oh Jesus, Lord, yours is the glory: Jesus Jesus holy holy holy; oh my God, my God, glory to God; hallelujah hallelujah hallelujah; in the name of Jesus do not wait, Father reveal yourself, do not wait, Lord, do not wait; oh holy holy Jesus, you are all love, peace and charity; glory glory glory glory.

The prayers, which are always spontaneous, take place in a choral environment which intensifies, assisting in the expression of emotion; when the worshippers attain a certain paroxysm, some of them begin to 'detach' themselves vocally from the group, talking 'in tongues' by using vocal inflexions which do not resemble their everyday pronunciation, going from high to low pitch, or raising their voice to the extent that the building trembles. They accompany their glossolalic speech with a total physical participation, which expresses itself by gestures and movements – flailing and tensing arms, cracking fingers, clapping hands, moving bodies – which they execute solely in that context. Although the missionary insists that those present favour and 'support' the worshipper in a glossolalic trance by curbing their own participation, no one actually remains silent once one person has started speaking 'in tongues'. On the contrary, that appears to stimulate them, since there are always several who then glossolalize or put themselves into a trance.

Having attended such glossolalic events several times, we have found in our material two episodes which seem to merit closer analysis. The first involves the missionary. The total duration of the glossolalic episode is approximately four minutes, and breaks into a prayer to Jesus delivered in Italian. Thus, while the worshippers implore and declaim, '*Gloria, halleluia, Santo Signore, Gesù mio, Gesù, Gesù*', the missionary demands:

> /Îaria assi vassia Îanana Îamama issia
> vorissia ianaši aria komessia komeviene
> adevanti ? ši ši o o klê klê klebeko
> Îaleluia/

interspersing this with some '*Gloria, Gloria*'.

The sequence of phenomena which she proclaims, which are without meaning in either Italian or English (the two languages which the missionary speaks fluently), are not far removed from the sounds of those two languages, and remain within the phonetic heritage of those languages. The second example of glossolalia was provided by the sister of the missionary. It is an episode which lasts five minutes, and which subsequently evolved into a sort of prayer spoken in a tone of very moving imploration:

/abaýato didirina amama areratoria
Îaleluia Jesu Kristo abbaýene ab'oria
Hermona oin Îamama/

This second chain without meaning in Italian is intriguing, more so than the first, because the aspirated 'h' which the sister uses, which is more characteristic of English, rather suggests an unconscious imitation of the glossolalic output of the first speaker. The missionary, who represents the righteous path, sainthood, the attainment of perfection, must have struck the imagination of her audience through the use of the aspirated 'h'. Normally, even outside the glossolalic moment, the members of *Il Tempio di Cristo* say '*Hallelujah*' with the 'h', contrary to common Italian language use and the local dialect, which lacks an aspirated 'h'.

For our premise it is useful to translate and analyse briefly the content of the spontaneous prayer spoken by the sister of the missionary during the long period of glossolalic trance we discussed above. Precisely because it is spontaneous and at an almost subconscious level, it can enlighten us on the symbolic subtext which feeds the imagination of this follower, and gives us an additional measure of the assimilation of the new doctrine:

> Blood of Jesus hallelujah / clothe us / reclothe us / clothe us / give me love / count [. . .] / long live the blood / of Jesus Chris / Jesus hallelujah / *Îêman didiš Îai* / Blood of Jesus / Cover us / Glory Jesus / Glory, glory, glory / glory, glory / Glory, glory, glory / Jesus, Jesus, Jesus / love, love, love / Lord you are love / God / *batta* / *amamon kømõ* / God, God, God / God, God, / the streets of God / are God / God / you love him / you love the Good / send him Lord / to you / that I love God / *silo silomos* / Jesus, our God / help us / [. . .] send [. . .] / send Lord the worker / that you know Lord / we need him / Lord / to be taught / by God and by glory / spare us [. . .] / from the evil spirit / Lord / you are the way / the rock / talk to me [. . .] / the rock Lord / you give us grace / day after day / you are / a great God / [. . .] / you give us / benedictions / you cover us / underneath your precious mantle / Lord / I thank the Lord / to be called again / in these days Lord, / God / to thank [. . .] / Lord / [. . .] God / blessed be his name eternally / Lord / [. . .] / Day after day / and

> you let us know Jesus / Lord / we have eternal life / Lord / you are the life among us / Heavenly Father / [. . .] / you give us strength / do not forget Jesus / to sanctify us, Lord / *ama'* / love of God / mother of God / how good she is / and how precious / [. . .] our Lord / Jesus Christ / [. . .] / Saint you are Lord Jesus / I thank you Lord / for giving us strength / to search / for your face / how joyful it is / day after day / Lord / you show us the way / Lord / you are amongst us / way / Jesus holy way / give us the freedom to pray / Lord / you are the way / eternal O Lord / you are unique / Jesus, hallelujah / Jesus holy holy / holy you are Lord / send us benedictions / on these [. . .] / [. . .] Lord / [. . .] / You are life Lord / and like the angels [. . .] / give us strength / in life / in our path / to set us in motion / with your permission / Lord / Hallelujah Jesus holy / holy holy holy / glory Jesus glory / glory glory glory / glory glory glory / hallelujah, hallelujah, hallelujah / hallelujah, hallelujah, hallelujah / Jesus Jesus Jesus Jesus / Holy! Glory!!

The terms employed by the worshippers in the *corpus* at our disposal to designate the addressee of the prayer are numerous and constantly repeated. Counting the number of times the same term is used, we notice that '*Signore*' is said twenty-five times, '*Gesù*' twenty-one times, '*Dio*' sixteen times, '*Gesù Cristo*' twice, '*Signore Gesù*' twice, '*Padre*' once and '*Iddio*' once. The speaker belongs to a unitary Pentecostal group which baptizes its followers solely in the name of Jesus. If one disregards the term 'Lord' (twenty-five times), which can equally designate the Father or the Son, we note that Jesus has been named twenty-five times in total, while God has been named eighteen times. That seems to indicate that the old Catholic religion maintains a hold which the followers find difficult to shake off in their own speech. This hold also receives confirmation at a different moment of the prayer, when the follower, addressing the mother of Jesus, declaims: 'Mother of God, how good and precious she is!' An amalgamation seems to take place in the spirit of the follower, without the division between the old belief and the new one asserting itself directly.

Anthropological interpretations of the glossolalic phenomenon

We are tempted to think *a priori* that glossolalia is a natural expression of humanity in certain mystical manifestations, a spontaneous act, at the outside perhaps an archetype of the behaviour of humankind facing the divine. But this is not the case. True, this phenomenon, which flourished particularly in the ancient world, is found again in certain regions (the Christian part of the ancient world, Africa, Siberia, Malaysia, Indonesia, China, Japan, Australia and the Philippines). However, on the other hand it is completely absent from other regions: the Muslim part of North Africa and Asia minor, in the new world mainly the plains, the northwest coast and the adjacent part of the Arctic (May 1956: 89–92).

This interesting fact, which places the glossolalic phenomenon only in certain geographic areas, would demand some assessment of the specific characteristics of societies where the phenomenon takes place. Carlyle May limits himself to saying that glossolalia and other associated phenomena develop in societies open to receiving them, because 'there seems to be considerable truth in the assertion that people do not speak in tongues unless they have heard about speaking-in-tongues, and this should be added that on the whole they become glossolalists only if their customs permit them to' (May 1956: 90).

So the phenomenon is not readily described in terms of cultural imprint and the capacity of societies to absorb that imprint. If these assertions are justified to explain the appearance of this phenomenon in certain societies, they do not explain sufficiently the phenomenon itself. Indeed, these explanations can easily be applied to our area of research. Effectively, Apulia has been and still is the land of the *tarantate* (De Martino 2005). The *tarantate*, mainly women, are usually bitten by a tarantula, which injects its venom; they mark this possession by dancing at fixed intervals – almost year on year until the possession has been expelled – for several days and nights, accompanied by a small local ensemble which plays the *tarantella*, the preferred tune of the tarantula.[3] Apulia – like the whole Mediterranean – is an area where the *lamento funebre* was strongly ingrained. It is a rite of collective or individual lamentation, a technique (De Martino 1958) practised largely by women on the death or at the funeral of a close or distant relative, or that of a *paesano.* Always in Apulia, and in the rest of the Mediterranean, one finds ritual practices linked to the evil eye. These practices have different aims, as they serve either to set out the fact of the *malocchio* or to diagnose it or to banish it. Depending on the stated aim, they are different both in their incantation and in the accompanying gestures. These gestures and phrases are familiar to all women both in meaning and practice. It is on this cultural *humus* that Pentecostalism flourishes when it arrives in Apulia, for it is clearly fertile ground. And it is on this rich past that the Pentecostalists draw when they express themselves: gestures, words, phrases, rhythms which are ingrained in their culture, and which they adapt to the new situation and graft onto the new acquisitions brought by the missionary.

Anthropological scholarship provides other interpretations of the glossolalic phenomenon. I. M. Lewis, for example, underlines the context in which this phenomenon evolves: 'New faiths may announce their advent with a flourish of ecstatic revelations, but once they become securely established they have little time or tolerance for enthusiasm' (Lewis 1971: 34). He continues: 'Where, however, such cults do not attain a comparable degree of acceptance, or are passively opposed or even actively persecuted, as long as they retain the support of oppressed sections of the community, possessional inspiration is likely to continue with unabated vigour' (Lewis 1971: 132). So these are short-lived phenomena, which are not institutionalised, part of the moment as well as the place, attaining longevity only if resisted.

Others see these as phenomena of reaction to adversity and oppression. The 'speaking in tongues' is a way of expressing oneself without being understood in a society outside the group or sect. Women, oppressed people, the poor of the third world are viewed as the proponents of the spread of these sects and cults in underdeveloped regions (Lanternari 1960; Muhlmann 1968; Pereira de Queiroz 1968). On the other hand, this phenomenon can be viewed as a means of integration into the fold of a structured group where the equality between members is theoretically a given. We also see that in the United States, Canada, Latin America, etc. the Pentecostal sects attract recent immigrants mainly because of the removal of all language barriers (Wilson 1970).

To summarize, glossolalia is not a general phenomenon, because it only exists in certain specific regions; it develops in societies where local customs allow it to, and by borrowing from other societies; it is the expression of enthusiasm of followers faced with new beliefs; as soon as these beliefs have become institutionalized, these expressions are banished and only continue at times of persecution; this phenomenon is closely linked to cults and sects which develop among oppressed populations, who express in this way their rejection of the world and their oppression; and, finally, it can be a method of integration into host societies.

These explanations, all interesting and in some cases very pertinent, are centred mainly on the social function of the phenomenon. None of them provides any theories on the reasons why certain societies manage this type of physical and vocal conduct, which takes place at specific moments, or why this rationalization of behaviour which appears spontaneous uses an unidentifiable language. These issues are for historians, who bring to them the objective judgement we currently lack (de Certeau 1980), and for psychologists and linguists, who can interpret the 'void' of meaning in an appropriate manner (Samarin 1972; Godin 1975).

The glossolalic phenomenon in rural southern Italy amongst the members of Oneness and Trinitarian Pentecostal groups we visited appears to have a function of distinction as well as of levelling. In the group of Accadia, followers must conform to the behaviour of the missionary and, as a result, almost all succeed in 'speaking in tongues'. Conversely, in other groups the believers do not acquire the 'gift' of glossolalia precisely because the missionaries and pastors discourage it in order that they retain the exclusivity of the 'gift'. Thus the phenomenon of glossolalia seems to serve the interests of the leader of the group, since she or he 'uses' it to stimulate equality among his members or to attain a dominant position in the group.

Our data is not statistically significant, and one cannot deduce from it that this opposition arises from the fact that a group, in terms of glossolalic expression, is united because it is directed by a woman, even if other divergences seem to flow from this gender difference in the orientation of the group. Even so, it seems to us that the interiorization of the 'subordinate' status of the woman, which is common in the Italian *meridione*, prevents the missionary of Accadia from imagining herself 'superior' to the men in her group, and therefore prompts her to instigate 'parity' within the group. In the other cases, the male missionaries and pastors of other Pentecostal groups insert themselves between the followers and God, as they have always seen done by Catholic priests, to preserve the 'superiority' inherent in their masculine state. The practice of glossolalia in southern Italy is therefore snapped up by the prevalent ideology, as Italians in rural areas use it to manage the problems of domination and hierarchy with which they concern themselves. It serves to make viable a strategy which could have taken a more tortuous and therefore risky path to get the same result.

Notes

* Original French: 'Langues et possession: le cas des pentecôtistes en Italie méridionale', in *Annales ESC (Oral/écrit)*, 1988, 43(4): 897–907.

1 It seems useful to start with the definition of 'glossolalia' in the *Enciclopaedia Universalis* (1975: 790), somewhat modified to come closer to our understanding of the term.

2 The Pentecostal religion presented here is illustrated primarily on the basis of material gathered in Accadia (Foggia), a village in Apulia – the center of Oneness Pentecostalism – in which, as far as we could determine, the number of converts did not exceed 70–100 people. The study was conducted in 1973, 1974 and 1975, for a total of ten months. It bore mainly on the members of this group, split almost equally between men and women. The earliest converts were mostly peasants, whereas artisans and merchants were to be found among the second and third generations.

3 The phenomenon of possession known under the name of *tarantisme* affects mainly single women. Bitten by a tarantula in summer, they exorcise the venom through a choreographic cycle by 'dressing up' in a colour reflecting the species of the possessing tarantula and doing a ritual dance over several days. They are accompanied by a small group of musicians who play only the themes – generally tarantellas – which the *tarantate* recognize as being those preferred by their own tarantula, until the possession is ended. On 29 June, the day of the feast of Saint Peter and Saint Paul, the *tarantate* go to the chapel of Saint Paul, in Galatina (Apulia), to thank the saint, protector against venomous bites, for grace received or, if possession is ongoing, to plead for relief. The following year, at the same time, the *tarantate* 'relive' their first bite by repeating the cycle of possession and exorcism, as thanks to the saint. (See Di Bella 2007.)

References

Cassin, Elena (1956) 'Quelques facteurs historiques et sociaux de la diffusion du protestantisme en Italie méridionale', *Archives de Sociologie des Religions* 2: 55–72.

Castiglione, Myriam (1972) 'Aspetti della diffusione del movimento pentecostale in Puglia', *Uomo e cultura* 9: 102–18.

de Certeau, Michel (1980) 'Utopies vocales: glossolalies', *Traverses* 20: 26–37.
De Martino, Ernesto (1958 [1975]) *Morte e pianto rituale dal lamento funebre antico al pianto di Maria*, Turin: Boringhieri.
—— (2005) *The Land of Remorse: A Study of Southern Italian Tarantism*, London: Free Association Books (originally Published as *La terra del rimorso: Contributo a una storia religiosa del Sud*, Milan: Il Saggiatore, 1961).
Di Bella, Maria Pia (1982) 'Un culte pentecôtiste en Apulie', *Les Temps modernes* 435: 824–33.
—— (1987) 'Maladie et guérison dans les groupes pentecôtistes de l'Italie méridionale', *Social Compass* (*Religion, santé et guérison*) XXXIV 4: 465–74.
—— (2007) 'Literature of Anthropology', in G. Marrone (gen ed.) *Encyclopedia of Italian Literary Studies*, New York: Routledge, vol. I, pp. 52–5.
Enciclopaedia Universalis (1975) 'Glossolalie', *Enciclopaedia Universalis France*, Paris, vol. 19, pp. 790–1.
Godin, André (1975) 'Moi perdu ou moi retrouvé dans l'expérience charismatique: perplexité des psychologues', *Archives de sciences sociales des religions* 40: 31–52.
Lanternari, Vittorio (1960) *Movimenti religiosi di libertà e di salvezza dei popoli oppressi*, Milan: Feltrinelli.
—— (1969) 'Religione popolare e contestazione: Riflessioni storico-sociali sul dissenso religioso', *Testimonianze* 118: 708–29.
Lewis, I. M. (1971) *Ecstatic Religion. An Anthropological Study of Spirit Possession and Shamanism*, Harmondsworth: Penguin.
May, Carlyle L. (1956) 'A Survey of Glossolalia and Related Phenomena in Non-Christian Religions', *American Anthropologist* 1: 75–96.
Miegge, Giovanni (1959) 'La Diffusion du protestantisme dans les zones sous-développées de l'Italie méridionale', *Archives de sociologie des religions* 8: 81–96.
Muhlmann, W. E. (1968) *Messianismes révolutionnaires du tiers monde*, Paris: Galllimard.
Pereira de Queiroz, M. I. (1968) *Réforme et révolution dans les sociétés traditionnelles: Histoire et ethnologie des mouvements messianiques*, Paris: Editions Anthropos.
Samarin, William J. (1972) *Tongues of Men and Angels: The Religious Language of Pentecostalism*, New York: Macmillan.
Wilson, Bryan R. (1970) *Les Sectes religieuses*, Paris: Hachette.

Part 13

NEGOTIATING RELIGIOUS AND POLITICAL COMPETITION

49

THE LORD OF HEAVEN VERSUS JESUS CHRIST

Christian sectarian violence in late-nineteenth-century South China

Joseph Tse-Hei Lee

Source: *positions*, 8(1) (2000), 77–99.

This article draws on a case study of communal conflicts between the Baptist and Catholic segments of the Li lineage in a southern Chinese village known as Kuxi (stream of hardship), in the late nineteenth century. The conflict originated from a complaint made by the French Catholic missionaries to their American Baptist counterparts in the treaty port of Shantou. Charges were lodged against the Baptist villagers in Kuxi who had attacked the local Catholic church and kidnapped Chen Aming, a Catholic catechist, on the evening of 6 March 1896. Despite the difference in time and geographical setting, the incident draws our attention to the impact of Christian sectarianism on a Chinese village and the escalation of intralineage conflicts into interreligious violence.

The following study reveals that the American Baptist and French Catholic missions had consistently competed with one another through collaboration with the rival lineage segments in Kuxi. Seeing the temporal advantages of associating themselves with either Christian mission the rival lineage segments made use of the political resources of missionaries in the intralineage conflicts. Lying between the missionaries and local Christians were the Baptist evangelists and Catholic catechists, who were not simply the propagators of the Baptist Christianity and Catholicism. They, in fact, operated as active political agents in merging intralineage disputes with Christian sectarian rivalries and reproducing the conditions and resources conducive to the outbreak of violence. Here, the central question is why the junior segment of the Li lineage identified itself with the American Baptist mission, whereas the senior segment of the same lineage joined the Catholic church.[1] These diverse patterns of religious identification, of the ongoing conflicts between the rival lineage segments, and of the changing power relations will be the foci of discussion. The significance of this development lies in the fact that it enables us to reflect on the operation of external and internal mediating forces in the colonizing project in a remote corner of late imperial China. This case study highlights the transformation of two rival lineage segments into two antagonistic Christian groups at the village level. In so doing, it helps us better understand how the external and internal forces had drawn these Christian villagers into a web of power relations that bound them closely to the American Baptist and French Catholic missions.

This article begins with a brief discussion of the tension and conflict associated with the Baptist and Catholic expansion in Kuxi. This is followed by a study of the historical setting of the village in the late nineteenth century. The core of this article is a detailed analysis of the making of two antagonistic Christian communities and the outbreak of sectarian violence. The analysis is based on the accounts of William Ashmore, the American Baptist missionary in Shantou in 1896.

Tension and conflict as integrated parts of Baptist and Catholic expansion in Kuxi

The conventional understanding of Christian missions as a single, coherent, and unifying institutional body seems no longer valid. This case study brings into sharp focus the specific historical moments of severe tension and conflict that characterized the Baptist and Catholic movements in Kuxi. This adds support to the view that, throughout the process of the missionary expansion, the impulse for competition and confrontation always coexisted with the concerns for unity and stability. It is therefore important to investigate under what circumstances the Baptist and Catholic missions preferred competition and rivalry to compromise and cooperation.

In the Chaoyang district, where Kuxi was situated, the American Baptist Missionary Society and the Paris Foreign Missions had begun to evangelize village communities during the second half of the nineteenth century. Owing to doctrinal differences, the Baptist and Catholic missions tended to ridicule and compete with one another in the field as elsewhere.[2] They even used separate Chinese terms to refer to Christianity, namely, *jidujiao* or *yesujiao* (religion of Christ) versus *tianzhujiao* (religion of the lord of heaven). This practice further confused Chinese villagers' understanding of Chrisitianity, creating an impression that Catholicism and Protestantism were two rather different religions and that missionaries from both sides were more than likely rivals, if not antagonists.[3]

As the Baptist and Catholic denominations began to take shape in local society, they merged with existing communal divisions and rivalries. This development can be clearly discerned from the many Catholic and Protestant missionary writings complaining about Chinese village converts shifting from one denomination to another and seeking missionary support in disputes. For example, both the Haifeng and Lufeng districts of eastern Guangdong were notorious for communal feuds among converts belonging to the Roman Catholic, American Baptist, and German Basel missions throughout the 1890s and 1900s.[4] As a result of Christian sectarian rivalries, interreligious clashes broke out more frequently in areas with a long tradition of intervillage or interlineage conflicts than under any other circumstances.

In other words, the Catholic and Protestant missions not only became entangled in longstanding conflicts in Chinese society, but they also created two rival Christian denominations and provided a new outlet for communal confrontations. It is against this background that the Kuxi case will be examined in detail.

The world of Kuxi in the late nineteenth century

To begin with, a brief sketch of the historical setting of Kuxi will help us to situate this study in the context of the late nineteenth century. The village, known as Kho-Knoi in the Chaozhou dialect and Kuxi in Mandarin, is located nine miles southwest of the city of Chaoyang and eighteen miles in the same direction from the treaty port of Shantou. It lies in the Lian River Valley, through which the Lian River flows from the eastern part of the Puning district into the Chaoyang district, where it passes through Haimen Bay and enters the South China Sea.[5] Due to its well-developed inland river systems and long coastal line, the Lian River Basin is deeply integrated into what G. William Skinner has called the "Southeast Coast" macroregion of Fujian, and closely linked to the Lingnan macroregion of Guangdong.[6] It was through its inland river networks that the American Baptist and French Catholic missions were able to penetrate into Kuxi during the second half of the nineteenth century.

The area surrounding Kuxi was then a rich, grain-growing region known as the agricultural heartland of the district.[7] The amount of grain production in the Chaozhou prefecture as a whole was estimated to have increased from 838 *catties/mu* in 1754 to 1062 *catties/mu* in 1761 and then to have dropped slightly to 1,038 *catties/mu* in 1873.[8] The production of such considerable amounts of grain had much to do with a rapid increase of population. In Chaoyang, for example, the population increased from 110,000 in 1757 to 250,000 in 1815, an annual average rate of population growth of 13.5 percent.[9] If grain production can be seen as an indicator of the balance between supply and demand for foodstuffs, the fast-growing population was surely the major reason for the increase of demand for grain production.

After harvest, rice and cash crops could be taken from Kuxi to Wuya (market of crows) and Xiashan (trading port of Xia Mountain), two nearby market towns. Apart from being commercial centers for inhabitants in

Kuxi, these market towns were also the seats of subdistrict officials in the area. Both police officers and assistant magistrates were stationed there.[10] These subdistrict officials were local lineage headmen and merchants, not civil degree holders. In contrast to the Chaoyang district magistrate, these lineage headmen and merchants had few political and military resources with which to deal with social disorder and communal violence. This explains why they were severely criticized by the American Baptist and French Catholic missionaries for being so ineffective in restoring law and order during the violence between Baptist and Catholic villagers in Kuxi in 1896.

Kuxi is a multisurname, walled village (*zhai*).[11] Physically, it is composed of *zhainei* (inner area) and *zhaiwai* (outer area). When the American Baptist and French Catholic missions arrived there, they did not enter an empty political landscape. Kuxi was already a world of inherent tension and conflict. Political power was distributed among four surnames, namely, Guo, Li, Yao, and Zheng.[12] According to the Chaoyang district magistrate writing in March 1896, "On the first day of the second moon [14 March 1896] . . . in the village of Kho-Knoi [Kuxi], persons of *four different clans* banded together not to obey the magistrate, and not to fear the Western people [i.e., the American Baptist Missionaries]."[13] Prior to the outbreak of violence between Baptist and Catholic communities in 1896, Kuxi was estimated by the Baptist missionaries to have "a population of about fifteen hundred [inhabitants]."[14] These inhabitants, most of whom were members of the Li and Yao lineage segments, made Kuxi a densely populated settlement.

Internal divisions among the four surnames were expressed along territorial, kinship, and religious lines. The inner area was largely occupied by temple worshipers, namely the Yao and Li lineages, whose ancestral halls were located in the northeastern and southwestern parts of the inner area, respectively. The areas surrounding the Li and Yao halls were densely inhabited by their own lineage members. When the junior and senior segments of the Li lineage converted to the Baptist faith and Catholicism in the late nineteenth century, only small numbers of the Li lineage remained as temple worshipers. From that time, the northeastern corner of the inner area was occupied by the Baptist lineage members, whereas the southeastern corner was settled by the Catholic ones. Having acquired much wealth in local trade, some Baptist and Catholic households began to move out of the walled village to settle in the outer area. The Baptist villagers expanded from the inner area of the walled village to the riverside to the north, whereas their Catholic neighbors occupied the eastern and southern parts of the outer area. Within these new settlements the power bases of the Baptist and Catholic communities were established in the north and south, respectively. The Zheng and Guo surnames, who made up fewer than fifty households altogether outside the western gate of the village, were temple worshipers like the Yao lineage and several Li households still inside the walled village.

The fact that Baptist and Catholic churches were erected outside the walled village suggests that none of the Christian missions was able to win the consent of the dominant Yao lineage to acquire land in the inner area for church construction. The location of the churches would also seem to indicate a strong sense of discontent on the part of temple worshipers with the Christian presence inside the walled village. The coexistence of various religious communities highlights the close linkage between territorial division and religious affiliation. Even today, the temple worshipers mainly have Yao, Guo, and Zheng surnames or come from the few Li households inside the walled village. Baptist members still live along the riverside in the north, while their Catholic counterparts continue to reside in the southeastern corner of the walled village and outside the eastern and southern entrances. This joint religious and kinship identity serves to prove the point that the Baptist and Catholic communities were originally created on the basis of the preexisting territorial and intralineage divisions. Also through these internal divisions both Christian communities were gradually transformed from having strong affiliations with the Christian missions to being deeply integrated into the separate segments of the Li lineage.

The making of two antagonistic Christian communities in Kuxi

Before the opening of the mission station in 1880, the Christian villagers always attended the Sunday service at the Baptist chapel in Dabu, a larger village settlement four miles away.[15] After the first believer from Kuxi, a man named Li Yan, was baptized in 1879, he and his family withdrew from Dabu and established their own village church. Once it was erected in 1880, the Kuxi Baptist church attracted many members of the junior segment of the Li lineage and developed into "a flourishing mission station."[16] Nowhere can the Baptist penetration of Kuxi be better illustrated than in the massive conversions of the junior segment. Membership in the church increased considerably in the first few years following the founding of the church, from one member in 1879 to five in 1880 and then to ten in 1881 and 1882.[17] Of these twenty-six people, sixteen were male members of the junior segment of the Li lineage and ten were female outsiders who had married into that segment. All of these church members were related to one another in kinship terms. They came from one large family consisting of Li Yan, his four brothers, and his elderly uncle, Li Xiaolao, with his own five married sons and sons-in-law.[18] That the initial stage of conversion to Baptist Christianity was successfully handled by Li Yan's family highlights the importance of kinship networks as effective channels of religious propogation. While the Baptist missionaries and Chinese evangelists from outside were often treated by village insiders with suspicion and hostility, evidently it was easier for Christian villagers to evangelize their relatives and friends.

One initial consequence of this increased Baptist presence was the rise of hostility toward the Baptist community. Though no instance of violence against the Baptist villagers was reported before 1896, potential conflict with the non-Christian party was a daily concern faced by Li Yan and Li Xiaolao, the lay leaders of the Baptist community. For example, while undertaking the project of church construction, the Baptist leaders were reported to be obliged to act a "little cautiously, owing to the animosity of their heathen [fellow] villagers."[19] That the project had been postponed several times during the 1880s and that not until 1894 had the new chapel been built on a plot of land donated by Li Xiaolao, outside the northern gate of the walled village, serve to underline this point.

According to William Ashmore, the Baptist villagers had always been on good terms with their Catholic neighbors, and through the help of the Baptist community a Catholic merchant, Li Zhiye, was able to secure sufficient funds to acquire a building outside the northern gate of the village and convert it into a Roman Catholic chapel.[20] Ashmore's account also suggests that the harmonious relation between the Baptist and Catholic villagers began to deteriorate only after the arrival of Chen Aming, the Catholic catechist, in February 1896. If that was the case, Chen was to blame for much if not all of the trouble that afflicted the Baptist community. Nevertheless, Ashmore's account has to be tested against the available archival sources and local historical materials.

In fact, evidence from local sources suggests that the Catholic penetration of Kuxi should be understood against the backdrop of a series of communal conflicts between the senior and junior segments of the Li lineage.[21] The question of why the junior segment identified with the Baptist mission and the senior group joined the Catholic church draws our attention to two important issues. One issue involves the presence of the rival missionary enterprises and their abilities to interfere, on behalf of their own converts, in communal politics. Another issue concerns the material considerations of Christian villagers, who saw the temporal advantages in the Christian presence, and what concessions and requests they made to the missionary enterprises. The relationship of these two issues plays itself out in a series of intralineage conflicts that shaped the course of the Baptist and Catholic movements in Kuxi.

The first incident was a ritual dispute in which the rival Li lineage segments argued with each other over which founding ancestor, *laogong* (the spirit of old dad) or *laomu* (the spirit of old mum), should be worshiped in the ancestral hall. While the senior segment preferred *laogong*, the junior worshiped *laomu*. Seeing no hope of reaching any agreement, the junior group, which had recently joined the Baptist church decided that its members would no longer participate in the annual ancestral worship. Interpreting this protest as a challenge to its leadership, the senior segment deprived the Baptist villagers of their right to share the use of ancestral resources.

Closely related to this ritual dispute was property conflict over the use of firewood in "the hilly ground." The senior and junior segments had at one time shared access to a hill considered to be ancestral property. It was arranged that for alternate three-year periods each group had the right to collect firewood there. Disregarding this agreement, however, some members of the senior segment went to collect the firewood while this ancestral property was still under the junior segment's management. With the support of the Baptist missionaries, the junior group protested, but the offending branch made no apology or concession.

A third instance, although unrelated to these intralineage rivalries, nonetheless directly influenced the senior segment's decision to convert to Catholicism. In 1886 the Zheng households intended to erect their own lineage hall inside the walled village. Such a project, however, was widely seen as disrupting the geomantic harmony between the Li lineage hall and its surrounding environment. The senior Li segment therefore mobilized all its subsegments to obstruct the project. As they were small in number, the Zheng households appealed to other Zheng settlements in nearby areas for help. Eventually the Zheng took their case to the *yamen* (office of the district magistrate). Meanwhile, the senior branch of the Li asked the Baptist villagers to share the cost of litigation against the Zheng, their common enemy; the Baptists, however, refused to do so. By chance the *yamen* runners came to Kuxi to investigate the dispute on a Sunday. When they reached the Baptist church, the runners went inside to see what was going on. When the American Baptist missionary criticized the runners for disrupting the Sunday service, the investigators immediately apologized to him. Seeing the practical effects of the support and protection of the missionary, the senior group recognized the temporal advantages of the Christian presence and soon began to approach the Catholic missionaries.

Around this time Li Zhiye, a member of the senior group, converted to Catholicism in Baileng (Pok-ling) village, at the border of the Huilai and Lufeng districts.[22] His conversion was a typical example of Christian propagation through family and lineage networks. Zhiye often traveled to his mother's native village of Baileng to trade in Chinese herbal medicine. There he came into contact with Catholicism through his mother's relatives. After his conversion Li Zhiye asked the French Catholic priest to establish a mission station in Kuxi. With the help of Li Ao, a powerful member of the senior segment, the Catholic chapel was erected on a plot of land in southern Kuxi in 1891.[23]

The Baptist and Catholic penetration of Kuxi highlights the close connection between the intralineage disputes and the massive Christian conversions. Because the junior segment had already strengthened itself by associating with the American Baptist missionaries, the senior branch had little choice but to join the French Catholic church to counter the American influence. Central to this phenomenon is the fact that throughout the course of their intralineage disputes, the junior and senior segments of the Li lineage began to identify certain issues of antagonism between them. As they continued to quarrel over these issues, they emerged as two mutually hostile religious communities. The core leadership of the Baptist community was composed of Li Yan, Li Xiaolao, and Li Duan from the junior segment, while the leadership on the Catholic side included Li Zhiye and Li Ao. This sharp division of leadership heightened the intralineage disputes and marked the beginning of the crystallization of two antagonistic Christian communities in Kuxi.

From intralineage dispute to Christian sectarian violence

Against this background of intralineage conflicts we may examine the escalation of anti-Baptist sentiment into interreligious violence in Kuxi. This phenomenon raises several important questions. First, if relations between the Baptist and Catholic villagers had previously always been harmonious, as suggested in Ashmore's account, why would some Catholic villagers suddenly turn so hostile and even violent toward their Baptist neighbors? Second, why did some Catholic villagers become involved in the anti-Baptist violence under the leadership of Chen Aming, then the newly appointed Catholic catechist? And what kind of institutional conditions made it possible for Chen Aming to mobilize a group of Catholic militants against the Baptist community? Let us start with the second and third questions by looking at how Chen Aming was appointed to assist the Catholic community in Kuxi and by what means he was able to recruit large numbers of Catholic converts shortly after his arrival.

According to testimony given by the *dibao* (police constable) from Oukeng (Au-Khe), Chen Aming was a native of that village, a Chen lineage settlement about one *li* (one-third of a mile) from Kuxi. Chen Aming was a member of the powerful third segment of the Chen lineage and had his own group of followers. He had once been involved in a property dispute, which escalated into a fight, with another branch of the Chen lineage. As a result a reward was posted by the *dibao* for his arrest in 1895. He then fled to Baileng, a village in the Huilai district. There he met Li Zhiye and his mother, natives of Kuxi, both of whom were Catholics. Through Li Zhiye, Chen Aming was introduced to the Catholic mission in Huilai. After his conversion Chen accompanied a Chinese priest from the St. Joseph's mission in Shantou on a visit to Kuxi and its neighboring villages. While in Kuxi they stayed on the premises recently bought by Li Zhiye and Li Ao. In the meantime Chen Aming had been entrusted with the task of looking after local Catholic interests.[24] Indeed, Chen Aming's had been a rather quick conversion to Catholicism and an even quicker promotion to catechist. Although no information is given as to why Chen went to Kuxi instead of Oukeng, his home village, the decision to stay at Kuxi most likely had to do with his new assignment to take care of the Catholic community there. Without the opportunity offered by the St. Joseph's mission in Shantou, a socially marginal outsider such as Chen would have found it extremely difficult, if not impossible, to establish a foothold in Kuxi. But with such an appointment, Chen would have been able to take advantage of the institutional resources of the local Catholic church in Kuxi and the support of the Catholic mission in Shantou to establish his new power base, rather than returning to Oukeng to begin from scratch.

Relying on the support of the Catholic church, Chen Aming frequently traveled from place to place to recruit new converts, declaring that "by entering the Church and paying one dollar, people need not pay their debts, nor rents, nor taxes, and need not fear the magistrates."[25] The strategy of offering financial and legal protection in return for religious conversion was extremely effective in winning large numbers of followers, from Kuxi and from nearby villages and market towns. Like Chen Aming, many of the new converts came from marginal sectors of the local society; they included destitute male villagers, lawbreakers, and gamblers. In Kuxi there was even a strong militance within the Catholic community. In correspondence with the U.S. diplomats in Shantou, Ashmore made the following remarks:

> Certain persons, among them . . . Li A O [Li Ao], Li Sam Hi, [and] Li Chin Hong [Li Jinfeng], . . . will all now be found within a week's time figuring on some high-handed operations under A Meng's [Chen Aming's] direction. . . . Terrorism and lawlessness and extortion and violence and kidnapping and midnight assault and open-day attack with murderous weapons and murderous intent, were all within the same short week of seven consecutive days to be exercised by these men, toward a helpless and unoffending agriculturalist, toward a village magistrate [the *dibao* in Wuya market] who had displeased him, toward an American Baptist chapel which they charged with being heretical, and toward the worshippers in that chapel because they dared to defend themselves against unprovoked assault.[26]

Ashmore's remarks give the impression that Chen and his followers had long been plotting against the local Chinese authorities in the area. These remarks in fact have much in common with official Chinese descriptions of the typical behavior of social rebels. Since Ashmore based his judgment purely on information given by the Baptist villagers, who had an inherent anti-Catholic bias, he predictably emphasized Chen's criminal practices of gathering people to form a militant group, collecting membership subscription fees, defying local authorities, breaking laws, and disturbing the peace. It is very likely that, given their primary concern with the threat posed by the ever growing Catholic community, the Baptist villagers were eager to win support and sympathy from both the American missionaries and Chinese local officials by portraying Chen Aming and his followers as subversives poised to overthrow the local government.

In spite of anti-Catholic bias, the above remarks have several implications for our understanding of the dispute. First is the fact of predominant support that Chen received from the senior segment of the Li lineage. Though Ashmore did not investigate how Li Ao, Li Sam Hi, and Li Jinfeng were related to each other in kinship terms, it is certain that these Catholic converts came from the senior Li lineage segment. Only by relying heavily on this lineage subgroup was Chen able to recruit large numbers of followers and to assemble fighters against the Baptist church and its settlement quarters.

The second implication involves the way in which a marginal outsider such as Chen could establish a stronghold in Kuxi. It is important to take a closer look at how he took advantage of his new opportunities to win support under rapidly changing circumstances. Specifically, three opportunities can be discerned in the Baptist missionaries' account. The first opportunity for Chen Aming to demonstrate his power and influence came when an inhabitant from Wuya market volunteered to join the Catholic church. That individual, who owed another person 17,200 Chinese cash (57 pounds Sterling or 229 Spanish dollars), was compelled by the *dibao* in Wuya market to pay the debt. After paying the money, the man urged Chen Aming and his followers to take revenge on the *dibao* on his behalf. As a result, the *dibao*'s son was kidnapped and taken to the lower part of Kuxi, which was the Catholic stronghold. In return for his son's release, the *dibao* had to set off 2,000 firecrackers in public acknowledgment of his fault in the handling of the case.[27]

Chen's second opportunity came when a complaint was made by Li Jinfeng and Li Ao, both Catholics, against Li Yan (Li A Tarn), the first Baptist convert, whose buffalo had entered their sugarcane fields and damaged the crop. Threatened by Chen Aming's followers, Li Yan eventually paid for the damages and arranged a puppet show for the Catholic villagers in apology.[28]

In his third opportunity, Chen Aming sent an ultimatum to the Baptist villagers before staging an attack on the Baptist church. In the early evening of Friday, 6 March 1896, between ten and twenty Baptist villagers had assembled at the church for the regular evening prayer meeting. While the pastor was preaching, Chen suddenly broke into the church with two other Catholic villagers, Li Jinfeng and Li Ao. Chen reportedly issued the verbal insult "Where there is Lord of Heaven teaching, there can be no Jesus teaching."[29] The three Catholics then left, and the Baptist villagers carried on their meeting.

Instead of waiting for the Catholics to attack, the Baptist villagers organized a dozen men armed with spears, bamboo poles, swords, and two pistols for a midnight assault on the Catholic church. At the entrance of the Catholic church, a fight broke out in which the two sides exchanged gunshots; one Baptist and one Catholic were severely wounded. During the fight Chen Aming himself was knocked down by a blow from a bamboo pole and captured by the Baptists. Seeing their leader taken hostage, the Catholic militants withdrew to the Li ancestral hall. The next morning, as the *yamen* runners were arriving at Kuxi, the Baptist villagers handed Chen Aming over to the magistrate for the Chaoyang district. Rather than telling the American Baptist missionaries that they had in fact attacked the Catholic church and captured Chen Aming there, the Baptist villagers claimed Chen had initiated the skirmish at the Baptist church, where they maintained they had apprehended him. Thus, the Baptist villagers were able to secure the support of the American Baptist missionaries and to persuade them to put pressure on the magistrate to punish Chen Aming and the dominant segment for the incident and the injuries.

To press for the release of Chen Aming, the Catholic militants turned their anger toward the Baptist villagers and created a fighting tower at the northwestern part of the inner area, from which they threatened to attack the Baptist households. Not until the arrival of a Chinese Catholic priest from Shantou a few days later did these militants agree to withdraw and await the outcome of the case and the Chaoyang magistrate's judgment.[30]

These three incidents reveal a number of interesting aspects of the dynamics of communal politics in Kuxi. First, that both Christian communities had obtained firearms bears witness to the intensity of competitive violence in the area. In such an environment, the Christian institutions consistently served as protective organizations. For instance, prior to the outbreak of violence, the Baptist chapel had already acquired some firearms for defensive purposes. It was, as we have seen, in fear of a potential attack by the Catholic militants that some Baptist villagers had taken the initiative to attack the Catholic church and capture its Chinese lay leader.

Furthermore, these events shed light on the role that an evangelistic agent such as Chen Aming played in escalating intralineage disputes into interreligious violence. In such a deeply divided multilineage community, the only means of recruiting followers was to take advantage of the preexisting lineage divisions. As far as Chen Aming was concerned, his ability to call for foreign support and to exempt local converts from Chinese imperial jurisdiction was essential for securing large numbers of followers in the area. To the potential Catholic converts in Kuxi and nearby communities, Chen Aming had to present himself as a strong leader and the Catholic church as an effective protective organization. To the Catholic villagers in Kuxi, he had to present himself as a defender of correct religious teaching. This dual identity was clearly expressed in a sequence of actions undertaken by Chen Aming and his militants to intimidate the Baptist villagers. Nevertheless, the strategy of promising security in exchange for religious conversion was bound to create difficulties in the long run. Before Chen's arrival, intralineage disputes were simply a problem of local law and order. After Chen's arrival, however, the Catholic misson was able to establish a powerful presence in Kuxi and to become an integral part of the senior segment of the Li lineage. This development added an external dimension to the ongoing conflicts and, significantly, paved the way for foreign interference.

The third aspect of communal politics that the incident reveals is the extent of the involvement of the rival Li lineage segments in the outbreak of violence. That Chen Aming came into contact with Catholicism through the senior branch confirms the importance of the sublineage network as a channel of religious conversion and communal mobilization. Despite Chen's arrest, the Catholic militants reorganized themselves inside the Li ancestral hall and continued to threaten the Baptist villagers. The implication is very clear that those anti-Baptist members of the senior segment, especially Li Ao and Li Jinfeng, hijacked the Catholic movement in order to strengthen their own position in local power conflicts. In so doing, they could express their anti-Baptist sentiments under the cover of the Catholic church and take advantage of the French missionary protection at the higher level of local politics.

The intervention of external forces: American Baptist and French Catholic missionaries

During the months following the arrest of Chen Aming, the Chaoyang district magistrate was faced with considerable pressure from both the American Baptist and French Catholic missionaries. Whereas the French Catholic missionaries in Shantou urged the release of Chen Aming through the French minister in Beijing, the American Baptist missionaries sought to have him severely punished by the Chinese authorities and accordingly appealed to the U.S. minister in Beijing for support, in an attempt to counter the French diplomatic influence. Rather than presenting a narrative of the diplomatic encounters among these various players, this section analyzes the arguments presented by different parties during the process of conflict resolution.

Let us begin with the arguments of the French missionaries and diplomats. Primarily concerned with Chen's release, the French priest, Father Serdet, rejected all the allegations made by the Baptist missionaries. In fact, Serdet accused the Baptist villagers of an unprovoked attack on the Catholic church and of taking Chen as a hostage without cause. Serdet also suggested that the incident was the result of religious conflict between Catholicism and Protestantism and that it had broken out due to a recent property dispute involving the Baptist and Catholic villagers. According to Serdet, "The trouble arose simply from a dispute about [Christian] doctrines, and . . . Li Yan's revenge against an unjust penalty recently imposed on him [because of damage to the sugarcane fields] had sparked the violence."[31] Having pointed out that the Kuxi case was essentially a religious conflict between the two rival Christian enterprises, the French priest suggested that the matter be resolved by negotiations between the missionaries concerned and not by the Chinese officials. In short, the Chaoyang authorities should immediately release Chen Aming and let the missionaries decide what should be done to ensure the harmonious relations between the rival Christian communities.

The American Baptist missionaries were well aware of the Catholics' attempt to reduce the Kuxi case to a religious conflict over Catholic versus Protestant doctrines. To get the local Chinese officials and the U.S. diplomats' support, the Baptist missionaries toned down their anti-Catholic rhetoric even as they condemned the French Catholic enterprise as an obstacle to the progress of Baptist evangelistic work in Kuxi. They instead portrayed the incident as a community feud in the context of which Chen Aming had led a group of Catholic militants to attack the Baptist villagers and their settlement quarters. Nowhere is this attitude better illustrated than in a statement made by Ashmore in his correspondence with the U.S. minister in Beijing. Ashmore wrote, "It was not a case against A Meng [Chen Aming] as a Roman Catholic, but against A Meng as a ruffian and a robber, who attacked our chapel at midnight."[32] This statement stands in stark contrast to the anti-Catholic sentiment that Ashmore had expressed in the annual report of the American Baptist Union.[33] Such inconsistency of attitude should be understood as a shift of tactics rather than a change of opinion. By portraying Chen Aming as a destructive, disruptive element of local society, the American missionaries had a better chance of persuading the U.S. consul to urge the Chaoyang magistrate to impose a harsh penalty on Chen. Whereas it was important for Ashmore to exploit the anti-Catholic feeling of supporters at home, in his communications with the American diplomats in China he had to reframe the conflict, shifting the emphasis from the Catholic threat to the danger of widespread social disorder and to criminality and the inadequacy of local Chinese official protection for the Baptist villagers.

But unlike the French minister in Beijing, who strongly supported the French Catholic priest's request for the release of Chen, the U.S. minister there was not keen to become involved in the dispute on behalf of the Baptist missionaries. In fact, the American officials favored a compromise with the French, preferring to avoid a direct confrontation. The U.S. minister and consul both resisted being used by the Baptist missionaries as a political weapon against the French. The consul had urged the Baptist missionaries to work out their differences with the French Catholics, but the Baptists found that tactic unacceptable. Unable to count on their country's diplomats in China, the Baptist missionaries appealed directly to the U.S. secretary of state in Washington, urging him to send a commission to Kuxi to investigate the extent of damages suffered by the Baptist villagers. The missionaries' request, however, was rejected by the secretary. With little diplomatic support, the American Baptist missionaries were unable to gain the upper hand or to effectively counter the French Catholic influence with the Chaoyang magistrate court. Under these circumstances the magistrate yielded to the Catholic pressure and released Chen Aming. The magistrate was obviously in a dilemma, torn between the traditional duty to ensure justice for his subjects and the official obligation to observe the extraterritoriality of Chinese Catholic converts. But since the French Catholics exercised more influence on the court than the American Baptists, the Chinese magistrate had little choice but to favor the Catholic over the Baptist villagers in his decision. The fact that the stronger Christian party had prevailed with the Chinese justice system seemed to confirm what Chen Aming had said, that is, that after joining the Catholic church one need not fear the magistrate. But in December 1896 Chen Aming was rearrested by the Guangdong provincial authorities because of his part in riots against the local government.[34] Although there is no direct evidence that the Guangdong authorities in fact acted under pressure from the American Baptist mission and U.S. diplomatic channels, the rearrest of Chen Aming certainly undermined the strength of the Catholic community in Kuxi.

Conclusion

This article has used a historical case study to explore how two rival segments of the Li lineage in Kuxi employed a range of internal and external political resources in local power struggles. In particular, it concentrates on the process by which these rival segments transformed themselves via conversions to the Baptist Christianity and Catholicism, into two antagonistic Christian communities. During this process they drew the American Baptist and French Catholic missionaries into an existing web of communal power relations. By interfering in communal politics, the Baptist and Catholic missionaries became entangled in the longstanding intralineage conflicts. The missionaries' intervention reproduced Christian sectarian rivalries at the village and reinforced the conditions and resources that were conducive to the outbreak of violence. This complicated process of interaction between the Christian sectarianism and intralineage conflict played itself out in Kuxi in 1896. In addressing this historical process, it is important to bear in mind that Western missionaries and Chinese converts never operated and interacted with one another in an empty political landscape. Their interaction was largely shaped by a range of preexisting disputes and a sophisticated web of communal power relations that had long predated and indeed even shaped the arrival of the Baptist and Catholic missions.

Notes

1 The Li lineage in Kuxi divides into a number of sublineages (*fang*), which trace their descent from different sons of the common ancestor. Each sublineage further divides into several segments made up of dozens of households. For convenience, the lineage segment that converted to Baptism is classified as the junior segment, while the segment that joined the Catholic church is referred to as the senior segment.

2 American Baptist Missionary Union, comp., *Eighty-Third Annual Report with the Proceedings of the Annual Meeting, Held at Pittsburgh, PA, May 24 and 25, 1897* (Boston: Missionary Rooms, Tremont Temple, 1897), 144, and *Eighty-Fourth Annual Report with the Proceedings of the Annual Meeting, Held at Rochester, NY, May 17 and 18, 1898* (Boston: Missionary Rooms, Tremont Temple, 1898), 158–159. For archival materials that shed light on the issue see Council for World Mission Archive at the SOAS (School of Oriental and African Studies) Library, University of London, pamphlets on China, vol. 1, *Roman Catholic Proclamation against Protestants [in Shanghai]* (no author or date of publication given), and vol. 72, pamplet no. 10, Rev. Dr. Williamson, "Some Points on the Distinction Observable in China Between Protestant and Catholic Missions," in *Analysis of the Circular of the Chinese Government Missions*, comp. Foreign Mission Committee of the Presbyterian Church of England (London: Ranken, 1871), 20.

3 For historians' comments on the issue see Tao Feiya, "The Cultural Background for the Growth of Late Qing Intellectuals' Anti-Christian Sentiments," *Shijie zongjiao yanjiu* (Studies in world religion), no. 3 (1988): 89; Yao Xinzhong, "Success or Failure? Christianity in China," *History Today* 44, no. 9 (September 1994): 4; and Jessie G. Lutz, "Chinese Christianity and Christian Missions, Western Literature: the State of the Field," *Journal of the History of Christianity in Modern China* 1 (March 1998): 34–35.

4 Fernando Galbiati, *P'eng P'ai and the Hai-lu-feng Soviet* (Stanford: Stanford University Press, 1985), 26, and Vincent Lau, comp., *Haifeng tianzhujiao qishiwunian dashiji* (The chronicle of the seventy-five years' events of the Catholic church in Haifeng) (Hong Kong: Hong Kong Catholic Social Communication Centre, 1991), 30–31.

5 For more information on the Lian River see *Chaoshan baike quanshe* (The Chaoshan encyclopaedia) (Beijing: Zhongguo da baike quanshe chubanshe, 1994), 325. See also Guangdong sheng Chaoyang shi dimingzhi bianzuan weiyuanhui (The editorial committee of the dictionary of place names of Chaoyang City in Guangdong Province) comp., *Guangdong sheng Chaoyang shi dimingzhi* (Guangzhou: Guangdong keiji chubanshe [Guangdong Technological Press], 1996), 4, 164–165.

6 William Skinner, "Presidential Address: The Structure of Chinese History," *Journal of Asian Studies* 104, no. 2 (February 1985): 275–280, and Richard Louis Edmonds, "Geography and Natural Resources," in *Guangdong: China's Promised Land*, ed. Brian Hook, Regional Development in China Series No. 1 (Hong Kong: Oxford University Press, 1996), 76–77.

7 Zhou Heng, comp., *Chaoyang Xianzhi* [Gazetteer of Chaoyang District] facsimile of the 1884 edition of Zhongguo fanzhi congshu (Collection of gazetteers of China) No. 12 (Taipei: Chengwen chubanshe, 1966), 43.

8 Huang Ting and Du Jingguo, "A Preliminary Estimation of the Grain Production in Chaozhou-Shantou Region during the Yuan, Ming and Qing Dynasties," *Chaoxue yanjiu* (Chaozhou-Shantou cultural research), no. 3 (1995): 130. As units of measurement in the late nineteenth-century China, one *catty* of grain products was 1.33 lb., and one *mu* of land was 0.165 acre.

9 Huang Ting and Du Jingguo, "Research on Commercial and Trading Ports in Ancient Chaozhou-Shantou," *Chaoxue yanjiu*, no. 1 (1994): 59, 74–75 n. 32.

10 Zhou Heng, *Chaoyang Xianzhi*, 46–47, 172.

11 In the Chaoyang district, a village is often referred to as *zhai*. A *zhai* can be either a single-surname/single-lineage or a multisurname/multilineage community. Many of the single-surname/single-lineage communities are often named after the resident surname. For details see Fang Liewen, ed., *Chaoshan minsu daguan*

[Dictionary of Chaoshan folk customs] (Shantou: Shantou daxue chubanshe, 1996), 188–189.

12 Contemporary local source materials state that Kuxi is made up of five surnames: Cai, Guo, Li, Yao, and Zheng. Information I gathered during my fieldwork suggests that the Cai surname settled as tenants in the outer area of the village only during the early twentieth century. For details see the Chaoyang City Archive, *Lishi ziliao* [Historical materials], C(5)/19: Section on "Surname Communities in Liangying Commune," in "Chaoyang xian xingshi diaocha ziliao" (The investigation materials of different surnames in Chaoyang District), comp. Cai Yehai (unpublished manuscript, 1964).

13 William Ashmore, "Outrages on the American Baptist Mission at Kho-Knoi [Kuxi]," pt. 1, *Chinese Recorder and Missionary Journal*, vol. 27, no. 8 (August 1896): 372.

14 Doc. No. 80, 7 November 1896, in *American Diplomatic and Public Papers: The United States and China*, ed. Jules Davids, series 3: The Sino-Japanese War to the Russo-Japanese War, 1984–1905, vol. 11 (Wilmington, Del.: Scholarly Resources, 1981), 288.

15 "History of the Chapel in Kuxi," in *Lingdong jinhui qishi zhounian jinian taihui tecon* [Special issue on the seventieth anniversary of the Lingdong Baptist Church], comp. Chen Peiren (Shantou: Lingdong Baptist Church, 1932), 15–16. See also the American Baptist Society of Foreign Mission microfilms of Sophia A. Norwood's correspondence from 1878 to 1886 (herinafter *FM*74–4): Sophia A. Norwood, 1878 to 1886, Sophia A. Norwood's published letters, 27 October 1881.

16 Ashmore, "Outrages," pt. 1, 365.

17 Shantou City Archive, *Mingguo ziliao*, C184: "List of Names of Church Members of the Longdong Baptist Church from 1860 to 1910," in *Lingdong jiayin: Lingdong jinxinhui lishi tekan* [Lingdong good news: special issue on the history of the Lingdong Baptist Church], vols. 10, 11, and 12 (combined issue, 20 December 1936).

18 Norwood's published letter, 27 October 1881.

19 Ibid.

20 Doc. No. 80.

21 Shantou City Archive, *Zongjiaoju dangan* [The archive of the Department of Religious Affairs], 85-1-83: Cai Kaizhen, "Instances of Feud between Baptists and Catholics in Kuxi in Chaoyang" 17 January 1966, in *Shantou shi fojiao tianzhujiao shangceng renyuan suoxie youguan henshi fojiao tianzhiujiao shiliao* [Materials written by the senior buddhist and Catholic leaders in Shantou concerning the history of Buddhism and Catholicism in this city], 349–361.

22 Shantou City Archive, *Zongjiaoju dangan*, 85-1-83: "Historical Materials Concerning the Catholic Church in Huilai District," 216–222. Baileng village is the second oldest and largest Catholic settlement in the coastal section of Chaozhou. It was founded by Catholic settlers from nearby villages sometime in the eighteenth century. The exact date of the arrival of Catholic missionaries is not known, but the graves of some local Catholic villagers can be dated as early as A.D. 1750 (the fifteenth year of the emperor Qianlong).

23 Shantou City Archive, *Zongjiaoju dangan*, 85-1-83: Cai Kaizhen, "Instances of Feud," 351, and Li Xufeng, *Chaoyang xian wenwu zhi* ([Dictionary of Historical Antiques in Chaoyang District] (Chaoyang City: Chaoyang xian wenhuaju bowuguan, 1985), 139–140.

24 Ashmore, "Outrages," pt. 1, 370–371; Doc. No. 1054, 7 December 1896, in *JWJAD* (Jiaowu jiaoandang), ed. Lu Shiqiang, series 6, vol. 3, p. 1547; and *Lingdong ribao*

[Lingdong daily news], 7 January 1904 [the twentieth day of the eleventh moon of the twenty-ninth year of Emperor Guangxu], 3.

25 Ashmore, "Outrages," pt. 1, 371.

26 Ibid. and Doc. No. 80, 289–291.

27 Ashmore, "Outrages," pt. 1, 424–427.

28 Ibid., 369–370, and Doc. No. 80, 299.

29 This was romanized in the Chaozhou dialect by Ashmore as "U Thien Chu ka, bai Ia-so ka."

30 William Ashmore, "Outrages on the American Baptist Mission at Kho-Knoi," pt. 2, *Chinese Recorder*, 27, no. 9 (September 1896): 424–427.

31 Doc. No. 80, 299.

32 Ibid., 296.

33 American Baptist Union, *Eighty-Third Annual Report*, 144, and *Eighty-Fourth Annual Report*, 158–159.

34 Doc. No. 1054, 1547.

50

REVOLUTIONARY ANTICLERICALISM AND HEGEMONIC PROCESSES IN AN ANDALUSIAN TOWN, AUGUST 1936

Richard Maddox

Source: *American Ethnologist*, 22(1) (1995), 125–43.

Anthropologists and social historians have debated whether the participants in violent attacks on the church and clergy in Spain during the Civil War period were "millenarian" protestants whose actions sprang from a premodern sociopolitical mentality or were pragmatic radicals whose actions simply represented a series of well-calculated attacks on a key ideological institution. In analyzing the events leading to anticlerical violence in an Andalusian town, this article argues that the attacks were the outcome of hegemonic processes of differing scope, intensity, and duration. Neither pure traditionalists nor modernists, the revolutionary anticlericals of August 1936 sought to define the specific character of the present in ways that were gauged to have the maximum effect on their allies and adversaries alike. The article discusses implications of these findings for analyses of "tradition," "modernity," and contemporary sociopolitical movements.

During the late 19th and early 20th centuries, strong class divisions were evident in the Andalusian town of Aracena, located in the Sierra Morena of Huelva province, Spain, about 90 kilometers northwest of Seville. Although the population of Aracena and its dependent hamlets never exceeded 9,000, the town was a regional marketing center and the seat of a judicial district. As a result, many of the largest landowners of the northern third of the province, who had grown wealthy by raising hogs and harvesting cork, chose to reside in the town. These proprietors, together with the professionals and business people who served them, created a remarkably urbane way of life for themselves. In contrast, most of the remaining 85 percent of the population of the township struggled to survive as agrarian day laborers and artisans. This situation led an editorialist for a local periodical to lament that "by the great wealth that God has given it, Aracena has individual fortunes like no other *pueblo*, but considered collectively, it is the poorest population in Spain" (*El Distrito* 1913c).

The editorialist was exaggerating, but not much. In Aracena, as elsewhere in rural Spain, the chasm separating the lives of the rich from the lives of the poor generated class antagonisms that persisted for decades. By 1936, the antagonisms in Aracena had become so intense that only a spark was needed to set the smoldering resentments and hatreds ablaze. This spark was provided when news reached the town that General Franco's troops in north Africa had risen in rebellion against the Second Republic on July 18. During the next three weeks in Aracena, the radical left seized control of the municipal government, took steps to defend the town from Franco's troops, and initiated a social revolution.

On August 10, 1936, just 23 days after the beginning of the Civil War, a crowd of 200 to 300 leftist radicals gathered in front of Aracena's 16th-century parish church of Santa María de la Asunción. It seemed at first that municipal guards were going to prevent anyone from entering the church. But then a group of 10 or 15 men stepped forward, and after a few minutes of heated discussion, the guards withdrew. Accompanied by other members of the crowd, the leaders entered the sanctuary and began to strip the walls, altars, chapels, and treasuries of their images, paintings, chalices, crucifixes, and other furnishings that had been the gifts and donations of generations of the town's agrarian gentry. All of these objects were gathered into a great pile in the center of the church and set ablaze. As the flames rose, dynamite charges exploded. Although the weakened stone walls did not collapse, the whole edifice was gutted.

In succession, the other churches and chapels of the town met a similar fate. The church of Santa Catalina lost at least 50 paintings, and the church of Santo Domingo and the chapels of San Pedro, San Roque, and Santa Lucia were stripped and severely damaged. The religious furnishings of El Carmen, the new revolutionary command post, were piled in carts, taken to the edge of town, and burned. For the most part, the anticlericals went about their job in a calm, orderly, and systematic way, with their work occasionally punctuated by curses and jibes that mocked the church, priests, and even God, the Virgin, and the saints. In the course of the day, the chapel of the school of the Esclavas Concepcionistas (an order of nuns who taught the children of the town's elite) was ruined, and the sisters of the convents of Santa Catalina and Jesús, María, y José were expelled from their cloisters.

While not physically harmed, the nuns were taunted and forced to put on secular dress. The sacristan and priests were saved from a similar or possibly much worse fate because they were already in the custody of jailers sworn to protect them. In all of the churches, the images of the lay religious brotherhoods, the most important objects of popular devotion in Aracena, were destroyed. In the late afternoon, the church of "El Castillo," for centuries a center of popular devotion, was sacked, and the image of the town's patron saint, La Virgen del Mayor Dolor, was also condemned to the flames. By the end of the day, only the chapel and nuns of the old people's home were left unmolested.

This composite description of the events of August 10, 1936, in Aracena is primarily based on interviews conducted in 1982 with numerous men and women who were between 17 and 22 years old when they witnessed the church burnings. Their accounts and the recollections of several other townspeople who had heard about the church burnings from older friends and relatives indicate that what happened in Aracena on August 10 was part of a much larger pattern.[1] Similar, although often more violent, attacks against both the church and the clergy were occurring in almost all of the surrounding towns and villages of Huelva province (see Collier 1987 and Ordóñez Márquez 1968 for detailed descriptions), throughout Andalusia, and in many parts of northern Spain as well. With the exception of the Holocaust and perhaps the recent war in Bosnia, these attacks represent the most severe religious violence witnessed in any European country during the 20th century (Payne 1984:168). Indeed, in his fine historical account of the religious politics of the Spanish Civil War, José María Sánchez claims that the violent deaths of nearly 7,000 Spanish priests, nuns, monks, and seminarians, most of whom were killed during the early months of the conflict, represent "the greatest clerical bloodletting in the entire history of the Christian church" (1987:8).

Early studies of violent anticlericalism strongly associated the phenomenon with anarchism and regarded it as one of the virtually diagnostic signs that rural radicalism represented a premodern and often irrational political mentality. Elaborating on the themes of Juan Díaz del Moral's (1984[1928]) discussion of anarchism in turn-of-the-century Córdoba, Gerald Brenan (1960: 189–190), for example, noted the highly moralistic character of working-class ideologies and argued that rural radicals could be considered millenarian heretics whose fanaticism sprang from the view that the Catholic church represented the Antichrist. In his influential account in *Primitive Rebels*, Eric Hobsbawm (1965) considerably refined Brenan's characterization but concurred with his general point of view. Less concerned than Brenan with drawing direct parallels to the Protestant Reformation, Hobsbawm nonetheless regarded anarchism as "the most impressive example of a modern mass millenarian or quasi millenarian movement" and argued that anarchism was "a form of peasant movement almost incapable of effective adaptation to modern conditions" (1965:90, 92). In Hobsbawm's account, church burning and anticlericalism represented a quasi-religious rejection of the "evil world" and embodied the "primitivism" and "ritualism" to which social movements lacking modern forms of party organization and discipline are prone (1965: 83–84, 150).

Several subsequent accounts of rural Spanish radicalism, including those of Temma Kaplan (1977) and Jerome Mintz (1982), have challenged the millenarian theory.[2] These studies stress the immediate sociopolitical contexts, rational planning, considerable degree of organization, ideological motives, and pragmatic aims of working-class actions in order to counter the impression that phenomena such as anticlerical violence and strikes represent spontaneous outbursts of revolutionary fanaticism. Kaplan (1977:90), for example, treats "spontaneity" as an expression of a libertarian philosophy rather than a symptom of millenarianism and argues that Andalusian radicals instrumentally adapted old cultural and religious forms to teach new patterns of social relations. According to Kaplan (1977:86), the similarities that exist between such practices as anarchist initiation ceremonies and Catholic baptism reflect the ingenuity of the anarchists and not their religious fervor. Mintz (1982:5), who also challenges Hobsbawm's "evolutionary model of prepolitical primitive rebels" in his detailed account of the rebellion of 1934 in Casas Viejas, claims that local radicals clearly distinguished clerical authority from religious faith and argues that, far from being millenarians, they were only secondarily concerned with the fate of religion or the church. In his study, Mintz (1982:63–77) cites one anarchist who maintained that Catholicism would naturally collapse when social justice was achieved.

Kaplan and Mintz both succeed in challenging the millenarian theory by giving a far more complex and detailed picture of rural radicalism than that offered by Brenan or Hobsbawm. But the analytic force of the Kaplan and Mintz accounts is weakened by two factors. First, since the accounts do not provide an alternative to Hobsbawm's model of political evolution, it is easy to read them as arguing that rural Spanish radicals were simply more advanced, pragmatic, and secular than Hobsbawm and Brenan believed and that these radicals should therefore be regarded as thoroughly "modern," political actors. Second, since the accounts do not discuss the real violence and intensity of the passions involved in radical anticlericalism, they tend to lead readers to the rather flat and unilluminating conclusion that assaults on the church and clergy can be satisfactorily understood as incidental attacks on the property and representatives of a key ideological institution.

As a result, the millenarian theory has by no means been wholly discredited. On the contrary, there has even been a revitalization of approaches that lend support to it and have been advocated in recent years by scholars whose primary motivation often seems to be to put culture (or social psychology) back into the study of politics. Examples include the provocative work of John Corbin (1986), Bruce Lincoln (1985), and Timothy Mitchell (1988), who have analyzed ritualized aspects of violence in working-class movements during the Civil War period. Mitchell (1988:192), for instance, treats anticlericalism as the violent behavioral manifestation of a deeply embedded archaic Spanish cultural structure involving the ritual victimization or expulsion of a scapegoat by a social in-group. Lincoln, after developing a wide-ranging, comparative analysis of anticlerical violence as "iconoclastic rituals of collective obscenity and status inversion," concludes that anticlerical violence in Spain was anti-institutional rather than anti-religious and that it represented "the horrific foundation ritual of a new religion" inspired by a millenarian creed (1985:259–260).

In this article, I provide an alternative to the millenarian and instrumentalist approaches to the study of revolutionary anticlericalism and argue that the church burners in Aracena in 1936 were neither frenzied fanatics nor coldhearted ideologues. Instead, they were highly self-conscious radicals whose motives were complex and whose actions were intended to have the maximum cultural and political impact on their adversaries and allies alike.

My arguments stem in part from the recent work in cultural studies and historical anthropology that has transformed many contemporary analysts' views of the dynamics of domination and resistance. In particular, I embrace Stuart Hall's (1986, 1988) conviction that hegemonic and counterhegemonic processes center on the struggles of contending groups to articulate meanings and representations from heterogeneous sources in a manner that allows them to form or consolidate effective political and social alliances. To develop this approach further, I draw on Marshall Sahlins's (1981, 1985) framework for analyzing historical events in terms of practical contingencies, conjunctural situations, and structures of the long run.[3] In the case presented here, I examine the events in Aracena on August 10 in terms of a threefold articulation of relations of domination and resistance. First, I describe church burning as a contingent practice that Aracena's radical leaders initiated more or less on the spur of the moment in accordance with their understanding of the immediate revolutionary crisis facing the town. Second, I explore how medium-range conjunctural factors, such as the shifts in church-state relations that occurred during the 19th and early 20th centuries in Spain, led local conservatives and radicals alike to develop strategies of ideological representation that both accelerated processes of class polarization and made the town's churches a focal point of political agitation in the years before the Civil War. Third, I show that the local radicals who burned the churches sought to undermine a once-dominant cultural formation that had been structured by the discourses of religion, honor, and patronage and had legitimated relations of inequality for centuries in the town. Having demonstrated that the events of August 10 were shaped by cultural and political processes of differing scope, intensity, and duration, I conclude with the argument that understanding church burning in Aracena as a response to multiple hegemonic pressures and constraints not only casts light on the "ideological" shortcomings of the millenarian and instrumentalist approaches to revolutionary anticlericalism but also provides guidelines useful in the critical analysis of contemporary sociopolitical movements in Eastern Europe and elsewhere.

Church burning and revolutionary crisis

To understand the practical dynamics driving revolutionary anticlericalism in Aracena, it is critical to know who participated in the events of August 10, 1936. When I recently asked townspeople about this, they usually responded with one of two answers: "a few fanatics" or "the Marxist hordes." Such stock responses clearly reflect the ideological pressures exerted during the long postwar period of the Franco dictatorship and should be treated with some caution.[4] More extended accounts of the day, however, substantially agree that the crowd was primarily composed of many young men from surrounding rural hamlets and a smaller number from Aracena ("the hordes") who were led by radicals from Aracena's Society of Agrarian Workers and Peasants and a group of Socialist workers from the mines of Río Tinto 30 kilometers to the south of Aracena. These leaders ("the fanatics") orchestrated the day's events and directed the small nucleus of men who actually stripped and burned the sanctuaries. The church burnings thus brought the most organized, committed, and knowledgeable radicals into extended contact with the least experienced and most ill-organized and isolated *campesinos* (peasants, agrarian workers) of the sierra. The more moderate Socialists and left-wing Republicans of Aracena's Popular Front town council were hardly represented among the participants.

The composition of the crowd who burned the churches suggests a great deal about the immediate motivations of the revolutionary anticlericals because it both reflected and transcended the political tensions existing within the left. In the weeks after the outbreak of the war, a social revolution had occurred in Aracena. Despite the opposition of the Popular Front town council, miners and local revolutionaries with the support of the great majority of the agrarian workers had managed to initiate a *reparto* (redistribution) of land, had organized a popular militia, and had jailed many members of the local gentry. Even so, there were divisions in the revolutionary left, particularly over the issue of how the captive members of the gentry were to be dealt with: many campesinos had argued for the summary execution of landowners and conservative politicians, while most of their leaders had urged restraint and taken steps to establish a revolutionary tribunal of justice. Thus, despite the considerable achievements of the first weeks of the war, the left was threatened by disunity and factionalism. From this perspective, church burning can be seen as a political rally staged by leaders whose authority was informal and whose effectiveness was heavily dependent on gaining the support of a large number of followers.

Moreover, there was a pressing need to rekindle revolutionary ardor and unite the various subgroups that constituted the popular forces in the town on August 10. For some days before, the left had been demoralized by rumors of easy Nationalist victories in the provinces of Seville and Huelva. In these circumstances, the revolutionary leaders evidently decided that some morale-building militant act was needed. In recent discussions with a number of men who were sympathetic to the aims of the miners and town revolutionaries at the time, a common explanation for the church burnings was that the principal people involved wanted to "unify," "wake up," and even "ignite" the masses. One aging working-class man underscored this rationale by associating the church burnings in Aracena with events of the same day in the neighboring town of Higuera de la Sierra, where a group of miners had killed six members of the Guardia Civil in the course of an attack on their barracks. According to this man, Aracena's radicals were aroused by news of the battle in Higuera and undertook the assault on the churches both as a sort of victory celebration and in anticipation of imminent combat. Words and plans alone were no longer sufficiently persuasive; it was time for great deeds to supplant them. Burning the churches was an irreversible act—a crossing of the Rubicon—that directly communicated this message and irrevocably sealed the commitment of leaders and followers to one another and to the aims and ideals of social revolution.

Burning the churches also provided an ideal means of further intimidating the conservative gentry. By August 10, 1936, the estates of the gentry had already been effectively seized, and most members of the local elite either were in jail or had been barricaded in their houses for some weeks. Nevertheless, many on the left believed that plots were still being hatched. The atmosphere of fear and suspicion in Aracena in the days just before the church burnings is well conveyed in the recollections of Don Manuel Siurot, a highly respected visiting Catholic educator, who had been trapped in the town by the war:

> The privation of liberty had reached such an extreme that one could not laugh, because this was a provocation; one could not be serious, because this was for some purpose; one could not open the window onto the street, because this was espionage; and one could not close it, because this was conspiracy. In the hotel, we lived always surrounded by *comunistas* [communists]; bombs, rifles, dynamite, and blasphemies were our house companions. . . . With the jail full of honorable men, what sort of death would be given the prisoners was discussed around the table of the hotel's dining room. In this discussion, I applauded in my soul those from Nerva and Río Tinto [that is, the miners] because they tenaciously opposed killing the poor detainees without a previous judgment, while those from Aracena wanted to burn them alive with no trial. When things were at this

> height, the communist revolutionary committee ordered that I was to be conducted to the jail willingly or by force, because as a Catholic I was highly dangerous. They did not imprison me for being a political man, but for being a Catholic.
>
> [quoted in Ordóñnez Márquez 1968:184]

In fact, no conservatives were burned alive or killed in Aracena. But with the prospect of fighting before them, the revolutionaries had every reason to see to it that the adversaries within their midst remained passive. Short of murder, there was no more forceful means available for demonstrating control of the town than burning and sacking the churches. This was so because generations of the town's elite had donated the paintings, images, and other furnishings sheltered inside the churches and thought of themselves as the patrons and guardians of the churches' artistic treasures. Thus, for the working-class militants to enter and sack what they sometimes called "the houses of the rich" was not only to destroy the most visible representation of the elite's cultural and political values but also was symbolically tantamount to entering the homes and violating the persons of the gentry. It was a way of chastising and humiliating them by demonstrating their vulnerability and impotence.

By all accounts, burning the churches succeeded in cowing the gentry, who believed that the working class had "gone crazy with hatred." Given the circumstances, however, it seems likely that the supposed fanaticism of the church burners was at least partly a matter of consciously adopting dramatic poses in order to generate a particular audience response. Indeed, viewed from a short-term, practical political perspective, church burning represented less an outburst of spontaneous ardor than a tactical maneuver at the most critical juncture in decades of class struggles and escalating ideological conflict. It offered a relatively low-risk and easy victory that rallied the popular forces, terrorized the elite, and satisfied working-class demands for action and revenge but did not involve needless bloodshed.

Church burning and ideological polarization

But how did the almost complete identification of the church with the gentry elite come about? To answer this, it is necessary to understand the events of August 10 in Aracena from the perspective of medium-range conjunctural processes of political polarization and ideological displacement.[5] During the Ancient Regime, the church had been the key social and cultural institution of Aracena, and it had remained so as late as the 1820s, when the clergy had mustered the township's populace to fight liberalism and support an absolutist monarchy. By the last decades of the 19th century, however, liberalism was triumphant, the situation of the church had radically changed, and virtually the whole working class had been alienated from orthodox religion.

A number of factors contributed to the deterioration of the power and authority of the church within the new liberal regime in Aracena.[6] Most important was the enforcement of disentailment legislation, which resulted in the sale of thousands of hectares of ecclesiastical land and other church properties in the period from 1836 to 1870. The disentailment was accompanied by a sharp decline in the number of parish clergy. In 1822, there were 27 parish clergy in the township, but their number fell to 11 by the late 1840s and declined still further in succeeding years. In addition, by mid-century the laws designed to eliminate the influence of the religious orders in Spain had dealt a severe blow to Aracena's convents and monasteries. Although a few nuns remained in the convents of Santa Catalina and Jesús, María, y José, the Dominican and Carmelite monasteries had been deserted (Mádoz 1845–50). The decline in the number of clergy led to an increasing lack of church involvement in many aspects of social life, especially in the hamlets and smaller pueblos of the sierra. Two other developments exacerbated the impact of this more or less forced clerical withdrawal on popular attitudes toward the church and formal religion.

First, the local clergy and ex-clergy of the town acted in ways that underscored a growing popular perception of abandonment by the church. After the collapse of the traditionalist resistance to liberalism, many members of the clergy came to identify their own interests with those of the local gentry who had already set about procuring the ecclesiastical and communal "patrimonies of the poor." There was nothing very surprising in this. Tax records of the incomes of 27 parish clergy in 1822 indicate that although no clerics were truly wealthy, half of them were enjoying sufficient incomes to fall in the upper-middle range of taxpayers and were clearly comfortably well-off. Not only these wealthier clergymen but also most of the poorer priests of the township were related to leading gentry families and were inclined to support the interests of their kinspeople. Moreover, several priests and former members of the clergy became substantial private landholders themselves when they inherited patrimonial lands or became the owners of properties that were previously part of endowed chaplaincies. Thus, those clergy or ex-clergy who were able to maintain or secure incomes through the period of disentailment became property holders whose interests were for the most part in opposition to the majority of their poor parishioners, and this no doubt contributed to the popular sense of abandonment by the church.

Second, these sentiments were intensified by the alliance forged between the church and the most conservative elements of national and local liberalism in the late 19th century. With the Concordance of 1851, the church accepted the confiscations of ecclesiastical property and agreed to the restrictions on the activities and number of religious orders in return for the recognition of Spain as an officially Catholic country, the provision of state salaries for priests, and the right of the church to acquire property in the future. From this time forward, the church devoted most of its energies to defending these and related privileges (such as its decisive role in elementary and secondary education) from the threats of radical liberals and republicans who regarded the church as the principal barrier to social and cultural progress. In the struggles with the left wing of liberalism, the church became the ally and supporter of the conservative liberal oligarchy. Thus, by the last decades of the 19th century, the landowning elite of Aracena had fervently reembraced the church as a bulwark of the social order and had begun to sponsor new orders of nuns, religious education, and all sorts of devotional and lay organizations. However, this revitalization of local Catholicism did nothing to narrow the distance between the church and the rural poor of the sierra, who were almost entirely illiterate and were hardly aroused by the supposed evils of social anarchy, Protestantism, and secular humanism. On the contrary, the identification of institutional religion with oligarchic interests added an active perception of betrayal to an already strong sense of abandonment that was further exacerbated by the fact that the more remote villages of the sierra had become notorious dumping grounds for bad priests by the turn of the century (see Ordóñez Márquez 1968). These conditions laid the foundations for the anticlericalism of the agrarian laborers of the sierra and most working-class townspeople of Aracena in the first decades of the 20th century.

However, the direct politicization of religion in Aracena was more the responsibility of the agrarian gentry than it was of the working class. In the 1890s, Aracena's gentry began to embrace the social doctrines and political ideology of "Catholic mutualism," a concept inspired by Catholic social thought as expounded by Pope Leo XIII in his encyclical on social justice and as explicated in Spain by the leading thinkers of Acción Católica. Mutualism was based on the premise that to fulfill the injunction to love one's neighbor under the conditions of liberal society, all social classes had to give up the pursuit of separate class interests and to respect the "obligations of each class to the others." The practical vehicles of mutualism in Aracena were to be the "agricultural syndicates" of proprietors and laborers, organizations whose governing bodies were to mediate labor disputes and promote the local economy. It was hoped that workers linked to these organizations would be instilled with a belief in "the sacred principle of authority," "the sacred rights of property," and the value of voluntary "free associations" and "social harmony." According to the contributors to *El Distrito* (1912), the local newspaper that hawked mutualist thought in the town and the sierra, the goal was "evolutionary progress" guided by "Science and Faith."

Mutualism was initially greeted with overwhelming enthusiasm as a solution to the "social problem"—at least by the local gentry: "At last the pueblo has been awakened by the call of Acción Católica. Fortifying themselves with religion and Christian law, generous men show the pueblo that what all our little brothers ask for in chorus like little birds in the nest can be immediately advanced" (*El Distrito* 1913b). The "little birds," however, were singing their own song, and neither in Aracena nor, for that matter, in the rest of Andalusia did mutualism win many working-class converts. The failure of mutualism to strike a responsive chord among the working class or to develop practical means of ameliorating social conditions meant that it soon degenerated into a set of ideological postures whose purpose was to provide a rationale for the authority and power of the agrarian gentry. The social crisis of the rural poor came to be viewed as a result of their ignorance, lack of understanding, and vulgarity, and any change in the status quo was made dependent upon a long process of moral education. In the meantime, the bedrock stance of the gentry and their allies on the critical "agrarian social question" was summarized as follows: "The patron needs strong workers for his exploitations and so he should protect and favor them. The worker requires his daily subsistence from the patron and should serve, respect, and honor him" (*El Distrito* 1914).

The working class of Aracena saw these mutualist principles as evidence that the church had given its imprimatur to social subordination and had sanctified poverty and exploitation. Indeed, so close was the identification of the interests of the gentry with those of the church that all conservative political groups were often referred to simply as "the party of the priest." In reaction to this perceived seamless alliance of church and gentry, the working classes of Aracena became more and more disaffected from religion as class antagonisms increased. Thus, during the 1910s and 1920s, strikes and protests over agrarian working conditions were accompanied, evidently for the first time, by extensive vandalism of church property.

The final and critical phase of this conjunctural process of ideological reorientation, however, began in the township only around 1930, when working-class militants started to preach regularly against the evils of Catholicism. Especially in the outlying hamlets, Socialist leaders actively spoke out against the church and promoted secular practices such as civil marriage and burial. As a result, many working-class couples refused to have their marriages sanctified or their children baptized, and the proportion of hamlet dwellers who rejected or neglected the last sacraments ranged from 50 to 90 percent (Ordóñez Márquez 1968:178–179). In light of these circumstances, a concerned Catholic declared that "the Christian life is almost dead" among the working class of the sierra (quoted in Ordóñez Márquez 1968:179).

The progressive widening of an ideological and cultural split following class lines laid the foundation for the direct and open attacks on the church that occurred in Aracena during the Second Republic when national disputes arose over the role of the church in education. In 1932, for example, an anticlerical riot was only narrowly averted when a group of Catholics marched to the town hall to deliver a petition protesting an order to remove all crucifixes from the schoolrooms. On a few minutes' notice, local radicals mustered 800 road workers armed with picks and shovels to block the delivery of the petition. Only the intervention of the Guardia Civil prevented bloodshed. Incidents such as this made the revolutionary leaders of 1936 highly conscious that anticlerical actions could galvanize their followers.

But this is not the whole story of the attitudes and processes that led to the church burnings of August 10. To regard anticlerical violence largely in terms of the direct tactics and conjunctural dynamics of class warfare still leaves many questions about the events unanswered. Why, for example, did the revolutionaries take great pains to destroy the most important images of popular devotion when it would seem that burning the church buildings would have accomplished the pragmatic ends discussed above? The question may seem trivial, but it is, in fact, of vital importance. One of the most striking features of accounts of the day is how shocked many working-class people were by the destruction of certain images of the saints, Christ, and the Virgin, especially the image of La Virgen del Mayor Dolor, the patron saint of Aracena. This discord within the working classes on the matter of the popular images indicates that anticlerical violence entailed something more than immediate revolutionary tactics and mid-range strategies of ideological and class warfare. To understand the significance of this discord and the broader motivations of the church burners, it is necessary to gain a sense of how the conjunctural dynamics of "revolutionary anticlericalism" were related to the transformation of long-term institutionalized structures of cultural authority that indirectly shaped the character of "popular anticlericalism" in towns such as Aracena.[7]

Church burning and structures of the long run

Throughout the early modern period in Aracena, the authority of the dual institutional formations of church and monarchy was legitimated through the promulgation of what can be termed the discourses of the spirit and flesh. Society was represented as a spiritual and corporal hierarchy whose members were bound together through the critical sociomoral relations of patronage that were imagined to exist between unequals in rank, power, and virtue. Such relationships could be construed either in terms of an ascetic religious morality of self-sacrifice for the sake of others or in terms of an aesthetic nobiliary social morality of honor (see Maravall 1986) that required the weak to cleave faithfully to the strong in order to ensure themselves a modicum of dignity and integrity in an agonistic, fallen, and dangerous world. Thus, cultural hegemony was exercised by assuming the role of patron and rendering social relations significant in terms of the adjustment of the life of the flesh to the life of the spirit and vice versa.

During the Ancient Regime, the hierarchical values of religious orthodoxy and codes of honor were broadly communicated to the general population through customary forms of interaction between social unequals, through elaborate cultural and religious performances (such as the baroque rituals and processions dedicated to the worship of patron saints), and through secular spectacles and fiestas (such as the *corrida de toros*, or "bullfight"). In modified versions, these rituals and celebrations dominated Andalusian popular culture well into the 20th century, and they have continued to exert a great influence on how many Andalusians view the world down to this day. Indeed, although the liberal revolutions of the 19th century largely eliminated aristocratic privileges, weakened the church, and altered the formal and legal bases upon which discriminations of honor and relationships of patronage had been grounded, traditional values and idealized forms of representing personhood (for example, the Virgin Mother, the protective patriarch, the brave young *torero*, and the modest daughter) still remain important in defining what it means to be a member of a family and a community.

Within this once-dominant cultural tradition, however, there have always been oppositional tendencies, one of which is popular anticlericalism. For most of its long history, popular anticlericalism has represented—and indeed to a limited extent still represents—an undercurrent of resistance, grounded in everyday concerns and practices and primarily focused on the politics of interpersonal relations rather than on broader social and political issues. And although popular anticlericalism has varied considerably in its intensity and modes of expression, one of its central themes has always been the hypocritical worldliness of the clergy. Common and widespread criticisms of the church have been expressed through direct complaints about the venality, abuse of privilege, greed, and arrogance of members of the ecclesiastical hierarchy and also through the countless stories and jokes whose theme is the misadventures, and especially the sexual dalliances, of ordinary priests and exalted prelates alike.

The reputed lapses of the clergy from ideal standards of behavior are significant largely because tales of clerical corruption and frailty have been used (explicitly or implicitly) to challenge the notion that taking a vow or exercising ritual functions can alter or suspend human nature in a way that justifies the priests' claims to a special authority to instruct laypeople, absolve them from sin, and intervene with God or the saints on their behalf. Thus, anticlericalism has embodied a particular strategy of social, moral, and spiritual leveling, and the principal practical manifestation of this leveling strategy has ordinarily been the refusal of the great majority of rural Andalusian men and many women to comply with orthodox religious practices, especially those practices that most smack of submission and subordination to priests, such as confession and communion. These ritual forms of compliance with religious authority are resisted because they set cultural limits to personal autonomy and make it nearly impossible for most laypeople to regard or approach priests as moral equals.

In spite of the fact that popular anticlericalism has egalitarian sentiments at its core, however, it has been nearly as much a vehicle of hegemonic domination as a mode of resistance to it. This is largely because the egalitarian implications of popular anticlericalism have been diffused and neutralized by preoccupations with other concerns, particularly notions of male prestige, honor, and patriarchal authority and fears and suspicions of women's sexuality and spirituality. The socioerotic aspect of anticlericalism is readily apparent in the comment of one man who explained his refusal to receive the sacraments by saying, "The priest gives the bread and wine with the same hands he uses to embrace other men's women." The association of communion and cuckoldry and other analogous representations indicate that popular anticlericalism is often a double-edged sword whose main functions are to undercut the moral distinction of priests from laymen and to defend men's prerogatives to control the actions of their wives and daughters in the course of everyday life. By creating doubts about both priests' and women's capacities to achieve a higher state of spiritual and moral purity through the sacrifice and control of bodily desires, popular anticlericalism reaffirms the secular, agonistic, intensely personalistic ethos of honor at the core of representations of masculine identity and thereby generates a diffused sense of solidarity among laymen of all social classes.[8] However, it does so at the cost not only of reproducing ideologies of gender inequality but also of deflecting attention from other patterns of domination and the differences in power, wealth, and prestige that shape class relations among laymen and laywomen alike.

The emergence of revolutionary anticlericalism in Aracena and elsewhere entailed a partial but important transformation of this popular anticlerical tradition. The conjunctural processes of ideological rearticulation discussed in the preceding section led not only to a direct politicization of the church and orthodox religion but also to a shift in the focus of popular anticlericalism, a shift that is critical to understanding why the revolutionary anticlericals chose the images of the community's patron saints as one of their targets. The militant Socialists who strove to organize the town's working-class neighborhoods and outlying hamlets during the early 1930s did not limit their ideological attacks to the orthodox church; they also criticized popular religious customs and faith. Indeed, the radicals' constant diatribes against popular religious traditions quickly led to a sharp decline in the memberships of lay religious brotherhoods, and, as a result of the disruptions and counterdemonstrations staged by the most committed anticlericals, many processions in honor of local patron saints on days of fiestas were suspended during the 1930s.

In these circumstances, relations with the divine necessarily became an increasingly private matter among the considerable number of working-class people who were devoted to Christ, the Virgin, and the saints, if not to the church. Moreover, since women—by reputation and probably in fact—comprised the great majority of the most devout members of the working class, the actions of the militants presented many of them with a more difficult dilemma than that faced by most working-class men. Nevertheless, in terms of their public behavior, the choice they made seems clear. By 1932, only 50 women among the roughly 2,000 parishioners of Aracena's hamlets complied with the Easter duty, regular attendance at mass was limited to a handful of elderly women, and many shrines and churches that working-class women had once maintained in Aracena and its hamlets had fallen into a state of abandonment and disrepair. In effect, the militants had made hostility or at least apparent indifference to religion an acid test of political solidarity among the working class and had thereby redefined the cultural politics of gender entailed in women's religiosity by directly subordinating hitherto subpolitical aspects of popular anticlericalism to the overriding demands of class struggle. Even so, it is clear that many people of the township who sympathized with the political aims of the radical leaders and were hostile to the official church remained faithful to their religious convictions and devoted to the images of the town's patron saints. Thus, in the years preceding the Civil War, the militants' attacks on popular religious practices had only partially succeeded in linking anticlerical attitudes to antireligious ones. From this perspective, to burn the images of the saints was an attempt to clear up unfinished business.

To understand fully the importance of the attacks against the images of popular devotion, however, it is important to recognize that the irreligious attitudes of the radical anticlericals themselves were influenced more by enduring modes of thought and expression related to popular anticlerical traditions than by skeptical, secular notions of disbelief in the supernatural. In particular, the actions of the anticlericals must be understood in light of what it meant to be irreligious in everyday life. Though popular anticlericalism by no means necessarily entailed a lack of faith in God or the saints—and indeed tended to strengthen certain aspects of religious practices by stressing their communitarian as opposed to priestly character—anticlerical attitudes have nonetheless always been closely linked with irreligious ones.

The principal forms of irreligious expression involve blasphemous statements and curses such as the following: "Man, I tell you that there is not a day that goes by that I don't shit in the milk of *la puta madre* [the whore mother, meaning here the Virgin Mary] for this lack of rain that is ruining me." In this and similar curses, a verbal defilement of spiritual purity takes the form of a direct insult delivered in response to an evident lack of divine patronage, protection, and favors. Although such remarks are frequently spontaneous outbursts uttered because of some immediate frustration and are often made quite casually, their effect (and often enough their intent) is to level the moral difference between the divine and the human, to overturn at least provisionally the notion of a spiritual-corporal hierarchy, and to convert a perception of religious estrangement into a defiant assertion of personal autonomy. Thus, while popular anticlericalism reflects hostility and resentment concerning priestly mediation between the human and the divine, blasphemy extends the logic of anticlericalism to the domain of unmediated spiritual relationships as well; and, like popular anticlericalism, it represents an effort to restore or reassert the values of honor by rejecting a religious subordination that appears to be without moral justification or practical benefits.[9]

Blasphemous curses expressing intensely personalized, direct accusations against the divine were far more central to revolutionary anticlericalism as a mode of thought and feeling than were coldhearted refusals to assent to sacred doctrines for intellectual or political reasons. Among the handful of older, vehemently anticlerical people who still live in Aracena, hatred of priests and the church is accompanied by a conviction that all religious practices and devotions are pointless and futile. When these people are asked to explain why the churches and the images of popular devotion were destroyed, the responses that seem most deeply felt are those that express a sense of religious alienation and evoke a painful feeling of the absence of divine love and mercy. These responses frequently incorporate the curses and blasphemies that punctuate ordinary male working-class speech:

> You don't understand why the images of the Virgin were burned? . . . I will tell you. Because the Virgin was a shameless whore and God had no sense of justice. . . . A mother who sees her children go hungry and turns away is a whore. . . . What a little mother she is. . . . Tell me, has she ever answered [your prayers]? Does she speak to you? Has she helped you? No? Well, now you understand [why the images were burned]. It's all lies. Those images were lies and lies have to be destroyed for the truth to live.

Although the rhetoric of this explanation of revolutionary anticlericalism resonates with both the androcentric and blasphemous elements in popular anticlericalism, its sense is quite different from that of the latter, not only because of the notion of disbelief implied by the contrast between "lies" and "truth" but also because of a difference in affective tone that distinguishes this diatribe from ordinary anticlerical and blasphemous tales, jokes, and curses. The impassioned and bitter irony of the man's remarks are different from the usual disdainful and sardonic mockery of popular anticlericalism but are virtually identical in feeling and forcefulness to the expressions of moral outrage that were at the heart of working-class ideological representations of the gentry as false, immoral, and hypocritical patrons of working-class families. Compare this man's statement to the following response of an elderly working-class man when he was asked about the role of the rich as patrons of the community and benevolent "friends" of the poor in the period before the Civil War:

> *Patrón? Patrón* is only a word. *Sí, patrón. No, patrón.* It meant nothing. . . . Some friends! Those who worked you to death and paid

> nothing. Sons of whores! We were their slaves, I tell you. They had us working in their houses, and they did nothing and paid us nothing. They were thieves—they robbed us of life.

The convergence of the anticlerical, the irreligious, and the hypermoralistic elements of working-class culture into a single current of cultural resistance was the key characteristic of revolutionary anticlericalism in Aracena. By means of an inversion of religious rhetoric, working-class radicals were able to link the general evils of the regnant social and cultural order of class domination to townspeople's sense that the local gentry had betrayed their immediate obligations as members of an intimate face-to-face moral community and had failed to provide for the material well-being and preserve the honor and dignity of working-class individuals and families. For this reason, the most striking anticlerical statements of working-class radicals reinterpret the significance of core religious images such as that of the figure of Christ in ways which suggest that the indifference and failures of the divine are of the same moral order as the venality, pride, and hypocrisy of the gentry and their priestly allies in their day-to-day relations with the poor.

This critical aspect of revolutionary anticlericalism is exemplified by the ironic rejoinder that one older radical offered to a passage from a catechism favored by Aracena's elite in the years before the Civil War. The passage declared, "The patrón will treat his workers like sons of God, and the workers will serve the patrón as if they served God" (*El Distrito* 1913a). To this injunction, the man responded, "Yes, clearly we were like sons of God to them; they saw us dying and did not save us." For this man, the figure of the crucified Son signified the extreme of human suffering imposed upon the poor by God and humankind alike, rather than signifying an act of redemptive sacrifice. In a similar vein, another man, when asked why he and his anticlerical friends refused to take communion, gave this response: "*Qué barbaridad!* [How barbarous! How ridiculous!] This body of Christ thing . . . the little bits of wine and bread of the priest are not food for a man. From God you receive even less than from the rich, and God wants everything. You know what happened to His son."

Through such blasphemous inversions of orthodox doctrine, religious discourse was used to put forth a moral indictment that was not only shaped by but also molded class antagonisms by recasting them in terms of the domestic values of working-class individuals and families. Revolutionary anticlericalism stripped away the supernatural and otherworldly aspects of religious culture in order to drive home the contradiction between legitimating ideals of beneficent patronage and the perceived reality of antagonistic social relations that denied working-class people minimal dignity. By combining the various strains of working-class resistance to sociopolitical and cultural domination, it challenged fundamental notions of patronage (whether human or divine), insisted on the unacceptability of continuing human suffering, and reasserted the moral claims to power that notions of spiritual hierarchy, authority, and doctrinal orthodoxy had served to deny the poor.

Even so, by August 10, 1936, it was clear to most people that the popular forces in Aracena were unlikely to withstand the onslaught of the approaching Nationalist troops.[10] In this context, the attack on religion was probably not initiated as an attempt to bring about a new age of equality, justice, and freedom but, rather, to achieve a partial but irrevocable break with the past by destroying the physical artifacts and symbolic foundations of local culture. This destruction could not in itself accomplish a revolution, and it is unlikely that the revolutionaries thought that it would. But by destroying or permanently defacing the principal monuments of a hegemonic cultural formation, the revolutionaries made a declaration that the dominant order was not eternal, inevitable, or invincible. What those who burned the churches and popular images hoped to achieve was not a new religion or even, in the short run, a new political regime; it was a reparto of meanings that would outlast the temporary and doomed reparto of land and seizure of political power by the revolutionary forces of the town and sierra and open a road to a better future.

The key to understanding the nature of this reparto of meanings lies in appreciating the difficulty of what the church burners were trying to accomplish. For the revolutionary anticlericals to realize in full the possibilities involved in a transvaluation of cultural and ideological elements was no easy matter. To achieve a rupture with the past at a moment of revolutionary crisis pitted them not only against the gentry but also against many culturally conservative members of other classes who were sympathetic to the popular political cause. This indirect struggle with their allies seemed necessary because, in addition to undermining the explicit ideology of Catholic mutualism, the church burners were attempting to break the religious attachments of some of their supporters while at the same time reviving the townspeople's desire for social justice. Moreover, destroying the images of popular devotion probably also went against some of the revolutionaries' own deeply entrenched predispositions: the force of saint worship and indeed of the whole cultural formation of paternalist patronage had profoundly penetrated and become embedded in daily life, while the images of personhood, family, and community that derived from the Ancient Regime had continued to shape fundamental social relations such as those between parents and children and those between men and women. In these circumstances, the iconoclastic act of burning the images of the saints marked the momentary collapse of religious culture and not simply the official church as a vehicle of hegemonic domination in Aracena. The long process of political and ideological class polarization that reached a crisis point in the summer of 1936 had brought to the fore residual and radically egalitarian aspects of popular anticlericalism and had enabled the revolutionaries to transform religion into an affair of honor.

Church burning, sociopolitical movements, and the dialectics of modernity and tradition

Although what occurred in Aracena on August 10, 1936, appears to have been consistent with events in other towns of the sierra and Huelva province, revolutionary anticlericalism elsewhere in Spain and particularly in large cities and those rural areas less immediately threatened by Nationalist forces probably had a somewhat different overall dynamic. No doubt the manner of articulation and the character of the practical, conjunctural, and structural forces involved in local anticlerical actions varied significantly from place to place, and these variations must be examined more systematically before a fully convincing account of Spanish anticlericalism can be constructed.

Thus far, however, neither the proponents of the millenarian thesis, who regard revolutionary anticlericalism as the manifestation of an archaic political and cultural mentality, nor their critics, who stress the instrumental political logic of an attack on a key ideological institution, have paid sufficient attention to the complex local political and cultural dynamics of church burning. Indeed, their general approaches prepare them poorly for the task. Although their arguments are poles apart, representatives of both approaches share the twin faults of overdrawing the distinction between symbolic and pragmatic action and of overlooking the range of intentions and understandings evident among revolutionary anticlericals. As a result, their analyses are weakened by a common tendency to place the intentions of the anticlerical group into narrow and opposed conceptual straitjackets despite their often compelling accounts and interpretations of many aspects of the culture and politics of the period.

Ultimately, however, the analysts' tendency to underanalyze critical aspects of the cultural and political dynamics of revolutionary anticlericalism and to oversimplify the motivational and affective structure of the phenomenon is probably best understood as an unintended consequence of their inclination to represent revolutionary anticlericalism in terms of a reductive logic of tradition versus modernity. Succumbing to the desire to discover the universal lesson in the particular case, the instrumentalist critics of the millenarian theory largely represent the revolutionaries as the foes of tradition, superstition, and mystification and identify them with the forward historical march of secular reason; thus, they emphasize the revolutionaries' efficient organization and pragmatic goals. In contrast, the proponents of millenarian theory are inclined to describe matters in more transhistorical terms and romantic tropes, by associating Spanish anticlericalism not only with the Protestant Reformation but also with a wide variety of other iconoclastic social movements that have arisen at different times and in different places. Within this comparative framework, they see the actions of the anticlericals as a tradition-bound response to an experience of existential alienation engendered by out-of-control social forces and as an attempt to overcome a crisis of meaning by creating a new religious dispensation; thus, the millenarian theorists emphasize the emotionally charged and ritualized forms of symbolic action.

It seems mistaken, however, to view revolutionary anticlericalism as primarily either a tradition-bound response to modernity or a highly rationalized modernist critique of traditional ideologies and institutions. The concrete historical relations of the discourses and practices of "tradition" and "modernity" cannot be adequately represented in terms of simple relations of exclusion, substitution, or alteration. This is so because neither nation-states nor capitalist economies are adequately self-legitimated by the pragmatic rationalities essential to their operation. (Nor, for that matter, are they effectively delegitimated solely by appeals to tradition-based ideals and values.) Rather, as Habermas observed some time ago, classic forms of "bourgeois culture" are "dependent on motivationally effective supplementation by traditional world-views" and feed "parasitically on the remains of tradition" (1975:76–77). Largely for this reason, "modernists can never be done with the past" (Berman 1988:346; see also Baudrillard 1987).

This was clearly the case with the ideology of Catholic mutualism and other aspects of gentry culture in Aracena in the period from 1900 to 1936. Aracena's gentry consistently sought to evade urgent working-class demands for radical social reform by defining the contemporary historical moment either in terms of a conservative project of preserving and protecting a sociomoral and spiritual hierarchy of distinction based on patronage or in terms of a liberal project of promoting education and economic development in order to ameliorate social conditions and gradually move toward a new social order of justice, prosperity, and social harmony beyond the horizon. Thus, the members of the gentry attempted to legitimate sociopolitical immobility by representing themselves as cultural mediators of the forces of tradition and modernity who were capable of acting both as the defenders of the spiritual legacy of the past and as the prophets of freedom and progress.

The unacknowledged irony involved in this effort to preserve the present social order by rushing to embrace particular versions of both the past and the future was clearly not lost on Aracena's working-class radicals. Indeed, church burning was in large measure a counter-hegemonic strategy devised in response to this dominant ideological and cultural formation. The radicals aimed to define the present in terms different from those of their adversaries. For them, the present represented the opportunity to struggle for the establishment of a new sociopolitical regime based on leftist ideologies of equality and social justice and the opportunity to fight for the restoration of the integrity, autonomy, and, above all, the honor of ordinary people.

One of the key ways in which they engaged in this struggle was by attacking the churches and images of popular devotion. Like their class adversaries, the church burners were neither pragmatic modernists nor enthusiastic traditionalists. Rather, they used cultural elements embedded in the past in an effort to clarify the specific character of the present. Both the millenarian theorists and their critics miss this key aspect of anticlericalism because they devote little attention to analyzing the relationship between the anticlericals' actions and the anticlericals' firm grasp of the dominant ideologies whose representational strategies they strove almost point by point to overcome.

It is attention to this relationship that can lead us beyond the limited search for fellow travelers of the church burners among religious fanatics of differing ages and cultures or, alternatively, among pragmatic political radicals. With respect to actions and understandings of dominant ideologies, it might be promising, for example, to compare the church burners with some of the avatars of the antibourgeois avant-garde subcultures of high modernism. After all, dadaists and surrealists such as George Grosz, Luis Bunuel, and Louis Aragon also envisioned the process of creating new forms of expression and ways of life as inextricably enmeshed with the willful and violent breakdown and reconstruction of dominant conventions and genres (see Morris 1972; Motherwell 1981). Indeed, with respect to religious sentiments, Federico García Lorca, who in 1936 was to meet the same violent death as many of the church burners of Aracena (see Maddox 1986, 1993), seems virtually to have been speaking for them when he wrote the following as a novice poet: "This is the kingdom of sorrow / And the God of Love they paint for us / Does not exist. / We guess the impossibility of God, / God the eternally mute, / God the unfeeling, the uncouth, / The abyss. / The God who Christ says lives / In Heaven is unjust."[11]

In contrast to this sort of immediate, highly tuned, and engaged response to cultural and social crisis, the analyses advanced by the proponents of millenarian and instrumentalist approaches to revolutionary anticlericalism tend—in spite of the sympathies of their authors for the plight of the exploited and oppressed—to reproduce as much as to expose the strategies of legitimation that are involved in representations of tradition and modernity and are vital to the maintenance of contemporary politicoeconomic formations. In this respect, their work can be criticized on many of the same grounds as that of contemporary commentators on sociopolitical movements in Eastern Europe and the former Soviet Union. Most of what currently appears in leading newspapers and political journals describes the complex cultural and political processes occurring in Eastern Europe and elsewhere in bipolar cultural terms. On the one hand, there are the dangers of the return of the repressed and the eruption of religious, ethnic, and nationalist hatreds in forms reminiscent of millenarian movements. On the other hand, we are encouraged to hope that such disasters can be avoided if only the rule of reason can be revitalized through efficient free market mechanisms, technobureaucratic reforms of state structures, and the reorganization of civil society by means of rationalized organizations such as political parties.[12]

In these circumstances, one of the most critical tasks for historical ethnographers is to point out how such accounts confound understanding. In complex state societies, the crucial (though usually unacknowledged) relation of whatever counts as tradition to whatever counts as modernity—or postmodernity, for that matter—is ironic and paradoxical. Discourses and images that various cultural authorities formally constitute as opposed and autonomous generally turn out to be something very different—that is, the mutually conditioning and strategically implicated means of struggling for ascendancy or regulating what Michel Foucault called "the hazardous play of dominations" (1984:83). A full understanding of this play of dominations requires that new analytic perspectives be developed to clarify how hegemonic processes of differing scope, intensity, and duration produce a range of effects of power and meaning. A principal virtue of developing such perspectives is that they will undermine the representation of complex acts and motives as merely the products of the elementary emotions or of the alleged calculations of simple historical subjects.

Acknowledgments

I am grateful to George Collier, Jane Collier, Sharon Keller Maddox, Peter Kivisto, Roger Rouse, the participants in seminars of the departments of anthropology of the University of Chicago and the University of Iowa, and the reviewers and editors of *American Ethnologist* for comments on earlier versions of this article. Research in Spain was supported by grants from the Commission for Educational Exchange between the United States of America and Spain, the Social Science Research Council and the American Council of Learned Societies, and the National Science Foundation (grant no. BNS 81-07146). Any opinions, findings, and conclusions or recommendations expressed in this publication are, of course, my own and do not necessarily reflect the views of the agencies acknowledged above.

Notes

1 Although the people who described the events of August 10, 1936, to me disagreed about the particular order in which the numerous churches of Aracena were sacked and burned, their accounts were otherwise remarkably consistent with one another and were generally supported by other townspeople who had heard about the events at second hand. For reasons of confidentiality, I cannot offer more details about the informants.

2 See also the well-balanced accounts of radical anticlericalism by Cilmore (1986, 1989) and Sánchez (1987), who suggest a number of useful lines of inquiry.

3 From Foucault (1984) to Scott (1985), the literature on relations of domination and resistance has become vast and varied. Nevertheless, in my own and many other people's judgment, the Gramscian concepts of hegemony and hegemonic processes remain central to understanding such relations and to the overall development of a historical anthropology of culture. However, many problems concerning hegemonic processes still need to be addressed. Recently, Ortner (1989) and Comaroff and Comaroff (1991) have proposed what appear to be sharply contrasting approaches. In her account of Sherpa Buddhism, Ortner (1989: 195–197) defines hegemony primarily in terms of ideological legitimation and the symbolic mediation of structural contradictions. But in their account of Tswana colonial history, Comaroff and Comaroff (1991:19–32) distinguish hegemony from ideology and primarily identify hegemony with taken-for-granted, homogenizing, naturalizing, and muted practices. While there is much to be learned from either perspective, some further efforts at synthesis seem in order. An approach to this task, which may avoid some of the pitfalls of abstract theoretical debate, is to find better ways to delineate how complex sociopolitical and cultural processes shape particular events and generate a range of legitimizing, polarizing, muting, and other effects for different people. In attempting to do this for the events of August 10 in Aracena, I have found the threefold framework for historical analysis (structure, conjuncture, event) offered by Sahlins (1981, 1985) to be most helpful because it enables me to sort out hegemonic processes and effects of differing scope, intensity, and duration.

4 The ideological tags of "fanatics" and "hordes" were imposed by the Franco regime, but the (usually qualified or ironic) use of these terms by many townspeople in Aracena in the early 1980s reflected a widespread and real contemporary perplexity concerning the church burners of 1936. Although most people had little desire to dredge up old animosities and personal grudges, they were nevertheless willing and quite able to defend their own political actions or those of family members and of others on the left who resisted the Nationalist uprising in 1936. The destruction of the churches and their artistic legacy, however, was a different matter. While a small group of key informants recalled the circumstantial factors and the emotional atmosphere of hatred and anxiety that made burning the churches seem justifiable and appropriate to the revolutionaries of 1936, the attitude of many of the elderly informants was one of distanced and somewhat puzzled sympathy for the church burners, mixed with genuine regret for the destruction of the town's cultural heritage. These contemporary perplexities among the older generation and the considerable degree of indifference among younger people with respect to the events of the 1930s inevitably raise the question of the ultimate efficacy or futility of revolutionary anticlericalism as a counterhegemonic strategy. Although this problem is beyond the scope of my article, it is worth noting that, especially during the most repressive years of the post-Civil War period, the ruins of the churches seemed to have served as a symbol of hope for many working-class people in spite of the imposition of the ideologies of National Catholicism. These days, however, the destruction of the churches is viewed by most townspeople as an indication of how different the present is from the past. While anticlericalism is not a primary focus of George Collier's (1987) study of revolutionaries, his work has provided valuable insights on the vicissitudes of cultural memory and the impact of the 1936 struggles on the lives of rural Andalusians in the decades following the Civil War. For a historically sensitive account of anticlericalism in contemporary Spain, see Behar 1990.

5 For a more detailed narrative account of the party politics and ideological dynamics and events surrounding the burning of the churches in Aracena, see Maddox 1986 and 1993.

6 For general accounts of the role of the church and anticlericalism in Spanish life and especially in the constitutional and party politics of the liberal regimes of the 19th and early 20th centuries, see Lannon 1987 and Ullman 1968 and 1983.

7 Hobsbawm (1965) described anticlerical and popular attitudes and even insurrections as "prepolitical" in character. I would substitute the term "popular" for the term "prepolitical." "Prepolitical" is misleading because some degree of politicization was often present in the popular form as well as the revolutionary form of anticlericalism, although the degree of politicization of popular anticlericalism waxed and waned over time and its manifestations varied, ranging from widespread refusal to attend mass to popular participation in debates, riots, or insurrections. Nevertheless, popular anticlericalism, even when it took the form of violent insurrection, was aimed primarily at reforming the practices of the church and clergy or promoting political and ideological agendas such as eliminating the influence of the church over state-funded schools. In contrast, revolutionary anticlericalism included such goals but was also intended to effect a radical transformation of virtually all aspects of culture. For a long-range historical account of the various strains of anticlericalism in Spain, see Caro Baroja 1980. For early and more recent ethnographic discussions of popular anticlericalism in rural Iberian towns and villages, see Lison-Tolosana 1983, Pitt-Rivers 1961, and Riegelhaupt 1973 and 1984.

8 Brandes (1980) and Cilmore (1986, 1989) have discussed Andalusian misogyny, machismo, and notions of homosexuality at considerable length and analyzed their relation to anticlericalism, politics, and other matters. They and others have argued that ribald tales and anecdotes of priestly seduction of other men's wives reflect deep-seated anxieties and fears concerning the lack of autonomy or the tenuous control of working-class men over their wives and daughters, their households, and their political and economic lives.

9 For another perspective on the relation of blasphemy to the politics of resistance in the Mediterranean, see Herzfeld 1984. For an account of how religious symbols and experiences could unite Spanish conservative forces during the Civil War period, see Christian 1987.

10 In fact, less than a week after the churches were burned, the town was conquered by a column of Franco's legionnaires. In the next few months, dozens, perhaps hundreds, of revolutionaries and moderate supporters of the Second Republic in Aracena and the sierra were executed. In the course of the Civil War, the gentry ideology of Catholic mutualism was stripped of its liberal elements and transformed into the reactionary ideology of National Catholicism.

11 These lines, translated by Ian Gibson, are from one of Lorca's first poems. For the Spanish text, see Gibson 1989:65.

12 An example of this sort of commentary culled almost randomly from the news is John Burns's "A Chance to Say Yes or No to Fresh Disaster," which appeared in the *New York Times*. In this editorial on the possibilities for sustaining the Yugoslav peace process, Burns (1992:1) begins by declaring that "atavistic passions have too frequently triumphed over sober calculations of self-interest" and that "the population of the six Yugoslav republics has been ruined in an explosion of bitterness and anger that has defied every standard of humanity, reason, and common sense." He goes on to discuss the prospects for the success of the United Nations in its role as a peacekeeper and mediator between contending

nationalities. Tragic and atrocious as the events in the former Yugoslavia are, Burns's invocation of atavistic passion versus pragmatic reason illuminates almost nothing about either the past of the region or how the people embroiled in the present conflict understand their situation. It does, however, convey the message that "they" would be better off if they only tried harder to be more like "us."

References cited

Baudrillard, Jean
1987 Modernity. Canadian Journal of Political and Social Theory 11: 63–72.

Behar, Ruth
1990 The Struggle for the Church: Popular Anticlericalism and Religiosity in Post-Franco Spain. *In* Religious Orthodoxy and Popular Faith in European Society. Ellen Badone, ed. Pp. 76–112. Princeton: Princeton University Press.

Berman, Marshall
1988 All That Is Solid Melts into Air: The Experience of Modernity. New York: Penguin Books.

Brandes, Stanley
1980 Metaphors of Masculinity: Sex and Status in Andalusian Folklore. Philadelphia: University of Pennsylvania Press.

Brenan, Gerald
1960 The Spanish Labyrinth: An Account of the Social and Political Background of the Spanish Civil War. Cambridge, MA: Cambridge University Press.

Burns, John F.
1992 A Chance to Say Yes or No to Fresh Disaster. New York Times, March 8: Week in Review Section, 1–2.

Caro Baroja, Julio
1980 Introducción a una historia contemporanea del anticlericalismo español. (Introduction to a Contemporary History of Spanish Anticlericalism.) Madrid: Istmo.

Christian, William
1987 Tapping and Defining New Power: The First Months of Visions at Ezquiroga, July 1931. American Ethnologist 14:140–166.

Collier, George A.
1987 Socialists of Rural Andalusia: Unacknowledged Revolutionaries of the Second Republic. Stanford, CA: Stanford University Press.

Comaroff, Jean, and John Comaroff
1991 Of Revelation and Revolution: Christianity, Colonialism, and Consciousness in South Africa, 1. Chicago: University of Chicago Press.

Corbin, John
1986 Insurrections in Spain: Casas Viejas 1933 and Madrid 1981. *In* The Anthropology of Violence. David Riches, ed. Pp. 28–49. Oxford: Basil Blackwell.

Díaz del Moral, Juan
1984[1928] Historia de las agitaciones campesinas andaluzas: Córdoba. (History of the Andalusian Rural Agitations: Córdoba.) Madrid: Alianza Editorial.

El Distrito. Aracena, Spain: La Liga para el Fomento de los Intereses Morales y Materiales de Aracena y su Distrito. (The League for the Fomentation of the Moral and Material Interests of Aracena and Its District.)
1912 El Distrito, January 6.
1913a El Distrito, January 15.
1913b El Distrito, February 15.
1913c El Distrito, August 25.
1914 El Distrito, May 11.

Foucault, Michel
1984 Nietzsche, Genealogy, History. *In* The Foucault Reader. Paul Rabinow, ed. Pp. 76–100. New York: Pantheon Books.

Gibson, Ian
1989 Federico García Lorca: A Life. New York: Pantheon Books.

Gilmore, David
1986 Andalusian Anti-Clericalism: An Eroticized Rural Protest. Anthropology 3:31–43.
1989 The Anticlericalism of Andalusian Rural Proletarians. *In* La religiosidad popular, 1. Carlos Alvarez Santaló, María Jesús Buxó i Rey, and Salvador Rodríguez Becerra, eds. Pp. 478–498. Barcelona: Anthropos.

Habermas, Jurgen
1975 Legitimation Crisis. Thomas McCarthy, trans. Boston: Beacon Press.

Hall, Stuart
1986 On Postmodernism and Articulation: An Interview with Stuart Hall. Journal of Communications Inquiry 10:45–60.
1988 The Toad in the Garden: Thatcherism among the Theorists. *In* Marxism and the Interpretation of Culture. Lawrence Grossberg and Cary Nelson, eds. Pp. 35–74. Urbana: University of Illinois Press.

Herzfeld, Michael
1984 The Significance of the Insignificant: Blasphemy as Ideology. Man 19:653–664.

Hobsbawm, Eric
1965 Primitive Rebels: Studies in Archaic Forms of Social Movements in the Nineteenth and Twentieth Century. New York: Norton.

Kaplan, Temma
1977 Anarchists of Andalusia, 1868–1903. Princeton: Princeton University Press.

Lannon, Frances
1987 Privilege, Persecution, and Prophecy: The Catholic Church in Spain, 1875–1975. Oxford: Clarendon.

Lincoln, Bruce
1985 Revolutionary Exhumations in Spain, July 1936. Comparative Studies in Society and History 2:241–260.

Lison-Tolosana, Carmelo
1983 Belmonte de los Caballeros: Anthropology and History in an Aragonese Community. Princeton: Princeton University Press.

Maddox, Richard
1986 Religion, Honor, and Patronage: A Study of Culture and Power in an Andalusian Town. Ph.D. dissertation, Stanford University, University Microfilms.

1993 El Castillo: The Politics of Tradition in an Andalusian Town. Urbana: University of Illinois Press.

Mádoz, Pascual, ed.

1845–50 Diccionario geográfico-estadístico-histórico de España y sus posesiones de ultramar. (Geographical-Statistical-Historical Dictionary of Spain and Its Overseas Possessions.) 16 vols. Madrid.

Maravall, José Antonio

1986 Culture of the Baroque: Analysis of a Historical Structure. Terry Cochran, trans. Minneapolis: University of Minnesota Press.

Mintz, Jerome R.

1982 The Anarchists of Casas Viejas. Chicago: University of Chicago Press.

Mitchell, Timothy

1988 Violence and Piety in Spanish Folklore. Philadelphia: University of Pennsylvania Press.

Morris, C. B.

1972 Surrealism and Spain, 1920–1936. Cambridge: Cambridge University Press.

Motherwell, Robert, ed.

1981 The Dada Painters and Poets: An Anthology. Boston: Hall.

Ordóñez Márquez, Juan

1968 La apostasía de las masas y la persecución religiosa en la provincia de Huelva, 1931–1936. (The Apostasy of the Masses and the Religious Persecution in the Province of Huelva, 1931–1936.) Madrid: Consejo Superior de Investigaciones Científicas.

Ortner, Sherry

1989 High Religion: A Cultural and Political History of Sherpa Buddhism. Princeton: Princeton University Press.

Payne, Stanley C.

1984 Spanish Catholicism: An Historical Overview. Madison: University of Wisconsin Press.

Pitt-Rivers, Julian A.

1961 The People of the Sierra. Chicago: University of Chicago Press.

Riegelhaupt, Joyce

1973 Festas and Padres: The Organization of Religious Action in a Portuguese Parish. American Anthropologist 75:835–852.

1984 Popular Anticlericalism and Religiosity in Pre-1974 Portugal. *In* Religion, Power, and Protest in Local Communities: The Northern Shore of the Mediterranean. Eric R. Wolf, ed. Pp. 93–114. Berlin: Mouton.

Sahlins, Marshall

1981 Historical Metaphors and Mythical Realities: Structure in the Early History of the Sandwich Islands Kingdom. Ann Arbor: University of Michigan Press.

1985 Islands of History. Chicago: University of Chicago Press.

Sánchez, José María

1987 The Spanish Civil War as a Religious Tragedy. Notre Dame, IN: University of Notre Dame Press.

Scott, James

1985 Weapons of the Weak: Everyday Forms of Peasant Resistance. New Haven, CT: Yale University Press.

Ullman, Joan Connelly
1968 The Tragic Week: A Study of Anticlericalism in Spain, 1875–1912. Cambridge, MA: Harvard University Press.
1983 The Warp and Woof of Parliamentary Politics in Spain, 1808–1939: Anticlericalism versus "Neo-Catholicism." European Studies Review 13:145–176.

51

ORTHODOX MISSION IN TROPICAL AFRICA

Stephen Hayes

Source: *Missionalia*, 24 (1996), 383–98.

Most histories of Christian mission in Africa, even those that are ostensibly ecumenical or pan-Christian, make little or no mention of Orthodox Church missions in Africa.[1]

There are several possible reasons for this, among them a bias on the part of many mission historians in favour of missions that were established before 1950 (Fiedler 1995:92). Most, though not all, Orthodox missions in tropical Africa began after that date. Another possible reason is that even those Orthodox missions that began before 1950 were not regarded as "mainstream" by the established Roman Catholic and Protestant missions, because they were identified with African independent church movements, which at that time were regarded by the Western churches as a problem for mission rather than a form of mission. The identification of Orthodoxy with the struggle against colonialism was also an embarrassment at that time. One Kenyan, writing of such attitudes, referred to "those who in their calculated ignorance misinterpret African-Christian-Orthodoxy as 'paganism' " (Lemopoulos 1993:123).

Much of what has been published in English has been fragmentary, dealing with a particular place or period. Orthodox mission in tropical Africa has had its ups and downs, and the situation has changed rapidly, so that descriptions of what was happening at times in the past may not apply today. Orthodox mission today is characterised by a huge variety. Just about every mission method ever found in any part of the world, at any time in Christian history, can be found here. The purpose of this article, therefore, is to try to give a broad survey of Orthodox mission in this part of the world. It is primarily historical and descriptive, rather than an analysis of the theology of mission. Obviously such a survey must be lacking in detail, but it should at least provide the context for interpreting other more specialised studies.

The Orthodox Church in Africa falls under the jurisdiction of the Pope and Patriarch of Alexandria and All Africa, and its history goes back to the first century. The tradition of the patriarchate is that it was established by St Mark in AD 62. In the first few centuries it was confined to North Eastern Africa. The North Western part was under the jurisdiction of the Pope of Rome. At first Christianity had only a rather precarious toe-hold on the African continent, but towards the end of the second century it became indigenous, and spread rapidly among the native Egyptian population (rather than the Graeco-Roman ruling class). The third and fourth centuries were marked by the ascendancy of Alexandrian Christianity. The churches of Alexandria, Antioch and Rome were the three most influential churches. In the fourth century Jerusalem and Constantinople were also recognised as patriarchates, and Constantinople, the new imperial capital, was given precedence over Alexandria. This led to a certain amount of rivalry, which tended to exacerbate some of the theological disputes in the following centuries.

It was in this period that the Patriarchate of Alexandria was the originator of two developments that influenced the entire Christian world for centuries to come. The first was the development of monasticism, which soon spread to other places, and became the main instrument of mission for over a thousand years. The second was the Arian controversy, which led to the formulation of the "Nicene Creed", which, with some variations, has been accepted as the basic statement of faith of Christians in most parts of the world.

In the fifth century, following the Council of Chalcedon, there was a split in the Church of Alexandria, and since then there have been two rival popes in Alexandria, the Coptic and the Byzantine (see Isichei 1995:29). The Byzantine Patriarchate of Alexandria remained in communion with the other patriarchates of Rome, Constantinople and Antioch, while the Coptic patriarchate did not. The schism affected mission. Ethiopia, which had been evangelised in the fourth century, was affiliated with the Coptic Patriarchate, while two rival missions were sent to Nubia. The Arab conquest of Egypt in the seventh century put an end to any further mission efforts for centuries to come. Both the Byzantine and Coptic Patriarchates were engaged in a struggle for survival. In this article I deal mainly with the Byzantine patriarchate.

Below the Tropic of Cancer, Christian influence only began to be felt when Western Christians (who were by then separated from the Orthodox, and divided among themselves into Roman Catholic and Protestant groups), began sailing round the sea coasts of Africa. Their main interest was Asian trade, and Africa remained incidental to their concerns until the plantation economy of the Americas made the trans-Atlantic trade in African slaves lucrative. Christian missions from those countries gradually fostered an aversion to the slave trade, and sought to introduce "legitimate commerce", but national rivalries led to the "scramble for Africa" and the parcelling out of most of sub-Saharan Africa among the European powers by the end of the nineteenth century.

Immigrant Greek communities

Among those from Europe who settled in Africa were traders from Orthodox countries, mainly from Greece. The churches in their countries of origin initially showed little interest in their emigrant flock. The immigrant communities, however, formed themselves into "koinotites" (communities), which sought to meet the needs of the immigrants, cultural, educational, recreational and religious. Clergy were sent to minister to these communities, initially by the Ecumenical Patriarchate in Constantinople, which was responsible for the Orthodox Christians who were beyond any other Orthodox jurisdiction. Eventually, however, all such communities in Africa were transferred to the jurisdiction of the Patriarchate of Alexandria.

Southern Africa

In 1908 such a priest, Father Nicodemus Sarikas, was sent to the community in Johannesburg, in the recently-conquered British colony of the Transvaal. Fr Nicodemus, however, was also interested in mission beyond the confines of the Greek community, and in this his views were at variance with those of the community, which expected him to function purely as a chaplain to the immigrants. After a few years, Fr Nicodemus left, and settled in what is now Tanzania.

A few years earlier another development took place in the Johannesburg area. In 1892 a group of black Methodists, unhappy with racism in the Methodist Church, broke away to form the Ethiopian Church. The Ethiopian Church later split into several groups, some of which were interested in episcopacy, and formed links with the African Methodist Episcopal Church of the USA, or with the (Anglican) Church of the Province of South Africa. In the 1920s one of the clergy of the Ethiopian Church, Daniel William Alexander, made contact with the African Orthodox Church, which had recently been formed in the USA, and eventually was ordained a bishop of that church.

The African Orthodox Church (AOC) was the offspring of the Pan African movement, one of the leading figures of which was Marcus Garvey, the founder of the Universal Negro Improvement Association (UNIA). Some of the clergy associated with the movement conceived the idea of forming a single black church, and one of the main proponents of this view was an Anglican priest, George Macguire, who sought affiliation with the Orthodox Church as a black ethnic jurisdiction (Platt 1989:474ff). He approached the Russian Orthodox bishop in the USA, but at that time, immediately after the Bolshevik Revolution in Russia, the Orthodox Church in

America was in a difficult position. The Russian bishop was also concerned about the ethnic exclusiveness that Macguire seemed to want. George Macguire was eventually ordained bishop by Rene Joseph Vilatte, an *episcopus vagans* who had himself been consecrated in dubious circumstances by a Syrian Jacobite bishop in India (Anson 1964:105ff). In 1935 the Syrian Jacobite Patriarchate of Antioch declared his episcopal orders null and void.

Daniel William Alexander was nevertheless consecrated bishop by Patriarch Macguire of the African Orthodox Church, and returned to South Africa, and established the African Orthodox Church among his followers there. The African Orthodox Church was one of the few African independent churches to receive government recognition. Recognition gave certain advantages, one of the chief of which was the legal authority to buy wine for communion (before 1962 blacks in South Africa were prohibited from buying "white" liquor). This was one factor that led other groups, such as some from the Ethiopian Catholic Church in Zion, to join the African Orthodox Church.[2] In early 1993 some of the bishops and clergy of the African Orthodox Church in southern Africa were received into membership of the Coptic Patriarchate of Alexandria, and became known as the African Coptic Orthodox Church.[3] Not all the members or clergy of the AOC joined the Coptic Church, however.

Uganda and Kenya

In the early 1930s Bishop Alexander travelled to Uganda at the invitation of Reuben Sseseya Mukasa (later known as Fr Reuben Spartas, and in 1973 he was consecrated as Bishop Christopherous of Nilopolis) and Obadiah Bassajjikitalo, two former Anglicans whose reading had led them to seek to join the Orthodox Church. Apparently they had discovered the address of Patriarch Macguire in an American publication, and written to him, and he in turn had asked Bishop Alexander to visit them. Alexander spent nine months in Uganda, from October 1931 to July 1932 teaching and baptising and ordained Mukasa and Bassajjikitalo before returning to South Africa (Zoe 1964:377). Among those he baptised was the daughter of a Greek living in Kampala, who said that the service used was unfamiliar. He encouraged the priests to make contact with the Patriarchate of Alexandria, and later in 1932 Fr Nicodemus Sarikas visited Uganda from Tanzania.

Alexander's visit aroused the suspicions of the colonial authorities. Uganda was then a British Protectorate, and Kenya was a colony. The colonial secret police wrote to the South African authorities asking about his background, and informing them of his movements. Alexander returned to South Africa through Kenya, travelling on the train from Kampala to Mombasa. In Mombasa he spoke to a postal clerk, James Beutah, who came from the Central Province, and he asked Alexander what denomination he belonged to, because the Gikuyu (Kikuyu) people did not want to join foreign missions with colonial connections. Beutah informed Jomo Kenyatta, the future president of Kenya who was in then in England, of this meeting, and persuaded Alexander to return to Nairobi.[4]

In 1929 the Kikuyu of the Central Province of Kenya had formed two educational associations in protest against a missionary ban on female circumcision. Education in Kenya at that time was almost entirely under the control of foreign missions. The missions, led by John Arthur of the Church of Scotland Mission (CSM) announced that their African "agents" (who were mainly teachers) must sign a written declaration denouncing circumcision and membership of the Kikuyu Central Association (KCA), a body opposed to colonial rule (Natsoulas 1988:220).[5] This had led to the formation of the Kikuyu Karing'a Educational Association (KKEA), and the Kikuyu Independent Schools Association (KISA), which sought to establish schools outside the control of foreign missions. Up till then all the schools in Kenya had been church schools, and so these bodies, having started schools, looked for a church. Bishop Alexander seemed to offer a solution, and the president of KISA wrote to Alexander, asking him to return to Kenya (Githieya 1992:156). Alexander replied, and also wrote to the Orthodox bishop of Johannesburg, asking for a letter of introduction to the Orthodox priest at Moshi, Tanganyika, and expressing an interest in a merger with the Greek Orthodox Church in South Africa (Githieya 1992:158).

Alexander returned to East Africa in November 1935. He founded a seminary where he trained eight students, seven sponsored by the KISA and one by the KKEA (Githieya 1992:160). He subsequently ordained two priests, Arthur Gatungu Gathuna and Philip Kianda Magu, and two deacons, Daudi Maina Kiragu and Harrison Gacukia Kiranga.

Alexander then returned to South Africa, but was unable to visit East Africa again because of the Second World War, and later the apartheid policy of the South African government. There was a strong perception among Africans in Kenya that the white rulers did not want them to know about Orthodoxy, since it was not associated with the colonial powers.[6]

In the meantime, the contact between the African Orthodox Church in Uganda and the Patriarchate of Alexandria was continuing. The Second World War made non-military travel difficult, but in 1942 Metropolitan Nikolaos of Axum visited East Africa, and wrote a report for the Holy Synod of the Patriarchate of Alexandria about the situation of the African Orthodox Churches there. The report was eventually published in book form.[7]

Fr Reuben Spartas and Fr Obadiah Bassajjikitalo of Uganda came to know of the Orthodox group in Kenya through newspaper reports, and visited Kenya, and encouraged the Kenyans to join the Patriarchate of Alexandria. There were two groups in Kenya. The African Orthodox Church, led by Gathuna, which was associated with the KKEA, and the African Independent Pentecostal Church, associated with the KISA. It was the former that sought linkswith the Patriarchate. They wrote a letter to Pope Meletios of

Alexandria. The patriarch replied positively, but died before anything further could be done. They then wrote again to Pope Christopherous II and applied to be received into the patriarchate as a canonical Orthodox Church.[8] This was officially done in 1946.

Meanwhile in Uganda Fr Nicodemus Sarikas had taken two young men back to Tanganyika to teach them the Orthodox faith, and in 1939 sent them to Pope Christopherous in Alexandria for further study. They were ordained and sent back to Uganda, but one of them died soon after their return. The other, Fr Irenaeus Magimbi, continued teaching for many years (Zoe 1964:379). In 1945 Fr Spartas sent another group of four young men to Egypt. After studying in Greek high schools in Egypt they went on to study theology at the University of Athens. Among them was Theodore Nankyamas, who is now Metropolitan of Uganda (Zoe 1964:379).

In Kenya, after the Second World War, the struggle against colonial rule intensified, and in 1952 the colonial authorities declared a state of emergency as a result of the activities of the Mau Mau guerrillas. The Orthodox Church was banned and its schools and temples were closed by the colonial regime. Many churches were burnt down by the armed forces, and the clergy put in concentration camps (Githieya 1992:181). During that period the Orthodox Church in Kenya was treated by the British colonial regime in the same fashion as the Bolsheviks treated the Russian Orthodox Church. Immediately after the Second World War the Orthodox Church had been growing rapidly, until it was banned in the 1950s. Orthodox Christians regarded the Roman Catholic and Protestant missions as collaborators with the regime, who sought to discredit and belittle the Orthodox Church, and conducted hostile propaganda against it.[9]

A similar struggle against colonial rule in Cyprus was being led by Archbishop Makarios, who in March 1956 was exiled to the Seychelles. In April 1957 he was released, and returned via Kenya, where people were still engaged in the struggle against colonial rule. He celebrated the Divine Liturgy in the Orthodox cathedral in Nairobi, and preached against colonialism (Lemopoulos 1993:122). This was a tremendous encouragement to the leaders of the Kenya independence struggle, many of whom (with the Orthodox clergy) were still in prison at the time. It also caused consternation among the British authorities, and questions were asked in the British parliament about why Archbishop Makarios had been allowed to preach in Kenya.[10]

A close friendship developed between Archbishop Makarios and Jomo Kenyatta, the future president of Kenya. Cyprus became independent in 1960, and Kenya in 1963, and in 1970 Archbishop Makarios, the first President of Cyprus, was invited to Kenya on a state visit by President Kenyatta of Kenya. Archbishop Makarios, as well as being President of Cyprus, was head of the autocephalous Church of Cyprus, and as such had no ecclesiastical jurisdiction in East Africa. But though he was visiting Kenya in his capacity of head of state, he also met church leaders, and visited Orthodox churches in various parts of Kenya.

Archbishop Makarios was struck by the poverty of the church and the people, and wrote to the Patriarchate of Alexandria offering to help. President Kenyatta provided a site for an Orthodox seminary at Riruta, on the outskirts of Nairobi, and Archbishop Makarios raised the money for the buildings. In 1971 he visited Kenya again to lay the foundation stone for the new seminary, though the patriarchate was not in a position to staff it and utilise it until 1982. At Kagira he baptised 5000 people, and at Nyeri he baptised 5000 more. These were both places where Bishop Alexander had visited and taught nearly 40 years previously.[11]

In 1958 the Patriarchate of Alexandria appointed a Metropolitan of Irinoupolis (Dar es Salaam) to care for Orthodox Christians in Tanzania, Kenya and Uganda. Metropolitan Nikolaos moved his headquarters to Kampala, but visited the other countries from there (Zoe 1964:379). In 1960 Archimandrite Chrysostom Papasarantopoulos went to Kampala, where he worked for ten years before moving to Zaire to begin a new mission there (Lemopoulos 1993:67). Through correspondence he also encouraged others to become involved in mission, among them the present Bishop Makarios of Riruta, Kenya. At that time the help of external missionaries in East Africa was greatly needed. After ten years of repression by the British colonial regime and the disingenuous propaganda of the Roman Catholic and Protestant missionaries who supported it, the Orthodox Church was in a parlous state (Zoe 1964:384–384).[12]

Metropolitan Nikolaos was elected Patriarch in 1968, and his successor as Metropolitan was Nicodemus, who ordained several new priests. The seminary site was blessed during his time.

He was succeeded in 1972 by Metropolitan Frumentius, who died in March 1981. There was little development during his time, and in fact there were some reverses, as Bishop George Gathuna (one of the original priests ordained by Daniel Alexander) was defrocked by the Holy Synod of the Patriarchate. He nevertheless continued to act as a bishop, and went into schism. He and his group became affiliated to a schismatic Old Calendrist group in Greece.

The leader of the Old Calendrist group, Cyprian of Fili, then consecrated a Bishop Kigundu, who became the leader when Gathuna died in 1986. Kigundu, however, was himself defrocked by the Old Calendrists when they found that he had secretly married, contrary to the canons. Most of the priests ordained by Gathuna and Kigundu after the schism have returned to the Orthodox Church. Some of them have been reordained.[13]

For several years there was no Metropolitan, but Bishop Anastasios Yannoulatos was appointed acting Metropolitan.[14] Bishop Anastasios is one of the foremost Orthodox missiologists of the twentieth century, and since the 1950s had been encouraging a revival of interest in mission in the Orthodox Church.[15]

The seminary in Nairobi opened in Bishop Anastasios's time, and it began with 19 students. It was originally only for students from East Africa, but in 1995 it began taking students from other African countries as well, and there were 42 students from seven countries – Kenya, Uganda, Tanzania, Cameroun, Nigeria, Zimbabwe and Madagascar. The aim is that the seminary should be a pan-African institution, and should foster a sense of unity in the Patriarchate. This decision has not been without its teething problems, however. The students from outside East Africa have suffered considerably from culture shock, and find the East African food difficult to cope with.

It is often said that Orthodox mission is centripetal rather than centrifugal, with people being attracted to Orthodoxy from the outside, rather than Orthodox churches sending missionaries out (Bosch 1991:207). The growth of Orthodoxy in Kenya and Uganda certainly seems to bear this out. It was largely the result of people in those countries seeking Orthodoxy, rather than Orthodox missionaries from elsewhere seeking them. The Orthodox Church in those countries may truly be said to be an African initiated church.[16]

Tanzania and Zimbabwe

In Tanzania the same pattern may be seen, but with some variations. As I noted earlier, Fr Nicodemus Sarikas went to Tanganyika from Johannesburg, partly because the Greek community in Johannesburg was not interested in mission. In East Africa he played an important role in enabling the African Orthodox Church in Uganda to become canonically Orthodox. There was a fairly large Greek community in the Arusha district of Tanganyika, but he was also engaged in evangelistic outreach among the local people, though with little lasting result, and in north-east Tanganyika the Orthodox community has diminished.

In North Western Tanganyika, however, the Orthodox Church has grown quite rapidly, and there is now a bishop at Bukoba, on the western shore of Lake Victoria. The Orthodox Church there was mainly the result of contact with the Church in Uganda.

In another part of Tanzania, just south of Lake Victoria, a Greek employee in a factory was asked by a fellow employee what his religion was. After hearing about Orthodoxy, this young man, Paul Budala, wrote to the Orthodox Church in Uganda, and a priest from there, Fr Theodore Nankyamas (now Metropolitan of Kampala) visited the places and baptised twenty people he had instructed (Zoe 1964:369).

In Zimbabwe, Orthodoxy was for a long time confined to immigrants from Orthodox countries, mainly those of Greek descent. A young Zimbabwean, Raphael Ganda, went to Greece for an army officer's training course. There he learnt Greek, and also learnt about Orthodoxy through the services at the army bases. On his return to Zimbabwe, he began attending services at the Orthodox cathedral in Harare, and in September 1994 he and his family and some others he had gathered were baptized. Three months later he was sent to the seminary in Nairobi. On completing his course, he plans to be a rural missionary, and is working on the translation of the Divine Liturgy and other services into Shona.[17]

In these instances, the methods of mission appear to resemble those of the pre-Nicene Church. From the fourth century onward, most Christian missionaries were monks, but in East Africa and Zimbabwe, monastic mission has not been much in evidence.

Zaire and Madagascar

In Zaire and Madagascar there has been some evidence of "centrifugal" mission, and also of monastic mission. Archimandrite Chrysostom Papasarantopoulos, after working in Uganda for ten years, moved to Zaire in the early 1970s and began new mission work in the capital (Lemopoulos 1993:67). In Kolwezi another Archimandrite was evangelising, and in 1975 he was joined by a young man, Yannis Aslanidis, who in 1978 returned to Greece to become a monk on Mount Athos. He later returned to Zaire as Fr Cosmas Grigoriatis, and initiated an agricultural development programme, in which he succeeded in adapting and growing various kinds of crops that other agriculturalists had failed to do. The farm is recognised as a model farm for the Shaba province (Lemopoulos 1993:69). Thus a monastery of Mount Athos was sending missionaries to Zaire, though the mission did not result in the founding of a monastery, but rather an agricultural development project.

In Madagascar the Greek community built a church in the capital, Antananarive, in 1953. In 1972, following political disturbances, the priest left, and the church was closed. In 1994, after reading a magazine article about appeals from the Greek community there, Archimandrite Nectarios Kellis went to Madagascar as a missionary priest from Australia. He has actively gone out evangelising, visiting towns and villages in various parts of the country, explaining the Orthodox Christian faith to anyone interested. Already a number of new congregations have been started in this way, and the services of the church are being translated into local languages.[18] The Orthodox Church in Madagascar is under the jurisdiction of the Metropolitan of Zimbabwe, and a local priest, trained by the Archimandrite, has already been ordained, and a student has been sent to the seminary in Nairobi.

West Africa

In West Africa, Orthodox mission shows as much variety as it does in East Africa and Central Africa. In both Ghana and Nigeria there were independent non-canonical Orthodox Churches calling themselves Orthodox. In Ghana there was an African Orthodox Church, which, like those of the same name in East and Southern Africa, traced its origin to the *episcopus vagans* Rene Joseph Vilatte. Unlike them, however, there was no apparent connection to the Garvey movement in the USA. The leader of a Ghanaian group, Bressi-Ando, had travelled to Europe and met Vilatte there.[19]

In the town of Larteh a group that had formerly belonged to the Salvation Army joined the African Orthodox Church, and, after reading Bishop Kallistos Ware's book *The Orthodox Church*, began to have doubts about their canonical status. On hearing that a World Council of Churches meeting was being held in Accra, a group of three young members of the church travelled there to meet some of the Orthodox representatives. As a result of this meeting, one of them, Joseph Kwame Labi, travelled to the USA, where he attended St Vladimir's Orthodox Seminary. He was later ordained and served as a priest in Larteh.

In Nigeria there was a similar group, though with different origins, calling itself the "Greek Orthodox Church". It was started by another *episcopus vagans* from America, Abuna Abraim, who later sent a bishop to ordain priests and deacons. This group was fairly well-established when it made contact with the Patriarchate of Alexandria. Two of its leaders travelled to Alexandria, and the Metropolitan of Accra, Archbishop Irenaeus, travelled to Nigeria and baptised them in 1985. He ordained the leaders of the group.[20]

The Metropolitan of Accra is actually based in Yaounde, Cameroun, and his archdiocese covers 22 countries in West Africa. When Archbishop Irenaeus became Metropolitan in 1976, he began extending Orthodoxy in Cameroun, which had previously been confined to the Greek community. The Greek community was dwindling through emigration, and many were moving to France, where their children were educated. There were people from the Toubouri tribe on the Chad border, many of whom worked in unskilled jobs, such as farm labourers or gardeners, for members of the Greek community. One of these who was interested in Orthodoxy became a catechist, and was ordained in 1981. Initially the Archbishop gave teaching and celebrated the Divine Liturgy in French, with Fr Justin translating, as the Archbishop did not understand Toubouri. Later some students who went to the university and knew French translated the Liturgy into the Toubouri language. The Archbishop would hold garden parties at his home 3–4 times a year, at which catechumens would be baptised. These feasts were customary in the African community on special occasions, and though most members of the Greek community were not directly involved in mission, they helped by providing food for these feasts.

By 1990, when Archbishop Irenaeus was transferred to Carthage, there were 8 parishes among the Toubouri-speaking people along the Chad border, and there is now a priest in Chad itself.[21]

Some general observations and summary

While the Orthodox Church in Africa is fairly static outside the tropics, in tropical Africa there has been significant growth since the Second World War, when the Patriarchate of Alexandria first received the African Orthodox Church in Kenya and Uganda. For the next fifteen years the position of Orthodox Christians was precarious, as churches were closed by the colonial governments in those countries. The establishment of an Archbishopric in 1958, and the independence of Kenya and Uganda relieved these pressures.

Since 1980 there has been rapid growth, not only in Kenya and Uganda, but in Central and West Africa as well. This growth has been characterised by an amazing variety of mission activities and methods. In certain times and places, Christian mission is often noted for particular approaches that are characteristic of that time and place, and are rare or non-existent at other times. In Orthodox mission in tropical Africa, however, one may find just about every mission method and approach that has ever been tried anywhere.

Perhaps the commonest method is the pre-Nicene method of "gossiping the gospel". People hear about the Orthodox Church from friends, family, or colleagues at work, and their interest is aroused. Even this happens in a great many different ways: a Zimbabwean army officer undergoing training in Greece or a factory worker talking to an Orthodox colleague. In Kiboine, in the Rift Valley Province of Kenya, the local chief of the Nandi people encountered Orthodoxy among the Luahs in Western Kenya, who had in turn got it from Uganda. He became a church reader and catechist, and in that area the Orthodox Church is the predominant Christian group.[22] This is also reminiscent in some ways of the conversion of Prince Vladimir of Kiev in the tenth century, whose people followed him in becoming Christian.

Some have joined the Orthodox Church from other denominations. A Luo Anglican school teacher had a problem of pupils being bewitched in the high school where he taught. An Orthodox charismatic evangelist, Charles Omuroka, who is based at Kakamega in Western Kenya, came to the school and prayed for some of the pupils, who were healed.[23] Such methods are usually associated with Pentecostal Protestant missionaries rather than with Orthodox missions.

In Konyabuguru, near Bukoba in Tanzania, a priest, Fr Sosthenes Kiyonga, came to the village in 1974 to teach the Orthodox faith. The people there had to walk 8 kilometres to fetch water. He prayed, and a spring appeared in the village, which has not dried up since then. This caused many, including pagans, Anglicans and Roman Catholics, to join the Orthodox Church.[24] Such methods are usually associated with Celtic missionaries of the seventh century rather than with Africa in the twentieth century.

There have been several instances of people reading about the Orthodox Church in books, and then travelling, often for long distances at great expense, to try to find the church. This was the case with Reuben Spartas and those in Ghana as well. One Lutheran seminarian, having learnt from the study of church history in the seminary that the Orthodox Church was the original one, decided to find the Orthodox Church and join it.[25] This could be described as "literature evangelism", except that most of the literature they read was not written with evangelism in mind.

A Kikuyu family moved to Labere, in a Turkana-speaking area of Kenya. One of the members of the family was attending the Orthodox seminary in Nairobi, and invited the seminary there to teach. A group of local Turkana-speaking people gathered under a tree to hear about the Orthodox faith. There was one blind man who could translate from English to Turkana. When the first group of people was baptised, Swahili and Kikuyu were used in the Liturgy, and the Bible readings were translated orally, as there was no Turkana Bible available then (1982). Since then the services have been translated into Turkana.[26]

This is similar to the "people-group" approach advocated by the Protestant missiologist Donald McGavran, though there is one major difference: the seminary consciously tries to be multinational and intertribal. When students go out on missions or to visit parishes, they go in groups comprising different nationalities or language-groups, and this is pointed out to the congregation. The church is not Luo or Kikuyu or Haya or Turkana or Greek, but is composed of people of all nationalities and cultures. McGavran's idea of planting churches for homogeneous people groups has therefore been modified. While in cases like this, evangelism may be aimed at a specific group, such as Turkana-speaking people, there is considerable emphasis on the idea of the church as an inclusive fellowship. One of the greatest obstacles to Orthodox mission in the last few centuries has been the ethnic insularity of Orthodox Christians themselves, and so a deliberate attempt is being made to counteract that.

The approach least in evidence is the one that has often been most prominent in Orthodox mission elsewhere – monastic mission. There are no Orthodox monasteries in tropical Africa. Yet several monks, male and female, have been sent by their monasteries to work in various parts of Africa and Madagascar.

The "classical" methods used by Roman Catholic and Protestant missionaries are also to be found – educational and medical services. The beginnings of the Orthodox Church in Kenya are tied up with the Kikuyu Karing'a Educational Association, and in many places in Kenya, Tanzania and Uganda, clinics and dispensaries have been built. Community development programmes have also not been lacking. The agricultural development work in Zaire is an example, and in 1988 the Uganda Orthodox Church drew up an ambitious development programme for reconstruction and development after the devastating civil wars and upheavals of the last 25 years. Health services and schools are virtually non-existent, and the church was trying to play its part in rebuilding them. The implementation of the programmes has been patchy. Progress has been made in some places, while in others, nothing has happened. In such projects, assistance has often been given by the Churches of Finland, Greece and Cyprus, and by the Orthodox Christian Mission Center in the USA. Teams of short-term volunteers have travelled from those countries to help the local people in the building and equipping of clinics, dispensaries, schools and churches.

Another aspect of mission, mission as liberation, is, as I have pointed out, closely bound up with the history of the Orthodox Church in Kenya, and the Orthodox Church was seen by many Kenyans (and the British colonial rulers) as the church of *uhuru*.

Thus Orthodox mission in tropical Africa has been initiated by people of all kinds: an archbishop in northern Cameroun, a charismatic evangelist in western Kenya, a priest in north-western Tanzania, and many others, bishops, priests and laity in all kinds of places. Mission has been both centripetal and centrifugal. It has been characterised by a great variety of methods and approaches, but it has largely been the result of African initiative, and it differs from many Western missions in that African clergy have been ordained rapidly, and predominate. Apart from the seminary in Nairobi, and a few cathedrals built by Greeks in some of the big cities, there is little of the elaborate infrastructure, or heavy investment in buildings and equipment, found in many Western mission bodies, that are so visible in cities like Nairobi. A large proportion of students at the seminary are children of peasant farmers, and many of the clergy themselves are peasant farmers, living in the communities where they have always lived.

Notes

1 For example Anderson's (1981) "The church in East Africa 1840–1974" makes only two disconnected references to the Orthodox Church, one of which is a rather patronising aside about "the 'protest cathedral' of Reuben Spartas' African Orthodox Church". References in Hastings (1979:33f) and Isichei (1995:248f) are less patronising, but still not very informative.

2 Information from an interview with the Revd. Johannes Motau, of the African Orthodox Church in Atteridgeville, Pretoria.

3 Personal knowledge, as I myself was present on that occasion.

4 Interview with Fr Eleftherios Ndwaru, Nairobi, 1995-11-16.

5 It is perhaps worth noting that one of the strongest objections to the Mau Mau guerrilla movement on the part of the Western missions and the colonial government was that involved "oathing", and this was regarded as one of the most heinous features of their activities. More than 20 years before, however, the Protestant missions, at the instigation of Arthur, had already established their own oathing ceremonies (see also Githieya 1992:141).

6 Interview with Fr Eleftherios Ndwaru, Nov 1975.

7 Interview with Bishop Makarios of Riruta, November 1995.

8 Interview with Fr Eleftherios Ndwaru, November 1995.

9 Interview, Fr Eleftherios Ndwaru, Nov 1995.

10 Interview, Bishop Makarios of Riruta, Nov. 1995.

11 Interview, Bishop Makarios of Riruta, Nov. 1995.
12 For the support of the Western missionaries for the colonial regime, see e.g. Anderson (1981:130–131). Some of the Western missionaries claimed that the Orthodoxy being preached by Fr Reuben Spartas was simply his own invention.
13 Interview, Bishop Makarios of Riruta, Nov. 1995.
14 He was not a full Metropolitan as he was not from the Patriarchate, but from another autocephalous church, the Church of Greece.
15 Orthodox mission had been largely dormant since 1920, when the Russian Orthodox Church's mission work was drastically curtailed as a result of the Bolshevik Revolution.
16 Githieya (1992:12ff) classifies the AOC as an African Independent Church of the "Ethiopian" type, using Sundkler's categories. Indeed the AOC of Kenya regards itself as an African Independent Church, and uses that terminology (Githieya 1992:270ff; 359; 375). Wentink (1961:3), too, calls them "independent" churches, noting that this term is less derogatory than Sundkler's term "separatist", but nevertheless regards them as "schismatics". In Orthodox ecclesiology, however, "independent" would imply that the Church in those countries was autocephalous, choosing its own head. The metropolitans of Irinoupolis and Kampala, however, are approved by the Holy Synod of the Patriarchate of Alexandria. It would therefore be better to speak of them as "African initiated churches".
17 Interview, Raphael Ganda, November 1995.
18 Interview, Jean Christos Tsakanias, November 1995.
19 Interview with Andrew Anderson, August 1995.
20 Interview, Fr Bede Osuji, Nov 1995.
21 Interview, Archbishop Irenaeus, November 1995.
22 Interview, Thomas Maritim, November 1995.
23 Interview, Fr Charles Otieno, November 1995.
24 Interview, Paul Kadoma, November 1995.
25 Interview, Thomas Shuza, November 1995.
26 Interview, Bishop Makarios of Riruta, November 1995.

Bibliography

Anson, Peter F. 1964. *Bishops at large.* London: Faber & Faber.

Bosch, David J. 1991. *Transforming mission: paradigm shifts in theology of mission.* Maryknoll: Orbis.

Brokensha, David. 1966. *Social change at Larteh, Ghana.* Oxford: Clarendon.

Corfield, F. D. 1960. *Historical survey of the origins and growth of Mau Mau.* London: Her Majesty's Stationery Office.

Debrunner, Hans W. 1967. *A history of Christianity in Ghana.* Accra: Waterville.

Fiedler, Klaus, 1995. Post-classical missions and churches in Africa: identity and challenge to missiological research, in *Missionalia*, Vol. 23(1) April. Page 92–107.

Githieya, Francis Kimani. 1992. The new people of God: the Christian community in the African Orthodox Church (Karing'a) and the Arathi (Agikuyu Spirit Churches). USA: Emory University, Ph.D. dissertation.

Hastings, Adrian. 1979. *A history of African Christianity 1950–1975.* Cambridge: Cambridge University Press.

Isichei, Elizabeth. 1995. *A history of Christianity in Africa from antiquity to the present.* Grand Rapids: Eerdmans.

Lemopoulos, George (ed). 1993. *You shall be my witnesses.* Tertios: Katerini, Greece.
Natsoulas, Theodore, 1981. Patriarch McGuire and the spread of the African Orthodox Church to Africa, in *Journal of Religion in Africa*, Vol. 12(2). Page 81–104.
Natsoulas, Theodore, 1988. The rise and fall of the Kikuyu Karing'a Education Association of Kenya, 1929–1952, in *Journal of Asian and African Studies*, Vol. 23(3–4). Page 219–233.
Platt, Warren C., 1989. The African Orthodox Church: an analysis of its first decade, in *Church History*, Vol. 58(4). Page 474–488.
Welbourn, Frederick Burkewood. 1961. *East African rebels: a study of some independent churches.* London: SCM.
Wentink, D. E., 1968. The Orthodox Church in East Africa, in *The Ecumenical Review*, Vol. (20). Page 33–43.

52

THE SPIRIT AND THE SCAPULAR

Pentecostal and Catholic interactions in Northern Nyanga District, Zimbabwe in the 1950s and early 1960s*

David J. Maxwell

Source: *Journal of Southern African Studies*, 23(2) (1997), 283–300.

Introduction

It was fitting that in a recent editorial of the *Journal of Religion in Africa* Adrian Hastings should recognise Terry Ranger's contribution, not only to the study of Zimbabwe's religious history, but also to scholarship on African religion in general.[1] Ranger's long scholarly engagement with the complex relationship between traditional Zimbabwean religion, Christianity and their socio-political context, combined with his presidency of numerous conference discussions of African religion has made Zimbabwean religious studies a sort of flagship character for the wider field.[2] Over that period of well over thirty years, he has moved from viewing Zimbabwean religious change in terms of the nationalist paradigm of collaboration and resistance to a position which takes more seriously the idioms and symbols of the adherents themselves: a position which nevertheless raises issues of rural politics and consciousness.[3]

In particular, Ranger has come to develop the notion of 'popular Christianity'. In an essay on African Christian identity he argues that the development of a popular Christianity in eastern Zimbabwe depended on three main factors: first, the seizing of the local landscape by symbolically sensitive missionaries who created new centres of spiritual power; secondly, the reliance of missionaries upon African agents – teachers, evangelists and catechists – who healed, made rain and founded their own Christian villages; and thirdly, the adoption of Christian symbols and powers and Christian literacy by Africans because these had practical utility in relating to the colonial economy.[4] Elsewhere, Ranger acknowledges that this dialectical 'interaction between missionary and African consciousness' often produced ironic and unexpected results.[5]

The bulk of Ranger's conclusions on popular Christianity stem from his research on the predominantly Manyika people of Zimbabwe's Makoni district, whose vigorous adoption of Christianity in the first two decades of the twentieth century had the appearance of a religious movement. This paper, about a Christian movement amongst the Hwesa people of the Katerere Chiefdom in eastern Zimbabwe in the 1950s, extends further our understanding of the social history of African Christianity. It takes Ranger's propositions about popular Christianity and tests them in another setting, adjacent to Makoni but very different: the northern part of Nyanga district. Although northern Nyanga's Christian movement involved some of the Manyika people about whom Ranger writes, their combination with a very different cocktail of missionaries and ethnic groups, in another geographical and socio-economic context, produced a popular Christianity distinct from that of Makoni district.

The history of mission Christianity in Katerere is full of ironic variations upon the theme of the local and the global. Although representatives of a world religion, the mission movements which arrived there in the 1950s took a profoundly local form. Missionaries were initially thin on the ground, and the foundation of a popular Christianity which accompanied their presence was as much the product of African agents as of missionaries' own idiosyncrasies. Moreover, although the missions which established themselves were representative of perhaps the two most dynamic forces in modern world Christianity – crusading Roman Catholicism and its systematic opposite, Protestant Pentecostalism – the form which these forces assumed in Katerere had a paradoxical and imported localism. Catholicism was represented by nationalist Irish Carmelites, predominantly from southern Ireland, and Protestantism by Ulster Pentecostals. The introverted battles of Ireland were re-fought in Katerere, giving an extra edge to the inevitable clash between two totally contrasting Christianities. The end result of Pentecostal/Catholic rivalries and of local Hwesa receptions and seizures of Christianity was a mosaic of competing Christian factions somewhat analogous to the political factions which dominated pre-colonial Hwesa politics. For Christianity in Katerere, whether Catholic or Pentecostal, was intensely rooted in the local environment.

The socio-economic context of missionisation in Katerere[6]

Before considering the ideas and social sources of the two missionary movements which entered Katerere in the 1950s it is worth sketching the rapidly transforming economic and political context which they were to encounter. Located on the north east border of Zimbabwe, Katerere was only brought under the rule of the British South Africa Company in 1904 after a show of force. Even then, the Rhodesian state was not present on a daily basis. Its major concern with the Hwesa, and Barwe refugees from Portuguese East Africa who lived in Katerere, was to ensure the maintenance of law and order, taxation and labour supply. State officials made no attempt to centralise peasant agriculture because Katerere's arid climate and poor soils, and distance from markets, made peasant production appear almost impossible. The majority of males were obliged to enter the migrant labour economy. Their long absences from Katerere weakened its already precarious economic base by depriving it of vital hunting and gathering components. Predominantly female producers were left to maintain a subsistence agriculture, now even more vulnerable to baboons and predators which male hunters had previously kept under control. Already subject to cyclical famines, Katerere experienced prolonged agro-ecological stress between *ca.* 1900–1950. There were numerous famines, and infant mortality was about 50%–60%.

Throughout the 1930s and early 1940s successive native commissioners (NCs) for Inyanga district resisted the implementation of the Land Apportionment Act because the eviction of Manyika from what was now deemed to be 'European' land to Katerere appeared untenable. But after 1945 the arrival of ex-servicemen seeking land, and the post-war boom in commercial agriculture meant that Inyanga NCs could hold out no longer. In 1946 the first group of Manyika peasants were removed to Nyamaropa reserve to the south of Katerere. Evictions continued, and by 1952 there was no alternative to Katerere. The Rhodesian Wattle Company's expansion finally pushed evicted Manyika into the Hwesa chiefdom.

The 1950s also heralded a period of greater state interest in reserves, exemplified by the Native Land Husbandry Act which enforced agricultural rules. The state also developed the infrastructure of reserves. Weirs, bridges, drains and irrigation schemes were rapidly constructed in Katerere. It was with a view to developing the medical resources of Inyanga North reserve that Meredith, the NC Inyanga in 1951, helped persuade the Elim missionaries, Drs. Cecil and Mary Brien, to pioneer a station in Katerere. A year later the Irish Carmelites arrived there to start Avila mission, going on to found Regina Coeli mission in Nyamaropa reserve in 1955. It is clear that the Rhodesian state was keen to include these late missionary pioneers in its strategy for technical development but, as we shall see, the Hwesa also had their own agendas for the missionaries.

The two Christianities: Ulster Pentecostalism and Southern Irish Catholicism

The near synchronised arrival of the Elim movement and the Carmelite Catholics in Katerere in the early 1950s had a certain explosive quality about it. This was as much due to the similarities between the two movements as to their differences. Although theological opposites, both missionary organisations were fundamentalist in their sense of their own mission.

Although scholars are beginning to take cognisance of contemporary Pentecostal movements sweeping across Africa,[7] little attention has been paid to their missionary forebears.[8] Part of the explanation for this scholarly neglect of Pentecostalism is that, relative to the established and non-conformist missions, it is a new phenomenon representing a third twentieth century wave of mission activity. Pentecostalism arose within an ambience of interrelated waves of 'revivalist' activity, which occurred between 1900 and 1910 in places as diverse as Azusa Street in California, Oslo in Norway, and the Welsh valleys, in what became known as the Pentecostal Movement.[9] This new Christian religion was a fusion of four theological antecedents: first, salvation, comprising the belief that forgiveness follows an act of repentance in the light of God's grace; secondly, sanctification, a second work of grace received by baptism in the Holy Spirit; thirdly, divine healing; fourthly, adventism, the belief in the imminent return of Christ.[10] It was this fourth strand, the imminence of the Second Coming, that rapidly transformed a western derived church into a missionary movement. More generally, Pentecostalism, along with Conservative Evangelicalism represented the only expanding sectors of a generally declining Protestant missionary movement.[11] Thus, Elim was not the only Pentecostal movement to enter Southern Rhodesia in the quarter of a century following the Second World War. It was joined by the Pentecostal Assemblies of Canada, the South African and American Assemblies of God, and a variety of smaller bodies.

The specific origins of Elim Pentecostalism are described by Bryan Wilson:

> The Elim Foursquare Gospel Church originally developed in Ireland about the time of the First World War, a period of great uncertainty in Irish History. It arose in an atmosphere of insecurity concerning political changes, and amid marked religious tensions. It was nourished by the old revivalist tensions of Ulster, and it spread by use of revivalist techniques in England and Wales in a period of economic unrest and depression in the twenties and early thirties, at a time when religion generally, and non-conformity in particular, were experiencing decline.[12]

The second movement, southern Irish Carmelite Catholicism, was part of a wider revival of Catholic missionary activity throughout Africa, which began with the Papacy of Pius XI in 1922. Within this movement the Irish played a leading role.[13] But despite being a twentieth century phenomenon, the Catholic resurgence was little influenced by liberal theology or secularising influences. Hastings outlines the movement's features:

> narrowly neo-scholastic, papalist, Marian. Hell was not questioned, Protestants hardly noticed except as rivals, social and political issues avoided unless they were greatly affecting Catholics or the

> conversion process. The element of control and unquestioned obedience internal to the system was decisive. It was highly self-sacrificing, unself-questioning, supremely confident in the mission committed to it and the divine approbation of every element of the Catholic Church exactly as it stood.[14]

Both the Elim Pentecostals and the Irish Carmelites were riding high on waves of recent expansion from within their own movements. In the first five years following the end of the Second World War, Elim had doubled its missionary effort.[15] Missionaries had gone to India, South America and Africa. And the Irish Carmelites, within their impressively extensive tradition, were also enjoying relatively recent success with missionary endeavours. Provinces had been founded in Australia and New York, and the order had reestablished itself in England and Wales.[16] Both missions believed in the imperative of evangelism. Elim did so because of its strongly adventist theology,[17] the Catholic impulse came from their belief in the absolute orthodoxy of their religion and the inadequacy of all others as a means to salvation.[18]

The movements also shared a sense of their own self-importance, both seeing themselves as part of great Christian traditions, even if they were somewhat invented. Elim claimed descent from the evangelical tradition of Wesley and Spurgeon and the revivalist tradition of Finney, Moody and Torrey.[19] The Carmelites associated their mission enterprise with the '"Golden Age of Irish Civilisation" and specifically with its missionary content'.[20] Despite historical evidence to the contrary, it was asserted that the modern Irish Catholic resurgence was a revival of an ancient missionary tradition which had cradled Christianity during the Barbarian invasions of the Roman Empire, later re-introducing it to Europe in the eighth century. An editorial in a 1946 edition of the Carmelite journal, *White Friars*, contended:

> What Ireland did for Europe in those ages she must do for the whole world today. The work of Jesus Christ must be done and we are the nation most favourably placed to do it. Surely it is the supreme honour to be placed in such a position, to be the chosen nation for so great a work.[21]

Indeed the Irish nationalism that informed, and was informed by, Carmelite Catholicism offers another clue to the intense contestation between the two movements. As Wilson noted, the Elim movement emerged from Ulster in the 1920s in a period marked by religious tensions, in part defining itself through opposition to the Catholic threat. Hence the Elim movement's exegesis of Revelation cast the Roman Catholic Church as the real entity symbolised by the Mother of Harlots drunk with the blood of the Saints.[22] Whilst the *Elim Evangel*, the journal of the movement, asserted the existence of a 'Roman Catholic Curtain' which kept the people of Spain subject to a systematic religious oppression coordinated by Rome,[23] Irish Carmelites triumphally proclaimed:

> Irishmen can stand before mankind with a clear conscience on many things. We have never figured in history as persecutors of our fellow men, either in the interests of politics or religion. We cannot be accused of having political ambitions overseas.[24]

Nonetheless, despite the bold rhetoric of both movements, their initial interactions with the Katerere were shaped by local agendas and local legacies.

Pentecostal interactions: the localisation of Ulster Protestantism

The sacred texts of the Elim movement, those written by or about its founder George Jeffreys and his brother Stephen, provide excellent insight into the character of Ulster Pentecostalism. It was strongly dualistic in nature. There were only two possible sources of spiritual power,[25] two possible masters of the body,[26] and two sources of disease.[27]

Despite its appearance, like other fundamentalist movements Elim was 'quintessentially modern'[28] in that it offered a response to contemporary conditions and events by means of demonising the perceived threat and defining itself in opposition to this 'notional and significant "other"'.[29] One significant 'other' was Roman Catholicism. The second was more nebulous, referring to the menacing modern world which the Pentecostals fought desperately to keep at bay. As late as the 1950s, even perhaps the 1960s,[30] secularising forces outside and within the church were identified, and became the object of Pentecostal vitriol. Such influences were cinema and public house owners, and clergy who allowed their churches to become places for dancers and players of cards, billiards and bagatelle.[31] Not surprisingly the movement's leaders and preachers were extremely adversarial in their defence of all that was good and Pentecostal. Thus victims of secularisation along with its agents were identified and castigated: 'Sinners of the deepest dye . . . Magdalens, drunkards, lovers of pleasures and religious journalists'.[32]

Cecil Brien was no newcomer to evangelical campaigning. In Belfast he had spent much of his spare time distributing religious tracts, along with his best friend, a bus conductor. In Rhonda, in Wales he had scandalised medical practice colleagues by preaching in the open air.[33] In Katerere, different categories of enemy were constructed, representing new threats. The spirit world replaced secularising influences, and Shona 'traditionalists' supplanted the British working classes. In this vein Cecil Brien referred to the Hwesa as 'bound by Satan' or 'worshipping Satan'.[34] Others were more adept in their turn of phrase. Katerere was 'the heart of savagedom and witchcraft' and the Hwesa were 'dirty uneducated, spirit worshippers, bound by witchcraft and superstition' who participated in the 'beating of drums and the wild frenzy of devil orgies'.[35]

New rituals were also found to emphasise the transformation of loyalties that conversion to Pentecostal Christianity brought. Substances that polluted the life of the British working classes were replaced with those which defiled the Shona. The rituals of burning pipes and tobacco pouches and of pouring home-made wine down the sink which accompanied British Elim campaigns[36] were transformed, under local initiative into the burning of charms, fetishes and bracelets outside the church and hospital.[37] The public confession of sin, the day and night long meetings, the destruction of polluted objects gave Elim's initial interaction with the Hwesa and Barwe the appearance of a witchcraft cleansing movement, not unlike the Mchape movement which had entered Katerere twenty years earlier during its spread throughout east and central Africa. Describing a weekend of special meetings in 1954 which was attended by over 400 people, Elim Missionary, Winnie Loosemore wrote: 'we saw men and women coming forward; some to repent, some with greater desire to follow the Lord Jesus, whilst others bound by evil spirits were delivered and their witchcraft burnt'.[38] Meetings of over 500 were not uncommon in the early years of Elim's presence in Katerere.

For the first four years of its existence, Elim mission was staffed by just three missionaries, the Briens and Nurse Winnie Loosemore. Under the pressure of a rapidly expanding medical work these missionaries were heavily dependent on African input into evangelism, and influenced by local agendas. This local Christian reshaping of Elim had a number of sources. The initial encounter between missionaries and Hwesa traditional authorities was arranged and mediated by Pentecostal labour migrants from the Apostolic Faith Mission who had returned from the gold mines at Gatooma (Kadoma) to found a Christian village in Katerere in 1946.[39] The Pentecostal ambience was added to by itinerant Methodists from Manyika Christian strongholds in Makoni district, whose zeal for revival has been well documented by Terence Ranger.[40] The Briens were also reliant on two black evangelists: Obed, and Buxton who was also a Methodist. Finally, there was a large input from women and youth, keen to exploit Pentecostalism's potential to subvert male gerontocratic control.[41]

In interview, Mary Brien provided insights into how her theology could arise out of dialogue with local Christians:

> I was once sitting with an African woman . . . and I said to her 'where are the spirits?' And she sat up and looked and said 'they are never beside water, but you see, where there's no water, where its very dry, that's where the spirits reside.' And the bible says the same: 'When a spirit goes out of a man, it will go looking for a new place and it will always seek a dry place'.[42]

In a similar manner her perception that African beer was just a nourishing drink was changed by an itinerant black Methodist pastor, together with some local women, to a more 'Pentecostal' view that it was a polluting substance associated with ancestor veneration.[43]

There was another reason why the Elim movement lent itself so easily to localisation. The missionaries' acceptance of the supernatural, and their Pentecostal practice, had immediate resonances with Shona cosmology. The Briens' own narrative of their journey to Katerere took the form of a sequence of divinely inspired prophecies, visions and dreams;[44] phenomena equally familiar to the Hwesa, but alien to many mainline missionaries. The Briens were also no strangers to the exorcisms, baptism in the spirit and tongues which they encountered in the Katerere. They had experienced this Pentecostal power in Elim's British campaigns in Wigan before coming to Southern Rhodesia to work for the Evangelical Africa Mission on the Zambezi Escarpment in 1946.[45] Thus, as Cecil and Mary Brien, along with their nurse Winnie Loosemoore, began their medical mission amongst the Hwesa, they proved extremely amenable to dialogue with local perceptions of evil. Perhaps the most remarkable Christian form to emerge out of this symbiosis between Elim Pentecostalism and local demand and creativity was a unique and powerful package of divine healing.

The Doctors Brien: medical science and Pentecostalism join forces

In Hwesa oral history, the surgeon Cecil Brien is remembered as a wonder-working figure. He is described in the same terms as an African prophet. The key to his beatification lies in the symbolic innovation he made in the domain of healing. Together with his wife, an anaesthetist, he brought to Katerere a sophisticated package of bio-medicine. But this knowledge of medical science was supplemented by a profound belief in divine healing.

The Briens' practise of divine healing had a dual pedigree. Its first line of descent came from George Jeffreys, the founder of the Elim movement, whose evangelistic campaigns in the 1920s and 1930s in the British Isles caught the attention of the national press because they were accompanied by extra-ordinary healings. The histories of the movement abound with citations from the national press describing the abandoned bath-chairs and crutches which resulted from the evangelist's ministry.[46] Jeffreys' own writings on the subject of divine healing locate it within a heritage which he traced back through Andrew Murray to George Fox and John Wesley.[47] The second pedigree had already been tried and tested in Southern Rhodesia in 1910–1920. Whilst in Swansea the Briens lived in a Bible college run by Rees Howells. A product of the great Welsh Revival, and a noted healer, Howells had worked at the South Africa General Mission in Rusitu which was renowned for its scenes of revival in the years 1915–1920. More importantly, in the post-war influenza pandemic, the mission station became transformed into a divinely protected zone, free from the virus, to which local chiefs and people fled for refuge.[48] The Briens were profoundly influenced by Howells.[49]

In the Briens' hands, Pentecost and medical science joined forces. Clinics were preceded by religious services and the hospital was transformed each morning into a place of singing, dancing, prayer, and the Word. But the process went far deeper than this. In 1952 Mary Brien wrote in the *Elim Evangel* of their response to cases considered 'medically hopeless'; a woman with peritonitis, her kidneys diseased beyond medical repair, a woman with puerperal infection not responding to drugs. Here the only option was the laying on of hands. Miraculous healings apparently followed.[50] In many cases of divine healings, the patient and even their family would join the church.[51]

Local perceptions of the Briens' medical practice often conflated it with divine healing, thereby greatly increasing the latter's spiritual efficacy. When in 1952 Cecil Brien revived a newly born baby, which had appeared to have been dead for forty minutes, the local headman and his wife, whose child it was, believed that the doctor had breathed life into it.[52] Informants viewed as 'miraculous' the ability of Drs Cecil and Mary Brien to cut open a woman and remove a child from her womb. Such surgical expertise would rarely have been encountered even in the southern portion of the district.

When contextualised within the half century of agro-ecological stress in Katerere, medical practice combined with divine healing had a remarkable relevance. As Mary Brien put it: 'As soon as the women saw their babies living, they started coming to church'.[53] A woman's capacity to produce children for her husband enhanced her status both within polygamous household and the wider community. And failure to reproduce greatly diminished a woman's sense of self,[54] and could lead to her rejection by her husband's family. Women who had received the Brien's medical treatment rapidly spread the news to others. It is not surprising that Mary Brien's *ruwadzano* – women's group – became one of the engines of church growth.[55]

But the Brien's healing had a far wider appeal. Those who had for many years been troubled with aching teeth flooded into clinics for their extraction during the mission's early days.[56] Others who had problems with sight and hearing were also helped.[57] Indeed this Pentecostal power intending 'to deal with pain and disease, sorrow and trials'[58] appeared very compelling, especially to Elim's staunchest enemies. Perceiving that the old religious system was no longer meeting the popular need, some local traditional leaders who practised traditional medicine converted to Christianity. Thus for instance, when a *n'anga* – traditional healer – found his wife's life had been saved in childbirth by Cecil Brien, he arrived at the hospital demanding to see the white doctor who was 'like Jesus'. He subsequently abandoned traditional healing, walking thirteen miles to church every Sunday.[59]

The Elim missionaries' package of bio-medicine and divine healing complicates scholarly understanding of Pentecostal/healing churches. In an essay entitled 'Medical Science and Pentecost: The Dilemma of Anglicanism in Africa' Terence Ranger argues that Pentecostal Christianity redefined the meaning of African perceptions of disease by abolishing the dichotomy between diseases of God and diseases of man. He writes:

> What African Pentecostalism did was to make available the healing power of the Holy Spirit to counter all other spiritual agencies. Thus God was brought into the diseases of Man, not as willing them nor as eradicating them, but as regularly combatting them through the openness of human beings to His Spirit. At the same time African Pentecostalism redefined the other category of diseases of God, where hitherto recourse had been both to traditional and Western medicine. Here, too, the Holy Spirit alone had power. African Pentecostals repudiated all medicines. Thus the dichotomy was abolished.[60]

Pentecostalism *per se* does abolish the dichotomy between diseases of God and diseases of man, but the example of the Briens also abolished the dichotomy between medical science and Pentecostalism.

Possessing the land: the demise of Chikumbirike

As well as transforming the bodies of its adherents, Elim Pentecostalism could also transform perceptions of the landscape. Their method of re-sacralising of the land, of seizing hold of the spiritual centre, differed radically from Ranger's accounts of this process in Makoni. Whilst Makoni Anglicans 'created cemeteries as focal points of the new religion', and 'American Methodists developed the "holy ground" of the sites at which their annual camp meetings were held',[61] the Elimites 'redeemed space'. The chroniclers of the history of the Elim Church in the British Isles record with sheer delight the irritation its evangelistic campaigns caused cinema owners and publicans, whose numbers dwindled due to the presence of George Jeffreys and his evangelistic team in an area. E. C. W. Boulton, author of *George Jeffreys. A Ministry Of The Miraculous*, wrote with joy concerning the movement's ability to restore a picture palace in Belfast, previously a Methodist Chapel, to its former glory, by turning it into an Elim Tabernacle. He notes in a postscript that after the first prayer meeting there, the caretaker and his wife (presumably unsavoury characters) 'developed a sudden desire to leave the premises, and as result made their departure under the cover of midnight darkness'.[62] The redemption of space occurred through contestation as chapter headings of Boulton's book illustrate; their titles include 'Invading England', 'Glorious Triumphs', and 'South Coast Conquests'.

In a similar vein, Winnie Loosemore wrote an article in the *Elim Evangel* entitled 'Possessing The Land'. Drawing on imagery from Deuteronomy of the Jewish occupation, she wrote:

> We have come to possess the land of Katerere, Inyanga North Reserve . . . Many who were groping in the darkness of heathenism have been liberated from the chains that bound them and have been brought into the glorious light of the Gospel. We are so sad to see so many coming to the hospital weighed down with heathen charms and so obviously under the power of Satan . . .[63]

Cecil Brien shared a similar vision. One of his African evangelists described for me how the Doctor declared 'war' on the people of Gande, the nearest village to the mission:

> That was his object lesson almost every Sunday. On certain occasions at certain times of the year, when they would beat their drums all night appeasing the ancestors and so forth, the next Sunday you would know that this would be Dr Brien's sermon. So he would preach and hammer very hard.[64]

Every member of Gande village who came to the hospital was chided by Dr Brien for taking his medicine yet refusing his message.

The local representatives of the old order came under considerable pressure from their Pentecostal adversaries. The mission site by the Manjanja river in Ruangwe had strong associations with a *mhondoro*[65] spirit, initially causing many to avoid attending church and hospital. Occasionally pots of beer were left along the upper reaches of the river.[66] The *mhondoro* in question was Chikumbirike, and his host, Razau Kaerezi, lived just outside the perimeter of the mission. The coming of the Pentecostals spelt disaster for Kaerezi. First, his wife converted and refused to brew him beer. He beat and persecuted her only to find his two daughters converting through their attendance at the secondary school. Things grew steadily worse: the pools along the river where pots of beer had once been placed became places of baptism, testimony and open air services. Later still the river was dammed. This great source of fertility was now clearly controlled by the Pentecostals.[67] None of the later missionaries knew that Kaerezi was a medium, but one could speculate that Cecil Brien at least understood something of his significance. He offered him a job as a school cook in the 1960s in order to win him.

Whilst around the mission, Kaerezi was a sociable man, but at home he was known to fall into a trance, Chikumbirike would then speak, seeming to address the missionaries: 'What are you here for? You are disturbing us, our people are not following our traditions because of this teaching'.[68] Kaerezi soon left his job. Having seized the centre of his spirit ward, the missionaries had severely curtailed his activities around the mission. His powers were only restored during the liberation war, through the agency of ZANLA guerrillas who relocated him. Around Elim the drums used to summon the spirits fell silent.

Catholic interactions: different models of inculturation

The account of Carmelite interactions in Katerere is as ironic as the Pentecostal one. It is a story of contrasts, the significance of which can only be grasped through the reconstruction of the social history of Catholic mission in the southern part of Inyanga district and Makoni district prior to the Carmelite's arrival in 1949.

The process of the foundation of a popular Catholicism in Makoni and southern Inyanga district has been reconstructed by Terence Ranger. Like the Pentecostals, Catholic missionaries also seized hold of the mystical landscape, this time by taking hold of 'every dominant feature of the local terrain with shrines and perambulations'.[69] But in distinct contrast to the Pentecostals there was also a strong emphasis on veneration. The three orders who worked consecutively in Manicaland, German Trappists, German Jesuits and Irish Carmelites, each had a different form of veneration. But as Ranger notes:

> One emphasis however remained constant: the emphasis upon the Virgin of the 19th and 20th century apparitions. At Triashill both the Trappists and the Jesuits erected a Lourdes grotto and held torch-light processions to it. The Carmelites, of course, made the feast of Our Lady of Mount Carmel the highlight of their liturgical year.[70]

In 1950, the Manicaland Catholic identity was further enhanced with a new Carmelite flavour through the founding of Brown Scapular Confraternities at Umtali, Triashill, St Barbaras and St Killians.[71] That the scapular (a monastic vestment) could be confused by some for a 'Papal Blessing' did not bother some priests, for along with the rosary it was eagerly taken up by the young and even the older generation, supplanting the metal bracelets that had hitherto been used to warn off evil spirits. Its use spread rapidly in the first few years of the Carmelite presence in the region.[72] Another Carmelite initiative was to share in the visit of the pilgrim statue of Our Lady of Fatima to Africa in 1950. In Rusape such large crowds turned out to venerate the statue that an outside altar had to be erected.[73]

One of the three Carmelite pioneers to Southern Rhodesia explained that the early missionaries had no formal instruction in missiology, nevertheless they were trained priests with the New Testament as their handbook. Hence they were to be exploratory.[74] This left much to each priest's initiative. Generally the early Carmelites worked with what was familiar to them, developing in Manicaland the Catholic symbolism and ritual imported from southern Ireland.

Irish Carmelite practice in Southern Rhodesia was not without effect. Its symbolic potential was explicitly recognised by its missionary priests. In an essay on 'mission' appearing in 1960 in *Zelo*, the journal of Carmelite novices, Father Tony Clarke wrote:

> Sacramentals, besides being efficacious, have a tremendous appeal to African people and can help us greatly in our battle to break the power of the witch-doctor and superstition . . . A priest, when he goes to a village, should always be armed with the Ritual, ready to bless the sick, to bless the homes of the people, their animals, their crops, their children . . . In time of drought processions should be organised to plead for rain . . . If the rains are exceptionally heavy, there is a blessing to prevent floods. For every occasion there is a blessing.[75]

Clarke was not advocating the open contestation with the leaders and practitioners of traditional religion practised by the Pentecostals, but rather that Carmelite Catholicism should supplant their major functions, rendering them redundant. Thus when he founded Avila mission in September 1953, a statue of Our Lady of Mt Carmel was erected at the entrance to the mission and local people wearing the scapular were encouraged to pray at this shrine.[76]

However, the founding of Avila and Regina Coeli missions, in the north of Manicaland, came at the end of an era. Clarke left Avila in 1959 and the new Carmelites who replaced him had very different missiological goals. These new men were profoundly influenced by the debates, deliberations and final proclamations of the Second Vatican Council. They were horrified by the brand of Catholicism they encountered in the southern portion of the district. One priest commented:

> I suppose when we went to Rhodesia we were shocked to see the things that were part of Catholicism in particular areas like Triashill for instance; that they were no different from a white European colonial church. We took the church from Ireland and planted it in Triashill with all the trappings of a pre-Vatican church – the Latin hymns . . . We came at the end of that era and the beginning of a new one. It was a different type of evangelisation . . . there was a move towards Africanisation, inculturation.[77]

Although the nineteenth century Ultramontanist peasant cults, tried and tested in rural Ireland, had great appeal to the Manicaland peasantry, it was these 'non-essentials' which were the first religious forms to be dropped by the new men. The later priests did not realise the extent to which they had already been indigenised, and the degree to which they played a vital role in the founding of a folk Catholicism.

The strength of folk Catholicism in the south became apparent in the late 1940s and 1950s when hundreds of Manyika Catholic families evicted from the vicinity of Triashill mission, arrived not only with their rosaries, brown scapulars and statues, but also with their own 'native' schools with distinctive saints' names. Village Christianities were exported wholesale from the south during the eviction process. Other Manyika Catholics who had formed themselves into societies for the veneration of specific saints retained these sub-religious identities as well.[78] African Catholics thus introduced their own brand of inculturation, from below.[79] The resilience of their local gatherings in the face of evictions meant that the migrants were later able to demand mission schools and hospitals, and other Christian infrastructures from ecclesiastical hierarchies initially removed from these processes. Around Elim, the Hwesa imitated these modernising Manyika peasants not only in their agricultural technique but also their Christian practice. At Avila, where there were no resettled Manyika peasants, the task of the missionary was far harder.

But the post-Vatican II Carmelites had very different views on inculturation. Father Luke MacCabe, doctor at Regina Coeli mission in the 1960s and 1970s, provided insights into his perception of the process. Unlike the Briens who were at war with the *n'anga* – traditional healers – MacCabe believed that these healers were able to heal people from 'acute mental psychosis' and that they had some 'quite good medicines'. He never preached against ancestor veneration because, like many post-Vatican II missionaries, he saw a direct parallel between this and the veneration of the saints. In his doctoral thesis on medicine he wrote: 'Pagan beliefs have many ethical points in common with Christianity; even the pagan concept of God is notably lofty and not far removed from the Christian concept'.[80] MacCabe also assisted Michael Gelfand in his ethnographic survey of the Nyamaropa area.[81] More generally, words like 'pagan' and 'heathen' disappeared from the rhetoric of the movement in the 1960s as it strove to reappraise local culture and religion. In a similar vein, Father Berthold Dowd produced a series of learned articles on Shona religion for the Order's journal.[82]

There was also a conscious desire to develop African symbols and forms of worship in church. Thus catechists from Regina Coeli returned there from weekend liturgical seminars with drums previously banned from services. Priests pre-empted pastoral decree in allowing their use. In the same vein came Father Peter Egan's architectural masterpiece – the round church with thatched roof, in Hwesa style, constructed at Avila mission.[83]

Inculturation had unexpected, even ironic results. The development of African forms of worship was a slow process and there seemed little to show for it before the mid 1970s. In comparison with the older folk Catholicism in the south, Catholicism in the north of the district, particularly around Avila mission which had few Manyika immigrants, appeared bleak and dry, devoid of the symbols which many of its non-literate practitioners could draw upon. It seemed as if the older pre-Vatican II priests, admittedly able to build upon the traditions of their German Trappist and Jesuit predecessors, were more successful in founding a popular Catholicism.

In the southern part of Inyanga district and Makoni, Catholic priests had constructed a more 'totalising' religion by controlling the lives of adherents living on their vast mission farms. The missionaries made demands not too dissimilar from those made by Pentecostals. Comparing life on the mission station with life in the reserves, Father Mel Hill made the following observations:

> It is not uncommon for the whole village to be drunk for a week. In a place like Triashill Mission where the Prior is the Landlord and the natives are his tenants, some sort of check can be kept on the beer, but in the Natives Reserves things are completely wild. . . . If the parents refuse to send their children to learn they are threatened with expulsion from the farm. . . . The whole atmosphere of their village life militates against any sort of learning or religion . . . Very few families say night prayers or even mention the name of Christ in their villages.[84]

On the mission station, Catholics attended daily mass and prayers. Priests monitored weddings and funerals and intervened if they did not consider the rituals suitably Christian.[85]

However, almost in spite of the later Carmelites' missiology, zones of popular Christianity were created around Avila and Regina Coeli missions through the agency of the Manyika. Nevertheless, the Carmelite missionaries did identify with Africans in ways the Pentecostals could not. This was because of the social context of southern Irish Catholicism. First, the rural background of many priests greatly enhanced their ability to relate to peasants. Some priests won great respect for their ability to irrigate previously infertile areas of Katerere and create vegetable gardens. Secondly, the Carmelite's strong sense of Irish Nationalism freed them from close association with the colonial state and offered greater opportunity for identification with the colonised people – a characteristic which was to become much more apparent during the liberation struggle.[86]

The sect from the Black North meets the mother of drunken harlots: the global export of a local struggle

Pentecostalism emerged at the turn of the twentieth century, in opposition to what it saw as the corrupting influences of priestly supremacy and liberal theology in the established churches. It made a particular object lesson of Catholicism. Jesse Williams, the first Elim missionary to Southern Rhodesia, was in no doubt about the veracity of his pre-Reformation stereotypes of Catholic practice. In a 1952 report he wrote: '[The Priest] takes a bucket of water and sprinkles them, thus making them members of their Church of Rome. Sometimes he gives them a medal to hang around their necks. These poor souls do not know what they believe'.[87] But the Carmelites were equally assured of their own cause. Their Irish Provincial's letter to *White Friars* set the tone of their work:

> The Fathers say that they are surrounded by schools under the care of Anglicans, American Methodists and Dutch Reform. These Fathers realise that they must do everything possible to keep the True Faith burning vigorously at St. Killian's mission and they appeal most earnestly for benefactors.[88]

The inevitable conflict between the two movements was intensified by their social sources: Ulster Pentecostalism and predominantly Southern Irish Catholicism. As Bryan Wilson rightly observes, Elim Pentecostals had a general disdain for and disinterest in social and political issues.[89] Their fundamentalist/evangelical theology tended to depoliticise issues by focusing on individual transformation. However, when it came to the Irish Question, Ulster Elimites were prepared to make an exception, because 'they just knew they were right'.[90] Elim was to clash with Carmelites who were unabashed in their promotion of the Irish cause. *Zelo* describes how the three Irish Pioneers celebrated their first St Patrick's Day in Southern Rhodesia in 1947. These 'true Irishmen' taught mission choirs to sing 'Hail Glorious St Patrick' and 'The Dear Little Shamrock', and choreographed a procession which culminated in the unfurling of the Irish Tricolour.[91] A decade later one of the few Northern Irish Carmelites, Donal Lamont, was consecrated Bishop of Umtali. The new bishop used the opportunity to pontificate on recent political developments in Central Africa. His speech, reported in *White Friars*, provides fascinating insight into how he viewed Colonial developments through Irish Nationalist spectacles:

> the Federation did not now need the Motherly care of England to the extent that she did when a small child, as it were. While she would not like to see her Mother attacked, she would still say 'Leave us alone,' and amid general laugher, 'As we would say in Ireland, "Sinn Fein!"'[92]

The battle lines were drawn in Ireland but Katerere was the site of this holy war between Pentecostals and Catholics. As soon as the Carmelites arrived on the scene, Elim missionaries moved onto the offensive. One missionary wrote in the *Elim Evangel*: 'The Catholics are fighting us desperately and have appealed to the government for school sites all over the reserve'.[93] In the following edition, the Briens issued an 'S.O.S. for Prayer' against the Roman Catholics not too dissimilar from the Irish Provincial's exhortation of his faithful to prayer.[94] Whilst Elim sought preferential treatment in Katerere,[95] the Catholics felt aggrieved that their northward expansion throughout Manicaland had been thwarted. One Carmelite missionary indignantly wrote of the 'Elim Sect' stepping into Katerere whilst the Catholics were still pursuing negotiations.[96]

The contest was intensified on the ground by the personalities involved. The Elim missionaries were led by Cecil Brien, a staunch Ulster Protestant who informed *Elim Evangel* readers in 1952 that 'Unless we get permission to go in [to Katerere] before the Catholics the whole of this vast unevangelised area will be shut of from the Gospel and all these tribes will remain in utter darkness'.[97] His opposition to Tony Clarke, the able and determined southern Irish priest based at Avila mission, was implacable and even reached the annals of Carmelite history. A recent biography of James Carmel O'Shea, a leading Irish Carmelite at the time, notes: 'He was very anxious about Anthony Clarke who had moved up to a new area, Katerere where he was experiencing particular difficulties from a Protestant mission, the directors of which were doing their utmost to prevent him from establishing schools there'.[98]

The struggle between the two movements reached almost comic proportions. On one occasion a missionary couple prayed that God would give the Pentecostals victory over the Catholics' 'crack football team'.[99] On another, Cecil Brien summoned the local NC informing him that the Catholic mission at Avila had built a school within Elim's three mile radius – a serious breach of missionary protocol. The Doctor insisted on pacing it out accompanied by the NC and the Catholic priest in question – Tony Clarke. At one stage of the journey the proceedings became particularly heated when Brien argued that they should walk straight through bush and scrub rather than around it for the sake of accuracy. The Catholics were found to have transgressed. Their newly erected school was torn down. It was hardly surprising that Carmelite Priests complained bitterly to the NC Inyanga about the 'man from the Black North'.[100]

The struggle between the missions also took the form of an extended argument over the number and location of schools each organisation could build. The struggle was so fraught because in the 1950s and 1960s schools were viewed as the major means of evangelism.[101] Evangelism was, of course, the primary concern of both missions. The struggle for schools inevitably drew the state into the conflict, not least because the Catholics believed that the Inyanga NC, Meredith, preferred the Pentecostals.[102] As evidence they cited the NC's failure to refute Jesse Williams' allegation, made at a meeting of the two missions, that Catholic priests murdered 'indigenous natives' in Portuguese East Africa.[103] The conflict widened as the fiery Donal Lamont went over Meredith's head, writing a thunderous letter of complaint to the Native Affairs Department, questioning both the NC's competence and impartiality.[104] Finding the 'prevailing spirit . . . quite un-Christian',[105] the exasperated Meredith wryly noted in a report to the provincial native commissioner, Umtali: 'It may also not be irrelevant to mention that Dr Brien is an Orangeman and the Roman missions are staffed by Southern Irishmen'.[106]

The Catholic and Pentecostal missionaries who later emerged onto the scene were not from Ireland and found this rivalry between the movements distasteful. But by then it had already affected the nature of the interactions between mission Christianity and local religious and political institutions. In a very obvious manner, Elim's strict adherence to the three mile rule forced the Catholics at Avila to construct schools at unsuitable sites often isolated from natural centres of population, thus affecting the latter's ability to evangelise. African reaction to Carmelite-Pentecostal rivalry was varied. NC Meredith thought it might have confused Africans,[107] but as we have seen many quickly developed their own local versions of Christianity. One response from chiefs and headmen was to manipulate the rivalries to ensure a school in the vicinity of their villages.[108]

Another effect of missionary rivalry was to create African enemies. Elim's desire for doctrinal purity caused missionaries to intervene in the prospective marriages of their teachers. In 1964, the mission received a letter signed by 'Zimbabwean Sons of the Soil',[109] attributed to local inhabitants who were members of the nationalist movement ZAPU (Zimbabwe African Peoples Union) in Salisbury.[110] The writers singled out for criticism the Schools Superintendent, whom they said had chased off a school teacher for marrying a Roman Catholic girl. What was significant about the letter was not that it was anti-Christian – it even quoted scripture in one place – but that it strongly disapproved of missionary sectarianism:

> Do you think that we Africans come from Rome or Elim? We are all Africans, don't split us by your political churches. We Africans marry Africans; Colonials marry Colonials . . . Do you think that your political club Elim is the only church which is loyal to God . . . all the European Churches shall be disbanded and form an African United Church.[111]

These early nationalists resented the fact that they were being used as cannon fodder in an imported local struggle which was not of their making.

The final African reaction was to vote with their feet. Throughout the 1950s an African controlled Pentecostal church, the *Vapostori* – Apostles of Johanna Marange – had spread like 'grass-fire' northwards throughout Manicaland.[112] The movement was initially unable to gain a foothold in Katerere, which already had its own strong Pentecostal heritage. However, in 1962 the *Vapostori* managed to establish themselves in Ruangwe, Katerere, in the shadow of Elim mission. Indeed, there is strong evidence that those 'Sons of the Soil' who wrote to protest about Elim's dismissal of its school teacher over his choice of bride may well also have been *Vapostori*. Their letter finished by recommending a passage of scripture – Deuteronomy 14:1–12, and the question: 'Do you ever preach these?' The biblical text cited concerns Hebrew food taboos – a text central in the definition of *Vapostori* identity. Thus, this group of African-led Pentecostals were also intent on challenging the legitimacy of Elim's popular Christianity.

Conclusion

When Elim Pentecostalism arrived in Katerere, it had the appearance of a religious movement. Africans rapidly adhered to the church as it legitimated itself in local terms, re-sacralising the landscape in Christian fashion, pitting itself against local demons, and making resonances with local concepts of illness. Likewise, the Catholic church literally followed a movement of popular Catholicism north, as Manyika migrants from the south arrived with their medals, scapulars and village schools, demanding the founding of Regina Coeli mission along with priest-led churches. In the two mission Christianities different concepts of Africanisation were at work. Carmelite Catholics first sought to replace traditional rituals and symbols with their own, and then after Vatican II, to incorporate them into Catholic practice. In contrast the Pentecostals arrived at Africanisation through the exclusion of traditional religious components by exorcism, demonisation and the destruction of sacred objects. By so doing, the Elimites were perpetuating an African tradition of cyclical societal cleansing.

Whilst much of Katerere's Christian movement happened in Christian villages, away from missionary supervision, this paper powerfully illustrates why it is necessary to appreciate the social sources of mission in order to understand local patterns of Christianity. Finally what is remarkable about Katerere's Christian movement is not that it happened, but that it occurred so late. Similar accounts of rapid Christian adherence to missions in southern and central Africa date from the final decades of the nineteenth century to the first decades of the twentieth century. It was with this in mind that Bengt Sundkler described nineteenth Christianisation as a 'youth movement' and twentieth century Christianisation as a 'woman's movement'.[113] That the two processes should occur in tandem in Katerere, and so late, was a product of the chiefdom's marginality, and of course, the belated pioneering zeal of the two mission movements which arrived there in the early 1950s.

Pioneer missionaries are generally seen as something of an exception in Africa of the 1950s. Much of the continent had been Christianised, and missionaries were now concerned with the management of their vast institutions, and the education of a tiny elite.[114] It is true that Katerere's Christian movement rapidly institutionalised as Pentecostal and Catholic missionaries built schools and hospitals to catch the spirit of the missionary age. Nevertheless other parts of Southern Rhodesia also experienced their first encounter with mission organisations in the 1950s, producing a similar popular response.[115] The periodisation of pioneer mission work needs to be adjusted to accommodate post-war movements of revived missionary Catholicism, and movements of Evangelical and Pentecostal revivalism. But more importantly, this paper adds to a new wave of scholarship[116] on the hitherto neglected social history of mission. It demonstrates that missionary ideas and practices must be taken seriously, but gives equal weight to exploring how they were adapted and repackaged in local contexts by African Christians.

Notes

* I am grateful to Adrian Hastings and Deborah Gaitskell for comments on earlier drafts of this paper.

1 A. Hastings, 'Editorial', *Journal of Religion in Africa*, 25, 3 (August 1995), p. 225.
2 *Ibid.*
3 T. O. Ranger, 'Religious Movements and Politics in Sub-Saharan Africa', *African Studies Review*, 29, 2 (June 1986), pp. 1–69, particularly the appendix.
4 T. O. Ranger, 'Religion, Development and African Christian Identity', in Kirsten Holst-Peterson (ed), *Religion, Development and African Identity* (Uppsala, 1987), pp. 37–41.
5 T. O. Ranger, 'An Africanist Comment', *American Ethnologist*, 14, 1 (1987), pp. 182–185.
6 The bulk of this section is drawn from D. J. Maxwell, 'A Social and Conceptual History of North East Zimbabwe 1890–1990' (DPhil, Oxford University, 1994), chaps 1 and 2.
7 R. Marshall, '"Power in the Name of Jesus": Social Transformation and Pentecostalism in Western Nigeria "Revisited"', in T. O. Ranger and O. Vaughan (eds), *Legitimacy and the State in 20th Century Africa* (Oxford, 1993); P. Gifford, *The New Crusaders: Christianity and the New Right in Southern Africa* (London, 1991).
8 N. Etherington, 'Missionaries and the Intellectual History of Africa: A Historical Survey,' *Itinerario*, vii, 2, (1983), p. 129. Except, perhaps South Africa, see B. Sundkler's, *Zulu Zion and Some Swazi Zionists* (London, 1976).
9 W. Hollenweger, *The Pentecostals* (London, 1972); G. McGee, 'The Azuza Street Revival and Twentieth-Century Missions', *International Bulletin of Missionary Research*, 12, 2 (1988), pp. 58–61.
10 D. Dayton, *Theological Roots of Pentecostalism* (Michigan, 1987), chap 1.
11 A. Hastings, *The Church in Africa 1450–1950* (Oxford, 1994), p. 567.
12 B. Wilson, *Sects and Societies: A Sociological Study of Three Religious Groups in Britain* (London, 1961), p. 15.
13 Hastings, *The Church in Africa*, pp. 559–561.
14 *Ibid.*, pp. 559–560.
15 *Elim Evangel*, 13 March 1950.
16 *White Friars*, September–October 1946.
17 Wilson, *Sects and Society*, p. 27.
18 Interview, Tony Clark, the Carmelite Priory, Mutare, 21 April 1989.
19 Wilson, *Sects and Society*, p. 15. G. Jeffreys, *Pentecostal Rays: The Baptism and Gifts of the Holy Spirit* (London, 1933), pp. 192–212.
20 E. Hogan, *The Irish Missionary Movement: A Historical Survey 1830–1980* (Dublin, 1990), p. 151.
21 *White Friars*, November–December 1946.
22 Wilson, *Sects and Society*, pp. 15, 94.
23 *Elim Evangel*, 'Elim Penetrates the R. C Curtain', 1 February 1958.
24 *White Friars*, November–December 1946.
25 Jeffreys, *Pentecostal Rays*, p. 148.
26 G. Jeffreys, *Healing Rays*, (London, 1932), p. 49.

27 *Ibid.*, pp. 37–46.
28 L. Caplan, 'Introduction', in L. Caplan (ed) *Studies in Religious Fundamentalism* (London, 1987), p. 5.
29 *Ibid.*, p. 20.
30 An excellent account of the social teachings and practices of British Elim churches in the 1950s is found in Wilson, *Sects and Society*, pp. 77–88. Jeanette Winterson's work of faction, *Oranges are Not the Only Fruit* (London, 1985), is based on her childhood experiences in an Elim Church in Lancashire in the 1960s. The Elim movement questioned the accuracy of her account.
31 E. Jeffreys, *Stephen Jeffreys: The Beloved Evangelist* (London, 1946), pp. 30, 51, 57.
32 E. C. Boulton, *George Jeffreys: A Ministry of The Miraculous* (London, 1928), p. 19.
33 Interview, Peter Griffiths, Mt Pleasant, Harare, 15 August 1987.
34 Cecil Brien, 'Meet Our Missionaries', *Elim Evangel*, 14 January 1961.
35 Dr and Mrs Brien, 'Gospel Advances in Southern Rhodesia', *Elim Evangel*, 3 December 1951. Winnie Loosemore, 'Demon Possessed Africans Delivered', *Elim Evangel*, 11 December 1954. A. Nicholson, 'Living Epistles', *Elim Evangel*, 7 September 1963.
36 Boulton, *George Jeffreys*, p. 21.
37 Interview, Mary Brien, Elim mission, 13 June 1988. *Elim Evangel*, 10 November 1956, Brenda Hurrell, 'Journey to Katerere', *Elim Missionary Evangel*, July–September 1957.
38 Winnie Loosemore, 'Demon Possessed Africans Delivered', *Elim Evangel*, 11 December 1954.
39 See Maxwell, 'A Social and Conceptual History', chapter 3.
40 T. O. Ranger, 'Protestant Missions in Africa: The Dialectic of Conversion in the American Episcopal Church in Eastern Zimbabwe, 1900–1950', in Thomas D. Blakely, Walter E. A. van Beek and Dennis L. Thomson (eds), *Religion in Africa: Experience and Expression* (London, 1994).
41 See Maxwell, 'A Social and Conceptual History', chapter 4.
42 Interview, Mary Brien, Elim mission, 13 June 1988.
43 *Ibid.*
44 Interview, Peter Griffiths, Mt Pleasant, Harare, 15 August 1987.
45 Elim Archives, Cheltenham (hereafter EAC), Elim missionaries A–J to 1966, Mary Brien to Elim HQ, 12 December 1950. Cecil Brien to Pastor L. Green, *ca.* 1950, EAC. *Elim Evangel*, 23 April 1951.
46 Boulton, *George Jeffreys*. Jeffreys, *Stephen Jeffreys*.
47 Jeffreys, *Healing Rays*, pp. 122–137.
48 N. Grubb, *Rees Howells, Intercessor* (London, 1973), chap. 24.
49 Interview, Peter Griffiths, Mt Pleasant, Harare, 15 August 1987.
50 Mary Brien, 'Healing of the Sick', *Elim Evangel*, 7 July 1952.
51 *Elim Evangel*, 3 January 1953. Mary Brien, 'Healing the Sick.'
52 *Elim Evangel*, 3 July 1953.
53 Sermon, Mary Brien, Elim Mission, 12 June 1988.
54 Motherhood is one of the dominant themes of Hwesa folk tale and proverb. Samson Mudzudza, 1994, Minority Languages Project, University of Zimbabwe.
55 Interview, Janet Nyamudeza, Nyamaropa, 31 April 1991.
56 Dr and Mrs C. Brien, 'Gospel Advances In Southern Rhodesia', *Elim Evangel*, 3 December 1951.
57 Interview, James Kaerezi, Gande village, 27 May 1989.
58 Jeffreys, *Stephen Jeffreys*, p. 26.

59 *Elim Evangel*, 25 June, 1955.
60 T. O. Ranger, 'Medical Science and Pentecost: The Dilemma of Anglicanism in Africa', in W. J. Sheils (ed), *The Church and Healing* (Oxford, 1982), pp. 339–341.
61 Ranger, 'Religion', p. 37.
62 Boulton, *George Jeffreys*, p. 43.
63 Winnie Loosemore, 'Possessing the Land', *Elim Evangel*, 5 May 1956.
64 Interview, Paul Makanyanga, Alexander Park, Harare, 7 January 1989.
65 Spirit of a royal ancestor responsible for the political, moral and ecological well-being of a spirit ward or wider region. See Maxwell, 'A Social and Conceptual History', chaps 1 and 2.
66 Interview, Peter Griffiths, Mt Pleasant, Harare, 15 August 1987.
67 Personal correspondence from Augustine Mabvira (Comrade Ranga), 13 July 1990. For evidence of Pentecostal activity along the river see *Elim Evangel*, 4 March 1961 and 23 January 1971.
68 Interview, Paul Makanyanga, Alexander Park, Harare, 7 January 1989.
69 Ranger, 'Religion', p. 37.
70 Ranger, 'Medical Science', p. 348.
71 *Zelo*, Summer 1958.
72 Mel Hill, 'The Scapular in Africa', *While Friars*, July–August 1950.
73 *Zelo*, Summer 1958.
74 Interview, Bishop Donal Lamont, Terenure College, Dublin, 8 September 1990.
75 Tony Clarke, 'Our Missions and some Methods', *Zelo*, Autumn 1960, pp. 81–82.
76 *White Friars*, July–August 1959.
77 Interview, Father Paddy Stornton, the Carmelite Priory, Dundrum, 11 September 1990.
78 Interview, Cyprian Pasipanodya and Camillo Mudondo, Bumhira school, Nyamaropa, 3 June 1991.
79 A statement on 'Faith and Inculturation' issued by the International Theological Commission of the Catholic Church in 1987 stated: 'The process of inculturation may be defined as the Church's efforts to make the message of Christ penetrate a given socio-cultural milieu, calling upon the latter to grow according to all its particular values, as long as these are compatible with the Gospel'. Cited in J. Sherer and S. Bevans (eds), *New Directions on Mission and Evangelisation 1: Basic Statements 1974–1991* (New York, 1992), p. 87.
80 R. MacCabe, 'Medicine in Nyamaropa: A Study of the Pattern of Disease among Africans living in a Remote Part of Rhodesia', (PhD, University College, Dublin, 1972), p. 26.
81 Interview, Father Luke MacCabe, (Dr R. J. MacCabe), the Carmelite Priory, Dundrum, 7 September 1991.
82 Berthold Dowd, 'Mashona Tribal Beliefs', October–November 1960; 'Carmelite African Mission', February–March 1961; 'A World of Spirits', December 1961–January 1962 in *The Scapular*.
83 Interview, Paddy Stornton, the Carmelite Priory, Dundrum, 11 September 1990. For the wider context see A. J. Dachs and W. F. Rea, *The Catholic Church and Zimbabwe 1879–1979* (Gwelo, 1979), chaps 14 and 16.
84 Mel Hill, 'Young Africa', *The Sword*, Summer 1953.
85 Anselm Corbett, 'The Feast', *White Friars*, November–December 1947.
86 Interview, Father Paddy Stornton, the Carmelite Priory, Dundrum, 11 September 1990. See I. Linden, *The Catholic Church and the Struggle for Zimbabwe* (London, 1980), pp. 32–34, for a more general consideration of how the varied

social sources of the Catholic Church's missionary organisations affected patterns of missionisation.

87 EAC, J. Williams, Report, 30 April 1952, file, J. Williams.
88 *White Friars*, July–August 1949.
89 Wilson, *Sects and Society*, p. 89.
90 This point was wryly related to me by Peter Griffiths who, as a Welsh socialist, was something of an exception in the movement.
91 Cathal O hAinle, 'Carmelites in Africa', *Zelo*, Spring 1958.
92 'Consecration Ceremony', *White Friars*, August–September 1957.
93 Mrs J. Williams, 'Southern Rhodesia', *Elim Evangel*, 9 June 1952.
94 Dr and Mrs C. Brien, 'Southern Rhodesia: An S.O.S. for Prayer', *Elim Evangel*, 23 June 1953.
95 National Archives of Zimbabwe (hereafter NAZ), S2810/4203, Acting Secretary to the PNC, Manicaland, 6 June 1952.
96 Cathal O'hAinle, 'Carmelites in Africa', *Zelo*, Summer 1958, p. 85.
97 Cecil Brien, *Elim Evangel*, 10 March 1952.
98 P. O'Dwyer, *James Carmel O'Shea, O'Carm* (Dublin, 1989) p. 39.
99 EAC, mission correspondence 1944–57, Mrs A. Nicolson to Elim HQ, 30 July 1956.
100 Interview, Mary Brien, Elim mission, 13 June 1988.
101 Tony Clarke, 'Our Missions And Some Methods', *Zelo*, Autumn 1960, p. 71. A. Nicholson, 'Africa', *Elim Evangel*, 7 July, 1956.
102 NAZ, S2810/4023, Secretary for Native Affairs to PNC Manicaland, 10 August 1953.
103 NAZ, S2810/4023, Donal Lamont to Mr Gardener, 4 June 1952.
104 *Ibid.*
105 NAZ, S2827/2/2/3, Annual Report, Inyanga, 1955.
106 NAZ, NC Inyanga to PNC Umtali, 5 April 1956.
107 NAZ, S2827/2/2/4, Annual Report, Inyanga, 1956.
108 For example, EAC, mission correspondence, 1944–1957, A. Nicholson to Elim HQ, 31 May 1956. *Elim Evangel*, 22 November 1951, 31 May 1956.
109 EAC, Elim missionaries A–J to 1966, Zimbabwean Sons of the Soil to The Missionaries, 1 March 1964.
110 EAC, Elim missionaries A–J to 1966, Cecil Brien to Reverend Gorman, Elim HQ, 26 March and 31 March 1964.
111 EAC, Elim missionaries A–J to 1966, Zimbabwean Sons of the Soil to The Missionaries, 1 March 1964.
112 Interview, Paul Makanyanga, Alexander Park, Harare, 7 January 1989.
113 B. Sundkler, 'African Church History in a New Key', in Kirsten Holst-Peterson (ed), *Religion Development and African Identity* (Uppsala, 1987), p. 83.
114 Hastings, *The Church in Africa*, p. 555.
115 Jocelyn Alexander and Terence Ranger, 'Competition and Integration in the Religious History of North Western Zimbabwe', *Journal of Religion in Africa* (forthcoming).
116 See J. and J. Comaroff, *Of Revelation and Revolution. Christianity, Colonialism and Consciousness in South Africa* (Chicago, 1991), and P. Landau, *The Realm of the Word: Language, Gender and Christianity in a Southern African Kingdom* (London, 1995).